Fourth Canadian Edition

MANAGEMENT INFORMATION SYSTEMS
Managing the Digital Firm

Kenneth C. Laudon
New York University

Jane P. Laudon
Azimuth Information Systems

Canadian adaptation by
Mary Elizabeth Brabston
I. H. Asper School of Business
University of Manitoba

PEARSON
Prentice
Hall

Toronto

Library and Archives Canada Cataloguing in Publication

Laudon, Kenneth C., 1944–
    Management information systems : managing the digital firm / Kenneth C. Laudon, Jane P. Laudon; Canadian adaptation by Mary Elizabeth Brabston.—4th Canadian ed.

Includes bibliographical references and index.
ISBN 978-0-13-159843-0

1. Management information systems.   2. Information technology—Management.   I. Laudon, Jane Price   II. Brabston, Mary Elizabeth, 1948–   III. Title.

T58.6.L38 2009   658.4′038   C2007-905253-3

ISBN-13: 978-0-13-159843-0
ISBN-10: 0-13-159843-0

Vice President, Editorial Director: Gary Bennett
Acquisitions Editor: Don Thompson
Marketing Manager: Leigh-Anne Graham
Developmental Editor: Eleanor MacKay
Production Editor: Imee Salumbides
Copy Editor: Emma Gorst
Proofreader: Deborah Cooper-Bullock
Production Coordinator: Andrea Falkenberg
Composition: Integra
Photo and Permissions Research: Sandy Cooke
Cover and Interior Design: Alex Li
Cover Image: Stockbyte/Getty Images

2 3 4 5   12 11 10 09

Printed and bound in the United States of America.

In *MyMISLab* you are treated as an individual with specific learning needs.

Personalized Study Plan

Pre-Tests

At the beginning of each chapter, take the Pre-Test to see how much you know about the subject of the chapter. If the results of your Pre-Test indicate you need help on a specific topic, you will be directed to the relevant sections of the eText where you can review those concepts.

Post-Tests

At the end of each chapter, take the Post-Test to gauge your understanding of the context in the chapter. If the results of your Post-Test indicate you need help on a specific topic, you will be directed to the relevant sections of the eText where you can review those concepts.

Other Student Resources

MyMISLab also includes additional interactive media, cases, and exercises that allow for further exploration.

eText

Study without leaving the online environment. Access the eText online while you study

Get a Better Grade

Use MyMISLab to prepare for tests and exams and go to class ready to learn

For Erica and Elisabeth

—K.C.L AND J.P.L

For my father (who died June 2007) and my mother (who died March 1996), both of whom taught me to value teaching and excellence

—M.E.B.

About the Authors

Kenneth C. Laudon is a Professor of Information Systems at New York University's Stern School of Business. He holds a B.A. in Economics from Stanford and a Ph.D. from Columbia University. He has authored twelve books dealing with electronic commerce, information systems, organizations, and society. Professor Laudon has also written over forty articles concerned with the social, organizational, and management impacts of information systems, privacy, ethics, and multimedia technology.

Professor Laudon's current research is on the planning and management of large-scale information systems and multimedia information technology. He has received grants from the National Science Foundation to study the evolution of national information systems at the Social Security Administration, the IRS, and the FBI. Ken's research focuses on enterprise system implementation, computer-related organizational and occupational changes in large organizations, changes in management ideology, changes in public policy, and understanding productivity change in the knowledge sector.

Ken Laudon has testified as an expert before the United States Congress. He has been a researcher and consultant to the Office of Technology Assessment (United States Congress), Department of Homeland Security, and to the Office of the President, several executive branch agencies, and Congressional Committees. Professor Laudon also acts as an in-house educator for several consulting firms and as a consultant on systems planning and strategy to several Fortune 500 firms.

At NYU's Stern School of Business, Ken Laudon teaches courses on Managing the Digital Firm, Information Technology and Corporate Strategy, Professional Responsibility (Ethics), and Electronic Commerce and Digital Markets. Ken Laudon's hobby is sailing.

Jane Price Laudon is a management consultant in the information systems area and the author of seven books. Her special interests include systems analysis, data management, MIS auditing, software evaluation, and teaching business professionals how to design and use information systems.

Jane received her Ph.D. from Columbia University, her M.A. from Harvard University, and her B.A. from Barnard College. She has taught at Columbia University and the New York University Graduate School of Business. She maintains a lifelong interest in Oriental languages and civilizations.

The Laudons have two daughters, Erica and Elisabeth, to whom this book is dedicated.

About the Canadian Adapter

Mary Elizabeth Brabston is Associate Professor of Management Information Systems at the University of Manitoba's I.H. Asper School of Business. Prior to the Asper School, Dr. Brabston taught at the University of Tennessee at Chattanooga. Dr. Brabston received her doctorate from Florida State University. Having spent her working life as a banker, political staffer, development officer, and academic, Dr. Brabston brings a comprehensive view to her analysis of how information systems can help organizations to achieve their potential. Her teaching and research interests involve strategic planning and applications of information systems and information resource management, as well as electronic commerce, including ethical and legal issues associated with advancing information technology. Her work has appeared in such publications as the *Journal of Computing and Information Technology*, *Journal of Computer Information Systems*, *Journal of Information Systems Education*, and *Human Relations*, and in several books. Dr. Brabston is also faculty advisor to the Asper School's Co-operative Education Program and the school's chapter of Beta Gamma Sigma, the business school honorary.

Brief Contents

Contents

PART III   Developing and Managing Information Systems 297

CHAPTER 9   Systems Development 298

OPENING CASE: Protecting Patients by Tracking Instruments 298

CHAPTER 10   Information Resource Management and Project Management   333

PART IV   How Digital Businesses Use Information and Systems   405

CHAPTER 13   E-Commerce: Digital Markets and Digital Goods   434

Integrating Business with Technology

By completing the projects in this text, students will be able to demonstrate business knowledge, application software proficiency, and Internet skills. These projects can be used by instructors as learning assessment tools and by students as demonstrations of business, software, and problem-solving skills to future employers. Here are some of the skills and competencies students using this text will be able to demonstrate:

Business Application Skills: Use both business and software skills in real-world business applications. Demonstrates both business knowledge and proficiency in spreadsheet, database, and Web page creation tools.

Internet Skills: Ability to use Internet tools to access information, conduct research, or perform online calculations and analysis.

Analytical, Writing, and Presentation Skills: Ability to research a specific topic, analyze a problem, think creatively, suggest a solution, and prepare a clear written or oral presentation of the solution, working either individually or with others in a group.

Business Application Skills

Business Skills	Software Skills	Chapter and Page
Finance and Accounting		
Financial statement analysis	Spreadsheet charts and formulas	Chapter 2, p. 61
Financial statement analysis	Spreadsheet formulas	
	Spreadsheet downloading and formatting	Chapter 13, p. 464
Pricing hardware and software	Spreadsheet formulas	Chapter 5, p. 186
Technology Total Cost of Ownership analysis	Spreadsheet formulas	Chapter 5, p. 186
Analyzing telecommunications services and costs	Spreadsheet formulas	Chapter 7, p. 260
Risk assessment	Spreadsheet charts and formulas	Chapter 8, p. 291
Retirement planning	Spreadsheet formulas and logical functions	Chapter 15, p. 528
Capital budgeting	Spreadsheet formulas	Chapter 10, p. 368, 369
Human Resources		
Employee training and skills tracking	Database design, querying, and reporting	Chapter 9, p. 329
Job posting database and Web page	Database design Web page design and creation	Chapter 11, p. 397
Manufacturing and Production		
Analyzing supplier performance and pricing	Spreadsheet functions Data filtering Database functions	Chapter 2, p. 62
Inventory management	Importing data into a database Database querying and reporting	Chapter 6, p. 217
Bill of materials cost sensitivity analysis	Spreadsheet data tables Spreadsheet formulas	Chapter 14, p. 493
Sales and Marketing		
Sales trend analysis	Database querying and reporting	Chapter 1, p. 26

Internet Skills

Analytical, Writing, and Presentation Skills

Real-World Companies

Here are some of the real-world companies you'll find in the boxed material, examples, and cases.

Preface

We wrote this book for business school students who want an in-depth look at how business firms use information technologies and systems to achieve corporate objectives. Information systems are one of the major tools available to business managers for achieving operational excellence, developing new products and services, improving decision making, and achieving competitive advantage.

When interviewing potential employees, business firms often look for new hires who know how to use information systems and technologies for achieving bottom-line business results. Regardless of whether you are an accounting, finance, management, human resources, operations management, marketing, or information systems major, the knowledge and information you find in this book will be valuable throughout your business career.

A New World of Business

A continuing stream of information technology innovations from the Internet to wireless networks to digital phone and cable systems is continuing to transform the business world. These innovations are enabling entrepreneurs and innovative traditional firms to create new products and services, develop new business models, destroy old business models, disrupt entire industries, build new business processes, and transform the day-to-day conduct of business.

New avenues of telecommunication, such as high-speed wireless Wi-Fi networks, cellular phone networks, high-speed telecommunications service to the home and small business, coupled with entirely new hardware platforms, such as smart phones, personal digital assistants, and very powerful wireless laptop computers, are changing how people work, where they work, and what they do when they work. In the process, some old businesses, even industries, are being destroyed while new businesses are springing up.

For instance, the emergence of online music stores—driven by millions of consumers who prefer iPods and MP3 players to CDs—has forever changed the older business model of distributing music on physical devices, such as records and CDs. The emergence of online DVD rentals has transformed the old model of distributing films through theatres and then through DVD rentals at physical stores. New high-speed broadband connections to the home have supported these two business changes, and in addition, permanently altered the marketing and advertising worlds as newspaper advertising declines and Internet advertising explodes.

The management of business firms has also changed: With new mobile phones and computers based on high-speed digital networks, remote salespeople on the road are only seconds away from their managers' questions and oversight. The growth of enterprise-wide information systems with extraordinarily rich data means that managers no longer operate in a fog of confusion, but instead have online, nearly instant, access to the really important information they need for accurate and timely decisions. In addition to their public uses on the Web, wikis and blogs are becoming important corporate tools for communication, collaboration, and information sharing.

These changes are leading to fully digital firms where nearly all significant business processes and relationships with customers and suppliers are digitally enabled. In digital firms, information is available any time and anywhere in the organization to support decisions in the value chain. New products and services, such as music and video on demand, photo-sharing services, and social networking communities, are increasingly based on digital technology. For these reasons, we have made *Managing the Digital Firm* the subtitle of this text.

The Fourth Canadian Edition: The Comprehensive Solution for the MIS Curriculum

Since its inception, this text, in its various global editions, has helped to define the MIS course around the globe. Now translated into more than a dozen languages, the fourth Canadian edition continues to be authoritative and comprehensive but is also more customizable, flexible, and geared to meeting the needs of different colleges, universities, and individual instructors. This book is now part of a complete learning package that includes the core text and our Pearson Education Canada MyMISLab. The core text consists of 15 chapters with hands-on projects covering the most essential topics in MIS. Our MyMISLab provides additional case studies, supplementary material, and data files. MyMISLab also provides an online source for career resources.

The Core Text

The core text provides an overview of fundamental MIS concepts using an integrated framework for describing and analyzing information systems. This framework depicts information systems being composed of management, organization, and technology elements. This view of information systems is reinforced in student projects and case studies.

More than 100 Canadian business and public organizations are featured in our real-world examples throughout the text to illustrate MIS concepts. Case studies and in-text discussions use companies familiar to students, such as Great West Life, Nygård, Chapters.Indigo, Royal Bank of Canada, Zeller's, Canadian Tire, and Boeing.

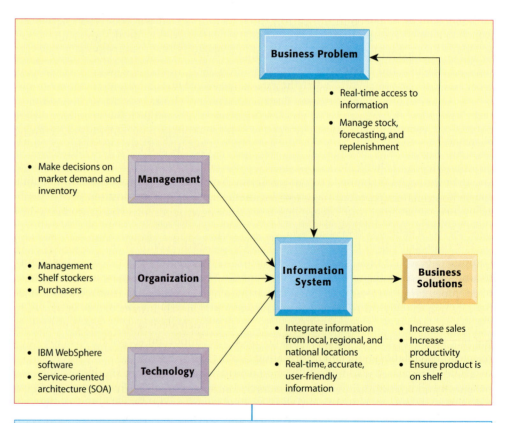

A diagram accompanying each chapter-opening case graphically illustrates how management, organization, and technology elements work together to create an information system solution to the business challenges discussed in the case.

Each chapter contains the following elements:

- A chapter-opening case describing a real-world organization to establish the theme and importance of the chapter
- A diagram analyzing the opening case in terms of the management, organization, and technology model used throughout the text
- A series of Learning Objectives to identify learning outcomes
- Two "Window on . . ." sections featuring management, organizational, or technology issues affecting real-world companies with To Think About questions and MIS in Action projects.
- A Hands-on MIS Application Exercises section featuring the Dirt Bikes Canada running case project, a hands-on application software project, and a project to develop Internet skills
- A chapter Summary keyed to the Learning Objectives
- A list of Key Terms students can use to review key concepts
- Review Questions for students to test their comprehension of chapter material
- Discussion Questions raised by the broader themes of the chapter
- A Teamwork project to help students develop teamwork and presentation skills
- A Learning Track Module section summarizing the Learning Track Module or Modules available on our MyMISLab for each chapter
- A chapter-ending case study illustrating important chapter themes
- A part-end CBC video case study illustrating important chapter concepts

---

HANDS-ON MIS   Application Exercises

The projects in this section give you hands-on experience in using spreadsheet software to help a real-world company make a rent vs. buy decision about new manufacturing software, using spreadsheet software to evaluate alternative desktop systems, and using Web research to budget for a sales conference.

Improving Decision Making: Making the Rent vs. Buy Decision for Software

Software skills: Spreadsheet formulas, electronic presentation software (optional)
Business skills: Technology rent vs. buy decision

This project provides an opportunity for you to help a real-world company make a decision about whether to rent or buy new technology. You will use spreadsheet software to compare the total three-year cost of licensing and maintaining new manufacturing software or renting the software from an application service provider.

Dirt Bikes Canada would like to implement new production planning, quality control, and scheduling software for use by 25 members of its manufacturing staff. Management is trying to determine whether to purchase the software from a commercial vendor along with any hardware required to run the software or to use a hosted software solution from an application service provider. (The hosted software runs on the ASP's computer.) You have been asked to help management with this rent vs. buy decision by calculating the total cost of each option over a three-year period.

The costs of purchasing the software (actually for purchasing a licence from the vendor to use its software package) include the initial purchase price of the software (a licensing fee of $100 000 paid in the first year), the cost of implementing and customizing the software in the first year ($20 000), one new server to run the software (a first-year purchase of $4000), one information systems specialist devoted half-time to supporting the software ($55 000 in full-time annual salary and benefits, with a 3 percent annual salary increase each year after the first year), user training in the first year ($10 000), and the cost of annual software upgrades ($5000).

The costs of renting hosted software are the rental fees ($2500 annually per user), implementation and customization costs ($12 000 in the first year), and training ($10 000 in the first year).

1. Use your spreadsheet software to calculate the total cost of renting or purchasing this software over a three-year period. Identify the lowest-price alternative that meets Dirt Bikes Canada's requirements.

2. What other factors should Dirt Bikes Canada consider besides cost in determining whether to rent or buy the hardware and software?

3. (Optional) If possible, use electronic presentation software to summarize your findings for management.

Each Dirt Bikes Canada running case project requires students to use application software, Web tools, or analytical skills to solve a problem encountered by this simulated company.

Key Features in The Fourth Canadian Edition

We have enhanced the core text to make it more interactive, instructor-friendly and leading-edge. The fourth Canadian edition includes the following new features:

Interactivity There is no better way to learn about MIS than by doing MIS! We provide different kinds of hands-on projects where students can work with real-world business scenarios and data and learn first-hand what MIS is all about. These projects heighten student involvement in this exciting subject.

- **Hands-on MIS Application Exercises**. Each chapter concludes with a Hands-on MIS Application Exercises section containing three types of projects: a running case project about a simulated company called Dirt Bikes Canada, a hands-on application software exercise using Microsoft Excel or Access, and a project that develops Internet business skills.
- **Window on . . . Sections**. Two short features in each chapter have been redesigned to be used in the classroom (or on Internet discussion boards) to stimulate student interest and active learning. Each feature concludes with two types of activities: To Think About questions and an MIS in Action project. The questions provide topics for class discussion, Internet discussion, or written assignments. The MIS in Action project features hands-on Web activities for exploring the issues they discuss in more depth.

Improving Decision Making:
Using Spreadsheet Software for Capital Budgeting for a New CAD System

Software skills: Spreadsheet formulas and functions
Business skills: Capital budgeting

This project provides you with an opportunity to use spreadsheet software to use the capital budgeting models discussed in this chapter to analyze the return on an investment for a new computer-aided design (CAD) system.

Your company would like to invest in a new CAD system that requires purchasing hardware, software, and networking technology, as well as expenditures for installation, training, and support. MyMISLab for Chapter 10 contains tables showing each cost component for the new system as well

as annual maintenance costs over a five-year period. You believe the new system will produce annual savings by reducing the amount of labour required to generate designs and design specifications, thus increasing your firm's annual cash flow.

1. Using the data provided in these tables, create a worksheet that calculates the costs and benefits of the investment over a five-year period and analyzes the investment using the four capital budgeting models presented in this chapter.
2. Is this investment worthwhile? Why or why not?

Improving Decision Making:
Using Web Tools for Buying and Financing a Home

Software skills: Internet-based software
Business skills: Financial planning

This project will develop your skills using Web-based software for searching for a home and calculating mortgage financing for that home.

You have found a new job in Saint John, New Brunswick, and would like to purchase a home in that area. Ideally, you would like to find a single-family house with at least three bedrooms and one bathroom that costs between $150 000 and $225 000 and you want to finance it with a 30-year fixed rate mortgage. You can afford a down payment that is 20 percent of the value of the house. Before you purchase a house, you would like to find out what homes are available in your price range, find a mortgage, and determine the amount of your monthly payment. You would also like to see how much of your mortgage payment represents principal and how much represents interest. Use the Multiple Listing Service (www.mls.ca) site to help you with the following tasks:

1. Locate homes in your price range in Saint John, New Brunswick. Find out as much information as you can about the houses, including the real estate listing agent, condition of the house, number of rooms, and school district.
2. Find a mortgage for 80 percent of the list price of the home. Compare rates from at least three sites. (Use search engines to find sites other than MLS.)
3. After selecting a mortgage, calculate your closing costs.
4. Calculate the monthly payment for the mortgage you select.
5. Calculate how much of your monthly mortgage payment represents principal and how much represents interest, assuming you do not plan to make any extra payments on the mortgage.
6. When you are finished, assess the ease of use of the site and your ability to find information about houses and mortgages; the breadth of choice of homes and mortgages; and how helpful the whole process would have been for you if you were actually in the situation described in this project.

Students practice using software for achieving operational excellence and enhancing decision making in real-world settings.

WINDOW ON MANAGEMENT

Monitoring Employees on Networks: Unethical or Good Business?

As Internet use has exploded worldwide, so has the use of e-mail and the Web for personal business at the workplace. A number of studies have concluded that at least 25 percent of employee online time is spent on non-work-related Web surfing, and perhaps as many as 90 percent of employees receive or send personal e-mail at work.

Many companies have begun monitoring their employee use of e-mail and the Internet, often without employee knowledge. Although North American companies have the legal right to monitor employee Internet and e-mail activity, is such monitoring unethical, or is it simply good business?

Managers worry about the loss of time and employee productivity when employees are focusing on personal rather than company business. A 2003 survey by Ipsos Reid found that the average Canadian worker wastes more than 4.5 hours per week surfing the Internet for personal reasons while at work (Evron, 2003). If personal traffic on company networks is too high, it can also clog the company's network so that business work cannot be performed. Downloading music or video files can severely limit the speed of the company's Internet traffic.

Too much time on personal business, on the Internet or not, can mean lost revenue or over-billed clients. Some

---

Each chapter contains two Window on . . . sections on Management, Organizations, or Technology, which use real-world companies to illustrate chapter concepts and issues.

Assessment and AACSB Assessment Guidelines The Association to Advance Collegiate Schools of Business (AACSB) is a not-for-profit corporation comprised of educational institutions, corporations, and other organizations that seeks to improve business education primarily by accrediting university business programs. As a part of its accreditation activities, the AACSB has developed an Assurance of Learning Program designed to ensure that schools do in fact teach students what they promise. Schools are required to state a clear mission, develop a coherent business program, identify student learning objectives, and then prove that students actually achieve the objectives.

We have attempted in this book to support the AACSB efforts to encourage assessment-based education. Our Integrating Business with Technology feature before the Preface in this book identifies skills the students will learn while conducting the exercises at the end of each chapter.

Companies that allow employees to use personal e-mail accounts at work could face legal and regulatory trouble if they do not retain those messages. E-mail today is an important source of evidence for lawsuits, and companies are now required to retain all their e-mail messages for longer periods than in the past. Courts do not discriminate about whether e-mails involved in lawsuits were sent via personal or business e-mail accounts. Not producing those e-mails could result in a five- to six-figure fine.

Companies have the legal right to monitor what employees are doing with company equipment during business hours. The question is whether electronic surveillance is an appropriate tool for maintaining an efficient and positive workplace. Some companies try to ban all personal activities on corporate networks—zero tolerance. Others block employee access to specific Web sites or limit personal time on the Web using software that enables IT departments to track the Web sites employees visit, the amount of time employees spend at these sites, and the files they download. Some firms have fired employees who have stepped out of bounds. Nearly one-third of the companies surveyed in a Forrester Consulting study had fired at least one employee within the last year for breaking company e-mail rules.

No solution is problem-free, but many consultants believe companies should write corporate policies on employee e-mail and Internet use. The policies should include explicit ground

To Think About

1. Should managers monitor employee e-mail and Internet usage? Why or why not?

2. Describe an effective e-mail and Web use policy for a company.

MIS in Action

Explore the Web site of a company selling online employee-monitoring software such as NetVizor (www.netvizor.net), SpyAgent (www.spy-software-solutions.com/), or Activity Monitor (www.softactivity.com/), and answer the following questions.

1. What employee activities does this software track? What can an employer learn about an employee by using this software?

2. How can businesses benefit from using this software?

3. How would you feel if your employer used this software where you work to monitor what you are doing on the job? Explain your response.

Sources: Alex Mindlin, "You've Got Someone Reading Your E-Mail," *The New York Times*, June 12, 2006; Darrell Dunn, "Who's Watching Now?" *InformationWeek*, February 27, 2006; and Jack M. Germain, "Monitoring Employee Communications in the Enterprise," *NewsFactor Network*, April 10, 2006.

MIS in Action projects in each Window on . . . section encourage students to learn more about the companies and issues discussed in these features.

Customization and Flexibility: Learning Track Modules Summary and Chapters A new **Learning Track Modules** summary section at the end of each chapter directs students to supplementary material on MyMISLab. Instructors can choose the topics they want to cover in greater depth. These Learning Track Modules deal with such topics as entity-relationship diagramming and normalization (Chapter 6), general and application controls (Chapter 8), and how to create pivot tables to enhance decision making (Chapter 14).

Career Orientation Career resources are integrated throughout and show students how the text and the course are directly useful in their future business careers.

- **Heads Up.** A new section at the beginning of each chapter shows why students need to know the contents of the chapter and how their knowledge of it will help them in their future careers in finance and accounting, human resources, information systems, management, manufacturing and production, and sales and marketing.
- **Digital Portfolio.** The new Digital Portfolio feature on our MyMISLab shows how you can use your knowledge to build a digital portfolio, which will demonstrate the business knowledge, application software proficiency, and Internet skills you have acquired from using this text. You can include the portfolio in a resume or job application or use it as a learning assessment tool.

Chapter on Project Management and Information Resource Management Our chapter on project management and information resource management highlights the importance of project management for ensuring successful system implementations that deliver genuine business value. This chapter also highlights the importance of managing the information system function like a business department to ensure that its business value is maximized.

Global Emphasis This edition has even more global emphasis than previous editions. There is a full chapter on Managing Global Systems (Chapter 11) and coverage in other chapters of global issues such as global supply chains (Chapter 12), offshore outsourcing (Chapters 5 and 11), the Internet and globalization (Chapter 3), managing global and virtual teams (Chapters 3 and 11), and global competition (Chapter 3).

Business Processes Without the right business process, investing in information systems leads to poor returns and less than optimal business performance. Using information systems correctly almost always involves changing basic, everyday business processes and management behaviour. This edition expands coverage of business processes, starting in Chapters 1 and 2. Throughout the text are numerous examples of how information systems enable new business processes that are much more efficient and which can be the basis for entirely new business models.

New Leading-Edge Topics This edition includes new coverage of the following leading-edge topics:

Ajax

Blogs

Inshore outsourcing

Multicore processing

Offshore outsourcing

RSS

Social bookmarking

Social networking

Social shopping

Software mashups

Virtualization
Web 2.0
Wikis

MyMISLab for Students

The Laudon, Laudon, and Brabston text is supported by an excellent online resource—MyMISLab. MyMISLab reinforces and enhances the text material by providing you with the opportunity to explore concepts and subjects presented in the text more thoroughly, master new management and software skills, and discover new topics of interest. You will find additional material on the Dirt Bikes Canada running case, CBC video cases, data files for the Hands-on MIS Application Exercises, career resources, additional study resources, additional case studies, and a special PowerPoint slide show on IT Careers custom-prepared by Ken Laudon.

- **Dirt Bikes Canada Running Case Material:** You will find important information to assist you with the Dirt Bikes Canada exercises in the book. You will learn more about the company's history and background, employees, organizational structure, products and services, sales and marketing strategies, and financial status.
- **Video Cases:** An MIS-related CBC video or videos accompany each of the part-end CBC Canadian Case Studies. Each case illustrates chapter concepts from that part and is tied to the chapter content through a series of questions that help students apply what they have learned to the case.
- **Additional Study Resources:** The additional study questions will help you review what you have learned in each chapter.
- **Career Guidelines:** Our career guidelines will help you understand the information systems skills required of accounting, finance, management, marketing, operations management, and information systems majors.
- **Additional Cases:** You will find additional cases with application questions to help you apply the concepts you have learned in the chapter.
- **Learning Track Modules:** The Learning Track Modules are short essays that accompany each chapter. They explore MIS topics, concepts, and debates more comprehensively; review basic technology concepts in database design, telecommunications, and other areas; or provide additional hands-on software instruction.
- **MIS Learning Track Chapter:** An entire additional chapter on building and using PivotTables in Microsoft Excel.

MyMISLab for Instructors

Instructor's Resource CD-ROM

Most of the support materials described in the following sections are conveniently available for adopters on the Instructor's Resource CD-ROM. The CD includes the Instructor's Manual, Test Item File, TestGen software, PowerPoint slides, and the helpful lecture tool "Image Library."

Instructor's Manual (on Web and Instructor's Resource CD-ROM)

The Instructor's Manual features not only answers to review, discussion, case study, and group project questions but also an in-depth lecture outline, teaching objectives, key terms, teaching suggestions, and Internet resources. This supplement can be downloaded from the secure faculty section of MyMISLab and is also available on the Instructor's Resource CD-ROM.

Test Item File (on Web and Instructor's Resource CD-ROM)

The Test Item File is a comprehensive collection of true-false, multiple-choice, fill-in-the-blank, and essay questions. The questions are rated by difficulty level and the answers are referenced by section. This supplement can be downloaded from the secure faculty section of MyMISLab and is also available using the TestGen software on the Instructor's Resource CD-ROM. The authors have worked closely with skilled test item writers to ensure that higher level cognitive skills are tested. Test bank multiple-choice questions include questions on content but also include many questions that require analysis, synthesis, and evaluation skills.

PowerPoint Slides (on Web and Instructor's Resource CD-ROM)

Electronic color slides are available in Microsoft PowerPoint. The slides illuminate and build on key concepts in the text. Faculty can download the PowerPoint slides from MyMISLab, and they are also provided on the Instructor's Resource CD-ROM.

Image Library (on Instructor's Resource CD-ROM)

The Image Library is an impressive resource to help instructors create vibrant lecture presentations. Almost every figure and photo in the text is provided and organized by chapter for convenience. These images and lecture notes can be imported easily into Microsoft PowerPoint to create new presentations or to add to existing ones.

Videos (on DVD, VHS, and Pearson Canada's Video Central

Four videos from CBC broadcasts are available to be used in conjunction with the four part-ending case studies. Each case study can be used with or without the videos being presented in class. As well, each video also lends itself to discussion with or without the case study, depending on instructor preference.

Acknowledgments

The production of any book involves valued contributions from a number of persons. We would like to thank all of our editors for encouragement, insight, and strong support over many years. Eleanor MacKay did a wonderful job guiding the development of this edition. We remain grateful to Don Thompson for his support and role in managing the project.

We praise Imee Salumbides for overseeing production for this project and thank Emma Gorst for her fine edit of the final manuscript. We extend a special thanks to Anthony Leung for his beautiful design work. Our special thanks also go to all of our supplement authors including Dale Foster (Memorial University) and Franca Giacomelli (Humber College Institute of Technology and Advanced Learning) for their contributions. Special thanks go to colleagues at the I.H. Asper School of Business at the University of Manitoba.

Finally, we also want especially to thank all of our reviewers whose suggestions helped to improve this text. The reviewers for this edition are:

Victor Bilodeau, Grant MacEwan College
David Chan, York University

Mary Furey, Memorial University of Newfoundland

Franca Giacomelli, Humber College Institute of Technology and Advanced Learning

Sherrie Komiak, Memorial University of Newfoundland

Ricky A. Menking, Trinity Western University

Jennifer Percival, University of Ontario Institute of Technology

Ken Sekhon, Camosun College

John H. Walker, Brock University

Cameron Welsh, University of Calgary

PART I

Organizations, Management, and the Networked Enterprise

CHAPTER 1

Information Systems in Global Business Today

After completing this chapter, you will be able to do the following:

1. Explain why information systems are so essential in business today.
2. Define an information system from both a technical and a business perspective.
3. Identify and describe the three dimensions of information systems.
4. Assess the complementary assets required for information technology to provide value to a business.
5. Identify and describe contemporary approaches to the study of information systems, and distinguish between computer literacy and information systems literacy.

OPENING **CASE** | Smart Systems and Smart Ways of Working Help Toyota Become Number One

Toyota Motor Corporation is about to surpass General Motors as the world's largest auto-maker, selling more than nine million vehicles in 2006. It is also considered the world's best auto-maker. The quality and reliability of Toyota vehicles are the gold standard of the industry, even among its lower-priced models. Customer loyalty is so high that Toyota can make sales without heavy discounting.

Toyota stands head and shoulders above fierce competition because it has been so skillful at combining quality with efficiency. One key to Toyota's success is its vaunted Toyota Production System, which is based on lean production—eliminating waste while optimizing value. Toyota has based its business processes and information systems on the principles of just-in-time delivery, quality, and continuous improvement.

By organizing its business processes and information systems around these principles, Toyota delivers value to the customer at a competitive price. As Ludo Vandervelden, vice-president of Finance and Accounting, Information Systems, and Vehicle Logistics for Toyota Motor Europe, points out, "You can achieve cost reductions and, at the same time, make your customers happy through implementation of smarter business processes."

Toyota Motor Europe and other Toyota divisions around the world use information systems to support these business processes. Vehicle production is based on actual customer orders rather than best guesses of what to stock in dealer showrooms, so the company only builds cars that customers want, when they want them, without additional delays or quality problems.

Toyota Motor Europe uses a vehicle orders management system based on Oracle E-Business Suite software to reduce the time it takes between placing a customer order and delivering the vehicle to the

customer. The software integrates easily with the company's existing systems and also with those of Toyota's independent dealerships and national marketing and sales companies, which run their own separate information systems based on a variety of technologies.

This system encompasses several business processes. It starts with the customer selecting a car and various options, such as tinted windows or a navigation system. The dealer uses the system to configure a car with all the selected options in front of the customer and then locates the best available car and options in the Toyota supply chain, including vehicles scheduled for production in the future. The dealer then uses the system to place the order through national distributors, who consolidate the order with those of their other retailers and place an order through Toyota Motor Europe. Toyota Motor Europe consolidates orders from

the national distributors and places an order with Toyota's factories. Each car is then shipped and invoiced from the factory to headquarters to national distributors to retailers, triggering all related accounting processes at each step. National distributors can use the system to monitor their orders and those of different dealers and even to "swap" cars with various retailers.

The vehicle order management system has helped Toyota reduce production time and the cost of maintaining materials and finished cars in inventory, while increasing customer service and satisfaction. According to Vandervelden, "with improved information transparency, we would be able to better readjust . . . our allocation of available product to markets that would be in high demand . . . and to reduce stock."

Sources: Katheryn Potterf, "Ready to Roll," *Profit Magazine*, May 2006; Ian Rowley, "No Traffic Ahead for Toyota," *BusinessWeek*, February 6, 2006; and "Triumphs & Trip-Ups in 2004," *Baseline Magazine*, December 20, 2004.

Toyota has flourished in a highly competitive environment because it has created a set of finely tuned business processes and information systems that simultaneously promote agility, efficiency, and quality. It can respond instantly to customers and changes in the marketplace as events unfold while working closely with suppliers and retailers. The experience of Toyota and other companies described in this text will help you

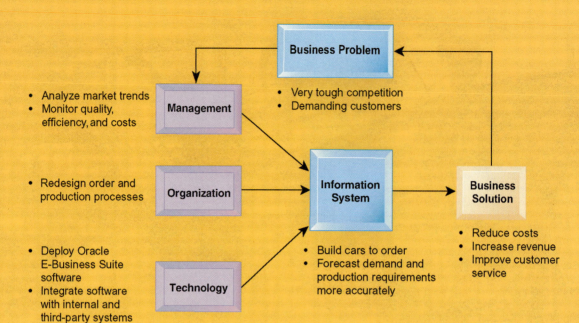

learn how to make your own business more competitive, efficient, and profitable.

The chapter-opening Business Challenges diagram highlights important points raised by this case and this chapter. As part of its ongoing effort to monitor quality, efficiency, and costs, Toyota management saw there was an opportunity to use information systems to improve business performance. Technology alone would not have provided a solution. Toyota had to carefully revise its business processes to support a build-to-order production model that based vehicle production on actual customer orders rather than "best guesses" of customer demand. Once that was accomplished, Oracle E-Business software was useful for coordinating the flow of information among disparate internal production, ordering, and invoicing systems within the company and with systems of retailers and suppliers.

By helping Toyota build only the cars customers have ordered, its vehicle order management system reduces inventory costs because the company and its dealers do not have to pay for making and storing vehicles customers did not want. The system also increases customer satisfaction by making it easier for customers to buy exactly the model, make, and options they desire. Information provided by the system helps management monitor trends and forecast demand and production requirements more accurately.

HEADS **UP**

This chapter introduces you to the roles that information systems and technologies play in business firms. All firms today, large and small, local and global, use information systems to achieve important business objectives, such as operational efficiency, customer and supplier intimacy, better decision making, and new products and services. You will need to know how to use information systems and technologies to help your firm solve problems and overcome challenges.

■ If your career is in finance or accounting, you will need information systems to summarize transactions, organize data, and perform financial analysis.

■ If your career is in human resources or management, you will need information systems to communicate with employees, maintain employee records, and coordinate work activities.

■ If your career is in information systems, you will be working with management and other business professionals to develop and support new systems that serve the needs of the business.

■ If your career is in manufacturing, production, or operations management, you will need information systems for planning, forecasting, and monitoring production and services.

■ If your career is in sales and marketing, you will need information systems for branding, promotions, processing orders, and providing customer service.

1.1 The Role of Information Systems in Business Today

It is not business as usual in North America any more, or for the rest of the global economy. In 2006, North American businesses will spend more than $1.9 trillion on information systems hardware, software, and telecommunications equipment. They will spend another $1.8 trillion on business and management consulting and services, much of which involves redesigning firms' business operations to take advantage of these new technologies. Figure 1-1 shows that between 1997 and 2006, investment in the information and communication technology (ICT) sector, consisting of hardware, software, and communications equipment, grew from 45 percent to 59 percent of all invested capital (Industry Canada, 2007).

As managers, most of you will work for firms that are intensively using information systems and making large investments in information technology. You will certainly want to know how to invest this money wisely. If you make wise choices, your firm can outperform competitors. If you make poor choices, you will be wasting valuable capital. This book is dedicated to helping you make wise decisions about information technology and information systems.

How Information Systems Are Transforming Business

You can see the results of the massive spending on information technology and systems around you every day just by observing how people conduct business. More wireless cell phone accounts were opened in 2005 than telephone land lines were installed. Cell phones, BlackBerrys, handhelds, e-mail, online conferencing, and international teleconferencing over the Internet have all become essential tools of business. In 2006, more than 38 percent of Canadian businesses had dot-com Internet sites registered. Sixty-three percent of Canadians are Internet users, and 44 percent of Canadians have broadband access at home. Fully 81 percent of Canadian Internet users shop online, while 56 percent actually buy online (eMarketer, 2006).

In 2005, FedEx shipped more than 100 million packages around the world, mostly overnight, and United Parcel Service (UPS) moved more than 380 million packages as businesses sought to sense and respond to rapidly changing customer demand, reduce inventories to the lowest possible levels, and achieve higher levels of operational efficiency, especially in their supply chains.

The responsiveness of this new "FedEx economy" has led many experts to believe the era of massive recessions and booms of the typical business cycle is over and has been replaced by much smaller contractions and expansions, and strong, long-term growth.

There has been a massive shift in media markets. Although newspaper readership continues to decline, more than 35 million people receive their news online. According to the Environics Research Group, 7 percent of Canadians have written their own blogs while

FIGURE 1-1 *Information and communication technology sector Gross Domestic Product, 1997–2006*

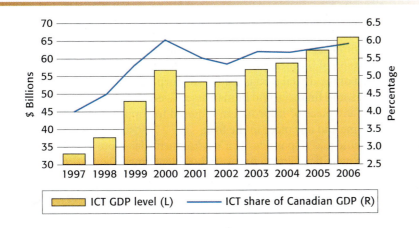

ICT GDP level (L)   ICT share of Canadian GDP (R)

Information and communication technology gross domestic product (GDP), defined as hardware, software, and communications equipment, grew from 45 percent to 59 percent between 1997 and 2006.

Source: Reproduced with the permission of the Minister of Public Works and Government Services, 2008, from Industry Canada. Information and Communication Technologies, ICT Sector Statistical Reports, "Canadian ICT Sector Profile," retrieved June 1, 2007, from http://strategis.ic.gc.ca/epic/site/ict-tic.nsf/en/h_it07229e.html.

9 percent claim they have posted a response to one. Canadian youth appear to be spurring the blogging trend, with 39 percent stating they read blogs on a regular basis. Fifteen percent of Canadians aged 18 to 24 say they also write their own blogs.

This change has created an explosion of new writers and new forms of customer feedback that did not exist five years ago (Environics, 2006).

E-commerce and Internet advertising are also booming: Google's online advertising revenues surpassed $6 billion in 2005, and Internet advertising continues to grow at more than 30 percent a year, reaching more than $11 billion in revenues in 2005.

Meanwhile, new federal security and accounting laws require many businesses to keep e-mail messages for a long period of time while existing occupational and health laws require firms to store various data about employees for many years. Together, these factors are spurring the growth of digital information: annual data storage is now estimated to be 5 exabytes, a previously unimaginable volume.

Globalization Opportunities

A growing percentage of the North American economy—and other advanced industrial economies in Europe and Asia—depend on imports and exports. Foreign trade, both exports and imports, accounts for more than 25 percent of the goods and services produced in North America, and an even higher portion of products and services in countries such as Japan and Germany.

The emergence of the Internet into a full-blown international communications system has drastically reduced the costs of operating on a global scale. Customers can now shop in a worldwide marketplace, obtaining price and quality information reliably 24 hours a day. Firms can achieve extraordinary cost reductions by finding low-cost suppliers and by managing production facilities in other countries. Digital content firms that produce Hollywood movies are able to sell millions more copies of DVDs of popular films by using foreign markets. Internet service firms, such as Google and eBay, are able to replicate their business models and services in multiple countries without having to redesign their expensive fixed-cost information systems infrastructure.

The Emerging Digital Firm

All the changes we have just described, coupled with equally significant organizational redesign, have created the conditions for a fully digital firm.

A **digital firm** can be defined along several dimensions. A digital firm is one in which nearly all the organization's *significant business relationships* with customers, suppliers, and employees are digitally enabled and mediated. Its *core business processes* are accomplished through digital networks spanning the entire organization or linking multiple organizations.

Business processes refer to the set of logically related tasks and behaviours that organizations develop over time to produce specific business results, and the unique manner in which these activities are organized and coordinated. Toyota's vehicle order management system changed Toyota's processes, enabling the company to reduce costs while improving customer service. Developing a new product, generating and fulfilling an order, creating a marketing plan, and hiring an employee are examples of business processes, and the ways organizations accomplish their business processes can be a source of competitive strength. (A detailed discussion of business processes can be found in Chapter 2.)

Another aspect of the digital firm is that its key corporate assets—intellectual property, core competencies, and financial and human assets—are managed through digital means. In a digital firm, any piece of information required to support key business decisions is available at any time and any place in the firm.

Digital firms sense and respond to their environments far more rapidly than traditional firms, giving them more flexibility to survive in turbulent times. Digital firms offer extraordinary opportunities for more flexible global organization and management. In digital firms, both *time shifting* and *space shifting* are the norm. Time shifting refers to business being conducted continuously, 24 × 7, rather than in narrow "work day" time bands of 9 a.m. to 5 p.m.

Digital firm

Business processes

Space shifting means that work takes place in a global workshop, as well as within national boundaries. Work is accomplished physically wherever in the world it is best accomplished.

Toyota Motor Company, described in the chapter-opening case, illustrates some of these features. Electronically integrating key business processes in vehicle ordering and inventory management has made this company much more agile and adaptive to customer demands and changes in its supplier and dealer network. A few firms, such as Cisco Systems or Dell Computer, are close to becoming digital firms, using the Internet to drive every aspect of their businesses. Most other companies are not fully digital, but they are moving toward close digital integration with suppliers, customers, and employees.

The Window on Organizations section in this chapter describes another example. Accenture is a global consulting services and outsourcing firm with more than 129 000 employees serving clients in 48 different countries. It has no operational headquarters and no formal branches, encouraging its employees to work on site with clients. Managers use e-mail, phones, the Web, and other information technologies to manage virtually, often while they are travelling themselves. As you read this case, try to identify the problems facing this company, how information systems are helping it solve them, and the management, organization, and technology issues it must address.

Strategic Business Objectives of Information Systems

What makes information systems so essential today? Why are businesses investing so much in information systems and technologies? In Canada, most managers and workers in the labour force rely today on information systems to conduct business. Information systems are essential for conducting day-to-day business in Canada and most other developed countries, as well as for achieving strategic business objectives.

Entire sectors of the economy would be nearly inconceivable without substantial investments in information systems. E-commerce firms such as Amazon, eBay, Google, and E*TRADE simply would not exist. Today's service industries—finance, insurance, and real estate, as well as personal services such as travel, medicine, and education—could not operate without information systems. Similarly, retail firms such as Wal-Mart and Sears, and manufacturing firms such as General Motors and General Electric require information systems to survive and prosper. Just as offices, telephones, filing cabinets, and efficient tall buildings with elevators were once the foundations of business in the twentieth century, information technology is a foundation for business in the twenty-first century.

There is a growing interdependence between a firm's ability to use information technology and its ability to implement corporate strategies and achieve corporate goals (see Figure 1-2). What a business would like to do in five years often depends on what its systems will be able to do. Increasing market share, becoming the high-quality or low-cost producer, developing

FIGURE 1-2   *The interdependence between organizations and information systems*

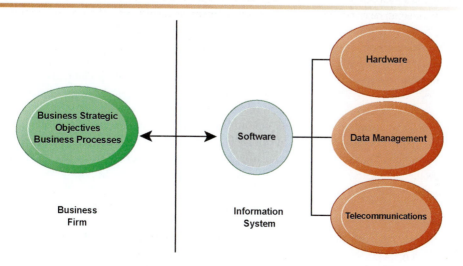

There is a growing interdependence between a firm's information systems and its business capabilities. Changes in strategy, rules, and business processes increasingly require changes in hardware, software, databases, and telecommunications. Often, what the organization would like to do depends on what its systems will permit it to do.

new products, and increasing employee productivity depend more and more on the kinds and quality of information systems in the organization. The more you understand about this relationship, the more valuable you will be as a manager.

Business firms invest heavily in information systems to achieve six strategic business objectives: operational excellence; new products, services, and business models; customer and supplier intimacy; improved decision making; competitive advantage; and survival.

Operational Excellence Businesses continuously seek to improve the efficiency of their operations in order to achieve higher profitability. Information systems and technologies are some of the most important tools available to managers for achieving higher levels of efficiency and productivity in business operations, especially when coupled with changes in business practices and management behaviour.

Wal-Mart, the largest retailer on Earth, exemplifies the power of information systems coupled with brilliant business practices and supportive management to achieve world-class operational efficiency. In 2005, Wal-Mart attained more than $330 billion in sales—nearly one-tenth of retail sales in the United States—in large part because of its RetailLink system, which digitally links its suppliers to every one of Wal-Mart's 5289 stores worldwide. As soon as a customer purchases an item, the supplier monitoring the item knows to ship a replacement to the shelf. Wal-Mart is the most efficient retail store chain in the industry, achieving sales of more than $32 per square foot, compared to its closest competitor, Target, at sales of $26 per square foot, and other retail firms selling less than $14 per square foot.

WINDOW ON ORGANIZATIONS

Virtual Management at Accenture

Accenture is a global management consulting, technology services, and outsourcing company, with over 129 000 employees in 48 countries. It specializes in helping businesses and governments improve their performance. Its information systems and business processes are designed so that consultants can work from virtually any location.

Accenture has no operational headquarters and no formal branches. Its chief financial officer lives in Silicon Valley, California, while the head of human resources is in Chicago and its chief technology officer is based in Germany. Accenture's thousands of management and technology consultants are constantly on the move, on site with clients or working temporarily in offices that the company leases in more than 150 locations around the world.

When a new consultant is hired, Accenture's system automatically sets up an e-mail account and instructions on where to pick up a laptop. Managers rely heavily on telephone and e-mail to keep up with their staff, and many of them are constantly in motion.

Every day, Accenture employees log on to the company's internal Web site, which they can access from anywhere in the world. They use this system to record where they are working and to access e-mail, phone messages, and their files. The system enables them to share documents and other data with Accenture colleagues and to conduct videoconferences when more face-to-face interaction is needed.

If a consultant or manager is about to travel to London, Chicago, or Beijing, he or she uses the system to find a cubicle with a desk in that location. Clients who call a manager whose

home base is Vancouver are automatically routed to his or her current working location, even if it is several time zones away.

To print a document, a person uses the Accenture internal Web site to click on the country where he or she is currently working. This action brings up a list of offices. After selecting an office, the employee selects a floor, which brings up a floor plan of the building and displays all of the available printers. When the employee clicks on a printer, it automatically prints the employee's documents.

Employees cannot pop into co-workers' offices for informal meetings. Participants in a specific project may be working from many different locations and time zones around the world, so scheduling phone conferences may require a few employees to give up some sleep. For global phone conferences, the best time appears to be around 1 p.m. London time, which is 9 p.m. in Beijing, midnight in Australia, and 5 a.m. in California. For executives who are constantly on the go, jet lag adds to the problem.

Accenture outsources about 82 percent of the information technology it uses. It hires other companies to manage its network, computer centres, and help desk, as well as technologies used at specific locations. External vendors provide the support for Accenture's PCs and conference call technology.

Accenture also outsources other parts of its business, such as the management of employee travel. Its travel vendors are able to track employee movements. When a major client in Copenhagen asked to see Accenture's chief operating officer Steve Rohleder in person, Accenture was able to locate Rohleder just as his plane was landing in Nice, France, en route from New York to India. Rohleder was able to change planes and head directly to Copenhagen.

Some problems, however, require Accenture managers and clients to "be there in person." When London-based Adrian Lajtha, who heads Accenture's financial services group, learned that a project team in the U.S. felt bogged down, he made an impromptu visit to their work site and staged a three-hour meeting. Personal contact is especially useful when sensitive personnel matters must be addressed or when employees need extra motivation and encouragement during hard times. That means more travel and conferences around the clock for Accenture virtual executives. During the last economic slowdown, for example, Lajtha held 280 meetings in 18 months with groups of the 12 000 employees he oversees.

Despite these challenges, Accenture believes virtual management works. The company does not have to maintain overhead costs for large headquarters, which it believes would amount to much more than its extensive travel expenses. Managers see many benefits to spending time in the field where clients are located. Managers meeting with lower-level employees who work with the clients obtain information that would not be available if they remained at headquarters. And their presence helps cement client relationships. Almost 85 percent of Accenture's 100 largest accounts have been its clients for 10 years or more.

To Think About

1. What are the advantages of working in a virtual environment like the one created by Accenture? What are the disadvantages?

2. Would you like to work in a company like Accenture? Why or why not? Explain your answer.

3. What kinds of companies could benefit from being run virtually like Accenture? Could all companies be run virtually like Accenture?

MIS in Action

1. Go to the Accenture Canadian Web site (www.accenture.com/Countries/Canada). On the home page, Accenture promises to help its clients achieve "high performance." According to Accenture, how does information technology help create high-performance organizations? Hint: Click on the "High Performance Business" link on the home page. Or, enter "information technology" into the search box on the home page, and read one of the articles linking IT with high-performance businesses. Write several paragraphs on Accenture's definition of a "high-performance" organization and the role of information systems in enabling such organizations.

2. Time to look for a job. What kinds of business and information system skills is Accenture looking for in recent college graduates? Hint: Click on the Careers tab and review the desired skills for customer care and SAP-related positions in Canada. Make a list of these skills in electronic presentation software for your class.

Sources: Carol Hymowitz, "Have Advice, Will Travel," *Wall Street Journal*, June 5, 2006; Rachel Rosmarin, "Accenture CIO Frank Modruson," *Forbes*, June 2, 2006; and www.accenture.com, accessed June 15, 2006.

New Products, Services, and Business Models Information systems and technologies are a major enabling tool for firms to create new products and services, as well as entirely new business models. A **business model** describes how a company produces, delivers, and sells a product or service to create wealth.

For example, today's music industry is vastly different from the industry in 2000. Apple Computer transformed an old business model of music distribution based on vinyl records, tapes, and CDs into an online, legal distribution model based on its own iPod technology platform. Apple has prospered from a continuing stream of iPod innovations, including the original iPod, the iPod nano, the iTunes music service, the iPod video player, and the iPhone.

Likewise, Netflix transformed the video rental business with a new Internet-enabled business model that makes more than 60 000 DVD titles (just about the entire population of DVD titles) available by postal mail to millions of users in the U.S. A typical Blockbuster video store, in contrast, stocks about 1200 titles (see the case study concluding Chapter 3).

Customer and Supplier Intimacy When a business really knows its customers and serves them well, the way they want to be served, the customers generally respond by returning and purchasing more. This raises revenues and profits. Likewise with suppliers: the more a business engages its suppliers, the better the suppliers can provide vital inputs. This lowers costs. How to really know your customers or suppliers is a central problem for businesses with millions of offline and online customers and suppliers.

Fairmont Hotels & Resorts, based in Toronto, and other high-end hotels exemplify the use of information systems and technologies to achieve customer intimacy. These hotels use computers to keep track of guests' preferences, such as their preferred room temperature, check-in time, frequently dialed telephone numbers, and television

Business model

Apple's iPod, iPod nano, iPod video player, and iPhone are popular new products based on information technology that are transforming the music and entertainment industries.

programs, and store this data in a giant data repository. Individual rooms in the hotels are networked to a central network server computer so that they can be remotely monitored or controlled. When a customer arrives at one of these hotels, the system automatically changes the room conditions, such as dimming the lights, setting the room temperature, or selecting appropriate music, based on the customer's digital profile. The hotels also analyze their customer data to identify their best customers and to develop individualized marketing campaigns based on customers' preferences.

Nygård, a Canadian-based clothing manufacturer, informs its suppliers electronically of its needs and expects just-in-time delivery of inventory from halfway around the world. In other words, Nygård's material inventory is near zero, as is the cost of storing it.

Improved Decision Making Many business managers operate in an information fog bank, never really having the right information at the right time to make an informed decision. Instead, managers rely on forecasts, best guesses, and luck. The result is overproduction or underproduction of goods and services, misallocation of resources, and poor response times. These poor outcomes raise costs and lose customers. In the past 10 years, information systems and technologies have made it possible for managers to use real-time data from the marketplace when making decisions.

For example, Trimac, a large Canadian trucking firm, uses an assessment of key performance indicators that it calls its "dashboard project." According to Matt Hines (*SearchCRM*, 2002), "The idea is to create consistent reporting across every level of the organization so that when an individual wants to know the effectiveness of any particular tool, person, or function, they can more easily identify the necessary data on a company-wide or divisional level." An example of a digital dashboard may be seen in Figure 1-3.

Competitive Advantage When firms achieve one or more of these business objectives—operational excellence; new products, services, and business models; customer and supplier intimacy; and improved decision making—chances are they have already achieved a competitive advantage. Doing things better than your competitors, charging

FIGURE 1-3   *Business Objects digital dashboard*

Business Objects digital dashboard delivers comprehensive and accurate information for decision making. The graphical overview of key performance indicators helps managers quickly spot areas that need attention.

less for superior products, and responding to customers and suppliers in real time all add up to higher sales and higher profits that your competitors cannot match.

Perhaps no other company exemplifies all these attributes leading to competitive advantage more than Dell Computer. In a period when PC prices have been falling by 25 percent a year, forcing most manufacturers into losses, Dell has shown consistent profitability during its lifespan of 25 years. Although recently its margins have fallen as competitors improve their own business processes, Dell remains the most efficient producer of PCs in the world. A large part of Dell's operational efficiency results from "mass customization," staying close to the customer by using a Web-based order entry model that can build and ship a customized PC to any of its millions of consumers in only a few days, even overnight if the customer is really in a hurry. Dell has used its commanding position to introduce many new products and services, especially to corporate customers, such as a custom Dell Web page for corporate accounts.

Survival Business firms also invest in information systems and technologies because they are necessities of doing business. Sometimes these necessities are driven by industry-level changes. For instance, after Citibank introduced the first automatic teller machines (ATMs) in the New York region in 1977 to attract customers through higher service levels, its competitors rushed to provide ATMs to their customers to keep up with Citibank. Today, virtually all banks in the world have regional ATMs and link to national and international ATM networks, such as CIRRUS. Providing ATM services to retail banking customers is simply a requirement of being in and surviving in the retail banking business.

There are many federal and provincial statutes and regulations that create a legal duty for companies and their employees to retain records, including digital records. The Canadian Rules on the Sarbanes-Oxley Act, more commonly known as the C-SOX Act, which was intended to improve the accountability of public firms and their auditors, requires certified public accounting firms that audit public companies to retain audit working papers and records, including all e-mails, for a number of years. Many other pieces of federal and provincial legislation in healthcare, financial services, education, and privacy protection impose significant information retention and reporting requirements on Canadian businesses and other organizations. Firms turn to information systems and technologies to provide the capability to respond to these requirements.

1.2   Perspectives on Information Systems

So far we have used *information systems* and *technologies* informally without defining the terms. **Information technology (IT)** consists of all the hardware and software that a firm needs to use in order to achieve its business objectives. This includes not only computers, printers, handheld personal digital assistants, and, yes, even iPods (where they are used for a business purpose) but also software, such as the Windows or Linux operating systems, the Microsoft Office desktop productivity suite, and the many thousands of computer programs that can be found in a typical large firm. Information systems are more complex and can be best understood by being viewed from both a technology and a business perspective.

What Is an Information System?

An **information system** can be defined technically as a set of interrelated components that collect (or retrieve), process, store, and distribute information to support decision making and control in an organization. In addition to supporting decision making, coordination, and control, information systems may also help managers and workers analyze problems, visualize complex subjects, and create new products.

Information systems contain information about significant people, places, and things within the organization or in the environment surrounding it. By **information** we mean data that have been shaped into a form that is meaningful and useful to human beings. **Data**, in contrast, are streams of raw facts (representing events occurring in organizations or the

Information technology (IT)

Information system

Information

Data

FIGURE 1-4   *Data and information*

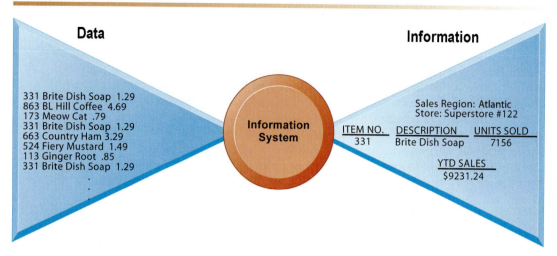

Raw data from a supermarket checkout counter can be processed and organized to produce meaningful information, such as the total unit sales of dish detergent or the total sales revenue from dish detergent for a specific store or sales territory.

physical environment) before they have been organized and arranged into a form that people can effectively understand and use.

A brief example contrasting information and data illustrates the difference between them. Supermarket checkout counters scan millions of pieces of data, such as bar codes, that describe the product. These pieces of data can be totalled and analyzed to provide meaningful information, such as the total number of bottles of dish detergent sold at a particular store, which brands of dish detergent were selling the most rapidly at that store or sales territory, or the total amount spent on that brand of dish detergent at that store or sales region (see Figure 1-4).

Four activities in an information system produce the information that organizations need to make decisions, control operations, analyze problems, and create new products or services. These activities are input, processing, output, and feedback (see Figure 1-5). **Input** captures or collects raw data from within the organization or from its external environment.

FIGURE 1-5   *Functions of an information system*

An information system contains information about an organization and its surrounding environment. Four basic activities—input, processing, output, and feedback— produce the information organizations need. Environmental actors, such as customers, suppliers, competitors, stockholders, and regulatory agencies, interact with the organization and its information systems.

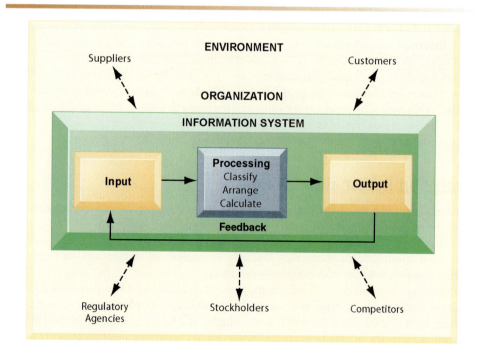

Processing converts this raw input into a meaningful form. **Output** transfers the processed information to the people who will use it or to the activities for which it will be used. Information systems also require **feedback**, which is output that is returned to appropriate members of the organization to help them evaluate or correct the input stage.

In Toyota's vehicle orders management system, the raw input consists of customer order data including the dealer identification number, model, colour, and optional features of each car ordered. Toyota's computers store this data and process it to locate the models with options specified by the customer that are either in inventory or under production, to place orders to national distributors, to consolidate the orders, and then to transmit them to factories. Toyota's production systems then tell its factories how many vehicles to manufacture for each model, colour, and option package, how much to bill for each vehicle, and where to ship the vehicles. The output consists of shipping instructions, invoices, and production reports. The system provides meaningful information, such as which models, colours, and options are selling in which locations, the most popular models and colours, and which dealers sell the most cars.

Although **computer-based information systems (CBIS)**—information systems that rely on computer hardware and software for processing and disseminating information—use computer technology to process raw data into meaningful information, there is a sharp distinction between a computer and a computer program on the one hand and an information system on the other. Electronic computers and related software programs are the technical foundation—the tools and materials—of modern information systems. Computers provide the equipment for storing and processing information. Computer programs, or software, are sets of operating instructions that direct and control computer processing. Knowing how computers and computer programs work is important in designing solutions to organizational problems, but computers are only part of an information system.

A house is an appropriate analogy for an information system. Houses are built with hammers, nails, and wood, but these tools do not make a house. The architecture, design, setting, landscaping, and all the decisions that lead to the creation of these features are part of the house and are crucial for solving the problem of putting a roof over one's head. Computers and programs are the hammer, nails, and lumber of CBISs, but alone they cannot produce the information a particular organization needs. To understand information systems, you must understand the problems they are designed to solve, their architectural and design elements, and the organizational processes that lead to these solutions.

Dimensions of Information Systems

To fully understand information systems, you must understand the broader organization, management, and information technology dimensions of systems (see Figure 1-6)

FIGURE 1-6 *Information systems are more than computers*

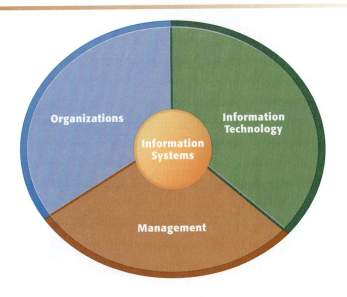

Using information systems effectively requires an understanding of the organization, management, and information technology shaping the systems. An information system creates value for the firm as an organizational and management solution to challenges posed by the environment.

Processing
Output
Feedback
Computer-based information systems (CBIS)

and their power to provide solutions to challenges and problems in the business environment. We refer to this broader understanding of information systems, which encompasses an understanding of the management and organizational dimensions of systems as well as the technical dimensions of systems, as **information systems literacy**. Information systems literacy includes a behavioural as well as a technical approach to studying information systems. **Computer literacy**, in contrast, focuses primarily on knowledge of information technology.

The field of **management information systems (MIS)** tries to achieve this broader information systems literacy. MIS deals with behavioural issues as well as technical issues surrounding the development, use, and impact of information systems used by managers and employees in the firm.

Let us examine each of the dimensions of information systems—organizations, management, and information technology.

Organizations Information systems are an integral part of organizations. Indeed, for some companies, such as credit reporting firms, without an information system, there would be no business. The key elements of an organization are its people, structure, business processes, politics, and culture. We introduce these components of organizations here and describe them in greater detail in Chapters 2 and 3.

Organizations have a structure that is composed of different levels and specialties. Their structures reveal a clear-cut division of labour. Authority and responsibility in a business firm are organized as a hierarchy, or a pyramid structure, of rising authority and responsibility. The upper levels of the hierarchy consist of managerial, professional, and technical employees while the lower levels consist of operational personnel.

Senior management makes long-range strategic decisions about products and services as well as ensures financial performance of the firm. **Middle management** carries out the programs and plans of senior management, and **operational management** is responsible for monitoring the daily activities of the business. **Knowledge workers**, such as engineers, scientists, or architects, design products or services and create new knowledge for the firm while **data workers**, such as secretaries or clerks, assist with paperwork at all levels of the firm. **Production or service workers** actually produce the product and deliver the service (see Figure 1-7).

Experts are employed and trained for different business functions. The major **business functions**, or specialized tasks performed by business organizations, consist of sales and marketing, manufacturing and production, finance and accounting, and human resources (see Table 1-1). Chapter 2 provides more detail on these business functions and the ways in which they are supported by information systems.

An organization coordinates work through its hierarchy and through its business processes, which we defined earlier in this chapter. Most organizations' business processes

Information systems literacy

Computer literacy

Management information systems (MIS)

Senior management

Middle management

Operational management

Knowledge workers

Data workers

Production or service workers

Business functions

FIGURE 1-7   *Levels in a firm*

Business organizations are hierarchies consisting of three principal levels: senior management, middle management, and operational management. Information systems serve each of these levels. Scientists and knowledge workers often work with middle management.

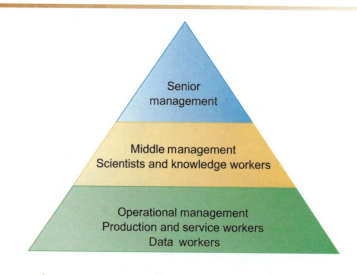

TABLE 1-1   *Major Business Functions*

FUNCTION	PURPOSE
Sales and marketing	Selling the organization's products and services
Manufacturing and production	Producing products and services
Finance and accounting	Managing the organization's financial assets and maintaining the organization's financial records
Human resources	Attracting, developing, and maintaining the organization's labour force; maintaining employee records

include formal rules that have been developed over a long time for accomplishing tasks. These rules guide employees in a variety of procedures, from writing an invoice to responding to customer complaints. Some of these business processes have been written down, but others are informal work practices, such as a requirement to return telephone calls from co-workers or customers, that are not formally documented. Information systems automate many business processes. For instance, how a customer receives credit or how a customer is billed is often determined by an information system that incorporates a set of formal business processes.

Each organization has a unique **culture**, or fundamental set of assumptions, values, and ways of doing things, that has been accepted by most of its members. You can see organizational culture at work by looking around your university or college. Some bedrock assumptions of university life are that professors know more than students, classes follow a regular schedule, and the reason students attend school is to learn.

Parts of an organization's culture can always be found embedded in its information systems. For instance, UPS's concern with placing service to the customer first is an aspect of its organizational culture that can be found in the company's package tracking systems, which we describe later in this section.

Different levels and specialties in an organization create different interests and points of view. These views often conflict over how the company should be run and how resources and rewards should be distributed. Conflict is the basis for organizational politics. Information systems come out of this cauldron of differing perspectives, conflicts, compromises, and agreements that are a natural part of all organizations. In Chapter 3, we examine these features of organizations and their role in the development of information systems in greater detail.

Management Management's job is to make sense out of the many situations faced by organizations, make decisions, and formulate action plans to solve organizational problems. Managers perceive business challenges in the environment; they set the organizational strategy for responding to those challenges; and they allocate the human and financial resources to coordinate the work and achieve success. Throughout, they must exercise responsible leadership. The business information systems described in this book reflect the hopes, dreams, and realities of real-world managers.

But managers must do more than manage what already exists. They must also create new products and services and even recreate the organization from time to time. A substantial part of management responsibility is creative work driven by new knowledge and information. Information technology can play a powerful role in helping managers design and deliver new products and services and redirecting and redesigning their organizations. Chapter 3 describes managerial activities, and Chapter 14 treats management decision making in detail.

Information Technology Information technology is one of many tools managers use to cope with change. **Computer hardware** is the physical equipment used for input, processing, output, and feedback activities in an information system. It consists of the following: computers of various sizes and shapes; various input, output, and storage devices; and telecommunications devices that link computers together.

Culture

Computer hardware

Computer software consists of the detailed, preprogrammed instructions that control and coordinate the computer hardware components in an information system. Chapter 5 describes the contemporary software and hardware platforms used by firms today in greater detail.

Data management technology consists of the software governing the organization of data on physical storage media. More detail on data organization and access methods can be found in Chapter 6.

Networking and telecommunications technology, consisting of both physical devices and software, links the various pieces of hardware and transfers data from one physical location to another. Computers and communications equipment can be connected in networks for sharing voice, data, images, sound, and video. A **network** links two or more computers to share data or resources, such as a printer.

The world's largest and most widely used network is the **Internet**. The Internet is a global "network of networks" that uses universal standards (described in Chapter 7) to connect millions of different networks with more than 350 million host computers in more than 200 countries around the world.

The Internet has created a new "universal" technology platform on which to build new products, services, strategies, and business models. This same technology platform has internal uses, providing the connectivity to link different systems and networks within the firm. Internal corporate networks based on Internet technology are called **intranets**. Private intranets extended to authorized users outside the organization are called **extranets**, and firms use such networks to coordinate their activities with other firms for making purchases, collaborating on design, and other interorganizational work. For most business firms today, using Internet technology is both a business necessity and a competitive advantage.

The **World Wide Web** is a service provided by the Internet that uses universally accepted standards for storing, retrieving, formatting, and displaying information in a page format on the Internet. Web pages contain text, graphics, animations, sound, and video and are linked to other Web pages. By clicking on highlighted words or buttons on a Web page, you can link to related pages to find additional information and links to other locations on the Web. The Web can serve as the foundation for new kinds of information systems such as UPS's Web-based package tracking system described in the following Window on Technology section.

All these technologies, along with the people required to run and manage them, represent resources that can be shared throughout the organization and constitute the firm's **information technology (IT) infrastructure**. The IT infrastructure provides the foundation, or *platform*, on which the firm can develop its specific information systems. Each organization must carefully design and manage its information technology infrastructure so that it has the set of technology services it needs for the work it wants to accomplish with information systems. Chapters 5 through 8 of this text examine the major technology components of information technology infrastructure and show how they all work together to create the technology platform for the organization.

Computer software

Data management technology

Networking and telecommunications technology

Network

Internet

Intranets

Extranets

World Wide Web

Information technology (IT) infrastructure

WINDOW ON TECHNOLOGY

Technology

UPS Competes Globally with Information Technology

United Parcel Service (UPS) is the world's largest air and ground package-distribution company. It started out in 1907 in a closet-sized basement office. Jim Casey and Claude Ryan—two teenagers from Seattle with two bicycles and one phone—promised the "best service and lowest rates." UPS has used this formula successfully for more than 90 years.

Today UPS delivers more than 14.1 million parcels and documents each day worldwide. The firm has been able to maintain leadership in small-package delivery services despite stiff competition from FedEx and Airborne Express (since purchased by DHL) by investing heavily in advanced information technology. During the past decade, UPS has poured billions of dollars into technology and systems to boost customer service while keeping costs low and streamlining its overall operations.

Using a handheld computer called a Delivery Information Acquisition Device (DIAD), a UPS driver can automatically capture customers' signatures along with pickup, delivery, and time-card information. The driver then places the DIAD into the UPS truck's vehicle adapter, an information-transmitting device that is connected to the cellular telephone network. Package tracking information is then transmitted to UPS computer network for storage and processing by UPS's main computers in Mahwah, New Jersey, and Alpharetta, Georgia. From there, the information can be accessed worldwide to provide proof of delivery to customers or to respond to customer queries.

Through its automated package tracking system, UPS can monitor packages throughout the delivery process. At various points along the route from sender to receiver, bar code devices scan shipping information on the package label; the information is then fed into the central computer. Customer service representatives can check the status of any package from desktop computers linked to the central computers and are able to respond immediately to inquiries from customers. UPS customers can also access this information from the company's Web site using their own computers or wireless devices, such as pagers and cell phones.

Anyone with a package to ship can access the UPS Web site to track packages, check delivery routes, calculate shipping rates, determine time in transit, and schedule a pickup. Businesses can use the Web site to arrange UPS shipments and bill the shipments to the company's UPS account number or to a credit card. The data collected at the UPS Web site are transmitted to the UPS central computer and then back to the customer after processing. UPS also provides tools that enable customers, such as Cisco Systems, to embed UPS functions, such as tracking and cost calculations, into their own Web sites so that they can track shipments without visiting the UPS site.

Information technology has helped UPS reinvent itself and keep growing. UPS has implemented a suite of custom-built software that uses operations research and mapping technology to optimize the way packages are loaded and delivered. Because UPS delivers 14 million small packages each day, the resulting information is cutting the distance that delivery trucks travel by more than 100 million miles each year.

UPS is now leveraging its decades of expertise managing its own global delivery network to manage logistics and supply-chain management for other companies. It has created a UPS Supply Chain Solutions division that provides a complete bundle of standardized services to subscribing companies at a fraction of what it would cost to develop their own systems

and infrastructure. These services include supply-chain design and management, freight forwarding, customs brokerage, mail services, multimodal transportation, and financial services, in addition to logistics services.

Adidas America, based in Portland, Oregon, is one of many companies benefiting from these services. Every three months, the company introduces as many as 10 000 new apparel items and 4000 new footwear items. It must handle orders for many thousands of retailers for these orders, and many of these orders are priority requests that must be fulfilled within one or two days. UPS Supply Chain Solutions consolidated what was previously handled by multiple third-party logistics providers into a single streamlined network outfitted with automated inventory and order fulfillment systems. By having UPS coordinate and manage distribution, Adidas America increased its order accuracy rate, boosted on-time deliveries, and improved customer service.

To Think About

1. What are the inputs, processing, and outputs of UPS's package tracking system?

2. What technologies are used by UPS? How are these technologies related to UPS's business strategy?

3. What problems do UPS's information systems solve? What would happen if these systems were not available?

MIS in Action

Explore the UPS Web site (www.ups.ca), and answer the following questions:

1. What kinds of information and services does the Web site provide for individuals, small businesses, and large businesses? List these services, and write several paragraphs describing one of them, such as customs and brokerage services or Automated Shipment Processing. Explain how you or your business would benefit from the service.

2. Explain how the Web site helps UPS achieve some or all of the strategic business objectives we described earlier in this chapter. What would be the impact on UPS's business if this Web site were not available?

Sources: "Adidas Goes for the Gold in Customer Service," www.ups.com, accessed June 14, 2006; United Parcel Service, *Round UPS*, Winter 2006; and Dave Barnes, "Delivering Corporate Citizenship," *Optimize*, September 2005.

The Window on Technology section describes some of the typical technologies used in CBISs today. UPS invests heavily in information systems technology to make its business more efficient and customer oriented. It uses an array of information technologies including bar-code scanning systems, wireless networks, large mainframe computers, handheld computers, the Internet, and many different pieces of software for tracking packages, calculating fees, maintaining customer accounts, and managing logistics.

Let us identify the organization, management, and information technology elements in the UPS package tracking system we have just described. The organization element anchors the package tracking system in UPS's sales and production functions (the main

Using a handheld computer called a Delivery Information Acquisition Device (DIAD), UPS drivers automatically capture customers' signatures along with pickup, delivery, and time-card information. UPS information systems use these data to track packages while they are being transported.

product of UPS is a service—package delivery). It specifies the required procedures for identifying packages with both sender and recipient information, taking inventory, tracking the packages en route, and providing package status reports for UPS customers and customer service representatives.

The system must also provide information to satisfy the needs of managers and workers. UPS drivers need to be trained in both package pickup and delivery procedures and in how to use the package tracking system so that they can work efficiently and effectively. UPS customers may need some training to use UPS in-house package tracking software or the UPS Web site.

UPS's management is responsible for monitoring service levels and costs and for promoting the company's strategy of combining low-cost and superior service. Management has decided to use automation to increase the ease of sending a package using UPS and checking its delivery status, thereby reducing delivery costs and increasing sales revenues.

The technology supporting this system consists of handheld computers, bar code scanners, wired and wireless communications networks, desktop computers, UPS's central computer, storage technology for the package delivery data, UPS in-house package tracking software, and software to access the Internet. The result is an information system solution to the business challenge of providing a high level of service with low prices in the face of mounting competition.

It Isn't Just Technology: A Business Perspective on Information Systems

Managers and business firms invest in information technology and systems because they provide real economic value to the business. The decision to develop or maintain an information system assumes that the returns on the investment will be superior to other investments in buildings, machines, or other assets. These superior returns will be expressed as increases in productivity, increases in revenues (which will increase the firm's stock market value), or perhaps superior long-term strategic positioning of the firm in certain markets (which produces superior revenues in the future).

We can see that from a business perspective, an information system is an important instrument for creating value for the firm. Information systems enable the firm to increase its revenue or decrease its costs by providing information that helps managers make better decisions or that improves the execution of business processes. For example, the information system for analyzing supermarket checkout data illustrated in Figure 1-4 can increase firm profitability by helping managers make better decisions on which products to stock and promote in retail supermarkets and as a result increase business value.

Every business has an information value chain, illustrated in Figure 1-8, in which raw data is systematically acquired and then transformed through various stages that add value to that information. The value of an information system to a business, as well as the decision to invest in any new information system, is, in large part, determined by the extent to which the system will lead to better management decisions, more efficient business processes, and higher firm profitability. Although there are other reasons why systems are developed, their primary purpose is to contribute to corporate value.

The business perspective calls attention to the organizational and managerial nature of information systems. An information system represents an organizational

FIGURE 1-8   *The business information value chain*

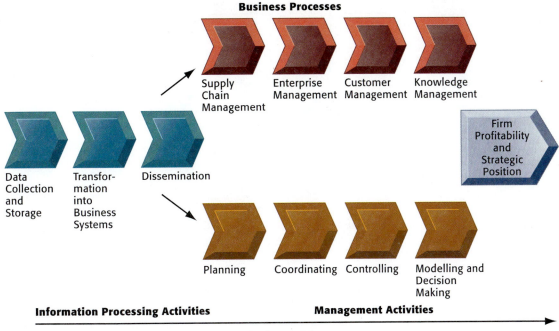

From a business perspective, information systems are part of a series of value-adding activities for acquiring, transforming, and distributing information that managers can use to improve decision making, enhance organizational performance, and, ultimately, increase firm profitability.

and management solution, based on information technology, to a challenge or problem posed by the environment. Every chapter in this book begins with a short case study that illustrates this concept. A diagram at the beginning of each chapter illustrates the relationship between a business challenge and resulting management and organizational decisions to use IT as a solution to that challenge. You can use this diagram as a starting point for analyzing any information system or information system problem you encounter.

Review the diagram at the beginning of the chapter that reflects this expanded definition of an information system. The diagram shows how Toyota's vehicle orders management system solves the business challenge presented by fierce competition and rapidly changing consumer preferences. The system creates value for Toyota by making its ordering and production processes more efficient and effective. The diagram also illustrates how management, technology, and organizational elements work together to create the system.

Complementary Assets: Organizational Capital and the Right Business Model

Awareness of the organizational and managerial dimensions of information systems can help us understand why some firms achieve better results from their information systems than others. Studies of returns from information technology investments show that there is considerable variation in the returns firms receive (see Figure 1-9). Some firms invest a great deal and receive a great deal (quadrant 2); others invest an equal amount and receive few returns (quadrant 4). Still other firms invest little and receive much (quadrant 1) while others invest little and receive little (quadrant 3). This suggests that investing in information technology does not by itself guarantee good returns. What accounts for this variation among firms?

Although, on average, investments in information technology produce returns far above those returned by other investments, there is considerable variation across firms.

Source: Erik Brynjolfsson and Lorin M. Hitt, "Beyond Computation: Information Technology, Organizational Transformation and Business Performance," *Journal of Economic Perspectives* 14, no. 4 (Fall 2000).

FIGURE 1-9 *Variation in returns on information technology investment*

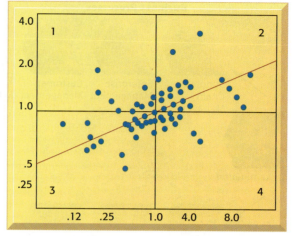

IT Capital Stock (relative to industry average)

Some firms fail to adopt the right business model that suits the new technology or seek to preserve an old business model that is doomed by new technology. For instance, recording label companies refused to change their old business model, which was based on physical music stores for distribution, rather than adopt a new online distribution model. As a result, online legal music sales are dominated not by record companies but by Apple Computer, a technology company.

In another example, Blockbuster has invested millions in new Internet sites and technologies to compete with Netflix, the mail-order video champion. But Blockbuster has refused to give up its physical distribution business model and maintains thousands of stores around the country. Blockbuster's share price has fallen with its earnings while Netflix continues to set revenue records. You can read more about Netflix and business models in the Chapter 3 ending case study.

Complementary assets are those assets required to derive value from a primary investment (Teece, 1998). For instance, to realize value from automobiles requires substantial complementary investments in highways, roads, gasoline stations, repair facilities, and a legal regulatory structure to set standards and control drivers.

Recent research on business information technology investment indicates that firms that support their technology investments with investments in complementary assets, such as new business models, new business processes, management behaviour, organizational culture, or training, receive superior returns while those firms failing to make these complementary investments receive less or no returns on their information technology investments (Brynjolfsson, 2003; Brynjolfsson and Hitt, 2000; Davern and Kauffman, 2000; Laudon, 1974). These investments in organization and management are also known as **organizational and management capital**.

Table 1-2 lists the major complementary investments that firms need to make to realize value from their information technology investments. Some of this investment involves tangible assets, such as buildings, machinery, and tools. However, the value of investments in information technology depends to a large extent on complementary investments in management and organization.

Key organizational complementary investments are a supportive business culture that values efficiency and effectiveness, an appropriate business model, efficient business processes, decentralization of authority, highly distributed decision rights, and a strong information system (IS) development team.

Important managerial complementary assets are strong senior management support for change, incentive systems that monitor and reward individual innovation, an emphasis on teamwork and collaboration, training programs, and a management culture that values flexibility and knowledge.

Complementary assets

Organizational and management capital

TABLE 1-2 *Complementary Social, Managerial, and Organizational Assets Required to Optimize Returns from Information Technology Investments*

ORGANIZATIONAL ASSETS	Supportive organizational culture that values efficiency and effectiveness
	Efficient business processes
	Appropriate business model
	Decentralized authority
	Distributed decision-making rights
	Strong IS development team
MANAGERIAL ASSETS	Strong senior management support for technology investment and change
	Incentives for management innovation
	Teamwork and collaborative work environments
	Training programs to enhance management decision skills
	Management culture that values flexibility and knowledge-based decision making
SOCIAL ASSETS	The Internet and telecommunications infrastructure
	IT-enriched educational programs raising labour force computer literacy
	Standards (both government and private sector)
	Laws and regulations creating fair, stable market environments
	Technology and service firms in adjacent markets to assist implementation

Important social investments (not made by the firm but by the society at large, other firms, governments, and other key market actors) are the Internet and the supporting Internet culture, educational systems, network and computing standards, regulations and laws, and the presence of technology and service firms.

Throughout the book, we emphasize a framework of analysis that considers technology, management, and organizational assets and their interactions. Perhaps the single most important theme in the book, reflected in case studies and exercises, is that managers need to consider the broader organization and management dimensions of information systems to understand current problems as well as to derive substantial above-average returns from their information technology investments. As you will see throughout the text, firms that can address these related dimensions of the IT investment are, on average, richly rewarded.

1.3 Contemporary Approaches to Information Systems

The study of information systems is a multidisciplinary field. No single theory or perspective dominates. Figure 1-10 illustrates the major disciplines that contribute problems, issues, and solutions in the study of information systems. In general, the field can be divided into technical and behavioural approaches. Information systems are sociotechnical systems. Though they are composed of machines, devices, and "hard" physical technology, they require substantial social, organizational, and intellectual investments to make them work properly.

Technical Approach

The technical approach to information systems emphasizes mathematically based models to study information systems as well as the physical technology and formal capabilities of these

FIGURE 1-10   *Contemporary approaches to information systems*

The study of information systems deals with issues and insights contributed from technical and behavioural disciplines.

systems. The disciplines that contribute to the technical approach are computer science, management science, and operations research.

Computer science is concerned with establishing theories of computability, methods of computation, and methods of efficient data storage and access. Management science emphasizes the development of models for decision making and management practices. Operations research focuses on mathematical techniques for optimizing selected parameters of organizations, such as transportation, inventory control, and transaction costs.

Behavioural Approach

An important part of the information systems field is concerned with behavioural issues that arise in the development and long-term maintenance of information systems. Issues such as strategic business integration, design, implementation, utilization, and management cannot be explored usefully with the models used in the technical approach. Other behavioural disciplines contribute important concepts and methods.

For instance, sociologists study information systems with an eye toward how groups and organizations shape the development of systems and also how systems affect individuals, groups, and organizations. Psychologists study information systems with an interest in how human decision makers perceive and use formal information. Economists study information systems with an interest in understanding the production of digital goods, the dynamics of digital markets, and understanding how new information systems change the control and cost structures within the firm.

The behavioural approach does not ignore technology. Indeed, information systems technology is often the stimulus for a behavioural problem or issue. But the focus of this approach is generally not on technical solutions. Instead, it concentrates on changes in attitudes, management and organizational policy, and behaviour.

Approach of This Text: Sociotechnical Systems

Throughout this book, you will find a rich story with four main actors: suppliers of hardware and software (the technologists); business firms making investments and seeking to obtain value from the technology; managers and employees seeking to achieve business value (and other goals); and the contemporary legal, social, and cultural context (the firm's environment). Together these actors produce what we call *management information systems*.

The study of management information systems (MIS) arose in the 1970s to focus on the use of CBISs in business firms and government agencies (Laudon, 1974; Davis and Olson, 1985). MIS combines the work of computer science, management science, and operations research with a practical orientation toward developing system solutions to real-world problems and managing information technology resources. It is also concerned with behavioural issues surrounding the development, use, and impact of information systems, which are typically discussed in the fields of sociology, economics, and psychology.

Our experience as academics and practitioners leads us to believe that no single approach effectively captures the reality of information systems. The successes and failures of information are rarely all technical or all behavioural. Our best advice to students is to understand the perspectives of many disciplines. Indeed, the challenge and excitement of the information systems field is that it requires an appreciation and tolerance of many different approaches.

The view we adopt in this book is best characterized as the **sociotechnical view** of systems. In this view, optimal organizational performance is achieved by jointly optimizing both the social and technical systems used in production.

Adopting a sociotechnical systems perspective helps to avoid a purely technological approach to information systems. For instance, the fact that information technology is rapidly declining in cost and growing in power does not necessarily or easily translate into productivity enhancement or bottom-line profits. The fact that a firm has recently installed an enterprise-wide financial reporting system does not necessarily mean that it will be used or used effectively. Likewise, the fact that a firm has recently introduced new business procedures and processes does not necessarily mean employees will be more productive in the absence of investments in new information systems to enable those processes.

In this book, we stress the need to optimize the firm's performance as a whole. Both the technical and behavioural components need attention. This means that technology must be changed and designed in such a way as to fit organizational and individual needs. Sometimes, the technology may have to be "de-optimized" to accomplish this fit. For instance, mobile phone users adapt that technology to their personal needs, and as a result, manufacturers quickly seek to adjust the technology to conform with user expectations (Lee, 2003; Sawyer and Allen, 2003; Bautsch et al., 2001). Organizations and individuals must also be changed through training, learning, and planned organizational change to allow the technology to operate and prosper (Lamb et al., 2004; Orlikowski and Baroudi, 1991; Orlikowski, 1992). Figure 1-11 illustrates this process of mutual adjustment in a sociotechnical system.

Sociotechnical view

FIGURE 1-11 *A sociotechnical perspective on information systems*

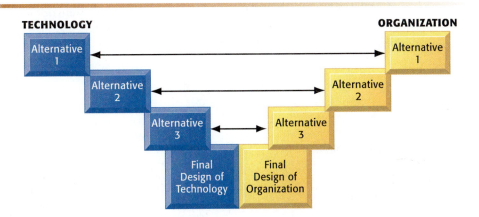

In a sociotechnical perspective, the performance of a system is optimized when both the technology and the organization mutually adjust to each other until a satisfactory fit is obtained.

Summary

1. *Explain why information systems are so essential in business today.*

   Information systems are a foundation for conducting business today. In many industries, survival and even existence is difficult without extensive use of information technology. Information systems have become essential for helping organizations operate in a global economy. Organizations are trying to become more competitive and efficient by transforming themselves into digital firms where nearly all core business processes and relationships with customers, suppliers, and employees are digitally enabled. Businesses today use information systems to achieve six major objectives: operational excellence; new products, services, and business models; customer and supplier intimacy; improved decision making; competitive advantage; and day-to-day survival.

2. *Define an information system from both a technical and a business perspective.*

   From a technical perspective, an information system collects, stores, and disseminates information from an organization's environment and internal operations to support organizational functions and decision making, communication, coordination, control, analysis, and visualization. Information systems transform raw data into useful information through four basic activities: input, processing, output, and feedback. From a business perspective, an information system provides a solution to a problem or challenge facing a firm and provides real economic value to the business.

3. *Identify and describe the three dimensions of information systems.*

   An information system represents a combination of management, organization, and information technology elements. The management dimension of information systems involves leadership, strategy, and management behaviour. The information technology dimension consists of computer hardware, software, data management technology, and networking and telecommunications technology (including the Internet). The organization dimension of information systems involves the organization's hierarchy, functional specialties, business processes, culture, and political interest groups.

4. *Assess the complementary assets required for information technology to provide value to a business.*

   An information system is a set of value-adding activities for acquiring, transforming, and distributing information to improve management decision making, enhance organizational performance, and, ultimately, increase firm profitability. Information technology cannot provide this value unless it is accompanied by supportive changes in organization and management, called complementary assets. These complementary assets include new business models, new business processes, a supportive organizational culture, incentives for management support and innovation, training, and social assets such as standards, laws and regulations, and telecommunications infrastructure. Firms that make appropriate investments in these complementary assets, also known as organizational and management capital, receive superior returns on their information technology investments.

5. *Identify and describe contemporary approaches to the study of information systems, and distinguish between computer literacy and information systems literacy.*

   The study of information systems deals with issues and insights contributed from technical and behavioural disciplines. The disciplines that contribute to the technical approach are computer science, management science, and operations research. The disciplines contributing to the behavioural approach are psychology, sociology, and economics.

   Information systems literacy requires an understanding of the organizational and management dimensions of information systems as well as the technical dimensions addressed by computer literacy. Information systems literacy draws on both technical and behavioural approaches to studying information systems. The field of MIS promotes information systems literacy by combining all these disciplines with a practical orientation toward developing system solutions to real-world problems, and managing information technology resources.

Key Terms

Business functions, 14
Business model, 9
Business processes, 6
Complementary assets, 20
Computer-based information systems (CBIS), 13
Computer hardware, 15
Computer literacy, 14
Computer software, 16

Culture, 15
Data, 11
Data management technology, 16
Data workers, 14
Digital firm, 6
Extranets, 16
Feedback, 13
Information, 11

Information system, 11
Information systems literacy, 14
Information technology (IT), 11
Information technology (IT) infrastructure, 16
Input, 12
Internet, 16
Intranets, 16

Review Questions

1. *Describe three ways in which information systems are transforming business.*

2. *Describe the qualities of a digital firm. Why are digital firms so powerful?*

3. *List and describe six reasons why information systems are so important for business today.*

4. *What is an information system? What activities does it perform?*

5. *What is the difference between data and information?*

6. *What is information systems literacy? How does it differ from computer literacy?*

7. *List and describe the organizational, management, and technology dimensions of information systems.*

8. *What are the Internet and the World Wide Web? How have they changed the role played by information systems in organizations?*

9. *What is the purpose of an information system from a business perspective? What role does it play in the business information value chain?*

10. *Why do some firms obtain greater value from their information systems than others? What role do complementary assets and organizational and management capital play?*

11. *Distinguish between a behavioural and a technical approach to information systems in terms of the questions asked and the answers provided. What major disciplines contribute to an understanding of information systems?*

Discussion Questions

1. *Information systems are too important to be left to computer specialists. Do you agree? Why or why not?*

2. *It has been said that Toyota's most valuable asset is "The Toyota Way." Discuss the implications of this statement for the role of information systems in that company.*

3. *Read the Learning Track Module of Nicholas Carr's article on whether information systems matter or not. Discuss whether or not you think that information systems are* mere commodities or utilities, such as electricity or water, or whether they add value and how.

4. *How has the advent of online computing influenced your school? Think of specific information systems that are used by your school. How much computer literacy does your school require of its students? Its employees? Why are these requirements mandated for most (certainly not all) jobs?*

Teamwork: Analyzing a Business System

In a group with three or four classmates, find a description in a computer or business magazine of an information system used by an organization. Look for information about the company on the Web to gain further insight into the company, and prepare a brief description of the business.

Describe the system you have selected in terms of its inputs, processes, and outputs and in terms of its organization, management, and technology features and the importance of the system to the company. If possible, use electronic presentation software to present your analysis to the class.

Learning Track Module

How Much Does IT Matter? In May 2003, Nicholas Carr, an editor at *Harvard Business Review*, wrote an article titled "IT Doesn't Matter." This and subsequent articles with a similar theme created a vigorous debate about the potential and actual role of information technology and systems in creating business strategic advantage. If you would like to participate in this debate and learn more about it, you will find a Learning Track Module on this topic at MyMISLab site for this chapter. You can also find more information about the current state of this debate on the Web. Just Google "IT Doesn't Matter" and read several rebuttals, one of the best being an article by Robert M. Metcalfe, inventor of Ethernet, a major networking technology, called "Why I.T. Matters," *MIT Technology Review*, January 2004. It's free at Technologyreview.com on the Internet. IT really does matter!

For online exercises, please visit www.pearsoned.ca/mymislab.

HANDS-ON MIS   Application Exercises

The projects in this section give you hands-on experience developing a knowledge management systems strategy for a real-world company, using expert system or spreadsheet tools to create a simple expert system and using intelligent agents to research products for sale on the Web.

Understanding Information System Requirements

Dirt Bikes CANADA

Software skills: Presentation software
Business skills: Management analysis and information system recommendations

How do you know what information systems are really needed by a business and which are the most important? How should a company's structure or culture affect the development and use of information systems?

The Dirt Bikes Canada case describes a real-world company that makes dirt bikes—a kind of motorcycle that is used off-road and often raced in competition. This case appears in every chapter with different assignments linked to the chapter contents. There is a complete description of the company, including its organizational structure, culture, management, and goals on MyMISLab. The case contains spreadsheets and databases that complete the description of the company. Throughout the text, you will be asked to act as either a consultant or employee of Dirt Bikes Canada to help the company make decisions about its products and services, marketing, and customer service, as well as its financing and information system. An illustration of the company's organization chart is on the next page.

Dirt Bikes Canada's management has asked you to prepare a management analysis of the company to help it assess the firm's current situation and future plans. Review Dirt Bikes' company history, organization chart, products and services, and sales and marketing in the Introduction to Dirt Bikes Canada found on MyMISLab. Then prepare a report that addresses these questions:

1. What are the company's goals and culture?

2. What products and services does Dirt Bikes Canada provide? How many types of products and services are available to customers? How does Dirt Bikes Canada sell its products?

3. How many employees are managers, production workers, or knowledge or information workers? Are there levels of management?

4. What kinds of information systems and technologies would be the most important for a company such as Dirt Bikes Canada? (Optional) Use electronic presentation software to summarize for management your analysis of Dirt Bikes Canada's performance.

Improving Decision Making: Using Databases to Analyze Sales Trends

Software skills: Database querying and reporting
Business skills: Sales trend analysis

You can find out how information systems improve management decision making in this exercise. Rather than guessing or relying on estimates and experience, managers today rely on information stored in databases. In this project, you will start out with raw transactional sales data and use Microsoft Access database software to develop queries and reports that help managers make better decisions about product pricing, sales promotions, and inventory replenishment.

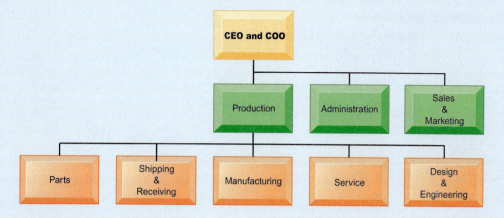

Dirt Bikes Canada Organization Chart

On MyMISLab for Chapter 1, you will find a Store and Regional Sales Database developed in Microsoft Access. A part of the database is shown below. The database contains raw data on weekly store sales of computer equipment in various sales regions. You will be using Access to manage the data and turn it into useful business information.

The database includes fields for record number, store identification number, sales region, item number, item description, unit price, units sold, and the weekly sales period when the sales were made.

Develop several reports and queries to make this information more useful for running the business. Sales and

production managers want answers to the following questions:

1. Which products should be restocked?
2. Which stores and sales regions would benefit from a promotional campaign and additional marketing?
3. When (what time of year) should products be offered at full price, and when should discounts be used?

You can easily modify the database table to find and report your answers. Print your reports and results of queries.

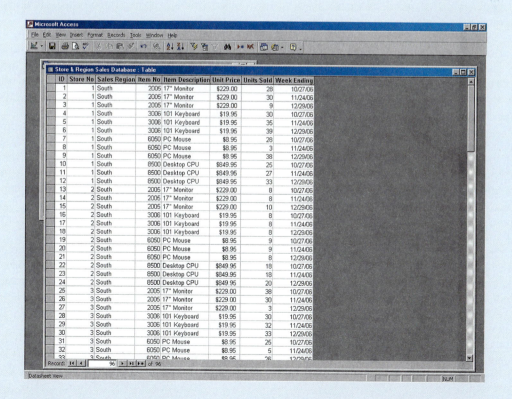

Achieving Operational Excellence:
Using Internet Software to Budget for Shipping Costs

Software skills: Internet-based software
Business skills: Information-driven decision making and cost management

The Internet provides some marvellous tools for driving down business costs both because of the powerful Internet software tools available and because vendors compete with one another in a transparent electronic marketplace. The result is lower costs to businesses that use these services.

In this exercise, you will use the same online software tools that businesses use to calculate and budget for shipping costs. Using these tools, you will choose the best shipper for your business. "Best" does not necessarily mean lowest cost but includes a consideration of other factors, such as scheduling, ease of use, and compatibility with your business schedule.

Assume you are the shipping clerk of a small firm that prints, binds, and ships popular books for a mid-level publisher. Your production facilities are located in Kitchener, Ontario (postal code N2M 2Y4). Your customers' warehouses are located in Calgary, Alberta (T2E 0B3); Halifax, Nova Scotia (B3P 2L5); Richmond, British Columbia (V7E 3M1); Montréal, Québec (H1Y 2G5); and St. John's, Newfoundland (A1E 2X1). The production facility operates 250 days per year. Your books are usually shipped in one of two package sizes:

- A: 23 cm tall by 33 cm long by 43 cm wide, weighing 20 kg
- B: 25 cm tall by 15 cm long by 30 cm wide, weighing 7 kg

Every day, the company ships about four of the A boxes and about eight of the B boxes to each warehouse.

What is the best shipper for your company? Go on the Web and compare three shippers, such as Federal Express (**www.fedex.ca**), UPS (**www.ups.ca**), and Canada Post (**www.canadapost.ca**). Consider not only costs but also such issues as delivery speed, pickup schedules, drop-off locations, tracking ability, and ease of use of the Web site. Which service did you select? Explain why in a slide presentation.

CASE STUDY | How the Royal Canadian Golf Association Cut Costs and Improved Customer Service

The Royal Canadian Golf Association (RCGA) supports more than 375 000 members at 1650 golf clubs across Canada and supervises more than 20 golf tournaments annually. The RCGA publishes the Rules of Golf and handicapping and course ratings. It supports turfgrass and environmental research, the Canadian Golf Hall of Fame and Museum, and Canada's junior golf program. Golf tournaments supervised by the RCGA include the Canadian Open, the CN Canadian Women's Open, and six regional and 10 amateur tournaments along with the CN Canadian Women's Tour. The RCGA was founded in 1895 and has very traditional roots and culture.

Until 2003, the RCGA used a local personal computer located at national headquarters in Oakville, Ontario, to manage all its tournaments. After organizers entered players' names, the system would generate the foursomes and choose their starting times for each tournament. If there were delayed starting times, or changes—such as the year Tiger Woods dropped out of the Canadian Open the week before the tournament—changes could only be made in Oakville on the local computer. Brent McLaughlin, RCGA director of amateur competitions, explains: "Anything, from a player who drops out due to bad weather, can affect a tournament. With our previous system, nothing was live, and we had no ability to accommodate changes on-site, where the action was taking place." Players had to apply by filling out paper forms and either faxing or mailing them to the Oakville office, where each application was entered into the system by hand.

Realizing the lack of efficiency in this system, the RCGA contracted with Martron, Inc., which has offices in Kitchener, Ontario, and Winnipeg, Manitoba. Meanwhile, the RCGA realized that its Web site was also inadequate and wanted a more sophisticated, user-friendly site that would be easy to update and search.

"Our first step was to take the scores from a local application to a Web site. Then we proposed the development of a Web-based application," says a senior account manager with Martron, Inc. Using the .NET framework (discussed in Chapter 5), the new application allows the RCGA to manage its tournaments from a single, Web-based application. A live scoring module permits the RCGA to upload players' scores to the Web site in real time. Kyocera smart phones can be used to access the application and upload scores from the golf course.

The RCGA can make changes to the tournament on the fly. For example, organizers can cancel a round due to a rain delay and reschedule the players, posting the new starting times on the Web in real time. "We now have the ability to be in Newfoundland and operate a tournament in Vancouver using this system and make changes accordingly," says McLaughlin. The RCGA can now also offer online player registration, enabling immediacy in correspondence and response between players and the RCGA. All this results in lower costs and better player and fan service.

"From a customer service standpoint, the answers are immediate now. Everything has been streamlined, and it filters all the way through the process, down to our volunteers. We employ approximately 12 000 volunteers over the course of a year, and because they all have access to the application via our Web site, they all have the most current data, at all times," says McLaughlin.

The system also cut, by more than half, printing and mailing costs for entry forms that would be mailed out. Now the entry forms are available on the Web. Overall, the new Web site for the RCGA is very user-friendly, with easy-to-find information. The RCGA also hosts other Web sites, such as those devoted to golfers who travel in Canada (**www.rcganetworktravel.org**), to junior golfers (**www.future-links.org**), and to RCGA member clubs and their members (**www.rcganetwork.org**). Each of these

Web sites stands on its own but is run by the RCGA, which has developed the capability to develop and manage these sophisticated Web sites.

Sources: "Stephen Ross Fired as RCGA Executive Director," March 9, 2007, **www.fairwaysgolf.ca/news.php?id=290&what=news**, accessed June 1, 2007; "RCGA Case Study," April 21, 2005, **www.martron.com**, accessed June 1, 2007; and "RCGA Cuts Costs and Improves Customer Service with Microsoft® .NET-based Online Tournament Program," **www.microsoft.com/canada/casestudies/rcga.mspx?pf=true**, accessed June 1, 2007.

CASE STUDY QUESTIONS

1. Why did the RCGA invest in information technology?

2. What were the disadvantages of the old system?

3. What do you think might have been the obstacles to overcome in developing the new tournament application?

4. How do you think the new Web sites help the RCGA to fulfill its mission and strategy?

How Businesses Use Information Systems

After completing this chapter, you will be able to do the following:

1. Define and describe business processes and their relationship to information systems.

2. Describe the information systems supporting the major business functions: sales and marketing, manufacturing and production, finance and accounting, and human resources.

3. Evaluate the role played by systems serving the various levels of management in a business and their relationship to one another.

4. Explain how enterprise applications and intranets promote business process integration and improve organizational performance.

5. Assess the role of the information systems function in a business.

OPENING CASE | Information Systems Join the Tupperware Party

Earl Tupper patented the airtight Tupper seal for food storage containers in 1947, but it was not catching on in retail stores. He turned to an engaging single mother, Brownie Wise, to help him sell his Tupperware through home demonstration parties. The strategy worked: Tupperware grew into a $1.3 billion company that sells through home parties using an independent sales force of one million members.

A Tupperware party begins every two seconds somewhere in the world.

In 2005, Tupperware faced another challenge. The company changed its North American operations from a distributorship model to a multilevel compensation structure. Tupperware's North American sales force mushroomed from three levels of compensation (sales consultant, manager, and distributor) to a dozen levels. Sales consultants are paid a commission for their own sales plus a smaller commission based on sales of consultants whom they recruited to the business.

As a sales consultant became successful and recruited more people to the business, that person was also responsible for her paperwork, plus paperwork from the people she had recruited to her downline sales team. There was not enough time left for the really important job of selling and recruiting. Tupperware's order entry system was not able to handle peak demand during sales promotions and busy times of the year. To support growth and improve business processes for both the sales force and corporate staff, Tupperware needed a system that

could handle an additional 5000 users each month, send e-mail messages to 50 000 recipients at a time, and allow restricted access to documents based on an employee's job position in the company.

In 2004, Tupperware began implementing an integrated Web-based order management system called My.Tupperware.ca in Canada that relieves distributors from the task of entering the orders from everyone they recruited. Now each sales consultant enters his or her own orders.

The Web-based system serves as a portal that integrates with Tupperware's existing systems so that authorized users can access information from related systems with a single sign-on. Different groups in the company, such as sales promotion, training, and Web support, have tools to publish and retire Web content for specific audiences in the company on their own without requiring help from the company's information systems staff. The system also streamlines communications among corporate managers, support staff, and sales consultants and provides better support to sales consultants in promoting product sales, recruiting new sales consultants, and managing downline sales teams.

The portal provides four levels of access. There is a home page accessible to consumers, which provides information on Tupperware products and increases brand awareness. A second level gives all

sales consultants access to order entry, e-mail, a calendar, training materials, and list functions. A third level offers sales consultants, who wish to pay a fee, additional marketing and promotional features and tools to create their own e-commerce Web sites linked to My.Tupperware.ca. The highest level lets users perform additional promotional activities and links to higher compensation opportunities. Any sales consultant can choose any level of accessibility she wishes.

Tupperware chose Oracle Collaboration Suite and Oracle Portal software as the platform for the system because they enabled the company to integrate functions for data management, financial systems, calendar, and e-mail into a single secure environment that could scale up to meet future growth in Tupperware sales and sales consultants. The company had also been using other Oracle software for a decade, so it felt comfortable with Oracle products.

Tupperware finished rolling out My.Tupperware.com and My.Tupperware.ca to 50 000 North American users in the final months of 2004. Reaction to the system has been very positive. Tupperware is now enhancing the system to provide online Web conferencing and voice and text messaging.

Sources: Molly Rose Teuke, "Sealing Success," *Profit Magazine*, February 2006; **www.tupperware.ca**, accessed May 8, 2007; and **www.tupperware.com**, accessed June 21, 2006.

Tupperware's experience illustrates how much companies today rely on information systems to run their businesses and drive growth and profitability. Tupperware has a unique business model based on selling food storage and preparation products at home parties using a large independent sales force. But its information systems were inadequate for supporting its new multilevel compensation structure and continuing growth.

The chapter-opening Business Challenges diagram calls attention to important points raised by this case and this chapter. Tupperware's old business model was outdated. When it changed its business model, moving toward a multilevel compensation structure, its sales agents were overwhelmed with paperwork. Tupperware management identified an opportunity to use information systems to solve this challenge and greatly improve business performance. Tupperware needed to change its technology, management, and organizational processes. The Oracle software made it possible to support additional levels of Tupperware consultants and gave individual consultants tools to process their own orders and set up personal e-commerce sites. To make the system effective, Tupperware had to revise its business processes for placing orders and compensating consultants. Tupperware's new ordering and compensation systems have increased employee productivity and provided a new channel for reaching customers on the Web.

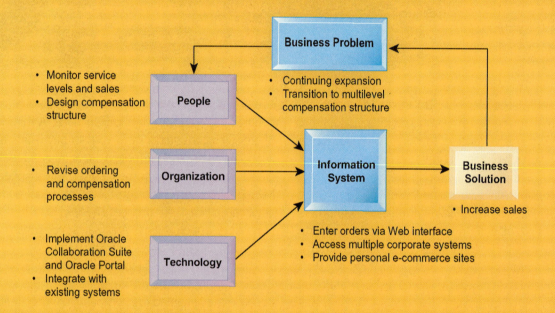

HEADS UP

This chapter provides you with a quick overview of the significant role of information systems in a business. You will learn about the different types of information systems used by businesses, including systems based on the Internet, and how these systems support the firm's core business processes. Many of the topics introduced here are covered in greater detail in later chapters. The basic information systems concepts introduced here prepare you for later chapters.

- If your career is in finance and accounting, you will be working with systems that keep track of your company's assets, fund flows, and overall financial performance.

- If your career is in human resources, information systems will help you develop staffing requirements; identify potential new employees; maintain employee records; track employee training, skills, and job performance; and design appropriate plans for employee compensation and career development.

- If your career is in information systems, you will be responsible for supplying and overseeing the hardware, software, and other technologies used by the various types of systems in organizations.

- If your career is in manufacturing and production, information systems will help you solve problems related to the planning, development, and delivery of products and services and control the flow of production.

- If your career is in sales and marketing, information systems will help you promote products, contact customers, track sales, identify profitable customers, provide ongoing service and support, and analyze the performance of the firm's sales staff.

2.1 Business Processes and Information Systems

In order to operate, businesses must deal with many different pieces of information about suppliers, customers, employees, invoices and payments, and of course, their products and services. They must organize work activities that use this information to operate efficiently and enhance the overall performance of the firm. Information systems make it possible for firms to manage all their information, make better decisions, and improve the execution of their business processes.

Business Processes

Information systems are all about improving business processes, which lie at the very heart of a business. So it is important to understand just what is meant by "business processes."

Business processes, which we introduced in Chapter 1, refer to the manner in which work is organized, coordinated, and focused to produce a valuable product or service. Business processes are workflows of material, information, and knowledge—sets of activities. Business processes also refer to the unique ways in which organizations coordinate work, information, and knowledge and the ways in which management chooses to coordinate work. Every business can be seen as a collection of business processes. Some of these processes are part of larger encompassing processes.

For example, almost every business has a way to hire employees. The process of hiring employees is a business process in the sense that it is a set of activities that a firm uses to hire new employees. The business process of hiring can be broken down into a number of different steps such as placing advertisements, contacting employment agencies, collecting resumes, reviewing resumes, interviewing candidates, ranking candidates, making the employment decision, and enrolling employees in employment systems such as payroll, health, and pension. In some businesses, this process can be slow and inefficient while in others it can be swift and highly efficient. One of the major purposes of information systems is to enable highly efficient business processes.

To a large extent, the performance of a business firm depends on how well its business processes are designed and coordinated. A company's business processes can be a source of competitive strength if they enable the company to innovate or to execute better than its rivals. Business processes can also be liabilities if they are based on outdated ways of working that impede organizational responsiveness and efficiency.

Many business processes are tied to a specific functional area. **Business functions** are specialized tasks performed in a business organization, including manufacturing and production, sales and marketing, finance and accounting, and human resources. For example, the sales and marketing function would be responsible for identifying customers, and the

Business functions

TABLE 2-1 *Functional Business Processes*

FUNCTIONAL AREA	BUSINESS PROCESS
Manufacturing and production	Assembling the product Checking for quality Producing bills of materials
Sales and marketing	Identifying customers Making customers aware of the product Selling the product
Finance and accounting	Paying creditors Creating financial statements Managing cash accounts
Human resources	Hiring employees Evaluating employees' job performance Enrolling employees in benefits plans

human resources function would be responsible for hiring employees. Table 2-1 describes some typical business processes for each of the functional areas of business.

Other business processes cross many different functional areas and require coordination across departments. For instance, consider the seemingly simple business process of fulfilling a customer order (see Figure 2-1). Initially, the sales department would receive the sales order. The order will pass first to accounting to ensure the customer can pay for the order either by a credit verification or request for immediate payment prior to shipping. Once the customer credit is established, the production department has to pull the product from inventory or produce the product. Then the product will need to be shipped (and this may require working with a logistics firm, such as UPS, DHL, or FedEx). A bill or invoice will then have to be generated by the accounting department, and a notice will be sent to the customer indicating that the product has shipped. Sales will have to be notified of the shipment and prepare to support the customer by answering calls or fulfilling warranty claims.

While at first appearing to be a simple process, fulfilling an order turns out to be a very complicated series of business processes that require the close coordination of major

FIGURE 2-1 *The order fulfillment process*

Fulfilling a customer order involves a complex set of steps that requires the close coordination of the sales, accounting, and manufacturing functions.

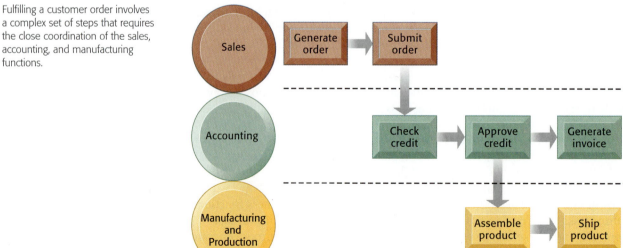

functional groups in a firm. Moreover, efficiently performing all these steps in the order fulfillment process requires a great deal of information. The required information must flow rapidly within the firm, with business partners, such as delivery firms, and with the customer. Information systems make this possible.

How Information Technology Enhances Business Processes: Efficiency and Transformation

Exactly how do information systems enhance business processes? Primarily in two ways: increasing the efficiency of existing processes and enabling entirely new processes that are capable of transforming the business. Information systems automate many steps in business processes that were formerly performed manually, such as checking a client's credit, or generating an invoice and shipping order. But today, information technology can do much more. New technology can actually change the flow of information, making it possible for many more people to access and share information, replacing sequential steps with tasks that can be performed simultaneously in parallel, and eliminating delays in decision making. In other words, information can enable entirely new business processes. It can even transform the way the business works and drive entirely new business models. Ordering a book online from Amazon.ca or downloading a music track from iTunes.ca are entirely new business processes based on new business models that would be inconceivable without information technology. Both iTunes and Amazon represent business transformations.

That is why it is so important to pay close attention to business processes, both in your information systems course and in your future career. By analyzing business processes in your firm, you can achieve a very clear understanding of how your business actually works. For instance, by analyzing the customer service process, you will learn how long it takes to answer a customer request for service, how many steps are involved, how many people are involved, and how much it costs. Moreover, by conducting a business process analysis, you will also begin to understand how to change the business to make it more efficient or effective. Throughout this book, we examine business processes with a view to understanding how they might be changed, or replaced, by using information technology to achieve greater efficiency, innovation, and customer service.

2.2   Types of Business Information Systems

Now that you understand business processes, it is time to look more closely at the many types of information systems that support the business processes of the firm. Because a business may have tens or even hundreds of different business processes, and because there are different people, specialties, and levels in an organization, there are different kinds of systems. No single system can provide all the information an organization needs. In fact, large- and medium-size firms have thousands of computer programs and hundreds of different systems. Even small firms have a collection of different systems: a system for conducting e-mail campaigns to customers, a system for monitoring advertisements placed on Google, a system for keeping track of basic sales transactions, a system for keeping track of vendors, and so forth. At first glance, it can be difficult to comprehend all the different systems in a business and even more difficult to understand how they relate to one another.

We attempt to describe this complex situation by looking at all these different systems from two different perspectives: a functional perspective identifying systems by their major business function, and a constituency perspective that identifies systems in terms of the major organizational groups that they serve.

TABLE 2-2 *Examples of Sales and Marketing Information Systems*

SYSTEM	DESCRIPTION	GROUPS SERVED
Order processing	Enter, process, and track orders	Operational management and employees
Pricing analysis	Determine prices for products and services	Middle management
Sales trend forecasting	Prepare five-year sales forecasts	Senior management

Systems from a Functional Perspective

We will start by describing systems using a functional perspective because this is how you will likely first encounter systems in a business. For instance, if you are a marketing major and take a job in marketing, you will be working on the job first with marketing information systems. If you are an accounting major, you will be working with accounting and financial systems first. From a historical perspective, functional systems were the first kinds of systems developed by business firms. These systems were located in specific departments, such as accounting, marketing and sales, production, and human resources. Let us take a close look at systems from this functional perspective.

Sales and Marketing Systems The sales and marketing function is responsible for selling the organization's products or services. Marketing is concerned with identifying the customers for the firm's products or services, determining what customers need or want, planning and developing products and services to meet their needs, and advertising and promoting these products and services. Sales is concerned with contacting customers, selling the products and services, taking orders, and following up on sales. These activities can be thought of as business processes. **Sales and marketing information systems,** such as the Tupperware applications described earlier in this chapter, support these business processes.

Table 2-2 shows that information systems are used in sales and marketing in a number of ways. Sales and marketing systems help senior management monitor trends affecting new products and sales opportunities, support planning for new products and services, and monitor the performance of competitors. Sales and marketing systems aid middle management by supporting market research and by analyzing advertising and promotional campaigns, pricing decisions, and sales performance. Sales and marketing systems assist operational management and employees in locating and contacting prospective customers, tracking sales, processing orders, and providing customer service support.

Figure 2-2 illustrates a sales information system used by retailers, such as The Bay or Canadian Tire. Point-of-sale devices (usually handheld scanners at the checkout counter) capture data about each item sold, which update the sales system's figures about sales and send data about items sold to related systems dealing with items remaining in inventory and with production. These businesses use this information to track which items have been sold, to determine sales revenue, and to identify hot-selling items and other sales trends.

Manufacturing and Production Systems The manufacturing and production function is responsible for actually producing the firm's goods and services. Manufacturing and production systems deal with the planning, development, and maintenance of production facilities; the establishment of production goals; the acquisition, storage, and availability of production materials; and the scheduling of equipment, facilities, materials, and labour required to fashion finished products. **Manufacturing and production information systems** support these activities.

Table 2-3 shows some typical manufacturing and production information systems for each major organizational group. Senior management uses manufacturing and production

Sales and marketing information systems

Manufacturing and production information systems

FIGURE 2-2   *Example of a sales information system*

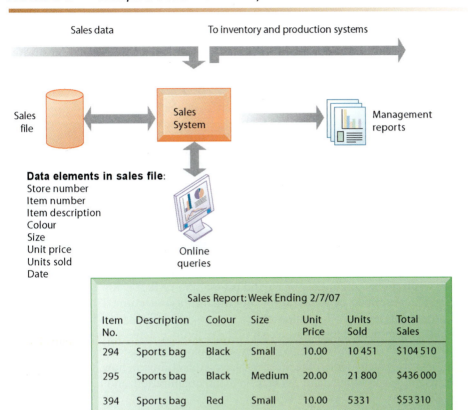

This system captures sales data at the moment the sale takes place to help the business monitor sales transactions and to provide information to help management analyze sales trends and the effectiveness of marketing campaigns.

Data elements in sales file:
Store number
Item number
Item description
Colour
Size
Unit price
Units sold
Date

Online queries

Sales Report: Week Ending 2/7/07

Item No.	Description	Colour	Size	Unit Price	Units Sold	Total Sales
294	Sports bag	Black	Small	10.00	10 451	$104 510
295	Sports bag	Black	Medium	20.00	21 800	$436 000
394	Sports bag	Red	Small	10.00	5331	$53 310

systems that deal with the firm's long-term manufacturing goals, such as where to locate new plants or whether to invest in new manufacturing technology. Manufacturing and production systems for middle management analyze and monitor manufacturing and production costs and resources. Operational management uses manufacturing and production systems that deal with the status of production tasks.

Most manufacturing and production systems use some sort of inventory system, as illustrated in Figure 2-3. Data about each item in inventory, such as the number of units depleted because of a shipment or purchase or the number of units replenished by reordering or returns, are either scanned or keyed into the system. The inventory master file contains basic data about each item, including the unique identification code for each item, a description of the item, the number of units on hand, the number of units on order, and the reorder point (the number of units in inventory that triggers a decision to reorder to prevent a stockout). Companies can estimate the number of items to reorder, or they can use a formula for calculating the least expensive quantity to reorder, called the *economic order quantity*. The system produces reports that give information about such things as the number of each item available in inventory, the number of units of each item to reorder, or items in inventory that must be replenished.

TABLE 2-3   *Examples of Manufacturing and Production Information Systems*

SYSTEM	DESCRIPTION	GROUPS SERVED
Machine control	Controls the actions of machines and equipment	Operational management
Production planning	Decides when and how many products should be produced	Middle management
Facilities location	Decides where to locate new production facilities	Senior management

FIGURE 2-3 *Overview of an inventory system*

This system provides information about the number of items available in inventory to support manufacturing and production activities.

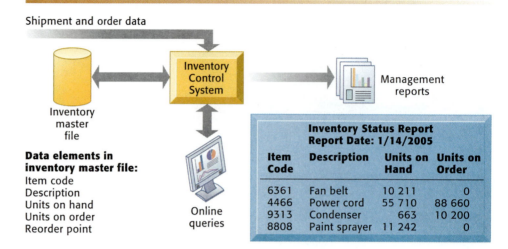

Shipment and order data

Inventory master file

Data elements in inventory master file:
Item code
Description
Units on hand
Units on order
Reorder point

Online queries

Inventory Control System

Management reports

Inventory Status Report
Report Date: 1/14/2005

Item Code	Description	Units on Hand	Units on Order
6361	Fan belt	10 211	0
4466	Power cord	55 710	88 660
9313	Condenser	663	10 200
8808	Paint sprayer	11 242	0

Another example of a manufacturing and production system is Kia Motors's quality control system described in the Window on Organizations section. This system helps identify sources of defects in Kia automobiles. Kia uses the information from the system to improve its production processes to eliminate or reduce defects. Improving vehicle quality lowers Kia's costs for warranty repairs while increasing customer satisfaction. As you read this case, try to identify the problems facing this company, how information systems are helping it solve them, and the management, organization, and technology issues it must address.

Finance and Accounting Systems The finance function is responsible for managing the firm's financial assets, such as cash, stocks, bonds, and other investments, to maximize the return on these financial assets. The finance function is also in charge of managing the capitalization of the firm (finding new financial assets in stocks, bonds, or other forms of debt). To determine whether the firm is getting the best return on its investments, the finance function must obtain a considerable amount of information from sources external to the firm.

The accounting function is responsible for maintaining and managing the firm's financial records—receipts, disbursements, depreciation, payroll—to account for the flow of funds in a firm. Finance and accounting share related problems—how to keep track of a firm's financial assets and fund flows. They provide answers to questions such as these: What is the current inventory of financial assets? What records exist for disbursements, receipts, payroll, and other fund flows?

WINDOW ON ORGANIZATIONS

Information Systems Help Kia Solve Its Quality Problems

A decade ago, few Americans had heard of the Korean car company Kia Motors. The company started selling cars in North America only in 1994, promising high-quality vehicles at prices well below the competition. That year, Kia sold 12 163 vehicles. In 2004, Kia sold 270 000 cars and expects to sell 500 000 annually in the U.S. market alone by 2010. Kias are 10 to 15 percent cheaper than comparable vehicles by competitors.

From a marketing and sales standpoint, Kia has been a phenomenal success. But until 2002, Kia ranked at the bottom of J.D. Power and Associates' annual initial-quality survey of new vehicle owners. In 1997, when the average North American car had 1.1 defects per vehicle, Kia had 2.75. In 2002, Kia had improved to 2.12 defects per vehicle, but the industry average was 1.33. Kia had a long way to go, and this was affecting its ability to sell cars, retain customers, and keep operational costs down.

Kia has tried to keep customers happy despite its quality problems by offering a 10-Year/100 000-Mile Warranty Program, which provides coverage until either the yearly or total mileage figure is reached, whichever occurs first. That means that Kia must pay for repairs on all warrantied items in its vehicles for many more years than its competitors are willing to do for their products, which raises operating costs and eats into profits.

Like all manufacturers of vehicles sold in North America, Kia had to create a system by December 1, 2003, to report any defects, accidents, or injuries involving its vehicles to the U.S. National Highway Traffic Safety Administration. This was a major challenge for the company. The information Kia had to report was stored in at least seven different systems run by Kia's warranty, parts, consumer, and legal affairs departments.

Fragmentation of this information in different systems prevented Kia from getting a complete picture of defects. Parts sales are the first indicator of a defect, warranty claims the second, and consumer complaints the third. Looking at parts sales alone will not provide an answer. A sudden increase in brake pad orders from Kia dealers making repairs indicates there might be a problem with a particular pad.

By examining warranty claims, Kia might discover that brake pads were being ordered only for four-wheel drive models of one of its vehicles and not for two-wheel drive models. This additional information might show that the problem was actually a result of excess vibration caused by the vehicle's design rather than the brake pads.

Kia could have created a series of stopgap software programs to extract the required information out of these various computer systems and collate it manually. But this would have been time-consuming and would not provide any other benefits to the company. So Kia's management decided instead to create a defect early warning system that could identify potential problems, such as faulty brake parts, by combining warranty claims, parts orders, field reports, and consumer complaints.

Kia enlisted Infogain, a Los Gatos, California, software consulting firm, to help it design a new information systems solution. Infogain created a software "engine" that examines six Kia systems for warranty claims, parts sales, vehicle identification number master storage files, and vehicle inventories, and stores the essential information in a single common data repository. The system automatically breaks down and categorizes reports based on individual components, such as steering assemblies or headlights, and links to Kia's Clarify customer relationship management system, tracking consumer complaints received by phone, e-mail, or postal mail.

Once data have been stored in a single place, Kia can use Crystal Analysis software to analyze the data with an early warning dashboard to highlight events such as spikes in warranty claims related to a particular vehicle model, unusual increases in parts orders, or high numbers of accidents resulting in serious injury or death. Managers are able to analyze the data by daily, weekly, or monthly reporting periods and by specific car models, model years, and components. They also can break down the data in detail to see how many complaints or warranty claims are associated with a specific item, such as a steering assembly.

Information from this system is helping Kia pinpoint the sources of defects and determine what percentage of its vehicles is likely to have problems. The company can then improve its production processes before the problems become more widespread, thus lowering costs for warranty repairs. This information also helps Kia determine the most cost-effective strategy for dealing with its quality problems. For example, should Kia recall all batteries if battery defects occur in extreme heat or limit recalls to vehicles sold in hotter climates?

Kia's quality has indeed improved. In quality rankings released on May 18, 2005, J.D. Power reported that Kia had 1.40 problems per vehicle, finishing second for quality in the compact-car category behind the Toyota Prius. According to Hirofumi Yokoi, an analyst with auto industry consulting firm CSM Worldwide, today "Kia quality is relatively comparable" with more established auto-makers.

To Think About

1. Why was it so difficult for Kia to identify sources of defects in the cars it produced?

2. What was the business impact of Kia not having an information system to track defects? What other business processes besides manufacturing and production were affected?

3. How did Kia's new defect-reporting system improve the way it ran its business?

4. What management, organization, and information technology issues did Kia have to address when it adopted its new quality control system?

5. What new business processes were enabled by Kia's new quality control system?

MIS in Action

1. Visit the Autobytel Web site (www.autobytel.com – or check out www.autobytel.ca, which leads you to www.gotcar.ca), and select a Kia model for your research. Investigate the retail price, warranties, and any relevant reviews and safety data. Select a comparable model (suggested by Autobytel) from another automobile manufacturer, and gather the same data for that make and model.

2. Visit the J.D. Power Web site (www.jdpower.com), and explore the Brand Ratings section. Examine Kia's overall quality rating and the quality ratings for overall quality-manufacturing, mechanical quality-manufacturing, and body and interior quality-manufacturing. Compare Kia's quality ratings to the quality ratings for the competing automaker you have been researching.

3. Create a table comparing the two cars you have selected on the basis of price, warranties, and quality. Would you select the Kia? Why or why not?

Sources: Craig Simons, "Kia Makes U.S. Inroads and Builds for Future Growth," Cox News Service, March 14, 2006; Mel Duvall, "Kia Motors America: Lemon Aid," *Baseline Magazine*, June 2005; and www.kia.com, accessed June 18, 2006.

Kia uses information systems to help it identify sources of defects in cars so it can improve vehicle quality, reduce warranty repair costs, and increase customer satisfaction.

Table 2-4 shows some of the typical **finance and accounting information systems** found in large organizations. Senior management uses finance and accounting systems to establish long-term investment goals for the firm and to provide long-range forecasts of the firm's financial performance. Middle management uses systems to oversee and control the firm's financial resources. Operational management uses finance and accounting systems to track the flow of funds in the firm through transactions, such as paycheques, payments to vendors, securities reports, and receipts.

Figure 2-4 illustrates an accounts receivable system, which keeps track of what customers who have made purchases on credit owe to a company. Every invoice generates an "account receivable"—that is, the customer owes the firm money. Some customers pay immediately in cash, but others are granted credit. The accounts receivable system records each invoice in a master file that also contains information on each customer, including that person's credit rating. The system also keeps track of all the bills outstanding and can produce a variety of output reports, both on paper and on the computer screen, to help the business collect bills. The system also answers queries about a customer's credit rating and payment history.

Human Resources Systems The human resources function is responsible for attracting, developing, and maintaining the firm's workforce. **Human resources information systems** support activities such as identifying potential employees, maintaining complete records on existing employees, and creating programs to develop employees' talents and skills.

Human resources systems help senior management identify the human resources requirements (skills, educational level, types of positions, number of positions, and cost) for meeting the firm's long-term business plans. Middle management uses human resources systems to monitor and analyze the recruitment, allocation, and compensation of employees. Operational management uses human resources systems to track the recruitment and placement of the firm's employees (see Table 2-5).

Figure 2-5 illustrates a typical human resources system for employee record keeping. It maintains basic employee data, such as the employee's name, age, gender, marital

Finance and accounting information systems

Human resources information systems

TABLE 2-4 *Examples of Finance and Accounting Information Systems*

SYSTEM	DESCRIPTION	GROUPS SERVED
Accounts receivable	Tracks money owed the firm	Operational management
Budgeting	Prepares short-term budgets	Middle management
Profit planning	Plans long-term profits	Senior management

FIGURE 2-4   *An accounts receivable system*

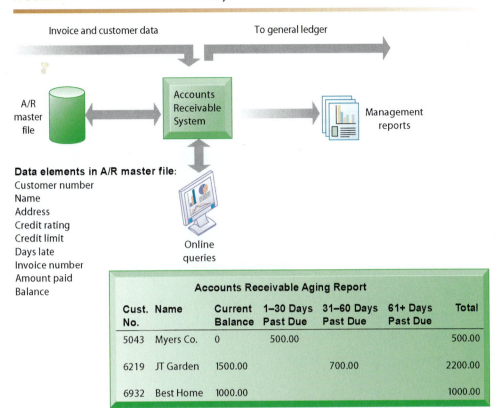

An accounts receivable system tracks and stores important customer data, such as payment history, credit rating, and billing history.

status, address, educational background, salary, job title, date of hire, and date of termination. The system can produce a variety of reports, such as lists of newly hired employees, employees who are terminated or on leaves of absence, employees classified by job type or educational level, or employee job performance evaluations. These systems are typically designed to provide data that can satisfy federal and provincial record-keeping requirements for Equal Employment Opportunity (EEO) and other purposes.

Systems from a Constituency Perspective

Although a functional perspective is very useful for understanding how business systems serve specific functions, this perspective does not tell us how systems help managers manage

TABLE 2-5   *Examples of Human Resources Information Systems*

System	Description	Groups Served
Training and development	Tracks employee training, skills, and performance appraisals	Operational management
Compensation analysis	Monitors the range and distribution of employee wages, salaries, and benefits	Middle management
Human resources planning	Plans the long-term labour force needs of the organization	Senior management

FIGURE 2-5 *An employee record-keeping system*

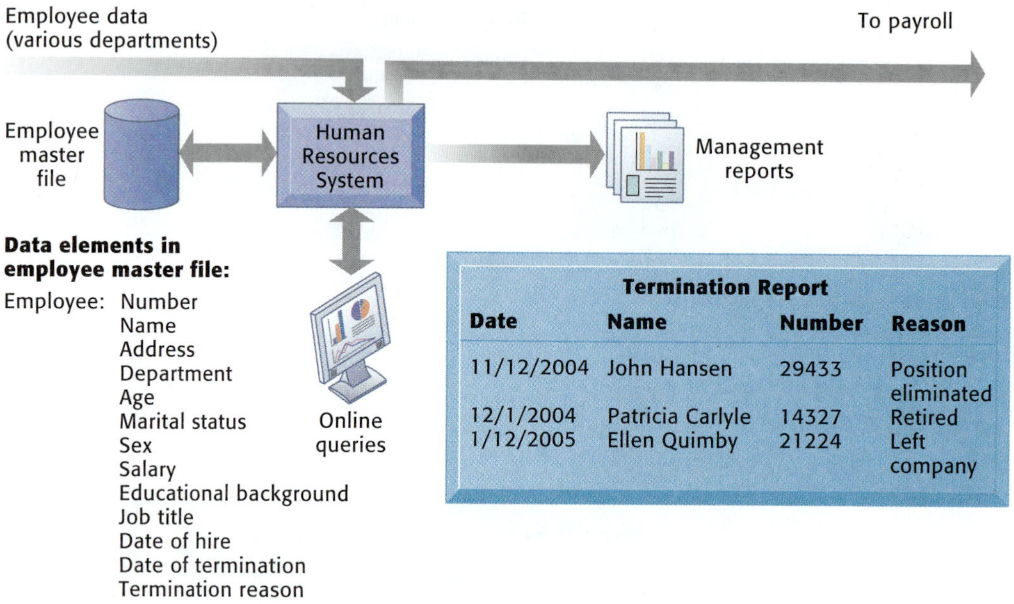

Employee data
(various departments)

To payroll

Employee master file

Human Resources System

Management reports

Data elements in employee master file:

Employee: Number
Name
Address
Department
Age
Marital status
Sex
Salary
Educational background
Job title
Date of hire
Date of termination
Termination reason

Online queries

Termination Report

Date	Name	Number	Reason
11/12/2004	John Hansen	29433	Position eliminated
12/1/2004	Patricia Carlyle	14327	Retired
1/12/2005	Ellen Quimby	21224	Left company

This system maintains data on the firm's employees to support the human resources function.

the firm. Here we need a perspective that examines systems in terms of the various levels of management and types of decisions that they support.

Each of these levels has different information needs given their different responsibilities, and each can be seen as a major information constituent. Senior managers need summary information that can quickly inform them about the overall performance of the firm, such as gross sales revenues, sales by product group and region, and overall profitability. Middle managers need more specific information on the results of specific functional areas and departments of the firm, such as sales contacts by the sales force, production statistics for specific factories or product lines, employment levels and costs, and sales revenues for each month or even each day. Operational managers need transaction-level information, such as the number of parts in inventory each day or the number of hours logged on Tuesday by each employee. Knowledge workers may need access to external scientific databases or internal databases with organizational knowledge. Knowledge workers may work with knowledge work systems or knowledge management systems, which we discuss further in Chapter 15. Finally, production or service workers need access to information from production machines, and service workers need access to customer records in order to take orders and answer questions from customers. Each of the groups we described in Chapter 1 uses a different type of system to deliver the information required to manage the company.

Transaction Processing Systems Operational managers need systems that keep track of the elementary activities and transactions of the organization, such as sales, receipts, cash deposits, payroll, credit decisions, and the flow of materials in a factory. **Transaction processing systems (TPS)** provide this kind of information. A transaction processing system is a computerized system that performs and records the daily routine transactions necessary to conduct business, such as sales order entry, hotel reservations, payroll, employee record-keeping, and shipping.

The principal purpose of systems at this level is to answer routine questions and to track the flow of transactions through the organization. How many parts are in inventory? What happened to Mr. Williams' payment? To answer these kinds of questions, information generally must be easily available, current, and accurate.

Transaction processing systems (TPS)

At the operational level, tasks, resources, and goals are predefined and highly structured. The decision to grant credit to a customer, for instance, is made by a lower-level supervisor according to predefined criteria. All that must be determined is whether the customer meets the criteria. The systems illustrated in Figures 2-4 and 2-5 are transaction processing systems (TPS).

Managers need TPS to monitor the status of internal operations and the firm's relations with the external environment. TPS are also major producers of information for the other types of systems. (For example, the accounts receivable system illustrated in Figure 2-4, along with other accounting TPS, supplies data to the company's general ledger system, which is responsible for maintaining records of the firm's income and expenses and for producing reports such as income statements and balance sheets.)

Transaction processing systems are often so central to a business that a TPS failure for a few hours can lead to a firm's demise and perhaps that of other firms linked to it. Imagine what would happen to UPS if its package tracking system were not working! What would the airlines do without their computerized reservation systems?

Management Information Systems and Decision-Support Systems Middle management needs systems to help with monitoring, controlling, decision-making, and administrative activities. The principal question addressed by such systems is this: Are things working well?

In Chapter 1, we defined management information systems as the study of information systems in business and management. The term **management information systems (MIS)** also designates a specific category of information systems serving middle management. MIS provide middle managers with reports on the organization's current performance. This information is used to monitor and control the business and predict future performance.

MIS summarize and report on the company's basic operations using data supplied by transaction processing systems. The basic transaction data from TPS are compressed and/ or summarized and usually presented in reports that are produced on a regular schedule. Today, many of these reports are delivered online. Figure 2-6 shows how a typical MIS transforms transaction-level data from inventory, production, and accounting into MIS files that are used to provide managers with reports. Figure 2-7 shows a sample report from this system.

Management information systems (MIS)

FIGURE 2-6   *How management information systems obtain their data from the organization's TPS*

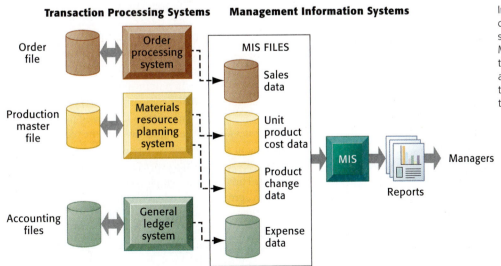

In the system illustrated by this diagram, three TPS supply summarized transaction data to the MIS reporting system at the end of the time period. Managers gain access to the organizational data through the MIS, which provides them with the appropriate reports.

FIGURE 2-7   *A sample MIS report*

This report, showing summarized annual sales data, was produced by the MIS in Figure 2-6.

Consolidated Consumer Products Corporation Sales by Product and Sales Region, 2005

PRODUCT CODE	PRODUCT DESCRIPTION	SALES REGION	ACTUAL SALES	PLANNED	ACTUAL versus PLANNED
4469	Carpet Cleaner	Central	4 066 700	4 800 000	0.85
		Atlantic	3 778 112	3 750 000	1.01
		Prairies	4 867 001	4 600 000	1.06
		Western	4 003 440	4 400 000	0.91
	TOTAL		16 715 253	17 550 000	0.95
5674	Room Freshener	Central	3 676 700	3 900 000	0.94
		Atlantic	5 608 112	4 700 000	1.19
		Prairies	4 711 001	4 200 000	1.12
		Western	4 563 440	4 900 000	0.93
	TOTAL		18 559 253	17 700 000	1.05

MIS serve managers primarily interested in weekly, monthly, and yearly results, although some MIS enable managers to drill down to see daily or hourly data if required. MIS generally provide answers to routine questions that have been specified in advance and have a predefined procedure for answering them. For instance, MIS reports might list the total pounds of lettuce used this quarter by a fast-food chain or, as illustrated in Figure 2-7, compare total annual sales figures for specific products to planned targets. These systems generally are not flexible and have little analytical capability. Most MIS use simple routines, such as summaries and comparisons, as opposed to sophisticated mathematical models or statistical techniques.

The Window on Management section describes an MIS that has helped companies monitor and control employee travel and entertainment expenses and reduce their operational costs. MarketStar is one of many firms using the Concur Expense Service system to automate its processes for reporting, auditing, and analyzing travel and entertainment expenses. As you read this case, try to identify the problems facing this company, how information systems are helping it solve them, and the management, organization, and technology issues it must address.

WINDOW ON MANAGEMENT

Managing Travel Expenses: New Tools, New Savings

Business travel and entertainment are requirements of many jobs and often a hefty component of corporate expenses. According to American Express and Concur Technologies, travel and entertainment expenditures for North American companies amount to more than $212 billion each year. In 2004, IBM spent $524 million on airline tickets alone while General Electric spent $297 million.

Processing travel and entertainment expense reports adds to the cost. According to Aberdeen Group Consulting in Boston, the cost to process a single expense report is US $48 dollars. Aberdeen found that an employee typically takes 57 minutes to complete an expense report.

Processing travel and entertainment expenditures is especially burdensome for smaller companies whose processes tend to be paper-based. MarketStar, a U.S.-based provider of outsourced sales and marketing services to other companies was drowning in a sea of expense reports. About 650 of its 1200 employees regularly file expense reports to its accounting department. Three full-time employees were required to manually approve, process, and audit 300 expense reports per week, most from remote locations. Expense disbursements were delayed for several weeks.

Jeff Jones, MarketStar's controller, likened this process to building "a dam when the flood waters were rising around your knees. We could never get ahead of the curve, and it was all we could do to just keep pace." In addition to processing reports, MarketStar's staff were also required to audit every single expense report to ensure that reports were accurately tabulated and all expenses were properly coded.

MarketStar decided to implement Concur Expense Service software, which automates the travel and entertainment expense-reporting process. Employees can input their expense data via a Web interface from wherever they are working with a computer or by telephone or Palm handheld device. The system also automatically imports travel and expense data from corporate credit cards. Electronic receipt imaging uses any available fax machine to digitize and attach receipts to expense reports.

Managers approve reports with just a mouse click, cutting processing time in half while boosting accuracy and productivity. Reports produced by the system help managers keep tabs on travel spending as transactions occur.

Control and compliance tools help firms minimize fraud and maximize compliance with company policies and government regulations such as CSOX or Sarbanes-Oxley (see Chapter 8). The system captures a firm's business rules about corporate travel policies, such as the maximum amount allowed for airfare, hotel rooms, and meals. A built-in audit feature automatically flags expenses that are not in compliance with these policies. This feature helps companies identify employees who are not booking airline flights with their companies' preferred vendors, those who are "padding" their expense accounts with fictitious expenses for taxis and tips, or even those who use their expense accounts for unauthorized purchases.

Corporate executives assert that instant feedback of information helps curb pervasive abuses. If, for example, the system shows a red flag on a Delta Airlines booking when a cheaper Southwest flight is available, the traveller can be alerted to rebook or pay the difference.

Concur software can be customized. MarketStar bills approximately 80 percent of its employee expenses back to its clients, who have their own expense policies. So it had to build special rules into its travel management application. MarketStar employees frequently work on a variety of projects at one time, and the software enables them to tie their expenses to a specific project as well as to a specific client.

Since implementing Concur Expense Service in early 2001, MarketStar was able to reduce staff for travel and expense processing down to one person and reduce the time to reimburse employees to a few days. It has used information provided by the system to negotiate better rates from preferred vendors, saving more than $155 000. Altogether MarketStar has realized more than $1 million in savings, representing a return on investment of 19 percent per year.

Many other companies have benefited from Concur and competing expense reporting systems. For instance, Mercer HR Consulting reduced the number of auditors required to process and audit employee expense spending by 75 percent, and Dell Computer reduced the cost of processing an expense report to less than $2. And corporate customers of Air Canada are now able to use Concur Technologies' Web-based booking tool, Cliqbook Travel, in order to book flight passes and a growing number of other services from Air Canada. According to Graham Wareham, general manager of product distribution for Air Canada, "The Cliqbook Travel tool will provide corporate Canada [with] efficient access to all of Air Canada's offerings."

To Think About

1. What kinds of systems are described here? What valuable information do they provide for employees and managers? What decisions do they support?

2. What problems do automated expense reporting systems solve for companies? How do they provide value for companies that use them?

3. Compare MarketStar's manual process for travel and entertainment expense reporting with its new process based on Concur Expense Service. Diagram the two processes.

4. What management, organization, and technology issues did MarketStar have to address when adopting Concur Expense Service?

5. Are there any disadvantages to using computerized expense processing systems? Explain your answer.

MIS in Action

Explore the Concur Technologies Web site (www.concur.com), and answer the following questions:

1. What kind of services does Concur Technologies (www.concur.com) provide for businesses? What kinds of businesses would benefit from using its software?

2. Compare Concur's services with those of another travel expense management vendor, such as American Express (www.americanexpress.ca). If you were trying to manage your company's travel and entertainment expenses, which service would you prefer?

Sources: Paul Burnham Finney, "Tools Can Catch Expense-Account Padders (and Make Filing Easier)," *New York Times*, June 27, 2006; "All Air Canada Content Now Available Through Concur Technologies' Cliqbook Travel," Concur Public Relations, March 22, 2007, www.concur.com/about/news/press.html?id=109, accessed May 8, 2007; and "Corporate Expense Management Case Study: MarketStar Stays Ahead of the ROI Curve with Concur Expense," www.concur.com/about/customers/case_studies/marketstar.html, accessed June 28, 2006.

Decision-support systems (DSS) support nonroutine decision making for middle management. They focus on problems that are unique and rapidly changing, for which the procedure for arriving at a solution may not be fully predefined in advance. They try to answer questions such as these: What would be the impact on production schedules if we were to double sales in the month of December? What would happen to our return on investment if a factory schedule were delayed for six months?

Although DSS use internal information from TPS and MIS, they often bring in information from external sources, such as current stock prices or product prices of competitors. These systems use a variety of models to analyze data, or they condense large amounts of data into a form in which decision makers can analyze them. DSS are designed so that users can work with them directly; these systems explicitly include user-friendly software.

One DSS changing the face of health care in Canada is e-MDS, a software used to assess Ontario patients in long-term care at home or in nursing homes. e-MDS uses standardized categories, developed by the University of Waterloo, the University of Alberta, and Toronto's Med e-care Consulting (www.mede-care.com), to assess patients. Patients' records can also be transmitted electronically from one agency to another as needed, such as when a patient moves from home health care to a nursing home. Patients can be assessed frequently to determine how they are responding over time. Among the data elements assessed in the *minimum data set* (MDS) standard categories are cognitive abilities (such as memory), depression, history of falls, pressure ulcers, and incontinence. Using the assessment tools, patient care can be planned before the patient even arrives at the nursing home. Med e-care is also partnering with Winnipeg's Momentum Software to provide MDS software for nursing homes throughout North America. Figure 2-8 illustrates the type of DSS now being developed. Interestingly, by using MDS and other standards currently being developed for patient assessment, many vendors can develop a variety of DSS tools for long-term care applications.

Med e-care's patient assessment DSS draws heavily on analytical models. Other types of DSS are less model-driven, focusing instead on extracting useful information to support decision making from large amounts of data.

For example, Intrawest—the largest ski operator in North America—collects and stores customer data from its Web site, call centre, lodging reservations, ski schools, and ski equipment rental stores. It uses several software programs to analyze these data to determine the value, revenue potential, and loyalty of each customer so managers can make better decisions on how to target their marketing programs. The system segments customers into seven categories based on needs, attitudes, and behaviours, ranging from "passionate experts" to "value-minded family vacationers." The company

Decision-support systems (DSS)

FIGURE 2-8   *Patient assessment decision-support system*

This DSS is used daily by health care professionals responsible for providing health care to patients who require long-term care.

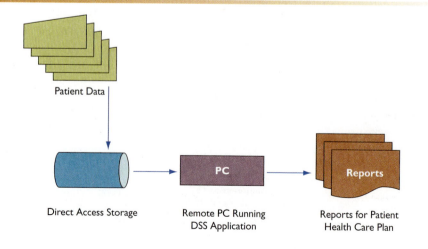

then e-mails video clips that would appeal to each segment to encourage more visits to its resorts.

Sometimes you may hear DSS referred to as *business intelligence systems* because they focus on helping users make better business decisions. You'll learn more about them in Chapters 6 and 14.

Executive Support Systems Senior managers need systems that address strategic issues and long-term trends, both in the firm and in the external environment. They are concerned with questions such as these: What will employment levels be in five years? What are the long-term industry cost trends, and where does our firm fit in? How well are competitors performing? What products should we be making in five years? What new acquisitions would protect us from cyclical business swings?

Executive support systems (ESS) help senior management make these decisions. ESS address nonroutine decisions requiring judgment, evaluation, and insight because there is no agreed-on procedure for arriving at a solution. ESS provide a generalized computing and communications capacity that can be applied to a changing array of problems.

ESS are designed to incorporate data about external events, such as new tax laws or competitors, but they also draw summarized information from internal MIS and DSS. They filter, compress, and track critical data, displaying the data of greatest importance to senior managers. For example, the CEO of Leiner Health Products, the largest manufacturer of private-label vitamins and supplements in the U.S., has an ESS that provides on his desktop a minute-to-minute view of the firm's financial performance as measured by working capital, accounts receivable, accounts payable, cash flow, and inventory.

ESS present graphs and data from many sources through an interface that is easy for senior managers to use. Often the information is delivered to senior executives through a **portal**, which uses a Web interface to present integrated personalized business content. You will learn more about other applications of portals in Chapters 12 and 15.

Figure 2-9 illustrates a model of an ESS. It consists of workstations with menus, interactive graphics, and communications capabilities that can be used to access historical and competitive data from internal corporate systems and external databases such as Dow Jones News/Retrieval or Ipsos Reid, the Canadian polling firm. More details on leading-edge applications of DSS and ESS can be found in Chapter 14.

Executive support systems (ESS)

Portal

FIGURE 2-9   *Model of an executive support system*

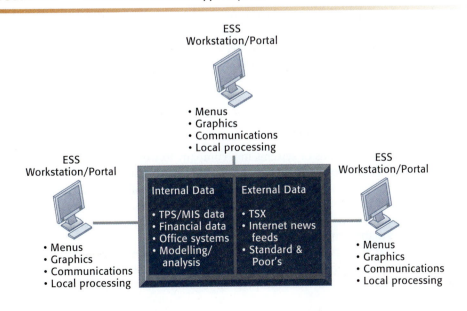

This system pools data from diverse internal and external sources and makes them available to executives in an easy-to-use form.

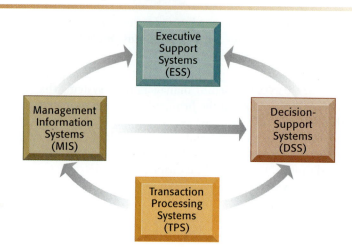

FIGURE 2-10 *Interrelationships among systems*

The various types of systems in the organization have interdependencies. TPS are major producers of information that is required by many other systems in the firm, which, in turn, produce information for other systems. These different types of systems are loosely coupled in most business firms, but firms are increasingly using new technologies to integrate information that resides in many different systems.

Relationship of Systems to One Another

Ideally, the systems we have just described are interrelated, as illustrated in Figure 2-10. TPS are typically a major source of data for other systems while ESS are primarily a recipient of data from lower-level systems.

The other types of systems may exchange data with one another as well. Data also may be exchanged among systems serving different functional areas.

For example, an order captured by a sales system may be transmitted to a manufacturing system as a transaction for producing or delivering the product specified in the order or to an MIS for financial reporting. In reality, in most business firms, these systems are only loosely integrated. As in the Kia case described earlier in the Window on Organizations on page 38, many firms are unable to quickly move data from one system to another and, therefore, are unable to respond rapidly to challenges in the business environment. But this situation is changing because of new networking technologies and enterprise-wide software systems described in the next section.

2.3   Systems That Span the Enterprise

Reviewing all the different types of systems we have just described, you might wonder how a business can manage all the information in these different systems. You might also wonder how costly it is to maintain so many different systems. And you might wonder how these different systems can share information. In fact, these are all excellent questions and challenges for businesses today.

Enterprise Applications

Getting all the different kinds of systems in a company to work together is a major challenge. Typically, corporations are put together both through normal "organic" or internal growth and through acquisition of smaller firms. After periods of acquisition, corporations end up with a collection of systems, most of them older, and face the challenge of getting them all to "talk" with one another and work together as one corporate system. There are several solutions to this problem.

One solution is to implement **enterprise applications**, which are systems that span functional areas, focus on executing business processes across the business firm, and include all levels of management. Enterprise applications help businesses become more

Enterprise applications

FIGURE 2-11   *Enterprise application architecture*

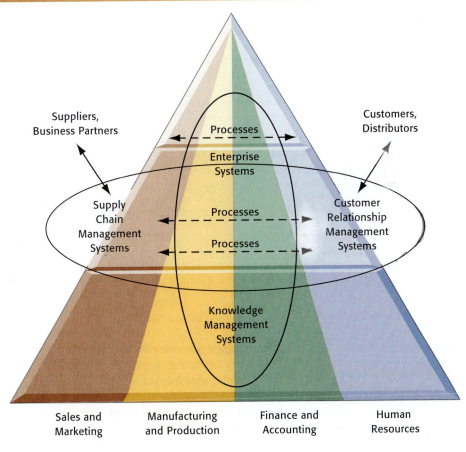

Enterprise applications automate processes that span multiple business functions and organizational levels and may extend outside the organization.

flexible and productive by coordinating their business processes more closely and integrating groups of processes so they focus on efficient management of resources and customer service.

There are four major enterprise applications: enterprise systems, supply chain management systems, customer relationship management systems, and knowledge management systems. Each of these enterprise applications integrates a related set of functions and business processes to enhance the performance of the organization as a whole. Figure 2-11 shows that the architecture for these enterprise applications encompasses processes spanning the entire organization and, in some cases, extending beyond the organization to customers, suppliers, and other key business partners.

Enterprise Systems A large organization typically has many different kinds of information systems built around different functions, organizational levels, and business processes that cannot automatically exchange information. Managers might have a hard time assembling the data they need for a comprehensive, overall picture of the organization's operations. For instance, sales personnel might not be able to tell at the time they place an order whether the items that were ordered are in inventory; customers may not be able to track their orders; and manufacturing might not communicate easily with finance to plan for new production. This fragmentation of data in hundreds of separate systems degrades organizational efficiency and business performance.

For example, Alcoa, the world's leading producer of aluminium products with operations spanning 41 countries and 500 locations, had initially been organized around multiple lines of business, each of which had its own set of information systems. Many of these

FIGURE 2-12   *Enterprise systems*

Enterprise systems integrate the key business processes of an entire firm into a single software system that enables information to flow seamlessly throughout the organization. These systems focus primarily on internal processes but may include transactions with customers and vendors.

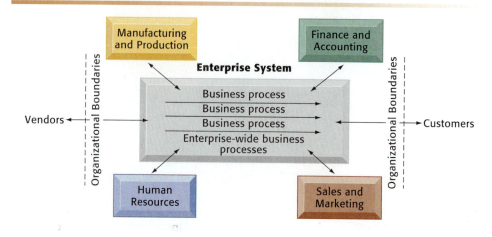

systems were redundant and inefficient. Alcoa's costs for executing requisition-to-pay and financial processes were much higher, and its cycle times were longer than those of other companies in its industry. (*Cycle time* refers to the total elapsed time from the beginning to the end of a process.) The company could not operate as a single worldwide entity (Oracle, 2005; Sullivan, 2005).

Enterprise systems, also known as *enterprise resource planning (ERP) systems*, solve this problem by collecting data from various key business processes in manufacturing and production, finance and accounting, sales and marketing, and human resources and storing the data in a single central data repository. This makes it possible for information that was previously fragmented in different systems to be shared across the firm and for different parts of the business to work more closely together (see Figure 2-12).

Enterprise systems speed communication of information throughout the company, making it easier for businesses to coordinate their daily operations. When a customer places an order, the data flow automatically to other parts of the company that are affected by them. The order transaction triggers the warehouse to pick the ordered products and schedule shipment. The warehouse informs the factory to replenish whatever has been depleted.

The accounting department is notified to send the customer an invoice. Customer service representatives track the progress of the order through every step to inform customers about the status of their orders.

Enterprise systems give companies the flexibility to respond rapidly to customer requests while producing and stocking inventory only with what is needed to fulfill existing orders. Their ability to increase accurate and on-time shipments, minimize costs, and increase customer satisfaction adds to firm profitability.

After implementing enterprise software from Oracle, Alcoa eliminated many redundant processes and systems. The enterprise system helped Alcoa reduce requisition-to-pay cycle time (the total elapsed time from the time a purchase requisition is generated to the time the payment for the purchase is made) by verifying receipt of goods and automatically generating receipts for payment. Alcoa's accounts payable transaction processing dropped 89 percent. Alcoa was able to centralize financial and procurement activities, which helped the company reduce nearly 20 percent of its worldwide costs. The company expects continued use of the enterprise system to reduce inventory by 25 percent, increase productivity by 15 percent, reduce materials costs by 5 percent, and improve customer service by 20 percent.

Enterprise systems provide valuable information for improving management decision making. Corporate headquarters has access to up-to-the-minute data on sales, inventory, and production and uses this information to create more accurate sales and production forecasts. Enterprise systems provide company-wide information to help managers

Enterprise systems

analyze overall product profitability or cost structures. For example, Alcoa's new enterprise system includes functionality for global human resources management that shows correlations between investment in employee training and quality; measures the company-wide costs of delivering services to employees; and measures the effectiveness of employee recruitment, compensation, and training.

Supply Chain Management Systems **Supply chain management (SCM) systems** help businesses manage relationships with their suppliers. These systems provide information to help suppliers, purchasing firms, distributors, and logistics companies share information about orders, production, inventory levels, and delivery of products and services so that they can source, produce, and deliver goods and services efficiently. The ultimate objective is to get the right amount of their products from their source to their point of consumption with the least amount of time and with the lowest cost.

If a company and its supply network do not have accurate information, they will most likely be saddled by excessive inventories, inaccurate manufacturing plans, and missed production schedules. Inability to move products efficiently through the supply chain raises costs while degrading customer service.

For example, until it implemented a supply chain management system from SAP, Montréal-based Alcan Packaging had trouble fulfilling customer orders for its packaging materials for food, pharmaceuticals, and cosmetics. It did not have the information to make good decisions about how much to produce, how to allocate personnel, or how to meet the delivery dates requested by customers. The company would work employees overtime one month and cut back staff the next. It could not accurately project when it would meet shipment requirements (SAP, 2005).

Table 2-6 describes how firms can benefit from supply chain management systems. These systems increase firm profitability by lowering the costs of moving and making products and by enabling managers to make better decisions about how to organize and schedule sourcing, production, and distribution. Alcan expects its supply chain management system to reduce overtime by 25 percent, reduce setup costs by up to 7.5 percent, and reduce carrying inventory by up to 10 percent.

Supply chain management systems are one type of **interorganizational system** because they automate the flow of information across organizational boundaries. You might not know it, but when you purchase a book or DVD from Amazon.ca and then trace the shipping of your order at Amazon, the information is being supplied to Amazon (and you) by the shipper's tracking system through the Amazon Web site. When you book a flight at Expedia.ca, Travelocity.ca, or Hotels.com, you are in fact dealing with several interorganizational systems that link reservation systems on the Web with flight and room inventory systems maintained by airlines and hotels. Interorganizational systems are increasingly common as firms combine their capabilities to offer customers an integrated online shopping experience. You will find examples of other types of interorganizational information systems throughout this text.

Supply chain management (SCM) systems

Interorganizational system

TABLE 2-6 *How Information Systems Facilitate Supply Chain Management*

INFORMATION FROM SUPPLY CHAIN MANAGEMENT SYSTEMS HELPS FIRMS ...
Decide when and what to produce, store, and move
Rapidly communicate orders
Track the status of orders
Check inventory availability and monitor inventory levels
Reduce inventory, transportation, and warehousing costs
Track shipments
Plan production based on actual customer demand
Rapidly communicate changes in product design

FIGURE 2-13 *Example of a supply chain management system*

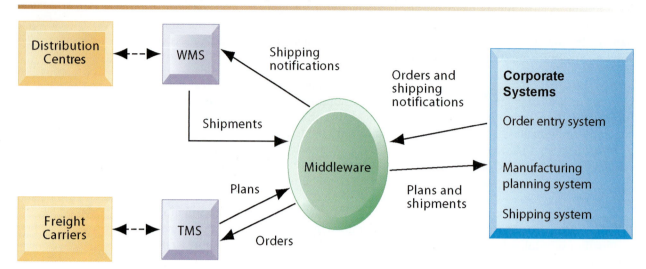

Customer orders, shipping notifications, optimized shipping plans, and other supply chain information flow among Haworth's Warehouse Management System (WMS), Transportation Management System (TMS), and its back-end corporate systems.

Figure 2-13 illustrates supply chain management systems used by Haworth Incorporated, a world-leading manufacturer and designer of office furniture. Haworth's 15 North American manufacturing facilities are located in North Carolina, Arkansas, Michigan, Mississippi, Texas, Ontario, Alberta, and Quebec. These facilities supply inventory to distribution centres in Michigan, Pennsylvania, Georgia, and Arkansas.

Haworth's Transportation Management System (TMS) examines customer orders, factory schedules, carrier rates and availability, and shipping costs to produce optimal lowest-cost delivery plans. These plans are generated daily and updated every 15 minutes. The TMS works with Haworth's Warehouse Management System (WMS), which tracks and controls the flow of finished goods from Haworth's distribution centres to its customers. Acting on shipping plans from TMS, WMS directs the movement of goods based on immediate conditions for space, equipment, inventory, and personnel. Haworth uses special "middleware" software to link its TMS and WMS to order entry, manufacturing planning, and shipping systems. The middleware passes customer orders, shipping plans, and shipping notifications among the applications.

Customer Relationship Management Systems Customer relationship management (CRM) systems help firms manage their relationships with customers. CRM systems provide information to coordinate all of the business processes that deal with customers in sales, marketing, and service to optimize revenue, customer satisfaction, and customer retention. This information helps firms identify, attract, and retain the most profitable customers; provide better service to existing customers; and hopefully increase sales.

In the past, a firm's processes for sales, service, and marketing were highly compartmentalized, and these departments did not share essential customer information. Some information on a specific customer might be stored and organized in terms of that person's account with the company. Other pieces of information about the same customer might be organized by products that were purchased. There was no way to consolidate all this information to provide a unified view of a customer across the company.

CRM systems try to solve this problem by integrating the firm's customer-related processes and consolidating customer information from multiple communication channels. A **channel** is the link by which data or voice are transmitted between sending and receiving devices in a network; for example, telephone, e-mail, wireless devices, retail outlets, or the Web. Detailed and accurate knowledge of customers and their preferences helps firms increase the effectiveness of their marketing campaigns and provide higher-quality

Customer relationship management (CRM) systems

Channel

customer service and support. A good CRM system can enable a company to have a 360-degree view of each customer, including prior service-related questions and all the marketing communication the customer had ever received. The company can track the status of leads that have been referred by others (i.e., referred leads) by monitoring events, such as a salesperson's initial call to a customer and the scheduling and completion of a customer visit. The systems provide detailed information to measure the sales results of specific leads, and target leads are directed more precisely to the right salespeople at the right locations. Figure 2-14 gives a snapshot of CRM system software.

Knowledge Management Systems The value of a firm's products and services is based not only on its physical resources but also on intangible knowledge assets. By some estimates, over half the stock market value of firms results from intangible assets, a large part of which is knowledge. Some firms perform better than others because they have better knowledge about how to create, produce, and deliver products and services. This firm knowledge is difficult to imitate, it is unique, and it can be leveraged into long-term strategic benefits. **Knowledge management systems (KMS)** enable organizations to better manage processes for capturing and applying knowledge and expertise. These systems collect all relevant knowledge and experience in the firm and make it available wherever and whenever it is needed to improve business processes and management decisions. They also link the firm to external sources of knowledge.

KMS support processes for acquiring, storing, distributing, and applying knowledge, as well as processes for creating new knowledge and integrating it into the

Knowledge management systems (KMS)

FIGURE 2-14   *Salesforce.com's CRM software*

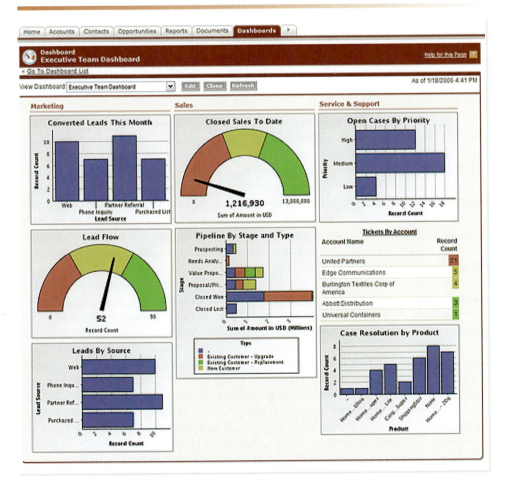

Illustrated here are some of the capabilities of Salesforce.com, a market-leading provider of on-demand customer relationship management (CRM) software. CRM systems integrate information from sales, marketing, and customer service.

organization. They include enterprise-wide systems for managing and distributing documents, graphics, and other digital knowledge objects; systems for creating corporate knowledge directories of employees with special areas of expertise; office systems for distributing knowledge and information; and knowledge work systems to facilitate knowledge creation. Other knowledge management applications use intelligent techniques that codify knowledge for use by other members of the organization and tools for knowledge discovery that recognize patterns and important relationships in large pools of data.

We examine enterprise systems and systems for supply chain management and customer relationship management in greater detail in Chapter 12 and describe knowledge management applications in Chapter 15.

Intranets and Extranets

Enterprise applications create deep-seated changes in the way a firm conducts its business, and they are often costly to implement. Companies that do not have the resources to invest in enterprise applications can still achieve some measure of information integration by using intranets and extranets, which we introduced in Chapter 1.

Intranets and extranets are really more technology platforms than specific applications, but they deserve mention here as one of the tools firms use to increase integration and expedite the flow of information within the firm and with customers and suppliers. Intranets are internal networks built with the same tools and communication standards as the Internet and are used for the internal distribution of information to employees and as repositories of corporate policies, programs, and data. Extranets are intranets extended to authorized users outside the company. We describe the technology for intranets and extranets in more detail in Chapter 7.

An intranet typically presents information to users through a private portal that provides a single point of access to information from several different systems and to documents using a Web interface. Just as Yahoo!'s public portal combines information from multiple sources and can be customized to user preferences, corporate portals can be customized to suit the information needs of specific business groups and individual users. They also typically feature e-mail, collaboration tools, and tools for searching for internal corporate systems and documents.

For example, SwissAir's corporate intranet for sales provides its salespeople with sales leads, fares, statistics, libraries of best practices, access to incentive programs, discussion groups, and collaborative workspaces. The intranet includes a Sales Ticket capability that displays bulletins about unfilled airplane seats around the world to help the sales staff work with colleagues and with travel agents who can help them fill those seats.

Companies can connect their intranets to internal company transaction systems, enabling employees to take actions central to a company's operations, such as checking the status of an order or granting a customer credit. SwissAir's intranet connects to its reservation system. GUESS Jeans has an intranet called ApparelBuy.com that links to its core order processing systems.

Extranets expedite the flow of information between the firm and its suppliers and customers. SwissAir uses an extranet to provide travel agents with fare data from its intranet electronically. GUESS Jeans allows store buyers to order merchandise electronically from ApparelBuy.com. The buyers can use this extranet to track their orders through fulfillment or delivery.

Extranets allow different firms to work collaboratively on product design, marketing, and production. Engineers at Johnson Controls and Daimler-Chrysler used an extranet design and collaboration system to design part of the Jeep Liberty interior together. Hewlett-Packard (HP) Laserjet Imaging Systems uses an extranet workgroup collaboration system to share information with its contract manufacturers, distribution centres, and resellers. The application makes parts plans from HP's internal production system available on a shared electronic workspace that can be accessed by suppliers. Suppliers then adjust their plans to coordinate their inventory with that of HP.

E-Business, E-Commerce, and E-Government

The systems and technologies we have just described are transforming firms' relationships with customers, employees, suppliers, and logistic partners into digital relationships using networks and the Internet. So much business is now enabled by or based upon digital networks that we use the terms *electronic business* and *electronic commerce* frequently throughout this text. **Electronic business**, or **e-business**, refers to the use of digital technology and the Internet to execute the major business processes in the enterprise. E-business includes activities for the internal management of the firm and for coordination with suppliers and other business partners. It also includes **electronic commerce,** or **e-commerce**. E-commerce is the part of e-business that deals with the buying and selling of goods and services over the Internet. It also encompasses activities supporting those market transactions, such as advertising, marketing, customer support, security, delivery, and payment.

The technologies associated with e-business have also brought about similar changes in the public sector. Governments on all levels are using Internet technology to deliver information and services to citizens, employees, and businesses with which they work. **E-government** refers to the application of the Internet and networking technologies to digitally enable government and public sector agencies' relationships with citizens, businesses, and other arms of government. In addition to improving delivery of government services, e-government can make government operations more efficient and also empower citizens by giving them easier access to information and the ability to network electronically with other citizens. For example, Canadian citizens can conduct most of their passport application process online. The Internet has become a powerful tool for instantly mobilizing interest groups for political action and fundraising.

2.4 The Information Systems Function in Business

We have seen that businesses need information systems to operate today and that they use many different kinds of systems. But who is responsible for running these systems? Who is responsible for making sure the hardware, software, and other technologies used by these systems are running properly and are up-to-date? End users manage their systems from a business standpoint, but managing the technology requires a special information systems function.

In all but the smallest of firms, the **information systems department** is the formal organizational unit responsible for information technology services.

The information systems department is responsible for maintaining the hardware, software, data storage, and networks that comprise the firm's IT infrastructure. We describe IT infrastructure in detail in Chapter 5.

The Information Systems Department

The information systems department consists of specialists, such as **programmers**, systems analysts, project leaders, and information systems managers. Programmers are highly trained technical specialists who write the software instructions for computers. **Systems analysts** constitute the principal liaisons between the information systems groups and the rest of the organization.

It is the systems analyst's job to translate business problems and requirements into information requirements and systems. **Information systems managers** are leaders of teams of programmers and analysts, project managers, physical facility managers, telecommunications managers, or database specialists. They are also managers of computer operations and data entry staff. Also, external specialists, such as hardware vendors

Electronic business (e-business)
Electronic commerce (e-commerce)
E-government
Information systems department
Programmers
Systems analysts
Information systems managers

and manufacturers, software firms, and consultants, frequently participate in the day-to-day operations and long-term planning of information systems.

In many companies, the information systems department is headed by a **chief information officer (CIO).** The CIO is a senior manager who oversees the use of information technology in the firm.

End users are representatives of departments outside of the information systems group for whom applications are developed. These users are playing an increasingly large role in the design and development of information systems.

In the early years of computing, the information systems group was composed mostly of programmers who performed very highly specialized but limited technical functions. Today, a growing proportion of staff members are systems analysts and network specialists, with the information systems department acting as a powerful change agent in the organization. The information systems department suggests new business strategies and new information-based products and services and coordinates both the development of the technology and the planned changes in the organization.

In the past, firms generally developed their own software and managed their own computing facilities. Today, many firms are turning to external vendors to provide these services (see Chapters 5 and 9) and are using their information systems departments to manage these service providers.

Organizing the Information Systems Function

There are many types of business firms, and there are many ways in which the IS function is organized within the firm (see Figure 2-15). A very small company with fewer than 100 employees will not have a formal information systems group. It will have one or two employees who are responsible for keeping its networks and applications running, or it might use consultants for these services. Larger companies will have a separate information systems department, which may be organized along several different lines, depending on the nature and interests of the firm.

Sometimes you will see a decentralized arrangement where each functional area of the business has its own information systems department and management that typically reports to a senior manager or chief information officer. In other words, the marketing department would have its own information systems group, as would manufacturing and each of the other business functions. The job of the CIO is to review information technology investments and decisions in the functional areas. The advantage of this approach is that systems are developed that directly address the business needs of the functional areas; however, central guidance is weak, and the danger is high that many incompatible systems will be developed, increasing costs as each group makes its own technology purchases.

In another arrangement, the information systems function operates as a separate department similar to the other functional departments with a large staff, a group of middle managers, and a senior management group that fights for its share of the company's resources. You will see this approach in many large firms. This central information systems department makes technology decisions for the entire company, which is more likely to produce more compatible systems and more coherent long-term systems development plans.

Very large "Fortune 1000"-size firms with multiple divisions and product lines might allow each division (such as the Consumer Products Division or the Chemicals and Additives Division) to have its own information systems group. All these divisional information systems groups report to a high-level central information systems group and CIO. The central IS group establishes corporate-wide standards, centralizes purchasing, and develops long-term plans for evolving the corporate computing platform. This model combines some divisional independence with some centralization.

Chief information officer (CIO)

End users

FIGURE 2-15   *Organization of the information systems function*

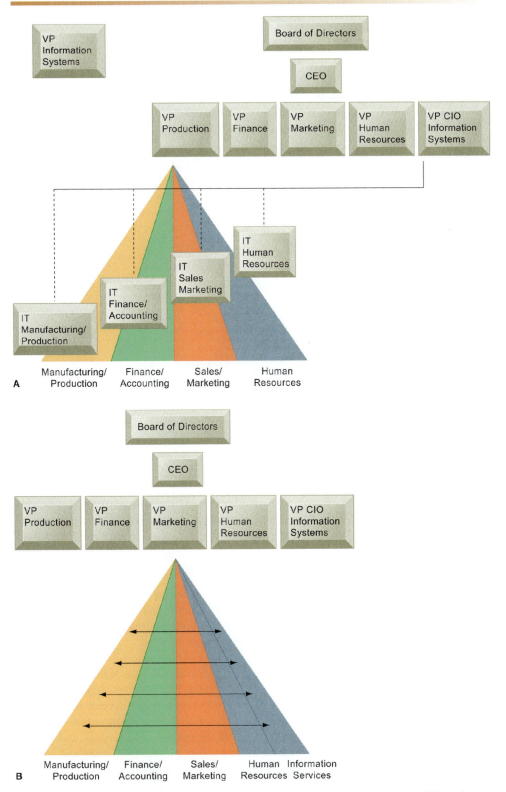

There are alternative ways of organizing the information systems function within the business: within each functional area (A), as a separate department under central control (B), or represented in each division of a large multidivisional company but under centralized control (C).

FIGURE 2-15   *Organization of the information systems function (continued)*

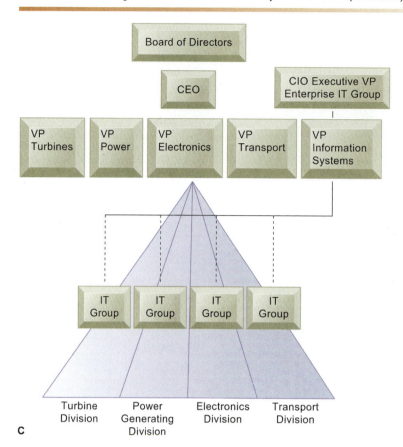

C

Summary

1. Define and describe business processes and their relationship to information systems.

A business process is a logically related set of activities that define how specific business tasks are performed; a business can be viewed as a collection of business processes. Business processes are concrete workflows of material, information, and knowledge. They also represent unique ways in which organizations coordinate work, information, and knowledge, and the ways in which management chooses to coordinate work. Managers need to pay attention to business processes because they determine how well the organization can execute its business, and thus be a potential source of strategic success or failure. Although each of the major business functions has its own set of business processes, many other business processes are cross-functional, such as order fulfillment. Information systems can help organizations achieve great efficiencies by automating parts of these processes or by helping organizations redesign and streamline them. Firms can become more flexible and efficient by coordinating their business processes closely, and, in some cases, integrating these processes so they are focused on efficient management of resources and customer service.

2. Describe the information systems supporting the major business functions: sales and marketing, manufacturing and production, finance and accounting, and human resources.

At each level of the organization, information systems support the major functional areas of the business. Sales and marketing systems help the firm identify customers for the firm's products or services, develop products and services to meet customers' needs, promote the products and services, sell the products and services, and provide ongoing customer support. Manufacturing and production systems deal with the planning, development, and production of products and services, and control the flow of production. Finance and accounting systems keep track of the firm's financial assets and fund flows. Human resources systems maintain employee records; track employee skills, job performance, and training; and support planning for employee compensation and career development.

3. *Evaluate the role played by systems serving the various levels of management in a business and their relationship to one another.*

There are four major types of information systems in contemporary organizations serving operational, middle, and senior management. Systems serving operational management are transaction processing systems (TPS), such as payroll or order processing, that track the flow of the daily routine transactions necessary to conduct business. Management information systems (MIS) and decision support systems (DSS) provide middle management with reports and access to the organization's current performance and historical records. Most MIS reports condense information from TPS and are not highly analytical. DSS support management decisions when these decisions are unique, rapidly changing, and not easily specified in advance. They have more advanced analytical models and data analysis capabilities than MIS and often draw on information from external as well as internal sources. Executive support systems (ESS) support senior management by providing data of greatest importance to senior management decision makers, often in the form of graphs and charts delivered via portals. They have limited analytical capabilities but can draw on sophisticated graphics software and many sources of internal and external information.

4. *Explain how enterprise applications and intranets promote business process integration and improve organizational performance.*

Enterprise applications, such as enterprise systems, supply chain management systems, customer relationship management systems, and knowledge management systems, are designed to support organization-wide process coordination and integration so that the organization can operate efficiently. They span multiple functions and business processes and may be tied to the business processes of other organizations. Enterprise systems integrate the key internal business processes of a firm into a single software system so that information can flow throughout the organization, improving coordination, efficiency, and decision making. Supply chain management systems help the firm manage its relationship with suppliers to optimize the planning, sourcing, manufacturing, and delivery of products and services. Customer relationship management uses information systems to coordinate all the business processes surrounding the firm's interactions with its customers to optimize firm revenue and customer satisfaction. Knowledge management systems enable firms to optimize the creation, sharing, and distribution of knowledge to improve business processes and management decisions.

Intranets and extranets use Internet technology and standards to assemble information from various systems and present it to the user in a Web page format. Extranets make portions of private corporate intranets available to outsiders.

5. *Assess the role of the information systems function in a business.*

The information systems department is the formal organizational unit responsible for information technology services. The information systems department is responsible for maintaining the hardware, software, data storage, and networks that comprise the firm's IT infrastructure. The information systems department consists of specialists, such as programmers, systems analysts, project leaders, and information systems managers, and is often headed by a CIO.

There are alternative ways of organizing the IT function within the firm. A very small company will not have a formal information systems group. Larger companies will have a separate information systems department, which may be organized along several different lines, depending on the nature and interests of the firm. Each functional area of the business may have its own information systems department, overseen by a corporate CIO. The information systems function may be run as a separate department similar to the other functional departments. A third arrangement found in very large firms with multiple divisions and product lines is to have an information systems department for each division reporting to a high-level central information systems group and CIO.

Key Terms

Business functions, 33	Enterprise applications, 48	Management information systems (MIS), 43
Channel, 52	Enterprise systems, 50	Manufacturing and production information
Chief information officer (CIO), 56	Executive support systems (ESS), 47	systems, 36
Customer relationship management (CRM)	Finance and accounting information	Portal, 47
systems, 52	systems, 40	Programmers, 55
Decision-support systems (DSS), 46	Human resources information systems, 40	Sales and marketing information
Electronic business (e-business), 55	Information systems department, 55	systems, 36
Electronic commerce (e-commerce), 55	Information systems managers, 55	Supply chain management (SCM) systems, 51
E-government, 55	Interorganizational system, 51	Systems analysts, 55
End users, 56	Knowledge management systems (KMS), 53	Transaction processing systems (TPS), 42

Review Questions

1. What are business processes? What role do they play in organizations? How are they enhanced by information systems?

2. List and describe the information systems serving each of the major functional areas of a business.

3. What are the characteristics of transaction processing systems? What role do they play in a business?

4. What are the characteristics of MIS? How do MIS differ from TPS? From DSS?

5. What are the characteristics of DSS? How do they differ from those of ESS?

6. Describe the relationship between TPS, MIS, DSS, and ESS.

7. Why are organizations trying to integrate their business processes? What are the four key enterprise applications?

8. What are enterprise systems? How do they benefit businesses?

9. What are supply chain management systems? How do they benefit businesses?

10. What are customer relationship management systems? How do they benefit businesses?

11. What is the role of knowledge management systems in the enterprise?

12. Describe how the information systems function supports a business. What roles are played by programmers, systems analysts, information systems managers, and the chief information officer (CIO)?

13. Describe alternative ways of organizing the information systems function in a business.

Discussion Questions

1. How could information systems be used to support the order fulfillment process illustrated in Figure 2-1 on page 34? What are the most important pieces of information these systems should capture? Explain your answer.

2. Adopting an enterprise application is a key business decision as well as a technology decision. Do you agree? Why or why not? Who should make this decision?

3. Discuss the differences in information needed by the different types of workers in an organization. Do not forget to include the various levels of management in your discussion.

4. Discuss whether you think all information systems function jobs are technical. Which jobs do you think are more technical, and which are more managerial? Do you think this can make for communication problems? If you think there could be communication problems, describe how you think they might happen and what could be done to alleviate these problems.

Teamwork: Describing Management Decisions and Systems

With a group of three or four other students, find a description of a manager in a corporation in *The National Post, The Globe and Mail, Canadian Business*, or another business magazine. Write a description of the kinds of decisions this manager has to make and the kind of information the manager would need for those decisions. Suggest how information systems could supply this information. If possible, use presentation software to present your findings to the class.

Learning Track Module

Challenges of Using Business Information Systems. This Learning Track Module provides a brief overview of the central management issues raised by information systems and their potential solutions. This module also provides a useful introduction to IS implementation issues that are described throughout the book. You can find the Learning Track Module on MyMISLab.

For online exercises, please visit www.pearsoned.ca/mymislab.

HANDS-ON **MIS**   **Application Exercises**

The projects in this section give you hands-on experience analyzing a company's financial and sales data to assess business performance and profitability, using a spreadsheet to improve decision making about suppliers, and using Internet software to plan efficient transportation routes.

Analyzing Financial Performance

Software skills: Spreadsheet charts and formulas
Business skills: Financial statement analysis

In this exercise, you will use spreadsheet software to analyze company financial statements and create graphs of important financial data.

As part of your analysis of the company, you have been asked to analyze data on Dirt Bikes Canada's financial performance and prepare a report for management. Review Dirt Bikes Canada's selected financial data in the Introduction to Dirt Bikes Canada, which can be found on MyMISLab. There you will find Dirt Bikes Canada's income statement and summary balance sheet data from 2005 to 2007, annual sales of bike models between 2003 and 2007, and total domestic versus international sales between 2003 and 2007.

Use your spreadsheet software to create graphs of Dirt Bikes Canada's sales history from 2003 to 2007 and its domestic versus international sales from 2003 to 2007. Select the type of graph that is most appropriate for presenting the data you are analyzing.

Use the instructions on MyMISLab and your spreadsheet software to calculate the gross and net margins in income statements from 2004 to 2006. You can also create graphs

showing trends in selected pieces of Dirt Bikes Canada's income statement and balance sheet data if you wish. (You may want to rearrange the historical ordering of the data if you decide to do this.)

Your management report should answer these questions:

1. What are Dirt Bikes Canada's best- and worst-performing products? What is the proportion of domestic to international sales? Have international sales grown relative to domestic sales?

2. Are sales (revenues) growing steadily, and, if so, at what rate? What is the cost of goods sold compared to revenues? Is it increasing or decreasing?

3. Are the firm's gross and net margins increasing or decreasing? Are the firm's operating expenses increasing or decreasing? Is the firm heavily in debt? Does it have sufficient assets to pay for operational expenses and to finance the development of new products and information systems?

4. (Optional) Prepare a slide show that summarizes your analysis of Dirt Bikes's performance.

Microsoft Excel - Sales by Model

File Edit View Insert Format Tools Data Window Help Acrobat

N31

	A	B	C	D	E	F	G
1		Dirt Bikes Sales by Model					
2	**Model**	**2002**	**2003**	**2004**	**2005**	**2006**	
3	Enduro 250	1201	1663	2291	2312	2195	
4	Enduro 550	2832	3290	3759	4078	3647	
5	Moto 300	1755	1932	2454	2615	2627	
6	Moto 450	463	598	661	773	823	
7	**TOTAL**	6251	7483	9165	9778	9292	
8							
9	Amounts are in thousands of dollars						
10							

Improving Decision Making:
Using a Spreadsheet to Select Suppliers

Software skills: Spreadsheet date functions, data filtering, DAVERAGE function
Business skills: Analyzing supplier performance and pricing

In this exercise, you will learn how to use spreadsheet software to improve management decisions about selecting suppliers. You will start with raw transactional data about suppliers organized as a large spreadsheet list. You will use Microsoft Excel software to filter the data based on several different criteria to select the best suppliers for your company.

You run a company that manufactures aircraft components. You have many competitor companies that are trying to offer lower prices and better service to customers, and you are trying to determine whether you can benefit from better supply chain management.

On MyMISLab, you will find a spreadsheet file that contains a list of all the items that your firm has ordered

from its suppliers during the past three months. The fields in the spreadsheet file include vendor name, vendor identification number, purchaser's order number, item identification number, and item description (for each item ordered from the vendor), cost per item, number of units of the item ordered (quantity), total cost of each order, vendor's accounts payable terms, order date, and actual arrival date for each order.

Prepare a recommendation of how you can use the data in this spreadsheet database to improve your decisions about selecting suppliers. Some criteria to consider for identifying preferred suppliers include the supplier's track record for on-time deliveries, suppliers offering the best accounts payable terms, and suppliers offering lower pricing when multiple suppliers can provide the same item. Prepare a report to support your recommendations.

Microsoft Excel – MIS10ch02_questionfile

File   Edit   View   Insert   Format   Tools   Data   Window   Help

Arial   10   B I U

Reply with Changes... End Review...

L32

Orders and Suppliers

Vendor No.	Order No.	Item No.	Item Description	Item Cost	Quantity	Cost per order	A/P Terms	Order Date	Arrival Date
2	A0111	6489	O-Ring	$ 3.00	900	$ 2,700.00	25	10/10/06	10/18/05
6	A0115	5319	Shielded Cable/ft.	$ 1.10	17,500	$ 19,250.00	30	08/20/06	08/31/06
6	A0123	4312	Bolt-nut package	$ 3.75	4,250	$ 15,937.50	30	08/25/06	09/01/06
6	A0204	5319	Shielded Cable/ft.	$ 1.10	16,500	$ 18,150.00	30	09/15/06	10/05/06
6	A0205	5677	Side Panel	$ 195.00	120	$ 23,400.00	30	11/02/06	11/13/06
6	A0207	4312	Bolt-nut package	$ 3.75	4,200	$ 15,750.00	30	09/01/06	09/10/06
5	A0223	4224	Bolt-nut package	$ 3.95	4,500	$ 17,775.00	30	10/15/06	10/20/06
5	A0433	5417	Control Panel	$ 255.00	500	$ 127,500.00	30	10/20/06	10/27/06
5	A0443	1243	Airframe fasteners	$ 4.25	10,000	$ 42,500.00	30	08/08/06	08/14/06
5	A0446	5417	Control Panel	$ 255.00	406	$ 103,530.00	30	09/01/06	09/10/06
2	A0533	9752	Gasket	$ 4.05	1,500	$ 6,075.00	25	09/20/06	09/25/06
2	A0555	6489	O-Ring	$ 3.00	1,100	$ 3,300.00	25	10/05/06	10/10/06
2	A0622	9752	Gasket	$ 4.05	1,550	$ 6,277.50	25	09/25/06	10/05/06
2	A0666	5125	Shielded Cable/ft.	$ 1.15	15,000	$ 17,250.00	25	10/01/06	10/15/06
2	A0777	6489	O-Ring	$ 3.00	1,050	$ 3,150.00	25	10/29/06	11/10/06
2	A1222	4111	Bolt-nut package	$ 3.55	4,200	$ 14,910.00	25	09/15/06	10/15/06
3	A1234	9399	Gasket	$ 3.65	1,250	$ 4,562.50	45	10/01/06	10/06/06
3	A1235	9399	Gasket	$ 3.65	1,450	$ 5,292.50	45	10/03/06	10/08/06
3	A1344	5454	Control Panel	$ 220.00	550	$ 121,000.00	45	10/09/06	10/14/06
3	A1345	9399	Gasket	$ 3.65	1,470	$ 5,365.50	45	10/07/06	10/12/06
3	A1346	9399	Gasket	$ 3.65	1,985	$ 7,245.25	45	10/05/06	10/11/06
2	A1444	4111	Bolt-nut package	$ 3.55	4,250	$ 15,087.50	25	09/20/06	10/10/06
2	A1445	4111	Bolt-nut package	$ 3.55	4,200	$ 14,910.00	25	09/25/06	10/25/06
2	A1449	4111	Bolt-nut package	$ 3.55	4,600	$ 16,330.00	25	10/05/06	10/19/06
3	A1456	5454	Control Panel	$ 220.00	500	$ 110,000.00	45	10/15/06	10/20/06

Achieving Operational Excellence:
Using Internet Software to Plan Efficient Transportation Routes

In this exercise, you will use the same online software tool that businesses use to map out their transportation routes and select the most efficient route.

The MapQuest (**www.mapquest.com**) Web site includes interactive capabilities for planning a trip. The software on this Web site can calculate the distance between two points and provide itemized driving directions to any location.

You have just started working as a dispatcher for Cross-Country Transport, a new trucking and delivery service based in Red Deer, Alberta. Your first assignment is to plan a delivery of office equipment and furniture from Kelowna, British Columbia (at the corner of Wilson Ave. and Pheasant Street), to Sackville, New Brunswick (at the corner of Main Street and Faucett Street). To guide your trucker, you need to know the most efficient route between the two cities. Use MapQuest to find the route that is the shortest distance between the two cities. Use MapQuest again to find the route that takes the least time. Compare the results. Which route should Cross-Country use? Prepare a one-page analysis of this problem and your answer.

CASE STUDY   Zellers Merchandises Better through Information Systems and Business Intelligence

In Canadian retail, staying competitive is always challenging. Margins are narrow, and profits can be found in the details of knowing your business. For Canadian retail businesses to succeed, management needs the ability to "see" into operations, and retailers are now using technology to provide managers with the insight that they need. This is certainly true of the Hudson's Bay Company.

Hudson's Bay Company (HBC) is Canada's oldest corporation, as well as being Canada's largest diversified retail organization and one of the country's largest employers. Established in 1670 as a fur trading company, HBC employs almost 70 000 people today and has an extensive array of goods and services available through its 94 Bay stores, 281 Zellers stores, 60 Home Outfitters stores, 151 Fields outlets, and 9 Designer Depots.

Zellers is HBC's mass merchandise retail chain, and, not surprisingly, improved technology has changed the way Zellers conducts business every day. Managing inventory is an ever-present challenge for Zellers staff: they must know when to restock their shelves, and up-to-the-minute inventory levels must be accessible.

It wasn't too many years ago that store personnel used a pen and paper to perform stockroom inventory checks. As part of their daily work, sales associates would examine the shelves, write down any merchandise that was low, and later replenish the shelves from the stockroom. Keeping records of stocks levels was done manually on a spreadsheet.

Gone are those days! Identifying the inaccuracy and inefficiency of this system, the IT department worked with IBM to develop a computerized inventory system for all the Zellers stores. The resulting system was dubbed the Listed Inventory Database System 2 (LID 2), and it gave employees the ability to track more accurately the movement of merchandise from the stockroom to the sales floor.

LID 2 had some serious drawbacks, however. The new system was still time-consuming and did not present management with the data they needed to analyze store operations. LID 2 still required sales associates to check and restock the shelves, make records of low-stock items, and print out reports that would itemize the merchandise needing to be replenished in the stockroom. Also, because each store maintained its own reports, with no access to a centralized database, numbers were often outdated and incomplete by the time they reached head office.

"LID 2 was an improvement over the previous system but it was still an inefficient system," said Chris Marinis, senior manager, Development Services, HBC. "From a management perspective, reports were not easy to obtain, and they often had to approach the IT team to produce these reports. Since many reports had to be printed on the weekend and did not reflect the flow of inventory on those days, reports were also not as accurate as they could be. That meant that the information our management team received per store was not reflective of the activity during the weekend, which is typically the busiest time of the week."

HBC management knew that inventory levels in the stockroom had to be closely aligned with sales to minimize inventory-holding costs. They also needed to know which merchandise was selling well to avoid stockouts and lost sales. Consolidating data from point-of-sale terminals and stockroom inventory data was a key objective for the proposed new system.

The inventory management systems had to be improved, and management needed to be able to gain better insight into operations at Zellers stores. So HBC worked with Microsoft Canada and T4G Ltd. to develop a new version of its LID application. Making use of the Microsoft SQL Server 2000 Reporting Services as well as IBM's Data Integration Facility, they were able to integrate data so that store personnel could receive reports on what merchandise needed to be replenished on the floor, not once but twice each day. These reports included a picking list, so that personnel could efficiently find and take merchandise from the stockroom to the floor. The improved software even took into account shelf capacity and location.

LID 3, the resulting proprietary wireless integrated replenishment and stockroom management system, used a centralized database integrated with the supply chain and point-of-sale systems. Zellers' RF Symbol technology was used, while HBC's central computing facility housed the application and data. LID 3 enabled Zellers to achieve annual cost savings of $5 million for the following reasons: automating shelf replenishment meant product was always in stock; inventory allocation among Zellers outlets was optimized; and more personnel were available on the sales floor to serve customers and facilitate sales.

HBC knew that the business intelligence (BI) capabilities of SQL Server Reporting Services would provide LID 3 with the means to gain insight into its Zellers operations. With this capability, management could get a clearer picture of the flow of inventory within the chain, helping them to make better business decisions. After implementing the inventory management system at Zellers, HBC realized many benefits, including time savings and improved productivity.

Another of LID 3's strengths was that it enabled Zellers to track inventory the moment it arrived and also when it left the store. Integrated with the point-of-sale systems as well as with wireless devices used by sales associates to track inventory on the floor and in the stockroom, LID 3 captured all the information in real time and sent it to the centralized database.

"As soon as a truck arrives at the store, the system knows what merchandise is getting there before we actually slot that merchandise in the stockroom. [. . .] As we begin selling merchandise, those pieces of information are integrated into the system so that we can replenish the shelves and always keep them full for customers. That's key to our business [. . .] But what's really critical to the whole system is the fact that we can now take the information that is captured in the centralized database and use that information more effectively through the creation of reports," explained HBC manager Chris Marinis.

With LID 3's reporting capability, HBC could collect and organize data coming in from the supply chain and point-of-sale systems to give users specialized reports based on their particular needs. Reports could also be delivered to key personnel in a format with which they were comfortable, making it easy for them to access the information they needed to make quick, informed decisions. Reports could be sent as an e-mail attachment, viewed using a Web browser, or even exported to a Microsoft Excel spreadsheet.

One type of report created for Zellers was used at the store level. The report enabled sales associates starting a shift to obtain a report indicating what merchandise was currently on the sales floor, what had been moved to the sales floor during the last shift, and what was still in the stockroom. Without physically walking the sales floor, sales associates had the information they needed to make sure the shelves were well-stocked. Store managers also accessed these reports to give them an accurate picture of the flow of merchandise inside the store throughout the day, week, or month. They could make informed decisions about purchasing and staffing, and they could easily send this information to district and regional managers.

The second type of report was for management at the head office, giving them a clear picture of Zellers operations, whether at an individual store, in a specific district, in an entire region, or across the whole chain. Management was able to identify quickly any trends within the Zellers chain—positive or negative—and respond with better decisions, based on accurate, up-to-date information. "With this system," explained Marinis, "because the data is centralized, we can create reports in real time. If management says they need it in an hour, we can deliver it. Our reporting capabilities have definitely become more agile as a result of implementing SQL Server Reporting Services."

The improvement in productivity was evident—LID 3's reporting capabilities reduced the amount of work by about two hours per store per day, seven days a week. In financial terms, the system paid for itself during the first year of LID 3's operation, with return on investment calculated at 100 percent.

"In the past, management had little visibility into operations," Marinis elaborated. "What visibility they did have was always outdated. Since we had data in 300 locations, we would only go and pull this data once a week. We would pull it on Friday night and develop the report over the weekend. On Monday morning, when head office came in, they would have some visibility as to what was happening in the stores. However, of course by then, the picture had changed, and therefore, the information was never totally up to date." With 300 stores, there were at least 600 reports.

In addition to the improved reporting capabilities and the increased productivity at store level, IT personnel were freed up for further enhancing the system. LID 3's centralized database allowed employees to access reports themselves without having to contact IT.

The success of the new system was evident in the stores themselves. Marinis explained, "Obviously customers can only find merchandise on the sales floor, not in the stockroom. From a presentation point of view, as a store, you have more merchandise to sell or available for sale on the sales floor. What this system translates to is fuller shelves and better services for customers."

And better service for customers is what retail is all about!

Sources: "Hudson's Bay Company Gains More Accurate Business Snapshot of its Zellers Operations with Microsoft SQL Server 2000 Reporting Services," October 12, 2004, **www.microsoft. com/canada/casestudies/hbc.mspx**, accessed May 10, 2007. See also Ryan Patrick, "HBC Puts LID Technology on Zellers Inventory," IT World Canada, **www.itworldcanada.com/Mobile/ViewArticle. aspx?title=&id= idgml-2726a919-81bd-4628&s=395692**, accessed May 10, 2007; Neil Sutton, "HBC Puts IT Smarts into Its Merchandising Strategy," IT Business Canada, **www.itbusiness.ca,it/ client/en/Home/News.asp?id=40143&bsearch=True**, accessed May 10, 2007; and "Hudson's Bay Company Creates an Award-Winning Inventory Solution," **www.xtremeretail.com/ studies/hbcfinal.pdf**, accessed May 10, 2007.

CASE STUDY QUESTIONS

1. Describe and diagram the previous process for inventory control and the new process. What are the differences between the new and old processes?

2. What improvement may be seen with the implementation of LID 3? How do wireless devices and wireless transmission help this process?

3. Should all retail stores switch to inventory management control systems such as LID 3? Why or why not?

4. What management, organization, and technical factors would you want to take into account before implementing a new inventory control system?

CHAPTER 3

Information Systems, Organizations, and Strategy

OPENING CASE | Information on Demand for Canadian Tire

Canadian Tire is a Canadian icon. The company was founded in 1922 by the Billes brothers. According to the Canadian Tire Web site, "nine out of ten adult Canadians shop at Canadian Tire at least twice a year, and 40 percent of Canadians shop at Canadian Tire every week. Eighty-five percent of the Canadian population lives within a 15-minute drive of their local Canadian Tire store." There are more than 1000 Canadian Tire stores and gas bars, including the company's Mark's Work Wearhouse locations. The company employs more than 48 000 staff. Canadian Tire combines three specialty stores under one roof—automotive, leisure, and home products.

With this diverse a customer population and this broad a geographic range, Canadian Tire had developed information systems to provide information at the local, regional, and national levels for decision making and to entice customers to buy a wide variety of products. However, a smorgasbord of 50 separate platforms, applications, databases, protocols, and data entry points made it difficult for both management and IT staff at Canadian Tire to know if the information they were looking at was accurate and timely. According to Ken Dschankilic, enterprise architect at Canadian Tire, "We have a technology roach motel. We check all the stuff in, but it never, ever gets checked out. It leaves us with an inflexible architecture that's costly to maintain and difficult to leverage for new opportunities."

Management at Canadian Tire realized that information needed to be presented in a user-friendly format. Canadian Tire needed real-time access to sales and order status, in-store kiosks, and service

desk enhancements to differentiate the Canadian Tire brand from its competitors. At the same time, the company needed to manage stock, forecasting, and replenishment to ensure that products that were selling were on the shelves when customers wanted them and that products that were not selling were not held over in inventory.

To address the issue of the diverse range of systems, platforms, and standards, Canadian Tire's IT management decided to implement service-oriented architecture (SOA) that would permit the various applications and platforms to speak to each other and exchange information.

Canadian Tire employed IBM Information on Demand solutions and IBM's WebSphere application to implement the service-oriented architecture (see Chapter 5 for more on SOA). As a result of these changes to Canadian Tire's system, market-demand and inventory information are now accurate and accessible. This has greatly improved decision making and helped Canadian Tire stay focused on the customer. Using SOA and Websphere, Canadian Tire has differentiated its systems from its competitors and improved its revenues while reducing inventory and IT costs.

Sources: IBM Corporation, "Canadian Tire Fuels Business Innovation with Information on Demand Initiative," **www.306.ibm.com/software/success/cssdb.nsf/CS/HSAZ-6M2UBV?OpenDocument&Site=software**, February 15, 2006, accessed May 10, 2007; and Canadian Tire Corporation, "Company Profile," **www2.canadiantire.ca/CTenglish/h_ourstory.html**, accessed August 3, 2007.

Canadian Tire's experience illustrates the interdependence of business environments, organizational culture, business processes, business strategy, and the development of information systems. The new information systems integrate Canadian Tire's data to support the company's strategy. Obviously, Canadian Tire's systems changes cannot succeed without a significant amount of organizational and management change.

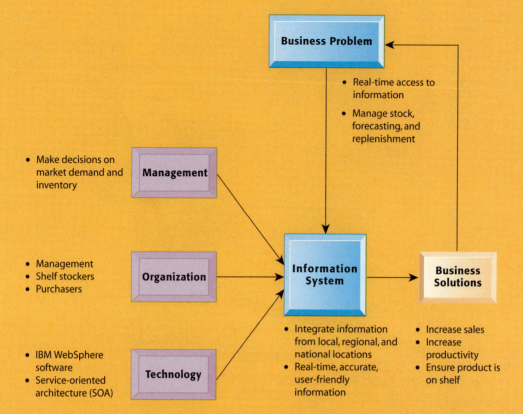

The chapter-opening Business Challenges diagram calls attention to important points raised by this case and this chapter. Canadian Tire faces intense pressure from retail competitors and from rising inventory costs. Their new IT platform, SOA, required investments in information systems and changes in management and organization. The new integrated systems provide value to customers by competing on both price and quality service. It is easy to see that such changes are not easy to make and require changes not just on the part of IT staff but also changes on the part of Canadian Tire's management, who would have to change the way they access and interpret information.

HEADS UP

As a manager, you will need to know about the relationship between organizations, information systems, and business strategy. This chapter first introduces the features of organizations that you will need to understand when you design, develop, and operate information systems. Then it examines the problems firms face from competition and the various ways in which information systems can provide competitive advantage. Every business student and future manager should know about these strategic uses of information technology.

- If your career is in finance and accounting, you will be developing and managing strategic products and services that are largely based on information systems, such as wealth management, financial advising, risk management systems, online financial services, and credit services.

- If your career is in human resources, you will be working with systems that could give your firm a strategic edge by providing information and communication capabilities that lower the cost of managing employees or by organizing jobs and work assignments to reduce operational costs.

- If your career is in information systems, you will be working with managers from all the other business areas to identify opportunities for strategic information systems and their technology requirements.

- If your career is in manufacturing and production, you will be developing production systems based on information technology and systems that help your firm compete by lowering supply chain costs, improving quality, and enabling the firm to design and bring new products to market more rapidly.

- If your career is in sales and marketing, you will be working with information systems and technologies that create strategic advantages

for your firm, such as customer relationship management systems, online Web site monitoring tools, and business analytics tools that can help you understand your customers better.

3.1 Organizations and Information Systems

Information systems and organizations influence one another. Information systems are developed by managers to serve the interests of the business firm. At the same time, in order to benefit from the new technologies the organization must be aware of and open to the influences of them.

The interaction between information technology and organizations is complex and is influenced by many mediating factors, including the organization's structure, business processes, politics, culture, surrounding environment, and management decisions (see Figure 3-1). You will need to understand how information systems can change social and work life in your firm. You will not be able to design new systems successfully or understand existing systems without understanding your own business organization.

As a manager, you will be the one to decide which systems will be developed, what they will do, and how they will be implemented. You may not be able to anticipate all of the consequences of these decisions. Some of the changes that occur in business firms because of new information technology (IT) investments cannot be foreseen and have results that may or may not meet your expectations. Who would have imagined ten years ago, for instance, that e-mail and instant messaging would become a dominant form of business communication and that many managers would be inundated with more than 200 e-mail messages each day (Walker, 2004)?

What Is an Organization?

An **organization** is a stable, formal social structure that takes resources from the environment and processes them to produce outputs. This technical definition focuses on three

Organization

FIGURE 3-1   *The two-way relationship between organizations and information technology*

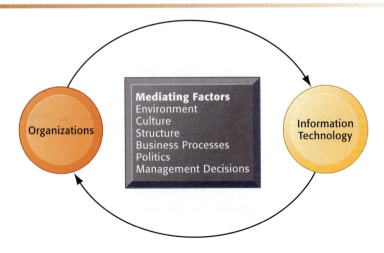

This complex two-way relationship is mediated by many factors, not the least of which are the decisions made—or not made—by managers. Other factors mediating the relationship include the organizational culture, structure, politics, business processes, and environment.

FIGURE 3-2   *The technical microeconomic definition of the organization*

In the microeconomic definition of organizations, capital and labour (the primary production factors provided by the environment) are transformed by the firm through the production process into products and services (outputs to the environment). The products and services are consumed by the environment, which supplies additional capital and labour as inputs in the feedback loop.

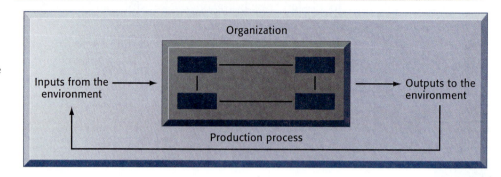

elements of an organization. Capital and labour are primary production factors provided by the environment. The organization (the firm) transforms these inputs into products and services in a production function. The products and services are consumed by environments in return for supply inputs (see Figure 3-2).

An organization is more stable than an informal group (such as a group of friends that meets every Friday for lunch) in terms of longevity and routine. Organizations are formal legal entities with internal rules and procedures that must abide by laws. Organizations are also social structures because they are a collection of social elements, much as a machine has a structure—a particular arrangement of valves, cams, shafts, and other parts.

This definition of organizations is powerful and simple, but it is not very descriptive or even predictive of real-world organizations. A more realistic behavioural definition of an organization is that it is a collection of rights, privileges, obligations, and responsibilities that is delicately balanced over a period of time through conflict and conflict resolution (see Figure 3-3).

In this behavioural view of the firm, people who work in organizations develop customary ways of working; they gain attachments to existing relationships; and they make arrangements with subordinates and superiors about how work will be done, the amount of work that will be done, and under what conditions work will be done. Most of these arrangements and feelings are not discussed in any formal rulebook.

How do these definitions of organizations relate to information systems technology? A technical view of organizations encourages us to focus on how inputs are combined to

FIGURE 3-3   *The behavioural view of organizations*

The behavioural view of organizations emphasizes group relationships, values, and structures.

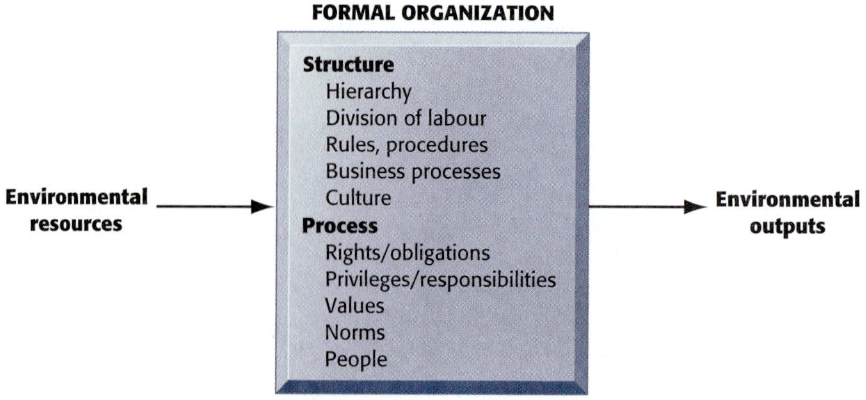

FORMAL ORGANIZATION

Structure
  Hierarchy
  Division of labour
  Rules, procedures
  Business processes
  Culture
Process
  Rights/obligations
  Privileges/responsibilities
  Values
  Norms
  People

Environmental
resources → [FORMAL ORGANIZATION] → Environmental
outputs

create outputs when technology changes are introduced into the company. The firm is seen as infinitely malleable, with capital and labour substituting for each other quite easily. But the more realistic behavioural definition of an organization suggests that developing new information systems or redeveloping old ones involves much more than a technical rearrangement of machines or workers. In behavioural terms, an **organization** is a collection of rights, privileges, obligations, responsibilities, and feelings that have been established and balanced over a long period of time. Changing information systems requires changing that balance.

Changing an organization can therefore take a long time, be very disruptive, and require more resources to support training and learning. For instance, the length of time required to effectively implement a new information system is much longer than usually anticipated simply because there is a lag between implementing a technical system and teaching employees and managers how to use the system.

Technological change requires changes in who owns and controls information; who has the right to access and update that information; and who makes decisions about whom, when, and how. This more complex view forces us to look at the way work is designed and the procedures used to achieve outputs.

The technical and behavioural definitions of organizations are not contradictory. Indeed, they complement each other: The technical definition tells us how thousands of firms in competitive markets combine capital, labour, and information technology while the behavioural model takes us inside the individual firm to see how that technology affects the organization's inner workings. Section 3.2 describes how each of these definitions of organizations can help explain the relationships between information systems and organizations.

Features of Organizations

All modern organizations have certain characteristics. They are bureaucracies with clear-cut divisions of labour and specialization. Organizations arrange specialists in a hierarchy of authority in which everyone is accountable to someone and authority is limited to specific actions governed by abstract rules or procedures. These rules create a system of impartial and universal decision making. Organizations try to hire and promote employees on the basis of technical qualifications and professionalism (not personal connections).

The organization is devoted to the principle of efficiency: maximizing output using limited inputs. Other features of organizations include their business processes, organizational culture, organizational politics, surrounding environments, structure, goals, constituencies, and leadership styles. All these features affect the kinds of information systems used by organizations.

Routines and Business Processes

All organizations, including business firms, become very efficient over time because individuals in the firm develop **routines** for producing goods and services. Routines—sometimes called *standard operating procedures*—are precise rules, procedures, and practices that have been developed to cope with virtually all expected situations. As employees learn these routines, they become highly productive and efficient, and the firm is able to reduce its costs over time as efficiency increases. For instance, when you visit a doctor's office, receptionists have a well-developed set of routines for gathering basic information from you; nurses have a different set of routines for preparing you for an interview with a doctor; and the doctor has a well-developed set of routines for diagnosing you. *Business processes*, which we introduced in Chapters 1 and 2, are collections of such routines. A business firm in turn is a collection of business processes (Figure 3-4).

Organization

Routines

FIGURE 3-4 *Routines, business processes, and firms*

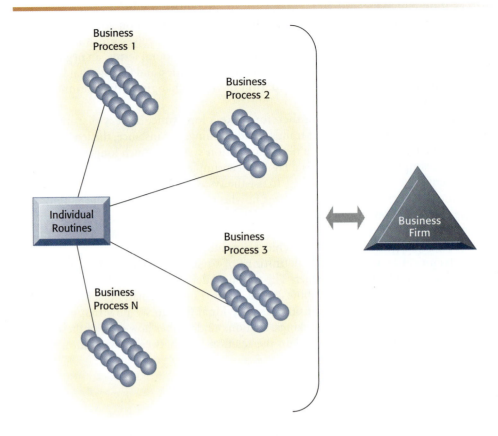

All organizations are composed of individual routines and behaviours, a collection of which make up a business process. A collection of business processes makes up the business firm. New information system applications require that individual routines and business processes change to achieve high levels of organizational performance.

Organizational Politics

People in organizations occupy different positions with different specialties, concerns, and perspectives. As a result, they naturally have divergent viewpoints about how resources, rewards, and punishments should be distributed. These differences matter to both managers and employees, and they result in political struggles for resources, competition, and conflict within every organization. Political resistance is one of the great difficulties of bringing about organizational change, especially the development of new information systems. Virtually all large information systems investments by a firm that bring about significant changes in strategy, business objectives, business processes, and procedures become politically charged events. Managers who know how to work with the politics of an organization will be more successful than less-skilled managers in implementing new information systems. Throughout this book, you will find many examples of internal politics defeating the best-laid plans for an information system.

Organizational Culture

All organizations have bedrock—unassailable, unquestioned (by the members) assumptions that define their goals and products. Organizational culture encompasses this set of assumptions about what products the organization should produce, how it should produce them, where, and for whom. Generally, these cultural assumptions are taken totally for granted and are rarely publicly announced or spoken about. Business processes—the actual way business firms produce value—are usually ensconced in the organization's culture.

You can see organizational culture at work by looking around your university or college. Some bedrock assumptions of university life are that professors know more than students, classes follow a regular schedule, and the reason students attend college is to learn.

Organizational culture is a powerful unifying force that restrains political conflict and promotes common understanding, agreement on procedures, and common practices. If we all share the same basic cultural assumptions, agreement on other matters is more likely.

At the same time, organizational culture is a powerful restraint on change, especially technological change. Most organizations will do almost anything to avoid making changes in basic assumptions. Any technological change that threatens commonly held cultural assumptions usually meets a great deal of resistance. However, there are times when the only sensible way for a firm to move forward is to employ a new technology that directly opposes an existing organizational culture. When this occurs, the technology is often stalled while the culture slowly adjusts.

Organizational Environments

Organizations reside in environments from which they draw resources and to which they supply goods and services. Organizations and environments have a reciprocal relationship. On the one hand, organizations are open to, and dependent on, the social and physical environment that surrounds them. Without financial and human resources—people willing to work reliably and consistently for a set wage or revenue from customers—organizations could not exist. Organizations must respond to legislative and other requirements imposed by government, as well as the actions of customers and competitors. On the other hand, organizations can influence their environments. For example, business firms form alliances with other businesses to influence the political process, and they advertise to influence customer acceptance of their products.

Figure 3-5 illustrates the role of information systems in helping organizations perceive changes in their environments and also in helping organizations act on their environments. Information systems are key instruments for *environmental scanning*, helping managers identify external changes that might require an organizational response.

Environments generally change much faster than organizations. The main reasons for organizational failure are an inability to adapt to a rapidly changing environment and a lack of resources, which make it hard for firms—particularly young firms—to survive even brief periods of troubled times. New technologies, new products, and changing public tastes and values (many of which result in new government regulations) strain any organization's culture, politics, and people. Most organizations do not cope well with large environmental shifts. The inertia built into an organization's standard operating procedures, the political

FIGURE 3-5   *Environments and organizations have a reciprocal relationship*

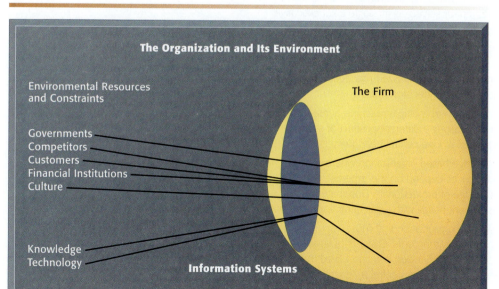

Environments shape what organizations can do, but organizations can influence their environments and decide to change environments altogether. Information technology plays a critical role in helping organizations perceive environmental change and in helping organizations act on their environment.

conflict raised by changes to the existing order, and the threat to closely held cultural values typically inhibit organizations from making significant changes. It is not surprising that only 10 percent of the Fortune 500 companies in 1919 still exist today.

Organizational Structure

Organizations all have a structure or shape. Mintzberg's classification, described in Table 3-1, identifies five basic kinds of organizational structure (Mintzberg, 1979).

The kind of information systems you find in a business firm—and the nature of problems with these systems—often reflects the type of organizational structure. For instance, in a professional bureaucracy such as a hospital, it is not unusual to find parallel patient record systems, one operated by the administration, another by doctors, and another by other professional staff such as nurses and social workers. In small entrepreneurial firms, you will often find poorly designed systems developed in a rush that often outgrow their usefulness quickly. In huge multidivisional firms operating in hundreds of locations, you will often find there is not a single integrating information system, but instead each locale or each division has its set of information systems.

Other Organizational Features

Organizations have goals and use different means to achieve them. Some organizations (e.g., prisons) have coercive goals; others (e.g., businesses) have utilitarian goals. Still others (e.g., universities and religious groups) have normative goals. Organizations also serve different groups or have different constituencies, and some organizations primarily benefit their members while others benefit clients, stockholders, or the public. The nature of leadership differs greatly from one organization to another—some organizations may be more democratic or authoritarian than others. Another way organizations differ is by the tasks they perform and the technology they use. Some organizations perform primarily routine tasks that can be reduced to formal rules requiring little judgment (such as manufacturing auto parts) while others (such as consulting firms) work primarily with nonroutine tasks.

TABLE 3-1 *Organizational Structures*

Organizational Type	Description	Examples
Entrepreneurial structure	Young, small firm in a fast-changing environment. It has a simple structure and is managed by an entrepreneur serving as its single chief executive officer.	Small start-up business
Machine bureaucracy	Large bureaucracy existing in a slowly changing environment, producing standard products. It is dominated by a centralized management team and centralized decision making.	Midsize manufacturing firm
Divisionalized bureaucracy	Combination of multiple machine bureaucracies, each producing a different product or service, all topped by one central headquarters.	Fortune 500 firms, such as General Motors
Professional bureaucracy	Knowledge-based organization where goods and services depend on the expertise and knowledge of professionals. Dominated by department heads with weak centralized authority.	Law firms, school systems, hospitals
Adhocracy	Task force organization that must respond to rapidly changing environments. Consists of large groups of specialists organized into short-lived multidisciplinary teams and has weak central management.	Consulting firms, such as EDS Canada

3.2 How Information Systems Impact Organizations and Business Firms

Information systems have become integral, online, interactive tools deeply involved in the minute-to-minute operations and decision making of large organizations. Over the last decade, information systems have fundamentally altered the economics of organizations and greatly increased the possibilities for organizing work. Theories and concepts from economics and sociology help us understand the changes brought about by IT.

Economic Impacts

From the point of view of economics, IT changes both the relative costs of capital and the costs of information. Information systems technology can be viewed as a factor of production that can be substituted for traditional capital and labour. As the cost of information technology decreases, it is substituted for labour, which historically has been a rising cost. Hence, information technology should result in a decline in the number of middle managers and clerical workers as information technology substitutes for their labour.

As the cost of information technology decreases, it also substitutes for other forms of capital, such as buildings and machinery, which remain relatively expensive. Hence, over time we should expect managers to increase their investments in IT because of its declining cost relative to other capital investments.

IT also obviously affects the cost and quality of information and changes the economics of information. Information technology helps firms contract in size because it can reduce transaction costs, that is, the costs incurred when a firm buys on the marketplace what it cannot make itself. According to **transaction cost theory**, firms and individuals seek to economize on transaction costs, much as they do on production costs. Using markets is expensive (Coase, 1937; Williamson, 1985) because of costs such as locating and communicating with distant suppliers, monitoring contract compliance, buying insurance, obtaining information on products, and so forth. Traditionally, firms have tried to reduce transaction costs through vertical integration, by getting bigger, hiring more employees, or buying their own suppliers and distributors, as both General Motors and Ford used to do.

Information technology, especially the use of networks, can help firms lower the cost of market participation (transaction costs), making it worthwhile for firms to contract with external suppliers instead of using internal sources. For instance, by using computer links to external suppliers, the Chrysler Corporation can achieve economies by obtaining more than 70 percent of its parts from the outside. Information systems make it possible for companies such as Cisco Systems and Dell Computer to outsource their production to contract manufacturers such as Flextronics instead of making their products themselves.

Figure 3-6 shows that as transaction costs decrease, firm size (the number of employees) should shrink because it becomes easier and cheaper for the firm to contract for the purchase of goods and services in the marketplace rather than to make the product or offer the service itself. Firm size can stay constant or contract even if the company increases its revenues. For example, when Eastman Chemical Company split off from Kodak in 1994, it had $3.8 billion in revenue and 24 000 full-time employees. By 2005, it generated $8.1 billion in revenue with only 12 000 employees.

Information technology also can reduce internal management costs. According to **agency theory**, the firm is viewed as a "nexus of contracts" among self-interested individuals rather than as a unified, profit-maximizing entity (Jensen and Meckling, 1976). A principal (an owner) employs "agents" (employees) to perform work on his or her behalf. However, agents need constant supervision and management; otherwise, they will tend to pursue their own interests rather than those of the owners. As firms grow in size and scope, agency costs or coordination costs rise because owners must expend more and more effort supervising and managing employees.

Transaction cost theory

Agency theory

FIGURE 3-6 *The transaction cost theory of the impact of information technology on the organization*

Firms traditionally grow in size to reduce transaction costs. IT potentially reduces the costs for a given size, shifting the transaction cost curve inward, opening up the possibility of revenue growth without increasing size or even revenue growth accompanied by shrinking size.

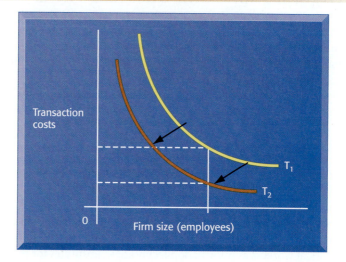

Information technology, by reducing the costs of acquiring and analyzing information, permits organizations to reduce agency costs because it becomes easier for managers to oversee a larger number of employees. The Canadian Tire system discussed at the beginning of this chapter is an example of such a system. Figure 3-7 shows that by reducing overall management costs, information technology enables firms to increase revenues while shrinking their number of middle managers and clerical workers. We have seen examples in earlier chapters where information technology expanded the power and scope of small organizations by enabling them to perform coordinating activities such as processing orders or keeping track of inventory with very few clerks and managers.

Organizational and Behavioural Impacts

Theories based on the sociology of complex organizations also provide some understanding about how and why firms change with the implementation of new IT applications.

IT Flattens Organizations Large, bureaucratic organizations, which primarily developed before the computer age, are often inefficient, slow to change, and less competitive

FIGURE 3-7 *The agency cost theory of the impact of information technology on the organization*

As firms grow in size and complexity, traditionally they experience rising agency costs. IT shifts the agency cost curve down and to the right, enabling firms to increase size while lowering agency costs.

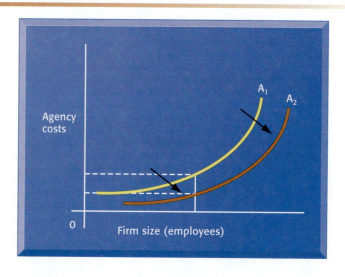

FIGURE 3-8   *Flattening organizations*

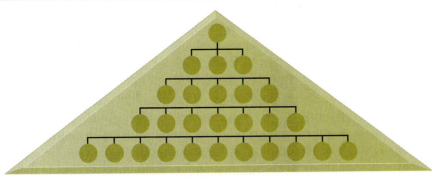

A traditional hierarchical organization with many levels of management

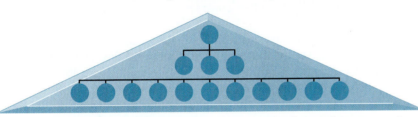

An organization that has been "flattened" by removing layers of management

Information systems can reduce the number of levels in an organization by providing managers with information to supervise larger numbers of workers and by giving lower-level employees more decision-making authority.

than newly created organizations. Some of these large organizations have downsized, reducing the number of employees and the number of levels in their organizational hierarchies.

Behavioural researchers have theorized that information technology facilitates flattening of hierarchies by broadening the distribution of information to empower lower-level employees and increase management efficiency (see Figure 3-8). IT pushes decision-making rights lower in the organization because lower-level employees receive the information they need to make decisions without supervision. (This empowerment is also possible because of higher educational levels among the workforce, which give employees the capabilities to make intelligent decisions.) Because managers now receive so much more accurate information on time, they become much faster at making decisions, so fewer managers are required. Management costs decline as a percentage of revenues, and the hierarchy becomes much more efficient.

These changes mean that the management span of control has also been broadened, enabling higher-level managers to manage and control more workers spread over greater distances. Many companies have eliminated thousands of middle managers as a result of these changes.

Postindustrial Organizations Postindustrial theories based more on history and sociology than economics also support the notion that IT should flatten hierarchies. In postindustrial societies, authority increasingly relies on knowledge and competence and not merely on formal positions. Hence, the shape of organizations flattens because professional workers tend to be self-managing, and decision making should become more decentralized as knowledge and information become more widespread throughout the firm (Drucker, 1988).

Information technology may encourage task force–networked organizations in which groups of professionals come together, face-to-face or electronically, for short periods of time to accomplish a specific task (e.g., designing a new automobile); once the task is accomplished, the individuals join other task forces. The global consulting service Accenture, described in Chapter 1, is an example. It has no operational headquarters and no formal branches. Many of its 129 000 employees move from location to location to work on projects at client sites in 48 different countries.

Who makes sure that self-managed teams do not head off in the wrong direction? Who decides which person works on which team and for how long? How can managers evaluate the performance of someone who is constantly rotating from team to team? How do people know where their careers are headed? New approaches for evaluating, organizing, and informing workers are required, and not all companies can make virtual work effective.

Understanding Organizational Resistance to Change Information systems inevitably become bound up in organizational politics because they influence access to a key resource—namely, information. Information systems can affect who does what, when, where, and how in an organization. Many new information systems require changes in personal, individual routines that can be painful for those involved and require retraining and additional effort that may or may not be compensated. Because information systems potentially change an organization's structure, culture, business processes, and strategy, there is often considerable resistance to them when they are introduced.

There are several ways to visualize organizational resistance. Leavitt (1965) used a diamond shape to illustrate the interrelated and mutually adjusting character of technology and organization (see Figure 3-9). Here, changes in technology are absorbed, deflected, and defeated by organizational task arrangements, structures, and people. In this model, the only way to bring about change is to change the technology, tasks, structure, and people simultaneously. Other authors have spoken about the need to "unfreeze" organizations before introducing an innovation, quickly implementing it, and "refreezing" or institutionalizing the change (Kolb, 1970).

Because organizational resistance to change is so powerful, many information technology investments flounder and do not increase productivity. Indeed, research on project implementation failures demonstrates that the most common reason for failure of large projects to reach their objectives is not the failure of the technology, but organizational and political resistance to change. Chapter 10 treats this issue in detail. Therefore, as a manager involved in future IT investments, your ability to work with people and organizations is just as important as your technical awareness and knowledge.

The Internet and Organizations

The Internet, especially the World Wide Web, is beginning to have an important impact on the relationships between firms and external entities, and even on the organization of business processes inside a firm. The Internet increases the accessibility, storage, and

FIGURE 3-9   *Organizational resistance and the mutually adjusting relationship between technology and the organization*

Implementing information systems has consequences for task arrangements, structures, and people. According to this model, to implement change, all four components must be changed simultaneously.

Source: Leavitt (1965)

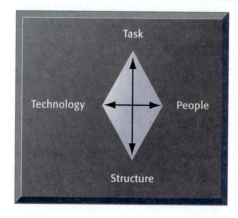

distribution of information and knowledge for organizations. In essence, the Internet is capable of dramatically lowering the transaction and agency costs facing most organizations. For instance, brokerage firms and banks in New York can now deliver their internal operations procedures manuals to their employees at distant locations by posting them on the corporate intranet, saving millions of dollars in distribution costs. A global sales force can receive nearly instant price product information updates using the Web or instructions from management sent by e-mail. Vendors of some large retailers can access retailers' extranets directly to find up-to-the-minute sales information and to initiate replenishment orders instantly.

Businesses are rapidly rebuilding some of their key business processes based on Internet technology and making this technology a key component of their IT infrastructures. If prior networking is any guide, one result will be simpler business processes, fewer employees, and much flatter organizations than in the past.

Implications for the Design and Understanding of Information Systems

To deliver genuine benefits, information systems must be developed with a clear understanding of the organization in which they will be used. In our experience, the central organizational factors to consider when planning a new system are the following:

- the environment in which the organization must function;
- the structure of the organization: hierarchy, specialization, routines, and business processes;
- the organization's culture and politics;
- the type of organization and its style of leadership;
- the principal interest groups affected by the system and the attitudes of workers who will be using the system; and
- the kinds of tasks, decisions, and business processes that the information system is designed to assist.

3.3 Using Information Systems to Achieve Competitive Advantage

In almost every industry you examine, you will find that some firms do better than most others. There is almost always a stand-out firm. In the automotive industry, Toyota is considered a superior performer. In pure online retail, Amazon.com is the leader. In off-line retail, Wal-Mart, the largest retailer on Earth, is the leader. In online music, Apple's iTunes is considered the leader with more than 75 percent of the downloaded music market, and in the related industry of digital music players, the iPod is the leader. In Web search, Google is considered the leader.

Firms that "do better" than others are said to have a competitive advantage over others. They either have access to special resources that others do not, or they are able to use commonly available resources more efficiently—usually because of superior knowledge and information assets. In any event, they do better in terms of revenue growth, profitability, or productivity growth (efficiency), all of which ultimately translate into higher stock market valuations than their competitors.

But why do some firms do better than others, and how do they achieve competitive advantage? How can you analyze a business and identify its strategic advantages? How can you develop a strategic advantage for your own business? And how do information systems contribute to strategic advantages? One answer to that question is Michael Porter's competitive forces model.

Porter's Competitive Forces Model

Arguably, the most widely used model for understanding competitive advantage is Michael Porter's **competitive forces model** (see Figure 3-10). This model provides a general view of the firm, its competitors, and the firm's environment. Earlier in this chapter, we described the importance of a firm's environment and the dependence of firms on environments. Porter's model is about the firm's general business environment. In this model, five competitive forces shape the fate of the firm.

Traditional Competitors All firms share market space with other competitors that are continuously devising new, more efficient ways to produce by introducing new products and services, and attempting to attract customers by developing their brands and imposing switching costs on their customers.

New Market Entrants In a free economy with mobile labour and financial resources, new companies are always entering the marketplace. In some industries, there are very low barriers to entry while in other industries, entry is very difficult.

For instance, it is fairly easy to start a pizza business or just about any small retail business, but it is much more expensive and difficult to enter the computer chip business, which has very high capital costs and requires significant expertise and knowledge that is hard to obtain. New companies have several possible advantages: They are not locked into old plants and equipment; they often hire younger workers who are less expensive and perhaps more innovative; they are not encumbered by old, worn-out brand names; and they are "more hungry" (more highly motivated) than traditional occupants of an industry. These advantages are also their weakness: They depend on outside financing for new plants and equipment, which can be expensive; they have a less experienced workforce; and they have little brand recognition.

Substitute Products and Services In just about every industry, there are substitutes that your customers might use if your prices become too high. New technologies create new substitutes all the time. Even oil has substitutes: Ethanol can substitute for gasoline in cars; vegetable oil for diesel fuel in trucks; and wind, solar, coal, and hydro power can be used for industrial electricity generation. Likewise, Internet telephone service can substitute for traditional telephone service, and fibre optic telephone lines to the home can substitute for cable TV lines. And, of course, an Internet music service that allows you to download music tracks to an iPod is a substitute for CD-based music stores. The more substitute products and services in your industry, the less you can control pricing and the lower your profit margins.

Customers A profitable company depends in large measure on its ability to attract and retain customers (while denying them to competitors), and charge high prices. The

Competitive forces model

FIGURE 3-10   *Porter's competitive forces model*

In Porter's competitive forces model, the strategic position of the firm and its strategies are determined not only by competition with its traditional direct competitors, but also by four forces in the industry's environment: new market entrants, substitute products, customers, and suppliers.

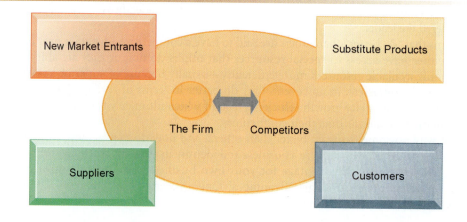

power of customers grows if they can easily switch to a competitor's products and services, or if they can force a business and its competitors to compete on price alone in a transparent marketplace where there is little **product differentiation**, and all prices are known instantly (such as on the Internet). For instance, in the used college textbook market on the Internet, students (customers) can find multiple suppliers of just about any current college textbook. In this case, online customers have extraordinary power over used-book firms.

Suppliers The market power of suppliers can have a significant impact on firm profits, especially when the firm cannot raise prices as fast as suppliers can. The more different suppliers a firm has, the greater control it can exercise over suppliers in terms of price, quality, and delivery schedules. For instance, manufacturers of laptop PCs almost always have multiple competing suppliers of key components, such as keyboards, hard drives, and display screens.

Information System Strategies for Dealing with Competitive Forces

What is a firm to do when it is faced with all these competitive forces? And how can the firm use information systems to counteract some of these forces? How do you prevent substitutes and inhibit new market entrants? There are four generic strategies, each of which often is enabled by using information technology and systems: low-cost leadership, product differentiation, focus on market niche, and strengthening customer and supplier intimacy.

Low-Cost Leadership Use information systems to achieve the lowest operational costs and the lowest prices. The classic example is Wal-Mart. By keeping prices low and shelves well stocked using a legendary inventory replenishment system, Wal-Mart became the leading retail business in North America. Wal-Mart's continuous replenishment system sends orders for new merchandise directly to suppliers as soon as consumers pay for their purchases at the cash

Wal-Mart's continuous inventory replenishment system uses sales data captured at the checkout counter to transmit orders to restock merchandise directly to its suppliers. The system enables Wal-Mart to keep costs low while fine-tuning its merchandise to meet customer demands.

register. Point-of-sale terminals record the bar code of each item passing the checkout counter and send a purchase transaction directly to a central computer at Wal-Mart headquarters. The computer collects the orders from all Wal-Mart stores and transmits them to suppliers. Suppliers can also access Wal-Mart's sales and inventory data using Web technology.

Because the system replenishes inventory with lightning speed, Wal-Mart does not need to spend much money on maintaining large inventories of goods in its own warehouses. The system also enables Wal-Mart to adjust purchases of store items to meet customer demands. Competitors, such as Sears, have been spending 24.9 percent of sales on overhead. But by using systems to keep operating costs low, Wal-Mart pays only 16.6 percent of sales revenue for overhead. (Operating costs average 20.7 percent of sales in the retail industry.)

Wal-Mart's continuous replenishment system is also an example of an efficient customer response system. An **efficient customer response system** directly links consumer behaviour to distribution and production and supply chains. Wal-Mart's continuous replenishment system provides such an efficient customer response. Dell Computer's assemble-to-order system, described in the following discussion, is another example of an efficient customer response system.

Product differentiation

Efficient customer response system

Product Differentiation Use information systems to promote a company's new products and services or significantly improve customer convenience in using its existing products and services. For instance, Google continuously introduces new and unique search services on its Web site, such as Google Maps. By purchasing PayPal, an electronic payment system, in 2003, eBay made it much easier for customers to pay sellers and expanded use of its auction marketplace. Apple created iPod, a unique portable digital music player, plus a unique online Web music service, iTunes, where songs can be purchased for 99 cents. Continuing to innovate, Apple recently introduced a portable iPod video player and the new iPhone, a combination cell phone, iPod, and Internet device.

Manufacturers and retailers are using information systems to create products and services that are customized and personalized to fit the precise specifications of individual customers. Dell sells directly to customers using assemble-to-order manufacturing. Individuals, businesses, and government agencies can buy computers directly from Dell, customized with the exact features and components they need. They can place their orders directly using a toll-free telephone number or by accessing Dell's Web site. Once Dell's production control receives an order, it directs an assembly plant to assemble the computer using components from an on-site warehouse based on the configuration specified by the customer.

Lands' End customers can use its Web site to order jeans, dress pants, chino pants, and shirts custom-tailored to their own specifications. Customers enter their measurements into a form on the Web site, which then transmits each customer's specifications over a network to a computer that develops an electronic made-to-measure pattern for that customer. The individual patterns are then transmitted electronically to a manufacturing plant, where they are used to drive fabric-cutting equipment. There are almost no extra production costs because the process does not require additional warehousing, production overruns, and inventories, and the cost to the customer is only slightly higher than that of a mass-produced garment. Fourteen percent of Lands' End shirt and pants sales are now customized. This ability to offer individually tailored products or services using the same production resources as mass production is called **mass customization**.

Table 3-2 lists a number of companies that have developed IS-based products and services that other firms have found difficult to copy, or at least took a long time to copy.

Mass customization

TABLE 3-2   *IS-Enabled New Products and Services Providing Competitive Advantage*

One-click shopping: Amazon.com	Amazon holds a patent on one-click shopping that it licenses to other online retailers.
Online music: Apple iPod and iTunes	An integrated handheld player backed up with an online library of two million songs; one billion songs downloaded so far.
Search engine advertising: Google	Online search engine integrated with online advertising using text ads; two billion searches per month; Google holds several patents on its PageRank method of search response.
Golf club customization: Ping	Customers can select from more than one million different golf club options; a build-to-order system ships their customized clubs within 48 hours.
Online bill payment: epost.ca	More than two million households pay their bills online through epost, as of 2005.
Online person-to-person payment: PayPal.com	Enables transfer of money between individual bank accounts and between bank accounts and credit card accounts.

Focus on Market Niche Use information systems to enable a specific market focus and serve this narrow target market better than competitors. Information systems support this strategy by producing and analyzing data for finely tuned sales and marketing techniques. Information systems enable companies to analyze customer buying patterns, tastes, and preferences closely so that they efficiently pitch advertising and marketing campaigns to smaller and smaller target markets.

The data come from a range of sources—credit card transactions, demographic data, purchase data from checkout counter scanners at supermarkets and retail stores, and data collected when people access and interact with Web sites. Sophisticated software tools find patterns in these large pools of data and infer rules from them to guide decision making. Analysis of the data drives one-to-one marketing that creates personal messages based on individualized preferences. Contemporary customer relationship management (CRM) systems feature analytical capabilities for this type of intensive data analysis (see Chapters 12 and 14).

Information systems make it possible for Ping Inc. to offer customers more than one million custom golf club options with different combinations of club heads, grips, shafts, and lie angles. Ping is able to fill many orders within 48 hours.

Hilton Hotels uses a customer information system called OnQ, which contains detailed data about active guests in every property across the eight hotel brands owned by Hilton. Employees at the front desk tapping into the system instantly search through 180 million records to find out the preferences of customers checking in and their past experiences with Hilton so they can give these guests exactly what they want. OnQ establishes the value of each customer to Hilton, based on personal history and on predictions about the value of that person's future business with Hilton. OnQ can also identify customers who are clearly not profitable. Profitable customers receive extra privileges and attention, such as the ability to check out late without paying additional fees. After Hilton started using the system, the rate of staying at Hilton Hotels rather than at competing hotels soared from 41 percent to 61 percent (Kontzer, 2004).

The Window on Technology section shows how 7-Eleven improved its competitive position by wringing more value out of its customer data. This company's early growth and strategy had been based on face-to-face relationships with its customers and intimate knowledge of exactly what they wanted to purchase. As the company grew over time, it was no longer able to discern customer preferences through personal face-to-face relationships. A new information system helped it obtain intimate knowledge of its customers once again by gathering and analyzing customer purchase transactions.

WINDOW ON TECHNOLOGY

7-Eleven Stores Ask the Customer by Asking the Data

There is probably a 7-Eleven store in your neighbourhood, and it is a convenient place for picking up a can of Coke or a quick ham-and-cheese sandwich. It is the largest convenience retailer in the world and the number one convenience store chain in North America, with 7100 stores.

This company started out about 75 years ago as an ice-dock operator. When refrigerators started replacing iceboxes, the manager of each store asked customers one by one what items they would like to stock in their new appliances. By asking customers directly and stocking only the items customers most wanted, the company grew and prospered.

Over time, the company moved away from its roots, losing touch with customers along the way. It had no means of knowing what sold in each store and allowed vendors to decide what to stock on its shelves. Although large vendors, such as Coca-Cola and Frito-Lay, had powerful information systems for analyzing what they sold in individual stores, other vendors did not have such systems. Moreover, the vendors' systems were designed to maximize opportunities for their businesses, not for 7-Eleven.

7-Eleven stores are not all alike. What their customers want depends a great deal on the neighbourhood and region of the country where they are located. What sells well in Charlottetown may not work in Whistler.

Without detailed knowledge of its customer and sales patterns, 7-Eleven was unable to determine which items were selling well or which items were most profitable to sell in the first place. This made a difference to the company's bottom line because of missed sales opportunities, lower profits, and excess store inventory, some of which consisted of perishable goods that had a very short shelf life. Profit margins are very thin in the convenience store business, so a quarter-point increase in sales volume can spell the difference between success and failure.

In 2004, 7-Eleven installed Hewlett-Packard servers and networking switches in all its U.S. stores to implement a Retail Information System. This system collects data from point-of-sale terminals in every store about each purchase made daily by its six million North American customers and transmits the information in real time to a 7-terabyte Oracle database operated by Electronic Data Systems (EDS).

With this database, 7-Eleven keeps track of its purchase transactions and analyzes them to amass information about customer demand, pricing, and interest in new products, such as the Diet Pepsi Slurpee. Analysis of the data shows which items are selling well in which stores, in which items customers are most interested, seasonal demand for items, and which items are most profitable to sell in the first place.

Management use this information to identify sales trends, improve product assortment, eliminate slow-moving products from inventory, and increase same-store sales by stocking products that are high in demand. Insights gleaned from the data also help 7-Eleven develop new products such as its fresh-food offerings that attract new customers and increase transaction size.

The system provides store managers with information on daily, weekly, and monthly sales of each item to help them determine which items to order and the exact quantities they will need for their stores. Managers use this information plus their on-the-spot knowledge of the neighbourhood to make final ordering decisions.

Store managers enter orders into workstations or handheld computers by 10 a.m. each day. The system consolidates these orders and transmits them to 7-Eleven's suppliers. Orders are consolidated four times daily, one for each U.S. time zone in which 7-Eleven stores operate. 7-Eleven's orders for fresh food items are aggregated at 7-Eleven headquarters and transmitted to fresh food suppliers and bakeries for preparation and delivery the next day.

Thanks to information technology, 7-Eleven has come full circle in its ability to respond to the needs of the customer. By tracking and analyzing its data, it knows its customers as intimately as it did when store owners talked to each customer face-to-face. According to 7-Eleven President and CEO James Keyes, "Now we can use technology as a surrogate for being able to talk to every customer who walks in the door."

To Think About

1. Why is knowing about the customer so important to a company such as 7-Eleven?

2. What are the benefits of 7-Eleven's Retail Information System?

3. In terms of Porter's model, what strategic forces does the Retail Information System seek to address?

4. Which of the strategies described in the chapter does the Retail Information System support?

MIS in Action

Visit a nearby 7-Eleven store. You can find your nearest 7-Eleven store by logging on to www.7-eleven.com and using the site's store locator. Observe the items available for sale and the sales process at the store.

1. What technologies does the store use to process a purchase? Do you see any other technologies being used at the store?

2. Do you think the selection of items for sale is appropriate for the neighbourhood and location of the particular 7-Eleven store you are visiting? What items might the Retail Information System have suggested for this store? Do you see any items that appear to be selling poorly at this store?

3. How well do you think 7-Eleven's Retail Information System works in stocking items for this store?

Sources: Oracle Corporation, "Streamlining Convenience," 2006 Shared Strategy Study and "7-Eleven Inc.," www.oracle.com, accessed July 15, 2006; Christopher Koch, "Who's Minding the Store?" *CIO*, May 15, 2005; James Keyes, "Data on the Fly," *Baseline*, August 2005; Laurie Sullivan, "Fine-Tuned Pricing," *InformationWeek*, August 15/22, 2005; 7-Eleven Inc., "About 7-Eleven," www.7-eleven.com/about/history.asp, accessed May 11, 2007; and Steven Marlin, "The 24-Hour Supply Chain," *InformationWeek*, January 26, 2004.

Strengthen Customer and Supplier Intimacy Use information systems to tighten linkages with suppliers and develop intimacy with customers. Chrysler Corporation uses information systems to facilitate direct access from supplies to production schedules and even permits suppliers to decide how and when to ship supplies to Chrysler factories. This allows suppliers more lead time in producing goods. On the customer side, Chapters.Indigo.ca keeps track of user preferences for book and CD purchases and can recommend titles purchased by others to its customers. Strong linkages to customers and suppliers increase **switching costs** (the cost of switching from one product to a competing product), and loyalty to your firm. Table 3-3 summarizes the competitive strategies we have just described.

7-Eleven stores use a point-of-sale system to capture data about customer purchases and to analyze it to learn more about customer preferences and sales trends.

Some companies focus on one of these strategies, but you will often see companies pursuing several of them simultaneously. For example, Dell Computer tries to emphasize low cost as well as the ability to customize its personal computers. Chapters.Indigo.ca is trying to compete with personalization of services as well as low cost.

The Internet's Impact on Competitive Advantage

The Internet has nearly destroyed some industries and has severely threatened more. The Internet has also created entirely new markets and formed the basis for thousands of new businesses. The first wave of e-commerce transformed the business world of books, music, and air travel.

In the second wave, eight new industries are facing a similar transformation scenario: telephone services, movies, television, jewellery, real estate, hotels, bill payments, and software. The breadth of e-commerce offerings grows, especially in travel, information clearinghouses, entertainment, retail apparel, appliances, and home furnishings.

Switching costs

TABLE 3-3 *Four Basic Competitive Strategies*

STRATEGY	DESCRIPTION	EXAMPLE
Low-cost leadership	Use information systems to produce products and services at a lower price than competitors while enhancing quality and level of service.	Wal-Mart Dell Computer
Product differentiation	Use information systems to differentiate products and enable new services and products.	Google, eBay, Apple, Lands' End
Focus on market niche	Use information systems to enable a focused strategy on a single market niche; specialize.	Hilton Hotels Harrah's
Customer and supplier intimacy	Use information systems to develop strong ties and loyalty with customers and suppliers.	Chrysler Corporation Chapters.Indigo.ca

TABLE 3-4   *Impact of the Internet on Competitive Forces and Industry Structure*

COMPETITIVE FORCE	IMPACT OF THE INTERNET
Substitute products or services	Enables new substitutes to emerge with new approaches to meeting needs and performing functions.
Customers' bargaining power	Availability of global price and product information shifts bargaining power to customers.
Suppliers' bargaining power	Procurement over the Internet tends to raise bargaining power over suppliers; suppliers can also benefit from reduced barriers to entry and from the elimination of distributors and other intermediaries standing between them and their users.
Threat of new entrants	Reduces barriers to entry, such as the need for a sales force, access to channels, and physical assets; it provides a technology for driving business processes that makes other things easier to do.
Positioning and rivalry among existing competitors	Widens the geographic market, increasing the number of competitors and reducing differences among competitors; makes it more difficult to sustain operational advantages; adds pressure to compete on price.

For instance, the printed encyclopedia industry and the travel agency industry have been nearly decimated by the availability of substitutes over the Internet. Likewise, the Internet has had a significant impact on the retail, music, book, brokerage, and newspaper industries. At the same time, the Internet has enabled new products and services, new business models, and new industries to spring up every day, from eBay and Amazon.com to iTunes and Google. In this sense, the Internet is "transforming" entire industries, forcing firms to change how they do business.

Because of the Internet, the traditional competitive forces are still at work, but competitive rivalry has become much more intense (Porter, 2001). Internet technology is based on universal standards that any company can use, making it easy for rivals to compete on price alone and for new competitors to enter the market. Because information is available to everyone, the Internet raises the bargaining power of customers, who can quickly find the lowest-cost provider on the Web. Profits have been dampened. Some industries, such as the travel industry and the financial services industry, have been more impacted than others. Table 3-4 summarizes some of the potentially negative impacts of the Internet on business firms identified by Porter.

However, contrary to Porter's somewhat negative assessment, the Internet also creates new opportunities for building brands and building very large and loyal customer bases that are willing to pay a premium for the brand, for example, Yahoo!, eBay, BlueNile, RedEnvelope, Overstock.com, Amazon.com, Google, and many others. In addition, as with all IT-enabled business initiatives, some firms are far better than other firms at using the Internet, which creates new strategic opportunities for the successful firms.

The Business Value Chain Model

Although the Porter model is very helpful for identifying competitive forces and suggesting generic strategies, it is not very specific about what exactly to do, and it does not provide a methodology to follow for achieving competitive advantages. If your goal is to achieve operational excellence, where do you start? Here is where the business value chain model is helpful.

The **value chain model** highlights specific activities in the business where competitive strategies can best be applied (Porter, 1985) and where information systems are most likely to have a strategic impact. This model identifies specific, critical-leverage

Value chain model

FIGURE 3-11   *The value chain model*

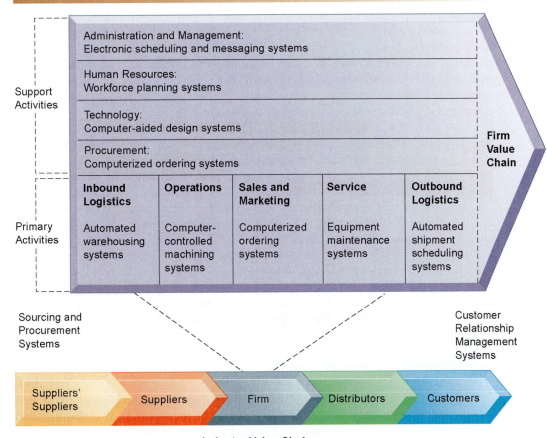

This figure provides examples of systems for both primary and support activities of a firm and of its value partners that can add a margin of value to a firm's products or services.

points where a firm can use information technology most effectively to enhance its competitive position. The value chain model views the firm as a series or chain of basic activities that add a margin of value to a firm's products or services. These activities can be categorized as either primary activities or support activities (see Figure 3-11).

Primary activities are most directly related to the production and distribution of the firm's products and services that create value for the customer. Primary activities include inbound logistics, operations, outbound logistics, sales and marketing, and service. Inbound logistics include receiving and storing materials for distribution to production. Operations transforms inputs into finished products. Outbound logistics entails storing and distributing finished products. Sales and marketing includes promoting and selling the firm's products. The service activity includes maintenance and repair of the firm's goods and services.

Support activities make the delivery of the primary activities possible and consist of organization infrastructure (administration and management), human resources (employee recruiting, hiring, and training), technology (improving products and the production process), and procurement (purchasing input).

Now you can ask at each stage of the value chain, "How can we use information systems to improve operational efficiency and improve customer and supplier intimacy?" This question will force you to critically examine how you perform

Primary activities

Support activities

value-adding activities at each stage and how the business processes might be improved. You can also begin to ask how information systems can be used to improve the relationship with customers and with suppliers who lie outside the firm value chain but belong to the firm's extended value chain, where they are absolutely critical to your success. Here, supply chain management systems that coordinate the flow of resources into your firm and customer relationship management systems that coordinate your sales and support employees with customers are two of the most common system applications that result from a business value chain analysis. We discuss these enterprise applications in detail later in Chapter 12.

Using the business value chain model will also cause you to consider benchmarking your business processes against your competitors or others in related industries and to identify industry best practices. **Benchmarking** involves comparing the efficiency and effectiveness of your business processes against strict standards and then measuring performance against those standards. Industry **best practices** are usually identified by consulting companies, research organizations, government agencies, and industry associations as the most successful solutions or problem-solving methods for consistently and effectively achieving a business objective.

Once you have analyzed the various stages in the value chain at your business, you can come up with candidate applications of information systems. Then, once you have a list of candidate applications, you can decide which to develop first. By making improvements in your own business value chain that your competitors might miss, you can achieve competitive advantage by attaining operational excellence, lowering costs, improving profit margins, and forging a closer relationship with customers and suppliers. If your competitors are making similar improvements, then at least you will not be at a competitive disadvantage—the worst of all cases!

Extending the Value Chain: The Value Web

Figure 3-11 on page 87 shows that a firm's value chain is linked to the value chains of its suppliers, distributors, and customers. After all, the performance of most firms depends not only on what goes on inside a firm but also on how well the firm coordinates with direct and indirect suppliers, delivery firms (logistics partners, such as FedEx or UPS), and, of course, customers.

How can information systems be used to achieve strategic advantage at the industry level? By working with other firms, industry participants can use information technology to develop industry-wide standards for exchanging information or business transactions electronically, which force all market participants to subscribe to similar standards. These efforts increase efficiency, making product substitution less likely and perhaps raising entry costs—thus discouraging new entrants. Also, industry members can build industry-wide, IT-supported consortia, symposia, and communications networks to coordinate activities concerning government agencies, foreign competition, and competing industries.

Looking at the industry value chain encourages you to think about how to use information systems to link up more efficiently with your suppliers, strategic partners, and customers. Strategic advantage derives from your ability to relate your value chain to the value chains of other partners in the process. For instance, if you are Amazon.com, you want to develop systems that do the following:

- Make it easy for suppliers to display goods and open stores on the Amazon site.
- Make it easy for customers to pay for goods.
- Develop systems that coordinate the shipment of goods to customers.
- Develop shipment tracking systems for customers.

In fact this is exactly what Amazon has done to become one of the Web's most satisfying online retail shopping sites. The Window on Organizations section discusses how Amazon.com developed and executes this business strategy. It also shows that Amazon.com had to revise its strategy several times in order to remain competitive.

Benchmarking

Best practices

Internet technology has made it possible to create highly synchronized industry value chains called value webs. A **value web** is a collection of independent firms that use information technology to coordinate their value chains to produce a product or service for a market collectively. It is more customer driven and operates in a less linear fashion than the traditional value chain.

Value web

WINDOW ON ORGANIZATIONS

Organization

Amazon.com: An Internet Giant Fine-Tunes Its Strategy

Amazon.com made Internet history as one of the first large-scale retail companies to sell over the Web: in 2004 it hit $4.6 billion in online revenues, and by 2006, its sales guidance estimates $12 billion in revenue. It has grown to become one of the largest Internet retailers on Earth. But the real significance of Amazon for this chapter is Amazon's continuous innovation in business strategy and information systems. In fact, the two are closely connected at Amazon: Its business innovations are all driven by huge investments in information systems.

In 1995, former investment banker Jeff Bezos took advantage of new business opportunities created by the Internet by setting up a Web site to sell books directly to customers online. There were three million titles in print, and any one physical bookstore could only stock a fraction of them.

A "virtual" bookstore offers a much larger selection of titles. Bezos believed consumers did not need to actually "touch and feel" a book before buying it, and Amazon.com provided online synopses, tables of contents, and reviews to help with selection. Amazon.com was able to charge lower prices than physical bookstores because it maintained very little of its own inventory (relying instead on distributors) and did not have to pay for maintaining physical storefronts or a large retail sales staff.

Amazon tried to provide superior customer service through e-mail and telephone customer support, automated order confirmation, online tracking and shipping information, and the ability to pay for purchases with a single click of the mouse using credit card and personal information a customer had provided during a previous purchase. This was called "1-Click" express shopping, and it made the shopping experience even more convenient. Amazon even received a patent for its 1-Click technology.

In 1998, Amazon started selling music, CDs, videos, and DVDs, revising its business strategy "to become the best place to buy, find, and discover any product or service available online"—the online Wal-Mart. Its offerings grew to include electronics, toys, home improvement products, video games, apparel, gourmet food, travel services, personal care, and jewellery. It also introduced Amazon.com Auctions (similar to those offered by eBay), and zShops (online storefronts for small retailers).

To service these new product lines, Amazon significantly expanded its warehouse and distribution capabilities and hired large numbers of employees. These moves strained its ability to adhere to its original vision of being a "virtual" retailer with lean inventories, low head count, and significant cost savings over traditional bookstores.

In 2001 and 2002, Amazon tried to increase revenue by cutting prices, offering free shipping, and leveraging its technology infrastructure to provide e-commerce services to other businesses. Amazon's Merchants@ and Amazon Marketplace allow other businesses to fully integrate their Web sites into Amazon's site to sell their branded goods using Amazon's fulfillment and payment systems. Nordstrom, The Gap, and Target stores use Amazon to sell their goods and then pay Amazon commissions and fees. In the Amazon Marketplace program, individuals are encouraged to sell their used or new goods on Amazon's Web site even when they compete directly with Amazon's sales of the same goods. Sales by third parties now represent 25 percent of Amazon's revenues.

Amazon refined its business model further to focus more on efficient operations while maintaining a steady commitment to keeping its 49 million customers satisfied. In early 2001, Amazon closed two of its eight warehouses, laid off 15 percent of its workforce, and consolidated orders from around the country prior to shipping to reduce shipping costs. Amazon used six sigma quality measures to reduce errors in fulfillment. These measures reduced fulfillment costs from 15 percent of revenue in 2000 to 10 percent by 2003.

Amazon finally became profitable in 2003 and remains an online retailing powerhouse growing at over 60 percent a year! It continues to innovate with IT-enabled services such as free unlimited two-day shipping for $79 a year (Amazon Prime). Amazon entered the dry goods grocery business in 2006. These innovations increased its costs and reduced its profits, much to the disappointment of the stock market, which has depressed Amazon's stock from a high of $100 in 2000 down to the mid $20 range in 2006.

Amazon faces powerful online retail competitors such as eBay and Yahoo!, which are also very adept at using information systems to develop new products and services. Google is emerging as a competitor because so many consumers use its search engine—six billion searches are performed each month at Google—and in the process are exposed to search engine ads. Google is expanding into other shopping services: Google Base offers free classified listings of goods for sale, and Google Checkout provides an online service that stores users' financial information to facilitate purchases from participating Internet vendors. Amazon is countering with new offerings, such as a digital mapping service with street-level photographs, a grocery store for non-perishable items sold in bulk, and selling short stories online for 49 cents apiece, along with additional expenditures to improve customer convenience and the shopping experience.

Like Google, eBay, Yahoo!, AOL, and other Web giants, Amazon has a Canadian Web site, amazon.ca, which includes almost identical elements, products, and services as its U.S.-based site. The Canadian site is offered in both English and French, and shipping charges are for within-Canada shipping, a true benefit for Canadian customers.

Recently, the company's profits have started to drop. The question is whether Amazon can turn its leadership in e-commerce into genuine long-term success. Can Amazon keep adapting its strategy to remain profitable and powerful?

To Think About

1. Analyze Amazon.com using the competitive forces and value chain models. How has it responded to pressures from its competitive environment? How does it provide value to its customers?

2. Describe Amazon's evolving business strategy.

3. Why did the company change its strategy?

4. Do you think Amazon can continue to be successful? Explain your answer.

MIS in Action

Search for an iPod nano on Amazon.ca, eBay.ca, and Yahoo! Shopping (**http://ca.shopping.yahoo.com/**). Compare the shopping experience at these sites to answer the following questions.

1. Evaluate how each site offers information about a product, including information about the reliability of the vendor (seller).

2. Evaluate each of the sites in terms of how many sources for the product they offer.

3. Evaluate the sites in terms of pricing and availability of the product you have selected.

4. Which site would you choose for shopping for your nano? Why?

Sources: Mary Crane, "Child's Play? Amazon Takes On Toys," Forbes.com, July 5, 2006; "Amazon Adds Groceries To Its Site," *The Wall Street Journal*, June 15, 2006; Randall Stross, "Trying to Get a Read on Amazon's Books," *The New York Times*, February 12, 2006; Bob Tedeschi, "Making Several Stops at Shops Online, but Paying All at Google," *The New York Times*, July 17, 2006; Gary Rivlin, "A Retail Revolution Turns 10," *The New York Times*, July 10, 2005; and Shaheen Pasha, "Amazon Has New Stories to Tell," *CNN Money*, August 22, 2005.

FIGURE 3-12   *Jeff Bezos, founder of Amazon.com*

Jeff Bezos is the founder, president, CEO, and chairman of the board of Amazon.com. Amazon.ca, which was launched in June 2002, is an early e-commerce leader that has adjusted its strategy multiple times. It is trying to become a one-stop source for online shoppers.

FIGURE 3-13　*The value web*

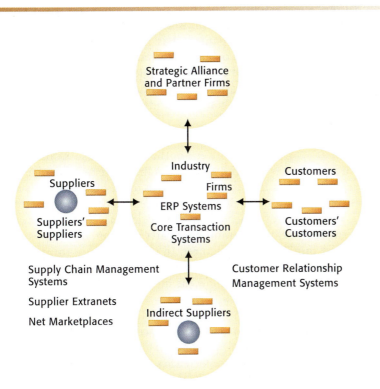

The value web is a networked system that can synchronize the value chains of business partners within an industry to respond rapidly to changes in supply and demand.

Figure 3-13 shows a value web that synchronizes the business processes of customers, suppliers, and trading partners among different companies in an industry or in related industries. These value webs are flexible and adapt to changes in supply and demand. Relationships can be bundled or unbundled in response to changing market conditions. Firms will accelerate time to market and to customers by optimizing their value web relationships to make quick decisions on who can deliver the required products or services at the right price and location.

Synergies, Core Competencies, and Network-Based Strategies

A large corporation is typically a collection of businesses. Often, the firm is organized financially as a collection of strategic business units, and the returns to the firm are directly tied to the performance of all the strategic business units. Information systems can improve the overall performance of these business units by promoting synergies and core competencies.

Synergies The idea of synergies is that when the output of some units can be used as inputs to other units, or two organizations pool markets and expertise, these relationships lower costs and generate profits. Recent bank and financial firm mergers, such as the mergers of Toronto Dominion Bank and Canada Trust, Great West Life and Canada Life, and Assante Corporation and IQON Financial, occurred precisely for this purpose, as did the acquisition by Hudson's Bay Company of Kmart Canada.

One use of information technology in these synergy situations is to tie together the operations of disparate business units so that they can act as a whole. For example, when Air Canada and Canadian Airlines merged, Air Canada not only eliminated the competition, it also gained access to new airport landing gates and customers, including the customers' profiles and loyalty card (i.e., frequent flyer program) data. After an initial problematic implementation of the information systems of these two Canadian giants, the loyalty card programs were merged, with Canadian's flyers having Air Canada miles. For other companies, it is not so easy. Both Great West Life Assurance and Investors Group are owned by the Power Corporation, but they cannot take advantage of the synergies that could be possible due to privacy issues. There is no mechanism to merge their information systems since doing so would open customer files of one company to the other company and its representatives—without their customers' permission.

Enhancing Core Competencies Yet another way to use information systems for competitive advantage is to think about ways that systems can enhance core competencies. The argument is that the performance of all business units will increase insofar as these business units develop or create a central core of competencies. A **core competency** is an activity for which a firm is a world-class leader. Core competencies may involve being the world's best miniature parts designer, the best package delivery service, or the best thin-film manufacturer. In general, a core competency relies on knowledge that is gained over many years of experience and a first-class research organization or simply key people who follow the literature and stay abreast of new external knowledge.

Any information system that encourages the sharing of knowledge across business units enhances competency. Such systems might encourage or enhance existing competencies and help employees become aware of new external knowledge; such systems might also help a business leverage existing competencies to related markets.

For example, Procter & Gamble (P&G), a world leader in brand management and consumer product innovation, uses a series of systems to enhance its core competencies. P&G uses an intranet called InnovationNet to help people working on similar problems share ideas and expertise. The system connects those working in research and development (R&D), engineering, purchasing, marketing, legal affairs, and business information systems around the world, using a portal to provide browser-based access to documents, reports, charts, videos, and other data from various sources. In 2001, InnovationNet added a directory of subject-matter experts who can be tapped to give advice or collaborate on problem solving and product development and created links to outside research scientists and 150 entrepreneurs who are searching for new, innovative products worldwide.

P&G sells more than 300 different branded products, with separate lines of business for Fabric and Home Care, Baby and Family Care, Beauty Care, Health Care, and Snacks and Beverages. It now uses custom-developed marketing management software to help all these groups share marketing ideas and data for marketing campaigns. This system supports strategic planning, research, advertising, direct mail, and events, and it is able to analyze the impact of marketing projects on the business.

Network-Based Strategies The availability of Internet and networking technologies has inspired strategies that take advantage of firms' abilities to create networks or network with one another. Network-based strategies include the use of network economics, a virtual company model, and business ecosystems.

Network Economics   Business models based on a network may help firms strategically by taking advantage of **network economics**. In traditional economics—the economics of factories and agriculture—production experiences diminishing returns.

The more any given resource is applied to production, the lower the marginal gain in output, until a point is reached where the additional inputs produce no additional outputs. This is the law of diminishing returns, and it is the foundation for most of modern economics.

Core competency

Network economics

In some situations, the law of diminishing returns does not work. For instance, in a network, the marginal costs of adding another participant are about zero while the marginal gain may be substantial. The larger the number of subscribers in a telephone system or on the Internet, the greater the value to all participants because each user can interact with more people. It is no more expensive to operate a television station with 1000 subscribers than with 10 million subscribers. The value of a community of people grows with size while the cost of adding new members is inconsequential.

From this network economics perspective, information technology can be strategically useful. Internet sites can be used by firms to build communities of users—like-minded customers who want to share their experiences. This builds customer loyalty and enjoyment and builds unique ties to customers. eBay, the giant online auction site, and iVillage, an online community for women, are examples. Both businesses are based on networks of millions of users, and both companies have used the Web and Internet communication tools to build communities. The more people offering products on eBay, the more valuable the eBay site is to everyone because more products are listed, and more competition among suppliers lowers prices. Network economics also provides strategic benefits to commercial software vendors. The value of their software and complementary software products increases as more people use them, and there is a larger installed base to justify continued use of the product and vendor support.

Virtual Company Strategy   Another network-based strategy uses the model of a virtual company to create a competitive business. A **virtual company**, also known as a virtual organization, uses networks to link people, assets, and ideas, enabling it to ally with other companies to create and distribute products and services without being limited by traditional organizational boundaries or physical locations. One company can use the capabilities of another company without being physically tied to that company. The virtual company model is useful when a company finds it cheaper to acquire products, services, or capabilities from an external vendor or when it needs to move quickly to exploit new market opportunities and lacks the time and resources to respond on its own.

Fashion companies, such as GUESS, Ann Taylor, Levi Strauss, and Reebok, enlist Hong Kong-based Li & Fung to manage production and shipment of their garments. Li & Fung handles product development, raw material sourcing, production planning, quality assurance, and shipping. Li & Fung does not own any fabric, factories, or machines; it outsources all its work to a network of more than 7500 suppliers in 37 countries all over the world. Customers place orders with Li & Fung over its private extranet. Li & Fung then sends instructions to appropriate raw material suppliers and factories where the clothing is produced. The Li & Fung extranet tracks the entire production process for each order. Working as a virtual company keeps Li & Fung flexible and adaptable so that it can design and produce the products ordered by its clients in short order to keep pace with rapidly changing fashion trends. Canadian-based Nygård International does the same with its suppliers based mainly in Asia. Nygård uses a company extranet to place orders for fabric with overseas suppliers, which must then deliver the goods by a tight deadline specified under contract. The deadline ensures that fabrics arrive just in time for Nygård to manufacture the clothes that use the material.

Business Ecosystems: Keystone and Niche Firms   The Internet and the emergence of digital firms call for some modification of the industry competitive forces model. The traditional Porter model assumes a relatively static industry environment; relatively clear-cut industry boundaries; and a relatively stable set of suppliers, substitutes, and customers, with the focus on industry players in a market environment. However,

Virtual company

FIGURE 3-14   *An ecosystem strategic model*

The digital firm era requires a dynamic view of the boundaries among industries, firms, customers, and suppliers, with competition occurring among industry sets in a business ecosystem. In the ecosystem model, multiple industries work together to deliver value to the customer. IT plays an important role in enabling a dense network of interactions among the participating firms.

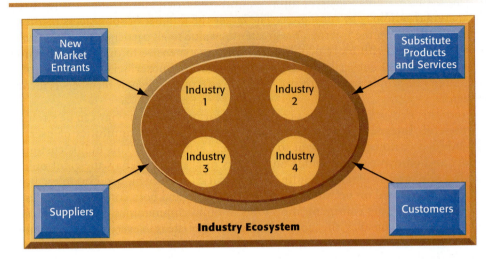

instead of participating in a single industry, some of today's firms are much more aware that they participate in industry sets—collections of industries that provide related services and products (see Figure 3-14). Business ecosystem is another term for these loosely coupled but interdependent networks of suppliers, distributors, outsourcing firms, transportation service firms, and technology manufacturers (Iansiti and Levien, 2004).

The concept of a business ecosystem builds on the idea of the value web described earlier, the main difference being that cooperation takes place across many industries rather than many firms. For instance, both Microsoft and Wal-Mart provide platforms composed of information systems, technologies, and services that thousands of other firms in different industries use to enhance their own capabilities. Microsoft has estimated that more than 40 000 firms use its Windows platform to deliver their own products, support Microsoft products, and extend the value of Microsoft's own firm. Wal-Mart's order entry and inventory management system is a platform used by thousands of suppliers to obtain real-time access to customer demand, track shipments, and control inventories.

Business ecosystems can be characterized as having one or a few keystone firms that dominate the ecosystem and create the platforms used by other niche firms. Keystone firms in the Microsoft ecosystem include Microsoft and technology producers such as Intel and IBM. Niche firms include thousands of software application firms, software developers, service firms, networking firms, and consulting firms that both support and rely on the Microsoft products.

Information technology plays a powerful role in establishing business ecosystems. Obviously, many firms use information systems to develop into keystone firms by building IT-based platforms that other firms can use.

For instance, eBay has created a platform for auctions and online stores used by more than 400 000 small businesses every day. Amazon.com and portals such as Yahoo! have created online store business platforms used by Fortune 500 firms such as Dell (and thousands of smaller firms) to sell directly to the public. In the digital firm era, we can expect greater emphasis on the use of IT to build industry ecosystems because the costs of participating in these ecosystems will fall and the benefits to all firms will increase rapidly as the platform grows.

Individual firms should consider how their information systems will enable them to become profitable niche players in larger ecosystems created by keystone firms. For instance, in making decisions about which products to build or which services to offer, a firm should consider the existing business ecosystems related to these products and how it might use IT to enable participation in these larger ecosystems.

3.4 Using Systems for Competitive Advantage: Management Issues

Strategic information systems often change the organization as well as its products, services, and operating procedures, driving the organization into new behavioural patterns. Successfully using information systems to achieve a competitive advantage is challenging and requires precise coordination of technology, organizations, and management.

Sustaining Competitive Advantage

The competitive advantages strategic systems confer do not necessarily last long enough to ensure long-term profitability. Because competitors can retaliate and copy strategic systems, competitive advantage is not always sustainable. Markets, customer expectations, and technology change; globalization has made these changes even more rapid and unpredictable. The Internet can make competitive advantage disappear very quickly because virtually all companies can use this technology. Classic strategic systems, such as American Airlines's SABRE computerized reservation system, Citibank's ATM system, and FedEx's package tracking system, benefited by being the first in their industries. Then rival systems emerged. Amazon.com, discussed earlier in this chapter, was an e-commerce leader but now faces competition from eBay, Yahoo!, and Google. Information systems alone cannot provide an enduring business advantage. Systems originally intended to be strategic frequently become tools for survival—a competitive necessity rather than a competitive advantage, required by every firm to stay in business—or they may inhibit organizations from making the strategic changes essential for future success.

Performing a Strategic Systems Analysis

Managers interested in using information systems for competitive advantage will need to perform a strategic systems analysis. To identify the types of systems that provide a strategic advantage to their firms, managers should ask the following questions:

1. What is the structure of the industry in which the firm is located?
   - What are some of the competitive forces at work in the industry? Are there new entrants to the industry? What is the relative power of suppliers, customers, and substitute products and services over prices?
   - Is the basis of competition quality, price, or brand?
   - What are the direction and nature of change within the industry? From where are the momentum and change coming?
   - How is the industry currently using information technology? Is the organization behind or ahead of the industry in its application of information systems?

2. What are the business, firm, and industry value chains for this particular firm?
   - How is the company creating value for the customer—through lower prices and transaction costs or higher quality? Are there any places in the value chain where the business could create more value for the customer and additional profit for the company?
   - Does the firm understand and manage its business processes using the best practices available? Is it taking maximum advantage of supply chain management, customer relationship management, and enterprise systems?
   - Does the firm leverage its core competencies?
   - Are the industry supply chain and customer base changing in ways that benefit or harm the firm?

• Can the firm benefit from strategic partnerships and value webs?
• Where in the value chain will information systems provide the greatest value to the firm?

Managing Strategic Transitions

Adopting the kinds of strategic systems described in this chapter generally requires changes in business goals, relationships with customers and suppliers, and business processes. These sociotechnical changes, affecting both social and technical elements of the organization, can be considered **strategic transitions**—a movement between levels of sociotechnical systems.

These changes often entail blurring organizational boundaries, both external and internal. Suppliers and customers must become intimately linked and may share each other's responsibilities. Managers will need to devise new business processes for coordinating their firms' activities with those of customers, suppliers, and other organizations. The organizational change requirements surrounding new information systems are so important that they merit attention throughout this text. Chapter 10 examines organizational change issues in more detail.

Strategic transitions

Summary

1. *Identify and describe important features of organizations that managers need to know about to develop and use information systems successfully.*

Managers need to understand certain essential features of organizations to build and use information systems successfully. All modern organizations are hierarchical, specialized, and impartial, using explicit routines to maximize efficiency. All organizations have their own cultures and politics arising from differences in interest groups, and they are affected by their surrounding environment. Organizations differ in goals, groups served, social roles, leadership styles, incentives, types of tasks performed, and type of structure. These features help explain differences in organizations' use of information systems.

2. *Evaluate the impact of information systems on organizations.*

Information systems and the organizations in which they are used interact with and influence one another. The introduction of a new information system will affect organizational structure, goals, work design, values, competition between interest groups, decision making, and day-to-day behaviour. At the same time, information systems must be designed to serve the needs of important organizational groups and will be shaped by the organization's structure, tasks, goals, culture, politics, and management. Information technology can reduce transaction and agency costs, and these changes have been accentuated in organizations using the Internet.

Information systems are closely intertwined with an organization's structure, culture, and business processes. New systems disrupt established patterns of work and power relationships, so there is often considerable resistance to them when they are introduced. The complex relationship between information systems, organizational performance, and decision making must be carefully managed.

3. *Demonstrate how Porter's competitive forces model and the value chain model help businesses use information systems for competitive advantage.*

In Porter's competitive forces model, the strategic position of the firm, and its strategies, are determined by competition with its traditional direct competitors but they are also greatly affected by new market entrants, substitute products and services, suppliers, and customers. Information systems help companies compete by maintaining low costs, differentiating products or services, focusing on market niche, strengthening ties with customers and suppliers, and increasing barriers to market entry with high levels of operational excellence.

The value chain model highlights specific activities in the business where competitive strategies and information systems will have the greatest impact. The model views the firm as a series of primary and support activities that add value to a firm's products or services. Primary activities are directly related to production and distribution while support activities make the delivery of primary activities possible. A firm's value chain can be linked to the value chains of its suppliers, distributors, and customers. A value web consists of information systems that enhance competitiveness at the industry level by promoting the use of standards and industry-wide consortia and by enabling businesses to work more efficiently with their value partners.

4. *Demonstrate how information systems help businesses use synergies, core competencies, and network-based strategies to achieve competitive advantage.*

Because firms consist of multiple business units, information systems achieve additional efficiencies or enhanced services by tying together the operations of disparate business units. Information systems help businesses leverage their core competencies by promoting the sharing of knowledge across business units. Information systems facilitate business models based on large networks of users or subscribers that take advantage of network economics. A virtual company strategy uses networks to link to other firms so that a company can use the capabilities of other companies to build, market, and distribute products and services. In business ecosystems, multiple industries work together to deliver value to the customer. Information systems support a dense network of interactions among the participating firms.

5. *Assess the challenges posed by strategic information systems and management solutions.*

Implementing strategic systems often requires extensive organizational change and a transition from one sociotechnical level to another. These changes are called strategic transitions and are often difficult and painful to achieve. Moreover, not all strategic systems are profitable, and they can be expensive to develop. Many strategic information systems are easily copied by other firms so that strategic advantage is not always sustainable. A strategic systems analysis is helpful.

Key Terms

Agency theory, 75	Network economics, 92	Switching costs, 85
Benchmarking, 88	Organization, 69, 71	Transaction cost theory, 75
Best practices, 88	Primary activities, 87	Value chain model, 86
Competitive forces model, 80	Product differentiation, 81	Value web, 89
Core competency, 92	Routines, 71	Virtual company, 93
Efficient customer response system, 81	Strategic transitions, 96	
Mass customization, 82	Support activities, 87	

Review Questions

1. *What is an organization? Compare the technical definition of organizations with the behavioural definition.*

2. *Identify and describe the features of organizations that help explain differences in organizations' use of information systems.*

3. *Describe the major economic theories that help explain how information systems affect organizations.*

4. *Describe the major behavioural theories that help explain how information systems affect organizations.*

5. *Why is there considerable organizational resistance to the introduction of information systems?*

6. *What is the impact of the Internet on organizations?*

7. *What is Porter's competitive forces model? How does it work? What does it explain about competitive advantage?*

8. *What are four competitive strategies enabled by information systems that firms could pursue? How do information systems support each of these competitive strategies? Give examples.*

9. *What is the value chain model? How can it be used to identify opportunities for strategic information systems?*

10. *What is the value web? How is it related to the value chain? How does it help identify opportunities for strategic information systems?*

11. *How has the Internet changed competitive forces and competitive advantage?*

12. *How do information systems promote synergies and core competencies? How does this enhance competitive advantage?*

13. *How can businesses benefit by using network economics?*

14. *What is a virtual company? What are the benefits of pursuing a virtual company strategy?*

15. *Describe the management challenges posed by strategic information systems in organizations and suggest some ways of dealing with them.*

Discussion Questions

1. *It has been said that there is no such thing as a sustainable strategic advantage. Do you agree? Why or why not?*

2. *It has been said that the advantage that leading-edge retailers such as Dell and Wal-Mart have over their competition is not technology; it is their management. Do you agree? Why or why not?*

3. *Do you believe that information systems can in and of themselves yield a strategic advantage, or do you believe*

that they are only tools for achieving that advantage? Discuss your ideas regarding your belief.

4. *Do you think that all companies can benefit in a strategic way from information systems? Which companies are more likely targets than others? Are there any companies, or classes of companies, that cannot use information systems to establish a strategic advantage?*

Teamwork: Identifying Opportunities for Strategic Information Systems

With a group of three or four students, select a company described in the *Financial Post, The Globe and Mail, Canadian Business,* or another business publication. Visit the company's Web site to find additional information about that company and to see how the firm is using the Web. On the basis of this information, analyze the business. Include a description of the organization's features, such as important business processes, culture, structure, and environment, as well as its business strategy. Suggest strategic information systems appropriate for that particular business, including those based on Internet technology, if appropriate. Use electronic presentation software to present your findings to the class.

Learning Track Module

The Changing Business Environment for Information Technology. This Learning Track Module surveys the major changes in the global business environment facing firms today. You can find the Learning Track Module on MyMISLab for this chapter.

For online exercises, please visit www.pearsoned.ca/mymislab.

HANDS-ON MIS   Application Exercises

The projects in this section give you hands-on experience analyzing a company's competitive strategy, using a database to improve decision making about business strategy, and using Web tools to configure and price an automobile.

Analyzing Competitive Strategy

Software skills: Web browser software and presentation software
Business skills: Value chain and competitive forces analysis, business strategy formulation

This project provides an opportunity for you to develop the competitive strategy for a real-world business. You will use the Web to identify Dirt Bikes Canada's competitors and the competitive forces in its industry. You will use value chain analysis to determine what kinds of information systems will provide the company with a competitive advantage.

Dirt Bikes Canada's management wants to be sure it is pursuing the right competitive strategy. You have been asked to perform a competitive analysis of the company using the Web to find the information you need. Prepare a report that analyzes Dirt Bikes Canada using the value chain and competitive forces models.

You report should include the following:

1. Which activities at Dirt Bikes Canada create the most value? [Hint: Review company description.]

2. How does Dirt Bikes Canada provide value to its customers? [Hint: Review company description.]

3. Who are Dirt Bikes Canada's major competitors? How do their products compare in price to those of Dirt Bikes

Canada? What are some of the product features they emphasize?

4. What are the competitive forces that can affect the industry? [Hint: Research the dirt bikes and motorcycle industry online.]

5. What competitive strategy should Dirt Bikes Canada pursue? [Hint: Review discussion of Porter in this chapter.]

6. What information systems best support that strategy?

7. (Optional) Use electronic presentation software to summarize your findings for management.

Improving Decision Making: Using a Database to Clarify Business Strategy

Software skills: Database querying and reporting; database design
Business skills: Reservation systems; customer analysis

In this exercise, you will use database software to analyze the reservation transactions for a hotel and use that information to fine-tune the hotel's business strategy and marketing activities.

The Queen's Inn is a small three-storey hotel on the Atlantic Ocean in St. John's, Newfoundland, a popular tourist resort. Ten rooms overlook side streets, 10 rooms have bay windows that offer limited views of the ocean, and the remaining 10 rooms in the front of the hotel face the ocean. Room rates are based on room choice, length of stay, and number of guests per room. Room rates are the same for one to four guests. Fifth and sixth guests must pay an additional $20 charge each per day. Guests staying for seven days or more receive a 10 percent discount on their daily room rates.

Business has grown steadily during the past 10 years. Now totally renovated, the inn uses a romantic weekend package to attract couples, a vacation package to attract young families, and a weekday discount package to attract business travellers. The owners currently use a manual reservation and bookkeeping system, which has caused many problems. Sometimes two families have been booked in the same room at the same time. Management does not have immediate data about the hotel's daily operations and income.

On MyMISLab for Chapter 3, you will find a database for hotel reservation transactions developed in Microsoft Access. Illustrated below are some sample records from that database.

Develop several reports in Access that provide information to help management make the business more competitive and profitable. Your reports should answer the following questions:

1. What is the average length of stay per room type?

2. What is the average number of visitors per room type?

3. What is the base income per room (i.e., length of visit multiplied by the daily rate) during a specified period of time?

After answering these questions, write a brief report describing what the database information reveals about the current business situation. Which specific business strategies might be pursued to increase room occupancy and revenue? How could the database be improved to provide better information for strategic decisions?

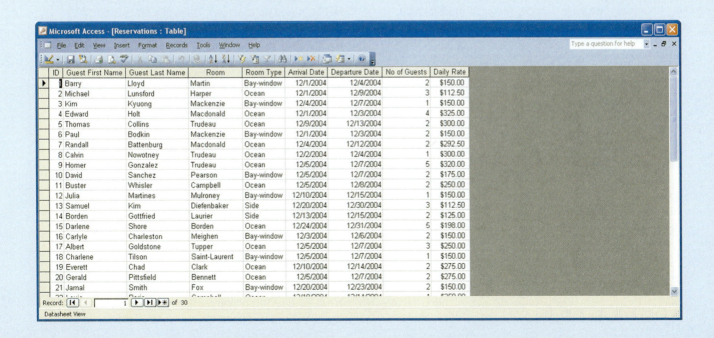

Improving Decision Making:
Using Web Tools to Configure and Price an Automobile

Software skills: Internet-based software
Business skills: Researching product information and pricing

The Web is an online library of consumer information besides being a marketplace where goods and services are purchased. The Web has an extraordinary influence on off-line purchases: more than 80 percent of new car buyers research their dream cars online first (Laudon and Traver, 2006).

In this exercise, you will use software at Web sites for selling cars to find product information about a car of your choice and use that information to make an important purchase decision. You will also evaluate two of these sites as selling tools.

Let us assume your seven-year-old car has tried your patience one too many times, and you have decided to purchase a new automobile. You have been interested in a Ford family car and want to investigate the Ford Fusion (if you are personally interested in another car, domestic or foreign, investigate that one instead). Go to the Web site of CarsDirect (**www.carsdirect.com**), and begin your investigation. Locate the car model you have chosen. Research the various specific automobiles available in that model, and determine which you prefer. Explore the full details about the specific car, including pricing, standard features, and

options. Locate and read at least two reviews if possible. Investigate the safety of that model based on the U.S. government crash tests performed by the National Highway Traffic Safety Administration if those test results are available. You should also look at *Consumer Reports* online car guide to see what it offers (**www.crcanadacars.org**). Unfortunately, the *Consumer Reports* site requires a fee to give you information. Explore the features for locating a vehicle in inventory and purchasing directly. Finally, explore the other capabilities of the CarsDirect site or a Canadian site for financing.

Having recorded or printed the information you need from CarsDirect for your purchase decision, surf the Web site of the manufacturer, in this case Ford (**www.ford.com**). Compare the information available on Ford's Web site with that of CarsDirect for the Ford Fusion. Be sure to check the price and any incentives being offered (which may not agree with what you found at CarsDirect). Next, find a dealer on the Ford site (**www.ford.ca**) so that you can view the car before making your purchase decision. Try to locate the lowest price for the car you want in a local dealer's inventory. Which site would you use to purchase your car? Why? Suggest improvements for the sites of CarsDirect and Ford.

CASE STUDY   Blockbuster vs. Netflix: Which Will Win Out?

When Blockbuster entered the video rental business in 1985, the industry consisted mostly of independent, mom-and-pop-style stores whose entire reach may have been two towns or a few city blocks. In its first 20 years of business, the rental giant opened 9100 stores in 25 countries, including Canada, gaining a market share that has been enjoyed by few companies in any industry.

Blockbuster equipped each of its video rental stores with custom software it had designed to simplify rental and sale transactions. An automated point-of-sale system uses a laser bar code scanner to read data from items being rented or sold and from a Blockbuster customer's identification card. These data are transmitted to Blockbuster's corporate computer centre. Management uses the data to monitor sales and to analyze the demographics, and rental and sales patterns for each store to improve its marketing decisions.

Blockbuster's success was based on video tape rentals and sales and rentals of DVDs. By 2004, Blockbuster possessed a 40-percent share of the U.S. video rental market, estimated to range from $8 billion of business per year to $10 billion; Blockbuster also had video sales of around $18 billion.

The greatest threat to Blockbuster's viability came from the emergence of a new business model in the video rental market. Launched in 1998, Netflix Inc. was intended to cater to those video rental customers who valued convenience

above all else. First, the upstart eliminated the need for a physical store. All interactions between Netflix and its customers took place on the Internet and through the postal service. Users could go online and create a wish list of movies they wanted to rent. For a monthly service fee, Netflix mailed up to three movies at a time, which the customer could keep for as long as he or she wanted without incurring late charges. When finished with a movie, the customer mailed it back to Netflix in prestamped packaging provided by the company. Returning a movie prompted Netflix to send the next title on the customer's wish list. For US $19.95 a month, Netflix customers had access to thousands of movie titles without leaving their homes.

According to Kagan Research LLC, revenues from online movie rentals, which were basically nonexistent in 1998, rose to $604 million in 2004. Kagan projected that the total revenue would approach $1.2 billion in 2005 and $3.5 billion by 2009. As Netflix caught on and its subscription model became popular, Netflix's gains in market share, from 2 to 7 percent between 2003 and 2004, gave Blockbuster true cause for concern.

To compete in the changing marketplace, Blockbuster made some dramatic changes in its business beginning in 2003. It added an online rental service; Movie Pass, a monthly subscription service for in-store customers; Game

Pass, a subscription service for video games; a trading service for movies and games; and the infamous "No More Late Fees" program.

The entire question of how to address a new source of competition was a complicated matter. Blockbuster could have chosen to launch an online rental store similar to Netflix and leave it at that, or, the company could have focused only on its traditional business in an attempt to lure customers back from the rising online tide. Instead, with the initiatives previously mentioned, Blockbuster tried to do both.

Blockbuster's $116 million increase in capital expenditures from 2003 to 2004 hints at the scale of the restructuring of the business. Many of those millions found their way to the information technology department, which took Netflix on directly by establishing the information systems supporting Blockbuster's own online subscription service.

This venture required Blockbuster to construct a new business model within its existing operations. Rather than meld the two channels, Blockbuster created a new online division with its own offices near corporate headquarters in Dallas. Part of Blockbuster's initial strategy for defeating the competition was to undercut Netflix in both pricing and distribution. Blockbuster set the price for its three-movies-at-a-time monthly subscription at US $19.99, which was, at the time, two dollars less than Netflix's competing plan. Blockbuster had a strategic advantage in distribution as well. Netflix was serving its customers from 35 distribution centres around the U.S. Blockbuster had 30 such facilities but also had 4500 stores in the U.S. to deliver DVDs to most of its customers in only a day or two at lower shipping costs. Blockbuster also enticed online customers to maintain a relationship with the physical stores by offering coupons for free in-store rentals. Blockbuster's original intent was to integrate the online and in-store services so that customers could float back and forth between the two channels with no restrictions; however, the disparate requirements for revenue recognition (i.e., what is revenue and when it should be recognized on financial statements and for tax purposes) and inventory management have so far been too complex to make the plan a reality.

After a year in existence, the report card on Blockbuster's online store was mixed. The service had acquired one million subscribers, and the company hoped to double that number within seven months or so. At the same time, Netflix had surpassed three million subscribers and was on its way to four million by the end of the year. Blockbuster continued to pursue gains through pricing, at one point lowering its three-movie plan to US $14.99 per month versus US $17.99 at Netflix. Both companies offer plan variations such as unlimited rentals of one DVD at a time for US $5.99 per month and two at a time with a limit of four per month for US $11.99.

In September 2005, research firm SG Cowen declared that Blockbuster's online DVD rental service "remains inferior" to Netflix. The researcher stated that Blockbuster had improved on movie availability but actually fell further behind in ratings of its user interface. The evaluation by SG Cowen came on the heels of rocky financial reports for Blockbuster. Blockbuster's most costly change was likely the "No More Late Fees" campaign it launched in January 2005. The goal of the program was to lure more customers and

position Blockbuster better in the market alongside Netflix, which never charged late fees. However, the program may have created more problems than it solved. Blockbuster did measure an increase in in-store rentals after eliminating late fees, but early returns did not suggest that the increase offset the $290 million to $345 million in annual late fee revenue that was no longer being collected.

Well-known corporate raider Carl Icahn took advantage of Blockbuster's low share price and acquired 9 percent of the company, entitling him to a position on the board of directors. Icahn harshly criticized CEO John Antico's business strategy. Icahn believed that Blockbuster's new initiatives, such as online rentals, were too expensive and too risky. He believed that the company should take advantage of its prevailing position in the bricks-and-mortar rental industry, even if that industry were slowly dying. Despite the presence of Icahn, Antico maintained that online rentals were the only segment of the industry open to growth.

Both Blockbuster and Netflix now face a new set of challenges. Fifteen million cable subscribers use video-on-demand (VOD) technology to watch movies and programs that are not yet available on DVD. TiVo and similar digital video recorders combined with VOD could make the rental of movies obsolete. Some analysts still insist that the economics do not make sense for movie studios to abandon DVD sales, which account for 50 percent of their profits, in favour of VOD. And technology does not currently permit the bandwidth for VOD suppliers to provide nearly the number of titles that Blockbuster can. Down the road, however, Blockbuster likely will have to address VOD, especially if the studios can eliminate companies such as Blockbuster as an intermediary.

In April 2006, the Internet as a channel for movie distribution finally came into focus. Six movie studios, including Warner Brothers, Sony Pictures, Universal, MGM, and Paramount, reached an agreement with Movielink, another Web company, to sell movies online via download. Until that time, Movielink had offered movie downloads as rentals, which, like the VOD model, the customer could watch for only 24 hours. Sony, MGM, and Lions Gate also reached agreements with a Movielink competitor, CinemaNow, which is partially owned by Lions Gate. Warner Brothers also expanded its presence by entering into relationships with Guba.com and BitTorrent. The studios moved to build on the momentum created by the success of the iTunes music store, which demonstrated that consumers were very willing to pay for legal digital downloads of copyrighted material. At the same time, they hoped that entering the download sales market would enable them to confront the piracy issue in their industry earlier in its development than the music industry was able to do.

While the studios' commitment to these ventures appeared clear, what remained a question was whether they could replicate the success of iTunes. The initial pricing schemes certainly did not offer the same appeal as Apple's $0.99 per song or $9.99 per CD. Movielink set the price for new movies at US $20 to US $30. Older movies were discounted to US $10. Movielink was counting on the fact that customers would pay more for the immediacy of downloading a movie in their homes, as opposed to visiting a bricks-and-mortar store such as Wal-Mart or an online store such as Amazon.ca, both of which sell new DVDs for less than Blockbuster or Netflix.

However, even if customers were willing to pay a little extra, they were getting less for their money. Most movie downloads did not come with the extra features that are common with DVD releases. Moreover, the downloaded movies were programmed for convenient viewing on computer screens, but transporting them from the computer to the TV screen involved a more complicated process than most consumers were willing to tackle. Neither Movielink nor CinemaNow offered a movie format that could be burned to a DVD and played on a regular DVD player. In fact, CinemaNow downloads were limited to use on a single computer. To watch these movies on a television screen, users would need to have Windows Media Center, which is designed to connect to a TV, or special jacks and cables.

An additional obstacle for both the technology and the consumer to overcome was bandwidth. Even using a broadband Internet connection, high-quality movie files, which generally surpassed 1 gigabyte in file size, required in the neighbourhood of 90 minutes to download completely.

Considering these issues, the near-term outlook for the legal digital distribution of movies remains cloudy. Movielink, with only 75 000 downloads per month, was struggling to sustain itself. Neither Blockbuster nor Netflix seemed in a panic to adjust to this new source of competition. While locked in legal battles over patents and antitrust concerns, the two companies had few specific plans related to downloading although Netflix was widely believed to be considering a set-top box. Netflix said only that downloading was part of its future plans, but expressed dissatisfaction with the terms the movie studios were offering in early discussions.

The one development that has the potential to force the hands of Blockbuster and Netflix is the entrance of Apple into the movie download market. Apple's iTunes store, like Netflix, already had a satisfied and loyal customer base, not to mention a pervasive "cool" factor. And it was iTunes's successful transition from music-only to music and television downloads that paved the way for Movielink and CinemaNow to sell movie downloads in the first place. Apple is said to be on the verge of adding movies to its store and sticking to its flat-rate pricing model. Industry rumours indicated that Apple CEO Steve Jobs would sell downloads of all movies for $9.99. Industry experts characterized Apple's involvement as a possible "tipping point" for online movie distribution.

Meanwhile, the list of Blockbuster's Canadian competitors is growing. Canflix is a Canadian online DVD rental company that charges $21.95 per month for its service (Netflix does not operate in Canada). Similar Canadian companies include Zip.ca ($24.95 monthly), Videomatica.ca ($29.95 monthly), and Starflix ($24.95 monthly). The game is the same; the competition offered to bricks-and-mortar video rental stores by online DVD rental services is changing the face of rental entertainment nationally and internationally.

In the meantime, Antico wants Blockbuster to stay very close to the cutting edge of technology in his industry. Doing so, he believes, will enable the company to replace directly any rental revenues lost to new technology. Meanwhile, add Amazon to the list of competitive threats on which Blockbuster must also keep a careful eye. Amazon.com already operates an online movie rental service in the United Kingdom. Could there be another player to compete with Blockbuster and Netflix? Or could a new partnership shake up the industry again?

Sources: Saul Hansell, "At Last, Movies to Keep Arrive on the Internet," *The New York Times*, April 3, 2006; Sarah McBride, "Movie Debut: Films for Sale by Download," *The Wall Street Journal*, April 3, 2006; Nate Mook, "Netflix Mulls Movie Download Service," BetaNews.com, June 21, 2006; "Guba Sells Sony Films," RedHerring.com, July 11, 2006; Michael Greeson, "iTunes' Movie Downloads the 'Tipping Point' for Online Movie Distribution," DigitalTrends.com, June 22, 2006; Mark Glaser, "Movie Download Services Still Need Work," PBS.org, June 30, 2006; Mike Snider, "Movie Downloads Can Be Fun, and the Technology Is Advancing," *USA Today*, accessed via **Citizen-Times.com**, July 4, 2006; "Guba to Distribute Warner Bros. Movies," Reuters, accessed via Yahoo! News, June 26, 2006; "Online DVD Rental Guide," **http://onlinedvdrentalguide.ca**, accessed May 11, 2007; and Janet Rae-Dupree, "Blockbuster: Movie Business Remains a Moving Target," *CIO Insight*, August 10, 2005.

CASE STUDY QUESTIONS

1. What is Blockbuster's business model? How successful has it been?

2. What industry and technology forces have challenged that business model? What problems have they created?

3. Is Blockbuster developing successful solutions to its problems? Are there other solutions it should have considered?

4. How successful is Netflix's business model?

5. Do you think Blockbuster or Netflix will succeed in the future? Explain your answer.

CHAPTER 4

Social, Legal, and Ethical Issues in the Digital Firm

LEARNING OBJECTIVES

After completing this chapter, you will be able to do the following:

1. Analyze the relationships among ethical, social, and political issues that are raised by information systems.

2. Identify the main moral dimensions of an information society and specific principles for conduct that can be used to guide ethical decisions.

3. Evaluate the impact of contemporary information systems and the Internet on the protection of individual privacy and intellectual property.

4. Assess how information systems have affected everyday life.

OPENING **CASE** | Israel's Trojan Horse Corporate Scandal

It started out as a family feud. But a small-time computer break-in erupted into Israels biggest business scandal in decades, reaching into some of the country's powerful corporate suites and jolting the cozy world of the industrial elite. Top Israeli blue-chip companies, including a high-tech giant that trades in New York, are suspected of using illicit surveillance software to steal information from their rivals and enemies.

The list of victims is equally impressive, ranging from a cigarette importer to the local operations of the Ace hardware chain to Hewlett-Packard Company. Even a well-known TV entertainment reporter is caught up in the affair, claiming hackers invaded his computer to get celebrity phone numbers.

The investigation has shed an unflattering light on the Israeli business world, where cutthroat competition in a small market, high-tech sophistication, and the secretive traditions of the army form a volatile mix. The case is also attracting the attention of top security software makers. Software firms have been updating their products to defend against similar outbreaks.

Police say they stumbled upon the case after author Amnon Jacont discovered excerpts of a book he was still writing on the Internet. When more documents from his computer began appearing on the Internet, and someone tried to use his banking information to make transactions, Jacont realized his computer had been invaded. He told police he suspected the spy was his stepdaughter's ex-husband, Michael Haephrati.

In a newspaper interview, Jacont said Haephrati became "vengeful and obsessive" after the collapse of his marriage. Police subsequently found surveillance software, a Trojan horse, on Jacont's machine. Nir Nateev, head of the police computer and cyber crime department in Tel Aviv, said the discovery snowballed into an international investigation involving British,

German, and American authorities. "We never saw this in the past," he said. "They were very, very, very surprised by the size of the case and helped us a lot in this."

Investigators determined that Haephrati sold customized copies of his Trojan horse program to three Israeli private investigators. The private investigators then used this technology to spy on and gather information about businesses that were in competition with their clients. As a result, Haephrati, who reportedly lives in London and Germany, has been arrested together with his wife Ruth, 28, in London and is currently awaiting extradition hearings so he can stand trial in Israel.

Sever Plocker, a leading Israeli economic commentator, said the scandal could have "unpleasant consequences" for foreign investment. "People don't like to invest in countries where companies do some very unethical things," he said. "I think it is bad for Israel, bad for the image of Israel, and nothing to be proud about."

The "Trojan horse" scandal, named after the monitoring software secretly planted on the corporate computers, was front-page news after police lifted the gag order. Police say 22 people have been arrested, and more arrests are expected.

"It's getting bigger every day," said Nateev, who added that 100 computers have been confiscated.

"In the end, there will be dozens [of companies] involved."

The scandal sent a shudder through the business world. The country's central bank chief, American economist Stanley Fischer, warned that the case could harm foreign investment. Amir Barnea, a business professor at the Interdisciplinary Center, a prestigious Israeli university, attributed the scandal to the hypercompetitive business atmosphere in a tiny market of 7 million people. "Unfortunately some managers may lose the distinction between a legitimate fight for survival and doing illegal acts," he said.

Others said the combination of Israel's high-tech culture, fine-tuned in secretive military units, and a penchant for independent thinking, made the scandal inevitable. Some of the world's top computer security companies, including Check Point Software Technologies Ltd., are Israeli.

Some versions of the spy software tempted victims into installing it by posing as a package of confidential documents delivered via e-mail. Once installed, the software recorded every keystroke and collected business documents and e-mails on the victim's PC and transmitted information to a server computer registered in London.

An unidentified lawyer, right, discusses the case with private investigators Zvika Krochmal, second right, and Ofer Fried, second left, both of whom were arrested in the Trojan horse investigation.

"This was not designed very well," said Robert Sandilands, the head of the virus research lab for Authentium Inc., a Florida security firm. "This does not seem to be the work of an experienced virus writer."

The suspects in Israel include senior executives from three prominent private investigation firms, among them a former top military investigator, a retired Shin Bet security agent, and former police officers. Eleven private investigators—hired by the companies to conduct the industrial espionage—have been arrested in addition to some eight senior executives from Israel's leading companies—including Cellcom, YES, Pelephone, Meir Car Imports, and the Tami-4 mineral water retailer.

The list of clients implicated in the affair reads like a Who's Who of Israeli blue chips: Amdocs Ltd., a business-software maker that trades on the New York Stock Exchange; the Cellcom phone carrier and three subsidiaries of the Bezeq phone monopoly—a long-distance carrier, a cell phone provider, and a satellite TV firm. Most of the companies have denied wrongdoing or said they were unaware of the tactics used by investigators they hired.

Lawyers for the suspects said their clients acknowledged ordering the private investigators to gather information on their rivals but did not know that the information was obtained illegally. Police dismissed the claim, asserting that the information obtained for the companies was valuable to the extent that the victims lost competitive bids and thousands of customers as a result of the espionage.

"The software is totally legal," said Ofir Katz Neriah, the lawyer for one of the suspects. "The question is if the use that my client made of the software was illegal—and the answer is definitely not."

The alleged victims, meanwhile, reportedly include Hewlett-Packard and the Ace Hardware chain, as well as the Globe's business daily, Strauss-Elite food group, the HOT cable company, and the Bezeq parent company. Police said they had evidence linking the Israeli industrial espionage affair to similar cases across Europe. Police refused to name the companies, claiming they had "yet to inform them of the espionage."

Ira Winkler, author of the book *Spies Among Us*, said Trojan horses are a relatively new tactic in a growing epidemic of global high-tech espionage. He said the break in the case—tracing the scandal to a vindictive relative—was typical. "Never underestimate the stupidity of criminals."

Sources: "Israeli 'Trojan Horse' Scandal Widens," Associated Press, June 1, 2005, available **www.msnbc.msn.com/id/8064757/**, accessed June 1, 2007; and Yaakov Katz, "Trojan Horse Also Hit Major International Firms," *The Jewish Post*, May 30, 2005, **www.jpost.com/servlet/Satellite?pagename=JPost/JPArticle/ ShowFull&cid=1117333096614**, accessed June 1, 2007.

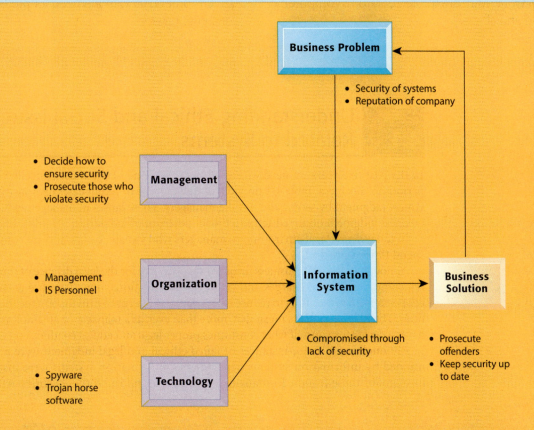

The chapter-opening Business Challenges diagram draws attention to important points raised in this case and in this chapter. Creating a Trojan horse is not illegal, but using it is illegal as well as unethical. Not only is the programmer who sold the Trojan horse software guilty of a criminal act, but so are the private investigation firms that bought the software and used it for their clients to spy on unsuspecting companies. The investigation firms' clients, who undoubtedly knew that this critical, confidential information was being gathered, are also culpable.

HEADS UP

Information systems raise new and often perplexing ethical problems. This is truer today than ever before because of the challenges posed by the Internet and electronic commerce to the protection of privacy and intellectual property. Other ethical issues raised by widespread use of information systems include establishing accountability for the consequences of information systems, setting standards to safeguard system quality that protects the safety of individuals and society, and preserving values and institutions considered essential to the quality of life in an information society. Whether you run your own business or work in a large company, you will be confronting these issues, and you'll need to know how to deal with them.

- If your career is in finance and accounting, you will need to ensure that the information systems you work with are protected from computer fraud and abuse.

- If your career is in human resources, you will be involved in developing and enforcing a corporate ethics policy and in providing special training to sensitize managers and employees to the new ethical issues surrounding information systems.

- If your career is in information systems, you will need to make management aware of the ethical implications of the technologies used by the firm and help management establish a code of ethics for information systems.

- If your career is in manufacturing, production, or operations management, you will need to deal with data quality and software problems that could interrupt the smooth and accurate flow of information among disparate manufacturing and production systems and among supply chain partners.

- If your career is in sales and marketing, you will need to balance systems that gather and analyze customer data with the need for protecting consumer privacy.

4.1 Understanding Ethical and Social Issues Related to Systems

In the past five years we have witnessed, arguably, one of the most ethically challenging periods for business. Table 4-1 provides a small sample of recent cases demonstrating failed ethical judgment by senior and middle managers. These lapses in management ethical and business judgment occurred across a broad spectrum of industries.

In today's new legal environment, managers who violate the law and are convicted may spend time in prison.

Although in the past, business firms would often pay for the legal defence of their employees enmeshed in civil charges and criminal investigations, now firms are encouraged to cooperate with prosecutors to reduce charges against the entire firm for obstructing investigations. These developments mean that, more than ever, as a manager or an employee, you will have to decide for yourself what constitutes proper legal and ethical conduct.

Although these major instances of failed ethical and legal judgment were not masterminded by information systems departments, information systems were instrumental in many of these frauds. In many cases, the perpetrators of these crimes artfully used

TABLE 4-1   Examples of Failed Ethical Judgment by Managers

Government of Canada	Sponsorship scandal, wherein the government apparently paid favoured marketing firms for services that were either not needed or not provided.
Enron	Top three executives convicted for misstating earnings using illegal accounting schemes and making false representations to shareholders. Bankruptcy declared in 2001.
WorldCom	Second-largest U.S. telecommunications firm. Chief executive convicted for improperly inflating revenue by billions using illegal accounting methods. Bankruptcy declared in July 2002 with $43 billion in debts.
Merrill Lynch	Indicted for assisting Enron in the creation of financial vehicles that had no business purpose, enabling Enron to misstate its earnings.
Parmalat	Italy's eighth-largest industrial group indicted for misstating more than $5 billion in revenues, earnings, and assets over several years; senior executives indicted for embezzlement.
Bristol-Myers Squibb	Pharmaceutical firm agreed to pay a fine of $158 million for misstating its revenues by $1.5 billion and inflating its stock value.
KPMG LLP, Ernst & Young, and PricewaterhouseCoopers	Senior tax accountants of three of the leading "Big Four" public accounting firms are indicted by the Justice Department over the selling of abusive tax shelters to wealthy individuals in the period 2000–2005. This case is frequently referred to as the "largest tax fraud case in history."

financial reporting information systems to bury their decisions from public scrutiny in the vain hope they would never be caught.

We deal with the issue of control in information systems in Chapter 8. In this chapter, we talk about the ethical dimensions of these and other actions based on the use of information systems.

Ethics refers to the principles of right and wrong that individuals, acting as free moral agents, use to make choices to guide their behaviours. Information systems raise new ethical questions for both individuals and societies because they create opportunities for intense social change, and thus threaten existing distributions of power, money, rights, and obligations. Like other technologies, such as steam engines, electricity, the telephone, and the radio, information technology can be used to achieve social progress, but it can also be used to commit crimes and threaten cherished social values. The development of information technology will produce benefits for many and costs for others.

Ethical issues in information systems have been given new urgency by the rise of the Internet and electronic commerce. Internet and digital firm technologies make it easier than ever to assemble, integrate, and distribute information, unleashing new concerns about the appropriate use of customer information, the protection of personal privacy, and the protection of intellectual property. Insiders with special knowledge can "fool" information systems by submitting phony records and diverting cash on a scale unimaginable in the pre-computer era.

Other pressing ethical issues raised by information systems include establishing accountability for the consequences of information systems, setting standards to safeguard system quality that protects the safety of the individual and society, and preserving values and institutions considered essential to the quality of life in an information society. When using information systems, it is essential to ask, "What is the ethical and socially responsible course of action?"

A Model for Thinking about Ethical, Social, and Political Issues

Ethical, social, and political issues are closely linked. The ethical dilemma you may face as a manager of information systems typically is reflected in social and political debate. One way to think about these relationships is given in Figure 4-1. Imagine society as a more or less

FIGURE 4-1   *The relationship between ethical, social, and political issues
in an information society*

The introduction of new information technology has a ripple effect, raising new ethical, social, and political issues that must be dealt with on individual, social, and political levels. These issues have five moral dimensions: information rights and obligations, property rights and obligations, system quality, quality of life, and accountability and control.

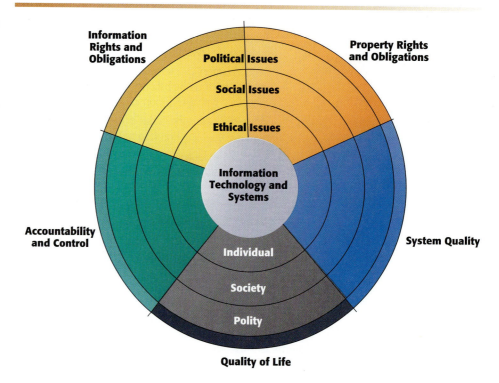

calm pond on a summer day, a delicate ecosystem in partial equilibrium with individuals and with social and political institutions. Individuals know how to act in this pond because social institutions (family, education, organizations) have developed well-honed rules of behaviour, and these are supported by laws developed in the political sector that prescribe behaviour and promise sanctions for violations. Now toss a rock into the centre of the pond. But imagine instead of a rock that the disturbing force is a powerful shock of new information technology and systems hitting a society more or less at rest. What happens? Ripples, of course.

Suddenly individual actors are confronted with new situations often not covered by the old rules. Social institutions cannot respond overnight to these ripples—it may take years to develop etiquette, expectations, social responsibility, politically correct attitudes, and approved rules. Political institutions also require time before developing new laws and often require the demonstration of real harm before they act. In the meantime, you may have to act. You may be forced to act in a legal grey area.

We can use this model to illustrate the dynamics that connect ethical, social, and political issues. This model is also useful for identifying the main moral dimensions of the information society, which cut across various levels of action—individual, social, and political.

Five Moral Dimensions of the Information Age

The major ethical, social, and political issues raised by information systems include the following moral dimensions:

Information rights and obligations. What information rights do individuals and organizations possess with respect to themselves? What can they protect? What obligations do individuals and organizations have concerning this information?

Property rights and obligations. How will traditional intellectual property rights be protected in a digital society in which tracing and accounting for ownership are difficult and ignoring such property rights is so easy?

Accountability and control. Who can and will be held accountable and liable for the harm done to individual and collective information and property rights?

System quality. What standards of data and system quality should we demand to protect individual rights and the safety of society?

Quality of life. What values should be preserved in an information- and knowledge-based society? Which institutions should we protect from violation? Which cultural values and practices are supported by the new information technology?

We explore these moral dimensions in detail in Section 4.3.

Key Technology Trends That Raise Ethical Issues

Ethical issues long preceded information technology. Nevertheless, information technology has heightened ethical concerns, taxed existing social arrangements, and made some laws obsolete or severely crippled. Information technologies and systems have also created new opportunities for criminal behaviour and mischief. There are four key technological trends responsible for these ethical stresses, and they are summarized in Table 4-2.

The doubling of computing power every 18 months has made it possible for most organizations to use information systems for their core production processes. As a result, our dependence on systems and our vulnerability to system errors and to poor data quality have increased. The very same information systems that lead to high levels of productivity also create opportunities for abuse. Social rules and laws have not yet adjusted to this dependence. Standards for ensuring the accuracy and reliability of information systems (see Chapter 8) are not universally accepted or enforced.

Advances in data storage techniques and rapidly declining storage costs have been responsible for the multiplying of databases on individuals—employees, customers, and potential customers—maintained by private and public organizations. These advances in data storage have made the routine violation of individual privacy both cheap and effective. Already, massive data storage systems are cheap enough for regional and even local retailing firms to use in identifying customers. For instance, the major search firms such as Google, America Online (AOL), MSN, and Yahoo! maintain detailed search histories on the more than 100 million people who use Internet search engines everyday and who generate more than 200 million searches each day. These huge collections of "consumer intentions" become the natural targets of government agencies, private investigators, and private firms looking for market advantage.

Advances in data analysis techniques for large pools of data are another technological trend that heightens ethical concerns because companies and government agencies are able to find out much detailed personal information about individuals. With contemporary data management tools (see Chapter 6), companies can assemble and combine the myriad pieces of information about individuals stored on computers much more easily than in the past.

TABLE 4-2 *Technology Trends That Raise Ethical Issues*

TREND	IMPACT
Computing power doubles every 18 months	More organizations depend on computer systems for critical operations.
Data storage costs are rapidly declining	Organizations can easily maintain detailed databases on individuals.
Data analysis advances	Companies can analyze vast quantities of data gathered on individuals to develop detailed profiles of individual behaviour.
Networking advances and the Internet	Copying data from one location to another and accessing personal data from remote locations are much easier.

Think of all the ways you generate computer information about yourself—credit card purchases; telephone calls; magazine subscriptions; video rentals; mail-order purchases; banking records; local, provincial, and federal government records (including court and police records); and visits to Web sites to read Web materials, use search engines, and write blogs (see Chapter 13). Put together and mined properly, this information could reveal not only your credit information but also your driving habits, your tastes, your associations, intended purchases, political views, and interests. What you thought was private, in fact, can quickly become public.

Companies selling products purchase relevant information from these sources to help them more finely target their marketing campaigns. Chapters 3 and 6 describe how companies can analyze large pools of data from multiple sources to rapidly identify buying patterns of customers and suggest individual responses. The use of computers to combine data from multiple sources and create electronic dossiers of detailed information on individuals is called **profiling**.

For example, hundreds of Web sites allow DoubleClick (www.doubleclick.net), an Internet advertising broker, to track the activities of their visitors in exchange for revenue from advertisements based on visitor information DoubleClick gathers. DoubleClick uses this information to create a profile of each online visitor, adding more detail to the profile as the visitor accesses an associated DoubleClick site. Over time, DoubleClick can create a detailed dossier of a person's spending and computing habits on the Web that can be sold to companies to help them target their Web ads more precisely.

Credit card purchases can make personal information available to market researchers, telemarketers, and direct-mail companies. Advances in information technology facilitate the invasion of privacy.

ChoicePoint, described in the Window on Management section, gathers data from police, criminal, and motor vehicle records; credit and employment histories; current and previous addresses; professional licences; and insurance claims to assemble and maintain electronic dossiers on almost every adult in the United States. The company sells this personal information to businesses and government agencies. Demand for personal data is so enormous that data broker businesses such as ChoicePoint are booming. The Georgia-based company has even purchased the voting records of Mexico's 65 million citizens along with data on 6 million Mexico City drivers. The implications for Canada and Canadians are obvious: ChoicePoint, or companies providing similar services, may assemble and maintain electronic files on almost all Canadians before very long.

A new data analysis technology called **nonobvious relationship awareness (NORA)** has given both the government and the private sector even more powerful profiling capabilities. NORA can take information about people from many disparate sources, such as employment applications, telephone records, customer listings, and "wanted" lists, and correlate relationships to find obscure hidden connections that might help identify criminals or terrorists (see Figure 4-2). For instance, an applicant for a government security job might have received phone calls from a person wanted by the police. This dyad (grouping of two) might also share the same religion, attend the same church, and be part of a small group with frequent telephone contacts.

NORA technology scans data and extracts information as the data are being generated so that it could, for example, instantly discover a man at an airline ticket counter who shares a phone number with a known terrorist before that person boards an airplane. The

Profiling

Nonobvious relationship awareness (NORA)

FIGURE 4-2   *Nonobvious Relationship Awareness (NORA)*

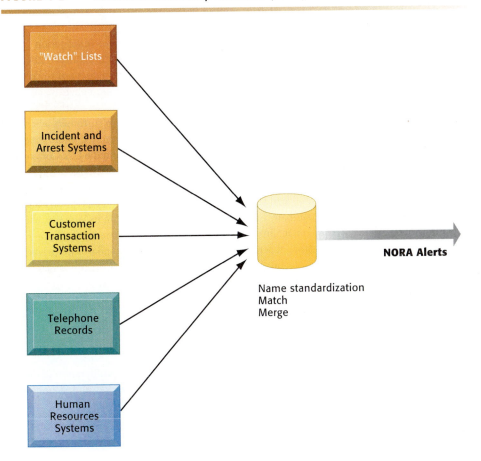

NORA technology can take information about people from disparate sources and find obscure, nonobvious relationships. It might discover, for example, that an applicant for a job at a casino shares a telephone number with a known criminal and could then issue an alert to the hiring manager.

technology is considered a valuable tool for national security but does have privacy implications because it can provide such a detailed picture of the activities and associations of a single individual.

Finally, advances in networking, including the Internet, promise to greatly reduce the costs of moving and accessing large quantities of data, and open the possibility of mining large pools of data remotely using small desktop machines, permitting an invasion of privacy on a scale and with a precision heretofore unimaginable. If computing and networking technologies continue to advance at the same pace as in the past, by 2023, large organizations will be able to devote the equivalent of a contemporary desktop personal computer to monitoring each of the individuals who will then be living in Canada (Farmer and Mann, 2003).

WINDOW ON MANAGEMENT

Data for Sale

Want a list of 3877 charity donors in Detroit? You can buy it from USAData for $489. Through USAData's Web site, which is linked to large databases maintained by Acxiom and Dun & Bradstreet, anyone with a credit card can buy marketing lists of consumers broken down by location, demographics, and interests. The College Board sells data on graduating high school seniors to 1700 colleges and universities for 28 cents per student. These businesses are entirely legal. Also selling data are businesses that obtain credit card and cell phone records illegally and sell to private investigators and law enforcement. The buying and selling of personal data has become a multibillion-dollar business that is growing by leaps and bounds.

Unlike banks or companies selling credit reports, these private data brokers are largely unregulated. There has been little or no federal or provincial oversight of how they collect, maintain, and sell their data. But they have been allowed to flourish because there is such a huge market for personal information, and they provide useful services for insurance companies, banks, employers, and federal, provincial, and local government agencies.

For example, in the U.S., the Internal Revenue Service and departments of Homeland Security, Justice, and State paid data brokers US $30 million in 2005 for data used in law enforcement and counterterrorism. The Internal Revenue Service signed a five-year, US $200 million deal to access ChoicePoint's databases to locate assets of delinquent taxpayers. After the September 11, 2001, terrorist attacks, ChoicePoint helped the U.S. government screen candidates for the new federally controlled airport security workforce.

ChoicePoint is one of the largest data brokers, with more than 5000 employees serving businesses of all sizes as well as federal, state, and local governments. In 2004, ChoicePoint performed more than seven million background checks. It processes thousands of credit card transactions every second.

ChoicePoint builds its vast repository of personal data through an extensive network of contractors who gather bits of information from public filings, financial-services firms, phone directories, and loan application forms. The contractors use police departments, school districts, the department of motor vehicles, and local courts to fill their caches. All the information is public and legal.

ChoicePoint possesses 19 billion records containing personal information on the vast majority of American adult consumers. According to Daniel J. Solove, associate professor of law at George Washington University, the company has collected information on nearly every adult American and "these are dossiers that J. Edgar Hoover (the former FBI director notorious for collecting information on dissidents) would be envious of."

The downside to the massive databases maintained by ChoicePoint and other data brokers is the threat they pose to personal privacy and social well being. The quality of the data they maintain can be unreliable, causing people to lose their jobs and their savings. In one case, Boston Market fired an employee after receiving a background check from ChoicePoint that showed felony convictions; however, the report had been wrong. In another, a retired General Electric assembly-line worker was charged a higher insurance premium because another person's driving record, with multiple accidents, had been added to his ChoicePoint file.

ChoicePoint came under fire in early 2005 for selling information on 145 000 customers to criminals posing as legitimate businesses. The criminals then used the identities of some of the individuals on whom ChoicePoint maintained data to open fraudulent credit card accounts.

Since then ChoicePoint curtailed the sale of products that contain sensitive data, such as social security and driver's license ID numbers, and limited access by small businesses, including private investigators, collection agencies, and non-bank financial institutions. ChoicePoint also implemented more stringent processes to verify customer authenticity.

Marc Rotenberg of the Electronic Privacy Information Center in Washington, D.C., believes that the ChoicePoint case is a clear demonstration that self-regulation does not work in the information business and that more comprehensive laws are needed. California, 22 other states, and New York City have passed laws requiring companies to inform customers when their personal data files have been compromised. More than a dozen data security bills were introduced in the U.S. Congress in 2006 and some type of federal data security and privacy legislation will likely result. In Canada, when privacy has been breached at banks and other major companies, typically the company issues a notice to its customers on its Web site, with a contact link. Canadian privacy advocates are hoping for a broad federal law with a uniform set of standards for privacy protection practices that goes beyond PIPEDA (discussed later in this chapter).

To Think About

1. Do data brokers pose an ethical dilemma? Explain your answer.

2. What are the problems caused by the proliferation of data brokers? What management, organization, and technology factors are responsible for these problems?

3. How effective are existing solutions to these problems?

4. Should the federal government regulate private data brokers? Why or why not? What are the advantages and disadvantages of doing so?

MIS in Action

Explore the Web sites of USAData (www.usadata.com) and ChoicePoint (www.choicepoint.com). At USAData, click on Order Mailing Lists/Sales Leads to start the process of ordering a consumer mailing list online, but do not use your credit card to pay for the list. Answer the following questions:

1. What kind of data does USAData provide? How does it obtain the data?

2. Who uses the data sold by USAData and ChoicePoint? Are there any restrictions on who can use the data?

3. What kind of information can you obtain by ordering a mailing list online? How detailed is this information? How easy is it to purchase this information? Can someone use this online capability to find out how much money you make?

4. Does the capability of USAData and ChoicePoint raise privacy issues? What are they?

5. If your name and other personal information were in this database, what limitations on access would you want in order to preserve your privacy? Consider the following data users: (a) government agencies, (b) your employer, (c) private business firms, (d) other individuals.

6. At ChoicePoint, determine how to order your own personal data so that you could verify it. Is there a charge for this service? What safeguards does ChoicePoint have in place to protect you from ChoicePoint providing your personal information to someone else as though it were their own information?

Sources: Rick Whiting, "Who's Buying and Selling Your Data? Everybody," *InformationWeek*, July 10, 2006; Christopher Wolf, "Dazed and Confused: Data Law Disarray," *Business Week*, June 8, 2006; Evan Perez and Rick Brooks, "For Big Vendor of Personal Data, A Theft Lays Bare the Downside," *The Wall Street Journal*, May 3, 2005; and "ChoicePoint Toughens Data Security," *CNN/Money*, July 5, 2005.

The development of global digital communication networks widely available to individuals and businesses poses many ethical and social concerns. Who will account for the flow of information over these networks? Will you be able to trace information collected about you? What will these networks do to the traditional relationships between family, work, and leisure? How will traditional job designs be altered when millions of "employees" become subcontractors using mobile offices for which they themselves must pay? In the next section, we consider some ethical principles and analytical techniques for dealing with these kinds of ethical and social concerns.

4.2 Ethics in an Information Society

Ethics is a concern of humans who have freedom of choice. Ethics is about individual choice: When faced with alternative courses of action, what is the correct moral choice? What are the main features of ethical choice?

Basic Concepts: Responsibility, Accountability, and Liability

Ethical choices are decisions made by individuals who are responsible for the consequences of their actions. **Responsibility** is a key element of ethical action. Responsibility means that you accept the potential costs, duties, and obligations for the decisions you make.

Accountability is a feature of systems and social institutions. It means that mechanisms are in place to determine who took responsible action and who is responsible for what occurred. Systems and institutions in which it is impossible to find out who took what action are inherently incapable of ethical analysis or ethical action. Liability extends the concept of responsibility further to the area of laws. **Liability** is a feature of political systems in which a body of laws is in place that permits individuals to recover the damages done to them by other actors, systems, or organizations. **Due process** is a related feature of law-governed societies and is a process in which laws are known and understood and there is an ability to appeal to higher authorities to ensure that the laws are applied correctly.

These basic concepts form the underpinning of an ethical analysis of information systems and those who manage them. First, information technologies are filtered through social institutions, organizations, and individuals. Systems do not have impacts by themselves. Whatever information system impacts exist are products of institutional, organizational, and individual actions and behaviours. Second, responsibility for the consequences of technology falls clearly on the institutions, organizations, and individual managers who choose to use the technology. Using information technology in a socially responsible manner means that you can and will be held accountable for the consequences of your actions. Third, in an ethical, political society, individuals and others can recover damages done to them through a set of laws characterized by due process.

Ethical Analysis

When confronted with a situation that seems to present ethical issues, how should you analyze it? The following five-step process should help.

Responsibility
Accountability
Liability
Due process

1. *Identify and describe clearly the facts.* Find out who did what to whom, and where, when, and how. In many instances, you will be surprised at the errors in the initially reported facts, and often you will find that simply getting the facts straight helps define the solution. It also helps to get the opposing parties involved in an ethical dilemma to agree on the facts.

2. *Define the conflict or dilemma, and identify the higher-order values involved.* Ethical, social, and political issues always reference higher values. The parties to a dispute all claim to be pursuing higher values (e.g., freedom, privacy, protection of property, and the free enterprise system). Typically, an ethical issue involves a dilemma: two diametrically opposed courses of action that support worthwhile values.

3. *Identify the stakeholders.* Every ethical, social, and political issue has stakeholders: players in the game who have an interest in the outcome, who have invested in the situation, and usually who have vocal opinions. Find out the identity of these groups and what they want. This will be useful later when designing a solution.

4. *Identify the options that you can reasonably take.* You may find that none of the options satisfy all the interests involved, but that some options do a better job than others. Sometimes arriving at a good or ethical solution may not always be a balancing of consequences to stakeholders.

5. *Identify the potential consequences of your options.* Some options may be ethically correct but disastrous from other points of view. Other options may work in one instance but not in other similar instances. Always ask yourself, "What if I choose this option consistently over time?"

Candidate Ethical Principles

Once your analysis is complete, what ethical principles or rules should you use to make a decision? What higher-order values should inform your judgment? Although you are the only one who can decide which among many ethical principles you will follow, and how you will prioritize them, it is helpful to consider some ethical principles with deep roots in many cultures that have survived throughout recorded history.

1. Do unto others as you would have them do unto you (the **Golden Rule**). Putting yourself into the place of others and thinking of yourself as the object of the decision can help you think about fairness in decision making.

2. If an action is not right for everyone to take, it is not right for anyone (**Immanuel Kant's Categorical Imperative**). Ask yourself, "If everyone did this, could the organization or society survive?"

3. If an action cannot be taken repeatedly, it is not right to take at all (**Descartes' rule of change**). This is the slippery-slope rule: An action may bring about a small change now that is acceptable, but if it is repeated, it would bring unacceptable changes in the long run. In the vernacular, it might be stated as "Once started down a slippery path, you may not be able to stop."

4. Take the action that achieves the higher or greater value (the **Utilitarian Principle**). This rule assumes you can prioritize values in a rank order and understand the consequences of various courses of action.

5. Take the action that produces the least harm or the least potential cost (**Risk Aversion Principle**). Some actions have extremely high failure costs of very low probability (e.g., building a nuclear generating facility in an urban area) or extremely high failure costs of moderate probability (speeding and automobile accidents). Avoid these high-failure-cost actions, and pay greater attention to actions that are likely to have high-failure-cost potential.

6. Assume that virtually all tangible and intangible objects are owned by someone else unless there is a specific declaration otherwise. (This is the **ethical "no free lunch" rule**.) If something someone else has created is useful to you, it has value, and you should assume the creator wants compensation (or credit) for this work.

Golden Rule

Immanuel Kant's Categorical Imperative

Descartes' rule of change

Utilitarian Principle

Risk Aversion Principle

Ethical "no free lunch" rule

Although these ethical rules cannot be guides to action, actions that do not easily pass these rules deserve some very close attention and a great deal of caution. The appearance of unethical behaviour may do as much harm to you and your company as actual unethical behaviour.

Professional Codes of Conduct

When groups of people claim to be professionals, they take on special rights and obligations because of their special claims to knowledge, wisdom, and respect. Professional codes of conduct are promulgated by associations of professionals, such as the Canadian Medical Association (CMA), the Canadian Bar Association (CBA), the Canadian Information Processing Society (CIPS), and the Association of Computing Machinery (ACM). These professional groups take responsibility for the partial regulation of their professions by determining entrance qualifications and competence. Codes of ethics are promises by professions to regulate themselves in the general interest of society.

Some Real-World Ethical Dilemmas

Information systems have created new ethical dilemmas in which one set of interests is pitted against another. For example, many large telephone companies are using information technology to reduce the sizes of their workforces. Voice recognition software reduces the need for human operators by enabling computers to recognize a customer's responses to a series of computerized questions. Many companies also monitor what their employees are doing on the Internet to prevent them from wasting company resources on non-business activities (see the Chapter 7 Window on Management section on page 244). SurfControl (see Figure 4-3) is software used to monitor employee Internet use.

In each ethical dilemma, you can find competing values at work, with groups lined up on either side of a debate. A company may argue, for example, that it has a right to use information systems to increase productivity and reduce the size of its workforce to lower

FIGURE 4-3   *SurfControl monitoring software*

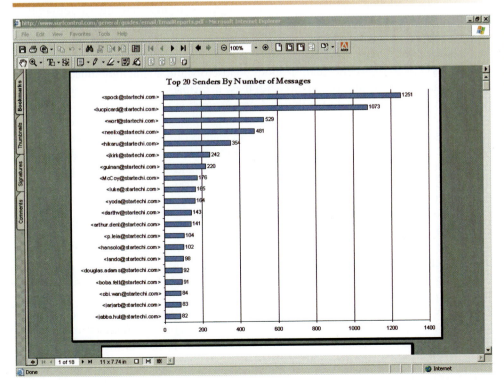

SurfControl offers tools for tracking Web and e-mail activity and for filtering unauthorized e-mail and Web site content. The benefits of monitoring employee e-mail and Internet use should be balanced with the need to respect employee privacy.

Source: © 2007 SurfControl, Inc.

costs and stay in business. Employees displaced by information systems may argue that employers have some responsibility for their welfare. Business owners might feel obligated to monitor employee e-mail and Internet use to minimize drains on productivity. Employees might believe they should be able to use the Internet for short personal tasks in place of the telephone. A close analysis of the facts can sometimes produce compromised solutions that give each side "half a loaf." Try to apply some of the principles of ethical analysis described to each of these cases. What is the right thing to do?

4.3 The Moral Dimensions of Information Systems

In this section, we take a closer look at the five moral dimensions of information systems first described in Figure 4-1 on page 108. In each dimension, we identify the ethical, social, and political levels of analysis and use real-world examples to illustrate the values involved, the stakeholders, and the options chosen.

Information Rights: Privacy and Freedom in the Internet Age

Privacy is the claim of individuals to be left alone, free from surveillance or interference from other individuals or organizations, including the state. Claims to privacy are also involved at the workplace: Millions of employees are subject to electronic and other forms of high-tech surveillance (Ball, 2001). Information technology and systems threaten individual claims to privacy by making the invasion of privacy cheap, profitable, and effective.

The claim to privacy is protected in the Canadian, U.S., and German constitutions in a variety of different ways and in other countries through various statutes. In Canada, the claim to privacy is protected primarily by the right to be secure against unreasonable search or seizure, found in the Charter of Rights and Freedoms. In addition, in 2000, Parliament passed PIPEDA, Canada's modern privacy law. The **Personal Information Protection and Electronic Documents Act** (**PIPEDA**) establishes the following principles to govern the collection, use, and disclosure of personal information: accountability, identifying the purposes for the collection of personal information, obtaining consent, limiting collection, limiting use, disclosure and retention, ensuring accuracy, providing adequate security, making information management policies readily available, providing individuals with access to information about themselves, and giving individuals a right to challenge an organization's compliance with these principles.

PIPEDA further provides for the Privacy Commissioner to receive complaints concerning contraventions of the principles, to conduct investigations, and to attempt to resolve such complaints. Unresolved disputes relating to certain matters can be taken to the Federal Court for resolution. This act complements the 1983 Privacy Act, which imposes rules on how federal government departments and agencies collect, use, and disclose personal information.

Every Canadian province and territory has enacted legislation parallel to the federal Privacy Act and the Access to Information Act. These laws prevent the unnecessary distribution of one's personal information and guarantee access to unrestricted government information.

Some of the provincial laws apply only to information held by the public sector. "Public sector" organizations under the privacy laws include public or private companies that are regulated by the government, such as financial institutions, air transportation companies, and broadcast media. The only province with a privacy law governing the private sector is Quebec. It is also the only province that meets European Union private-sector privacy law standards. That is significant for international trade, which increasingly concerns information, not hard products. Interestingly, United States legislation does not meet those standards.

Privacy

Personal Information Protection and Electronic Documents Act (PIPEDA)

Due process has become a key concept in defining privacy. Due process requires that a set of rules or laws exist that clearly define how information about individuals will be treated and what appeal mechanisms are available. Perhaps the best statement in Canada of due process in record keeping is given by the *Canadian Standards Association's Model Privacy Code.* Published in March 1996, the Code establishes 10 basic principles for all organizations that collect or use personal information. Retailers, direct marketers, financial institutions, telecommunications companies, product manufacturers, service providers, schools, universities, hospitals, personnel departments, and government agencies are potential users.

By choosing to adopt the voluntary Code, organizations demonstrate that they are following fair, nationally accepted principles. The Code is also an important resource for consumers, employees, patients, and other "data subjects," says Professor Jim Savary, former vice-president of Policy and Issues at the Consumers' Association of Canada. "The Code is a vehicle for challenging an organization's behaviour. You can refer to these principles if you are uneasy about the information you are asked to supply or how it will be used."

The 10 practices in the Code, very similar to what was enacted in PIPEDA, are as follows:

- Accountability
- Identifying purposes
- Consent
- Limiting collection
- Limiting use, disclosure, and retention
- Accuracy
- Safeguards
- Openness
- Individual access
- Challenging compliance

Most American and European privacy law is based on a regime called Fair Information Practices (FIP) first set forth in a report written in 1973 by a U.S. federal government advisory committee (U.S. Department of Health, Education, and Welfare, 1973). **Fair Information Practices (FIP)** is a set of principles governing the collection and use of information about individuals. FIP principles are based on the notion of a mutuality of interest between the record holder and the individual. The individual has an interest in engaging in a transaction, and the record keeper—usually a business or government agency—requires information about the individual to support the transaction. Once information is gathered, the individual maintains an interest in the record, and the record may not be used to support other activities without the individual's consent.

Fair Information Practices (FIP)

TABLE 4-3 *Federal Trade Commission Fair Information Practice Principles*

1. *Notice/awareness* (core principle). Web sites must disclose their information practices before collecting data. Includes identification of collector; uses of data; other recipients of data; nature of collection (active/inactive); voluntary or required status; consequences of refusal; and steps taken to protect confidentiality, integrity, and quality of the data.
2. *Choice/consent* (core principle). There must be a choice regime in place allowing consumers to choose how their information will be used for secondary purposes other than supporting the transaction, including internal use and transfer to third parties.
3. *Access/participation*. Consumers should be able to review and contest the accuracy and completeness of data collected about them in a timely, inexpensive process.
4. *Security*. Data collectors must take responsible steps to assure that consumer information is accurate and secure from unauthorized use.
5. *Enforcement*. There must be in place a mechanism to enforce FIP principles. This can involve self-regulation, legislation giving consumers legal remedies for violations, or federal statutes and regulations.

In 1998, the U.S. Federal Trade Commission (FTC) restated and extended the original FIP to provide guidelines for protecting online privacy. Table 4-3 describes the FTC's Fair Information Practice principles. U.S. laws are important because Canadian companies doing business in the U.S. need to follow American privacy laws regarding data collected in the U.S. on American customers.

The European Directive on Data Protection In Europe, privacy protection is much more stringent than in North America. Unlike the United States, but similar to Canada, European countries do not allow businesses to use personally identifiable information without consumers' prior consent. On October 25, 1998, the European Commission's Directive on Data Protection went into effect, broadening privacy protection in the European Union (EU) nations. The directive requires companies to inform people when they collect information about them and disclose how it will be stored and used. Customers must provide their informed consent before any company can legally use data about them, and they have the right to access that information, correct it, and request that no further data be collected. **Informed consent** can be defined as consent given with knowledge of all the facts needed to make a rational decision. EU member nations must translate these principles into their own laws and cannot transfer personal data to countries such as the U.S. that do not have similar privacy protection regulations.

Working with the European Commission, the U.S. Department of Commerce developed a safe harbour framework for U.S. firms. A **safe harbour** is a private, self-regulating policy and enforcement mechanism that meets the objectives of government regulators and legislation but does not involve government regulation or enforcement.

U.S. businesses doing business with Europeans are allowed to use personal data from EU countries if they develop privacy protection policies that meet EU standards. Enforcement occurs in the U.S. using self-policing, regulation, and government enforcement of fair trade statutes. Firms must be certified by public accounting firms to be "safe harbour" for personal data on Europeans, and this certification is recognized (but not enforced) by the Department of Commerce. With this safe harbour policy, the Americans and Europeans have been able to overcome their differences on privacy matters and permit trade to take place. Prior to PIPEDA, Canadian companies also made use of the safe harbour framework.

Internet Challenges to Privacy Internet technology has posed new challenges for the protection of individual privacy. Information sent over this vast network of networks may pass through many different computer systems before it reaches its final destination. Each of these systems is capable of monitoring, capturing, and storing communications that pass through it.

It is possible to record all online activities of literally tens of millions of people, including which online newsgroups or files a person has accessed, which Web sites and Web pages he or she has visited, and what items that person has inspected or purchased over the Web. Much of this monitoring and tracking of Web site visitors occurs in the background without the visitor's knowledge. Tools to monitor visits to the World Wide Web have become popular because they help organizations determine who is visiting their Web sites and how to better target their offerings. Some firms also monitor the Internet usage of their employees to see how they are using company network resources. Web retailers now have access to software that lets them "watch" the online shopping behaviour of individuals and groups while they are visiting a Web site and making purchases. The commercial demand for this personal information is virtually insatiable.

Web sites can learn the identities of their visitors if the visitors voluntarily register at the site to purchase a product or service or to obtain a free service, such as information. Web sites can also capture information about visitors without their knowledge using cookie technology.

Cookies are tiny files deposited on a computer hard drive when a user visits certain Web sites. Cookies identify the visitor's Web browser software and track visits to the Web

Informed consent

Safe harbour

Cookies

FIGURE 4-4   *How cookies identify Web visitors*

Windows XP
IE
jdoe123@aol.ca

1

Cookie   **2**

3   931032944 Previous buyer

Welcome back, Jane Doe!   **4**

User   **Server**

Cookies are written by a Web site on a visitor's hard drive. When the visitor returns to that Web site, the Web server requests the ID number from the cookie and uses it to access the data stored by the server on that visitor. The Web site can then use the data to display personalized information.

1. The Web server reads the user's Web browser and determines the operating system, browser name, version number, Internet address, and other information.
2. The server transmits a tiny text file with user identification information called a cookie, which the user's browser receives and stores on the user's computer hard drive.
3. When the user returns to the Web site, the server requests the contents of any cookie it deposited previously in the user's computer.
4. The Web server reads the cookie, identifies the visitor, and calls up data on the user.

site. When the visitor returns to a site that has stored a cookie, the Web site software will search the visitor's computer, find the cookie, and know what that person has done in the past. It may also update the cookie, depending on the activity during the visit. In this way, the site can customize its contents for each visitor's interests. For example, if you purchase a book on the Amazon.ca Web site and return later from the same browser, the site will welcome you by name and recommend other books of interest based on your past purchases. DoubleClick, described earlier in this chapter, uses cookies to build its dossiers with details of online purchases and to examine the behaviour of Web site visitors. Figure 4-4 illustrates how cookies work.

Web sites using cookie technology cannot directly obtain visitors' names and addresses; however, if a person has registered at a site, that information can be combined with cookie data to identify the visitor. Web site owners can also combine the data they have gathered from cookies and other Web site monitoring tools with personal data from other sources, such as offline data collected from surveys or paper catalogue purchases, to develop very detailed profiles of their visitors.

There are now even more subtle and surreptitious tools for surveillance of Internet users. Marketers use **Web bugs** as another tool to monitor online behaviour. Web bugs are tiny graphic files embedded in e-mail messages and Web pages that are designed to monitor who is reading the e-mail message or Web page and transmit that information to another computer. Other **spyware** can secretly install itself on an Internet user's computer by piggybacking on larger applications. Once installed, the spyware calls out to Web sites to send banner ads and other unsolicited material to the user, and it can also report the user's movements on the Internet to other computers. Spyware can also log user keystrokes and send the information to other sites on the Web without the user's knowledge. More information is available about Web bugs, spyware, and other intrusive software in Chapter 8.

Google has been using tools to scan the contents of messages received by users of its free Web-based e-mail service called Gmail. Ads that users see when they read their e-mail are related to the subjects of these messages. Google's service offers users 1 gigabyte of storage space—far more than any of its competitors—but privacy advocates find the practice offensive.

While the U.S. has allowed businesses to gather transaction information generated in the marketplace and then use that information for other marketing purposes without obtaining the informed consent of the individual whose information is being used, PIPEDA changed that practice in Canada. While U.S. e-commerce sites are largely content

Web bugs

Spyware

to publish statements on their Web sites informing visitors about how their information will be used, Canadian firms must not only publish their privacy statements, they must also have contact information for individuals to inquire about the privacy policy and their own data, as well as a method for the individual to "opt-in" to the company's data collection about the individual. Some U.S. companies have added opt-out selection boxes to these information policy statements. An **opt-out** model of informed consent permits the collection of personal information until the consumer specifically requests that the data not be collected. Privacy advocates would like to see wider use of an **opt-in** model of informed consent in which a business is prohibited from collecting any personal information unless the consumer specifically takes action to approve information collection and use. PIPEDA requires individuals to opt-in in Canada.

The online industry has preferred self-regulation to privacy legislation for protecting consumers. In 1998, the online industry formed the Online Privacy Alliance to encourage self-regulation and develop a set of privacy guidelines for its members. The group promotes the use of online seals, such as that of TRUSTe, certifying Web sites that claim to adhere to certain privacy principles. Some Canadian organizations, such as Air Canada and the Law Society of Upper Canada, are registered with TRUSTe. Members of the advertising network industry, including DoubleClick, have created an additional industry association called the Network Advertising Initiative (NAI) to develop its own privacy policies to help consumers opt out of advertising network programs and provide consumers redress from abuses.

While nearly all the top 100 Web sites have privacy policies, you will quickly discover upon reading them that there are few limitations these firms place on their use of your personal information. In turn, consumers do not do as much as they could or should to protect themselves. Many companies with Web sites do not have privacy policies. Of the companies that do post privacy polices on their Web sites, about half do not monitor their sites to ensure they adhere to these policies. While the vast majority of online customers claim they are concerned about online privacy, less than half read the privacy statements on Web sites (Laudon and Traver, 2006).

Opt-out

Opt-in

FIGURE 4-5   *Use of the TRUSTe seal*

Web sites are now posting their privacy policies for visitors to review. The TRUSTe seal designates Web sites that have agreed to adhere to TRUSTe's established privacy principles of disclosure, choice, access, and security.

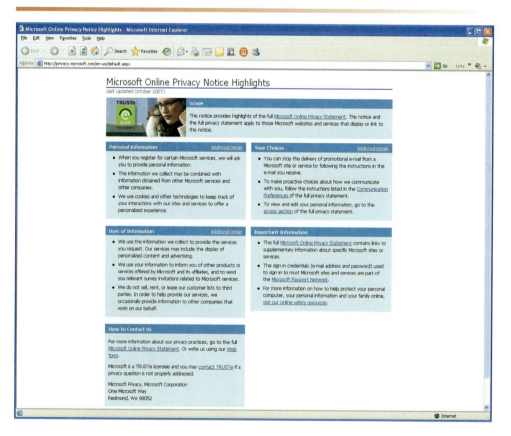

Technical Solutions In addition to legislation, new technologies are available to protect user privacy during interactions with Web sites. Many of these tools are used for encrypting e-mail, for making e-mail or surfing activities appear anonymous, for preventing client computers from accepting cookies, or for detecting and eliminating spyware.

There are now tools to help users determine the kind of personal data that can be extracted by Web sites. The Platform for Privacy Preferences, known as P3P, enables automatic communication of privacy policies between an e-commerce site and its visitors. **P3P** provides a standard for communicating a Web site's privacy policy to Internet users and for comparing that policy to the user's preferences or to other standards, such as the U.S. FTC's new Fair Information Practice guidelines or the European Directive on Data Protection. Users can use P3P to select the level of privacy they wish to maintain when interacting with the Web site.

The P3P standard allows Web sites to publish privacy policies in a form that computers can understand. Once it is codified according to P3P rules, the privacy policy becomes part of the software for individual Web pages (see Figure 4-6). Users of Microsoft Internet Explorer Web browsing software can access and read the P3P site's privacy policy and a list of all cookies coming from the site. Internet Explorer enables users to adjust their computers to screen out all cookies or let in selected cookies based on specific levels of privacy. For example, the "medium" level accepts cookies from first-party host sites that have opt-in or opt-out policies but rejects third-party cookies that use personally identifiable information without an opt-in policy.

However, P3P works only with Web sites of members of the World Wide Web Consortium that have translated their Web site privacy policies into P3P format. The technology will display cookies from Web sites that are not part of the consortium, but users will not be able to obtain sender information or privacy statements. Many users may also need to be educated about interpreting company privacy statements and P3P levels of privacy.

Property Rights: Intellectual Property

Contemporary information systems have severely challenged existing law and social practices that protect private intellectual property. **Intellectual property** is considered to be intangible property created by individuals or corporations. Information technology has made it difficult to protect intellectual property because computerized information can be so easily copied or distributed on networks. Intellectual property is subject to a variety of protections under three different legal traditions: trade secrets, copyright, and patent law.

P3P

Intellectual property

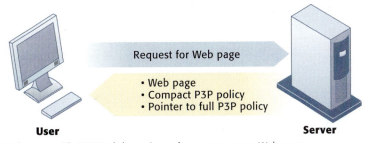

1. The user with P3P Web browsing software requests a Web page.
2. The Web server returns the Web page along with a compact version of the Web site's policy and a pointer to the full P3P policy. If the Web site is not P3P-compliant, no P3P data are returned.
3. The user's Web browsing software compares the response from the Web site with the user's privacy preferences. If the Web site does not have a P3P policy or the policy does not match the privacy levels established by the user, it warns the user or rejects the cookies from the Web site. Otherwise, the Web page loads normally.

P3P enables Web sites to translate their privacy policies into a standard format that can be read by the user's Web browser software. The user's Web browser software evaluates the Web site's privacy policy to determine whether it is compatible with the user's privacy preferences.

Trade Secrets Any intellectual work product—a formula, device, pattern, or compilation of data—used for a business purpose can be classified as a **trade secret**, provided it is not based on information in the public domain. Trade secret law has arisen out of the broad "duty of good faith" and the principle of equity that whoever "has received information in confidence shall not take unfair advantage of it." The Supreme Court of Canada has stated that the test for whether there has been a breach of confidence consists of three elements:

1. The information conveyed must be confidential (that is, it must not be public knowledge);
2. The information must have been communicated in confidence; and
3. The information must have been misused by the party to whom it was communicated.

As trade secret law in Canada is a matter of provincial jurisdiction, the drafting and interpretation of agreements that contain trade secret provisions must be carried out by a lawyer in the province that governs the agreement in question. Similarly, the assessment of whether a breach of confidence has occurred must be carried out by a lawyer in the province that governs the obligation of confidence. In general, trade secret laws grant a monopoly on the ideas behind a work product, but it can be a very tenuous monopoly.

Software that contains novel or unique elements, procedures, or compilations can be included as a trade secret. Trade secret law protects the actual ideas in a work product, not only their manifestation. To make this claim, the creator or owner must take care to bind employees and customers with nondisclosure agreements and to prevent the secret from falling into the public domain.

The limitation of trade secret protection is that although virtually all software programs of any complexity contain unique elements of some sort, it is difficult to prevent the ideas in the work from falling into the public domain when the software is widely distributed.

Copyright **Copyright** is a statutory grant that protects creators of intellectual property from having their work copied by others for any purpose for a period of at least 50 years. The Copyright Office registers copyrights and enforces copyright law in Canada. Parliament has extended copyright protection to books, periodicals, lectures, dramas, musical compositions, maps, drawings, artwork of any kind, and motion pictures. The intent behind copyright law has been to encourage creativity and authorship by ensuring that creative people receive the financial and other benefits of their work. Most industrial nations have their own copyright laws, and there are several international conventions and bilateral agreements through which nations coordinate and enforce their laws.

Copyright law in Canada is one of the principal means of protecting computer software in Canada. Canadian copyright law is governed by the Copyright Act, which protects original literary, artistic, musical, and dramatic works. Computer software is protected in Canada as a literary work. Canadian copyright comes into existence automatically, and in the case of software, it comes into existence at the time the software was created and continues until the end of the calendar year in which the author of the software dies (regardless of whether the author has sold or assigned the copyright in the software or not) and continues for an additional period of 50 years following the end of that calendar year.

"Moral" rights are also protected under Canadian copyright law. Moral rights in Canada include the right of the author of a piece of software to be associated with the software by name or pseudonym and the right to remain anonymous. They also include the author's right to the integrity of the software (that is, the author's right to stop the software from being distorted, mutilated or modified, to the prejudice of the author's honour or reputation, or from being used in association with a product, service, cause, or institution).

Moral rights remain with the author of a piece of software, even where the software, or the copyright in the software, has been sold or assigned; regardless of whether the author created the software in the employ of someone else, or created it under contract, or otherwise.

Trade secret

Copyright

Copyright protection is clear-cut: It protects against copying of entire programs or their parts. Damages and relief are readily obtained for infringement. The drawback to copyright protection is that the underlying ideas behind a work are not protected, only their manifestation in a work. A competitor can use your software, understand how it works, and develop new software that follows the same concepts without infringing on a copyright.

"Look and feel" copyright infringement lawsuits are about the precise distinction between an idea and its expression. Most of this type of copyright infringement has occurred in the United States. For instance, in the early 1990s, Apple Computer sued Microsoft Corporation and Hewlett-Packard Inc. for infringement of the *expression* of Apple's Macintosh interface. Among other claims, Apple claimed that the defendants copied the expression of overlapping windows. The defendants counterclaimed that the idea of overlapping windows can only be expressed in a single way and, therefore, was not protectable under the "merger" doctrine of copyright law. When ideas and their expression merge, the expression cannot be copyrighted. In general, courts appear to be following the reasoning of a 1989 U.S. case—*Brown Bag Software* vs. *Symantec Corp.*—in which the court dissected the elements of software alleged to be infringing. The court found that neither similar concept, function, general functional features (e.g., drop-down menus), nor colours are protected by copyright law (*Brown Bag* vs. *Symantec Corp.*, 1992).

Patents   A **patent** grants the owner an exclusive monopoly on the ideas behind an invention for between 17 and 20 years. The intent behind patent law is to ensure that inventors of new machines, devices, or methods receive the full financial and other rewards of their labour and yet still make widespread use of the invention possible by providing detailed diagrams for those wishing to use the idea under licence from the patent's owner. The granting of a patent is determined by the Canadian Patent Office and relies on court rulings.

The key concepts in patent law are originality, novelty, and invention. The Canadian Patent Office does not accept applications for software patents because software is considered to fall under Canadian copyright law. The U.S. Patent Office did not routinely issue patents on software in the U.S. until a 1981 Supreme Court decision that held that computer programs could be a part of a patentable process. Since that time, hundreds of U.S. software patents have been granted, and thousands await consideration.

The strength of patent protection is that it grants a monopoly on the underlying concepts and ideas of software. The difficulty is passing stringent criteria of nonobviousness (e.g., the work must reflect some special understanding and contribution), originality, and novelty as well as years of waiting to receive protection.

Challenges to Intellectual Property Rights   Contemporary information technologies, especially software, pose severe challenges to existing intellectual property regimes and, therefore, create significant ethical, social, and political/legal issues. Digital media differ from physical media such as books, periodicals, CDs, and newspapers in terms of ease of replication; ease of transmission; ease of alteration; difficulty in classifying a software work as a program, book, or even music; compactness—making theft easy; and difficulties in establishing uniqueness.

The proliferation of electronic networks, including the Internet, has made it even more difficult to protect intellectual property. Before the widespread use of networks, copies of software, books, magazine articles, or films had to be stored on physical media, such as paper, computer disks, or videotape, creating some hurdles to distribution. Using networks, information can be more widely reproduced and distributed. A study conducted by the International Data Corporation for the Business Software Alliance found that more than one-third of the software worldwide was counterfeit or pirated, and the Business Software Alliance reported US $29 billion in yearly losses from software piracy (Geitner, 2004; Lohr, 2004).

The Internet was designed to transmit information freely around the world, including copyrighted information. With the World Wide Web in particular, you can easily copy and distribute virtually anything to thousands and even millions of people around the world,

Patent

even if they are using different types of computer systems. Information can be illicitly copied from one place and distributed through other systems and networks even though these parties do not willingly participate in the infringement.

Individuals have been illegally copying and distributing digitized MP3 music files on the Internet for a number of years. File sharing services such as Napster, and, later, Grokster, Kazaa, and Morpheus, sprung up to help users locate and swap digital music files, including those protected by copyright. Illegal file-sharing became so widespread that it threatened the viability of the music recording industry.

The recording industry won significant legal battles against Napster, and later against Grokster and all commercial P2P networks. The U.S. Supreme Court found in June 2005 that file-sharing networks that intentionally profited from illegal distribution of music could be held liable for their actions. This decision forced most of the large-scale commercial P2P networks to shut down or to seek legal distribution agreements with the music publishers.

Despite these victories in court, illegal music file sharing abounds on the Internet: In the U.S., more than 36 million Americans report downloading music from illegal sites. This is down from 2002. The good news—if there is any in this area—is that legal music downloads from sites such as iTunes have expanded to more than 43 percent of Internet users in the U.S. (Madden and Rainie, 2005). As more and more homes adopt high-speed Internet access, illegal file sharing of videos will pose similar threats to the motion picture industry.

Mechanisms are being developed to sell and distribute books, articles, and other intellectual property legally on the Internet, and the U.S. **Digital Millennium Copyright Act (DMCA)** of 1998 is providing some copyright protection. The DMCA implemented a World Intellectual Property Organization Treaty that makes it illegal to circumvent technology-based protections of copyrighted materials. Internet service providers (ISPs) are required to take down sites of copyright infringers that the ISPs are hosting, once they are notified of the problem.

What effect did the DMCA have on Canadian copyright legislation? The DMCA set the agenda for copyright discussions in Canada in the following areas:

- Technological tampering—devices or conduct
- ISP liability
- Library provisions to be examined
- Database protection

The Speech from the Throne in the fall of 2002 sought to establish policy to bring Canada into alignment with the World Intellectual Property Organization (WIPO) and also to look at some other long-term aims of copyright legislation in Canada. Compliance with WIPO would include short-term goals of technological measures protection and digital rights management as well as the liability of the Internet service provider when its users infringe copyright. The government also decided to look at the blank recording levy currently in place. This levy is incorporated into the price of blank media and its profits aggregated and split among various recording industry figures, such as publishers and artists. Another goal was to examine the fair use part of the Copyright Act and whether it could or should be expanded. Canadian lawmakers are currently looking at the duration of copyright and whether it should be increased to life plus 70 years, as has taken place in the United States. In the longer term, protection of native folklore and oral histories will be examined.

Microsoft and 1400 other software and information content firms are represented by the Software and Information Industry Association (SIIA), which lobbies for new laws and the enforcement of existing laws to protect intellectual property around the world. SIIA was formed on January 1, 1999, from the merger of the Software Publishers Association (SPA) and the Information Industry Association (IIA). The SIIA runs an anti-piracy hotline for individuals to report piracy activities and has educational programs to help organizations combat software piracy. The SIIA has also published guidelines for employee use of software.

Digital Millennium Copyright Act (DMCA)

Accountability, Liability, and Control

Along with privacy and property laws, new information technologies are challenging existing liability law and social practices for holding individuals and institutions accountable. If a person is injured by a machine controlled, in part, by software, who should be held accountable and, therefore, held liable? Should a public bulletin board or an electronic service, such as AOL (as broadcasters), permit the transmission of pornographic or offensive material, or should they be held harmless against any liability for what users transmit (as is true of common carriers, such as the telephone system)? What about the Internet and what can be found on Web sites? Should those who posted illegal or offensive material be held liable, and by whom should they be held liable? If you outsource your information processing, can you hold the external vendor liable for injuries done to your customers? Some real-world examples may shed light on these questions.

Computer-Related Liability Problems On November 28, 2000, a double failure in Sprint Canada's network shut down trading on Vancouver's Canadian Venture Exchange for more than two hours. Three hundred thousand Rogers@Home cable customers were left without service recently when a rodent chewed through cables that were exposed during routine repairs. And in November 1998, a railway backhoe operator accidentally cut an AT&T Canada fibre cable along the rail line between Toronto and Windsor, crashing computers, knocking out phone lines, and generally disrupting communications in southern Ontario. The main branch of the Bank of Nova Scotia was computerless as a result.

In the U.S., during the weekend of March 15, 2002, tens of thousands of Bank of America customers in California, Arizona, and Nevada were unable to use their paycheques and social security payments that had just been deposited electronically. Cheques bounced. Withdrawals were blocked because of insufficient funds. Because of an operating error at the bank's computer centre in Nevada, a batch of direct-deposit transactions was not processed. The bank lost track of money that should have been credited to customers' accounts, and it took days to rectify the problem (Carr and Gallagher, 2002). Who is liable for any economic harm caused to individuals or businesses that could not access their full account balances in this period?

These cases reveal the difficulties faced by information systems executives who ultimately are responsible for any harm done by systems developed by their staffs. In general, insofar as computer software is part of a machine that injures someone physically or economically, the producer of the software and the operator can be held liable for damages. Insofar as the software acts like a book, storing and displaying information, courts have been reluctant to hold software authors liable for contents (the exception being in instances of fraud or defamation). In general, it is very difficult (if not impossible) to hold software producers liable for their software products when those products are considered like books, regardless of the physical or economic harm that results. Historically, print publishers, books, and periodicals have not been held liable by the courts because of fears that liability claims would interfere with rights guaranteeing freedom of expression.

What about software as service? ATM machines are a service provided to bank customers. Should this service fail, customers will be inconvenienced and perhaps harmed economically if they cannot access their funds in a timely manner. Should liability protections be extended to software publishers and operators of defective financial, accounting, simulation, or marketing systems?

Software is very different from books. Software users may develop expectations of infallibility about software; software is less easily inspected than a book, and it is more difficult to compare with other software products for quality; finally, software claims actually to perform a task rather than describe a task, as a book does; and people come to depend on services essentially based on software. Given the centrality of software to everyday life, the chances are excellent that liability law will extend its reach to include software even when the software merely provides an information service.

Telephone systems have not been held liable for the messages transmitted because they are regulated common carriers. In return for their right to provide telephone service, they must provide access to all at reasonable rates, and achieve acceptable reliability. But broadcasters and cable television systems are subject to a wide variety of federal and local constraints on content and facilities. Organizations can be held liable for offensive content on their Web sites; and online services, such as MSN or AOL, might be held liable for postings by their users. Although courts have increasingly exonerated Web sites and ISPs for posting material by third parties, the threat of legal action still has a chilling effect on small companies or individuals who cannot afford to take their cases to trial.

System Quality: Data Quality and System Errors

The debate over liability and accountability for unintentional consequences of system use raises a related but independent moral dimension: What is an acceptable, technologically feasible level of system quality? At what point should system managers say, "Stop testing, we've done all we can to perfect this software. Ship it!" Individuals and organizations may be held responsible for avoidable and foreseeable consequences, which they have a duty to perceive and correct. The reason this is a grey area is that some system errors are foreseeable and correctable only at very great expense, an expense so great that pursuing this level of perfection is not feasible economically—achieving it would mean that no one could afford the product.

For example, although software companies try to debug their products before releasing them to the marketplace, they knowingly ship buggy products because the time and cost of fixing all minor errors would prevent these products from ever being released. What if the product was not offered on the marketplace—would social welfare as a whole not advance and perhaps even decline? Carrying this further, just what is the responsibility of a producer of computer services—should it withdraw the product that can never be perfect, warn the user, or forget about the risk (let the buyer beware)?

Three principal sources of poor system performance are (1) software bugs and errors, (2) hardware or facility failures caused by natural or other causes, and (3) poor input data quality. In general, zero defects in software code of any complexity cannot be achieved due to the complexity of most software, and therefore the seriousness of remaining bugs cannot be estimated. Hence, there is a technological barrier to perfect software, and users must be aware of the potential for catastrophic failure. The software industry has not yet arrived at testing standards for producing software of acceptable but not perfect performance.

Although software bugs and facility catastrophes are likely to be widely reported in the press, by far the most common source of business system failure is data quality. Few companies routinely measure the quality of their data, but studies of individual organizations report data error rates ranging from 0.5 to 30 percent (Gilhooly, 2005).

Quality of Life: Equity, Access, and Boundaries

The negative social costs of introducing information technologies and systems are beginning to mount along with the power of the technology. Many of these negative social consequences are not property crimes or violations of individual rights. Nevertheless, these negative consequences can still be extremely harmful to individuals, societies, and political institutions. Computers and information technologies can potentially destroy valuable elements of our culture and society even while they bring us benefits. If there is a balance of good and bad consequences of using information systems, whom do we hold responsible for the bad consequences? Next, we briefly examine some of the negative social consequences of systems, considering individual, social, and political responses.

Balancing Power: Centre versus Periphery An early fear of the computer age was that huge, centralized mainframe computers would centralize power at corporate headquarters and in the nation's capital, resulting in a Big Brother society, as was suggested in George Orwell's novel *1984*. The shift toward highly decentralized computing, coupled with an ideology of empowerment of thousands of workers, and the decentralization of decision-making to lower organizational levels, has reduced the fears of power centralization in institutions. Yet much of the empowerment described in popular business magazines is trivial. Lower-level employees may be empowered to make minor decisions, but the key policy decisions may be as centralized as in the past.

Rapidity of Change: Reduced Response Time to Competition Information systems have helped to create much more efficient national and international markets. The now-more-efficient global marketplace has reduced the normal social buffers that permitted businesses many years to adjust to competition. Time-based competition has an ugly side: The business you work for may not have enough time to respond to global competitors and may be wiped out in a year, along with your job. We stand the risk of developing a "just-in-time" society with "just-in-time" jobs and "just-in-time" workplaces, families, and vacations.

Maintaining Boundaries: Family, Work, and Leisure Parts of this book were produced on trains and planes, as well as on family vacations and during what otherwise might have been "family" time. The danger to ubiquitous computing, telecommuting, nomad computing, and the "do anything anywhere any time" computing environment is that it might actually come true. If so, the traditional boundaries that separate work from family and just plain leisure will be weakened.

Although authors have traditionally worked just about anywhere (typewriters have been portable for nearly a century), the advent of information systems, coupled with the growth of knowledge-work occupations, means that more and more people will be working when traditionally they would have been playing or communicating with family and friends. The work umbrella now extends far beyond the eight-hour day.

Although some people enjoy the convenience of working at home, the "do anything anywhere any time" computing environment can blur the traditional boundaries between work and family time.

Even leisure time spent on the computer threatens these close social relationships. Extensive Internet use, even for entertainment or recreational purposes, takes people away from their family and friends. The Window on Organizations section explores what happens to children and teenagers when time spent online is excessive or inappropriate.

Weakening these institutions poses clear-cut risks. Family and friends historically have provided powerful support mechanisms for individuals, and they act as balance points in society by preserving private life, providing a place for people to collect their thoughts, allowing people to think in ways contrary to their employer, and allowing them to dream.

Organization **WINDOW ON ORGANIZATIONS**

The Internet: Friend or Foe to Children?

The Internet has so much to offer people of all ages, including children. School-age children typically use the Internet for school assignments, for downloading music, playing games, and for connecting with others. A child might use e-mail or instant messaging to stay in touch with friends who have moved away or family members in distant locations. Shy children may find an online community and set of "friends" with whom to share feelings that they are unable to express in person. Children living in rural areas can stay in touch with others who are isolated geographically.

But there is a dark side to all that Internet use. The Internet can also socially isolate children and expose them to unhealthy activities and experiences.

According to child and adolescent psychiatrist Dr. David Bassler, certain children become too isolated as a result of heavy Internet use. A shy or overweight child can become a football star in an online game or a persona in MySpace. Bassler believes that "a degree of this is healthy, but if it starts to become the primary focus, it can become a problem." Staying online for long periods of time may make a shy or depressed child even more shy or depressed.

When children spend too much time online, they do not do their homework or cannot focus on their work in school because their online activities have drained their energy. They miss out on sports and other activities, and they do not spend enough time with their real-world peers and family members.

E-mail and instant messaging can help youngsters stay in touch with friends and family but they have also become instruments for cyberbullying. Kids will use these tools to send insulting remarks to one another or to distribute personal details meant for a few close friends to a wide circle of strangers. One 16-year-old boy whose girlfriend had broken up with him over the telephone was shocked to find a detailed explanation for her actions on her instant messenger profile. She had used instant messaging to tell their entire network of social contacts, including friends of friends in different high schools, details about the reasons for the breakup. The boy was so upset he skipped school the next day. In Canada, a cyberbullying incident at the University of Manitoba resulted in suspensions and other penalties for the several dozen students involved in describing another student as (among other terms) "creepy."

Ten million young people use the Internet each day in the U.S., and one in five have been solicited or approached by a sexual predator, according to the U.S. FBI. Federal arrests in the U.S. for online exploitation of children doubled from 863 to 1649 between 2003 and 2005. Fifty percent of child victims of online sex abuse are in the seventh through ninth grades.

Online predators monitor screen names and scrutinize personal information on social networking sites such as MySpace, Friendster, and Facebook to find youngsters with self-esteem problems. They'll ask youngsters questions such as "Do you like this band? Can I help you with your homework?" Then they will try to arrange a physical meeting with these juveniles.

Dr. Robert Kraut, a professor at Carnegie-Mellon University who has studied online behaviour for more than a decade, found that the more people use the Internet, the less they socialize and the less they communicate with family members. High Internet usage among teenagers is associated with a decline in social support. Many hours spent online in casual conversation with other strangers do not translate into meaningful relationships.

Obesity, now an epidemic in North America, is especially prevalent among youngsters who sit at their computers for hours at a time munching on snack food. And there are plenty of Web sites encouraging them to do just that.

Food companies aggressively use Internet games and other perks such as screen-saver downloads to entice children into buying their brands. Their Web sites offer childrens' games linked to snacks, such as Chips Ahoy Soccer Shootout, Pop-Tart Slalom, and Lucky Charms Wild Chocolate Mine. A Kaiser Family Foundation study found that, between June and November 2005, more than 12.2 million children had visited 77 food company Web sites it examined.

According to the study's lead researcher Vicky Rideout, Internet advertising "still doesn't have the reach TV advertising has. But [those] who it does reach, it reaches more deeply." This study is the first to investigate the scope of Internet advertising aimed at children.

To Think About

1. Does use of the Internet by children and teenagers pose an ethical dilemma? Why or why not?

2. Should parents restrict use of the Internet by children or teenagers? Why or why not?

MIS in Action

Visit Nabiscoworld.com or another food company Web site featuring games or other interactive features of interest to children and teenagers. Explore the site and answer the following questions.

1. What kinds of games and interactive features are available at this site? Are there any restrictions on who can play?

2. How do these sites help the company pitch food products to children?

3. Do these sites collect personal information? What kind of information?

4. Are these sites at all beneficial to consumers? What are the benefits?

5. Do these sites represent an ethical dilemma? Why or why not?

Sources: Johanna Ambrosio, "Connected to Nowhere," *InformationWeek*, May 1, 2006; Jennifer B. McKim, "Keep Your Child Safe from Online Predators," *Orange County Register*, July 18, 2006; and Curtis L. Taylor, "Kids Swallowing Online Food Company Lures," *Newsday*, July 20, 2006.

Dependence and Vulnerability Today, our businesses, governments, schools, and private associations, such as churches, are incredibly dependent on information systems and are, therefore, highly vulnerable if these systems fail. With systems now as ubiquitous as the telephone system, it is startling to remember that there are no regulatory or standard-setting forces in place that are similar to telephone, electrical, radio, television, or other public-utility technologies. The absence of standards and the criticality of some system applications will probably call forth demands for national standards and perhaps regulatory oversight.

Computer Crime and Abuse New technologies, including computers, create new opportunities for committing crime by creating new valuable items to steal, new ways to steal them, and new ways to harm others. The Israeli Trojan Horse Scandal described at the beginning of this chapter is an example of this type of crime. **Computer crime** is the commission of illegal acts through the use of a computer or against a computer system. Computers or computer systems can be the object of the crime (i.e., destroying a company's computer centre or a company's computer files), as well as the instrument of a crime (i.e., stealing computer lists by illegally gaining access to a computer system using a home computer). Simply accessing a computer system without authorization or with intent to do harm, even by accident, is now a federal crime. Chapter 8 provides more detail on this topic.

Computer abuse is the commission of acts involving a computer that may not be illegal but that are considered unethical. The popularity of the Internet and e-mail has turned one form of computer abuse—spamming—into a serious problem for both individuals and businesses. **Spam** is junk e-mail sent by an organization or individual to a mass audience of Internet users who have expressed no interest in the product or service being marketed. Spammers tend to market pornography, fraudulent deals and services, outright scams, and other products not widely approved in most civilized societies. Some countries have passed laws to outlaw spamming or to restrict its use. In North America, it is still legal if it does not involve fraud and the sender and subject of the e-mail are properly identified.

Spamming has mushroomed because it only costs a few cents to send thousands of messages advertising wares to Internet users. Hundreds of CDs for sale on the Web offer spammers millions of e-mail addresses harvested by software robots that read message boards, chat rooms, and Web sites, or spammers may use their own harvesting tools for this purpose. The industry of combatting spam has also generated new products such as McAfee's SpamKiller (see Figure 4-7). Spam now accounts for 70 percent of Internet e-mail traffic worldwide. Figure 4-8 provides data on the scope of spamming and the types of industries most affected by the practice.

Spam costs for businesses are very high (an estimated $50 billion per year) because of the computing and network resources consumed by billions of unwanted e-mail messages

Computer crime
Computer abuse
Spam

FIGURE 4-7 *Spam filtering software*

Spam consists of unsolicited e-mail messages, which can be bothersome, offensive, and even a drain on office worker productivity. Spam filtering software such as McAfee's SpamKiller blocks suspicious e-mail.

FIGURE 4-8   *The spamming problem*

Spam for Everyone

Spam e-mail messages hawking many kinds of products and services, including scams, clog inboxes of employees in many industries.

What is being offered . . .   . . . and to whom

Products and services being sold with spam e-mail messages   Average number of spam e-mail messages received daily per user

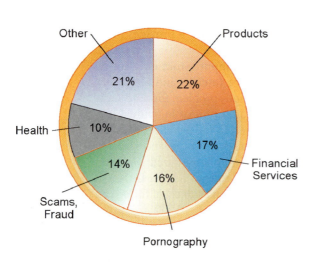

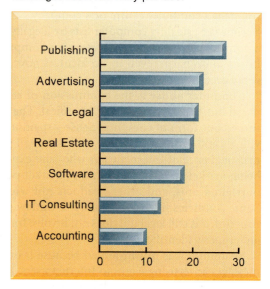

This figure shows the major types of products and services hawked through spam e-mail messages, and the industries that receive the most spam.

and the time required to deal with them. Internet service providers and individuals can combat spam by using spam filtering software to block suspicious e-mail before it enters a recipient's e-mail inbox. However, spam filters may block legitimate messages, and many spammers skirt around filters by continually changing their e-mail accounts. Many spam messages are sent from one country while another country hosts the spam Web site.

Spamming is more tightly regulated in Europe than in North America. On May 30, 2002, the European Parliament passed a ban on unsolicited commercial messaging. Electronic marketing can be targeted only to people who have given prior consent.

In the U.S., the CAN-SPAM Act of 2003, which went into effect on January 1, 2004, does not outlaw spamming but does ban deceptive e-mail practices by requiring commercial e-mail messages to display accurate subject lines, identify the true senders, and offer recipients an easy way to remove their names from e-mail lists. It also prohibits the use of fake return addresses. A few people have been prosecuted under the law, but spamming increased after it went into effect.

Employment: Trickle-Down Technology and Reengineering Job Loss

Reengineering work is typically hailed in the information systems community as a major benefit of new information technology. It is much less frequently noted that redesigning business processes could potentially cause millions of mid-level managers and clerical workers to lose their jobs. One economist has raised the possibility that we will create a society run by a small "high tech elite of corporate professionals . . . in a nation of the permanently unemployed" (Rifkin, 1993).

Other economists are much more sanguine about the potential job losses. They believe relieving bright, educated workers from reengineered jobs will result in these workers moving to better jobs in fast-growth industries. Missing from this equation are unskilled, blue-collar workers and older, less well-educated middle managers. It is not clear that these groups can be retrained easily for high-quality (high-paying) jobs. Careful planning and sensitivity to employee needs can help companies redesign work to minimize job losses.

Equity and Access: Increasing Racial and Social Class Cleavages Does everyone have an equal opportunity to participate in the digital age?

Will the social, economic, and cultural gaps that exist in North America and other societies be reduced by information systems technology? Or will the cleavages be increased, permitting the better off to become even more better off relative to others?

These questions have not yet been fully answered because the impact of systems technology on various groups in society has not been thoroughly studied. What is known is that information, knowledge, computers, and access to these resources through educational institutions and public libraries are inequitably distributed along ethnic and social class lines, as are many other information resources. Several studies have found that certain ethnic and income groups in North America are less likely to have computers or online Internet access, particularly broadband access, even though computer ownership and Internet access have soared in the past five years. Although the gap is narrowing, higher-income families in each ethnic group are still more likely to have home computers and Internet access than lower-income families in the same group.

A similar **digital divide** exists in North American schools, with schools in high-poverty areas less likely to have computers, high-quality educational technology programs, or Internet access availability for their students. Left uncorrected, the digital divide could lead to a society of information haves, computer-literate and skilled, versus a large group of information have-nots, computer-illiterate and unskilled. Public interest groups want to narrow this digital divide by making digital information services—including the Internet—available to virtually everyone, just as basic telephone service is now.

Health Risks: RSI, CVS, and Techno-stress The most rampant occupational disease today is **repetitive stress injury (RSI)**. RSI occurs when muscle groups are forced through repetitive actions often with high-impact loads (such as tennis) or tens of thousands of repetitions under low-impact loads (such as working at a computer keyboard).

The single largest source of RSI is computer keyboards. The most common kind of computer-related RSI is **carpal tunnel syndrome (CTS)**, in which pressure on the median nerve through the wrist's bony structure, called a carpal tunnel, produces pain. The pressure is caused by constant repetition of keystrokes—in a single shift, a data entry clerk may perform 23 000 keystrokes. Symptoms of carpal tunnel syndrome include numbness, shooting pain, inability to grasp objects, and tingling. Millions of workers have been diagnosed with carpal tunnel syndrome.

RSI is avoidable. Designing workstations for a neutral wrist position (using a wrist rest to support the wrist), proper monitor stands, and footrests all contribute to proper posture and reduced RSI. New, ergonomically correct

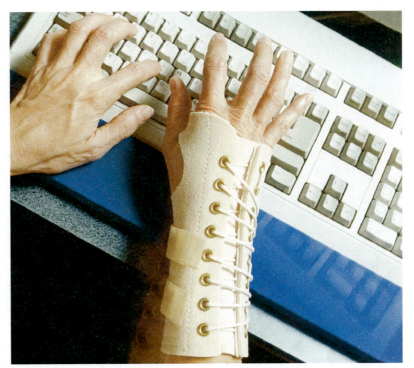

Repetitive stress injury (RSI) is the leading occupational disease today. The single largest cause of RSI is computer keyboard work.

keyboards are also an option. These measures should be supported by frequent rest breaks and rotation of employees to different jobs.

RSI is not the only occupational illness computers cause. Back and neck pain, leg stress, and foot pain also result from poor ergonomic designs of workstations.

Digital divide
Repetitive stress injury (RSI)
Carpal tunnel syndrome (CTS)

Computer vision syndrome (CVS) refers to any eyestrain condition related to computer display screen use. Its symptoms, which are usually temporary, include headaches, blurred vision, and dry and irritated eyes.

The newest computer-related malady is **technostress**, which is stress induced by computer use. Its symptoms include aggravation, hostility toward humans, impatience, and fatigue. According to experts, humans working continuously with computers come to expect other humans and human institutions to behave like computers, providing instant responses, attentiveness, and an absence of emotion. Technostress is thought to be related to high levels of job turnover in the computer industry, high levels of early retirement from computer-intense occupations, and elevated levels of drug and alcohol abuse.

The incidence of technostress is not known but is thought to be in the millions and growing rapidly in North America. Computer-related jobs now top the list of stressful occupations, based on health statistics in several industrialized countries.

To date, the role of radiation from computer display screens in occupational disease has not been proved. Video display terminals (VDTs) emit nonionizing electric and magnetic fields at low frequencies. These rays enter the body and have unknown effects on enzymes, molecules, chromosomes, and cell membranes. Long-term studies are investigating low-level electromagnetic fields and birth defects, stress, low birth weight, and other diseases.

All manufacturers have reduced display screen emissions since the early 1980s, and European countries, such as Sweden, have adopted stiff radiation emission standards.

The computer has become a part of our lives—personally as well as socially, culturally, and politically. It is unlikely that the issues and our choices will become easier as information technology continues to transform our world. The growth of the Internet and the information economy suggests that all the ethical and social issues we have described will be heightened further as we move into the first digital century.

Computer vision syndrome (CVS)

Technostress

Summary

1. Analyze the relationships among ethical, social, and political issues that are raised by information systems.

Information technology has raised new possibilities for behaviour for which laws and rules of acceptable conduct have not yet been developed. Information technology is introducing changes that create new ethical issues for societies to debate and resolve. Increasing computing power, storage, and networking capabilities—including the Internet—can expand the reach of individual and organizational actions and magnify their impacts. The ease and anonymity with which information can be communicated, copied, and manipulated in online environments are challenging traditional rules of right and wrong behaviour. Ethical, social, and political issues are closely related. Ethical issues confront individuals who must choose a course of action, often in a situation in which two or more ethical principles are in conflict (a dilemma). Social issues spring from ethical issues as societies develop expectations in individuals about the correct course of action. Political issues spring from social conflict and are mainly concerned with using laws that prescribe behaviour to create situations in which individuals behave correctly.

2. Identify the main moral dimensions of an information society and specific principles for conduct that can be used to guide ethical decisions.

The moral dimensions of information systems centre on information rights and obligations, property rights and obligations, accountability and control, system quality, and quality of life.

Six ethical principles are available to judge conduct. These principles are derived independently from several cultural, religious, and intellectual traditions and include the Golden Rule, Immanuel Kant's Categorical Imperative, Descartes' rule of change, the Utilitarian Principle, the Risk Aversion Principle, and the ethical "no free lunch" rule. These principles should be used in conjunction with an ethical analysis to guide decision making. Ethical analysis involves identifying the facts, values, stakeholders, options, and consequences of actions. Once completed, you can consider which ethical principle to apply to a situation to arrive at a judgment.

3. Evaluate the impact of contemporary information systems and the Internet on the protection of individual privacy and intellectual property.

Contemporary information systems technology, including Internet technology, challenges traditional regimens for protecting individual privacy and intellectual property. Data storage and data analysis technology enables companies to easily gather personal data about individuals from many different sources and analyze these data to create detailed electronic profiles about individuals and their behaviours. Data flowing over the Internet can be monitored at many points. The activities of Web site visitors can be closely tracked using cookies and other Web monitoring tools. Not all Web sites have strong privacy protection policies, and they do not always allow for informed consent regarding the use of personal information. The online industry prefers self-regulation to the government tightening privacy protection legislation.

Traditional copyright laws are insufficient to protect against software piracy because digital material can be copied so easily. Internet technology also makes intellectual property even more difficult to protect because digital material can be copied easily and transmitted to many different locations simultaneously over the Internet. Web pages can be constructed easily using pieces of content from other Web sites without permission.

4. ***Assess how information systems have affected everyday life.***

Although computer systems have been sources of efficiency and wealth, they have some negative impacts. It is impossible to eradicate all errors in large computer systems. Computer errors can cause serious harm to individuals and organizations, and existing laws and social practices are often unable to establish liability and accountability for these problems. Less serious errors are often attributable to poor data quality, which can cause disruptions and losses for businesses. Jobs can be lost when computers replace workers or tasks become unnecessary in reengineered business processes. The ability to own and use a computer may be exacerbating socioeconomic disparities among different racial groups and social classes. Widespread use of computers increases opportunities for computer crime and computer abuse. Computers can also create health problems, such as repetitive stress injury, computer vision syndrome, and technostress.

Key Terms

Accountability, 113

Carpal tunnel syndrome (CTS), 131

Computer abuse, 129

Computer crime, 129

Computer vision syndrome (CVS), 132

Cookies, 118

Copyright, 122

Descartes' rule of change, 114

Digital divide, 131

Digital Millennium Copyright Act (DMCA), 124

Due process, 113

Ethical "no free lunch" rule, 114

Ethics, 107

Fair Information Practices (FIP), 117

Golden Rule, 114

Immanuel Kant's Categorical Imperative, 114

Informed consent, 118

Intellectual property, 121

Liability, 113

Nonobvious relationship awareness (NORA), 110

Opt-in, 120

Opt-out, 120

P3P, 121

Patent, 123

Personal Information Protection and Electronic Documents Act (PIPEDA), 116

Privacy, 116

Profiling, 110

Repetitive stress injury (RSI), 131

Responsibility, 113

Risk Aversion Principle, 114

Safe harbour, 118

Spam, 129

Spyware, 119

Technostress, 132

Trade secret, 122

Utilitarian Principle, 114

Web bugs, 119

Review Questions

1. *In what ways are ethical, social, and political issues connected? Give some examples.*

2. *What are the key technological trends that heighten ethical concerns?*

3. *What are the differences between responsibility, accountability, and liability?*

4. *What are the five steps in an ethical analysis?*

5. *Identify and describe six ethical principles.*

6. *What is a professional code of conduct?*

7. *What are meant by privacy and fair information practices? What is PIPEDA?*

8. *How is the Internet challenging the protection of individual privacy?*

9. *What role can informed consent, legislation, industry self-regulation, and technology tools play in protecting the individual privacy of Internet users?*

10. *What are three regimes other than PIPEDA that protect intellectual property rights? What challenges to intellectual property rights does the Internet pose?*

11. *Why is it so difficult to hold software services liable for failure or injury?*

12. *What is the most common cause of system quality problems?*

13. *Name and describe four quality-of-life impacts of computers and information systems.*

14. *What is technostress, and how would you identify it?*

15. *Name three management actions that could reduce RSI injuries.*

Discussion Questions

1. *Should producers of software-based services, such as ATMs, be held liable for economic injuries suffered when their systems fail?*

2. *Should companies be responsible for unemployment caused by their information systems? Why or why not?*

3. *Do you believe that practising good ethics pays off? Why or why not?*

4. *What do you believe the role of government should be in policing the practice of good ethics by businesses and other organizations?*

Teamwork: Developing a Corporate Ethics Code

With three or four of your classmates, develop a corporate ethics code on privacy that addresses both employee privacy and the privacy of customers and users of the corporate Web site. Be sure to consider e-mail privacy and employer monitoring of worksites, as well as corporate use of information about employees concerning their off-the-job behaviour (e.g., lifestyle, marital arrangements, and so forth). If possible, use electronic presentation software to present your ethics code to the class.

Learning Track Module

Developing a Corporate Code of Ethics for Information Systems. This Learning Track Module describes the outline for a corporate code of ethics in information systems. What should be in a code of ethics? What ethical dimensions should be included? The Learning Track Module is available on MyMISLab.

For online exercises, please visit www.pearsoned.ca/mymislab.

HANDS-ON MIS   Application Exercises

The projects in this section give you hands-on experience in developing a privacy policy for a real-world company, using Web page development tools to design and create a simple Web site, and using Internet newsgroups for market research.

Developing a Web Site Privacy Policy

Software skills: Web browser software and presentation software
Business skills: Corporate privacy policy formulation

Dirt Bikes Canada's management wants to make sure it has policies and procedures in place to protect the privacy of visitors to its Web site. You have been asked to develop Dirt Bikes Canada's Web site privacy policy. The TRUSTe Web site at www.truste.org has Model Privacy Disclosures in its Privacy Resources that you can download and review to help you draft Dirt Bikes Canada's privacy policy. You can also examine specific companies' privacy policies by searching for Web site privacy policies on Yahoo!, Google,

or another search engine. Prepare a report for management that addresses the following issues: How much data should Dirt Bikes Canada collect on visitors to its Web site? What information could it discover by tracking visitors' activities at its Web site?

1. What value would this information provide the company? What are the privacy problems raised by collecting such data?

2. Should Dirt Bikes Canada use cookies? What are the advantages of using cookies for both Dirt Bikes Canada

and its Web site visitors? What privacy issues do they create for Dirt Bikes?

3. Should Dirt Bikes Canada join an organization such as TRUSTe to certify that it has adopted approved privacy practices? Why or why not?

4. Should Dirt Bikes Canada design its site so that it conforms to P3P standards? Why or why not?

5. Should Dirt Bikes Canada adopt an opt-in or opt-out model of informed consent?

6. Include in your report a short (two to three pages) privacy statement for the Dirt Bikes Canada Web site. You can use the categories of the TRUSTe Model Privacy Disclosures as a guideline if you wish.

7. (Optional) Use electronic presentation software to summarize your recommendations for management.

Achieving Operational Excellence:
Creating a Simple Web Site Using Web Page Development Tools

Software skills: Web page creation
Business skills: Web page design

In this project, you will learn how to develop a simple Web site of your own design for a business using the Web page creation function of Microsoft Word, Macromedia Dreamweaver, Microsoft FrontPage, or a Web page development tool of your choice.

Develop a simple Web site for a business. The Web site should include a home page with a description of your business and at least one picture or graphic. From the home page, you must be able to link to a second Web page and, from there, link to a third Web page. Make the home page long enough so that when you arrive at the

bottom of the page, you can no longer see the top. At the bottom of your Web page, include a link back to the top. Also include a link to one of the secondary Web pages. On the secondary page, include a link to the top of that page and a link back to the top of the home page. Also include a link to the third page, which should contain a link to its own top and a link back to the top of the home page. Finally, on one of the secondary pages, include another picture or graphic, and on the other page include an object that you create using Microsoft Excel or other spreadsheet software. MyMISLab includes instructions for completing this project. If you have tested every function and all work to your satisfaction, save the pages for submission to your instructor.

Improving Decision Making:
Using Internet Newsgroups for Online Market Research

Software skills: Web browser software and Internet newsgroups
Business skills: Using Internet newsgroups to identify potential customers

This project will help develop your Internet skills in using newsgroups for marketing. It will also ask you to think about the ethical implications of using information in online discussion groups for business purposes.

You are producing hiking boots that you are selling through a few stores at this time. You think your boots are more comfortable than those of your competition. You believe you can undersell many of your competitors if you can significantly increase your production and sales. You would like to use Internet discussion groups interested in hiking, climbing, and camping both to sell your boots and to make them well known. Visit Google's Usenet archives (**http://groups.google.com**), which stores discussion postings from many thousands of newsgroups. Through this site you can locate all relevant newsgroups and search

them by keyword, author's name, forum, date, and subject. Choose a message and examine it carefully, noting all the information you can obtain, including information about the author.

1. How could you use these newsgroups to market your boots?

2. What ethical principles might you be violating if you use these messages to sell your boots? Do you think there are ethical problems in using newsgroups this way? Explain your answer.

3. Next use Google.ca or Yahoo.ca to search for the hiking boots industry and locate sites that will help you develop other new ideas for contacting potential customers.

4. Given what you have learned in this and previous chapters, prepare a plan to use newsgroups and other alternative methods to begin attracting visitors to your site.

CASE STUDY   Tech Data Helps to Fight Software Piracy

What is the cost of software piracy in Canada? With the piracy rate pegged at 38 percent, there are more than 30 000 jobs that have been lost, resulting in about $1 billion in wages and salaries lost and more than $255 million in tax revenues lost.

Putting the hard numbers to what seems an innocent—although illegal and unethical—practice makes it real. Software piracy is bad for business.

Today most companies in North America have computer usage policies that tell employees to use only software that has been properly leased or purchased; by implication, this also tells managers not to purchase software that they believe may be pirated for use by their employees. It would be good if we could rely on employees and managers—as well as friends, students, and even children—to use only legal software, but unfortunately we cannot. It is this author's feeling that students, who pirate software to save money and because their friends do so, will continue these practices after they enter the workplace. We need to educate our students on the facts: Piracy costs businesses money in the long run, and is plain wrong in the short run.

The Canadian Alliance Against Software Theft (CAAST) has conducted surveys on piracy and attitudes toward software piracy in Canada. Fully half of all Canadians think that pirating software for individual use is acceptable. Paradoxically, three-quarters of all Canadians think that it is unacceptable for organizations to pirate software, and more than 85 percent of Canadians believe that "there is something wrong with downloading illegal software." And according to a survey conducted on behalf of the Entertainment Software Association of Canada by Nielsen Interactive in 2005, 34 percent of video game consumers admitted to having acquired, either through purchase and/or download, a video game which was knowingly "copied" or "pirated."

CAAST conducts an annual survey of software piracy. In the 2007 survey of 102 countries, 62 countries reportedly reduced their rate of piracy from the previous year. However, half of the countries surveyed reported a piracy rate of 62 percent or higher, an astounding statistic. Even though China has taken great steps to reduce piracy, it still has a piracy rate of 82 percent!

Worldwide, for every $2 worth of legally bought software, $1 was illegally bought. Yet in half the countries in the CAAST survey, the reverse was true: For every $1 of legally bought software, $2 of software was bought illegally—another astounding statistic. Fortunately for Canadians, Canada had one of the lowest piracy rates (34 percent) and was ranked 15th among 20 countries. Armenia had the highest piracy rate: an absurd 95 percent.

To truly understand the impact of piracy, consider the following. According to IDC, a leading IT research organization, for every $1.00 that is spent on software, there is at least an additional $1.25 spent on software services to design, create, install, and support the software, and most of the $1.25 goes to local firms, not the big software firms. In other words,

Canadian firms stand to suffer worse financial losses from piracy than multinationals do.

According to Nielsen Interactive, the Canadian video game piracy rate was up by 6 percent over 2004, while the U.S. rate decreased. And in its annual Report on Piracy, the International Intellectual Property Alliance (IIPA) recently recommended that Canada be included once again on the U.S. Trade Representative's watch list of countries considered to be a haven for pirated and counterfeit goods. The IIPA estimates that piracy was responsible for a loss of $40 billion globally in 2005. While Canada's specific share of that loss is unknown, it is nonetheless an amount that demands the urgent attention of Canadian government and business leaders.

Sullying Canada's reputation within the business community could be devastating. Legitimate companies and Canadian consumers stand to suffer the consequences, such as a stunted software industry's impact on the job market, and potential trade sanctions by U.S. Sanctions could cost Canada millions of dollars each year, just to start.

One company trying to fight software piracy in Canada is Tech Data Canada Inc., a leading distributor of hardware and software to more than 9000 wholesalers and retailers across Canada. Let's take a look at Tech Data and see what they are doing to fight piracy.

Founded 33 years ago, Tech Data Corporation is now ranked 109th on the Fortune 500 list. The company and its subsidiaries (of which Tech Data Canada Inc. is one) serve more than 90 000 technology resellers around the world in more than 100 countries. The company generated $21.4 billion in sales for the fiscal year ended January 31, 2007, a record for the technology giant. Tech Data employs more than 8000 staff worldwide and ships more than 70 000 shipments in a year. Tech Data Canada (TDC) was established in 1989. Today it employs more than 500 people in Canada and sells thousands of brand-name products, including components (including mass storage, enterprise storage, networking, peripherals, software, supplies, and systems).

Although TDC is a large company, it sells only to qualified computer resellers and retailers, not to individual customers. With that kind of a background, how can TDC fight software piracy? TDC decided that many of its customers may not understand software piracy and how to recognize it, thereby leaving the customers open to commit piracy unknowingly, perhaps by buying from an unscrupulous vendor of pirated software. "We would receive calls from customers who said they could get, for example, a Microsoft software product for a considerable amount less than the actual cost," said Irene Buchan, Director, Product Management and Software Business Unit at TDC. "It was important for us to make our customers realize how software piracy affected their businesses and what they could do to help reduce it."

TDC wanted both its customers and its employees to be able to recognize pirated software and to know how to report it appropriately. To this end, TDC launched an anti-piracy program to educate its customers and its sales representatives.

Having learned of TDC's anti-piracy program, Microsoft— one of the companies most severely affected by piracy— pledged financial support and material for the information seminars that TDC wanted to run across Canada. Microsoft helped TDC conduct training sessions for its sales representatives, and provided questions for TDC's software piracy customer checklist.

The anti-piracy program included distributing a 16-page guide, sponsored by vendors such as Microsoft, to more than 20 000 resellers across Canada. The guide details the impact of piracy on the Canadian economy and businesses and features articles from several vendors. TDC also published a one-page question-and-answer checklist for resellers and placed the checklist on its Web site. The questions were used as an early warning guide. The checklist even gives the contact information for the Canadian Alliance Against Software Theft (CAAST) as well as Microsoft's toll-free hotline so that resellers could report suspected acts of piracy.

As part of the sales representatives' training, a "mystery caller" would telephone sales representatives to offer them supposedly pirated software. This helped sales reps learn how to recognize and respond to a call offering pirated software. "Our anti-piracy program really focuses on bringing greater awareness to our customers and employees by providing them with the skills needed to identify pirated software," said Buchan. "We will definitely renew our program each year."

The TDC anti-piracy program has seen results. Not only do both TDC customers and sales representatives claim to be more knowledgeable about piracy, TDC's customers have seen revenues increase and losses decrease. According to Buchan, "Sales reps have the knowledge to tell resellers, 'That price is too good to be true, I think you bought pirated software.' And resellers can easily reach CAAST or call the toll-free hotline if they believe they have pirated software. Our program benefits everyone in the industry."

Sources: Danielle Labossiere, "The Hidden Cost of Piracy in Canada," *The Globe and Mail*, May 5, 2006; Canadian Alliance Against Software Theft, "Canadians Find Falsified Resumes a Bigger Offence than Using Pirated Software," **www.caast.com/resources/ 2006_national_study.pdf**, accessed June 1, 2007; Canadian Alliance Against Software Theft, "Fourth Annual BSA and ICD Global Software Piracy Study," **www.caast.com/resources/piracy_study_2007.pdf**, accessed June 1, 2007; Canadian Alliance Against Software Theft, "About CAAST," **www.caast.com/about/default.asp?load=content**, accessed June 1, 2007; Microsoft Corporation, "Tech Data Canada Equips its Resellers and Employees with Tools to Help Fight Software Piracy," **www.microsoft.com/canada/casestudies/techdata.mspx**, accessed June 1, 2007; Tech Data, "Welcome to Tech Data," **www.techdata.com/content/cen/about/companyinfo.main.aspx**, accessed June 1, 2007; and "Tech Data Ranks 109th on 2007 Fortune 500," **www.portfolio.com/resources/company-profiles/TECD/ press/2007/04/16/tech-data-ranks-109th-on-2007-fortune-500r**, accessed June 1, 2007.

CASE STUDY QUESTIONS

1. Do you agree that software piracy is a bad thing? Explain your answer.
2. Apply an ethical analysis to the issue of software piracy.
3. What are the ethical, social, and political issues raised by software piracy?
4. What is the responsibility of a business such as Tech Data in reducing or eliminating software piracy?

Part I CANADIAN CASE STUDY:
Can Canada Can Spam?

"Spam spam spam spam!" So sang Eric Idle, Graham Chapman, and Terry Jones of the British comedy group Monty Python, as they revealed their loathing for the mystery meat mixture. Because of the popularity of this very funny comedy skit, the junk e-mail that we all receive in massive doses on a daily basis is called "spam."

During World War II, spam was one of the few meats exempted from rationing in England. Rationing continued long after the war was over, and British people got sick of it and spam. The Monty Python sketch was thus created to lament the ubiquitous presence of spam on every menu. The word *spam* later came to be used to describe junk mail with advertising messages that flooded Usenet newsgroups and individuals' e-mails. "Spamming" referred to the repetitive and unwanted presence of these e-mails.

The maker of Spam, Hormel, was supportive of Monty Python's skit but was not thrilled about the association of their product with unwanted e-mails. However, they did release a special Spam issue for the Broadway premiere of Eric Idle's hit musical *Spamalot*.

So, what is this e-mail called spam? According to **www.whatis.com**, even though spam is considered unsolicited junk e-mail by users of the Internet, the sender sees it as merely a form of bulk mail sent to names on distribution lists. These lists of names are obtained from companies that specialize in creating these lists. Spammers expect only a fraction of the millions of their list members to respond positively to their offers.

Spam originates from almost every country around the world. The U.S. is the worst spam-offending country, but Canada is ranked eighth of the top 10 worst spam origin countries. Of the top 10 worst spammers, none are from Canada, and one is from the U.S. The rest are from Russia, the Ukraine, Israel, Hong Kong, and Australia. Of course, an Internet service provider (ISP) has to permit the spammer to send spam. Of the top 10 ISPs who are the worst for allowing spam, none are located in Canada. However, Canada is not immune to spam and the need for measures to curb spam.

Unlike telemarketing or direct mail, spam has an extremely low per-message cost. Many spammers send their spam through worm- or virus-infected computers owned by other people or companies. Because of the resulting low per-message cost, it is easy for a spammer to make a profit off of a very small response rate. There is almost no additional cost for additional spam with the possibility of a larger return.

While the sender profits, the user does not. Spam is somewhat like telemarketing calls, but unlike incoming phone calls, these e-mails cost the user to a certain extent, because everyone has to pay for the cost of maintaining the Internet.

Spamming has become a significant problem for all Internet users.

Let's look at the statistics on spam. As recently as 2002, e-mail traffic reports indicated that spam amounted to only about 10 percent of e-mail volume. By the end of 2006—only four years later—spam accounted for more than 90 percent of e-mail volume. The phenomenal growth of spamming has now forced companies that offer Internet services to factor it into their pricing.

The cost of spamming has to be borne not only by organizations that conduct business electronically but also by individuals who use the Internet for personal communication.

In Canada, Internet users received an average of 121 unsolicited e-mails per week in 2006. Surveys reveal that 53 percent of users have become leery of e-mails, and 22 percent use e-mail less frequently overall.

The threat from spam goes beyond draining users' resources and taking up bandwidth on the Internet. Spam can deliver greater dangers such as spyware, viruses, phishing, and botnets, as well as a host of other threatening technologies.

Phishing is e-mail fraud whereby the perpetrator sends e-mails that appear to come from well-known and trustworthy Web sites in an attempt to gather personal and financial information from the recipient. MessageLabs, which keeps tabs on the spam invasion, reported seeing 18 million phishing e-mails in 2004. A phishing expedition, like the fishing expedition it is named for, is a speculative venture: the phisher puts out the bait hoping to lure at least a few of the prey that encounter it. Web sites that are frequently spoofed by phishers include PayPal, eBay, MSN, Yahoo!, BestBuy, and America Online. Banks and financial institutions, including the Royal Bank and Bank of Montreal, are also frequently spoofed by phishers.

Spam can also deliver spyware—software that collects personal information about users and may sometimes even alter a computer's operation without users' knowledge or consent. According to a 2004 study, 89 percent of users infected by spyware had not been aware of the presence of the spyware in their computers.

Spam has significantly undermined users' confidence in the Internet as a safe means of communication and

business transactions. Therefore, in May 2004, the Minister of Industry introduced the "Anti-spam Action Plan for Canada" to combat spamming. A task force was set up to implement the action plan within a year. This task force, led by Industry Canada, brought together experts and key people from the three groups mainly affected by spam: businesses, consumers, and Internet service providers. The first challenge the task force faced was to determine the effectiveness of current Canadian legislation on spam.

Canadians watched with bemused interest as the U.S.-touted "CanSpam" Act completely failed to reduce spam. Maintaining the balance among privacy, freedom of expression and stopping spam is not easy, as the American attempts to thwart spam have shown. Nevertheless, many of those involved in the task force on spam felt that existing Canadian legislation—when properly and diligently enforced—could greatly reduce the volume of spam. Existing Canadian laws that could be used to reduce spam include the Personal Information Protection and Electronic Documents Act (PIPEDA), the Competition Act, and the Criminal Code of Canada.

PIPEDA prohibits the release of personal information (such as e-mail addresses) without consent and specifies that any information can be used only for its intended purpose, requiring consent for additional uses, such as spam. The Competition Act deals with the deceptive and misleading representations often found in spam. The Criminal Code of Canada prohibits unauthorized access to computer systems and networks, fraud, and harming data. Finally, the Telecommunications Act may have provisions that apply to sending spam wirelessly through a short message service (SMS) network. Together, these laws should address the issue of viruses, Trojan horses, spyware, and phishing.

The task force found that, though the legal apparatus exists, there has only been limited overall enforcement of Canadian laws that apply to spam. The agencies responsible for enforcing these laws have limited resources and competing priorities. They also frequently do not have the technical expertise to track down, investigate, and prosecute spam perpetrators. Determining who has jurisdiction is another challenge: Is jurisdiction established by the location of the spammer, the location of the Internet servers delivering the spam, or the location of the users who receive the spam?

The task force on spam also compared existing Canadian law related to spam with similar laws in several countries: the United States, Australia, the United Kingdom, France, and the European Union, all of which have spam laws. In doing so, they identified gaps in Canadian law and have proposed new legislation to address these gaps.

What has been done so far to fight spam? Two cases have been heard by the Privacy Commissioner of Canada under the jurisdiction of PIPEDA. In the first case, Michael Geist received two e-mail solicitations to purchase season tickets from a community football team. The team's office had obtained his e-mail address from university and law firm Web sites. He filed a complaint with the Privacy Commissioner after he received the second e-mail, which was sent after Geist requested that he not be sent any more e-mails. The Office of the Privacy Commissioner found that a business address, such as that found on the law firm's Web site, is, in fact, personal information and therefore protected by PIPEDA. This information can be gathered and used without consent—but only for its intended purpose, and not for unwanted solicitation through e-mail.

In the second case, Suzanne Morin received e-mail solicitations at her business e-mail address. Her e-mail address was collected from an online professional association's membership directory. She filed a complaint with the Privacy Commissioner, who again found that the solicitation at her business address represented a violation of personal information use in contravention of the Act. In both cases, the organizations (a community football team and a marketing company) apologized for their actions, removed the e-mail addresses from their e-mail marketing lists, and amended their internal practices in accordance with the Commissioner's findings.

Only one such case has been heard so far by the Competition Bureau. Performance Marketing Ltd. made false claims about two weight-loss patches, Zyapex and Dyapex. The claims were made in e-mails. Performance Marketing Ltd. had failed to enforce its own anti-spam policy, which allowed its affiliates using spam to sell these products. The Competition Bureau's Project FairWeb, aimed at combatting misleading and deceptive advertising on the Internet, pursued the case. In a consent agreement issued in December 2004, Performance Marketing agreed to ensure that spam will not be used as a vehicle for marketing its products. The company will also post a notice on its Web site correcting the claims and provide a full refund to the purchasers of the diet patches.

Unfortunately, where spam is concerned, these three cases represent only the tip of the iceberg. Every day, spammers think up new ways to spam. Immediately after the devastation of Hurricane Katrina in late August 2005, spammers masquerading as charitable organizations started firing off spam, simply including the word "Katrina" in their subject lines. Commtouch, an anti-spam technology company, reported that these spam e-mails used subject lines such as: "Claim your stock car racing gift Katrina," "Enter now for a complimentary trip to Maui Katrina," "Today's Headlines: Hurricane Katrina slams into Gulf coast; dozens are dead," and "Instantly Track Katrina's Progress."

According to Commtouch, while some spam may have masqueraded as messages relating to Katrina, the real spam content for August 2005—based on 1.5 billion spam messages—was similar to those of other months. Pharmaceuticals lead the list of spam content (29 percent), followed by financing schemes (21 percent), and sex enhancers (14 percent). Commtouch's spam detection centre identified almost 28 million new spam examples in that same month, averaging almost a million per day. Believe it or not, that is a slight decrease from the previous month. Still, it was a 38-percent increase over August 2004. Mirapoint, a competitor of Commtouch, found that pornography was the third highest subject of spam. Another competitor, Clearswift, found that gambling-related spam increased 1500 percent over the previous year—presumably caused by the popularity of poker shows on reality television.

As the CBC video that accompanies this case study relates, there is now more junk e-mail than legitimate e-mail. It takes about 1.5 seconds, at a minimum, to delete a spam message, costing businesses around the world billions of dollars a year, at the rate of about $1000 per employee per year. Other studies show that spam does not cost so much but is still expensive. Some Web sites even host spam cost calculators, such as Computer Mail Services, Inc. (**www.cmsconnect.com**). These statistics do not, however, count the cost of losing an important message along with all the spam you are deleting—something everyone has probably done at one time or another.

It is estimated that most spam comes from 200 big spammers, while the rest comes from spammers who work from home—a sort of "cottage industry."

All this—cost, threats to computers, bandwidth reduction—has resulted in the rise of the anti-spam industry. In Canada alone, there are more than 700 businesses involved in anti-spam and anti-virus activities. Fighting spam and viruses has become a $1.5 billion industry. The more spam is blocked, the more creative the spammers become—and the more creative the anti-spammers must become. That is why Carleton University received a $10-million grant to teach students how to combat viruses and spam: so that their graduates could find jobs in the industry doing exactly that.

What can individuals do to thwart spam? Do not give out your e-mail address over the Internet without knowing how it will be used. Ensure that Web sites you deal with have privacy policies, and check to see what their policies say they do with your data. Use spam filters provided by your Internet service provider, and download and use spam filters on your own computer.

Canadian consumers can also sign up for a free service of the Canadian Marketing Association (offered in conjunction with the U.S. Direct Marketing Association) to opt out of commercial spam. The user registers at **www.e-mps.org**, allowing his or her e-mail address to be compared against a company's marketing e-mail solicitation lists. If the company is a member of the Direct Marketing Association or of the Canadian Marketing Association, the company will comply with the opt-out request and delete the registered user's e-mail address from its lists. However, marketers are not required to remove the names of their existing customers, and the service does not apply to marketers using opt-in lists, which involve individuals self-selecting to receive the companies' e-mail solicitations.

The problem with any spam filter is that it will actually do one of two things: either permit too much spam to get through to your e-mail or send too much legitimate e-mail to your spam folder, where you can retrieve it after sifting through all the real spam. Various Web sites post reviews and comparisons of the most popular spam filter programs; you should check out these reviews and then pick a spam filter.

What about organizations? What can they do to fight spam? The advice for organizations is similar to that for individuals. Aggressive filtering of spam helps. Running other software to thwart viruses, spyware, and other technologies, such as Web bugs (see page 119), helps, too.

In June 2007, the Coalition Against Unsolicited Commercial E-mail (CAUCE) Canada and its CAUCE counterpart in the U.S. merged to form CAUCE North America. In addition to the efforts of this group, governments are continuing to work on the problem of spam. The Canadian Association of Internet Providers (CAIP) mandates members to follow its "Fair Practices Document," which includes the following clause: "CAIP members will not knowingly allow their services to be used for the transmission of unsolicited bulk e-mail especially unsolicited commercial bulk e-mail between parties that have had no previous commercial relationship." The Canadian Marketing Association mentioned above, which represents about 80 percent of direct marketers in Canada, also mandates members to follow its code of ethics, which includes a clause against sending unsolicited e-mail to any addresses other than existing customers'.

Governments believe that spam could be used by terrorists and criminals as well as those simply trying to make a buck. In May 2004, the Canadian government announced the creation of a joint government–private sector task force to combat spam. Various governments have created sites to report spam. In Canada, the Privacy Commissioner's Office and the Competition Bureau are two such offices. The U.S. has its "Can-Spam" law; the European Union mandates all EU members to adopt strong anti-spam legislation; and the Organisation for Economic Co-operation and Development (of which Canada is a member) has developed "Guidelines for Consumer Protection in the Context of Electronic Commerce" and is working on specific guidelines for spam. Even Google has set up spamreport@google.com to handle spam reporting.

Still, most businesses today will probably have to make computer security a priority. It is too easy for spammers to get into a company's computers and dump in viruses and a host of other threats. Organizations that make security a top priority and instill that focus throughout the organization will find it easier to survive the spam era than those that ignore the threat.

Sources: Canadian Inter@ctive Reid Report, Fourth Quarter Winter 2006, **www.ipsos.ca/reid/interactive/ifg.cfm**, accessed July 16, 2007; "Commtouch Reports August Spam Trends: Spammers Seek to Profit from Katrina," **www.commtouch.com//Site/News_Events/** pr_content.asp?news_id=449&cat_id=1, accessed October 2, 2005; Government of Canada, "What is Spam?" Industry Canada, **http://3-com.ic.gc.ca/epic/internet/inecic-ceac.nsf/en/ h_gv00170e.html**, accessed July 16, 2007; Computer Mail Services, Inc., "The Cost of Spam," **www.cmsconnect.com/Marketing/ spamcalc.htm**, accessed October 2, 2005; Enid Burns, "The Deadly Duo: Spam and Viruses, August 2005," **www.clickz.com/stats/ sectors/e-mail/print.php/3549111**, accessed October 2, 2005; Government of Canada, "Stopping Spam: Creating a Stronger, Safer Internet," Industry Canada, May 2005, **http://e-com.ic.gc.ca/epic/ internet/inecic-ceac.nsf/vwapj/stopping_spam_May2005.pdf/ $file/stopping_spam_May2005.pdf**, accessed October 2, 2005; MessageLabs Ltd., "Spam Intercepts," **www.messagelabs.com/ default.aspx, accessed October 2, 2005; "Spam (Monty Python)," September 30, 2005,** http://en.wikipedia.org/wiki/ Spam_(Monty_Python), accessed October 2, 2005; "Average Global Ratio of Spam in E-mail Scanned by MessageLabs," **www.messagelabs.com/portal/server.pt/gateway/ PTARGS_0_0_453_454_-454_43/http%3B/0120-0176- CTC1%3B8080/publishedcontent/publish/ _dotcom_libraries_en/files/monthly_reports/ messagelabs_intelligence_report__spam_intercepts_timeline_j uly_2005_us_5.pdf**, accessed October 2, 2005; "Spamhaus Statistics: The Top 10," **www.spamhaus.org/statistics/countries. lasso**, accessed July 16, 2007; Matt Vernhout, "Where Does Spam Come from? Why?" **www.cauce.net/archives/49-Where-does- spam-come-from-Why.html**, accessed July 16, 2007; "Spam-o-Meter Statistics by Percentage, **www.junk-o-meter.com/stats/ index.php**, accessed July 16, 2007; "Spam E-Mail," **www.rcmp=grc. gc.ca/scams/spam_e.htm**, accessed July 16, 2007; "Welcome to CAUCE North America," **www.cauce.org/**, accessed July 16, 2007; and "Canadian Internet Policy and Public Interest Clinic (CIPPIC)," **www.cippic.ca/en/faqs-resources/spam**, accessed July 16, 2007.

Video Resource

"The Spammed (Life of the Spammed)." *Venture* 910. Canadian Broadcasting Corporation. January 18, 2004.

CASE STUDY QUESTIONS

1. Why would someone send spam? Give at least three different, unrelated reasons to send spam.

2. Why has spam become so costly to both individuals and organizations? Can you calculate the cost to business of spam? What factors and costs would go into your calculation?

3. Why is it so easy for spammers to avoid prosecution?

4. What can organizations do to stop spam? What can lawmakers do to stop spam?

PART II

Information Technology Infrastructure

PART II Canadian Case Study
Wi-Fi in Canada: The Good, the Bad, and the Ugly

CHAPTER 5

IT Infrastructure and Emerging Technologies

LEARNING OBJECTIVES

After completing this chapter, you will be able to do the following:

1. Define IT infrastructure and describe the components and levels of IT infrastructure.
2. Identify and describe the stages of IT infrastructure evolution.
3. Identify and describe the technology drivers of IT infrastructure evolution.
4. Assess contemporary computer hardware platform trends.
5. Assess contemporary software platform trends.
6. Evaluate the challenges of managing IT infrastructure and possible management solutions.

OPENING CASE | Frantic Films and DreamWorks Animation Turn to Technology for Production Support

Can technology help DreamWorks Animation do better? How has information technology enabled a small Canadian company, Frantic Films, to build its market around the world? These are two key questions answered by the entrepreneurs in their initial visions for their companies.

At Frantic Films, the creative use and development of new technologies has enabled management to open offices in Winnipeg, Vancouver, Los Angeles, and Sydney, Australia. The company does pre- and post-production visual effects and design, animation, and live action. In addition, the company develops its own visual effects software, including a fluid simulator for simulating floods and tidal waves, and enhanced special effects using a crystal growth simulator.

Frantic Films' special effects have been seen in movies as varied as *Poseidon*, *Superman Returns*, *The Italian Curse*, two *X-Men* movies, *Scooby-Doo 2: Monsters Unleashed*, Wes Craven's *Cursed*, and a host of television movies and specials. Frantic Films also produces documentaries for PBS, CanWest Global, the History Channel, History Television, and Life Network.

The use of information technology at Frantic Films has enabled rapid growth for this Winnipeg-based company. IT has enhanced the company's reputation and its ability to market its services in a broad array of broadcast projects. Recently, Frantic Films received two celebrated national honours, for talent and innovation in technology. The National Research Council of Canada has even named Frantic one of Canada's Innovation Leaders.

At DreamWorks, management certainly sees technology as a key factor in their success. It uses world-class creative talent and advanced computer technology to produce such successful computer-generated (CG) animated films as *Shrek*, *Shrek 2*, *Shark Tale,* and *Madagascar*. To date, *Shrek 2* is the third-highest-grossing movie ever and the number one animated film of all time.

Nevertheless, DreamWorks has plenty of competition. Pixar Studios, DreamWorks' arch-rival in computer animation, has prospered from a string of six blockbuster hits, including *The Incredibles, Finding Nemo,* and *Monsters Inc*. Computer animation house Blue Sky Studios is another competitor, as is Disney. Sony Pictures Entertainment and Lucasfilm have also begun producing computer-animated films.

To gain an edge in this fiercely competitive market, DreamWorks Animation has set out to make entertaining films that appeal to all audiences, while leveraging the latest technology and finest talent available. With this strategy in mind, the company established a very ambitious production schedule, one that no

other studio has ever tried before—the release of two animated movies per year. In order to meet this schedule, DreamWorks' staff often find themselves working on more than one movie at the same time, sharing technology among the various projects, and scaling up to work on multiple features.

How is DreamWorks able to make this happen? One of the solutions is to use the finest technology available. DreamWorks has implemented a high-speed network to link the powerful computers required for animation for three key animation pipelines: two in Los Angeles and one in Redwood City, California. A sophisticated video-teleconferencing system that projects nearly life-size images on the wall enables all three groups to collaborate as never before.

Additionally, DreamWorks animators use proprietary software developed in-house called EMO for nearly every stage of their work. In DreamWorks' *Madagascar*, this software enabled animators to adopt traditional "squash and stretch" techniques and place their characters in a digital environment. The software made each frame in *Madagascar* exquisitely detailed, right down to the animals' fur. According to the company's CEO Jeffrey Katzenberg, "Technically, we couldn't have made this movie a year ago."

DreamWorks Animation's management believes that its exclusive software and other technology infrastructure investments will not only pay off but will also provide a strategic advantage. DreamWorks Animation's investments in technology are leveraged across all pipelines and all future films as well.

To render a CG film, DreamWorks technicians use a network of 2700 Hewlett-Packard (HP) processors running the Linux operating system, which are organized to act as a single computer system that is distributed among the company's studios and an HP research lab facility in Palo Alto, California.

At the end of the day, it takes approximately 400 artists, animators, and technicians, over 200 characters modelled and surfaced, 15 terabytes of disk storage, 2700 processors, over 10 million CPU rendering hours and 18 months of core production to complete any one film. DreamWorks Animation has orchestrated its people, processes, and physical assets into an effective balance that produces world class CG content effectively and efficiently.

Sources: Ed Leonard, "I.T. Gets Creative at DreamWorks," *Optimize Magazine*, April 2006; Aaron Ricadela, "High-Tech Reveries," *InformationWeek*, May 23, 2005; DreamWorks Animation, **www.dreamworksanimation.com**, accessed September 29, 2005; Laura Bracken, "Frenzy of Success for Frantic Films," *Playback*, May 24, 2004, **www.playbackmag.com/articles/magazine/20040524/frantic.html**, accessed February 23, 2007; and Frantic Films, **www.franticfilms.com**, accessed February 23, 2007.

Frantic Films and DreamWorks Animation have enviable track records in creating successful high-quality CG animated films. But they also have a series of formidable competitors and a finicky mass audience to please. Frantic Films decided to outclass its competitors by investing heavily in computer hardware and software that increased animation quality and enabled it to produce animated films more rapidly. DreamWorks began their business with that same philosophy of investing heavily in hardware and software at the forefront of their strategy. This case highlights the critical role that hardware and software investments can play in improving business performance and achieving strategic advantages by using information technology to create differentiated products more rapidly than your competitors.

The chapter-opening Business Challenges diagram calls attention to important points raised by this case and this chapter. Computer-generated filmmaking requires an extraordinary amount of computing power and collaborative work. These CG firms' management both decided that investing in superior information technology would enable them to create higher-quality animations and accelerate the pace at which films were produced.

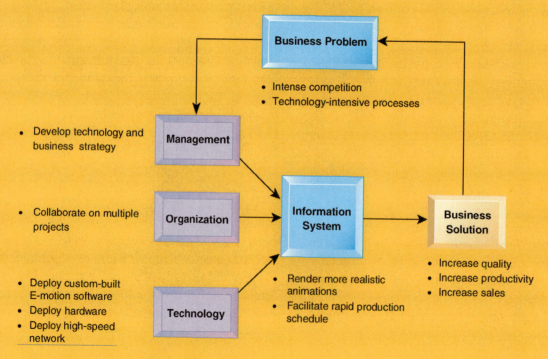

HEADS UP

As a manager, you will face many decisions about investments in hardware, software, and other elements of IT infrastructure that are necessary for your firm to conduct its business—and which may even give your firm new capabilities to surge ahead of competitors. This chapter provides an overview of the technology and service components of IT infrastructure, leading technology vendors, and the most important trends in hardware and software platforms.

- If your career is in accounting and finance, you will be working with application software packages for corporate accounting, tax calculations, payroll processing, or investment planning and helping management calculate the total cost of ownership (TCO) of technology assets.

- If your career is in human resources, you will be evaluating software productivity tools for employees and arranging for training so that employees can use hardware and software effectively.

- If your career is in information systems, you will be managing and operating the firm's IT infrastructure and providing end users with technology services.

- If your career is in manufacturing, production, or operations management, you will be using applications based on client/server computing to control the flow of work on the factory floor and you will be using supply chain management systems that use XML standards.

- If your career is in sales and marketing, you will be using hardware and software technologies that provide customers and sales staff with rapid access to data via Web sites enhanced by Java, XML, and HTML.

5.1 IT Infrastructure

In Chapter 1, we defined *information technology (IT) infrastructure* as the shared technology resources that provide the platform for the firm's specific information system applications. IT infrastructure includes investment in hardware, software, and services—such as consulting, education, and training—that are shared across the entire firm or across business units in the firm.

A firm's IT infrastructure provides the foundation for serving customers, working with vendors, and managing internal firm business processes (see Figure 5-2 on page 149).

Supplying Canadian firms with IT infrastructure hardware is more than a $10.2 billion industry when telecommunications, networking equipment and telecommunications services (Internet, telephone, and data transmission) are included (Statistics Canada, 2006a). Investments in infrastructure account for between 15 and 20 percent of information technology expenditures in large firms (Statistics Canada, 2006b).

The Computer System

A **computer** is a physical device that receives data from users as input, processes the data according to stored instructions, and outputs the processed information. A contemporary computer system consists of a central processing unit, primary storage, secondary storage, input devices, output devices, and communications devices (see Figure 5-1).

The **central processing unit** manipulates data into a more useful form and controls the other parts of the computer system. **Primary storage** temporarily stores data and program instructions while **secondary storage** devices (magnetic and optical disks, magnetic

Computer
Central processing unit
Primary storage
Secondary storage

FIGURE 5-1   *Hardware components of a computer system*

A contemporary computer system is composed of six major components. The central processing unit manipulates data and controls the other parts of the computer system; primary storage temporarily stores data and program instructions during processing; secondary storage stores data and instructions permanently; input devices convert data and instructions from their input form for processing in the computer; output devices present data in a form that people can understand; and communications devices control the transfer of information to and from different computers on communications networks.

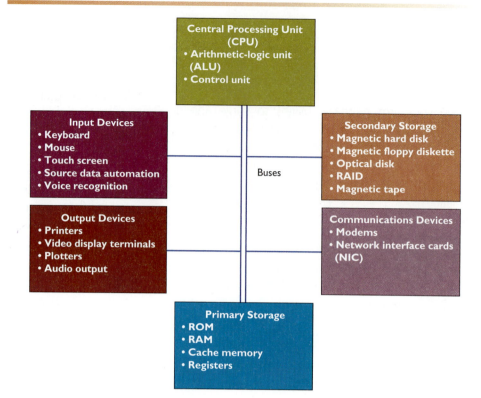

tape) store data and programs even when the computer is not turned on. **Input devices**, such as a keyboard or mouse, convert data and instructions into electronic form for input into the computer. **Output devices**, such as printers and video display terminals, convert electronic data produced by the computer system and display them in a form that people can understand. **Communications devices** provide connections between the computer and communications networks. Buses are circuitry paths for transmitting data and signals among the parts of the computer system.

In order for information to flow through a computer system and be in a form suitable for processing, all symbols, pictures, or words must be reduced to a string of binary digits. A binary digit is called a **bit** and represents either a 0 or a 1. In the computer, the presence of an electronic or magnetic signal means 1, and its absence signifies 0. Digital computers operate directly with binary digits, either singly or strung together to form bytes. A string of 8 bits that the computer stores as a unit is called a **byte.** Each byte can be used to store a decimal number, a symbol, a character, or part of a picture.

The CPU and Primary Storage   The central processing unit (CPU) is the part of the computer system where the manipulation of symbols, numbers, and characters occurs, and it controls the other parts of the computer system. Located near the CPU is primary storage (sometimes called primary or main memory), where data and program instructions are stored temporarily during processing while the computer is on. Buses provide pathways for transmitting data and signals between the CPU, primary storage, and the other devices in the computer system. The characteristics of the CPU and primary storage are very important in determining a computer's speed and capabilities.

Primary storage has three functions. It stores all or part of the software program that is being executed. Primary storage also stores the **operating system** programs that manage the operation of the computer. The operating system manages the interface between the computer hardware, software, and the end user. It includes utilities for printing, copying, and deleting files as well as many more functions. Finally, the primary storage area holds data that the program is using. Internal primary storage is often called **RAM,** or

Input devices
Output devices
Communications devices
Bit
Byte
Operating system

random access memory. It is called RAM because it can directly access any randomly chosen location in the same amount of time.

Primary memory is divided into storage locations called *bytes*. Each location contains a set of eight binary switches or devices, each of which can store one bit of information. The set of eight bits found in each storage location is sufficient to store one letter, one digit, or one special symbol (such as $). Each byte has a unique address, similar to a mailbox, indicating where it is located in RAM. The computer can remember where the data in all of the bytes are located simply by keeping track of these addresses. Computer storage capacity is measured in bytes. Table 5-1 lists the primary measures of computer storage capacity and processing speed.

Primary storage is composed of *semiconductors*, which are integrated circuits made by printing thousands and even millions of tiny transistors on small silicon chips. There are several different kinds of semiconductor memory used in primary storage. RAM is used for short-term storage of data or program instructions. RAM is *volatile*: Its contents will be lost when the computer's electric supply is disrupted by a power outage or when the computer is turned off. **ROM**, or **read-only memory**, can only be read from; it cannot be written to and is non-volatile; its contents are present even when the computer is turned off. ROM chips come from the manufacturer with programs already burned in, or stored, although some ROM chips can be updated electronically. ROM is used in general-purpose computers to store important or frequently used programs.

Computer Processing

The processing capability of the CPU plays a large role in determining the amount of work that a computer system can accomplish.

Microprocessors and Processing Power Contemporary CPUs use semiconductor chips called **microprocessors**, which integrate all the memory, logic, and control circuits for an entire CPU onto a single chip. The speed and performance of a computer's microprocessors help determine a computer's processing power and are based on the number of bits that can be processed at one time (*word length*), the amount of data that can be moved between the CPU, primary storage, and other devices (data bus width), and cycle speed, measured in **megahertz**. (Megahertz is abbreviated MHz and stands for millions of cycles per second).

Random access memory (RAM)

Read-only memory (ROM)

Microprocessors

Megahertz

TABLE 5-1 *Key Measures of Computer Storage Capacity and Processing Speed*

TIME	ABBREVIATION	SECONDS
Millisecond	ms	1/1000
Microsecond	mus	1/1 000 000
Nanosecond	ns	1/1 000 000 000
Picosecond	ps	1/1 000 000 000 000
STORAGE CAPACITY	**ABBREVIATION**	**NUMBER OF BYTES**
Byte	B	1*
Kilobyte	KB	1000**
Megabyte	MB	1 000 000
Gigabyte	GB	1 000 000 000
Terabyte	TB	1 000 000 000 000

* String of eight bits
** Actually 1024 bytes

Microprocessors can be made faster by using **reduced instruction set computing (RISC)** in their design. Conventional chips, based on complex instruction set computing, have several hundred or more instructions hard-wired into their circuitry, and they may take several cycles to execute a single instruction. If the seldom-used instructions are eliminated, the remaining instructions can execute much faster. RISC computers have only the most frequently used instructions embedded in them. A RISC CPU can execute most instructions in a single machine cycle and sometimes multiple instructions at the same time. RISC technology is often used in scientific and workstation computing. A variety of faster chips with additional features such as security or lower power requirements are being developed by chip manufacturers such as IBM, Intel, and Advanced Micro Devices (AMD).

MyMISLab has more about how a computer system actually processes information and the various types of storage, input, and output technologies.

Connections to the Central Computer Unit

All *peripheral* devices (located outside the central computer unit) must be connected in some way to the central computer unit, usually through a **port**. Ports determine which devices can be used based on their connectors and *drivers* (software that manages the interface between the peripheral device and the central computer unit), as well as which cables can be used for the connection.

There are many different kinds of ports. Many keyboards and computer mice use a *PS/2* port while display screens use a video display port found on the graphics adapter card in the central computer unit. Microphone and headset/speaker ports are found on sound cards. Other ports can be used by a variety of devices. A **serial port** sends a signal along the cable one bit at a time while a **parallel port** sends the signal multiple bits at a time, much faster than the serial connection.

Recent technology has sped up port connections. **Firewire**, also known as IEEE1824, is available on all newer Apple computers and is now available on PCs as well; it can transfer data much faster than older ports. **Universal serial bus (USB) ports** are available on most computers today. USB technology permits up to 128 devices to be "daisy-chained" through only one USB port by use of USB hubs. USB ports and hubs can also provide power to peripheral devices, adding convenience as well as speed. Finally, *wireless ports* permit laptops and palmtop computers to be *synchronized* with desktop computers without using cables. They can also connect computers on a network as we will see in Chapter 7.

Defining IT Infrastructure

IT infrastructure consists of a set of physical devices and software applications that are required to operate the entire enterprise. But IT infrastructure is also a set of firmwide services budgeted by management and comprising both human and technical capabilities (Weill, Subramani, and Broadbent, 2002). These services include the following:

- Computing platforms used to provide computing services that connect employees, customers, and suppliers into a coherent digital environment, including large mainframes, desktop and laptop computers, personal digital assistants (PDAs), and Internet appliances.

- Telecommunications services that provide data, voice, and video connectivity to employees, customers, and suppliers.

- Data management services that store and manage corporate data and provide capabilities for analyzing the data.

- Application software services that provide enterprise-wide capabilities such as enterprise resource planning, customer relationship management, supply chain management, and knowledge management systems that are shared by all business units.

Reduced instruction set computing (RISC)
Port
Serial port
Parallel port
Firewire
Universal serial bus (USB) ports

FIGURE 5-2   *Connection between the firm, IT infrastructure, and business capabilities*

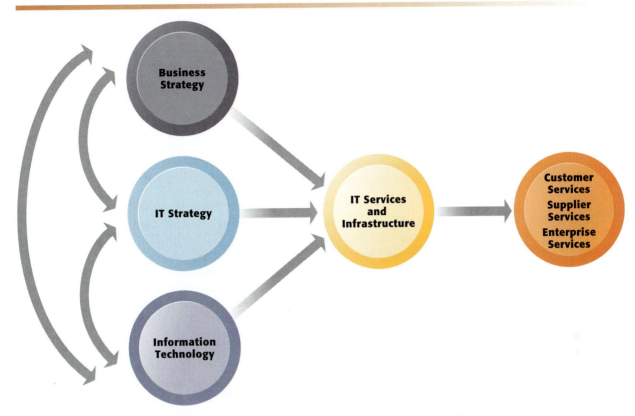

The services a firm is capable of providing to its customers, suppliers, and employees are a direct function of its IT infrastructure. Ideally, this infrastructure should support the firm's business and information systems strategy. New information technologies have a powerful impact on business and IT strategies, as well as the services that can be provided to customers.

- Physical facilities management services that develop and manage the physical installations required for computing, telecommunications, and data management services.

- IT management services that plan and develop the infrastructure, coordinate with the business units for IT services, manage accounting for IT expenditures, and provide project management services.

- IT standards that provide the firm and its business units with policies that determine which information technology will be used and when, and how it will be used.

- IT education services that provide training in system use to employees and offer managers training in how to plan for and manage IT investments.

- IT research and development services that provide the firm with research on potential future IT projects and investments that could help the firm differentiate itself in the marketplace.

This "service platform" perspective makes it easier to understand the business value provided by infrastructure investments. For instance, the real business value of a fully loaded personal computer operating at 3 gigahertz (that costs about $1000) or a high-speed Internet connection is hard to understand without knowing who will use it and how it will be used. When we look at the services provided by these tools, however, their value becomes more apparent: The new PC makes it possible for a high-cost employee making $100 000 a year to connect to all the company's major systems and the public Internet. The high-speed Internet service saves this employee about one hour per day in reduced wait time for Internet information. Without this PC and Internet connection, the value of this one employee to the firm might be cut in half.

Evolution of IT Infrastructure: 1950–2007

The IT infrastructure in organizations today is an outgrowth of more than 50 years of evolution in computing platforms. We have identified five stages in this evolution, each representing a different configuration of computing power and infrastructure elements (see Figure 5-3). The five periods are automated special-purpose machines, general-purpose mainframe and minicomputer computing, personal computers, client/server networks, and enterprise and Internet computing.

These periods do not necessarily end for all organizations at the same time, and the technologies that characterize one period may also be used in another time period for other purposes. For example, some companies still run traditional mainframe or minicomputer systems. Mainframe computers today are used as massive servers supporting large Web sites and corporate enterprise applications.

Electronic Accounting Machine Period (1930 to 1950)
The first period of business computing used specialized machines that could sort computer cards into bins, accumulate totals, and print reports (Columbia University, 2006). Although the electronic accounting machine was an efficient processor of accounting tasks, the machines were large and cumbersome. Software programs were hardwired into circuit boards, and they could be changed by altering the wired connections on a patch board. There were no programmers, and a human machine operator was the operating system, controlling all system resources.

General-Purpose Mainframe and Minicomputer Period (1959 to Present)
The first commercial all-electronic vacuum tube computers appeared in the early 1950s with the introduction of the UNIVAC computers and the IBM 700 Series. Not until 1959 with the introduction of IBM transistorized machines did widespread commercial use of **mainframe** computers begin in earnest. In 1965, the general-purpose commercial mainframe computer truly came into its own with the introduction of the IBM 360 series. The 360 was the first commercial computer with a powerful operating system that could provide time sharing, multitasking, and virtual memory.

Mainframe computers eventually became powerful enough to support thousands of online remote terminals connected to the centralized mainframe using proprietary communication protocols and proprietary data lines. The first airline reservation systems appeared in 1959 and became the prototypical online, real-time interactive computing system that could scale to the size of an entire nation.

IBM dominated mainframe computing from 1965 onward and still dominates this $31.3 billion global market. Today IBM mainframe systems can work with a wide variety of different manufacturers' computers and multiple operating systems on client/server networks and networks based on Internet technology standards.

The mainframe period was a period of highly centralized computing under the control of professional programmers and systems operators (usually in a corporate data centre), with most elements of infrastructure provided by a single vendor, the manufacturer of the hardware and the software. This pattern began to change with the introduction of the **minicomputer** produced by Digital Equipment Corporation (DEC) in 1965. DEC minicomputers offered powerful machines at far lower prices than IBM mainframes, making possible decentralized computing, customized to the specific needs of individual departments or business units rather than time-sharing on a single huge mainframe.

Personal Computer Period (1981 to Present)
Although the first truly personal computers (PCs) appeared in the 1970s (the Xerox Alto, MIT's Altair, and the Apple I and II, to name a few), these machines had only limited distribution to computer enthusiasts. The appearance of the IBM PC in 1981 is usually considered the beginning of the PC period because this machine was the first to be widely adopted by American businesses. At first using the DOS operating system, a text-based command language, and later the Microsoft Windows operating system, the **Wintel PC** computer (Windows operating system software on a computer with an Intel microprocessor) became the standard

Mainframe

Minicomputer

Wintel PC

FIGURE 5-3   *Periods in IT infrastructure evolution*

Stages in IT Infrastructure Evolution

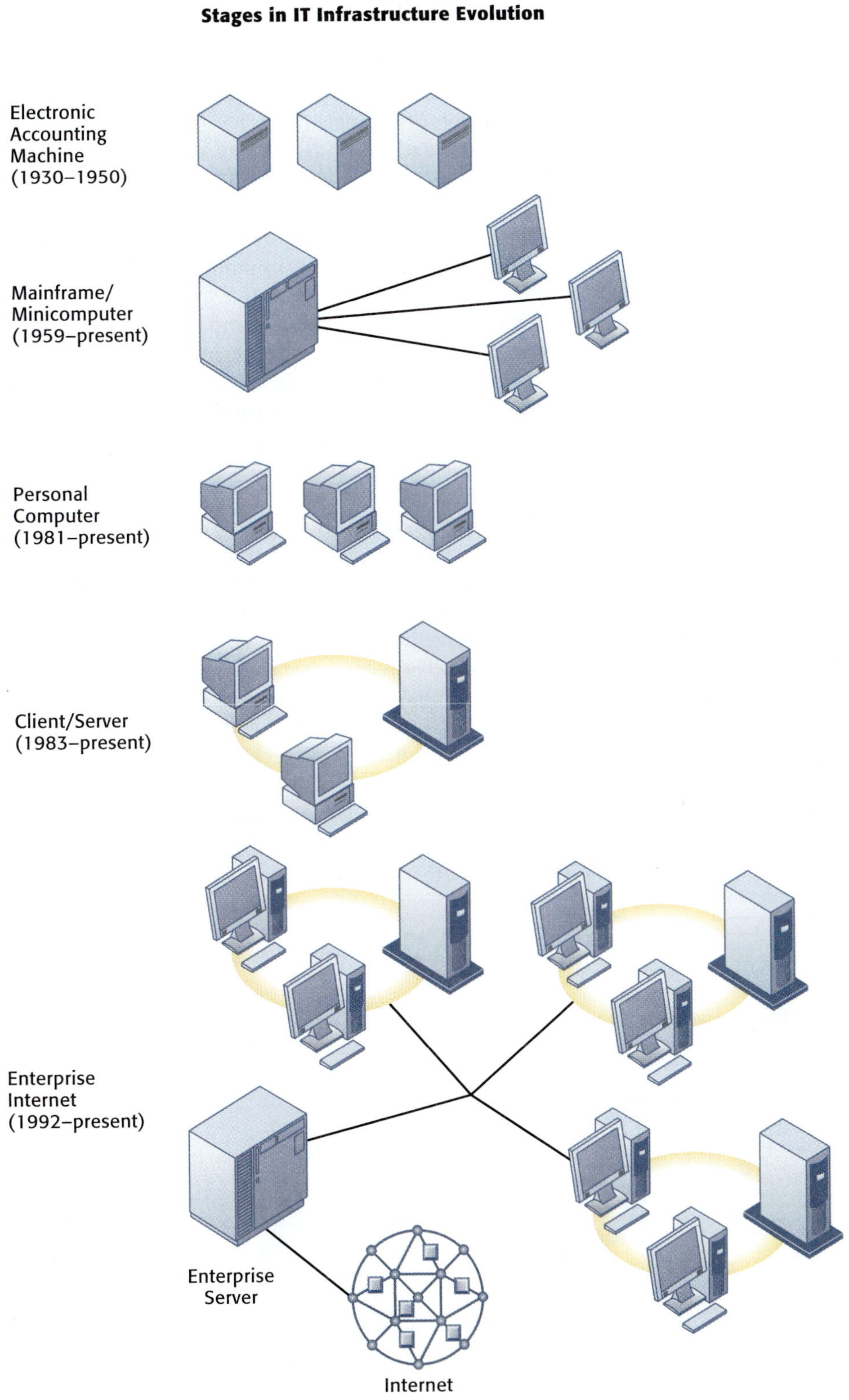

Illustrated here are the typical computing configurations characterizing each of the five periods of the IT infrastructure evolution.

Electronic Accounting Machine (1930–1950)

Mainframe/ Minicomputer (1959–present)

Personal Computer (1981–present)

Client/Server (1983–present)

Enterprise Internet (1992–present)

Enterprise Server

Internet

desktop personal computer. Today, 95 percent of the world's estimated 1 billion computers use the Wintel standard.

Proliferation of PCs in the 1980s and early 1990s launched a spate of personal desktop productivity software tools—word processors, spreadsheets, electronic presentation software, and small data management programs—that were very valuable to both home and corporate users. These PCs were stand-alone systems until PC operating system software in the 1990s made it possible to link them into networks.

Client/Server Period (1983 to Present)

In **client/server computing**, desktop or laptop computers called **clients** are networked to powerful **server** computers that provide the client computers with a variety of services and capabilities. Computer processing work is split between these two types of machines. The client is the user point of entry while the server typically processes and stores shared data, serves up Web pages, or manages network activities. The term server refers to both the software application and the physical computer on which the network software runs. The server could be a mainframe, but today server computers typically are more powerful versions of personal computers, based on inexpensive Intel chips and often using multiple processors in a single computer box.

The simplest client/server network consists of a client computer networked to a server computer, with processing split between the two types of machines. This is called a two-tiered client/server architecture. While simple client/server networks can be found in small businesses, most corporations have more complex, **multitiered** (often called **N-tier**) **client/server architectures** in which the work of the entire network is balanced over several different levels of servers, depending on the kind of service being requested (see Figure 5-4).

For instance, at the first level a **Web server**, a computer that uses Web server software to house Web pages for a Web site, will serve a Web page to a client in response to a request for service. Web server software is responsible for locating and managing stored Web pages. If the client requests access to a corporate system (a product list or price information, for instance), the request is passed along to an application server. **Application server software** handles all application operations between a user and an organization's back-end business systems. The application server may reside on the same computer as the Web server or on its own dedicated computer. Chapters 6 and 7 provide more detail on other pieces of software that are used in multitiered client/server architectures for e-commerce and e-business.

Client/server computing enables businesses to distribute computing work across a series of smaller, inexpensive machines that cost much less than minicomputers or centralized mainframe systems. The result is an explosion in computing power and applications throughout the firm.

Client/server computing

Clients

Server

Multitiered (N-tier) client/server
  architectures

Web server

Application server software

FIGURE 5-4   *A multitiered client/server network (N-tier)*

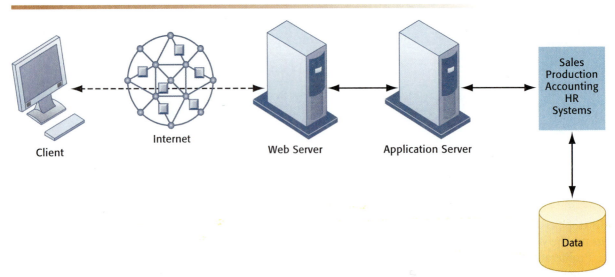

In a multitiered client/server network, different levels of servers handle client requests for service.

Novell Netware was the leading technology for client/server networking at the beginning of the client/server period. Today Microsoft is the market leader, with its **Windows** operating systems (Windows Server, Windows Vista, Windows XP, Windows 2000), dominating 78 percent of the local area network market.

Enterprise Internet Computing Period (1992 to Present)

The success of the client/server model posed a new set of problems. Many large firms found it difficult to integrate all their local area networks (LANs) into a single, coherent corporate computing environment. Applications developed by local departments and divisions in a firm, or in different geographic areas, could not communicate easily with one another and share data.

In the early 1990s, firms turned to networking standards and software tools that could integrate disparate networks and applications throughout the firm into an enterprise-wide infrastructure. As the Internet developed into a trusted communications environment after 1995, business firms began using the *Transmission Control Protocol/Internet Protocol* (*TCP/IP*) networking standard to tie their disparate networks together. We discuss TCP/IP in detail in Chapter 7.

The resulting IT infrastructure links different pieces of computer hardware and smaller networks into an enterprise-wide network so that information can flow freely across the organization and between the firm and other organizations. It can link different types of computer hardware, including mainframes, servers, PCs, mobile phones, and other handheld devices, and it includes public infrastructures such as the telephone system, the Internet, and public network services.

The enterprise infrastructure also requires software to link disparate applications and enable data to flow freely among different parts of the business. Chapters 2 and 12 describe how enterprise applications perform this function. Other solutions for enterprise integration include enterprise application integration software, Web services, and outsourcing to external vendors that provide hardware and software for a comprehensive enterprise infrastructure. We discuss these solutions in detail in Section 5.4.

The enterprise period promises to bring about a truly integrated computing and IT services platform for the management of global enterprises. The hope is to deliver critical business information painlessly and seamlessly to decision-makers as needed to create customer value. The reality is wrenchingly difficult because most firms have a huge tangled web of inherited hardware systems and software applications. This makes achieving this level of enterprise integration a difficult, long-term process that can last perhaps as long as a decade and cost large companies hundreds of millions of dollars. Table 5-2 compares each period on the infrastructure dimensions introduced.

Technology Drivers of Infrastructure Evolution

The changes in IT infrastructure we have just described have resulted from developments in computer processing, memory chips, storage devices, telecommunications and networking hardware and software, and software design that have exponentially increased computing power while exponentially reducing costs. Let's look at the most important developments.

Moore's Law and Microprocessing Power

In 1965, Gordon Moore, former director of Fairchild Semiconductor's Research and Development Laboratories, an early manufacturer of integrated circuits and co-founder in 1968 of Intel Corporation, the world's largest computer chip manufacturer, wrote in *Electronics* magazine that since the first microprocessor chip was introduced in 1959, the number of components on a chip with the smallest manufacturing costs per component (generally transistors) had doubled each year. This assertion became the foundation of **Moore's Law**. Moore later reduced the rate of growth to a doubling every two years (Tuomi, 2002).

This law would later be interpreted in multiple ways. There are at least three variations of Moore's Law, none of which Moore ever stated: (1) the power of microprocessors

Windows

Moore's Law

TABLE 5-2 *Stages in the IT Infrastructure Evolution*

INFRASTRUCTURE DIMENSION	ELECTRONIC ACCOUNTING MACHINE ERA (1930–1950)	MAINFRAME ERA (1959 TO PRESENT)	PC ERA (1981 TO PRESENT)	CLIENT/SERVER ERA (1983 TO PRESENT)	ENTERPRISE ERA (1992 TO PRESENT)
SIGNATURE FIRM(S)	IBM Burroughs NCR	IBM	Microsoft/Intel Dell HP IBM	Novell Microsoft	SAP Oracle PeopleSoft
HARDWARE PLATFORM	Programmable card sorters	Centralized mainframe	Wintel computers	Wintel computers	Multiple: • Mainframe • Server • Client
OPERATING SYSTEM	Human operators	IBM 360 IBM 370 Unix	DOS/Windows Linux IBM 390	Windows 3.1 Windows Server Linux	Multiple: • Unix/Linux • OS 390 • Windows Server
APPLICATION AND ENTERPRISE SOFTWARE	None; application software created by technicians	Few enterprise-wide applications; departmental applications created by in-house programmers	No enterprise connectivity; boxed software	Few enterprise-wide applications; boxed software applications for workgroups and departments	Enterprise-wide applications linked to desktop and departmental applications: • mySAP • Oracle E-Business Suite
NETWORKING/ TELECOMMUNICATIONS	None	Vendor-provided: • Systems Network Architecture (IBM) • DECNET (Digital) • AT&T voice	None or limited	Novell NetWare Windows Server Linux AT&T voice	LAN Enterprise-wide area network (WAN) TCP/IP Internet standards-enabled
SYSTEM INTEGRATION	Vendor-provided	Vendor-provided	None	Accounting and consulting firms Service firms	Software manufacturer Accounting and consulting firms System integration firms Service firms
DATA STORAGE AND DATABASE MANAGEMENT	Physical card management	Magnetic storage Flat files Relational databases	DBase II and III Access	Multiple database servers with optical and magnetic storage	Enterprise database servers
INTERNET PLATFORMS	None	Poor to none	None at first Later browser-enabled clients	None at first Later: • Apache server • Microsoft IIS	None in the early years Later: • Intranet- and Internet-delivered enterprise services • Large server farms

FIGURE 5-5   *Moore's Law and microprocessor performance*

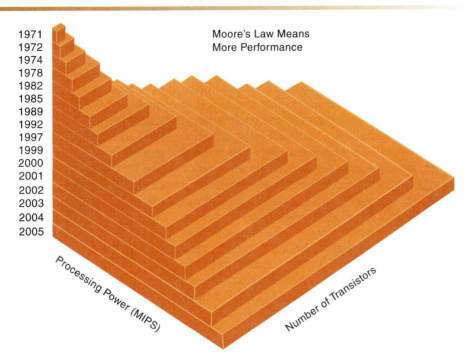

Packing more transistors into a tiny microprocessor has exponentially increased processing power.

Source: Intel Corporation, 2004; updated by the authors.

doubles every 18 months (Gates, 1996); (2) computing power doubles every 18 months; and (3) the price of computing falls by half every 18 months.

Figure 5-5 illustrates the relationship between the number of transistors on a microprocessor and millions of instructions per second (MIPS), a common measure of processor power. Figure 5-6 shows the exponential decline in the cost of transistors and rise in computing power.

FIGURE 5-6   *Falling cost of chips*

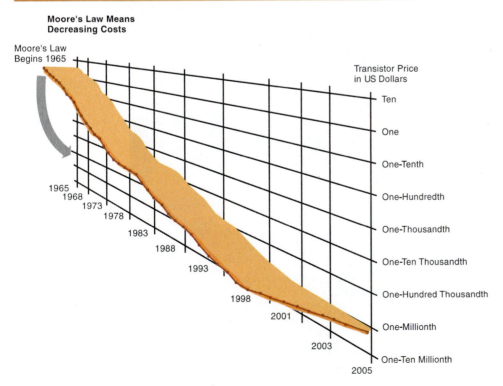

Packing more transistors into less space has driven down transistor cost dramatically as well as the cost of the products in which they are used. An Intel® process today can contain as many as 1 billion transistors, run at 3.2 GHz and higher, deliver over 10 000 MIPS, and be manufactured in high volumes with transistors that cost less than 1/10 000th of a cent. That's a little less than the cost of one printed character in this book.

Source: © 2004 Intel. All rights reserved.

There is reason to believe the exponential growth in the number of transistors and the power of processors coupled with an exponential decline in computing costs will continue into the future. Chip manufacturers continue to miniaturize components. Intel changed its manufacturing process from 0.13-micron component size (a micron is a millionth of a metre), introduced in 2002, to a newer 90-nanometre process in 2004 (a nanometre is a billionth of a metre). Both IBM and AMD, the other large manufacturers of processor chips, began producing 90-nanometre chips in 2006. With a size of about 50 nanometres, today's transistors should no longer be compared to the size of a human hair but rather to the size of a virus, the smallest form of organic life.

By using nanotechnology, Intel believes it can shrink the size of transistors down to the width of several atoms. **Nanotechnology** uses individual atoms and molecules to create computer chips and other devices that are thousands of times smaller than current technologies permit. IBM and other research labs have created transistors from nanotubes and other electrical devices and have developed a manufacturing process that could produce nanotube processors economically (Figure 5-7). Other new technologies include strained silicon, 300-millimetre production wafers (which decrease the costs of production), and denser interconnections among components.

While the first Pentium microprocessors operated at 75 megahertz, today's Pentiums are available with close to 4-gigahertz speeds. However, increasing processor speeds at the same exponential rate as in the past may no longer be possible. As processor speeds increase, heat is generated that cannot be dissipated with air fans.

Another brake on future increases in microprocessor speed is consumer interest in low power consumption for longer battery life and low weight to increase laptop and handheld computer portability. For this reason, Intel and other firms are designing the next generation of chips to be less power hungry and lower in weight even if they are the same or even slower speeds. Other options include putting multiple processors on a single chip.

Nanotechnology

FIGURE 5-7   *Examples of nanotubes*

Nanotubes are tiny tubes about 10 000 times thinner than a human hair. They consist of rolled up sheets of carbon hexagons. Discovered in 1991 by researchers at NEC, they have potential uses as minuscule wires or in ultrasmall electronic devices and are very powerful conductors of electrical current.

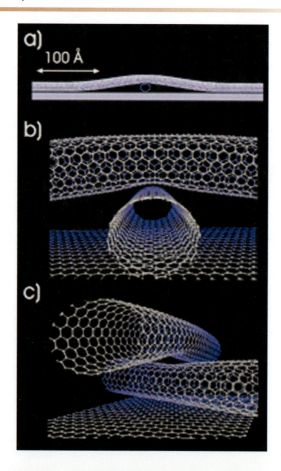

FIGURE 5-8   *The capacity of hard disk drives grows exponentially (1980 to 2007)*

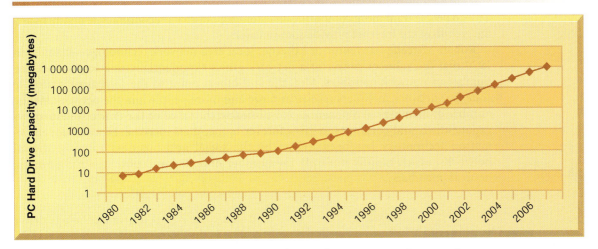

From 1980 to 1990, hard disk drive capacities for PCs grew at the rate of 25 percent annual compound growth, but after 1990, growth accelerated to more than 65 percent each year.

The Law of Mass Digital Storage   A second technology driver of IT infrastructure change is the Law of Mass Digital Storage. The world produces as much as 5 exabytes of unique information per year (an exabyte is a billion gigabytes, or 10^{18} bytes). The amount of digital information is roughly doubling every year (Lyman and Varian, 2003). Almost all this information growth involves magnetic storage of digital data, and printed documents account for only 0.003 percent of the annual growth.

Fortunately, the cost of storing digital information is falling at an exponential rate of 100 percent a year. Figure 5-8 shows that PC hard drive capacity—beginning with a Seagate 506 in 1980 that had 5 megabytes of memory—has grown at a compound annual growth rate of 25 percent in the early years to more than 60 percent a year since 1990. Today's PC hard drives have storage densities approaching 1 gigabyte per square inch and total capacities of more than 500 gigabytes.

Figure 5-9 shows that the number of kilobytes that can be stored on magnetic disks for one dollar from 1950 to 2005 roughly doubled every 15 months.

FIGURE 5-9   *The cost of storing data declines exponentially (1950 to 2007)*

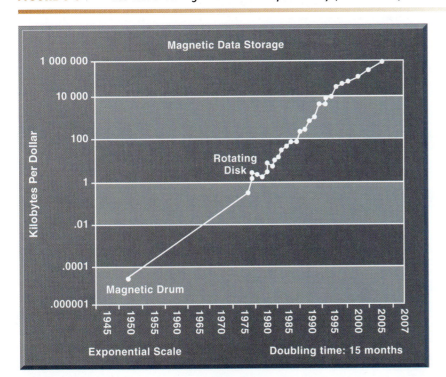

Since the first magnetic storage device was used in 1955, the cost of storing a kilobyte of data has fallen exponentially, doubling the amount of digital storage for each dollar expended every 15 months on average.

Source: Kurzweil, 2003; updated by the authors.

Metcalfe's Law and Network Economics Moore's Law and the Law of Mass Storage help us understand why computing resources are now so readily available. But why do people want more computing and storage power? The economics of networks and the growth of the Internet provide some answers.

Robert Metcalfe—inventor of Ethernet local area network technology—claimed in 1970 that the value or power of a network grows exponentially as a function of the number of network members. Metcalfe and others point to the *increasing returns to scale* that network members receive as more and more people join the network. As the number of members in a network grows linearly, the value of the entire system grows exponentially and continues to grow forever as members increase. Demand for information technology has been driven by the social and business value of digital networks, which rapidly multiply the number of actual and potential links among network members.

Declining Communications Costs and the Internet A fourth technology driver transforming IT infrastructure is the rapid decline in the costs of communication and the exponential growth in the size of the Internet. An estimated 1.1 billion people worldwide now have Internet access, with more than 19 million of these being located in Canada. Almost 40 percent of private sector firms have a Web site while 95 percent of public sector organizations have a Web site. More than 75 percent of Canadian private sector firms now use e-mail while almost 100 percent of public sector organizations use e-mail (Statistics Canada, 2006b). Figure 5-10 illustrates the exponentially declining cost of communication both over the Internet and over telephone networks (which increasingly are based on the Internet). As communication costs fall and approach 0, utilization of communication and computing facilities explodes.

To take advantage of the business value associated with the Internet, firms must greatly expand their Internet connections, including wireless connectivity, and greatly expand the power of their client/server networks, desktop clients, and mobile computing devices. There is every reason to believe these trends will continue.

Standards and Network Effects Today's enterprise infrastructure and Internet computing would be impossible—both now and in the future—without agreements among manufacturers and widespread consumer acceptance of **technology standards**. Technology standards are specifications that establish the compatibility of products and the ability to communicate in a network (Stango, 2004).

Technology standards

FIGURE 5-10 *Exponential declines in Internet communications costs*

One reason for the growth in the Internet population is the rapid decline in Internet connection and overall communication costs. The cost per kilobit of Internet access has fallen exponentially since 1995. Digital Subscriber Line (DSL) and cable modems now deliver a kilobit of communication for a retail price of less than 2 cents.

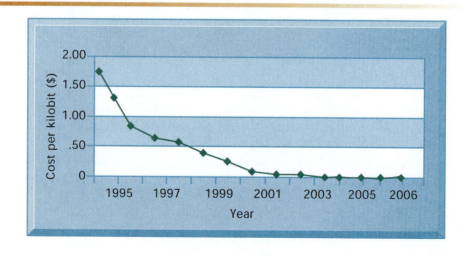

Technology standards unleash powerful economies of scale and result in price declines as manufacturers focus on products built to a single standard. Without these economies of scale, computing of any sort would be far more expensive. Table 5-3 describes just a few important standards that have shaped IT infrastructure. In fact there are hundreds of additional standards that are beyond the focus of this textbook.

Beginning in the 1990s, corporations started moving toward standard computing and communications platforms. The Wintel PC with the Windows operating system and Microsoft Office desktop productivity applications became the standard desktop and mobile client computing platform. Widespread adoption of **Unix** (a machine-independent operating system) as the enterprise server operating system of choice made possible the replacement of proprietary and expensive mainframe infrastructure. In telecommunications, the Ethernet standard enabled PCs to connect together in small local area networks (LANs; see Chapter 7), and the TCP/IP standard enabled these LANs to be connected into firmwide networks, and ultimately, to the Internet.

Unix

TABLE 5-3 *Some Important Standards in Computing*

STANDARD	SIGNIFICANCE
American Standard Code for Information Interchange (ASCII)(1958)	Made it possible for computer machines from different manufacturers to exchange data; later used as the universal language linking input and output devices such as keyboards and mice to computers. Adopted by the American National Standards Institute in 1963.
Common Business Oriented Language (COBOL) (1959)	An easy-to-use software language that greatly expanded the ability of programmers to write business-related programs and reduced the cost of software. Sponsored by the Defense Department in 1959.
Unix (1969–1975)	A powerful multitasking, multiuser, portable operating system initially developed at Bell Labs (1969) and later released for use by others (1975). It operates on a wide variety of computers from different manufacturers. Adopted by Sun, IBM, HP, and others in the 1980s and became the most widely used enterprise-level operating system.
Transmission Control Protocol/Internet Protocol (TCP/IP) (1974)	Suite of communications protocols and a common addressing scheme that enables millions of computers to connect together in one giant global network (the Internet). Later, it became the default networking protocol suite for local area networks and intranets. Developed in the early 1970s for the U.S. Department of Defense.
Ethernet (1973)	A network standard for connecting desktop computers into local area networks that enabled the widespread adoption of client/server computing and local area networks and further stimulated the adoption of personal computers.
IBM/Microsoft/Intel Personal Computer (1981)	The standard Wintel design for personal desktop computing based on standard Intel processors and other standard devices, Microsoft DOS, and later Windows software. The emergence of this standard, low-cost product laid the foundation for a 25-year period of explosive growth in computing throughout all organizations around the globe. Today, more than 1 billion PCs power business and government activities every day.
World Wide Web (1989–Present)	Standards for storing, retrieving, formatting, and displaying information as a worldwide web of electronic pages incorporating text, graphics, audio, and video that enable the creation of a global repository of billions of Web pages.

Infrastructure Components

IT infrastructure today is composed of seven major components. Figure 5-11 illustrates these infrastructure components and the major vendors within each component category. These components are investments that must be coordinated with one another to provide the firm with a coherent infrastructure.

In the past, technology vendors supplying these components were often in competition with one another, offering purchasing firms a mixture of incompatible, proprietary, partial solutions. But increasingly the vendor firms have been forced by large customers to cooperate in strategic partnerships with one another. For instance, a hardware and services provider such as IBM cooperates with all the major enterprise software providers, has strategic relationships with system integrators (often accounting firms), and promises to work with whichever database products its client firms wish to use (even though it sells its own database management software called DB2). Let's examine the size and dynamics of each of these infrastructure components and their markets.

Computer Hardware Platforms

U.S. firms will spend about US $145 billion in 2005 on computer hardware. This component includes client machines (desktop PCs, mobile computing devices such as

FIGURE 5-11   *The IT infrastructure ecosystem*

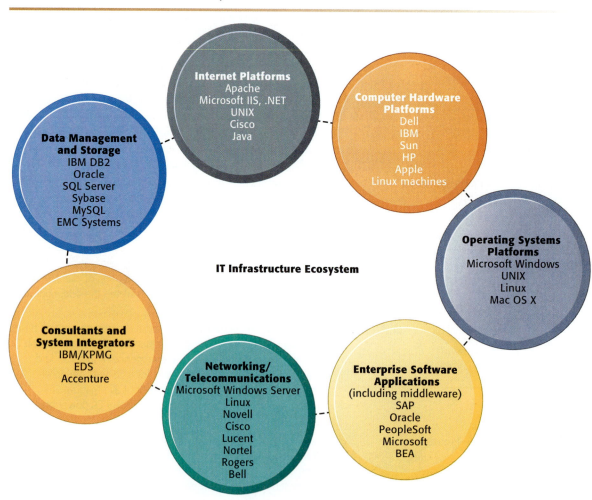

There are seven major components that must be coordinated to provide the firm with a coherent IT infrastructure. Listed here are major technologies and suppliers for each component.

PDAs and laptops) and server machines. The client machines use primarily Intel or AMD microprocessors. Both DreamWorks and Frantic Films, discussed at the beginning of the chapter, use high-end client machines called workstations for their intensive level of graphics computing. In 2005, 155 million PCs were shipped to U.S. customers, and US $30 billion was spent on clients (eMarketer, 2005).

The server market is more complex, using mostly Intel or AMD processors in the form of blade servers in racks, but also including Sun SPARC microprocessors and

A blade server is a thin, modular processing device that is intended for a single dedicated application (such as serving Web pages) that can be easily inserted into a space-saving rack (as shown here) with many similar servers.

IBM PowerPC chips specially designed for server use. **Blade servers** are ultrathin computers consisting of a circuit board with processors, memory, and network connections that are stored in racks. They take up less space than traditional box-based servers. Secondary storage may be provided by a hard drive in each blade server or by very large external mass-storage drives.

The marketplace for computer hardware has increasingly become concentrated in top firms such as IBM, HP, Dell, and Sun Microsystems, which produce 90 percent of the machines, and three chip producers, Intel, AMD, and IBM, which account for more than 90 percent of the processors sold. The industry has collectively settled on Intel as the standard processor, with major exceptions in the server market for Unix and Linux machines, which might use SUN or IBM Unix processors.

Mainframes have not disappeared. The mainframe market has actually grown steadily over the last decade although the number of providers has dwindled to one: IBM. IBM has also repurposed its mainframe systems so they can be used as giant servers for massive enterprise networks and corporate Web sites. A single IBM mainframe can run up to 17 000 instances of Linux or Windows server software and is capable of replacing thousands of smaller blade servers.

Operating System Platforms

At the client level, 95 percent of PCs and 45 percent of handheld devices use some form of Microsoft Windows operating system (such as Windows XP, Windows 2000, or Windows CE). In contrast, in the server marketplace, more than 85 percent of the corporate servers in the U.S. use some form of Unix or **Linux**, an inexpensive and robust open-source relative of Unix. Although Microsoft Windows Server 2003 is capable of providing enterprise-wide operating system and network services, it is generally not used when there are more than 3000 client computers in a network.

Unix and Linux constitute the backbone of corporate infrastructure throughout much of the world because they are scalable, reliable, and much less expensive than mainframe operating systems. They can also run on many different types of processors. The major providers of Unix operating systems are IBM, HP, and Sun, each with slightly different and partially incompatible versions.

Although Windows continues to dominate the client marketplace, many corporations have begun to explore Linux as a low-cost desktop operating system. Linux is provided by

Blade servers

Linux

commercial vendors such as RedHat and is available in free versions downloadable from the Internet as **open-source software**, i.e., software created and updated by a worldwide community of programmers and available for free (see Section 5.4 below for more on open-source platforms).

Enterprise and Other Software Applications

After telecommunications services, software is the largest single component of IT infrastructure. A large portion of the software budget of medium-large-sized companies will be spent on enterprise system software. The largest providers of enterprise application software are SAP and Oracle (which acquired PeopleSoft and many other smaller enterprise software firms in recent years). Also included in this category is middleware software supplied by vendors such as BEA Systems for achieving firmwide integration by linking the firm's existing application systems. We describe both types of software in detail in Section 5.3.

Microsoft is attempting to move into the lower ends of this market by focusing on small and medium-sized businesses. In general, most traditional large firms have already implemented enterprise applications and have developed long-term relationships with their providers. Once a firm decides to work with an enterprise vendor, switching can be difficult and costly, though not impossible.

Data Management and Storage

There are few choices for enterprise database management software, which is responsible for organizing and managing the firm's data so that it can be efficiently accessed and used. Chapter 6 describes this software in detail. The leading database software providers are IBM (DB2), Oracle, Microsoft (SQL Server), and Sybase (Adaptive Server Enterprise), which supply a large portion of the database management and storage marketplace. A growing new entrant is MySQL, a Linux open-source relational database product available for free on the Internet and increasingly supported by HP and others.

The physical data storage market is dominated by EMC Corporation for large-scale systems and a small number of PC hard disk manufacturers led by Seagate, Maxtor, and Western Digital. In addition to traditional disk arrays and tape libraries, large firms are turning to network-based storage technologies. **Storage area networks (SANs)** connect multiple storage devices on a separate high-speed network dedicated to storage. The SAN creates a large central pool of storage that can be rapidly accessed and shared by multiple servers.

The amount of new digital information in the world is doubling every three years, driven in part by e-commerce, e-business, and statutes and regulations requiring firms to invest in extensive data storage and management facilities. Consequently, the market for digital data storage devices has been growing at more than 15 percent annually over the last five years.

Networking/Telecommunications Platforms

Canadian firms spend an enormous amount annually on networking and telecommunications hardware and services. The vast part of this budget is for telecommunications services (consisting mainly of telecommunications, cable, and telephone company charges for voice lines and Internet access; these are not included in this discussion but certainly could be counted as part of the firm's infrastructure). Chapter 7 is devoted to an in-depth description of the enterprise networking environment, including the Internet. Windows Server is predominantly used as local area network operating system, followed by Novell, Linux, and Unix. Large enterprise-wide area networks primarily use some variant of Unix. Nearly all local area networks, as well as wide area enterprise networks, use the TCP/IP protocol suite as a standard (see Chapter 7).

Open-source software

Storage area networks (SANs)

The leading networking hardware providers are Cisco, Lucent, Nortel, and Juniper Networks. Telecommunications platforms are typically provided by telecommunications/telephone services companies that offer voice and data connectivity, wide area networking, and Internet access. Leading telecommunications service vendors include Shaw, Rogers, Primus, and regional telephone companies such as Manitoba Telecommunication Services (MTS). As noted in Chapter 7, this market is exploding with new providers of cellular wireless, Wi-Fi, and Internet telephone services.

Internet Platforms

Internet platforms overlap with, and must relate to, the firm's general networking infrastructure and hardware and software platforms. Expenditures for Internet-related infrastructure are for hardware, software, and management services to support a firm's Web site, including Web hosting services, and for intranets and extranets. A **Web hosting service** maintains a large Web server, or series of servers, and provides fee-paying subscribers with space to maintain their Web sites. This category of technology expenditures is growing by approximately 10 percent per year.

The Internet revolution of the late 1990s led to a veritable explosion in server computers, with many firms collecting thousands of small servers to run their Internet operations. Since then, there has been a steady push toward server consolidation, reducing the number of server computers by increasing the size and power of each. The Internet hardware server market has become increasingly concentrated in the hands of Dell, HP, and IBM as prices have fallen dramatically.

The major Web software application development tools and suites are supplied by Microsoft, IBM, and Sun Microsystems. Microsoft offers FrontPage and the Microsoft.NET family of development tools used to create Web sites using Active Server Pages for dynamic content, IBM has its WebSphere line of Internet management tools, and Sun's Java is the most widely used tool for developing interactive Web applications on both the server and client sides. Competing with these big players are a host of independent software developers, including Adobe (Flash, Dreamweaver, and Acrobat), RealNetworks (Real Media). Windows and Apple also compete in the media distribution field with products such as iTunes and Windows Media Player. Chapter 7 describes the components of a firm's Internet platform in greater detail.

Consulting and System Integration Services

Although 20 years ago it might have been possible for a large firm to implement all its own IT infrastructure, today this is far less common. Even large firms do not have the staff, skills, budget, or necessary experience to do so. Implementing new infrastructure requires significant changes in business processes and procedures, training and education, and software integration (as noted in Chapters 3 and 10). For these reasons, firms spend more each year on consulting services and system integrators.

Software integration means ensuring the new infrastructure works with the firm's older, so-called legacy systems and ensuring the new elements of the infrastructure work with one another. A **legacy system** is generally an older transaction processing system created for mainframe computers that continues to be used to avoid the high cost of replacement or redesign. Replacing legacy systems is cost-prohibitive and generally unnecessary if these older systems can be integrated into a contemporary infrastructure.

Most companies in the past relied on their accounting firms to provide consulting and system integration services simply because the accounting firms were the only ones that truly understood a company's business processes and had the expertise to change its software. Many Canadian accounting firms have followed the practice of U.S. accounting firms, which have been prohibited by law from providing these services. In the U.S., many accounting firms have consequently split off consulting services into separate

Web hosting service
Legacy system

entities, such as Accenture (formerly part of Arthur Andersen) and PwC Consulting (split off from the Pricewaterhouse Coopers accounting firm and now part of IBM). Interestingly, most of these firms have since re-added new consulting service components to their services. Some Canadian firms, on the other hand, have maintained their consulting practices while others have abandoned them or outsourced them to a strategic partner.

5.2 Hardware Platform Trends and Emerging Technologies

Although the cost of computing has fallen exponentially, the cost of the IT infrastructure has actually expanded as a percentage of corporate budgets. Why should this be? The costs of computing services (consulting, systems integration) and software are high, and the intensity of computing and communicating has increased as other costs have declined. For example, employees now use much more sophisticated applications, requiring more powerful and expensive hardware of many different types (such as laptop, desktop, handheld, and tablet computers).

Firms face a number of other challenges. They need to integrate information stored in different applications and on different platforms (telephone, legacy systems, intranet, Internet sites, desktop, and mobile devices). Firms also need to build resilient infrastructure that can withstand huge increases in peak loads and routine assaults from hackers and viruses while conserving electrical power. Because customer and employee expectations for service are increasing, firms need to increase their service levels to meet customer demands. The trends in hardware and software platforms we now describe address some or all of these challenges.

The Integration of Computing and Telecommunications Platforms

Arguably, the most dominant theme in hardware platforms today is the convergence of telecommunications and computing platforms to the point where computing increasingly takes place over the network. You can see this convergence at several levels.

The Palm Treo 700w combines a mobile phone, e-mail, messaging, personal organizer, Web access, digital camera, video recorder, and digital music player all in one device. Convergence of computing and communications technologies has turned cell phones into mobile computing platforms.

At the client level, communication devices such as cell phones are taking on functions of handheld computers while handheld personal digital assistants (PDAs) are taking on cell phone functions. For instance, the Palm Treo 700w digital handheld integrates phone, camera, digital music player, and handheld computer in one device. High-end cell phones come equipped for downloading music and video clips and for playing 3-D games. Television, radio, and video are moving toward all-digital production and distribution. There is little doubt that personal computers of some sort will be the core of the home entertainment centre and the mobile personal entertainment centre of the next five years as a storage device and operating system.

At the server and network level, the growing success of Internet telephone systems (now the fastest-growing type of telephone service) demonstrates how historically separate telecommunications and computing platforms are converging toward a single network—the Internet. Chapter 7 describes the convergence of computing and telecommunications in greater depth.

Other major trends in hardware platforms described here are based in large part on computing over high-capacity networks. The network in many respects is becoming the source of computing power, enabling business firms to expand their computing power greatly at very little cost.

Grid Computing

Grid computing involves connecting geographically remote computers into a single network to create a virtual supercomputer by combining the computational power of all computers on the grid. Grid computing takes advantage of the fact that most computers use their central processing units on average only 25 percent of the time for the work they have been assigned, leaving these idle resources available for other processing tasks. Grid computing was impossible until high-speed Internet connections enabled firms to connect remote machines economically and move enormous quantities of data.

Grid computing requires software programs to control and allocate resources on the grid, such as open-source software provided by Globus Alliance (www.globus.org) or private providers. Client software communicates with a server software application. The server software breaks data and application code into chunks that are then parcelled out to the grid's machines. The client machines can perform their traditional tasks while running grid applications in the background.

The business case for using grid computing involves cost savings, speed of computation, and agility. For example, Royal Dutch/Shell Group is using a scalable grid computing platform that improves the accuracy and speed of its scientific modelling applications to find the best oil reservoirs. This platform, which links 1024 IBM servers running Linux, in effect creates one of the largest commercial Linux supercomputers in the world. The grid adjusts to accommodate the fluctuating data volumes that are typical in this seasonal business. Royal Dutch/Shell Group claims the grid has enabled the company to cut processing time for seismic data, while improving output quality and helping its scientists pinpoint problems in finding new oil supplies.

On-Demand Computing (Utility Computing)

On-demand computing refers to firms off-loading peak demand for computing power to remote, large-scale data processing centres. In this manner, firms can reduce their investment in IT infrastructure by investing just enough to handle average processing loads and paying for only as much additional computing power as the market demands. Another term for on-demand computing is **utility computing**, which suggests that firms purchase computing power from central computing utilities and pay only for the amount of computing power they use, much as they would pay for electricity. IBM, HP, Oracle, and Sun Microsystems all offer utility computing services on demand.

In addition to lowering the cost of owning hardware resources, on-demand computing gives firms greater agility to use technology and greatly reduces the risk of over-investing in IT infrastructure. On-demand computing shifts firms from having a fixed infrastructure capacity toward a highly flexible infrastructure, some of it owned by the firm, and some of it rented from giant computer centres owned by computer hardware vendors. This arrangement frees firms to launch entirely new business processes that they would never attempt with a fixed infrastructure.

DreamWorks, described in the chapter-opening case, has used HP utility computing services for about four years. The company's demand for computing resources is cyclical and tied to events such as tight production deadlines for new films. Rather than purchase additional infrastructure to handle this peak load, DreamWorks rents this capacity when it needs it from HP (Krazit, 2005).

Grid computing
On-demand computing
Utility computing

Autonomic Computing

Computer systems have become so complex today that some experts believe they may not be manageable in the future. With operating systems, enterprise applications, and database software weighing in at millions of lines of code, and with large systems encompassing many thousands of networked devices, the problem of managing these systems looms very large (Kephart and Chess, 2003).

It is estimated that one-third to one-half of a company's total IT budget is spent preventing or recovering from system crashes. About 40 percent of these crashes are caused by operator error. The reason is not that operators are not well trained or do not have the right capabilities. Rather, it is that the complexities of today's computer systems are too difficult to understand, and IT operators and managers are under pressure to make decisions about problems in seconds.

One approach to dealing with this problem from a computer hardware perspective is to employ autonomic computing. **Autonomic computing** is an industry-wide effort to develop systems that can configure themselves, optimize and tune themselves, heal themselves when broken, and protect themselves from outside intruders and self-destruction. Imagine, for instance, a desktop PC that could know it was invaded by a computer virus. Instead of blindly allowing the virus to invade, the PC would identify and eradicate the virus or, alternatively, turn its workload over to another processor and shut itself down before the virus destroyed any files. Table 5-4 explains some of the capabilities autonomic computing provides.

A few of these capabilities are present in desktop operating systems. For instance, virus and firewall protection software can detect viruses on PCs, automatically defeat the viruses, and alert operators. A **firewall** is hardware or software placed in between an organization's internal network and external networks to prevent outsiders from invading private networks. These programs can be updated automatically as the need arises by connecting to an online virus protection service such as McAfee. IBM and other vendors are starting to build autonomic features into products for large systems (IBM, 2005).

Edge Computing

Autonomic computing
Firewall
Edge computing

Edge computing is a multitier, load-balancing scheme for Web-based applications in which significant parts of Web site content, logic, and processing are performed by smaller, less expensive servers located nearby the user in order to increase responsiveness and resilience while lowering technology costs. In this sense, edge computing is another technique like grid

TABLE 5-4 *Four Aspects of Self-Management as They Are Now and Would Be with Autonomic Computing*

CONCEPT	CURRENT COMPUTING	AUTONOMIC COMPUTING
Self-configuration	Corporate data centres have multiple vendors and platforms. Installing, configuring, and integrating systems is time-consuming and error-prone.	Automated configuration of components and systems follows high-level policies. Rest of system adjusts automatically and seamlessly.
Self-optimization	Systems have hundreds of manually set, nonlinear tuning parameters, and their number increases with each release.	Components and systems continually seek opportunities to improve their own performance and efficiency.
Self-healing	Problem determination in large, complex systems can take a team of programmers weeks.	System automatically detects, diagnoses, and repairs localized software and hardware problems.
Self-protection	Detection of and recovery from attacks and cascading failures is manual.	System automatically defends against malicious attacks or cascading failures. It uses early warning to anticipate and prevent systemwide failures.

FIGURE 5-12   *Edge computing platform*

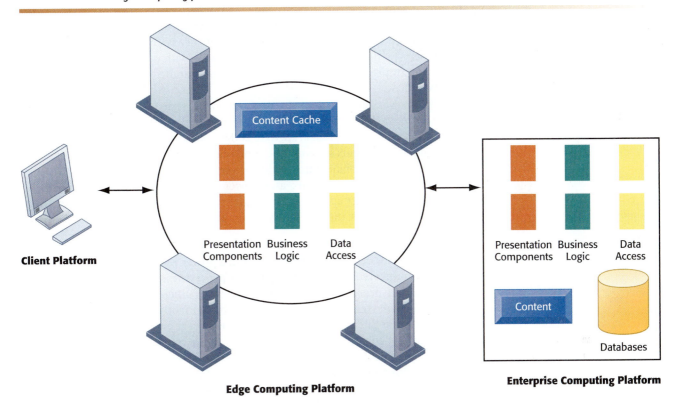

Edge Computing Platform

Client Platform

Enterprise Computing Platform

Edge computing involves the use of the Internet to balance the processing load of enterprise platforms across the client and edge computing platform.

computing and on-demand computing for using the Internet to share the workload experienced by a firm across many computers located remotely on the network.

Figure 5-12 illustrates the components of edge computing. There are three tiers in edge computing: the local client; the nearby edge computing platform, which consists of servers positioned at any Internet service providers; and enterprise computers located at the firm's main data centre. The edge computing platform is owned by a service firm such as Akamai Technologies, which employs more than 15 000 edge servers around North America.

In an edge platform application, edge servers initially process requests from the user client computer. The edge server delivers to the client presentation components such as static Web page content, reusable code fragments, and interactive elements gathered on forms. Database and business logic elements are delivered by the enterprise computing platform.

Virtualization and Multicore Processors

As companies deploy hundreds or thousands of servers, many have discovered that they are spending more on electricity to power and cool their systems than they did on acquiring the hardware. Google is building a new data centre in Oregon in part because electricity costs are far cheaper there than other parts of the United States. Cutting power consumption in data centres is now a priority for most CIOs.

One way of curbing hardware proliferation and power consumption is to use virtualization to reduce the number of computers required for processing. **Virtualization** is the process of presenting a set of computing resources (such as computing power or data storage) so that they can all be accessed in ways that are not restricted by physical configuration or geographic location. Server virtualization enables companies to run more than one operating system at the same time on a single machine. Most servers run at just 10 to 15 percent of capacity, and virtualization can boost server utilization rates to 70 percent

Virtualization

or higher. Higher utilization rates translate into fewer computers required to process the same amount of work.

For example, Camelot Group PLC, the licensed operator of the UK National Lottery, was faced with a tremendous increase in server capacity needs. By purchasing two storage area network servers, they added 10 terabytes of storage with decreased computing and utility costs; the improved storage area network can handle 1200 percent of normal capacity (IBM, 2006).

Server virtualization software runs between the operating system and the hardware, masking server resources, including the number and identity of physical servers, processors, and operating systems, from server users. VMware is the leading server virtualization software vendor for Windows and Linux systems. Microsoft offers its own Virtual Server product and has built virtualization capabilities into the newest version of Windows Server.

In addition to reducing hardware and power expenditures, virtualization allows businesses to run their legacy applications on older versions of an operating system on the same server as newer applications. Virtualization also facilitates centralization of hardware administration.

Multicore Processors Another way to reduce power requirements and hardware sprawl is to use multicore processors. A **multicore processor** is an integrated circuit that contains two or more processors. In the past, chip makers increased the speed of processors by increasing their frequency, from a few megahertz to today's chips which operate at gigahertz frequencies. But this strategy increased both heat and power consumption to the point where very high gigahertz chips require water cooling. Dual-core processors combine two or more slower processors in a single chip. This technology enables two processing engines with reduced power requirements and heat dissipation to perform tasks faster than a resource-hungry chip with a single processing core.

Intel and AMD now make dual-core microprocessors and are introducing quad-core processors. Sun Microsystems sells servers using its eight-core UltraSparc T1 processor.

The Tokyo Institute of Technology used dual-core processors to create the largest super-computer in Japan. Using single-core processors would have required a data centre that was twice as large as the Institute's current facility and would have generated nearly twice the heat. The dual-core implementation required half as many servers as the single-core approach and is less costly to maintain because there are fewer systems to monitor (Dunn, 2005).

5.3 Software Platform Trends and Emerging Technologies

There are five major themes in contemporary software platform evolution:

- Linux and open-source software
- Java
- Enterprise software
- Web services and service-oriented architecture
- Software outsourcing

The Rise of Linux and Open-Source Software

Open-source software is software produced by a community of several hundred thousand programmers around the world. According to the leading open-source professional association, OpenSource.org, open-source software is free and can be modified by users. Works derived from the original code must also be free, and the software can be redistributed by the user without additional licensing. Open-source software is by definition not restricted to any specific operating system or hardware technology, although most open-source software is currently based on a Linux or Unix operating system (Open Source Development Lab, 2004).

Open-source software is based on the premise that it is superior to commercially produced proprietary software because thousands of programmers around the world, working for no pay, can read, perfect, distribute, and modify the source code much faster, and with more reliable results, than small teams of programmers working for a single software company.

Although it may seem that contributors to open-source software receive nothing in return, in fact they receive respect, prestige, and access to a network of knowledgeable programmers. Open-source contributors are dedicated professionals who have a well-defined organizational structure and set of procedures for getting the work done. The open-source movement has been evolving for more than 30 years and has demonstrated after many years of effort that it can produce commercially acceptable, high-quality software, such as the MySQL database and Apache Web server software.

Now thousands of open-source programs are available from hundreds of Web sites. The range of open-source software extends from operating systems to desktop productivity suites, Web browsers, and games. Major hardware and software vendors, including IBM, HP, Dell, Oracle, and SAP, now offer Linux-compatible versions of their products. You can find out more about the Open Source Definition from the Open Source Initiative and the history of open-source software on MyMISLab.

Linux Perhaps the most well known open-source software is Linux, an operating system related to Unix. Linux was created by the Finnish programmer Linus Torvalds and was first posted on the Internet in August 1991. Linux is now the world's fastest-growing client and server operating system. In North America, Linux was installed in nearly 6 percent of new shipments of PCs in 2005, and this number is expected to grow to more than 20 percent of new PC shipments by 2010 (Bulkeley, 2004). In Russia and China, more than 40 percent of new PCs are shipped with Linux although in part this reflects a very high percentage of users who install pirated editions of Microsoft Windows on much less expensive Linux PCs.

Applications for the Linux operating system are rapidly growing also. Many of these applications are embedded in cell phones, PDAs, and other handheld devices. Although Linux is currently a small but rapidly growing presence on the desktop, it plays a major role in the back office, running local area networks and Web servers for companies such as ING Canada (see the Window on Technology below). In the server market, Linux is the most rapidly growing LAN server, with an approximately 23 percent market share, up from 1 percent in 1998.

IBM, HP, Intel, Dell, and Sun have made Linux a central part of their offerings to corporations. More than two dozen countries in Asia, Europe, and Latin America have adopted open-source software and Linux. Cost is a major driver, as discussed in Window on Technology, as are reliability and flexibility. However the benefits are not always automatic, and managers need to carefully assess whether open-source software will meet their business and computing requirements.

Scalability

WINDOW ON TECHNOLOGY

Is It Time for Open-Source?

The largest provider of property and casualty insurance in Canada, ING Canada, uses Linux for its Web services applications. Because ING Canada recently experienced multiple mergers and acquisitions, the company's systems operated on multiple platforms around the world. ING therefore contracted with IBM

to provide upgrades, including moving its Web services to one mainframe running Linux; this move was to enable scalability for ING's Web services depending on customer demand. **Scalability** means having the ability to scale up, or add capacity (typically storage space in the form of additional servers), so that users receive fast, reliable access during times of heightened activity. Scalability also requires that capacity can be easily decreased, or scaled down, at times of reduced activity. ING also plans to use its new Linux capability to create virtual servers to support the increase in demand.

One company that successfully used Linux to scale down is E*Trade Financial. During the late 1990s, when E*Trade Financial's trading volume was mushrooming, the online trading company managed its growth by adding capacity in the form of large servers from Sun Microsystems running Sun Solaris, Sun's proprietary version of Unix, at a cost of US $250 000 each. By the fall of 2001, the stock market was cooling, and trading volumes—and E*Trade's cash flow—dropped precipitously. The company decided to switch to Linux running on inexpensive Intel processor–based IBM x335 servers to rein in costs.

Preliminary tests running E*Trade's applications on Linux showed that each Linux server could handle about 180 users at a time, compared to 300 to 400 users simultaneously on one of the Sun 4500 servers. More than 180 users degraded performance, but with 180 users or fewer, the Linux server performed faster than the Sun server. However, even though each Linux computer could handle only 180 people at a time, it cost only US $4000. E*Trade needed to purchase only two Linux computers at a total cost of US $8000 to provide the same processing capabilities for 400 users as the expensive Sun machine. Using Linux on small inexpensive servers saves E*Trade US $13 million annually while increasing computer performance. E*Trade's Sun servers were reallocated, retired, or sold to other companies.

Another obvious benefit of open-source is access to source code that companies can use to integrate Linux with their existing business applications and improve it for their purposes. Siegenia-Aubi KG, a German maker of windows, doors, and ventilating equipment, replaced the Windows operating system on its Compaq servers with Linux to run mySAP customer relationship management software, the open-source Apache Web server, and the MySQL database. Being able to manipulate Linux source code makes it easier to integrate with business applications the company uses. Linux is also more reliable than Windows, at least according to its supporters. Previously, the company had to reboot its Compaq servers every two weeks when they were running Windows because the operating system malfunctioned. Siegenia-Aubi is now trying to move more of its business systems to Linux.

Against these benefits, managers must weigh the issues and challenges that accompany the incorporation of open-source into an IT infrastructure. Arguably, a successful open-source deployment requires more to be spent on support and mainte-nance because the Linux tool set is not as well developed as that for Microsoft Server, and the skills required of support staff are more esoteric and therefore more expensive. If companies do not have access to resources that can provide support inexpensively, they may negate the advantages they gained by adopting open-source. Larry Kinder, CIO of Cendant, reflects, "You're always weighing the value of having a company like Microsoft behind you or relying on an open-source community you have no control over." If you are a

large Microsoft Fortune 1000 user and you have a problem with Microsoft products, Microsoft can supply an army of support technicians to solve your problem, often free of charge. The same cannot be said of RedHat Linux or free Linux downloaded from the Web.

Kamal Nasser, vice president of IT strategy for Nielsen Media Research, notes that adoption of Linux at his company has not progressed freely because the knowledge base of the IT staff is Sun Solaris. Florian Kainz, computer graphics principal engineer at Industrial Light & Magic, asserts that companies migrating from Unix to Linux are more likely to have better results than companies migrating from Windows because the technical support skills for Unix and Linux are similar. Vendors of open-source applications can provide support but may be stymied if customers have altered program code and created problems whose origins cannot be easily uncovered.

Communities that develop open-source applications are decentralized and unregulated. When an upgrade is released, mission-critical features may have disappeared without warn-ing because the developers determined they lacked value.

The undefined structure of the development community also exposes companies to legal issues that they do not con-front when using commercial applications. Large businesses fear that intellectual property lawsuits could result from using a product developed by, in some cases, thousands of people across the globe who may claim ownership. Licence agreements for open-source do not always grant complete freedom for distributing and modifying code. Yahoo! and United Parcel Service (UPS), major adopters of Linux servers, both scrutinize and manage the usage rights and licences of the open-source software they deploy.

Companies also need to ensure that the open-source offerings will fit into their operating environments. Most companies are not ripping out the commercial software in which they have invested quite heavily. For example, Yahoo! uses open-source to create and support the services that its users are most drawn to, such as e-mail and Web page templates. However, Yahoo! has no plans to abandon the commercial applications that run its search technology, customer billing, and online ads. UPS, however, expects to run all of the traffic on UPS.com through Linux servers.

According to a survey conducted by Saugatuck Research, almost half of all organizations will use Linux for their mission-critical application within five years even though only about 18 percent of businesses will use Linux for these applications by the end of 2007.

To Think About

1. What problems do Linux and other open-source software address? How does open-source software help solve these problems?

2. What issues and challenges does open-source software present? What can be done to address these issues?

3. What are the business as well as the technology issues that should be addressed when deciding whether to use open-source software?

The rise of open-source software, particularly Linux and the applications it supports, has profound implications for corporate software platforms: cost reduction, reliability and resilience, and integration, because Linux works on all the major hardware platforms from mainframes to servers to clients. Linux has the potential to break Microsoft's desktop monopoly. Sun's StarOffice has an inexpensive Linux-based version that competes with Microsoft's Office productivity suite. And Web-based office applications now promoted by Google (see page 175) that do not require a Windows operating system will offer Microsoft some competition in the coming years. However, the transition to open-source and Web-based office applications will take many years because of the sunk costs of billions of spreadsheets, Word documents, and PowerPoint presentations, which cannot be easily converted to open-source office productivity suites.

Java Is Everywhere

Java is an operating system–independent, processor-independent, object-oriented programming language that has become the leading interactive programming environment for the Web. If an object moves on the Web or takes input from the user, a Java applet is likely behind it.

Java was created by James Gosling and the Green Team at Sun Microsystems in 1992 as a programming environment to support interactive cable television content delivery. Widespread use of Java began in 1995 when large numbers of people started using the World Wide Web and Internet. Nearly all Web browsers come with a Java platform built in. More recently, the Java platform has migrated into cell phones, automobiles, music players, game machines, and finally, into set-top cable television systems serving interactive content and pay-per-view services.

Java software is designed to run on any computer or computing device, regardless of the specific microprocessor or operating system the device uses. A Macintosh PC, an IBM PC running Windows, a Sun server running Unix, and even a smart cell phone or personal digital assistant can share the same Java application. For each of the computing environments in which Java is used, Sun has created a Java Virtual Machine that interprets Java programming code for that machine. In this manner, the code is written once and can be used on any machine for which there exists a Java Virtual Machine.

Java is particularly useful in network environments such as the Internet. Here, Java is used to create miniature programs called applets that are designed to reside on centralized network servers. The network delivers to client computers only the applets required for a specific function. With Java applets residing on a network, a user can download only the software functions and data that he or she needs to perform a particular task, such as analyzing the revenue from one sales territory. The user does not need to maintain large software programs or data files on his or her desktop machine.

Java is also a very robust language that can handle text, data, graphics, sound, and video, all within one program if needed. Java enables PC users to manipulate data on

Java

networked systems using Web browsers, reducing the need to write specialized software. A **Web browser** is an easy-to-use software tool with a graphical user interface for displaying Web pages and for accessing the Web and other Internet resources. Microsoft's Internet Explorer, Mozilla Firefox, and Netscape Navigator are examples. At the enterprise level, Java is being used for more complex e-commerce and e-business applications that require communication with an organization's back-end transaction processing systems.

The rapid deployment of Java was hindered in the past because of disagreements between Sun Microsystems and Microsoft over Java standards. In April 2004, under pressure from major customers such as General Motors, Microsoft agreed to stop distributing the Microsoft Java Virtual Machine (MSJVM) it had developed for its proprietary version of Java and to cooperate with Sun in the development of new technologies, including Java.

Software for Enterprise Integration

Without a doubt, the single most urgent software priority for North American firms is integration of existing legacy software applications with newer Web-based applications into a coherent single system that can be rationally managed. In the past, business firms typically developed their own custom software and made their own choices about their software platform. This strategy produced hundreds of thousands of computer programs that frequently could not communicate with other software programs, were difficult and expensive to maintain, and were nearly impossible to change quickly as business models changed.

One solution is to replace isolated systems that cannot communicate with enterprise applications for customer relationship management, supply chain management, knowledge management, and enterprise systems, which integrate multiple business processes. Chapter 12 provides a detailed description of these enterprise applications and their roles in digitally integrating the enterprise.

Not all firms can jettison all their legacy systems to convert to enterprise-wide platforms. These existing legacy mainframe applications are essential to daily operations and are very risky to change, but they can become more useful if their information and business logic can be integrated with other applications.

Some integration of legacy applications can be achieved by using special software called middleware to create an interface or bridge between two different systems. **Middleware** is software that connects two otherwise separate applications, enabling them to communicate with each other and to exchange data.

Firms may choose to write their own software to connect one application to another, but increasingly they are purchasing **enterprise application integration (EAI) software** packages to connect disparate applications or application clusters. This software enables multiple systems to exchange data through a single software hub rather than building countless custom software interfaces to link each system (see Figure 5-13). WebMethods, Tibco, SeeBeyond, BEA, and Vitria are leading enterprise application integration software vendors.

Web Services and Service-Oriented Architecture (SOA)

Enterprise application integration software tools are product-specific, meaning that they can work only with certain pieces of application software and operating systems. For example, one EAI tool to connect a specific piece of sales order entry software to manufacturing, shipping, and billing applications might not work with another vendor's order entry software. A middleware program developed by BEA systems, a large systems integrator, may not be able to communicate with another vendor's middleware application that was purchased in previous years without a large expenditure of programming and design resources. Web services seek to provide a standardized alternative for dealing with integration problems such as these by creating a communications environment that is vendor-neutral.

Web services are a set of loosely coupled software components that exchange information with one another using typical Web communication standards and languages. They can exchange information between two different systems regardless of the operating

Web browser
Middleware
Enterprise application integration
  (EAI) software
Web services

FIGURE 5-13 *Enterprise application integration (EAI) software versus traditional integration*

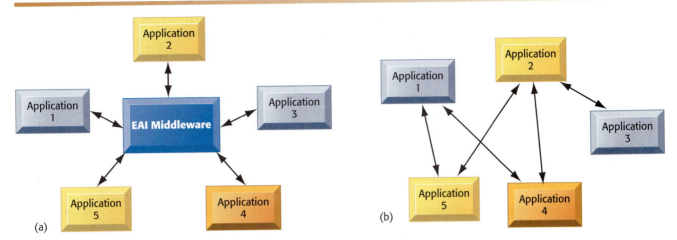

EAI software (a) uses special middleware that creates a common platform with which all applications can freely communicate with each other. EAI requires much less programming than traditional point-to-point integration (b).

systems or programming languages on which the systems are based. They can be used to develop open-standard Web-based applications linking systems of two different organizations, and they can also be used to create applications that link disparate systems within a single company. Web services are not tied to any one operating system or programming language, and different applications can use them to communicate with each other in a standard way without time-consuming custom coding.

The foundation technology for Web services is **XML**, which stands for **Extensible Markup Language**. This language was developed in 1996 by the World Wide Web Consortium (W3C, the international body that oversees the development of the Web) as a more powerful and flexible markup language than hypertext markup language (HTML) for Web pages. **Hypertext Markup Language (HTML)** is a page description language for specifying how text, graphics, video, and sound are placed on a Web page document. While HTML is limited to describing how data should be presented in the form of Web pages, XML can perform presentation, communication, and storage of data. In XML, a number is not simply a number; the XML tag specifies whether the number represents a price, a date, or a postal code. Table 5-5 provides some sample XML statements.

By tagging selected elements of the content of documents for their meanings, XML makes it possible for computers to manipulate and interpret their data automatically and perform operations on the data without human intervention. Web browsers and computer programs, such as order processing or enterprise resource planning (ERP) software, can follow programmed rules for applying and displaying the data. XML provides a standard format for data exchange, enabling Web services to pass data from one process to another.

Web services communicate through XML messages over standard Web protocols. **SOAP**, which stands for **Simple Object Access Protocol**, is a set of rules for structuring messages that enables applications to pass data and instructions to one another.

Extensible Markup Language (XML)
Hypertext Markup Language (HTML)
Simple Object Access Protocol (SOAP)

TABLE 5-5 *Examples of XML*

PLAIN ENGLISH	XML
Subcompact	<AUTOMOBILETYPE="Subcompact">
4 passenger	<PASSENGERUNIT="PASS">4</PASSENGER>
$16 800	<PRICE CURRENCY="CAD">$16 800</PRICE>

WSDL stands for **Web Services Description Language**; it is a common framework for describing the tasks performed by a Web service and the commands and data it will accept so that it can be used by other applications. **UDDI**, which stands for **Universal Description, Discovery, and Integration**, enables a Web service to be listed in a directory of Web services so that it can be easily located. Companies discover and locate Web services through this directory much as they would locate services in the yellow pages of a telephone book. Using these protocols, a software application can connect freely to other applications without custom programming for each different application with which it wants to communicate, since every application shares the same standards.

The collection of Web services that are used to build a firm's software systems constitutes what is known as a service-oriented architecture. A **service-oriented architecture (SOA)** is set of self-contained services that communicate with one another to create a working software application. Business tasks are accomplished by executing a series of these services. Software developers reuse these services in other combinations to assemble other applications as needed. In other words, SOA is an entirely new way of developing software for a firm. In the past, firms used to develop software applications to serve a specific purpose, such as calculate invoices and send out printed invoices. Often, there would be multiple programs that performed parts of or all of a task but used different code to accomplish their objectives. None of the programs could talk to one another.

An SOA environment operates more efficiently than this. For example, an "invoice service" can be written that is the only program in the firm responsible for calculating invoice information and reports. Whenever a different program in the firm needs invoice information, it can make use of this pre-defined, single invoice service.

If you want to see SOA at work in a single firm, go to Amazon.com for a demonstration. Amazon uses SOA to create a sales platform with 55 million active customers, and more than one million retail partners worldwide. Until 2001, Amazon ran a monolithic application on a Web server that created the customer interface, the vendor interface, and catalogue that operated on a single database in the backend. By 2001 this approach could not scale up, was very inflexible, and was vulnerable to failures at critical points. Today, Amazon's operation is a collection of hundreds of services delivered by a number of application servers that provide the customer interface, customer service interface, the seller interface, billing, and many third-party Web sites that run on Amazon's platform. So what you see on Amazon is the direct result of SOA services (Grey, 2006).

Here's a real-world example of an *inter-organizational* SOA at work. Dollar Rent A Car's systems use Web services for its online booking system with Southwest Airlines' Web site. Although both companies' systems are based on different technology platforms, a person booking a flight on SouthwestAir.com can reserve a car from Dollar without leaving the airline's Web site. Instead of struggling to get Dollar's reservation system to share data with Southwest's information systems, Dollar used Microsoft.NET Web services technology as an intermediary. Reservations from Southwest are translated into Web services protocols, which are then translated into formats that can be understood by Dollar's computers.

Other car rental companies have linked their information systems to airline companies' Web sites before. But without Web services, these connections had to be developed one at a time. Web services provide a standard way for Dollar's computers to talk to other companies' information systems without having to develop special links to each one. Dollar is now expanding its use of Web services to link directly to the systems of a small tour operator and a large travel reservation system as well as a wireless Web site for mobile phones and PDAs. It does not have to write new software code for each new partner's information systems or each new wireless device (see Figure 5-14).

Virtually all major software vendors such as IBM, Microsoft, Oracle, SAP, Sun, and HP provide tools and entire platforms for developing and integrating software applications using Web services. IBM includes Web service tools in its WebSphere e-business software platform, and Microsoft has incorporated Web services tools in its Microsoft. NET platform. SOA is not a universal salve for all firms, and it does raise other issues. It is not clear what services to develop at first, and even Web service applications need to be re-written

Web Services Description Language (WSDL)

Universal Description, Discovery, and Integration (UDDI)

Service-oriented architecture (SOA)

FIGURE 5-14 *How Dollar Rent A Car uses Web services*

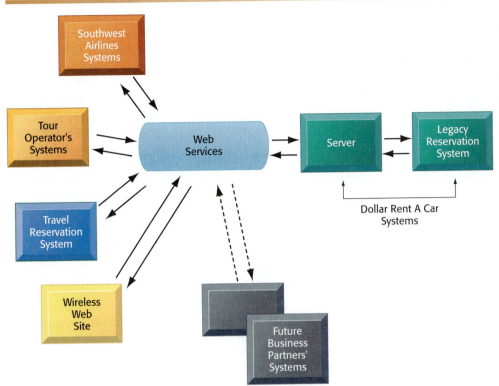

Dollar Rent A Car uses Web services to provide a standard intermediate layer of software to "talk" to other companies' information systems without having to build a separate link to each firm's systems.

as business firms develop and change. Once re-written, all the programs that use these Web services need to be tested. In addition, SOA requires IT staff to master a whole new set of tools and a new mentality about software development.

Software Trends: Ajax, Mashups, Web 2.0, and Web-Based Software Applications

Ever fill out a Web order form, make a mistake, then have to start all over again after a long wait for a new order form page to appear on your screen? Ever visit a map site, click the North arrow once, and then wait some time for an entire new page to load? Ajax is a new software technique that prevents all this inconvenience and makes the user experience more seamless. Ajax (Asynchronous JavaScript and XML) is a technique for allowing your client and the server you are working with to hold a conversation in the background, transferring your entries as they are made to the server without your awareness. Click North on a map site, such as Google Maps, and the server downloads just that part of the application that changes with no wait for an entirely new map. Google Earth, composed of photos laid out around the world similar to a map, goes even further, permitting your computer (through Ajax technology) to handle the movement around the map. Make a mistake on forms at the iHotelier.com, TJMaxx.com, or HomeGoods.com Web sites, and you will be prompted just for clarifications on those entries and will not be forced to start over again. Ajax and a related set of techniques called RIA (rich Internet applications) use JavaScript or Macromedia Flash programs downloaded to your client to maintain a nearly continuous conversation with the server you are using. While making the life of consumers much easier, Ajax and RIA are even more important for another new software development: Web-based applications.

Imagine that instead of purchasing a suite of software tools in a box for word processing and spreadsheet development, you could go out to the Web and do all your writing and calculating online using free software, in the form of Web-based tools. In fact, you don't have to imagine anymore. In 2006 Google began delivering on its promise to provide online spreadsheet and word processing, along with calendar, e-mail, and instant messaging in a suite called Google Apps for Your Domain. While initially aimed at small businesses, there is no reason that, once the bugs are worked out, Google would not try to extend this product to the same mass market where Microsoft's Office dominates (more than 90 percent of the 1.5 billion PCs worldwide). Google will encourage people to share their Microsoft Word documents and spreadsheets with one another, but first they will have to translate those documents into Google formats. Once that happens, users will no longer be so dependent on Word and Excel formats. They may end up dependent on Google formats, but Google promises to release all the tools necessary to users so they can integrate their Google applications and files into their existing infrastructure (e.g., Microsoft Office software and Microsoft Windows networks). Google will be using Ajax and related RIA tools to ensure that every time you move a cursor, or change a spreadsheet cell, you won't have to wait for the whole page to refresh itself! Besides Google, there are many enterprise software firms such as SalesForce.com, SAP, Oracle, and others that are delivering software services over the Web to client computers at their customers' sites. Increasingly over the next few years, software functionality will be delivered on the Web. Adobe's Dreamweaver Web publishing software already incorporates Ajax technology.

On a smaller scale, entrepreneurs are creating new software applications and services based on combining different online software applications. Called **mashups**, these new combined applications depend on high-speed data networks, universal communication standards, and open-source code. The idea is to take different sources and produce a new work that is "greater than" the sum of its parts.

Part of a movement called Web 2.0, and in the spirit of musical mashups, Web mashups combine the capabilities of two or more online applications to create a kind of hybrid that provides more customer value than the original sources alone. One area of great innovation is the mashup of mapping and satellite image software with local content. For instance, Paul Rademacher, a Silicon Valley programmer, opened a Web site called housingmaps.com that makes it possible to display real estate listings in local areas from Craigslist.com overlaid on Google Maps, with pushpins showing the location of each listing. The site has attracted more than half a million visitors and receives about 10 000 visits a day.

Although building communication links among software applications using Web services is not new, online mapping applications are driving a whole new set of recombinant applications. Other map- and satellite-image-based mashups are in the works, encouraged by Google and Yahoo!, both of which in 2005 released to programmers the application programming interfaces (APIs) that allow other applications to pull in information from Google's and Yahoo!'s map and satellite images. Microsoft's competing map and satellite service is called Virtual Earth. Google has also made a Javascript library called the Google AJAX Search API widely available so that its search technology can be embedded in and used by other online services—such as those offered by Toronto-based NAC Geographic Products Inc. NAC has developed a mapping and address mashup standard called Natural Area Code. Using a precise string of digits, the system will be used to locate any building anywhere. By making their service work with Google, NAC hopes to gain additional market share (Sutton, 2006).

Google's service has simplified the process of using its mapping data down to the level of inserting four lines of Javascript into a program. This simplification has made the process of integrating maps into other applications extremely easy for thousands of Web site designers. Publicly available APIs provide programmers with the tools for pulling data from many different Web sites and combining them with other information to make an entirely new Web service. The result is that instead of the Web being a collection of pages, it becomes a collection of capabilities, a platform where thousands of programmers can create new services quickly and inexpensively.

As we stated above, Web mashups are part of a movement called **Web 2.0**, second-generation interactive Web services. Web 2.0 is an expression of all the changes discussed

Mashups

Web 2.0

above, plus other changes in the way people and businesses use the Web and think about human interaction on the Web. Coined by O'Reilly Media and MediaLive International after the dot.com bubble burst in 2001, the term Web 2.0 is used to refer to newer Web applications such as blogs, wikis, RSS (rich site summary) and social bookmarking. The main differences between Web 1.0 and Web 2.0 are the new technology (such as Ajax and RSS) and the new emphasis on collaboration.

Web 2.0 applications and developers do the following (O'Reilly, 2005):

- Offer services, not packaged software, with cost-effective scalability
- Allow control over unique, hard-to-recreate data sources that get richer as more people use them
- Trust users as co-developers
- Harness collective intelligence
- Leverage the so-called long tail economy, wherein the break-even point for sales is met by ever-smaller quantities of any item, books included, that are available for sale, through customer self-service
- Provide software above the level of a single device
- Have lightweight user interfaces, development models, and business models

Software Outsourcing

Today most business firms continue to operate their legacy systems that continue to meet a business need and that would be extremely costly to replace. But they will purchase most of their new software applications from external sources.

Changing Sources of Software

In the past, most software was developed inside the firm by teams of programmers. While firms still retain sizable IT staffs, they are no longer exclusively in the software business. Instead firms today will turn over about one-third of their software development to outside developers, including enterprise software firms who will sell them pre-packaged solutions customized to their needs. Most of the outsourcing of software development is performed in Canada and the U.S., but a growing portion of outsourced software projects are completed in off-shore, low-wage regions such as India, China, Eastern Europe, Africa, and Latin America. In addition, another 15 percent of the functional software will be obtained not by buying the software but by purchasing the service—letting someone else develop the software. For instance, firms will purchase payroll processing services from application service providers, as well as sales force management services from Web providers such as SalesForce.com.

Software Packages and Enterprise Software We have already described software packages for enterprise applications as one of the major types of software components in contemporary IT infrastructures.

If **application software** is a program written for a specific application to perform functions specified by end users, an **application software package** is a prewritten commercially available set of software programs that eliminates the need for a firm to write its own software programs for certain functions, such as payroll processing or order handling.

Enterprise application software vendors such as SAP and Oracle-PeopleSoft have developed powerful software packages that can support the primary business processes of a firm worldwide, from warehousing, customer relationship management, supply chain management, and finance, to human resources. These large-scale enterprise software systems provide a single, integrated, worldwide software system for firms at a cost much less than they would pay if they developed it themselves. These systems are so complex and require so much experience that very few corporations

Application software
Application software package

have the expertise required to develop these packages. Chapter 12 discusses enterprise systems in detail.

Application Service Providers   A second external source of software is online application service providers (ASPs). An **application service provider (ASP)** is a business that delivers and manages applications and computer services from remote computer centres to multiple users using the Internet or a private network. Instead of buying and installing software programs, subscribing companies can rent the same functions from these services. Users pay for the use of this software either on a subscription per-user or per-transaction basis.

The ASP's solution combines packaged software applications and all the related hardware, system software, network, and other infrastructure services that the customer otherwise would have to purchase, integrate, and manage independently. The ASP customer interacts with a single entity instead of an array of technologies and service vendors.

The time-sharing services of the 1970s, which ran applications such as payroll on their computers for other companies, were an earlier version of this application-hosting. But today's ASPs run a wider array of applications than these earlier services and deliver many of these software services over the Web. As Web-based services, servers perform the bulk of the processing, and the only essential program needed by users is a desktop computer running either thin client software (operating systems for a minimally furnished computer) or a Web browser.

Large- and medium-sized businesses are using ASPs for enterprise systems, sales force automation, or financial management, and small businesses are using them for functions such as invoicing, tax calculations, electronic calendars, and accounting. ASP vendors are starting to provide tools to integrate the applications they manage with clients' internal systems or with applications hosted by different vendors. In addition, enterprise software vendors such as SAP and Oracle have developed ASP versions of their enterprise software packages (such as www.mysap.com) for small- and medium-sized firms that do not want to run enterprise software on their own servers.

Some companies find it much easier to rent software from the ASP firm and avoid the expense and difficulty of installing, operating, and maintaining the hardware and software for complex systems, such as enterprise resource planning (ERP) systems. The ASP contracts guarantee a level of service and support to ensure that the software is available and working at all times. Today's Internet-driven business environment is changing so rapidly that getting a system up and running in three months instead of six could mean the difference between success and failure.

Application service providers also enable small- and medium-sized companies to use applications that they otherwise could not afford. Small and midsize businesses have been drawn to these software-as-service solutions because the costs per user tend to be much less expensive than licensed on-premise software, which can cost anywhere from several hundred thousand dollars to several million dollars up front. But application service providers are not necessarily the best solution, even for these small companies. The Window on Technology explores this issue by examining two companies' experiences with hosted software, and why the results were so different.

Software Outsourcing   A third external source of software is **outsourcing**, in which a firm contracts custom software development or maintenance of existing legacy programs to outside firms, frequently firms that operate offshore in low-wage areas of the world. According to the Gartner Group, worldwide outsourcing totalled more than $723 billion in 2005 (McDougall, 2006). The largest expenditure here is paid to domestic firms providing middleware, integration services, and other software support that are often required to operate larger enterprise systems.

For example, in early 2003, BP Canada outsourced many of its applications to EDS, a global IT outsourcing and consulting company. BP Canada needed to replace its mainframe and mainframe applications. EDS moved BP Canada to a Web-based solution, decreasing costs of one application, payroll, by half while maintaining quality (EDS, 2007).

Application service provider (ASP)

Outsourcing

WINDOW ON MANAGEMENT

Air Canada Uses Neoware to Streamline Its Airline Reservation System

Air Canada flies more than 25 million passengers to more than 150 destinations on more than 325 aircraft. Its 40 000 employees around the world include those who handle reservations in person, over the telephone, and online. It is no wonder that Air Canada's reservation system is its heart and soul—without a well-functioning reservation system, Air Canada would be left with half-filled airplanes and unhappy customers.

Air Canada's reservation system was first upgraded back in 1961, and the complexity of the system grew almost as fast as Air Canada itself. In the 1970s, the green-screen terminals required robust protocols to communicate with the mainframe housing the reservation system. Without existing appropriate standards, Air Canada developed their own: ALC100. Then, in the 1980s and 1990s, the technology field exploded. By the new millennium Air Canada's reservation system had become outdated. It was using a wide variety of communication standards and green-screen terminals that were not upgradeable. Many of the terminal parts were no longer manufactured.

In 2001 Air Canada sought out an outsourcer and consultant to address issues of outdated hardware and lack of standardization on appropriate—and generally accepted—communication protocols. IBM was hired, and the result was a decision to move to TCP/IP. Bob Eardley, Air Canada's senior director of IT transformation solutions, says, "There was a great opportunity to further re-enable the airline. We determined that moving to Internet Protocol (IP) was the best vehicle to do so."

The Internet Protocol was developed in the early 1970s by Vinton Cerf and Robert Kahn under contract to the U.S. government. Today, the two protocols known as TCP/IP (Transmission Control Protocol and Internet Protocol) are the most widely accepted communication protocols around the world and are the protocols on which the Internet is based.

Air Canada also realized that their employees typically needed access to computers with a limited range of functions. "We didn't really require fully functional PCs [for people] with highly specialized functions where we can control the information," said Eardley. Most Air Canada employees do not need a broad variety of applications or functions to do their jobs, so Air Canada decided to change its architecture to one based on **thin clients**, PCs without large hard drives or much RAM, which have just enough resources to do the jobs for which they were intended.

With the new thin clients, Air Canada staff can access manuals, parts for repair, or data, all through their desktops—even though the information is stored on the company network. Air Canada decided to replace about 2000 green-screen terminals and PCs—about 15 per cent of its desktops, located at about 300 service points—with thin client network devices.

With IBM's support, Air Canada chose Neoware thin client devices at its passenger, cargo, and operational facilities and its reservation centres in North America, Asia, and Europe. Grant Fengstad, Director of IT Architecture and Strategy at Air Canada, said, "It was critical to maintain access to existing legacy systems while migrating our IT infrastructure. Neoware was able to customize a solution that included our Java-based emulator software."

Thin clients have few, if any, moving parts to wear out or break, making them a much better investment than PCs, which have moving parts that age quickly. According to Fengstad, "Our thin client appliances never go down, and they are quicker to boot up." Fengstad says the total cost of ownership of a thin client device is 20 to 30 per cent lower than for a typical PC. The users still get the same functionality they need, and, with the new network architecture, users can now access the Internet and Air Canada's Web-based applications.

Neoware makes use of a variety of thin-client specific utilities that permit software and operating system upgrades to be made over the Web. And like Air Canada, it's taking off. Neoware was listed by IT Business.ca as one of the "top 5 vendors to watch in 2007."

To Think About

1. What were the main reasons Air Canada decided to replace both its network architecture and the communication protocols being used?

2. Why was the total cost of ownership for the thin clients less than for the PCs? What management, organization, and technology factors account for this difference?

3. If your company was considering using thin client technology, what management, organization, and technology factors should be addressed when making your decision?

MIS in Action

Explore the Web sites of RightNow (**www.rightnow.com**) and Siebel CRM on Demand (**www.oracle.com/crmondemand/index.html**) offered by Oracle.

1. Compare the services offered by both companies.

2. How could a business benefit from using these services?

3. What steps would a business need to take to use these hosted CRM systems?

Sources: Patrick Boake, "Neoware Streamlines Air Canada Reservation System," *The Globe and Mail*, June 2, 2004; IT Business.ca, "Five Vendors to Watch in 2007," **www.itbusiness.ca/it/client/en/CDN/DetailNewsPrint.asp?id=42203**, accessed August 1, 2007; and Neoware, "Case Study: Air Canada," available **www.neoware.com/solutions/canada.html**; Neoware, **www.neoware.com**, accessed August 1, 2007.

Offshore firms provide a growing proportion of software services, about 2 percent of the combined software plus software services budget. Up until recently, this type of software development involved lower-level maintenance, data entry, and call centre operations, but with the growing sophistication and experience of offshore firms, particularly in India, more and more new-program development is taking place offshore. Chapter 9 discusses offshore software outsourcing in greater detail.

5.4 Management Issues

Creating and managing a coherent IT infrastructure raises multiple challenges: dealing with scalability and technology change, management and governance, and making wise infrastructure investments.

Dealing with Infrastructure Change

As firms grow, they can quickly outgrow their infrastructure. As firms shrink, they can get stuck with excessive infrastructure purchased in better times. How can a firm remain flexible when most of the investments in IT infrastructure are fixed-cost purchases and licences? How well does the infrastructure scale up or down?

Management and Governance

A long-standing issue among information system managers and CEOs has been the question of who will control and manage the firm's IT infrastructure. Should departments and divisions have the responsibility of making their own information technology decisions, or should IT infrastructure be centrally controlled and managed? What is the relationship between central information systems management and business unit information systems management? How will infrastructure costs be allocated among business units? Each organization will need to arrive at answers based on its own needs.

Making Wise Infrastructure Investments

IT infrastructure is a major investment for the firm. If too much is spent on infrastructure, it lies idle and constitutes a drag on the firm's financial performance. If too little is spent, important business services cannot be delivered and the firm's competitors (who spent just the right amount) will outperform the underinvesting firm. How much should the firm spend on infrastructure? This question is not easy to answer.

A related question is whether a firm should purchase its own IT infrastructure components or rent them from external suppliers. As we discussed earlier, a major trend in computing platforms—both hardware and software—is to outsource to external providers. The decision either to purchase your own IT assets or rent them from external providers is typically called the *rent versus buy* decision.

Competitive Forces Model for IT Infrastructure Investment Figure 5-15 illustrates a competitive forces model you can use to address the question of how much your firm should spend on IT infrastructure.

Market Demand for your Firm's Services Make an inventory of the services you currently provide to customers, suppliers, and employees. Survey each group, or hold focus groups to find out if the services you currently offer are meeting the needs of each group. For example, are customers complaining of slow responses to their queries about price and availability? Are employees complaining about the difficulty of finding the right information for their jobs? Are suppliers complaining about the difficulties of discovering your production requirements?

Thin clients

FIGURE 5-15   *Competitive forces model for IT infrastructure*

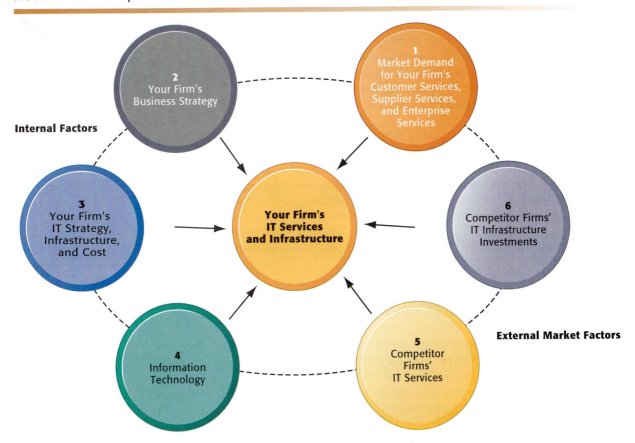

There are six factors you can use to answer the question, "How much should our firm spend on IT infrastructure?"

Your Firm's Business Strategy   Analyze your firm's five-year business strategy, and try to assess what new services and capabilities will be required to achieve strategic goals.

Your Firm's IT Strategy, Infrastructure, and Cost   Examine your firm's information technology plans for the next five years, and assess its alignment with the firm's business plans. Determine total IT infrastructure costs. You will want to perform a *total cost of ownership* analysis (see the discussion on page 182). If your firm has no IT strategy, you will need to devise one that takes into account the firm's five-year strategic plan.

Information Technology Assessment   Is your firm behind the technology curve or at the bleeding edge of information technology? Both situations are to be avoided. It is usually not desirable to spend resources on advanced technologies that are still experimental, often expensive, and sometimes unreliable. You want to spend on technologies for which standards have been established, where IT vendors are competing on cost, not design, and where there are multiple suppliers. However, you do not want to put off investment in new technologies or allow competitors to develop new business models and capabilities based on the new technologies.

Competitor Firms' IT Services   Try to assess what technology services competitors offer to customers, suppliers, and employees. Establish quantitative and qualitative measures to compare them to those of your firm. If your firm's service levels fall short, your company is at a competitive disadvantage. Look for ways your firm can excel at service levels.

Competitor Firms' IT Infrastructure Investments   Benchmark your expenditures for IT infrastructure against your competitors. Many companies are quite public about their innovative expenditures on IT. If competing firms try to keep IT expenditures secret, you may be able to find IT investment information in public companies' 52-109F1 management information circular annual reports to the federal government when those expenditures impact a firm's financial results.

Your firm does not necessarily need to spend as much as, or more than, your competitors. Perhaps it has discovered much less expensive ways of providing services, and this can lead to a cost advantage. Alternatively, your firm may be spending far less than competitors and experiencing commensurate poor performance and losing market share.

Total Cost of Ownership of Technology Assets In benchmarking your firm's expenditures on IT infrastructure with that of your competitors, you will need to consider a wide range of costs. The actual cost of owning technology resources includes the original cost of acquiring and installing hardware and software, as well as ongoing administration costs for hardware and software upgrades, maintenance, technical support, training, and even utility and real estate costs for running and housing the technology. The **total cost of ownership (TCO)** model can be used to analyze these direct and indirect costs to help firms determine the actual cost of specific technology implementations.

Table 5-6 describes the most important TCO components to consider in a TCO analysis.

When all these cost components are considered, the TCO for a PC might run up to three times the original purchase price of the equipment. Hidden costs for support staff, downtime, and additional network management can make distributed client/server architectures—especially those incorporating handheld computers and wireless devices—more expensive than centralized mainframe architectures.

Hardware and software acquisition costs account for only about 20 percent of TCO, so managers must pay close attention to administration costs to understand the full cost of the firm's hardware and software. It is possible to reduce some of these administration costs through better management. Many large firms are saddled with redundant, incompatible hardware and software because their departments and divisions have been allowed to make their own technology purchases.

These firms could reduce their TCO through greater centralization and standardization of their hardware and software resources. Companies could reduce the size of the

Total cost of ownership (TCO)

TABLE 5-6 *Total Cost of Ownership (TCO) Cost Components*

INFRASTRUCTURE COMPONENT	COST COMPONENTS
Hardware acquisition	Purchase price of computer hardware equipment, including computers, terminals, storage, and printers
Software acquisition	Purchase or licence of software for each user
Installation	Cost to install computers and software
Training	Cost to provide training for information systems specialists and end users
Support	Cost to provide ongoing technical support, help desks, and so forth
Maintenance	Cost to upgrade the hardware and software
Infrastructure	Cost to acquire, maintain, and support related infrastructure, such as networks and specialized equipment (including storage backup units)
Downtime	Cost of lost productivity if hardware or software failures cause the system to be unavailable for processing and user tasks
Space and energy	Real estate and utility costs for housing and providing power for the technology

information systems staff required to support their infrastructure if they minimize the number of different computer models and pieces of software that employees are allowed to use. In a centralized infrastructure, systems can be administered from a central location, and troubleshooting can be performed from that location (David, Schuff, and St. Louis, 2002).

Summary

1. **Define IT infrastructure and describe the components and levels of IT infrastructure.**

   IT infrastructure is the shared technology resources that provide the platform for the firm's specific information system applications. IT infrastructure includes hardware, software, and services that are shared across the entire firm. Major IT infrastructure components include computer hardware platforms, operating system platforms, enterprise software platforms, networking and telecommunications platforms, database management software, Internet platforms, and consulting services and systems integrators. You can better understand the business value of IT infrastructure investments by viewing IT infrastructure as a platform of services as well as a set of technologies.

2. **Identify and describe the stages of IT infrastructure evolution.**

   There are five stages of IT infrastructure evolution. IT infrastructure in the earliest stage consisted of specialized "electronic accounting machines" that were primitive computers used for accounting tasks (1930 to 1950). IT infrastructure in the mainframe period (1959 to present) consists of a mainframe performing centralized processing that could be networked to thousands of terminals and eventually some decentralized and departmental computing using networked minicomputers. The personal computer period (1981 to present) in IT infrastructure has been dominated by the widespread use of stand-alone desktop computers with office productivity tools. The predominant infrastructure in the client/server period (1983 to present) consists of desktop or laptop clients networked to more powerful server computers that handle most of the data management and processing. The enterprise Internet computing period (1992 to present) is defined by large numbers of PCs linked into local area networks, and by the growing use of standards and software to link disparate networks and devices into an enterprise-wide network so that information can flow freely across the organization.

3. **Identify and describe the technology drivers of IT infrastructure evolution.**

   A series of technology developments has driven the continuing transformation of IT infrastructure. Moore's Law deals with the exponential increase in processing power and decline in the cost of computer technology, stating that every 18 months the power of microprocessors doubles and the price of computing falls by half. The Law of Mass Digital Storage deals with the exponential decrease in the cost of storing data, stating that the number of kilobytes of data that can be stored on magnetic media for $1 doubles roughly every 15 months. Metcalfe's Law helps explain the mushrooming use of computers by showing that a network's value to participants grows exponentially as the network takes on more members. Also driving exploding computer use is the rapid decline in costs of communication and growing agreement in the technology industry to use computing and communications standards.

4. **Assess contemporary computer hardware platform trends.**

   Contemporary hardware and software platform trends address the overwhelming need to reduce IT infrastructure costs, to use computing resources more efficiently, to integrate information across platforms, and to provide a higher level of flexibility and service to the firm and its customers. The integration of computing and telecommunications platforms, grid computing, edge computing, and on-demand computing demonstrate that, increasingly, computing is taking place over a network. Grid computing involves connecting geographically remote computers into a single network to create a computational grid that combines the computing power of all the computers on the network to attack large computing problems. Edge computing balances the processing load for Web-based applications by distributing parts of the Web content, logic, and processing among multiple servers. On-demand computing also depends on networks for firms to purchase additional processing power from large computer service firms and to have that power delivered when they need it over a network. In autonomic computing, computer systems have capabilities for automatically configuring and repairing themselves. Virtualization organizes computing resources so that their use is not restricted by physical configuration or geographic location. Server virtualization enables companies to run more than one operating system at the same time. A multicore processor is a microprocessor to which two or more processors have been attached for enhanced performance, reduced power consumption and more efficient simultaneous processing of multiple tasks.

5. *Assess contemporary software platform trends.*

Contemporary software platform trends include the growing use of Linux, open-source software, Java; software for enterprise integration, and software outsourcing. Open-source software is produced and maintained by a global community of programmers and is downloadable for free. Linux is a powerful, resilient open-source operating system that can run on multiple hardware platforms and is used widely to run Web servers. Java is an operating system– and hardware-independent programming language that is the leading interactive programming environment for the Web. Software for enterprise integration includes enterprise applications and middleware such as enterprise application integration (EAI) software and Web services. Unlike EAI software, Web services are loosely coupled software components based on open Web standards that are not product-specific and can work with any application software and operating system. They can be used as components of Web-based applications to link the systems of two different organizations or to link disparate systems of a single company. Mashups are new software applications and services based on combining different online software applications using high-speed data networks, universal communication standards, and open-source code. Companies are purchasing their new software applications from outside sources, including software packages, by outsourcing custom application development to an external vendor (that may be offshore) or by renting software services from an application service provider.

6. *Evaluate the challenges of managing IT infrastructure and possible management solutions.*

Major infrastructure challenges include dealing with infrastructure change, agreeing on infrastructure management and governance, and making wise infrastructure investments. Solution guidelines include using a competitive forces model to determine how much to spend on IT infrastructure and where to make strategic infrastructure investments and establishing the total cost of ownership (TCO) of information technology assets. The total cost of owning technology resources includes not only the original cost of computer hardware and software but also costs for hardware and software upgrades, maintenance, technical support, and training.

Key Terms

Application server software, 152
Application service provider (ASP), 178
Application software, 177
Application software package, 177
Autonomic computing, 166
Bit, 146
Blade servers, 161
Byte, 146
Central processing unit (CPU), 145
Client/server computing, 152
Clients, 152
Communications device, 146
Computer, 145
Edge computing, 166
Enterprise application integration (EAI) software, 172
Extensible Markup Language (XML), 173
Firewall, 166
Firewire, 148
Grid computing, 165
Hypertext Markup Language (HTML), 173
Input Device, 146
Java, 171
Legacy systems, 163
Linux, 161

Mainframe, 150
Mashup, 176
Megahertz, 147
Microprocessors, 147
Middleware, 172
Minicomputers, 150
Moore's Law, 153
Multicore processor, 168
Multitiered (N-tier) client/server architecture, 152
Nanotechnology, 156
On-demand computing, 165
Open-source software, 162
Operating system, 146
Output Device, 146
Outsourcing, 178
Parallel port, 148
Port, 148
Primary Storage, 145
Random access memory (RAM), 147
Read-only memory (ROM), 147
Reduced instruction set computing (RISC), 148
Scalability, 169
Secondary Storage, 145

Serial port, 148
Server, 152
Service-oriented architecture (SOA), 174
Simple Object Access Protocol (SOAP), 173
Storage area network (SAN), 162
Technology standards, 158
Thin clients, 179
Total cost of ownership (TCO), 182
Universal Description, Discovery, and Integration (UDDI), 174
Universal serial bus (USB) port, 148
Unix, 159
Utility computing, 165
Virtualization, 167
Web 2.0, 176
Web browser, 172
Web hosting service, 163
Web server, 152
Web Services Description Language (WSDL), 174
Web services, 172
Windows, 153
Wintel PC, 150

Review Questions

1. *Define IT infrastructure from both a technology and a services perspective. Which services does IT infrastructure comprise?*

2. *List each of the eras in IT infrastructure evolution, and describe their distinguishing characteristics.*

3. *Define and describe the following: Web server, application server, multitiered client/server architecture.*

4. *What are Moore's Law and the Law of Mass Digital Storage? What aspects of infrastructure change do they help explain?*

5. *How do network economics, declining communications costs, and technology standards affect IT infrastructure and the use of computers?*

6. *List and describe the components of IT infrastructure that firms need to manage.*

7. *Compare grid computing and edge computing.*

8. *How can businesses benefit from on-demand computing? From autonomic computing?*

9. *How can businesses benefit from virtualization and multi-core processors?*

10. *Define and describe open-source software and Linux. How can they benefit businesses?*

11. *What is Java? Why is it important today?*

12. *What is the difference between enterprise application integration software and Web services? What role is played by XML in Web services?*

13. *What are software mashups? How do they benefit businesses?*

14. *Name and describe the three external sources for software.*

15. *Name and describe the management challenges posed by IT infrastructure.*

16. *How would using a competitive forces model and calculating the total cost of ownership (TCO) of technology assets help firms make infrastructure investments?*

Discussion Questions

1. *Why is selecting computer hardware and software for the organization an important management decision? What management, organization, and information technology issues should be considered when selecting computer hardware and software?*

2. *Should organizations use application service providers (ASPs) for all their software needs? Why or why not? What management, organization, and information technology factors should be considered when making this decision?*

3. *What should be the role of open-source software in an organization? What organizational factors (e.g., size, support) should enter into the decision to use open-source software?*

4. *How can newer technologies, such as the technologies found in Web 2.0, best be used by organizations? How does management ensure that these technologies fit in with the organization's mission?*

Teamwork: Evaluating Server Operating Systems

Form a group with three or four of your classmates. One group should research and compare the capabilities and costs of Linux versus the most recent version of the Windows operating system for servers. Another group should research and compare the capabilities and costs of Linux versus Unix. Each group should present its findings to the class, using electronic presentation software if possible.

Learning Track Modules

How Computer Hardware and Software Work. If you would like to review basic hardware and software concepts, you will find a Learning Track Module on this topic on MyMISLab.

The Open-Source Software Initiative. If you want to learn more about the Open Source Definition from the Open Source Initiative and the history of open-source software, you will find a Learning Track Module on this topic on MyMISLab.

For online exercises, please visit www.pearsoned.ca/mymislab.

HANDS-ON **MIS**   **Application Exercises**

The projects in this section give you hands-on experience in using spreadsheet software to help a real-world company make a rent vs. buy decision about new manufacturing software, using spreadsheet software to evaluate alternative desktop systems, and using Web research to budget for a sales conference.

Improving Decision Making:
Making the Rent vs. Buy Decision for Software

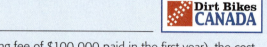

Software skills: Spreadsheet formulas, electronic presentation software (optional)
Business skills: Technology rent vs. buy decision

This project provides an opportunity for you to help a real-world company make a decision about whether to rent or buy new technology. You will use spreadsheet software to compare the total three-year cost of licensing and maintaining new manufacturing software or renting the software from an application service provider.

Dirt Bikes Canada would like to implement new production planning, quality control, and scheduling software for use by 25 members of its manufacturing staff. Management is trying to determine whether to purchase the software from a commercial vendor along with any hardware required to run the software or to use a hosted software solution from an application service provider. (The hosted software runs on the ASP's computer.) You have been asked to help management with this rent vs. buy decision by calculating the total cost of each option over a three-year period.

The costs of purchasing the software (actually for purchasing a licence from the vendor to use its software package) include the initial purchase price of the software (a licensing fee of $100 000 paid in the first year), the cost of implementing and customizing the software in the first year ($20 000), one new server to run the software (a first-year purchase of $4000), one information systems specialist devoted half-time to supporting the software ($55 000 in full-time annual salary and benefits, with a 3 percent annual salary increase each year after the first year), user training in the first year ($10 000), and the cost of annual software upgrades ($5000).

The costs of renting hosted software are the rental fees ($2500 annually per user), implementation and customization costs ($12 000 in the first year), and training ($10 000 in the first year).

1. Use your spreadsheet software to calculate the total cost of renting or purchasing this software over a three-year period. Identify the lowest-price alternative that meets Dirt Bikes Canada's requirements.

2. What other factors should Dirt Bikes Canada consider besides cost in determining whether to rent or buy the hardware and software?

3. (Optional) If possible, use electronic presentation software to summarize your findings for management.

Improving Decision Making:
Using a Spreadsheet to Evaluate Hardware and Software Options

Software skills: Spreadsheet formulas
Business skills: Technology pricing

In this exercise, you will use spreadsheet software to calculate the cost of alternative desktop systems.

You have been asked to obtain pricing information on hardware and software for an office of 30 people. Using the Internet, get pricing for 30 PC desktop systems (monitors, computers, and keyboards) manufactured by IBM, Dell, and HP/Compaq as listed at their respective corporate Web sites. (For the purposes of this exercise, ignore the fact that desktop systems usually come with preloaded software packages.) Also obtain pricing on 15 monochrome desktop printers manufactured by HP and by Xerox. Each desktop system must satisfy the minimum specifications shown in the following table:

Minimum Desktop Specifications

Processor speed	3 GHz
Hard drive	250 GB
RAM	1 GB
CD-ROM speed	48 speed
Monitor (diagonal measurement)	17 inches

Each desktop printer must satisfy the minimum specifications shown in the following table:

Minimum Monochrome Printer Specifications

Print speed	12 pages per minute
Print resolution	600 x 600
Network ready?	Yes
Maximum price/unit	$1000

After pricing the desktop systems and printers, obtain pricing on 30 copies of the most recent versions of Microsoft Office, Lotus SmartSuite, and Sun StarOffice desktop productivity packages, and on 30 copies of Microsoft Windows XP Professional Edition or Windows Vista. The application software suite packages come in various versions, so be sure that each package contains programs for word processing, spreadsheet analysis, database analysis, graphics preparation, and e-mail.

Prepare a spreadsheet showing your research results for the desktop systems, for the printers, and for the software. Use your spreadsheet software to determine the desktop system, printer, and software combination that will offer both the best performance and pricing per worker. Because every two workers will share one printer (15 printers/30 systems), assume only half a printer cost per worker in the spreadsheet. Assume that your company will take the standard warranty and service contract offered by each product's manufacturer.

Which configuration has the lowest cost? What other issues should you consider in deciding which configuration to purchase?

Improving Decision Making:
Using Web Research to Budget for a Sales Conference

Software skills: Internet-based software
Business skills: Researching transportation and lodging costs

In this exercise, you will use software at various online travel sites to arrange transportation and lodging for a large sales force to attend a sales conference at two alternative locations. You will use that information to calculate total travel and lodging costs and decide where to hold the conference.

The Foremost Composite Materials Company is planning a two-day sales conference for October 15 and 16, starting with a reception on the evening of October 14. The conference consists of all-day meetings that the entire sales force, numbering 125 sales representatives and their 16 managers, must attend. Each sales representative requires his or her own room, and the company needs two common meeting rooms, one large enough to hold the entire sales force plus a few visitors (200) and the other able to hold half the force (75). Management has set a budget of $85 000 for the representatives' room rentals. The hotel must also have such services as overhead and computer projectors as well as business centre and banquet facilities. It also should have facilities for the company representatives to be able to work in their rooms and to enjoy themselves in a swimming pool or gym facility. This year, the company would like to hold the conference in either Fredericton or Saint John, New Brunswick.

Foremost usually likes to hold such meetings in Hilton- or Marriott-owned hotels. Use the Hilton and Marriott Web sites to select a hotel in whichever city that will enable the company to hold its sales conference within its budget.

Link to the two sites' home pages, and search them to find a hotel that meets Foremost's sales conference requirements. Once you have selected the hotel, locate flights arriving the afternoon prior to the conference because the attendees will need to check in the day before and attend the reception the evening prior to the conference. Your attendees will be coming from Vancouver (54), Calgary (32), Edmonton (22), Montreal (19), and Halifax (14). Determine costs of each airline ticket from these cities. When you are finished, create a budget for the conference. The budget will include the cost of each airline ticket, the room cost, and $60 per attendee per day for food.

1. What is your final budget?
2. Which did you select as the best hotel for the sales conference and why?

CASE STUDY **Edge Computing Powers MuchMusic and Much More**

What would you do if your Web site had surges when it was pushed beyond capacity, but most of the time was readily accessible by the average number of visitors? Edge computing can provide the means to deal with access surges.

CHUM Limited, a Canadian subsidiary of CTVglobemedia specializing in entertainment, owns MuchMusic. CHUM's original content is also seen in more than 120 countries, on television stations other than MuchMusic, which include CityTV,

A-Channel, Canadian Learning Television (CLT), Book Television, and Bravo!, in addition to MuchMusic and MuchMusic Retro. When special events, such as breaking news and events, push CHUM's Web servers beyond their limits, CHUM's subsidiaries—32 radio stations, 12 local television stations, and 21 specialty channels—rely on edge computing to provide the excess server capacity needed to meet demand.

Before the move to edge computing, CHUM's Web site almost crashed during the Pope's 2002 visit to Toronto, when many Ontarians were logging on to keep up with the breaking news about the Pope's visit. CHUM now uses Akamai EdgeSuite Delivery, a package to push access demand out to edge servers to increase traffic by 20 percent on their news site. According to Dale Fallon, Manager of Operations at CHUM Interactive, "By transferring our infrastructure demands to Akamai, we improved the site's performance which resulted in an increase in traffic." The change also had financial benefits, said Fallon: "Akamai enabled us to handle traffic surges during special live events, like the 2003 SARS Relief Concert with the Rolling Stones and AC/DC and the MuchMusic Video Awards, without spending money on maintenance and infrastructure."

CHUM's Web site doubled its speed using EdgeSuite Delivery and achieved a 20 percent savings in infrastructure and maintenance costs, up to $5000 per month. Akamai offloaded about 80 percent of CHUM's streaming traffic (whereby CHUM can permit visitors to download news, music, and program videos).

So what is Akamai, and how does its EdgeSuite Delivery application work?

Akamai is a U.S.-based company founded by Danny Lewin, a young computer whiz who received his master's degree from MIT. After working at IBM, Lewin founded Akamai in the late 1990s. Lewin was killed on September 11, 2001, when the flight he was on, American Airlines Flight 11, crashed into the World Trade Center in New York. His company has since continued to flourish under new leadership.

Akamai uses a platform of 20 000 servers located in 71 countries. These servers are specially equipped to provide edge computing to its clients. Akamai handles tens of billions (yes—billions!) of Web interactions for more than 2000 private and public organizations. But these interactions are critical for Akamai's clients. According to the Boston Consulting Group, "28 percent of Web users do not return to a company's Web site if it does not perform sufficiently well, and a further 6 percent do not even go to the affiliated retail store anymore." It is easy to see that having a fast Web site that is easy to access is critical to today's digital organizations. Akamai has the world's largest distributed computing platform, which uses applied mathematics and algorithms to distribute their clients' workload.

Two companies whose Web services have enhanced by Akamai would include CGA-Canada and Cathay Pacific Airways. Cathay Pacific increased online booking and extranet adoption while saving about US $1 000 000 annually. With nearly 35 000 travel agents regularly accessing Cathay Pacific's Web site, performance degraded, forcing users to wait a long time for reservations and other travel information; this led to abandonment (as predicted by Boston Consulting Group, above) and lost business. After the move to edge computing, Cathay Pacific saw online bookings increase by 100 percent annually; with more online sales, Cathay Pacific was also able to save about US $1 500 000 on their call centre.

When the Certified General Accountants Association of Canada (CGA-Canada) decided to move from CD-based education to online content delivery, they turned to Akamai to beef up their Web site performance. Now they deliver the educational portion of their program via distance education to 24 000 students in Canada, China, Hong Kong, and the Caribbean. Today their Web site can handle 3.5 million hits while delivering 14 GB of data, all through the use of edge computing. The move to edge computing reduced the CGA's infrastructure costs by 40 percent and virtually eliminated system crashes.

Akamai is not the only vendor to offer edge computing services. Sun Microsystems also offers this capability. Saskatoon's Black Sun, an Internet service provider with more than 5000 customers, uses Sun's edge platform to provide the company with increased speed, low prices, and low repair costs.

As Web traffic increases annually, more and more organizations, both public and private, may need to consider using edge computing as the platform for their Web infrastructure. Increased speed, capacity, and reliability, along with reduced costs, are potential benefits of edge computing. Edge computing appears to provide a true "web" of servers for the Web for many organizations.

Sources: Sun Microsystems, "Computing at the Edge," **www.sun.com/software/grid/whitepaper.edge.pdf**, accessed March 2, 2007; Akamai, "Case Study: CGA-Canada Delivers 24/7 Interactive Online Learning to Students Worldwide While Reducing Infrastructure Costs by 40%." **www.akamai.com/html/customers/case_study_cga_ canada.html**, accessed February 27, 2007; Akamai, "Cathay Pacific Airways Increases Online Bookings and Extranet Adoption—Saving Over $1,000,000 Annually," **www.akamai.com/html/customers/case_study_cathay.html**, accessed February 27, 2007; Akamai, "EdgeSuite Delivery," **www.akamai.com/html/solutions/edgesuite_delivery.html**, accessed February 27, 2007; "About Akamai," **www.akamai.com/html/about/index.html**, accessed February 27, 2007; "Akamai Remembers Danny Lewin," **www.akamai.com/html/about/management_dl.html**, accessed February 27, 2007; "Case Study: Akamai Helps Canadian Media Company Boost Traffic, Reduce Costs," **www.streamingmedia.com/article.asp?id=9134&page=2&c=1**accessed February 27, 2007; "High Performance Streaming Increases Site Traffic and Reduces Costs," **www.akamai.com/html/customers/case_study_chum.html**, accessed February 27, 2007; "CHUM Limited Overview," **www.chumlimited.com**, accessed February 27, 2007; and "Company Information,**www.chumlimited.com/corporate/investorrelations.asp**, accessed April 11, 2007.

CASE STUDY QUESTIONS

1. Why did CHUM need to modify its Web infrastructure?

2. What is the relationship of information technology to CHUM's business strategy? How is edge computing related to that strategy?

3. Evaluate CHUM's decision to use edge computing? What are the advantages to offloading their infrastructure needs to Akamai? Are there any disadvantages? Was doing so a good solution? Explain your answer.

4. What other organizations could benefit from implementing edge computing?

CHAPTER 6

Databases and Information Management

LEARNING OBJECTIVES

After completing this chapter, you will be able to do the following:

1. Describe basic file organization concepts and the problems of managing data resources in a traditional file environment.

2. Describe the principles of a database management system and the features of a relational database.

3. Apply important database design principles.

4. Evaluate tools and technologies for providing information from databases to improve business performance and decision making.

5. Assess the role of information policy, data administration, and data quality assurance in the management of organizational data resources.

OPENING **CASE** | Bonjour Québec

Bonjour Québec.com is the main portal for those travelling in Quebec. By using the Quebec tourism Web site (see page 191), visitors can access information and make reservations for hotels and other forms of housing, restaurants, festivals, and entertainment. Tourists can also see a wealth of images of what their trip will be like. Bonjour Québec.com is a partnership between Tourisme Québec and Bell Canada, with Bell Canada running the technology. At the heart of the Web site is a massive database that contains all the information needed to run the site.

This portal for travellers to Quebec, now the largest in the Canadian travel industry, is driven by sophisticated database technology.

Although the promotional budget for Tourisme Québec was decreasing, the technology budget was being significantly increased. This permitted Tourisme Québec to overhaul their Web site and add reservations capability. It took almost a year and a half to develop the partnership that became Bonjour Québec, with Bell Canada employing four subcontractors to work on the project during start-up. Those suppliers couldn't meet the deadlines and requirements of the project and so did not continue with the project.

Bell Canada's former subsidiary, Travellinks, was not suitable for most of the Bonjour Québec.com development, but in working with Tourisme Québec, Bell Canada was able to use some of the technological enhancements they had already developed for Travellinks. Although Travellinks did not have a satisfactory search engine, there were many other features it was able to implement. Dynamic mapping,

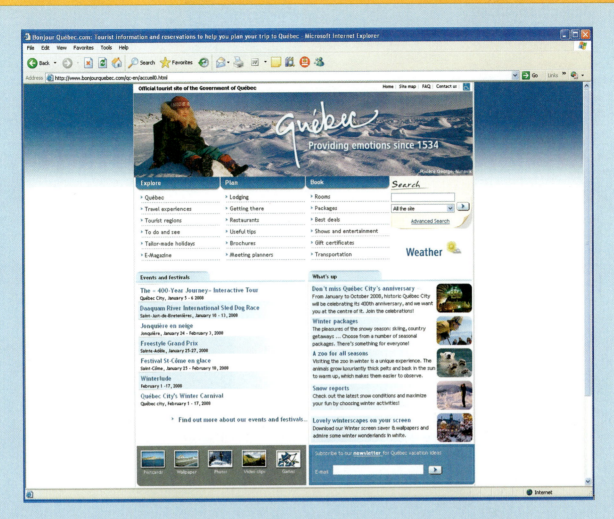

such as geographic cross-referral, enables visitors to pick a region or even a specific neighbourhood to find accommodation, restaurants, and lists of festivals and activities to attend. There is also an online library. All this requires a large and very sophisticated database, capable of cataloguing different types of data, such as photographs, graphical images, addresses, and links to the reservations system and individual Web sites of the places and activities it is presenting to the visitor. The database used by Bonjour Québec.com is the largest in the Canadian tourism industry.

Many sites like Bonjour Québec exist, and most permit businesses (e.g., hotels, restaurants, etc.) to register themselves online. This often results in distortions and inaccuracies in the data. At Bonjour Québec.com, however, clerks enter the data, thereby ensuring the uniformity of records. Data capture and the system's many functions can be performed in 99 languages.

Bonjour Québec.com measures its success by several methods, one of which is Web traffic. The updated Web site has reduced telephone traffic by 30 percent, saving Tourisme Québec money by reducing the number of tourist service operators required to answer inquiries. The Web site has more than 9 million visitors annually, with many linking from it into the reservation system.

The project has met with some resistance from other Web sites and travel agencies that are more or less in competition with Bonjour Québec.com for the travellers' dollars. But by developing a multimedia database that can handle customer information as well as business and not-for-profit information, Bonjour Québec.com was able to meet the needs of Tourisme Québec in promoting tourism in the province.

Sources: Vincent Sabourin, Michel Vézina, and Louise Côté, "The Adoption of Electronic Affairs in the Tourism Industry: Success Key Factors and Barriers to Adoption," **www.cefrio.qc.ca/english/projets/Documents/ bonjour_eng_fnl.pdf,** accessed March 25, 2007; Government of Canada, "Bonjour Québec.com—E-Business Case Study," **strategis.ic.gc.ca/epic/site/ dsib-tour.nsf/en/qq00113e.html**, accessed March 25, 2007; "Reserve Québec with Bonjour Québec.com," **www.bulletin.enligne.gouv.qc.ca/ archives/2004/07_juillet_aout/english/print_en/p_index.html**, accessed March 25, 2007; and "Travel Canada," **www.metrocanada.com/ travelcanada.htm**, accessed March 25, 2007.

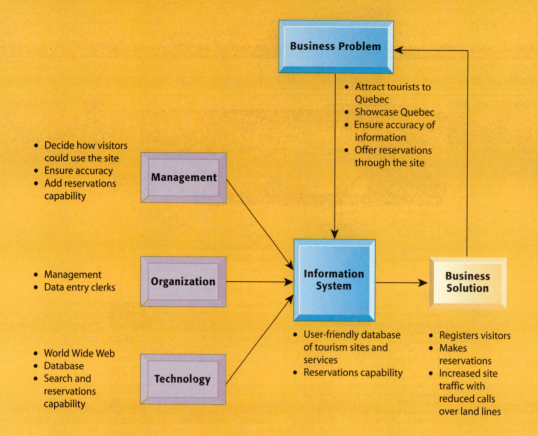

- **Business Problem**
  - Attract tourists to Quebec
  - Showcase Quebec
  - Ensure accuracy of information
  - Offer reservations through the site

- Decide how visitors could use the site
- Ensure accuracy
- Add reservations capability

Management

- Management
- Data entry clerks

Organization

- World Wide Web
- Database
- Search and reservations capability

Technology

Information System

- User-friendly database of tourism sites and services
- Reservations capability

Business Solution

- Registers visitors
- Makes reservations
- Increased site traffic with reduced calls over land lines

Bonjour Québec.com's experience described in the opening case illustrates the importance of data management and database systems for business. This tourist Web site has experienced phenomenal growth. But its future growth and business performance depend on what it can or can't do with its customer data. How businesses store, organize, and manage their data has a tremendous impact on organizational effectiveness.

The chapter-opening Business Challenges diagram calls attention to important points raised by this case and

this chapter. Data about Quebec businesses and potential tourists has been stored in a number of different databases that can now be merged for e-mailing tourists with news and special announcements for registered businesses. Management decided that the tourism site's business strategy needed to focus on creating ease of use for the customer and ease of finding requested information, which necessitated development of the massive, multimedia database.

HEADS UP

This chapter focuses on data management and how businesses use database technology to achieve their objectives. Once businesses use database management systems to properly organize their data, the data can be analyzed. The resulting information can be used to develop new businesses, achieve operational excellence, inform management decision making, and help the firm fulfill its regulatory reporting requirements. Entire businesses, such as United Parcel Service, credit card companies, and Google, are based on databases.

It would not be an overstatement to say that databases are the foundation of business today and that most businesses would fail should their databases cease to exist.

- If your career is in finance and accounting, you will be working with databases of financial transactions, such as payments, invoices, or credit history. If your job is in finance, you will work with massive databases housing data about securities prices, investment portfolios, and economic statistics.

- If your career is in human resources, you will work with databases maintaining data on employees, benefits plans, compensation plans, training programs, and compliance with governmental regulations on health, safety, and equal employment opportunity.

- If your career is in information systems, you will play a key role in providing data management tools and expertise to the firm. You will design databases, implement and maintain database technology, and help promote data administration policies and procedures.

- If your career is in manufacturing, production, logistics, or operations management, you will be working with large databases with data on finished goods, raw materials in inventory, suppliers, product components, product quality, schedules, and goods in transit that can be used for supply chain management.

- If your career is in sales and marketing, you will be using databases for tracking customer purchases, analyzing customer data for targeted marketing campaigns, or identifying profitable customers and products.

6.1 Organizing Data in a Traditional File Environment

An effective information system provides users with accurate, timely, and relevant information. Accurate information is free of errors. Information is timely when it is available to decision makers when it is needed. Information is relevant when it is useful and appropriate for the types of work and decisions that require it.

You might be surprised to learn that many businesses do not have timely, accurate, or relevant information because the data in their information systems have been poorly organized and maintained. That's why data management is so essential. To understand the problem, we will look at how information systems arrange data in computer files and traditional methods of file management.

File Organization Concepts

A computer system organizes data in a hierarchy that starts with bits and bytes and progresses to fields, records, files, and databases (see Figure 6-1). A *bit* represents the smallest unit of data a computer can handle. A group of bits, called a *byte*, represents a single character, which can be a letter, a number, or another symbol. A grouping of characters into a word, a group of words, or a complete number (such as a person's name or age) is called a **field**. A group of related fields, such as the student's name, the course taken, the date, and the grade, comprises a **record**; a group of records of the same type is called a **file**.

For example, the records in Figure 6-1 could constitute a student course file. A group of related files makes up a **database**. The student course file illustrated in Figure 6-1 could be grouped with files on students' personal histories and financial backgrounds to create a student database.

A record describes an entity. An **entity** is a person, place, thing, or event about which we store and maintain information. Each characteristic or quality describing a particular entity is called an **attribute**. For example, Student_ID, Course, Date, and Grade are attributes of the entity COURSE. The specific values that these attributes can have are found in the fields of the record describing the entity COURSE.

Problems with the Traditional File Environment

In most organizations, data files and systems tended to grow independently without a company-wide plan. Accounting, finance, manufacturing, human resources, and sales and

Field
Record
File
Database
Entity
Attribute

FIGURE 6-1 *The data hierarchy*

A computer system organizes data in a hierarchy that starts with the bit, which represents either a 0 or a 1. Bits can be grouped to form a byte to represent one character, number, or symbol. Bytes can be grouped to form a field, and related fields can be grouped to form a record. Related records can be collected to form a file, and related files can be organized into a database.

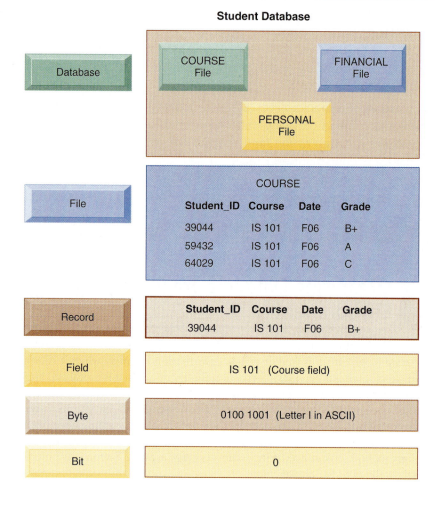

FIGURE 6-2 *Traditional file processing*

The use of a traditional approach to file processing encourages each functional area in a corporation to develop specialized applications and files. Each application requires a unique data file that is likely to be a subset of the master file. These subsets of the master file lead to data redundancy and inconsistency, processing inflexibility, and wasted storage resources.

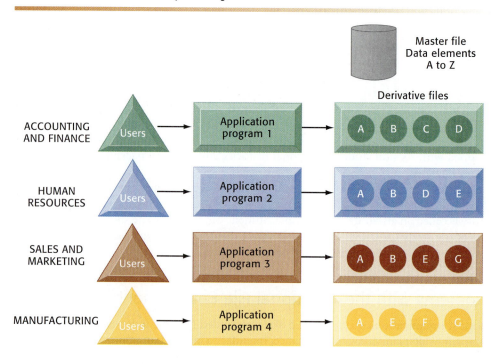

marketing all developed their own systems and data files. Figure 6-2 illustrates the traditional approach to information processing.

Each application, of course, required its own files and its own computer program to operate. For example, the human resources department might have a personnel master file, a payroll file, a medical insurance file, a pension file, a mailing list file, and so forth, until tens, perhaps hundreds, of files and programs existed. The finance department might also have a payroll file, a pension file, and an employee master list to run the payroll. In the company as a whole, this process led to multiple master files created, maintained, and operated by separate divisions or departments. As this process goes on for 5 or 10 years, the organization is saddled with hundreds of programs and applications that are very difficult to maintain and manage. The resulting problems are data redundancy and inconsistency, program-data dependence, inflexibility, poor data security, and an inability to share data among applications.

Data Redundancy and Inconsistency **Data redundancy** is the presence of duplicate data in multiple data files so that the same data are stored in more than one place or location. Data redundancy occurs when different groups in an organization independently collect the same piece of data and store it independently of one another. Data redundancy wastes storage resources and also leads to **data inconsistency**, where the same attribute may have different values. For example, in instances of the entity COURSE illustrated in Figure 6-1, the Date may be updated in some systems but not in others. The attribute Student_ID may have different names in different systems throughout the organization. Some systems might use Student_ID, and others might use ID, for example.

Additional confusion might result from using different coding systems to represent values for an attribute. For instance, the sales, inventory, and manufacturing systems of a clothing retailer might use different codes to represent clothing size. One system might represent clothing size as "extra large," while another might use the code "XL" for the same purpose. The resulting confusion would make it difficult for companies to create customer relationship management, supply chain management, or enterprise systems that integrate data from different sources.

Program-Data Dependence **Program-data dependence** refers to the coupling of data stored in files and the specific programs required to update and maintain those files such that changes in programs require changes to the data. Every traditional computer program has to describe the location and nature of the data with which it works. In a traditional file environment, any change in a software program could require a change in the data accessed by that program. One program might be modified from a six-digit to a nine-digit postal code. If the original data file were changed from six-digit to nine-digit postal codes, then other programs that required the six-digit postal code would no longer work properly. Such changes could cost millions of dollars to implement properly.

Lack of Flexibility A traditional file system can deliver routine scheduled reports after extensive programming efforts, but it cannot deliver ad hoc reports or respond to unanticipated information requirements in a timely fashion. The information required by ad hoc requests is somewhere in the system but may be too expensive to retrieve. Several programmers might have to work for weeks to put together the required data items in a new file.

Poor Security Because there is little control or management of data, access to and dissemination of information may be out of control. Management may have no way of knowing who is accessing or even making changes to the organization's data.

Lack of Data Sharing and Availability Because pieces of information in different files and different parts of the organization cannot be related to one another, it is virtually impossible for information to be shared or accessed in a timely manner. Information cannot flow freely across different functional areas or different parts of the organization. If users find different values of the same piece of information in two different systems, they may not want to use these systems because they cannot trust the accuracy of their data.

Data redundancy

Data inconsistency

Program-data dependence

6.2 The Database Approach to Data Management

Database technology cuts through many of the problems of traditional file organization. A more rigorous definition of a **database** is a collection of data organized to serve many applications efficiently by centralizing the data and controlling redundant data. Rather than storing data in separate files for each application, data are stored so as to appear to users as being stored in only one location. A single database services multiple applications. For example, instead of a corporation storing employee data in separate information systems and separate files for personnel, payroll, and benefits, the corporation could create a single common human resources database.

Database Management Systems

A **database management system (DBMS)** is software that permits an organization to centralize data, manage the data efficiently, and provide access to the stored data by application programs. The DBMS acts as an interface between application programs and the physical data files. When the application program calls for a data item, such as gross pay, the DBMS finds this item in the database and presents it to the application program. Using traditional data files, the programmer would have to specify the size and format of each data element used in the program and then tell the computer exactly where they were located.

The DBMS relieves the programmer or end user from the task of understanding where and how the data are actually stored by separating the logical and physical views of the data. The *logical view* presents data as they would be perceived by end users or business specialists while the *physical view* shows how data are actually organized and structured on physical storage media.

The database management software makes the physical database available for different logical views required by users. For example, for the human resources database illustrated in Figure 6-3, a benefits specialist might require a view consisting of the employee's name, social insurance number, and supplemental health insurance coverage. A payroll department staff member might need data such as the employee's name, social insurance number, gross pay, and net pay. The data for all these views are stored in a single database, where they can be more easily managed by the organization.

Database (rigorous definition)

Database management system (DBMS)

FIGURE 6-3   *Human resources database with multiple views*

A single human resources database provides many different views of data, depending on the information requirements of the user. Illustrated here are two possible views, one of interest to a benefits specialist and one of interest to a member of the company's payroll department.

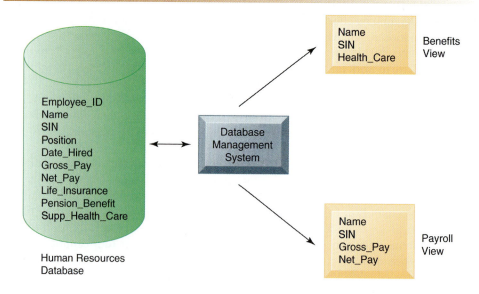

How a DBMS Solves the Problems of the Traditional File Environment

A DBMS reduces data redundancy and inconsistency by minimizing isolated files in which the same data are repeated. The DBMS may not enable the organization to eliminate data redundancy entirely, but it can help control redundancy. Even if the organization maintains some redundant data, using a DBMS eliminates data inconsistency because the DBMS can help the organization ensure that every occurrence of redundant data has the same values.

The DBMS uncouples programs and data, enabling data to stand on their own. Access and availability of information will be increased and program development and maintenance costs reduced because users and programmers can perform ad hoc queries of data in the database. The DBMS enables the organization to centrally manage data, their use, and security.

Relational DBMS Contemporary DBMS use different database models to keep track of entities, attributes, and relationships. The most popular type of DBMS today for PCs as well as for larger computers and mainframes is the **relational DBMS**. Relational databases represent data as two-dimensional tables (called relations). Tables may be referred to as files. Each table contains data on an entity and its attributes. Microsoft Access is a relational DBMS for desktop systems while DB2, Oracle Database, and Microsoft SQL Server are relational DBMS for large mainframes and midrange computers. MySQL is a popular open-source DBMS, and Oracle Database Lite is a DBMS for small handheld computing devices.

Now we will look at how a relational database organizes data about suppliers and parts (see Figure 6-4). The database has a separate table for the entity SUPPLIER and a table for

Relational DBMS

FIGURE 6-4   *Relational database tables*

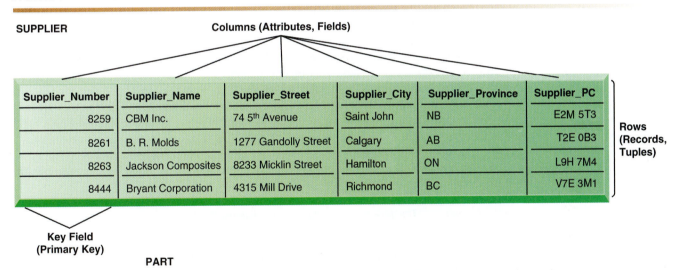

A relational database organizes data in the form of two-dimensional tables. Illustrated here are tables for the entities SUPPLIER and PART showing how they represent each entity and its attributes. Supplier_Number is a primary key for the SUPPLIER table and a foreign key for the PART table.

the entity PART. Each table consists of a grid of columns and rows of data. Each individual element of data for each entity is stored as a separate field, and each field represents an attribute for that entity. Fields in a relational database are also called columns. For the entity SUPPLIER, the supplier number, name, street, city, province, and postal code are stored as separate fields within the SUPPLIER table and each field represents an attribute for the entity SUPPLIER.

The actual information about a single supplier that resides in a table is called a row. Rows are commonly referred to as records, or in very technical terms, as **tuples**. Data for the entity PART have their own separate table.

The field for Supplier_Number in the SUPPLIER table uniquely identifies each record so that the record can be retrieved, updated, or sorted, and it is called a **key field**. Each table in a relational database has one field that is designated as its **primary key**. This key field is the unique identifier for all the information in any row of the table, and this primary key cannot be duplicated. Supplier_Number is the primary key for the SUPPLIER table, and Part_Number is the primary key for the PART table. Note that Supplier_Number appears in both the SUPPLIER and PART tables. In the SUPPLIER table, Supplier_Number is the primary key. When the field Supplier_Number appears in the PART table, it is called a **foreign key** and is essentially a look-up field to look up data about the supplier of a specific part.

Operations of a Relational DBMS Relational database tables can be combined easily to deliver data required by users, provided that any two tables share a common data element. Suppose we wanted to find in this database the names and addresses of suppliers that could provide us with part number 137 or part number 150. We would need information from two tables: the SUPPLIER table and the PART table. Note that these two files have a shared data element: Supplier_Number.

In a relational database, three basic operations, as shown in Figure 6-5, are used to develop useful sets of data: select, project, and join. The *select* operation creates a subset consisting of all records (rows) in the table that meet stated criteria. In our example, we want to select records (rows) from the PART table where the Part_Number equals 137 or 150. The *join* operation combines relational tables to provide the user with more information than is available in individual tables. In our example, we want to join the now-shortened PART table (only parts 137 or 150 will be presented) and the SUPPLIER table into a single new table.

The *project* operation creates a subset consisting of columns in a table, permitting the user to create new tables that contain only the information required. In our example, we

Tuples
Key field
Primary key
Foreign key

FIGURE 6-5   *The three basic operations of a relational DBMS*

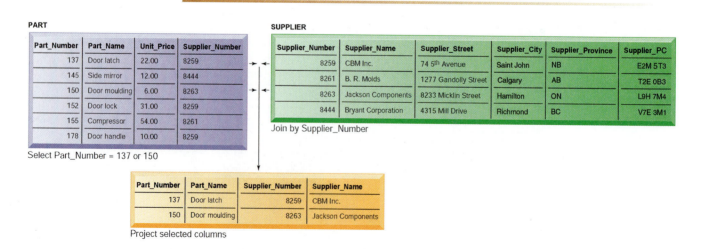

The select, project, and join operations enable data from two different tables to be combined and only selected attributes to be displayed.

want to extract from the new table only the following columns: Part_Number, Part_Name, Supplier_Number, and Supplier_Name.

Hierarchical and Network DBMS You may run across older systems that use a hierarchical or network DBMS. A hierarchical DBMS models one-to-many relationships while a network DBMS models many-to-many relationships. Hierarchical and network DBMS are no longer used for building new database applications. They are much less flexible than relational DBMS and do not support ad hoc, natural language-like inquiries for information.

Relational DBMS have much more flexibility in providing data for ad hoc queries, combining information from different sources, and adding new data and records without disturbing existing programs and applications. However, these systems slow down if they require many accesses to the data stored on disk to carry out the select, join, and project commands. Of course, the database can be fine-tuned to speed up prespecified queries.

Object-Oriented DBMS Many applications today, such as that for Bonjour Québec described at the beginning of the chapter, require databases that can store and retrieve not only records containing numbers and characters, but also drawings, images, photographs, voice, and full-motion video. DBMS designed for organizing structured data into rows and columns are not well suited to handling graphics-based or multimedia applications. Object-oriented databases are better suited for this purpose. For instance, an architectural firm deals mostly with objects and drawings rather than structured text records.

An **object-oriented database management system (OODBMS)** stores the data and procedures that act on those data as objects that can be automatically retrieved and shared. OODBMS are becoming popular because they can be used to manage the various multimedia components or Java applets used in Web applications, which typically integrate pieces of information from a variety of sources.

Although object-oriented databases can store more complex types of information than relational DBMS, they are relatively slow compared with relational DBMS for processing large numbers of transactions or records. Hybrid **object-relational DBMS** systems are now available to provide capabilities of both object-oriented and relational DBMS.

Capabilities of Database Management Systems

A DBMS includes capabilities and tools for organizing, managing, and accessing the data in the database. The most important are its data definition language, data dictionary, and data manipulation language.

DBMS have a **data definition** language to specify the structure of the content of the database. It is used to create database tables and define the characteristics of the fields in each table. This information about the database would be documented in a **data dictionary**. A data dictionary is an automated or manual file that stores definitions of data elements and their characteristics.

Microsoft Access and most other database management software have a built-in rudimentary data dictionary capability that displays information about the name, description, size, type, format, and other properties of each field in a table when it is in Design view or when the Documenter capability is employed. Data dictionaries for large corporate databases may capture additional information, such as ownership (who in the organization is responsible for maintaining the data); authorization; security; and the individuals, business functions, programs, and reports that use each data element (see Figure 6-6).

Querying and Reporting DBMS includes tools for accessing and manipulating information in databases. Most DBMS have a specialized language called a **data manipulation language** that is used to add, change, delete, and retrieve the data in the database.

Object-oriented database management system (OODBMS)

Object-relational DBMS

Data definition

Data dictionary

Data manipulation language

FIGURE 6-6 *Sample data dictionary report*

The sample data dictionary report for a human resources database provides helpful information, such as the size of the data element, which programs and reports use it, and which group in the organization is the owner responsible for maintaining it.

NAME: Salary

DESCRIPTION: Employee's annual salary
SIZE: 9 bytes
TYPE: N (Numeric)
DATE CHANGED: 1/1/05
OWNERSHIP: Compensation

UPDATE SECURITY: Site Personnel
ACCESS SECURITY: Manager, Compensation Planning
Manager, Human Resources Planning
Manager, Equal Opportunity Affairs
Manager, Benefits Department

BUSINESS FUNCTIONS USED BY: Compensation
HR Planning
Employment
Insurance
Pension and RPP
PROGRAMS USING: PI01000
PI02000
PI03000

REPORTS USING: Salary Increase Tracking Report
Salary Review Listing
Pension Reference Listing

This language contains commands that permit end users and programming specialists to extract data from the database to satisfy information requests and develop applications. The most prominent data manipulation language today is **Structured Query Language**, or **SQL**. Figure 6-7 illustrates the SQL query that would produce the results found in Figure 6-5.

Users of DBMS for large and midrange computers, such as DB2, Oracle, or SQL Server, would employ SQL to retrieve information they needed from the database. Microsoft Access also uses SQL, but it provides its own set of user-friendly tools for querying databases and for organizing data from databases into more polished reports. In fact most other database management systems, including those housed on mainframes and midrange computers, also have these tools available.

In Microsoft Access, you will find Query Wizard and Query Design View features that enable users to create queries by identifying the tables, fields, and results they want, and then selecting the rows from the database that meet particular criteria. These actions in turn are translated into SQL commands to be used by the "back-end" of MS Access.

Structured Query Language (SQL)

FIGURE 6-7 *Example of an SQL query*

Illustrated here are the SQL statements for a query to select suppliers for parts 137 or 150. They produce a list with the same results as Figure 6-5.

```
SELECT PART.Part_Number, PART.Part_Name, SUPPLIER.Supplier_Number,
SUPPLIER.Supplier_Name
FROM PART, SUPPLIER
WHERE PART.Supplier_Number = SUPPLIER.Supplier_Number AND
Part_Number = 137 OR Part_Number = 150;
```

FIGURE 6-8   *An Access query*

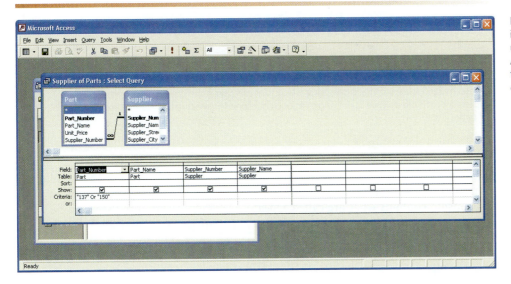

Illustrated here is how the query in Figure 6-7 would be constructed using query-building tools in the MS Access Query Design View. It shows the tables, fields, and selection criteria used for the query.

Figure 6-8 illustrates how the same query as the SQL query to select parts and suppliers would be constructed using the Query Design View.

Microsoft Access and other DBMS include capabilities for report generation so that the data of interest can be displayed in a more structured and polished format than would be possible just by querying. Crystal Reports is a popular report generator for large corporate DBMS that can also be used with Access. Access also has capabilities for developing desktop system applications. These include tools for creating data entry screens, reports, and developing the logic for processing transactions.

Designing Databases

To create a database, you must understand the relationships among the data, the type of data that will be maintained in the database, how the data will be used, and how the organization will need to change to manage data from a company-wide perspective. The database requires both a conceptual design and a physical design. The conceptual, or logical, design of a database is an abstract model of the database from a business perspective, while the physical design shows how the database is actually arranged on direct-access storage devices.

Normalization and Entity-Relationship Diagrams

The conceptual database design describes how the data elements in the database are to be grouped. The design process identifies relationships among data elements and the most efficient way of grouping data elements together to meet business information requirements. This process also identifies redundant data elements and the groupings of data elements required for specific application programs. Groups of data are organized, refined, and streamlined until an overall logical view of the relationships among all the data elements in the database emerges.

To use a relational database model effectively, complex groupings of data must be streamlined to minimize redundant data elements and awkward many-to-many relationships. The process of creating small, stable, yet flexible and adaptive data structures from complex groups of data is called **normalization**. Figures 6-9 and 6-10 illustrate this process.

In the particular business modelled here, an order can have more than one part, but only one supplier provides each part. If we build a relation called ORDER with all the

Normalization

FIGURE 6-9   *An unnormalized relation for order*

ORDER (Before Normalization)

| Order_Number | Order_Date | Part_Number | Part_Name | Unit_Price | Part_Quantity | Supplier_Number | Supplier_Name | Supplier_Street | Supplier_City | Supplier_Province | Supplier_PC |

An unnormalized relation contains repeating groups. For example, there can be many parts and suppliers for each order. There is only a one-to-one correspondence between Order_Number and Order_Date.

fields included here, we would have to repeat the name and address of the supplier for every part on the order, even though the order is for parts from a single supplier. This relationship contains what are called *repeating data groups* because there can be many parts on a single order to a given supplier. A more efficient way to arrange the data is to break down ORDER into smaller relations, each of which describes a single entity. If we go step by step and normalize the relation ORDER, we end up with the relations illustrated in Figure 6-10.

Database designers document their data model with an **entity-relationship diagram**, illustrated in Figure 6-11. This diagram illustrates the relationship between the entities ORDER, LINE_ITEM, PART, and SUPPLIER. The boxes represent entities. The lines connecting the boxes represent relationships.

A line connecting two entities that ends in two short marks designates a one-to-one relationship. A line connecting two entities that ends with a crow's foot topped by a short mark indicates a one-to-many relationship. Figure 6-11 shows that one ORDER can contain many LINE_ITEMs. (A PART can be ordered many times and appear many times as a line item in a single order.) Each PART can have only one SUPPLIER, but many PARTs can be provided by the same SUPPLIER.

It cannot be emphasized enough: If the business does not get its data model right, the system will not be able to serve the business well. The company's systems will not be as effective as they could be because they will have to work with data that may be inaccurate, incomplete, or difficult to retrieve. Understanding the organization's data and how they should be represented in a database is perhaps the most important lesson you can learn from this course.

Entity-relationship diagram

FIGURE 6-10   *Normalized tables created from order*

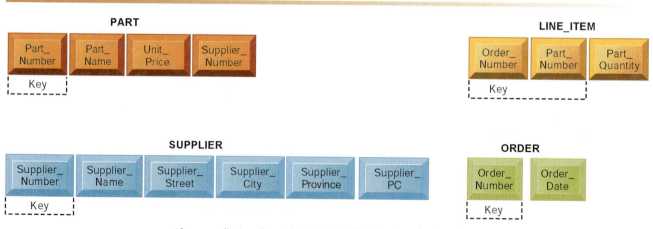

PART

| Part_Number | Part_Name | Unit_Price | Supplier_Number |
| Key | | | |

LINE_ITEM

| Order_Number | Part_Number | Part_Quantity |
| Key | | |

SUPPLIER

| Supplier_Number | Supplier_Name | Supplier_Street | Supplier_City | Supplier_Province | Supplier_PC |
| Key | | | | | |

ORDER

| Order_Number | Order_Date |
| Key | |

After normalization, the original relation ORDER has been broken down into four smaller relations. The relation ORDER is left with only two attributes and the relation LINE_ITEM has a combined, or concatenated, key consisting of Order_Number and Part_Number.

FIGURE 6-11   *An entity-relationship diagram*

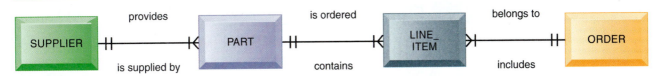

This diagram shows the relationships between the entities ORDER, LINE_ITEM, PART, and SUPPLIER that might be used to model the database in Figure 6-10.

Distributing Databases Database design also considers how the data are to be distributed. Information systems can be designed with a centralized database that is used by a single central processor or by multiple processors in a client/server network. Alternatively, the database can be distributed. A **distributed database** is one in which data is stored in more than one physical location.

There are two main methods of distributing a database (see Figure 6-12). In a *partitioned* database, parts of the database are stored and maintained physically in one location and other parts are stored and maintained in other locations (see Figure 6-12a) so that each remote processor has the necessary data to serve its local area. Changes in local files can be justified with the central database on a batch basis, often at night. Another strategy is to *replicate* (that is, duplicate in its entirety) the central database (Figure 6-12b) at all remote locations. For example, Lufthansa Airlines replaced its centralized mainframe database with a replicated database to make information more immediately available to flight dispatchers. Any change made to Lufthansa's Frankfurt DBMS is automatically replicated in New York and Hong Kong. This strategy also requires updating the central database during off-hours.

Distributed systems reduce the vulnerability of a single, massive central site. They increase service and responsiveness to local users and often can run on smaller, less-expensive computers; however, local databases can sometimes depart from central data standards and definitions, and they pose security problems by widely distributing access to sensitive data. Database designers need to weigh these factors in their decisions.

Distributed database

FIGURE 6-12   *Distributed databases*

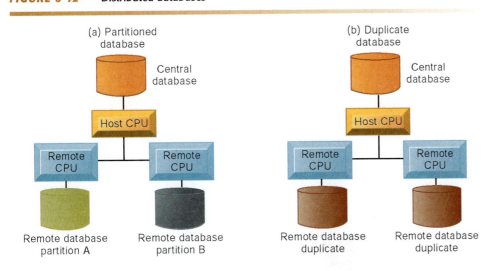

There are alternative ways of distributing a database. The central database can be partitioned (a) so that each remote processor has the necessary data to serve its own local needs. The central database also can be replicated (b) at all remote locations.

6.3

Using Databases to Improve Business Performance and Decision Making

Businesses use their databases to keep track of basic transactions, such as paying suppliers, processing orders, keeping track of customers, and paying employees. But they also need databases to provide information that will help the company run the business more efficiently and help managers and employees make better decisions. If a company wants to know which product is the most popular or who is its most profitable customer, the answer lies in the data.

For example, by analyzing data from customer credit card purchases, Earls Restaurants, a Western Canadian restaurant chain, might learn that quality was more important than price for most of its customers, who were college-educated and liked fine wine. Acting on this information, the chain could introduce more vegetarian dishes, more seafood selections, and more expensive wines, raising sales significantly.

In a large company, with large databases or large systems for separate functions, such as manufacturing, sales, and accounting, special capabilities and tools are required for analyzing vast quantities of data and for accessing data from multiple systems. These capabilities include data warehousing, data mining, and tools for accessing internal databases through the Web.

Data Warehouses

Suppose you wanted concise, reliable information about current operations, trends, and changes across the entire company. If you worked in a large company, obtaining this might be difficult because data are often maintained in separate systems, such as sales, manufacturing, and accounting. Some of the data you need might be found in the sales system, and other pieces might be in the manufacturing system. Many of these systems are older legacy systems that use outdated data management technologies or file systems where information is difficult for users to access.

You might have to spend an inordinate amount of time locating and gathering the data you need, or you would be forced to make your decision based on incomplete knowledge. If you want information about trends, you might also have trouble finding data about past events because most firms only make their current data immediately available. Data warehousing addresses these problems.

What Is a Data Warehouse? A **data warehouse** is a mammoth database that stores current and historical data of potential interest to decision makers throughout the company. The data originate in many core operational transaction systems, such as systems for sales, customer accounts, and manufacturing, and may include data from Web site transactions. The data warehouse consolidates and standardizes information from different operational databases so that the information can be used across the enterprise for management analysis and decision making.

Figure 6-13 illustrates how a data warehouse works. The data warehouse makes the data available for anyone to access as needed, but it cannot be altered. A data warehouse system also provides a range of ad hoc and standardized query tools, analytical tools, and graphical reporting facilities. Many firms use intranet portals to make the data warehouse information widely available throughout the firm.

Data warehouse
Data mart

Data Marts Companies often build enterprise-wide data warehouses, where a central data warehouse serves the entire organization, or they may create smaller, decentralized warehouses called data marts. A **data mart** is a subset of a data warehouse in which a summarized or highly focused portion of the organization's data is placed in a separate database for a specific population of users. For example, a company might develop marketing and sales data marts to deal with customer information. A data mart typically focuses on a single subject area or line of business, so it usually can be constructed more rapidly and at a lower cost than an enterprise-wide data warehouse.

FIGURE 6-13   *Components of a data warehouse*

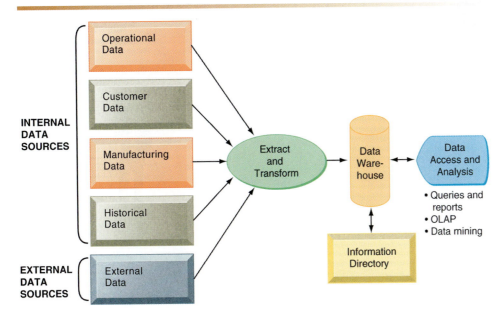

The data warehouse extracts current and historical data from multiple operational systems inside the organization. These data are combined with data from external sources and reorganized into a central database designed for management reporting and analysis. The information directory provides users with information about the data available in the warehouse.

Business Intelligence, Multidimensional Data Analysis, and Data Mining

Once data have been captured and organized in data warehouses and data marts, they are available for further analysis. A series of tools enables users to analyze these data to see new patterns, relationships, and insights that are useful for guiding decision making. These tools for consolidating, analyzing, and providing access to vast amounts of data to help users make better business decisions are often referred to as **business intelligence (BI)**. Principal tools for business intelligence include software for database query and reporting, tools for multidimensional data analysis (online analytical processing), and data mining.

When we think of *intelligence* as applied to humans, we typically think of people's ability to combine learned knowledge with new information and change behaviours in such a way that they succeed at their task or adapt to a new situation. Likewise, business intelligence provides firms with the capability to amass information; develop knowledge about customers, competitors, and internal operations; and change decision-making behaviour to achieve higher profitability and other business goals.

For instance, the Best Western Heidelberg Inn, located in Lethbridge, Alberta, is a member of one of the world's largest hotel chains. Wayne Dwornik is responsible for developing long-lasting business relationships with corporate clients to increase hotel occupancy rates. Using Maximizer, customer-relationship management (CRM) software that is based on a finely tuned database of customer data, Best Western saw its occupancy rate increase by 12 percent in only one year. Dwornik can target his contacts with e-mail messages containing information they may find valuable, keeping Best Western in the forefront of his potential clients' thinking. According to Dwornik, "the best way of reaching out and contacting corporate travellers including construction firms, federal employees, oil and gas pipeline operators, is via e-mail." The CRM software tracks details of past stays, telephone conversations, responses to previous e-mails, and special events such as birthdays or anniversaries; this helps to further adapt the message that goes to the clients. This type of business intelligence quickly becomes part of a business' strategy.

Figure 6-14 illustrates how business intelligence works. The firm's operational databases keep track of the transactions generated by running the business. These databases feed data to the data warehouse. Managers use business intelligence tools to find patterns and meanings in the data. Managers then act on what they have learned from analyzing the data by making more informed and intelligent business decisions.

Business intelligence (BI)

FIGURE 6-14   Business intelligence

A series of analytical tools works with data stored in databases to find patterns and insights for helping managers and employees make better decisions to improve organizational performance.

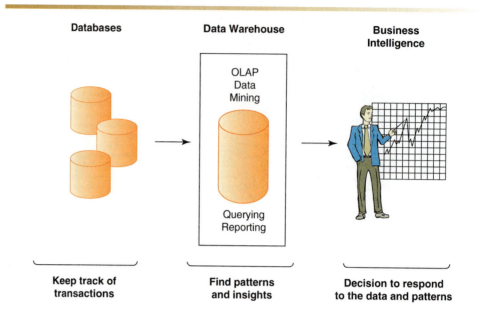

This section will introduce you to the most important business intelligence technologies and tools. We'll provide more detail about business intelligence applications in Chapter 14.

Online Analytical Processing (OLAP) Suppose your company sells four different products—nuts, bolts, washers, and screws—in the East, West, and Prairie regions. If you wanted to ask a fairly straightforward question, such as how many washers sold during the past quarter, you could easily find the answer by querying your sales database. But what if you wanted to know how many washers were sold in each of your sales regions and compare actual results with projected sales?

To obtain the answer, you would need **online analytical processing (OLAP)**. OLAP supports multidimensional data analysis, enabling users to view the same data in different ways using multiple dimensions. Each aspect of information—product, pricing, cost, region, or time period—represents a different dimension. So a product manager could use a multidimensional data analysis tool to learn how many washers were sold in the East in June, how that compares with the previous month and the previous June, and how it compares with the sales forecast. OLAP enables users to obtain online answers to ad hoc questions such as these in a fairly rapid amount of time, even when the data are stored in very large databases, such as sales figures for multiple years.

Figure 6-15 shows a multidimensional model that could be created to represent products, regions, actual sales, and projected sales. A matrix of actual sales can be stacked on top of a matrix of projected sales to form a cube with six faces. If you rotate the cube 90 degrees one way, the face showing will be product versus actual and projected sales. If you rotate the cube 90 degrees again, you will see region versus actual and projected sales. If you rotate 180 degrees from the original view, you will see projected sales and product versus region. Cubes can be nested within cubes to build complex views of data. A company would use either a specialized multidimensional database or a tool that creates multidimensional views of data in relational databases.

Data Mining Traditional database queries answer such questions as, "How many units of product number 403 were shipped in February of this year?" OLAP, or multidimensional analysis, supports much more complex requests for information, such as, "Compare sales of product 403 relative to the plan by quarter and sales region for the past two years." With OLAP and query-oriented data analysis, users need to have a good idea about the information for which they are looking.

FIGURE 6-15 *Multidimensional data model*

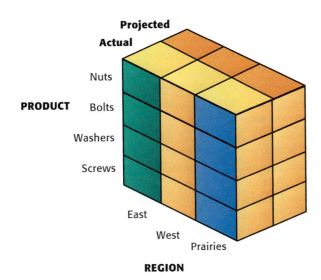

The view that is showing is product versus region. If you rotate the cube 90 degrees, the face that will show is product versus actual and projected sales. If you rotate the cube 90 degrees again, you will see region versus actual and projected sales. Other views are possible.

Data mining is more discovery-driven. Data mining provides insights into corporate data that cannot be obtained with OLAP by finding hidden patterns and relationships in large databases and inferring rules from them to predict future behaviour. The patterns and rules are used to guide decision making and forecast the effect of those decisions. The types of information obtainable from data mining include associations, sequences, classifications, clusters, and forecasts.

- *Associations* are occurrences linked to a single event. For instance, a study of supermarket purchasing patterns might reveal that, when corn chips are purchased, a cola drink is purchased 65 percent of the time, but when there is a promotion, cola is purchased 85 percent of the time. This information helps managers make better decisions because they have learned the profitability of a promotion.

- In *sequences*, events are linked over time. We might find, for example, that if a house is purchased, a new refrigerator will be purchased within two weeks 65 percent of the time, and an oven will be bought within one month of the home purchase 45 percent of the time.

- *Classification* recognizes patterns that describe the group to which an item belongs by examining existing items that have been classified and by inferring a set of rules. For example, businesses such as credit card or telephone companies worry about the loss of steady customers. Classification helps discover the characteristics of customers who are likely to leave and can provide a model to help managers predict who those customers are so that the managers can devise special campaigns to retain such customers.

- *Clustering* works in a manner similar to classification when no groups have yet been defined. A data mining tool can discover different groupings within data, such as finding affinity groups for bank cards or partitioning a database into groups of customers based on demographics and types of personal investments.

- Although these applications involve predictions, *forecasting* uses predictions in a different way. It uses a series of existing values to forecast what other values will be. For example, forecasting might find patterns in data to help managers estimate the future value of continuous variables, such as sales figures.

These systems perform high-level analyses of patterns or trends, but they can also drill down to provide more detail when needed. There are data mining applications for all the functional areas of business and for government and scientific work. One popular use for

Data mining

data mining is to provide detailed analyses of patterns in customer data for one-to-one marketing campaigns or for identifying profitable customers.

For example, Virgin Mobile Australia uses a data warehouse and data mining to increase customer loyalty and roll out new services. The data warehouse consolidates data from its enterprise system, customer relationship management system, and customer billing systems in a massive database. Data mining has enabled management to determine the demographic profile of new customers and relate it to the handsets they purchased. It has also helped management evaluate the performance of each store and point-of-sale campaign, consumer reactions to new products and services, customer attrition rates, and the revenue generated by each customer.

Predictive analysis uses data mining techniques, historical data, and assumptions about future conditions to predict outcomes of events, such as the probability a customer will respond to an offer or purchase a specific product. For example, the Dutch insurance company FBTO Verzekeringen, with about 500 000 customers and more than a million car, health, home, and life insurance policies, needed to reduce its direct mailing costs while increasing the efficiency of its marketing campaigns and cross-selling existing customers. FBTO used predictive analysis to identify customers and prospects with a better-than-average probability of purchasing one of their products. In doing so, FBTO reduced direct mail costs by 35 percent and increased conversion rates (from prospects to customers) by 40 percent. Today FBTO's marketing team can simulate different scenarios and calculate conversion rates and mailing costs in advance.

Data mining is both a powerful and profitable tool, but it poses challenges to the protection of individual privacy. Data mining technology can combine information from many diverse sources to create a detailed "data image" about each of us—our income, our driving habits, our hobbies, our families, and our political interests. The question of whether companies should be allowed to collect such detailed information about individuals is discussed in Chapter 4. The following Window on Technology section explores the debate about whether large databases housing DNA profiles used in crime fighting pose a threat to privacy and social well-being.

Predictive analysis

WINDOW ON TECHNOLOGY

DNA Databases: Crime-Fighting Weapon or Threat to Privacy?

In 1969, David Milgaard, then 16 years old, was on a road trip with friends across Canada, fuelled by a small amount of drugs and a few petty thefts. One of his companions would later testify against him in the murder case of a 20-year-old nursing student, Gail Miller, in Saskatoon, who was found dead on a snow bank while Milgaard was in Saskatoon. Based on somewhat questionable testimony and little concrete evidence, in 1970 Milgaard was sentenced to life in prison. Although he appealed his verdict several times, he remained in prison until 1992, when he was released without being formally acquitted. It was only in 1997 that sophisticated DNA testing proved Milgaard did not commit the murder.

In a similarly stunning travesty of justice, Thomas Sophonow was convicted of the 1981 murder of 16-year-old waitress Barbara Stoppel in Winnipeg. Although he was released from prison after four years, it was not until 2000 that DNA evidence finally cleared Sophonow of the murder charges. Other notorious Canadian cases include those of James Driskell, Guy Paul Morin, and Simon Marshall.

To avoid such miscarriages of justice here in Canada and around the world, DNA evidence has become a potent crime-fighting tool, allowing a criminal to be identified by his or her own genes. Computer analysis can discover the identity of a criminal by matching DNA from blood, hair, saliva, or other bodily fluids left at a crime scene with a DNA profile in a database. A laboratory creates a profile of specific agreed-upon genetic segments of the DNA molecule for a specific individual and stores that information in a database. To identify a particular individual, the laboratory compares the profile produced from a sample of unknown DNA with the profile produced from a sample belonging to an identified individual to see if there is a match.

In Canada, the National DNA Data Bank was created by the DNA Identification Act in 2000. Since its inception, the NDDB has assisted in more than 6000 investigations, including almost 400 murders. The blood or saliva samples on which the DNA profiles are primarily based are collected at crime scenes by law enforcement training in DNA evidence collection. All Canadian local law enforcement agencies work with the NDDB to assist in solving crimes.

DNA can help to solve crimes, but it is also helpful in proving innocence. Lawyer Barry Scheck's Innocence Project at the Cardozo School of Law in Yeshiva University has used DNA identification to free more than 100 people who had been wrongly convicted. According to Joseph M. Polisar, president of the International Association of Chiefs of Police, DNA testing "is the fingerprint technology of this century. . . . The potential for us in the criminal justice field to solve crimes with this technology is boundless."

Despite all their benefits, DNA databases remain controversial. Privacy advocates and defense lawyers believe genetic databases pose risks if they contain data on people who are not convicted criminals. In some instances, DNA has been collected from witnesses or others to eliminate them from police inquiries. DNA has also been collected from families of suspects to determine whether suspects should continue to be pursued.

Most people are not violent criminals, including those who commit misdemeanours, and their inclusion in a national DNA database exposes them to risks they would not otherwise face. People who collect and analyze DNA can make mistakes. (Sloppy DNA collection and laboratory procedures resulted in at least one wrongful conviction in Houston, Texas, and may have affected the outcome of the California trial of O.J. Simpson.) There may be valid reasons for an innocent person's DNA to be at a crime scene, and police might choose to disregard those reasons. Innocent people may be caught up in a criminal investigation when their DNA from a single hair or spot of saliva on a drinking glass appears in a public or private place where they had every right to be.

The Canadian National DNA Data Bank has security policies in place to protect the privacy of innocent individuals. Yet during parliamentary hearings prior to enacting the DNA Identification Act, the Privacy Commissioner of Canada voiced

concern about the protection of the privacy of individuals whose biological samples are in the DNA Data Bank. The DNA Identification Act itself specifies harsh penalties for unauthorized use of the data or the DNA samples themselves. Like many newer technologies and their applications, DNA identification is a two-edged sword: It helps law enforcement both convict and exonerate suspects, but it also has serious long-term privacy implications.

To Think About

1. What are the benefits of DNA databases?
2. What problems do DNA databases pose?
3. Who should be included in a national DNA database? Should it be limited to convicted felons? Explain your answer.
4. Who should be able to use DNA databases?

MIS in Action

Explore the Web site for the National DNA Data Bank of Canada (www.nddb-bndg.org/main_e.htm), and answer the following questions.

1. How does the NDDB work? How is it designed?
2. What information does NDDB maintain?
3. Who is allowed to use the NDDB?
4. How does the NDDB aid criminal investigations?

Sources: Susan Munroe, "Canadian Murder Rate Stays Low without Capital Punishment," *Canada Online*, www.canadaonline.com/od/crime/a/abolitioncappun.htm, accessed March 25, 2007; "Caught Up in DNA's Growing Web," *The New York Times*, March 17, 2006; "Genetic Privacy," www.epic.org, accessed August 3, 2006; CBC News, "Wrongfully Convicted," www.cbc.ca/news/background/wrongfullyconvicted/, accessed March 25, 2007; "Privacy and Security," www.nddb-bndg.org/pri_secu_e.htm, accessed March 25, 2007; and National DNA Data Bank of Canada, www.nddb-bndg.org/images/brochure_e.pdf, accessed March 25, 2007.

Databases and the Web

Have you ever tried to use the Web to place an order or view a product catalogue? If so, you were probably using a Web site linked to an internal corporate database. Many companies now use the Web to make some of the information in their internal databases available to customers and business partners.

Suppose, for example, a customer with a Web browser wants to search an online retailer's database for pricing information. Figure 6-16 illustrates how that customer might access the retailer's internal database over the Web. The user accesses the retailer's Web site over the Internet using Web browser software on his or her client PC. The user's Web browser software requests data from the organization's database, using HTML commands to communicate with the Web server.

Because many "back-end" databases cannot interpret commands written in HTML, the Web server passes these requests for data to middleware software that translates HTML commands into SQL so that they can be processed by the DBMS working with the database. In a client/server environment, the DBMS resides on a dedicated computer called a **database server**. The DBMS receives the SQL requests and provides the required data. The middleware transfers information from the organization's internal database back to the Web server for delivery in the form of a Web page to the user.

Database server

FIGURE 6-16   *Linking internal databases to the Web*

Users access an organization's internal database through the Web using their desktop PCs and Web browser software.

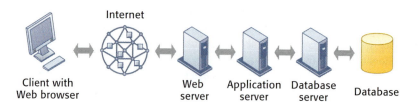

Figure 6-16 shows that the middleware working between the Web server and the DBMS could be an application server running on its own dedicated computer (see Chapter 5). The application server software handles all application operations, including transaction processing and data access, between browser-based computers and a company's back-end business applications or databases. The application server takes requests from the Web server, runs the business logic to process transactions based on those requests, and provides connectivity to the organization's back-end systems or databases. Alternatively, the software for handling these operations could be a custom program or a CGI script. A CGI script is a compact program using the *Common Gateway Interface (CGI)* specification for processing data on a Web server.

There are a number of advantages to using the Web to access an organization's internal databases. First, Web browser software is much easier to use than proprietary query tools. Second, the Web interface requires few or no changes to the internal database. It costs much less to add a Web interface in front of a legacy system than to redesign and rebuild the system to improve user access.

Accessing databases through the Web is creating new efficiencies, opportunities, and business models. ThomasNet.com provides an up-to-date online directory of more than 650 000 suppliers of industrial products, such as chemicals, metals, plastics, rubber, and automotive equipment. Formerly called Thomas Register, the company used to send out huge paper catalogues with this information. iGo.com is an Internet-based business that sells batteries and accessories for mobile phones and computing devices. Its Web site links to a giant relational database with product information about batteries and peripherals for nearly every brand and model of mobile computer and portable electronic device. Figure 6-17 shows the home page from the ThomasNet Web site.

FIGURE 6-17   *The ThomasNet.com Web site*

The ThomasNet Web site is a massive database that includes information about industrial products, services, brand names, and suppliers from across Canada and the U.S.

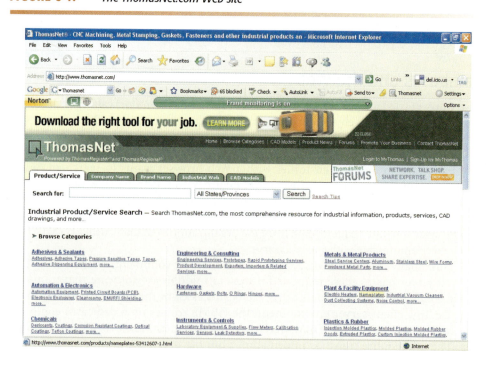

6.4 Managing Data Resources

Setting up a database is only the start. In order to make sure that the data for your business remain accurate, reliable, and readily available to those who need it, your business will need special policies and procedures for data management.

Establishing an Information Policy

Every business, large and small, needs an information policy. Your firm's data are an important resource, and you do not want people doing whatever they want with them. You need to have rules on how the data are to be organized and maintained, and who is allowed to view the data or change them.

An **information policy** specifies the organization's rules for sharing, disseminating, acquiring, standardizing, classifying, and inventorying information. An information policy lays out specific procedures and accountabilities, identifying which users and organizational units can share information, where information can be distributed, and who is responsible for updating and maintaining the information. For example, a typical information policy would specify that only selected members of the payroll and human resources department would have the right to change and view sensitive employee data, such as an employee's salary or social security number, and that these departments are responsible for making sure that such employee data are accurate.

If you work in a small business, the information policy would be established and implemented by the owners or managers. In a large organization, managing and planning for information as a corporate resource often requires a formal data administration function. **Data administration** is responsible for the specific policies and procedures through which data can be managed as an organizational resource. These responsibilities include developing an information policy, planning for data, overseeing logical database design and data dictionary development, and monitoring how information systems specialists and end-user groups use data.

You may hear the term **data governance** used to describe many of these activities. Promoted by IBM, data governance deals with the policies and processes for managing the availability, usability, integrity, and security of the data employed in an enterprise, with special emphasis on promoting privacy, security, data quality, and compliance with government regulations.

A large organization will also have a database design and management group within the corporate information systems division that is responsible for defining and organizing the structure and content of the database and maintaining the database. In close cooperation with users, the design group establishes the physical database, the logical relations among elements, and the access rules and security procedures. The functions it performs are called **database administration**.

Ensuring Data Quality

A well-designed database and information policy will go a long way toward ensuring that the business has the information it needs; however, additional steps must be taken to ensure that the data in organizational databases are accurate and remain reliable.

What would happen if a customer's telephone number or account balance were incorrect? What would be the impact if the database had the wrong price for the product you sold? Data that are inaccurate, untimely, or inconsistent with other sources of information lead to incorrect decisions, product recalls, and even financial losses.

The Gartner Group consultants reported that more than 25 percent of the critical data in large Fortune 1000 companies' databases is inaccurate or incomplete, including bad product codes and product descriptions, faulty inventory descriptions, erroneous financial data, incorrect supplier information, and incorrect employee data. Gartner believes

Information policy
Data administration
Data governance
Database administration

that customer data degrades at a rate of 2 percent per month, making poor data quality a major obstacle to successful customer relationship management (Gage and McCormick, 2002; Klau, 2003).

Think of all the times you have received several pieces of the same direct mail advertising on the same day. This is very likely the result of having your name maintained multiple times in a database. Your name may have been misspelled, or you used your middle initial on one occasion and not on another, or the information was initially entered onto a paper form and not scanned properly into the system. Because of these inconsistencies, the database would treat you as different people! One author often receives redundant mail addressed to Mary Brabson (no T!).

If a database is properly designed and enterprise-wide data standards established, duplicate or inconsistent data elements should be minimal. Most data quality problems, however, such as misspelled names, transposed numbers, or incorrect or missing postal codes, stem from errors during data input. The incidence of such errors is rising as companies move their businesses to the Web and allow customers and suppliers to enter data into their Web sites that directly update internal systems.

Before a new database is in place, organizations need to identify and correct their faulty data and establish better routines for editing data once their database is in operation. Analysis of data quality often begins with a **data quality audit**, which is a structured survey of the accuracy and level of completeness of the data in an information system. Data quality audits can be performed by surveying entire data files, surveying samples from data files, or surveying end users for their perceptions of data quality.

Data cleansing, also known as *data scrubbing*, consists of activities for detecting and correcting data in a database that are incorrect, incomplete, improperly formatted, or redundant. Data cleansing not only corrects errors but also enforces consistency among different sets of data that originated in separate information systems. Specialized data-cleansing software is available to automatically survey data files, correct errors in the data, and integrate the data in a consistent company-wide format.

The Window on Management describes some companies that experienced data quality problems and looks at how they tried to solve them. These problems were multi-faceted. As you read this section, look for the managerial, organizational, and technology factors that produced these data quality problems and how they were addressed.

Data quality audit

Data cleansing

WINDOW ON MANAGEMENT

What Can Be Done about Data Quality?

BT Group, formerly British Telecom, struggled with data quality problems for a number of years. Poor product inventory data and customer billing errors were hindering its interactions with suppliers and customers. BT Group was spending too much time and effort correcting data.

BT Group started taking data quality seriously in 1997. Nigel Turner, project lead manager for BT data quality programs, identified a data quality "champion" in each of BT's major lines of business to lead an information management forum. Each information management group targeted specific projects with demonstrable returns on investment, such as improving private-inventory recordkeeping to increase the number of disconnected circuits returned to stock for reuse or correcting names and addresses in marketing data to reduce the number of letters sent to the wrong people. As the project expanded, Turner's group

centralized data management and developed a data quality methodology that incorporated best practices from inside and outside the company.

By improving the quality of its data, BT Group saved as much as $1.27 billion from improved inventory data and interactions with customers and suppliers and increased revenue through more accurate billing. To maintain a high level of data quality in its databases, BT Group uses data profiling and cleansing tools from Trillium Software to identify and remove erroneous data on an ongoing basis.

Canadian Tire Corporation (CTC) was faced with integrating more than fifty disparate applications and multiple platforms, databases, data entry points, and transaction processing protocols. Business and IT staff at CTC, which has 1100 stores and gas bars across Canada, were concerned with the accessibility and accuracy of information.

For each new application, CTC developers had to write code to share information between applications and supporting data sources. Even off-the-shelf applications often needed to be customized. And each time application changes were made or new software versions released, the code would need to be rewritten. These processes were time-consuming and expensive, and slowed the company's ability to respond to market opportunities. Different applications often pulled and updated data to and from different sources. It meant the existence of multiple versions of key reference, customer, and vendor information. Executives worried that the lack of consistent data could affect certification and legal reporting processes as well as the overall accuracy of decision making.

"We have a technology roach motel," said Ken Dschankilic, enterprise architect for Canadian Tire. "We check all the stuff in, but it never, ever gets checked out. It leaves us with an inflexible architecture that's costly to maintain and difficult to leverage for new opportunities."

CTC leveraged a service-oriented architecture (see Chapter 5) in which applications would be autonomous from information sources and would not share any database directly. Knowledge of interconnections would be removed from both the source application and the target data source and stored centrally.

CTC also resolved some data inconsistencies and identified where bad data resides. According to Dschankilic, this is CTC's first step to gaining control over its master data. CTC plans to use IBM Information Management software solutions to help validate content and route changes back to the source of the application.

"There is a high cost associated with bad data," says Dschankilic. "The new solutions will help us move beyond application integration to actually synchronize data and create a single source of information that is as accurate as possible."

Bank of America had maintained a centralized data warehouse with account data from multiple sources used for marketing and cross-selling for a number of years. In 2002, it had to re-examine its data quality efforts to make sure it complied with the anti-money-laundering provisions of the Patriot Act. The bank established a common set of practices for capturing, integrating, and managing the data. Management designated data stewards in business units and the bank's information systems department to meet monthly and resolve data quality problems. The bank uses both commercial and home-grown data profiling and matching tools to examine and correct data sent to the warehouse.

To Think About

1. What was the impact of data quality problems on the companies described in this case study? What management, organization, and technology factors caused these problems?

2. How did the companies described in this case study solve their data quality problems? What management, organization, and technology issues had to be addressed?

3. It has been said that the biggest obstacle to improving data quality is that business managers view data quality as a technical problem. Discuss how this statement applies to the companies described in this case study.

MIS in Action

Visit the Web site of a data quality software vendor such as Dataflux (www.dataflux.com), Cognos (www.cognos.com), Trillium Software (www.trilliumsoftware.com), or Group 1 (www.g1.com). Explore the site and answer the following questions:

1. What are the capabilities of the software for ensuring data completeness, accuracy, and consistency?

2. What steps would your business need to take to use this software?

Sources: IBM, "Case Study: Canadian Tire Fuels Business Innovation with Information On Demand Initiative," www-306.ibm.com/software/success/cssdb.nsf/CS/HSAZ-6M2UBV?OpenDocument&Site=corp&cty=en_us, accessed March 29, 2007; Rick Whiting, "Aaww, Rubbish!" *InformationWeek*, May 8, 2006; and Kym Gilhooly, "Dirty Data Blights the Bottom Line," *Computerworld*, November 7, 2005.

Summary

1. *Describe basic file organization concepts and the problems of managing data resources in a traditional file environment.*

   A computer system organizes data in a hierarchy that starts with bits and bytes and progresses to fields, records, files, and databases. Traditional file management techniques make it difficult for organizations to keep track of all of the pieces of data they use in a systematic way and to organize these data so that they can be easily accessed. Different functional areas and groups were allowed to develop their own files independently. Over time, this traditional file management environment creates problems such as data redundancy and inconsistency, program-data dependence, inflexibility, poor security, and lack of data sharing and availability.

2. *Describe the principles of a database management system and the features of a relational database.*

   A database management system (DBMS) consists of software that permits centralization of data and data management so that businesses have a single consistent source for all their data needs.

   A single database services multiple applications. The most important feature of the DBMS is its ability to separate the logical and physical views of data. The user works with a logical view of data. The DBMS retrieves information so that the user does not have to be concerned with its physical location.

The principal capabilities of a DBMS include a data definition capability, a data dictionary capability, and a data manipulation language. The data definition capability specifies the structure and content of the database. The data dictionary is an automated or manual file that stores information about the data in the database, including names, definitions, formats, and descriptions of data elements. The data manipulation language, such as SQL, is a specialized language for accessing and manipulating the data in the database.

The relational database is the primary method for organizing and maintaining data today in information systems. It organizes data in two-dimensional tables with rows and columns called relations. Each table contains data about an entity and its attributes. Each row represents a record and each column represents an attribute or field. Each table also contains a key field to uniquely identify each record for retrieval or manipulation.

3. *Apply important database design principles.*

Designing a database requires both a logical design and a physical design. The logical design models the database from a business perspective. The organization's data model should reflect its key business processes and decision-making requirements. The process of creating small, stable, flexible, and adaptive data structures from complex groups of data when designing a relational database is termed normalization. A well-designed relational database will not have many-to-many relationships, and all attributes for a specific entity will apply only to that entity. An entity-relationship diagram graphically depicts the relationship between entities (tables) in a relational database. Database design also considers whether a complete database or portions of the database can be distributed to more than one location to increase responsiveness and reduce vulnerability and costs. There are two major types of distributed databases: replicated databases and partitioned databases.

4. *Evaluate tools and technologies for providing information from databases to improve business performance and decision making.*

Powerful tools are available to analyze and access the information in databases. A data warehouse consolidates current and historical data from many different operational systems in a central database designed for reporting and analysis. Data warehouses support multidimensional data analysis, also known as online analytical processing (OLAP). OLAP represents relationships among data as a multidimensional structure, which can be visualized as cubes of data and cubes within cubes of data, enabling more sophisticated data analysis. Data mining analyzes large pools of data, including the contents of data warehouses, to find patterns and rules that can be used to predict future behaviour and guide decision making. Conventional databases can be linked via middleware to the Web or a Web interface to facilitate user access to an organization's internal data.

5. *Assess the role of information policy, data administration, and data quality assurance in the management of organizational data resources.*

Developing a database environment requires policies and procedures for managing organizational data as well as a good data model and database technology. A formal information policy governs the maintenance, distribution, and use of information in the organization. In large corporations, a formal data administration function is responsible for information policy, as well as for data planning, data dictionary development, and monitoring data usage in the firm.

Data that are inaccurate, incomplete, or inconsistent create serious operational and financial problems for businesses because they may create inaccuracies in product pricing, customer accounts, and inventory data, and lead to inaccurate decisions about the actions that should be taken by the firm. Firms must take special steps to make sure they have a high level of data quality. These include using enterprise-wide data standards, databases designed to minimize inconsistent and redundant data, data quality audits, and data cleansing software.

Key Terms

Attribute, 193
Business intelligence (BI), 205
Data administration, 211
Data cleansing, 212
Data definition, 199
Data dictionary, 199
Data governance, 211
Data inconsistency, 195
Data manipulation language, 199
Data mart, 204
Data mining, 207
Data quality audit, 212
Data redundancy, 195

Data warehouse, 204
Database, 193
Database (rigorous definition), 196
Database administration, 211
Database management system (DBMS), 196
Database server, 209
Distributed database, 203
Entity, 193
Entity-relationship diagram, 202
Field, 193
File, 193
Foreign key, 198
Information policy, 211

Key field, 198
Normalization, 201
Object-oriented database management system (OODBMS), 199
Object-relational DBMS, 199
Online analytical processing (OLAP), 206
Predictive analysis, 208
Primary key, 198
Program-data dependence, 195
Record, 193
Relational DBMS, 197
Structured query language (SQL), 200
Tuples, 198

Review Questions

1. Why is file management important for overall system performance?

2. List and describe each of the components in the data hierarchy.

3. Define and explain the significance of entities, attributes, and key fields.

4. List and describe the problems of the traditional file environment.

5. Define a database and a database management system.

6. List some benefits of a DBMS and the solutions it provides for the problems of a traditional file environment.

7. What is a relational DBMS? How does it organize data? What are the three operations of a relational DBMS?

8. Name and briefly describe the capabilities of a DBMS.

9. What is normalization? How is it related to the features of a well-designed relational database?

10. What is a distributed database, and what are the two main ways of distributing data?

11. What is a data warehouse? How can it benefit organizations?

12. What is business intelligence? How is it related to database technology?

13. Describe the capabilities of online analytical processing (OLAP).

14. What is data mining? How does it differ from OLAP? What types of information can be obtained from data mining?

15. How can users access information from a company's internal databases through the Web?

16. What are the roles of information policy and data administration in information management?

17. Why are data quality audits and data cleansing essential?

Discussion Questions

1. It has been said that you do not need database management software to create a database environment. Discuss.

2. To what extent should end users be involved in the selection of a database management system and database design?

3. Is it important for end users and managers to know details about what type of database management software is being used and where the data are being housed? Why or why not?

4. What are the implications for privacy, corruption, theft, and updating of data that are housed on the Web and available over intranets, extranets, or the Internet? Is there a difference in whether the data are housed on an intranet, extranet, or the Internet?

Teamwork: Identifying Entities and Attributes in an Online Database

With a group of two or three of your fellow students, select an online database to explore, such as AOL Music, iGo.com, or the Internet Movie Database. Explore these Web sites to see what information they provide. Then list the entities and attributes that they must keep track of in their databases. Diagram the relationship between the entities you have identified. If possible, use electronic presentation software to present your findings to the class.

Learning Track Modules

Database Design, Normalization, and Entity-Relationship Diagramming. A well-designed relational database follows certain principles, which are described in this Learning Track Module along with instructions on how to create an entity-relationship diagram. This module can be found on MyMISLab for this chapter.

Introduction to SQL. SQL is the standard data manipulation language for relational database systems. This Learning Track Module, which can be found on MyMISLab for this chapter, describes basic SQL syntax and shows you how to construct a SQL query.

Hierarchical and Network Data Models. Many legacy systems still use these older data models. The Learning Track Module, which can be found on MyMISLab for this chapter, describes how these data models represent relationship, their strengths, and their limitations.

For online exercises, please visit www.pearsoned.ca/mymislab.

HANDS-ON MIS   Application Exercises

The projects in this section give you hands-on experience in redesigning a customer database for targeted marketing, creating a database for inventory management, and using the Web to search online databases for overseas business resources.

Improving Decision Making: Redesigning the Customer Database

Software skills: Database design, querying, and reporting
Business skills: Customer profiling

Companies maintain data on their customers that could provide valuable insights about customer interests and buying preferences. Often, however, customer databases may not be capturing the right pieces of data for marketing decisions, or their design may not allow the data to be analyzed. In this project, you will redesign a customer database so that it provides useful information for targeted marketing.

Dirt Bikes Canada sells primarily through its distributors. It maintains a small customer database with the following data: customer name, address, telephone number, model purchased, date of purchase, and distributor.

The database is illustrated below and you can find it on MyMISLab for Chapter 6. These data are collected by its distributors when they make a sale and are then forwarded to Dirt Bikes Canada. Dirt Bikes Canada would like to be able to market more aggressively to its customers.

The marketing department would like to be able to send customers e-mail notices of special racing events and of sales on parts. It would also like to learn more about customers' interests and tastes: their ages, years of schooling, another sport in which they are interested, and whether they attend dirt bike racing events. Additionally, Dirt Bikes Canada would like to know whether customers own more than one motorcycle. (Some Dirt Bikes Canada customers own two or three motorcycles purchased from Dirt Bikes Canada or other manufacturers.) If the customer purchased a motorcycle from Dirt Bikes Canada, the company would like to know the date of purchase, model purchased, and distributor. If the customer owns a non–Dirt Bikes Canada motorcycle, the company would like to know the manufacturer and model of the other motorcycle (or motorcycles) and the distributor from whom the customer purchased that motorcycle.

1. Design Dirt Bikes Canada's customer database so that it can store and provide the information needed for marketing. You will need to develop a design for the new customer database and then implement that design using database software. Consider using multiple tables in your new design. Populate each new table with 10 records.

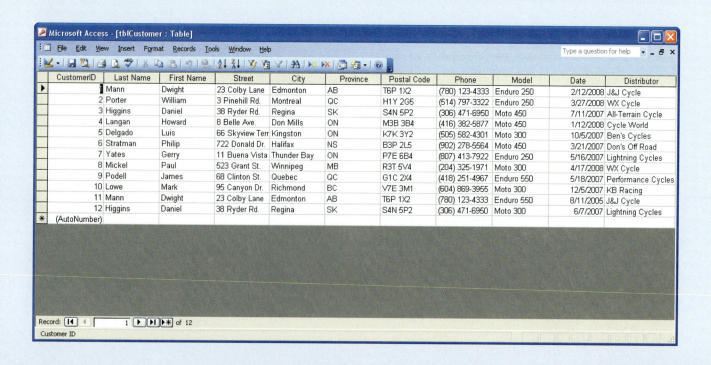

CustomerID	Last Name	First Name	Street	City	Province	Postal Code	Phone	Model	Date	Distributor
1	Mann	Dwight	23 Colby Lane	Edmonton	AB	T6P 1X2	(780) 123-4333	Enduro 250	2/12/2008	J&J Cycle
2	Porter	William	3 Pinehill Rd.	Montreal	QC	H1Y 2G5	(514) 797-3322	Enduro 250	3/27/2008	WX Cycle
3	Higgins	Daniel	38 Ryder Rd.	Regina	SK	S4N 5P2	(306) 471-6950	Moto 450	7/11/2007	All-Terrain Cycle
4	Langan	Howard	8 Belle Ave.	Don Mills	ON	M3B 3B4	(416) 382-5877	Moto 450	1/12/2008	Cycle World
5	Delgado	Luis	66 Skyview Terr	Kingston	ON	K7K 3Y2	(505) 582-4301	Moto 300	10/5/2007	Ben's Cycles
6	Stratman	Philip	722 Donald Dr.	Halifax	NS	B3P 2L5	(902) 278-5564	Moto 450	3/21/2007	Don's Off Road
7	Yates	Gerry	11 Buena Vista	Thunder Bay	ON	P7E 6B4	(807) 413-7922	Enduro 250	5/16/2007	Lightning Cycles
8	Mickel	Paul	523 Grant St.	Winnipeg	MB	R3T 5V4	(204) 325-1971	Moto 300	4/17/2008	WX Cycle
9	Podell	James	68 Clinton St.	Quebec	QC	G1C 2X4	(418) 251-4967	Enduro 550	5/18/2007	Performance Cycles
10	Lowe	Mark	95 Canyon Dr.	Richmond	BC	V7E 3M1	(604) 869-3955	Moto 300	12/5/2007	KB Racing
11	Mann	Dwight	23 Colby Lane	Edmonton	AB	T6P 1X2	(780) 123-4333	Enduro 550	8/11/2005	J&J Cycle
12	Higgins	Daniel	38 Ryder Rd.	Regina	SK	S4N 5P2	(306) 471-6950	Moto 300	6/7/2007	Lightning Cycles

2. Develop several reports that would be of interest to Dirt Bikes Canada's marketing and sales department (for example, lists of repeat Dirt Bikes Canada's customers, Dirt Bikes Canada customers who attend racing events, or the average ages and years of schooling of Dirt Bikes Canada customers) and print them out.

Achieving Operational Excellence:
Building a Relational Database for Inventory Management

Software skills: Database design, querying, and reporting
Business skills: Inventory management

Businesses today depend on databases to provide reliable information about items in inventory, items that need restocking, and inventory costs. In this exercise, you will use database software to design a database for managing inventory for a small business.

Sylvester's Bike Shop, located in Hamilton, Ontario, sells road, mountain, hybrid, leisure, and children's bicycles. Currently, Sylvester's purchases bikes from three suppliers but plans to add new suppliers in the near future. This rapidly growing business needs a database system to manage this information.

Initially, the database should house information about suppliers and products. The database will contain two tables: a supplier table and a product table. The reorder level refers to the number of items in inventory that triggers a decision to order more items to prevent a stockout. (In other words, if the number of units of a particular inventory item falls below the reorder level, the item should be reordered.) The user should be able to perform several queries and produce several managerial reports based on the data contained in the two tables.

Using the information found in the tables on MyMISLab for Chapter 6, build a simple relational database for Sylvester's. Once you have built the database, perform the following activities:

1. Prepare a report that identifies the five most expensive bicycles. The report should list the bicycles in descending order from most expensive to least expensive, the quantity on hand for each, and the markup percentage for each.
2. Prepare a report that lists each supplier, its products, the quantities on hand, and associated reorder levels. Sort the report alphabetically by supplier. Within each supplier category, the products should be sorted alphabetically.
3. Prepare a report listing only the bicycles that are low in stock and need to be reordered. The report should provide supplier information for the items identified.
4. Write a brief description of how the database could be enhanced to further improve management of the business. What tables or fields should be added? What additional reports would be useful?

Improving Decision Making:
Searching Online Databases for Overseas Business Resources

Software skills: Online databases
Business skills: Researching services for overseas operations

Internet users have access to many thousands of Web-enabled databases with information on services and products in faraway locations. This project develops skills in searching these online databases.

Your company is located in Calgary, Alberta, and manufactures office furniture of various types. You have recently acquired several new customers in Australia, and a study you commissioned indicates that, with a presence there, you could greatly increase your sales. Moreover, your study indicates that you could do even better if you actually manufactured many of your products locally (in Australia). First, you need to set up an office in Melbourne to establish a presence, and then you need to begin importing from Canada. You can then plan to start producing locally.

You will soon be travelling to the area to make plans to actually set up an office, and you want to meet with organizations that can help you with your operation. You will need to engage people or organizations that offer many services necessary for you to open your office,

including lawyers, accountants, import-export experts, telecommunications equipment and support, and even trainers who can help you to prepare your future employees to work for you. Start by searching for Canada Department of Commerce advice and other Canadian agency advice on doing business in Australia. Then try the following online databases to locate companies that you would like to meet with during your coming trip: Australian Business Register (http://abr.gov.au), AustraliaTradeNow.com, and the Nationwide Business Directory of Australia (www.nationwide.com.au). If necessary, you could also try search engines such as Yahoo! and Google.

1. List the companies you would contact to interview on your trip to determine whether they can help you with functions you think are vital to establishing your office.
2. Rate the databases you used for accuracy of name, completeness, ease of use, and general helpfulness.
3. What does this exercise tell you about the design of databases?

CASE STUDY

More and More and More Data—and What the RCMP Does with It

When we think of crime, we think of law enforcement. With the variety of crime lab shows on television, we assume that all law enforcement agencies should have access to the latest and greatest technologies, not only in laboratory technologies, but also in databases. A quick look at what the Royal Canadian Mounted Police (RCMP) are doing with data certainly supports that view. Let's look at two different data applications the RCMP have implemented and how they work: the DNA database and crime analysis database.

The national DNA database used by most Canadian law enforcement agencies is called the National DNA Data Bank (NDDB). Also available to foreign law enforcement agencies, the NDDB uses the Sample Tracking and Control System (STaCS) to automate and track processing DNA samples of those convicted of crimes for which DNA was part of the evidence. While criminals can wear gloves to avoid leaving fingerprints at the scenes of their crimes, it is a lot harder to avoid leaving DNA in the form of hairs or epithelial cells. DNA is the newest form of evidence that can be analyzed to identify criminals, and it can be used in court to convict those guilty of a variety of crimes, from sex crimes to murders and robberies.

The NDDB is located in Ottawa and uses the same CODIS (Combined DNA Index System) software that is used by the U.S. FBI and that is so frequently referenced on television shows such as *CSI: Criminal Science Investigation*. STaCS software works with the CODIS software to ensure that data can be shared between the two systems and also to ensure privacy for those whose DNA is in the database.

In addition to the issues discussed in the Window on Technology section on page 208, there are a number of scientific, legislative, and ethical issues associated with using DNA in solving crime. Is the DNA actually from a specific person? When was it left at the crime scene? Can DNA be used in court? How close a match must the DNA be to certify that it is a match, a legal as well as probability issue? Does collecting DNA violate the privacy of the individual giving the DNA sample? What legal and ethical considerations must be thought through before seeking or granting a search warrant on an individual's DNA? What is an appropriate "margin of error" for processing a DNA sample and linking it to a specific individual?

A number of strategies were developed in order to reduce margin of error and improve accountability. The STaCS system, developed by the RCMP in conjunction with Anjura Technology, is intended to track, control, and document every step in the process that converts the biological DNA sample into simplified numeric DNA profiles. The process must be transparent so that anyone can see exactly the process the DNA sample went through, ensuring that it is in fact the sample that started the process and that it has not been tampered with, so there is an audit trail of every activity that takes place in the system. STaCS includes a

report portal to permit everyone using the system to see where a DNA sample is in process and what the results are, as well as machine maintenance records and workload on the system.

In developing STaCS, the RCMP gained the licence to the software. They have since earned revenue from selling the licence to other law enforcement agencies, such as the Florida Department of Law Enforcement. Anjura has the right to market and sell STaCS, but the royalties the RCMP receives are to be used to upgrade the system to maintain the highest level of bioinformatics tools. (Bioinformatics relates to the information about a person's physical characteristics, including DNA, fingerprints, and retinal scans.)

Dr. Ron Fourney, the Officer in Charge of the NDDB, RCMP, states, "The National DNA Data Bank has become the number one tool in the forensic investigative toolbox for good reason. STaCS provides the ability to develop turnkey solutions at half the cost, run by half the staff, at double the efficiency." For example, STaCS' plug-and-play design could be used by a host of other DNA-type applications, from animal husbandry to paternity cases.

In addition to DNA analysis and tracking with the NDDB, the RCMP uses a variety of other data applications to help them prevent, solve, track, and report crimes. All law enforcement agencies want to know where crimes are occurring and how often, and what kinds of crime are occurring in specific locations.

Law enforcement officers who want to gather information about the types and frequency of specific criminal activities typically have to do the research manually—sifting through files, and then using their handwritten findings to place coloured pins on a map to indicate the number and type of crimes occurring in a particular area. A number of pins in one area would indicate a trend in criminal activity. To automate this process, the RCMP implemented CADVIEW, a data application to track criminal activity. CADVIEW yields better, more timely information, and its data can be mined to provide reports that can indicate where more law enforcement officers may need to be sent in advance of surges in criminal activity in that area.

The data in CADVIEW comes from computer-aided dispatch. Integrating geographic information system data along with tabular data about crimes permits the system to help law enforcement to focus on areas where crime is high— so-called "hot spots." The RCMP dispatch system sends the data to CADVIEW, where a PowerBuilder-based database application developed by xwave, a consulting firm and subdivision of Bell Aliant, stores the data and permits it to be mined by an intuitive interface. Onscreen reports can show frequency, number of all crimes in an area, types of crimes in an area, or even the sequence of crimes in an area. This visual representation is extremely helpful not only for the RCMP but also for the community—for example, it shows what is happening to a Block Watch meeting of concerned citizens. This application has been deployed to the RCMP's 35 communication centres across Canada.

Nancy MacDonald, the xwave developer who developed the CADVIEW program, explains how the CADVIEW map can be used at shift change briefings. "At some detachments, the map is also used as a 'pin map' that is handed out to the officers at the start of their shift. They can see what is happening in their jurisdiction. As the officers go on duty, they know exactly what sort of crimes occurred and what investigations are in progress."

Thinking of data as dry and dense helps us to realize that dry, dense data can be used to better society and to support law enforcement in protecting us from crime. The use of the National DNA Data Bank, STaCS, and CADVIEW systems certainly shows that data can come to life and help protect human life.

Sources: Microsoft, "The Royal Canadian Mounted Police: Microsoft Software Helps Solve Crimes," available **www.microsoft.com/canada/casestudies/rcmp.mspx**, accessed April 10, 2007; Microsoft, "2005 Computerworld Honors Case Study: CADVIEW," **www.cwhonors.org/laureates/government/20055332.pdf**, accessed April 10, 2007; and Government Technology, "Case Study: Royal Canadian Mounted Police," **www.govtech.net/digitalcommunities/studies/sybase_RCMPv2.pdf**, accessed April 10, 2007.

CASE STUDY QUESTIONS

1. Evaluate the RCMP's reasons for implementing STaCS and CADVIEW. Compare the need for efficiency with the need for effectiveness. Were both efficiency and effectiveness key factors in these solutions?

2. What management, organization, and information technology factors were responsible for the decision to implement these systems?

3. What problems were to be addressed by these systems? How did data management address these problems? How effective are these solutions?

4. What are the privacy issues that arise from the use of these two databases? Are there simple solutions to these issues, or are the privacy issues complex, requiring the courts to adjudicate them?

CHAPTER 7

Telecommunications, the Internet, and Wireless Technology

LEARNING OBJECTIVES

After completing this chapter, you will be able to do the following:

1. Describe the features of telecommunications networks and identify key networking technologies.

2. Evaluate alternative transmission media, types of networks, and network services.

3. Demonstrate how the Internet and Internet technology work and how they support communication and e-business.

4. Identify and describe the principal technologies and standards for wireless networking, communication, and Internet access.

5. Assess the business value of wireless technology and important wireless applications in business.

OPENING CASE | Hyatt Regency Osaka Uses Wireless Networking for High-Touch Service

Hyatt Hotels are known for the "Hyatt Touch," and the Hyatt Regency Osaka (HRO) is no exception. This urban resort hotel in the Hyatt International hotel chain is located in the new Cosmo Square business district some distance from central Osaka. It features approximately 500 guest rooms and 19 rooms for conferences and other functions spread over 28 floors. With the hotel industry increasingly competitive, HRO searched for ways to provide a superior environment for guests and encouraging repeat visits despite its less convenient location. The hotel turned to technology for a solution.

Working with Nomura Research Institute and Intel Corporation, HRO implemented a mobile wireless local area network (LAN) using Internet standards to provide integrated voice and data coverage across the entire

hotel. The hotel initially deployed 25 wireless-enabled notebook computers using Intel Centrino mobile technology and 60 handheld mobile devices based on Intel XScale technology. Both types of devices can handle voice phone calls as well as data communication, and their quality of service is comparable to HRO's wired voice system. The wireless infrastructure also provides guests with high-speed Internet access.

Before this system was installed, HRO staff members were only able to communicate using fixed-line telephones and pagers. The new wireless network enables these employees to communicate via handheld wireless personal digital assistants (PDAs) or notebook PCs wherever they are working. HRO estimates its wireless network has saved 60 hours per year per staff member or a total of 4800 hours annually. This

time saved by higher employee productivity can be spent on more personal attention to guests.

The ability to access information online from anywhere in the hotel allows every employee to "act as a concierge," responding accurately and immediately to guest inquiries. If, for example, a guest asks a bell captain a question, the bell captain can access the information from HRO's intranet using a wireless PDA and reply to the guest on the spot. The ability to share and access information also makes it easier to provide customized services to guests. For example, if a guest reports she prefers a different kind of pillow than the one in her room, the staff can immediately check online the information maintained about that guest from past visits and provide exactly what she wants on the spot. That sort of memorable service makes guests want to visit again.

The wireless LAN has been a big hit with guests, who use it to access the Internet from the hotel lobbies, conference centre, meeting rooms, and guest rooms. Increasingly, the availability of high-speed Internet access in conference facilities has become an essential requirement for corporate conventions and seminars. Providing wireless Internet service for conferences could potentially generate several million yen (tens of thousands of Canadian dollars) in additional revenue for the hotel.

Sources: Intel Corporation, "VoIP Enables VIP Service at Hyatt Regency Osaka," 2006; Intel Corporation, "Pilot Project Using Mobile IP-Centrex to Build an Integrated Voice and Data Environment," www.intel.com, accessed August 14, 2006; and Meru Networks, "Hyatt Regency Osaka Deploys Hotel-Wide Wireless VoIP System: New System Rivals Wired Dial-Tone Quality," 2005.

Hyatt Regency Osaka (HRO) illustrates some of the powerful new capabilities—and opportunities—provided by contemporary networking technology. HRO used Internet and wireless networking technology to provide staff and guests with voice and data communication capabilities, as well as wireless Internet access,

anywhere in the hotel. The technology enabled HRO to provide superior customer service and made it a hotel of choice, even though its location is somewhat inconvenient.

The chapter-opening Business Challenges diagram calls attention to important points raised by this case and

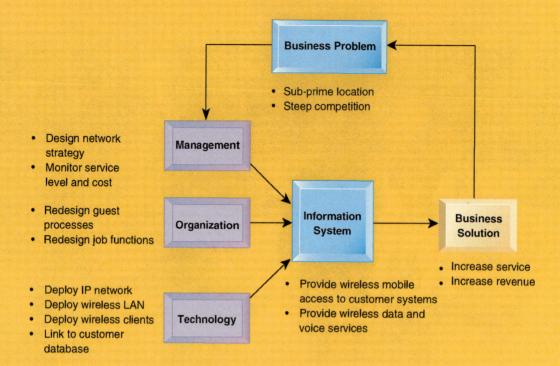

this chapter. The hotel industry is exceptionally competitive. HRO's management chose a strategy of focusing on a superior customer experience to distinguish it from competitors. Limitations of outdated networking and voice technology made it difficult to provide this experience.

Using networks based on the Internet protocol and wireless technology saved staff time, which was redirected to serving customers, and HRO had to redesign its processes for serving guests and redesign employee jobs to take advantage of the new technology.

HEADS UP

This chapter describes the key technologies for digital networking and communications and shows how they help business firms achieve operational excellence, strategic advantage, and close relationships with suppliers and customers. Businesses today could not survive without their computer and telecommunications networks.

- If your career is in finance or accounting, you will be working with networked systems and the Internet to access and update account information, research financial markets, trade securities, and transfer funds.

- If your career is in human resources, you will be using private corporate networks and intranets to access employee records and the Internet to research benefits and compensation plans.

- If your career is in information systems, you will be supporting your company's network infrastructure and Web site and recommending new networking technologies and applications.

- If your career is in manufacturing and production, you will be working with networked systems for monitoring the factory floor, for scheduling work, for supply chain management, and for warehousing and delivery. Some of these systems will be based on intranets and extranets.

- If your career is in sales and marketing, you will be working with online sales systems that obtain order transactions from private networks or the Web and with marketing systems that use data generated by Web sites.

7.1 Telecommunications and Networking in Today's Business World

If you work in a business, chances are you have already learned that you cannot stay in business without networks. You need to communicate rapidly with your customers, suppliers, and employees. Until about 1990, you would have used the postal system or telephone system with voice or fax for business communication. Today, however, you and your employees use computers and e-mail, instant messages, the Internet, cell phones, and mobile computers connected to wireless networks for this purpose. Networking and the Internet are now nearly synonymous with doing business.

Networking and Communication Trends

Firms in the past used two fundamentally different types of networks: telephone networks and computer networks. Telephone networks historically handled voice communication, and computer networks handled data traffic. Telephone networks were built by telephone companies throughout the twentieth century using voice transmission technologies (hardware and software), and these companies almost always operated as regulated monopolies throughout the world. Computer networks were originally built by computer companies seeking to transmit data between computers in different locations.

Thanks to continuing telecommunications deregulation and information technology innovation, telephone and computer networks are slowly converging into a single digital network using shared Internet-based standards and equipment. Telecommunications providers such as Bell Canada today offer data transmission, Internet access, wireless telephone service, and television programming as well as voice service. Cable companies such as Shaw Communications now offer voice service and Internet access. Computer networks have expanded to include Internet telephone and limited video services. Increasingly, all these voice, video, and data communications are based on Internet technology.

Both voice and data communication networks have also become more powerful (faster), more portable (smaller and mobile), and less expensive. For instance, the typical Internet connection speed in 2000 was 56 kilobits per second (Kbps). Today more than 60 percent of North American Internet users have high-speed broadband connections provided by telephone and cable TV companies running at one million bits per second. The cost for this service has fallen exponentially, from around 25 cents in 2000, to less than 1 cent today.

Increasingly, voice and data communication as well as Internet access are taking place over broadband wireless platforms, such as cell phones, handheld digital devices, and PCs in wireless networks (Macklin, 2005). In fact, wireless broadband access is the fastest-growing form of Internet access, growing at approximately 28 percent a year.

What Is a Computer Network?

If you had to connect the computers for two or more employees together in the same office, you would need a computer network. Exactly what is a network? In its simplest form, a network consists of two or more connected computers. Figure 7-1 illustrates the major hardware, software, and transmission components used in a simple network: a client computer and a dedicated server computer, network interfaces, a connection medium, network operating system software, and either a hub or a switch. Each computer on the network contains a network interface device called a network interface card (NIC). Most personal computers today have this card built into the motherboard. The connection medium for linking network components can be a telephone wire, coaxial cable, fibre optic cable, or radio signal in the case of cell phone and wireless local area networks (Wi-Fi networks).

FIGURE 7-1   *Components of a simple network*

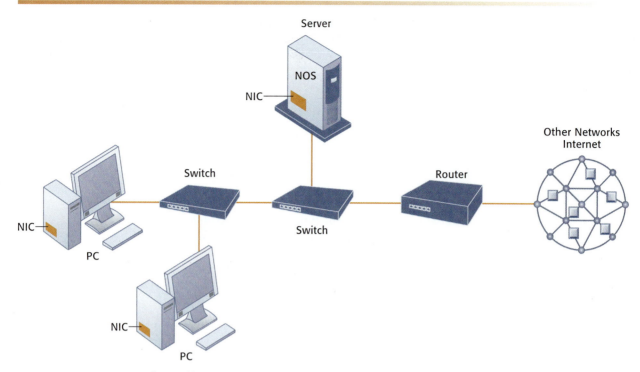

Illustrated here is a very simple computer network, consisting of computers, a network operating system residing on a dedicated server computer, cable (wiring) connecting the devices, network interface cards (NICs), switches, and a router.

The **network operating system (NOS)** routes and manages communications on the network and coordinates network resources. It can reside on every computer in the network, or it can reside primarily on a dedicated server computer for all the applications on the network. A **dedicated server computer** is a computer on a network that performs important network functions for client computers, such as serving up Web pages, storing data, and storing the network operating system (and hence controlling the network). Network operating systems such as Linux, Microsoft Windows Server, and Novell NetWare, are the most widely used network operating systems.

Most networks also contain a switch or a hub acting as a connection point between the computers. **Hubs** are simple devices that connect network components, sending a packet of data to all other connected devices. A **switch** has more intelligence than a hub and can filter and forward data to a specified destination on a local area network (LAN). Hubs and switches link up the devices on a LAN.

But what if you want to communicate with another network (such as the Internet)? **Routers** are network devices that connect two or more networks. So for instance, the cable modem in your house that brings you broadband Internet service is also a router that connects your LAN to the Internet. Routers are fairly intelligent devices that have to figure out where the packets of information you send are supposed to go. Routers maintain a routing table internally that keeps track of the addresses of destinations to which you frequently send packets. There are more than one billion people connected to the Internet, and more than five billion Internet addresses. Routers make sure your messages get to the right address.

Networks in Large Companies   The network we have just described might be suitable for a small business, but what about large companies with many different locations and thousands of employees? As a firm grows, and collects hundreds of small LANs, these networks are linked together into a corporate-wide networking infrastructure. The network infrastructure for a large corporation consists of a large number of these small LANs

Network operating system (NOS)
Dedicated server computer
Hubs
Switch
Routers

FIGURE 7-2   *Corporate network infrastructure*

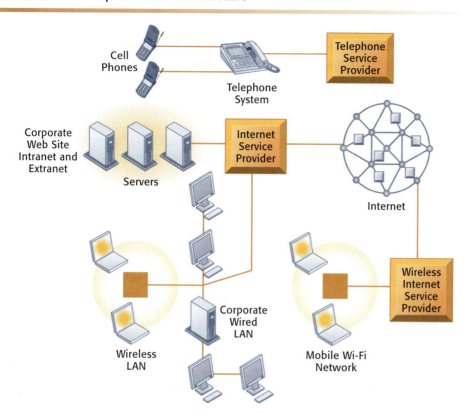

Today's corporate network infrastructure is a collection of many different networks from the public switched telephone network to the Internet to corporate local area networks linking workgroups, departments, or office floors.

linked to other LANs and to firm-wide corporate networks. A number of powerful servers support a corporate Web site, a corporate intranet, and perhaps an extranet. Some of these servers link to other large computers supporting back-end systems for sales transactions, financial transactions, order entries, and purchasing transactions.

Figure 7-2 provides an illustration of these more complex, larger-scale corporate-wide networks. Here you can see that the corporate network infrastructure supports a mobile sales force using cell phones; mobile employees linking to the company Web site, or internal company networks using mobile wireless LANs (Wi-Fi networks); and a videoconferencing system to support managers across the world. In addition to these computer networks, the firm's infrastructure usually includes a separate telephone network that handles most voice data. Many firms are dispensing with their traditional telephone networks and using Internet telephones that run on their existing data networks (described below).

As you can see from this figure, a large corporate network infrastructure uses a wide variety of technologies—everything from ordinary telephone service and corporate data networks to Internet service, wireless Internet, and wireless cell phones. One of the major problems facing corporations today is how to integrate all the different communication networks and channels into a coherent system that enables information to flow from one part of the corporation to another, from one system to another. As more and more communication networks become digital and are based on Internet technologies, it will become easier to integrate them.

Key Digital Networking Technologies

Contemporary digital networks and the Internet are based on three key technologies: client/server computing, the use of packet switching, and the development of widely used communications standards (the most important of which is Transmission Control Protocol/Internet Protocol [TCP/IP]) for linking disparate networks and computers.

Client/Server Computing In Chapter 5, we introduced client/server computing. *Client/server computing* is a distributed computing model in which some of the processing power is located within small, inexpensive client computers under user control and resides literally on desktops, laptops, or in handheld devices. These powerful clients are linked to one another through a network that is controlled by a network server computer. The server sets the rule of communication for the network and provides every client with an address so others can find it on the network.

Client/server computing has largely replaced centralized mainframe computing in which nearly all the processing takes place on a central large mainframe computer. Client/server computing has extended computing to departments, workgroups, factory floors, and other parts of the business that could not be served by a centralized architecture. The Internet is the largest implementation of client/server computing.

Packet Switching **Packet switching** is a method of slicing digital messages into parcels called packets, sending the packets along different communication paths as they become available, and then reassembling the packets once they arrive at their destinations (see Figure 7-3). Prior to the development of packet switching, computer networks used leased, dedicated telephone circuits to communicate with other computers in remote locations. In circuit-switched networks, such as the telephone system, a complete point-to-point circuit is assembled, and then communication can proceed. These dedicated circuit-switching techniques were expensive and wasted available communications capacity—the circuit was maintained regardless of whether any data were being sent.

Packet switching makes much more efficient use of the communications capacity of a network. In packet-switched networks, messages are first broken down into small fixed bundles of data called packets. The packets include information for directing the packet to the right address and for checking transmission errors along with the data. The packets are transmitted over various communications channels using routers, each packet travelling independently. Packets of data originating at one source can be routed through many different paths and networks before being reassembled into the original message when they reach their destinations.

TCP/IP and Connectivity In a typical telecommunications network, diverse hardware and software components need to work together to transmit information. **Connectivity** is the ability of computers and computer-based devices to communicate with one another and share information in a meaningful way without human intervention. Different components in a network communicate with each other only by adhering to a common set of

Packet switching
Connectivity

FIGURE 7-3 *Packet-switched networks and packet communications*

Data are grouped into small packets, which are transmitted independently over various communications channels and reassembled at their final destination.

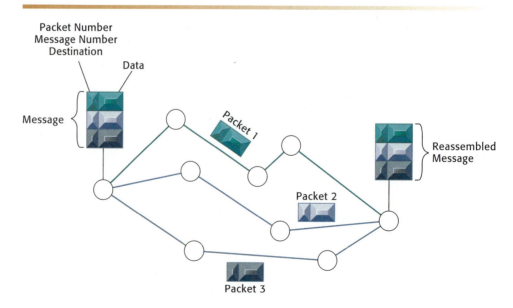

rules called protocols. A **protocol** is a set of rules and procedures governing transmission of information between two points in a network.

In the past, many diverse proprietary and incompatible protocols often forced business firms to purchase computing and communications equipment from a single vendor. Today, however, corporate networks are increasingly using a single, common, worldwide standard called Transmission Control Protocol/Internet Protocol. **Transmission Control Protocol/Internet Protocol (TCP/IP)** was developed during the early 1970s to support U.S. Department of Defense Advanced Research Projects Agency (DARPA) efforts to help scientists transmit data among different types of computers over long distances.

TCP/IP uses a suite of protocols, the main ones being TCP and IP. TCP refers to the Transmission Control Protocol (TCP), which handles the movement of data between computers. TCP establishes a connection between the computers, sequences the transfer of packets, and acknowledges the packets sent. IP refers to the Internet Protocol (IP), which is responsible for the delivery of packets and includes the disassembling and reassembling of packets during transmission. Figure 7-4 illustrates the four-layered reference model for TCP/IP.

1. **Application layer.** The application layer enables client application programs to access the other layers and defines the protocols that applications use to exchange data. One of these application protocols is the Hypertext Transfer Protocol (HTTP), which is used to transfer Web page files.

2. **Transport layer.** The transport layer is responsible for providing the application layer with communication and packet services. This layer includes TCP and other protocols.

3. **Internet layer.** The Internet layer is responsible for addressing, routing, and packaging data packets called IP datagrams. The Internet Protocol is one of the protocols used in this layer.

4. **Network interface layer.** At the bottom of the reference model, the network interface layer is responsible for placing packets on and receiving them from the network medium, which could be any networking technology.

Two computers using TCP/IP can communicate even if they are based on different hardware and software platforms. Data sent from one computer to the other passes downward through all four layers, starting with the sending computer's application layer and passing through the network interface layer. After the data reach the recipient host computer, they travel up the layers and are reassembled into a format the receiving computer can use. If the receiving computer finds a damaged packet, it asks the sending computer to retransmit it. This process is reversed when the receiving computer responds.

Protocol

Transmission Control Protocol/
Internet Protocol (TCP/IP)

FIGURE 7-4   *The Transmission Control Protocol/Internet Protocol reference model*

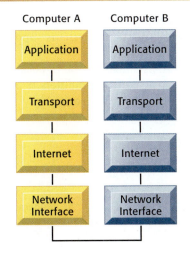

This figure illustrates the four layers of the TCP/IP reference model for communications.

7.2 Communications Networks

Now let us look more closely at the alternative networking technologies available to businesses.

Signals: Digital vs. Analog

The most basic distinction in communication networks is that between analog and digital signals. There are two ways to communicate a message: either an analog signal or a digital signal. An **analog signal** is represented by a continuous waveform that passes through a communications medium and is typically used for voice communication. The most common analog devices are the telephone handset, the speaker on your computer, or your iPod earphone, all of which create analog wave forms that your ear can hear. Oh yes, your ear is an analog device also.

A **digital signal** is a discrete, binary waveform, rather than a continuous waveform. Digital signals communicate information as strings of two discrete states: one bit and zero bits, which are represented as on-off electrical pulses. Computers use digital signals, so if you want to use the analog telephone system to send digital data, a device called a **modem** is required to translate digital signals into analog form and back again (see Figure 7-5). Modem stands for modulation/demodulation.

Types of Networks

There are many different kinds of networks and ways of classifying them. One way of looking at networks is in terms of their geographic scope (see Table 7-1).

Local Area Networks If you work in a business that uses networking, you are probably connecting to other employees and groups via a local area network. A **local area network (LAN)** is designed to connect personal computers and other digital devices within a half-mile or 500-metre radius. LANs typically connect a few computers in a small office, all the computers in one building, or all the computers in several buildings in close proximity. LANs interconnected within multiple buildings or a geographic area, such as a school campus or military base, create a **campus area network (CAN)**. LANs can link to long-distance wide area networks (WANs, described later in this section) and other networks around the world using the Internet.

Review Figure 7-1 on page 224, which could serve as a model for a small LAN that might be used in an office. One computer is a dedicated network file server, providing users with access to shared computing resources on the network, including software programs and data files. The server determines who gets access to what and in which sequence. The router connects the LAN to other networks, which could be the Internet or another corporate network, so that the LAN can exchange information with networks external to it. The most common LAN operating systems are Windows, Linux, and NetWare. Each of these network operating systems supports TCP/IP as their default networking protocol.

Ethernet is the dominant LAN standard at the physical network level, specifying the physical medium to carry signals between computers, access control rules, and a standardized frame or set of bits used to carry data over the system. Originally, Ethernet sup-

Analog signal

Digital signal

Modem

Local area network (LAN)

Campus area network (CAN)

FIGURE 7-5   *Functions of the modem*

A modem is a device that translates digital signals from a computer into analog form so that they can be transmitted over analog telephone lines. The modem also translates analog signals back into digital form for the receiving computer.

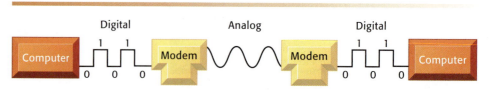

TABLE 7-1   *Types of Networks*

TYPE	AREA
Local area network (LAN)	Up to 500 metres; an office or floor of a building
Campus area network (CAN)	Up to 1000 metres; a college campus or corporate facility
Metropolitan area network (MAN)	A city or metropolitan area
Wide area network (WAN)	A transcontinental or global area

ported a data transfer rate of 10 megabits per second (Mbps). Newer versions, such as Fast Ethernet and Gigabit Ethernet, support data transfer rates of 100 Mbps and 1 gigabit per second (Gbps), respectively, and are used in network backbones.

The LAN illustrated in Figure 7-1 uses a client/server architecture where the network operating system resides primarily on a single file server, and the server provides much of the control and resources for the network. Alternatively, LANs may use a peer-to-peer architecture. A **peer-to-peer** network treats all processors equally and is used primarily in small networks with 10 or fewer users. The various computers on the network can exchange data by direct access and can share peripheral devices without going through a separate server.

In LANs using the Windows Server family of operating systems, the peer-to-peer architecture is called the *workgroup network model* in which a small group of computers can share resources, such as files, folders, and printers, over the network without a dedicated server. The Windows *domain network model*, in contrast, uses a dedicated server to manage the computers in the network.

Larger LANs have many clients and multiple servers, with separate servers for specific services, such as storing and managing files and databases (file servers or database servers), managing printers (print servers), storing and managing e-mail (mail servers), or storing and managing Web pages (Web servers).

Sometimes LANs are described in terms of the way their components are connected together, or their **topology**. There are three major LAN topologies: star, bus, and ring (see Figure 7-6).

Peer-to-peer
Topology

FIGURE 7-6   *Network topologies*

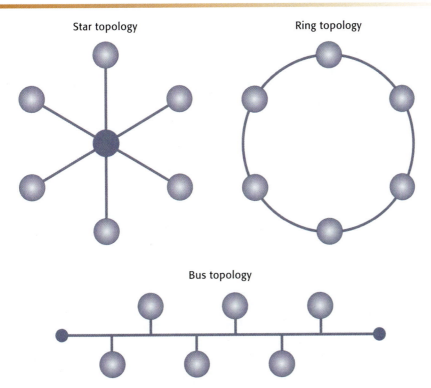

Star topology

Ring topology

Bus topology

The three basic network topologies are the bus, star, and ring.

In a simple **star network**, all network components connect to a single hub. All network traffic flows through the hub. In an *extended star network*, multiple layers or hubs are organized into a hierarchy.

In a bus topology, one station transmits signals, which travel in both directions along a single transmission segment. All the signals are broadcast in both directions to the entire network. All machines on the network receive the same signals, and software installed on the clients enables each client to listen for messages addressed specifically to it. The **bus network** is the most common Ethernet topology.

A ring topology connects network components in a closed loop. Messages pass from computer to computer in only one direction around the loop, and only one station at a time may transmit. A **ring network** is found primarily in older LANs using Token Ring networking software.

Metropolitan and Wide Area Networks   A **wide area network (WAN)** spans broad geographical distances—entire regions, provinces, countries, continents, or the entire globe. The most universal and powerful WAN is the Internet. Computers connect to a WAN through public networks, such as the telephone system or private cable systems, or through leased lines or satellites. A **metropolitan area network (MAN)** is a large computer network that spans a metropolitan area or campus. Its geographic scope falls between a WAN and a LAN. MANs provide Internet connectivity for LANs in a metropolitan region and connect them to WANs such as the Internet.

Physical Transmission Media

Networks use different kinds of physical transmission media, including twisted wire, coaxial cable, fibre optics, microwave, and other radio frequencies for wireless transmission. Each has advantages and limitations. A wide range of speeds is possible for any given medium depending on the software and hardware configuration.

Twisted Wire   **Twisted wire** consists of strands of copper wire twisted in pairs and is an older type of transmission medium. The telephone systems in buildings that had twisted wires installed for analog communication can use those wires for digital communication as well. Although an older form of physical media, most of today's LANs use twisted wires and can obtain speeds up to 1 Gbps. The most common LAN cabling today is CAT5 cable. CAT5 contains four pairs of copper wire and can transmit up to 1000 Mbps. Twisted-pair cabling is limited to a maximum recommended run of 100 metres.

Coaxial Cable   **Coaxial cable**, similar to that used for cable television, consists of a single, thickly insulated copper wire, which can transmit a larger volume of data than twisted wire. Coaxial cable was used in early LANs and is still used today for longer (more than 100 metres) runs in large buildings. Coaxial is often referred to as "solid" CAT5 and has speeds similar to twisted wire, up to 1000 Mbps.

Fibre Optics and Optical Networks   **Fibre-optic cable** consists of strands of clear glass fibre, each the thickness of a human hair, which are bound into cables. Data are transformed into pulses of light, which are sent through the fibre-optic cable by a laser device at rates varying from 500 kilobits to several trillion bits per second in experimental settings. Fibre-optic cable is considerably faster, lighter, and more durable than wire media, and is well suited to systems requiring transfers of large volumes of data; however, fibre-optic cable is more difficult to work with than wire media, more expensive, and harder to install.

Until recently, fibre-optic cable had been used primarily as the high-speed network backbone for the Internet, other WANs, and MANs while twisted wire and coaxial cable were used to connect the backbone to individual businesses and households. A **backbone** is the part of a network that handles the major traffic. It acts as the primary path for traffic flowing to or from other networks. Now, local cable companies and telephone companies are bringing fibre all the way into the basements of buildings and homes so they can provide a variety of new services to businesses and eventually residential customers.

Star network
Bus network
Ring network
Wide area network (WAN)
Metropolitan area network (MAN)
Twisted wire
Coaxial cable
Fibre-optic cable
Backbone

These **optical networks** can transmit all types of traffic—voice, data, and video—over fibre cables and provide the massive bandwidth needed for new types of services and software. Using optical networks, on-demand video, software downloads, and high-quality digital audio can be accessed using set-top boxes and other information appliances without severe degradation in quality or increased delays.

Existing optical networks can boost their capacity by using dense wavelength division multiplexing. **Multiplexing** enables a single communications channel to simultaneously carry data transmissions from multiple sources. This is accomplished by dividing a high-speed channel into multiple channels of slower speeds or by assigning each transmission source a very small slice of time for using a high-speed channel. **Dense wavelength division multiplexing (DWDM)** boosts transmission capacity by using many different colours of light, or different wavelengths, to carry separate streams of data over the same fibre strand at the same time. DWDM combines up to 160 wavelengths per strand and can transmit up to 6.4 terabits per second (Tbps) over a single fibre. This technology adds transmission capacity to an existing fibre-optic network without having to lay more fibre-optic cable. Before wavelength division multiplexing, optical networks could use only a single wavelength per strand.

Wireless Transmission Media and Devices Wireless transmission is based on radio signals of various frequencies. **Microwave** systems, both terrestrial and celestial, transmit high-frequency radio signals through the atmosphere and are widely used for high-volume, long-distance, point-to-point communication. Microwave signals follow a straight line and do not bend with the curvature of the earth; therefore, long-distance terrestrial transmission systems require that transmission stations be positioned about 60 kilometres apart, adding to the expense of microwave systems.

This problem can be solved by bouncing microwave signals off communication satellites, enabling them to serve as relay stations for microwave signals transmitted from terrestrial stations. **Satellites** are typically used for communications in large, geographically dispersed organizations that would be difficult to tie together through cabling media or terrestrial microwave transmission.

For instance, Petro-Canada has oil production facilities at the Terra Nova oil field, about 350 kilometres from St. John's, Newfoundland and Labrador. Petro-Canada's

Optical networks
Multiplexing
Dense wavelength division
multiplexing (DWDM)
Microwave
Satellites

FIGURE 7-7 *One of Petro-Canada's Floating Production Storage and Offloading vessels that operate in the Terra Nova oil field*

Petro-Canada uses ships like this one to process the oil it finds in the Terra Nova oil field and prepare it for offloading at a port.
Source: Courtesy of Petro-Canada

Floating Production Storage and Offloading (FPSO) ships process its oil and prepares is for offloading when in port (see Figure 7-7). In 2004, the Petro-Canada facility at Terra Nova had an oil spill. Petro-Canada tracked the spill through aerial and on-water surveillance, satellite imaging, and satellite-monitored tracking buoys. This precise tracking permitted Petro-Canada to deploy floating absorbent buoys, limiting the spill.

A **cellular telephone (cell phone)** works by using radio waves to communicate with radio antennas (towers) placed within adjacent geographic areas called cells. Cell phones operate in a defined radio spectrum from 800 to 2000 MHz (megahertz) depending on their generation. A telephone message is transmitted to the local cell by the cellular telephone and then is passed from antenna to antenna—cell to cell—until it reaches its destination cell, where it is transmitted to the receiving telephone. As a cellular signal travels from one cell into another, a computer that monitors signals from the cells switches the conversation to a radio channel assigned to the next cell.

Older cellular systems are analog and used primarily for voice transmission. Contemporary cellular systems are digital, supporting data transmission as well as voice transmission.

Wireless transmission technology has matured to the point where wireless networks are supplanting traditional wired networks for many applications and creating new applications, services, and business models. In Section 7.4, we provide a detailed description of the applications and technology standards driving the "wireless revolution."

Transmission Speed The total amount of digital information that can be transmitted through any telecommunications medium is measured in bits per second (bps). One signal change, or cycle, is required to transmit one or several bits; therefore, the transmission capacity of each type of telecommunications medium is a function of its frequency. The number of cycles per second that can be sent through that medium is measured in **hertz**—one hertz is equal to one cycle of the medium.

The range of frequencies that can be accommodated on a particular telecommunications channel is called its bandwidth. The **bandwidth** is the difference between the highest and lowest frequencies that can be accommodated on a single channel. The greater the range of frequencies, the greater the bandwidth and the greater the channel's transmission capacity. Table 7-2 compares the transmission speeds of the major types of media.

Broadband Network Services and Technologies

Cellular telephone (cell phone)

Hertz

Bandwidth

Frame relay

A number of network services and technologies are available to companies that need high-speed transmission or access to the Internet.

Frame relay is a shared network service that is faster and less expensive than packet switching and can achieve transmission speeds ranging from 56 Kbps to more than 40 Mbps. Frame relay packages data into frames similar to packets but takes advantage

TABLE 7-2 *Typical Speeds of Telecommunications Transmission Media*

MEDIUM	SPEED
Twisted wire (unshielded)	Up to 1000 Mbps (1 Gbps)
Microwave	Up to 600+ Mbps
Satellite	Up to 600+ Mbps
Coaxial cable	Up to 1 Gbps
Fibre-optic cable	Up to 6+ Tbps

Mbps = megabits per second
Gbps = gigabits per second
Tbps = terabits per second

of higher-speed, more reliable digital circuits that require less error checking than packet switching. The major telecommunications carriers provide frame relay services. Many organizations use frame relay services in their international data communication networks.

A technology called **Asynchronous Transfer Mode (ATM)** can handle many types of network traffic and provides transmission speeds ranging from 1.5 Mbps to more than 9 Gbps. Like frame relay, ATM takes advantage of high-bandwidth digital circuits, parcelling information into fixed 53-byte cells, of which 48 bytes are for data and 5 are for header information. ATM can pass data among computers from different vendors and is popular for transmitting data, video, and audio over the same network. Many telecommunications carriers and large enterprise backbone networks use ATM.

Integrated Services Digital Network (ISDN) is an older, international telephone standard for network access that integrates voice, data, image, and video services. It is still very effective for supporting interactive teleconferencing over long distances (say, Montreal to Sao Paulo, Brazil). There are two levels of ISDN service: basic rate ISDN (which can transmit at 128 Kbps) and primary rate ISDN (which can transmit at 1.5 Mbps).

Other high-capacity services include digital subscriber line technologies, cable, and T1 lines. Like ISDN, **digital subscriber line (DSL)** technologies also operate over existing telephone lines to carry voice, data, and video, but they have higher transmission capacities than ISDN. (By 2005, most small businesses had converted from ISDN to either cable or DSL Internet services, which are cheaper and more powerful.) There are several categories of DSL. Asymmetric digital subscriber lines (ADSLs) support a transmission rate of 1.5 to 9 Mbps when receiving data and over 700 Kbps when sending data. Symmetric digital subscriber lines (SDSLs) support the same transmission rate for sending and receiving data at speeds up to 3 Mbps.

Cable Internet connections provided by cable television vendors use digital cable coaxial lines to deliver high-speed Internet access to homes and businesses. They can provide high-speed access to the Internet of up to 10 Mbps. The Canadian population is relatively equally split between broadband cable access and broadband telephone line (i.e., DSL) access (Statistics Canada, 2006).

But what if you have large amounts of very sensitive information to send from one continent to another? Would you use the Internet or a public telephone service? Chances are you would not use either because the risk of failure or security losses is too great. The Internet does not guarantee any level of service, just "best effort." Most Fortune 1000 firms that have high-security or guaranteed service level requirements lease high-speed data lines from communication providers, typically long-distance telephone companies. These lines are designated as **T lines**.

T1 lines offer up to 24 64-Kbps channels that can support a total data transmission rate of 1.54 Mbps. Each of these 64-Kbps channels can be configured to carry voice or data traffic. A T3 line is a very high-speed connection capable of transmitting data at around 45 Mbps, a whopping rate of 45 million bps. You will rarely encounter a T3 line unless you work in the networking department of a major corporation or university. For instance, the Internet backbone operates using multiple T3 lines. Leasing a T1 line costs about $1000 per month while T3 line costs start around $10 000 per month. Table 7-3 summarizes these network services.

7.3 The Internet

We all use the Internet, and many of us cannot do without it. It has become an indispensable personal and business tool. But what exactly is the Internet? How does it work, and what does Internet technology have to offer for business? Let us now look at the most important Internet features.

Asynchronous Transfer Mode (ATM)

Integrated Services Digital Network (ISDN)

Digital subscriber line (DSL)

Cable Internet connections

T lines

TABLE 7-3   *Broadband Network Services*

SERVICE	DESCRIPTION	BANDWIDTH
Frame relay	Packages data into frames for high-speed transmission over reliable circuits that require less error checking than packet switching	56 Kbps to 40+ Mbps
Asynchronous Transfer Mode (ATM)	Parcels data into uniform 53-byte cells for high-speed transmission; can transmit data, video, and audio over the same network	1.5 Mbps to 9+ Gbps
Integrated Services Digital Network (ISDN)	Dial-up network access standard that can integrate voice, data, and video services	Basic rate ISDN: 128 Kbps Primary rate ISDN: 1.5 Mbps
Digital Subscriber Line (DSL)	Dedicated telephone network broadband Internet access	ADSL: Up to 9 Mbps for receiving and over 700 Kbps for sending data SDSL: Up to 3 Mbps for both sending and receiving
Cable Internet connection	Dedicated cable network broadband access	Up to 10 Mbps
T lines	Dedicated lines for high-speed data transmission and Internet connection	T1: 1.544 Mbps T3: 45 Mbps

What Is the Internet?

The Internet has become the world's most extensive public communication system and now rivals the global telephone system in reach and range. It is also the world's largest implementation of client/server computing and internetworking, linking hundreds of thousands of individual networks all over the world and more than 1 billion people worldwide. The word *Internet* derives from the word **internetworking**, or the linking of separate networks, each of which retains its own identity, into an interconnected network. This gigantic network of networks began in the early 1970s as a U.S. Department of Defense network to link scientists and university professors around the world.

Individuals connect to the Internet in two ways. Most homes connect to the Internet by subscribing to an Internet service provider. An **Internet service provider** (**ISP**) is a commercial organization with a permanent connection to the Internet that sells temporary connections to retail subscribers. Telephone lines, cable lines, or wireless connections can provide these connections. Major ISPs include the major Canadian telecommunications companies along with myriad local ISPs. Individuals also connect to the Internet through their business firms, universities, or research centres that have designated Internet domains, such as www.pearsoned.ca.

Internet Addressing and Architecture

The Internet is based on the TCP/IP networking protocol suite described earlier in this chapter. Every computer on the Internet is assigned a unique **Internet Protocol** (**IP**) **address**, which currently is a 32-bit number represented by four strings of numbers ranging from 0 to 255 separated by periods. For instance, the IP address of www.microsoft.com is 207.46.250.119.

When a user sends a message to another user on the Internet, the message is first decomposed into packets using the TCP protocol. Each packet contains its destination address. The packets are then sent from the client to the network server, then to a local router, and from there on to as many other routers and servers as necessary to arrive at a specific computer with the correct IP address. At the destination address, the packets are reassembled into the original message.

The Domain Name System   Because it would be incredibly difficult for Internet users to remember strings of 12 numbers, a **Domain Name System** (**DNS**) converts IP addresses to

Internetworking

Internet service provider (ISP)

Internet Protocol (IP) address

Domain Name System (DNS)

FIGURE 7-8   *The Domain Name System*

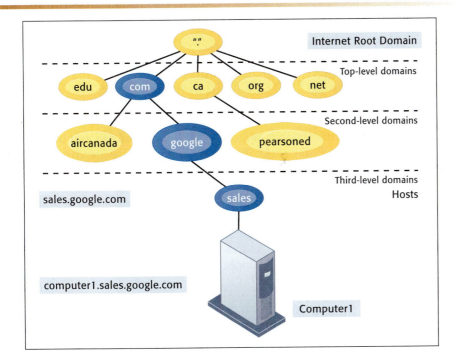

The Domain Name System is a hierarchical system with a root domain, top-level domains, second-level domains, and host computers at the third level.

domain names. The **domain name** is the English-like name that corresponds to the unique 32-bit numeric IP address for each computer connected to the Internet. DNS servers maintain a database containing IP addresses mapped to their corresponding domain names. To access a computer on the Internet, users need only specify its domain name.

DNS has a hierarchical structure (see Figure 7-8). At the top of the DNS hierarchy is the root domain. The child domain of the root is called a top-level domain, and the child domain of a top-level domain is called is a second-level domain. Top-level domains are two- and three-character names you are familiar with from surfing the Web, for example, .com, .edu, .gov, and the various country codes such as .dk for Denmark or .it for Italy. Second-level domains have two parts—designating a top-level name and a second-level name—such as buy.com, dal.ca, or amazon.ca. A host name at the bottom of the hierarchy designates a specific computer on either the Internet or a private network, such as communicationsandmarketing.dal.ca.

The most common domain extensions currently available and officially approved are shown in the following list. Countries also have domain names such as .uk, .au, and .fr (United Kingdom, Australia, and France, respectively). In the future, this list will expand to include many more types of organizations and industries.

.aero Aviation

.biz Business organizations

.com Commercial organizations/businesses

.coop Cooperative organizations

.edu Educational institutions

. gc Canadian government agencies

.info Information providers

.int International organizations

.mil U.S. military

.mus Museums

.name Personal

Domain name

.net Network computers

.org Nonprofit organizations and foundations

.pro Professional organizations

Internet Architecture and Governance Internet data traffic is carried by transcontinental high-speed backbone networks that generally operate today in the range of 45 Mbps to 2.5 Gbps (see Figure 7-9). These trunk lines are typically owned by long-distance telephone companies (called *network service providers*) or by national governments. Local connection lines are owned by regional telephone and cable television companies that connect retail users in homes and businesses to the Internet. The regional networks lease access to ISPs, private companies, and government institutions.

No one "owns" the Internet, and it has no formal management. However, worldwide Internet policies are established by a number of professional organizations and government bodies, including the Internet Architecture Board (IAB), which helps define the overall structure of the Internet; the Internet Corporation for Assigned Names and Numbers (ICANN), which assigns IP addresses; and the World Wide Web Consortium (W3C), which sets Hypertext Markup Language (HTML) and other programming standards for the Web.

These organizations influence government agencies, network owners, ISPs, and software developers with the goal of keeping the Internet operating as efficiently as possible. The Internet must also conform to the laws of the sovereign nation-states in which it operates, as well as the technical infrastructures that exist within the nation-states. Although in the early years of the Internet and the Web there was very little legislative or executive interference, this situation is changing as the Internet plays a growing role in the distribution of information and knowledge, including content that some find objectionable. In some countries, the Internet is censored just like traditional broadcast media.

The Internet is not "free," even though many people, such as students and employees, do not pay for their access. In fact, everyone who uses the Internet pays some fee—hidden

---

FIGURE 7-9 *Internet network architecture*

The Internet backbone connects to regional networks, which in turn provide access to Internet service providers, large firms, and government institutions. Network access points (NAPs) and metropolitan area exchanges (MAEs) are hubs where the backbone intersects regional and local networks and where backbone owners connect with one another. MAEs are also referred to as Internet Exchange Points.

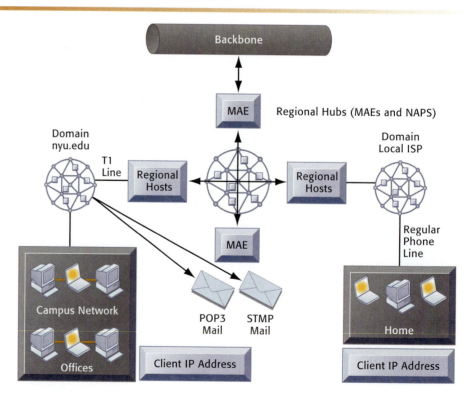

or otherwise—to maintain the network. Each organization and business firm pays for its own networks and its own local Internet connection services, a part of which is paid to the long-distance trunk line owners. The costs of e-mail and other Internet connections tend to be far lower than equivalent voice, postal, or overnight delivery costs, making the Internet a very inexpensive communications medium. It is also a very fast method of communication, with messages arriving anywhere in the world in a matter of seconds, or a minute or two at most.

The Future Internet: IPv6 and Internet2 The Internet was not originally designed to handle the transmission of massive quantities of data and billions of users. Because many corporations and governments have been given large blocks of millions of IP addresses to accommodate current and future workforces, and because of sheer Internet population growth, the world is running out of available IP addresses using the existing addressing convention called IPv4. IPv4 uses a 32-bit addressing scheme and contains only 4.5 billion addresses, not enough for each of the 6.5 billion people on Earth, not to mention businesses, governments, and other organizations.

Internet engineers believe the world will start running out of addresses beginning in 2009. To avoid this unpleasant outcome, the Internet Engineering Task Force adopted a new Internet Protocol Version 6 (IPv6), which uses a 128-bit addressing scheme and produces 3.4×10^{38} addresses. This is a large enough number to give each person on Earth several million addresses.

The existing Internet has many shortcomings, chief among which are poor security, no service level guarantees, no differential service, no differential pricing, and bandwidth limitations that would prevent the emergence of wide-scale Internet television or Internet video distribution. **Internet2** and Next-Generation Internet (NGI) are consortia representing 200 universities, private businesses, and government agencies in the U.S. that are working on a new, robust, high-bandwidth version of the Internet. They have established several new high-performance backbone networks with bandwidths ranging from 2.5 Gbps to 9.6 Gbps. CANARIE is the Canadian equivalent of Internet2. CANARIE has already deployed various versions of **CA*net4**, the national backbone for Canada with one drop (or high-speed router) per province. Currently, CA*net facilitates innovation by connecting regional networks, universities, and schools, which can collaborate to create new, advanced applications such as tele-learning and grids of interested researchers who can use the "grid" similarly to grid computing, to connect securely to each other on an ad hoc basis. The goal is to promote an "innovation culture." Today, CA*net has evolved to CA*net4, based on optical networking technologies; CA*net4 allows the fastest speeds available over the Internet and is used primarily for research and education purposes.

The CANARIE and Internet2 research groups are developing and implementing new technologies for more effective routing practices, different levels of service (depending on the type and importance of the data being transmitted), and advanced applications for purposes such as distributed computation, virtual laboratories, digital libraries, distributed learning, and teleimmersion. These networks will not replace the public Internet, but they do provide test beds for leading-edge technology that may eventually migrate to the public Internet. Figure 7-10 illustrates the latest CANARIE CA*net4 infrastructure map.

Internet Services

The Internet is based on client/server technology. Individuals using the Internet control what they do through client applications on their computers, such as Web browser software. The data, including e-mail messages and Web pages, are stored on servers. A client uses the Internet to request information from a particular Web server on a distant computer, and the server sends the requested information back to the client over the Internet. Chapters 5 and 6 describe how Web servers work with application servers and database servers to access information from an organization's internal information systems applications and their associated databases.

Internet2

CA*net4

FIGURE 7-10 *CA*net4 infrastructure*

The CA*net4 infrastructure describes how this advanced Internet infrastructure works, not only across Canada but also with links to the U.S.

Source: Reprinted with the permission of CANARIE Inc.

Client platforms today include not only PCs and other computers but also cell phones, small handheld digital devices, and other information appliances. An **information appliance** is a device, such as an Internet-enabled cell phone or a TV Internet receiver for Web access and e-mail, that has been designed to perform a few specialized computing tasks well with minimal user effort. People are increasingly relying on these easy-to-use specialized information appliances to connect to the Internet.

A client computer connecting to the Internet has access to a variety of services. These services include e-mail, electronic discussion groups (Usenet newsgroups), chatting and instant messaging, Telnet, File Transfer Protocol (FTP), and the World Wide Web. Table 7-4 provides a brief description of these services.

Information appliance

TABLE 7-4 *Major Internet Services*

CAPABILITY	FUNCTIONS SUPPORTED
E-mail	Person-to-person messaging; document sharing
Usenet newsgroups	Discussion groups on electronic bulletin boards
Chatting and instant messaging	Interactive conversations
Telnet	Logging on to one computer system and doing work on another
File Transfer Protocol (FTP)	Transferring files from computer to computer
World Wide Web	Retrieving, formatting, and displaying information (including text, audio, graphics, and video) using hypertext links

FIGURE 7-11   *Client/Server computing on the Internet*

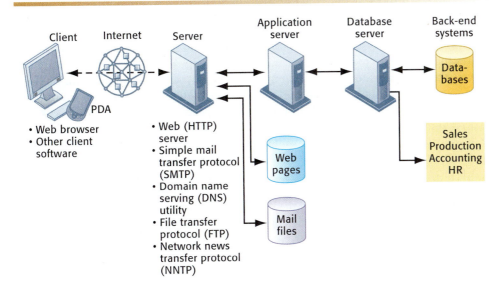

Client computers running Web browser and other software can access an array of services on servers over the Internet. These services may all run on a single server or on multiple specialized servers.

Each Internet service is implemented by one or more software programs. All the services may run on a single server computer, or different services may be allocated to different machines. Figure 7-11 illustrates one way that these services might be arranged in a multitiered client/server architecture.

The World Wide Web

You have probably used the World Wide Web to download music, to find information for a term paper, or to obtain news and weather reports. The Web is the most popular Internet service. It is a system with universally accepted standards for storing, retrieving, formatting, and displaying information using a client/server architecture. Web pages are formatted using hypertext with embedded links that connect documents to one another and that also link pages to other objects, such as sound, video, or animation files. When you click a graphic and a video clip plays, you have clicked a hyperlink. Newer capabilities on the Web, discussed in the section on software trends in Chapter 5, are adding to the popularity of the Web; many of these technologies fall under what is being called Web 2.0, which we discuss further in this section.

Hypertext   Web pages are based on a standard Hypertext Markup Language (HTML), which formats documents and incorporates dynamic links to other documents and pictures stored in the same or remote computers (see Chapter 5). Web pages are accessible through the Internet because Web browser software operating your computer can request Web pages stored on an Internet host server using the Hypertext Transfer Protocol. **Hypertext Transfer Protocol (HTTP)** is the communications standard used to transfer pages on the Web. For example, when you type a Web address in your browser, such as www.pearsoned.ca, your browser sends an HTTP request to the pearsoned.ca server requesting the home page of pearsoned.ca.

HTTP is the first set of letters at the start of every Web address, followed by the domain name, which specifies the organization's server computer that is storing the document. Most companies have a domain name that is the same as or closely related to their official corporate name. The directory path and document name are two more pieces of information within the Web address that help the browser track down the requested page. Together, the address is called a **uniform resource locator (URL)**. When typed into a browser, a URL tells the browser software exactly where to look for the information. Consider the following URL:

http://www.megacorp.com/content/features/082602.html

Hypertext Transfer Protocol (HTTP)
Uniform resource locator (URL)

Http names the protocol used to display Web pages, www.megacorp.com is the domain name, content/features is the directory path that identifies where on the domain Web server the page is stored, and 082602.html is the document name and the type of file it is.

Web Servers   A Web server is software for locating and managing stored Web pages. It locates the Web pages requested by a user on the computer where they are stored and delivers the Web pages to the user's computer. Server applications usually run on dedicated computers although they can all reside on a single computer in small organizations.

The most common Web server in use today is Apache HTTP Server, which controls 70 percent of the market. Apache is an open-source product that is free of charge and can be downloaded from the Web. Microsoft's product Internet Information Services (IIS) is the second most commonly used Web server, with a 21 percent market share.

A typical **Web site** is a collection of Web pages linked to a **home page**—a text and graphical screen display that usually welcomes the user and provides a brief description of the organization that has established the Web site. Most home pages offer a way to contact the organization or individual. The person in charge of an organization's Web site is called a **Web master**.

Searching for Information on the Web   No one knows for sure how many Web pages there really are. The surface Web is the part of the Web that search engines visit and about which information is recorded. For instance, Google visited about 25 billion pages in 2006. But there is a "deep Web" that contains an estimated 800 billion additional pages, many of them proprietary (such as the pages of *The Wall Street Journal Online*, which cannot be visited without an access code) or that are stored in protected corporate databases.

Search Engines   Obviously, with so many Web pages, finding specific Web pages that can help you or your business, nearly instantly, is an important problem. The question is, how can you find the one or two pages you really want and need out of billions of indexed Web pages? **Search engines** solve the problem of finding useful information on the Web nearly instantly, and, arguably, they are the "killer app" of the Internet era. There are hundreds of different search engines in the world, but three top providers supply the vast majority of search results (see Figure 7-12).

Web search engines started out in the early 1990s as relatively simple software programs that roamed the nascent Web, visiting pages, and gathering information about the content of each page. These early programs were called variously crawlers, spiders, and wanderers. AltaVista, launched in 1995, was the first to allow "natural language" queries, such as "history of web search engines" rather than "history+web search+search engine."

The first search engines were simple keyword indexes of all the pages they visited. They would count the number of times a word appeared on the pages and store this information in an index, leaving the user with lists of pages that may not have been truly relevant to their search.

In 1994, Stanford University computer science students David Filo and Jerry Yang created a hand-selected list of their favourite Web pages and called it "Yet Another Hierarchical Officious Oracle," or Yahoo!. Yahoo! was never a real search engine but rather

Web site
Home page
Web master
Search engines

FIGURE 7-12   *Major Web search engines*

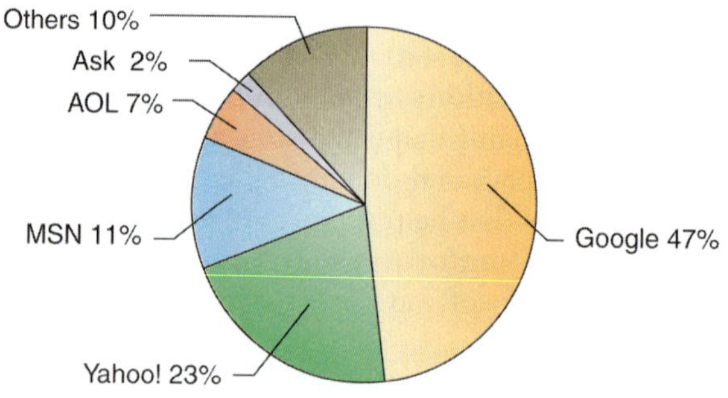

Google is the most popular search engine on the Web, handling nearly 50 percent of all Web searches.

Sources: **http://searchenginewatch. com**, accessed August 19, 2006; and Kevin J. Delaney, "Search Engines Find a Role for Humans," *The Wall Street Journal*, May 11, 2006.

Others 10%
Ask 2%
AOL 7%
MSN 11%
Google 47%
Yahoo! 23%

an edited selection of Web sites organized by categories the editors found useful. Yahoo! has since developed its own search engine capabilities.

In 1998, Larry Page and Sergey Brin, two other Stanford computer science students, released their first version of Google. This search engine was different: Not only did it index each Web page's words, but it also ranked search results based on the relevance of each page. Page patented the idea of a page ranking system (PageRank System), which essentially measures the popularity of a Web page by calculating the number of other sites that link to that page. Brin contributed a unique Web crawler program that indexed not only keywords on a page but also combinations of words (such as authors and the titles of their articles). These two ideas became the foundation for the Google search engine. Figure 7-13 illustrates how Google works.

Web sites for locating information, such as Yahoo!, Google, and MSN, have become so popular and easy to use that they now serve as major portals for the Internet (see Chapter 13). The search marketplace has become very competitive. Microsoft has unleashed its MSN search tool; Amazon.com has entered the fray with A9; and Overture.com (now owned by Yahoo!) transformed the search world by charging advertisers for placement and ranking.

The spectacular increase in Internet advertising revenues has made search engines major shopping tools by offering what is now called **search engine marketing**. When users enter a search term at Google, MSN, Yahoo!, or any of the other sites serviced by these search engines, they receive two types of listings: sponsored links, for which advertisers have paid to be listed (usually at the top of the search results page) and unsponsored "organic" search results. In addition, advertisers can purchase tiny text boxes on the right side of the Google and MSN search results page. The paid (sponsored) advertisements are

Search engine marketing

FIGURE 7-13   *How Google works*

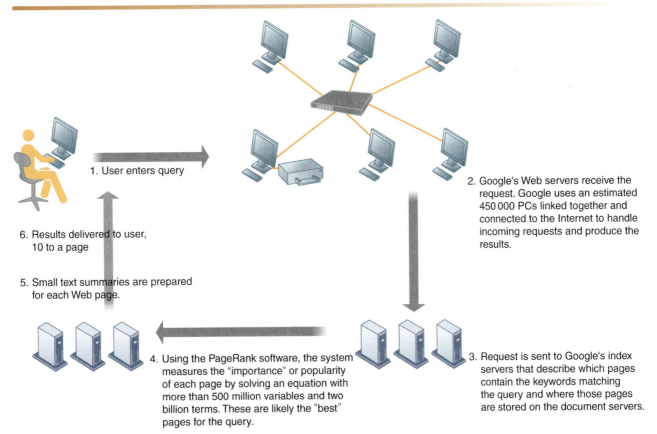

1. User enters query

2. Google's Web servers receive the request. Google uses an estimated 450 000 PCs linked together and connected to the Internet to handle incoming requests and produce the results.

6. Results delivered to user, 10 to a page

5. Small text summaries are prepared for each Web page.

4. Using the PageRank software, the system measures the "importance" or popularity of each page by solving an equation with more than 500 million variables and two billion terms. These are likely the "best" pages for the query.

3. Request is sent to Google's index servers that describe which pages contain the keywords matching the query and where those pages are stored on the document servers.

The Google search engine is continuously crawling the Web, indexing the content of each page, calculating its popularity, and storing the pages so that it can respond quickly to user requests to see a page. The entire process takes about one half second.

the fastest-growing form of Internet advertising and are powerful new marketing tools that precisely match consumer interests with advertising messages at the right moment (see the chapter-ending case study).

Search engines have become crucial tools within individual e-commerce sites. Customers can search easily for the product information they want with the help of an internal search program. However, within Web sites, the search engine is limited to finding matches from that one site.

Intelligent Agent Shopping Bots Chapter 15 describes the capabilities of software agents with built-in intelligence that can gather or filter information and perform other tasks to assist users. **Shopping bots** use intelligent agent software for searching the Internet for shopping information. Shopping bots such as MySimon or Froogle can help people interested in making a purchase filter and retrieve information about products of interest, evaluate competing products according to criteria the users have established, and negotiate with vendors for price and delivery terms. Many of these shopping agents search the Web for pricing and availability of products specified by the user and return a list of sites that sell the item along with pricing information and a purchase link.

Web 2.0 If you have shared photos over the Internet at Flickr or another photo site, blogged, looked up a word on Wikipedia, or contributed information yourself, you have used services that are part of Web 2.0. Today's Web sites do not just contain static content—they enable people to collaborate, share information, and create new services online. Web 2.0 refers to these second-generation interactive Internet-based services.

The innovations that distinguish **Web 2.0** are mashups, blogs, Rich Site Summary/ Really Simple Syndication (RSS), and wikis. Mashups, which we introduced in Chapter 5, are software services that enable users and system developers to mix and match content or software components to create something entirely new. For example, Yahoo!'s photo storage and sharing site Flickr combines photos with other information about the images provided by users and tools to make it usable within other programming environments.

With mashups, the Web is not just a collection of destination sites but a source of data and services that can be combined to create applications users need. Web 2.0 software applications run on the Web itself instead of the desktop and bring the vision of Web-based computing closer to realization.

A **blog**, the popular term for a Weblog, is an informal, yet structured Web site where subscribing individuals can publish stories, opinions, and links to other Web sites of interest. Blogs have become popular personal publishing tools, but they also have business uses (see Chapter 13).

If you are an avid blog reader, you might use RSS to keep up with your favourite blogs without constantly checking them for updates. **RSS**, which stands for Rich Site Summary or Really Simple Syndication, syndicates Web site content so that it can be used in another setting. RSS technology pulls specified content from Web sites and feeds it automatically to users' computers, where it can be stored for later viewing.

To receive an RSS information feed, you need to install aggregator or news reader software that can be downloaded from the Web. (For example, Microsoft Internet Explorer 7 includes RSS-reading capabilities.) Alternatively, you can establish an account with an aggregator Web site. You tell the aggregator to collect all updates from a given Web page, or list of pages, or gather information on a given subject by conducting Web searches at regular intervals. Once subscribed, you automatically receive new content as it is posted to the specified Web site. A number of businesses use RSS internally to distribute updated corporate information.

Blogs allow visitors to add comments to the original content, but they do not allow visitors to change the original posted material. A **wiki**, in contrast, is a collaborative Web site where visitors can add, delete, or modify content, including the work of previous authors. Wiki comes from the Hawaiian word for "quick." Probably the best-known wiki site is Wikipedia, the massive online open-source encyclopedia to which anyone can contribute.

Shopping bots

Web 2.0

Blog

RSS

Wiki

But wikis also are used for business. For example, investment bank Dresdner Kleinwort Wasserstein uses wikis instead of e-mail to create meeting agendas and post training videos for new hires.

Intranets and Extranets

Organizations use Internet networking standards and Web technology to create private networks called *intranets*. We introduced intranets in Chapter 1, explaining that an intranet is an internal organizational network that provides access to data across the enterprise. It uses the existing company network infrastructure along with Internet connectivity standards and software developed for the World Wide Web. Intranets create networked applications that can run on many different kinds of computers throughout the organization, including mobile handheld computers and wireless remote access devices.

While the Web is available to anyone, an intranet is private and is protected from public visits by **firewalls**—security systems with specialized software to prevent outsiders from entering private networks. Intranet software technology is the same as that of the World Wide Web. A simple intranet can be created by linking a client computer with a Web browser to a computer with Web server software using a TCP/IP network with software to keep unwanted visitors out.

Extranets A firm creates an extranet to allow authorized vendors and customers to have limited access to its internal intranet. For example, authorized buyers could link to a portion of a company's intranet from the public Internet to obtain information about the shipping and other details about their orders. The company uses firewalls to ensure that access to its internal data is limited and remains secure; firewalls also authenticate users, making sure that only authorized users access the site.

Both intranets and extranets reduce operational costs by providing the connectivity to coordinate disparate business processes within the firm and to link electronically to customers and suppliers. Extranets often are employed for collaborating with other companies for supply chain management, product design and development, and training efforts.

Technologies and Tools for Communication and E-Business

You have probably used e-mail and instant messaging at home and at work. They are some of the Internet-based tools that today's businesses use for communication and coordination. Others include electronic discussion groups, groupware, electronic conferencing, Internet telephony, and virtual private networks.

E-Mail, Chat, Instant Messaging, and Electronic Discussions **E-mail** enables messages to be exchanged from computer to computer, eliminating costly long-distance telephone charges while expediting communication among different parts of the organization. E-mail software has capabilities for routing messages to multiple recipients, forwarding messages, and attaching text documents or multimedia files to messages. Although some organizations operate their own internal electronic mail systems, a great deal of e-mail today is sent through the Internet.

Nearly 90 percent of U.S. workplaces have employees communicating interactively using **chat** or instant messaging tools. Chatting enables two or more people who are simultaneously connected to the Internet to hold live, interactive conversations. Chat groups are divided into channels, and each is assigned its own topic of conversation. Chat systems now support voice and video chat as well as written conversations. Many online retail businesses offer chat services on their Web sites to attract visitors, to encourage repeat purchases, and to improve customer service.

Instant messaging is a type of chat service that enables participants to create their own private chat channels. The instant messaging system alerts the user whenever someone on his or her private list is online so that the user can initiate a chat session with

Firewalls

E-mail

Chat

Instant messaging

other individuals. Instant messaging systems for consumers include Yahoo! Messenger, Windows Live Messenger, and AOL Instant Messenger. Companies concerned with security are building proprietary instant messaging systems with tools such as Lotus Sametime. Instant messaging has also migrated to cell phones and wireless handhelds.

Usenet newsgroups are worldwide discussion groups posted on Internet electronic bulletin boards on which people share information and ideas on a defined topic, such as radiology or rock bands. Anyone can post messages on these bulletin boards for others to read. Many thousands of groups exist that discuss almost all conceivable topics. Users can follow a "thread" in the discussion about a specific topic or conversation.

Employee use of e-mail, instant messaging, and the Internet is supposed to increase worker productivity, but the accompanying Window on Management section shows that this may not always be the case. Many company managers now believe they need to monitor their employees' online activity. Is this ethical? Although there are some strong business reasons why companies may need to monitor their employees' e-mail and Web activities, what does this mean for employee privacy?

Groupware and Electronic Conferencing   **Groupware** provides capabilities for supporting enterprise-wide communication and collaborative work. Individuals, teams, and workgroups at different locations in the organization use groupware for writing and commenting on group projects, sharing ideas and documents, conducting electronic meetings, tracking the status of tasks and projects, scheduling, and sending e-mail. Any group member can review the ideas of other group members at any time and add to them, or an individual can post a document for others to comment on or edit. Commercial groupware products, such as Lotus Notes and OpenText's LiveLink, are Internet-based. Microsoft Office Groove 2007 is an interesting groupware tool based on peer-to-peer technology that enables people to work directly with other people over the Internet without going through a central server, sharing files, conversations, and project documents.

A growing number of companies are using Internet conferencing tools to stage meetings, conferences, and presentations online. Web conferencing and collaboration software provide virtual conference tables for participants to view and modify documents and slides, write or draw on an electronic whiteboard, or share their thoughts and comments using chat or voice conferencing. The current generation of such tools from Lotus, Microsoft, and WebEx work through a standard Web browser. Web videoconferencing tools enable meeting participants equipped with Web cameras to see and talk to one another using their PCs and Web browsers. These forms of electronic conferencing are growing in popularity because they reduce the need for face-to-face meetings, saving travel time and cost.

Usenet newsgroups
Groupware

WINDOW ON MANAGEMENT

Monitoring Employees on Networks: Unethical or Good Business?

As Internet use has exploded worldwide, so has the use of e-mail and the Web for personal business at the workplace. A number of studies have concluded that at least 25 percent of employee online time is spent on non-work-related Web surfing, and perhaps as many as 90 percent of employees receive or send personal e-mail at work.

Many companies have begun monitoring their employee use of e-mail and the Internet, often without employee knowledge. Although North American companies have the legal right to monitor employee Internet and e-mail activity, is such monitoring unethical, or is it simply good business?

Managers worry about the loss of time and employee productivity when employees are focusing on personal rather than company business. A 2003 survey by Ipsos Reid found that the average Canadian worker wastes more than 4.5 hours per week surfing the Internet for personal reasons while at work (Evron, 2003). If personal traffic on company networks is too high, it can also clog the company's network so that business work cannot be performed. Downloading music or video files can severely limit the speed of the company's Internet traffic.

Too much time on personal business, on the Internet or not, can mean lost revenue or over-billed clients. Some employees may be charging time they spend trading their personal stocks online or pursuing other personal business to clients, thus overcharging the clients.

When employees use e-mail or the Web at employer facilities or with employer equipment, anything they do, including anything illegal, carries the company's name. Therefore, the employer can be traced and held liable. Management in many firms fear that racist, sexually explicit, or other potentially offensive material accessed or traded by their employees could result in adverse publicity and even lawsuits for the firm. Even if the company is found not to be liable, responding to lawsuits could cost the company tens of thousands of dollars. Companies also fear e-mail leakage of trade secrets.

Companies that allow employees to use personal e-mail accounts at work could face legal and regulatory trouble if they do not retain those messages. E-mail today is an important source of evidence for lawsuits, and companies are now required to retain all their e-mail messages for longer periods than in the past. Courts do not discriminate about whether e-mails involved in lawsuits were sent via personal or business e-mail accounts. Not producing those e-mails could result in a five- to six-figure fine.

Companies have the legal right to monitor what employees are doing with company equipment during business hours. The question is whether electronic surveillance is an appropriate tool for maintaining an efficient and positive workplace. Some companies try to ban all personal activities on corporate networks—zero tolerance. Others block employee access to specific Web sites or limit personal time on the Web using software that enables IT departments to track the Web sites employees visit, the amount of time employees spend at these sites, and the files they download. Some firms have fired employees who have stepped out of bounds. Nearly one-third of the companies surveyed in a Forrester Consulting study had fired at least one employee within the last year for breaking company e-mail rules.

No solution is problem-free, but many consultants believe companies should write corporate policies on employee e-mail and Internet use. The policies should include explicit ground rules that state, by position or level, under what circumstances employees can use company facilities for e-mail or Internet use. The policies should also inform employees whether these activities are monitored and explain why.

The rules should be tailored to specific business needs and organizational cultures. For example, although some companies may exclude all employees from visiting sites that have explicit sexual material, law firm or hospital employees may require access to these sites. Investment firms will need to allow many of their employees to access other investment sites. A company dependent on widespread information sharing, innovation, and independence could very well find that monitoring creates more problems than it solves.

To Think About

1. Should managers monitor employee e-mail and Internet usage? Why or why not?

2. Describe an effective e-mail and Web use policy for a company.

MIS in Action

Explore the Web site of a company selling online employee-monitoring software such as NetVizor (**www.netvizor.net**), SpyAgent (**www.spy-software-solutions.com/**), or Activity Monitor (**www.softactivity.com/**), and answer the following questions.

1. What employee activities does this software track? What can an employer learn about an employee by using this software?

2. How can businesses benefit from using this software?

3. How would you feel if your employer used this software where you work to monitor what you are doing on the job? Explain your response.

Sources: Alex Mindlin, "You've Got Someone Reading Your E-Mail," *The New York Times*, June 12, 2006; Darrell Dunn, "Who's Watching Now?" *InformationWeek*, February 27, 2006; and Jack M. Germain, "Monitoring Employee Communications in the Enterprise," *NewsFactor Network*, April 10, 2006.

Internet Telephony **Internet telephony** enables companies to use Internet technology for telephone voice transmission over the Internet or private networks. (Internet telephony products sometimes are called *IP telephony* products.) **Voice over IP (VoIP)** technology uses the Internet Protocol (IP) to deliver voice information in digital form using packet switching, avoiding the tolls charged by local and long-distance telephone networks (see Figure 7-14). Calls that would ordinarily be transmitted over public telephone networks would travel over the corporate network based on the Internet Protocol, or the public Internet. IP telephony calls can be made and received with a desktop computer equipped with a microphone and speakers or with a VoIP-enabled telephone.

VoIP is the fastest-growing form of telephone service in North America. During the first quarter of 2006, Statistics Canada data showed Canadians are indeed moving away from home phone use in favour of cell phones, VoIP, or a combination of the two. The 2006 Residential Telephone Service Survey says 615 000 Canadian households did not have home

Internet telephony
Voice over IP (VoIP)

FIGURE 7-14   *How IP telephony works*

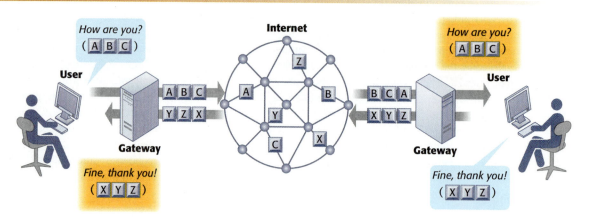

An IP phone call digitizes and breaks up a voice message into data packets that may travel along different routes before being reassembled at the final destination. A processor nearest the call's destination, called a gateway, arranges the packets in the proper order and directs them to the telephone number of the receiver or the IP address of the receiving computer.

phones, up 46 percent from 2005, which is attributable to increasing use of cell phones instead of land lines and to the increased use of VoIP. Skype, which offers free VoIP worldwide (computer-to-computer, with fee-based computer-to-land-line service) using a peer-to-peer network, has now been acquired by eBay while Google has its own similar free VoIP service.

Although there are up-front investments required for an IP phone system, VoIP can reduce communication and network management costs by 20 to 30 percent. For example, VoIP saves Virgin Entertainment Group $811 300 per year in long-distance bills (Hoover, 2006). In addition to lowering long-distance costs and eliminating monthly fees for private lines, an IP network provides a single voice-data infrastructure for both telecommunications and computing services. Companies no longer have to maintain separate networks or provide support services and personnel for each different type of network.

Another advantage of VoIP is its flexibility. Unlike the traditional telephone network, phones can be added or moved to different offices without rewiring or reconfiguring the network. With VoIP, a conference call is arranged by a simple click-and-drag operation on the computer screen to select the names of the conferees. Voice mail and e-mail can be combined into a single directory.

Virtual Private Networks   What if you had a marketing group charged with developing new products and services for your firm with members spread across North America. You would want to be able to e-mail one another and communicate with the home office without any chance that outsiders could intercept the communications. In the past, one answer to this problem was to work with large private networking firms who offered secure, private, dedicated networks to customers. But this was an expensive solution. A much less expensive solution is to create a virtual private network within the public Internet.

A **virtual private network (VPN)** is a secure, encrypted, private network that has been configured within a public network to take advantage of the economies of scale and management facilities of large networks, such as the Internet (see Figure 7-15). A VPN provides your firm with secure, encrypted communications at a much lower cost than the same capabilities offered by traditional non-Internet providers who use their private networks to secure communications. VPNs also provide a network infrastructure for combining voice and data networks.

Several competing protocols are used to protect data transmitted over the public Internet, including Point-to-Point Tunnelling Protocol (PPTP). In a process called tunnelling, packets of data are encrypted and wrapped inside IP packets. By adding this wrapper around a network message to hide its content, business firms create a private connection that travels through the public Internet.

Virtual private network (VPN)

FIGURE 7-15   *A virtual private network using the Internet*

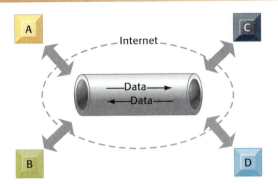

This VPN is a private network of computers linked using a secure "tunnel" connection over the Internet. It protects data transmitted over the public Internet by encoding the data and "wrapping" them within the Internet Protocol (IP). By adding a wrapper around a network message to hide its content, organizations can create a private connection that travels through the public Internet.

7.4   The Wireless Revolution

If you have a cell phone, do you use it for taking and sending photos, sending text messages, or downloading music clips? Do you take your laptop to class or to the library to link up to the Internet? If so, you are a part of the wireless revolution! Cell phones, laptops, and small handheld devices have morphed into portable computing platforms that let you perform some of the computing tasks you used to do at your desk.

Wireless communication helps businesses more easily stay in touch with customers, suppliers, and employees and provides more flexible arrangements for organizing work. Wireless technology has also created new products, services, and sales channels, which we discuss in Chapter 13.

Wireless Devices

If you require mobile communication and computing power or remote access to corporate systems, you can work with an array of wireless devices: PCs, cell phones, personal digital assistants (PDAs), e-mail handhelds, and smart phones. The Hyatt Regency Hotel in Osaka discussed at the beginning of the chapter is an example of a company using wireless devices for remote access from all areas of the hotel.

We introduced cell phones in Section 7.2. **Personal digital assistants (PDAs)** are small, handheld computers featuring applications such as electronic schedulers, address books, memo pads, and expense trackers. Many models feature e-mail messaging, wireless access to the Internet, voice communication, and digital cameras. **E-mail handhelds**, such as the BlackBerry Handheld, are a special type of handheld that is optimized for wireless text messaging. A hybrid device combining the functionality of a PDA with that of a digital cell phone is called a **smart phone**.

Cellular Systems

Chapter 5 explained that mobile phones are not only for voice communication—they have become mobile platforms for delivering digital data. Mobile phones enable many millions of people to communicate and access the Internet in Africa and other countries where conventional telephone or Internet service is expensive or unavailable.

Cellular Network Standards and Generations Digital cellular service uses several competing standards that are incompatible. This means that digital cellular handsets cannot work on networks that use another wireless standard.

In Europe and much of the rest of the world outside North America, the standard is **Global System for Mobile Communication (GSM)**. GSM's strength is its international roaming capability. Users have seamless same-number roaming in more than

Personal digital assistants (PDAs)

E-mail handhelds

Smart phone

Global System for Mobile Communication (GSM)

170 countries. Most GSM systems outside North America operate in the 900 MHz and 1.8 gigahertz (GHz) frequency bands. (In North America, they operate in the 1.9 GHz band.)

There are GSM cell phone systems in North America, including Rogers Wireless. However, the most widely used standard in North America is **Code Division Multiple Access (CDMA)**, which is the system used by Telus and Bell Mobility. The U.S. military developed CDMA during World War II. It transmits over several frequencies, occupies the entire spectrum, and randomly assigns users to a range of frequencies over time. In general, CDMA is cheaper to implement, is more efficient in its use of spectrum, and provides higher quality voice and data than GSM.

Cellular Generations

Most digital cellular systems today are used primarily for voice, but they are able to transmit data at rates ranging from 9.6 to 2 Mbps. Most cellular users in Canada with Web service adopt plans that offer 384 Kbps, which is acceptable for e-mail but not for downloading large files or entire Web pages. The most economical use of cellular technology for data transmission is SMS messaging. **Short message service (SMS)** is a text message service used by a number of digital cell phone systems to send and receive short alphanumeric messages less than 160 characters in length. Like e-mail, SMS messages can be forwarded and stored for later retrieval.

More powerful cellular networks called **third-generation (3G) networks** have transmission speeds ranging from 384 Kbps for mobile users in, say, a car, to more than 2 Mbps for stationary users. This is sufficient transmission capacity for video, graphics, and other rich media, in addition to voice, making 3G networks suitable for wireless broadband Internet access and always-on data transmission.

Wireless carriers have rolled out 3G services in many countries around the world including Canada. Those interested in high-speed Internet access and data transmission where 3G is unavailable are relying on an interim solution called 2.5G networks. **2.5G networks** use upgrades to the existing cellular infrastructure and feature data transmission rates ranging from 30 to 144 Kbps. However, an even newer type of service is now being developed. 4G (fourth generation) cellular communication systems will provide an end-to-end IP solution in which voice, data, and streaming multimedia can be served up at higher data rates anytime, anywhere. So far there is no formal definition of 4G, but its objective is to be a fully IP-based integrated system of systems and network of networks. In other words, 4G's goal is the convergence of wired and wireless networks, computers, consumer electronics, and communication technology, all at 100 Mbs and 1 Gbs, with only one billing.

Mobile Wireless Standards for Web Access

There are also multiple standards and technologies governing how cellular phones access the Internet and the World Wide Web. **Wireless Application Protocol (WAP)** is a system of protocols and technologies that enables cell phones and other wireless devices with tiny display screens, low-bandwidth connections, and minimal memory to access Web-based information and services. WAP uses Wireless Markup Language (WML), which is based on XML (see Chapter 5) and optimized for tiny displays.

A person with a WAP-compliant phone uses the built-in microbrowser to make a request in WML. A **microbrowser** is an Internet browser with a small file size that works with the low-memory constraints of handheld wireless devices and the low bandwidth of wireless networks. The request is passed to a WAP gateway, which retrieves the information from an Internet server in either standard HTML format or WML. The gateway translates HTML content back into WML for the WAP client to receive it. WAP (see Figure 7-16) supports most wireless network standards and operating systems for handheld computing devices.

I-mode is a wireless service offered by Japan's NTT DoCoMo mobile phone network that uses a different set of standards. Instead of using WAP, i-mode uses compact HTML to deliver content, making it easier for businesses to convert their HTML Web sites to mobile service. I-mode enables users to be connected constantly to the network and

Code Division Multiple Access (CDMA)

Short message service (SMS)

Third-generation (3G) networks

2.5G networks

Wireless Application Protocol (WAP)

Microbrowser

I-mode

FIGURE 7-16   *Wireless Application Protocol versus i-mode*

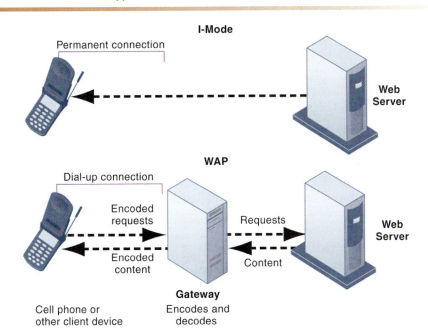

WAP and i-mode use alternative standards for accessing information from the wireless Web.

content providers to broadcast relevant information to users. (WAP users have to dial in to see if a site has changed—see Figure 7-16).

Wireless Computer Networks and Internet Access

If you have a laptop computer, you might be able to use it to access the Internet as you move from room to room in your dorm, or table to table in your university library. An array of technologies provides high-speed wireless access to the Internet for PCs and other wireless handheld devices as well as for cell phones. These new high-speed services have extended Internet access to numerous locations that could not be covered by traditional wired Internet services.

In rural areas, such as Alberta, base station wireless towers can be used to provide broadband access to the Internet and other services. Motorola's Canopy solution offers this type of technology. This permits those located outside highly populated areas to have broadband access the same as their more urban counterparts.

The Institute of Electrical and Electronics Engineers (IEEE) has established a hierarchy of complementary standards for wireless computer networks. These standards include IEEE 802.15 for the personal area network (Bluetooth), IEEE 802.11 for the local area network (LAN; Wi-Fi), and IEEE 802.16 for the metropolitan area network (MAN; WiMax).

Bluetooth **Bluetooth** is the popular name for the 802.15 wireless networking standard, which is useful for creating small personal area networks (PANs). It links up to eight devices within a 10-metre area using low-power, radio-based communication and can transmit up to 722 Kbps in the 2.4-GHz band.

Wireless phones, pagers, computers, printers, and computing devices using Bluetooth communicate with each other and even operate each other without direct user intervention (see Figure 7-17). For example, a person could direct a notebook computer to send a document file wirelessly to a printer. Bluetooth connects wireless keyboards and mice to PCs or cell phones to earpieces without wires. Bluetooth has low-power requirements, making it appropriate for battery-powered handheld computers, cell phones, or PDAs.

Bluetooth

FIGURE 7-17   *A Bluetooth network (personal area network)*

Bluetooth enables a variety of devices, including cell phones, PDAs, wireless keyboards and mice, PCs, and printers, to interact wirelessly with one another within a small 10-metre area. In addition to the links shown, Bluetooth can be used to network similar devices to send data from one PC to another, for example.

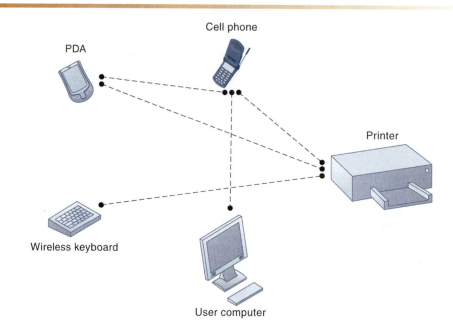

Although Bluetooth lends itself to personal networking, it has uses in large corporations. For example, Federal Express drivers use Bluetooth to transmit the delivery data captured by their handheld PowerPad computers to cellular transmitters, which forward the data to corporate computers. Drivers no longer need to spend time docking their handheld units physically in the transmitters, and Bluetooth has saved FedEx $31 800 000 per year.

Wi-Fi   The IEEE set of standards for wireless LANs is the 802.11 family, also known as **Wi-Fi** (for wireless fidelity). There are three standards in this family: 802.11a, 802.11b, and 802.11g. The 802.11n standard is an emerging standard for increasing the speed and capacity of wireless networking.

The 802.11a standard can transmit up to 54 Mbps in the unlicensed 5 GHz frequency range and has an effective distance of 10 to 30 metres. The **802.11b** standard can transmit up to 11 Mbps in the unlicensed 2.4 GHz band and has an effective distance of 30 to 50 metres, although this range can be extended outdoors by using tower-mounted antennas. The 802.11g standard can transmit up to 54 Mbps in the 2.4 GHz range. 802.11n will transmit at more than 200 Mbps.

Because 802.11b and 802.11g operate in the 2.4 GHz frequency, products built for either of these two standards are compatible. Products designed for the 802.11a specification will not work with either 802.11b or 802.11g because 802.11a uses a different frequency band.

802.11b was the first wireless standard to be widely adopted for wireless LANs and wireless Internet access. 802.11g is increasingly used for this purpose, and dual-band systems capable of handling 802.11b and 802.11g are available.

A Wi-Fi system can operate in two different modes. In infrastructure mode, wireless devices communicate with a wired LAN using access points. An **access point** is a box consisting of a radio receiver/transmitter and antennas that link to a wired network, router, or hub.

In ad hoc mode, also known as peer-to-peer mode, wireless devices communicate with each other directly and do not use an access point. Most Wi-Fi communication uses infrastructure mode. (Ad hoc mode is used for very small LANs in the home or small business offices.)

Figure 7-18 illustrates an 802.11 wireless LAN operating in infrastructure mode that connects a small number of mobile devices to a larger wired LAN. Most wireless devices

Wi-Fi

802.11b

Access point

FIGURE 7-18   *An 802.11 wireless local area network*

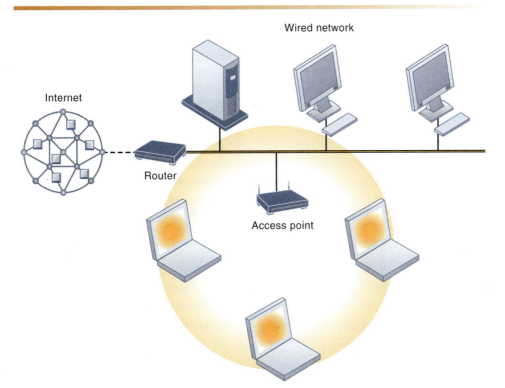

Mobile laptop computers equipped with network interface cards link to the wired LAN by communicating with the access point. The access point uses radio waves to transmit network signals from the wired network to the client adapters, which convert them into data that the mobile device can understand. The client adapter then transmits the data from the mobile device back to the access point, which forwards the data to the wired network.

are client machines. The servers that the mobile client stations need to use are on the wired LAN. The access point controls the wireless stations and acts as a bridge between the main wired LAN and the wireless LAN. (A bridge connects two LANs based on different technologies.) The access point also controls the wireless stations.

Mobile wireless stations often need an add-in card called a wireless **network interface card (NIC)** that has a built-in radio and antenna. **Wireless NICs** can be credit card–size cards that snap into the Personal Computer Memory Card International Association (PCM-CIA) card slot on a PC or external adapters that plug into the PC's universal serial bus (USB) port. Newer laptop PCs come equipped with chips that can receive Wi-Fi signals.

Wi-Fi and Wireless Internet Access   The 802.11 standard also provides wireless access to the Internet using a broadband connection. In this instance, an access point plugs into an Internet connection, which could come from a cable TV line or DSL telephone service. Computers within a range of the access point use it to link wirelessly to the Internet.

Large corporations and small businesses are using Wi-Fi networks to provide low-cost wireless LANs and Internet access. Wi-Fi hotspots are springing up in hotels, airport lounges, libraries, cafes, and college campuses to provide mobile access to the Internet. Carleton University is one of many campuses where students now use Wi-Fi for research, course work, and entertainment.

A **hotspot** typically consists of one or more access points positioned on a ceiling, wall, or other strategic spot in a public place to provide maximum wireless coverage for a specific area. Users in range of a hotspot are able to access the Internet from their laptops. Some hotspots are free or do not require any additional software to use; others may require activation and the establishment of a user account by providing a credit card number over the Web.

Wi-Fi technology poses several challenges, however. Right now, users cannot freely roam from hotspot to hotspot if these hotspots use different Wi-Fi network services. Unless the service is free, users need to log on to separate accounts for each service, each with its own fees.

Network interface card (NIC)

Wireless NIC

Hotspot

One major drawback of Wi-Fi is its weak security features, which make these wireless networks vulnerable to intruders. We provide more detail about Wi-Fi security issues in Chapter 8.

Another drawback of Wi-Fi networks is susceptibility to interference from nearby systems operating in the same spectrum, such as wireless phones, microwave ovens, or other wireless LANs. Wireless networks based on the 802.11n specification will solve this problem by using multiple wireless antennas in tandem to transmit and receive data and technology called MIMO (multiple input multiple output) to coordinate multiple simultaneous radio signals.

WiMax A surprisingly large number of areas in North America and throughout the world do not have access to Wi-Fi or fixed broadband connectivity. The range of Wi-Fi systems is no more than 91 metres from the base station, making it difficult for rural groups without cable or DSL service to find wireless access to the Internet.

The IEEE has developed a new family of standards known as WiMax to deal with these problems. **WiMax**, which stands for Worldwide Interoperability for Microwave Access, is the popular term for IEEE Standard 802.16, known as the "Air Interface for Fixed Broadband Wireless Access Systems." WiMax has a wireless access range of up to 50 kilometres, compared to 91 metres for Wi-Fi and 10 metres for Bluetooth, and a data transfer rate of up to 75 Mbps. The 802.16 specification has robust security and quality-of-service features to support voice and video.

WiMax antennas are powerful enough to beam high-speed Internet connections to rooftop antennas of homes and businesses that are kilometres away. Nortel is building Canada's first WiMax network in Alberta to support video, video calling, and other data-intensive wireless services for rural areas in the province. Intel has developed a special chip that facilitates WiMax access from mobile computers.

Broadband Cellular Wireless and Emerging Wireless Services Suppose your sales force needs to access the Web or use e-mail but cannot always find a convenient Wi-Fi hotspot? You can now plug a small card into your laptop and use your PC on a cellular network. Major cellular telephone carriers have configured their 3G networks to provide anytime, anywhere broadband access for PCs and other handheld devices. Bell Mobility and Rogers Wireless now offer wireless 3G access based on a technology called EV-DO, which stands for Evolution Data Optimized. **EV-DO** provides wireless access to the Internet over a cellular network at an average speed of 300 to 500 Kbps.

Cell phones, wireless PDAs, and laptops increasingly offer the ability to switch from one type of network to another. For example, most new cell phone handsets now have Bluetooth capabilities or the ability to support wireless calls over the Internet. These technologies can be used in mobile commerce, which is discussed in detail in Chapter 13.

Radio Frequency Identification and Wireless Sensor Networks

Mobile technologies are creating new efficiencies and ways of working throughout the enterprise. In addition to the wireless systems we have just described, radio frequency identification (RFID) systems and wireless sensor networks are having a major impact.

Radio Frequency Identification **Radio frequency identification (RFID)** systems provide a powerful technology for tracking the movement of goods throughout the supply chain. RFID systems use tiny tags with embedded microchips containing data about an item and its location to transmit radio signals over a short distance to special RFID readers. The RFID readers then pass the data over a network to a computer for processing. Unlike bar codes, RFID tags do not need line-of-sight contact to be read.

The transponder, or RFID tag, is electronically programmed with information that can uniquely identify an item plus other information about the item, such as its location, where and when it was made, or its status during production. Embedded in the tag is a microchip for storing the data. The rest of the tag is an antenna that transmits data to the reader.

WiMax

EV-DO

Radio frequency identification (RFID)

FIGURE 7-19   *How radio frequency identification works*

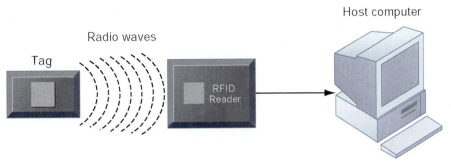

Radio waves

Tag

Host computer

RFID
Reader

RFID uses low-powered radio transmitters to read data stored in a tag at distances ranging from 2.54 centimetres to 30 metres. The reader captures the data from the tag and sends them over a network to a host computer for processing.

Contains a microchip that holds data, including an identification number. The rest of the tag is an antenna that transmits data to a reader.

Has an antenna that constantly transmits. When it senses a tag, it wakes it up, interrogates it, and decodes the data. Then it transmits the data to a host system over wired or wireless connections.

Processes the data from the tag that have been transmitted by the reader.

The reader unit consists of an antenna and radio transmitter with a decoding capability attached to a stationary or handheld device. The reader emits radio waves in ranges anywhere from 2.54 centimetres to 30 metres, depending on its power output, the radio frequency employed, and surrounding environmental conditions. When an RFID tag comes within the range of the reader, the tag is activated and starts sending data. The reader captures these data, decodes them, and sends them back over a wired or wireless network to a host computer for further processing (see Figure 7-19). Both RFID tags and antennas come in a variety of shapes and sizes. The most recent RFID chips to be developed are 0.05 millimetres square and look like bits of powder. They are so thin they could be embedded in a piece of paper.

RFID systems operate in a number of unlicensed frequency bands worldwide. Low-frequency systems (30 to 500 kHz) have short reading ranges (centimetres to a few metres); lower system costs; and are often used in security, asset tracking, or animal identification applications. High-frequency RFID systems (850 to 950 MHz and 2.4 to 2.5 GHz) offer reading ranges that can extend beyond 27 metres and are useful for applications such as railroad car tracking or automated toll collection for highways or bridges.

In inventory control and supply chain management, RFID systems capture and manage more detailed information about items in warehouses or in production than bar coding systems. If a large number of items are shipped together, RFID systems track each pallet, lot, or even unit item in the shipment. Manufacturers using RFID will be able to track the production history of each product for a better understanding of product defects and successes.

RFID has been available for decades, but widespread use was held back by the expense of the tags, which ranged from just under $1.00 to $20.00 each. Now the cost of a tag has dropped to about 20 cents and will drop to 5 cents within a few years. At these prices for tags, RFID becomes cost effective for many companies.

In addition to installing RFID readers and tagging systems, companies may need to upgrade their hardware and software to process the massive amounts of data produced by RFID systems—transactions that could add up to tens or hundreds of terabytes.

Special middleware is required to filter, aggregate, and prevent RFID data from overloading business networks and system applications. Applications will need to be redesigned to accept massive volumes of RFID-generated data frequently and to share those data with other applications. Major enterprise software vendors, including SAP and Oracle-PeopleSoft, now offer RFID-ready versions of their supply chain management applications.

The following Window on Organizations section deals with these issues. Wal-Mart now requires some of its top suppliers to use passive RFID tags on cases and pallets shipped to its stores to help it track and record inventory flow. Suppliers have been proceeding slowly because of difficulties in RFID implementation.

WINDOW ON ORGANIZATIONS

Organization

Wal-Mart Grapples With RFID

On February 1, 2005, Wal-Mart began rolling out its first RFID applications in seven of its Texas stores. Wal-Mart had ordered its top suppliers to place RFID tags on all products shipped to specific distribution centres. The objective was to reduce out-of-stock items by tracking item location more precisely as goods moved from the receiving dock to store shelves.

Wal-Mart wanted RFID readers installed at store receiving docks to record the arrival of cases of goods that were shipped with RFID tags. The RFID reader would read the tags a second time just as the cases were brought to the sales floor from back-room storage areas. Software would use sales data from Wal-Mart's point-of-sale systems and the RFID data about the number of cases brought out to the sales floor to figure out which items would soon be depleted, and automatically generate a list of items to pick in the warehouse to replenish store shelves. This information would help Wal-Mart reduce out-of-stock items, increase sales, and further reduce costs.

Wal-Mart is sharing all its RFID data with suppliers through its Retail Link extranet. The RFID data improve inventory management because suppliers know exactly where their goods are located within 30 minutes of the goods' movement from one part of a Wal-Mart store to another. Sales improve because the system allows Wal-Mart to always have products in stock.

Despite these benefits, the RFID implementations did not go exactly as planned. In late 2004, Wal-Mart scaled back its original demands, requiring suppliers to attach RFID tags to only 65 percent of their products. Even then, not all suppliers could comply. Only 30 percent made the major technology and business process changes to integrate RFID into their IT infrastructures and information systems. The rest were practising what is called "slap and ship," sticking an RFID tag to a small percentage of cases and pallets slated for Wal-Mart. They did not make further changes to their systems so that they could actually use the data generated by RFID to track product movement and inventory costs.

Why was there such supplier resistance to RFID? Some industry analysts believe Wal-Mart tried to impose a top-down mandate for suppliers to use RFID before the technology matured and was cost-effective. "We don't have a business case for RFID," commented a supply chain executive for one of the world's largest consumer goods manufacturers who did not want to be identified. "Because the standards are not complete, the equipment isn't developed. . . . I can't fulfill Wal-Mart's demand," he said.

RFID tags in early 2005 were costing suppliers between 26 and 78 cents each, still too expensive to be cost-effective. RFID-tagging a case of goods might easily cost a supplier an additional 42 to 53 cents per case—about 21 to 33 cents for the tag, and the remainder for labour costs to affix the tags. A large supplier that shipped 15 million cases and pallets to Wal-Mart each year would be spending an extra $7 million in tag costs.

Wal-Mart wanted all the cases on a pallet RFID-tagged and did not distinguish between a case containing video games or one containing toothpaste. RFID tagging would obviously contribute much more to costs for suppliers of low-cost items than for suppliers of high-value merchandise.

Moreover, RFID tags, particularly the least expensive types, may not perform properly when they are near certain liquids, metals, or porous objects. Kimberly-Clark's baby wipes absorbed radio-frequency signals, and Unilever had similar problems with liquid-containing products. To ensure accuracy and proper performance, suppliers may have to use more expensive tags. Integrating the new RFID data with legacy systems amplifies the costs.

Acknowledging these difficulties, Wal-Mart is working with suppliers individually to help them get up to speed. Today, Wal-Mart has more than 600 suppliers (only 3 percent of Wal-Mart's suppliers) that use RFID tags on cases and pallets. Over 1000 Wal-Mart stores handle more than 3 million RFID-tagged cases and pallets per week. RFID helped Wal-Mart reduce out-of-stock merchandise in its stores by 30 percent in the fall of 2005 compared with a year earlier.

To Think About

1. How is RFID technology related to Wal-Mart's business model? How does it benefit suppliers?

2. What management, organization, and technology factors explain why Wal-Mart suppliers had trouble implementing RFID systems?

3. What conditions would make adopting RFID more favourable for suppliers?

4. Should Wal-Mart require all its suppliers to use RFID? Why or why not? Explain your answer.

MIS in Action

Explore the RFID Privacy Page at the Electronic Privacy Information Center (EPIC) (**www.epic.org/privacy/rfid**) and answer the following questions.

1. Describe some RFID applications that might pose a threat to privacy. What information does RFID enable them to track?

2. How do these applications threaten personal privacy? How serious is this threat?

3. Should these RFID applications be deployed? Why or why not? Justify your answer.

Sources: Laurie Sullivan, "Hey, Wal-Mart, New Case of Pampers Is on the Way," *InformationWeek*, January 23, 2006; Elena Malykhina, "RFID: Beyond the Pallet," *InformationWeek*, June 19, 2006; Mark Roberti, "Wal-Mart Begins RFID Process Changes, *RFID Journal*, February 1, 2005; and Thomas Wailgum, "Tag, You're Late," *CIO Magazine*, November 15, 2004; and Mary Hayes Weier, "RFID: Hold the Revolution, Pass the Incremental Change," *InformationWeek*, April 2, 2007.

Wireless Sensor Networks If your company wanted state-of-the art technology to monitor building security or detect hazardous substances in the air, it might deploy a wireless sensor network. **Wireless sensor networks (WSNs)** are networks of interconnected wireless devices that are embedded into the physical environment to provide measurements of many points over large spaces. These devices have built-in processing, storage, and radio frequency sensors and antennas. They are linked into an interconnected network that routes the data they capture to a computer for analysis.

These networks range from hundreds to thousands of nodes. Because wireless sensor devices are placed in the field for years at a time without any maintenance or human intervention, they must have very low power requirements and batteries capable of lasting for years.

Sensor networks typically have a tiered architecture, such as that used by the wireless security system illustrated in Figure 7-20. This particular wireless sensor network starts with low-level sensors and progresses toward nodes for high-level data aggregation, analysis, and storage. Both simple and complex data are routed over a network to an automated facility that provides continuous building monitoring and control.

Wireless sensor networks are valuable in areas such as monitoring environmental changes, monitoring traffic or military activity, protecting property, efficiently operating and managing machinery and vehicles, establishing security perimeters, monitoring supply chain management, or detecting chemical, biological, or radiological material.

Wireless sensor networks (WSNs)

FIGURE 7-20   *A wireless sensor network for a security system*

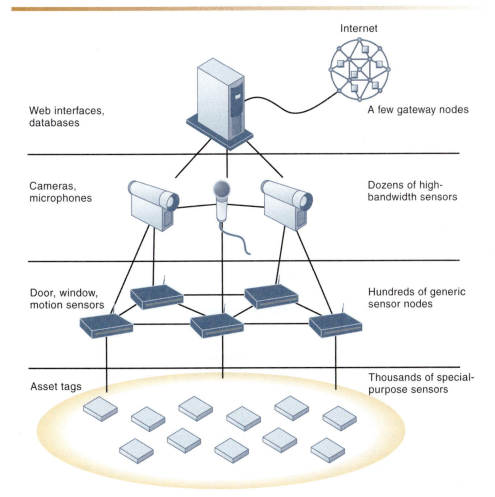

Internet

Web interfaces, databases

A few gateway nodes

Cameras, microphones

Dozens of high-bandwidth sensors

Door, window, motion sensors

Hundreds of generic sensor nodes

Asset tags

Thousands of special-purpose sensors

Each level of this wireless sensor network handles different types of sensing. Lower-level sensors for monitoring events, such as doors opening and closing, motion, and breakage of windows and doors, are complemented by a small group of more advanced sensors placed in key locations, such as cameras and acoustic and chemical detectors.

Source: From Jason Hill, Mike Horton, Ralph Kling, and Lakshman Krishamurthy, "The Platforms Enabling Wireless Sensor Networks," *Communications of the ACM 47*, no. 6 (June 2004).

Summary

1. ***Describe the features of telecommunications networks and identify key networking technologies.***

   A simple network consists of two or more connected computers. Basic network components include computers, network interfaces, a connection medium, network operating system software, and either a hub or a switch. The networking infrastructure for a large company relies on both public and private infrastructures to support the movement of information across diverse technological platforms. It includes the traditional telephone system, mobile cellular communication, wireless local area networks (LANs), videoconferencing systems, a corporate Web site, intranets, extranets, and an array of local and wide area networks, including the Internet. This collection of networks evolved from two fundamentally different types of networks: telephone networks and computer networks.

   Contemporary networks have been shaped by the rise of client/server computing, the use of packet switching, and the adoption of Transmission Control Protocol/Internet Protocol (TCP/IP) as a universal communications standard for linking disparate networks and computers. Client/server networks have distributed much of the organization's computing power to the desktop and factory floor. Packet switching makes more efficient use of network communications capacity by breaking messages into small packets that are sent independently along different paths in a network and then reassembled at their destinations. Protocols provide a common set of rules that enable communication among diverse components in a telecommunications network. TCP/IP is a suite of protocols that is the connectivity model used for the Internet.

2. ***Evaluate alternative transmission media, types of networks, and network services.***

   The principal physical transmission media are twisted copper telephone wire, coaxial copper cable, fibre-optic cable, and wireless transmission. The choice of transmission medium depends on the distance and volume of communication required by the organization and on its financial resources. Twisted wire enables companies to use existing wiring for telephone systems for digital communication. Fibre-optic and coaxial cable are used for high-volume transmission but are expensive to install. Microwave and satellite are used for wireless communication over long distances. The transmission capacity of a medium, known as the bandwidth, is determined by the range of frequencies it can accommodate.

   There are different types of networks and network services available to organizations. Network selection and design should be based on the organization's information requirements and the distance required for transmission. LANs connect PCs and other digital devices together within a 500-metre radius and are used today for many corporate computing tasks. Network components may be connected together using a star, bus, or ring topology. Wide area networks (WANs) span broad geographical distances, ranging from several kilometres to continents, and are private networks that are independently managed. Metropolitan area networks (MANs) span a single urban area while campus area networks (CANs) span a campus of buildings or a military base.

   A number of network services are available to organizations requiring high-bandwidth transmission. Frame relay is a shared network service with transmission speeds ranging from 56 Kbps to more than 40 Mbps; it relies on digital circuits that require less error checking than packet switching. Asynchronous Transfer Mode (ATM) provides transmission speeds of 1.5 Mbps to more than 9 Gbps, parcelling data into fixed 53-byte cells. ATM can pass data between computers from different vendors and is popular for transmitting data, video, and audio over the same network. Integrated Services Digital Network (ISDN) is an international standard for dial-up network access that uses existing local telephone lines to integrate voice, data, image, and video services. Basic-rate ISDN can transmit data at a rate of 128 Kbps.

   Digital subscriber line (DSL) technologies, cable Internet connections, and T1 lines are often used for high-capacity Internet connections. Like ISDN, DSL technologies also operate over existing copper telephone lines to carry voice, data, and video, but they have higher transmission capacities than ISDN. Asymmetric Digital Subscriber Line (ADSL) supports a transmission rate of 1.5 to 9 Mbps when receiving data and up over 700 Kbps when sending data. Symmetric Digital Subscriber Line (SDSL) supports the same transmission rate for sending and receiving data of up to 3 Mbps.

   Cable Internet connections provide high-speed access to the Web or corporate intranets at speeds of up to 10 Mbps. T lines are high-speed data lines leased from communications providers. A T1 line supports a data transmission rate of 1.544 Mbps.

3. ***Demonstrate how the Internet and Internet technology work and how they support communication and e-business.***

   The Internet is a worldwide network of networks that uses the client/server model of computing and the TCP/IP network reference model. Every computer on the Internet is assigned a unique numeric IP address. The Domain Name System (DNS) converts IP addresses to domain names so that users need only to specify a domain name to access a computer on the Internet instead of typing in the numeric IP address. No one owns the Internet, and it has no formal management organization. However, worldwide Internet policies are established by organizations and government bodies, such as the Internet Architecture Board and the World Wide Web Consortium. The Internet must also conform to the laws of the sovereign nation-states in which it operates as well as the technical infrastructures that exist within the nation-state.

Major Internet services include e-mail, Usenet, chatting, instant messaging, Telnet, FTP, and the World Wide Web. Web pages are based on Hypertext Markup Language (HTML) and can display text, graphics, video, and audio. Web site directories, search engines, and Rich Site Summary or Really Simple Syndication (RSS) technology help users locate the information they need on the Web. RSS, blogs, and wikis are features of Web 2.0. Web technology and Internet networking standards provide the connectivity and interfaces for internal private intranets and private extranets that can be accessed by many different kinds of computers inside and outside the organization.

Internet-based groupware and electronic conferencing software provide tools to support communication and collaboration when people work together in groups or work teams, often in different locations. Firms are also starting to realize economies by using Internet telephony, which enables Internet technology to be used for telephone voice transmission. Internet technology can also reduce communication costs by enabling companies to create virtual private networks (VPNs) as low-cost alternatives to private WANs.

4. *Identify and describe the principal technologies and standards for wireless networking, communication, and Internet access.*

Cellular networks have evolved from slow-speed (1G) analog networks to high-speed, high-bandwidth, digital, third-generation (3G) networks with speeds ranging from 144 Kbps to more than 2 Mbps for data transmission. Second-generation (2G) cellular networks are digital circuit-switched networks used primarily for voice transmission, but they can also transmit data at rates ranging from 9.6 to 14.4 Kbps. 2.5G networks are packet switched, use many existing infrastructure elements, and have data transmission rates ranging from 50 to 144 Kbps.

Major cellular standards include Code Division Multiple Access (CDMA), which is used primarily in North America, and Global System for Mobile Communication (GSM), which is the standard in Europe and much of the rest of the world but is also spreading throughout North America. Alternative standards governing the way wireless mobile devices access the Internet

and the World Wide Web include Wireless Application Protocol (WAP) and i-mode.

Standards for wireless computer networks include Bluetooth (802.15) for small personal area networks (PANs), Wi-Fi (802.11) for LANs, and WiMax (802.16) for metropolitan area networks (MANs). Bluetooth can link up to eight devices within a 10-metre area using low-power, radio-based communication and can transmit up to 722 Kbps in the 2.4 GHz band. Wireless phones, keyboards, computers, printers, and PDAs using Bluetooth can communicate with each other and even operate each other without direct user intervention.

The most popular of the 802.11 standards are 802.11b and 802.11g. The 802.11b standard can transmit up to 11 Mbps in the unlicensed 2.4 GHz band. The 802.11g standard can transmit up to 54 Mbps in the same frequency range. The 802.11b standard has been the most widely used standard for creating wireless LANs and providing broadband wireless Internet access. However, 802.11b is vulnerable to penetration by outsiders and interference from other wireless devices in the same frequency spectrum.

WiMax has a wireless access range of up to 50 kilometres and a data transfer rate of up to 75 Mbps, making it suitable for providing broadband Internet access in areas lacking DSL and cable lines. The 802.16 specification also has robust security and quality-of-service features to support voice and video.

Major cellular carriers are also upgrading their networks to provide wireless broadband access to the Internet at an average speed of 300 to 500 Kbps. A new technology called EV-DO provides relatively fast Internet access over a cellular network.

5. *Assess the business value of wireless technology and important wireless applications in business.*

Wireless technology increases productivity and worker output by providing anytime, anywhere communication and access to information, including the information resources of the Internet. Wireless communication helps businesses stay in touch more easily with customers, suppliers, and employees and provides more flexible arrangements for organizing work.

Mobile wireless technology facilitates supply chain management by capturing data on the movement of goods as these events take place and by providing detailed, immediate information as goods move among supply chain partners. Radio frequency identification (RFID) systems provide a powerful technology for this purpose. These systems use tiny tags that have embedded microchips that contain data about an item and its location. The tags transmit radio signals over a short distance to special RFID readers. The RFID readers then pass the data over a network to a computer for processing.

Wireless sensor networks (WSNs) are networks of interconnected wireless devices with some processing and radio-transmitting capability that are embedded into the physical environment to provide measurements of many points over large spaces. Wireless sensor networks are valuable for monitoring environmental changes, traffic patterns, security incidents, or supply chain events.

Key Terms

2.5G networks, 248	Global System for Mobile Communication (GSM), 247	Ring network, 230
802.11b, 250		Router, 224
Access point, 250	Groupware, 244	RSS, 242
Analog signal, 228	Hertz, 232	Satellite, 231
Asynchronous Transfer Mode (ATM), 233	Home page, 240	Search engine, 240
Backbone, 230	Hotspot, 251	Search engine marketing, 241
Bandwidth, 232	Hubs, 224	Shopping bots, 242
Blog, 242	Hypertext Transfer Protocol (HTTP), 239	Short message service (SMS), 248
Bluetooth, 249	I-mode, 248	Smart phone, 247
Bus network, 230	Information appliance, 238	Star network, 230
Cable Internet connections, 233	Instant messaging, 243	Switch, 224
Campus area network (CAN), 228	Integrated Services Digital Network (ISDN), 233	T lines, 233
CA*net4, 237	Internet Protocol (IP) address, 234	Third-generation (3G) networks, 248
Cellular telephone (cell phone), 232	Internet service provider (ISP), 234	Topology, 229
Chat, 243	Internet telephony, 245	Transmission Control Protocol/Internet Protocol (TCP/IP), 227
Coaxial cable, 230	Internet2, 237	
Code Division Multiple Access (CDMA), 248	Internetworking, 234	Twisted wire, 230
Connectivity, 226	Local area network (LAN), 228	Uniform resource locator (URL), 239
Dedicated server computer, 224	Metropolitan area network (MAN), 230	Usenet newsgroups, 244
Dense wavelength division multiplexing (DWDM), 231	Microbrowser, 248	Virtual private network (VPN), 246
	Microwave, 231	Voice over IP (VoIP), 245
Digital signal, 228	Modem, 228	Web 2.0, 242
Digital subscriber line (DSL), 233	Multiplexing, 231	Web site, 240
Domain name, 235	Network interface card (NIC), 251	Web master, 240
Domain Name System (DNS), 234	Network operating system (NOS), 224	Wide area network (WAN), 230
E-mail, 243	Optical network, 231	Wi-Fi, 250
E-mail handheld, 247	Packet switching, 226	Wiki, 242
EV-DO, 252	Peer-to-peer, 229	WiMax, 252
Fibre-optic cable, 230	Personal digital assistant (PDA), 247	Wireless Application Protocol (WAP), 248
Firewall, 243	Protocol, 227	Wireless NIC, 251
Frame relay, 232	Radio frequency identification (RFID), 252	Wireless sensor networks (WSNs), 255

Review Questions

1. Describe the features of a simple network and the network infrastructure for a large company.

2. Name and describe the principal technologies and trends that have shaped contemporary telecommunications systems.

3. What is a local area network (LAN)? What are the components of a typical LAN? What are the functions of each component?

4. Name and describe the principal network topologies.

5. Name the different types of physical transmission media and compare them in terms of speed and cost.

6. Define the following: WAN, MAN, 3G, modem, protocol, optical network, bandwidth, and Internet2.

7. List and describe the various broadband network services.

8. What is the Internet? How does it work? How does it provide business value?

9. Explain how the domain name and IP addressing system work.

10. List and describe the principal Internet services.

11. List and describe alternative ways of locating information on the Web.

12. What are intranets and extranets? How do they provide value to businesses?

13. Name and describe the principal technologies and tools that support communication and electronic business.

14. What are Internet telephony and virtual private networks? How do they provide value to businesses?

15. Compare Bluetooth, Wi-Fi, WiMax, and EV-DO. What are their capabilities? For what types of applications is each best suited?

16. Compare the WAP and i-mode standards for wireless access to the Web.

17. What is RFID? How does it work? How does it provide value to businesses?

18. What are wireless sensor networks? How do they work? What applications use them?

Discussion Questions

1. *Network design is a key business decision as well as a technology decision. Why?*

2. *Should all major retailing and manufacturing companies switch to RFID? Why or why not?*

3. *Should organizations with little or no technical support (e.g., smaller organizations) implement wireless technologies? Why or why not?*

4. *What do you think are the future business applications of 4G cellular networks?*

Teamwork : Comparing Mobile Internet Access Devices

Form a group with three or four of your classmates. Evaluate mobile devices with Internet access from two different vendors, such as Palm, BlackBerry, Nokia, Samsung, or Motorola. Your analysis should consider the purchase cost of each device, the wireless networks where each device can operate, the cost of wireless Internet services, and what other services are available for each device. You should also consider other capabilities of each device, including the ability to integrate with existing corporate or PC applications. Which device would you select? What criteria would you use to guide your selection? If possible, use electronic presentation software to present your findings to the class.

Learning Track Modules

Computing and Communications Services Provided by Commercial Telecommunications Vendors. The Learning Track Module on MyMISLab for Chapter 7 describes the communication and computing services from major telecommunications vendors that are now available to individuals and businesses.

Cellular System Generations. This Learning Track Module on MyMISLab for Chapter 7 compares the transmission technologies and capacities of first-, second-, and third-generation wireless cellular systems.

Wireless Applications for CRM, SCM, and Health Care. The Learning Track Module on MyMISLab for Chapter 7 describes how wireless systems are used in customer relationship management, supply chain management, and health care.

For online exercises, please visit www.pearsoned.ca/mymislab.

HANDS-ON MIS   Application Exercises

The projects in this section give you hands-on experience designing Internet applications to increase employee efficiency, using spreadsheet software to improve selection of telecommunications services, and using Web search engines for business research.

Achieving Operational Excellence:
Using Internet Tools to Increase Efficiency and Productivity

Software skills: Web browser software and presentation software
Business skills: Employee productivity analysis

In this project, you will suggest applications of Internet technology to help employees at a real-world company work more efficiently.

Dirt Bikes Canada's management is concerned about how much money is being spent communicating with people inside and outside the company and on obtaining information about developments in the motorcycle industry and the global economy. You have been asked to investigate how Internet tools and technology could be used to help Dirt Bikes Canada's employees communicate and obtain information more efficiently. Dirt Bikes Canada provides Internet access to all its employees who use desktop computers.

1. How could the various Internet tools help employees at Dirt Bikes Canada? Create a matrix showing what types of employees and business functions would benefit from using each type of tool and why.

2. How could Dirt Bikes Canada benefit from intranets for its sales and marketing, human resources, and manufacturing and production departments? Select one of these departments and describe the kind of information that could be provided by an intranet for that department. How could this intranet increase efficiency and productivity for that department?

3. (Optional) Use electronic presentation software to summarize your findings for management.

Improving Decision Making:
Using Spreadsheet Software to Evaluate Wireless Services

Software skills: Spreadsheet formulas, formatting
Business skills: Analyzing telecommunications services and costs

In this project, you will use the Web to research alternative wireless services and use spreadsheet software to calculate wireless service costs for a sales force.

You would like to equip your sales force of 35 based in St. John's, Newfoundland, with mobile phones that have capabilities for voice transmission, text messaging, and taking and sending photos. Use the Web to select a wireless service provider that provides nationwide service as well as

good service in your home area. Examine the features of the mobile handsets offered by each of these vendors. Assume that each of the 35 salespeople will need to spend three hours per day during business hours (8 a.m. to 6 p.m.) on mobile voice communication, and send 30 text messages per day and five photos per week. Use your spreadsheet software to determine the wireless service and handset that will offer the best pricing per user over a two-year period. For the purposes of this exercise, you do not need to consider corporate discounts.

Achieving Operational Excellence:
Using Web Search Engines for Business Research

Software skills: Web search tools
Business skills: Researching new technologies

This project will help develop your Internet skills in using Web search engines for business research.

With the price of home heating oil and natural gas skyrocketing, you believe that fuel cells might be a reasonable, cost-effective alternative for home heating systems as well as co-generation of electricity; however, you don't know much about fuel cells, their current cost per kilowatt of output, or their BTU heat output. You would like to explore a possible new business model for supplying heating and electricity to homes. Your first step will be to figure out how

fuel cells work. Second, you want some information on the economics of small fuel cells. For instance, how much do they cost? Finally, you want to know how much heat and electricity could small fuel cells potentially generate for a home. Use the following four search engines to obtain that information: Yahoo!, Google, MSN, and Ask.com. If you wish, try some other search engines as well. Compare the volume and quality of information you find with each search tool. Which tool is the easiest to use? Which produced the best results for your research? Why do the results differ if all search engines search the same Web?

CASE STUDY Google Takes on the World

The rise of Google, whose capitalization now tops $6.4 billion, has been fast and fierce. Founders Sergey Brin and Larry Page met in 1995 as Stanford University graduate students. They created a search engine that combined the technologies of

Page's PageRank system, which evaluates a page's importance based on the external links to it, and Brin's Web crawler, which visits Web sites and records a summary of their content. Because Google was so effective, it quickly became the search engine of choice for Web users. Today, Google handles nearly 50 percent of Web searches.

Google stopped displaying the number of Web pages it indexed after the number surpassed 8 billion in 2005, but some estimates now place the number at 25 billion. Google's index also includes one billion images and one billion Usenet newsgroup messages. In addition to searching for Web pages, Google users can search for PDF, PostScript, text, Microsoft Office, Lotus, PowerPoint, and Shockwave files. Google claims to be one of the five most popular sites on the Internet with more than 380 million unique users per month and more than 50 percent of its traffic coming from outside the United States.

Google's IT infrastructure is a closely guarded secret because it is part of its competitive advantage. The best guess is that Google has up to 450 000 servers spread over at least 25 locations around the world. These servers use inexpensive off-the-shelf hardware to run a customized version of the Linux operating system and other critical pieces of custom software. These include MapReduce, a programming model to simplify processing and create large data sets; Google WorkQueue, a system that groups queries and schedules them for distributed processing; and the Google File System, which keeps copies of data in several places so that the data will always be available even if a server fails.

According to a widely cited estimate, Google needs only to spend $1 for every $3 each of its competitors spends to deliver a comparable amount of computing power. This inexpensive, flexible infrastructure explains the speed of Google Web searches and its ability to provide its users with such a vast array of Web-based services and software tools.

Most of Google's revenue comes from online advertising and online search services. Google Search Services enable organizations to include the Google search engine on their own Web pages. This is a straightforward technology licensing arrangement—not groundbreaking, but profitable.

The side of Google that has driven its phenomenal growth and profits is its advertising program. In a fraction of a second, Google's technology can evaluate millions of variables about its users and advertisers, correlate them with millions of potential ads, and deliver the message to which each user is most likely to respond. Because this technology makes ads more relevant, users click on ads 50 to 100 percent more often on Google than on Yahoo!, creating a better return for advertisers. According to *eMarketer*, Google grabbed about 70 percent of all paid search advertising.

In 2000, Google launched AdWords, a self-service advertising program in which vendors bid to have their ads placed alongside the search results for specific keyword queries. In 2002, AdWords Select introduced cost-per-click (CPC) pricing so that advertisers pay for their ads only when users actually click on them. Google determines the placement of ads through a combination of the CPC and click-through (total number of clicks) rates so that the most relevant ads for a keyword string appear in the most prominent positions. The keyword-targeted ads appear throughout the Google Network, which includes America Online, Shopping.com, Ask.com, *The New York Times* on the Web, and many other high-profile Web sites.

AdWords has come under some fire for being vulnerable to a practice known as click-fraud. A business whose ad receives thousands of clicks from sources that have no intention of making a purchase may run through its marketing budget quickly and have to drop out of the ad game altogether. Unscrupulous businesses have tried to use click fraud to drive up the cost of competitors' ads and put them at a competitive disadvantage.

Google and its competitor, Yahoo!, have been criticized for their vague response to the problem. Google credits customers for invalid clicks. It also has a system in place to detect click-fraud before customers are charged. Google does not disclose details about its antifraud methods to advertisers because of security concerns.

Although advertising customers are worried about fraud attacks, Google must be concerned with legitimate offensives from its rivals. Yahoo! has been sponsoring prominent academic economists and other researchers to find new ways of using its data about online consumer behaviour to increase market share for its services and the revenue generated by its searches.

Another competitor, Microsoft, has a history of diminishing or destroying its competitors by exploiting the fact that its Microsoft Windows operating system can be found on 95 percent of the world's personal computers. Netscape Navigator, Lotus 1-2-3, and WordPerfect have all been defeated in this manner.

Microsoft launched MSN Search in November 2004, but this search service made only a marginal dent in the market, accounting for 13 percent of worldwide search requests. Still, that 13 percent could double now that Microsoft's Windows Vista operating system has entered the marketplace. Microsoft plans to integrate search technology into Windows Vista and into upcoming versions of Office.

Two other areas where Microsoft can vault ahead of Google are context-aware searches and "Deep Web" searches. By personalizing search technology, a search engine can return results that accurately match the context of the user's query, producing more relevant search outcomes. Because Microsoft has the capital to purchase the rights to copyrighted material and owns powerful digital rights management software, the company is considered a good candidate to become the gateway to the Deep Web's massive quantity of documents and data that are not indexed by search engines.

Microsoft's battle for Google's market share goes beyond search engines. To Microsoft, Google has ceased being a search technology company and is now a software company, capable of infringing on the markets that Microsoft dominates. In the past, Microsoft has thwarted competition through strategic pricing and feature enhancements, as well as by tying its products together so that they are the most convenient to use. Microsoft may not find it so easy to thwart Google. Other software manufacturers had to rely on Windows as a platform on which to run their products. Since Google's applications are Web-based and not tied to the Windows operating system, Microsoft cannot use its operating system monopoly to limit access to Google. Google is giving away its Linux-based programs over the Internet for free.

In the spring of 2006, Google introduced Google Spreadsheets, a Web-based spreadsheet application, and also acquired the company Writely, which offers a Web-based word processor. In late August of that year, Google offered a package targeting businesses called Google Apps for Your Domain that bundles e-mail, calendar, instant messaging, and Web page creation services that run on Google's computers. Competition with Microsoft will intensify when Google adds its online spreadsheet, word-processing, and collaboration applications to the Apps suite and markets the whole package to large companies.

How far Google can eat into Microsoft's software franchise is uncertain, but Microsoft fears that Google's Web-based computing model could make it possible for computer users to bypass its products entirely.

Google is constantly looking for new ways to grow. Its AdSense program scans Web pages for target words and displays appropriate advertisements, enabling Web site operators to generate revenue from their sites. Google introduced the Google Toolbar, which enables Web surfers to search the Google index without visiting the Google home page. The toolbar also provided one of the Web's earliest defences against pop-up ads. Google's image search index launched in 2001 and now archives more than one billion images. In 2002, Google News appeared, becoming the first Internet news service compiled completely by computer algorithms, and offering customized news alerts by e-mail.

In April 2004, Google announced Gmail, its Web-based e-mail service, offering free online storage to users. Google made headlines later that year when it released Google Desktop Search, a downloadable program for searching personal files on a computer, including e-mail, productivity files, browsing history, and instant message conversations. The latest version of Google Desktop introduced Gadgets, small applications that bring specific content such as news, weather, or cartoons, along with highly targeted ads, directly to the user's desktop.

Other popular services that Google has introduced include Froogle, a consumer product locator; Google Maps, which includes dynamic online mapping and satellite pictures of searchable addresses; and Google Earth, which includes photographs that can be zoomed in and out for almost the entire Earth. Google also acquired and improved Picasa digital photo management software, which is downloadable free of charge, and introduced a free instant messaging and voice communication service for personal computers called Google Talk. Instant messaging is now fully integrated with Gmail so users can chat in the same window in which they compose and read e-mail. Taking advantage of the social networking craze started by Web sites such as Friendster and MySpace, Google partnered with Nike to create an online, invitation-only community for soccer fans worldwide called **Joga.com**.

Not all of Google's products have been met with unanimous enthusiasm. Gmail, for instance, raised the ire of privacy advocates because it uses the same technology as AdSense to place advertisements alongside messages. The selection of ads is based on the actual text of the messages, meaning that every Gmail message is read by an automated scanner.

Google Checkout, which stores users' credit card numbers and shipping information to facilitate online purchases, is forging new relationships with online merchants, who receive a more favourable transaction charge from Google than they would get from credit card companies. Google's roster of paying advertisers continues to grow.

Google Video allows users to search for and then purchase TV shows, sports broadcasts, film clips, and music videos. In this area, Google has less experience than Yahoo! in negotiating with content providers, who are particularly concerned with piracy in the digital age. Eric Schmidt, Google's CEO, says that video search and its corresponding rights issues "will be a major story for Google for years." In the meantime, profits continue to soar, and Google will continue to innovate. Schmidt estimates that Google will need 300 years to organize all of the information in the world.

Sources: Thomas Claburn, "Google Revealed," *InformationWeek*, August 28, 2006; Ben Worthen, "The Enterprise Gets Googled," *CIO Magazine*, May 1, 2006; Thomas Claburn, "Google Goes to Work," *InformationWeek*, February 27, 2006; Ben Elgin and Jay Greene, "The Counterattack on Google," *Business Week*, May 8, 2006; Steve Lohr and Saul Hansell, "Microsoft and Google Set to Wage Arms Race," *The New York Times*, May 2, 2006; David F. Carr, "How Google Works," *Baseline*, July, 2006; Kevin J. Delaney, "Hoping to Overtake Its Rivals, Yahoo Stocks Up on Academics," *The Wall Street Journal*, August 25, 2006 and "Google Bundles Package of Tools for Business, Education Markets," *The Wall Street Journal*, August 28, 2006; Saul Hansell, "Your Ads Here (All of Them)," *The New York Times*, October 30, 2005; John Markoff, "Google to Offer Instant Messaging and Voice Communications on Web," *The New York Times*, August 24, 2005; Fred Vogelstein, "Search and Destroy," *Fortune*, May 2, 2005; Kevin J. Delaney, "Web Start-Ups Vie to Detect 'Click Fraud,'" *The Wall Street Journal*, June 9, 2005; and Kevin J. Delaney and Mylene Mangalindan, "Google Plans Online-Payment Service," *The Wall Street Journal*, June 20, 2005.

CASE STUDY QUESTIONS

1. Evaluate Google using the competitive forces and value chain models described in Chapter 3.

2. What are Google's sources of competitive advantage? How does it provide value to its users?

3. What problems and challenges does Google face in this case? What management, organization, and technology factors are responsible for these problems and challenges?

4. Does Google's business strategy effectively address these challenges? Explain your answer.

5. How successful do you think Google will be in the future?

CHAPTER 8

Securing Information Systems

LEARNING OBJECTIVES

After completing this chapter, you will be able to do the following:

1. Analyze why information systems need special protection from destruction, error, and abuse.

2. Assess the business value of security and control.

3. Design an organizational framework for security and control.

4. Evaluate the most important tools and technologies for safeguarding information resources.

OPENING CASE | Phishing: A Costly New Sport for Internet Users

Elizabeth Owen almost lost her identity. A frequent eBay user, she received an e-mail that appeared to come from eBay's payment service PayPal asking her to update her credit information or be barred from future purchases. She immediately started assembling the data. Right before she was to transmit it, she stopped. Her office, the National Association of Consumer Agency Administrators, had received constant complaints of e-mail scams. Even with this knowledge, she had almost become a victim of a special type of identify theft called phishing.

A phishing attack sends e-mail that claims to be from a bank, credit card company, retailer, or other company directing the recipient to a Web site where that person is asked to enter vital information, such as bank account numbers, social security numbers, credit card details, or online passwords. The Web site appears to be legitimate, but it's actually bogus. Scam

artists use information obtained through phishing to drain bank or credit card accounts or sell the information to others to do the same.

According to FraudWatch International, a vendor of anti-phishing products, Bank of Montreal, Royal Bank of Canada, TD Canada Trust, and CIBC top the list of Canadian financial brand names hijacked by phishers. Most phishing losses have been absorbed by the banks and credit card companies, but fear of identity theft has discouraged a significant number of people from using online financial services.

What can be done to combat phishing and prevent confidence from disappearing?

A number of approaches are helpful. First, companies can educate their consumers about phishing scams. All the major Canadian banks (and probably the smaller ones, too) warn their Web site visitors about the dangers of phishing along with providing

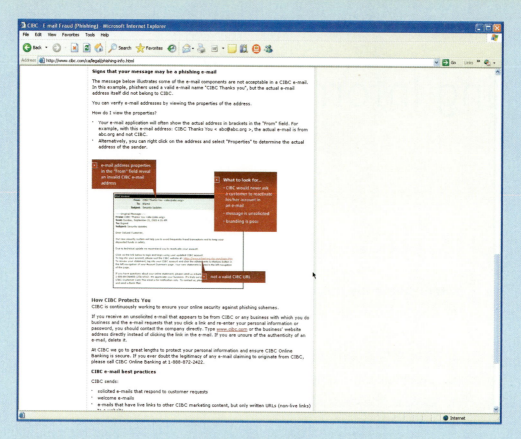

warning signs of potentially fraudulent e-mails. Most assert that they will never send customers e-mail requesting sensitive information.

Individual Web sites and Internet service providers (ISPs) have started using anti-phishing products and services. Some services sift through junk e-mail. Others scour the Web for bogus sites, issuing blacklists of known phishing sites to warn consumers about them. Some monitor online banking sites for signs the sites are being cased as possible targets and even contact Internet service providers to remove offending sites.

Banks are starting to blunt phishing attacks by requiring two-factor authentication of online customers—i.e., their user names and passwords plus something extra, such as a tiny, unique photo. In the U.S., Bank of America has implemented a system called SiteKey that requires Internet customers to choose a digital image (such as a picture of a cat) from an archive, name that image, and answer various secret questions, such as "What is your first pet's name?" to help the bank verify their identity. The software will not allow users to enter their password into the bank's Web site until they see and acknowledge their image, which proves they are on the real Bank of America site rather than a bogus site.

However, other banks are hesitant to adopt such measures, for fear that they will make Internet banking too difficult. Even Bank of America itself has experienced some problems. Although SiteKey cut down on phishing attacks, the bank experienced a spike in customer service calls because online users forgot their answers to the secret questions.

Sources: Sarah D. Scalet, "Two-Factor Too Scarce at Consumer Banks," *CIO Magazine*, July 11, 2006; Deborah Gage, "Helping Customers Help Themselves," *Baseline Magazine*, May 15, 2006; Robin Arnfield, "Online Banking: How Safe Is Your Money?" NewsFactor Network, January 20, 2006; and Kimberly Morrison, "Internet Sees Increase in 'Phishing' for Online Victims," *Knight Ridder Newspapers*, February 28, 2005.

The problems created by phishing for companies such as Bank of Montreal, eBay, and PayPal as well as for individual consumers illustrate some of the reasons why businesses need to pay special attention to information system security. Phishing and identity theft have cost banks and financial services billions of dollars and individual victims much agony and worry. They also discourage individuals from making Internet purchases or from using online financial services, thereby lowering revenues and profits.

The chapter-opening Business Challenges diagram calls attention to important points raised by this case and this chapter. Phishing has proliferated because so many people

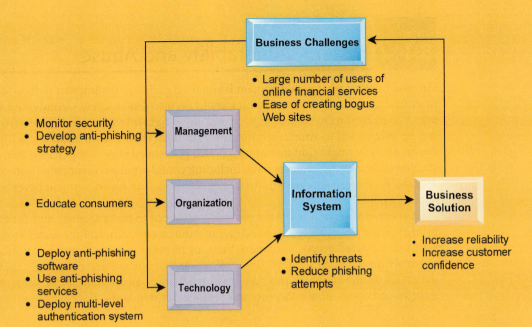

use online financial services and because the technology for phishing is readily available. Combatting phishing is a complex problem that involves multiple approaches, including education, new tools and technologies, and better authentication procedures. No single approach is sufficient. Moreover, approaches such as multi-step authentication procedures are helpful, but problematic in that they may make it more difficult to visit a Web site or use a system.

This is true not only of anti-phishing efforts but for information system security as a whole. Securing information systems from unauthorized access, abuse, destruction, or tampering of assets requires a combination of training, procedures, and technologies. The cost and difficulty of using all these must be balanced with the net benefits to the business in the form of greater customer trust, uninterrupted operations, compliance with government regulations, and protection of financial assets.

HEADS UP

This chapter focuses on how to secure your information systems and the information inside them. As e-commerce and e-business have grown to encompass so much of our lives, we have all become much more aware of the need to secure digital information. Your customers expect you to keep their digital private information secure and confidential. As your business increasingly relies on the Internet, you will become vulnerable to a variety of attacks against your systems that could, if successful, put you out of business in a very short time. To protect your business, you will need to pay more attention to security and control than ever before.

- If your career is in finance or accounting, you will need to work with information system controls to prevent errors, fraud, and disruption of services that lead to large monetary losses and the erosion of customer confidence.

- If your career is in human resources, you will be dealing with "people factors," which are as important as technology in establishing the security and reliability of the firm's information systems. Many security breaches and system errors are caused by legitimate company insiders, and the human resources function is responsible for training programs and establishing security awareness among employees.

- If your career is in manufacturing and production or operations management, you will be concerned with preventing security breaches and downtime as your firm links with the systems of other firms for supply chain management.

- If your career is in information systems, you will be working with technologies and procedures to ensure your company's systems are reliable and secure.

- If your career is in sales and marketing, you will be concerned with secure payment systems for online purchases, as well as measures for ensuring that customer data are secure and properly used.

8.1 System Vulnerability and Abuse

Can you imagine what would happen if you tried to link to the Internet without a firewall or antivirus software? Your computer could be disabled in a few seconds, and it might take you many days to recover. If you used the computer to run your business, you might not be able to sell to your customers or place orders with your suppliers while it was down. And you might find that outsiders had penetrated your computer system, perhaps stealing or destroying valuable data, including confidential payment data from your customers. If too much data were destroyed or divulged, your business might never be able to operate again!

In short, if you operate a business today, you need to make security and control a top priority. **Security** refers to the policies, procedures, and technical measures used to prevent unauthorized access, alteration, theft, or physical damage to information systems. **Controls** consist of all the methods, policies, and organizational procedures that ensure the safety of the organization's assets, the accuracy and reliability of its accounting records, and operational adherence to management standards.

Why Systems Are Vulnerable

When large amounts of data are stored in electronic form, they are vulnerable to many more kinds of threats than when they existed in manual form. Through communications networks, information systems in different locations are interconnected. The potential for unauthorized access, abuse, or fraud is not limited to a single location but can occur at any access point in the network.

Figure 8-1 illustrates the most common threats against contemporary information systems. They can stem from technical, organizational, and environmental factors compounded by poor management decisions. In the multitier client/server computing environment illustrated here, vulnerabilities exist at each layer and in the communications between the layers. Users at the client layer can cause harm by introducing errors, accessing the system without authorization, or unknowingly downloading spyware and viruses. Hackers can, through a variety of ruses, access data flowing over networks, steal valuable data during transmission, or alter messages without authorization. Needless to say, the Internet and other networks are highly vulnerable to disruptions from radiation. Intruders can launch denial-of-service attacks or malicious software to disrupt the

FIGURE 8-1 *Contemporary security challenges and vulnerabilities*

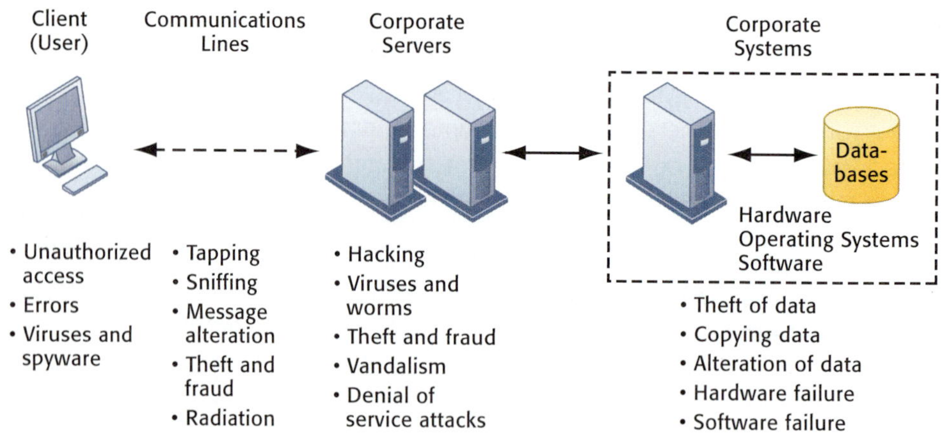

The architecture of a Web-based application typically includes a Web client, a server, and corporate information systems linked to databases. Each of these components presents security challenges and vulnerabilities. Floods, fires, power failures, and other electrical problems can cause disruptions at any point in the network.

Client (User)	Communications Lines	Corporate Servers	Corporate Systems
• Unauthorized access • Errors • Viruses and spyware	• Tapping • Sniffing • Message alteration • Theft and fraud • Radiation	• Hacking • Viruses and worms • Theft and fraud • Vandalism • Denial of service attacks	Hardware Operating Systems Software • Theft of data • Copying data • Alteration of data • Hardware failure • Software failure

operation of Web sites. Those capable of penetrating corporate systems can destroy or alter corporate data stored in databases or files.

Systems malfunction if computer hardware breaks down, is not configured properly, or is damaged by improper use or criminal acts. Errors in programming, improper installation, or unauthorized changes cause computer software to fail. Power failures, floods, fires, or other natural disasters can also disrupt computer systems.

Domestic or offshore partnering with another company adds to system vulnerability if valuable information resides on networks and computers outside the organization's control. Without strong safeguards, valuable data could be lost or destroyed, or could fall into the wrong hands, revealing important trade secrets or information that violates personal privacy.

Internet Vulnerabilities Large public networks, such as the Internet, are more vulnerable than internal networks because they are open to anyone. The Internet is so huge and so fast that when abuses do occur, they can have an enormously widespread impact in a matter of minutes. When corporate networks link to the Internet, the firm's information systems are vulnerable to attacks from outsiders.

High-speed broadband networks do not help matters. Computers that are constantly connected to the Internet by cable or digital subscriber line (DSL) modems are more open to penetration by outsiders than older dial-up lines. Computers with high-speed access are typically connected for a greater number of hours per day; attacks can take place much faster; and for DSL lines that offer clients fixed IP addresses, the identity of the local computer is easier to establish. A fixed Internet address creates a fixed target for hackers.

Telephone service based on Internet technology (see Chapter 7) can be more vulnerable than the switched voice network if it does not run over a secure, private network. Most Voice over IP (VoIP) traffic over the public Internet is not encrypted, so hackers can potentially listen in on conversations at a number of points from the local area network (LAN) modem to neighbourhood servers. Hackers can intercept conversations to obtain credit card and other confidential personal information or shut down voice service by flooding servers supporting VoIP with bogus traffic.

Vulnerability has also increased from widespread use of e-mail and instant messaging (IM). E-mail may contain attachments that serve as springboards for malicious software or unauthorized access to internal corporate systems. Employees may use e-mail messages to transmit valuable trade secrets, financial data, or confidential customer information to unauthorized recipients. Popular instant messaging applications for consumers do not use a secure layer for text messages, so they can be intercepted and read by outsiders during transmission over the public Internet. IM activity over the Internet can in some cases be used as a back door to an otherwise secure network.

Wireless Security Challenges Is it safe to log onto a wireless fidelity (Wi-Fi) hotspot network at an airport, library, or other public location? Generally not, because these networks are "open" and "unsecured," meaning that anyone can gain access, and the communication between your laptop and the wireless server is not encrypted. In spite of its availability, encryption is not frequently used to secure wireless networks in homes, and hackers passing by in cars or on bicycles can easily use your network and listen to your communications using your wireless router. Even Bluetooth communication devices have notorious holes in the security of their communications.

Although the range of Wi-Fi networks is only less than 100 metres, it can be extended up to 500 metres using external antennae. Outsiders armed with laptops, wireless cards, external antennae, and hacking software can easily penetrate LANs using the 802.11 standard. Hackers use these tools to detect unprotected networks, monitor network traffic, and, in some cases, gain access to the Internet or to corporate networks.

Wi-Fi transmission technology was designed to make it easy for stations to find and hear one another. The service set identifiers (SSIDs) identifying the access points in a

FIGURE 8-2   *Wi-Fi security challenges*

Many Wi-Fi networks can be penetrated easily by intruders using sniffer programs to obtain an address to access the resources of a network without authorization.

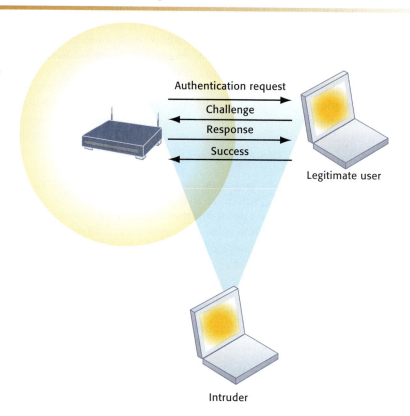

Wi-Fi network are broadcast multiple times and can be picked up fairly easily by intruders' sniffer programs (see Figure 8-2). Wireless networks in many locations do not have basic protections against **war driving**, in which eavesdroppers drive by buildings or park outside and try to intercept wireless network traffic.

A hacker can employ an 802.11 analysis tool to identify the SSID. (Windows XP has capabilities for detecting the SSID used in a network and automatically configuring the radio network interface card [NIC] within the user's device.) An intruder that has associated with an access point by using the correct SSID can then access other resources on the network, using the Windows operating system to determine which other users are connected to the network, access their computer hard drives, and open or copy their files.

An intruder may also use the information gleaned to set up a rogue access point in a location close to a user. The intruder then broadcasts on a different radio channel in order to force the user's radio NIC to associate with the rogue access point. Once this association occurs, hackers using the rogue access point can capture the names and passwords of unsuspecting users.

The initial security standard developed for Wi-Fi, called Wired Equivalent Privacy (WEP), is not very effective. WEP is built into all standard 802.11 products, but its use is optional. Many users neglect to use WEP security features, leaving them unprotected. The basic WEP specification calls for an access point and all its users share the same 40-bit encrypted password, which can be easily decrypted by hackers from a small amount of traffic. Manufacturers of wireless networking products are now beefing up their security by offering stronger encryption and authentication systems.

Malicious Software: Viruses, Worms, Trojan Horses, and Spyware

Malicious software programs are referred to as **malware** and include a variety of threats, such as computer viruses, worms, and Trojan horses. **Spyware** is technology that aids in gathering information about a person or organization without their knowledge.

War driving

Malware

Spyware

A **computer virus** is a rogue software program that attaches itself, usually without user knowledge or permission, to other software programs or data files in order to be executed. Most computer viruses deliver a "payload." The payload may be relatively benign, such as the instructions to display a message or image, or it may be highly destructive—destroying programs or data, clogging computer memory, reformatting a computer's hard drive, or causing programs to run improperly. Viruses typically spread from computer to computer when users take an action, such as sending an e-mail attachment or copying an infected file.

Most recent attacks have come from **worms**, which are independent computer programs that copy themselves from one computer to other computers over a network. Unlike viruses, worms operate on their own without attaching to other computer program files. They rely less on human behaviour in order to spread from computer to computer. This explains why computer worms spread much more rapidly than computer viruses. Worms destroy data and programs as well as disrupt or even halt the operation of computer networks.

Worms and viruses are often spread over the Internet from files of downloaded software, files attached to e-mail, compromised e-mail messages, or instant messaging. Viruses have also invaded computerized information systems from "infected" disks or infected machines. E-mail worms are currently the most problematic.

Now viruses and worms are spreading to wireless computing devices. For example, the Cabir worm, which first appeared in early 2005, targets mobile devices running the popular Symbian mobile operating system and spreads through Bluetooth wireless networks. Cabir continually seeks other Bluetooth devices and eventually runs down a device's battery. Mobile device viruses pose serious threats to enterprise computing because so many wireless devices are now linked to corporate information systems.

Computer virus

Worms

TABLE 8-1   *Examples of Malicious Code*

NAME	TYPE	DESCRIPTION
Sasser.ftp	Worm	First appeared in May 2004. Spread over the Internet by attacking random IP addresses. Causes computers to continually crash and reboot, and infected computers to search for more victims. Affected millions of computers worldwide, disrupting British Airways flight check-ins, operations of British coast guard stations, Hong Kong hospitals, Taiwan post office branches, and Australia's Westpac Bank. Sasser and its variants caused an estimated $17 billion to $21 billion in damages worldwide.
MyDoom.A	Worm	First appeared January 26, 2004. Spreads as an e-mail attachment. Sends e-mail to addresses harvested from infected machines, forging the sender's address. At its peak, this worm lowered global Internet performance by 10 percent and Web page loading times by as much as 50 percent. Was programmed to stop spreading after February 12, 2004.
Bagle	Worm	First appeared January 18, 2004. Infected PCs via an e-mail attachment, then used the PC e-mail addresses for replicating itself. Infected PCs and their data could be accessed by remote users and applications. Bagle.B stopped spreading after January 28, 2004, but other variants are still active. Has caused tens of millions of dollars in damage already.
Sobig.F	Worm	First detected on August 19, 2003. Spreads via e-mail attachments and sends massive amounts of mail with forged sender information. Deactivated itself on September 10, 2003, after infecting more than 1 million PCs and doing $6 to $12 billion in damage.
ILoveYou	Virus	First detected on May 3, 2000. Script virus written in Visual Basic script and transmitted as an attachment to e-mail with the subject line ILOVEYOU. Overwrites music, image, and other files with a copy of itself and did an estimated $12 billion to $17 billion in damage.
Melissa	Macro virus/worm	First appeared in March 1999. Word macro script mailing an infected Word file to first 50 entries in user's Microsoft Outlook address book. Infected 15 to 29 percent of all business PCs, causing $350 million to $700 million in damage.
CIH (Chernobyl)	Virus	Unleashed in June 1998. Infected Windows executable files and overwrote the data on a PC's hard drive. Destroyed huge amounts of PC data, creating $22 to $88 million in damage worldwide.

Table 8-1 describes the characteristics of some of the most harmful worms and viruses that have appeared to date.

Over the past decade, worms and viruses have caused billions of dollars of damage to corporate networks, e-mail systems, and data. Among the companies surveyed in the ICSA Labs Tenth Annual Virus Prevalence Survey, recovering from virus and malware attacks took respondents an average of seven person days and cost an average of $150 000 per respondent (ICSA Labs, 2005).

A **Trojan horse** is a software program that appears to be benign but then does something unexpected. The Trojan horse is not itself a virus because it does not replicate but is often a way for viruses or other malicious code to be introduced into a computer system. The term Trojan horse is based on the huge wooden horse used by the Greeks to trick the Trojans into opening the gates to their fortified city during the Trojan War. Once inside the city walls, Greek soldiers hidden in the horse revealed themselves and captured the city.

An example of a modern-day Trojan horse is DSNX-05, detected in early 2005. It was unleashed by a bogus e-mail message appearing to come from Microsoft, which directed recipients to visit a Web site designed to look like the Microsoft Windows Update page. The Web site downloaded and installed malicious code on the compromised computer. Once this Trojan horse was installed, hackers could access the computer remotely without detection and use it for their own purposes.

Some types of spyware also act as malicious software. These small programs install themselves surreptitiously on computers to monitor user Web surfing activity and serve up advertising. Thousands of forms of spyware have been documented. Harris Interactive found that 92 percent of the companies surveyed in its Web@Work study reported detecting spyware on their networks (Mitchell, 2006).

Spyware is not just annoying. It offers outsiders the possibility of invading your privacy and stealing your personal identity, including PIN codes, logins, and account information. **Key loggers** record every keystroke made on a computer to steal serial numbers for software, to launch Internet attacks, to gain access to e-mail accounts, to obtain passwords to protected computer systems, or to pick up personal information such as credit card numbers. Other spyware programs reset Web browser home pages, redirect search requests, or slow computer performance by taking up too much memory.

Hackers and Cybervandalism

A **hacker** is an individual who intends to gain unauthorized access to a computer system. Within the hacking community, the term **cracker** is typically used to denote a hacker with criminal intent although in the public press, the terms hacker and cracker are used interchangeably. Hackers and crackers gain unauthorized access by finding weaknesses in the security protections employed by Web sites and computer systems, often taking advantage of various features of the Internet that make it an open system that is easy to use.

Hacker activities have broadened beyond mere system intrusion to include theft of goods and information, as well as system damage and **cybervandalism**, the intentional disruption, defacement, or even destruction of a Web site or corporate information system. For example, on August 20, 2006, hackers broke into the computer hosting the Web site of Kevin Mitnick, an ex-hacker turned security consultant, and replaced the home page with one displaying a vulgar message (Evers, 2006).

Spoofing and Sniffing Hackers attempting to hide their true identities often try **spoofing**, or misrepresenting, themselves by using fake e-mail addresses or masquerading as someone else. Spoofing also may involve redirecting a Web link to an address different from the intended one, with the site masquerading as the intended destination.

For example, if hackers redirect customers to a fake Web site that looks almost exactly like the true site, they can then collect and process orders, effectively stealing business as well as sensitive customer information from the true site. We provide more detail on other forms of spoofing in our discussion of computer crime.

A **sniffer** is a type of eavesdropping program that monitors information travelling over a network. When used legitimately, sniffers help identify potential network trouble spots

Trojan horse
Key loggers
Hacker
Cracker
Cybervandalism
Spoofing
Sniffer

or criminal activity on networks, but when used for criminal purposes, they can be damaging and very difficult to detect. Sniffers enable hackers to steal proprietary information from anywhere on a network, including e-mail messages, company files, and confidential reports.

Denial-of-Service Attacks In a **denial-of-service (DoS) attack**, hackers flood a network server or Web server with many thousands of false communications or requests for services to crash the network. The network receives so many queries that it cannot keep up with them and is thus unavailable to service legitimate requests.

A **distributed denial-of-service (DDoS) attack** uses hundreds or even thousands of computers to inundate and overwhelm a network from numerous launch points.

Although DoS attacks do not destroy information or access restricted areas of a company's information systems, they often cause a Web site to shut down, making it impossible for legitimate users to access the site. For busy e-commerce sites, these attacks are costly; while the site is shut down, customers cannot make purchases. Especially vulnerable are small and midsize businesses whose networks tend to be less protected than those of large corporations.

Perpetrators of DoS attacks often use thousands of "zombie" PCs infected with malicious software without their owners' knowledge and organized into a botnet. Hackers create these **botnets** infecting other people's computers with bot malware that opens a back door through which an attacker can give instructions. The infected computer then becomes a slave, or zombie, serving a master computer belonging to someone else. Once a hacker infects enough computers, he or she can use the amassed resources of the botnet to launch distributed denial-of-service attacks, phishing campaigns, or unsolicited "spam" e-mail (see Chapter 4).

Experts estimate that there are over three million bots active around the world in any given day, and each day those bots infect hundreds of thousands of Internet-connected devices (Gage and Nash, 2006). The Window on Technology section describes some of these bot attacks, illustrating their scope and severity.

Figure 8-3 illustrates the estimated worldwide damage from all forms of digital attack, including hacking, malware, and spam between 1999 and 2005.

Denial-of-service (DoS) attack
Distributed denial-of-service (DDos) attack
Botnets

FIGURE 8-3 *Worldwide damage from digital attacks*

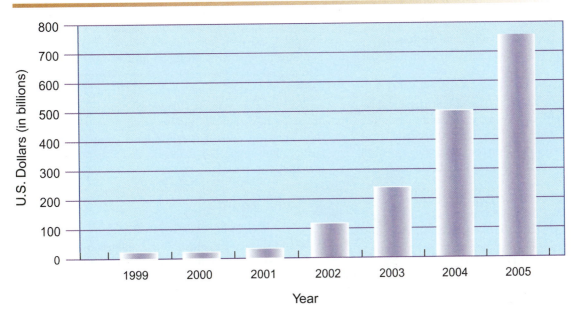

This chart shows estimates of the average annual worldwide damage from hacking, malware, and spam since 1999. These data are based on figures from mi2G and the authors.

WINDOW ON TECHNOLOGY

Bot Armies and Network Zombies

On July 7, 2004, Gary Chiacco reported to federal authorities that customers had difficulty accessing his Jersey-Joe.com online sports apparel site for several days. Unable to conduct business, Jersey-Joe lost hundreds of thousands of dollars in sales.

Jersey-Joe had become the victim of a denial-of-service attack, in which the Web site was bombarded by so many requests that the site overloaded and went offline. As investigators worked on the case into the fall of 2004, the attacks worsened to such a degree that the company hosting the Jersey-Joe Web site asked Chiacco to take his site elsewhere because the attacks were affecting service to other Web sites hosted by the company.

Investigators discovered that the attacks came from computers belonging to college students in Massachusetts and Pennsylvania that were infected with software that made them "zombies." These computers were receiving instructions from a user whose IP address was traced to a high school student in Edison, New Jersey, named Jasmine Singh.

The teenager had been hired to launch these attacks by 18-year-old Jason Arabo, another online seller of sports apparel who wanted to harm his competition. The government gave Singh a five-year prison sentence, which it believes was justified by the widespread harm to Chiacco and other businesses affected by Singh and Arabo's actions. Arabo could be imprisoned for up to ten years.

Building and selling bots for malicious purposes has become a serious money-making enterprise. James Ancheta, a self-taught computer expert, pleaded guilty in a Los Angeles court on January 23, 2006, to building and selling bots and using his network of thousands of bots to commit crimes. His botnet infected at least 400 000 computers, including machines at two U.S. Department of Defense facilities, and had installed unauthorized adware that earned him more than US $60 000.

Adware companies pay other companies for each digital advertisement they install on a PC. The adware tries to display pop-up ads related to the user's activity, such as the terms the user searched for at Google. Ancheta abused this system by instructing his bots to install ads on computers they had taken over so he could collect fees for placing the ads—as much as 40 cents per successful placement.

Ancheta also rented or sold bots to people interested in using them to send spam or launch DoS attacks to disable specific Web sites. Ancheta's botz4sale Web site offered access to up to 10 000 compromised PCs at one time for as little as 4 cents each. He even provided his "customers" with tips for using his product.

To outwit law enforcement, Ancheta continually changed e-mail addresses, ISPs, domain names, and instant messaging handles. Eventually, his luck ran out. The FBI arrested him on November 3, 2005, and shut down his operations. Ancheta was sentenced to 57 months in a U.S. federal prison.

Could bot attacks such as these be prevented? It is getting increasingly difficult. According to Michael Lines, chief security officer at credit reporting firm TransUnion, "There is no single technology or strategy to [solve] the problem." Even if people use antivirus and antispyware software and patch software vulnerabilities, new bots appear that target different vulnerabilities. In 2005, 175 new bots were detected.

Hackers do not even have to write their own bot programs. They can download bot toolkits for free on the Internet. Ancheta modified Rxbot, a bot strain available for download at several Web sites, and had his bots report to an Internet Relay Chat (IRC) channel that he controlled. And as the Ancheta case revealed, people can even buy access to bots.

Having a strategy in place before a bot attack hits is crucial to mitigating the damage of the attack. When DNS servers that keep track of Internet addresses and domain names at Akamai Technologies (mentioned in Chapter 5) were flooded in June 2004 with bogus requests for connections from a zombie army, the damage to Akamai's business could have been severe; however, the staff at Akamai was prepared to respond.

When Akamai's Network Operations Command Center (NOCC) detected spikes in traffic volume on company DNS servers, Akamai's first-response team, known as the White Hat team, initiated its emergency response procedure. The team made its initial diagnosis of who and what was under attack, and then the team split into subgroups. One group was put in charge of capturing the incoming requests, decoding their patterns, creating a profile of the attack, and recommending countermeasures. A second group began notifying federal law enforcement officials and Internet service providers, who offered guidance and helped shut down secondary attacks. Another group measured the impact of the attack on customers. Still another group deployed a custom-built application to identify and filter the bogus incoming data packets.

To Think About

1. What is the business impact of botnets?

2. What management, organization, and technology factors should be addressed in a plan to prevent botnet attacks?

3. How easy would it be for a small business to combat botnet attacks? A large business?

MIS in Action

Read the article on "Robot Wars—How Botnets Work" by Massimiliano Romano, Simone Rosignoli, and Ennio Giannini at WindowsSecurity.com. Prepare an electronic presentation that summarizes your answers to the following questions:

1. What are botnets, and how do they work?

2. What features do the most popular botnets offer?

3. How does a bot infect and control a host computer?

4. How can a bot attack be prevented?

Sources: Deborah Gage and Kim S. Nash, "When Bots Attack," *BaselineMagazine*, April 2006; Robert Lemos, "Major Prison Time for Bot Master," Security Focus, May 9, 2006; "Computer Attacks-Jason Salah Arabo," Federal Crimes Blog, April 13, 2006; and Cassell Bryan-Low, "Tech-Savvy Blackmailers Hone a New Form of Extortion," *The Wall Street Journal*, May 5, 2005.

Computer Crime and Cyberterrorism

Most hacker activities are criminal offenses, and the vulnerabilities of systems we have just described make them targets for other types of computer crime as well. Computer crime, which we introduced in Chapter 4, is defined by the U.S. Department of Justice as "any violations of criminal law that involve a knowledge of computer technology for their perpetration, investigation, or prosecution." Table 8-2 provides examples of the computer as a target of crime and as an instrument of crime.

No one knows the magnitude of the computer crime problem—how many systems are invaded, how many people engage in the practice, or the total economic damage. According to one study by the Computer Crime Research Center, U.S. companies lose approximately $16 billion annually to cybercrimes. Canadian statistics are not available although the Canadian Centre for Justice Statistics (CCJS) is considering how to collect such data. Many companies are reluctant to report computer crimes because the crimes may involve employees or the company fears that publicizing its vulnerability will hurt its reputation. The most economically damaging kinds of computer crime are DoS attacks, introducing viruses, theft of services, and disruption of computer systems.

Identity Theft With the growth of the Internet and electronic commerce, identity theft has become especially troubling. **Identity theft** is a crime in which an imposter obtains key pieces of personal information, such as social security insurance numbers, driver's licence numbers, or credit card numbers, to impersonate someone else. The information may be used to obtain credit, merchandise, or services in the name of the victim or to provide the thief with false credentials. According to statistics gathered by Phonebusters, almost 8000 Canadians were victims of identity theft in 2006 and they suffered losses totalling more than $16 million.

Identify theft has flourished on the Internet. Credit card files are a major target of Web site hackers. Moreover, e-commerce sites are wonderful sources of customer personal

Identity theft

TABLE 8-2 *Examples of Computer Crime*

COMPUTERS AS TARGETS OF CRIME	COMPUTERS AS INSTRUMENTS OF CRIME
Breaching the confidentiality of protected computerized data	Theft of trade secrets and unauthorized copying of software or copyrighted intellectual property, such as articles, books, music, and video
Accessing a computer system without authority	Schemes to defraud
Knowingly accessing a protected computer to commit fraud	Using e-mail for threats or harassment
Intentionally accessing a protected computer and causing damage, negligently or deliberately	Intentionally attempting to intercept electronic communication
Knowingly transmitting a program, program code, or command that intentionally causes damage to a protected computer	Illegally accessing stored electronic communications, including e-mail and voice mail
Threatening to cause damage to a protected computer	Transmitting or possessing child pornography using a computer

information—name, address, and phone number. Armed with this information, criminals can assume new identities and establish new credit for their own purposes.

One increasingly popular tactic is a form of spoofing called phishing, which we described in the chapter-opening case. **Phishing** involves setting up fake Web sites or sending e-mail messages that look like those of legitimate businesses to ask users for confidential personal data. The e-mail message instructs recipients to update or confirm records by providing social insurance numbers, bank and credit card information, and other confidential data either by responding to the e-mail message, by entering the information at a bogus Web site, or by calling a telephone number.

Phishing scams have posed as PayPal, the online payment service; online service provider America Online (AOL); Royal Bank of Canada; Bank of Montreal; American Express; the Bank of England; and other banks around the world. Phishing is increasing at an alarming rate. In May 2006 alone, the Anti-Phishing Working Group received reports of 20 109 phishing e-mail messages, 11 976 phishing Web sites, and 137 "hijacked" brands (Anti-Phishing Working Group, 2006).

New phishing techniques called evil twins and pharming are harder to detect. **Evil twins** are wireless networks that pretend to offer trustworthy Wi-Fi connections to the Internet, such as those in airport lounges, hotels, or coffee shops. The bogus network looks identical to a legitimate public network. Fraudsters try to capture passwords or credit card numbers of unwitting users who log on to the network.

Pharming redirects users to a bogus Web page, even when the individual types the correct Web page address into his or her browser. This is possible if pharming perpetrators gain access to the Internet address information stored by Internet service providers to speed up Web browsing and the ISP companies have flawed software on their servers that allows the fraudsters to hack in and change those addresses.

Parliament has yet to directly address the issue of computer crime, largely because most of the issues that would be addressed by new laws are already in place under existing law. Violations of copyright and privacy, hacking, phishing, and promoting pornography or hate and most other issues are already covered by various non-computer parts of the Canadian Criminal Code, such as Part VI, Invasion of Privacy. Nonetheless, as you can see from the opening discussion in this chapter, phishing is still a serious problem in Canada. Many provinces have also enacted privacy and other laws related to computer crime. The U.S. Congress addressed the threat of computer crime in 1986 with a specific law, the Computer Fraud and Abuse Act. This act makes it illegal to access a computer system without authorization. Most states have similar laws, and nations in Europe have comparable legislation. Congress also passed the National Information Infrastructure Protection Act in 1996 to make virus distribution and hacker attacks intended to disable Web sites federal crimes. U.S. legislation, such as the Wiretap Act, Wire Fraud Act, Economic Espionage Act, Electronic Communications Privacy Act, E-Mail Threats and Harassment Act, and Child Pornography Act, covers computer crimes involving intercepting electronic communication, using electronic communication to defraud, stealing trade secrets, illegally accessing stored electronic communications, using e-mail for threats or harassment, and transmitting or possessing child pornography. In spite of the plethora of U.S. laws, Canadian law appears to cover the gamut of these crimes without the need for additional legislation.

Click Fraud When you click on an ad displayed by a search engine, the advertiser typically pays a fee for each click, which is supposed to direct potential buyers to its products. **Click fraud** occurs when an individual or computer program fraudulently clicks on an online ad without any intention of learning more about the advertiser or making a purchase. Click fraud has become a serious problem at Google and other Web sites that feature pay-per-click online advertising (see the case study concluding Chapter 7).

Some companies hire third parties (typically from low-wage countries) to fraudulently click on a competitor's ads to weaken them by driving up their marketing costs. Click fraud can also be perpetrated with software programs doing the clicking, and bot networks are often used for this purpose (for example, see the Window on Technology on page 272). Search engines such as Google attempt to monitor click fraud but have been reluctant to publicize their efforts to deal with the problem. However, some, including

Phishing
Evil twins
Pharming
Click fraud

Google executives, believe click fraud is the single largest threat to search engine marketing. The percentage of clicks that are fraudulent is estimated to vary from less than 5 percent to more than 20 percent, with some keywords exceeding 25 percent on occasion.

Cyberterrorism and Cyberwarfare Concern is mounting that the vulnerabilities of the Internet or other networks could be exploited by terrorists, foreign intelligence services, or other groups to create widespread disruption and harm. Such cyberattacks might target the software that runs electrical power grids, air traffic control systems, or networks of major banks and financial institutions. At least 20 countries are believed to be developing offensive and defensive cyberwarfare capabilities. According to David McMahon, a cyberneticist with EWA-Canada, most Canadian government Web sites have been hacked or compromised, but no more so than private industry (Richardson, 1999). In Canada, the Canadian Security Intelligence Service (CSIS) and the Royal Canadian Mounted Police are charged with dealing with this threat.

Internal Threats: Employees

We tend to think the security threats to a business originate outside the organization. In fact, company insiders pose serious security problems. Employees have access to privileged information, and in the presence of sloppy internal security procedures, they are often able to roam throughout an organization's systems without leaving a trace.

Studies have found that user lack of knowledge is the single greatest cause of network security breaches. Many employees forget their passwords to access computer systems or allow co-workers to use them, which compromises the system. Malicious intruders seeking system access sometimes trick employees into revealing their passwords by pretending to be legitimate members of the company in need of information. This practice is called **social engineering**.

Both end users and information systems specialists are also a major source of errors introduced into information systems. End users introduce errors by entering faulty data or by not following the proper instructions for processing data and using computer equipment. Information systems specialists may create software errors as they design and develop new software or maintain existing programs.

Software Vulnerability

Software errors pose a constant threat to information systems, causing untold losses in productivity. Symantec, a leading vendor of security software, found 3758 vulnerabilities in software in 2005, up 42 percent from the previous year (Vara, 2006). Commercial software often contains flaws that create not only performance but also security vulnerabilities that open networks to intruders. These vulnerabilities enable malware to slip past antivirus defences. A great deal of malware has been trying to exploit vulnerabilities in the Microsoft Windows operating system and other Microsoft products, but malware targeting the Linux operating system is on the rise as well.

To correct software flaws once they are identified, software vendors create a small piece of software called a **patch** to repair the flaws without disturbing the proper operation of the software. An example is Microsoft's XP Service Pack 2 (SP2) introduced in 2004, which features added firewall protection against viruses and intruders, capabilities for automatic security updates, and an easy-to-use interface for managing the security applications on the user's computer. It is up to users of the software to track these vulnerabilities, test, and apply all patches. This process is called patch management.

Because a company's IT infrastructure is typically laden with multiple business applications, operating system installations, and other system services, maintaining patches on all devices and services used by a company is often time-consuming and costly. Malware is being created so rapidly that companies have very little time to respond between the time a vulnerability and a patch are announced and the time malicious software appears to exploit the vulnerability.

Social engineering

Patch

Business Value of Security and Control

Many firms are reluctant to spend heavily on security because it is not directly related to sales revenue. Protecting information systems is so critical to the operation of the business, however, that it deserves a second look.

Companies have very valuable information assets to protect. Systems often house confidential information about individuals' taxes, financial assets, medical records, and job performance reviews. They also can contain information on corporate operations, including trade secrets, new product development plans, and marketing strategies. Government systems may store information on both company and individual taxes, passport information, and pension information. These information assets have tremendous value, and the repercussions can be devastating if they are lost, destroyed, or placed in the wrong hands. A recent U.S. study estimated that when the security of a large firm is compromised, the company loses approximately 2.1 percent of its market value within two days of the security breach, which translates into an average loss of almost $2 billion in stock market value per incident (Cavusoglu, Mishra, and Raghunathan, 2004).

Inadequate security and control can also create serious legal liability. Businesses must protect not only their own information assets but also those of customers, employees, and business partners. Failure to do so may open the firm to costly litigation for data exposure or theft. An organization can be held liable for needless risk and harm created if the organization fails to take appropriate protective action to prevent loss of confidential information, data corruption, or breach of privacy (see the chapter-ending case study). A sound security and control framework that protects business information assets can thus produce a high return on investment.

Legal and Regulatory Requirements for Electronic Records Management

Recent Canadian government laws and regulations, particularly CSOX (discussed below) and PIPEDA (which we discussed in Chapter 4), are forcing Canadian companies to take security and control more seriously. These acts mandate the protection of data from abuse, exposure, and unauthorized access. Firms face new legal obligations for electronic records management and document retention as well as for privacy protection. **Electronic records management (ERM)** consists of policies, procedures, and tools for managing the retention, destruction, and storage of electronic records.

ERM is a key item in CSOX. **CSOX (Canadian Rules for Sarbanes-Oxley Act, Bill 198)** imposes responsibility on companies and their management to safeguard the accuracy and integrity of financial information that is used internally and released externally. The legislation is based on a U.S. law, the Public Company Accounting Reform and Investor Protection Act of 2002, better known as the **Sarbanes-Oxley Act** (SOX). SOX got its name from its sponsors, Senator Paul Sarbanes of Maryland and Representative Michael Oxley of Ohio. It was designed to protect U.S. investors from financial scandals, such as those at Enron, WorldCom, and other public companies. Canadian publicly traded companies were required to develop a plan for action for CSOX compliance by December 31, 2006, and to put that plan into action by the end of 2007.

CSOX and SOX are fundamentally about ensuring that internal controls are in place to govern the creation and documentation of information in financial statements. Because information systems are used to generate, store, and transport such data, the legislation requires firms to consider information systems security and other controls required to ensure the integrity, confidentiality, and accuracy of their data. Each system application that deals with critical financial reporting data requires controls to make sure the data are accurate. Controls to secure the corporate network, prevent unauthorized access to

Electronic records management (ERM)

CSOX (Canadian Rules for Sarbanes-Oxley Act, Bill 198)

Sarbanes-Oxley Act

systems and data, and ensure data integrity and availability in the event of disaster or other disruption of service are essential as well.

Electronic Evidence and Computer Forensics

Security, control, and electronic records management have become essential for responding to legal actions. Today, much of the evidence for stock fraud, embezzlement, theft of company trade secrets, computer crime, and many civil cases is in digital form. In addition to information from printed or typewritten pages, legal cases today increasingly rely on evidence represented as digital data stored on portable floppy disks and USB drives, CDs and DVDs, and computer hard disk drives, as well as in e-mail, instant messages, and e-commerce transactions over the Internet. E-mail is currently the most common type of electronic evidence.

In a legal action, a firm is obligated to respond to a discovery request for access to information that may be used as evidence, and the company is required by law to produce those data. The cost of responding to a discovery request can be enormous if the company has trouble assembling the required data or the data have been corrupted or destroyed. Likewise, the cost of not responding is very high. Courts now impose financial and even criminal penalties for improper destruction of electronic documents, failure to produce records, and failure to store records properly.

An effective electronic document retention policy ensures that electronic documents, e-mail, and other records are well organized, accessible, and neither retained too long nor discarded too soon. It also reflects an awareness of how to preserve potential evidence for computer forensics. **Computer forensics** is the scientific collection, examination, authentication, preservation, and analysis of data held on or retrieved from computer storage media in such a way that the information can be used as evidence in a court of law. It deals with the following problems: recovering data from computers while preserving evidential integrity, securely storing and handling recovered electronic data, finding significant information in a large volume of electronic data, and presenting the information to a court of law.

Electronic evidence may reside on computer storage media in the form of computer files and as ambient data, i.e., data that are not visible to the average user. An example of ambient data might be a file that has been deleted on a PC hard drive. Data that a computer user may have deleted on computer storage media can be recovered through various techniques, and computer forensics experts try to recover this type of hidden data for presentation as evidence.

An awareness of computer forensics should be incorporated into a firm's contingency planning process. The CIO, security specialists, information systems staff, and corporate legal counsel should all work together to have a plan in place that can be executed if a legal need arises.

8.3 Establishing a Framework for Security and Control

Technology is not the key issue in information systems security and control. The technology provides a foundation, but in the absence of intelligent management policies, even the best technology can easily be defeated.

For instance, experts believe that more than 90 percent of successful cyberattacks could have been prevented by technology available at the time. Inadequate human attention made these attacks so prevalent.

Protection of information resources requires a sound security policy and set of controls. **ISO 17799**, an international set of standards for security and control, provides helpful guidelines. It specifies best practices in information systems security and control, including security policy, business continuity planning, physical security, access control, compliance, and creating a security function within the organization.

Computer forensics

ISO 17799

Risk Assessment

Before your company commits resources to security, it must know which assets require protection and the extent to which these assets are vulnerable. A risk assessment helps answer these questions and determine the most cost-effective set of controls for protecting assets.

A **risk assessment** determines the level of risk to the firm if a specific activity or process is not properly controlled. Business managers working with information systems specialists can determine the value of information assets, points of vulnerability, the likely frequency of a problem, and the potential for damage. For example, if an event is likely to occur no more than once a year, with a maximum of a $1000 loss to the organization, it is not feasible to spend $20 000 on the design and maintenance of a control to protect against that event; however, if that same event could occur at least once a day, with a potential loss of more than $300 000 a year, $100 000 spent on a control might be entirely appropriate.

Table 8-3 illustrates sample results of a risk assessment for an online order processing system that processes 30 000 orders per day. The likelihood of each exposure occurring over a one-year period is expressed as a percentage. The next column shows the highest and lowest possible loss that could be expected each time the exposure occurred and an average loss calculated by adding the highest and lowest figures together and dividing by two. The expected annual loss for each exposure can be determined by multiplying the average loss by its probability of occurrence.

This risk assessment shows that the probability of a power failure occurring in a one-year period is 30 percent. Loss of order transactions while power is down could range from $5000 to $200 000 (averaging $102 500) for each occurrence, depending on how long processing is halted. The probability of embezzlement occurring over a yearly period is about 5 percent, with potential losses ranging from $1000 to $50 000 (and averaging $25 500) for each occurrence. User errors have a 98 percent chance of occurring over a yearly period, with losses ranging from $200 to $40 000 (and averaging $20 100) for each occurrence.

Once the risks have been assessed, system builders will concentrate on the control points with the greatest vulnerability and potential for loss. In this case, controls should focus on ways to minimize the risk of power failures and user errors because anticipated annual losses are highest for these areas.

Security Policy

Once you have identified the main risks to your systems, your company will need to develop a security policy for protecting the company's assets. A **security policy** consists of statements ranking information risks, identifying acceptable security goals, and identifying the mechanisms for achieving these goals. What are the firm's most important information assets? Who generates and controls this information in the firm? What existing security policies are in place to protect the information? What level of risk is management willing to accept for each of these assets? Is management willing, for instance, to lose customer credit data once every 10 years? Or will it build a security system for credit card data that can withstand the once-in-a-decade disaster? Management must estimate how much it will cost to achieve this level of acceptable risk.

In larger firms, you may see a formal corporate security function headed by a chief security officer. The security group educates and trains users, keeps management aware of

Risk assessment

Security policy

TABLE 8-3 *Online Order Processing Risk Assessment*

Exposure	Probability of Occurrence (%)	Loss Range/Average ($)	Expected Annual Loss ($)
Power failure	30%	$5000–$200 000 ($102 500)	$30 750
Embezzlement	5%	$1000–$50 000 ($25 500)	$1275
User error	98%	$200–$40 000 ($20 100)	$19 698

security threats and breakdowns, and maintains the tools chosen to implement security. The **chief security officer (CSO)** is responsible for enforcing the firm's security policy.

The security policy drives policies determining acceptable use of the firm's information resources and which members of the company have access to its information assets. An **acceptable use policy (AUP)** defines acceptable uses of the firm's information resources and computing equipment, including desktop and laptop computers, wireless devices, telephones, and the Internet. The policy should clarify company policy regarding privacy, user responsibility, and personal use of company equipment and networks. A good AUP defines unacceptable and acceptable actions for every user and specifies consequences for noncompliance.

Authorization policies determine differing levels of access to information assets for different levels of users. **Authorization management systems** establish where and when a user is permitted to access certain parts of a Web site or a corporate database. Such systems allow each user access only to those portions of a system that person is permitted to enter, based on information established by a set of access rules.

The authorization management system knows exactly what information each user is permitted to access as shown in Figure 8-4. This figure illustrates the security allowed for two sets of users of an online personnel database containing sensitive information, such as employees' salaries, benefits, and medical histories. One set of users consists of all employees who perform clerical functions, such as inputting employee data into the system.

All individuals with this type of profile can update the system but can neither read nor update sensitive fields, such as salary, medical history, or earnings data. Another profile applies to a divisional manager, who cannot update the system but who can read all employee data fields for his or her division, including medical history and salary. These profiles are based on access rules supplied by business groups. The system illustrated in Figure 8-4 provides very fine-grained security restrictions, such as allowing authorized personnel users to inquire about all employee information except that in confidential fields, such as salary or medical history.

Chief security officer (CSO)
Acceptable use policy (AUP)
Authorization policies
Authorization management systems

FIGURE 8-4   *Security profiles for a personnel system*

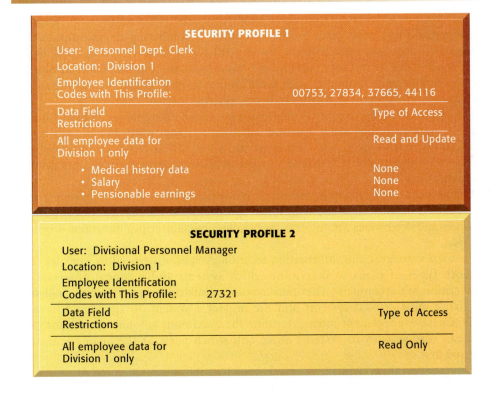

These two examples represent two security profiles or data security patterns that might be found in a personnel system. Depending on the security profile, a user would have certain restrictions on access to various systems, locations, or data in an organization.

Ensuring Business Continuity

As companies increasingly rely on digital networks for revenue and operations, they need to take additional steps to ensure that their systems and applications are always available. Firms such as those in the airline and financial services industries, with critical applications requiring online transaction processing, have traditionally used fault-tolerant computer systems for many years to ensure 100 percent availability. In **online transaction processing**, transactions entered online are immediately processed by the computer. Multiple changes to databases, reporting, and requests for information occur each instant.

Fault-tolerant computer systems contain redundant hardware, software, and power supply components that create an environment that provides continuous, uninterrupted service. Fault-tolerant computers use special software routines or self-checking logic built into their circuitry to detect hardware failures and automatically switch to a backup device. Parts from these computers can be removed and repaired without disruption to the computer system.

Fault tolerance should be distinguished from high-availability computing. Both fault tolerance and high-availability computing try to minimize downtime. **Downtime** refers to periods of time in which a system is not operational. However, **high-availability computing** helps firms recover quickly from a system crash while fault tolerance promises continuous availability and the elimination of recovery time altogether. High-availability computing environments are a minimum requirement for firms with heavy electronic commerce processing or for firms that depend on digital networks for their internal operations.

High-availability computing requires backup servers, distribution of processing across multiple servers, high-capacity storage, and good disaster recovery and business continuity plans. The firm's computing platform must be extremely robust with scalable processing power, storage, and bandwidth.

Researchers are exploring ways to make computing systems recover even more rapidly when mishaps occur, an approach called **recovery-oriented computing**. This work includes designing systems that recover quickly and implementing capabilities and tools to help operators pinpoint the sources of faults in multicomponent systems and easily correct their mistakes (Fox and Patterson, 2003).

Disaster Recovery Planning and Business Continuity Planning

Disaster recovery planning devises plans for the restoration of computing and communications services after they have been disrupted by an event such as an earthquake, flood, or terrorist attack. Disaster recovery plans focus primarily on the technical issues involved in keeping systems up and running, such as which files to back up and the maintenance of backup computer systems or disaster recovery services.

For example, disaster recovery firms provide hot sites housing spare computers at locations far away from the "home" location where subscribing firms can run their critical applications in an emergency. Goodman and Carr, LLP, a large Toronto law firm, contracted with Fusepoint Managed Services to provide site replication on a minute-by-minute basis.

Business continuity planning focuses on how the company can restore business operations after a disaster strikes. The business continuity plan identifies critical business processes and determines action plans for handling mission-critical functions if systems go down.

Business managers and information technology specialists need to work together on both types of plans to determine which systems and business processes are most critical to the company. They must conduct a business impact analysis to identify the firm's most critical systems and the impact a system outage would have on the business. Management must determine the maximum amount of time the business can survive with its systems down and which parts of the business must be restored first.

Online transaction processing
Fault-tolerant computer systems
Downtime
High-availability computing
Recovery-oriented computing
Disaster recovery planning
Business continuity planning

For example, in April 2007, Research In Motion (RIM)'s BlackBerry data centre in Southwestern Ontario went dark for 14 hours. Millions of users in North America were unable to connect their BlackBerrys to receive and send e-mail or to access the Internet. There are eight million BlackBerry users around the world, including Dimitri Soudas, Press Secretary to Prime Minister Stephen Harper. Soudas says he receives between 600 and 700 BlackBerry messages per day. U.S. White House spokesperson Tony Fratto joked: "I apologize to a number of you who tried e-mailing over the last 14 hours. We're 14 hours into no BlackBerry, so you can imagine how things are" (Meyerson, 2007). Soudas said that if the BlackBerry outage had lasted longer, "I'd probably be stuck in my office monitoring my computer all day." As it turns out, the BlackBerry outage was caused by a software update at company headquarters that had not been properly tested. All this means that companies need to include mobile devices in their business continuity planning for just such an eventuality.

Security Outsourcing Many companies, especially small businesses, lack the resources or expertise to provide a secure high-availability computing environment on their own. They can outsource many security functions to **managed security service providers (MSSPs)** that monitor network activity and perform vulnerability testing and intrusion detection. Guardent, Counterpane, VeriSign, MX-Logic, ISS, and Symantec are leading providers of MSSP services. Symantec has an MSSP office in Ontario.

The Role of Auditing

How does management know that information systems security and controls are effective? To answer this question, organizations must conduct comprehensive and systematic audits. An **MIS audit** examines the firm's overall security environment as well as controls governing individual information systems. The auditor should trace the flow of sample transactions through the system and perform tests, using, if appropriate, automated audit software.

Managed security service providers (MSSPs)

MIS audit

Security audits review technologies, procedures, documentation, training, and personnel. A thorough audit will even simulate an attack or disaster to test the response of the technology, information systems staff, and business employees.

The audit lists and ranks all control weaknesses and estimates the probability of their occurrence. It then assesses the financial and organizational impact of each threat. Figure 8-5 is a sample auditor's listing of control weaknesses for a loan system. It includes a section for notifying management of such weaknesses and for management's response. Management is expected to devise a plan for countering significant weaknesses in controls.

An auditor often traces the flow of sample transactions through an information system and may perform tests using automated audit software. MIS audits help management identify security vulnerabilities and determine whether information system controls are effective.

FIGURE 8-5   *Sample auditor's list of control weaknesses*

This chart is a sample page from a list of control weaknesses that an auditor might find in a loan system in a local commercial bank. This form helps auditors record and evaluate control weaknesses and shows the results of discussing those weaknesses with management, as well as any corrective actions taken by management.

Function: Loans Location: Peoria, IL	Prepared by: J. Ericson Date: June 16, 2007		Received by: T. Benson Review date: June 28, 2007	
Nature of Weakness and Impact	Chance for Error/Abuse		Notification to Management	
	Yes/No	Justification	Report date	Management response
User accounts with missing passwords	Yes	Leaves system open to unauthorized outsiders or attackers	5/10/07	Eliminate accounts without passwords
Network configured to allow some sharing of system files	Yes	Exposes critical system files to hostile parties connected to the network	5/10/07	Ensure only required directories are shared and that they are protected with strong passwords
Software patches can update production programs without final approval from Standards and Controls group	No	All production programs require management approval; Standards and Controls group assigns such cases to a temporary production status		

8.4   Technologies and Tools for Security

An array of tools and technologies are available to secure systems and data. They include tools for authentication, firewalls, intrusion detection systems, antivirus and antispyware software, and encryption.

Access Control

Access control consists of all the policies and procedures a company uses to prevent improper access to systems by unauthorized insiders and outsiders.

To gain access, a user must be authorized and authenticated. **Authentication** refers to the ability to know that a person is who he or she claims to be. Access control software is designed to allow only authorized users to use systems or to access data using some method for authentication.

Authentication is often established by using passwords known only to authorized users. An end user uses a password to log on to a computer system and may also use passwords for accessing specific systems and files; however, users often forget passwords, share them, or choose poor passwords that are easy to guess, which compromises security. Password systems that are too rigorous hinder employee productivity. When employees must change complex passwords frequently, they often take shortcuts, such as choosing passwords that are easy to guess or writing down their passwords at their workstations in plain view. Passwords can also be "sniffed" if transmitted over a network or stolen through social engineering.

New authentication technologies, such as tokens, smart cards, and biometric authentication, overcome some of these problems. A **token** is a physical device, similar to an identification card, that is designed to prove the identity of a single user. Tokens are small gadgets that typically fit on key rings and display passcodes that change frequently. A **smart card** is a device about the size of a credit card that contains a chip formatted with access permission and other data. (Smart cards are also used in

Access control

Authentication

Token

Smart card

electronic payment systems.) A reader device interprets the data on the smart card and allows or denies access.

Biometric authentication is based on the measurement of a physical or behavioural trait that makes each individual unique. It compares a person's unique characteristics, such as the fingerprints, face, or retinal image, against a stored set profile of these characteristics to determine whether there are any differences between these characteristics and the stored profile. If the two profiles match, access is granted. The technology is expensive, and fingerprint and facial recognition technologies are just beginning to be used for information system security applications.

There are a few concerns with biometric authentication. Sometimes the technology does not recognize a valid user. For example, one of the authors was travelling through the Minneapolis airport and used a locker that recorded a fingerprint image. It took four attempts to open the locker before the software could match the fingerprint. Another concern is that measures cannot be changed, even if a criminal obtains or compromises the biometric data. For example, an individual may be able to change a password or get an access card, but he cannot change his retina or fingerprint. An additional concern is privacy: It is important to consider how the biometric information is used—for example, for time cards or library access. Finally, there is the risk of criminals kidnapping an individual to use fingerprint or retina data, for access to bank accounts and other valuable information.

Biometric identification uses technologies that read and interpret individual human traits, such as fingerprints, voices, or facial images, in order to grant or deny access to systems.

Firewalls, Intrusion Detection Systems, and Antivirus Software

Without protection against malware and intruders, connecting to the Internet would be very dangerous. Firewalls, intrusion detection systems, and antivirus software have become essential business tools.

Firewalls Chapter 7 describes the use of firewalls to prevent unauthorized users from accessing private networks. A firewall is a combination of hardware and software that controls the flow of incoming and outgoing network traffic. It is generally placed between the organization's private internal networks and distrusted external networks, such as the Internet, although firewalls can also be used to protect one part of a company's network from the rest of the network (see Figure 8-6).

The firewall acts like a gatekeeper who examines each user's credentials before access is granted to a network. The firewall identifies names, IP addresses, applications, and other characteristics of incoming traffic. It checks this information against the access rules that have been programmed into the system by the network administrator. The firewall prevents unauthorized communication into and out of the network.

In large organizations, the firewall often resides on a specially designated computer separate from the rest of the network, so no incoming request directly accesses private network resources. There are a number of firewall screening technologies, including static packet filtering, stateful inspection, Network Address Translation, and application proxy filtering. They are frequently used in combination to provide firewall protection.

Packet filtering examines selected fields in the headers of data packets flowing back and forth between the trusted network and the Internet, examining individual packets in isolation. This filtering technology can miss many types of attacks. **Stateful inspection** provides additional security by determining whether packets are part of an ongoing dialogue between a sender and a receiver. It sets up state tables to track information over multiple packets. Packets are accepted or rejected based on whether they are part of an approved conversation or whether they are attempting to establish a legitimate connection.

Network Address Translation (NAT) can provide another layer of protection when static packet filtering and stateful inspection are employed. NAT conceals the IP addresses

Biometric authentication
Packet filtering
Stateful inspection
Network Address Translation (NAT)

FIGURE 8-6   *A corporate firewall*

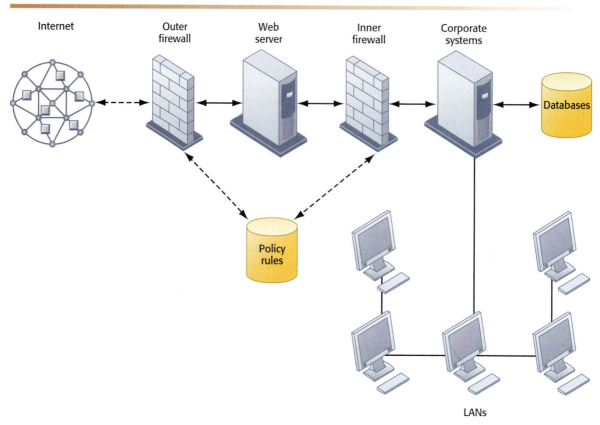

Internet   Outer firewall   Web server   Inner firewall   Corporate systems   Databases

Policy rules

LANs

The firewall is placed between the firm's private network and the public Internet or another distrusted network to protect against unauthorized traffic.

of the organization's internal host computer(s) to prevent sniffer programs outside the firewall from ascertaining them and using that information to penetrate internal systems.

Application proxy filtering examines the application content of packets. A proxy server stops data packets originating outside the organization, inspects them, and passes a proxy to the other side of the firewall. If a user outside the company wants to communicate with a user inside the organization, the outside user first "talks" to the proxy application, and the proxy application communicates with the firm's internal computer. Likewise, a computer user inside the organization goes through the proxy to talk with computers on the outside.

To create a good firewall, an administrator must maintain detailed internal rules identifying the people, applications, or addresses that are allowed or rejected. Firewalls can deter, but not completely prevent, network penetration by outsiders and should be viewed as one element in an overall security plan.

Intrusion Detection Systems In addition to firewalls, commercial security vendors now provide intrusion detection tools and services to protect against suspicious network traffic and attempts to access files and databases. **Intrusion detection systems** feature full-time monitoring tools placed at the most vulnerable points or hotspots of corporate networks to detect and deter intruders continually. The system generates an alarm if it finds a suspicious or anomalous event. Scanning software looks for patterns indicative of known methods of computer attacks, such as bad passwords, checks to see if important files have been removed or modified, and sends warnings of vandalism or system administration errors. Monitoring software examines events as they are happening to discover security attacks in progress. The intrusion detection tool can also be customized to shut down a particularly sensitive part of a network if it receives unauthorized traffic.

Application proxy filtering
Intrusion detection systems

Antivirus and Antispyware Software Defensive technology plans for both individuals and businesses must include antivirus protection for every computer. **Antivirus software** is designed to check computer systems and drives for the presence of computer viruses. Often the software eliminates the virus from the infected area. However, most antivirus software is effective only against viruses already known when the software was written. To remain effective, the antivirus software must be continually updated.

Leading antivirus software vendors, such as McAfee, Symantec, and Trend Micro, have enhanced their products to include protection against spyware. Antispyware software tools such as Ad-Aware, Spybot, and Spyware Doctor are also very helpful.

Securing Wireless Networks

Despite its flaws, WEP provides some margin of security if Wi-Fi users remember to activate it. Corporations can further improve Wi-Fi security by using it in conjunction with virtual private network (VPN) technology when accessing internal corporate data.

In June 2004, the Wi-Fi Alliance industry trade group finalized the 802.11i specification that tightens security for wireless LAN products. It replaces the static encryption keys used in WEP with much longer keys that continually change, making them harder to crack. A central authentication server authenticates each user on the network. 802.11i also employs mutual authentication so that a wireless user does not get pulled into a rogue network that might steal the user's network credentials. Data packets are checked to make sure they are part of a current network session and not repeated by hackers to fool network users.

To be effective, wireless security technology should be accompanied by appropriate policies and procedures for using wireless devices securely. The Window on Management section shows how Rogers Communications, Nortel, and Unilever PLC handle this issue.

Antivirus software

WINDOW ON MANAGEMENT

Do You Really Need to Secure Mobile Devices?

In 2005, Rogers Communications launched a wireless offering for mobile workforces to enable them to use mobile "forms" when handling field service and sales calls, eliminating the need for paper forms. The target market for the Rogers mForms program is the three million Canadians who perform field service work as part of their jobs. This could be a security nightmare, but Rogers and its partner TrueContext, which furnishes the software for the mobile devices, stress security as part of the program. According to TrueContext President and CEO Alvaro Pombo, all transmissions go through a secure channel and can be encrypted if ordered by the customer company. The devices are also fully managed, so that if a device is lost or stolen, all information on the device can be deleted wirelessly.

Communications giant Nortel also has a comprehensive corporate policy for mobile and wireless security. Nortel mobile users must have passwords for user access to their devices. A "device-kill" policy is also enabled in wireless machines. Device-kill is a function of the operating system that deletes all files contained in the device in the event that the password is keyed incorrectly after a prescribed number of attempts.

Compare these companies' policies with Unilever. Unilever PLC is a $54 billion global manufacturer and supplier of fast-moving consumer goods, including brands such as Q-Tips, Lipton tea, and Dove personal care products. It operates in 57 countries, with regional teams for Europe, the Americas, and Asia/Africa (including Australia.) Unilever also has teams for its Foods and Home and Personal Care products.

This global giant is known for its ability to leverage products and brands throughout the world by tailoring them to local conditions and for its commitment to top-quality management. Unilever recruits its managers from all over the world and carefully trains them to serve as a unifying force for its operations.

In March 2004, Unilever's senior management ordered the company's thousand top executives to be equipped with mobile handheld devices to increase their productivity. The devices had to provide both voice and data transmission, operate on different wireless networks, be able to view e-mail attachments, such as Word files, and run on battery power for more than four hours.

The company selected BlackBerry 7100, 7290, and 8700 handhelds from Research in Motion because they were the leader in their category and they worked with heterogeneous e-mail servers and multiple wireless network standards, including CDMA and Wi-Fi.

Selecting the handheld was the easy part. The hard part was making sure Unilever's handhelds were secure. Wireless handhelds are easy to lose or steal because they are so portable. For example, in London, England, more than 63 000 mobile phones, 5838 PDAs, and 4973 laptops were left in taxis during a six-month period in 2006. Mobile devices are also penetrable by hackers and other outsiders. PDAs and smart phones, especially those used by senior executives, often store sensitive corporate data such as sales figures, social security numbers, customer names, phone numbers, and e-mail addresses. Unauthorized users may be able to access internal corporate networks through these devices. Downloading unauthorized data or messages may introduce disabling malware.

Tony Farah, Unilever's director of global solutions, and his team were charged with developing the security for these mobile devices to make sure Unilever did not suffer any data theft or financial losses. The team decided that a mobile handheld required the same level of security as Unilever's laptops. Under Unilever's corporate security policy, every employee equipped with a laptop or handheld must use a company-specified device. Users who log onto the corporate network must be able to identify themselves using a password or some other method of authentication.

BlackBerry devices use a proprietary operating system that allows an information technology manager to establish automated restrictions, such as not allowing users to open e-mail attachments sent from their desktops. This reduces the chances of a virus infecting the company network. The security settings also prevent the use of alternative e-mail or Web browser services. All e-mail and browser traffic are routed through BlackBerry Enterprise Servers, which use strong data encryption technology. Applications running on the BlackBerry operating system cannot open both internal and external connections to the Internet, which would allow a malicious application to gather data from inside the company firewall and transmit the data outside the firewall without any auditing.

Unilever's firewall monitors all traffic and tracks user attempts to forward their e-mail to non-corporate accounts. If the firewall detects an employee who is doing this, the company orders the employee to stop. E-mail that passes from a person's home network to Unilever's corporate network is not secure.

Unilever configured the BlackBerrys so that users could not install any third-party applications. The handheld devices must be cradled every 30 days to create a new security key. The handhelds were set to time out after being idle for 15 minutes. After that amount of time has elapsed, a user must re-enter his or her password to regain access to e-mail or the telephone.

Another security feature triggers a lockout and complete wipe of the device after ten unsuccessful attempts to log in or submit a password.

Although an overwhelming majority of Unilever executives believed that the BlackBerry security procedures were reasonable, not everyone was pleased. Some executives balked at having to enter a password when using the BlackBerry as a phone. Although management originally stipulated that the BlackBerrys were to be used both as phones and for data transmission, Unilever allows recalcitrant executives to use their BlackBerry for data and a cell phone or smart phone for voice transmission.

Unilever's wireless handheld security program costs US $70 000 annually to support more than 450 executives. An additional 550 executives were added in 2006. Although there have been a few lost or stolen handhelds, Unilever has not experienced any security breaches.

To Think About

1. How are Unilever and Nortel executives' wireless handhelds related to the company's business performance?

2. Discuss the potential impact of a security breach at Unilever or Nortel.

3. What management, organization, and technology factors had to be addressed in developing security policies and procedures for Unilever's wireless handhelds? Are these the same factors for every company?

4. Is it a good idea to allow Unilever executives to use both BlackBerrys and cell phones? Why or why not?

MIS in Action

Explore the BlackBerry Web site (www.blackberry.com or www.rim.com), paying particular attention to the security features of the BlackBerry Enterprise Solution. Then answer these questions:

1. What security does BlackBerry provide for wireless data and stored data?

2. How do BlackBerry Enterprise Solution tools help protect BlackBerry devices against malware?

Sources: Beth McFadden, "Security from Scratch," *Baseline Magazine*, May 15, 2006; Mary Lisbeth D'Amico, "Call Security," *The Wall Street Journal*, February 13, 2006; www.unilever.com, accessed August 25, 2006; Mari-Len De Guzman, "Security: Keeping Mobile Workers Safe from Highway Robbery," *CIO Canada*, October 1, 2006; and Mari-Len De Guzman, "Company Offers Canadian Field Workers Mobile Device," *Computerworld Canada*, November 30, 2005.

Encryption and Public Key Infrastructure

Many businesses use encryption to protect digital information that they store, physically transfer, or send over the Internet. **Encryption** is the process of transforming plain text or data into cipher text that cannot be read by anyone other than the sender and the intended receiver. Data are encrypted by using a secret numerical code, called an encryption key, that transforms plain data into cipher text. The receiver must decrypt the message.

Encryption

Two methods for encrypting network traffic on the Web are SSL and S-HTTP. **Secure Sockets Layer (SSL)** and its successor **Transport Layer Security (TLS)** enable client and server computers to manage encryption and decryption activities as they communicate with each other during a secure Web session. **Secure Hypertext Transfer Protocol (S-HTTP)** is another protocol used for encrypting data flowing over the Internet, but it is limited to individual messages while SSL and TLS are designed to establish a secure connection between two computers.

The capability to generate secure sessions is built into Internet client browser software and servers. The client and the server negotiate what key and what level of security to use. Once a secure session is established between the client and the server, all messages in that session are encrypted.

There are two alternative methods of encryption: symmetric key encryption and public key encryption. In symmetric key encryption, the sender and receiver establish a secure Internet session by creating a single encryption key and sending it to the receiver so both the sender and receiver share the same key. The strength of the encryption key is measured by its bit length. Today, a typical key will be 128 bits long (a string of 128 binary digits).

The problem with all symmetric encryption schemes is that the key itself must be shared somehow among the senders and receivers, which exposes the key to outsiders who might just be able to intercept and decrypt the key. A more secure form of encryption called **public key encryption** uses two keys: one shared (or public) and one totally private, as shown in Figure 8-7. The keys are mathematically related so that data encrypted with one key can be decrypted using only the other key. To send and receive messages, communicators first create separate pairs of private and public keys. The public key is kept in a directory and the private key must be kept secret. The sender encrypts a message with the recipient's public key. On receiving the message, the recipient uses his or her private key to decrypt it.

Digital signatures and digital certificates further help with authentication. A **digital signature** is an encrypted message (such as the sender's name) that only the sender using his or her private key can create. A digital signature is used to verify the origin and contents of a message. It provides a way to associate a message with a sender, performing a function similar to a written signature.

Digital certificates are data files used to establish the identity of users and electronic assets for protection of online transactions (see Figure 8-8). A digital certificate system uses a trusted third party, known as a certificate authority (CA), to validate a user's identity. There are many CAs in Canada and around the world, including Grid Canada, Cancert, IdenTrust, and Australia's KeyPost.

The CA verifies a digital certificate user's identity offline. This information is put into a CA server, which generates an encrypted digital certificate containing owner identification information and a copy of the owner's public key. The certificate authenticates that the public key belongs to the designated owner. The CA makes its own public key available publicly either in print or perhaps on the Internet. The recipient of an encrypted message uses the CA's public key to decode the digital certificate attached to the message, verifies it was

Secure Sockets Layer (SSL)

Transport Layer Security (TLS)

Secure Hypertext Transfer Protocol (S-HTTP)

Public key encryption

Digital signature

Digital certificates

FIGURE 8-7   *Public key encryption*

A public key encryption system can be viewed as a series of public and private keys that lock data when they are transmitted and unlock the data when they are received. The sender locates the recipient's public key in a directory and uses it to encrypt a message. The message is sent in encrypted form over the Internet or a private network. When the encrypted message arrives, the recipient uses his or her private key to decrypt the data and read the message.

FIGURE 8-8 *Digital certificates*

Digital certificates help establish the identity of people or electronic assets. They protect online transactions by providing secure, encrypted, online communication.

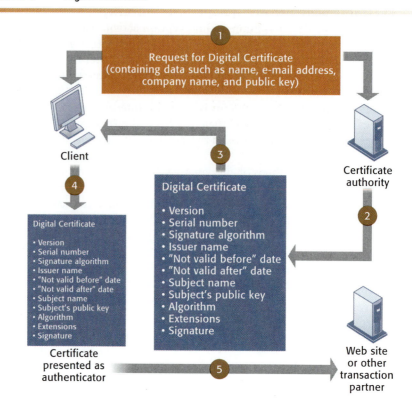

issued by the CA, and then obtains the sender's public key and identification information contained in the certificate. Using this information, the recipient can send an encrypted reply. The digital certificate system would enable, for example, a credit card user and a merchant to validate that an authorized and trusted third party issued their digital certificates before they exchange data. **Public key infrastructure (PKI)**, the use of public key cryptography working with a certificate authority, is now widely used in e-commerce.

Public key infrastructure (PKI)

Summary

1. **Analyze why information systems need special protection from destruction, error, and abuse.**

   With data concentrated into electronic form and many procedures invisible through automation, computerized information systems are vulnerable to destruction, misuse, error, fraud, and hardware or software failures. Corporate systems using the Internet are especially vulnerable because the Internet is designed to be an open system and makes internal corporate systems more vulnerable to actions from outsiders. Hackers can unleash denial-of-service (DoS) attacks or penetrate corporate networks, causing serious system disruptions. Intruders using sniffer programs can easily penetrate Wi-Fi networks to obtain an address to access the resources of the network. Computer viruses and worms can spread rampantly from system to system, clogging computer memory or destroying programs and data.

   Software presents problems because software bugs may be impossible to eliminate and because hackers and malicious software can exploit software vulnerabilities. End users can introduce errors.

2. **Assess the business value of security and control.**

   Security and control are important but often-neglected areas for information systems investment. Firms relying on computer systems for their core business functions can lose sales and productivity. Information assets, such as confidential employee records, trade secrets, or business plans, lose much of their value if they are revealed to outsiders or if they expose the firm to legal liability. New laws, such as CSOX and PIPEDA, require companies to practise stringent electronic records management and adhere to strict standards for security, privacy, and control. Legal actions requiring electronic evidence and computer forensics also require firms to pay more attention to security and electronic records management.

3. ***Design an organizational framework for security and control.***

Firms need to establish an appropriate organizational and managerial framework for security and control to use technologies effectively to protect their information resources. A risk assessment evaluates information assets, identifies control points and control weaknesses, and determines the most cost-effective set of controls.

Firms must also develop a coherent corporate security policy and plans for continuing business operations in the event of disaster or disruption. The security policy includes policies for acceptable use and authorization. A disaster recovery plan provides procedures and facilities for restoring computing and communication services after they have been disrupted while a business continuity plan focuses on how the company can restore business operations. Comprehensive and systematic MIS auditing helps organizations determine the effectiveness of security and controls for their information systems.

4. ***Evaluate the most important tools and technologies for safeguarding information resources.***

Companies require special measures to support electronic commerce and digital business processes. They can use fault-tolerant computer systems or create high-availability computing environments to make sure that their information systems are always available and performing without interruptions. Firewalls are placed between an organization's private network and external networks, such as the Internet, to prevent unauthorized users from accessing the private network. Intrusion detection systems monitor private networks from suspicious network traffic and attempts to access corporate systems. Passwords, tokens, smart cards, and biometric authentication are used to authenticate system users. Antivirus software checks computer systems for infections by viruses and worms and often eliminates the malicious software, while antispyware software combats intrusive and harmful spyware programs. Encryption, the coding and scrambling of messages, is a widely used technology for securing electronic transmissions over the Internet and over Wi-Fi networks. Digital certificates combined with public key encryption provide further protection of electronic transactions by authenticating a user's identity.

Key Terms

Acceptable use policy (AUP),   279
Access control,   282
Antivirus software,   285
Application proxy filtering,   284
Authentication,   282
Authorization management systems,   279
Authorization policies,   279
Biometric authentication,   283
Botnet,   271
Business continuity planning,   280
Chief security officer (CSO),   279
Click fraud,   274
Computer forensics,   277
Computer virus,   269
Controls,   266
Cracker,   270
CSOX (Canadian Rules for Sarbanes-Oxley Act, Bill 198),   276
Cybervandalism,   270
Denial-of-service (DoS) attack,   271
Digital certificate,   287
Digital signature,   287

Disaster recovery planning,   280
Distributed denial-of-service (DDoS) attack,   271
Downtime,   280
Electronic records management (ERM),   276
Encryption,   286
Evil twins,   274
Fault-tolerant computer systems,   280
Hacker,   270
High-availability computing,   280
Identity theft,   273
Intrusion detection systems,   284
ISO 17799,   277
Key logger,   270
Malware,   268
Managed security service provider (MSSP),   281
MIS audit,   281
Network Address Translation (NAT),   283
Online transaction processing,   280
Packet filtering,   283
Patch,   275
Pharming,   274

Phishing,   274
Public key encryption,   287
Public key infrastructure (PKI),   288
Recovery-oriented computing,   280
Risk assessment,   278
Sarbanes-Oxley Act,   276
Secure Hypertext Transfer Protocol (S-HTTP),   287
Secure Sockets Layer (SSL),   287
Security,   266
Security policy,   278
Smart card,   282
Sniffer,   270
Social engineering,   275
Spoofing,   270
Spyware,   268
Stateful inspection,   283
Token,   282
Transport Layer Security (TLS),   287
Trojan horse,   270
War driving,   268
Worms,   269

Review Questions

1. *Why are computer systems so vulnerable? Describe the most common threats against contemporary information systems.*

2. *Why are the Internet and Wi-Fi networks so difficult to secure?*

3. *What is malware? Distinguish among a virus, a worm, and a Trojan horse.*

4. *What is a hacker? How do hackers create security problems and damage systems?*

5. *How can software affect system reliability and security?*

6. *What is computer crime? Provide two examples of crime in which computers are targets and two examples in which computers are used as instruments of crime.*

7. *What is identity theft? Why is it such a big problem today? How does phishing promote identity theft?*

8. *How can computer systems and networks be used for cyberterrorism and cyberwarfare?*

9. *What security problems are created by employees?*

10. *Define security and control. How do they provide business value? How are security and control related to recent U.S. government regulatory requirements and to computer forensics?*

11. *What is the function of risk assessment? How is it conducted for information systems?*

12. *Define and describe the following: security policy, acceptable use policy, authorization policy.*

13. *Distinguish between fault-tolerant and high-availability computing, and between disaster recovery planning and business continuity planning.*

14. *How does MIS auditing promote security and control?*

15. *Name and describe three authentication methods.*

16. *Describe the roles of firewalls, intrusion detection systems, and antivirus software in promoting security.*

17. *How can encryption be used to protect information? Describe the role of encryption and digital certificates in a public key infrastructure.*

Discussion Questions

1. *Security is not simply a technology issue, it is a business issue. Discuss.*

2. *If you were developing a business continuity plan for your company, where would you start? What aspects of the business would the plan address?*

3. *Do all organizations need a risk assessment and business continuity plan? Why or why not?*

4. *With computer threats changing and increasing every day and with ways to fight those threats changing every day as well, how can organizations stay on top of these security issues?*

Teamwork: Evaluating Security Software Tools

With a group of three or four students, use the Web to research and evaluate security products, such as antivirus software, firewalls, or antispyware software, from two competing vendors. For each product, describe its capabilities, the types of businesses to which it is best suited, and its cost to purchase and install. Which is the best product? Why? If possible, use electronic presentation software to present your findings to the class.

Learning Track Modules

General and Application Controls for Information Systems. If you want to learn more about the various types of controls used in information systems, you will find a Learning Track Module on general and application controls on MyMISLab for this chapter.

Management Challenges of Security and Control. If you want to learn more about management challenges and decisions concerning security and control, you will find a Learning Track Module on that topic on MyMISLab for this chapter.

Software Vulnerability and Reliability. If you want to learn more about software vulnerability and measures to ensure software reliability, you will find a Learning Track Module on these topics on MyMISLab for this chapter.

For online exercises, please visit www.pearsoned.ca/mymislab.

HANDS-ON MIS Application Exercises

The projects in this section give you hands-on experience designing Internet applications to increase employee efficiency, using spreadsheet software to improve selection of telecommunications services, and using Web search engines for business research.

Achieving Operational Excellence: Developing a Disaster Recovery Plan

Software skills: Web browser and presentation software
Business skills: Disaster recovery planning

This project requires you to develop a disaster recovery plan for a real-world company.

Management is concerned that Dirt Bikes Canada's computer systems could be vulnerable to power outages, vandalism, computer viruses, natural disasters, or telecommunications disruptions. You have been asked to perform an analysis of system vulnerabilities and disaster recovery planning for the company. Your report should answer the following questions:

1. What are the most likely threats to the continued operation of Dirt Bikes Canada's systems?

2. What would you identify as Dirt Bikes Canada's most critical systems? What is the impact on the company if these systems cannot operate? How long could the company survive if these systems were down? Which systems are the most important to back up and restore in the event of a disaster?

3. Use the Web to locate two disaster recovery services that could be used by a small business such as Dirt Bikes. Compare them in terms of the services they offer. Which should Dirt Bikes Canada use? Exactly how could these services help Dirt Bikes Canada recover from a disaster?

4. (Optional) If possible, use electronic presentation software to summarize your findings for management.

Improving Decision Making: Using Spreadsheet Software to Perform a Security Risk Assessment

Software skills: Spreadsheet formulas and charts
Business skills: Risk assessment

This project uses spreadsheet software to calculate anticipated annual losses from various security threats identified for a small company.

Mercer Paints is a small but highly regarded paint manufacturing company located in Saskatchewan. The company has a network in place linking many of its business operations. Although the firm believes that its security is adequate, the recent addition of a Web site has become an open invitation to hackers. Management requested a risk assessment. The risk assessment identified a number of potential exposures. These exposures, their associated probabilities, and average losses are summarized in the following table.

1. In addition to the potential exposures listed, you should identify at least three other potential threats to Mercer Paints, assign probabilities, and estimate a loss range.

2. Use spreadsheet software and the risk assessment data to calculate the expected annual loss for each exposure.

Mercer Paints Risk Assessment

Exposure	Probability of Occurrence (%)	Average Loss ($)
Malware attack	60%	$75 000
Data loss	12%	$70 000
Embezzlement	3%	$30 000
User errors	95%	$25 000
Threats from hackers	95%	$90 000
Improper use by employees	5%	$5000
Power failure	15%	$300 000

3. Present your findings in the form of a chart. Which control points have the greatest vulnerability? What recommendations would you make to Mercer Paints? Prepare a written report that summarizes your findings and recommendations.

Improving Decision Making:
Evaluating Security Outsourcing Services

Software skills: Web browser and presentation software
Business skills: Evaluating business outsourcing services

Businesses today have a choice of whether to outsource the information systems security function or maintain their own internal staff for this purpose. This project will help develop your Internet skills in using the Web to research and evaluate information system security outsourcing services.

As an information systems expert in your firm, you have been asked to help management decide whether to outsource security or keep the security function within the firm. Search the Web to find information to help you decide whether to outsource security and to locate security outsourcing services.

1. Present a brief summary of the arguments for and against outsourcing system security for your company.

2. Select two firms that offer system security outsourcing services, and compare them and their services.

3. Prepare an electronic presentation for management summarizing your findings. Your presentation should make the case on whether or not your company should outsource system security. If you believe your company should outsource, the presentation should identify which security outsourcing service should be selected and justify your selection.

CASE STUDY   Beware Wi-Fi Phishers at Airports and Elsewhere

It is almost impossible to travel anywhere now, by plane, train, or automobile, and not have access to a Wi-Fi pay-as-you-go network. That is the good news: You can be connected almost anywhere. But there is bad news, too.

"Sharing information via the Internet is a positive thing and doing so can reap a great deal of positive benefits," says Staff Sergeant Bruce Imrie, Pacific Regional coordinator for the RCMP's integrated technological crime unit. "But people need to be aware there are also risks involved . . . Many people consider WEP or wireless encryption programs to be secure when in fact they are relatively easily broken."

Ron O'Brien, senior security analyst for North America for Sophos, an international security company with offices in Vancouver, B.C., says, "Using your laptop in public over a wireless connection, particularly when it is free, is the same as letting someone look over your shoulder while you are punching in your banking PIN."

As always, if you build a technology, it is not only valid users who will make use of it; bad people will abuse it, too. For example, so-called phishers establish rogue wireless networks, or evil twins, that lure users to log on to them. These rogue networks may capture your data—including logon IDs, passwords, credit card numbers, and other vital but highly confidential information; download viruses to your computer; and even gain control of your computer.

So how does this happen? Let's imagine a hacker sitting in a café at the airport with the book bag or laptop case they brought with them. The hacker reads the paper and sips a cup of coffee. Inside the book bag is a laptop computer, wireless-enabled as an access point. The hacker's network is labelled "Free Tim Horton's Wi-Fi."

Sitting a short distance away at the McDonalds is another individual, a user. While browsing for free Internet access, the user sees "Free Tim Horton's Wi-Fi" available. Trusting this well-known brand, the user judges that the network found by his own laptop's wireless scan is safe; it is, after all, named after Tim Horton's.

The user logs on to the Free Tim Horton's Wi-Fi network and immediately is taken to a home Web page for that network. The Web page says the user will be permitted access after entering a valid credit card number and expiry date. What the user does not realize is that the host Wi-Fi computer is logging every keystroke from his laptop and storing personal data, including the credit card number and expiry date, for future use by the evil twin network and its hacker creator.

"Give me an encrypted wireless network, and in 10 minutes, I will give you the password," says Ryan Purita, a senior security consultant with Totally Connected Security, a security consulting firm in Vancouver, B.C. Even legitimate security-enabled sites can be cracked with hacker software that's freely available on the Internet.

"We are seeing an increase in this type of incident," Telus spokesman Shawn Hall said of schemes such as evil twin networks and man-in-the-middle interceptions. Hall says people often let their computers default to the strongest wireless signal and that may not necessarily be the one to trust. A hacker can fake a network to fool users.

Of course, this does not happen only in airport cafès; it could happen anywhere there is unsecure Wi-Fi access: your favourite bookstore, on campus, at your local Tim Horton's or Starbucks, or almost anywhere with public access.

And the individual may not be the only one affected. Most business travellers use company laptops when travelling. This means that company information, including logon IDs and passwords to the company's network, may be stolen. Viruses, spyware, and other malware may also be downloaded to the company's network when the laptop logs in to the corporate network, thereby infecting the entire corporate system.

This type of phishing can also lead to identity theft. The criminal evil twin network can enable a hacker to use your ID, password, and credit card information to charge merchandise to your account. If the evil twin hacker has obtained your social insurance number, he or she might also be able to take out a loan or cash advance in your name.

How do you stop this type of phishing and its dangerous consequences? The first method for protecting your Wi-Fi access is to log on to hotspot networks using passwords and only at Web sites that include a Secure Sockets Layer key at the bottom right of the Web browser. Hotspots should be used only for accessing the Internet (surfing) and not for online transactions where passwords or credit card information may be transmitted. When not using a hotspot, the user should turn off Wi-Fi access, either through menu-driven commands or by removing the wireless NIC. Users should also ensure that security software, such as firewalls and antivirus and anti-spyware software, is up to date.

Constant vigilance is required to prevent phishing and identity theft. It appears that evil twin hackers target the airport market more than other locations, presumably because there is a more affluent market, i.e., airline travellers, to hoodwink. In addition, travellers are much more likely to be watching for pickpockets or listening for boarding calls than they are to focus on wireless security. So, for now, when a friend tells you to "Travel safe!" you should include your laptop in that mandate—be vigilant in connecting safely while travelling with a wireless device.

Sources: Gillian Shaw, "What Evil Twin Lurks at Your WiFi Café?" *The Vancouver Sun*, November 4, 2006; Susan MacLean, "Preventing Mobile Data Theft," IT Focus, **www.itworldcanada.com/a/IT-Focus/b5f55476-c2a3-47e1-949d-dba0166a88b0.html**, accessed April 14, 2007; and Todd Weiss, "Wi-Fi Phishing Scam Targets Business Travelers," *Computerworld*, May 10, 2005.

CASE STUDY QUESTIONS

1. List and describe the security weaknesses involved in Wi-Fi transmission.

2. What management, organization, and technology factors—as well as individual or situational factors—contribute to these weaknesses?

3. How effective are the measures described above to protect wireless access?

4. Are there additional solutions you could suggest to prevent these security problems?

Part II CANADIAN CASE STUDY:
Wi-Fi in Canada: The Good, the Bad, and the Ugly

THE GOOD
More than two-thirds of Canadians are connected to the Internet today. It is interesting to note that about 15 percent of Canadians, or 23 percent of those Canadians connected to the Internet, use wireless fidelity, one of the newer standards for telecommunication.

As detailed earlier in this chapter, IEEE standard 802.11 governs wireless networking. It has three sub-standards: a, b, and g. Sub-standard 802.11a is not compatible with either 802.11b or 802.11g, but the latter two are compatible with each other. The 802.11b standard has been the most widely used standard for creating wireless LANs and providing wireless Internet access. However, 802.11g may become more popular in the next few years, and dual-band systems capable of handling 802.11b and 802.11g are expected to proliferate. Today most computers are sold with 802.11b or 802.11g networking capability built-in, either through a wireless networking card or, more recently, with a wireless motherboard chip that holds the processing and RAM chips. In this part-ending case study, we explore how Canadian businesses and individuals are using Wi-Fi, and what challenges they are encountering.

The Baycrest Centre for Geriatric Care, headquartered in Toronto, uses Wi-Fi to support more than 200 doctors, nurses, and administrators, who provide patients with a high standard of care. Services such as bedside charting, monitoring, and order entry are carried out using 50 wireless-enabled computers-on-wheels (COWs) to access Baycrest's Meditech System.

Baycrest realized a few years ago that its doctors, nurses, and administrators needed a single wireless network over which they could transmit data. However, they did not want to make the project costly and complex: IT staff were paid $100 per hour, so keeping costs to a minimum, even after implementation, was critical. Security, of course, was also of paramount concern. Meanwhile, the system would need to support a wide variety of wireless devices, from VoIP telephones to laptop computers, handheld personal digital assistants, and voice communication badges. The centre also considered implementing new applications, such as voice over wireless.

After some research, Baycrest implemented a wireless LAN switching system that included a suite of wireless applications. The system was relatively self-configuring, resulting in ease of use and easy addition or movement of the various nodes on the network. This makes it simple to add capacity as demand increases. The new wireless network also makes it easy to transmit very large files, such as those used in medical imaging.

On the security front, Baycrest implemented data encryption to meet the requirements of the federal Personal Information Protection and Electronic Documents Act (PIPEDA). In addition, virtual private networks are hosted on the wireless network, permitting staff to log in from home to leave patient orders or check on their patients' conditions.

Baycrest is one of many companies in the health-care field that are adopting wireless technologies.

The Royal Ottawa Hospital, which opened to patients in late 2006, provides a wireless network for telemedicine to serve all the hospital's facilities and grounds. Doctors, researchers, and hospital staff, numbering over a thousand, use the Nortel Mobility network to deliver the highest quality of care.

"Hospitals tend to be large facilities," says Brian McFadden, chief research officer of Nortel Networks. The network "allows connectivity to a network with broadband capabilities, wirelessly. It allows clinical staff to stay online throughout the facility regardless of the task being undertaken." According to Bruce Swan, CEO, Royal Ottawa Health Care Group, the network "builds in flexibility for clinicians." Wireless connectivity, he adds, "makes better use of people's time. It allows information to be recorded at the time of the procedure, rather than having clinicians go back to a workstation to input it."

According to Swan, the design of the Royal Ottawa Hospital building incorporated the ability to install a wireless network. This allowed the installation to proceed smoothly. "Positioning of the nodes required to transmit information where they will be the most practical is easier than retrofitting a hospital because you don't have to work around existing infrastructure." The network has wide implications for improved efficiency at the Royal Ottawa Hospital. Wireless-enabled laptops and other handheld devices can help clinical teams to access the hospital's internal network, patient records, the Internet, email, shared files, and other applications. "It is going to drastically reduce the potential for errors," according to McFadden.

Wi-Fi is also coming to consumers at their favourite places of business through Wi-Fi hotspots. A Wi-Fi hotspot is an area where consumers can log on to a wireless Internet connection, typically for a charge. VIA Rail Canada offers Wi-Fi connectivity on most trains with routes in southern Ontario and Quebec for VIA 1 (VIA's first class) passengers. VIA already offers Wi-Fi connectivity to VIA 1 and sleeper class passengers in its Panorama Lounges in many stations. Wireless service does not come cheaply for passengers, however. VIA 1 passengers can select from three different payment plans. They can select the pay-per-use plan, for which the first 15 minutes cost $3.99, and each additional minute cost $0.30; the daily access plan, with a flat rate of $8.95 for a 24-hour period; or the monthly access plan, which costs $46. Guy Faulkner, product manager for corridor service at VIA, believes Wi-Fi access gives the company a potential advantage over its competition. Faulkner anticipates that VIA passengers will have a growing interest in onboard Internet service.

Bell Canada, a division of BCE, Inc. in Montreal, is working with VIA to provide this wireless service. The satellite signals are fed into an onboard server and then to a wireless access point in the first-class car. Users can then access this point from their laptops or handhelds. The return signal from user devices is fed from the access point in the car to the server

and then over Bell's terrestrial CDMA network, with an average data rate of about 70 Kbs.

But you don't have to ride the rails to have mobile access to wireless Internet service. Hotspots are appearing in any number of retail outlets, primarily coffee shops and restaurants. In the U.S., Schlotzsky's Deli chain offers Wi-Fi access to its customers for free in 30 of its 600 locations. According to Schlotzsky's CEO John Wooley, the free Wi-Fi access results in an additional 15 000 visits per restaurant per year, by customers who spend an average of $7 per visit. That means Wi-Fi service brings in more than $117 000 per year per outlet in return for an investment of under $10 000. Experts speculate that once free Wi-Fi access is universal, the return on investment for that type of service will decrease.

Starbucks was one of the first retail companies to incorporate Wi-Fi hotspots into its outlets, finally partnering with Bell Canada in late 2005 to offer hotspots throughout Canada. Many Second Cup locations in Canada also offer Wi-Fi access through Rogers Wireless, Inc.; Second Cup customers can read their e-mail or surf the Web while drinking their cups of coffee. Rogers, along with its competitors Bell Mobility and TELUS Mobility, is creating a national standard to make roaming between competing hotspot locations possible. With the Rogers Connect plan, Rogers' cell phone customers can use the Wi-Fi service and charge the cost to their cell phone bill.

You have only to travel the 401 between Toronto and Kitchener to find hotspots at Tim Hortons and Wendy's. Many hotels are offering Wi-Fi access in their meeting rooms or conference areas so that conference attendees can connect during conference breaks. Some hotels are even offering Wi-Fi service—for a fee—from hotel rooms.

After the outbreaks of SARS and West Nile virus and a 30 percent drop in business, Toronto's Forest Hills' Business Improvement Area created a two-block-long stretch of wireless Internet access to try to lure customers. Wireless Internet access is available from any store or even outside on Spadina Road. The "village" uses an outdoor Wi-Fi access point with 20 times the regular range with a single business DSL connection. Before customers can actually surf the Web, though, they must sit through one minute of ads—a small price to pay for free access.

If you're from out of town, how do you know where to get your Wi-Fi access? Luckily there are even Web sites that list hotspots around the world. At a site such as **www. wi-fihotspotlist.com**, a user can simply enter the address where she wishes to access a hotspot, and have the Web site return a list of available hotspots. The list includes the actual address of the hotspot, and a further link detailing a little more about the type of store (if the hotspot is hosted by a store), the type of link, and other potentially useful information.

Canadian municipalities as well as companies have rolled out Wi-Fi networks to make themselves more attractive to businesses and technology-savvy citizens. In Ontario, hydro companies are looking at Wi-Fi as a potential backhaul system, or as a way to distribute information over a network—even a wired network that the Wi-Fi network hooks into—for the smart meters mandated by the provincial government. With the advent of WiMax, a new standard for wireless telecommunication that promises high-speed links over longer distances than Wi-Fi, wireless access may eventually be possible from almost anywhere. One of the key barriers to these advances, however, is the billing dilemma: How do you bill customers for Wi-Fi or WiMax access that is carried through cellular phone carriers? There is little incentive for cellular carriers to permit their customers to make calls over Wi-Fi since the carriers cannot bill customers for those calls. Somehow, a compromise must be reached in the area of billing to converge cellular and wireless broadband technologies.

WiMax, also known as IEEE standard 802.16, brings together the dual advantages of the fast data transfer rate of Wi-Fi type technology and the broad range of a cellular phone network. The first WiMax-enabled commercial products are to be released soon; development of WiMax product standards has stalled development for some time. WiMax, an Internet Protocol (IP)–based technology, makes it possible to move all types of communication, from voice to data to video, as packets over the same network. According to experts, WiMax will offer potential rates of 75 megabits per second over a distance of more than 50 km. However, as the range of WiMax is extended, the speed of transmission is reduced.

Sometimes the technology is ready even before the applications are ready. A Windows Pocket PC device turned into a dual-mode phone, with capabilities to send and receive both cellular and Wi-Fi calls through the same dialer, has been created by Cicero Softphone. Using Wi-Fi service, the Softphone routes calls across the Internet or defaults to the cellular connection. Skype, the free VoIP provider, now offers a mobile version, permitting Pocket PC devices with Wi-Fi access to make phone calls for free or for very low charges (for example, three cents per minute to almost anywhere in the world).

THE BAD

Most experts feel that, like the billing dilemma, the security of wireless networks is difficult to establish and manage. It has become so simple to install wireless routers that almost anyone can do it. In fact, many people installing their own home wireless networks never even refer to the user's manual for their wireless routers. They use the default setups found in the installation wizards and feel that they are safely connected throughout their homes. That's the problem. As the CBC video that accompanies this case study shows, wireless access is accessible over a specific geographic area, meaning that a person in a car (war-driver), on a bike (war-biker), or simply walking (war-chalker) can steal your wireless signal to log on to the Internet. Of course, they may not view it as stealing.

Many computer aficionados feel that all wireless service should be free. Perhaps you pay to have wireless access in your home and have even wondered yourself, where is the harm in sharing something that is already there? Just remember—allowing others to access your wireless signal means that interlopers can hack into your home network, steal your files, log on to the Internet, and download pornography or illegal material, while all the time masquerading as you.

Recently, Toronto police stopped a man for a traffic violation. They quickly realized the man, who was naked from the waist down, was using his laptop to access a pornographic video that he had downloaded and was watching over a residential wireless hotspot. He was eventually charged not only with the traffic violation but also with theft

of telecommunications—a first in Canada. The owners of the hotspot he used were not charged, but it may be only a matter of time until Internet service providers and owners of unsecured wireless networks in their own homes could be liable for permitting unlawful access to their networks.

Security on wireless networks is not so hard to establish: you simply need to read the network installation manual and follow the instructions to restrict access to your wireless network, including using logon IDs and passwords that are unique to your network.

As the video that accompanies this case shows, war-driving, war-biking, or war-chalking is easy to do with proper, inexpensive equipment. Chalked symbols on streets and sidewalks (put there by "war-chalkers") show others where they can access open wireless networks. According to research by WorldWide WarDrive, more than two-thirds of the approximately 88 100 access points found by war drivers around the world did not have basic security enabled.

Whether someone is gaining illegal wireless access while walking, biking, or driving, they are stealing a valuable service. It truly is theft: You should know that, according to Wartalking.com, someone was arrested for hacking into a court's wireless network just to prove that the court's network could be hacked.

A new wireless security standard called 801.11i was finalized in 2004 but has been slow to be implemented over the more popular, but less secure, WEP and WPA. Standard 802.11i requires firmware or driver support for both the wireless host and the wireless client. However, another solution to most wireless vulnerabilities is to make it easier to set up and turn on wireless security. It would be even simpler to have security enabled out-of-the box. But some experts feel that ease-of-setup is most important for Wi-Fi "newbies." They also think that if security were enabled to default settings, soon everyone would be using the default password. This would make hacking on a large scale even more likely and even more dangerous.

THE UGLY

Vancouver police detective Mark Fenton has told his superiors that the city's plans for a city-wide wireless Internet system, housing transit systems, traffic signals, and electric utility systems, puts the city at risk of a terrorist attack during the 2010 Winter Olympic games. The city wants to offer a free or low-cost wireless network available even before the Olympics starts. The plan calls for much of the city's infrastructure to use the platform for wireless communications and remote operations. "If you have an open wireless system across the city, as a bad guy, I could sit on a bus with a laptop and do global crime," Fenton stated. "It would be virtually impossible to find me."

The previous case study points to another serious problem: evil twin hotspots. In the financial district in London, England, many Wi-Fi networks lack basic security. NTA Monitor, a security testing company, recently used passive monitoring to determine that many internal resources, such as printer queues, could easily be found, and many even used no encryption whatsoever.

What is the future of Wi-Fi? Perhaps it will eventually give way to newer, faster technologies with a broader geographical reach, such as WiMax. But for now, Wi-Fi will be here for several years as the newer technologies mature and applications become available to make use of them.

Sources: Brian Eaton, "Ottawa—A Hospital Built for Mesh," *IT World Canada*, August 2, 2005, available **www.techworld.com/features/index.cfm?featureID=1607**, accessed September 24, 2005; Aruba Networks, "Secure Voice and Data over Wi-Fi Moves Baycrest to Switch to Aruba," April 2004, available **www.arubanetworks.com/pdf/baycrest_cs.pdf**, accessed September 24, 2005; Via Rail Canada, "Wireless Internet in Via 1 Class," available **www.viarail.ca/wirelessinternet/en_index.html**, accessed September 24, 2005; Bob Brewin, "All Aboard with Wi-Fi on Via Rail Canada," *Computerworld Canada*, July 10, 2003, available **www.computerworld.com/printthis/2003/0,4814,82940,00.html**, accessed September 24, 2005; B. Mann Consulting, "Computerworld: Free Hot Spots Pay Dividends," October 22, 2003, available **www.bmannconsulting.com/node/614**, accessed September 24, 2005; Tyler Hamilton, "Wi-Fi 'Hotspots' Coming to a Coffee Shop Near You," *Toronto Star*, February 18, 2005, **www.thestar.com**, accessed September 24, 2005; Michael Martin, "The Wi-Fi/Cell Conundrum," September 16, 2005, available **www.itworldcanada.com//Pages/Docbase/ViewArticle.aspx?ID=idgml-b2e4cb03-ddff-4c06-9aec-ad8679abf822**, accessed September 24, 2005; Peter Judge, "Converged Softphone Cuts Bill," September 8, 2005, available **www.itworldcanada.com/a/search/e10c3e79-22ad-4c3d-a8d4-47e0c1dc6123.html**, accessed September 24, 2005; Dan McLean, "Bluetooth and WiFi, Meet WiMAX Technology," August 4, 2005, available **www.itworldcanada.com/a/search/6fa973d9-511a-4d6c-a3e3-c9209578f0df.html**, accessed September 24, 2005; Rosie Lombardi, "Canadian Researchers Uncover New 'Wireless' Possibilities," July 29, 2005, available **www.itworldcanada.com/a/search/a8dd82dc-62b6-46d1-846f-6a50e74b24bf.html**, accessed September 24, 2005; Sean Carruthers, "Forest Hills Cuts the Cords," November 6, 2003, available **www.hubacanada.com/story_10783_4**, accessed September 26, 2005; "Wi-Fi Arrest Highlights Security Dangers," **http://news.zdnet.com**, accessed July 16, 2007; Randy Shore, "WiFi Could Pose Threat during Vancouver Olympics," **www.canada.com/topics/news/national/story.html?id=207f6d54-68fc-40da-8ae3-dc9f057c 2f54&k=25065**, access July 16, 2007; and John E. Dunn, "Wi-Fi Networks Still Insecure in London's City," Techworld,com, **www.itworldcanada.com/a/Enterprise-Infrastructure/4de93aab-8968-47ce-9611-05566a5ad095.html**, accessed July 16, 2007.

Video Resource: "Wireless Internet (WI-FI)." *Venture* 883. Canadian Broadcasting Corporation. June 8, 2003.

CASE STUDY QUESTIONS

1. What are the implications of having competing wireless standards, such as three 802.11 standards and WiMAX? Do you see convergence of these standards, one standard becoming prominent, or a newer standard coming forward in the next three to five years?

2. Do you think that the advent of wireless hot spots will change the way people compute? If people change the places and times that they use their computers, do you think that the hardware or type of computers people use will change? How will the hardware change?

3. Looking at the health care industry, what are some of the ways, in addition to those mentioned above, that health care professionals can make use of wireless technology? Are there any information technology uses for which wireless is not an appropriate telecommunications method?

4. What are some of the privacy and security considerations in thinking about or using wireless technologies? How can these concerns be addressed?

PART III

Developing and Managing Information Systems

PART III   Canadian Case Study
In Tech We Trust: The Story of SAP in Canada

CHAPTER 9

Systems Development

After completing this chapter, you will be able to do the following:

1. Demonstrate how developing new systems produces organizational change.
2. Identify and describe the core activities in the systems development process.
3. Evaluate alternative methods for developing information systems.
4. Compare alternative methodologies for modelling systems.
5. Identify and describe new approaches for systems development in the digital firm era.

OPENING **CASE** | Protecting Patients by Tracking Instruments

If you were to go to a hospital for a medical procedure, whether in the emergency room, elective surgery, or major surgery, could you envision that you might get an infection from one of the instruments used in your procedure? Or could you envision that the instrument that was needed for your procedure could not be found? This is a frightening prospect, one that could easily happen without the benefit of a hospital instrument tracking system.

For many hospitals, managing and tracking instruments through the different stages of storage, use, and sterilization, and back to storage again, is a manual, paper-based process rife with errors. These errors could lead to cross-contamination and infection. Like most hospitals, The Ottawa Hospital (TOH) once relied on a paper-based system, tracking instrument inventory using sheets and binders. Inaccuracies originated with hospital staff, whose primary job was not to carry out instrument inventory but to update the instrument inventory records. When the operating room department requested certain instruments, much time was spent on finding the correct paper-trail entry and then the correct instrument.

Sterilization technicians assemble sets of instruments on a tray based on the type of procedure. In the sterilization area, technicians had difficulties maintaining paper records and noting each instrument's place in the sterilization process of cleaning, sterilizing, reassembly, or storage.

To improve the tracking process, TOH decided to implement an established computer-based instrument tracking program, Alex Gold, by the software company TGX Medical.

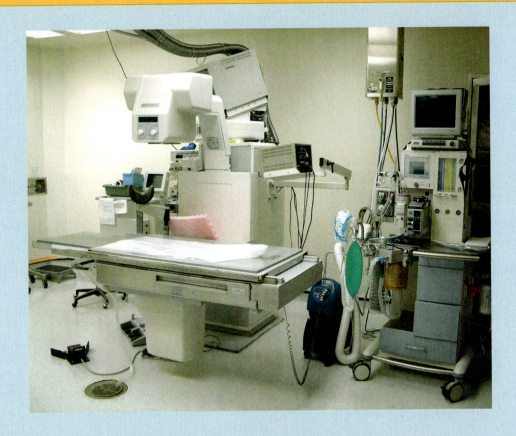

Lynne Trott, director of logistical services at TOH, made the decision to implement Alex Gold across all three hospital campuses. For her, lack of integrated information was a primary issue. "We couldn't guarantee we had accurate information on which tray was used for a specific patient. With Alex, we can now tie that [tray] to patient information."

Alex Gold coordinates every facet of instrument and equipment use within the healthcare facility, allowing doctors to have properly sterilized instrument sets at the right time and at the right location. The system uses Web-based technology to allow communication across all levels of users. Alex Gold tracks instruments from the operating room through sterilization to storage, ensuring that they have been properly cleaned, assembled, and maintained.

Before implementation of Alex Gold, the paper data had to be converted to electronic data in order to inventory all the hospital's instruments. The data were then placed in a database that included cleaning and sterilization instructions. These instructions differ based not only on the type of instrument, but even on the manufacturer. After data were converted, training

was given to sterilization technicians in how to use the new system.

The implementation took more than a year. The instruments had to be bar-coded, with special strips that could withstand the heat and chemicals involved in sterilization, so the instruments could be scanned and recorded at every step of the instrument cycle.

Michael Good, CEO of TGX Medical Systems, said, "We did a lot of custom work at TOH beyond what's in the packaged product." However, the work will pay off for TOH long-term because the new system reduces training time. According to Kay Lee, manager of instrument systems for the Codman Division of Johnson and Johnson, the Canadian distributor of Alex Gold, sterilization technicans (who are gloved and masked) have a hard time looking at paper records. Technicians "need extensive training [on paper-based systems], but that requirement drops dramatically with Alex," said Lee.

Using Alex Gold, TOH can even budget and track maintenance costs for the instruments. The new system flags instruments that need to be sent out for maintenance and lets the hospital monitor how many instruments are being processed. The system also allows TOH to determine proper staffing levels of sterilization technicians. TOH has seen a dramatic decrease in errors in instrument processing, and the system can quantify that improvement for TOH.

Sources: Rosie Lombardi, "From Paper Trail to Patient Care," **www.itworldcanada.com/a/E-Government/78a168dc-e318-4702-ada5-0c93c482afca.html**, accessed April 17, 2007; "The Ottawa Hospital Launches an Instrument Tracking System," *Summit Magazine*, **www.summitconnects.com/In_the_News/ARCHIVE/2005_10.htm**, accessed April 17, 2007; and TGX Medical Systems, "Alex Gold," **www.tgxmedical.com/products_and_services/alex_gold.asp**, accessed April 17, 2007.

The experience of TOH illustrates some of the steps required to design and develop new information systems. Developing the new system entailed analyzing the organization's problems with existing information systems, assessing people's information needs, selecting appropriate technology, and redesigning business processes and jobs. Management had to monitor the systems development effort and to evaluate its benefits and costs. The new information system represented a process of planned organizational change.

The chapter-opening Business Challenges diagram calls attention to important points raised by this case and this chapter. The TOH instrument tracking system was heavily manual and could not support the large number of instruments and processes that needed to be coordinated. Consequently, instrument processes, such as cleaning, sterilizing, and storing, had higher error rates than were desirable. The TOH instrument tracking process required many steps and coordination of multiple groups and campuses. Given the constraints of the problem, the best solution was to rapidly create a system using a vendor's application software package, with customization by both the hospital and the vendor. The new system reduces the amount of time, effort, and errors in the instrument tracking process. The Ottawa Hospital logistics leadership had to design a new instrument tracking process and manage the transition from the old manual instrument tracking processes to the new system.

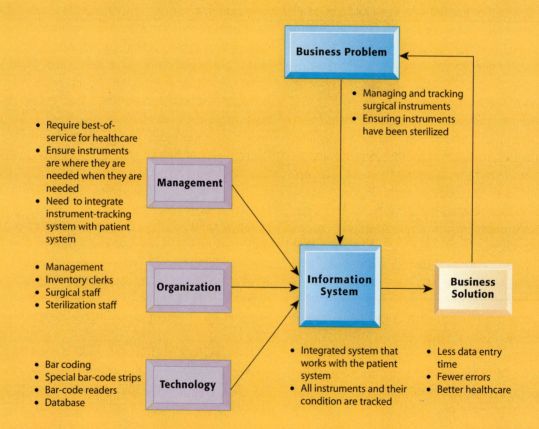

HEADS **UP**

During your career, you will undoubtedly be asked to work on the development of a new system to solve an important challenge for your firm. In the process of developing new systems, you will face many choices about hardware and software, and you will have to think about how to redesign business processes and jobs in order to maximize the value derived from the new system. You will also have to decide whether to develop your own software solution, or purchase packaged software or online Web services. But the most important decisions you will face involve understanding just exactly what it is you want the software to do and what value it will bring to your firm.

- If your career is in finance and accounting, you will help systems developers analyze the costs and benefits of new information system projects and assess their economic feasibility.

- If your career is in human resources, you will be analyzing changes in workflows and job responsibilities resulting from the new information systems and arranging for employee training in the new systems.

- If your career is in information systems, you will be working with end users to design new systems, choose appropriate hardware and software, and test these systems.

- If your career is in manufacturing, production, or operations management, you will work on process improvements and information systems that increase the quality of products or services.

- If your career is in sales and marketing, you will be helping to design and test new Web-based systems for online sales or a new customer relationship management system because these systems often receive high priority in many firms' information system plans.

9.1 Systems as Planned Organizational Change

Developing a new information system is one kind of planned organizational change. The introduction of a new information system involves much more than new hardware and software. It also includes changes in jobs, skills, management, and organization. When we design a new information system, we are redesigning the organization. System developers must understand how a system will affect specific business processes and the organization as a whole.

Systems Development and Organizational Change

Information technology can promote various degrees of organizational change, ranging from incremental to far-reaching. Figure 9-1 shows four kinds of structural organizational change that are enabled by information technology: (1) automation, (2) rationalization, (3) reengineering, and (4) paradigm shifts. Each carries different rewards and risks.

The most common form of IT-enabled organizational change is **automation**. The first applications of information technology involved assisting employees with performing their tasks more efficiently and effectively. Calculating paychecks and payroll registers, giving bank tellers instant access to customer deposit records, and developing a nationwide network of airline reservation terminals for airline reservation agents are all examples of early automation.

A deeper form of organizational change—one that follows quickly from early automation—is rationalization of procedures. Automation frequently reveals new bottlenecks in production and makes the existing arrangement of procedures and structures painfully cumbersome. **Rationalization of procedures** is the streamlining of standard

Automation
Rationalization of procedures

FIGURE 9-1   *Organizational change carries risks and rewards*

The most common forms of organizational change are automation and rationalization. These relatively slow-moving and slow-changing strategies present modest returns but little risk. Faster and more comprehensive change—such as reengineering and paradigm shifts—carries high rewards but offers substantial chances of failure.

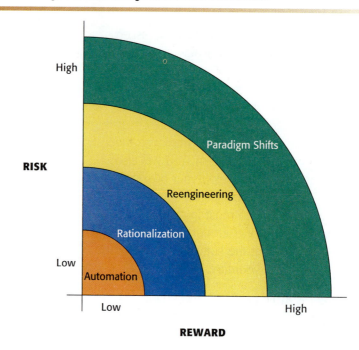

operating procedures. For example, The Ottawa Hospital's new instrument tracking system described in the chapter-opening case is effective not only because it uses computer technology but also because its design enables the organization to operate more efficiently. The hospital had to have standard identification codes for each type of instrument and each location, and standard rules for entering tracking information online. Without a certain amount of rationalization in The Ottawa Hospital's organization, its computer technology would have been useless.

A more powerful type of organizational change is business process reengineering, in which business processes are analyzed, simplified, and redesigned. Using information technology, organizations can rethink and streamline their business processes to improve speed, service, and quality. Business process reengineering reorganizes work flows, combining steps to cut waste and eliminating repetitive, paper-intensive tasks (sometimes the new design eliminates jobs as well). It is much more ambitious than rationalization of procedures, requiring a new vision of how the process is to be organized.

A widely cited example of business process reengineering is Ford Motor Company's invoiceless processing, which reduced headcount in Ford's North American accounts payable organization of 500 people by 75 percent. Accounts payable clerks used to spend most of their time resolving discrepancies between purchase orders, receiving documents, and invoices. Ford reengineered its accounts payable process so that the purchasing department enters a purchase order into an online database that can be checked by the receiving department when the ordered items arrive. If the received goods match the purchase order, the system automatically generates a cheque for accounts payable to send to the vendor. There is no need for vendors to send invoices.

Reengineering does not suit everyone affected by the reengineering project. It is radical change, change usually undertaken over a short period of time. Such radical change can meet with dissension and opposition. See the section in Chapter 10 on change management for a discussion of these issues.

Rationalizing procedures and redesigning business processes are limited to specific parts of a business. New information systems can ultimately affect the design of the entire organization by transforming how the organization carries out its business or even the nature of the business. For instance, the Canadian trucking and transportation firm Trans-X used new information systems to change its business model. Trans-X created a new business managing the logistics for other companies. This more radical form of business change is called a paradigm shift. A **paradigm shift** involves rethinking the nature of the business, defining a new business model, and often changing the very nature of the organization.

Paradigm shifts and reengineering often fail because extensive organizational change is so difficult to orchestrate (see Chapter 10). Why, then, do so many corporations contemplate such radical change? Because the rewards are equally high (see Figure 9-1). In many instances, firms seeking paradigm shifts and pursuing reengineering strategies achieve stunning, order-of-magnitude increases in their returns on investment (or productivity). Some of these success stories, and some failure stories, are included throughout this book.

Business Process Reengineering

Many companies today are focusing on developing new information systems that will improve their business processes. Some of these system projects represent radical restructuring of business processes while others entail more incremental process change.

If organizations rethink and redesign their business processes before developing information systems, they can potentially obtain very large payoffs from their investments in information technology. Let's look at how the home mortgage industry in Canada accomplished this.

The application process for a home mortgage used to take about six to eight weeks. Leading banks, such as Scotiabank and ING Direct, have redesigned the mortgage application process to reduce the cost and time to obtain a mortgage to less than one week.

In the past, a mortgage applicant filled out a paper loan application. A bank entered the application into its computer system. Specialists, such as credit analysts and underwriters from various departments, accessed and evaluated the application individually. If the loan application was approved, the closing was scheduled. After the closing, bank specialists dealing with insurance or funds in escrow serviced the loan. This "desk-to-desk" assembly-line approach might take weeks.

Today loan originators in the field, in "online offices," or in bank branches enter the mortgage application directly into their desktop or laptop computers. Software checks the application transaction to make sure that all the information is correct and complete.

At ING Direct, the Mortgage Application Processing Solution (MAPS) accepts mortgages from ING Direct's Web site or mortgage brokers and integrates with ING Direct's customer-relationship management software. The MAPS software then automatically integrates with other external entities to allow ING's mortgage underwriters to quickly assess applications. Meanwhile, mortgage applicants and clients can check online on the status of their applications, and any ING staff member can be in immediate contact with the client without leaving their computer. Once the application is approved, MAPS produces the commitment letter with the specifics of the mortgage and automatically images and associates the signed documents (which have been faxed back to ING by the customer) with the correct account and mortgage. Introducing MAPS to its outdated mortgage processing process cut the time required to underwrite a mortgage by more than 200 percent—from one week to a maximum of two days.

Like ING Direct, Scotiabank also felt pressured to meet its clients' demands for faster mortgage processing. Prior to automating the mortgage work flow process, Scotiabank personnel filled out mortgage applications and faxed them to a central mortgage processing unit, where the data from the application were manually keyed into a centralized database. It the data were incomplete, the entire process had to be repeated. Today, branch personnel or mortgage originators use workflow software to input, edit, and confirm mortgage data, after which the data are transmitted electronically to the central mortgage processing unit. Before automation, bank personnel who wanted to check on their clients' mortgage applications had to e-mail the central mortgage processing unit, where the request was printed out and manually distributed to an underwriter to respond to the request. Today, such requests are automatically transferred to an underwriter, who can respond quickly.

By rethinking their approaches to mortgage processing, mortgage banks have achieved remarkable efficiencies. They have not focused on redesigning a single business process,

Paradigm shift

but instead they have re-examined the entire set of logically connected processes required to obtain a mortgage.

To support the new mortgage application process, the banks have implemented work flow and document management software. **Work flow management** is the process of streamlining business procedures so that documents can be moved easily and efficiently. Work flow and document management software automates processes such as routing documents to different locations, securing approvals, scheduling, and generating reports. Two or more people can work simultaneously on the same document, allowing much quicker completion time. Work need not be delayed because a file is out or a document is in transit. And with a properly designed indexing system, users are able to retrieve files in many different ways, based on the content of the document.

The Window on Organizations section describes how the U.S. organization Small Business Administration (SBA) reengineered its processes for providing low-interest loans to disaster victims. When Hurricanes Katrina, Rita, and Wilma hit the southeastern United States in 2005, entire communities and regions were crushed. Besides the horrendous loss of life, thousands lost businesses and homes. This in turn led to an onslaught of applications to SBA for disaster assistance. Fortunately, SBA was ready with a new system that could handle the load: the Disaster Credit Management System (DCMS), a Web-enabled electronic loan processing system responsible for all federal government loans to those affected by disasters.

Work flow management

WINDOW ON ORGANIZATIONS

Organization

Business Process Redesign at the Small Business Administration

The Small Business Administration (SBA) is a government-funded organization that assists business people and property owners in the United States with funding and advice. Following a disaster or economic disruption, the agency provides low-interest, taxpayer-subsidized loans to businesses and homeowners. Businesses can qualify for loans of up to US $1.5 million, which cover repairs, inventory, machinery, and working capital. Homeowners can borrow US $200 000 for real estate losses and US $40 000 for replacing personal property.

SBA administers loans through its Office of Disaster Assistance (ODA). Prior to 2004, ODA was organized like many federal agencies in regional centres located in Atlanta, New York, Fort Worth, and Sacramento. At some point in history, this probably made sense, but no one could say today why this was necessary. Each of these centres was a duplicate of the others, except that each had its own IT infrastructure. Each centre had a small permanent crew that handled paperwork and routing while others were field workers who were needed to inspect properties.

Until November 2004, the SBA loan application process was almost totally paper-based. The only computerized system was an Automated Loan Control System (ALCS), which was outdated, cumbersome, unreliable, and not compliant with the current IT security requirements. ALCS was not really a loan control system that handled all the details of a loan, but just a tracking system that interfaced with the agency's mainframe that ran a program that actually funded and dispersed loans.

This is how the old system worked in the past: Once the Federal Emergency Management Agency (FEMA) declared a disaster, SBA officials mailed out applications to victims who requested them. Then they set up temporary centres in the affected areas to advise applicants and receive applications.

The applications were taken to the regional office where the data was entered into ALCS and a paper file was created. Then a manual credit report would be prepared. A Dun & Bradstreet credit report would be obtained for businesses, and other internal SBA systems were checked. These reports were stuffed into the file.

Once the physical file was prepared, it was shipped to the Loss Verification department and by overnight mail to a property inspector, who would inspect the property. Stuffed with reports and photos, the physical file would be sent back to a loan officer, who then made the final decision about granting a loan. In the process, files were lost, duplicate entries made, calculations were mistaken, and this all caused further delay. Prior to redesigning its business processes, the agency required 200 people just to control the files, and more than 3000 people on staff to feed the paper monster.

In November 2004, SBA consolidated the four centres into a single centre that created a single point of contact and base of command for IT support. All calls now go through one place rather than being routed based on geography. The Fort Worth office became a processing and disbursement centre where the loan and legal staffs actually make and disburse loans. SBA contracted with SuperSolutions Corporation and Oracle to install SuperSolutions's Daybreak Lending Suite, which automates the lending process. The software runs on an Oracle9i database.

To help speed up the data collection process and reduce errors and labour, SBA purchased Toshiba's Protégé M200 tablet PCs to take to disaster sites, and a Java-based custom application that helped inspectors do their jobs.

The process is simple: A loan request is created and keyed into the Oracle database. These requests are turned into assignments that are pushed out electronically to the inspectors' tablet PCs. They can enter data and inspection details directly into the tablet, and that data is then uploaded back to the database at the end of the day.

Rather than send reports by mail or FedEx, the inspectors enter their work and connect to the same Oracle database from which they receive their assignments. "They can go out independently without being connected to anything, perform their work, then go back to their hotel room, or anywhere with a Wi-Fi connection, and sync with the database. This process cuts days if not weeks out of the loan process.

Launched in November 2004, in the fall of 2005 DCMS underwent its first critical test: three large continental hurricanes in a year, including Katrina, the storm of the century. SBA workers in the hurricane-ravaged Gulf Coast were hampered by a damaged regional IT infrastructure. The new system worked, but not as fast as victims arrived asking for help. The system had some setbacks and received some Congressional criticism, but it survived.

By 2006, the new system was working extremely well. Before Hurricane Katrina hit in 2005, ODA handled about 100 applications per day. Today it handles about 7000 or 8000 daily. So far the system has processed well over 400 000 loan applications. The largest savings have come from salary and daily expense reductions. You do not need as many people if you can pull up a record electronically whenever and wherever you need it. Postage savings are huge, too, considering each file often made its way back and forth across the country several times.

In the future, SBA envisages reducing costs further by implementing self-service applications. Instead of having disaster victims go to a centre to fill out paper forms, individuals will go to the Internet and apply online. This would eliminate the need to key in from a paper-based application. Other applications include a staff management tool that can keep track of more than 5000 emergency workers who come on board in a

crisis. In the past, it was impossible to keep track of their hours, and paper vouchers were used.

To Think About

1. What was wrong with the existing computer system (ALCS), and why did SBA decide to replace it?

2. What was the purpose of re-organizing the ODA, centralizing IT in a single office, and centralizing other functions such as the call centre in a single office?

3. In what other ways could the agency use information systems to improve the process of loan application, approval, and maintenance?

4. Check out the Canadian government's small business loan program at http://strategis.ic.gc.ca/epic/site/csbfp-pfpec.nsf/en/Home. Can you determine if it uses a system similar to the one described for the U.S. Small Business Administration?

MIS in Action

1. Using any graphic tool available, diagram both the old and the new business process for loan applications at SBA. Try to identify the key decision-making points and persons, the amount of time SBA spends on their part of the process, and the cost of their labour. (You will have to estimate the time and labour cost elements because the case does not have enough detail.) When you are done, calculate the time it takes to make a decision about a loan, the number of people involved, and the cost of the labour involved. Compare the old and the new processes on the dimensions of time and resources required to process a single loan application.

2. Go to the SuperSolutions Web site (www.supersolution.com) and identify the features of the company's Daylight Lending Suite used by SBA. How were these features illustrated in the SBA case? What other features should SBA think about using?

3. At the SuperSolutions Web site, identify a success story, and describe how the firm using the Daylight Lending Suite redesigned its business processes in order to benefit from the new technology.

Sources: Karen J. Bannan, "A Helping Hand," *Profit Magazine*, February, 2006; Rob Thormeyer, "SBA weathers storm of criticism over loan processing," *Government Computing News*, October 5, 2006; and SRA, Inc., "Small Business Administration Disaster Credit Management System Support," October 2006, www.sra.com/about/index.asp?id=602 accessed September 1, 2007.

Steps in Effective Reengineering One of the most important strategic decisions that a firm can make is not deciding how to use information systems to improve business processes, but rather understanding what business processes need improvement. Businesses are composed of hundreds—sometimes thousands—of business processes. How can you decide which need to be changed and which could really benefit from information systems? When systems are used to strengthen the wrong business model or business processes, the business can become more efficient at doing what it should not do (Hammer, 2002). As a result, the firm becomes vulnerable to competitors who may have discovered the right business model. Considerable time and cost can also be spent improving business processes that have little impact on overall firm performance and revenue.

You will need to determine what business processes are the most important to focus on when applying new information technology, and how improving these processes will help the firm execute its strategy. It is typically senior management that determines which business processes need improvement and have the highest priority. This decision results from two considerations:

- Strategic analysis: Senior managers identify the business processes that are most important for the firm's success and focus efforts on these processes.
- Pain points: Senior managers identify the processes that produce the most complaints from vendors, customers, or employees and fix those first.

Once the proper business process has been selected, firms engage in the following activities:

- Identify the inputs and outputs to a business process.

  Inputs refer to tangible and intangible items that flow from the environment into the process, including customer requests for products or services from vendors. Outputs flow back into the environment and can include task orders, satisfied customers, cash, or materials.

- Identify the flow of products and/or services.

  All processes are composed of a flow of goods or services.

- Identify the network of activities and buffers in the process.

  Processes are collections of related business activities such as receiving requests from customers, filling orders, filing papers, and talking with vendors. Buffers are delay times built into the process to facilitate review and monitoring. All business processes consume time, as well as other resources.

- Identify all resources.

  All processes consume capital, labour, and time. Because cost reduction is a major objective of business process design, it is imperative that baseline costs be established. Baseline costs refers to the cost of the original business process in time and resources before any improvements are made.

- Identify the information structure and flow.

  Business processes are informed and supported by a flow of information required to make decisions.

- Identify the process owners.

  Processes are "owned" by decision makers who have primary responsibility for the process and decisions. In some cases, ownership is shared.

- Identify process actors and decision makers.
- Processes involve a network of activities and decisions.

Once firms are able to identify and describe the existing process, the next step is understanding how much the process costs and how long it takes to perform. Business processes are typically measured along the following dimensions:

- Process cost: The total cost of the business process for a "typical" transaction.
- Process time: The total decision and activity time of all actors.
- Process quality: The amount of time and money spent reworking defective parts and services.

- Process flexibility: The ability of the process to produce a variety of outputs, or change in the face of environmental pressures. "Flexibility" translates directly into better utilization of plants and equipment, and lower labour costs.

Once the existing business process has been thoroughly understood, the next step is to think about how to improve it. New information systems and technologies offer many opportunities for greatly reducing costs, increasing efficiency, and enhancing effectiveness and revenues. Here are some common principles that business process designers use:

- Replace sequential steps in the process with parallel steps;
- Enrich jobs by enhancing decision authority and concentrating information;
- Enable information sharing throughout among all participants;
- Eliminate buffers (decision delays and inventories);
- Transform batch processing and decision making into continuous flow processes; and
- Automate decision tasks where possible.

While it is difficult to separate the contributions of new information technology from the new business processes enabled by that new technology, it is widely believed that more than 50 percent of the improvements in organizational efficiency and business value occur because of improvements in business design, while the remainder results from the new technology, largely because it increases transparency, enables collaboration across the enterprise, and drastically reduces the cost of communication, information management, and business intelligence.

One result is that, today, a modern business organization would not attempt to install a new procurement system or other major enterprise system without doing a thorough documentation and analysis of its existing procurement processes. As an example of the power of business process redesign, consider the case of Cemex, the international provider of cement and ready-mix concrete. Prior to reengineering its delivery process, Cemex required an average time of three hours to make a delivery. After Cemex's processes were reengineered, average delivery time dropped to 20 minutes. Without measuring the baseline original process, you will have no way to judge improvements.

Following the steps described previously does not automatically guarantee that reengineering will always be successful for you and your firm. Many reengineering projects do not achieve breakthrough gains in business performance because the organizational changes are often very difficult to manage. Managing change is neither simple nor intuitive, and companies committed to reengineering need a good change management strategy (see Chapter 10).

Interorganizational processes, such as those for supply chain management, not only need to be streamlined but also coordinated and integrated with those of customers and suppliers. In such cases, reengineering will involve multiple companies working together to jointly redesign their shared processes. Reengineering expert James Champy calls the joint redesign of interorganizational business processes X-engineering, and it is even more challenging to implement successfully than reengineering processes for a single company (Champy, 2002). We examine the organizational change issues surrounding reengineering more carefully in Chapter 10.

Process Improvement: Business Process Management, Total Quality Management, and Six Sigma

Business process reengineering (BPR) is primarily a one-time effort, focusing on identifying one or two strategic business processes that need radical change. But organizations have many business processes and support processes that must be constantly revised to keep the business competitive. Business processes are not static but continually change as employees adjust to changes in the markets. Business process management and quality improvement programs provide opportunities for more incremental and ongoing types of business process change.

Business process reengineering (BPR)

Business Process Management Mergers and acquisitions, changes in business models, new industry requirements, and changing customer expectations all pose multiple process-related problems that continually confront organizations. **Business process management (BPM)** is an effort to help firms manage process changes that are required in many areas of the business. There are a variety of methods and tools that are intended to help a firm revise and optimize its business processes on an ongoing basis. The goal of BPM is to enable organizations to make continual improvements to many business processes and to use processes as the fundamental building blocks of corporate information systems.

BPM includes work flow management, business process modelling notation, quality measurement and management, change management, and tools for recasting the firm's business processes into a standardized form where they can be continually manipulated. Companies practising business process management use process-mapping tools to identify and document existing processes and to create models of improved processes that can then be translated into software systems. The process models might require entirely new systems or could be based on existing systems and data. Ideally, a business process can be expressed entirely in software and be accomplished with little or no human intervention. For instance, the process of clearing credit card transactions is entirely automated in online businesses. But obviously there are many business processes that are not as mechanistic as credit card transactions. For instance, identifying and securing a new customer can be supported by software, but in most cases still requires a human sales person.

BPM also includes process monitoring and analytics. Firms need to verify that process performance has been improved and measure the impact of process changes on key business performance indicators. A number of commercial software vendors, including IBM, BEA Systems, Vitria, FileNet, Tibco, and Fuego, supply business process management products.

Total Quality Management and Six Sigma Quality management is another area of continuous process improvement. In addition to increasing organizational efficiency, companies must fine-tune their business processes to improve the quality of their products, services, and operations. Many are using the concept of **total quality management (TQM)** to make quality the responsibility of all people and functions within an organization. TQM holds that the achievement of quality control is an end in itself. Everyone is expected to contribute to the overall improvement of quality—the engineer who avoids design errors, the production worker who spots defects, the sales representative who presents the product properly to potential customers, and even the secretary who avoids typing mistakes. TQM derives from quality management concepts developed by American quality experts such as W. Edwards Deming and Joseph Juran, but the Japanese people popularized it.

Another quality concept that is being widely implemented today is six sigma. **Six sigma** is a specific measure of quality, representing 3.4 defects per million opportunities. Most companies cannot achieve this level of quality but use six sigma as a goal to implement a set of methodologies and techniques for improving quality and reducing costs. Studies have repeatedly shown that the earlier in the business cycle a problem is eliminated, the less it costs the company. Thus, quality improvements not only raise the level of product and service quality, but they can also lower costs.

How Information Systems Support Quality Improvements TQM and six sigma are considered to be more incremental than business process reengineering. TQM typically focuses on making a series of continuous improvements rather than dramatic bursts of change. Six sigma uses statistical analysis tools to detect flaws in the execution of an existing process and make minor adjustments. Sometimes, however, processes may have to be fully reengineered to achieve a specified level of quality. Information systems can help firms achieve their quality goals by helping them simplify products or processes, make improvements based on customer demands, reduce cycle time, improve the quality and precision of design and production, and meet benchmarking standards.

Benchmarking consists of setting strict standards for products, services, and other activities, and then measuring performance against those standards. Companies may use external industry standards, standards set by other companies, internally developed high standards, or some combination of the three. L.L.Bean, the Freeport, Maine,

Business process management (BPM)

Total quality management (TQM)

Six sigma

Benchmarking

outdoor clothing company, used benchmarking to achieve an order-shipping accuracy of 99.9 percent. Its old batch order fulfillment system could not handle the surging volume and variety of items to be shipped. After studying German and Scandinavian companies with leading-edge order fulfillment operations, L.L.Bean carefully redesigned its order fulfillment process and information systems so that orders could be processed as soon as they were received, and shipped within 24 hours. You can find other examples of systems promoting quality improvements throughout this text. For example, The Ottawa Hospital had benchmarked their instrument tracking errors; we know this because they could tell that there had been a dramatic decrease in such errors after the implementation of the Alex Gold instrument tracking system.

9.2 Overview of Systems Development

New information systems are an outgrowth of a process of organizational problem solving. A new information system is developed as a solution to some type of problem or set of problems the organization perceives it is facing. The problem may be one in which managers and employees realize that the organization is not performing as well as expected, or it may come from the realization that the organization should take advantage of new opportunities to perform more successfully.

The activities that go into producing an information system solution to an organizational problem or opportunity are called systems development. **Systems development** is a structured kind of problem solving with distinct activities. These activities consist of systems analysis, systems design, programming, testing, conversion, and production and maintenance.

Figure 9-2 illustrates the systems development process. The systems development activities depicted here usually take place in sequential order, but some of the activities may need to be repeated or some may take place simultaneously, depending on the approach to systems development that is being employed (see Section 9.3).

Systems Analysis

Systems analysis is the analysis of a problem that an organization will try to solve with an information system. It consists of defining the problem, identifying its causes, specifying the solution, and identifying the information requirements that must be met by a system solution.

Systems development
Systems analysis

FIGURE 9-2   *The systems development process*

Developing a system can be broken down into six core activities.

The systems analyst creates a road map of the existing organization and systems, identifying the primary owners and users of data along with existing hardware and software. The systems analyst then details the problems of existing systems. By examining documents, work papers, and procedures; observing system operations; and interviewing key users of the systems, the analyst can identify the problem areas and objectives a solution would achieve. Often the solution requires developing a new information system or improving an existing one.

Systems analysis includes conducting a feasibility study to determine whether the proposed solution is feasible or achievable from a financial, technical, and organizational standpoint. The **feasibility study** determines whether the proposed system was a good investment, whether the technology needed for the system is available and can be handled by the firm's information systems specialists, and whether the organization can handle the changes introduced by the system.

Normally, the systems analysis process identifies several alternative solutions that the organization can pursue. The process then assesses the feasibility of each. A written systems proposal report describes the costs and benefits, advantages, and disadvantages of each alternative. It is up to management to determine which mix of costs, benefits, technical features, and organizational impacts represents the most desirable alternative.

Establishing Information Requirements Perhaps the most challenging task of the systems analyst is to define the specific information requirements that must be met by the system solution selected. At the most basic level, defining the **information requirements** of a new system involves identifying who needs what information where, when, and how (e.g., format, medium). Requirements analysis carefully defines the objectives of the new or modified system and develops a detailed description of the functions that the new system must perform. Faulty requirements analysis is a leading cause of systems failure and high systems development costs (see Chapter 10). A system designed around the wrong set of requirements will either have to be discarded because of poor performance or will need to undergo major modifications. Section 9.3 describes alternative approaches to eliciting requirements that help minimize this problem.

Some problems do not require an information system solution but instead need an adjustment in management, additional training, or refinement of existing organizational procedures. If the problem is information related, systems analysis still may be required to diagnose the problem and arrive at the proper solution.

Systems Design

Systems analysis describes what a system should do to meet information requirements, and **systems design** shows how the system will fulfill this objective. The design of an information system is the overall plan or model for that system. Like the blueprint of a building or house, it consists of all the specifications that give the system its form and structure.

The systems designer details the system specifications that will deliver the functions identified during systems analysis. These specifications should address all the managerial, organizational, and technological components of the system solution. Table 9-1 lists the types of specifications that would be produced during systems design.

Like houses or buildings, information systems may have many possible designs. Each design represents a unique blend of all technical and organizational components. What makes one design superior to others is the ease and efficiency with which it fulfills user requirements within a specific set of technical, organizational, financial, and time constraints.

The Role of End Users User information requirements drive the entire systems development effort. Users must have sufficient control over the design process to ensure that the system reflects their business priorities and information needs, not the biases of the technical staff. Working on design increases users' understanding and acceptance of the system. As we describe in Chapter 10, insufficient user involvement in the design effort

Feasibility study
Information requirements
Systems design

TABLE 9-1   *Design Specifications*

OUTPUT	CONTROLS
Medium	Input controls (characters, limit, reasonableness)
Content	Processing controls (consistency, record counts)
Timing	Output controls (totals, samples of output)
INPUT	Procedural controls (passwords, special forms)
Origins	**SECURITY**
Flow	Access controls
Data entry	Catastrophe plans
USER INTERFACE	Audit trails
Simplicity	**DOCUMENTATION**
Efficiency	Operations documentation
Logic	Systems documents
Feedback	User documentation
Errors	**CONVERSION**
DATABASE DESIGN	Transfer files
Logical data model	Initiate new procedures
Volume and speed requirements	Select testing method
File organization and design	Cut over to new system
Record specifications	**TRAINING**
PROCESSING	Select training techniques
Computations	Develop training modules
Program modules	Identify training facilities
Required reports	**ORGANIZATIONAL CHANGES**
Timing of outputs	Task redesign
MANUAL PROCEDURES	Job design
What activities	Process design
Who performs them	Organizational structure design
When	Reporting relationships
How	
Where	

is a major cause of system failure. Some systems require more user participation in design than others, however, and Section 9.3 shows how alternative systems development methods address the user participation issue.

Completing the Systems Development Process

The remaining steps in the systems development process translate the solution specifications established during systems analysis and design into a fully operational information system. These concluding steps consist of programming, testing, conversion, production, and maintenance.

Programming During the **programming** stage, system specifications that were prepared during the design stage are translated into software program code. Today, many organizations no longer do their own programming for new systems. Instead, they purchase the software that meets the requirements for a new system from external sources such as software packages from a commercial software vendor, software services from an application service provider, or outsourcing firms that develop custom application software for their clients (see Section 9.3).

Testing Exhaustive and thorough testing must be conducted to ascertain whether the system produces the right results. **Testing** answers the question, "Will the system produce the desired results under known conditions?"

The amount of time needed to answer this question has been traditionally underrated in systems project planning (see Chapter 10). Testing is time-consuming: Test data must be carefully prepared, results reviewed, and corrections made in the system. In some instances, parts of the system may have to be redesigned. The risks resulting from glossing over this step are enormous.

Testing an information system can be broken down into three types of activities: unit testing, system testing, and acceptance testing. **Unit testing**, or program testing, consists of testing each program separately in the system. It is widely believed that the purpose of such testing is to guarantee that programs are error-free, but this goal is realistically impossible. Testing should be viewed instead as a means of locating errors in programs, focusing on finding all the ways to make a program fail. Once they are pinpointed, problems can be corrected.

System testing tests the functioning of the information system as a whole. It tries to determine whether discrete modules will function together as planned and whether discrepancies exist between the way the system actually works and the way it was conceived. Among the areas examined are performance time, capacity for file storage and handling peak loads, recovery and restart capabilities, and manual procedures.

Acceptance testing provides the final certification that the system is ready to be used in a production setting. Systems tests are evaluated by users and reviewed by management. When all parties are satisfied that the new system meets their standards, the system is formally accepted for installation.

The systems development team works with users to devise a systematic test plan. The **test plan** includes all the preparations for the series of tests we have just described.

Figure 9-3 shows an example of a test plan. The general condition being tested is a record change. The documentation consists of a series of test-plan screens maintained on a database (perhaps a microcomputer database) that is ideally suited to this kind of application.

Conversion **Conversion** is the process of changing from the old system to the new system. Four main conversion strategies can be employed: the parallel strategy, the direct cutover strategy, the pilot study strategy, and the phased approach strategy.

Testing
Unit testing
System testing
Acceptance testing
Test plan
Conversion

When developing a test plan, it is imperative to include the various conditions to be tested, the requirements for each condition tested, and the expected results. Test plans require input from both end users and information systems specialists.

FIGURE 9-3   *A sample test plan to test a record change*

Procedure	Address and Maintenance "Record Change Series"		Test Series 2		
	Prepared By:		Date:	Version:	
Test Ref.	Condition Tested	Special Requirements	Expected Results	Output On	Next Screen
2.0	Change records				
2.1	Change existing record	Key field	Not allowed		
2.2	Change nonexistent record	Other fields	"Invalid key" message		
2.3	Change deleted record	Deleted record must be available	"Deleted" message		
2.4	Make second record	Change 2.1 above	OK if valid	Transaction file	V45
2.5	Insert record		OK if valid	Transaction file	V45
2.6	Abort during change	Abort 2.5	No change	Transaction file	V45

In a **parallel strategy**, both the old system and its potential replacement are run together for a time until everyone is assured that the new one functions correctly. This is the safest conversion approach because, in the event of errors or processing disruptions, the old system can still be used as a backup. However, this approach is very expensive, and additional staff or resources may be required to run the extra system.

The **direct cutover strategy** replaces the old system entirely with the new system on an appointed day. It is a very risky approach that can potentially be more costly than running two systems in parallel if serious problems with the new system are found. There is no other system to fall back on. Dislocations, disruptions, and the cost of corrections may be enormous.

The **pilot study strategy** introduces the new system to only a limited area of the organization, such as a single department or operating unit. When this pilot version is complete and working smoothly, it is installed throughout the rest of the organization, either simultaneously or in stages.

The **phased approach strategy** introduces the new system in stages, either by functions or by organizational units. If, for example, the system is introduced by functions, a new payroll system might begin with hourly workers who are paid weekly, followed six months later by adding salaried employees (who are paid monthly) to the system. If the management introduces the system by organizational units, corporate headquarters might be converted first, followed by outlying operating units four months later.

Moving from an old system to a new one requires that end users be trained to use the new system. Detailed **documentation** showing how the system works from both a technical and end-user standpoint is finalized during conversion for use in training and everyday operations. Lack of proper training and documentation contributes to system failure, so this portion of the systems development process is very important.

Production and Maintenance After the new system is installed and conversion is complete, the system is said to be in **production**. During this stage, both users and technical specialists will review the system to determine how well it has met its original objectives and to decide whether any revisions or modifications are in order.

In some instances, a formal **post-implementation audit** document is prepared. After the system has been fine-tuned, it must be maintained while it is in production to correct errors, meet requirements, or improve processing efficiency. Changes in hardware, software, documentation, or procedures to a production system to correct errors, meet new requirements, or improve processing efficiency are termed **maintenance**.

Studies of maintenance have examined the amount of time required for various maintenance tasks (Lientz and Swanson, 1980). Approximately 20 percent of the time is devoted to debugging or correcting emergency production problems; another 20 percent is concerned with changes in data, files, reports, hardware, or system software. But 60 percent of all maintenance work consists of making user enhancements, improving documentation, and recoding system components for greater processing efficiency. The amount of work in the third category of maintenance problems could be reduced significantly through better systems analysis and design practices. Table 9-2 summarizes the systems development activities.

Modelling and Designing Systems: Structured and Object-Oriented Methodologies

There are alternative methodologies for modelling and designing systems. Structured methodologies and object-oriented development are the most prominent.

Structured Methodologies Structured methodologies have been used to document, analyze, and design information systems since the 1970s. **Structured** refers to the fact that the techniques are step by step, with each step building on the previous one. Structured methodologies are top-down, progressing from the highest, most abstract level to the lowest level of detail, i.e., from the general to the specific.

Parallel strategy
Direct cutover strategy
Pilot study strategy
Phased approach strategy
Documentation
Production
Post-implementation audit
Maintenance
Structured

TABLE 9-2   *Systems Development*

CORE ACTIVITY	DESCRIPTION
Systems analysis	Identify problem(s) Specify solutions Establish information requirements
Systems design	Create design specifications
Programming	Translate design specifications into program code
Testing	Unit test Systems test Acceptance test
Conversion	Plan conversion Prepare documentation Train users and technical staff
Production and maintenance	Operate the system Evaluate the system Modify the system

Structured development methods are process-oriented, focusing primarily on modelling the processes or actions that capture, store, manipulate, and distribute data as the data flow through a system. These methods separate data from processes. A separate programming procedure must be written every time someone wants to take an action on a particular piece of data. The procedures act on data that the program passes to them.

The primary tool for representing a system's component processes and the flow of data between them is the **data flow diagram** (**DFD**). The data flow diagram offers a logical graphical model of information flow, partitioning a system into modules that show manageable levels of detail. A DFD rigorously specifies the processes or transformations that occur within each module and the interfaces that exist between them.

Figure 9-4 shows a simple data flow diagram for a mail-in university course registration system. The rounded boxes represent processes, which portray the transformation of data. The square box represents an external entity, which is an originator or receiver of

Data flow diagram (DFD)

FIGURE 9-4   *Data flow diagram for mail-in university registration system*

The system has three processes: Verify availability (1.0), Enroll student (2.0), and Confirm registration (3.0). The name and content of each of the data flows appear adjacent to each arrow. There is one external entity in this system: the student. There are two data stores: the student master file and the course file.

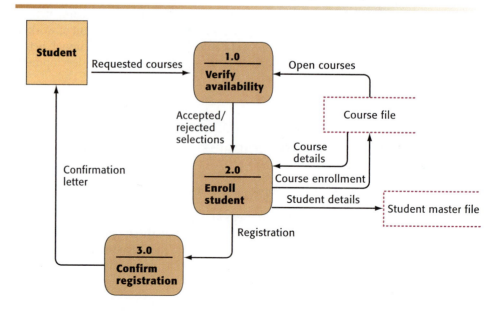

information located outside the boundaries of the system being modelled. The open rectangles represent data stores, which are either manual or automated inventories of data. The arrows represent data flows, which show the movement between processes, external entities, and data stores. They always contain packets of data with the name or content of each data flow listed beside the arrow.

This data flow diagram shows that students submit registration forms with their name, identification number, and the numbers of the courses they wish to take. In process 1.0, the system verifies that each course selected is still open by referencing the university's course file. The file distinguishes courses that are open from those that have been cancelled or filled. Process 1.0 then determines which of the student's selections can be accepted or rejected. Process 2.0 enrolls the student in the courses for which he or she has been accepted.

It updates the university's course file with the student's name and identification number and recalculates the class size. If maximum enrollment has been reached, the course number is flagged as closed. Process 2.0 also updates the university's student master file with information about new students or changes in address. Process 3.0 then sends each student applicant a confirmation-of-registration letter listing the courses for which he or she is registered, noting the course selections that could not be fulfilled.

The diagrams can be used to depict higher-level processes as well as lower-level details. Through levelled data flow diagrams a complex process can be broken down into successive levels of detail. An entire system can be divided into subsystems with a high-level data flow diagram. Each subsystem, in turn, can be divided into additional subsystems with second-level data flow diagrams, and the lower-level subsystems can be broken down again until the lowest level of detail has been reached.

Another tool for structured analysis is a data dictionary, which contains information about individual pieces of data and data groupings within a system (see Chapter 6). The data dictionary defines the contents of data flows and data stores so that systems developers understand exactly what pieces of data they contain. **Process specifications** describe the transformation occurring within the lowest level of the data flow diagrams. They express the logic for each process.

In structured methodology, software design is modelled using hierarchical structure charts. The **structure chart** is a top-down chart, showing each level of design, its relationship to other levels, and its place in the overall design structure. The design first considers the main function of a program or system, then breaks this function into subfunctions, and decomposes each subfunction until the lowest level of detail has been reached. Figure 9-5 shows a high-level structure chart for a payroll system. If a design has too many levels to fit onto one structure chart, it can be broken down further on more detailed structure charts. A structure chart may document one program, one system (a set of programs), or a part of one program.

Process specifications

Structure chart

FIGURE 9-5   *High-level structure chart for a payroll system*

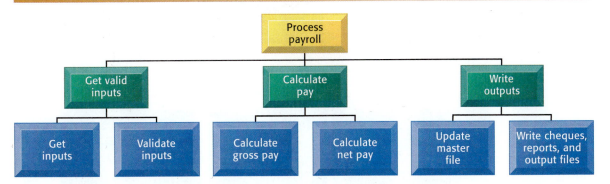

This structure chart shows the highest or most abstract level of design for a payroll system, providing an overview of the entire system.

Object-Oriented Development and Unified Modelling Language Structured methods are useful for modelling processes but do not handle the modelling of data well. They also treat data and processes as logically separate entities while in the real world such separation seems unnatural. Different modelling conventions are used for analysis (the data flow diagram) and for design (the structure chart).

Object-oriented development addresses these issues. **Object-oriented development** uses the object as the basic unit of systems analysis and design. An **object** combines data and the specific processes that operate on those data. Data encapsulated in an object can be accessed and modified only by the operations, or methods, associated with that object. Instead of passing data to procedures, programs send a message for an object to perform an operation that is already embedded in it. The system is modelled as a collection of objects and the relationships among them. Because processing logic resides within objects rather than in separate software programs, objects must collaborate with one another to make the system work.

Object-oriented modelling is based on the concepts of class and inheritance. Objects belonging to a certain class, or general categories of similar objects, have the features of that class. Classes of objects in turn can inherit all the structure and behaviours of a more general class and then add variables and behaviours unique to each object. New classes of objects are created by choosing an existing class and specifying how the new class differs from the existing class, instead of starting from scratch each time.

We can see how class and inheritance work in Figure 9-6, which illustrates the relationships among classes concerning employees and how they are paid. Employee is the common ancestor, or superclass, for the other three classes. Salaried, Hourly, and Temporary are subclasses of Employee. The class name is in the top compartment, the attributes for each class are in the middle portion of each box, and the list of operations is in the bottom portion of each box.

The features that are shared by all employees (ID, name, address, date hired, position, and pay) are stored in the Employee superclass while each subclass stores features that are specific to that particular type of employee. Specific to Hourly employees, for example, are their hourly rates and overtime rates. A solid line from the subclass to the superclass is a generalization path showing that the subclasses Salaried, Hourly, and Temporary have common features that can be generalized into the superclass Employee.

Object-oriented development

Object

FIGURE 9-6   *Class and inheritance*

This figure illustrates how classes inherit the common features of their superclass.

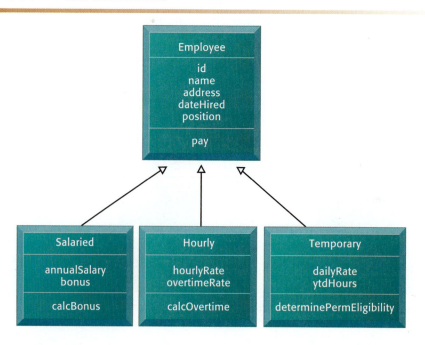

Object-oriented development is more iterative and incremental than traditional structured development. During analysis, systems developers document the functional requirements of the system, specifying its most important properties and what the proposed system must do. Interactions between the system and its users are analyzed to identify objects, which include both data and processes. The object-oriented design phase describes how the objects will behave and how they will interact with one other. Similar objects are grouped together to form a class, and classes are grouped into hierarchies in which a subclass inherits the attributes and methods from its superclass.

The information system is implemented by translating the design into program code, reusing classes that are already available in a library of reusable software objects, and adding new ones created during the object-oriented design phase. Implementation may also involve the creation of an object-oriented database. The resulting system must be thoroughly tested and evaluated.

Because objects are reusable, object-oriented development could potentially reduce the time and cost of writing software because organizations can reuse software objects that have already been created as building blocks for other applications. New systems can be created by using some existing objects, changing others, and adding a few new objects. Object-oriented frameworks have been developed to provide reusable, semicomplete applications that the organization can further customize into finished applications.

UML (Unified Modelling Language) is an industry standard language or notation, a way of communicating in writing and graphics, for the modelling of real-world objects that may be used as a first step in developing an object-oriented design. UML uses several models and diagrams, among which is a use case diagram, a chart that shows how users interact with a system, in effect showing the functional requirements of the system. The use case model uses "actors" and "use cases." An actor is a user who (or which) interacts with the system in some way, such as placing an order. A use case is a single interaction between a user and other (secondary) users and the system itself. The interaction is presented as a sequence of simple steps. The use case illustrates what exists in the system by following a specific, yet complete, flow in the system.

Computer-Aided Software Engineering Computer-aided software engineering (CASE) provides software tools to automate the methodologies we have just described to reduce the amount of repetitive work the developer needs to do. CASE tools also facilitate the creation of clear documentation and the coordination of team development efforts. Team members can share their work easily by accessing one another's files to review or modify what has been done. Modest productivity benefits can also be achieved if the tools are used properly. Many CASE tools are PC-based, with powerful graphical capabilities.

CASE tools provide automated graphics facilities for producing charts and diagrams, screen and report generators, data dictionaries, extensive reporting facilities, analysis and checking tools, code generators, and documentation generators. In general, CASE tools try to increase productivity and quality by doing the following:

- enforcing a standard development methodology and design discipline;
- improving communication between users and technical specialists;
- organizing and correlating design components and providing rapid access to them using a design repository;
- automating tedious and error-prone portions of analysis and design; and
- automating code generation and testing and controlling rollout.

Many CASE tools have been classified in terms of whether they support activities at the front end or the back end of the systems development process. Front-end CASE tools focus on capturing analysis and design information in the early stages of systems development, while back-end CASE tools address coding, testing, and maintenance activities. Back-end tools help convert specifications automatically into program code.

CASE tools automatically tie data elements to the processes where they are used. If a data flow diagram is changed from one process to another, the elements in the data

UML (Unified Modelling Language)

Computer-aided software engineering (CASE)

dictionary would be altered automatically to reflect the change in the diagram. CASE tools also contain features for validating design diagrams and specifications. CASE tools thus support iterative design by automating revisions and changes and providing prototyping facilities. A CASE information repository stores all the information defined by the analysts during the project. The repository includes data flow diagrams, structure charts, entity-relationship diagrams, data definitions, process specifications, screen and report formats, notes and comments, and test results.

To be used effectively, CASE tools require organizational discipline. Every member of a development project must adhere to a common set of naming conventions and standards as well as to a development methodology. The best CASE tools enforce common methods and standards, which may discourage their use in situations where organizational discipline is lacking.

9.3 Alternative Systems Development Approaches

Systems differ in terms of their size and technological complexity and in terms of the organizational problems they are meant to solve. A number of systems development approaches have been developed to deal with these differences. This section describes these alternative methods: the traditional systems life cycle, prototyping, application software packages, end-user development, and outsourcing.

Traditional Systems Life Cycle

The systems life cycle is the oldest method for developing information systems. The life cycle methodology is a phased approach to developing a system, dividing systems development into formal stages. Systems development specialists have different opinions on how to partition the systems development stages, but they roughly correspond to the stages of systems development that we have just described.

The **systems life cycle** methodology maintains a very formal division of labour between end users and information systems specialists. Technical specialists, such as system analysts and programmers, are responsible for much of the systems analysis, design, and implementation work; end users are limited to providing information requirements and reviewing the technical staff's work. The life cycle also emphasizes formal specifications and paperwork because many documents are generated during the course of a systems project.

The systems life cycle is still used for developing large complex systems that require a rigorous and formal requirements analysis, predefined specifications, and tight controls over the systems development process. However, the systems life cycle approach can be costly, time-consuming, and inflexible. Although systems developers can go back and forth among stages in the life cycle, the systems life cycle is predominantly a "waterfall" approach in which tasks in one stage are completed before work for the next stage begins. Activities can be repeated, but volumes of new documents must be generated and steps retraced if requirements and specifications need to be revised. This encourages freezing of specifications relatively early in the development process. The life cycle approach is also not suitable for many small desktop systems, which tend to be less structured and more individualized.

Prototyping

Prototyping consists of developing an experimental system rapidly and inexpensively for end users to evaluate. By interacting with the prototype, users can get a better idea of their information requirements. The prototype endorsed by the users can be used as a template to create the final system.

Systems life cycle

Prototyping

The **prototype** is a working version of an information system or part of the system, but it is meant to be only a preliminary model. Once operational, the prototype will be further refined until it conforms precisely to users' requirements. Once the design has been finalized, the prototype can be converted to a polished production system.

The process of developing a preliminary design, trying it out, refining it, and trying again has been called an **iterative** process of systems development because the steps required to develop a system can be repeated over and over again. Prototyping is more explicitly iterative than the conventional life cycle, and it actively promotes system design changes. It has been said that prototyping replaces unplanned rework with planned iteration, with each version more accurately reflecting users' requirements.

Steps in Prototyping Figure 9-7 shows a four-step model of the prototyping process, which consists of the following:

Step 1: Identify the user's basic requirements. The system designer (usually an information systems specialist) works with the user only long enough to capture the user's basic information needs.

Step 2: Develop an initial prototype. The system designer creates a working prototype quickly, using tools for rapidly generating software.

Step 3: Use the prototype. The user is encouraged to work with the system to determine how well the prototype meets his or her needs and to make suggestions for improving the prototype.

Step 4: Revise and enhance the prototype. The system developer notes all changes the user requests and refines the prototype accordingly. After the prototype has been revised, the cycle returns to step 3. Steps 3 and 4 are repeated until the user is satisfied.

When no more iterations are required, the approved prototype then becomes an operational prototype that furnishes the final specifications for the application. Sometimes the prototype is adopted as the production version of the system.

Prototype
Iterative

FIGURE 9-7 *The prototyping process*

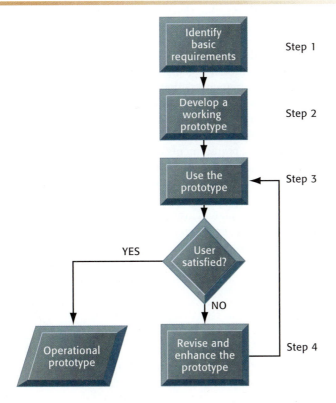

The process of developing a prototype can be broken down into four steps. Because a prototype can be developed quickly and inexpensively, systems developers can go through several iterations, repeating steps 3 and 4, to refine and enhance the prototype before arriving at the final operational one.

Advantages and Disadvantages of Prototyping Prototyping is most useful when there is some uncertainty about requirements or design solutions and is often used for designing an information system's **end-user interface** (the part of the system with which end users interact, such as online display and data-entry screens, reports, or Web pages). Because prototyping encourages intense end-user involvement throughout the systems development life cycle, it is more likely to produce systems that fulfill user requirements.

Rapid prototyping can gloss over essential steps in systems development, however. If the completed prototype works reasonably well, management may not see the need for reprogramming, redesign, or full documentation and testing to develop a polished production system. Some of these hastily constructed systems may not easily accommodate large quantities of data or a large number of users in a production environment. They may also have security vulnerabilities.

End-User Development

End users with little or no formal assistance can develop some types of information systems from technical specialists. This phenomenon is called **end-user development**. A series of software tools categorized as fourth-generation languages makes this possible. A **fourth-generation language** is a programming language that enables end users to create reports or develop software applications with minimal or no technical assistance. Some of these fourth-generation tools also enhance professional programmers' productivity.

Fourth-generation languages tend to be nonprocedural, or less procedural, than conventional programming languages. Procedural languages require specification of the sequence of steps or procedures that tell the computer what to do and how to do it. Nonprocedural languages need only specify what has to be accomplished rather than provide details about how to carry out the task.

Table 9-3 shows that there are seven categories of fourth-generation languages: PC software tools, query languages, report generators, graphics languages, application generators, application software packages, and very high-level programming languages. The table shows the tools ordered in terms of ease of use by nonprogramming end users. End users are most likely to work with PC software tools and query languages. A **query language** is a language that provides immediate online answers to requests for information that are not predefined, such as "Who are the highest-performing sales representatives?" Query languages are often tied to data management software and to database management systems (see Chapter 6).

On the whole, end-user-developed systems can be completed more rapidly than those developed through the conventional systems life cycle. Allowing users to specify their own business needs improves requirements gathering and often leads to a higher level of user involvement and satisfaction with the system. However, fourth-generation tools still cannot replace conventional tools for some business applications because they cannot easily handle the processing of large numbers of transactions or applications with extensive procedural logic and updating requirements or security requirements.

End-user computing also poses organizational risks because it occurs outside of traditional mechanisms for information systems management and control. When systems are created rapidly, without a formal development methodology, testing and documentation may be inadequate. Control over data can be lost in systems outside the traditional information systems department. To help organizations maximize the benefits of end-user applications development, management should control the development of end-user applications by requiring cost justification of end-user information system projects and by establishing hardware, software, and quality standards for user-developed applications.

End-user interface
End-user development
Fourth-generation language
Query language

Application Software Packages and Outsourcing

Chapter 5 points out that the software for most systems today is not developed in-house but is purchased from external sources. Firms can rent the software from an

TABLE 9-3   *Categories of Fourth-Generation Languages*

FOURTH-GENERATION TOOL	DESCRIPTION	EXAMPLE	
PC software tools	General-purpose application software packages for PCs	WordPerfect Microsoft Access	**Oriented toward end users**
Query languages	Language for retrieving data stored in databases or files. Capable of supporting requests for information that are not predefined	SQL	
Report generators	Extracts data from files or databases to create customized reports in a wide range of formats not routinely produced by an information system	Crystal Reports	
Graphics languages	Retrieves data from files or databases and display them in graphic format. Some graphics software can perform arithmetic or logical operations on data as well	SAS Graph Systat	
Application generators	Contains preprogrammed modules that can generate entire applications, including Web sites, greatly speeding development. A user can specify what needs to be done, and the application generator will create the appropriate program code for input, validation, update, processing, and reporting	FOCUS Microsoft FrontPage	
Application software packages	Software programs sold or leased by commercial vendors that eliminate the need for custom-written, in-house software	Oracle PeopleSoft HCM mySAP ERP	
Very high-level programming languages	Generates program code with fewer instructions than conventional languages, such as COBOL or FORTRAN. Designed primarily as productivity tools for professional programmers	APL Nomad2	**Oriented toward IS professionals**

application service provider, they can purchase or lease a software package from a commercial vendor, or they can have a custom application developed by an outside outsourcing firm.

Application Software Packages During the past several decades, many systems have been developed on an application software package foundation. Many applications are common to all business organizations—for example, payroll, accounts receivable, general ledger, or inventory control. For such universal functions with standard processes that do not change a great deal over time, a generalized system will fulfill the requirements of many organizations.

If a software package can fulfill most of an organization's requirements, the company does not have to write its own software. The company can save time and money by using the prewritten, predesigned, pretested software programs from the package. Package vendors supply much of the ongoing maintenance and support for the system, including enhancements to keep the system in line with ongoing technical and business developments.

If an organization has unique requirements that the package does not address, many packages include capabilities for customization. **Customization** features allow a software package to be modified to meet an organization's unique requirements without destroying the integrity of the package software. If a great deal of customization is required, additional programming and customization work may become so expensive and time-consuming that they negate many of the advantages of software packages. The Ottawa Hospital

Customization

instrument tracking system discussed at the beginning of this chapter is an example of a system that required customization.

When a system is developed using an application software package, systems analysis will include a package evaluation effort. The most important evaluation criteria are the functions provided by the package, flexibility, user friendliness, hardware and software resources, database requirements, installation and maintenance efforts, documentation, vendor quality, and cost. The package evaluation process often is based on a **request for proposal (RFP)**, which is a detailed list of questions submitted to packaged-software vendors.

When a software package solution is selected, the organization no longer has total control over the system design process. Instead of tailoring the system design specifications directly to user requirements, the design effort will consist of trying to mould user requirements to conform to the features of the package. If the organization's requirements conflict with the way the package works and the package cannot be customized, the organization will have to adapt to the package and change its procedures.

Outsourcing If a firm does not want to use its internal resources to develop or operate information systems, it can outsource the work to an external organization that specializes in providing these services. Application service providers (ASPs), which we describe in Chapter 5, are one form of outsourcing. Subscribing companies would use the software and computer hardware provided by the ASP as the technical platform for their systems. In another form of outsourcing, a company could hire an external vendor to design and create the software for its system, but that company would operate the system on its own computers. The outsourcing vendor might be domestic or in another country, and in Chapter 11 we discuss the special issues raised by offshore outsourcing.

Outsourcing has become popular because some organizations perceive it as providing more value than an in-house computer centre or information systems staff. The provider of outsourcing services benefits from economies of scale and complementary core competencies that would be difficult for a firm that does not specialize in information technology services to replicate (Levina and Ross, 2003). The vendor's specialized knowledge and skills can be shared with many different customers, and the experience of working with so many information systems projects further enhances the vendor's expertise. Outsourcing enables a company with fluctuating needs for computer processing to pay for only what it uses rather than build its own computer centre, which would be underutilized when there is no peak load. Some firms outsource because their internal information systems staff cannot keep pace with technological change or innovative business practices or because management wants to free up scarce and costly talent for activities with higher paybacks.

Not all organizations benefit from outsourcing, and outsourcing can create serious problems for organizations if it is not well understood and managed. Many firms underestimate costs for identifying and evaluating vendors of information technology services, for transitioning to a new vendor, and for monitoring vendors to make sure they are fulfilling their contractual obligations. These hidden costs can easily undercut anticipated benefits from outsourcing (Barthelemy, 2001). When a firm allocates the responsibility for developing and operating its information systems to another organization, it can lose control over its information systems function. If the organization lacks the expertise to negotiate a sound contract, the firm's dependence on the vendor could result in high costs or loss of control over technological direction. Firms should be especially cautious when using an outsourcer to develop or to operate applications that give it some type of competitive advantage.

A firm is most likely to benefit from outsourcing if it understands its own requirements, knows exactly how the outsourcing vendor will provide value, and identifies providers with capabilities and objectives that are best aligned with the firm's specific needs. The firm must also be able to design an outsourcing contract that allows it to manage the vendor relationship (Feeny, Lacity, and Willcocks, 2005; Lee, Miranda, and Kim, 2004). The Window on Management section provides more detail about these issues.

Request for proposal (RFP)

9.4 Application Development for the Digital Firm

In the digital firm environment, organizations need to be able to add, change, and retire their technology capabilities very rapidly to respond to new opportunities. Companies are adopting shorter, more informal development processes for many of their e-commerce and e-business applications, processes that provide fast solutions and that do not disrupt their core transaction processing systems and organizational databases. Companies are also developing more systems that tie the firm's business processes more closely to those of customers and suppliers. In addition to using software packages, application service providers, and other outsourcing services, businesses are relying more heavily on fast-cycle techniques such

WINDOW ON MANAGEMENT

How to Get Outsourcing Right: Avoid Getting It Wrong

Among large corporations in the last decade, there has been a stampede to turn over technology management, system ownership, customer service, and back-office functions to third parties. The leading motivation for outsourcing is the belief that it will save money for the company, but there are other reasons as well: to gain access to technology expertise, to avoid capital expenditures on infrastructure the firm uses sporadically, to free up internal staff, to keep headcount down, and so on. Of course, outsourcing vendor firms are in business to make money. They claim they can do the job better, faster, and cheaper than your internal staff and still make a profit. They claim to have the economies of scale to do the basic computing cheaper, and to have the complementary assets in the form of people and expertise that your firm needs.

It would seem we have a marriage of interests where both parties see advantage and where both parties should benefit. But the reality of outsourcing is not so simple. A staggering 50 percent of all outsourcing deals fall apart, many ending in court proceedings. In a recent survey of 420 business IT professionals, only one-third are neutral on outsourcing deals, and 17 percent called them complete disasters. Some recent bad outcomes include Sprint Nextel taking outsourcer IBM to court, claiming IBM owes Sprint 119 000 hours of work.

In Sprint's case, it was a US $400 million deal. After IBM failed to increase productivity by 6.4 percent, Sprint took 4500 outsourced call centre employees back. Sprint was then shocked to learn that it had greatly underestimated the value of its IT workers. When outsourcer IBM valued those services and sent a bill to Sprint management for the workers who had been "reclaimed," Sprint had severe sticker shock. In another case, Sears Kmart tore up its US $1.6 billion outsourcing contract with Computer Sciences Corporation (CSC) "for cause." CSC is suing Sears Kmart.

What's going on here? Why is it so difficult for large firms to get along with their outsourcing partners and cut a deal that makes sense for both parties? There are many sources of the problem, but chief among them are the failure of firms to adequately value their internal staffs and failure to understand their own cost structure. And when an outsourcer comes along and says "We can do it cheaper, faster, and better," managers in many firms really have no data to evaluate these claims. Once management signs the contract, they quickly learn that the vendor will charge for every hour of work. Management may find out it was cheaper to do the work in-house rather than pay market rates—plus a healthy profit margin—charged by vendors.

But there are also lessons here from the successful outsourcing deals. Ontario Power Generation (OPG) has had a long-term $1 billion relationship with consulting firm Capgemini, which provides 80 percent of the power company's IT services. In this case, the firms did something quite unique: They set up a joint venture company to perform the work and share the risks and the rewards. In this way, both firms had an incentive to save OPG money and do the work properly. In another example, Campbell Soup has had a successful outsourcing relationship with IBM since 1995, although the relationship has gone through periods of strain.

In both Campbell Soup's and OPG's cases, the firms have developed long-term strategic alliances with their vendors. Both parties have been able to take the other partner's interests into account as the relationship has evolved. Flexibility, trust, performance, and even self-sacrifice seem to be the key factors here. In these cases, it is not just about money; it is also about continuing a mutually beneficial relationship even if you sometimes pay a financial price. Some outsourcing deals are so big and so long-term that it is impossible to write ironclad contracts. "As these examples show, the bigger the outsourcing deal gets, the higher risk of failure—and the greater the possibility for success."

Researchers at MIT Center for Information Systems Research (CISR) have identified two other outsourcing models: transaction relationships and co-sourcing alliances.

In transaction relationships, the firm precisely understands its costs and has a well-defined understanding of the functions it wants to outsource. In these cases, writing contracts for relatively small chunks of IT services is more straightforward and less prone to later surprises and misinterpretations. In co-sourcing alliances, both the vendor and the firm co-manage and co-own the outsourcing project. Here, too, there tends to be a more precise understanding of costs and benefits, and a greater transparency because both partners "own" the outcome. Over two-thirds of transaction relationships and co-sourcing alliances work out successfully.

To Think About

1. What is the basis for vendor firms claiming they can provide IT services more economically than a firm's own IT staff?

2. Why is it difficult to write ironclad legal contracts specifying in detail strategic alliance outsourcing relationships?

3. Why do joint ventures and co-sourcing outsourcing relationships have a better chance of success?

MIS in Action

1. Capgemini is one of the largest IT service firms. Visit its Web site (www.capgemini.com). Identify and describe its outsourcing services. What are the benefits it promises to deliver?

2. At the Capgemini Web site, read one of the company's success stories of collaboration with a Canadian firm for providing IT services. Describe what is being outsourced and identify what type of outsourcing relationship is being used (strategic, transaction, or co-sourcing). Do you think this is the right model for the work being performed?

3. Review the article "In Depth: Customers Analyze Outsourcing Vendors and Strategies," by Paul McDougall, *InformationWeek*, June 19, 2006. This article is available at www.informationweek.com. What are the motivations for using outsourcing? Is outsourcing expected to grow, and why?

Sources: Stephanie Overby, "Big Deals, Big Savings, Big Problems," *CIO Magazine*, February 1, 2006 and "Simple Successful Outsourcing," *CIO Magazine*, October 1, 2005; and Paul McDougall, "In Depth: When Outsourcing Goes Bad," *InformationWeek*, June 19, 2006.

as joint application design, prototypes, and reusable standardized software components that can be assembled into a complete set of services for e-commerce and e-business. These fast-cycle techniques greatly reduce the amount of time to develop a completed system.

Rapid Application Development (RAD)

Object-oriented software tools, reusable software, prototyping, and fourth-generation language tools are helping systems developers create working systems much more rapidly than they could using traditional systems development methods and software tools. The term **rapid application development** (**RAD**) is used to describe this process of creating workable systems in a very short period of time. RAD can include the use of visual programming and other tools for developing graphical user interfaces, iterative prototyping of key system elements, the automation of program code generation, and close teamwork among end users and information systems specialists. Simple systems often can be assembled from pre-developed components. The process does not have to be sequential, and key parts of development can occur simultaneously.

Sometimes a technique called **joint application design** (**JAD**) is used to accelerate the generation of information requirements and to develop the initial systems design. JAD brings end users and information systems specialists together in an interactive session to discuss the system's design. Properly prepared and facilitated, JAD sessions can significantly speed up the design phase and involve users at an intense level.

Agile Development and Extreme Programming

Managers waiting on their systems to be developed and implemented successfully have always complained about the length of time between completing the specifications and seeing the new system. Typically they pressure IS managers to get the new systems out of the pipeline as quickly as possible. Toward that end, two new approaches to systems development and coding have been developed: agile software development and extreme programming.

Agile software development is a methodology that attempts to develop many versions, or iterations, of a software in a short period of time. According to Wikipedia, it "is

Rapid application development (RAD)

Joint application design (JAD)

Agile software development

a conceptual framework for undertaking software engineering projects that embraces and promotes evolutionary change throughout the entire life cycle of the project." An iteration of the software typically lasts from one to four weeks. At every iteration, developers meet with management. Financial risk is reduced because each iteration is a relatively small and flexible, hence the name "agile." Each iteration is essentially a small program that has a new feature added on and yet still enables the team to conduct planning, requirements analysis, design, code-writing, testing, and documentation. The iteration should be publishable, though it may not actually be released. This is particularly true when the software is Web-based. At the end of each iteration, the team re-evaluates project priorities.

Agile methods also emphasize working software as the primary measure of progress. This, combined with the preference for face-to-face communication, means that agile methods produce very little written documentation relative to other methods. The lack of documentation produced has resulted in criticism of agile methods as being undisciplined.

Extreme Programming (XP) is another pragmatic approach to program development that emphasizes business results first and takes an incremental, get-started approach to developing the application. XP is one of the methodologies used in agile software development. XP's focus is on using continual testing and revision. Kent Beck, who developed the concept of XP, emphasizes that a programmer must write a test for the programming code in order to know when the code has succeeded. Beck also believes that pairs of programmers should write code, as this forces the main programmer to describe the code to the other programmer and may stimulate additional ideas.

Component-Based Development and Web Services

We have already described some of the benefits of object-oriented development for developing systems that can respond to rapidly changing business environments, including Web applications. To further expedite software creation, groups of objects have been assembled to provide software components for common functions, such as a graphical user interface or online ordering capability that can be combined to create large-scale business applications. This approach to software development is called **component-based development**, and it enables a system to be developed by assembling and integrating existing software components. Businesses are using component-based development to create their e-commerce applications by combining commercially available components for shopping carts, user authentication, search engines, and catalogues with pieces of software for their own unique business requirements.

Web Services and Service-Oriented Computing Chapter 5 introduced Web services as loosely coupled, reusable software components deliverable using Extensible Markup Language (XML) and other open protocols and standards that enable one application to communicate with another with no custom programming required to share data and services.

In addition to supporting internal and external integration of systems, Web services can be used as tools for developing new information system applications or enhancing existing systems. Web services can create software components that are deliverable over the Internet and provide new functions for an organization's existing systems or create new systems that link an organization's systems to those of other organizations. Because these software services use a universal set of standards, they promise to be less expensive and less difficult to weave together than proprietary components.

Web services can perform certain functions on their own, and they can also engage other Web services to complete more complex transactions, such as checking credit, procurement, or ordering products. By creating software components that can communicate and share data regardless of the operating system, programming language, or client device, Web services can provide significant cost savings in systems development while opening up new opportunities for collaboration with other companies (Ferris and Farrell, 2003; Hagel and Brown, 2001; Patel and Saigal, 2002).

Extreme Programming (XP)

Component-based development

Summary

1. **Demonstrate how developing new systems produces organizational change.**

   Developing a new information system is a form of planned organizational change that involves many different people in the organization. Because information systems are sociotechnical entities, a change in information systems involves changes in work, management, and the organization. Four kinds of technology-enabled change are (a) automation, (b) rationalization of procedures, (c) business process reengineering, and (d) paradigm shift, with far-reaching changes carrying the greatest risks and rewards. Many organizations are attempting business process reengineering to redesign work flows and business processes in the hope of achieving dramatic productivity breakthroughs. Information systems can also be used to support business process management, total quality management (TQM), six sigma, and other initiatives for incremental process improvement.

2. **Identify and describe the core activities in the systems development process.**

   The core activities in systems development are systems analysis, systems design, programming, testing, conversion, production, and maintenance. Systems analysis is the study and analysis of problems of existing systems and the identification of requirements for their solutions. Systems design provides the specifications for an information system solution, showing how its technical and organizational components fit together. Programming is translating the previous steps into actual computer code, and testing is ensuring that the system is as error-free as possible and acceptable to users. Conversion is taking the previous system, whether paper- or computer-based, and moving the data and operations to the new system. Production is the activity when the system is actually operational, and maintenance is the process of keeping the system up to date and error-free after it has gone into production.

3. **Evaluate alternative methods for developing information systems.**

   There are a number of alternative methods for developing information systems, each suited to different types of problems. The oldest method for developing systems is the systems life cycle, which requires that information systems be developed in formal stages. The stages must proceed sequentially and have defined outputs; each requires formal approval before the next stage can commence. The system life cycle is useful for large projects that need formal specifications and tight management control over each stage of systems development. However, this approach is very rigid and costly and is not well suited for unstructured, decision-oriented applications for which requirements cannot be immediately visualized.

   Prototyping consists of developing an experimental system rapidly and inexpensively for end users to interact with and evaluate. The prototype is refined and enhanced until users are satisfied that it includes all their requirements and can be used as a template to create the final system. Prototyping encourages end-user involvement in systems development and iteration of design until specifications are captured accurately. The rapid creation of prototypes can result in systems that have not been completely tested or documented or that are technically inadequate for a production environment.

   Developing an information system using an application software package eliminates the need for writing software programs when developing an information system. Using a software package reduces the amount of design, testing, installation, and maintenance work required to develop a system. Application software packages are helpful if a firm does not have the internal information systems staff or financial resources to custom-develop a system. To meet an organization's unique requirements, packages may require extensive modifications that can substantially raise development costs.

   End-user development is the development of information systems by end users, either alone or with minimal assistance from information systems specialists. End-user-developed systems can be created rapidly and informally using fourth-generation software tools. The primary benefits of end-user development are improved requirements determination; reduced application backlog; and increased end-user participation in, and control of, the systems development process. However, end-user development, in conjunction with distributed computing, has introduced new organizational risks by propagating information systems and data resources that do not necessarily meet quality assurance standards and that are not easily controlled by traditional means.

   Outsourcing consists of using an external vendor to develop (or operate) a firm's information systems. The work is done by the vendor rather than by the organization's internal information systems staff. Outsourcing can save application development costs or enable firms to develop applications without an internal information systems staff; however, firms risk losing control over their information systems and becoming too dependent on external vendors.

   Selection of a systems development approach can have a big impact on the time, cost, and end product of systems development. Managers should be aware of the strengths and weaknesses of each systems development approach and the types of problems for which each is best suited. The impact of application software packages and of outsourcing should be carefully evaluated before they are selected because these approaches give organizations less control over the systems development process.

4. *Compare alternative methodologies for modelling systems.*

The two principal methodologies for modelling and designing information systems are structured methodologies and object-oriented development. Structured methodologies focus on modelling processes and data separately. The data flow diagram is the principal tool for structured analysis, and the structure chart is the principal tool for representing structured software design. Object-oriented development models a system as a collection of objects that combine processes and data. Object-oriented modelling is based on the concepts of class and inheritance.

5. *Identify and describe new approaches for systems development in the digital firm era.*

Businesses today are often required to develop e-commerce and e-business applications very rapidly to remain competitive. New systems are likely to have more interorganizational requirements and processes than in the past. Companies are turning to rapid application design, joint application design (JAD), and reusable software components to improve the systems development process. Rapid application development (RAD) uses object-oriented software, visual programming, prototyping, and fourth-generation tools for very rapid creation of systems. Component-based development expedites application development by grouping objects into suites of software components that can be combined to create large-scale business applications. Unified modelling language (UML) can help determine and communicate information and functional requirements. Agile software development methods, including extreme programming, can greatly reduce the time and cost of systems development.

Web services enable firms to obtain software application components delivered over the Internet for developing new systems or integrating existing systems. Web services provide a common set of standards that enable organizations to link their systems regardless of their technology platform through standard plug-and-play architecture.

Key Terms

Acceptance testing,   312
Agile software development,   324
Automation,   301
Benchmarking,   308
Business process management (BPM),   308
Business process reengineering (BPR),   307
Component-based development,   325
Computer-aided software engineering (CASE),   317
Conversion,   312
Customization,   321
Data flow diagram (DFD),   314
Direct cutover strategy,   313
Documentation,   313
End-user development,   320
End-user interface,   320
Extreme programming (XP),   325
Feasibility study,   310

Fourth-generation language,   320
Information requirements,   310
Iterative,   319
Joint application design (JAD),   324
Maintenance,   313
Object,   316
Object-oriented development,   316
Paradigm shift,   303
Parallel strategy,   313
Phased approach strategy,   313
Pilot study strategy,   313
Post-implementation audit,   313
Process specifications,   315
Production,   313
Programming,   311
Prototype,   319
Prototyping,   318
Query language,   320

Rapid application development (RAD),   324
Rationalization of procedures,   301
Request for proposal (RFP),   322
Six sigma,   308
Structure chart,   315
Structured,   313
System testing,   312
Systems analysis,   309
Systems design,   310
Systems development,   309
Systems life cycle,   318
Test plan,   312
Testing,   312
Total quality management (TQM),   308
UML (Unified Modelling Language),   317
Unit testing,   312
Work flow management,   304

Review Questions

1. *Describe each of the four kinds of organizational change that can be promoted with information technology.*

2. *What is business process reengineering? What steps are required to make it effective? How does it differ from business process management?*

3. *How do information systems support process changes that promote quality in an organization?*

4. *What is the difference between systems analysis and systems design? What activities does each process comprise?*

5. *What are information requirements? Why are they difficult to determine correctly?*

6. *Why is the testing stage of systems development so important? Name and describe the three types of testing for an information system.*

7. *What role do programming, conversion, production, and maintenance play in systems development?*

8. *Compare object-oriented and traditional structured approaches for modelling and designing systems.*

9. *What is the traditional systems life cycle? Describe each of its steps and its advantages and disadvantages for systems development.*

10. *What do we mean by information system prototyping? What are its benefits and limitations? List and describe the steps in the prototyping process.*

11. *What is an application software package? What are the advantages and disadvantages of developing information systems based on software packages?*

12. *What is meant by end-user development? What are its advantages and disadvantages? Name some policies and procedures for managing end-user development.*

13. *Under what circumstances should outsourcing be used for developing information systems?*

14. *What is rapid application development (RAD)? How can it help system developers?*

15. *How can component-based development and Web services help firms develop and enhance their information systems?*

Discussion Questions

1. *Why is selecting a systems development approach an important business decision? Who should participate in the selection process?*

2. *Some have said that the best way to reduce systems development costs is to use application software packages or fourth-generation tools. Do you agree? Why or why not?*

3. *How much end user input is necessary to develop a new system? Does the amount of end user input vary based on the type of project? What types of projects require more end-user support than others?*

4. *Discuss the view that there is no such thing as bug-free software. When should software be considered bug-free enough to release?*

Teamwork: Preparing Web Site Design Specifications

With three or four of your classmates, select a system described in this text that uses the Web. Review the Web site for the system you select. Use what you have learned from the Web site and the description in this book to pre-

pare a report describing some of the design specifications for the system you select.

If possible, use electronic presentation software to present your findings to the class.

Learning Track Modules

Unified Modelling Language (UML). In this Learning Track Module, you will learn more about standards for representing object-oriented systems and Unified Modelling Language (UML). You can find this Learning Track Module on MyMISLab for this chapter.

Primer on Business Process Design and Documentation. In this Learning Track Module, you can discover how to perform a business process analysis and apply this to a case study of ITC Corporation. You can find this Learning Track Module on MyMISLab for this chapter.

 For online exercises, please visit www.pearsoned.ca/mymislab.

HANDS-ON MIS   Application Exercises

The projects in this section give you hands-on experience preparing systems analysis reports, designing and developing an employee training and skills tracking system for a

real-world company, designing and developing a customer system for auto sales, and redesigning business processes for a company that wants to purchase goods over the Web.

Achieving Operational Excellence:
Designing an Employee Training and Skills Tracking System and Database

Software skills: Database design, querying, and reporting
Business skills: Employee training and skills tracking

This project requires you to perform a systems analysis and then design a system solution using database software.

Dirt Bikes Canada promotes itself as a "learning company." It pays for employees to take training courses or college courses to help them advance in their careers. As employees move on, their job positions become vacant, and Dirt Bikes Canada must quickly fill them to maintain its pace of production. Dirt Bikes Canada's human resources staff would like to find a way to quickly identify qualified employees who have the training to fill vacant positions. Once the company knows who these employees are, it has a better chance of filling open positions internally rather than paying to recruit outsiders. Dirt Bikes Canada would like to track each employee's years of education and the title and date completed of training classes that each employee has attended.

Dirt Bikes Canada currently cannot identify such employees. Its existing employee database is limited to basic human resources data, such as employee name, identification number, birth date, address, telephone number, marital status, job position, and salary. A portion of this database is illustrated here. You can find some sample records from this database on MyMISLab for Chapter 9. Dirt Bikes Canada's human resources staff keeps skills and training data in paper folders.

Prepare a systems analysis report describing Dirt Bikes Canada's problem and a system solution that can be implemented using PC database software. Then use the database software to develop a simple system solution. Your report should include the following:

1. Description of the problem and its organizational and business impact;

2. Proposed solution and solution objectives;

3. Information requirements to be addressed by the solution; and

4. Management, organization, and technology issues to be addressed by the solution, including changes in business processes.

On the basis of the requirements you have identified, design the solution using database software and populate it with at least 10 records per table. Consider whether you can use or modify the existing employee database in your design. Print out the design for each table in your new application. Use the system you have created to create queries and reports that would be of most interest to management, such as which employees have college education or which employees have training in project management or advanced computer-aided design (CAD) tools. A sample database is shown below.

If possible, use electronic presentation software to summarize your findings for management.

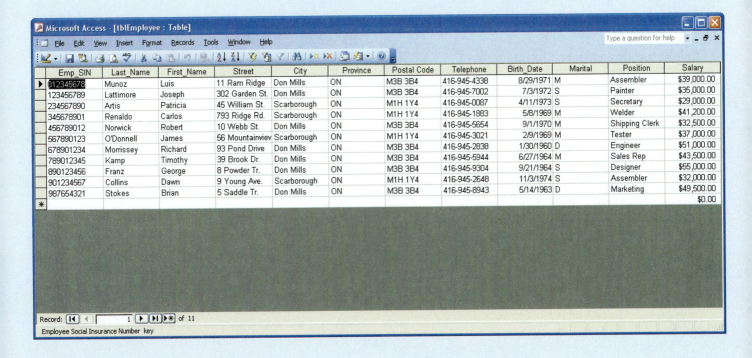

Improving Decision Making:
Using Database Software to Design a Customer System for Auto Sales

Software skills: Database design, querying, reporting, and form creation
Business skills: Sales lead and customer analysis

This project requires you to perform a systems analysis and then design a system solution using database software.

Ace Auto Dealers specializes in selling new vehicles from Subaru. The company advertises in local newspapers and also is listed as an authorized dealer on the Subaru Web site and other major Web sites for auto buyers. The company benefits from a good local word-of-mouth reputation and name recognition and is a leading source of information for Subaru vehicles in the Halifax, Nova Scotia, area.

When a prospective customer enters the showroom, an Ace sales representative greets him or her. The sales representative manually fills out a form with information such as the prospective customer's name, address, telephone number, date of visit, and make and model of the vehicle in which the customer is interested. The representative also asks where the prospect heard about Ace—whether it was from a newspaper ad, the Web, or word of mouth—and this information is noted on the form also. If the customer decides to purchase an auto, the dealer fills out a bill of sale form.

Ace does not believe it has enough information about its customers. It cannot easily determine which prospects have made auto purchases, nor can it identify which customer touch points have produced the greatest number of sales leads or actual sales so it can focus advertising and marketing more on the channels that generate the most revenue.

Are purchasers discovering Ace from newspaper ads, from word of mouth, or from the Web?

Prepare a systems analysis report detailing Ace's problem and a system solution that can be implemented using PC database management software. Then use database software to develop a simple system solution. Your systems analysis report should include the following:

1. Description of the problem and its organizational and business impact;

2. Proposed solution, solution objectives, and solution feasibility;

3. Costs and benefits of the solution you have selected. The company has a PC with Internet access and the full suite of Microsoft Office desktop productivity tools;

4. Information requirements to be addressed by the solution; and

5. Management, organization, and technology issues to be addressed by the solution, including changes in business processes.

On the basis of the requirements you have identified, design the database, and populate it with at least 10 records per table. Consider whether you can use or modify the existing customer database in your design. Print out the database design. Then use the system you have created to generate queries and reports that would be of most interest to management. Create several prototype data input forms for the system, and review them with your instructor. Then revise the prototypes.

Achieving Operational Excellence:
Redesigning Business Processes for Web Procurement

Software skills: Web browser software
Business skills: Procurement

This project requires you to decide how a business should be redesigned when it moves to the Web.

You are in charge of purchasing for your firm and would like to use the Acklands-Grainger.com (www.acklandsgrainger.com) B2B e-commerce site for this purpose. Find out how to place an order for painting supplies by exploring the capabilities of this site. Do not register at the site. Describe all the steps your firm would need to take to use this system to place orders online for 30 gallons of paint thinner. Include a diagram of what you think your firm's business process for purchasing should be and the pieces of information required by this process.

In a traditional purchase process, whoever is responsible for making the purchase fills out a requisition form and submits it

for approval based on the company's business rules. When the requisition is approved, a purchase order with a unique purchase order identification number is sent to the supplier.

The purchaser might want to browse supplier catalogues to compare prices and features before placing the order. The purchaser might also want to determine whether the items to be purchased are available. If the purchasing firm were an approved customer, that company would be granted credit to make the purchase and would be billed for the total cost of the items purchased and shipped after the order was shipped. Alternatively, the purchasing company might have to pay for the order in advance or pay for the order using a credit card. Multiple payment options might be possible. How might this process have to change to make purchases electronically from the Grainger site?

CASE STUDY — Lemontonic and NET: A Match Made on the Web

Lemontonic is not just another Canadian Web site developed within the Microsoft.NET environment. It is a Canadian online dating site that is active in Quebec, Ontario, and British Columbia, as well as around the world. It is interesting that in this information age, dating has moved to the Web, and the Web sites that provide this environment are interesting in and of themselves.

Based in Toronto, Lemontonic identified four challenges in the online dating industry for which the company felt instant messaging (IM) was the answer. These challenges were connectivity (eliminating blind dates), control (selecting who can communicate with you), comfort (sharing and involvement), and convenience (instant connection). Unlike other online dating services that use e-mail, Lemontonic decided that their Web presence would revolve around instant messaging.

Scott Rogers, Vice President of Marketing at Lemontonic, says: "The reason I was so keen on starting this business was that I saw from my time at another online dating service that a number of consumer needs weren't being satisfied. We wanted to make the online dating experience more life-like and realized we needed to create a dating application that had both a Web component and an instant messaging component." Rogers felt that these two features would provide a more realistic and enjoyable way through which individuals could meet online.

To do this, Lemontonic engaged Eidenai Innovations (EI), a Canadian company that provides software solutions, i.e., an outsourcing consulting firm. EI was founded in 1999 by Sunil Abraham and Orren Johnson, who each had experience working in IT in larger firms. Since its inception, EI has consulted for some of Canada's leading financial firms, such as CIBC and Bank of Montreal, telecommunications firms Vonage and Nortel, and Labatt Breweries. EI is a Microsoft Gold Certified and Managed Partner, and in 2003, EI became Microsoft's number two sub-contracted development partner in terms of revenue and contracts awarded in Canada. Based on EI's stellar track record, Lemontonic decided that EI provided the right skill set to develop the Web site and customer services for the online dating service. In less than a year from awarding the contract to EI, Lemontonic's Web presence and customer service site were online. This rapid application development cost Lemontonic about $6 million over a two-year period.

Because of the speed needed to get the Web site up and running, EI used the .NET environment. According to David Benoliel, Executive Vice President of EI, "We built a case for using .NET because we needed the ability to quickly deploy solutions. . . . We had a very short time-to-market schedule and had two large projects to finish: the Web site and the instant messaging application." The .NET platform also enabled these two applications to integrate with other .NET-compatible technologies.

The "Lemontonic Solution Platform" includes a Microsoft.NET-based rich-client IM application that is available for free download. The IM application integrates with the Web-based interface to give the user an enhanced interaction with the ability to have direct, real-time communication with prospective dates. There are also corporate functions including content validation and account management, as well as direct marketing, campaigning, and business reporting. The site can support 10 million registered users with 100 000 simultaneous active users.

EI used many Microsoft products to develop these applications, including ASP.NET and Visual C#® development tool in Visual Studio®.NET. EI also used Commerce Server 2002, enabling the company to quickly develop functionality such as billing, subscription, and promotions. Meanwhile, SQL Server 2000 provides the scalability needed for the rapid growth Lemontonic envisioned. Interestingly, EI also incorporated Microsoft Passport, used by many worldwide for logging into Hotmail and similar Microsoft-related sites, to authenticate users. By integrating Microsoft CRM, Microsoft's customer relationship management application, Lemontonic was also able to route user requests to the company's customer service representatives. In addition, the system was developed for high-availability computing, with fault tolerance built in throughout the IT infrastructure.

The result? In its first three months, Lemontonic signed up 60 000 members. Three months after the Web site was first launched, the instant messaging application went live. The IM application includes chat, video, and audio functionality, and even permits two users to jointly explore the Web in a shared browser. Rogers wanted this exploration capability to give the users a shared activity, in order to avoid those awkward silences after the first moments of saying hello online.

It is interesting that the most traditional of activities—finding and getting to know people to date—has been translated almost intact to the Web. However, instead of asking a potential date if they want to "hang out" or "go to the movies," individuals can ask potential dates if they want to "look at my favourite Web site with me," "meet up in a chat room," or "watch a video online together." Rogers's vision for Lemontonic has recognized and incorporated familiar dating activities into Lemontonic's Web presence, producing a site that has grown rapidly to more than five million users worldwide.

Sources: Microsoft, "Online Daters Get Up Close and Personal at Microsoft.NET-based Lemontonic.com," **www.microsoft.com/ canada/casestudies/lemontonic.mspx**, accessed April 19, 2007; "Lemontonic Appoints Kaleil Isaza Tuzman to Board," Newswire.ca, **www.newswire.ca/releases/archive/February2005/24/c7770. html?view=print**, accessed April 19, 2007; Eidenai Innovations, "EI Case Studies: Lemontonic," **www.eidenai.ca/EI/SiteContent/ CaseStudies/Pages/LemontonicCaseStudy.html**, accessed April 19, 2007; Eidenai Innovations, "About EI: Vision," **www.eidenai.ca/**

EI/SiteContent/About/Vision/, accessed April 19, 2007; Eidenai Innovations, "About EI: Clients," www.eidenai.ca/EI/SiteContent/About/Clients/, accessed April 19, 2007; and Lemontonic, "Lemontonic: The Revolution of Life Online," www.lemontonic.com, accessed April 19, 2007.

CASE STUDY QUESTIONS

1. Write a systems analysis report about the Lemontonic instant messaging system. What do you think may have been the problems with previous similar systems? What management, organization, and technology factors do you think caused the problems? What do you think was the impact of these problems? What are the objectives and information requirements of a new systems solution?

2. As part of your report, diagram the new member subscription process for joining Lemontonic. How could this process be improved?

3. Describe what you think the role of end users and technical specialists should have been in analyzing the Lemontonic situation and developing a solution.

CHAPTER 10

Information Resource Management and Project Management

After completing this chapter, you will be able to do the following:

1. Understand the various components of information resource management and the issues involved in each component.
2. Identify and describe the objectives of project management and why it is so essential in developing information systems.
3. Compare models for selecting and evaluating information systems projects and methods for aligning IS projects with the firm's business goals.
4. Evaluate models for assessing the business value of information systems.
5. Analyze the principal risk factors in information systems projects.
6. Select appropriate strategies for managing project risk and system implementation.

OPENING CASE | HSBC Malaysia: Master of Change Management

HSBC Malaysia Berhad is one of the oldest banks in Malaysia. It is a wholly owned subsidiary of HSBC Holdings, headquartered in London, which is one of the largest financial services companies in the world.

This bank has been a leader in introducing Internet banking and short message service (SMS)–based banking in Malaysia, as well as new value-added banking services for businesses. HSBC's V-Banking (Value Banking) provides new electronic services to retail customers while its Automate@HSBC initiative provides e-business and collaborative commerce technologies to local Malaysian small- and medium-sized businesses.

V-Banking provides retail customers with more than 30 telebanking and Internet banking services, consolidated portfolio summaries, and detailed account reconciliation. Customers can receive SMS Smart Alert notifications of returned cheques, credit card payment details, and birthday greetings.

These initiatives have made the bank's business processes more digital, with 96 percent of its transactions now handled online. In changing the way the bank delivers services to retail and corporate customers, these systems have naturally changed the way the bank works.

HSBC restructured bank branches across Malaysia to become personal financial services (PFS) centres. These PFS centres offer 24-hour electronic banking machines with more self-service options and fewer counters manned by tellers. Counter activities focus more on providing personal customer service rather

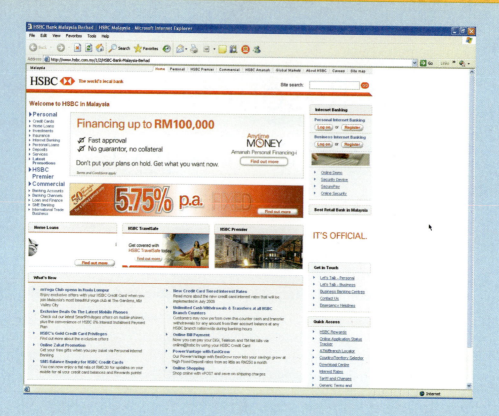

than traditional cash banking functions such as accepting cheques and deposits.

A portion of the HSBC Malaysia workforce had to change their job responsibilities from manual, labour-intensive tasks to working more closely with customers as "personal bankers." HSBC's customer relationship management systems and call centres were enhanced to handle the new customer demand for information across a variety of touch points.

Chief information officer Chu Hong Keong and his staff had to sell this new way of doing business to the rest of the organization. They tried to enlist support for the new business processes through meetings, demonstrations, and strategy discussions. The team ran retraining exercises to promote more customer-oriented attitudes among banking staff. To train customers in new banking habits, Chu's group stationed

V-Banking ambassadors at key branches to demonstrate how the new electronic banking services and Internet banking kiosks would save customers time and money. V-Banking succeeded because Chu and his managers understood the importance of changing the organization along with the technology. Chu and his Automate@HSBC/V-Banking initiative won several awards, but the initiative did not spread to other countries' HSBC subsidiaries; it has not yet reached Canada, where HSBC has 77 offices and several subsidiaries in addition to straight banking offices.

Sources: Raoul LeBlond, "Time as a Strategic Tool," *CIO Asia,* March 2004; HSBC, "Welcome to HSBC in Mayalsia" **www.hsbc.com.my**, accessed July 11, 2004; HSBC, "Home: HSBC Bank Canada" **www.hsbc.ca/hsbc**, accessed May 22, 2005; University Malaysia Sarawak, "eBario Wins AFACT's eASIA Award," **www.unimas.my/ebario/award4.htm**, accessed May 21, 2005; and A. Asohan, "MDC launches two new APICTA initiatives," August 2, 2003, **www.unrealmind.com/press_release_7.htm**, accessed May 21, 2005.

One of the principal challenges posed by information systems is ensuring they can deliver genuine business benefits. There is a very high failure rate among information systems projects because organizations have incorrectly assessed their business value or because firms have failed to manage the organizational change surrounding the introduction of new technology.

Chu Hong Keong and his team at HSBC Malaysia realized the nature of this challenge and took special pains to ensure the bank would obtain business value from the new system.

The chapter-opening Business Challenges diagram calls attention to important points raised by this case and this chapter. HSBC is in an information-intensive industry

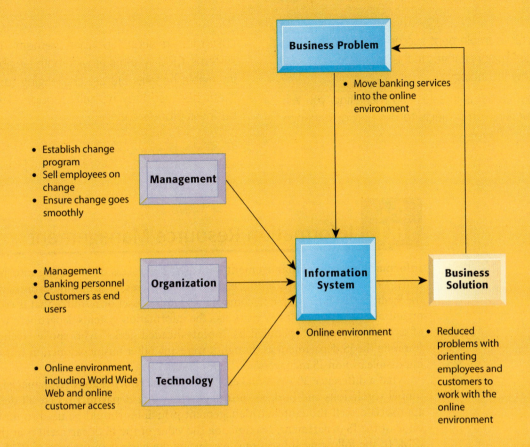

- Move banking services into the online environment

Business Problem

- Establish change program
- Sell employees on change
- Ensure change goes smoothly

Management

- Management
- Banking personnel
- Customers as end users

Organization

- Online environment, including World Wide Web and online customer access

Technology

Information System

- Online environment

Business Solution

- Reduced problems with orienting employees and customers to work with the online environment

where it must continually develop new systems and enhance existing systems to remain competitive. If HSBC were unable to manage its information systems projects properly, this would raise operating costs and prevent the company from realizing a good return on its IT investments. The company was able to successfully implement both the V-banking and Automate@HSBC systems only because close attention was paid to change management.

HEADS UP

During your career, you will undoubtedly be asked to work on information systems projects to solve an important challenge for your firm. Whether the project entails developing a new information system or enhancing an existing system, you will need to know how to measure the business benefits of these investments and how to make sure that these systems work successfully in your organization. The success of your project will depend on how well it is managed.

- If your career is in finance and accounting, you will help systems developers use financial models to justify investments in information systems projects.

- If your career is in human resources, you will be working with employees to help them adjust to new job responsibilities, reporting relationships, and other changes associated with new systems. You will also take part in hiring, training, and evaluating technical staff.

- If your career is in information systems, you will be evaluating the technology for new system projects and working with project management tools and software to document and monitor project plans. You will also take part in information resource management, the actual managing of the activities of the IST department.

- If your career is in manufacturing, production, or operations management, you will participate in projects to develop or enhance supply chain management systems and enterprise resource planning systems. These systems can provide significant benefits, but they are among the most difficult to implement successfully because they require major changes to the organization as well as new technology.

- If your career is in sales and marketing, you will be working on projects to develop or enhance customer relationship management (CRM) systems. CRM systems provide both tangible and intangible benefits but are challenging to implement because they typically require extensive business process change.

10.1 Information Resource Management

Information resource management (IRM) is the process of managing information systems—including hardware, software, data and databases, telecommunications, people, and the facilities that house these IS components—as an asset or resource that is critical to the organization. As recently as 30 years ago, the information systems department was thought of as an "ivory tower" peopled by "pointy-headed geeks" who spoke "technobabble." Running the IS department as though it were any other business function was considered impossible by non-IS managers.

What a difference 30 years makes! Today IS departments are well-managed, with personnel regulations and budgets, just like every other department. Like all departments, appropriate, well-thought-out management principles should be used to maximize the value of the IS department. Maximizing the value of the IS department is at the heart of IRM. In the following subsections, we review the basic components of IRM. While we assume that IS managers need to know these components, we also feel strongly that all managers should understand IRM in order to interact effectively and efficiently with the IS department. The IS department is a service provider to other departments and should be held accountable for the level of service provided. Managers who understand the components of IRM can accurately evaluate the level of service that the IS department provides to other departments.

The Information Systems Department

Almost every organization today has a computer. Whether there is only one computer and only one individual who uses it or whether there are thousands of computers located around the world, the duties and functions of the information systems department are vested in one or more individuals. Whether these duties are explicit, as they are in middle- to large-sized organizations, or implicit, as in a "mom-and-pop" shop, these duties must be handled. The IS department has the following duties and functions:

- Manage computer operations
- Manage systems development and systems development projects
- Manage IS personnel
- Budget for the department and others in the organization who use computers
- Plan for strategic, tactical, and operational level systems and for the IS department's operations
- Justify financial investment in information systems

IS departments are structured like other departments; they have managers at all levels, and frequently there is a division of duties and reporting responsibilities. A typical IS department will have divided its duties into several divisions, such as systems development, telecommunications, e-commerce/Web, database management, user relations/support, and operations. Each of these divisions might have subdivisions; for example,

Information resource management (IRM)

FIGURE 10-1   *A typical information systems department structure*

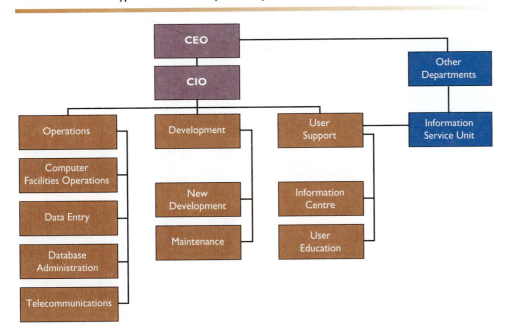

Each division has subdivisions to manage the overall departmental responsibilities.

systems development might have two subdivisions, such as new development and maintenance. Each division would have a manager and IS staff who report to the division manager. Division managers would report to the IS department manager. Figure 10-1 shows a typical IS department structure.

In some firms, the IS department manager may be the chief information officer. As a member of senior management, the **chief information officer (CIO)** is responsible for strategic level IS planning and for ensuring that all IS plans, systems, and operations support the organization's overall strategy. Some organizations have begun calling the CIO a chief technology officer (CTO) or chief knowledge officer (CKO).

In addition to having a CIO at the strategic level, the organization may also make use of a management information systems (MIS) Steering Committee. The **MIS Steering Committee** sets policy and priorities for the IS department, including approving budgets for major projects and hearing progress reports on those major projects. The MIS Steering Committee is usually composed of the CIO and other members of senior management. In the best-case scenario, the organization's CEO is also a member of the MIS Steering Committee. It is the responsibility of the CIO to represent the IS department on the MIS Steering Committee and to communicate effectively with the committee's membership, "selling" them and other top managers on the IS department's plans and projects.

Managing Planning, Strategy, and External Relations

Like every other department, the IS department should conduct periodic strategic, tactical, and operational planning. Strategic IS plans describe, from a broad perspective, the major strategic information systems that support or will support the organization's strategy. These long-range plans have a huge impact on the organization and on the IS department. Tactical IS plans have a more short-term focus and concentrate on breaking down the strategic IS plan into more detailed plans that middle-level managers can focus on implementing. Finally, operational-level IS plans detail how the strategic IS plan will be implemented during the coming short term, usually one year. Specific goals and objectives permit measurement of how the IS department is performing in supporting the organization's strategy. Each of these sets of IS plans—strategic, tactical, and operational—should be aligned with the organization's strategy and with the organization's strategic, tactical, and operational level plans (see Figure 10-2).

Chief information officer (CIO)

MIS Steering Committee

FIGURE 10-2 *How information systems strategy and planning are aligned with organizational strategy and planning*

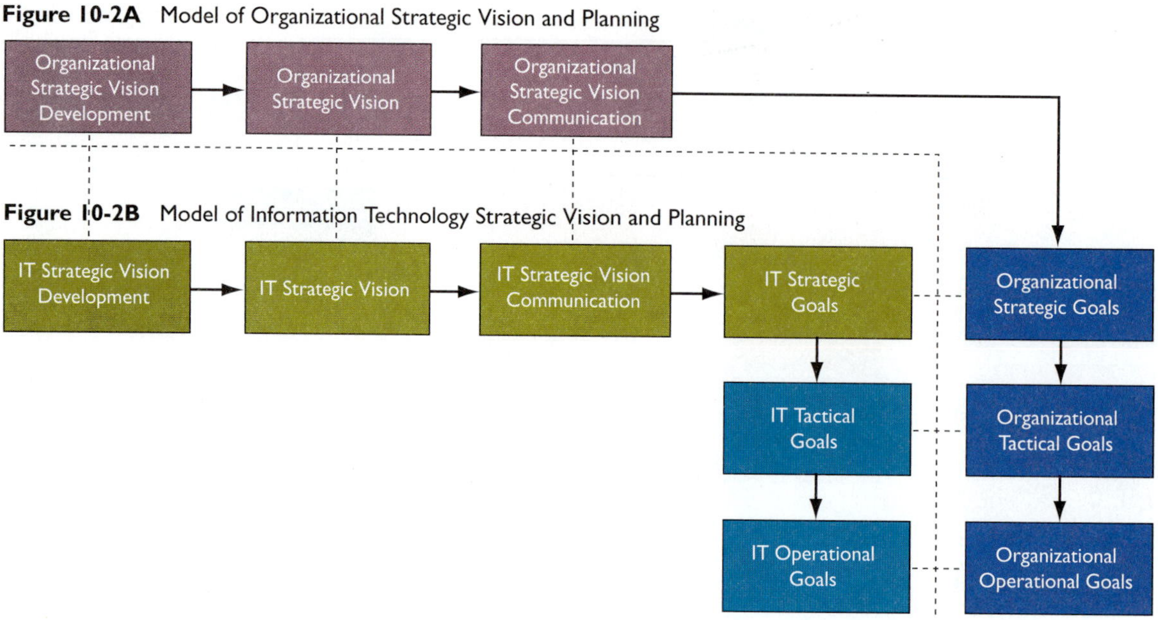

Figure 10-2A Model of Organizational Strategic Vision and Planning

Figure 10-2B Model of Information Technology Strategic Vision and Planning

Figure 10-2A represents the organization's strategy and planning steps and levels, while Figure 10-2B represents the IS department's strategy and planning steps and levels. The dashed lines represent alignment between the organizational and IS strategies and plans at all steps and levels.

Source: Mary Brabston, Robert Zmud, and John Carlson, "Strategic Vision for Information Technology," in *Strategic Information Technology: Opportunities for Competitive Advantage*, edited by Raymond Papp, Idea Group Publishing, 2000.

The CIO is responsible for ensuring that these plans are developed and aligned with the organization's plans. The CIO is also the major link to external parties, such as senior-level managers at vendor organizations and strategic partners' CIOs. Many CIOs have been promoted from the ranks of the IS department; however, because of the communication-intensive nature of the position, many CIOs come from other areas of the organization, such as finance or human resources.

Managing Systems Development

Systems development can be viewed from many perspectives. In Chapter 9, we looked at the systems development life cycle and at systems development as organizational change. In this chapter, we look at systems development in terms of managing the implemented system and in terms of personnel assignments to develop systems.

In Chapter 8, we discussed information systems quality, security, and control in detail. These topics are also part of information resource management. Once a system has been implemented, it is the IS department's responsibility to ensure that policies, guidelines, and decisions about the implemented systems are followed. These responsibilities include ensuring that backups are made, that IS audits are conducted when and where appropriate, that appropriate security processes and appropriate controls—such as passwords and locked doors—are maintained and followed. Included in this are network, database, and Web management, which ensure that organizational and department policies are followed in each of these areas and that these parts of the organization's information systems are secure, reliable, available, and accessible as needed.

In previous chapters, we also briefly discussed the role of systems analysts and programmers. However, IS departments also employ **systems operators** who run the hardware, including loading tape and disk drives, starting and stopping computer "jobs," and ensuring that backups are carried out as dictated by policy. **Data entry operators** enter data in computer-readable format and are managed by database managers. **Network managers**

Systems operators
Data entry operators
Network managers

supervise networks while Web masters handle the organization's Web-based presence. It is important to recall that every organization organizes its IS department and information system components differently. Every organization also gives different titles to the people who hold these generic positions. A network manager in one organization may be a LAN coordinator in another, but the employee's function is the same.

Many organizations centralize their information systems so that most of the information systems components, such as hardware and software, are located centrally and managed by a central IS department. These centralized IS departments make most of the decisions about information systems. Other organizations choose to decentralize their information systems, permitting organizational departments or divisions to make their own decisions about what information systems to develop or purchase. Individual departments may house their own networks, hardware, and software. Many of these decentralized organizations also employ extra IS staff who report to the decentralized unit.

Today, the trend is toward information service units and information centres. Figure 10-1 on page 337 depicts this modern type of IS department structure. An information service unit is located within a non-IS department, such as marketing, but is employed by and reports to the IS department. The IS unit handles local department requests for systems development, end-user support, and training and serves as an interface to the IS department. An information centre, also known as user support, is housed in the IS department but handles requests for support, training, assistance, and guidance from other departments. For example, if the marketing department needs to determine whether to upgrade their desktop computer operating system, marketing staff could call the information centre for advice.

Assigning Personnel to Develop Systems How does an IS manager decide who will be assigned to a particular systems development project? Should an experienced person be assigned to new projects or to maintaining those projects on which he or she has already worked? Should less experienced personnel be assigned to maintenance projects so that they may gain experience?

New systems development is considered to be creative and more desirable than maintenance, which is viewed similarly to semi-annual checkups with your dentist. It has to be done, but you'd rather not have to do it. Every organization handles the assignment of programmers and analysts to individual projects differently. Frequently, rotation is used, so that personnel may be assigned to new development for a project and, when that project is completed, move on to a maintenance project. Just as frequently, less experienced IS staff are partnered with more experienced staff, who act as mentors and help newer employees gain higher levels of expertise.

Finally, the IS department is a service department, providing systems development and other services to other departments. Many businesses have implemented service level agreements. According to this framework, the company has the IS department sign an agreement to develop a system for another department. The service level agreement specifies milestones, deadlines, budget, level of service to be achieved, and other requested benchmarks. The IS department agrees to these terms and is held accountable by corporate management for meeting these benchmarks.

Managing Personnel

We mentioned above that IS staff were formerly viewed as "pointy-headed geeks." Previous generations of hardware and software required a high level of technical knowledge and expertise. Today's systems permit lower levels of technical knowledge, enabling those with a middle level of technical expertise to succeed as programmers and analysts. This trend has opened IS career tracks to non-computer science majors.

While computer science focuses more on the technical side of information systems, the management information system (MIS) field focuses on the needs of business that can be met by computer-based information systems. Today's IS departments hire both computer science and MIS staff to fulfill their personnel requirements. In addition, yesterday's pointy-headed geeks receive education and training in business applications and how to communicate effectively. More and more, the language of the IS department is "business-ese" instead of technobabble.

The changing educational background of IS staff also affects questions of evaluation, since, like all other employees, IS staff must be evaluated periodically. Determining metrics on which to base IS staff evaluation is a difficult task. Should a programmer be evaluated on number of lines of code generated? The code could be inefficient and time-consuming to run. Should function points be used instead? Function points define where an actual function has been performed, but some functions are complex while others are not. Do you evaluate an analyst on how well the assigned user area is satisfied with their analyst? Or on how well the analyst works with his or her programming teams? This is not an easy issue. Determining what criteria should be used in evaluating IS staff is a difficult task because each staff member's job presents a different mix of the technical and behavioural elements. The differences in the combination of technical and behavioural elements depend on the specifics of the job, which makes it difficult to develop and use unchanging evaluation criteria. A detailed discussion of this topic is beyond the scope of this text, but all these issues must be considered when IS personnel are periodically evaluated and counselled on their performance.

The last 10 years have seen the salaries of IS staff increase rapidly and then level off. How does an organization recruit and retain IS staff when they cannot afford to give periodic raises that are as high as the local rate of increase for their classification? Some organizations have taken to giving bonuses based on work done, projects completed, or tenure in the organization. For example, in the late 1990s, NorthWest Company on occasion gave a "signing bonus" to new employees, accompanied by a retention bonus after one year on the job. Other organizations, such as the City of Winnipeg, have given their IS staff a year-end bonus, up to several thousand dollars, to those employees who have been there for several years. These loyalty bonuses serve to defuse the natural desire of IS staff to "follow the money." How does that fit the company's salary policy?

We hear in Canada about a "brain drain" to the South, in which skilled Canadians are being hired by U.S. companies at inflated salaries. Interestingly, there are experts on each side of the brain-drain issue. Some feel Canada is losing its best and brightest to the U.S., while others disagree, arguing that the "brain drain" is based only on almost mythical anecdotal evidence. Regardless of which opinion is correct, the bottom line for IRM is that IS managers must attempt to keep their employees happy. In a time when IS jobs are going unfilled, this makes sense. The slowing economy (particularly following the terrorist attacks on September 11, 2001, in the United States) combines with the recent trend toward dot-com failures to reduce the number of new IS jobs available. At least in this regard, perhaps the brain drain—if there ever was one—will subside. Today the number of IS jobs available has returned to pre-September 11 and dot-com bubble bursting levels; in fact, a shortfall in the number of qualified applicants for entry-level and mid-level IS jobs is predicted for the short and even longer term.

With technology advancing so rapidly, how do IS staff keep their skills up to date? IS departments need to develop policies for staff to receive training and to upgrade their skills. IS training policies need to address funding and time off to attend seminars, workshops, and courses; eligibility for funding and time off; the number of courses that can be taken in a given period; and the locus of the decision about continuing education, i.e., who decides which courses employees will take.

In addition to keeping employees' skills up to date, providing training opportunities is an excellent way to motivate and retain employees. The flip side of the coin is, of course, that the employees will now have advanced skills with which to seek other jobs. Maintaining a challenging, positive environment with a few "perks"—such as a day-care service, or the now-common casual day—also helps to retain employees.

Managing Budgets

How can an IS manager know what the budget for the IS department should be for the coming year? A detailed analysis of ongoing and forthcoming projects is required, along with determining the need to upgrade technologies. In light of the trend in IS salaries, the IS department must also examine the potential need for raises or exceptional performance bonuses to retain key IS staff. These are not easy calculations. IS projects are notorious for running over budget (see the discussion on change management later in this chapter.).

How do you know when you should upgrade hardware or software? What do you do when your most productive and effective analyst comes to you with a job offer in hand for a 10 percent raise, and requests only a 5 percent raise to stay in your organization? How does that fit within the budget? Every IS organization handles their budgeting issues differently.

Many IS departments receive revenue from other departments in the form of charge-backs, or internal transfers of funds to reflect payment for services rendered. Chargebacks can be calculated based on the other department's computer usage, the number of its LAN nodes, the number of employees or revenues generated by the department, or in myriad other ways. It is important that the method of chargeback is well communicated to department heads so that they understand the process and the charges.

Taken together, the topics discussed above comprise the major components of IRM. Being able to justify financial investments in information systems is also part of planning at all levels. The IS department must be able to explain and demonstrate that their budget and systems are worth the organization's financial commitment.

10.2 The Importance of Project Management

There is a very high failure rate among information systems projects. In nearly every organization, information systems projects take much more time and money to implement than originally anticipated, or the completed system does not work properly. When an information system fails to work properly or costs too much to develop, companies may not realize any benefit from their information system investment, and the system may not be able to solve the problems for which it was intended. The development of a new system must be carefully managed and orchestrated, and the way a project is executed is likely to be the most important factor influencing its outcome (Wallace and Keil, 2004). That's why it's essential to have some knowledge about how to manage information systems projects and about how and why they succeed or fail.

Runaway Projects and System Failure

How badly are projects managed? On average, private sector projects are underestimated by one-half in terms of budget and time required to deliver the complete system promised in the system plan. A very large number of projects are delivered with missing functionality that is promised for delivery in later versions. The Standish Group consultancy, which monitors IT project success rates, found that only 29 percent of all technology investments were completed on time, on budget, and with all features and functions originally specified (Levinson, 2006). Between 30 and 40 percent of all software projects are "runaway" projects that far exceed the original schedule and budget projections and fail to perform as originally specified (Keil, Mann, and Rai, 2000).

As illustrated in Figure 10-3, a systems development project without proper management will most likely suffer these consequences:

- Costs that greatly exceed budgets
- Unexpected time slippage
- Technical performance that is less than expected
- Failure to obtain anticipated benefits

The systems produced by failed information projects are often not used in the way they were intended, or they are not used at all. Users often have to develop parallel manual systems to make these systems work.

FIGURE 10-3 *Consequences of poor project management*

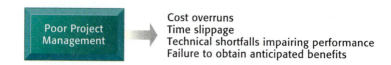

Without proper management, a systems development project takes longer to complete and most often exceeds the allocated budget. The resulting information system is most likely technically inferior and may not be able to demonstrate any benefits to the organization. Great ideas for systems often flounder on the rocks of implementation.

The actual design of the system may fail to capture essential business requirements or improve organizational performance. Information may not be provided quickly enough to be helpful; it may be in a format that is impossible to digest and use; or it may represent the wrong pieces of data.

The way in which nontechnical business users must interact with the system may be excessively complicated and discouraging. A system may be designed with a poor user interface. The **user interface** is the part of the system with which end users interact. For example, an online input form or data entry screen may be so poorly arranged that no one wants to submit data or request information. System outputs may be displayed in a format that is too difficult to comprehend (Speier and Morris, 2003).

Web sites may discourage visitors from exploring further if the Web pages are cluttered and poorly arranged, if users cannot easily find the information they are seeking, or if it takes too long to access and display the Web page on the user's computer.

Additionally, the data in the system may have a high level of inaccuracy or inconsistency. The information in certain fields may be erroneous or ambiguous, or it may not be organized properly for business purposes. Information required for a specific business function may be inaccessible because the data are incomplete.

Project Management Objectives

A **project** is a planned series of related activities for achieving a specific business objective. Information systems projects include the development of new information systems, enhancing existing systems, or projects for replacing or upgrading the firm's information technology (IT) infrastructure.

Project management refers to the application of knowledge, skills, tools, and techniques to achieve specific targets within specified budget and time constraints. Project management activities include planning the work, assessing risk, estimating resources required to accomplish the work, organizing the work, acquiring human and material resources, assigning tasks, directing activities, controlling project execution, reporting progress, and analyzing the results. As in other areas of business, project management for information systems must deal with five major variables: scope, time, cost, quality, and risk.

Scope defines what work is or is not included in a project. For example, the project scope for a new order processing system might include new modules for inputting orders and transmitting them to production and accounting but not any changes to related accounts receivable, manufacturing, distribution, or inventory control systems. Project management defines all the work required to complete a project successfully and should ensure that the scope of a project does not expand beyond what was originally intended.

Time is the amount of time required to complete the project. Project management typically establishes the amount of time required to complete major components of a project. Each of these components is then broken down into activities and tasks. Project management tries to determine the time required to complete each task and establish a schedule for completing the work.

Cost is based on the time to complete a project multiplied by the cost of human resources required to complete the project. Information systems project costs also include the cost of hardware, software, and work space. Project management develops a budget for the project and monitors ongoing project expenses.

Quality is an indicator of how well the end result of a project satisfies the objectives specified by management. The quality of information systems projects usually boils down

User interface

Project

Project management

Scope

to improved organizational performance and decision making. Quality also considers the system's ease of use, and the accuracy and timeliness of the information it produces.

Risk refers to potential problems that could threaten the success of a project. These potential problems might prevent a project from achieving its objectives by increasing time and cost, lowering the quality of project outputs, or preventing the project from being completed altogether. Section 10.5 describes the most important risk factors for information systems.

10.3 Selecting Projects

Companies typically are presented with many different projects for solving problems and improving performance. There are far more ideas for systems projects than there are resources. Firms will need to select from this group the projects that promise the greatest benefit to the business. Obviously the firm's overall business strategy should drive project selection.

Management Structure for Information Systems Projects

Figure 10-4 shows the elements of a management structure for information systems projects in a large corporation. Such a structure helps ensure that the most important systems projects are given priority.

At the apex of this structure is the corporate strategic planning group and the information system steering committee. The corporate strategic planning group is responsible for developing the firm's strategic plan, which may require the development of new systems.

The information systems steering committee is the senior management group with responsibility for systems development and operation. It is composed of department heads from both end-user and information systems areas. The steering committee reviews and approves plans for systems in all divisions, seeks to coordinate and integrate systems, and occasionally becomes involved in selecting specific information systems projects.

FIGURE 10-4   *Management control of systems projects*

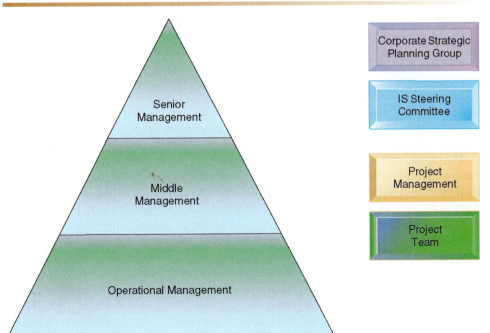

Each level of management in the hierarchy is responsible for specific aspects of systems projects, and this structure helps give priority to the most important systems projects for the organization.

The project team is supervised by a project management group composed of information systems managers and end-user managers responsible for overseeing several specific information systems projects. The project team is directly responsible for the individual systems project. The team consists of systems analysts, specialists from the relevant end-user business areas, application programmers, and perhaps database specialists. The mix of skills and the size of the project team depend on the specific nature of the system solution.

Linking Systems Projects to the Business Plan

In order to identify the information systems projects that will deliver the most business value, organizations need to develop an **information systems plan** that supports their overall business plan and incorporates strategic systems into top-level planning. The plan serves as a road map indicating the direction of systems development (the purpose of the plan), the rationale, the current systems/situation, new developments to consider, the management strategy, the implementation plan, and the budget (see Table 10-1).

The plan contains a statement of corporate goals and specifies how information technology will support the attainment of those goals. The report shows how general goals will be achieved by specific systems projects.

The IS plan identifies specific target dates and milestones that can be used later to evaluate the plan's progress in terms of how many objectives were actually attained in the time frame specified in the plan. The plan indicates the key management decisions concerning hardware acquisition; telecommunications; centralization/decentralization of authority, data, and hardware; and required organizational change. Organizational changes are also usually described, including management and employee training requirements; recruiting efforts; changes in business processes; and changes in authority, structure, or management practice.

In order to plan effectively, firms need to inventory and document all of their information system applications and IT infrastructure components. For projects whose benefits include improved decision making, managers should try to identify the decision improvements that would provide the greatest additional value to the firm. They should then develop a set of metrics to quantify the value of more timely and precise information on the outcome of the decision (see Chapter 14 for more detail on this topic).

Enterprise Analysis and Critical Success Factors

To develop an effective information systems plan, the organization must have a clear understanding of both its long- and short-term information requirements. Two principal methodologies for establishing the essential information requirements of the organization as a whole are enterprise analysis and critical success factors.

Enterprise Analysis (Business Systems Planning)

Enterprise analysis (also called *business systems planning*) argues that the firm's information requirements can be understood only by examining the entire organization in terms of organizational units, functions, processes, and data elements. Enterprise analysis can help identify the key entities and attributes of the organization's data.

The central method used in the enterprise analysis approach is to take a large sample of managers and ask them how they use information, where they get their information, what their objectives are, how they make decisions, and what their data needs are. The results of this large survey of managers are aggregated into subunits, functions, processes, and data matrices. Data elements are organized into logical application groups—groups of data elements that support related sets of organizational processes.

Figure 10-5 is an output of enterprise analysis conducted as part of a massive systems redevelopment effort. It shows what information is required to support a particular process, which processes create the data, and which use them. The shaded boxes in the figure indicate a logical application group. In this case, actuarial estimates, organization plans, and budget data are created in the planning process, suggesting that an information system should be developed to support planning.

Information systems plan

Enterprise analysis

TABLE 10-1 Information Systems Plan

1. PURPOSE OF THE PLAN

Overview of plan contents

Current business organization and future organization

Key business processes

Management strategy

2. STRATEGIC BUSINESS PLAN RATIONALE

Current situation

Current business organization

Changing environments

Major goals of the business plan

Firm's strategic plan

3. CURRENT SYSTEMS

Major systems supporting business functions and processes

Current infrastructure capabilities

Hardware

Software

Database

Telecommunications and Internet

Difficulties meeting business requirements

Anticipated future demands

4. NEW DEVELOPMENTS

New system projects

Project descriptions

Business rationale

Applications' role in strategy

New infrastructure capabilities required

Hardware

Software

Databases

Telecommunications and Internet

5. MANAGEMENT STRATEGY

Acquisition plans

Milestones and timing

Organizational realignment

Internal reorganization

Management controls

Major training initiatives

Personnel strategy

6. IMPLEMENTATION PLAN

Anticipated difficulties in implementation

Progress reports

7. BUDGET REQUIREMENTS

Requirements

Potential savings

Financing

Acquisition cycle

FIGURE 10-5   *Process/Data class matrix*

Group	PROCESSES	Actuarial estimates	Agency plans	Budget	Program regulations/policy	Administrative regulations/policy	Labour agreements	Data standards	Procedures	Automated systems documentation	Educational media	Public agreements	Intergovernmental agreements	Grants	External	Exchange control	Administrative accounts	Program expenditures	Audit reports	Organization/position	Employee identification	Recruitment/placement	Complaints/grievances	Training resources	Security	Equipment utilization	Space utilization	Supplies utilization	Workload schedules	Work measurement	Enumeration i.D.	Enumeration control	Earnings	Employer i.D.	Earnings control	Claims characteristics	Claims control	Decisions	Payment	Collection/waiver	Notice	Inquiries control	Quality appraisal
PLANNING	Develop agency plans	C	C	C	U	U									U																												
	Administer agency budget	C	C	C	U	U						U	U	U		U	U	U		U	U					U	U	U				U		U		U						U	U
	Formulate program policies	U	U		C				U							U				U		U														U							U
	Formulate administrative policies		U		U	C	C		U							U				U	U	U																					
	Formulate data policies		U	U		U		C	U	U																U	U	U	U														
	Design work processes		U		U	U			C	C		U	U							U																U							U
GENERAL MANAGEMENT	Manage public affairs		U		U	U			U		C	C	C																														
	Manage intergovernment affairs	U	U		U	U			U		U	C	C	C															U	U		U	U		U			U					
	Exchange data		U						U			U	U	U	U	C	U	U														U											
	Maintain administrative accounts		U		U						U	U				C		U								U	U	U								U		U					
	Maintain program accounts		U	U		U					U	U					C													U						U		U	U	U	U		U
	Conduct audits		U	U		U			U	U						U	U	C		U									U														
	Establish organizations		U		U				U											C	U								U	U													U
	Manage human resources		U		U	U			U											C	C	C	C	C																			
	Provide security				U	U			U	U	U	U													C	C	C	C		U													
	Manage equipment		U		U				U	U	U	U													C	C	C	C															
	Manage facilities		U		U				U																U	U	C																
	Manage supplies		U		U				U																C	U	U	C															
	Manage workloads	U		U	U	U			U						U											U	U	U	C	C		U		U		U		U				U	U
PROGRAM ADMINISTRATION	Issue Social Insurance Numbers								U			U		U																	C	C											
	Maintain earnings								U			U	U	U																		U		C	C	C	C	U					
	Collect claims information				U	U			U					U																	U	U		U		C	C	U	U	U			
	Determine eligibility/entitlement								U																						U	U	U		U	C	U	U					
	Compute payments				U				U									U													U		U		U	C	C						
	Administer debt management				U				U									U																	U	C							
SUPPORT	Generate notices								U			U																			U		U		U		U	U	U	U	C		
	Respond to program inquiries		U			U	U		U																						U		U	U	U		U	U	U	U	U	C	
	Provide quality assessment		U	U		U	U		U																						U		U		U		U				U	C

KEY: C = creators of data   U = users of data

This chart depicts which data classes are required to support particular organizational processes and which processes are the creators and users of data.

The weakness of enterprise analysis is that it produces an enormous amount of data that is expensive to collect and difficult to analyze. The questions frequently focus not on management's critical objectives and where information is needed, but rather on what existing information is used. The result is a tendency to automate whatever exists rather than developing entirely new approaches to conducting business.

Critical Success Factors The strategic analysis, or critical success factors, approach argues that an organization's information requirements are determined by a small number of **critical success factors (CSFs)** of managers. If these goals can be attained, success of the firm or organization is assured (Rockart, 1979). The industry, the firm, the manager, and the broader environment shape CSFs. For example, CSFs for the automobile industry might include styling, quality, and cost to meet the goals of increasing market share and raising profits. New information systems should focus on providing information that helps the firm meet these goals.

The principal method used in CSF analysis is three or four personal interviews in which a number of top managers identify their goals and the resulting CSFs. These personal CSFs are aggregated to develop a picture of the firm's CSFs. Then systems are

Critical success factors (CSFs)

FIGURE 10-6   *Using CSFs to develop systems*

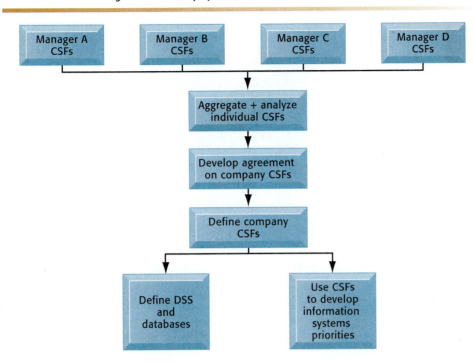

The CSF approach relies on interviews with key managers to identify their CSFs. Individual CSFs are aggregated to develop CSFs for the entire firm. Systems can then be developed to deliver information on these CSFs.

developed to deliver information about these CSFs. The method for developing CSFs in an organization is shown in Figure 10-6.

The strength of the CSF method is that it produces less data to analyze than does enterprise analysis. Only top managers are interviewed, and the questions focus on a small number of CSFs rather than requiring a broad inquiry into what information is used in the organization. It is especially suitable for top management and for the development of decision-support systems (DSSs) and executive support systems (ESSs). Unlike enterprise analysis, the CSF method focuses organizational attention on how information should be handled.

The method's primary weakness is that there is no particularly rigorous way in which individual CSFs can be aggregated into a clear company pattern.

In addition, interviewees (and interviewers) often become confused when distinguishing between individual and organizational CSFs. These types of CSFs are not necessarily the same. What may be considered critical to a manager may not be important for the organization as a whole. This method is clearly biased toward top managers, although it could be extended to elicit ideas for promising new systems from lower-level members of the organization.

Portfolio Analysis

Once strategic analyses have determined the overall direction of systems development, portfolio analysis can be used to evaluate alternative system projects. **Portfolio analysis** inventories all the organization's information systems projects and assets, including infrastructure, outsourcing contracts, and licences. This portfolio of information systems investments can be described as having a certain profile of risk and benefit to the firm (see Figure 10-7) similar to a financial portfolio.

Each information systems project carries its own set of risks and benefits. (Section 10.5 describes the factors that increase the risks of systems projects.) Firms try to improve the return on their portfolios of IT assets by balancing the risk and return from their systems investments. Although there is no ideal profile for all firms, information-intensive industries (e.g., finance) should have a few high-risk, high-benefit projects to ensure that they stay current with technology. Firms in non-information-intensive industries should focus on high-benefit, low-risk projects.

Most desirable, of course, are systems with high benefit and low risk. These promise early returns and low risks. Second, high-benefit, high-risk systems should be examined;

FIGURE 10-7 *A system portfolio*

Companies should examine their portfolio of projects in terms of potential benefits and likely risks. Certain kinds of projects should be avoided altogether and others developed rapidly. There is no ideal mix. Companies in different industries have different profiles.

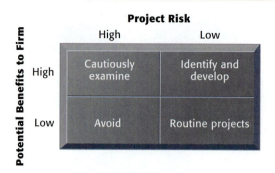

low-benefit, high-risk systems should be totally avoided; and low-benefit, low-risk systems should be reexamined for the possibility of redeveloping and replacing them with more desirable systems having higher benefits. By using portfolio analysis, management can determine the optimal mix of investment risk and reward for their firms, balancing riskier high-reward projects with safer lower-reward ones. Firms where portfolio analysis is aligned with business strategy have been found to have a superior return on their IT assets, better alignment of information technology investments with business objectives, and better organization-wide coordination of IT investments (Jeffrey and Leliveld, 2004).

Scoring Models

Scoring model

A **scoring model** is useful for selecting projects where many criteria must be considered. It assigns weights to various features of a system and then calculates the weighted totals. Using Table 10-2, the firm must decide between two alternative enterprise resource planning

TABLE 10-2 *Example of a Scoring Model for an ERP System*

CRITERIA	WEIGHT	ERP SYSTEM A %	ERP SYSTEM A SCORE	ERP SYSTEM B %	ERP SYSTEM B SCORE
1.0 Order Processing					
1.1 Online order entry	4	67	268	73	292
1.2 Online pricing	4	81	324	87	348
1.3 Inventory check	4	72	288	81	324
1.4 Customer credit check	3	66	198	59	177
1.5 Invoicing	4	73	292	82	328
Total Order Processing			1370		1469
2.0 Inventory Management					
2.1 Production forecasting	3	72	216	76	228
2.2 Production planning	4	79	316	81	324
2.3 Inventory control	4	68	272	80	320
2.4 Reports	3	71	213	69	207
Total Inventory Management			1017		1079
3.0 Warehousing					
3.1 Receiving	2	71	142	75	150
3.2 Picking/Packing	3	77	231	82	246
3.3 Shipping	4	92	368	89	356
Total Warehousing			741		752
Grand Total			3128		3300

(ERP) systems. The first column lists the criteria that decision makers will use to evaluate the systems. These criteria are usually the result of lengthy discussions among the decision-making group. Often the most important outcome of a scoring model is not the score but agreement on the criteria used to judge a system.

Table 10-2 shows that this particular company attaches the most importance to capabilities for sales order processing, inventory management, and warehousing. The second column in Table 10-2 lists the weights that decision makers attached to the decision criteria. Columns 3 and 5 show the percentage of requirements for each function that each alternative ERP system can provide. Each vendor's score can be calculated by multiplying the percentage of requirements met for each function by the weight attached to that function. ERP System B has the highest total score.

As with all "objective" techniques, there are many qualitative judgments involved in using the scoring model. This model requires experts who understand the issues and the technology. It is appropriate to cycle through the scoring model several times, changing the criteria and weights, to see how sensitive the outcome is to reasonable changes in criteria. Scoring models are used most commonly to confirm, rationalize, and support decisions, rather than as the final arbiters of system selection.

10.4 Establishing the Business Value of Information Systems

Even if a system project supports a firm's strategic goals and meets user information requirements, it needs to be a good investment for the firm.

The value of systems from a financial perspective essentially revolves around the issue of return on invested capital. Does a particular information system investment produce sufficient returns to justify its costs?

Information System Costs and Benefits

Table 10-3 lists some of the more common costs and benefits of systems. **Tangible benefits** can be quantified and assigned a monetary value. **Intangible benefits**, such as more efficient customer service or enhanced decision making, cannot be immediately quantified but may lead to quantifiable gains in the long run. Transaction and clerical systems that displace labour and save space always produce more measurable, tangible benefits than management information systems, decision-support systems, and computer-supported collaborative work systems.

Chapter 5 introduced the concept of total cost of ownership (TCO), which is designed to identify and measure the components of information technology expenditures beyond the initial cost of purchasing and installing hardware and software. However, TCO analysis provides only part of the information needed to evaluate an information technology investment because it does not typically deal with benefits, cost categories such as complexity costs, and "soft" and strategic factors discussed later in this section.

Capital Budgeting for Information Systems

Capital budgeting models are one of several techniques used to measure the value of investing in long-term capital investment projects. Firms invest in capital projects to expand production to meet anticipated demand or to modernize production equipment to reduce costs. Firms also invest in capital projects for many noneconomic reasons, such as installing pollution control equipment, converting to a human resources database to meet some government regulations, or satisfying nonmarket public demands. Information systems are considered long-term capital investment projects.

Tangible benefits

Intangible benefits

Capital budgeting

TABLE 10-3 *Costs and Benefits of Information Systems*

COSTS

Hardware

Telecommunications

Software

Services

Personnel

TANGIBLE BENEFITS (COST SAVINGS)

Increased productivity

Lower operational costs

Reduced workforce

Lower computer expenses

Lower outside vendor costs

Lower clerical and professional costs

Reduced rate of growth in expenses

Reduced facility costs

INTANGIBLE BENEFITS

Improved asset utilization

Improved resource control

Improved organizational planning

Increased organizational flexibility

More timely information

More information

Increased organizational learning

Legal requirements attained

Enhanced employee goodwill

Increased job satisfaction

Improved decision making

Improved operations

Higher client satisfaction

Better corporate image

The principal capital budgeting models for evaluating information technology projects are as follows:

- The payback method
- The accounting rate of return on investment (ROI)
- The net present value
- The internal rate of return (IRR)

Capital budgeting methods rely on measures of cash flows into and out of the firm. Capital projects generate cash flows into and out of the firm. The investment cost for information systems projects is an immediate cash outflow caused by expenditures for hardware, software, and labour. In subsequent years, the investment may cause additional cash outflows that will be balanced by cash inflows resulting from the investment. Cash inflows take the form of increased sales of more products (for reasons such as new products, higher quality, or increasing market share) or reduced costs in production and operations. The difference between cash outflows and cash inflows is used for calculating the financial worth of an investment. Once the cash flows have been established, several alternative methods are available for comparing different projects and deciding about the investment.

Case Example: Capital Budgeting for a New Supply Chain Management System

Let us look at how financial models would work in a real-world business scenario. Heartland Stores is a general merchandise retail chain operating across Canada. It has five regional distribution centres, 220 stores, and about 14 000 different products stocked in each store. The company is considering investing in new software and hardware modules to upgrade its existing supply chain management system to help it better manage the purchase and movement of goods from its suppliers to its retail outlets. Too many items in Heartland's stores are out of stock, even though many of these products are in the company's distribution centre warehouses.

Management believes that the new system would help Heartland Stores reduce the amount of items that it must stock in inventory, and thus its inventory costs, because it would be able to track precisely the status of orders and the flow of items in and out of its distribution centres. The new system would reduce Heartland's labour costs because the company would not need so many people to manage inventory or to track shipments of goods from suppliers to distribution centres and from distribution centres to retail outlets. Telecommunications costs would be reduced because customer service representatives and shipping and receiving staff would not have to spend so much time on the telephone tracking shipments and orders. Heartland Stores expects the system to reduce transportation costs by providing information to help it consolidate shipments to retail stores and to create more efficient shipping schedules. If the new system project is approved, implementation would commence in January 2009 and the new system would become operational in early January 2010.

The solution uses the existing IT infrastructure at the Heartland Stores but requires the purchase of additional server computers, PCs, database software, and networking technology, along with new supply chain planning and execution software. The solution also calls for new radio-frequency identification technology to track items more easily as they move from suppliers to distribution centres to retail outlets.

Figure 10-8 shows the estimated costs and benefits of the system. The system would have an actual investment cost of $11 467 350 in the first year (year 0) and a total cost over six years of $19 017 350. The estimated benefits total $32 500 000 after six years. Is the investment worthwhile? If so, in what sense? Financial models to evaluate the investment are depicted in Figure 10-9.

The Payback Method The simple **payback method** is a measure of the time required to pay back the initial investment of a project. The payback period is computed as follows:

$$\frac{\text{Original investment}}{\text{Annual net cash inflow}} = \text{Number of years to pay back}$$

In the case of Heartland Stores, it will take more than two years to pay back the initial investment. (Because cash flows are uneven, annual cash inflows are summed until they equal the original investment to arrive at this number.) The payback method is a popular method because of its simplicity and power as an initial screening method. It is especially good for high-risk projects in which the useful life of a project is difficult to determine. If a project pays for itself in two years, then it matters less how long after two years the system lasts.

The weakness of this measure is its virtue: The method ignores the time value of money, the amount of cash flow after the payback period, the disposal value (frequently zero with computer systems), and the profitability of the investment.

Payback Method

FIGURE 10-8   *Costs and benefits of the new supply chain management system*

	A	B	C	D	E	F	G	H	I	J	K
1	**Year :**					0	1	2	3	4	5
2						2007	2008	2009	2010	2011	2012
3	**Costs: Hardware**										
4		Servers			7@ 80 000	560 000					
5		Backup servers			4@ 80 000	320 000					
6		PCs at loading dock			100@ 1250	125 000					
7		Radio-frequency devices			1000@ $1175	1 175 000					
8		Storage				800 000					
9											
10	**Network Infrastructure**										
11		Routers and hubs			300@ 4100	1 230 000					
12		Firewalls			2@ 6300	12 600					
13		Wireless RF network				1 750 000					
14		Backup network system				1 150 000					
15		Telecom links				74 250	225 000	225 000	225 000	225 000	225 000
16											
17	**Software**										
18		Database				475 000					
19		Web servers (Apache)				0					
20		Supply chain planning & execution modules				1 187 500					
21											
22	**Labour**										
23		Business staff				425 000	115 000	115 000	115 000	115 000	115 000
24		IS staff				1 225 000	525 000	525 000	525 000	525 000	525 000
25		External consultants				576 000	95 000	95 000	95 000	95 000	95 000
26		Training (end users)				382 000	35 000	35 000	35 000	35 000	35 000
27	**Subtotal**					11 467 350	995 000	995 000	995 000	995 000	995 000
28											
29	**Maintenance and Support**										
30		Hardware maintenance & upgrades					240 000	240 000	240 000	240 000	240 000
31		Software maintenance & upgrades					275 000	275 000	275 000	275 000	275 000
32		Subtotal					515 000	515 000	515 000	515 000	515 000
33	**Total by Year**					11 467 350	1 510 000	1 510 000	1 510 000	1 510 000	1 510 000
34											
35	**Total Costs**					19 017 350					
36	**Benefits**										
37		Reduced labour costs					1 650 000	1 400 000	1 400 000	1 400 000	1 400 000
38		Reduced inventory costs					3 500 000	3 500 000	3 500 000	3 500 000	3 500 000
39		Reduced transportation costs					1 300 000	1 300 000	1 300 000	1 300 000	1 300 000
40		Reduced telecommunications costs					250 000	250 000	250 000	250 000	250 000
41											
42	**Subtotal**					0	6 700 000	6 450 000	6 450 000	6 450 000	6 450 000
43											
44	**Net Cash Flow**					−11 467 350	5 190 000	4 940 000	4 940 000	4 940 000	4 940 000
45											
46	**Total Benefits**					32 500 000					

This spreadsheet analyzes the basic costs and benefits of implementing supply chain management system enhancements for a midsize Canadian retailer. The costs for hardware, telecommunications, software, services, and personnel are analyzed over a six-year period.

Accounting Rate of Return on Investment (ROI) Firms make capital investments to earn a satisfactory rate of return. Determining a satisfactory rate of return depends on the cost of borrowing money, but other factors can enter into the equation also. These factors include the historic rates of return expected by the firm. In the long run, the desired rate of return must equal or exceed the cost of capital in the marketplace. Otherwise, no one will lend the firm money.

The **accounting rate of return on investment (ROI)** calculates the rate of return from an investment by adjusting the cash inflows produced by the investment for depreciation. It gives an approximation of the accounting income earned by the project.

To find the ROI, first calculate the average net benefit. The formula for the average net benefit is as follows:

Accounting rate of return on investment (ROI)

$$\frac{(\text{Total benefits} - \text{Total cost} - \text{Depreciation})}{\text{Useful life}} = \text{Net benefit}$$

FIGURE 10-9   *Financial models*

	A	B	C	D	E	F	G	H	I	J	K	L	M
								Financial Models					
1	Year:							0	1	2	3	4	5
2	Net Cash Flow (not including original investment) for years 2007–2012								$5 190 000.00	$4 940 000.00	$4 940 000.00	$4 940 000.00	$4 940 000.00
3	Net Cash Flow (including original investment) for years 2007–2012							–$11 467 350.00	$5 190 000.00	$4 940 000.00	$4 940 000.00	$4 940 000.00	$4 940 000.00
4													
5	Payback Period = 2.5 years					Cumulative Cash Flow							
6	Initial Investment =			Year 0	–$11 467 350.00	–$11 467 350.00							
7				Year 1	$5 190 000.00	–$6 277 350.00							
8				Year 2	$4 940 000.00	_$1 337 350.00							
9				Year 3	$4 940 000.00	$3 602 650.00							
10				Year 4	$4 940 000.00	$8 542 650.00							
11				Year 5	$4 940 000.00	$13 482 650.00							
12													
13	Accounting Rate of Return												
14	(Total Benefits – Total Costs – Depreciation)/Useful Life					Total Benefits	$32 500 000.00						
15						Total Costs	$19 017 350.00						
16	Total Initial Investment					Depreciation	$11 467 350.00						
17					Total Benefits–Total Costs–Deprec.		$2 015 300.00						
18													
19						Life	6 years						
20	Return on Investment (ROI) = 2.93%												
21													
22													
23													
24													
25													
26	Net Present Value =												
27			=NPV(0.05,H2:M2)–11 467 350				$10 158 359.99						
28													
29													
30													
31													
32	Internal Rate of Return												
33			= IRR(H3:M3)				33%						

Sheet1 Sheet2 Sheet3

To determine the financial basis for an information systems project, a series of financial models helps determine the return on invested capital. These calculations include the payback period, the accounting rate of return on investment (ROI), the net present value (NPV), and the internal rate of return (IRR).

This net benefit is divided by the total initial investment to arrive at ROI. The formula is as follows:

$$\frac{\text{Net benefit}}{\text{Total initial investment}} = \text{ROI}$$

In the case of Heartland Stores, the average rate of return on the investment is 2.93 percent. The weakness of ROI is that it can ignore the time value of money. Future savings are simply not worth as much in today's dollars as are current savings. However, ROI can be modified (and usually is) so that future benefits and costs are calculated in today's dollars. (The present value function on most spreadsheets can perform this conversion.)

Net Present Value Evaluating a capital project requires that the cost of an investment (a cash outflow usually in year 0) be compared with the net cash inflows that occur many years later. But these two kinds of cash flows are not directly comparable because of the time value of money. Money you have been promised to receive three, four, and five years from now is not worth as much as money received today. Money received in the future has to be discounted by some appropriate percentage rate—usually the prevailing interest rate or sometimes the cost of capital. **Present value** is the value in current dollars of a payment or stream of payments to be received in the future. It can be calculated by using the following formula:

$$\text{Payment} \times \frac{1 - (1 + 1 \text{ interest})^{-n}}{\text{Interest}} = \text{Present value}$$

Present value

Thus, to compare the investment (made in today's dollars) with future savings or earnings, you need to discount the earnings to their present value and then calculate the net present value of the investment. The **net present value (NPV)** is the amount of money an investment is worth, taking into account its cost, earnings, and the time value of money. The formula for net present value is this:

Present value of expected cash flows – Initial investment cost = Net present value

In the case of Heartland Stores, the present value of the stream of benefits is $21 625 709, and the cost (in today's dollars) is $11 467 350, giving a net present value of $10 158 359. In other words, for a $21 million investment today, the firm will receive more than $10 million. This is a fairly good rate of return on an investment.

Internal Rate of Return (IRR) **Internal rate of return (IRR)** is defined as the rate of return or profit that an investment is expected to earn, taking into account the time value of money. IRR is the discount (interest) rate that will equate the present value of the project's future cash flows to the initial cost of the project (defined here as negative cash flow in year 0 of $11 467 350). In other words, the value of R (discount rate) is such that Present value – Initial cost = 0. In the case of Heartland Stores, the IRR is 33 percent.

Results of the Capital Budgeting Analysis Using methods that take into account the time value of money, the Heartland Stores project is cash-flow positive over the time period under consideration and returns more benefits than it costs. Against this analysis, you might ask what other investments would be better from an efficiency and effectiveness standpoint and if all the benefits have been calculated.

Real Options Pricing Models

Some information systems projects are highly uncertain, especially investments in IT infrastructure. Their future revenue streams are unclear, and their upfront costs are high. Suppose, for instance, that a firm is considering a $20 million investment to upgrade its information technology infrastructure—its hardware, software, data management tools, and networking technology. If this upgraded infrastructure were available, the organization would have the technology capabilities to respond more easily to future problems and opportunities. Although the costs of this investment can be calculated, not all the benefits of making this investment can be established in advance. But if the firm waits a few years until the revenue potential becomes more obvious, it might be too late to make the infrastructure investment. In such cases, managers might benefit from using real options pricing models to evaluate information technology investments.

Real options pricing models (ROPMs) use the concept of options valuation borrowed from the financial industry. An option is essentially the right, but not the obligation, to act at some future date. A typical call option, for instance, is a financial option in which a person buys the right (but not the obligation) to purchase an underlying asset (usually a stock) at a fixed price (strike price) on or before a given date.

For instance, on June 5, 2008, for $3.00, you could purchase the right (a call option) maturing in January 2009 to buy a share of Bombardier Class B common stock for $10 per share. If, by the end of January 2009, the price of Bombardier Class B stock did not rise above $10 per share, you would not exercise the option, and the value of the option would fall to zero on the strike date. If, however, the price of Bombardier Class B common stock rose to, say, $15 per share, you could purchase the stock for the strike price of $10 and retain the profit of $5 per share minus the cost of the option. (Because the option is sold as a 100-share contract, the cost of the contract would be 100 × $3.00 before commissions, or $300, and you would be purchasing and obtaining a profit from 100 shares of Bombardier Class B common stock.) The stock option enables the owner to benefit from the upside potential of an opportunity while limiting the downside risk.

Real options pricing models value information systems projects similarly to stock options, where an initial expenditure on technology creates the right, but not the obligation, to obtain the benefits associated with further development and deployment of the

Net present value (NPV)
Internal rate of return (IRR)
Real options pricing models (ROPMs)

technology as long as management has the freedom to cancel, defer, restart, or expand the project. ROPMs give managers the flexibility to stage their IT investment or test the waters with small pilot projects or prototypes to gain more knowledge about the risks of a project before investing in the entire implementation. The disadvantages of this model are primarily in estimating all the key variables affecting option value, including anticipated cash flows from the underlying asset and changes in the cost of implementation. Models for determining option value of information technology platforms are being developed (Fichman, 2004; McGrath and MacMillan, 2000).

Limitations of Financial Models

The traditional focus on the financial and technical aspects of an information system tends to overlook the social and organizational dimensions of information systems that may affect the true costs and benefits of the investment. Many companies' information systems investment decisions do not adequately consider costs from organizational disruptions created by a new system, such as the cost to train end users, the impact that users' learning curves for a new system have on productivity, or the time managers need to spend overseeing new system-related changes. Social and organizational benefits, such as more timely decisions from a new system or enhanced employee learning and expertise, may also be overlooked in a traditional financial analysis (Ryan, Harrison, and Schkade, 2002).

10.5   Managing Project Risk

We have already introduced the topic of information system risks and risk assessment in Chapter 8. In this chapter, we describe the specific risks to information systems projects and show what can be done to manage them effectively.

Dimensions of Project Risk

Systems differ dramatically in their size, scope, level of complexity, and organizational and technical components. Some systems development projects are more likely to create the problems we have described earlier or to suffer delays because they carry a much higher level of risk than others. The level of project risk is influenced by project size, project structure, and the level of technical expertise of the information systems staff and project team.

Project size The larger the project—as indicated by the dollars spent, the size of the implementation staff, the time allocated for implementation, and the number of organizational units affected—the greater the risk. Very large-scale systems projects have a failure rate of 50 to 75 percent more than do other projects because large projects are more complex and difficult to control. The organizational complexity of the system—how many units and groups use it and how much it influences business processes—contribute to the complexity of large-scale systems projects just as much as technical characteristics, such as the number of lines of program code, length of project, and budget (Xia and Lee, 2004; Concours Group, 2000; Laudon, 1989). In addition, there are few reliable techniques for estimating the time and cost of developing large-scale information systems.

Project structure Some projects are more highly structured than others. Their requirements are clear and straightforward so outputs and processes can be easily defined. Users know exactly what they want and what the system should do; there is almost no possibility of the users changing their minds. Well-structured projects run a much lower risk than those with relatively undefined, fluid, and constantly changing requirements; with outputs that cannot be fixed easily because they are subject to users' changing ideas; or with users who cannot agree on what they want.

Experience with technology The project risk rises if the project team and the information system staff lack the required technical expertise. If the team is unfamiliar with the hardware, system software, application software, or database management system proposed for the project, it is highly likely that the project will experience technical problems or take more time to complete because of the need to master new skills.

Although the difficulty of the technology is one risk factor in information systems projects, the other factors are primarily organizational, dealing with the complexity of information requirements, the scope of the project, and how many parts of the organization will be affected by a new information system.

Risk Management and the IS Department

With the possibility of so much risk, whether from outsiders and insiders (see Chapter 8) or the technology itself failing, organizations need to exercise proper risk management when managing their information systems. Risk management includes the following steps: determining the possibility and probability of risk, identifying where risk could arise, evaluating how much a risk could cost the organization, deciding whether to respond to the risk, and then choosing whether to mitigate or eliminate the risk. There are policies and procedures as well as processes to help managers conduct proper risk management. In addition to using technology such as anti-virus software to help reduce or eliminate risk, proper project management techniques also help to mitigate against risk during systems development and implementation.

Change Management and the Concept of Implementation

The introduction or alteration of an information system has a powerful behavioural and organizational impact. Changes in the way that information is defined, accessed, and used to manage the organization's resources often lead to new distributions of authority and power. This internal organizational change breeds resistance and opposition and can lead to the demise of an otherwise good system.

A very large percentage of information systems projects stumble because the process of organizational change surrounding system development was not properly addressed. Successful system development requires careful **change management**, the management of organizational change associated with innovation such as the change management program implemented by HSBC that was discussed at the beginning of this chapter.

The Concept of Implementation To manage the organizational change surrounding the introduction of a new information system effectively, you must examine the process of implementation. **Implementation** refers to all organizational activities working toward the adoption, management, and routinization of an innovation, such as a new information system. In the implementation process, the systems analyst is a change agent. A **change agent** communicates with users, mediates between competing interest groups, and ensures that the organizational adjustment to such changes is complete. The analyst not only develops technical solutions but also redefines the configurations, interactions, job activities, and power relationships of various organizational groups. The analyst is the catalyst for the entire change process and is responsible for ensuring that all parties involved accept the changes created by a new system.

The Role of End Users System implementation generally benefits from high levels of user involvement and management support. User participation in the design and operation of information systems has several positive results. First, if users are heavily involved in systems design, they have more opportunities to mould the system according to their priorities and business requirements and more opportunities to control the outcome. Second, they are more likely to react positively to the completed system because they have been active participants in the change process and are more likely to feel a sense of ownership of the new system. Incorporating user knowledge and expertise leads to better solutions.

Change management

Implementation

Change agent

The relationship between users and information systems specialists has traditionally been a problem area for information systems implementation efforts. Users and information systems specialists tend to have different backgrounds, interests, and priorities. This is referred to as the **user-designer communications gap**. These differences lead to divergent organizational loyalties, approaches to problem solving, and vocabularies.

Information systems specialists, for example, often have a highly technical, or machine, orientation to problem solving. They look for elegant and sophisticated technical solutions in which hardware and software efficiency is optimized at the expense of ease of use or organizational effectiveness. Users prefer systems that are oriented toward solving business problems or facilitating organizational tasks. Often the orientations of both groups are so at odds that they appear to speak in different tongues.

These differences are illustrated in Table 10-4, which depicts the typical concerns of end users and technical specialists (information systems designers) regarding the development of a new information system. Communication problems between end users and designers are a major reason why user requirements are not properly incorporated into information systems and why users are driven out of the implementation process.

Systems development projects run a very high risk of failure when there is a pronounced gap between users and technical specialists and when these groups continue to pursue different goals. Under such conditions, users are often driven out of the implementation process. Because they cannot comprehend what the technicians are saying, users conclude that the entire project is best left in the hands of the information specialists alone.

Management Support and Commitment If an information systems project has the backing and commitment of management at various levels, it is more likely to be perceived positively by both users and the technical information services staff. Both groups will believe that their participation in the development process will receive higher-level attention and priority. They will be recognized and rewarded for the time and effort they devote to implementation. Management backing also ensures that a systems project receives sufficient funding and resources to be successful. Furthermore, to be enforced effectively, all the changes in work habits and procedures and any organizational realignments associated with a new system depend on management backing. If a manager considers a new system a priority, his or her subordinates will be more likely to treat the system that way.

Change Management Challenges for Business Process Reengineering, Enterprise Applications, and Mergers and Acquisitions Given the challenges of innovation and implementation, it is not surprising to find a very high failure rate among enterprise application and business process reengineering (BPR) projects, which typically require extensive organizational change and which may require replacing old technologies and legacy systems that are deeply rooted in many interrelated business processes. A number of studies have indicated that 70 percent of all business process reengineering projects fail to deliver promised benefits. Likewise, a high percentage of

User-designer communications gap

TABLE 10-4 *The User-Designer Communications Gap*

User Concerns	Designer Concerns
Will the system deliver the information I need for my work?	How much disk storage space will the master file consume?
How quickly can I access the data?	How many lines of program code will it take to perform this function?
How easily can I retrieve the data?	How can we cut down on CPU time when we run the system?
How much clerical support will I need to enter data into the system?	What is the most efficient way of storing the data?
How will the operation of the system fit into my daily business schedule?	What database management system should we use?

enterprise applications fail to be fully implemented or to meet the goals of their users even after three years of work.

Many enterprise application and reengineering projects have been undermined by poor implementation and change management practices that failed to address employees' concerns about change. Dealing with fear and anxiety throughout the organization; overcoming resistance by key managers; changing job functions, career paths, and recruitment practices; and training have posed greater threats to reengineering than the difficulties companies faced visualizing and designing breakthrough changes to business processes. All the enterprise applications require tighter coordination among different functional groups as well as extensive business process change (see Chapter 12).

Projects related to mergers and acquisitions have a similar failure rate. Mergers and acquisitions are deeply affected by the organizational characteristics of the merging companies as well as by their IT infrastructures. Combining the information systems of two different companies usually requires considerable organizational change and complex systems projects to manage. If the integration is not properly managed, firms can emerge with a tangled hodgepodge of inherited legacy systems developed by aggregating the systems of one firm after another. Without a successful systems integration, the benefits anticipated from the merger cannot be realized, or worse, the merged entity cannot execute its business processes and loses customers. The Window on Management section explores this topic.

Management | WINDOW ON MANAGEMENT

Managing IT in the Merger and Acquisition Game

Mergers and acquisitions (M&As) are on the rise in Canada. In the first three months of 2007, Ed Giacomellie of Crosbie & Co. counts 13 bids valued at more than $1 billion each. According to Giacomellie, "For the past seven quarters, we've been reporting activity of between 400 and 550 deals per quarter in Canada." "Due diligence" is the concept used to describe what acquirers should perform before they make an acquisition. Technically, for public firms, due diligence is a legal requirement of senior management to ensure the financial and business statements of firms they are acquiring are accurate and complete.

In the past, acquiring firms have lost a great deal of money by ignoring a very important element of the acquired firm's business, namely, its information systems. Because M&As are typically entered into for financial reasons (greater market share, elimination of competitors, greater efficiency and profitability), and are led by financial managers, it is understandable that sizing up the target company's IT infrastructure is last on the list of due diligence activities.

But there is a price to pay for ignoring the IT/IS element in mergers. There are a number of systems-related risks in M&As. The target company may have stopped spending on maintenance years ago to decrease costs and increase profits. It may have fallen behind competitors in new applications. Its software licences may not be transferable to the new company without significant new fees. The infrastructure may be outdated. The target company's systems may be totally incompatible with the acquirer's systems. For example, one important

reason Logicalis, a UK-based IT integration and consulting company, backed off acquiring a value-added reseller was that the company's customer relationship management system was incompatible with its own.

So how do companies perform due diligence in the information systems area? What are some management tactics for dealing with the merger of two or more very different IT infrastructures? The first step is to classify the assets your firm is about to acquire, create an inventory of these assets, and establish the value of these systems to the newly merged firm. For instance, you could divide the target firm's IT assets into four categories: transactional systems that perform the basic transactions of the firm; informational systems that inform management about the state of operations; strategic systems that differentiate the firm in the marketplace; and basic infrastructure that includes both the hardware and software installed as well as the services provided by the IS group to the business.

Once you have created an inventory of the target firm's IT assets, you will need to value their potential contribution to the new firm. There are four options: keep the target company systems if they are better than your own; keep your own systems and retire the target company systems if yours are better; choose the best of both companies' systems; or use the M&A to develop an entirely new infrastructure.

In general, firms rarely decide to develop a new infrastructure completely. Most commonly, the acquiring firms shut down systems of the acquired company and extend the reach of their own systems. Target firms are usually smaller and less capitalized than acquiring firms and have systems that lag behind those of the acquiring firm. Moreover, the financial rationale for many mergers is scale economies. The argument is that the existing IT/IS infrastructure of the acquiring firm can be expanded with minimal cost while the merged companies' revenues will increase many fold. The same fixed costs in infrastructure will be able to support a much larger and more profitable business.

But the evidence that managers at acquiring firms really understand the risks of mergers and acquisitions is not encouraging. Studies of M&A activity over the past 75 years show that about 60 percent actually destroy shareholder value and result in falling stock prices for the acquiring company. The reasons are that the acquiring firm overvalues the assets of the target firm and systematically underestimate the risks of the acquisition, especially the costs of merging the operational activities and information system infrastructures of two firms.

To Think About

1. What are some of the risks involved when one firm acquires another firm's IT infrastructure?

2. Why do firms often fail to take the target firm's information systems and IT infrastructure into account when purchasing other firms?

3. How would you go about assessing the value of another firm's IT infrastructure and operational capabilities? What questions would you ask?

MIS in Action

1. Bain and Company is one of the premiere international business consulting firms specializing in advice about mergers and acquisitions. Visit www.Bain.ca to learn about the company's Canadian operations, and explore the advice on the company's main Web site, www.bain.com, on how to conduct a successful merger by clicking on the "Consulting Expertise" tab, and then selecting "Mergers & Acquisitions." Read this page, then click on "Deals Done Right." Why does Bain advise managers to stay close to their "core business?" Why might this advice ease the change in information systems infrastructure when mergers take place? What does Bain recommend about "integration" of the business, and how would this affect IS/IT decisions?

2. On the Web, explore the IT/IS integration issues raised by one of these mega-mergers of the past few years: Great West Life/ Canada Life; Clarica/Sun Life; Toronto Dominion Bank/ Canada Trust Bank; UJF/Mitsubishi Tokyo Financial; HEXAL/ Novartis; or Kellogg/Keebler. You can explore these mergers using Google searches such as "Kellogg Keebler merger."

Sources: Eric Chabrow, "IT Plays Linchpin Role in High-Stakes M&As," *InformationWeek*, June 26, 2006; Spencer McIlmurray, "M&A Survival Kit: Relearning Enterprise Addition and Subtraction," *CIO Magazine*, October 24, 2006; Nick Moore, "The New Role of the CIO in M&A Due Diligence," Software Mag.com, July 2006; Dale Jackson, "You Can't Beat Barbarians, So Why Not Join the Invasion? A Money Manager Assesses Valuations to Predict Targets," *The Globe and Mail*, April 10, 2007; and "Canadian Corporate Takeovers That Made News," CBC.ca, www.cbc.ca/ news/background/mergers, accessed April 20, 2007.

Controlling Risk Factors

Various project management, requirements gathering, and planning methodologies have been developed for specific categories of implementation problems. Strategies have also been devised for ensuring that users play appropriate roles throughout the implementation period and for managing the organizational change process. Not all aspects of the implementation process can be easily controlled or planned. However, anticipating potential implementation problems and applying appropriate corrective strategies can increase the chances for system project success.

The first step in managing project risk involves identifying the nature and level of risk confronting the project (Schmidt, Lyytinen, Keil, and Cule, 2001). Implementers can then handle each project with the tools and risk-management approaches geared to its level of risk (Iversen, Mathiassen, and Nielsen, 2004; Barki, Rivard, and Talbot, 2001; McFarlan, 1981).

Managing Technical Complexity Projects with challenging and complex technology to master benefit from **internal integration tools**. The success of such projects depends on how well their technical complexity can be managed. Project leaders need both heavy technical and administrative experience. They must be able to anticipate problems and develop smooth working relationships among a predominantly technical team. The team should be under the leadership of a manager with a strong technical and project management background, and team members should be highly experienced. Team meetings should take place frequently. Essential technical skills or expertise not available internally should be secured from outside the organization.

Formal Planning and Control Tools Large projects benefit from appropriate use of **formal planning tools** and **formal control tools** for documenting and monitoring project

Internal integration tools
Formal planning tools
Formal control tools

plans. The two most commonly used methods for documenting project plans are Gantt charts and PERT charts. A **Gantt chart** lists project activities and their corresponding start and completion dates. The Gantt chart visually represents the timing and duration of different tasks in a development project as well as their human resource requirements (see Figure 10-10). It

Gantt chart

FIGURE 10-10 A Gantt chart

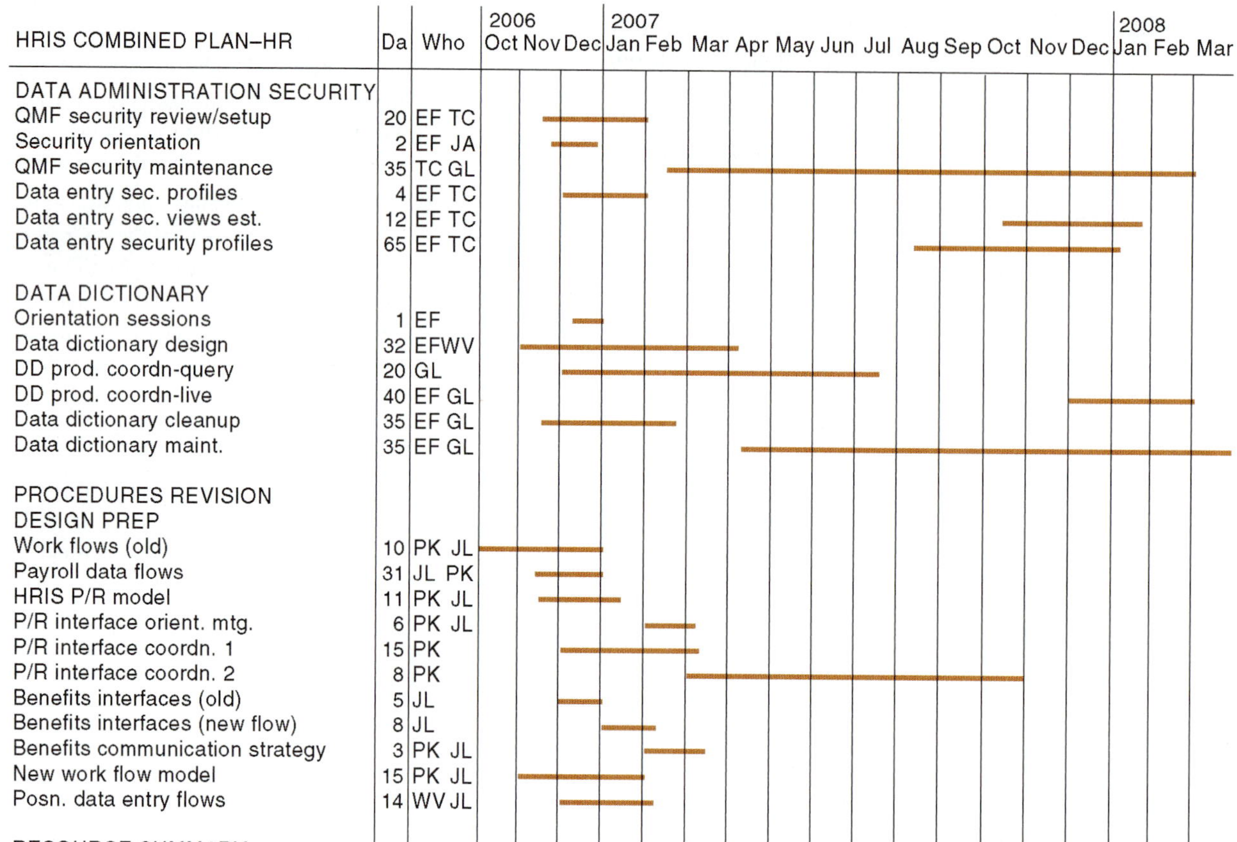

HRIS COMBINED PLAN–HR

Task	Da	Who
DATA ADMINISTRATION SECURITY		
QMF security review/setup	20	EF TC
Security orientation	2	EF JA
QMF security maintenance	35	TC GL
Data entry sec. profiles	4	EF TC
Data entry sec. views est.	12	EF TC
Data entry security profiles	65	EF TC
DATA DICTIONARY		
Orientation sessions	1	EF
Data dictionary design	32	EFWV
DD prod. coordn-query	20	GL
DD prod. coordn-live	40	EF GL
Data dictionary cleanup	35	EF GL
Data dictionary maint.	35	EF GL
PROCEDURES REVISION DESIGN PREP		
Work flows (old)	10	PK JL
Payroll data flows	31	JL PK
HRIS P/R model	11	PK JL
P/R interface orient. mtg.	6	PK JL
P/R interface coordn. 1	15	PK
P/R interface coordn. 2	8	PK
Benefits interfaces (old)	5	JL
Benefits interfaces (new flow)	8	JL
Benefits communication strategy	3	PK JL
New work flow model	15	PK JL
Posn. data entry flows	14	WV JL

RESOURCE SUMMARY (person-days per month; Oct–Dec = 2006, Jan–Dec = 2007, Jan–Mar = 2008)

Name	Rate	Init	Oct	Nov	Dec	Jan	Feb	Mar	Apr	May	Jun	Jul	Aug	Sep	Oct	Nov	Dec	Jan	Feb	Mar
Edith Farrell	5.0	EF	2	21	24	24	23	22	22	27	34	34	29	26	28	19	14			
Woody Vinton	5.0	WV	5	17	20	19	12	10	14	10	2							4	3	
Charles Pierce	5.0	CP		5	11	20	13	9	10	7	6	8	4	4	4	4	4			
Ted Leurs	5.0	TL		12	17	17	19	17	14	12	15	16	2	1	1	1	1			
Toni Cox	5.0	TC	1	11	10	11	11	12	19	19	21	21	21	17	17	12	9			
Patricia Knopp	5.0	PK	7	23	30	34	27	25	15	24	25	16	11	13	17	10	3	3	2	
Jane Lawton	5.0	JL	1	9	16	21	19	21	21	20	17	15	14	12	14	8	5			
David Holloway	5.0	DH	4	4	5	5	5	2	7	5	4	16	2							
Diane O'Neill	5.0	DO	6	14	17	16	13	11	9	4										
Joan Albert	5.0	JA	5	6			7	6	2	1				5	5	1				
Marie Marcus	5.0	MM	15	7	2	1	1													
Don Stevens	5.0	DS	4	4	5	4	5	1												
Casual	5.0	CASL		3	4	3			4	7	9	5	3	2						
Kathy Mendez	5.0	KM		1	5	16	20	19	22	19	20	18	20	11	2					
Anna Borden	5.0	AB					9	10	16	15	11	12	19	10	7	1				
Gail Loring	5.0	GL		3	6	5	9	10	17	18	17	10	13	10	10	7	17			
UNASSIGNED	0.0	X												9	236	225	230	14	13	
Co-op	5.0	CO		6	4				2	3	4	4	2	4	16			216	178	
Casual	5.0	CAUL									3	3	3							
TOTAL DAYS			49	147	176	196	194	174	193	195	190	181	140	125	358	288	284	237	196	12

The Gantt chart in this figure shows the task, person-days, and initials of each responsible person, as well as the start and finish dates for each task. The resource summary provides a manager with the total person-days for each month and for each person working on the project to manage the project successfully. The project described here is a data administration project.

shows each task as a horizontal bar whose length is proportional to the time required to complete it.

Although Gantt charts show when project activities begin and end, they do not depict task dependencies, how one task is affected if another is behind schedule, or how tasks should be ordered. That is where a PERT chart is useful. PERT stands for Program Evaluation and Review Technique, a methodology developed by the U.S. Navy during the 1950s to manage the Polaris submarine missile program. A **PERT chart** graphically depicts project tasks and their interrelationships. The PERT chart lists the specific activities that make up a project and the activities that must be completed before a specific activity can start, as illustrated in Figure 10-11.

The PERT chart portrays a project as a network diagram consisting of numbered nodes (either circles or rectangles) representing project tasks. Each node is numbered and shows the task, its duration, the starting date, and the completion date. The direction of the arrows on the lines indicates the sequence of tasks and shows which activities must be completed before the commencement of another activity.

This project team of professionals is using computing tools to enhance communication, analysis, and decision making.

PERT chart

FIGURE 10-11   A PERT chart

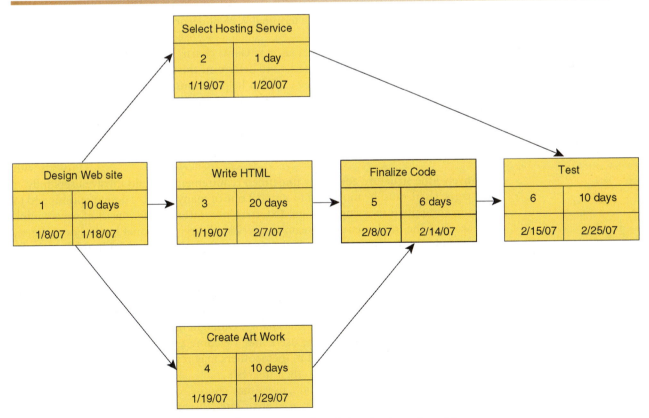

This is a simplified PERT chart for creating a small Web site. It shows the ordering of project tasks and the relationship of a task to preceding and succeeding tasks.

In Figure 10-11, the tasks in nodes 2, 3, and 4 are not dependent on one another and can be undertaken simultaneously, but each is dependent on completion of the first task. PERT charts for complex projects can be difficult to interpret, and project managers often use both techniques.

PERT charts are often used in the critical path method. The **Critical Path Method** **(CPM)**, also known as critical path analysis, is an algorithm used to schedule project activities. CPM is indispensable to good project management. It is used in many fields, such as research and development, construction, software, plant maintenance, and engineering. CPM can be used in any project with interdependent activities.

CPM involves making a model of the project with the following features:

1. A list of all project activities (a *Work Breakdown Structure*)
2. The duration of each activity
3. A list of dependencies between activities

CPM uses these three features to calculate the start and end times for each activity, determine which activities are mission critical, and reveal activities with "float time," i.e., those activities that are less critical. The sequence of critical activities is called the critical path. Project managers can determine through CPM which activities require ensuring that deadlines are met and which activities have a certain amount of slack time if needed.

One fundamental project management technique is work breakdown structure. A **Work Breakdown Structure (WBS)** uses a hierarchical tree structure to define and organize a project's full scope. The root node and Level 2 of the WBS tree structure define planned outcomes that represent 100 percent of the project scope. The children nodes also represent 100 percent of their parent node's scope. One feature of an effective WBS is that it describes planned outcomes (i.e., desired end results) rather than planned actions. Outcomes may be accurately predicted, whereas actions are part of the project plan and can be hard to predict. Another feature of a good WBS is that it facilitates the assignment of a project activity to a terminal WBS node, or the lowest level of activity that cannot be further subdivided.

Project management techniques such as Gantt charts, PERT charts, CPM, and WBS can help managers identify bottlenecks and determine the impact that problems will have on project completion times. They can also help systems developers partition projects into smaller, more manageable segments with defined, measurable business results. Standard control techniques can successfully chart the progress of the project against budgets and target dates, so deviations from the plan can be spotted.

Increasing User Involvement and Overcoming User Resistance

Increasing User Involvement and Overcoming User Resistance Projects with relatively little structure and many undefined requirements should involve users fully at all stages. Users must be mobilized to support one of many possible design options and to remain committed to a single design. **External integration tools** consist of ways to link the work of the implementation team to users at all organizational levels. For instance, users can become active members of the project team, take on leadership roles, and take charge of installation and training. The implementation team can demonstrate its responsiveness to users, promptly answering questions, incorporating user feedback, and showing their willingness to help (Gefen and Ridings, 2002).

Participation in implementation activities may not be enough to overcome the problem of user resistance to organizational change. Different users may be affected by the system in different ways. While some users may welcome a new system because it brings changes they perceive as beneficial to them, others may resist these changes because they believe the shifts are detrimental to their interests.

If the use of a system is voluntary, users may choose to avoid it; if use is mandatory, resistance will take the form of increased error rates, disruptions, turnover, and even sabotage. Therefore, the implementation strategy must not only encourage user participation and involvement, but it must also address the issue of counterimplementation (Keen,

Critical Path Method (CPM)

Work Breakdown Structure (WBS)

External integration tools

1981). **Counterimplementation** is a deliberate strategy to thwart the implementation of an information system or an innovation in an organization.

Strategies to overcome user resistance include user participation (to elicit commitment as well as to improve design), user education and training, management edicts and policies, and better incentives for users who cooperate. The new system can be made more user friendly by improving the end-user interface. Users will be more cooperative if organizational problems are solved prior to introducing the new system.

The Window on Organizations section illustrates how one company used these techniques to build user support for a new customer relationship management system (CRM). CRM system projects often encounter user resistance because they typically require marketing and sales staff to share information and change the way they work.

Counterimplementation

 # WINDOW ON ORGANIZATIONS

Getting Buy-In and ROI for CRM

The idea behind CRM seems simple enough: to centralize and share throughout the firm information about customers in order to maximize sales and profitability. For a variety of reasons—most having to do with implementation issues—achieving these objectives proves difficult.

Consider the case of Wallace, Welch & Willingham (WWW), a Florida-based insurance company. The firm decided to purchase a contemporary CRM system after its existing patchwork of file cards, rolodexes, and accounting packages failed to produce a coherent view of the customer. The job of implementing went to the IT Director, Kirstin Johnson. The firm has two lines of business: commercial and residential insurance, and a 20-person sales force. Each of the sales representatives kept their own customer information on index cards, and sales information was stored on their personal spreadsheets and then uploaded to an accounting application when sales were finally booked and payments received. There was no ability to share information. Sales representatives were paid on commission and received a percentage of the annual insurance revenue.

When sales people left the firm, they took the customer information with them, or just left it in their desks. The sales manager would assign a few sale representatives to search through the empty desks of departed employees to find potential "workable leads."

In the search for a vendor, Johnson faced two barriers: finding the right vendor and understanding the costs before committing to a single vendor. She spent several weeks interviewing CRM users in other firms to identify which vendors were most respected.

Cost was another matter: it was painfully difficult to figure out how much licensing a system would really cost in day-to-day use. There were per-seat models, pay-for-use models, and hosted "on-demand" solutions where you paid by the month depending on how much your sales force used the system.

She finally went with the on-demand solution because it did not involve installing any new software or hardware at WWW and seemed the least expensive way to go. The main vendors were Sage CRM's SalesLogix and salesforce.com. Ultimately, she chose SalesLogix because it allowed her a choice: she could start with an on-demand, online model and then later install the system on in-house servers if that became less expensive and more suitable.

Getting buy-in from the sales force was the most difficult barrier to implementation. For starters, she shut down the ability of sales people to use the accounting system for entering customer information, and forced them to enter customer data and establish files for all their customers on the SalesLogix system. If sales people did not file their customer prospecting information on the new system, it was assumed they were not doing their jobs, and this would show up in bi-annual performance reviews. Her logic was "If there's no driving force behind using the system, people can just ignore it."

Staff resistance sprung up immediately. Sales representatives worried their information would be lost on another firm's Web site; they felt the system could not handle all the information they wanted to put in it; many felt the system would "blow up" someday if SalesLogix went out of business or was purchased by another firm. The firm's largest revenue producing sales representative refused to use the new system. Instead, he printed out customer notes using a word processor and distributed them to other sales representatives. He created his own manual paper-based CRM! When other representatives saw this, they asked, "Why should I use the new system?" Everyone wanted to continue doing their own thing.

Recognizing that sales representatives do not like to take orders from the IT department, and that sales representatives in many firms are the major producers of revenue whom no one wants to disturb, Johnson called out to the sales manager for help. The sales manager was sympathetic and told the recalcitrant user to either use the SalesLogix system or face severe consequences. After that, the leading revenue-producing sales representative started using the system and in fact became its champion supporter.

After a year of training, educating, and cajoling, the implementation effort finally achieved its ambition of centralizing customer information, and creating a platform where the information could be shared and where it was protected from high turnover in the sales force. Customer information was, for the first time, information that belonged to the firm, not the sales representatives. This in itself was quite a revolution.

But other worries remain for Johnson and the firm. As system use goes up, so do costs, and it has been difficult to put a hard number on the benefits of information integration. How do you measure the benefits of CRM: the number of prospects contacted, sales made, customers retained, size of purchase, or some other metric? Not knowing ahead of time how you measure success often makes it difficult after the fact to claim success. How much is it worth for the firm to actually "own" the customer information and control it? Is this priceless, or is it just a nice thing?

For most enterprise implementations, the cost of implementing is typically two to three times the cost of the software and hardware. Once initial implementation is achieved, it does not end; instead there needs to be an ongoing training and education effort to explain new features and to ensure real value is produced for the firm. There are also concerns about vendors: what if the chosen vendor is not financially stable and you need to switch to another? The switching costs of enterprise software can be quite high. Eventually, the firm would like to integrate the information in the SalesLogix system with the sales information in the older financial accounting system, but there is no inexpensive way to do this.

To Think About

1. Why was the director of IT assigned the job of implementing a CRM system? Would the sales manager better perform this job?

2. Why were sales representatives reluctant to share customer information with other sales representatives? What strategies did Kirstin Johnson use to overcome user resistance? How would you recommend the firm overcome this problem?

3. What do you think the metrics for CRM success should be in a firm like this? How would you change the sales representative compensation plan to support more effective use of the CRM system?

MIS in Action

1. Go to the Sage CRM SalesLogix Web site at www.saleslogix .com. Explore the product description for SalesLogix. What kinds of firms is this product aimed at? What kinds of functionality are provided in the suite of SalesLogix programs? What is the advantage of a hosted solution versus an on-demand solution?

2. At the SalesLogix Web site, explore the company's mobile solutions by playing the mobile solution Flash demo. How could firms take advantage of SalesLogix mobile solutions? What are some of the risks of a mobile solution?

3. On the SalesLogix Web site, identify and review a success case study (usually displayed on the home page). What are the major themes emphasized in the case?

Sources: Colin Beasty, "Barriers to CRM Success," *CRM Magazine*, May 1, 2006; Susannah Patton, "Customer Service: Answering the Call," *CIO Magazine*, June 1, 2006; and Bill Donlan, "Anatomy of a Successful CRM Implementation," CIOupdate.com, July 11, 2005.

Although systems analysis and design activities are supposed to include an organizational impact analysis, this area has traditionally been neglected. An **organizational impact analysis** explains how a proposed system will affect organizational structure, attitudes, decision making, and operations. To integrate information systems successfully with the organization, thorough and fully documented organizational impact assessments must be given more attention in the development effort.

Designing for the Organization

Because the purpose of a new system is to improve the organization's performance, information systems projects must explicitly address the ways in which the organization will change when the new system is installed, including installation of intranets, extranets, and Web applications. In addition to procedural changes, transformations in job functions, organizational structure, power relationships, and the work environment should be carefully planned.

Organizational impact analysis

TABLE 10-5 *Organizational Factors in Systems Planning and Implementation*

Employee Participation and Involvement

Job design

Standards and performance monitoring

Ergonomics (including equipment, user interfaces, and the work environment)

Employee grievance resolution procedures

Health and safety

Government regulatory compliance

Areas where users interface with the system require special attention, with sensitivity to ergonomics issues. **Ergonomics** refers to the interaction of people and machines in the work environment. It considers the design of jobs, health issues, and the end-user interface of information systems. Table 10-5 lists the organizational dimensions that must be addressed when planning and implementing information systems.

Sociotechnical Design One way of addressing human and organizational issues is to incorporate sociotechnical design practices into information systems projects. Designers set forth separate sets of technical and social design solutions. The social design plans explore different workgroup structures, allocation of tasks, and the design of individual jobs. The proposed technical solutions are compared with the proposed social solutions. The solution that best meets both social and technical objectives is selected for the final design. The resulting **sociotechnical design** is expected to produce an information system that blends technical efficiency with sensitivity to organizational and human needs, leading to higher job satisfaction and productivity.

Project Management Software Tools

Commercial software tools that automate many aspects of project management facilitate the project management process. Project management software typically features capabilities for defining and ordering tasks, assigning resources to tasks, establishing starting and ending dates to tasks, tracking progress, and facilitating modifications to tasks and resources. Many automate the creation of Gantt and PERT charts.

Some of these tools are large, sophisticated programs for managing very large projects, dispersed work groups, and enterprise functions. These high-end tools can manage very large numbers of tasks and activities and complex relationships.

Microsoft Project has become the most widely used project management software today. It is PC-based, with capabilities for producing PERT and Gantt charts and for supporting critical path analysis, resource allocation, project tracking, and status reporting. Project Guide wizards are available to assist users in defining a project, listing tasks, setting deadlines, specifying workers and associated costs, choosing calendar templates, and saving a baseline version of the project plan. Project also tracks the way changes in one aspect of a project affect others.

Microsoft Project now has an Enterprise Project Management Solution version with a server component that helps large enterprises manage projects in many different locations. Project also provides a Web-based front end so that users can work with Web browser software to add project resources. Products such as EasyProjects.NET and Vertabase are also useful for firms that want Web-based project management tools.

Ergonomics

Sociotechnical design

Summary

1. Understand the various components of information resource management and the issues involved in each component.

The IS department may be structured in any of several ways: centralized as its own department, decentralized within other departments, or with personnel located both centrally and in various information service units and information centres. The CIO and MIS Steering Committee set IS policies and prioritize and review major projects. IS planning takes place at the strategic, tactical, and operational levels and should be aligned with organizational strategy at each level.

Systems development actually involves a number of IS personnel roles and includes the staff assignments to various projects as well as ensuring that security issues are addressed. IS personnel must be recruited, hired, retained, and evaluated and must be permitted to keep their skill sets up to date. Like every other department in an organization, the IS department must set a budget, which is difficult given the trend toward rapidly changing technology and escalating IS personnel salaries.

2. Identify and describe the objectives of project management and why it is so essential in developing information systems.

A high percentage of information systems projects take more time and money to implement than originally anticipated or are delivered with missing functionality. Good project management is essential for ensuring that systems are delivered on time and on budget and provide genuine business benefits. Project management activities include planning the work, assessing the risk, estimating and acquiring resources required to accomplish the work, organizing the work, directing execution, and analyzing the results. Project management must deal with five major variables: scope, time, cost, quality, and risk.

3. Compare models for selecting and evaluating information systems projects and methods for aligning IS projects with the firm's business goals.

Organizations need to identify and select IS projects that best support their business goals. They need an information systems plan that describes how information technology supports the attainment of their business goals and documents all their system applications and IT infrastructure components. Large corporations will have a management structure to ensure the most important systems projects receive priority. Once strategic analyses have determined the overall direction of systems development, enterprise analysis, critical success factors, portfolio analysis, and scoring models can be used to identify and evaluate alternative information systems projects.

4. Evaluate models for assessing the business value of information systems.

Information systems provide business value for a firm in many different ways, including increased profitability and productivity. Some, but not all, of these business benefits can be quantified and measured. Capital budgeting models are used to determine whether an investment in information technology produces sufficient returns to justify its costs. The principal capital budgeting models for evaluating systems projects are the payback method, accounting rate of return on investment (ROI), net present value, and internal rate of return (IRR). Real options pricing models, which apply the same techniques used for valuing financial options to systems investments, can be useful when considering highly uncertain IT investments.

5. Analyze the principal risk factors in information systems projects.

The level of risk in a systems development project is determined by three key dimensions: (1) project size, (2) project structure, and (3) experience with technology. A very large percentage of information systems fail to deliver benefits or solve the problems for which they were intended because the process of organizational change surrounding system development was not properly addressed. IS projects are more likely to fail when there is insufficient or improper user participation in the systems development process, lack of management support, and poor management of the implementation process. There is a very high failure rate among business process reengineering and enterprise application projects because they require extensive organizational change that is often resisted by members of the organization. System changes resulting from mergers and acquisitions are also difficult to implement successfully because they usually require far-reaching changes to business processes.

6. Select appropriate strategies for managing project risk and system implementation.

Developing an information system is a process of planned organizational change that must be carefully managed. The term implementation refers to the entire process of organizational change surrounding the introduction of a new information system. Especially important is the relationship between participants in the implementation process, notably the interactions between system designers and users. Eliciting user support and maintaining an appropriate level of user involvement at all stages of system development are essential.

Management support and control of the implementation process are essential, as are mechanisms for dealing with the level of risk in each new systems project. Project risk factors can be brought under some control by a contingency approach to project management. The risk level of each project determines the appropriate mix of external integration tools, internal integration tools, formal planning tools, and formal control tools to be applied. Appropriate strategies can be applied to ensure the correct level of user participation in the systems development process and to minimize user resistance. Information systems design and the entire implementation process should be managed as planned organizational change. Sociotechnical design aims for an optimal blend of social and technical design solutions.

Key Terms

Accounting rate of return on investment (ROI), 352
Capital budgeting, 349
Change agent, 356
Change management, 356
Chief information officer (CIO), 337
Counterimplementation, 363
Critical path method (CPM), 362
Critical success factors (CSFs), 346
Data entry operators, 338
Enterprise analysis, 344
Ergonomics, 365
External integration tools, 362
Formal control tools, 359
Formal planning tools, 359

Gantt chart, 360
Implementation, 356
Information resource management (IRM), 336
Information systems plan, 344
Intangible benefits, 349
Internal integration tools, 359
Internal rate of return (IRR), 354
MIS steering committee, 337
Net present value (NPV), 354
Network managers, 338
Organizational impact analysis, 364
Payback method, 351
PERT chart, 361

Portfolio analysis, 347
Present value, 353
Project, 342
Project management, 342
Real options pricing models (ROPMs), 354
Scope, 342
Scoring model, 348
Sociotechnical design, 365
Systems operators, 338
Tangible benefits, 349
User-designer communications gap, 357
User interface, 342
Work breakdown structure (WBS), 362

Review Questions

1. *Name and describe the components involved in information resource management.*

2. *Compare the role of the CIO with that of the MIS steering committee.*

3. *Name and describe the types or levels of IS planning.*

4. *Name and describe the various roles IS personnel have in the IS department.*

5. *Why is project management so important for information systems projects?*

6. *What kinds of information systems problems result from poor project management?*

7. *What is project management? List and describe the project management activities and variables addressed by project management.*

8. *Name and describe the groups responsible for the management of information systems projects.*

9. *What are the major categories of an information systems plan?*

10. *How can enterprise analysis and critical success factors be used for selecting information systems projects?*

11. *Describe how portfolio analysis and scoring models can be used to select information systems projects.*

12. *List and describe the major costs and benefits of information systems. What is the difference between tangible and intangible benefits?*

13. *Name and describe the principal capital budgeting methods used to evaluate information system projects.*

14. *How can real options pricing models help evaluate information technology investments?*

15. *What are the limitations of financial models for establishing the value of information systems?*

16. *What dimensions influence the level of risk in each information systems project?*

17. *Why do developers of new information systems need to address change management?*

18. *What is implementation and counterimplementation?*

19. *Why is eliciting support of management and end users so essential for successful implementation of information systems projects? What is the user-designer communications gap?*

20. *Why is there such a high failure rate among enterprise application implementations and business process reengineering (BPR) projects? What role do information systems play in the success or failure of mergers and acquisitions?*

21. *What project management techniques can be used to control project risk?*

22. *What organizational considerations should be addressed by information systems planning and implementation?*

23. *How do project management software tools contribute to successful project managment?*

Discussion Questions

1. *How much does project management impact the success of a new information system?*

2. *It has been said that most systems fail because systems developers ignore organizational behaviour problems. Why might this be so?*

3. *It has been said that an IS department is different from other organizational departments and should be treated differently as well. Discuss this viewpoint.*

4. *Why can it be difficult to estimate the value that a new information system can have for an organization? What can be done to make this process easier and its outcome more accurate?*

Teamwork: Identifying Implementation Problems

Form a group with two or three other students. Write a description of the implementation problems you might expect to encounter in one of the systems described in the chapter-opening or chapter-ending cases in this text.

Write an analysis of the steps you would take to solve or prevent these problems. If possible, use electronic presentation software to present your findings to the class.

Learning Track Module

Information Technology Investments and Productivity. Increases in business productivity from information technology investments have been difficult to measure. The

Learning Track Module on this topic describes why this is so. You can find it on MyMISLab for this chapter.

For online exercises, please visit www.pearsoned.ca/mymislab.

HANDS-ON MIS   Application Exercises

The projects in this section give you hands-on experience using spreadsheet software to perform capital budgeting

analyses for new information systems investments and using Web tools to analyze the financing for a new home.

Improving Decision Making:
Using Spreadsheet Software to Analyze the Return on a New System Investment

Software skills: Spreadsheet formulas and functions
Business skills: Capital budgeting

This project provides you with an opportunity to use spreadsheet software and the capital budgeting models discussed in this chapter to analyze the return on a new information system investment for a real-world company.

Dirt Bikes Canada's management would like to analyze the return on its investment in its employee training and skills tracking system described in Chapter 9.

The system runs on the human resources specialists' PCs using PC database software. Because the entire corporate administrative staff recently received new desktop PC systems with database and other productivity software, there are no additional hardware and software purchase costs. The main costs include the initial cost of designing and implementing the database (business staff cost of $5000; information systems staff cost of $15 000), gathering and adding employee skills and training data to the database ($5500 initial data conversion cost plus $1000 annual data entry costs), and ongoing maintenance and support ($3000 annually). Human resources staff members believe the new application could save each of them two hours of work per week. (Their annual salaries are $37 000 and $42 000 each.) The company would also save about $11 000 annually in employee recruiting costs because it would be able to fill many vacant positions with existing employees, thereby reducing its costs for recruiting outside the company. The system would not be installed until the end of 2009 and would return benefits from 2010 to 2014.

1. Prepare a report for management analyzing the return on the investment for this system over a five-year period using the following capital budgeting models: net present value, ROI, IRR, and payback method. Assume a 5 percent interest rate for your net present value calculations. Use spreadsheet software for your calculations.

2. (Optional) Use electronic presentation software to summarize your findings for management.

Improving Decision Making:
Using Spreadsheet Software for Capital Budgeting for a New CAD System

Software skills: Spreadsheet formulas and functions
Business skills: Capital budgeting

This project provides you with an opportunity to use spreadsheet software to use the capital budgeting models discussed in this chapter to analyze the return on an investment for a new computer-aided design (CAD) system.

Your company would like to invest in a new CAD system that requires purchasing hardware, software, and networking technology, as well as expenditures for installation, training, and support. MyMISLab for Chapter 10 contains tables showing each cost component for the new system as well

as annual maintenance costs over a five-year period. You believe the new system will produce annual savings by reducing the amount of labour required to generate designs and design specifications, thus increasing your firm's annual cash flow.

1. Using the data provided in these tables, create a worksheet that calculates the costs and benefits of the investment over a five-year period and analyzes the investment using the four capital budgeting models presented in this chapter.

2. Is this investment worthwhile? Why or why not?

Improving Decision Making:
Using Web Tools for Buying and Financing a Home

Software skills: Internet-based software
Business skills: Financial planning

This project will develop your skills using Web-based software for searching for a home and calculating mortgage financing for that home.

You have found a new job in Saint John, New Brunswick, and would like to purchase a home in that area. Ideally, you would like to find a single-family house with at least three bedrooms and one bathroom that costs between $150 000 and $225 000 and you want to finance it with a 30-year fixed rate mortgage. You can afford a down payment that is 20 percent of the value of the house. Before you purchase a house, you would like to find out what homes are available in your price range, find a mortgage, and determine the amount of your monthly payment. You would also like to see how much of your mortgage payment represents principal and how much represents interest. Use the Multiple Listing Service (www.mls.ca) site to help you with the following tasks:

1. Locate homes in your price range in Saint John, New Brunswick. Find out as much information as you can about the houses, including the real estate listing agent, condition of the house, number of rooms, and school district.

2. Find a mortgage for 80 percent of the list price of the home. Compare rates from at least three sites. (Use search engines to find sites other than MLS.)

3. After selecting a mortgage, calculate your closing costs.

4. Calculate the monthly payment for the mortgage you select.

5. Calculate how much of your monthly mortgage payment represents principal and how much represents interest, assuming you do not plan to make any extra payments on the mortgage.

6. When you are finished, assess the ease of use of the site and your ability to find information about houses and mortgages; the breadth of choice of homes and mortgages; and how helpful the whole process would have been for you if you were actually in the situation described in this project.

CASE STUDY Cargo Portal Services Brings Competitors Together

We have seen how UPS, Federal Express, and several other companies have taken advantage of the World Wide Web and the Internet to improve customer service and lower customer costs. By permitting customers to book online—and even be billed online—these companies have offered smaller shipping customers greatly improved service while lowering their own and their customers' costs.

Another company that is using the Web and Internet to its advantage is Cargo Portal Services (CPS), a company owned and run by Unisys, the computer manufacturer and consulting firm. CPS is an electronic booking and shipment management service for the air cargo industry. It was designed in cooperation with major carriers and forwarders (companies that arrange for the shipment of freight for other companies with which they have contracted). Access to CPS is free for forwarders through the Internet and through secure system-to-system connections. CPS serves more than 3333 branch offices of 1635 forwarding companies in 67 countries.

CPS is the first full-service Internet portal for the air cargo industry. It provides booking facilities, Cargo 2000 proactive shipment event management, and computer system-to-system communications. (Cargo 2000 is an interest group of 30 major airlines, freight forwarders and ground handling agents. Its goal is to implement a new quality management system for the worldwide air cargo industry and thereby improve its efficiency.) Pro-active shipment event management permits shippers and receivers to be notified of "events," such as delays during shipping.

Air cargo has struggled to enter the Internet age. Web-based solutions for booking space and managing shipments have either failed due to unrealistic visions or have been slowed down by complex IT integration issues. A major problem is the wide range of different legacy systems in use by airlines and their freight forwarder customers. Booking procedures also vary from airline to airline. Personal relationships remain important, preventing new technology take-up.

Three airlines—Northwest Airlines, United Airlines, and Air Canada—decided to break through that barrier. Putting aside their commercial rivalry, they agreed on an approach for a Web-based booking and shipment management system. In May 2002, they asked Unisys to create one. Unisys had an advantage in that it offered experience in the realities of the cargo business. Its air cargo system was used by two of the carriers, and Unisys had valuable Web development and integration expertise from other projects.

Once Unisys was appointed, the process of refining requirements was worked on intensively. The original broad design had to be refined into detailed specifications, a three-month process that required further setting aside of competitive issues and differences by the three carriers. The result was that before a line of code was written, the exact functionality of the portal had been clearly defined. "This was the most challenging aspect of the project," said Unisys project manager Dave Fischer.

Cost and speed were key factors in the implementation of CPS. With a rival platform already up and running, the three carriers were keen to bring their solution to market very quickly. After September 11, 2001, investments had also been slashed in the airline industry. Luckily, Unisys could draw on its existing air cargo solutions and expertise, and CPS was able to go live just six months after Unisys was appointed.

The big challenge was to devise a system that could work with the different procedures among airlines. These included not just divergent booking procedures but different attitudes to pricing. It was also important to create a solution that would be acceptable to other carriers. "Forwarders don't want to go to a large number of carrier sites; they want one portal they can use to book across airlines," said Mark Haeussler, director of cargo strategic planning and business development at United Airlines. The site had to make adoption easy for other carriers that would join after the portal went live.

The technology decisions made in implementing CPS were not unduly complex. XML was chosen because it was the best way to connect the portal with the diverse systems in the air cargo industry and allowed for future customization. "There is now recognition among carriers that XML is the way forward, even if they are progressing at different speeds," said Steve Schuppenhauer, Unisys technical architect. "We are taking advantage of that trend and driving it forward."

An object-oriented approach was also adopted to reuse existing modules from other Unisys projects. Other key technologies were a Weblogic server and a multitiered architecture using J2EE. This open approach was key, as one of the three launch carriers, United Airlines Cargo, used an in-house-developed cargo system that gave the development team an important test bed for their interface solutions.

Throughout the project implementation, the three carriers remained closely involved, each taking on project roles and holding weekly development meetings with Unisys. Forwarders—the users of the system, and the key to its success or failure—were also involved at all stages. "Early on we focused on a clear set of requirements," said Jim Friedel, president of NorthWest Airlines Cargo. "We hammered down our different wish lists to something achievable. That is a key reason why the project was able to succeed."

Involvement of forwarders also dated back to the early days of the project. A group of nine forwarders of varying sizes and scope had been consulted by the three carriers when drawing up their original plans. They continued to participate fully in the specification and development phases through a series of meetings and test sessions. This involvement was important to minimize the amount of reworking needed during the test phase. Glitches were ironed out at an early stage, and customer views were reflected in the final design.

Ideas from forwarders resulted in several enhancements to CPS. The most important was a function whereby multiple bookings could be loaded into the portal to reflect the way business often needs to be done. This functionality was incorporated into the launch version.

The real importance of forwarder participation came when the system went live in January 2003. The biggest barrier CPS had to overcome in the industry at large was a resistance to new technology: Front-line staff in forwarder offices remained fond of traditional booking methods such as the phone and fax.

Their solution was to undertake exhaustive testing of CPS' functionality with an advisory group of 10 forwarders throughout the development process. Too often, the real users are ignored when systems are being developed. CPS ensured that the portal was offering what booking staff needed and in the way that they needed it.

To save costs and speed up adoption, it was also important to minimize the need to train forwarder staff. "If you put the system in front of them, they should be able to use it straightaway," said Air Canada's manager of cargo marketing, sales planning and support, Gerald Simpson, who took charge of training for the portal. Early tests were successful. "After demonstration sessions in October and November 2002, we asked forwarders what training they needed," recalls Simpson. "They said that they were comfortable, after one viewing, that they could tell the rest of their staff how it worked."

The usability issue was the key to CPS' success. Advising the project throughout was Sam Racine, a Unisys usability expert who has a doctorate in interface design. Racine's focus on making sure the system helped users to do their jobs quickly and simply kept costs down by eliminating potential glitches at an early stage and reduced the amount of testing and reworking needed later.

Several usability issues arose during testing. One issue was the need to eliminate the mouse in site navigation. Screens were also made as comprehensive as possible, with minimal need to click through multiple screens. Care was also taken to include comprehensive information under help buttons in order to make new and existing users self-sufficient.

"The feedback we got is that the system is easy to understand and simple to use. People are at ease with it," said Simpson. Asked how he will know if the site is working, he added: "When forwarders start ringing up other carriers and saying 'get on this system too.'"

For Friedel, CPS represents a case study in successful project management. "Success was all about the people on the project team and the way they took decisions. We avoided transformational technology. We did not try and rebuild institutions—just to substitute technology for what is currently done by phone. Most of all, we kept the design simple for users. With a vision that simple and the team approach to the technical aspects, the odds of success were 100 percent."

Since opening the portal in 2003, CPS continues to increase functionality. In 2004, CPS added a template for recurring bookings and for waybill processing.

A waybill is a receipt for shipped goods. CPS introduced house waybill services in response to the new United States Customs and Border Patrol four-hour ruling. The ruling requires that airlines and forwarders provide the house waybill details of shipments no less than four hours in advance of flights arriving into the U.S. If this information is not provided to U.S. Customs, shipments will be delayed, often creating a domino effect because more than one flight segment may be required before a shipment arrives at its final destination.

Currently, most airlines receive house waybill data electronically via the industry standard consolidation list (FHL) message. Otherwise, they must manually enter the data into their cargo operational system using paper given to them by the forwarder. To save carriers data entry effort, and to help those small- to medium-sized forwarders who are unable to send the FHL message, CPS offers three ways in which carriers and forwarders can use the new house waybill service: via the Web, through an XML system-to-system interface with forwarder systems, or through an EDI-Internet interface.

CPS's new template for recurring bookings is called "recycle booking." It gives users an easy way to submit their permanent or recurring bookings. Previously, if a booking was repeated daily or weekly, all booking data needed to be re-entered from scratch. The CPS recycle booking service allows the user to store booking data in a template that can be used for a single recurring booking or an entire week of recurring bookings. Using the recycle booking service, a forwarder can quickly and accurately get confirmations for its consolidation allocations.

CPS opened for business in 2003 with only three carriers (Air Canada, United, and Northwest). To date, CPS offers transportation services from 430 cities in 117 countries through the global cargo networks of Air Canada, Austrian Airlines, KLM, Northwest Airlines, United Airlines, Continental Airlines, and American Airlines. CPS continues to add airline partners and freight forwarder clients to its portal. As can be seen by the recent introduction of additional service. CPS is attempting to be the "go-to" air cargo portal.

Sources: "Cargo Portal Services Launches Two New Services," *Enterprise Networks and Servers,* October 2004; Unisys, "Multi-carrier Web-Based Booking for Air Cargo," available **www.unisys.com/ transportation/clients/featured_case_studies/ northwest_airlines_c0_united_ airlines_and_air_canada_ case_study.htm** (accessed May 22, 2005); and "American Airlines Cargo to Join Unisys-Operated Cargo Portal Services," *Logistics Management,* May 2, 2005.

CASE STUDY QUESTIONS

1. How important are information systems for the air cargo industry?

2. Using the categories of the causes of system failure described in this chapter, classify and describe the problems CPS faced in trying to develop and launch its systems.

3. What management, organization, and technology factors caused the problems identified in question 2?

4. Evaluate the risks and key risk factors in implementing the air cargo portal project.

5. Originally, Air Canada was the only non-U.S. airline involved in CPS. Do you think it was a wise decision for Air Canada to proceed with the CPS project, or should they have let others be the guinea pigs for this project? Why do you feel that way?

6. What financial measures and justifications do you think were used in deciding how to proceed with this project?

Managing Global Systems

After completing this chapter, you will be able to do the following:

1. Identify the major factors driving the internationalization of business.
2. Compare strategies for developing global businesses.
3. Demonstrate how information systems can support different global business strategies.
4. Identify the challenges posed by global information systems and management solutions.
5. Evaluate the issues and technical alternatives to be considered when developing international information systems.

OPENING **CASE** | Think Global, Act Local: DHL Builds a Global IT Organization

Servicing more than 140 000 destinations in more than 220 countries with overnight and express package deliveries poses a unique problem: How do you work in very unique local environments, with different languages, cultures, and local knowledge while at the same time delivering this service on a global, time-intense platform? This is the question facing DHL, a logistics and parcel delivery business with worldwide operations. Founded in 1969 by Adrian Dalsey, Larry Hillblom, and Robert Lynn (the source of D, H, and L), DHL began as a service shuttling bills of lading between San Francisco and Honolulu. Now owned by Deutsche Post World Net, DHL operates a global system of 4400 local offices, 238 gateways, and more than 450 hubs, warehouses, and terminals. The company employs more than 170 000 people. The company offers 4.2 million customers worldwide

fast, reliable, and cost-efficient package delivery service around the world. More than 400 aircraft operate for or on behalf of DHL. Keeping track of its own operations, in addition to customer packages, is a major challenge for DHL.

For DHL, acting locally means that customers and employees can see on their computer screens information in their local language on their packages, databases contain important country regulations, and local information is current. Acting globally means that DHL computer systems around the world can check on the status and location of any DHL package and have that information be current and accurate within minutes of an event happening. If the information is delayed even more than a few seconds, or is wrong, scanners cannot operate, planes fly empty, and packages remain in warehouses.

Originally, DHL solved this problem by developing more than 50 different data centres in each of the major countries where it operated and by coordinating these loosely with a common set of core database applications that were installed in each of the countries. The core applications sat on top of a messaging and communications network so information could transfer from one country to another. The core applications included a master common shipment database that kept the tracking information, as well as e-mail programs, customer shipment, transit times, and billing details. The global databases allowed local countries' units to see only the data needed locally and required them to store only local data.

This arrangement of common global core systems that could be customized to local needs was adequate until traffic volume expanded rapidly in the last decade as global trade pushed the existing system to the limits. With 50 decentralized data centres running supposedly common programs, the risks that any one centre or several centres could fail might jeopardize shipments in several countries. Through painful experience, DHL learned that maintaining 50 different IS centres to a single global standard was difficult in many countries. The company also learned that "the information is more important than the package." Customers might understand and be sympathetic when hurricanes or tsunamis lead to lost packages, but they are intolerant of the idea that the DHL system failed and cannot tell them where their package is—even if it is at the bottom of the ocean.

In addition, the highly decentralized IS structure raised costs and slowed down change. Upgrades to software programs would have to be deployed in 50 different countries, taking over 18 months. Costs rose because, instead of maintaining the computers and programmers in one location, they had to be maintained in 50 locations.

When Managing Director of IT services, Stephen McGuckin, took over the Asian and Middle Eastern operation beginning in the late 1990s, management was increasingly strained by the existing organization of IT. Country managers were flying far too often to regional meetings with one another trying to coordinate policies, and McGuckin estimated that managers lost 20 percent of their productivity. The IT coordinating centres were headquartered in four different, expensive locations: London, Singapore, Hong Kong, and Bahrain. The software was all being developed in the United States, which also was very costly. A new set of management processes needed to be developed.

McGuckin started moving DHL toward a more centralized arrangement of systems to reduce its risks, decrease its costs, increase the speed with which it could deploy new applications, and raise the reliability of its systems. Beginning in 2000, DHL began concentrating its global computing infrastructure into three low-cost, regional global centres: Cyberjaya (Malaysia), Prague (Czech Republic), and Scottsdale, Arizona (United States). Each of these regional centres handles the information processing for a group of countries in the region.

In the process of consolidating, McGuckin also changed the management of software production. Initially outsourcing all software development to InfoSys, a large India-based outsourcing firm, DHL learned how to separate the design work (now done in the U.S.) from the implementation and execution work (now done in India). Costs declined, and quality was enhanced despite an early period of misunderstandings with their outsourcing firm.

By 2006, the consolidation was completed. So far the move seems to have been a success. Costs of maintaining the IT infrastructure have fallen by 40 percent; the time to deploy new applications has fallen to a matter of hours from months. New applications are developed in Arizona, deployed to the other two global centres, and then, in a matter of hours, deployed to customers and employees who access these centres for all their information needs.

Sources: Laurie Sullivan, "DHL Taps Several Vendors For RFID Project," *TechWeb News*, March 8, 2006; Michael Bloch and Marcus Schaper, "Building a Global IT Organization: An Interview with DPWN's Managing Director of IT," *The McKinsey Quarterly*, May 2006; **www.DHL-usa.com/company/history.htm**.

DHL's transition from a highly decentralized global logistics company toward a more regional global structure illustrates how global firms are adjusting their systems to support the rapid growth in world trade. This case also illustrates the tensions between the need to be locally responsive and the need to achieve a seamless flow of information across national boundaries in a truly global system.

The chapter-opening Business Challenges diagram calls attention to important points raised by this case and this chapter. DHL's original solution to developing a global logistics support system including package delivery was costly, slow, and difficult to manage. The solution consisted of three parts. DHL changed the organization of its systems by consolidating into three low-cost centres. It changed the management of its systems by also centralizing management in three centres, simplifying management communication, and changed how it managed software development by outsourcing implementation of software designs developed in the United States. The technology change involved moving core applications from 50 local servers onto three regional server centres and strengthening communication links with the local offices to ensure connectivity.

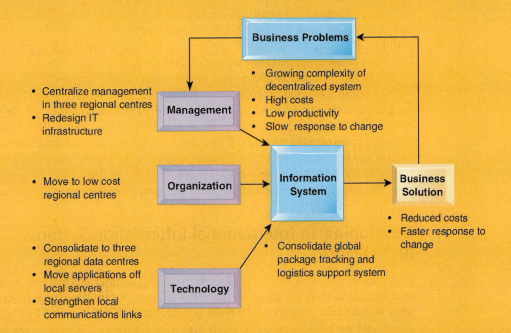

HEADS **UP**

During your career, you may work in a company that operates internationally. To be effective, you will need a global perspective on business and an understanding of the information systems needed to conduct business on an international scale. Special issues must be addressed when developing and managing global information systems. This chapter shows you how to organize, manage, and control the development of global systems.

- If your career is in finance or accounting, you will be using international systems to enable the flow of funds between corporate headquarters and operating units and to facilitate purchases in different countries.

- If your career is in human resources, you will be advising system developers about how to deal

with language and cultural differences affecting implementation and use of international systems.

- If your career is in information systems, you will be developing connectivity solutions to link disparate local systems with different technology platforms and working with management to develop standard data definitions and business processes to integrate these systems.

- If your career is in manufacturing, production, or operations management, you will be helping to implement standard supply chain management software or enterprise software to coordinate global manufacturing processes and supply chains.

- If your career is in sales and marketing, you will be setting up Web sites designed for global sales and marketing.

11.1 The Growth of International Information Systems

In earlier chapters, we describe the emergence of a global economic system and global world order driven by advanced networks and information systems. The new world order is sweeping away many national corporations, national industries, and national economies controlled by domestic politicians. Fast-moving networked corporations that transcend national boundaries will replace many localized firms. The growth of international trade has radically altered domestic economies around the globe. Today, the combined value of imports and exports from all nations is just over $20 trillion annually, a little less than one-third of the world's total GDP (Gross Domestic Product) of $70 trillion. While the world GDP is growing at about 4.7 percent a year, international trade is growing at an even faster rate of about 5.6 percent a year (CIA, 2006).

Today, the production and design of many high-end electronic products is parcelled out to a number of different countries. Consider the path to market for Hewlett-Packard's ProLiant ML150 server, which is illustrated in Figure 11-1. The idea for the product was hatched in Singapore, where the initial design work was done. HP headquarters in Houston approved the concept. Contractors in Taiwan did the machine's engineering design and initial manufacture. Final assembly of the server takes place in Singapore, China, India, and Australia (Buckman, 2004). None of this would be possible without powerful international information and communication systems.

Developing an International Information Systems Architecture

This chapter describes how to go about developing an international information systems architecture suitable for your international strategy. An **international information systems architecture** consists of the basic information systems required by organizations to coordinate worldwide trade and other activities. Figure 11-2 illustrates the reasoning we

International information systems architecture

FIGURE 11-1   *Global product development and production*

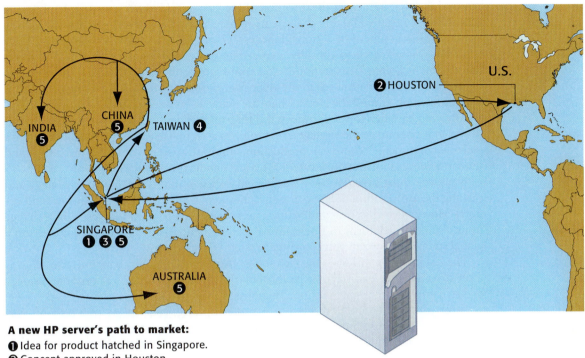

A new HP server's path to market:
❶ Idea for product hatched in Singapore.
❷ Concept approved in Houston.
❸ Concept design done in Singapore.
❹ Engineering design in Taiwan, where many computer components are made;
   initial manufacture by a Taiwanese contractor.
❺ Final assembly in Singapore, Australia, China, and India. Products made in Australia,
   China, and India are primarily for those markets; machines made in Singapore go to all of Southeast Asia.

Hewlett-Packard and other electronics companies assign distribution and production of high-end products to a number of different countries.

Source: © *The New York Times.* Used with Permission.

follow throughout the chapter and depicts the major dimensions of an international information systems portfolio.

The basic strategy to follow when developing an international system is to understand the global environment in which your firm is operating. This means understanding the

FIGURE 11-2   *International information systems architecture*

International Information Systems Architecture

The major dimensions for developing an international information systems architecture are the global environment, the corporate global strategies, the structure of the organization, the management and business processes, and the technology platform.

overall market forces, or business drivers, that are pushing your industry toward global competition. A **business driver** is a force in the environment to which businesses must respond and that influences the direction of the business. Likewise, examine carefully the inhibitors or negative factors that create management challenges—factors that could scuttle the development of a global business. Once you have examined the global environment, you will need to consider a corporate strategy for competing in that environment. How will your firm respond? You could ignore the global market and focus on domestic competition only, sell to the globe from a domestic base, or organize production and distribution around the globe. There are many in-between choices.

After you have developed a strategy, it is time to consider how to structure your organization so it can pursue the strategy. How will you accomplish a division of labour across a global environment? Where will production, administration, accounting, marketing, and human resource functions be located? Who will handle the systems function?

Next, you must consider the management issues in implementing your strategy and making the organization design come alive. Key here will be the design of business procedures. How can you discover and manage user requirements? How can you induce change in local units to conform to international requirements? How can you reengineer on a global scale, and how can you coordinate systems development?

The last issue to consider is the technology platform. Although changing technology is a key driving factor leading toward global markets, you need to have a corporate strategy and structure before you can rationally choose the right technology.

After you have completed this process of reasoning, you will be well on your way toward an appropriate international information systems architecture capable of achieving your corporate goals. Let us begin by looking at the overall global environment.

The Global Environment: Business Drivers and Challenges

Table 11-1 lists the business drivers in the global environment that are leading all industries toward global markets and competition.

The global business drivers can be divided into two groups: general cultural factors and specific business factors. Easily recognized general cultural factors have driven internationalization since World War II. Information, communication, and transportation technologies have created a global village in which communication (by telephone, television, radio, or computer network) around the globe is no more difficult and not much more expensive than communication down the block. The cost of moving goods and services to and from geographically dispersed locations has fallen dramatically.

The development of global communications has created a global village in a second sense: A **global culture** created by television, the Internet, and other globally shared media such as movies now permits different cultures and peoples to develop common expectations about right and wrong, desirable and undesirable, heroic and cowardly. The collapse of the Eastern bloc has enormously accelerated the growth of a world culture, increased support for capitalism and business, and considerably reduced the level of cultural conflict.

A last factor to consider is the growth of a global knowledge base. At the end of World War II, knowledge, education, science, and industrial skills were highly concentrated in

Business driver

Global culture

TABLE 11-1 *Global Business Drivers*

GENERAL CULTURAL FACTORS	SPECIFIC BUSINESS FACTORS
Global communication and transportation technologies	Global markets
Development of global culture	Global production and operations
Emergence of global social norms	Global coordination
Political stability	Global workforce
Global knowledge base	Global economies of scale

North America, Western Europe, and Japan, with the rest of the world euphemistically called the Third World. This is no longer true. Latin America, China, India, Southern Asia, and Eastern Europe have developed powerful educational, industrial, and scientific centres, resulting in a much more democratically and widely dispersed knowledge base.

These general cultural factors leading toward internationalization result in specific business globalization factors that affect most industries. The growth of powerful communications technologies and the emergence of world cultures create the condition for *global markets*—global consumers interested in consuming similar products that are culturally approved. Coca-Cola, American sneakers (made in Korea but designed in Los Angeles), and Cable News Network (CNN) programming can now be sold in Latin America, Africa, and Asia.

Responding to this demand, global production and operations have emerged with precise online coordination between far-flung production facilities and central headquarters thousands of kilometres away. The new global markets and pressure toward global production and operation have called forth whole new capabilities for global coordination of all factors of production. Not only production but also accounting, marketing and sales, human resources, and systems development (all the major business functions) can be coordinated on a global scale.

In health care, an example is telerobotic surgery. Using telerobotic surgery, a doctor in one location can guide a surgical robot (usually just two robotic hands) to perform surgery on an individual located at a far distance, even on a different continent. Two Ontario doctors in Hamilton recently used telerobotics to perform surgery on a North Bay General Hospital patient hundreds of kilometres away. The pilot was deemed a success by the surgical teams who performed this first-time-ever procedure. Telerobotic surgery has even been performed across oceans: a U.S. surgeon has already used telerobotics to operate on a patient in France. It is only a matter of time before this is commonplace.

In marketing, Frito-Lay might develop a marketing sales-force automation system in the U.S. and then try the same techniques and technologies in Spain. Micromarketing—marketing to very small geographic and social units—no longer means marketing to neighbourhoods in North America; neighbourhoods throughout the world may be targeted! These new levels of global coordination permit for the first time in history the location of business activity according to comparative advantage. Design should be located where it is best accomplished, as should marketing, production, and finance.

Finally, global markets, production, and administration create the conditions for powerful, sustained global economies of scale. Production driven by worldwide global demand can be concentrated where it can best be accomplished, fixed resources can be allocated over larger production runs, and production runs in larger plants can be scheduled more efficiently and can be more precisely estimated. Lower cost factors of production can be exploited wherever they emerge. The result is a powerful strategic advantage to firms that can organize globally. These general and specific business drivers have greatly enlarged world trade and commerce.

Not all industries are similarly affected by these trends. Clearly, manufacturing has been much more affected than services that still tend to be domestic and highly inefficient. However, the localism of services is breaking down in telecommunications, entertainment, transportation, financial services, and general business services, including law. Clearly, those firms within an industry that can understand the internationalization of the industry and respond appropriately will reap enormous gains in productivity and stability.

Business Challenges Although the possibilities of globalization for business success are significant, fundamental forces are operating to inhibit a global economy and to disrupt international business. Table 11-2 lists the most common and powerful challenges to the development of global systems.

Particularism means making judgments and taking action on the basis of narrow or personal characteristics, (religious, nationalistic, gender, ethnic, regionalism, geopolitical position). At a cultural level, particularism in all its forms rejects the very concept of a shared global culture and rejects the penetration of domestic markets by foreign goods

Particularism

TABLE 11-2 *Challenges and Obstacles to Global Business Systems*

GENERAL	SPECIFIC
Cultural particularism: Regionalism, nationalism, language differences	Standards: Different Electronic DataInterchange (EDI), e-mail, telecommunications standards
Social expectations: Brand-name expectations, work hours	Reliability: Phone networks not uniformly reliable
Political laws: Transborder data and privacy laws, commercial regulations	Speed: Different data transfer speeds,many slower than in North America
	Personnel: Shortages of skilled consultants

and services. Differences among cultures produce differences in social expectations, politics, and ultimately legal rules. In certain countries, such as Canada, consumers expect domestic name-brand products to be developed domestically and are disappointed to learn that much of what they thought of as domestically produced is in fact foreign-made.

Different cultures produce different political regimes. The many different countries of the world have different laws governing the movement of information, information privacy, origins of software and hardware in systems, and radio and satellite telecommunications. Even the hours of business and the terms of business trade vary greatly across political cultures. These different legal regimes complicate global business and must be considered when developing global systems.

For instance, European countries have very strict laws concerning transborder data flow and privacy. **Transborder data flow** is defined as the movement of information across international boundaries in any form. Some European countries prohibit the processing of financial information outside their boundaries or the movement of personal information to foreign countries. The European Union Data Protection Directive, which went into effect in October 1998, restricts the flow of any information to countries (such as Canada) that do not meet strict European information laws on personal information. Financial services, travel, and health care companies could be directly affected. In response, most multinational firms develop information systems within each European country to avoid the cost and uncertainty of moving information across national boundaries.

Cultural and political differences profoundly affect organizations' business processes and applications of information technology. A host of specific barriers arise from the general cultural differences, everything from differing reliability of phone networks to the shortage of skilled consultants.

National laws and traditions have created disparate accounting practices in various countries, which impact the ways profits and losses are analyzed. German companies generally do not recognize the profit from a venture until the project is completely finished and they have been paid. Conversely, British firms begin posting profits before a project is completed, when they are reasonably certain they will get the money.

These accounting practices are tightly intertwined with each country's legal system, business philosophy, and tax code. Canadian, British, U.S., and Dutch firms share a predominantly Anglo-Saxon outlook that separates tax calculations from reports to shareholders to focus on showing shareholders how fast profits are growing. Continental European accounting practices are less oriented toward impressing investors, focusing rather on demonstrating compliance with strict rules and minimizing tax liabilities. These diverging accounting practices make it difficult for large international companies to evaluate the performance of units in different countries.

Language remains a significant barrier. Although English has become a kind of standard business language, this is truer at higher levels of companies and not throughout the middle and lower ranks. Software may have to be developed with local language interfaces before a new information system can be successfully implemented.

Currency fluctuations can play havoc with planning models and projections. A product that appears profitable in Mexico or Japan may actually produce a loss because of changes in foreign exchange rates.

Transborder data flow

These inhibiting factors must be taken into account when designing and developing international systems. For example, companies trying to implement "lean production" systems spanning national boundaries typically underestimate the time, expense, and logistical difficulties of making goods and information flow freely across different countries.

State of the Art

One might think, given the opportunities for achieving competitive advantages as outlined previously, and given the interest in future applications, that most international companies have rationally developed marvellous international systems architectures. Nothing could be further from the truth. Most companies have inherited patchwork international systems from the distant past, often based on concepts of information processing developed in the 1960s—such as batch-oriented reporting from independent foreign divisions to corporate headquarters, and manual entry of data from one legacy system to another, with little online control and communication. Corporations in this situation increasingly face powerful competitive challenges in the marketplace from firms that have rationally designed truly international systems. Still other companies have recently developed technology platforms for international systems but have nowhere to go because they lack global strategy.

As it turns out, there are significant difficulties in developing appropriate international architectures. The difficulties involve planning a system appropriate to the firm's global strategy, structuring the organization of systems and business units, solving implementation issues, and choosing the right technical platform. Let us examine these problems in greater detail.

11.2 Organizing International Information Systems

Three organizational issues face corporations seeking a global position: choosing a strategy, organizing the business, and organizing the systems management area. The first two are closely connected, so we will discuss them together.

Global Strategies and Business Organization

Four main global strategies form the basis for global firms' organizational structure. These are domestic exporter, multinational, franchiser, and transnational. Each of these strategies is pursued with a specific business organizational structure (see Table 11-3). For simplicity's sake, we describe three kinds of organizational structure or governance: centralized (in the home country), decentralized (to local foreign units), and coordinated (all units participate as equals). Other types of governance patterns can be observed in specific companies (e.g., authoritarian dominance by one unit, a confederacy of equals, a federal structure balancing power among strategic units, and so forth).

TABLE 11-3 Global Business Strategy and Structure

BUSINESS FUNCTION	DOMESTIC EXPORTER	MULTINATIONAL	FRANCHISER	TRANSNATIONAL
Production	Centralized	Dispersed	Coordinated	Coordinated
Finance/Accounting	Centralized	Centralized	Centralized	Coordinated
Sales/Marketing	Mixed	Dispersed	Coordinated	Coordinated
Human Resources	Centralized	Centralized	Coordinated	Coordinated
Strategic Management	Centralized	Centralized	Centralized	Coordinated

The **domestic exporter** strategy is characterized by heavy centralization of corporate activities in the home country of origin. Nearly all international companies begin this way, and some move on to other forms. Production, finance/accounting, sales/marketing, human resources, and strategic management are set up to optimize resources in the home country. International sales are sometimes dispersed using agency agreements or subsidiaries, but even here, foreign marketing is totally reliant on the domestic home base for marketing themes and strategies. Heavy capital-equipment manufacturers fall into this category of firm.

The **multinational** strategy concentrates financial management and control in a central home base while decentralizing production, sales, and marketing operations to units in other countries. The products and services on sale in different countries are adapted to suit local market conditions. The organization becomes a far-flung confederation of production and marketing facilities in different countries. Many financial service firms, along with a host of manufacturers, such as Toyota, Great West Life, and Intel, fit this pattern.

Franchisers are an interesting mix of old and new. On the one hand, the product is created, designed, financed, and initially produced in the home country, but for product-specific reasons it must rely heavily on foreign personnel for further production, marketing, and human resources. Food franchisers such as Tim Horton's, McDonald's, and Mrs. Fields Cookies fit this pattern. McDonald's created a new form of fast-food chain in the U.S. and continues to rely largely on the U.S. for inspiration for new products, strategic management, and financing. Nevertheless, because the product must be produced locally—it is perishable—extensive coordination and dispersal of production, local marketing, and local recruitment of personnel are required.

Generally, foreign franchisees are clones of the mother country units, but fully coordinated worldwide production that could optimize factors of production is not possible. For instance, potatoes and beef can generally not be bought where they are cheapest on world markets but must be produced reasonably close to the area of consumption.

Transnational firms are the stateless, truly globally managed firms that may represent a larger part of international business in the future. Transnational firms have no single national headquarters but instead have many regional headquarters and perhaps a world headquarters. In a **transnational** strategy, nearly all the value-adding activities are managed from a global perspective without reference to national borders, optimizing sources of supply and demand wherever they appear, and taking advantage of any local competitive advantages. Transnational firms take the globe, not the home country, as their management frame of reference. The governance of these firms has been likened to a federal structure in which there is a strong central management core of decision making but considerable dispersal of power and financial muscle throughout the global divisions. Few companies have actually attained transnational status, but Nestlé, Citicorp, Sony, Ford, and others are attempting this transition.

Information technology and improvements in global telecommunications are giving international firms more flexibility to shape their global strategies. Protectionism and a need to serve local markets better encourage companies to disperse production facilities and at least become multinational. At the same time, the drive to achieve economies of scale and take advantage of short-term local advantage moves transnationals toward a global management perspective and a concentration of power and authority. Hence, there are forces of decentralization and dispersal, as well as forces of centralization and global coordination.

Global Systems to Fit the Strategy

Information technology and improvements in global telecommunications are giving international firms more flexibility to shape their global strategies. The configuration, management, and development of systems tend to follow the chosen global strategy (Ives, Jarvenpaa, and Mason, 1993; Roche, 1992; Ives and Jarvenpaa, 1991). Figure 11-3 depicts the typical arrangements. By systems, we mean the full range of activities involved in developing and operating information systems: conception and alignment with the strategic business plan, systems development, and ongoing operation and maintenance. For the sake of simplicity, we consider four types of systems configuration. Centralized systems are those in which systems development and operation occur totally at the domestic home base.

Domestic exporter

Multinational

Transnational

Duplicated systems are those in which development occurs at the home base, but operations are handed over to autonomous units in foreign locations. Decentralized systems are those in which each foreign unit designs its own unique solutions and systems. Networked systems are those in which systems development and operations occur in an integrated and coordinated fashion across all units.

As can be seen in Figure 11-3, domestic exporters tend to have highly centralized systems in which a single domestic systems development staff develops worldwide applications. Multinationals offer a direct and striking contrast: Here, foreign units devise their own systems solutions based on local needs with few if any applications in common with headquarters (the exceptions being financial reporting and some telecommunications applications). **Franchisers** have the simplest systems structure: Like the products they sell, franchisers develop a single system usually at the home base and then replicate it around the world. Each unit, no where it is located, has identical applications. Last, the most ambitious form of systems development is found in the transnational strategy: Networked systems are those in which there is a solid, singular global environment for developing and operating systems. This usually presupposes a powerful telecommunications backbone, a culture of shared applications development, and a shared management culture that crosses cultural barriers. The networked systems structure is the most visible in financial services where the homogeneity of the product—money and money instruments—seems to overcome cultural barriers.

Reorganizing the Business

How should a firm organize itself for doing business on an international scale? To develop a global company and information systems support structure, a firm needs to follow these principles:

1. Organize value-adding activities along lines of comparative advantage. For example, marketing/sales functions should be located where they can best be performed, for least cost and maximum impact—likewise with production, finance, human resources, and information systems.

2. Develop and operate systems units at each level of corporate activity—regional, national, and international. To serve local needs, there should be host country systems units of some magnitude. Regional systems units should handle telecommunications and systems development across national boundaries that take place within major geographic regions (North American, European, Asian). Transnational systems units should be established to create the linkages across major regional areas and coordinate the development and operation of international telecommunications and systems (Roche, 1992).

3. At world headquarters, establish a single office responsible for the development of international systems, a global chief information officer (CIO) position.

Franchisers

FIGURE 11-3   *Global strategy and systems configurations*

SYSTEM CONFIGURATION	Strategy			
	Domestic Exporter	Multinational	Franchiser	Transnational
Centralized	X			
Duplicated			X	
Decentralized	x	X	x	
Networked		x		X

The large Xs show the dominant patters, and the small Xs show the emerging patters. For instance, domestic exporters rely predominantly on centralized systems, but there is continual pressure and some development of decentralized systems in local marketing regions.

WINDOW ON ORGANIZATIONS

Avnet: Developing Systems to Support Global Strategy

You probably have not heard of Avnet Inc.—or its leading competitor Arrow Electronics—but chances are the computer you are using these days has some—if not all—of its components purchased from one of these distributors. Avnet is number 212 on the list of Fortune 500 firms, and number three on *InformationWeek*'s list of most innovative users of information systems. Avnet and Arrow are two American-based firms that together dominate the world market for electronic parts, connectors, components, and computers, with a 60-percent global market share. While locked in competition for the remaining 40 percent of the world market, Avnet and Arrow have each adopted different business strategies for future growth, and each has a different idea about how to use information systems to support corporate growth.

Beginning as a radio-parts distributor started by Charles Avnet in 1921 in New York City, Avnet went public in 1959 and was then managed by Charles Avnet's sons. Since 1991, the company has been on a growth spurt, purchasing 43 companies including British semiconductor distributor Access Group. About 60 percent of Avnet's business involves component distribution, and the rest is distributing computers that it purchases from computer manufacturers and resells to corporations and large retail outlets. Avnet, like Arrow, is an intermediary between manufacturers and end users. It is also a key supplier of industrial electronic components to the computer industries.

In 2001, Avnet completed its expansion in Europe and began moving into Asian markets by purchasing China's Sunrise Technology. In 2005, it purchased Memec Group Holdings, a $2-billion purchase of China's largest electronic components distributor.

Because it was so dependent on acquisitions and rapid integration of newly purchased companies, Avnet developed what it calls its "Cookbook" for acquisitions. Composed of more than 1000 pages stored on Avnet servers, the Cookbook contains Avnet's accumulated wisdom on how to integrate new companies into Avnet's business process and information systems. It has chapters on human resources, finances, IT/IS, logistics, materials, sales, and marketing. You can think of the Cookbook as an encyclopedia of business processes for Avnet.

Rather than force all its acquisitions to adopt Avnet's American systems, Avnet has divided the world into three regions, each with its own regional enterprise resource planning (ERP) and related systems. The goal was—in order to speed the integration of newly acquired companies—to integrate new acquisitions tightly and smoothly within each region and to allow regional managers a certain degree of freedom in choosing how they organized their business within the region. When acquiring new companies, Avnet tries to use the best systems from each company and not always its own. In the case of Memec, it chose to use the Avnet regional Asian system rather

than Memec's own global system because it would lower the costs of training Avnet employees, who otherwise would have to learn an entirely new system.

Avnet successfully integrated the Memec business and employees into its Asian system. Avnet now runs two regional ERP systems: SAP in Asia, and a custom-developed mainframe system called Genesis in the U.S. In Europe, Avnet runs 10 different SAP systems, nearly one for each European country where it does business, but it is attempting to consolidate them into a single European SAP system in the future.

The Cookbook has been very useful for ensuring commonality of business processes around the world despite different ERP systems in major regions and countries. The Cookbook goes into considerable detail on how to set up and process financial transactions, coordinate orders, pay accounts, and assign responsibility for transactions.

Arrow too has begun making acquisitions in Asia, most notably, purchasing a large Taiwanese distributor, Ultra Source Technology. Using a similar collection of best business practices it calls "the Playbook," Arrow once integrated a newly acquired company into the Arrow global systems in a single weekend. But Arrow, according to its executives, may rely less on acquisitions in Asia than on trading relationships with existing Asian distributors. They want to focus not just on revenue growth but profit growth. They believe the costs of acquisitions may outweigh the profit benefits. Unlike Avnet, Arrow is pursuing a one-world, one-system strategy. In 2007, Arrow plans to be using a single Oracle financial system and is working on plans for a single global ERP system to replace a hodgepodge of ERP systems that have sprung up around its global operations. "We want to move towards more conformity," explained one Arrow executive, "while trying to recognize the uniqueness of each market; we want to have a global view of the whole company when it makes sense for us." Without a single global system, they believe, it is difficult to view the company as a truly global entity.

To Think About

1. Review Table 11-3 on page 381, and then contrast and compare the global strategies of Avnet and Arrow. Are they the same or different?

2. Review Figure 11-3 on page 383, and compare and contrast the Avnet systems development strategy with that of Arrow. Has each company made the "correct" choice given their strategies?

3. Identify the risks that Avnet incurs by pursuing its regional strategy. What are the off-setting benefits?

4. For this product and market, do you believe that a multinational strategy is superior to a transnational strategy? Why or why not?

MIS in Action

1. Go to the Avnet Web site (www.avnet.com) and identify (a) how many countries in which it operates, and (b) how its revenues are divided among the major regions of North America, Europe, and Asia.

2. At the Avnet Web site, explore the sections on Avnet's Management Technologies and their logistics services. These are quite separate businesses from operating a global parts distribution system. Or are they? How is Avnet leveraging its investment in distribution systems?

3. Visit Avnet's largest competitor, Arrow Electronics Inc. (www.arrow.com). Compare Avnet's financial performance (revenue growth, operating margins, and net income) with that of Arrow over the last three years. Include their three-year stock price performance. Which of these companies has an edge in financial performance? How do their different global strategies and systems contribute to differences in their financial performance?

Sources: Edward Cone, "Avnet Tries Buying Its Way to the Top," *CIO Insight*, February 1, 2006 and www.avnet.com, accessed October 15, 2006.

Many successful companies have devised organizational systems structures along these principles. The success of these companies relies not only on the proper organization of activities, but also on a key ingredient—a management team that can understand the risks and benefits of international systems and that can devise strategies for overcoming the risks. We turn to these management topics next.

11.3 Managing Global Systems

Table 11-4 lists the principal management problems posed by developing international systems. It is interesting to note that these problems are the chief difficulties managers experience in developing ordinary domestic systems as well. But such problems are enormously complicated in the international environment.

A Typical Scenario: Disorganization on a Global Scale

Let us look at a common scenario. A traditional multinational consumer-goods company based in Canada and operating in Europe would like to expand into Asian markets and knows that it must develop a transnational strategy and a supportive information systems structure. Like most multinationals, it has dispersed production and marketing to regional and national centres while maintaining a world headquarters and strategic management in Canada. Historically, it has allowed each of the subsidiary foreign divisions to develop its own systems. The only centrally coordinated system is financial controls and reporting. The central systems group in Canada focuses only on domestic functions and production.

The result is a hodgepodge of hardware, software, and telecommunications. The e-mail systems between Europe and Canada are incompatible. Each production facility uses a different manufacturing resources planning system (or a different version of the same ERP system) and different marketing, sales, and human resources systems. Hardware and database platforms are very different. Communications between different sites are poor, given the high-cost European intercountry communications. Recently, the central systems

TABLE 11-4 Management Challenges in Developing Global Systems

Agreeing on common user requirements
Introducing changes in business processes
Coordinating applications development
Coordinating software releases
Encouraging local users to support global systems

group at headquarters in Canada was decimated and dispersed to the Canadian local sites in the hope of serving local needs better and reducing costs.

What do you recommend to the senior management leaders of this company, who now want to pursue a transnational strategy and develop an information systems architecture to support a highly coordinated global systems environment? Consider the problems you face by re-examining Table 11-4. The foreign divisions will resist efforts to agree on common user requirements; they have never thought about much other than their own units' needs. The systems groups in Canadian local sites, which have been enlarged recently and told to focus on local needs, will not easily accept guidance from anyone recommending a transnational strategy. It will be difficult to convince local managers anywhere in the world that they should change their business procedures to align with other units in the world, especially if this might interfere with their local performance. After all, local managers are rewarded in this company for meeting local objectives of their division or plant. Finally, it will be difficult to coordinate development of projects around the world in the absence of a powerful telecommunications network and, therefore, difficult to encourage local users to take on ownership in the systems developed.

Global Systems Strategy

Figure 11-4 lays out the main dimensions of a solution. First, consider that not all systems should be coordinated on a transnational basis; only some core systems are truly worth sharing from a cost and feasibility point of view. **Core systems** are systems that support functions that are absolutely critical to the organization. Other systems should be partially coordinated because they share key elements, but they do not have to be totally common across national boundaries. For such systems, a good deal of local variation is possible and desirable. A final group of systems is peripheral, truly provincial, and needed to suit local requirements only.

Define the Core Business Processes How do you identify core systems? The first step is to define a short list of critical core business processes. Business processes are defined and described in Chapter 2, which you should review. Briefly, business processes are sets of logically related tasks to produce specific business results, such as shipping out correct orders to customers or delivering innovative products to the market. Each

Core systems

Agency and other coordination costs increase as the firm moves from local option systems toward regional and global systems. However, transaction costs of participating in global markets probably decrease as firms develop global systems. A sensible strategy is to reduce agency costs by developing only a few core global systems that are vital for global operations, leaving other systems in the hands of regional and local units.

Source: From *Managing Information Technology in Multinational Corporations* by Edward M. Roche, © 1993. Adapted by permission of Prentice Hall, Inc., Upper Saddle River, N.J.

FIGURE 11-4   *Local, regional, and global systems*

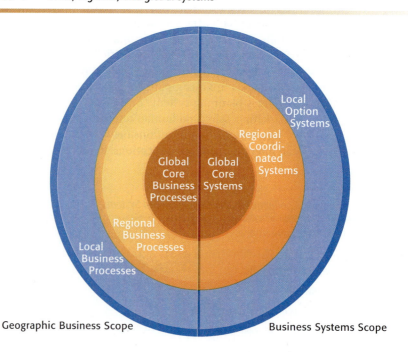

business process typically involves many functional areas communicating and coordinating work, information, and knowledge.

The way to identify these core business processes is to conduct a business process analysis. How are customer orders taken; what happens to them once they are taken; who fills the orders; how are they shipped to the customers? What about suppliers? Do they have access to manufacturing resource planning systems so that supply is automatic? You should be able to identify and set priorities in a short list of 10 business processes that are absolutely critical for the firm.

Next, can you identify centres of excellence for these processes? Is the customer order fulfillment superior in Canada, manufacturing process control superior in Germany, and human resources superior in Asia? You should be able to identify some areas of the company, for some lines of business, where a division or unit stands out in the performance of one or several business functions.

When you understand the business processes of a firm, you can rank-order them. You then can decide which processes should be core applications, centrally coordinated, designed, and implemented around the globe, and which should be regional and local. At the same time, by identifying the critical business processes, the really important ones, you have gone a long way to defining a vision of the future that you should be working toward.

Identify the Core Systems to Coordinate Centrally By identifying the critical core business processes, you begin to see opportunities for transnational systems. The second strategic step is to conquer the core systems and define these systems as truly transnational. The financial and political costs of defining and implementing transnational systems are extremely high. Therefore, keep the list to an absolute minimum, letting experience be the guide and erring on the side of minimalism. By dividing off a small group of systems as absolutely critical, you divide opposition to a transnational strategy. At the same time, you can appease those who oppose the central worldwide coordination implied by transnational systems by permitting peripheral systems development to progress unabated, with the exception of some technical platform requirements.

Choose an Approach: Incremental, Grand Design, Evolutionary A third step is to choose an approach. Avoid piecemeal approaches. These surely will fail for lack of visibility, opposition from all who stand to lose from transnational development, and lack of power to convince senior management that the transnational systems are worth it. Likewise, avoid grand design approaches that try to do everything at once. These also tend to fail, because of an inability to focus resources. Nothing gets done properly, and opposition to organizational change is needlessly strengthened because the effort requires huge resources. An alternative approach is to evolve transnational applications incrementally from existing applications with a precise and clear vision of the transnational capabilities the organization should have in five years. This is sometimes referred to as the "salami strategy," or one slice at a time. It permits systems development to evolve over time.

Make the Benefits Clear What is in it for the company? One of the worst situations to avoid is to develop global systems for the sake of developing global systems. From the beginning, it is crucial that senior management at headquarters and foreign division managers clearly understand the benefits that will come to the company as well as to individual units. Although each system offers unique benefits to a particular budget, the overall contribution of global systems lies in four areas.

Global systems—truly integrated, distributed, and transnational systems—contribute to superior management and coordination. A simple price tag cannot be put on the value of this contribution, and the benefit will not show up in any capital budgeting model. It is the ability to switch suppliers on a moment's notice from one region to another in a crisis, the ability to move production in response to natural disasters, and the ability to use excess capacity in one region to meet raging demand in another.

A second major contribution is vast improvement in production, operations, and supply and distribution. Imagine a global value chain, with global suppliers and a global distribution network. For the first time, senior managers can locate value-adding activities in regions where they are most economically performed.

Third, global systems mean global customers and global marketing. Fixed costs around the world can be amortized over a much larger customer base. This will unleash new economies of scale at production facilities.

Last, global systems mean the ability to optimize the use of corporate funds over a much larger capital base. This means, for instance, that capital in a surplus region can be moved efficiently to expand production of capital-starved regions; that cash can be managed more effectively within the company and put to use more effectively.

These strategies will not by themselves create global systems. You will have to implement what you strategize.

The Management Solution

We can now reconsider how to handle the most vexing problems facing managers developing the global information systems architectures that were described in Table 11-4 on page 385.

Agreeing on Common User Requirements Establishing a short list of the core business processes and core support systems will begin a process of rational comparison across the many divisions of the company, develop a common language for discussing the business, and naturally lead to an understanding of common elements (as well as the unique qualities that must remain local).

Introducing Changes in Business Processes Your success as a change agent will depend on your legitimacy, your actual raw power, and your ability to involve users in the change design process. **Legitimacy** is defined as the extent to which your authority is accepted on grounds of competence, vision, or other qualities. The selection of a viable change strategy, which we have defined as evolutionary but with a vision, should assist you in convincing others that change is feasible and desirable. Involving people in change and assuring them that change is in the best interests of the company and their local units is a key tactic.

Coordinating Applications Development Choice of change strategy is critical for this problem. At the global level, there is far too much complexity to attempt a grand design strategy of change. It is far easier to coordinate change by making small incremental steps toward a larger vision. Imagine a five-year plan of action rather than a two-year plan of action, and reduce the set of transnational systems to a bare minimum to reduce coordination costs.

Coordinating Software Releases Firms can institute procedures to ensure that all operating units convert to new software updates at the same time so that everyone's software is compatible.

Encouraging Local Users to Support Global Systems The key to this problem is to involve users in the creation of the design without giving up control over the development of the project to parochial interests. The overall tactic for dealing with resistant local units in a transnational company is cooptation. **Cooptation** is defined as bringing the opposition into the process of designing and implementing the solution without giving up control over the direction and nature of the change. As much as possible, raw power should be avoided. Minimally, however, local units must agree on a short list of transnational systems, and raw power may be required to solidify the idea that transnational systems of some sort are truly required.

How should cooptation proceed? Several alternatives are possible. One option is to permit each country unit the opportunity to develop one transnational application first in its home territory, and then throughout the world. In this manner, each major country systems group is given a piece of the action in developing a transnational system, and local units feel a sense of ownership in the transnational effort. On the downside, this assumes the ability to develop high-quality systems is widely distributed, and that a German team, for example, can successfully implement systems in France and Italy. This will not always be the case.

A second tactic is to develop new transnational centres of excellence, or a single centre of excellence. There may be several centres around the globe that focus on specific business

Legitimacy

Cooptation

processes. This is the approach taken by DHL discussed at the beginning of this chapter. These centres draw heavily from local national units, are based on multinational teams, and must report to worldwide management. Centres of excellence perform the initial identification and specification of business processes, define the information requirements, perform the business and systems analysis, and accomplish all design and testing. Implementation, however, and pilot testing are rolled out to other parts of the globe. Recruiting a wide range of local groups to transnational centres of excellence helps send the message that all significant groups are involved in the design and will have an influence.

Even with the proper organizational structure and appropriate management choices, it is still possible to stumble over technology issues. Choices of technology platforms, networks, hardware, and software are the final element in developing transnational information system architectures.

11.4 Technology Issues and Opportunities for Global Value Chains

Once firms have defined a global business model and systems strategy, they must select hardware, software, and networking standards along with key system applications to support global business processes. Many companies today are using teams in other countries to develop and run their software and hardware, so they will need to address the challenges of managing global teams and global technology services as well.

Technology Challenges of Global Systems

Hardware, software, and networking pose special technical challenges in an international setting. One major challenge is finding some way to standardize a global computing platform when there is so much variation from operating unit to operating unit and from country to country. Another major challenge is finding specific software applications that are user friendly and that truly enhance the productivity of international work teams. The universal acceptance of the Internet around the globe has greatly reduced networking problems. But the mere presence of the Internet does not guarantee that information will flow seamlessly throughout the global organization, because not all business units use the same applications, and the quality of Internet service can be highly variable (just as with telephone service). For instance, German business units may use a Linux-based collaboration tool to share documents and communicate, which is incompatible with Canadian headquarters teams that use Lotus Notes. Overcoming these challenges requires systems integration and connectivity on a global basis.

Computing Platforms and Systems Integration The development of a transnational information systems architecture based on the concept of core systems raises questions about how the new core systems will fit in with the existing suite of applications developed around the globe by different divisions, different people, and for different kinds of computing hardware. The goal is to develop global, distributed, integrated systems to support digital business processes spanning national boundaries. Briefly, these are the same problems faced by any large domestic systems development effort. However, the problems are magnified in an international environment. Just imagine the challenge of integrating systems based on the Windows, Linux, Unix, or proprietary operating systems running on IBM, Sun, Hewlett-Packard, and other hardware in many different operating units in many different countries!

Moreover, having all sites use the same hardware and operating system does not guarantee integration. Some central authority in the firm must establish data and other technical standards, with which sites are to comply. For instance, technical accounting terms, such as the beginning and end of the fiscal year, must be standardized (review the earlier discussion of the cultural challenges to building global businesses), as well as the acceptable interfaces between systems, communication speeds and architectures, and network software.

Connectivity Truly integrated global systems must have connectivity—the ability to link together the systems and people of a global firm into a single integrated network just like the phone system but capable of voice, data, and image transmissions. The Internet has provided an enormously powerful foundation for providing connectivity among the dispersed units of global firms; however, many issues remain.

The public Internet does not guarantee any level of service (even in Canada). Few global corporations trust the security of the Internet, and they generally use private networks to communicate sensitive data, and Internet-based virtual private networks (VPNs) for communications that require less security. Not all countries support even basic Internet service, which requires obtaining reliable circuits, coordinating among different carriers and the regional telecommunications authority, obtaining bills in a common currency standard, and obtaining standard agreements for the level of telecommunications service provided. Table 11-5 lists the major challenges posed by international networks.

An increasingly attractive alternative to using the public Internet is to create global networks based on the Internet and Internet technology. Companies can create global intranets for internal communication or extranets to exchange information more rapidly with business partners in their supply chains. They can use the public Internet to create global networks using VPNs from Internet service providers, which provide many features of a private network using the public Internet (see Chapter 7). However, VPNs may not provide the same level of quick and predictable response as private networks, especially during times of the day when Internet traffic is very congested, and they may not be able to support large numbers of remote users.

Low penetration of PCs and widespread illiteracy limit demand for Internet service in many developing countries (see Figure 11-5). Where an infrastructure exists in less-developed countries, it is often outdated, lacks digital circuits, and has very noisy lines. The purchasing power of most people in developing countries makes access to Internet services very expensive. Many countries monitor transmissions. Governments in China, Singapore, Iran, and Saudi Arabia monitor Internet traffic and block access to Web sites considered morally or politically offensive.

Software The development of core systems poses unique challenges for application software: How will the old systems interface with the new? Entirely new interfaces must be developed and tested if old systems are kept in local areas (which is common). These interfaces can be costly and messy to develop. If new software must be created, another challenge is to develop software that can be realistically used by multiple business units from different countries, given that these business units are accustomed to their own unique business processes and definitions of data.

Aside from integrating the new with the old systems, there are problems of human interface design and functionality of systems. For instance, to be truly useful for enhancing productivity of a global workforce, software interfaces must be easily understood and mastered quickly. Graphical user interfaces are ideal for this but presuppose a common language—often English. When international systems involve knowledge workers only, English may be the assumed international standard. But as international systems penetrate deeper into

TABLE 11-5 *Problems of International Networks*

Quality of Service
Security
Costs and tariffs
Network management
Installation delays
Poor quality of international service
Regulatory constraints
Network capacity

FIGURE 11-5 *Internet population in selected countries*

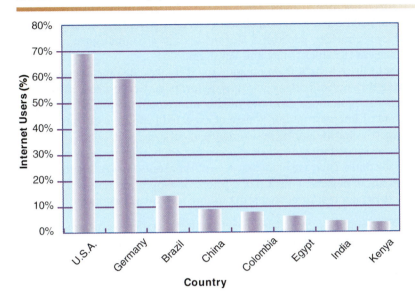

The percentage of the total population using the Internet in developing countries is much smaller than in the United States and Europe.

Source: *CIA World Factbook*, 2005.

management and clerical groups, a common language may not be assumed and human interfaces must be developed to accommodate different languages and even conventions.

What are the most important software applications? Many international systems focus on basic transaction and management reporting systems. Increasingly, firms are turning to supply chain management and enterprise systems to standardize their business processes on a global basis and to create coordinated global supply chains. However, these cross-functional systems are not always compatible with differences in languages, cultural heritages, and business processes in other countries (Martinsons, 2004; Liang et al., 2004; Davison, 2002). Company units in countries that are not technically sophisticated may also encounter problems trying to manage the technical complexities of enterprise applications.

Electronic Data Interchange (EDI) systems and supply chain management systems are widely used by manufacturing and distribution firms to connect to suppliers on a global basis. Groupware systems, e-mail, and videoconferencing are especially important worldwide collaboration tools for knowledge- and data-based firms, such as advertising firms, research-based firms in medicine and engineering, and graphics and publishing firms. Internet-based tools will be increasingly employed for such purposes.

Managing Global Software Development

Both global and domestic firms are increasingly managing their hardware and software resources using global teams. Sometimes these teams work for the firm at offshore locations, and in some instances, these teams are working for external vendors in offshore locations. This practice is called **offshore software outsourcing**, and it is becoming very popular. According to a Canadian Chamber of Commerce report, 75 000 of Canada's 550 000 IT sector jobs may be lost to offshore outsourcing (Canadian Chamber of Commerce, 2005). Forrester Research Group predicted that in 2007 U.S. firms would spend US $95 billion on offshore outsourcing to India (the largest recipient of outsourced jobs) of approximately 200 000 IT jobs. (Forrester Research, 2004; eMarketer, 2004). According to Gartner and other consulting groups, CIOs of major U.S. corporations are under considerable pressure to outsource as much of their non-strategic systems development work as feasible in order to reduce the cost of IS operations (McCue, 2006). The reasons for offshore outsourcing are very compelling: A skilled programmer in India or Russia earns about $12 000 per year, compared to a typical programmer in Canada, who makes $60 000 per year. The Internet has drastically lowered the cost of communicating with and coordinating offshore development teams. In addition to cost savings, outsourcing provides firms with access to world-class complementary technology assets and skills.

Offshore software outsourcing

There is a very strong chance that at some point in your career, you will be working with offshore outsourcers or global teams. Thus, it is very important to understand how offshore resources can best be managed. Not all work can be exported, special managerial and organizational issues must be addressed, and the savings are not as great as simple wage comparisons suggest (Krishna, Sahay, and Walsham, 2004).

Your firm is most likely to benefit from outsourcing if it takes the time to evaluate all the risks and to make sure outsourcing is appropriate for its particular needs. Any company that outsources its applications must thoroughly understand the project, including requirements, method of implementation, source of expected benefits, cost components of the project, and metrics for measuring performance.

Offshore outsourcing can reduce software development costs, but companies will not save as much as they initially think. There are hidden costs to offshore outsourcing, and these costs can increase the total cost of ownership (TCO) of offshore-developed software by more than 50 percent. Here are the major cost components of offshore software development:

- *Contract cost.* Most of this cost is for labour required by the project—programmers, software engineers, systems analysts, network specialists, project team managers.

- *Vendor selection costs.* With any outsourced service, the expense of selecting a service provider can run from 0.1 percent to 10 percent in addition to the cost of the contract. Companies will need to allocate resources for documenting requirements, sending out requests for proposal (RFPs), travel expenses, negotiating contracts, legal fees, and project management. A project leader may be assigned to work full-time on this, with others contributing, and these are lost labour costs. The entire vendor selection process can take three to six months to a year.

- *Transition management and knowledge transfer costs.* It takes from three months to a full year to completely transfer work to an offshore partner and make sure the vendor thoroughly understands your business. Users should be prepared to spend even more time with the offshore team than an in-house group to make sure the team fully understands their requirements. A certain number of outsourcer staff have to travel to the client company to analyze the client's technology and applications before they can begin the actual work. The client company's systems and specifications have to be thoroughly documented. The offshore employees have to work in parallel with costly in-house employees, and neither can produce very much during the training period. If not included in the outsourcing contract, additional travel costs and visa costs must be figured in. Companies should expect to spend an additional 2 to 3 percent of their contracts on transition costs.

- *Domestic human resources costs.* If your company has to lay off domestic employees as a result of the offshore outsourcing, you may have to pay laid-off workers severance pay and retention bonuses to keep them working long enough to share their knowledge with their offshore replacements. Layoffs can also adversely impact employee morale and productivity. The firm's staff may resist working with the outsourcer and resign, taking valuable knowledge with them. Layoffs and related costs can add an extra 3 to 5 percent.

- *Costs of improving software development processes.* If a company does not have solid in-house processes for software development, it will take much longer to coordinate work with the vendor.

Both parties should agree on the processes to be used. If the outsourcer has to follow your standards, make sure the offshore team thoroughly understands them.

North American firms often use rather informal methods for documenting and analyzing software projects. They may need to formalize their software development processes and adopt the methodology used by the offshore vendor. (Many Indian companies use the Capability Maturity Model [CMM] developed by Carnegie-Mellon as their software development methodology, and their clients may need to come up to speed on CMM to work effectively with Indian outsourcers.) Ability to write clear specifications is critical as well, and creating a good set of specifications is very time-consuming.

Quality assurance testing also must be beefed-up in an offshore arrangement. There must be a dedicated group of people in the client organization who are always available to develop test plans and review results as they are generated by the offshore team.

Companies outsourcing software development to external vendors should anticipate spending an additional 1 to 10 percent on improving software development processes.

- *Costs of adjusting to cultural differences.* Cultural differences can drain productivity. A seasoned Canadian employee cannot automatically be replaced by an offshore worker. Their values and attitudes are different. American workers tend to feel much more comfortable about speaking up and making suggestions. If something does not make sense or does not appear workable, they will voice concerns. But offshore programmers may keep these feelings to themselves, believing that their aim is to please and that this is what the client wants. The work then may take more time and money to complete and require extensive rework. Likewise, an application that makes sense to a Canadian worker, such as automatically logging all customer calls, may be a foreign concept offshore. Lags in productivity caused by the need to adjust to cultural differences can add as much as 20 percent of additional costs to the offshore contract during the first two years. There will probably be a need for more face-to-face interaction, or more time spent on Internet teleconferencing, or Skyping at odd hours, than originally anticipated because offshore workers do not interpret things the same way.

- *Cost of managing an offshore contract.* Managing the offshore relationship requires additional work—such as invoicing, auditing, additional telecommunications costs, ensuring work is billed correctly, and making sure time is properly recorded. Maintaining security merits special attention. Offshoring partners must agree on common procedures for data security, data recovery, protection of intellectual property rights, network security, and access control. For example, the EU Data Privacy Directive could prohibit an outsourcing agreement from transferring personal data to non-EU countries unless both parties satisfy EU data protection standards. Companies should expect to pay an additional 6 to 10 percent on managing the offshore contract.

Figure 11-6 shows best- and worst-case scenarios for the total cost of ownership of an outsourcing project. It shows how much hidden costs can affect the total cost of an outsourcing project. The best case reflects the lowest estimates for additional costs, and the worst case reflects the highest estimates for these costs. As you can see, hidden costs will increase the total cost of an outsourcing project by an extra 15 to 57 percent.

Even with these extra costs, many firms will benefit from offshore outsourcing if they manage the work well. The total cost of doing the software work in-house might run to $18 million, so even under the worse-case scenario, the firm would still save about 15 percent.

FIGURE 11-6 *Total cost of offshore outsourcing*

Cost of outsourcing contract			$10 000 000	
Hidden Costs	Best Case	Additional Cost ($)	Worst Case	Additional Cost ($)
1. Vendor selection	0.2%	20 000	2%	200 000
2. Transition costs	2%	200 000	3%	300 000
3. Layoffs & retention	3%	300 000	5%	500 000
4. Lost productivity/cultural issues	3%	300 000	27%	2 700 000
5. Improving development processes	1%	100 000	10%	1 000 000
6. Managing the contract	6%	600 000	10%	1 000 000
Total additional costs		**1 520 000**		**5 700 000**
	Outstanding Contract ($)	Additional Cost ($)	Total Cost ($)	Additional Cost
Total cost of outsourcing (TCO) best case	10 000 000	1 520 000	11 520 000	15.2%
Total cost of outsourcing (TCO) worst case	10 000 000	5 700 000	15 700 000	57.0%

If a firm spends $10 million on offshore outsourcing contracts, that company will actually spend 15.2 percent in extra costs even under the best-case scenario. In the worst-case scenario, where there is a dramatic drop in productivity along with exceptionally high transition and layoff costs, a firm can expect to pay up to 57 percent in extra costs on top of the $10 million outlay for an offshore contract.

Although offshore software outsourcing might benefit individual firms, its broader social impact is less clear and much more controversial in the countries that are shipping jobs to low-wage countries. Of course, in the countries that are the recipients of these outsourced jobs, the practice is celebrated not only as a powerful tool for economic development, but as a reflection of the natural order of international trade and comparative advantage. They argue that North America benefits from outsourcing because the cost of developing systems falls, and hence more systems can be developed. The fear in developed countries such as Canada and the U. S., which are creating tens of thousands of IT jobs in India and other low-wage countries, is that this practice lowers wages paid to North American technical and managerial workers in the IS area and, worse, may permanently damage the systems-development capabilities of North American workers. The Window on Management section looks at both sides of the debate.

WINDOW ON MANAGEMENT

Management

Offshore Outsourcing: Good, Bad, or Does Not Make a Difference?

When truck rental giant Penske buys a new truck and leases it out to commercial trucking companies, its Indian vendor Genpact remotely arranges for state titles, registrations, and permits electronically from Hyderabad, India. When the truck is rented and returned, the driver's log and taxes, fuel, and toll documents are sent to Genpact. The paperwork is sent to Genpact's office in Juarez, Mexico, where the information is entered into Penske's computer system. Other workers in Hyderabad complete entering data for tax filings and accounting purposes. Penske's practice of "componentizing" its business processes and sending out large chunks of business processes, including data entry and routine administration, is becoming standard practice in American service and manufacturing firms. It is part of a swelling movement toward offshore outsourcing, a term designating the movement of white-collar jobs abroad. Many other companies, including Delta Air Lines and American Express, have moved their call centres to India or the Philippines. The consulting firm Accenture has doubled its staff in India to 10 000. Procter & Gamble has 7000 workers handling payroll, travel, benefits administration, accounts payable, and invoice processing in offices in Costa Rica, the Philippines, and the United Kingdom. Mindcrest Incorporated of Chicago maintains a staff of 15 in Bombay to provide legal research for companies and law firms.

Canada has long prospered as a call-centre home for U.S. businesses, but that may be changing. Not only are Indian firms and firms from several other countries cheaper for firms to use as call centres; Canadian call centre firms may even be taken over by Indian firms. In 2006, TransWorks Information Services of India announced a $200-million takeover of Minacs Worldwide Inc. (TSX:MXW), a Toronto-based call centre specialist. TransWorks is part of the Aditya Birla Group, one of India's leading business process outsourcing companies. It employs more than 4200 employees in India and Canada.

An estimated 1.4 million call centre jobs, telemarketing jobs, financial analysts, and jobs in banking and insurance in North America have been steadily moving offshore. Also threatened are jobs in medical transcription, insurance applications and claims processing, and typesetting, as well as some jobs in accounting and tax preparation. Low-cost telecommunications networks and the Internet make it possible to communicate and exchange documents with people many thousands of kilometres away as inexpensively as if they were in the next town. Estimates differ greatly, but there are arguably more than 250 000 IT-related jobs from low-level programming to system administration, management, and design that used to be performed in North America but are now performed in India.

Forrester Research estimated that 3.3 million white-collar jobs will be transferred from the U.S. abroad by 2015. The impact of offshore outsourcing in the information technology industry could be especially severe: According to the Gartner Group, one out of 10 jobs in U.S. computer services may have already shifted to lower-cost countries such as Russia or India. Unfortunately, similar statistics are not available for Canada, but the trend appears to be growing.

In mid-July 2003, IBM set off a firestorm when news of its plans to move more white-collar and programming jobs overseas was leaked to the press. By 2006, IBM was employing more than 40 000 people in India. Hewlett-Packard has 5000 Indian employees in research, software development, and customer support. Many non-technology companies now use offshore programmers for much of their routine programming work, as well as low-level clerical jobs and some management jobs in human services, engineering, logistics, and procurement.

Critics claim that offshore outsourcing shifts jobs from high-wage countries to low-wage countries, taking jobs away from Canadian workers or pressuring them to take lower pay to remain working. These critics fear that highly trained and educated workers will be ground down by globalization, just as blue-collar workers were in the 1970s and 1980s.

But other experts point out that offshore outsourcers often provide better quality work at lower costs. Domestic firms also have a better chance of long-term survival if they can keep their costs low, and prices more competitive. Companies can pass these savings from outsourcing on to consumers or use them to expand the business and create new jobs that provide more value than those replaced. In addition, in Canada, outsourcing firms can offer lower costs for U.S. firms, resulting in the possibility of an additional 200 000 IT sector jobs in Canada (Canadian Chamber of Commerce, 2005).

Employment is growing as the labour force grows. Given the huge labour market, the number of jobs being outsourced to India is a drop in the bucket with respect to overall levels of employment, even though certain occupations (generally those requiring less education and lower pay) are hit particularly hard.

In the IT sector, over the next five years, Canadian businesses will have to fill no fewer than 90 000 new IT positions, said Stephen Ibaraki, vice-president, Canadian Information Processing Society (CIPS) and association of IT professionals in Toronto. However, according to a recent article, "Canadian colleges and universities will not produce the required number of qualified candidates for these positions. Of the 90 000 vacancies, around 60 000 will be newly created positions and an estimated 30 000 will result from retirement" (Arellano, 2007). Without help from India in the form of outsourcing, there would be a severe IT labour shortage in Canada, the cost of systems would rise, and firms would reduce spending on systems. With outsourcing, the cost of system development and operation might just stabilize, and relative to other capital goods, fall in price. This could result in more systems-development activity and growing demand for many higher-level IT employees.

To Think About

1. Does offshore outsourcing create an ethical dilemma? Why or why not?

2. Should offshore outsourcing be restricted? How? Why or why not?

3. How could the outsourcing of jobs lead to the creation of new jobs in Canada? Explain your reasoning.

MIS in Action

1. WIPRO is one of India's largest outsourcing firms. Visit www.wipro.com, click on "Investor," and read the financial portions of their current annual report. On a spreadsheet, chart their revenue, operating margin, and profit growth for the years reported. How fast did WIPRO grow in the last year? What are some of the limitations on this growth in the next five years?

2. There are many other countries where outsourcing is growing very rapidly. Why is this so? Read the article by Pete Engardio, "The Future of Outsourcing," *BusinessWeek*, January 30, 2006. Make a table containing three columns. In the left column, create a list of the top 10 outsourcing countries, and in the centre column, briefly explain the advantages of outsourcing to these countries. In the right column, briefly explain the risks of outsourcing to these countries.

3. *CIO Magazine* publishes an annual outsourcing guide. Go to the CIO.com Web site and read the "2006 Global Outsourcing Guide." You can search the site for this guide or go to www.cio.com/archive/071506/global_outsourcing.html. What is the "cost versus risk" equation discussed in this report? After reading this report, describe how you would balance the cost versus risk when choosing an offshore outsourcing firm.

Sources: Daniel Gross, "Why 'Outsourcing' May Lose Its Power as a Scare Word," *The New York Times*, August 13, 2006; Pete Engardio, "The Future of Outsourcing," *BusinessWeek*, January 30, 2006; Global Insight, "IT Outsourcing and the U.S. Economy," October, 2005; Charles Schultz, "Offshoring, Import Competition, and the Jobless Recovery," The Brookings Institute, Washington D.C., June 2004; Catherine Mann, "Globalization of IT Services and White Collar Jobs: the Next Wave of Productivity Growth," Institute for International Economics, December 2003; Stephen Baker and Manjeet Kripalani, "Software: Will Outsourcing Hurt America's Supremacy?" *BusinessWeek*, March 1, 2004; and Jesse Drucker and Ken Brown, "Press 1 for Delhi, 2 for Dallas," *Wall Street Journal*, March 9, 2004; Nestor E. Arellano, "Canadian IT Industry Needs Image Makeover, say Analysts," *ITWorld Canada*, January 24, 2007; Rita Trichur, "Transworks Takeover of Minacs Could Result in Some Jobs Going to India: Analyst," CBC News, June 26, 2006, www.cbc.ca/cp/business/060626/b062652.html, accessed August 11, 2007; and Nestor E. Arellano, "Canadian IT Industry Needs Image Makeover, say Analysts," *ITWorld Canada*, January 24, 2007.

Summary

1. *Identify the major factors driving the internationalization of business.*

   General cultural factors and specific business factors drive offshore expansion. The growth of cheap international communication and transportation has created a world culture with stable expectations or norms. Political stability and a growing global knowledge base that is widely shared also contribute to the world culture. These general factors create the conditions for global markets, global production, coordination, distribution, and global economies of scale.

2. *Compare strategies for developing global businesses.*

   There are four basic international strategies: domestic exporter, multinational, franchiser, and transnational. In a domestic exporter strategy, there is heavy centralization of corporate activities in the home country of origin. The multinational strategy concentrates financial management and control out of a central home base while decentralizing production, sales, and marketing operations to units in other countries. In a franchiser strategy, the product is created, designed, financed, and initially produced in the home country, but for product-specific reasons, must rely heavily on foreign personnel for further production, marketing, and human resources. In a transnational strategy, all factors of production are coordinated on a global scale. However, the choice of strategy is a function of the type of business and product.

3. *Demonstrate how information systems can support different global business strategies.*

There is a connection between firm strategy and information systems design. Transnational firms must develop networked system configurations and permit considerable decentralization of development and operations. Franchisers almost always duplicate systems across many countries and use centralized financial controls. Multinationals typically rely on decentralized independence among foreign units while there is some movement toward development of networks. Domestic exporters typically are centralized in domestic headquarters with some decentralized operations permitted.

4. *Identify the challenges posed by global information systems and management solutions.*

Global information systems pose challenges because cultural, political, and language diversity magnifies differences in organizational culture and business processes and encourages proliferation of disparate local information systems that are difficult to integrate. Typically, international systems have evolved without a conscious plan. The remedy is to define a small subset of

core business processes and focus on developing systems to support these processes. Tactically, managers will have to co-opt widely dispersed foreign units to participate in the development and operation of these systems, being careful to maintain overall control.

5. *Evaluate the issues and technical alternatives to be considered when developing international information systems.*

Implementing a global system requires a strategy that considers both business design and technology platforms. Typically, global systems have evolved without a conscious plan. The remedy is to define a small subset of core business processes and focus on developing systems that could support these processes. Tactically, you will have to co-opt widely dispersed foreign units to participate in the development and operation of these systems, being careful to maintain overall control.

The main hardware and telecommunications issues are systems integration and connectivity. The choices for integration are to go with either a proprietary architecture or open systems technology. Global networks are extremely difficult to develop and operate. Firms can develop their own global networks or they can create global networks based on the Internet (intranets or virtual private networks). The main software issue concerns developing interfaces to existing systems and selecting applications that can work with multiple cultural, language, and organizational frameworks.

Key Terms

Business driver, 378
Cooptation, 388
Core systems, 386
Domestic exporter, 382
Franchisers, 383

Global culture, 378
International information systems architecture 376
Legitimacy, 388
Multinational, 382

Offshore software outsourcing, 391
Particularism, 379
Transborder data flow, 380
Transnational, 382

Review Questions

1. *What are the five major factors to consider when developing an international information systems portfolio?*

2. *Describe the five general cultural factors leading toward growth in global business and the four specific business factors. Describe the interconnection among these factors.*

3. *What is meant by a global culture?*

4. *What are the major challenges to the development of global systems?*

5. *Why have firms not planned for the development of international systems?*

6. *Describe the four main strategies for global business and organizational structure.*

7. *Describe the four different system configurations that can be used to support different global strategies.*

8. *What are the major management issues in developing international systems?*

9. *What are three principles to follow when organizing the firm for global business?*

10. *What are three steps of a management strategy for developing and implementing global systems?*

11. *What is meant by cooptation, and how can it be used in developing global systems?*

12. *Describe the main technical issues facing global systems.*

13. *Describe some new technologies that help firms develop global systems.*

14. *What is offshore software outsourcing? What challenges does it pose? What are the cost components of offshore software development?*

Discussion Questions

1. *If you were a manager in a company that operates in many countries, what criteria would you use to determine whether an application should be developed as a global application or as a local application?*

2. *Describe ways the Internet can be used in international information systems.*

3. *What are the difficulties in managing a global system? What can be done to alleviate these difficulties?*

4. *As an organization grows, it may become global. What changes does the IS department need to make to be able to meet the challenge of "going global?"*

Teamwork: Identifying Technologies for Global Business Strategies

With a group of students, identify an area of information technology, and explore how this technology might be useful for supporting global business strategies. For instance, you might choose an area such as digital telecommunications (e.g., e-mail, wireless communications, value-added networks), enterprise systems, collaborative work group software, or the Internet. It will be necessary to choose a business scenario to discuss the technology. You might choose, for instance, an automobile parts franchise or a clothing retailer, such as Nygård, as an example. Which applications would you make global, which core business processes would you choose, and how would the technology be helpful? If possible, use electronic presentation software to present your findings to the class.

HANDS-ON MIS   Application Exercises

The projects in this section give you hands-on experience conducting international market research and developing a job posting database and Web page for an international company.

Achieving Operational Excellence: Expanding International Sales

Software skills: Web browser and electronic presentation software
Business skills: Identifying international markets

In this project, you will use the Web to research international markets for a small manufacturing company.

Management would like to expand international sales for Dirt Bikes Canada. You have been asked to analyze opportunities for global business expansion of the company, using the Web to find the information you need. Prepare a report for management that answers the following questions:

1. Which countries would provide the best markets for Dirt Bikes Canada's products? Your analysis should consider factors such as in which countries dirt bikes are popular and the per capita income of these countries.
2. How could Dirt Bikes Canada use the Web to increase international sales? What features should it place on its Web site to attract buyers from the countries it targets?
3. (Optional) If possible, use electronic presentation software to summarize your findings for management.

Achieving Operational Excellence: Developing a Job Database and Web Page for an International Consulting Firm

Software skills: Database and Web page design
Business skills: Human resources internal job postings

Companies with many overseas locations need a way to inform employees about available job openings in these locations. In this project, you will use database software to design a database for posting internal job openings and a Web page for displaying this information.

KTP Consulting operates in various locations around the world. KTP specializes in designing, developing, and implementing enterprise systems for medium- to large-size companies. KTP offers its employees opportunities to travel, live, and work in various locations throughout Canada, Europe, and Asia. The firm's human resources department has a simple database that enables its staff to track job vacancies. When an employee is interested in relocating, she or he contacts the human resources department for a list of KTP job vacancies. KTP also posts its employment opportunities on the company Web site.

1. What type of data should be included in the KTP job vacancies database? What information should not be included in this database? Based on your answers to these questions, develop a job vacancies database for KTP.

2. Populate the database with at least 20 records. You should also develop a simple Web page that incorporates job vacancy data from your newly created database. Submit a copy of the KTP database and Web page to your professor.

Improving Decision Making:
Conducting International Marketing and Pricing Research

Software skills: Internet-based software
Business skills: International pricing and marketing

When companies sell overseas, it is important to determine whether their products are priced properly for non-domestic markets. In this project, you will use the Web to research overseas distributors and customs regulations and use Internet-based software to calculate prices in foreign currencies.

You are in charge of marketing for a Canadian manufacturer of office furniture that has decided to enter the international market. You have been given the name of Sorin SRL, a major Italian office furniture retailer, but your source had no other information. You want to test the market by contacting this firm to offer it a specific desk chair that you have to sell

at about $125. Using the Web, locate the information needed to contact this firm and to find out how many European euros you would need to get for the chair in the current market. One source for locating European companies is the Europages Business Directory (**www.europages .com**). In addition, consider using the Universal Currency Converter Web site (**www.xe.net/ucc/**), which determines the value of one currency expressed in other currencies. Obtain both the information needed to contact the firm and the price of your chair in their local currency. Then locate and obtain customs and legal restrictions on the products you will export from Canada and import into Italy. Finally, locate a company that could represent you as a customs agent and gather information on shipping costs.

CASE STUDY Nestlé Tries for an All-for-One Global Strategy

Nestlé is the largest food and beverage company in the world. Headquartered in Vevey, Switzerland, the company has annual revenues in excess of $70 billion and nearly 250 000 employees at 500 facilities in 200 countries. Best known for its chocolate, coffee (it invented instant coffee), and milk products, Nestlé sells hundreds of thousands of other items, most of which are adapted to fit local markets and cultures.

Traditionally, this huge firm allowed each local organization to conduct business as it saw fit, taking into account the local conditions and business cultures. To support this decentralized strategy, it had 80 different information technology units that ran nearly 900 IBM AS/400 midrange computers, 15 mainframes, and 200 Unix systems, quite a hodgepodge of hardware and operating systems.

However, Nestlé's management found that allowing these local differences created inefficiencies and extra costs that could prevent the company from competing effectively in electronic commerce. The lack of standard

business processes prevented Nestlé from, for example, leveraging its worldwide buying power to obtain lower prices for its raw materials. Even though each factory used the same global suppliers, each negotiated its own deals and prices.

Several years ago, Nestlé embarked on a program to standardize and coordinate its information systems and business processes. The company initially installed SAP's R/3 enterprise resource planning (ERP) software to integrate material, distribution, and accounting applications in Canada, the United States, and Europe.

Nestlé then extended its enterprise systems strategy to all its facilities to make them act as a single-minded e-business. Once this project is completed, Nestlé will be able to use sales information from retailers on a global basis to measure the effectiveness of its promotional activities and will be able to reduce overstocking and spoilage caused by having products sit around too long on grocery shelves.

Achieving global standardization of operational processes has been a complex task. None of Nestlé's products is considered a truly global brand, with perhaps the exception of Nescafé, of which 100 million cups are served around the world each year. But even Nescafé is rebranded, repackaged, and reformulated to create more than 200 product versions for different regional preferences. This is just a small representation of the complexity that CEO Peter Brabeck wanted to address when he decided to bring a sense of order to the company's business operations.

In 1995, Nestlé facilities in 14 countries were running their businesses on SAP R/2, an older version of its ERP software. They all ran the software differently and used different schemes for formatting data and managing forms. The system disparity resulted in increasing maintenance costs. Compiling financial reports to gain a company-wide view of performance became more laborious.

Between 1994 and 1999, Nestlé increased its spending on information systems from $575 million to $750 million. Brabeck arrived in 1997, and while the technology budget was growing, he was actually decreasing the size of the company by selling off Nestlé brands. The cost of tracking the sales chain, as a percentage of total sales, rose from 1.2 percent in 1994 to 1.6 percent in 1999.

By April 2000, Brabeck had had enough of a corporate philosophy that allowed for thousands of differently configured supply chains, multiple methods of forecasting demand, and innumerable practices for invoicing customers and collecting payments. The inconsistencies and inefficiencies across the enterprise were chipping away at Nestlé's profits. Brabeck, Chief Financial Officer Mario Corti, and the entire executive board launched a $2.8 billion initiative to compel its market heads around the world to adopt a single set of business processes and systems for procurement, distribution, and sales management.

Chris Johnson, who was in charge of Nestlé's Taiwan market, was asked to lead the initiative that would come to be known as GLOBE (Global Business Excellence). Johnson was instructed to find a way to harmonize processes, standardize data, and standardize systems. All Nestlé's worldwide business units were to use the same processes for making sales commitments, establishing factory production schedules, billing customers, compiling management reports, and reporting financial results. The units would no longer be permitted to adhere to local customs for conducting business except in cases where the laws of a particular country required that they do so. Every Nestlé facility would format and store data identically, using the same set of information systems. Johnson would have to oversee the confluence of divergent processes into a "single source of truth." Johnson would have three and a half years to deploy the GLOBE strategy in 70 percent of the company's global markets.

Such an undertaking was unusual for Nestlé. Large projects, such as the construction of a coffee factory, generally cost the company in the range of $35 million to $46 million. Putting up billions of dollars to fund a project was risky, but for Brabeck, the potential benefits were too important. He could significantly curb IT spending, which was growing dangerously. In addition, he could gain an advantage over competitors such as Unilever and Kraft Foods in improving operational efficiency while continuing to grow with new markets and new products. Nestlé would also be able to reduce its number of suppliers from 600 000 to 167 000, and save hundreds of millions of dollars in the process. The savings would be reinvested in innovation, pleasing its largest customers such as Wal-Mart and Tesco, and further strengthening Nestlé's position among the other global food suppliers. It would be the first global enterprise to conduct business as though it were operating in a single country.

The goal was lofty, and previous attempts at cooperative standards had had mixed results. Technology experts from headquarters had emphasized standards and best practices to the 14 countries that deployed SAP in the past. The pleas for a unified corporate culture were largely ignored. On the other hand, market managers in Asia had come together to develop a common system for managing their supply chains using software from SSA Global. The Business Excellence Common Application flourished in Indonesia, Malaysia, the Philippines, and Thailand, and even spread to South Africa. The American division of Nestlé also standardized its practices using SAP software in a project known as BEST (Business Excellence through Systems Technology). However, it was the Asian effort that would serve as the model due to its success in crossing cultures and satisfying multiple market managers.

GLOBE, under the leadership of Johnson, launched on July 4, 2000. Johnson had support from Olivier Gouin, chief information officer for Nestlé in France, and a panel of 12 senior executives with various backgrounds who had been chosen specifically for the project. Even before beginning the likely difficult task of convincing market managers worldwide to adopt a centralized culture, the GLOBE team had a more pressing challenge to confront: Was it actually possible to convert 70 percent of the business to a common set of best practices and systems by the December 2003 deadline?

There were to be no shortcuts. Everything had to be standardized on the new mySAP Internet-based software. Moreover, the deadline had already appeared in a company newsletter, so changing the date could have damaged confidence in the project.

Johnson's team studied the experiences of competitors, and received feedback from consultants at PricewaterhouseCoopers and deployment experts at SAP. Johnson and Gouin were not surprised to determine that the parameters of the project would have to be adjusted. GLOBE required a larger staff, more funding, and a larger window of time than the executive board had allotted. The GLOBE team predicted that its staff would need to grow to a maximum of 3500 workers.

The team's projections also gave rise to the $2.4 billion budget. Gouin softened the blow of the cost by pointing out that the status quo, individual markets managing their own systems, was projected to cost $3.7 billion over five years. In the end, considering the scope of the project, Johnson's team also concluded that the schedule was too ambitious.

The schedule was revised so that a "majority of the company's key markets," rather than 70 percent, would be GLOBE-enabled by the end of 2005, instead of 2003.

Instead of selecting technology managers, Johnson tried to build his team from a diverse group of business managers who had experience in a variety of business sectors including manufacturing, finance, marketing, and human resources. He recruited from Nestlé offices all over the world. He went after the best of the best—managers who were considered "untouchables" because they were too valuable in their current capacities to be let go for new projects.

Johnson put his first team together in the fall of 2000. By the following winter, the team had added 400 executives with diverse career backgrounds at Nestlé covering 40 different countries. In February 2001, this core group began the critical process of compiling the GLOBE Best Practices Library. The 400 were knowledgeable in how the company actually conducted business. They would need to know the processes for everything from calculating product demand and managing the supply chain to generating an invoice and ordering office equipment. Many of these processes had never been documented and were simply passed down by word of mouth. Johnson described the task as converting Nestlé's oral history into decoding "the DNA of how Nestlé does business."

The 400 executives documented the best ways of performing each process. Then, the GLOBE team brought in experts in each area to challenge the processes, find their weaknesses, and pare the list down to the best practice for each process. In this way, the Best Practices Library evolved into an online database of step-by-step guides for 1000 processes, divided into 45 solution sets that focused on disciplines such as demand planning or financial reporting.

Some best practices, such as getting a product to market, were afforded a degree of flexibility to account for the wide variety of Nestlé products and the breadth of markets in which they were sold. Other practices, such as financial reporting, were given no wiggle room. Salespeople were to enter orders with precision in a standard format and by a specific date every month. Financial terms and recording dates were standardized across the enterprise. Johnson later described the accounting software as being "kind of like handcuffs in a way to make you do the right thing."

It became apparent to Johnson that the greatest challenge of GLOBE might not be technical, but personal. Despite clear support for the project from the highest-ranking executives, including Brabeck, managers resisted the idea of giving up control over their business processes to participate in a centralized solution. They feared the loss of decision-making power. Many thought that making back-office operations identical in so many different countries was impractical. They might agree to standardization, but only if it was their particular practices that were made the GLOBE standard. The resistance was fortified by the fact that each country's operations would have to spend its own money to pay for the project.

In the fall of 2001, Johnson was on the defensive. He was given a full day of a three-day meeting to convince market managers that falling in step with GLOBE was in their best interest and in the best interest of the company. The managers peppered him with questions that were intended to demonstrate how GLOBE would make their jobs more difficult and degrade the performance of their units. Johnson did the best he could to satisfy them and then took a frank approach. The project was going to proceed. If they did not

get behind GLOBE, he would be fired, and Brabeck would select one of them to head the massive undertaking. The other managers were not interested in that outcome.

Johnson did receive support that day from Jose Lopez, the head of the Malaysia and Singapore markets, which were being used to test GLOBE's back-office systems. It was too early to measure the benefits of the project, but Lopez expressed his belief in the premise and his willingness to cooperate.

A year and a half later, in the spring of 2003, the market heads had another opportunity to question Johnson. While there were still plenty of questions, a number of them described the operational efficiencies they had achieved since implementing GLOBE standards. For example, their financial reports and demand forecasts were better and faster.

By a third meeting in May 2005, 20 market heads were able to endorse the benefits of GLOBE. In the interim, however, an unwelcome financial problem arose. GLOBE was not controlling information technology costs as expected. As a percentage of sales, costs were approaching 2 percent. Brabeck instituted a cap on information technology expenses at 1.9 percent. In order to meet the cap, Johnson and Gouin revised the schedule of the project again. They set a goal of 80 percent of Nestlé being on the GLOBE system by the end of 2006. The extended schedule allowed the GLOBE team to maintain Brabeck's spending cap and protect the company's profits.

In the fall of 2005, the percentage of Nestlé units running GLOBE reached 25 percent, and costs were within the limit.

To help the rollouts along, Johnson asked each country to name a GLOBE manager who would facilitate the adoption of the system. These managers also provided value to one another by exchanging their experiences with the system and the solutions they employed for specific challenges. Johnson also established a steering committee at company headquarters to schedule and manage the rollouts. The steering committee oversaw the reduction of company data centres from 100 to four, including the centre in Vevey, which stored the GLOBE templates, Best Practices Library, and central functions.

One of Brabeck's biggest concerns was that the rollouts occur with no effect on customers. A rollout could only be a true success if no one outside the company noticed it. The initial test markets found this daunting because they would have to fix bugs and confront unanticipated problems during the deployment. Nestlé also had to implement the new business processes concurrently with the new systems. There was no opportunity to perfect the processes. And, finally, the managers and their workers had no time to train on the new systems before they deployed them and began using them. Despite these challenges, the test markets experienced few problems, and rollouts proceeded around the world. After the test markets, market managers had at least nine months to document their processes and perfect them until they conformed with the GLOBE templates.

Along the way, Nestlé did encounter some technical issues. For example, Canadian market managers used special promotions liberally to attract business from local and regional grocery chains. The mySAP software was not designed to accommodate the extra data points generated by so many promotions. Nestlé worked with SAP to develop a "multiple angles approach" to allow for such a difference. The approach enabled Nestlé to separate the storage of data by market. This way, a country such as Canada could have the extra storage space in the central system that it needed for its promotion data.

By the end of 2005, Nestlé had converted 30 percent of its business to GLOBE and had the capacity for one major rollout every month. The 80 percent goal, which had to be achieved by the end of 2006, still loomed far off, but the company had learned how to operate as a single unit on a global scale. Johnson was not entirely satisfied with the results, citing delayed and flawed summary reports compromising the work of factory and country managers. He was also eager to see reports made available instantly on a 24/7 basis rather than having to wait for them to be completed overnight each day.

To make sure that the data entering GLOBE's streamlined data centres are accurate and complete, each country has a data manager. Johnson believes that the system will never achieve perfection as long as time constraints remain a factor. However, Nestlé is much closer to achiev-

ing its goal of standardizing all processes, data, and systems. The closer the company comes to developing the perfect system, the better the company can serve its customers.

Sources: Tom Steinert-Threlkeld, "Nestlé Pieces Together Its Global Supply Chain," *Baseline Magazine*, January 20, 2006; "Nestlé Group in 2005: Record Sales and Profits—Higher Dividend Proposed," **www.nestle.com**, February 23, 2006; and The Associated Press, "Nestle Reports 14 Percent Rise in Sales," **MSNBC.com**, April 25, 2006, accessed October 11, 2006.

CASE STUDY QUESTIONS

1. Analyze Nestlé using the competitive forces and value chain models. What challenges did Nestlé face?

2. What type of global business and systems strategy did Nestlé adopt? Was this strategy appropriate for Nestlé's business model?

3. With what management, organization, and technology challenges did Nestlé have to deal to standardize its business processes and systems?

4. What strategies did Nestlé management use to deal with these challenges? How successful were these strategies. Explain your answer.

PART III CANADIAN CASE STUDY:
In Tech We Trust: The Story of SAP in Canada

The road to Enterprise Resources Planning (ERP) success is littered with the corpses of many a company and many a CIO who tried and failed at this complex and demanding undertaking. Why do ERP implementations go wrong? Is it information resource management (IRM) practices or change management? What steps can help put companies on the right track?

One question is whether there are certain factors about an organization—for example, its type (e.g., retail, utility, or manufacturing), size, or geographical dispersion—that make it harder or easier to implement an ERP system such as SAP. For example, Morrie Baker and Gary Lackstein plan to take their Ben & Jerry's ice cream "Scoop Shops" franchise operation from three to more than 100 shops in just a few years. Operating a handful (or scoopful) of three ice cream shops may seem like small potatoes, but multiply that number of shops by more than 30, and you have the makings of a small empire of frozen treats. With at least 18 flavours per mini-store, the logistics, inventory, human resources, and other service delivery aspects of this business could become overwhelming. Would SAP help to resolve these issues and make managing the Canada-wide operation easier? Let's look at some Canadian and other companies that have experienced problems and successes with SAP implementations before we return to the Ben & Jerry case.

NOVA Chemicals, a Calgary-based commodity firm, has reached a level of ERP maturity. NOVA produces styrenics

and olefins/polyolefins at 18 locations in Canada, the United States, France, the Netherlands, and the United Kingdom.

By the mid-1990s, NOVA had made a number of acquisitions and had gone through several reorganizations, resulting in a host of outdated legacy systems and a variety of systems running different parts of its business. The company was ripe for significant business process reengineering. Seeing some of its competitors already going the ERP route, NOVA decided to head in that direction as well.

In retrospect, some of NOVA's initial reasons for embarking on its ERP journey may not have been the right ones. As Senior Vice President and CIO John Wheeler observed, "NOVA is a commodity chemical company. We're not as big or as diverse as some of our competitors. But because of the commonality of our business, one of the things we can do is focus on best practices. So over time, it became apparent that ERP was not about technology. It wasn't even about information systems. It was really about building a company that could leverage best practices. It was about business process." When NOVA first embarked on ERP, however, that realization was still years away. Whether developing, purchasing, or outsourcing systems, the first step in the systems development life cycle should be to identify properly the needs of the company and what type of system solution should be planned to meet those needs. Nova failed to do that at first.

NOVA'S INITIAL IMPLEMENTATION

NOVA first took the ERP plunge in 1995 when it decided to implement SAP's new distributed R3 Version 2.2. SAP is the third-largest software company in the world and specializes in client/server enterprise application software modules (see Chapter 12 for a more complete description). That first plunge into ERP can be like taking a dip in a northern lake on a windy January day. NOVA attempted to do a pilot installation in a small U.S.-based styrenics business, but the project faltered and was abandoned. The company had to step back and regroup.

During that first installation, NOVA did not have a CIO. But after that initial setback, it was decided that a CIO was necessary, and the company's vice president and controller, Larry MacDonald, was given that responsibility.

Reflecting on the company's early experiences with ERP, MacDonald points to the newness of the SAP/R3 product and its integrated nature as two early stumbling blocks. "The distributed R3 version was brand new, and people weren't used to the complexity of SAP implementations," he said. "Having something that was so broad and touched on the business from beginning to end—the total supply chain—was something that we did not understand well. We didn't understand the complexities that integration brought to an implementation." With hindsight, we can appreciate that proper IRM practices would have helped Nova better prepare for implementation of its ERP. For example, one way in which NOVA failed to follow IRM practices was by not appointing a CIO early on. This is a sign that they underestimated the scope of the business process improvement and the need to get key people from across the business involved. NOVA also had to abandon the pilot project early. They had underestimated what it would take to deliver the project, train employees to use the software, and persuade employees to use it as well.

What complicated matters was that many of NOVA's business people failed to embrace SAP. NOVA was implementing all modules, so SAP was being installed virtually "wall to wall" throughout the business. The company did not spend enough time learning how to do the implementation. It needed to focus particularly on how to bring SAP into the culture of the organization. A lot of people resisted the early implementations, because they weren't receiving much value from them.

"The change that this was bringing to how people did their work was tremendous," notes MacDonald. "We really had to work on the cultural piece, the education piece, and then the technical piece of it." MacDonald's words suggest that an adequate change management program might have shown value to both management and line employees, and helped to change organizational culture.

In the end, consulting firm Deloitte & Touche became NOVA's main implementation partner. As experienced consultants, they brought a strong change-management capability, as well as strong project- and IT-management methodologies and a good knowledge of SAP. According to Wheeler, NOVA's strong operations and change-management capability today can be attributed to practices introduced by its consulting partner.

THE TURNAROUND

Rallying line management was crucial to the success of the implementation. MacDonald recalls, "Once providing resources to support the implementation became part of line management's job expectations and was clearly embedded in their performance requirements, we started to see a lot of progress. In the initial stages, it wasn't high on the priority list. It had to come from the president that this was important—we had to pay attention to it, and we had to dedicate resources to making this successful."

When John Wheeler was appointed as CIO, business support for ERP was still an issue. His goal was to strengthen support by moving ownership for the system toward the business. A significant measure of management's commitment to the success of NOVA's IT program was current CEO Jeff Lipton's appointment of Wheeler to the company's executive leadership team. Says Wheeler, "Being part of the senior team provides a clear understanding of the expectations of business leaders and an important forum to ensure that we work together to achieve the company's strategic goals."

Wheeler points out that ERP change needs to happen at all levels of an organization; it does not just involve rolling out new hardware and software. "In the early days, the criticism is usually that ERP is an IT implementation. You need to move that ownership toward the business and make IT the enabler. To the extent you can do that earlier rather than later, you'll be more successful," says Wheeler. "The truly mature IT program is the one in which the business owns the process, the system, the costs, and the value. IT's role is to be in partnership with the business, using technology to enable business needs."

Wheeler believes that ERP projects require full-time commitment from business people. And those full-time people should be quality people. "Sometimes the people you get turn out to be the people who are available, rather than the best people. And that's a mistake," he cautioned. "When you're changing your business process in a fundamental way, you cannot afford not to have your best people—and to have them relatively full-time."

SAP: THE COMPANY

Founded in 1972 by four former IBM employees, SAP (Systems, Applications, and Products in Data Processing—pronounced S - A - P) is a dynamic, Germany-based company that creates client/server enterprise application software modules. Today more than 12 million users in 41 200 companies in more than 120 countries run more than 121 000 installations of SAP software. The company has subsidiaries in more than 50 countries. SAP's former CEO and current chair of its supervisory board, Hasso Plattner, is the company's "visioneer," who sees all departments becoming one, not only across an organization, but across its environment as well. He calls this the "City of E."

SAP Canada Inc. was established in 1989 and is the fourth-largest company subsidiary of the parent SAP. SAP Canada has offices in Toronto, Montreal, Ottawa, Calgary, and Vancouver and has more than 900 employees who work with 720 Canadian customers. The Canadian SAP subsidiary is interested not just in making sales. State-of-the-art software products are created by SAP Labs Canada for the mySAP Business Suite family of solutions. The research centre in Montreal is an integral part of SAP's global development network. Developers in SAP Labs Canada software developers are constantly engaged in designing applications for SAP's CRM, Retail and Manufacturing, and Mobile Business solutions.

The two main versions of SAP are R/3 (Release 3) and mySAP, the latest Web-enabled version. Companies can buy entire ERP packages for their particular industry, such as SAP Retail, SAP Mining, or SAP Banking, or they can buy individual modules, such as human resources or financial applications. Implementation of SAP can run into the tens of millions of dollars, including hardware, software, networking, personnel, and consulting components. SAP will not permit a company to adopt its software unless there are SAP-certified programmers and consultants on board for the project. SAP's latest "version" is called Accelerated SAP and is targeted at companies with less than $250 million in sales. Accelerated Solutions are pre-configured, scaled-down versions of R/3. Accelerated SAP claims to have a four-month implementation schedule and is offered at a fixed cost, rather than a per-user cost.

SAP's ERP software can translate foreign currencies and languages and handle taxes that vary worldwide, making it a truly global application. It is a cradle-to-grave application that can cover the life of a product, from financing the production plant to payment from the customer after the product has arrived. But SAP follows the product in its own individual fashion.

SAP software implements "best practices" of companies it has studied, including its customers. Any organization—for profit, not-for-profit, governmental agency—that implements SAP must change its business processes to reflect those found in the way SAP's applications operate. Failure to do so is asking for implementation failure.

Consider Sobeys, Canada's second-largest supermarket chain, which in early 2001 pulled the plug on its SAP implementation after writing off an after-tax loss of about $50 million. Bill McEwan, president and CEO of Nova Scotia–based Sobeys Inc. said that the two-year-old project had "systemic problems of a much more serious nature" than the growing pains they had been led to expect. SAP implementation—after two years—resulted in "unprecedented" stockouts in December 2000 throughout eastern Canada. McEwan said, "The SAP Retail software couldn't effectively deal with the extreme, high number of transactions in our retail operating environment." Business operations were affected for four to five weeks while problems were reconciled.

Indigo Books & Music's story is related to Sobeys's. When Indigo was considering adopting SAP to improve its merchandise assortment planning, Indigo Chief Technical Officer Doug Caldwell called an old friend of his, an executive at Sobeys, to get his opinion on Sobeys's problems with SAP. The Sobeys executive admitted that many of the problems had been Sobey's problems, rather than problems with SAP. After talking with his friend, Caldwell decided to implement SAP at Indigo. SAP knows its customers talk to each other: SAP even sponsors an annual users' conference, partly to let SAP customers talk with each other.

Businesses need to look to their software vendors for support, says Michael Moreia, a technical consultant at ATI Technologies Inc. ATI is a graphics equipment manufacturer based in Markham, Ontario. ATI turned to SAP for more support in order to overcome the obstacles in its SAP implementation. Moreia, however, criticized SAP and its experts: he said SAP failed to bring more support people to Canada. The SAP advisors did help ATI, but the calls they made to Germany happened rather late by Eastern Standard Time. If SAP had utilized local help, it would have afforded more reasonable work hours for the ATI staff.

The City of Ottawa's implementation of SAP also had major growing pains. City staff members channelled their anger toward Deidre Stirling, the city manager of business application management. Stirling and her team were trying to install SAP across Ottawa's IT infrastructure. What added fuel to the fire was a municipal amalgamation process happening at the same time. The implementation was a lengthy and difficult process, but Stirling says, "I survived." Her project did, too. Ottawa spent $40 million on SAP software, but it has already saved $2 million in operational costs. It is expected that the new financial, HR, and property applications will save the city $8 million a year.

For employees of companies that have implemented SAP, one of the major changes is that they work mostly with data and software, rather than with people, according to Barry Hasler of Sony Canada. Another change is that employees cannot get the exact reports and information they were used to getting; SAP reports are standard and do the job, but staff must change the information they need as well as what they do with it in the SAP environment.

But for those who are willing to exercise appropriate change management initiatives—including changes to their policies and procedures, reporting relationships, and training—SAP does its job well. In other words, it's "The SAP Way, or No Way." Organizations that successfully implement SAP spend about one-third of their SAP budget on change management initiatives—training, communicating, consulting, and selling.

Returning to Ben & Jerry's expanding Canadian operation, what do you think—should Baker and Lackstein examine whether or not they should use an ERP system? Should they consider SAP?

Sources: David Carey, "Surviving the ERP Journey," *CIO Canada*, May 1, 2001; Rebecca Maxwell, "Rayovac Gets a Charge from Accelerated SAP," *Computerworld Canada*, September 10, 2000; Curtis Cook and Michelle Schoffro, "SAP Not Just for Big Companies," *Canada Computes*, October 9, 1999; Lucas Mearlan, "Sobeys Says Goodbye to SAP," *Computerworld Online*, February 2, 2001; SAP, "mySAP.com to Power Canada's National Newspaper, *The Globe and Mail*," **www.sap.com**, accessed August 13, 2001; **www.sap.com**, accessed October 1, 2005; **www.sap.com/Canada/company**, accessed October 1, 2005; Chris Conrath, "SAP is Sold on the Internet," *Network World Canada*, July 28, 2000; and Stefan Dubowski, "Book Retailer Spins Its Tale of SAP Tips," *Computerworld Canada*, June 10, 2005, **www.itworldcanada.com/a/search/6edebed9-0d6c-4909-b41a-204441899dcc.html**, accessed October 1, 2005.

Video Resources:

"In Tech We Trust." *Undercurrents* 113. Canadian Broadcasting Corporation. October 31, 1999; and "Ben & Jerry's Ice Cream Moves into Canada 'The Frozen Empire.'" *Venture* 935. Canadian Broadcasting Corporation. January 30, 2005.

CASE STUDY QUESTIONS

1. What sort of businesses should invest in SAP's ERP applications? Should a company adopt all the SAP modules? How does a company decide that it needs an ERP solution?

2. What specific change management actions might a company adopting SAP take to ensure implementation success?

3. Why does SAP consider it necessary for SAP-certified programmers and consultants to work with companies implementing SAP?

4. It has been said that SAP is a change management program or philosophy. Do you agree or disagree? Why? What might happen to implementation if a company chose to try to adapt SAP to its own processes rather than adapting its processes to SAP?

5. Do you believe that Ben & Jerry's Canadian operation should implement SAP? Why or why not?

PART IV

How Digital Businesses Use Information and Systems

PART IV Canadian Case Study
Second Life: A New Generation of Online Application

CHAPTER 12

Enterprise Applications to Manage Supply Chains and Respond to Customers

LEARNING OBJECTIVES

After completing this chapter, you will be able to do the following:

1. Demonstrate how enterprise systems achieve operational excellence by integrating and coordinating diverse functions and business processes in the firm.

2. Demonstrate how supply chain management systems coordinate planning, production, and logistics with suppliers.

3. Demonstrate how customer relationship management systems achieve customer intimacy by integrating all customer information and making it available throughout the firm.

4. Assess the challenges posed by enterprise applications.

5. Describe how enterprise applications can be used in platforms for new cross-functional services.

OPENING **CASE** | Sony Canada Fixes Its Supply Chain

Sony Canada is headquartered in Toronto and has sales offices in Montreal, Toronto, Calgary, and Vancouver, as well as distribution centres in Coquitlam, B.C., and Whitby, ON. The distribution centres employ 1100 people to support more than 70 Sony stores and a Canadian network of 3000 authorized dealers. Sony Canada has more than 1000 products to process through inventory along its demand chain.

With so many dealers and stores, Sony Canada found it increasingly hard to get the right product to the right place at the right time. Sony Canada needed to capture customer data to better understand its customers' buying trends.

Sony Canada has always been in the forefront of innovation. Almost 50 years ago, a Canadian retailer made the first purchase of a Sony product outside of Japan. Although Sony Canada is a wholly owned subsidiary of Sony Corporation headquartered in Tokyo, the Canadian subsidiary has been a proving ground for all other Sony subsidiaries.

In the late 1990s, Sony Canada had become one of the first Sony companies to implement SAP enterprise software, using SAP for financial, inventory management, and sales distribution functions. Because of the company's previous experience with SAP, Sony Canada chose the mySAP™ Customer Relationship Management (mySAP CRM) application. Sony Canada wanted to use the new SAP application to capture the life cycle of its customers from warranty registration to additional mail and e-mail promotions.

Sony Canada's call centre representatives handled customer inquiries using multiple systems, but with the implementation of mySAP CRM, the company was able to integrate its customer information at the call centres. In addition, the system captures all call centre call data, enabling a more consistent process than previously possible.

Trying to reduce inventory throughout its supply chain—from retailers and dealers to its own distribution centres—Sony Canada then implemented SAP's Advanced Planning and Optimization (SAP APO) module, enabling the company to conduct better demand planning and better vendor-managed inventory. By integrating SAP, electronic data interchange (EDI), and a third-party-run B2B Web site, Sony Canada today receives more than 90 percent of its orders electronically. Using the CRM module, Sony Canada can now "slice and dice the customer data to understand the demographics of who was buying what," according to CIO Wayne Ground.

Using yet another SAP module, this one on business intelligence, Sony Canada can use cus-

tomer analytics to launch targeted marketing campaigns that use SonyStyle, the company's business-to-consumer (B2C) Web site. With this business intelligence module, Sony Canada can connect to its key trading parties electronically to gather data for forecasting, thereby reducing inventory while still ensuring that the right product is at the right place at the right time. In essence, Sony Canada wanted to replace inventory with information. Sony Canada conducted a manual pilot test of the new concepts while implementing the project. The test results exceeded expectations in all areas including inventory levels and turns, revenue and margin improvements and customer service level improvements.

Sources: Sun Microsystems, "Customer Snapshot: Manufacturing: Sony of Canada," **www.sun.com/customers/servers/sony_ca.hml**, accessed May 1, 2007; Deloitte, "Sony Canada Launches New High Velocity Supply Chain," **www.deloitte.com/dtt/case_study/0,1005,sid%253D3648% 2526cid% 352D32458,00.html**, accessed May 1, 2007; and Sony Canada, "Sony and SAP Team Up to Keep Ahead in Competitive Retail Market," **www.sap.com/industries/hightech/pdf/CS_Sony_Canada.pdf**, accessed May 1, 2007.

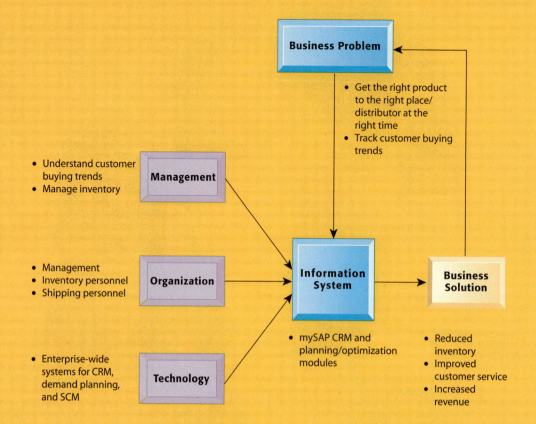

Sony's problems with its supply chain illustrate the critical role of supply chain management in business. Sony needed to provide more rapid, more effective inventory replenishment for its retailers. The company needed better control over its demand chain.

The chapter-opening Business Challenges diagram calls attention to important points raised by this case and this chapter. Like many large firms, Sony has several thousand intermediate customers (such as its own stores and authorized dealers), and these customers in turn have thousands of customers for Sony's products. Altogether, Sony Canada deals with a large number of locations that sell Sony products, from televisions to stereos to videocameras. Ensuring that the right products show up at the retailers at the right time and that the right amount of products were actually ordered are available was a major problem. Replacing outdated systems with supply chain management software from SAP improved Sony Canada's coordination of inventory with demand, which lowered costs and ultimately increased profitability.

HEADS UP

This chapter focuses on how firms use enterprise-wide systems to achieve operational excellence, customer intimacy, and improved decision making. Enterprise systems and systems for supply chain management and customer relationship management help companies integrate information from many different parts of the business, forge closer ties with customers, and coordinate firm activities with those of suppliers and other business partners.

- If your career is in finance and accounting, you will be working with enterprise resource planning systems with comprehensive financial modules that integrate financial information from manufacturing, marketing, and sales.

- If your career is in human resources, you will be helping your firm deal with the "people" issues that are critical to the successful implementation of enterprise applications, such as changing job responsibilities, new training, and overcoming resistance to change.

- If your career is in information systems, you will be evaluating and installing software for enterprise applications and helping your company redesign its business processes to work with the new software.

- If your career is in manufacturing, production, or operations management, you will be using enterprise systems and supply chain management systems to plan, make, and deliver products and services to customers more rapidly and accurately at lower cost.

- If your career is in sales and marketing, you will be using customer relationship management systems to plan marketing campaigns, identify profitable customers, advance new products and services, generate sales leads, and fine-tune customer service.

12.1 Enterprise Systems

Around the globe, companies are increasingly becoming more connected, both internally and with other companies. If you run a business, you want to be able to react instantaneously when a customer places a large order or when a shipment from a supplier is delayed. You may also want to know the impact of these events on every part of the business and how the business is performing at any point in time, especially if you are running a large company. Enterprise systems provide the integration to make this possible. Let us look at how they work and what they can do for the firm.

What Are Enterprise Systems?

Imagine that you had to run a business based on information from tens or even hundreds of different databases and systems, none of which could speak to one another. Imagine your company had 10 different major product lines, each produced in separate factories, and each with separate and incompatible sets of systems controlling production, warehousing, and distribution. Your decision making would often be based on manual hard copy reports, often out of date, and it would be difficult to really understand what was happening in the business as whole. You would have a very poor grasp of how profitable the firm was as a whole, or what your costs were. You now have a good idea of why firms need a special enterprise system to integrate information.

Chapter 2 introduced enterprise systems, also known as enterprise resource planning (ERP) systems, which are based on a suite of integrated software modules and a common central database. The database collects data from many different divisions and departments in a firm and from a large number of key business processes in manufacturing and production, finance and accounting, sales and marketing, and human resources, making the data available for applications that support nearly all of an organization's internal business activities. When new information is entered by one process, the information is made available immediately to other business processes (see Figure 12-1).

If a sales representative places an order for tire rims, for example, the system verifies the customer's credit limit, schedules the shipment, identifies the best shipping route, and reserves the necessary items from inventory. If inventory stock were insufficient to fill the order, the system schedules the manufacture of more rims, ordering the needed materials and components from suppliers. Sales and production forecasts are immediately updated. General ledger and corporate cash levels are automatically updated with the revenue and cost information from the order. Users could tap into the system and find out where that particular order was at any minute. Management could obtain information at any point in time about how the business was operating. The system could also generate enterprise-wide data for management analyses of product cost and profitability.

FIGURE 12-1 *How enterprise systems work*

Enterprise systems feature a set of integrated software modules and a central database that enables data to be shared by many different business processes and functional areas throughout the enterprise.

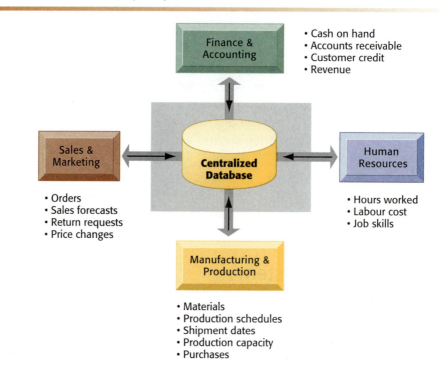

Enterprise Software

Enterprise software is developed around thousands of predefined business processes that reflect best practices. **Best practices** are the most successful solutions or problem-solving methods in an industry for consistently and effectively achieving a business objective. Best practices emerge from two sources: consulting firms that work for many firms in an industry and enterprise software firms that develop industry expertise working with many clients. When your firm hires a consulting company or enterprise software firm to help you develop your own enterprise system, you are in reality hiring the knowledge base of best practices accumulated by these companies over many years. Table 12-1 describes some of the major business processes supported by enterprise software.

Companies implementing this software would have to first select the functions of the system they wished to use and then map their business processes to the predefined business processes in the software. A firm would use configuration tables provided by the software to tailor a particular aspect of the system to the way it does business. For example,

Enterprise software

Best practices

TABLE 12-1 *Business Processes Supported by Enterprise Systems*

Financial and accounting processes, including general ledger, accounts payable, accounts receivable, fixed assets, cash management and forecasting, product-cost accounting, cost-centre accounting, asset accounting, tax accounting, credit management, and financial reporting

Human resources processes, including personnel administration, time accounting, payroll, personnel planning and development, benefits accounting, applicant tracking, time management, compensation, workforce planning, performance management, and travel expense reporting

Manufacturing and production processes, including procurement, inventory management, purchasing, shipping, production planning, production scheduling, material requirements planning, quality control, distribution, transportation execution, and plant and equipment maintenance

Sales and marketing processes, including order processing, quotations, contracts, product configuration, pricing, billing, credit checking, incentive and commission management, and sales planning the firm could use these tables to select whether it wants to track revenue by product line, geographical unit, or distribution channel.

If the enterprise software does not support the way the organization does business, companies can rewrite some of the software to support the way their business processes work. However, enterprise software is unusually complex, and extensive customization may degrade system performance, compromising the information and process integration that are the main benefits of the system. If companies want to reap the maximum benefits from enterprise software, they must change the way they work to conform to the business processes in the software.

Major enterprise software vendors include SAP, Oracle (with its acquisition of PeopleSoft), SSA Global, Lawson Software, and Microsoft (which sells the Dynamics software suite). There are versions of enterprise software packages designed for small businesses and versions obtained through application service providers over the Web. Although initially designed to automate the firm's internal back-office business processes, enterprise systems have become more externally oriented and capable of communicating with customers, suppliers, and other organizations.

Business Value of Enterprise Systems

Enterprise systems provide value both by increasing operational efficiency and by providing firm-wide information to help managers make better decisions. Large companies with many operating units in different locations have used enterprise systems to enforce standard practices and data so that everyone does business the same way worldwide.

Coca-Cola, for instance, implemented a SAP enterprise system to standardize and coordinate important business processes in 200 countries. Lack of standard, company-wide business processes prevented the company from leveraging its worldwide buying power to obtain lower prices for raw materials and from reacting rapidly to market changes.

Enterprise systems help firms respond rapidly to customer requests for information or products. Because the system integrates order, manufacturing, and delivery data, manufacturing is better informed about producing only what customers have ordered, procuring exactly the right amount of components or raw materials to fill actual orders, staging production, and minimizing the time that components or finished products are in inventory.

Enterprise software includes analytical tools for using data captured by the system to evaluate overall organizational performance. Enterprise system data have common standardized definitions and formats that are accepted by the entire organization. Performance figures mean the same thing across the company. Enterprise systems allow senior management to easily find out at any moment how a particular organizational unit is performing or to determine which products are most or least profitable.

12.2 Supply Chain Management Systems

If you manage a small firm that makes a few products or sells a few services, chances are you will have a small number of suppliers. You could coordinate your supplier orders and deliveries using a telephone and fax machine. But if you manage a firm that produces more complex products and services, then you will have hundreds or even thousands of suppliers, and your suppliers will each have their own set of suppliers. Suddenly, you are in a situation where you will need to coordinate the activities of many supplier firms in order to produce your products and services. Supply chain management systems, which we introduced in Chapter 2, are an answer to these problems of supply chain complexity and scale.

The Supply Chain

A firm's **supply chain** is a network of organizations and business processes for procuring raw materials, transforming these materials into intermediate and finished products, and

Supply chain

distributing the finished products to customers. It links suppliers, manufacturing plants, distribution centres, retail outlets, and customers to supply goods and services from source through consumption. Materials, information, and payments flow through the supply chain in both directions.

Goods start out as raw materials and, as they move through the supply chain, are transformed into intermediate products (also referred to as components or parts), and finally, into finished products. The finished products are shipped to distribution centres and from there to retailers and customers. Returned items flow in the reverse direction from the buyer back to the seller.

Let us look at the supply chain for Nike sneakers as an example. Nike designs, markets, and sells sneakers, socks, athletic clothing, and accessories throughout the world. Its primary suppliers are contract manufacturers with factories in China, Thailand, Indonesia, Brazil, and other countries. These companies fashion Nike's finished products.

Nike's contract suppliers do not manufacture sneakers from scratch. They obtain components for the sneakers—the laces, eyelets, uppers, and soles—from other suppliers and then assemble them into finished sneakers. These suppliers in turn have their own suppliers. For example, the suppliers of soles have suppliers for synthetic rubber, suppliers for chemicals used to melt the rubber for moulding, and suppliers for the moulds into which to pour the rubber. Suppliers of laces have suppliers for their thread, dyes, and for the plastic lace tips.

Figure 12-2 provides a simplified illustration of Nike's supply chain for sneakers. It shows the flow of information and materials among suppliers, Nike, and Nike's distributors, retailers, and customers. Nike's contract manufacturers are its primary suppliers. The suppliers of soles, eyelets, uppers, and laces are the secondary (Tier 2) suppliers. Suppliers to these suppliers are the tertiary (Tier 3) suppliers.

The *upstream* portion of the supply chain includes the company's suppliers, the suppliers' suppliers, and the processes for managing relationships with them. The *downstream* portion (sometimes called the "demand chain") consists of the organizations and processes for distributing and delivering products to the final customers. Companies doing manufacturing, such as Nike's contract suppliers of sneakers, also manage their own *internal supply chain* processes for transforming materials, components, and services furnished by their suppliers into finished products or intermediate products (components or parts) for their customers and for managing materials and inventory.

The supply chain illustrated in Figure 12-2 has been simplified. It shows only two contract manufacturers for sneakers and only the upstream supply chain for sneaker soles.

FIGURE 12-2   *Nike's supply chain*

This figure illustrates the major entities in Nike's supply chain and the flow of information upstream and downstream to coordinate the activities involved in buying, making, and moving a product. Shown here is a simplified supply chain, with the upstream portion focusing only on the suppliers for sneakers and sneaker soles.

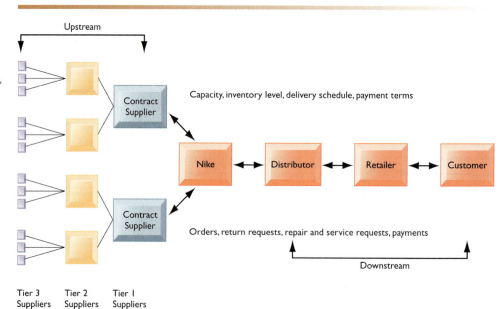

Nike has hundreds of contract manufacturers turning out finished sneakers, socks, and athletic clothing, each with its own set of suppliers. The upstream portion of Nike's supply chain would actually comprise thousands of entities. Nike also has numerous distributors and many thousands of retail stores where its shoes are sold, so the downstream portion of its supply chain is also large and complex.

Information and Supply Chain Management

Inefficiencies in the supply chain, such as parts shortages, underutilized plant capacity, excessive finished goods inventory, or high transportation costs, are caused by inaccurate or untimely information. For example, manufacturers may keep too many parts in inventory because they do not know exactly when they will receive their next shipments from their suppliers. Suppliers may order too few raw materials because they do not have precise information on demand. These supply chain inefficiencies waste as much as 25 percent of a company's operating costs.

If a manufacturer had perfect information about exactly how many units of product customers wanted, when they wanted them, and when they could be produced, it would be possible to implement a highly efficient **just-in-time** strategy. Components would arrive exactly at the moment they were needed, and finished goods would be shipped as they left the assembly line.

In a supply chain, however, uncertainties arise because many events cannot be foreseen—uncertain product demand, late shipments from suppliers, defective parts or raw materials, or production process breakdowns. To satisfy customers, manufacturers often deal with such uncertainties and unforeseen events by keeping more material or products in inventory than what they think they may actually need. The safety stock acts as a buffer for the lack of flexibility in the supply chain. Although excess inventory is expensive, low fill rates are also costly because business may be lost due to cancelled orders.

One recurring problem in supply chain management is the **bullwhip effect**, in which information about the demand for a product gets distorted as it passes from one entity to the next across the supply chain. A slight rise in demand for an item might cause different members in the supply chain—distributors, manufacturers, suppliers, secondary suppliers (suppliers' suppliers), and tertiary suppliers (suppliers' suppliers' suppliers)—to stockpile inventory so each has enough "just in case." These changes ripple throughout the supply chain, magnifying what started out as a small change from planned orders, creating excess inventory, production, warehousing, and shipping costs (see Figure 12-3).

For example, Procter & Gamble (P&G) found it had excessively high inventories of its Pampers disposable diapers at various points along its supply chain because of such distorted information. Although customer purchases in stores were fairly stable, orders from distributors would spike when P&G offered aggressive price promotions. Pampers and Pampers components accumulated in warehouses along the supply chain to meet demand that did not actually exist. To eliminate this problem, P&G revised its marketing, sales, and supply chain processes and used more accurate demand forecasting (Lee, Padmanabhan, and Wang, 1997).

The bullwhip is tamed by reducing uncertainties about demand and supply, i.e., when all members of the supply chain have accurate and up-to-date information. If all supply chain members share dynamic information about inventory levels, schedules, forecasts, and shipments, they have more precise knowledge about how to adjust their sourcing, manufacturing, and distribution plans. Supply chain management systems provide the kind of information that helps members of the supply chain make better purchasing and scheduling decisions. Figure 12-4 shows a software product that enables companies to forecast future demand for products.

Supply Chain Management Applications

Supply chain software is classified as either software to help businesses plan their supply chains (supply chain planning) or software to help them execute the supply chain steps

Just-in-time

Bullwhip effect

FIGURE 12-3   *The bullwhip effect*

Inaccurate information can cause minor fluctuations in demand for a product to be amplified as one moves further back in the supply chain. Minor fluctuations in retail sales for a product can create excess inventory for distributors, manufacturers, and suppliers.

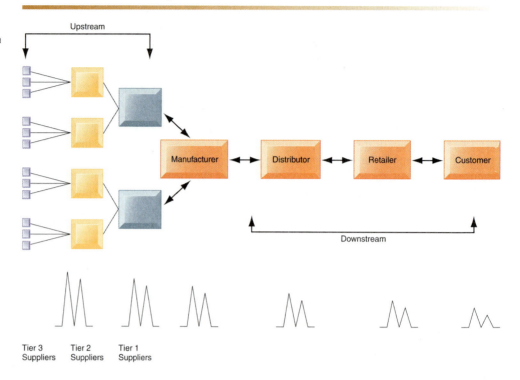

(supply chain execution). **Supply chain planning systems** enable the firm to generate demand forecasts for a product and to develop sourcing and manufacturing plans for that product. Such systems help companies make better operating decisions, such as determining how much of a specific product to manufacture in a given time period; establishing inventory levels for raw materials, intermediate products, and finished goods; determining where to store finished goods; and identifying the transportation mode to use for product delivery.

Supply chain planning systems

FIGURE 12-4   *A demand forecast graph from SmartForecasts software*

An important use of SmartForecasts demand planning software from Smart Software is to forecast future demand for products where demand is intermittent or irregular. Shown here is a forecast graph for the distribution of total cumulative demand for a spare part over a four-month lead time.

Source: Reprinted with permission of Smart Software, Inc.

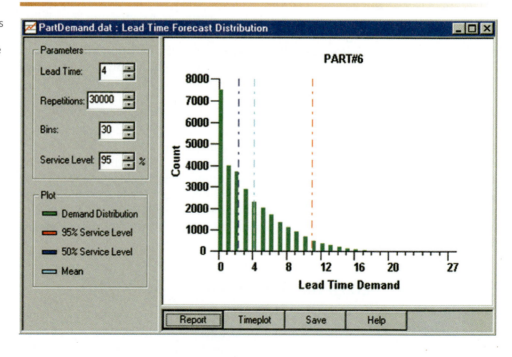

For example, if a large customer places a larger order than usual or changes that order on short notice, the change can have a widespread impact throughout the supply chain. Additional raw materials or a different mix of raw materials may need to be ordered from suppliers. Manufacturing may have to change job scheduling. A transportation carrier may have to reschedule deliveries. Supply chain planning software makes the necessary adjustments to production and distribution plans. Information about changes is shared among the relevant supply chain members so that their work can be coordinated. One of the most important—and complex—supply chain planning functions is **demand planning**, which determines how much product a business needs to make to satisfy all its customers' demands.

Supply chain execution systems manage the flow of products through distribution centres and warehouses to ensure that products are delivered to the right locations in the most efficient manner. They track the physical status of goods, the management of materials, warehouse and transportation operations, and financial information involving all parties. Manugistics (acquired by JDA Software Group) and i2 Technologies are major supply chain management software vendors, and enterprise software vendors SAP and Oracle-PeopleSoft offer supply chain management modules. Table 12-2 provides more details on supply chain planning and execution systems.

Supply Chain Management and the Internet

Before the Internet, supply chain coordination was hampered by the difficulties of making information flow smoothly among disparate internal supply chain systems for purchasing, materials management, manufacturing, and distribution. It was also difficult to share information with external supply chain partners because the systems of

Demand planning

Supply chain execution systems

TABLE 12-2 Supply Chain Planning and Execution Systems

CAPABILITIES OF SUPPLY CHAIN PLANNING SYSTEMS

Order planning. Select an order fulfillment plan that best meets the desired level of service to the customer given existing transportation and manufacturing constraints.

Advanced scheduling and manufacturing planning. Provide detailed coordination of scheduling based on an analysis of changing factors, such as customer orders, equipment outages, or supply interruptions. Scheduling modules create job schedules for the manufacturing process and supplier logistics.

Demand planning. Generate demand forecasts from all business units using statistical tools and business forecasting techniques.

Distribution planning. Create operating plans for logistics managers for order fulfillment based on input from demand and manufacturing planning modules.

Transportation planning. Track and analyze inbound, outbound, and intracompany movement of materials and products to ensure that materials and finished goods are delivered at the right time and place at the minimum cost.

CAPABILITIES OF SUPPLY CHAIN EXECUTION SYSTEMS

Order commitments. Enable vendors to quote accurate delivery dates to customers by providing more real-time detailed information on the status of orders from availability of raw materials and inventory to production and shipment status.

Final production. Organize and schedule final subassemblies required to make each final product.

Replenishment. Coordinate component replenishment work so that warehouses remainstocked with the minimum amount of inventory in the pipeline.

Distribution management. Coordinate the process of transporting goods from the manufacturer to distribution centres to the final customer. Provide online customer access to shipment and delivery data.

Reverse distribution. Track the shipment and accounting for returned goods or remanufactured products.

FIGURE 12-5 *Intranets and extranets for supply chain management*

Intranets integrate information from isolated business processes within the firm to help manage its internal supply chain. Access to these private intranets can also be extended to authorized suppliers, distributors, logistics services, and sometimes, to retail customers to improve coordination of external supply chain processes.

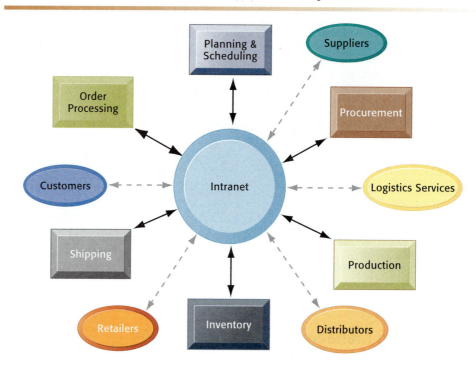

suppliers, distributors, or logistics providers were based on incompatible technology platforms and standards. Enterprise systems could supply some integration of internal supply chain processes, but they were not designed to deal with external supply chain processes.

Some supply chain integration is supplied inexpensively using Internet technology. Firms use *intranets* to improve coordination among their internal supply chain processes, and they use *extranets* to coordinate supply chain processes shared with their business partners (see Figure 12-5).

Using intranets and extranets, all members of the supply chain are instantly able to communicate with one another, using up-to-date information to adjust purchasing, logistics, manufacturing, packaging, and schedules. A manager will use a Web interface to tap into suppliers' systems to determine whether inventory and production capabilities match demand for the firm's products. Business partners will use Web-based supply chain management tools to collaborate online on forecasts. Sales representatives will access suppliers' production schedules and logistics information to monitor a customer's order status. Many companies now use suppliers from many different countries, and the Internet helps them coordinate overseas sourcing, transportation, communications, financing, and compliance with customs regulations.

Demand-Driven Supply Chains: From Push to Pull Manufacturing and Efficient Customer Response

In addition to reducing costs, supply chain management systems facilitate efficient customer response, enabling the workings of the business to be driven more by customer demand. (We introduced efficient customer response systems in Chapter 3.)

Earlier supply chain management systems were driven by a push-based model (also known as *build-to-stock*). In a **push-based model**, production master schedules are based on forecasts or best guesses of demand for products, and products are "pushed" to customers. With new flows of information made possible by Web-based tools, supply chain management more easily follows a pull-based model. In a **pull-based model**, also known

Push-based model
Pull-based model

FIGURE 12-6 *Push- versus pull-based supply chain models*

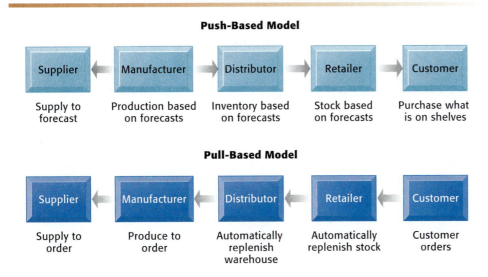

The difference between push- and pull-based models is summarized by the slogan "Make what we sell, not sell what we make."

as a *demand-driven model* or *build-to-order*, actual customer orders or purchases trigger events in the supply chain. Transactions to produce and deliver only what customers have ordered move up the supply chain from retailers to distributors to manufacturers and eventually to suppliers. Only products to fulfill these orders move back down the supply chain to the retailer. Manufacturers use only actual order demand information to drive their production schedules and the procurement of components or raw materials, as illustrated in Figure 12-6.

Wal-Mart's continuous replenishment system and Dell Computer's build-to-order system, both described in Chapter 3, are examples of the pull-based model.

The Internet and Internet technology make it possible to move from sequential supply chains, where information and materials flow sequentially from company to company, to concurrent supply chains, where information flows in many directions simultaneously among members of a supply chain network. Members of the network immediately adjust to changes in schedules or orders. Ultimately, the Internet could create a "digital logistics nervous system" throughout the supply chain. This system permits simultaneous, multidirectional communication of information about participants' inventories, orders, and capacities, optimizing the activities of individual firms and groups of firms interacting in e-commerce marketplaces (see Figure 12-7).

Business Value of Supply Chain Management Systems

You have just seen how supply chain management systems enable firms to streamline both their internal and external supply chain processes and provide management with more accurate information about what to produce, store, and move. By implementing a networked and integrated supply chain management system, companies match supply to demand, reduce inventory levels, improve delivery service, speed product time to market, and use assets more effectively.

Total supply chain costs represent the majority of operating expenses for many businesses and in some industries approach 75 percent of the total operating budget (Handfield and Nichols, 2002). Reducing supply chain costs may have a major impact on firm profitability.

In addition to reducing costs, supply chain management systems help increase sales. If a product is not available when a customer wants it, customers often try to purchase it from someone else. More precise control of the supply chain enhances the firm's ability to have the right product available for customer purchases at the right time, as illustrated by the chapter-opening vignette about Sony Canada.

FIGURE 12-7 *The future Internet-driven supply chain*

The future Internet-driven supply chain operates like a digital logistics nervous system. It provides multidirectional communication among firms, networks of firms, and e-marketplaces so that entire networks of supply chain partners can immediately adjust inventories, orders, and capacities.

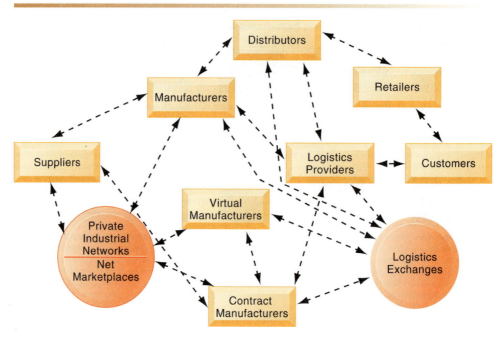

12.3 Customer Relationship Management Systems

You have probably heard phrases such as "the customer is always right" or "the customer comes first." Today these words ring more true than ever. Because competitive advantage based on an innovative new product or service is often very short lived, companies are realizing that their only enduring competitive strength may be their relationships with their customers. Some say that the basis of competition has switched from who sells the most products and services to who "owns" the customer, and that customer relationships represent a firm's most valuable asset. Even manufactured goods, such as automobiles, come with significant customer service and support content from warranties and roadside repairs and towing services built into the purchase price. The distinction between a manufactured product and a service is increasingly difficult to maintain.

What Is Customer Relationship Management?

What kinds of information would you need to develop and nurture strong, long-lasting relationships with customers? You would want to know exactly who your customers are, how to contact them, whether they are costly to service and sell to, in what kinds of products and services they are interested, and how much money they spend with your company. If you could, you would want to make sure you knew each of your customers well, as if you were running a small-town store. And you would want to make your good customers feel special.

In a small business operating in a neighbourhood, it is possible for business owners and managers to really know their customers on a personal, face-to-face basis. But in a large business operating on a metropolitan, regional, national, or even global basis, it is impossible to "know your customer" in this intimate way. In these kinds of businesses, there are too many customers and too many different ways that customers interact with the firm (over the Web, the phone, fax, and face to face). It becomes especially difficult to integrate information from all these sources and to deal with the large numbers of customers.

FIGURE 12-8 *Customer relationship management (CRM)*

CRM systems examine customers from a multifaceted perspective. These systems use a set of integrated applications to address all aspects of the customer relationship, including customer service, sales, and marketing.

This is where customer relationship management systems help. Customer relationship management (CRM) systems, which we introduced in Chapter 2, capture and integrate customer data from all over the organization, consolidate the data, analyze the data, and then distribute the results to various systems and customer touch points across the enterprise. A **touch point** (also known as a *contact point*) is a method of interaction with the customer, such as telephone, e-mail, customer service desk, conventional mail, Web site, wireless device, or retail store.

Well-designed CRM systems provide a single enterprise view of customers that is useful for improving both sales and customer service. CRM systems likewise provide customers with a single view of the company regardless of what touch point the customer uses (see Figure 12-8).

Good CRM systems provide data and analytical tools for answering questions such as these: "What is the value of a particular customer to the firm over his or her lifetime?" "Who are our most loyal customers?" (It can cost six times more to sell to a new customer than to an existing customer.) "Who are our most profitable customers?" and "What do these profitable customers want to buy?" Firms use the answers to these questions to acquire new customers, provide better service and support to existing customers, customize their offerings more precisely to customer preferences, and provide ongoing value to retain profitable customers.

The Window on Technology section describes how the International House of Pancakes (IHOP) used customer relationship management systems to learn more about its customers and improve customer communication. IHOP installed Oracle Corporation's Customer Data Hub to integrate customer data from multiple sources and Oracle Teleservice software to manage telephone communication about customer service.

Touch point

WINDOW ON TECHNOLOGY

Technology

IHOP Cooks Customer Data to Order

The International House of Pancakes (IHOP) is known best for serving an estimated three-quarter billion pancakes annually to diners across Canada and the United States. The chain, which is based in Glendale, California, has expanded its menu over the years to include a growing number of traditional lunch and dinner items as well. The promise of a simple, economical, and taste-bud-satisfying dining experience has enabled IHOP to maintain its position as one of the top family restaurant chains in North America. More than 90 percent of Americans are familiar with the IHOP brand name. The chain includes approximately 1200 restaurants, more than 90 percent of which are owned by independent franchisees.

IHOP's slogan is "Come Hungry, Leave Happy." But IHOP did not know as much as it wanted about its customers and how to make them happier. The company had been conducting extensive research into demographic trends, spending patterns, and customer preferences. However, according to Patrick Piccininno, IHOP's vice president of information technology, the information in its systems "wasn't available in a useful, easy-to-access way." Each IHOP division worked with a different slice of customer data. In fact, the company employed five different systems for processing sales data, and there was no method for synchronizing or cleansing the data. Piccininno had no idea if separate franchises were finding the same problems or trends.

What IHOP needed was a single, central company-wide repository of all its customer information that could provide a quantifiable picture of customer behaviour. "Instead of using gut feel and conjecture, we want to find out what is actually driving customers to us," Piccininno stated.

IHOP could have developed an entirely new system based on a centralized company-wide database that was a single source of customer information. This approach would have been prohibitively costly and complicated. Instead, it chose to use Oracle Customer Data Hub middleware to integrate its customer data from its various legacy systems.

Data hubs pull together data from many different applications and make them available for operational systems. Oracle's Customer Data Hub creates a single company-wide view of the customer so that every single customer touch point displays current and consistent information without disrupting existing systems. This integration makes it possible for a call centre representative, for instance, to find out whether the customer on the line does a lot of business with the company.

IHOP's Oracle's Customer Data Hub collects and integrates customer data from six point-of-sale systems, human resources, and financial systems based on Lawson software and an Oracle data warehouse. It also cleans and enriches the customer data as they are collected from source applications.

In the past, the company required separate data cleansing, support, and processing work for each of its systems, which was quite costly. Duplicate and inconsistent data have been eliminated.

IHOP adopted Oracle TeleService to improve communication with its customers through a call centre. Previously, diners communicated with IHOP via e-mail. However, the company lacked a central process for tracking the e-mail. Consequently, some e-mail was not dealt with in a timely manner. There was

no mechanism for knowing how long it would take to solve a problem or if specific problems that had been reported were ever solved at all.

With Oracle TeleService, IHOP receives comments and feedback from restaurant guests on a toll-free number. Its information systems department is able to log the calls, route the collected data to the appropriate resource, and track the progress of resolutions to customers' questions and problems. Now restaurant guests who report problems receive a resolution in three days, on average. The centralized and encompassing nature of TeleService also enables IHOP to notice trends among its clientele, based on its messages, and to take appropriate action to address the trends.

Individual franchisees have access to the CRM system through portals created with Oracle AS Portal 10g software. Users connect to the portal through a Web browser. IHOP restaurant franchisees are able to see daily sales data, the average check for each day, how promotions are performing, and figures on how well they manage their operations. The portal is customizable to help restaurant owners access the specific types of information they need while giving IHOP an improved ability to measure customer service.

To Think About

1. How does knowledge of customers impact IHOP's business performance?

2. Why did IHOP have trouble getting to know its customers?

3. How has the company chosen to improve its knowledge of customers? Analyze the management, organization, and technology dimensions of the solution.

4. Did IHOP choose the best solution? Explain your answer.

MIS in Action

Explore IHOP's Web site (www.ihop.com), and answer the following questions:

1. Does this Web site provide opportunities for IHOP to gather data about its customers? Describe the customer data collected at the Web site, and explain how IHOP can use the data to improve its business performance.

2. Is this Web site well-designed for interacting with customers and gathering customer data? What other customer data could this Web site collect?

3. How would you redesign the Web site to increase interactions with customers?

Sources: Oracle, "Fresh Guest Data Helps IHOP Franchises Thrive," www.oracle.com, accessed September 5, 2006; Colin Beasty, "CRM Where You Least Expect It," *Customer Relationship Management*, March 2005; Robert Westervelt, "Customer Data Hub Keeps IHOP Stats Hot," searchoracle.techtarget.com, accessed June 7, 2005; and Charles Babcock, "Customer-Data Hubs Inch Ahead," *InformationWeek*, April 25, 2005.

Customer Relationship Management Software

Commercial CRM software packages range from niche tools that perform limited functions, such as personalizing Web sites for specific customers, to large-scale enterprise applications that capture myriad interactions with customers, analyze them with sophisticated reporting tools, and link to other major enterprise applications, such as supply chain management and enterprise systems. The more comprehensive CRM packages contain modules for partner relationship management and employee relationship management.

Partner relationship management (PRM) software uses many of the same data, tools, and systems as customer relationship management to enhance collaboration between a company and its selling partners. If a company does not sell directly to customers but rather works through distributors or retailers, PRM helps these channels sell to customers directly. It provides a company and its selling partners with the ability to trade information and distribute leads and data about customers, integrating lead generation, pricing, promotions, order configurations, and availability. It also provides a firm with tools to assess its partners' performance so it can make sure its best partners receive the support they need to close more business.

Employee relationship management (ERM) software deals with employee issues that are closely related to CRM, such as setting objectives, employee performance management, performance-based compensation, and employee training. Major CRM application software vendors include Siebel Systems (acquired by Oracle Corp.), Clarify, and Salesforce.com. Enterprise software vendors, such as SAP and Oracle-PeopleSoft, are also active in customer relationship management and feature tools for integrating their enterprise system modules with their customer relationship management modules.

Customer relationship management systems typically provide software and online tools for sales, customer service, and marketing. We briefly describe some of these capabilities.

Sales Force Automation (SFA)
Sales force automation modules in CRM systems help sales staff increase their productivity by focusing sales efforts on the most profitable customers, those who are good candidates for sales and services. CRM systems provide sales prospect and contact information, product information, product configuration capabilities, and sales quote generation capabilities. SFA software can assemble information about a particular customer's past purchases to help the salesperson make personalized recommendations. CRM software enables sales, marketing, and delivery departments to easily share customer and prospect information. It increases each salesperson's efficiency in reducing the cost per sale as well as the cost of acquiring new customers and retaining old ones. CRM software also has capabilities for sales forecasting, territory management, and team selling.

Customer Service
Customer service modules in CRM systems provide information and tools to increase the efficiency of call centres, help desks, and customer support staff. They have capabilities for assigning and managing customer service requests.

One of these capabilities is an appointment or advice telephone line. When a customer calls a standard phone number, the system routes the call to the correct service person, who inputs information about that customer into the system only once. Once the customer's data are in the system, any service representative can handle the customer relationship. Improved access to consistent and accurate customer information helps call centres handle more calls per day and decrease the duration of each call. Thus, call centres and customer service groups achieve greater productivity, reduced transaction time, and higher quality of service at lower cost. The customer is happier because he or she spends less time on the phone restating his or her problem to customer service representatives.

CRM systems may also include Web-based self-service capabilities: The company Web site can be set up to provide inquiring customers personalized support information as well as the option to contact customer service staff by phone for additional assistance.

Marketing
CRM systems support direct-marketing campaigns by providing capabilities for capturing prospect and customer data, for providing product and service information,

Partner relationship management (PRM)

Employee relationship management (ERM)

Customer relationship management software provides a single point for users to manage and evaluate marketing campaigns across multiple channels, including e-mail, direct mail, telephone, the Web, and wireless messages.

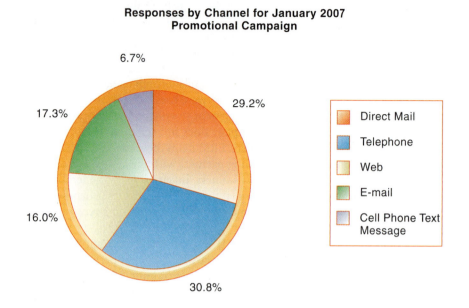

FIGURE 12-9 *How CRM systems support marketing*

for qualifying leads for targeted marketing, and for scheduling and tracking direct-marketing mailings or e-mail (see Figure 12-9). Marketing modules also include tools for analyzing marketing and customer data—identifying profitable and unprofitable customers, designing products and services to satisfy specific customer needs and interests, and identifying opportunities for cross-selling.

Cross-selling is the marketing of complementary products to customers. (For example, in financial services, a customer with a chequing account might be sold a money market account or a home improvement loan.) CRM tools also help firms manage and execute marketing campaigns at all stages, from planning to determining the rate of success for each campaign.

Figure 12-10 illustrates the most important capabilities for sales, service, and marketing processes that would be found in major CRM software products. Like enterprise software, this software is business-process driven, incorporating hundreds of business processes thought to represent best practices in each of these areas. To achieve maximum benefit, companies need to revise and model their business processes to conform to the best-practice business processes in the CRM software.

Figure 12-11 illustrates how a best practice for increasing customer loyalty through customer service might be modelled by CRM software. Directly servicing customers provides firms with opportunities to increase customer retention by singling out profitable long-term customers for preferential treatment. CRM software can assign each customer a score based on that person's value and loyalty to the company and provide that information to help call centres route each customer's service request to agents who can best handle that customer's needs. The system would automatically provide the service agent with a detailed profile of that customer that included his or her score for value and loyalty. The service agent would use this information to present special offers or additional service to the customer to encourage the customer to keep transacting business with the company.

Operational and Analytical CRM

All the applications we have just described support either the operational or analytical aspects of customer relationship management. **Operational CRM** includes customer-facing applications, such as tools for sales force automation, call centre and customer service support, and marketing automation. **Analytical CRM** includes applications that analyze

Cross-selling
Operational CRM
Analytical CRM

FIGURE 12-10   *CRM software capabilities*

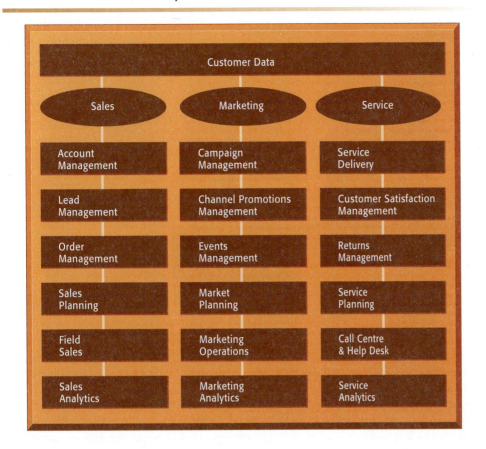

The major CRM software products support business processes in sales, service, and marketing, integrating customer information from many different sources. Included are support for both the operational and analytical aspects of CRM.

customer data generated by operational CRM applications to provide information for improving business performance.

Analytical CRM applications are based on data warehouses that consolidate the data from operational CRM systems and customer touch points for use with online analytical processing (OLAP), data mining, and other data analysis techniques (see Chapter 6). Customer data collected by the organization might be combined with data from other

FIGURE 12-11   *Customer loyalty management process map*

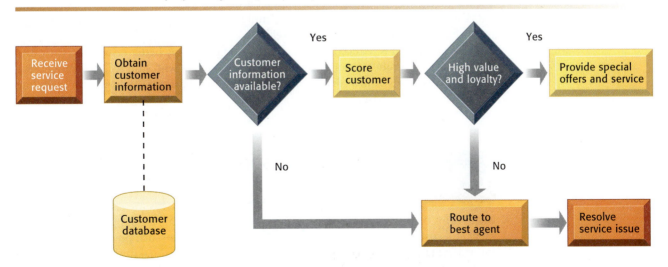

This process map shows how a best practice for promoting customer loyalty through customer service would be modelled by customer relationship management software. The CRM software helps firms identify high-value customers for preferential treatment.

FIGURE 12-12 *Analytical CRM data warehouse*

Analytical CRM uses a customer data warehouse and tools to analyze customer data collected from the firm's customer touch points and from other sources.

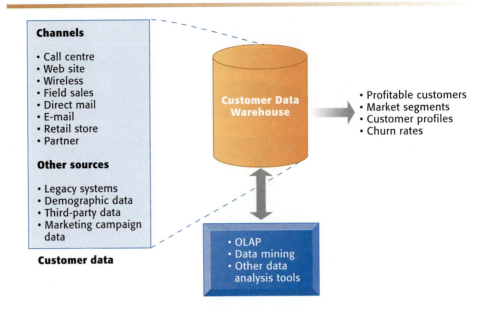

sources, such as customer lists for direct-marketing campaigns purchased from other companies or demographic data. These data are analyzed to identify buying patterns, to create segments for targeted marketing, and to pinpoint profitable and unprofitable customers (see Figure 12-12).

Another important output of analytical CRM is the customer's lifetime value to the firm. **Customer lifetime value (CLTV)** is based on the relationship between the revenue produced by a specific customer, the expenses incurred in acquiring and servicing that customer, and the expected life of the relationship between the customer and the company.

Business Value of Customer Relationship Management Systems

Companies with effective customer relationship management systems realize many benefits, including increased customer satisfaction, reduced direct-marketing costs, more effective marketing, and lower costs for customer acquisition and retention. Information from CRM systems increases sales revenue by identifying the most profitable customers and segments for focused marketing and cross-selling.

Customer churn is reduced as sales, service, and marketing better respond to customer needs. The **churn rate** measures the number of customers who stop using or purchasing products or services from a company. It is an important indicator of the growth or decline of a firm's customer base.

12.4 Enterprise Applications: New Opportunities and Challenges

Many firms have implemented enterprise systems and systems for supply chain management and customer relationship management because they are such powerful instruments for achieving operational excellence and enhancing decision making. But it is precisely because they are so powerful in changing the way the organization works that these systems are challenging to implement. Let us briefly examine some of these challenges as well as new ways of obtaining value from these systems.

Customer lifetime value (CLTV)

Churn rate

Enterprise Application Challenges

Promises of dramatic reductions in inventory costs, order-to-delivery time, as well as more efficient customer response and higher product and customer profitability make enterprise systems and systems for supply chain management and customer relationship management very alluring. But to obtain this value, you must clearly understand how your business has to change in order to use these systems effectively.

Enterprise applications involve complex pieces of software that are very expensive to purchase and implement. It might take a large company several years to complete a large-scale implementation of an enterprise system or a system for supply chain management or customer relationship management. The total implementation cost of a large system, including software, database tools, consulting fees, personnel costs, training, and perhaps hardware costs, might amount to four to five times the initial purchase price for the software.

Enterprise applications require not only deep-seated technological changes but also fundamental changes in the way the business operates. Companies must make sweeping changes to their business processes to work with the software. Employees must accept new job functions and responsibilities. They must learn how to perform a new set of work activities and understand how the information they enter into the system can affect other parts of the company. This requires new organizational learning.

Supply chain management systems require multiple organizations to share information and business processes. Each participant in the system may have to change some of its processes and the way it uses information to create a system that best serves the supply chain as a whole.

Some firms experienced enormous operating problems and losses when they first implemented enterprise applications because they did not understand how much organizational change was required. Canadian retail food giant Sobeys had trouble getting products to store shelves when it implemented supply chain management (SCM) software from SAP over a two-year period ending in 2001. Originally, Sobeys blamed the software while the software company blamed Sobeys's failure to change its processes to the SAP model. By 2004, both sides were sufficiently mollified to try again, and with additional change management programs in place, the implementation of SAP's SCM module went smoothly.

Hershey Foods Corporation's profitability also dropped when it tried to implement SAP enterprise software, Manugistics SCM software, and Siebel Systems CRM software on a crash schedule in 1999 without thorough testing and employee training. Shipments ran two weeks late and many customers did not receive enough candy to stock shelves during the busy Halloween selling period. Hershey lost sales and customers during that period, although the new systems eventually improved operational efficiency.

The Window on Organizations section describes another company's struggle to implement enterprise software. Novartis, a leading international pharmaceutical house, had trouble making some of the modules supplied by SAP perform properly. Its experience illustrates some of the problems that occur when a company tries to make enterprise software work with its unique business processes.

 WINDOW ON ORGANIZATIONS

Why Novartis Backed Off from Enterprise Software

Novartis A.G. is a leading global pharmaceutical and health care company headquartered in Basel, Switzerland. It operates in more than 140 countries around the world, employing about 77 200 people and producing nearly $29 billion in revenue in 2003.

Novartis is replacing legacy systems at Novartis offices in more than 50 countries with SAP enterprise software for human resources, supplier relationship management, and supply chain management. Management believes the SAP software will help the company cut down system integration costs as well as standardize and streamline administrative processes, work flow, and reporting in its worldwide operations. The SAP software will also help the company comply with U.S. Food and Drug Administration regulations on electronic records and signatures for the pharmaceutical industry.

A research survey conducted by Frost & Sullivan, a global consulting company specializing in emerging high-technology and industrial markets, recognized SAP as the dominant enterprise resource planning and supply chain management vendor for the global pharmaceuticals industry. Pharmaceutical companies seeking a single system that could tie together their operations in various countries were impressed by SAP's ability to address their industry-specific business requirements as well as the vendor's superior global service and support network.

Novartis had already adopted SAP's R/3 enterprise resource planning and financial modules for many of its operating units. Given the company's enthusiasm for enterprise systems and SAP, it was surprising to learn that the accounts payable department at Novartis Pharmaceuticals, the U.S. arm of the company, was having problems with its SAP enterprise system. Somewhere in the process of paying invoices, payments were being held, and a backlog of overdue bills was building. A few vendors even withheld credit from the company.

The accounts payable and strategic sourcing departments fingered a recent upgrade to the SAP R/3 financial modules as the source of their financial crisis. Novartis had insisted that SAP be its global standard, and the software just was not working for them. In frustration, these groups began meeting to figure out a way to redesign their requisition-to-pay process, even if it meant scrapping SAP modules that did not meet their needs. They did not want to work with the Novartis information systems department.

Novartis' information systems staff, on the other hand, believed the unpaid invoices were not entirely caused by the SAP software. The company's existing process for invoicing was inefficient, requiring manual approvals from many different managers. It was not a true integrated requisition-to-pay process. Work was still structured into silos and no one knew what was going on.

The information systems staff thought a recent implementation of the SAP R/3 software would solve the problem. It believed that if it let the SAP software handle as many business processes as possible, it would not have to deal with so many interfaces between different information systems. The information systems department had assigned special staff members to serve as business information managers (BIMs) who could work more closely with end-user departments to clarify and support business goals. Nevertheless, because of tight deadlines and limited budget, information systems specialists scrimped on training and did not pay sufficient attention to the new system's impact on business processes.

Something had to be done to get user and information systems groups to cooperate. Ray Pawlicki, Novartis's vice president for information and chief information officer, invited accounts payable and information systems groups to a six-month program to foster joint leadership. The groups met many times. Eventually, both groups finally started listening to each other and committed to two outcomes.

One was to create a new way for the information systems, accounts payable, and strategic sourcing departments to work together to facilitate rapid business transformation. The other outcome was a proposal to improve the purchasing process for Novartis departments so that they would no longer make independent purchases. Instead, all requisitions would be channelled through the strategic sourcing department. By centralizing purchases, the company would be able to obtain larger discounts from suppliers because it was buying in larger quantities. About $4.6 million to $5.8 million could be saved annually this way.

Business information managers (BIMs) from the information systems department emerged with a deeper appreciation of business requirements and how these matched up with SAP and other software providers. In the end, the information systems group agreed to what accounts payable and strategic sourcing had originally requested: a solution that was the "best of breed," irrespective of the software vendor, that would best support the company's redesigned purchasing process.

In May 2003, the information systems department agreed to update an old system from Ariba that would reduce late payments by automatically reconciling sourcing and accounts payable. The Ariba upgrade improved Novartis's purchasing process so much that $4.6 to $5.8 million in savings were achieved within six months.

To Think About

1. Why was Novartis having trouble with its requisition-to-pay process?

2. What management, organization, and technology factors were involved?

3. Was the solution to this problem a good one? Why or why not?

MIS in Action

Visit the Web sites of Ariba (www.ariba.com) and SAP (www.sap.com/canada/index.epx), and explore their "solutions" sections. Then answer the following questions:

1. List and describe the capabilities of the purchasing or sourcing solutions/modules.

2. How would these modules benefit a company such as Novartis? (www.novartis.com) Describe how Novartis could use these capabilities. What other modules do each of these companies have that could benefit Novartis?

Sources: Stephanie Overby, "Can't We All Just Get Along?" *CIO Australia,* March 10, 2004; and "SAP Chosen by Novartis as a Major Building Block," *EETimes,* June 16, 2003.

Enterprise applications also introduce "switching costs." Once you adopt an enterprise application from a single vendor, such as SAP, Oracle, or others, it is very costly to switch vendors, and your firm becomes dependent on the vendor to upgrade its product and maintain your installation.

Enterprise applications are based on organization-wide definitions of data. You'll need to understand exactly how your business uses its data and how the data would be organized in a customer relationship management, supply chain management, or enterprise system. CRM systems typically require some data cleansing work.

In a nutshell, it takes a lot of work to get enterprise applications to work properly. Everyone in the organization must be involved. Of course, for those companies that have successfully implemented CRM, SCM, and enterprise systems, the results have justified the effort.

Extending Enterprise Software

Today many experienced business firms are looking for ways to wring more value from their enterprise applications. One way is to make them more flexible, Web-enabled, and capable of integration with other systems. The major enterprise software vendors have created what they call *enterprise solutions, enterprise suites,* or *e-business suites* to make their customer relationship management, supply chain management, and enterprise systems work closely with one another and link to systems of customers and suppliers. SAP's mySAP and Oracle's E-Business Suite are examples. For some firms, such as Sony Canada, which we discussed at the beginning of this chapter, use of enterprise software starts with one module and is then followed by adding a module at a time.

Service Platforms Another way of leveraging investments in enterprise applications is to use them to create service platforms for new or improved business processes that integrate information from multiple functional areas. These enterprise-wide service platforms provide a greater degree of cross-functional integration than the traditional enterprise applications. A **service platform** integrates multiple applications from multiple business functions, business units, or business partners to deliver a seamless experience for the customer, employee, manager, or business partner.

For instance, the order-to-cash process involves receiving an order and seeing it all the way through obtaining payment for the order. This process begins with lead generation, marketing campaigns, and order entry, which are typically supported by CRM systems. Once the order is received, manufacturing is scheduled, and parts availability is verified—processes that are usually supported by enterprise software. The order then is handled by processes for distribution planning, warehousing, order fulfillment, and shipping, which are usually supported by supply chain management systems. Finally, the order is billed to the customer, and the order is handled by either enterprise financial applications or accounts receivable. If the purchase at some point required customer service, customer relationship management systems would again be invoked.

A service such as order-to-cash requires data from enterprise applications and financial systems to be further integrated into an enterprise-wide composite process. To accomplish this, firms need software tools that use existing applications as building blocks for new cross-enterprise processes (see Figure 12-13). Enterprise application vendors provide middleware and tools that use XML and Web services for integrating enterprise applications with older legacy applications and systems from other vendors.

Increasingly, these new services will be delivered through portals. Today's portal products provide frameworks for building new composite services. Portal software can integrate information from enterprise applications and disparate in-house legacy systems, presenting it to users through a Web interface so that the information appears to be coming from a single source.

Service platform

FIGURE 12-13 *Order-to-cash service*

Order-to-cash is a composite process that integrates data from individual enterprise applications and legacy financial applications. The process must be modelled and translated into a software system using application integration tools.

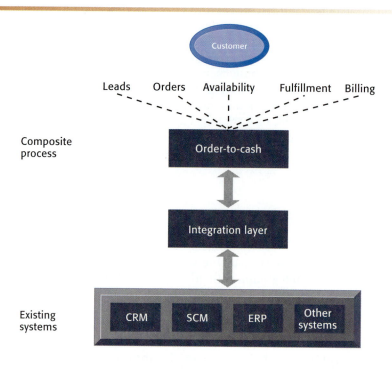

Summary

1. **Demonstrate how enterprise systems achieve operational excellence by integrating and coordinating diverse functions and business processes in the firm.**

   Enterprise systems integrate the key business processes of a firm into a single software system so that information can flow seamlessly throughout the organization, improving coordination, efficiency, and decision making. Enterprise software is based on a suite of integrated software modules and a common central database. The database collects data from and feeds the data into numerous applications that can support nearly all of an organization's internal business activities. When new information is entered by one process, the information is made available immediately to other business processes. Organizations implementing enterprise software would have to adopt the business processes embedded in the software and, if necessary, change their business processes to conform to those in the software.

   Enterprise systems support organizational centralization by enforcing uniform data standards and business processes throughout the company and a single unified technology platform. The firm-wide data generated by enterprise systems helps managers evaluate organizational performance. By integrating business processes in sales, production, finance, and logistics, the entire organization will more efficiently respond to customer requests for products or information, forecast new products, and build and deliver them as demand requires.

2. **Demonstrate how supply chain management systems coordinate planning, production, and logistics with suppliers.**

   Supply chain management systems automate the flow of information among members of the supply chain so they can use it to make better decisions about when and how much to purchase, produce, or ship. More accurate information from supply chain management systems reduces uncertainty and the impact of the bullwhip effect. The correct movement of information makes it possible to time orders, shipments, and production properly to minimize inventory levels and expedite deliveries to customers.

   Supply chain management software includes software for supply chain planning and for supply chain execution. Supply chain planning systems enable the firm to generate demand forecasts for a product and to develop sourcing, manufacturing, and distribution plans. Supply chain execution systems manage the flow of products through the final stages of production, distribution, and delivery. Firms can use intranets to improve coordination among their internal supply chain processes, and they can use extranets to coordinate supply chain processes shared with their business partners. Internet technology facilitates the management of global supply chains by providing the connectivity for organizations in different countries to share supply chain information. Improved communication among supply chain members also facilitates efficient customer response and movement toward a demand-driven model.

3. *Demonstrate how customer relationship management systems achieve customer intimacy by integrating all customer contact information and making it available throughout the firm.*

Customer relationship management (CRM) systems integrate and automate many customer-facing processes in sales, marketing, and customer service, providing an enterprise-wide view of customers. These systems track all the ways in which a company interacts with its customers and analyze these interactions to maximize customer lifetime value for the firm. CRM systems capture and integrate customer data from all over the organization, analyzing the data and distributing the results to customer-related systems and customer touch points across the enterprise. Companies can use this customer knowledge when they interact with customers to provide them with better service or to sell new products and services. These systems also identify profitable or nonprofitable customers and opportunities to reduce the churn rate.

The major customer relationship management software packages integrate customer-related processes in sales, marketing, and customer service and provide capabilities for both operational CRM and analytical CRM. They often include modules for managing relationships with selling partners (partner relationship management) and for employee relationship management.

If they are properly implemented, CRM systems help firms increase customer satisfaction, reduce direct-marketing costs, and lower costs for customer acquisition and retention. Information from CRM systems increases sales revenue by identifying the most profitable customers and segments for focused marketing and cross-selling. Customer churn will be reduced as sales, service, and marketing better respond to customer needs.

4. *Assess the challenges posed by enterprise applications.*

Enterprise applications are difficult to implement. They require extensive organizational change, large new software investments, and careful assessment of how these systems will enhance organizational performance. Enterprise applications create new interconnections among myriad business processes and data flows inside the firm (and in the case of supply chain management systems, between the firm and its external supply chain partners). Enterprise applications cannot provide value if they are implemented atop flawed processes or if firms do not know how to use these systems to measure performance improvements. Employees require training to prepare for new procedures and roles. Attention to data management is essential.

5. *Describe how enterprise applications can be used in platforms for new cross-functional services.*

Enterprise applications can serve as building blocks for new cross-functional services for customers, suppliers, or business partners. Service platforms integrate data and processes from the various enterprise applications (customer relationship management, supply chain management, and enterprise systems), as well as from disparate legacy applications to create new composite business processes. Application integration middleware or Web services tie various systems together. The new services are delivered through enterprise portals, which can integrate disparate applications so that information appears to be coming from a single source.

Key Terms

Analytical CRM, 422	Employee relationship management (ERM), 421	Push-based model, 416
Best practices, 410		Service platform, 427
Bullwhip effect, 413	Enterprise software, 410	Supply chain, 411
Churn rate, 424	Just-in-time, 413	Supply chain execution systems, 415
Cross-selling, 422	Operational CRM, 422	Supply chain planning systems, 414
Customer lifetime value (CLTV), 424	Partner relationship management (PRM), 421	Touch point, 419
Demand planning, 415	Pull-based model, 416	

Review Questions

1. *What is an enterprise system? How does enterprise software work?*

2. *How do enterprise systems provide value for a business?*

3. *What is a supply chain? What entities does it comprise?*

4. *What is the bullwhip effect? How can supply chain management systems deal with it?*

5. *What are supply chain planning systems and supply chain execution systems? What functions do they perform?*

6. *How can the Internet and Internet technology facilitate supply chain management?*

7. *Distinguish between a push-based and pull-based model of supply chain management. How can contemporary supply chain management systems facilitate a pull-based model?*

8. *How do supply chain management systems provide value for a business?*

9. What is customer relationship management? Why are customer relationships so important today?

10. How are partner relationship management (PRM) and employee relationship management (ERM) related to customer relationship management (CRM)?

11. Describe the tools and capabilities of customer relationship management software for sales, marketing, and customer service.

12. Distinguish between operational and analytical CRM.

13. Define the following terms and explain why they are important for customer relationship management: churn rate, customer lifetime value (CLTV), best practices.

14. What are the challenges posed by enterprise applications? How can these challenges be addressed?

15. How can enterprise applications be extended to provide more value to businesses? Describe the role of service platforms and portals.

Discussion Questions

1. Supply chain management is less about managing the physical movement of goods and more about managing information. Discuss the implications of this statement.

2. If a company wants to implement an enterprise application, it had better do its homework. Discuss the implications of this statement.

3. What are some of the problems likely to be encountered by organizations attempting to take their current systems and convert them to an enterprise system?

4. What are the ethical implications of CRM systems?

Teamwork: Analyzing Enterprise Application Vendors

With a group of three or four students, use the Web to research and evaluate the products of two vendors of enterprise application software. You could compare, for example, the SAP and Oracle enterprise systems, the supply chain management systems from i2 and JDA Software's Manugistics, or the customer relationship management systems of Oracle's Siebel Systems and salesforce.com. Use what you have learned from these companies' Web sites to compare the software packages you have selected in terms of business functions supported, technology platforms, cost, and ease of use. Which vendor would you select? Why? Would you select the same vendor for a small business as for a large one? If possible, use electronic presentation software to present your findings to the class.

Learning Track Module

SAP Business Process Map. If you want to learn more about how SAP enterprise software works, you will find a Learning Track Module on SAP's Business Process Map on MyMISLab for this chapter.

Best Practices Business Processes in CRM Software. If you want to learn more about customer-related business processes supported by CRM software, you will find a Learning Track Module on Siebel Systems' best practice business processes on MyMISLab for this chapter.

 For online exercises, please visit www.pearsoned.ca/mymislab.

HANDS-ON MIS   Application Exercises

The projects in this section give you hands-on experience evaluating supply chain management software for a real-world company, using database software to manage customer service requests, and evaluating supply chain management business services.

Achieving Operational Excellence:
Identifying Supply Chain Management Solutions

Software skills: Web browser and presentation software
Business skills: Locating and evaluating suppliers and SCM software

Businesses are always seeking suppliers that can fulfill orders promptly at the lowest possible cost. In this project, you will use the Web to identify the best suppliers for one component of a dirt bike and appropriate supply chain management software for a small manufacturing company.

A growing number of Dirt Bikes Canada's orders cannot be fulfilled on time because of delays in obtaining some important components and parts for its motorcycles, especially their fuel tanks. Complaints are mounting from distributors that fear losing sales if the dirt bikes they have ordered are delayed too long. Dirt Bikes Canada's management has asked you to help it address some of its supply chain issues.

1. Use the Internet to locate alternative suppliers for motorcycle fuel tanks. Identify two or three suppliers. Find out

the amount of time and cost to ship a fuel tank (weighing about three kilograms) by ground (surface delivery) from each supplier to Dirt Bikes Canada in Halifax, Nova Scotia. Which supplier is most likely to take the shortest amount of time and cost the least to ship the fuel tanks?

2. Dirt Bikes Canada's management would like to know if there is any supply chain management software for a small business that would be appropriate for Dirt Bikes Canada. Use the Internet to locate two supply chain management software providers for companies such as Dirt Bikes Canada. Briefly describe the capabilities of the two software applications, and indicate how they could help Dirt Bikes Canada. Which supply chain management software product would be more appropriate for Dirt Bikes Canada? Why?

3. (Optional) Use electronic presentation software to summarize your findings for management.

Improving Decision Making:
Using Database Software to Manage Customer Service Requests

Software skills: Database design, querying, and reporting
Business skills: Customer service analysis

Companies specializing in service need a way to monitor and manage the numerous requests for their services that they receive each day. It is usually advantageous while providing service to give priority to the customers who have generated the most revenue for the business. In this exercise, you will use database software to develop an application that tracks customer service requests and analyzes customer data to identify customers meriting priority treatment.

Prime Service is a large service company that provides maintenance and repair services for close to 1200 commercial businesses in Ontario and Quebec. Its customers include businesses of all sizes. Customers with service needs call into its customer service department with requests for repairing heating ducts, broken windows, leaky roofs, broken water pipes, and other problems.

The company assigns each request a number and writes down the service request number, identification number of the customer account, the date of the request, the type of equipment requiring repair, and a brief description of the problem. The service requests are handled on a first-come-first-served basis. After the service work has been completed, Prime calculates the cost of the work, enters the price on the service request form, and bills the client.

Management is not happy with this arrangement because the most important and profitable clients—those

with accounts of more than $70 000—are treated no differently from its clients with small accounts. It would like to find a way to provide its best customers with better service. Management would also like to know which types of service problems occur the most frequently so that it can make sure it has adequate resources to address them.

Prime Service has a small database (see page 432) with client account information, which can be found on the MyMISLab for Chapter 12. It includes fields for the account ID, company (account) name, street address, city, province, postal code, account size (in dollars), contact last name, contact first name, and contact telephone number. The contact is the name of the person in each company who is responsible for contacting Prime about maintenance and repair work. Use your database software to design a solution that would enable Prime's customer service representatives to identify the most important customers so that they can receive priority service. Your solution will require more than one table. Populate your database with at least 15 service requests. Create several reports that would be of interest to management, such as a list of the highest- and lowest-priority accounts or a report showing the most frequently occurring service problems. Create a report showing customer service representatives which service calls they should respond to first on a specific date.

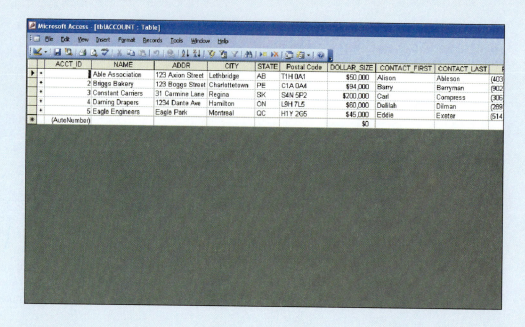

Achieving Operational Excellence: Evaluating Supply Chain Management Services

Software skills: Web browser and presentation software
Business skills: Evaluating supply chain management services

Trucking companies no longer merely carry goods from one place to another. Some also provide supply chain management services to their customers and help them manage their information. In this project, you will use the Web to research and evaluate two of these business services.

Investigate the Web sites of the two companies TransX and Schneider Logistics to see how these companies'

services can be used for supply chain management. Then respond to the following questions:

1. What supply chain processes can each of these companies support for their clients?
2. How can customers use the Web sites of each company to help them with supply chain management?
3. Compare the supply chain management services provided by these companies. Which company would you select to help your firm manage its supply chain? Why?

CASE STUDY   CCL Custom Manufacturing Uses Web Services to Speed Up Both Ends of Its Supply Chain

Toronto-based CCL Custom Manufacturing (CCLCM) is a division of CCL Industries, Inc. It is one of the largest contract manufacturers of consumer products globally, and many of its customers—such as Unilever, Johnson & Johnson, and Procter & Gamble—are larger than CCLCM. How does CCLCM stay in close contact with its customers? CCLCM's CIO Akhil Bhandari states that their Web portal makes communication both feasible and fast. The CCLCM Web portal is a self-service portal that customers can access, with more than 40 percent of the company's purchasing transactions being conducted through the portal.

CCLCM employs 7000 people and operates 35 production facilities in Europe and North and Central America. CCLCM provides both normal production runs and emergency production runs and overflow production for its customers. The company does not produce any products for itself; it is strictly an outsourcer for companies such as Unilever. In surveying its customers, CCLCM found one pressing need along its supply chain: improved business communication.

Bhandari says, "You're dealing with trading partners who may have disparate systems, different technologies. The challenge is to be able to flow the critical business information in an effective way." CCLCM was looking for a solution that would communicate across different systems without direct, one-to-one systems integration. However, CCLCM did not feel that it could dictate to its customers or suppliers—many of which are much larger than CCLCM—how they could communicate with CCLCM. The company started by working on supplier communication.

For a manufacturing company, one missing piece of the manufactured product can throw off the entire production schedule, leaving customers unhappy. According to Al Hintz, Director of Information Systems at CCLCM, "Because of the type of business we are in, we would often have to bring a supplier's system in-house, connecting to them only through their system. Not only did we have to enter order information into our own reporting system, but we had to enter the same information again for them, which added a lot of work on our end and created opportunities for mistakes."

Tom Tulk, CCLCM's business systems analyst, says: "It was difficult to manage the purchasing system when somebody would have to print the purchase order, then fax it over to the supplier, then phone to make sure they got it. We wasted a lot of time trying to contact someone, and it was easy to miss something important."

Simply creating a Web portal was not enough to address these issues. CCLCM needed its information systems to talk to the information systems of its suppliers, without human intervention. Management recognized that the company needed to use a widely accepted standard for its B2B communication system. It settled on Web services as that standard, combined with use of the .NET framework discussed in Chapter 5.

The new system takes purchase orders from CCLCM's five North American plants and posts them to the Web site so that suppliers can access the data. The system also e-mails the supplier to check the new purchase order online; the supplier then sends an e-mail back to CCLCM acknowledging the order and including a hyperlink for the supplier's representative to check the order. The new system also permits suppliers to respond with comments, such as only being able to fulfill a partial order, something the use of EDI (another standard for accomplishing this type of ordering system) cannot do. By using the .NET framework for this type of communication rather than EDI, CCLCM also saved the per-transaction fees associated with EDI. CCLCM also wanted to leverage the Internet, a universal standard available to all suppliers and customers.

But handling purchase orders was not enough. CCLCM still needed to let its suppliers' information systems interface with the systems at CCLCM. They employed XML Web services for this portion of the new system. Hintz says, "We embarked on a pilot program with one of our key suppliers, Dow Corning, where all our orders were being transmitted directly from our JD Edwards program into their SAP system by using XML."

Today CCLCM's enterprise resource planning (ERP) system downloads data into the Web portal, thereby keeping the ERP data secure while opening the data up to authorized users from the supplier side. The Web portal has its own database into which the ERP data is downloaded. By using the .NET platform, utilities such as messaging are available, which saves labour in creating a new messaging system.

More recent additions to the Web services-based portal include demand forecasts, purchase orders, change orders, and advance ship notices. Again, this saves time and errors. Dow Corning now processes 100 percent of its CCLCM orders and change orders through the system. The dollar value of business being conducted through the portal amounts to tens of millions of dollars.

This project was complex to develop. CCLCM employed Whitecap Canada, a developer of customized e-business solutions and Internet-based applications, to develop the portal. Whitecap used Web services standards such as SOAP, XML, and Microsoft's Message Queue technology. The use of SOAP required an added level of complexity since Whitecap had to build a layered security framework to provide privacy and authentication for documents that were being exchanged.

CCLCM plans to extend the new Web portal with Web services into its other divisions. "Based on the success of the pilot program, we want to expand the use of Web services within other divisions of CCL," says Bhandari. "We also want to use this platform for the system-to-system XML-based interface of key transactional data, which will improve the speed of business and reduce our costs . . . I would like to see us using this technology to enhance our collaborative processes with trading partners, [processes] such as product development, logistics, and capacity planning."

Sources: Stefan Dubrowski, "CCL Relies on Web-based Consensus," IT Focus, **www.itworldcanada.com/Pages/Docbase/ViewArticle. aspx?id=idgml-4d2eb4c0-fc13-4dd5-8e81-1080c036388d**, accessed May 3, 2007; Whitecap Canada, "Case Studies: CCL Industries, Inc.," **www.whitecapcanada.com/client_cs_ccl.aspx**, accessed May 3, 2007; and Microsoft, "Manufacturer Improves Customer Communication and Supply Chain Flow with Web Services," **http://download.microsoft.com/documents/customerevidence/ 20407_CCLCustom_CaseStudy_word.doc**, accessed May 3, 2007.

CASE STUDY QUESTIONS

1. Analyze CCLCM using the competitive forces and value chain models. How is supply chain management related to the company's business strategy?

2. Describe the supply chain management problems encountered by CCLCM in this case. What was their business impact?

3. What management, organization, and technology factors were responsible for these problems?

4. How did CCLCM solve these problems? What management, organization, and technology issues were addressed by the solution?

CHAPTER 13

E-Commerce: Digital Markets and Digital Goods

LEARNING OBJECTIVES

After completing this chapter, you will be able to do the following:

1. Describe the unique features of e-commerce, digital markets, and digital goods.
2. Analyze how Internet technology has changed value propositions and business models.
3. Describe the various types of e-commerce and how e-commerce has changed consumer retailing and business-to-business transactions.
4. Evaluate the role of m-commerce in business and describe the most important m-commerce applications.
5. Compare the principal payment systems for electronic commerce.

OPENING CASE | Major League Baseball Hits a Home Run with Information Systems

Technology is helping Major League Baseball (MLB) raise its batting average. MLB is responsible for operating the two top baseball leagues in North America—the National League and the American League. Although baseball is a sport, Major League Baseball is also a big business, requiring revenue from tickets, television broadcasts, and other sources to pay for its stadiums and teams. One of the functions of MLB is to promote and grow that business.

MLB has its own set of business challenges. As salaries for top players have ballooned, so have ticket prices. Many fans now watch games on television rather than attending them in person. Although some teams fill the stadiums, others, such as the Toronto Blue Jays, have seen their fan base dwindle. Shea Stadium, the home field of the New York Mets, was half empty most of the 2004 baseball season.

MLB still uses traditional print and broadcast media—newspapers, television, and radio—to publicize games, and it uses retail outlets and stadiums to sell baseball tickets and souvenirs. But its new emphasis is on using the Internet and information technology. It now runs a high-tech production/Internet spinoff based in New York City called MLB Advanced Media (MLBAM), which oversees MLB video productions, the Web sites for each of MLB's 30 teams, and its own Web site, MLB.com.

Bib Bowman, CEO and president of MLBAM, wants to find more customers and turn them into devoted fans who will go to more games and buy more baseball-related merchandise. "A lot of people just go to one game per year, and we need to encourage that

fan to be more active with his or her favourite team," he says. Teams such as the Blue Jays and the Mets, which had ranked seventeenth in attendance among MLB's 30 teams, have benefited. The MLB Web sites have helped publicize information about the Mets and increased season ticket sales.

It is easy to see why. At MLB.com, for example, fans can check game scores; purchase game tickets; shop for caps, jerseys, baseball cards, and memorabilia; post opinions on electronic message boards; use e-mail; and find out more about their favourite teams and players. The site features fantasy baseball games, where fans compete with one another by managing "fantasy teams" based on real players' statistics. About 800 000 subscribers pay US $79.95 per year for live streaming video of baseball games that play on their computers. During the baseball season, MLB.com streams 10 to 15 live baseball games a day.

MLBAM is trying to boost ticket sales further by broadcasting offers to fans' cell phones. For instance,

Blue Jays fans who have shown interest in ticket offers may receive a text message that there are still seats available for a Blue Jays game at Rogers Centre, and they can purchase tickets using their cell phones. If the fan purchases, a bar code is transmitted to his or her cell phone to use as a ticket that will be accepted at the gate. MLBAM also sold more than one million cell phone wallpapers, ring tones, and other content during that baseball season. It has started to offer live audio broadcast feeds of games and fantasy games to owners of colour-screen phones at all the major cellular services.

To learn more about who its customers are and what they want, MLBAM worked with SAS Inc. on software to collect and analyze its customer data. These data come from subscriptions; e-commerce transactions on MLB Web sites; and e-mail addresses collected from sweepstakes, online newsletters, and other offers. Special Web site tracking tools provide information on the most popular parts of MLB Web sites, which ball games participants watch or download, which online games they play, and which team merchandise or tickets they buy.

MLB has leveraged its expertise in streaming live video baseball games to offer streaming video services to other businesses. Major League Soccer, the World Championship Sports Network, and entertainer Jimmy Buffet have hired MLB.com to stream their video events. About 15 percent of MLB.com's total revenue of $226 million in 2005 came from managing Web sites and streaming video partnerships.

Sources: Bobby White, "Major League Baseball Steps Out as Coach in the Game of Web Video," *The Wall Street Journal*, March 27, 2006; Jon Surmacz, "In a League of Its Own," *CIO Magazine*, April 15, 2005; W. David Gardner, "Fans Say 'Take Me Out to the Web Site,'" *InformationWeek*, August 22, 2005; and Peter J. Howe, "Major League Baseball Pitches Cellphone Content," *Boston Globe*, March 14, 2005.

Major League Baseball's Web-based ventures show why e-commerce is becoming so important. The Internet has breathed new life into MLB, as well as many other organizations, by providing new online channels for reaching customers, new digital products and services, and new marketing tools. Internet technology has transformed its business model.

The chapter-opening Business Challenges diagram calls attention to important points raised by this case and this chapter. Baseball ticket prices have risen, costs are up, and baseball must compete with other forms of entertainment, including electronic games. MLB set up a series of Web sites that offer extensive information about teams, games, and players; video and audio broadcasts, the ability to purchase tickets via computer or cell phone; and the ability to purchase souvenirs and memorabilia over the Web. The Web sites include community-building features, such as e-mail and electronic messaging, and new products for sale, such as cell phone content and fantasy games, that are not available through traditional channels. Use of the Internet and the Web makes it possible for MLB to use new tools for analyzing customers. Knowledge of this technology has opened up a new line of business supplying technology services. Thanks to all these new e-commerce initiatives, MLB revenue has increased.

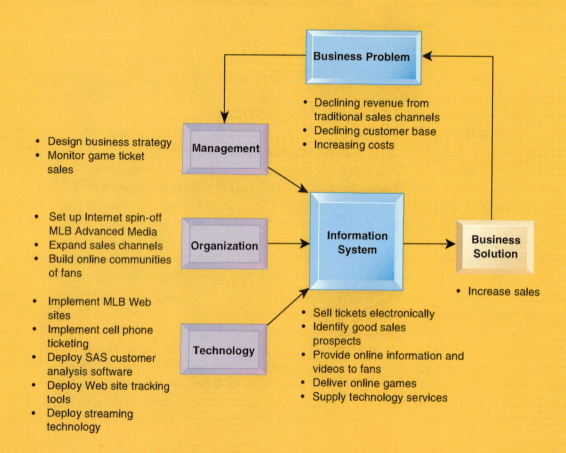

HEADS **UP**

This chapter focuses on e-commerce and how businesses use e-commerce to achieve operational excellence and customer intimacy. E-commerce is also transforming business and industries. E-commerce advertising revenues are growing faster than other forms of advertising. Every large company, and most medium and small companies, have Web sites that speak directly to customers. If you work in business today, you need to know about e-commerce.

- If your career is in finance and accounting, you will be working with systems for receiving payments electronically over the Internet and for delivering new online financial services based on the Web.

- If your career is in human resources, you will be using online job-hunting sites to attract new employees.

- If your career is in information systems, you will be helping to design and maintain e-commerce Web sites.

- If your career is in manufacturing, production, or operations management, you will be using the Internet for sourcing, and using a variety of network exchanges and private industrial networks for procurement and management of your supply chain.

- If your career is in sales and marketing, you will be using the Web to provide digital products and services and to sell and promote products by using personalization, customization, and community marketing techniques.

13.1 Electronic Commerce and the Internet

Have you ever downloaded music over the Web? Ever purchased books and CDs online? Have you ever used the Web to search for information about personal clothing items before you bought anything in a retail store? If so, you've participated in e-commerce. So have hundreds of millions of people around the globe. And although most purchases still take place through traditional channels, e-commerce continues to be the fastest growing form of retail trade and continues to transform the way companies do business.

E-Commerce Today

E-commerce refers to the use of the Internet and the Web to transact business. More formally, e-commerce is about digitally enabled commercial transactions between and among organizations and individuals. For the most part, this means transactions that occur over the Internet and the Web. Commercial transactions involve the exchange of value (e.g., money) across organizational or individual boundaries in return for products and services.

E-commerce began in 1995 when one of the first Internet portals, Netscape.com, accepted the first ads from major corporations and popularized the idea that the Web could be used as a new medium for advertising and sales. No one envisioned at the time what would turn out to be an exponential growth curve for e-commerce retail sales, which doubled and tripled in the early years. Only since 2006 has consumer e-commerce "slowed" to a 25 percent annual growth rate (see Figure 13-1).

Mirroring the history of commercial innovations, such as the telephone, radio, and television, the very rapid growth in e-commerce in the early years created a stock market bubble in e-commerce stocks. Like all bubbles, the "dot-com" bubble burst, in March 2001. A large number of e-commerce companies failed during this process. Yet for many others, such as Amazon, eBay, Expedia, and Google, the results have been more positive: soaring revenues, fine-tuned business models that produce profits, and rising stock prices.

FIGURE 13-1 *The growth of e-commerce*

Retail e-commerce revenues have grown exponentially since 1995 and have only recently "slowed" to a very rapid 25 percent annual increase, which is projected to remain the same until 2008.

Source: Based on data from eMarketer, 2006; Shop.org and Forrester Research, 2005; and authors.

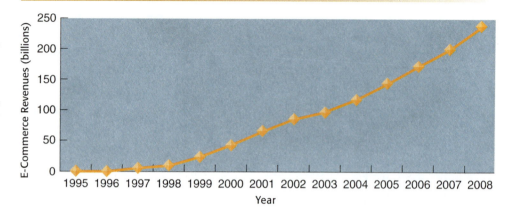

In 2007, the overall e-commerce revenues picture is very positive:

- Online consumer sales will increase by more than 23 percent in 2007 to an estimated $180 billion (including travel), with 106 million people purchasing online (eMarketer, 2006).

- In the world, more than 1 billion people are now connected to the Internet. Growth in the overall Internet population has spurred growth in e-commerce.

- On the average day, 70 million people go online, 140 million send e-mail, 5 million write on their blogs, 4 million share music on peer-to-peer networks, and 3 million use the Internet to rate a person, product, or service.

- The number of people who have purchased something online expanded to about 106 million, with additional millions shopping (gathering information) but not purchasing.

- B2B e-commerce—use of the Internet for business-to-business commerce—will continue to expand; in 2006, Canadian B2B e-commerce was $31.4 billion, or about 68 percent of total e-commerce by private firms (Statistics Canada, 2007).

The e-commerce revolution is still just beginning. Individuals and businesses will increasingly use the Internet to conduct commerce as more products and services come online and more households switch to broadband telecommunications. More industries will be transformed by e-commerce, including travel reservations, music and entertainment, news, software, education, and finance. Table 13-1 highlights these new e-commerce developments.

Why E-commerce Is Different

Why has e-commerce grown so rapidly? The answer lies in the unique nature of the Internet and the Web. Simply put, the Internet and e-commerce technologies are much richer and more powerful than previous technology revolutions. Table 13-2 describes the unique features of the Internet and Web as a commercial medium.

Let us explore each of these unique features in more detail.

Ubiquity In traditional commerce, a marketplace is a physical place, such as a retail store, that you visit to transact business. E-commerce is ubiquitous, meaning that it is available just about everywhere, at all times. It makes it possible to shop from your desktop, at home, at work, or even from your car, using mobile commerce. The result is called a **marketspace**—a marketplace extended beyond traditional boundaries and removed from a temporal and geographic location.

From a consumer point of view, ubiquity reduces transaction costs—the costs of participating in a market (see Chapter 3). To transact business, it is no longer necessary to spend time or money travelling to a market, and much less mental effort is required to make a purchase.

Marketspace

prices in a market; **cost transparency** refers to the ability of consumers to discover the actual costs merchants pay for products.

There are advantages for merchants as well. Online merchants can discover much more about consumers than in the past. This allows merchants to segment the market into groups who are willing to pay different prices and permits the merchants to engage in **price discrimination**—selling the same goods, or nearly the same goods, to different targeted groups at different prices. For instance, an online merchant can discover a consumer's avid interest in expensive, exotic vacations and then pitch high-end vacation plans to that consumer at a premium price, knowing the consumer is willing to pay extra for such a vacation. At the same time, the online merchant can pitch the same vacation plan at a lower price to a more price-sensitive consumer. Information density also helps merchants differentiate their products in terms of cost, brand, and quality.

Personalization/Customization E-commerce technologies permit **personalization**: Merchants can target their marketing messages to specific individuals by adjusting the message to a person's name, interests, and past purchases. The technology also permits **customization**—changing the delivered product or service based on a user's preferences or prior behaviour. Given the interactive nature of e-commerce technology, much information about the consumer can be gathered in the marketplace at the moment of purchase. With the increase in information density, a great deal of information about the consumer's past purchases and behaviour can be stored and used by online merchants.

The result is a level of personalization and customization unthinkable with traditional commerce technologies. For instance, you may be able to shape what you see on television by selecting a channel, but you cannot change the content of the channel you have chosen. In contrast, the *Wall Street Journal Online* allows you to select the type of news stories you want to see first and gives you the opportunity to be alerted when certain events happen.

Key Concepts in E-commerce: Digital Markets and Digital Goods

The location, timing, and revenue models of business are based in some part on the cost and distribution of information. When communication is limited to people moving along paths that connect villages, the cost of gathering information is extremely high, and village markets provide the location of business and the business model. The Internet has greatly reduced the cost of obtaining and distributing information and created a digital marketplace where millions of people are able to exchange massive amounts of information directly, instantly, and for free. As a result, the Internet has changed the way companies conduct business.

The Internet shrinks information asymmetry. **Information asymmetry** exists when one party in a transaction has more information that is important for the transaction than the other party. That information helps determine their relative bargaining power. In digital markets, consumers and suppliers can "see" the prices being charged for goods, and in that sense, digital markets are said to be more "transparent" than traditional markets.

For example, until auto retailing sites appeared on the Web, there was a pronounced information asymmetry between auto dealers and customers. Only the auto dealers knew the manufacturers' prices, and it was difficult for consumers to shop around for the best price. Auto dealers' profit margins depended on this asymmetry of information. Today's consumers have access to a legion of Web sites providing competitive pricing information, and three-fourths of North American auto buyers use the Internet to shop around for the best deal. Thus, the Web has reduced the information asymmetry surrounding an auto purchase. The Internet has also helped businesses seeking to purchase from other businesses reduce information asymmetries and locate better prices and terms.

Digital markets are very flexible and efficient because they operate with reduced search and transaction costs, lower **menu costs** (merchants' costs of changing prices), price discrimination, and the ability to change prices dynamically based on market conditions. In **dynamic pricing**, the price of a product varies depending on the demand characteristics of the customer or the supply situation of the seller.

Cost transparency
Price discrimination
Personalization
Customization
Information asymmetry
Menu costs
Dynamic pricing

These markets may either reduce or increase switching costs, depending on the nature of the product or service being sold, and they may cause some extra delay in gratification. Unlike a physical market, you cannot immediately consume a product such as clothing purchased over the Web (although immediate consumption is possible with digital music downloads and other digital products).

Digital markets provide many opportunities to sell directly to the consumer, bypassing intermediaries such as distributors or retail outlets. Eliminating intermediaries in the distribution channel can significantly lower purchase transaction costs. To pay for all the steps in a traditional distribution channel, a product may have to be priced as high as 135 percent of its original cost to manufacture.

Figure 13-2 illustrates the amount of savings that can result from eliminating each of these layers in the distribution process. By selling directly to consumers or reducing the number of intermediaries, companies are able to raise profits while charging lower prices. The removal of organizations or business process layers responsible for intermediary steps in a value chain is called **disintermediation.**

Disintermediation is also taking place in the market for services. Airlines and hotels operating their own reservation sites online earn more per ticket because they have eliminated travel agents as intermediaries. Table 13-3 summarizes the differences between digital markets and traditional markets.

Digital Goods The Internet digital marketplace has greatly expanded sales of digital goods. **Digital goods** are goods that can be delivered over a digital network. Music tracks, video, software, newspapers, magazines, and books can all be expressed, stored, delivered, and sold as purely digital products. Currently, most of these products are sold as physical goods, for example, CDs, DVDs, and hard copy books. But the Internet offers the possibility of delivering all these products on demand as digital products.

In general, for digital goods, the marginal cost of producing another unit is about zero (it costs nothing to make a copy of a music file). However, the cost of producing the original first unit is relatively high—in fact it is nearly the total cost of the product because there are few other costs of inventory and distribution. Costs of delivery over the Internet are very low; marketing costs remain the same; and pricing can be highly variable. (On the Internet, the merchant can change prices as often as desired because of low menu costs.)

The impact of the Internet on the market for these kinds of digital goods is nothing short of revolutionary, and we see the results around us every day. Businesses dependent on the physical products for sales—such as bookstores, book publishers, music labels, and film studios—face the possibility of declining sales and even destruction of their

FIGURE 13-2   *The benefits of disintermediation to the consumer*

The typical distribution channel has several intermediary layers, each of which adds to the final cost of a product, such as a sweater. Removing layers lowers the final cost to the consumer.

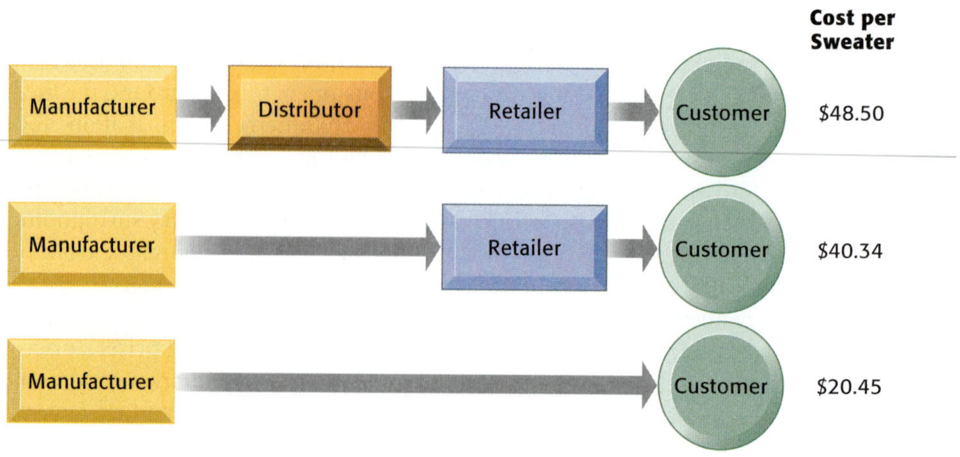

				Cost per Sweater
Manufacturer	Distributor	Retailer	Customer	$48.50
Manufacturer		Retailer	Customer	$40.34
Manufacturer			Customer	$20.45

Disintermediation
Digital goods

TABLE 13-3 Digital Markets Compared to Traditional Markets

	DIGITAL MARKETS	**TRADITIONAL MARKETS**
Information asymmetry	Asymmetry reduced	Asymmetry high
Search costs	Low	High
Transaction costs	Low (sometimes virtually nothing)	High (time, travel)
Delayed gratification	High (or lower in the case of a digital good)	Lower: purchase now
Menu costs	Low	High
Dynamic pricing	Low cost, instant	High cost, delayed
Price discrimination	Low cost, instant	High cost, delayed
Market segmentation	Low cost, moderate precision	High cost, less precision
Switching costs	Higher/lower (depending on product characteristics)	High
Network effects	Strong	Weaker
Disintermediation	More possible/likely	Less possible/unlikely

businesses. Newspapers and magazines are losing readers to the Internet, and losing advertisers. Record label companies are losing sales to Internet piracy and record stores are going out of business. Video rental firms, such as Blockbuster, based on a physical DVD market and physical stores, are losing sales to NetFlix using an Internet model (see the Chapter 3 ending case). Hollywood studios as well face the prospect that Internet pirates will distribute their product as digital streaming video, bypassing Hollywood's monopoly on DVD rentals and sales, which now accounts for more than half of industry film revenues. Table 13-4 describes digital goods and how they differ from traditional physical goods.

Internet Business Models

The bottom line result of these changes in the economics of information is nearly a revolution in commerce, with many new business models appearing and many old business models no longer tenable. Table 13-5 describes some of the most important Internet business models that have emerged. All, in one way or another, use the Internet to add extra value to existing products and services or to provide the foundation for new products and services.

TABLE 13-4 How the Internet Changes the Markets for Digital Goods

	DIGITAL GOODS	**TRADITIONAL GOODS**
Marginal cost/unit	Zero	Greater than zero, high
Cost of production	High (most of the cost)	Variable
Copying cost	Approximately 0	Greater than zero, high
Distributed delivery cost	Low	High
Inventory cost	Low	High
Marketing cost	Variable	Variable
Pricing	More variable (bundling, random pricing games)	Fixed, based on unit costs

TABLE 13-5 *Internet Business Models*

CATEGORY	DESCRIPTION	EXAMPLES
Virtual storefront	Sells physical products directly to consumers or to individual businesses.	Chapters.Indigo.ca EPM.com
Information broker	Provides product, pricing, and availability information to individuals and businesses. Generates revenue from advertising or from directing buyers to sellers.	Edmunds.com KBB.com Ehealthinsurance.com Insweb.com, Realtor.com
Transaction broker	Saves users money and time by processing online sales transactions and generating a fee each time a transaction occurs. Also provides information on rates and terms.	BayStreet.ca Expedia.ca TDAmeritrade.com
Online marketplace	Provides a digital environment where buyers and sellers can meet, search for products, display products, and establish prices for those products. Can provide online auctions or reverse auctions in which buyers submit bids to multiple sellers to purchase at a buyer-specified price as well as negotiated or fixed pricing. Can serve consumers or B2B e-commerce, generating revenue from transaction fees.	eBay.ca Priceline.com ChemConnect.com
Content provider	Creates revenue by providing digital content, such as digital news, music, photos, or video, over the Web. The customer may pay to access the content, or revenue may be generated by selling advertising space.	FinancialPost.com Yahoo.ca iTunes.ca Canada.com
Online service provider	Provides online service for individuals and businesses. Generates revenue from subscription or transaction fees, from advertising, or from collecting marketing information from users.	Streamload.com Xdrive.com, Ofoto.com salesforce.com
Virtual community	Provides an online meeting place where people with similar interests can communicate and find useful information.	YouTube.com Facebook.com, iVillage.com Kidshelp.sympatico.ca
Portal	Provides initial point of entry to the Web along with specialized content and other services.	Yahoo.ca MSN.ca, Canoe.ca

Communication and Community

Some of these new business models take advantage of the Internet's rich communication capabilities. eBay is an online auction forum that uses e-mail and other interactive features of the Web. The system accepts bids entered on the Internet, evaluates the bids, and notifies the highest bidder. eBay collects a small commission on each listing and sale. eBay has become so popular that its site serves as a huge trading platform for other companies, hosting hundreds of thousands of "virtual storefronts." The case study concluding this chapter discusses eBay and its business model in greater detail.

Business-to-business auctions have also emerged. GoIndustry, for instance, features Web-based auction services for business-to-business sales of industrial equipment and machinery.

The Internet has created online communities where people with similar interests exchange ideas from many different locations. Some of these virtual communities are providing the foundation for new businesses. iVillage.com provides an online community for women sharing similar interests, such as diet and fitness, pregnancy, parenting, home and garden, and food. Members participate in online discussions and join online "communities" with other like-minded people.

A major source of revenue for these communities involves providing ways for corporate clients to target customers, including the placement of banner ads and pop-up ads on their Web sites. A **banner ad** is a graphic display on a Web page used for advertising. The banner is linked to the advertiser's Web site so that a person clicking the banner is transported to a Web page with more information about the advertiser. **Pop-up ads** work in

Banner ad

Pop-up ads

the opposite manner. They automatically open up when a user accesses a specific Web site, and the user must click the ad to make it disappear.

Social networking sites are a type of online community that has become extremely popular. Social networking is the practice of expanding the number of one's business or social contacts by making connections through individuals. Social networking sites link people through their mutual business or personal connections, enabling them to mine their friends (and their friends' friends) for sales leads, job-hunting tips, or new friends. MySpace.com, Facebook.com, YouTube (Figure 13-3) and Friendster.com appeal to people who are primarily interested in extending their friendships, while LinkedIn.com focuses on job networking.

Members of social networking sites spend hours surfing pages, checking out other members, and exchanging messages, and they reveal a great deal of information about themselves. Businesses harvest this information to create carefully targeted promotions that far surpass the typical text and display ads found on the Web. They also use the sites to interact with potential customers. The most popular of these sites attract so many visitors and are so "sticky" that they have become very powerful marketing tools. The Window on Management section discusses MySpace as a business model.

Social networking sites

FIGURE 13-3   *YouTube streaming video*

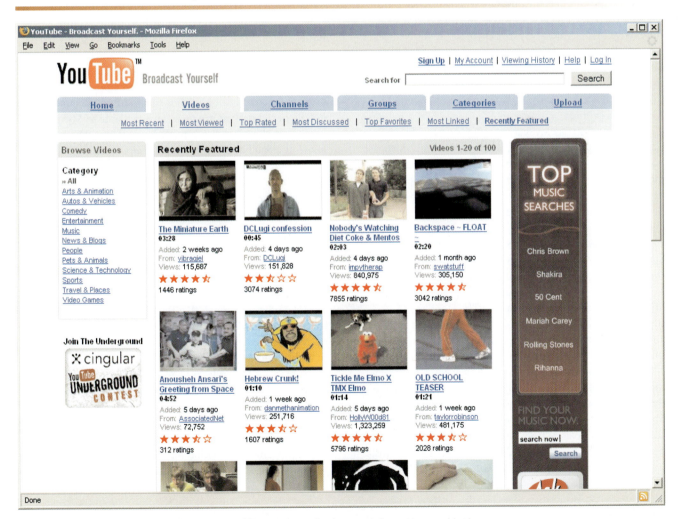

YouTube is a free online streaming video service enabling users to upload, tag, and share videos worldwide. Members can join and create video groups to connect to people with similar interests.

The Allure of MySpace

MySpace.com has become nothing short of a phenomenon. Next to Yahoo!, it is the most highly visited Web site in the U.S. and the destination of nearly 4.5 percent of all online visits. And it has only been in business since January 2004! Its chief rival is Facebook, another social networking site.

MySpace offers a rich array of features, including message boards, e-mail, instant messaging, video clips, classified ads, online games, blogs, job searches, music, and, of course, the ability to network with other people online and perhaps meet them in person. Although MySpace touts itself as a private community favouring bands and musicians seeking audiences for their music, it is also big business. News Corp. paid $672 million to acquire MySpace in late 2005.

Advertisers are enthralled with the opportunity to create personal relationships with millions of young people. "What we really struck upon is the power of friendship," said Michael Barrett, chief revenue officer for News Corp.'s Fox Interactive Media. And MySpace's circle of friends is huge. According to Nielsen/NetRatings, MySpace logged close to 457 million unique visitors in June 2006 alone, with users spending an average of nearly two hours on each visit to the site. By early August 2006, MySpace was hosting 100 million profiles.

Companies can pay MySpace to set up profiles of their products as if they were members of the community. MySpace users can become "friends" of Toyota's Yaris car or entire movies, such as *Fullmetal Alchemist*. Profile sponsors see exactly who is interested in their product and gather rich data on age, marital status, location language, gender, occupation, and personal interests.

Procter & Gamble used MySpace to launch its Secret Sparkle deodorant for 16- to 24-year-old women by linking the product to the Web pages of musicians that used MySpace and appealed to the same demographic group. When users listened to new songs by The Donnas and Bonnie McKey, they were exposed to ads for Secret Sparkle and offered a chance to participate in a Secret Sparkle sweepstakes.

On August 8, 2006, Google agreed to pay Fox Interactive Media $900 million to have MySpace use its search engine so that it could place text ads alongside search results generated by MySpace users. Besides the Google deal, MySpace will be able to generate revenue from display advertising, video advertising, and ads on key MySpace destinations such as the music page, the main comedy page, or the home page. Pali Research analyst Richard Greenfield expects MySpace to generate $347 million in revenue for fiscal year 2007 and at least $521 million the following year.

Sounds like good business—except that MySpace is also very controversial. Many teenage subscribers post suggestive photos of themselves and lie about their age. About one-fourth of all MySpace users are registered as minors under 18 years of age, but that number could be much larger. Parents, politicians, and police worry that sexual predators use MySpace to stalk potential victims. In June 2006, the mother of a 14-year-old girl who was sexually assaulted by a 19-year-old user sued MySpace and News Corp. for $35 million. The lawsuit, filed in Texas, claimed the 19-year-old lied about being a high school senior to gain the young girl's trust and phone number. Other similar incidents have been reported.

In response, MySpace is trying to restrict how adults contact its younger users. It already prohibits children under 13 from setting up accounts and displays only partial profiles of registered 14- or 15-year-olds unless the person viewing the profile is already on the teen's list of friends. (Partial profiles display gender, age, and city while full profiles describe hobbies, schools, and other personal details.) Friends' lists are no longer available to MySpace users over 18 unless they already know the youth's full name or e-mail address. However, users under 18 can still make contact, and MySpace has no mechanism for verifying that users submit their true age when registering. So adults can sign up as minors and join a 14-year-old's list of friends. MySpace is also fine-tuning its ad targeting to avoid displaying gambling and other adult-themed sites on minors' profile pages.

MySpace's chief rival, Facebook, was used recently to launch a cyber-bullying attack against a business student at a Canadian university. The student had apparently upset several students so much that they forgot what most of them had learned in their business classes about ethics and posted hostile messages to one another about the student. In addition to the students who posted these hostile messages, many other students viewed the messages and did not respond or alert school authorities. When Facebook was notified by the school, it took down the account that hosted the messages. All of which is to say that these sites can be used—even by business students—for good or not so good. Technology, including social networking sites, is what we make it.

To Think About

1. How do businesses benefit from MySpace? How do MySpace members benefit?

2. Does MySpace create an ethical dilemma? Why or why not?

3. Do parents' and schools' objections to MySpace have any merit? Should a site such as MySpace be allowed to operate? Why or why not?

4. Is there anything that MySpace management can do to make the site less controversial?

MIS in Action

Explore www.MySpace.com, examining the features and tools that are not restricted to registered members. View the profile created for a product such as the Toyota Yaris or a movie of your choice and related profiles about individuals who are "friends" of that product. Then answer the following questions:

1. What information can you find out about the product from its MySpace profile?

2. What features of the profile would attract teenage and college buyers? How does this profile differ from display advertising on the Web?

3. Explore some of the profiles of "friends" of this product. What kind of information is available about them?

4. Is using MySpace a good way to promote this product? Why or why not?

Sources: Elizabeth Holmes, "On MySpace, Millions of Users Make 'Friends' with Ads," *The Wall Street Journal*, August 7, 2006; Jessica Sebor, "MySpace Cadets," *Customer Relationship Management*, September 2006; Steve Rosenbush, "Fox to Make MySpace More Spacious," *Business Week*, August 8, 2006; Steve Rosenbush, "Socializing for Dollars," *Business Week*, April 10, 2006; "MySpace Plans New Age Restrictions," Associated Press, June 21, 2006; and Anick Jesdanun, "Online Age Verification May Prove Complex," Associated Press, July 17, 2006.

Social networking is so appealing that it has inspired a new type of e-commerce experience called **social shopping**. Social shopping sites such as Kaboodle, ThisNext, Wists.com, and StyleHive.com provide online meeting places for people to swap shopping ideas. These sites provide tools for users to create their own Web pages with information and images about items they like to help other shoppers.

Digital Content, Entertainment, and Services The ability to deliver digital goods and digital content over the Web has created new alternatives to traditional print and broadcast media. There are Web sites for digital versions of print publications, such as the *National Post* or *The Globe and Mail*, and for new online journals such as Salon.com.

Some of the most popular Web sites deliver entertainment in digital form. Online games attract huge numbers of players. For example, Blizzard Entertainment's online role-playing game World of Warcraft earned $1 billion in 2006 alone, from seven million players worldwide (*Wireless Week*, 2006).

You can listen online to some of your favourite radio channels, ranging from the CBC to independent channels such as CHWV 97.3 FM from Saint John, New Brunswick. Because the radio signal is relayed over the Internet, it is possible to access stations from anywhere in the world. Services such as Yahoo!'s LAUNCHcast and RealNetworks' Rhapsody even put together individualized radio channels for listeners.

Broadband connections now make it possible for Web sites to display full-length films and television shows. Apple, Amazon.com, Movielink, and CinemaNow have downloading services for full-length movies. The chapter-opening case describes online broadcasts of MLB baseball games. For viewers outside North America, the National Football League (NFL) has started streaming a full season of live games over the Internet.

Many of you use the Web to preview and download music. Although some of this Internet music is free of charge, Apple's iTunes and other sites are generating revenue by charging for each song or album downloaded from their Web sites. The phenomenal popularity of Apple's iTunes music service and Apple's iPod portable music player has inspired a new form of digital content delivery called *podcasting*. **Podcasting** is a method of publishing audio broadcasts via the Internet, allowing subscribing users to download audio files onto their personal computers or portable music players. Video clips designed to be downloaded and viewed on a portable device are called *vcasts*.

Podcasting enables independent producers to self-publish their own audio content and gives broadcast media a new distribution method. The "Canadian Banks 2007" podcast series (www.rogic.com/canadapodcasts) features PricewaterhouseCoopers Canada subject matter experts discussing topics related to the banking industry in Canada. Podcasts also have internal uses for businesses that want to distribute information in

Social shopping

Podcasting

audio form to their employees. Internet security firm SonicWall uses podcasts to demonstrate its expertise to customers and to provide new product information to its resellers.

The Web's information resources are so vast and rich that portals have emerged as an Internet business model. Portals help individuals and organizations locate information more efficiently and also seek to become destination sites by aggregating content on their sites. In Chapter 2, we defined a portal as a Web interface for presenting integrated, personalized information from a variety of sources. As an e-commerce business model, a *portal* is a "super site" that provides a comprehensive entry point for a huge array of resources and services on the Internet.

Yahoo! is an example. It provides capabilities for locating information on the Internet along with news, sports, weather, telephone directories, maps, games, shopping, e-mail, chat, discussion boards, and links to other sites. Portals also target regional groups. Canoe.ca and Canada.com provide news and social networking for Canadians. StarMedia.com is a portal customized for Latin American Internet users, and the portal Sina.com is customized for Chinese users.

Portals and Web content sites often combine content and applications from many different sources and service providers. Other Internet business models use syndication as well, providing additional value. For example, E*Trade, the discount Web trading site, purchases most of its content from outside sources such as Reuters (news) and BigCharts.com (charts). Online **syndicators**, which aggregate content or applications from multiple sources, package them for distribution, and resell them to third-party Web sites, have emerged as another variant of the online content provider business model. The Web makes it much easier for companies to aggregate, repackage, and distribute information and information-based services.

Chapter 5 describes application service providers, such as salesforce.com, that feature software that runs over the Web. They provide online services to subscribing businesses. Other online service providers offer services to individual consumers, such as remote storage of data at Xdrive.com or online photo storage printouts at Ofoto.com (recently purchased by Kodak). Service providers generate revenue through subscription fees or from advertising.

Most of the business models described in Table 13-5 above are called **pure-play** business models because they are based purely on the Internet. These firms did not have an existing bricks-and-mortar business when they designed their Internet business. However, many existing retail firms, such as Hudson's Bay Company (and its subsidiaries, Zeller's and Home Outfitters), L.L.Bean, Office Depot, and *The Globe and Mail*, have developed Web sites as extensions of their traditional bricks-and-mortar businesses. These businesses represent a hybrid **clicks-and-mortar** business model.

13.2 Electronic Commerce

Although most commercial transactions still take place through traditional retail channels, rising numbers of consumers and businesses are using the Internet for electronic commerce. Today, e-commerce revenue represents about 2 percent of all retail sales in North America, and there is tremendous upside potential for growth.

Types of Electronic Commerce

There are many ways to classify electronic commerce transactions. One is by looking at the nature of the participants in the electronic commerce transaction. The three major electronic commerce categories are business-to-consumer (B2C) e-commerce, business-to-business (B2B) e-commerce, and consumer-to-consumer (C2C) e-commerce.

- **Business-to-consumer (B2C) electronic commerce** involves retailing products and services to individual shoppers. Chapters.Indigo.ca, which sells books, videos, and music to individual consumers, is an example of B2C e-commerce. The Major League Baseball Web site discussed at the beginning of this chapter is another example of B2C e-commerce.

- **Business-to-business (B2B) electronic commerce** involves sales of goods and services among businesses. ChemConnect's Web site for buying and selling natural gas liquids,

Syndicators

Pure-play

Clicks-and-mortar

Business-to-consumer (B2C) electronic commerce

Business-to-business (B2B) electronic commerce

refined and intermediate fuels, chemicals, and plastics is an example of B2B e-commerce.

- **Consumer-to-consumer (C2C) electronic commerce** involves consumers selling directly to consumers. For example, eBay, the giant Web auction site, enables people to sell their goods to other consumers by auctioning the merchandise off to the highest bidder.

Another way of classifying electronic commerce transactions is in terms of the participants' physical connection to the Web. Until recently, almost all e-commerce transactions took place over wired networks. Now mobile phones and other wireless handheld digital appliances are Internet-enabled to send text messages and e-mail, access Web sites, and make purchases. Companies are offering new types of Web-based products and services that can be accessed by these wireless devices. The use of handheld wireless devices for purchasing goods and services from any location has been termed **mobile commerce** or **m-commerce**. Both business-to-business and business-to-consumer e-commerce transactions can take place using m-commerce technology, which we discuss in detail in Section 13.3.

Achieving Customer Intimacy: Interactive Marketing, Personalization, and Self-Service

The unique dimensions of e-commerce technologies that we have just described offer many new possibilities for marketing and selling. The Internet provides companies with additional channels of communication and interaction for closer yet more cost-effective relationships with customers in sales, marketing, and customer support.

Interactive Marketing and Personalization The Internet and e-commerce have helped some merchants achieve the holy grail of marketing: making personalized products for millions of consumers, an impossible task in traditional markets. Web sites, such as those for Lands' End (shirts and pants) and Staples (business cards, note cards, and labels), feature online tools that allow consumers to purchase products tailored to their individual specifications.

Web sites have become a bountiful source of detailed information about customer behaviour, preferences, needs, and buying patterns that companies can use to tailor promotions, products, services, and pricing. Some customer information may be obtained by asking visitors to "register" online and provide information about themselves, but many companies also collect customer information using software tools that track the activities of Web site visitors.

Clickstream tracking tools collect data on customer activities at Web sites and store them in a log. The tools record the site that users visited prior to coming to a particular Web site and where these users go when they leave that site. They also record the specific pages visited on the particular site, the time spent on each page of the site, the types of pages visited, and what the visitors purchased (see Figure 13-4). Firms analyze this information about customer interests and behaviour to develop precise profiles of existing and potential customers.

Such information enables firms to create unique personalized Web pages that display content or ads for products or services of special interest to each user, improving the customer's experience and creating additional value (see Figure 13-5). By using personalization technology to modify the Web pages presented to each customer, marketers achieve the benefits of using individual salespeople at dramatically lower costs.

One technique for Web personalization is **collaborative filtering**, which compares information gathered about a specific user's behaviour at a Web site to data about other customers with similar interests to predict what the user would like to see next. The software then makes recommendations to users based on their assumed interests. For example, Amazon.ca and Chapters.Indigo.ca use collaborative filtering software to prepare personalized book recommendations: "Customers who bought this book also bought. . . ." These recommendations are made just at the point of purchase, an ideal time to prompt a consumer into purchasing a related product.

Consumer-to-consumer (C2C) electronic commerce

Mobile commerce (m-commerce)

Clickstream tracking

Collaborative filtering

FIGURE 13-4 *Web site visitor tracking*

E-commerce Web sites have tools to track a shopper's every step through an online store. Close examination of customer behaviour at a Web site selling women's clothing shows what the store might learn at each step and what actions it could take to increase sales.

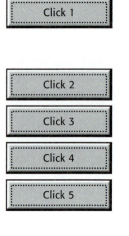

The shopper clicks on the home page. The store can tell that the shopper arrived from the Yahoo portal at 2:30 p.m. (which might help determine staffing for customer service centres) and how long she lingered on the home page (which might indicate trouble navigating the site).

The shopper clicks on blouses, clicks to select a woman's white blouse, then clicks to view the same item in pink. The shopper clicks to select this item in a size 10 in pink and clicks to place it in her shopping cart. This information can help the store determine which sizes and colours are most popular.

From the shopping cart page, the shopper clicks to close the browser to leave the Web site without purchasing the blouse. This action could indicate the shopper changed her mind or that she had a problem with the Web site's checkout and payment process. Such behaviour might signal that the Web site was not well designed.

Blogs Blogs, which we introduced in Chapter 7, have emerged as another promising Web-based tool for marketing. A blog, the popular term for a Weblog, is a personal Web page that typically contains a series of chronological entries (newest to oldest) by its author and links to related Web pages.

The blog may include a blogroll (a collection of links to other blogs) and TrackBacks (a list of entries in other blogs that refer to a post on the first blog). Most

FIGURE 13-5 *Web site personalization*

Firms can create unique personalized Web pages that display content or ads for products or services of special interest to individual users, improving the customer experience and creating additional value.

blogs allow readers to post comments on the blog entries as well. The act of creating a blog is often referred to as "blogging." Blogs are either hosted by a third-party site such as Blogger.com (owned by Google and formerly called Blogspot.com), LiveJournal.com, Typepad.com, and Xanga.com, or prospective bloggers can download software such as Moveable Type and bBlog to create a blog that is hosted by the user's ISP. Blog pages are usually variations on templates provided by the blogging service or software and hence require no knowledge of HTML. Therefore, millions of people without HTML skills of any kind can post their own Web pages and share content with friends and relatives. The totality of blog-related Web sites is often referred to as the **blogosphere**.

The content of blogs ranges from individual musings to corporate communications. Blogs have had a significant impact on political affairs, and have gained increasing notice for their role in breaking and shaping the news. Blogs have become hugely popular. Some research firms put the number of blogs at more than 25 million as of January 2006. According to comScore Networks, nearly 50 million Americans visited a blog during the first quarter of 2005, and around 7 percent of the U.S. online population (8 million people) have created blogs (comScore Networks, 2005; Pew Internet & American Life Project, 2005). In addition, it appears that about 7 percent (2.1 million) of Canadians blog while 9 percent have posted a response to a blog (Peralty, 2006).

Companies that maintain public blogs use them as a new channel for reaching customers. These corporate blogs provide a personal and conversational way for businesses to present information to the public and prospective customers about new products and services. Readers are often invited to post comments. The Window on Organizations section describes how organic yogourt company Stonyfield Farm Inc. and other organizations are taking advantage of these capabilities to create tighter relationships with their customers.

Marketers are starting to analyze blogs as well as chat groups and message boards to see what is being said online about new products, old brands, and ad campaigns. Blog-watching services that monitor popular blogs claim that "blog watching" can be cheaper and faster for analyzing consumer interests and sentiment than traditional focus groups and surveys. For example, Polaroid learned from blogs that consumers online frequently discuss photo longevity and archiving, prompting it to pay more attention to long-lasting photos in its product development. Companies are also posting ads on some of the most popular blogs published by individuals or by other organizations.

As of September 2006, about 6 percent of Fortune 500 companies had active public blogs. Many more, such as McDonald's and Cannondale Bicycle, use them for internal corporate communication. The Canadian Automobile Association (CAA) recently created a blog for use by members (blog.caa.ca). CAA staff post articles to the blog, and members can post responses. Nortel's CTO John Roese maintains a corporate blog accessible to the public (http://blogs.nortel.com/johnroese/). Also useful for internal communication are wikis (see Chapter 15).

Customer Self-Service Many companies use their Web sites and e-mail to answer customer questions or to provide customers with product information, reducing the need for human customer-support experts. For instance, Air Canada, American, Northwest, and other major airlines have created Web sites where customers can review flight departure and arrival times, seating charts, and airport logistics; check frequent-flyer miles; and purchase tickets online. Chapter 1 describes how customers of UPS use its Web site to track shipments, calculate shipping costs, determine time in transit, and arrange for a package pickup. Canada Post (see Figure 13-6), FedEx, DHL, and other package delivery firms provide similar Web-based services. Automated self-service or other Web-based responses to customer questions cost only a fraction of what a live customer service representative on the telephone would cost.

Blogosphere

FIGURE 13-6   *Canada Post self-service*

Visitors to the Canada Post Web site can calculate postage, find the nearest post office, and track shipments. Web sites for customer self-service are convenient for customers and help firms lower their customer service and support costs.

Source: Copied with the permission of Canada Post.

Organization   WINDOW ON ORGANIZATIONS

Stonyfield Farm and Tucows Blog for Profit

The story of Stonyfield Farm is something of a legend. In 1983, friends and social activists Gary Hirschberg and Samuel Kaymen started out with a great yogourt recipe, seven cows, and a dream. They set up an organic yogourt company in Wilton, New Hampshire, to capitalize on baby boomers' growing concerns with pure foods and health, and to revitalize the New England dairy industry. Stonyfield Farms has grown to become the third largest organic company in the world, with more than $58 million in annual sales in 50 states and also in Quebec. It produces more than 18 million cups of yogourt each month.

Stonyfield Farm's phenomenal growth is in part attributable to its ability to provide a product for a special niche market—people who treasure healthy foods and want to protect the environment. These values have become embedded in the company's "personality." Stonyfield pledges to use in its products only natural ingredients and milk that have not been produced with antibiotics, synthetic growth hormones, and toxic pesticides and fertilizers. The company donates 10 percent of its profits each year to efforts that help protect or restore the earth.

As the company expanded, management feared it would lose touch with its loyal and committed customer base. Traditional media-based advertising was expensive and would not really help the company "connect" with the kinds of people it was trying to reach. This company prefers word-of-mouth approaches that get its message to customers in ways that are more compatible with its grassroots, organic, activist people-friendly image. Stonyfield has several active e-mail newsletters with more than 500 000 subscribers, and it regularly places messages promoting causes it supports on

the lids of its yogourt cups. Now it is turning to blogs to further personalize its relationship with customers and reach even more people.

Inspired by Howard Dean's presidential campaign and tutorials from Dean's bloggers, CEO Hirschberg became convinced that Stonyfield could use blogs to create a more personal relationship with consumers that is different from the traditional selling relationship. "The blogs give us what we call a handshake with consumers" and "a little more access to us as a people with a mission," he says.

Stonyfield now publishes two different blogs on its Web site—Baby Babble and the Bovine Bugle. At one time, Stonyfield was managing five blogs but decided to retire three of them because they were not attracting enough readers.

Baby Babble provides a forum for Stonyfield employees and other parents of young children to meet and talk about child development and balancing work with family. Stonyfield started that blog because baby yogourts are one of its most popular product lines, and blogs about parenting seem to draw large numbers of readers.

The Bovine Bugle provides reports from Jonathan Gates's organic dairy farm in Franklin, Vermont, a member of the organic cooperative that supplies the milk for Stonyfield products. This blog elicits a large number of nostalgic comments from readers remembering their childhood on a farm. As organic foods go mainstream, these blogs help the company show how its brand differs from others and invite customers to help them in that effort.

Stonyfield continually posts new content to each of the blogs. Readers can subscribe to any of these blogs and automatically receive updates when they become available. And of course, they can respond to the postings.

At this point, the benefits of Stonyfield's blogs have not yet been quantified, but management has faith that there are real benefits. The blogs have created a positive response to the Stonyfield brand by providing readers with something that inspires them or piques their interest. If the blogs give readers new information, inspire them to take environmental actions, or ask for opinions, management believes they will remember the brand when they stand in front of the yogourt case at the super-market or grocery store and that they will reach for Stonyfield rather than a competing product when given the choice.

Stonyfield has a very large Web site. The blogs provide a way to highlight some of the Web content that might otherwise get lost. This, too, helps steer some blog readers to buy Stonyfield products.

Speaking of milk products and animals that give milk, how about a Canadian company named for those animals?

Toronto-based Tucows is an Internet services company that provides back-office solutions and wholesale Internet services to a global network of more than 7000 Web-hosting compa-nies, Internet service providers (ISPs), and other service providers worldwide. The original software download site, Tucows.com, earned its reputation early on for being the first to provide software on a "freeware" or "shareware" basis. Tucows currently hosts more than 40 000 software titles (all tested virus- and spyware-free) through its international net-work of partner (i.e., mirror) sites. These sites provide users with fast, local, and safe virus- and spyware-free downloads.

Most of Tucows' business rests on domain registration and downloading of freeware and shareware around the world. Second only to CNet in shareware downloading, Tucows President and CEO Elliot Noss wanted a way to let Tucows users know more about what was happening at the company, particularly in the area of downloads and acquisitions, and to find out from users what the impact of the company's growth, acquisitions, and service was on its customers. Tucows' blog consists of newsy articles about conferences Tucows' senior and technical staff have attended, tips and clues on how to work with the various software available from Tucows, and what is

going on at the company, particularly in terms of acquisition of new software packages for download. Users can—and do—respond, providing even more tips or more user-friendly ways to handle the software and commenting on the more editorial pieces, such as the appropriateness of sponsored blogs.

To Think About

1. What are Stonyfield Farm's business model and business strategy? What challenges and problems does the company face? What challenges face Tucows?

2. How do blogs help these companies solve these problems and compete in their industries?

3. What are the advantages and disadvantages of using blogs for companies such as Stonyfield Farm and Tucows?

MIS in Action

Visit Stonyfield Farm's Web site (www.stonyfield.com), and explore each of its blogs. Read some of the postings and related material. Then answer these questions:

1. Describe the kind of topics discussed on Stonyfield Farm's blogs. Are they closely related to Stonyfield's products? What kinds of people would they attract?

2. Is there any other content on the blog pages to promote Stonyfield products? Describe what you see and how it might help the company.

3. What types of content does Tucows have on its blog? Does Tucows need more than one blog? What additional blogs would you recommend for Tucows?

4. Should all companies use blogs to reach their customers? Why or why not?

Sources: "Stonyfield Farm's Chief Blogger Leaves," Backbone Corporate Blogging Survey, March 24, 2006; "Online Extra: Stonyfield Farm's Blog Culture," *Business Week*, May 2, 2005; Sarah Needleman, "Blogging Becomes a Corporate Job: Digital 'Handshake'?" *The Wall Street Journal*, May 31, 2005; www.stonyfieldfarms.com, accessed September 12, 2006; and Tucows Blog Site, http://blog.tucows.com/blog/, accessed May 6, 2007.

New software products are even integrating the Web with customer call centres, where customer service problems have been traditionally handled over the telephone. A **call centre** is an organizational department responsible for handling customer service issues by telephone and other channels. For example, a visitor to the Lands' End Web site can request a phone call from customer service by entering his or her telephone number. A call-centre system directs a customer service representative to place a voice telephone call to the user's phone.

Business-to-Business (B2B) Electronic Commerce: New Efficiencies and Relationships

About 80 percent of B2B e-commerce is still based on proprietary systems for **electronic data interchange (EDI)**, which enables the computer-to-computer exchange between two organizations of standard transactions such as invoices, bills of lading, shipment schedules,

Call centre

Electronic data interchange (EDI)

FIGURE 13-7   *Electronic data interchange (EDI)*

Companies use EDI to automate transactions for B2B e-commerce and continuous inventory replenishment. Suppliers can automatically send data about shipments to purchasing firms. The purchasing firms can use EDI to provide production and inventory requirements and payment data to suppliers.

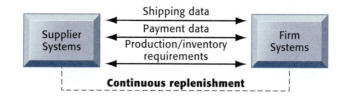

or purchase orders. Transactions are automatically transmitted from one information system to another through a network, eliminating the printing and handling of paper at one end and the inputting of data at the other. Each major industry in North America and much of the rest of the world has EDI standards that define the structure and information fields of electronic documents for that industry.

EDI originally automated the exchange of documents such as purchase orders, invoices, and shipping notices. Although some companies still use EDI for document automation, firms engaged in just-in-time inventory replenishment and continuous production use EDI as a system for continuous replenishment. Suppliers have online access to selected parts of the purchasing firm's production and delivery schedules and automatically ship materials and goods to meet prespecified targets without intervention by firm purchasing agents (see Figure 13-7).

Although many organizations still use private networks for EDI, companies are increasingly turning to the Internet for this purpose because it provides a much more flexible and low-cost platform for linking to other firms. Using the Internet, businesses are able to extend digital technology to a wider range of activities and broaden their circle of trading partners.

Take procurement, for example. **Procurement** involves not only purchasing goods and materials but also sourcing, negotiating with suppliers, paying for goods, and making delivery arrangements. Businesses can now use the Internet to locate the most low-cost supplier, search online catalogues of supplier products, negotiate with suppliers, place orders, make payments, and arrange transportation. They are not limited to partners linked by traditional EDI networks.

The Internet and Web technology enable businesses to create new electronic storefronts for selling to other businesses with multimedia graphic displays and interactive features similar to those for B2C commerce. Alternatively, businesses can use Internet technology to create extranets or electronic marketplaces for linking to other businesses for purchase and sale transactions.

Private industrial networks typically consist of a large firm using an extranet to link to its suppliers and other key business partners (see Figure 13-8). The network is owned by the buyer, and it permits the firm and designated suppliers, distributors, and other business partners to share product design and development, marketing, production

Procurement
Private industrial networks

FIGURE 13-8   *A private industrial network*

A private industrial network, also known as a private exchange, links a firm to its suppliers, distributors, and other key business partners for efficient supply chain management and other collaborative commerce activities.

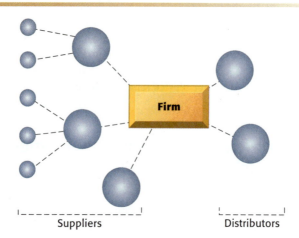

FIGURE 13-9   *A net marketplace*

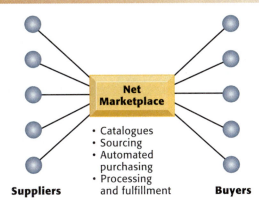

Net marketplaces are online marketplaces where multiple buyers can purchase from multiple sellers.

scheduling, inventory management, and unstructured communication, including graphics and e-mail. Another term for a private industrial network is a **private exchange**.

An example is VWGroupSupply.com, which links the Volkswagen Group and its suppliers. VWGroupSupply.com handles 90 percent of all global purchasing for Volkswagen, including all automotive and parts components.

Net marketplaces, which are sometimes called *e-hubs*, provide a single, digital marketplace based on Internet technology for many different buyers and sellers (see Figure 13-9). They are industry-owned or operate as independent intermediaries between buyers and sellers. Net marketplaces generate revenue from purchase and sale transactions and other services provided to clients. Participants in Net marketplaces can establish prices through online negotiations, auctions, or requests for quotations, or they can use fixed prices.

There are many different types of Net marketplaces and ways of classifying them. Some Net marketplaces sell *direct goods* and some sell *indirect goods*. Direct goods are goods used in a production process, such as sheet steel for autobody production. Indirect goods are all other goods not directly involved in the production process, such as office supplies or products for maintenance and repair. Some Net marketplaces support contractual purchasing based on long-term relationships with designated suppliers, and others support short-term spot purchasing, where goods are purchased based on immediate needs, often from many different suppliers.

Some Net marketplaces serve vertical markets for specific industries, such as automobiles, telecommunications, or machine tools while others serve horizontal markets for goods and services that can be found in many different industries, such as office equipment or transportation.

Exostar is an example of an industry-owned net marketplace, focusing on long-term contract purchasing relationships and on providing common networks and computing platforms for reducing supply-chain inefficiencies. This aerospace and defence industry-sponsored Net marketplace was founded jointly by BAE Systems, Boeing, Lockheed Martin, Raytheon, and Rolls-Royce PLC to connect these companies to their suppliers and facilitate collaboration on major projects. More than 16 000 trading partners in the commercial, military, and government sectors use Exostar's sourcing, e-procurement, and collaboration tools for both direct and indirect goods. Exostar includes capabilities for auctioning, purchase forecasting, issuing electronic payments and receipts, and linking to participants' internal corporate systems. Also featured are capabilities for collaboration on joint development projects and sharing engineering product data.

An **exchange** is an independently owned third-party Net marketplace that connects thousands of suppliers and buyers for spot purchasing. Many exchanges provide vertical markets for a single industry, such as food, electronics, or industrial equipment, and they primarily deal with direct goods. For example, FoodTrader.com (see Figure 13-10) automates spot purchases among buyers and sellers from more than 180 countries in the food and agriculture industry.

Exchanges proliferated during the early years of e-commerce, but many have failed. Suppliers were reluctant to participate because the exchanges encouraged competitive bidding that drove prices down and did not offer any long-term relationships with buyers

Private exchange

Net marketplaces

Exchange

FIGURE 13-10 *FoodTrader.com's Web site*

FoodTrader.com is a Net marketplace serving the food and agricultural industries. More than 100 000 growers, packers, processors, and retail chains in 170 countries use the site as a one-stop source to buy and sell food products directly.

or services to make lowering prices worthwhile. Many essential direct purchases are not conducted on a spot basis because they require contracts and consideration of issues such as delivery timing, customization, and quality of products.

13.3 M-Commerce

Wireless mobile devices are starting to be used for purchasing goods and services as well as for transmitting messages. Although m-commerce represents a small fraction of total e-commerce transactions, revenue has been steadily growing (see Figure 13-11). In 2006, there were an estimated more than two billion wireless and mobile subscribers worldwide.

FIGURE 13-11 *Global m-commerce revenue, 2000–2009*

M-commerce sales represent a small fraction of total e-commerce sales, but that percentage is steadily growing. (Totals for 2006–2009 are estimated.)

Sources: Jupiter Research; eMarketer, 2006; eMarketer, 2005; and authors.

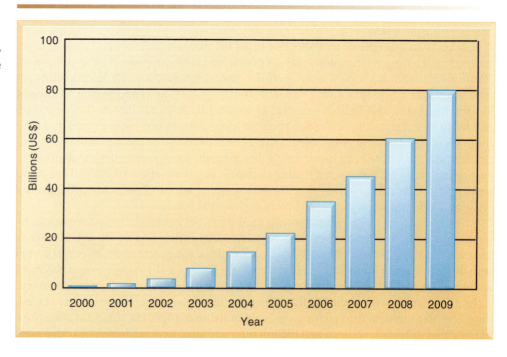

M-Commerce Services and Applications

M-commerce applications have taken off for services that are time-critical, that appeal to people on the move, or that accomplish a task more efficiently than other methods. They are especially popular in Europe, Japan, South Korea, and other countries where fees for conventional Internet usage are very expensive. Here are some examples.

Content and Location-Based Services Subscribers to NTT DoCoMo wireless services in Japan can access wireless Web sites to check train schedules, obtain movie listings, browse restaurant guides, purchase tickets on Japan Airlines, trade stocks, view new cartoons, and read Japan's largest daily newspaper. Go2 Mobile Directory, the most widely used mobile location-based directory and information service in the United States, enables users to search for local businesses, movie shows, and restaurants; obtain driving directions; check local weather forecasts; and find detailed information about hotels, airlines, and car rental agencies.

Banking and Financial Services The Bank of Montreal enables users to receive RSS news feeds and podcasts through Yahoo!, Google, or even their iPods. Citibank offers wireless alerts about changes in account information on digital cell phones that support text messaging or Web access. Customers of Bank Asia in Bangladesh can use their mobile phones to check account balances, transfer funds between accounts, and pay bills from their accounts. Most Canadian banks now permit customers to use their online banking services to transfer money to another individual or company; all that is needed is for the receiving party to have a chequing account with a Canadian bank. In April 2007, ClairMail announced a strategic partnership with TELUS, a Canadian telecommunications company, to enable retail banks, credit unions, brokerages, and credit card companies across Canada to offer mobile banking and payments services.

Wireless Advertising Wireless service providers are starting to include advertising on their sites. Yahoo! and go2 Directory Systems have arranged to put Yahoo!-sponsored listings on the go2 Mobile Directory search site carried by Verizon Wireless, Sprint, and Cingular Wireless. When consumers use go2 Mobile Directory to search for local restaurants or movie theaters, Yahoo!-sponsored advertisers appear in the list of search results.

Games and Entertainment Cell phones are quickly turning into portable entertainment platforms. Mobile phone services offer downloadable digital games and ringtones (digitized snippets of music that play on mobile phones when a user receives or places a call). Some handset models combine the features of a cell phone and a portable music player. Users of broadband services from the major wireless vendors can download on-demand movie clips, news clips, and weather reports. Bell Mobility, TELUS, and Rogers all offer mobile television content on cellphones. The content is in the form of short clips, sports, entertainment, and news updates, although no full-length content is offered yet. Rogers Communications

Nokia's N91 mobile handset combines the features of a cell phone and a portable music player. It can store up to 3000 songs.

was one of the first to offer this service to Canadian cell phone users; Rogers' content includes BBC World, MSNBC, CNBC, and live Toronto Blue Jays coverage. All three carriers' TV service is powered by MobiTV, the leading mobile television firm. Film companies are starting to produce short films exclusively designed to play on mobile phones.

Accessing Information from the Wireless Web

Although cell phones, PDAs, and other handheld mobile devices are able to access the Web at any time and from any place, the amount of information that they can actually handle at one time is very limited. Until 3G broadband service comes into widespread use, these devices will not be able to transmit or receive large amounts of data. The information must fit onto small display screens.

Some Web sites have been specifically designed for m-commerce. They feature Web pages with very few graphics and just enough information to fit on a small mobile handheld screen. Special **wireless portals** (also known as *mobile portals*) feature content and services optimized for mobile devices to steer users to the information they are most likely to need.

M-Commerce Challenges

The number of Wi-Fi hotspots for wireless Internet access has been mushrooming in many countries because the technology combines high-speed Internet access with a measure of flexibility and mobility. Rollout of mobile m-commerce services, however, has proved more problematic. Keyboards and screens on cell phones are still tiny and awkward to use. The data transfer speeds on second-generation cellular networks are very slow compared to dial-up and high-speed Internet connections for PCs. Each second waiting for data to download costs the customer money. Most Internet-enabled phones have limited memory and power supplies. M-commerce will benefit from 3G networks, other cellular broadband services, and standardized mobile payment systems.

13.4 Electronic Commerce Payment Systems

Special electronic payment systems have been developed to pay for goods electronically on the Internet. Electronic payment systems for the Internet include systems for digital credit card payments, digital wallets, accumulated balance digital payment systems, stored value payment systems, digital cash, peer-to-peer payment systems, digital chequing, and electronic billing presentment and payment systems.

Types of Electronic Payment Systems

Credit cards account for 80 percent of online payments in North America and about 50 percent of online purchases outside North America. The more sophisticated electronic commerce software has capabilities for processing credit card purchases on the Web. Businesses can also contract with services that extend the functionality of existing credit card payment systems. **Digital credit card payment systems** extend the functionality of credit cards so they can be used for online shopping payments. They make credit cards safer and more convenient for online merchants and consumers by providing mechanisms for authenticating the purchaser's credit card to make sure it is valid and by arranging for the bank that issued the credit card to deposit money for the amount of the purchase in the seller's bank account.

Wireless portals

Digital credit card payment
systems

Digital wallets make paying for purchases over the Web more efficient by eliminating the need for shoppers to enter their address and credit card information repeatedly each time they buy something. A **digital wallet** securely stores credit card and owner identification information and provides that information at an electronic commerce site's "checkout counter." The digital wallet enters the shopper's name, credit card number, and shipping information automatically when invoked to complete the purchase. Q*Wallet and Google Toolbar AutoFill are examples of digital wallets.

Micropayment systems have been developed for purchases of less than $10, such as downloads of individual articles or music clips, which would be too small for conventional credit card payments. Accumulated balance digital payment systems or stored value payment systems are useful for such purposes.

Accumulated balance digital payment systems enable users to make micropayments and purchases on the Web, accumulating a debit balance that they must pay periodically on their credit card or telephone bills. Qpass enables wireless customers to charge ringtones, games, and other digital products and services to their monthly phone bills.

Stored value payment systems such as Ecount enable consumers to make instant online payments to merchants and other individuals based on value stored in a digital account. Online value systems rely on the value stored in a consumer's bank, chequing, or credit card account, and some of these systems require the use of a digital wallet.

Smart cards are another type of stored value system used for micropayments. A smart card, which we introduced in Chapter 8, is a plastic card the size of a credit card that stores digital information. The smart card can store health records, identification data, or telephone numbers, or it can serve as an "electronic purse" in place of cash. The Mondex smart card (owned 51 percent by MasterCard), originally developed in the UK and famously piloted in Guelph, Ontario, contains electronic cash and can be used to transfer funds to merchants in physical storefronts and to merchants on the Internet. It requires use of a special card-reading device whenever the card needs to transfer cash to either an online or offline merchant.

Digital cash (also known as *electronic cash* or *e-cash*) can also be used for micropayments or larger purchases. **Digital cash** is currency represented in electronic form that moves outside the normal network of money (paper currency, coins, cheques, and credit cards). Users are supplied with client software and can exchange money with another e-cash user over the Internet or with a retailer accepting e-cash. ClearBIT is an example of a digital cash service. In addition to facilitating micropayments, digital cash can be useful for people who do not have credit cards and wish to make Web purchases.

New Web-based **peer-to-peer payment systems**, such as PayPal, serve people who want to send money to vendors or individuals who are not set up to accept credit card payments. The party sending money uses his or her credit card to create an account with the designated payment at a Web site dedicated to peer-to-peer payments. The recipient "picks up" the payment by visiting the Web site and supplying information about where to send the payment (a bank account or a physical address).

Digital chequing payment systems, such as eCheck, extend the functionality of existing chequing accounts so they can be used for online shopping payments. Digital cheques are less expensive than credit cards and much faster than traditional paper-based checking. These cheques are encrypted with a digital signature that can be verified and used for payments in electronic commerce. Electronic cheque systems are useful in business-to-business electronic commerce.

Electronic billing presentment and payment systems are used for paying routine monthly bills. They enable users to view their bills electronically and pay them through electronic fund transfers from bank or credit card accounts. These services support payment for online and physical store purchases of goods or services after the purchase has taken place. They notify purchasers about bills that are due, present the bills, and process the payments. Some of these services, such as CheckFree, consolidate subscribers' bills

Digital wallet

Micropayment

Accumulated balance digital payment systems

Stored value payment systems

Digital cash

Peer-to-peer payment systems

Digital chequing

Electronic billing presentment and payment systems

TABLE 13-6 Examples of Electronic Payment Systems for E-Commerce

PAYMENT SYSTEM	DESCRIPTION	COMMERCIAL EXAMPLE
Digital credit card payment systems	Secure services for credit card payments on the Internet protect information transmitted among users, merchant sites, and processing banks	eCharge
Digital wallet	Software that stores credit card and other information to facilitate form completion and payment for goods on the Web	MSN Wallet, Google Toolbar AutoFill
Accumulated balance digital payment systems	Accumulates micropayment purchases as a debit balance that must be paid periodically on credit card or telephone bills	Qpass, Valista, Peppercoin, Trivnet, PaymentOne
Stored value payment systems	Enables consumers to make instant payments to merchants based on value stored in a digital account	Ecount, Mondex card
Digital cash	Digital currency that can be used for micropayments or larger purchases	ClearBIT
Peer-to-peer payment systems	Sends money using the Web to individuals or vendors who are not set up to accept credit card payments	PayPal
Digital chequing	Electronic cheque with a secure digital signature	eCheck
Electronic billing presentment and payment systems	Supports electronic payment for online and physical store purchases of goods or services after the purchase has taken place	CheckFree, Yahoo! Bill Pay, epost

from various sources so that they can all be paid at one time. Table 13-6 summarizes the features of some of these e-commerce payment systems.

Digital Payment Systems for M-Commerce

With a Wi-Fi connection, you can take advantage of all existing forms of Internet payment—the fact that you are connected wirelessly should have no impact. Many m-commerce transactions, however, are small, frequent purchases for items such as soft drinks, sports scores, newspapers, or mobile games that require special micropayment systems.

Micropayment systems are working well in Europe and Asia, where mobile operators and Internet service providers handle small payments by adding them up and presenting them on a single bill, such as the mobile telephone bill. In London, you can buy Virgin Cola using a Virgin Mobile phone by simply dialing a number posted on the vending machine (the cost of the drink is simply charged to your cell phone account). eBay's PayPal Mobile Text2Buy service allows consumers to send payments to PayPal Mobile accounts, purchase items from select retailers, or donate money to some charities by punching a short text code into a cell phone. Japan's NTT DoCoMo offers a cell phone with a stored payment system for purchases in designated stores, restaurants, and vending machines and another handset model with an embedded credit card. Motorola, MasterCard, and Visa are developing mobile wallet services.

In both North America and Europe, individual micropayment service providers run their own separate payment systems. A common secure platform for wireless m-commerce payments would help m-commerce take off.

Summary

1. Describe the unique features of e-commerce, digital markets, and digital goods.

E-commerce involves digitally enabled commercial transactions between and among organizations and individuals. There are seven unique features of e-commerce technology: E-commerce technology is ubiquitous; it has global reach; it operates according to universal standards; it provides information richness; it is interactive; it increases information density; and it permits personalization and customization.

The Internet has created a digital marketplace where millions of people are able to exchange massive amounts of information directly, instantly, and for free. Digital markets are said to be more "transparent" than traditional markets. Information asymmetry is reduced. Digital markets are very flexible and efficient, with reduced search and transaction costs, lower menu costs, and the ability to change prices dynamically based on market conditions. Digital markets provide many opportunities to sell directly to the consumer, bypassing intermediaries, such as distributors or retail outlets.

Digital goods are goods, such as music, video, software, newspapers, magazines, and books, that can be delivered over a digital network. Once a digital product has been produced, the cost of delivering that product digitally is extremely low. New business models based on delivering digital goods are challenging bookstores, publishers, music labels, and film studios that depend on delivery of traditional goods.

2. Analyze how Internet technology has changed value propositions and business models.

The Internet radically reduces the cost of creating, sending, and storing information while making that information more widely available. Information is not limited to traditional physical methods of delivery. This unbundling of information from traditional value chain channels is having a disruptive effect on old business models, and it is creating new business models. Some of the traditional channels for exchanging product information have become unnecessary or uneconomical, and business models based on the coupling of information with products and services may no longer be necessary.

The Internet can help companies create and capture profits in new ways by adding extra value to existing products and services or by providing the foundation for new products and services. Many different business models for electronic commerce on the Internet have emerged, including virtual storefronts, information brokers, transaction brokers, Net marketplaces, content providers, online service providers, virtual communities, and portals. Business models that take advantage of the Internet's capabilities for communication, community-building capabilities, and digital goods distribution have become especially prominent.

3. Describe the various types of e-commerce and how e-commerce has changed consumer retailing and business-to-business transactions.

The three major types of electronic commerce are business-to-consumer (B2C), business-to-business (B2B), and consumer-to-consumer (C2C). Another way of classifying electronic commerce transactions is in terms of the participants' physical connections to the Web. Conventional e-commerce transactions, which take place over wired networks, can be distinguished from mobile commerce, or m-commerce, which is the purchase of goods and services using handheld wireless devices.

The Internet provides a universally available set of technologies for electronic commerce that can be used to create new channels for marketing, sales, and customer support and to eliminate intermediaries in buy-and-sell transactions. Interactive capabilities on the Web can be used to build closer relationships with customers in marketing and customer support. Firms can use various Web personalization technologies to deliver Web pages with content geared to the specific interests of each user, including technologies that deliver personalized information and ads through m-commerce channels. Companies can also reduce costs and improve customer service by using Web sites, as well as e-mail and even telephone access to customer service representatives, to provide helpful information.

B2B e-commerce generates efficiencies by enabling companies to locate suppliers, solicit bids, place orders, and track shipments in transit electronically. Businesses can use their own Web sites to sell to other businesses or use Net marketplaces or private industrial networks. Net marketplaces provide a single, digital marketplace based on Internet technology for many buyers and sellers. Net marketplaces can be differentiated by whether they sell direct or indirect goods, support spot or long-term purchasing, or serve vertical or horizontal markets. Private industrial networks link a firm with its suppliers and other strategic business partners to develop highly efficient supply chains and to respond quickly to customer demands.

4. Evaluate the role of m-commerce in business and describe the most important m-commerce applications.

M-commerce uses the Internet for purchasing goods and services as well as for transmitting messages using wireless mobile devices. It is especially well-suited for location-based applications, such as finding local hotels and restaurants, monitoring local traffic and weather, and providing personalized location-based marketing. Mobile phones and handhelds are being used for mobile bill payment; banking; securities trading; transportation schedule updates; and downloads of digital content, such as music, games, and video clips.

Wireless portals (mobile portals) feature content and services optimized for mobile devices to steer users to the information they are most likely to need. M-commerce requires special digital payment systems that can handle micropayments because most m-commerce purchases today are for very small amounts.

M-commerce represents a tiny fraction of all online purchases because wireless mobile devices cannot display merchandise very well. Mobile phones have tiny keyboards, small screens, and slow data transfer speeds (9.6 to 14.4 Kbps). M-commerce will benefit from interoperable payment systems for wireless devices and faster wireless networks to support more data-rich communication.

5. *Compare the principal payment systems for electronic commerce.*

The principal electronic payment systems for electronic commerce are digital credit card payment systems, digital wallets, accumulated balance digital payment systems, stored value payment systems, digital cash, peer-to-peer payment systems, digital chequing, and electronic billing presentment and payment systems. Accumulated balance systems, stored value systems (including smart cards), and digital cash are useful for small micropayments.

Key Terms

Accumulated balance digital payment
    systems,   459
Banner ad,   444
Blogosphere,   451
Business-to-business (B2B) electronic
    commerce,   448
Business-to-consumer (B2C) electronic
    commerce,   448
Call centre,   453
Clicks-and-mortar,   448
Clickstream tracking,   449
Collaborative filtering,   449
Consumer-to-consumer (C2C) electronic
    commerce,   449
Cost transparency,   441
Customization,   441
Digital cash,   459
Digital chequing,   459

Digital credit card payment systems,   458
Digital goods,   442
Digital wallet,   459
Disintermediation,   442
Dynamic pricing,   441
Electronic billing presentment and
    payment systems,   459
Electronic data interchange (EDI),   453
Exchange,   455
Information asymmetry,   441
Information density,   440
Market entry costs,   440
Marketspace,   438
Menu costs,   441
Micropayment,   459
Mobile commerce (m-commerce),   449
Net marketplace,   455
Peer-to-peer payment systems,   459

Personalization,   441
Podcasting,   447
Pop-up ads,   444
Price discrimination,   441
Price transparency,   440
Private exchange,   455
Private industrial networks,   454
Procurement,   454
Pure-play,   448
Richness,   440
Search costs,   440
Social networking sites,   445
Social shopping,   447
Stored value payment systems,   459
Syndicators,   448
Wireless portals,   458

Review Questions

1. *Name and describe four business trends and three technology trends shaping e-commerce today.*

2. *List and describe the seven unique features of e-commerce technology.*

3. *Define a digital market and describe its distinguishing features.*

4. *Define digital goods and describe their distinguishing features.*

5. *How is the Internet changing the economics of information and business models?*

6. *Name and describe six Internet business models for electronic commerce. Distinguish between a pure-play Internet business model and a clicks-and-mortar business model.*

7. *Name and describe the various categories of electronic commerce.*

8. *How can the Internet facilitate sales and marketing for individual customers? Describe the role played by Web personalization.*

9. *How can the Internet enhance customer service?*

10. *How can Internet technology support business-to-business electronic commerce?*

11. *What are Net marketplaces? Why do they represent an important business model for B2B e-commerce? How do they differ from private industrial networks?*

12. *List and describe important types of m-commerce services and applications.*

13. *How do wireless portals help users access information on the wireless Web?*

14. *What are some of the barriers to m-commerce?*

15. *Name and describe the principal electronic payment systems used on the Internet. What types of payment systems are used in m-commerce?*

Discussion Questions

1. *How does the Internet change consumer and supplier relationships?*

2. *The Internet may not make corporations obsolete, but the corporations will have to change their business models. Do you agree? Why or why not?*

3. *The Internet permits small firms to act like large, global firms and at the same time permits businesses to find and market to customer niches of perhaps even one customer. Discuss the implications of this for established businesses that have not yet gone online.*

4. *Canadian statistics show that workers spend 4.5 hours per day surfing the Internet for personal reasons. What company policies could be implemented to stop this? In your* *opinion, would these policies work? If not, what else do you recommend to increase productivity?*

Teamwork: Performing a Competitive Analysis of E-Commerce Sites

Form a group with three or four of your classmates. Select two businesses that are competitors in the same industry and that use their Web sites for electronic commerce. Visit these Web sites. You might compare, for example, the Web sites for iTunes and MSN Music, Amazon.ca and Chapters.Indigo.ca,

or TDAmeriTrade and Scottrade. Prepare an evaluation of each business's Web site in terms of its functions, user friendliness, and ability to support the company's business strategy. Which Web site does a better job? Why? Can you make some recommendations to improve these Web sites?

Learning Track Modules

E-Commerce Challenges: The Story of Online Groceries. This Learning Track Module explores the history of the online grocery business and examines the business model of FreshDirect, a new generation online grocery business. You can find this material on MyMISLab for this chapter.

Build an E-commerce Business Plan. This Learning Track Module outlines the process of building an e-commerce business plan, including the development of a marketing plan and a financial plan. You can find this material on MyMISLab for this chapter.

For online exercises, please visit www.pearsoned.ca/mymislab.

HANDS-ON MIS   Application Exercises

The projects in this section give you hands-on experience developing an e-commerce strategy for a real-world company, using spreadsheet software to analyze the profitability of an e-commerce company, and using Web tools to research and evaluate e-commerce hosting services.

Achieving Operational Excellence: Developing an E-Commerce Strategy

Software skills: Web browser software, Web page development software
Business skills: Strategic analysis

This project provides an opportunity for you to develop an e-commerce strategy for a real-world business and to use a Web page development tool to create part of the company's Web site.

Dirt Bikes Canada's management believes that the company could benefit from e-commerce. The company has sold motorcycles and parts primarily through authorized dealers. Dirt Bikes Canada advertises in various magazines catering to dirt bike enthusiasts and maintains booths at important off-road motorcycle racing events. You have been asked to explore how Dirt Bikes Canada could benefit from e-commerce and a Dirt Bikes Canada Web site.

Prepare a report for management that answers the following questions:

1. How could Dirt Bikes Canada benefit from e-commerce? Should it sell motorcycles or parts over the Web? Should it use its Web site primarily to advertise its products and services? Should it use the Web for customer service?
2. How would a Web site provide value to Dirt Bikes Canada? Use the Web to research the cost of an e-commerce site for a small- to medium-sized company. How much revenue or cost savings would the Web site have to produce to make it a worthwhile investment for Dirt Bikes Canada?
3. Prepare specifications describing the functions that should be performed by Dirt Bikes Canada's Web site.

Include links to other Web sites or other systems in your specifications.

4. (Optional) Design the home page for Dirt Bikes Canada's Web site and an important secondary page linked to the home page using the Web page creation capabilities of word processing software or a Web page development tool of your choice.

Improving Decision Making:
Using Spreadsheet Software to Analyze a Dot-Com Business

Software skills: Spreadsheet downloading, formatting, and formula generation
Business skills: Financial statement analysis

Publicly traded companies, including those specializing in e-commerce, are required to file financial data with the System for Electronic Document Analysis and Retrieval (SEDAR) operated for the Canadian Securities Administrators (CSA). By analyzing this information, you can determine the profitability of an e-commerce company and the viability of its business model.

Pick one Canadian company that conducts e-commerce on the Internet, for example, the Hudson's Bay Company. Study the Web pages that describe the company and explain its purpose and structure. Use the Web to find articles that comment on the company. Then visit the SEDAR Web site at **www.sedar.com**, select your company, and select View This Public Company's Documents to access the company's news releases and financial reports showing income statements and balance sheets. Select only the sections of the financial reports containing the desired portions of financial statements that you need to examine, and print them out and enter the data into your spreadsheet. Create simplified spreadsheets of the company's balance sheets and income statements for the past three years. (Note: The U.S. Securities and Exchange Commission filings can be downloaded into spreadsheets.)

1. Is the company a dot-com success, borderline business, or failure? What information forms the basis of your decision? Why? When answering these questions, pay special attention to the company's three-year trends in revenues, cost of sales, gross margins, operating expenses, and net margins. See MyMISLab for Chapter 13 for definitions of these terms and how they are calculated.

2. Prepare an overhead presentation (with a minimum of five slides), including appropriate spreadsheets or charts, and present your work to your professor and classmates.

Achieving Operational Excellence:
Evaluating E-Commerce Hosting Services

Software skills: Web browser software
Business skills: Evaluating e-commerce hosting services

This project will help develop your Internet skills in evaluating services for hosting an e-commerce site for a small startup company.

You would like to set up a Web site to sell towels, linens, pottery, and tableware from Portugal and are examining services for hosting small business Internet storefronts. Your Web site should be able to take secure credit card payments and to calculate shipping costs and taxes. Initially, you would like to display photos and descriptions of 40 different products. Visit Yahoo! Small Business, **netnation.com**, and **zenutech.ca** and compare the range of e-commerce hosting services they offer to small business, their capabilities, and costs. Also examine the tools they provide for creating an e-commerce site. Compare these services, and decide which you would use if you were actually establishing a Web store. Write a brief report indicating your choice and explaining the strengths and weaknesses of the choices.

CASE STUDY Can eBay Continue Growing?

eBay.com, together with its subsidiary, ebay.ca, is an online auction service whose business model is ideally suited to the Web. eBay stores no inventory and ships no products. Instead, it derives its revenue from the movement of information, an ideal task for the Internet. Since eBay was founded in 1995 by Pierre Omidyar and Jeff Skoll, the company has been profitable, attracting more than 200 million users by 2006. eBay now employs more than 8000 full-time workers and has operations in 32 countries, including an equity investment in MercadoLibre, which services Mexico and eight South American countries. In 2005, eBay users listed 1.8 billion items for auction, resulting in $46 billion worth of goods changing hands. The number of items listed in 2006 was expected to surpass two billion.

eBay has mass appeal because its fully automated auction service helps buyers and sellers trade high-end articles, such as fine art, automobiles, and jewellery, as well as more mundane and practical items, such as clothing, consumer electronics, and housewares. Users can list their goods under more than 30 main categories and tens of thousands of subcategories.

The success of eBay relies on a unique formula. eBay derives the bulk of its revenue from fees and commissions associated with its trading services. This revenue, however, is only made possible by the hundreds of thousands of people who put time and effort into selling goods on eBay but do not work for the company. Nearly half a million people rely on eBay auctions as their main source of income. The seller pays an insertion fee for listing goods; the fee operates on a sliding scale. For example, if the opening bid price starts between 1 cent and 99 cents, eBay charges the seller a 23-cent insertion fee. The fee increases as the opening price increases all the way up to $5.60 for goods starting at $600 or more. eBay also collects a fee from the seller when an auction is successful. The larger the closing price, the higher the final fee. eBay charges a sliding scale, starting at 5.25 percent of the first $30.

A portion of eBay's revenue also comes from direct advertising on the site as well as end-to-end service providers whose services increase the ease and speed of eBay transactions. The acquisition of PayPal, whose service enables the exchange of money between individuals over the Internet, brings additional transaction-based fee revenue. PayPal charges the recipients of payments a flat fee plus a percentage of the total transaction size and has more than 70 million user accounts.

eBay's growth strategy focuses on expansion in geography and scope and on continuing innovation to enhance the variety and appeal of products on its sites. eBay has taken its model to numerous foreign markets and been successful there, particularly in England, France, and Germany. It is also working hard to gain a foothold in the Chinese online auction market. Growth rates have been hindered somewhat by an increase in seller fees, but these losses have been covered by rapid growth in some countries. Although eBay's U.S. growth has slowed to about 20 to 30 percent annually, the company's international business is growing at 50 percent per year. By 2005, transactions completed on international Web sites, including eBay's Canadian Web site, accounted for approximately half of eBay's business.

In 2000, eBay introduced eBay Motors to encourage the sale of bulky items that are too expensive to ship. Critics believed that consumers would find purchasing a used car over the Web too risky. However, eBay added extra measures of protection in the form of used-vehicle warranties and purchase protection up to $2000. These measures, combined with the standard eBay seller feedback ratings, gave users enough security to buy one million cars within four years. eBay Motors now includes subcategories for boats, motorcycles, parts and accessories, and more.

Also in 2000, eBay implemented the "Buy It Now" feature, which enables sellers to name a price at which they would be willing to sell an item to any buyer. Buyers have the option to purchase the item instantly without waiting for an auction to end. Additionally, eBay acquired Half.com, which offers person-to-person selling of goods such as books, CDs, videos, and games without the auction process. On Half.com, listings are free, but eBay collects a commission for completed sales

In 2001, the company launched eBay Stores. eBay Stores enable sellers with a proven track record, a verified ID, or a PayPal account to set up an online storefront and offer fixed-price merchandise. eBay Store owners pay subscription fees (from $15.95 to $589.95 per month), insertion fees, and final value fees on a sliding scale.

In another attempt to reinvigorate its growth, eBay agreed to buy Shopping.com, an online shopping comparison site, for $718 million in mid-2005. In September of that year, eBay also acquired VoIP service provider Skype Technologies for $3 billion. Skype provides a service for free or low-cost voice calls over the Internet. eBay is betting heavily that Internet telephony will become an integral part of the e-commerce experience and accelerate trade on its Web site. The service could potentially generate $4 billion in revenue from markets that eBay traditionally had trouble penetrating, such as real estate, travel, new-car sales, and expensive collectibles. Those markets require more communication among buyers and sellers than eBay currently offers, and Skype will provide voice communication services to help. Internet companies such as Google and Microsoft are now offering VoIP services, and VoIP may become a required capability for all major companies that do business online.

However, some analysts report that many of eBay's top sellers aren't interested in adding voice calls to their sales models. They can barely keep up with the e-mail they receive on eBay and may like the simplicity and anonymity that eBay provided pre-Skype. VoIP could also stimulate eBay's "grey market," consisting of items sold outside the eBay structure to avoid seller fees.

eBay faces other challenges. Yahoo! is trying to edge it out of the Asian market by setting up competing auction sites. eBay's growing international presence may make it difficult to monitor compliance with the variety of laws and regulations that apply in different jurisdictions. For example, there are many unsettled legal issues related to the liability of providers of online services for the activities of their users. Even though eBay has taken steps to prohibit the listing of certain items, it may be liable if its members nonetheless manage to use it to sell unlawful goods, such as weapons, drugs, alcohol, adult material, and cigarettes, or if its members defame or libel one another in eBay's Feedback Forum.

In response to growing domestic and international competition, eBay has entered into a number of relationships with other major players in the e-commerce field, including competitors Yahoo! and Google. Google gained the exclusive right to display text advertisements on eBay's international auction sites despite having recently added shopping services that compete with eBay auctions. eBay was willing to look beyond its rivalry with Google to secure the potential windfall of revenue from Google's first-rate advertising technology. The deal with Google followed by just a few months a similar deal with Yahoo!, giving that company exclusive rights to provide advertisements for eBay's sites in the U.S. As part of that agreement, Yahoo! will promote PayPal on its sites. The pair reached the accord despite their battle for shares of the auction market in Asia.

eBay is optimistic that its partnership with Google will also enable the auction house to generate more revenue from its acquisition of Skype. The partnership includes the introduction of a "click-to-call" feature, which enables consumers to talk to merchants and advertisers directly using Skype by clicking a connection embedded in their ads. The strategy embraces the idea that some goods, such as mortgages and homes, are not well-suited to the traditional eBay transaction model. Advertisers of these goods seem willing to pay a fee, perhaps as much as $15, for each call received from a potential customer in order to establish better dialogues that are more likely to result in sales.

Meanwhile, eBay is competing directly with Google by introducing its AdContext service. The service is similar to Google AdSense in that it runs online contextual ads based on keywords in Web pages. eBay sellers can use AdContext to display contextual ads and auction promotions on linked Web sites.

Clearly, the largest threat to eBay is the question of its auctions' honesty and integrity, over which eBay has some—but not total—control. As eBay ventured into the realm of higher-priced antiques and collectibles, it opened itself up to lawsuits from buyers claiming to have been defrauded by online sellers. Some buyers have alleged that eBay does not do enough to prevent unscrupulous sellers from collecting inflated fees for goods that are not legitimate, or worse, do not exist. eBay users have also been the victims of identity theft scams that resulted in the unauthorized use of their accounts—and hundreds of thousands of dollars worth of fraudulent sales.

With online crime becoming more and more sophisticated, the onus is on eBay to provide its users with a secure trade environment. Some users and former users believe that the company has not adequately addressed the issue of fraud. The growing scale of eBay makes fraud protection prohibitive. eBay insists that the percentage of listings on its site that are fraudulent is tiny and that the success of the marketplace bears that out.

Another area in which the sheer size of eBay may be a hindrance is customer service. The company understandably struggles with the task of satisfying two types of "customers": online buyers and online sellers. What is good for one is not always good for the other. Fraud complaints often result in an automated response from eBay that encourages buyers and sellers to resolve disputes on their own. As eBay has seen, one unilateral policy decision can set off a negative chain reaction. When eBay Store fees were raised, some 7000 storeowners shut down their stores and looked for other means to conduct their businesses. But eBay is in a bind because addressing customer service issues costs money. The more money eBay spends, the more it cuts into its profits, which also makes Bay Street and Wall Street nervous.

eBay does make an effort to remain in touch with its community of users. A program called Voices brings buyers and sellers together 10 times a year at corporate headquarters. The users engage in two full days of give-and-take with company officials about the best and worst aspects of eBay's services. eBay also monitors every transaction and usage statistics in real time, enabling timely troubleshooting.

A Rules, Trust, and Safety committee judges whether questionable listings should be permitted on the site (human organs have been banned, for example). Indeed, the sustained growth of eBay may rely on the continued enhancement of the technology available to the eBay community rather than on major acquisitions. Recent partnerships with Google's JotSpot and Kaboodle seek to improve the overall value of the eBay experience for members of the community. JotSpot is a provider of wiki applications and, with eBay, is developing the eBay Community Wiki. The wiki serves as an information source that buyers and sellers can update and edit with entries on best practices and tips and tricks for effective auctioning. Kaboodle is teaming with eBay to create an online "social collecting" destination named MyCollectibles where users can promote and share information about the items they collect and trade.

Keeping the community happy is of utmost importance to the future of eBay. A loyal user base may be the company's most valuable asset and one which competitors will be challenged to replicate. While investors and analysts mostly maintain their confidence in the company's management, cries for change have gone up from the merchant population. Sellers are concerned about the declining number of transactions and a coinciding drop in sales prices. eBay must find a way to secure the confidence of its merchant population or it will risk losing business to other online marketplaces.

Sources: Mylene Mangalindan, "eBay Merchants Seek Management Change," *The Wall Street Journal*, August 21, 2006; Stacy Cowley, "eBay Turns to Partners, ISPs to Jack Up Sales," *InformationWeek*, July 24, 2006; Thomas Claburn, "eBay Is Sold on Wikis," *InformationWeek*, June 14, 2006; Thomas Claburn, "Analysis: eBay's Growth to Come from Community, Not Acquisitions," *InformationWeek*, June 19, 2006; Stacy Cowley, "eBay Opens More PayPal Tools to Developer Partners," *InformationWeek*," June 12, 2006; Saul Hansell, "eBay Gambles on Google Partnership for Success of Skype, the Internet Phone Service," *The New York Times*, August 29, 2006; Mylene Mangalindan, "eBay, Google Reach Overseas Text-Ad Alliance," *The Wall Street Journal*, August 28, 2006; Laurie Sullivan, "eBay to Go Head to Head Against Google for Online Ad Market," *InformationWeek*, June 12, 2006; Nicholas Hoover, "eBay Bets on VoIP, but Do Sellers Want to Chat?" *InformationWeek*, September 19, 2005; and CNBC, "Ten Things You Didn't Know About eBay," **msnbc.com**, accessed June 29, 2005.

CASE STUDY QUESTIONS

1. What is eBay's business model and business strategy? How successful has it been?

2. What are the problems that eBay is currently facing?

3. How is eBay trying to solve these problems? Are these good solutions? Are there any other solutions that eBay should consider?

4. What management, organization, and technology factors play a role in eBay's response to its problems?

5. Will eBay be successful in the long run? Why or why not?

CHAPTER 14

Enhancing Decision Making

After completing this chapter, you will be able to do the following:

1. Describe different types of decisions and the decision-making process.
2. Assess how information systems support the activities of managers and management decision making.
3. Demonstrate how decision-support systems (DSS) differ from MIS and how they provide value to the business.
4. Demonstrate how executive support systems (ESS) help senior managers make better decisions.
5. Evaluate the role of information systems in helping people working in a group make decisions more efficiently.

OPENING **CASE** | Procter & Gamble Restructures Its Supply Chain

Procter & Gamble (P&G) is one of the world's largest consumer goods companies, with annual revenues of $59 billion and 80 000 employees in 140 countries. The company sells more than 300 brands worldwide, including Crest, Charmin, Tide, Pringles, and Pampers. Although P&G is known for innovation and marketing muscle, it is always looking for ways to lower its costs, in response both to competitors and to pressure from large customers, such as Wal-Mart.

In the early 1990s, P&G started looking at ways to reduce supply chain costs and improve efficiency throughout its entire North American manufacturing and distribution network. Management wanted answers to questions such as, "How many plants should there be for a new product?" "Where should they be located?" "Where should distribution centres

be located?" and "How can we deliver these products faster and better to our major customers?"

Answers were not easy to obtain because P&G's supply chains are incredibly complex, with more than 100 000 suppliers. P&G's Global Beauty Care division alone has hundreds of combinations of suppliers, manufacturing facilities, and markets with which to deal, compounded by 10 to 15 new product launches per year. Each of the company's dozens of beauty care products has multiple sizes and package designs. A tiny change—and changes are constant—ripples through the supply chain, impacting inventory levels, service levels, and costs.

Jean Kinney, a P&G purchasing manager, recalls the launch of a new global health care product whose success depended on the choice of plant locations

and sources of raw materials. The problem was very complicated, and there were millions of possible solutions. If you asked the managers in the countries marketing this product, they would all say the plants should be located in their countries. Corporate experts, however, would say that scale is important and P&G should build a single megaplant instead of distributing production. In between were millions of other options. What was the best approach?

P&G turned to its IT Global Analytics group for a solution. IT Global Analytics constructed some models using Microsoft Excel spreadsheet software enhanced by LINDO Systems's What's*Best!* for more powerful optimization and Palisade's @RISK software for Monte Carlo simulation, which randomly generates values for uncertain variables. The models tried to maximize the value of the investment, considering manufacturing costs, freight costs, import/export duties, local wage rates, foreign exchange rates, taxes, and the cost of capital.

This model was one of a series of models developed by IT Global Analytics for restructuring P&G's supply chain. P&G used optimization models to determine how best to allocate supply chain resources, and it used simulation models to mathematically try out various options to see how they reacted to changes in important variables. In addition, the company used techniques, such as decision trees, that combined the possibilities of various outcomes with their financial results. Using these decision-support tools, IT Global Analytics found that the success of a supply chain is not necessarily based on the most optimal solution but rather a robust solution that would stand up under real-world conditions.

P&G uses a number of different software tools for implementing its models. In addition to Excel and add-on products, P&G also uses stand-alone software packages. These packages include Xpress-MP from Dash Optimization Inc. and Cplex from Ilog Inc. for building optimization models, and Extend from Imagine That Inc. for building simulation models. Most of the data for these decision-support systems come from a massive Oracle data warehouse with 36 months of data on supplier, manufacturing, customer, and consumer histories by region.

P&G's use of decision-support systems for restructuring its supply chain has paid off. The company consolidated North American plants by 20 percent and lowered supply chain costs by $232 million each year.

Sources: Gary H. Anthes, "Modeling Magic," *Computerworld*, February 7, 2005; Palisade, "Procter & Gamble Uses @ RISK and PrecisionTree World-Wide," **www.palisade.com**, accessed August 6, 2005; and **www.pg.com**, accessed October 10, 2006.

Procter & Gamble's use of information systems to restructure its supply chain illustrates how information systems improve decision making.

By improving decisions about how to restructure P&G's supply chain, information systems helped the company operate more efficiently, reduce its costs,

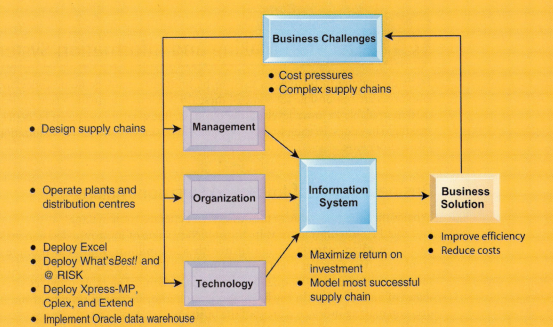

and increase responsiveness to customers and to the marketplace.

The chapter-opening Business Challenges diagram calls attention to important points raised by this case and this chapter. P&G management was unable to make good decisions about where to locate plants and distribution centres for new products because P&G's supply chain was extremely large, complex, and affected by many different variables. Bad decisions about where to locate plants and distribution centres increased costs to procure, manufacture, warehouse, and ship P&G products because plants and distribution centres did not operate efficiently. P&G solved this problem by implementing new, model-based, decision-support systems capable of evaluating large quantities of data and thousands of variables. These systems helped decision makers find an optimal design for P&G's supply chain and improve the allocation of supply chain resources.

HEADS UP

This chapter focuses on how business firms use information systems to improve decision making. A wide variety of information systems directly improves decision making throughout the firm, from the executive suite to the customer service centre and the factory floor. There are even systems to help customers make better decisions. It would not be an overstatement to say that a primary contribution of information systems to business firms has been to improve decision making at all levels.

■ If your career is in finance and accounting, you will be working with decision-support systems that use financial models for break-even analysis, profitability analysis, capital budgeting, and financial forecasting, and executive support systems (ESS) that provide overviews of firm-wide financial performance.

■ If your career is in human resources, you will use decision-support systems for analyzing the impact of employee compensation plans and for projecting the firm's long-term labour force requirements.

■ If your career is in information systems, you will be developing databases, models, and reporting capabilities for systems to support decision making.

■ If your career is in manufacturing, production, or operations management, you will be using decision-support systems to guide decisions about the optimization of sourcing, production, logistics, and maintenance that must evaluate many interrelated variables.

■ If your career is in sales and marketing, you will be working with decision-support systems to guide decisions about product pricing, sales forecasting, advertising and promotional campaigns, and location of retail outlets.

14.1 Decision Making and Information Systems

Decision making in businesses used to be limited to management. Today, lower-level employees are responsible for some of these decisions as information systems make information available to lower levels of the business. But what do we mean by better decision making? How does decision making take place in businesses and other organizations? Let us take a closer look.

Business Value of Improved Decision Making

What is the monetary value to the business of better decision making?

Table 14-1 attempts to measure the monetary value of improved decision making for a small Canadian manufacturing firm with $280 million in annual revenue and 140 employees. The firm has identified a number of key decisions where new system investments might improve the quality of decision making. The table provides selected estimates of annual value (in the form of cost savings or increased revenue) from improved decision making in selected areas of the business.

We can see from Table 14-1 that decisions are made at all levels of the firm and that some of these decisions are common, routine, and numerous. Although the value of improving any single decision may be small, improving hundreds of thousands of "small" decisions adds up to a large annual value for the business.

Types of Decisions

Chapter 2 showed that there are different levels in an organization. Each of these levels has different information requirements for decision support and responsibility for different types of decisions (see Figure 14-1). Decisions are classified as structured, semistructured, and unstructured.

Unstructured decisions are those in which the decision maker must provide judgment, evaluation, and insight to solve the problem. Each of these decisions is novel, important, and nonroutine, and there is no well-understood or agreed-on procedure for making them.

Structured decisions, by contrast, are repetitive and routine, and they involve a definite procedure for handling them so that they do not have to be treated each time as if they were new.

Unstructured decisions
Structured decisions

TABLE 14-1 *Business Value of Enhanced Decision Making*

EXAMPLE DECISION	DECISION MAKER	NUMBER OF ANNUAL DECISIONS	ESTIMATED VALUE TO FIRM OF A SINGLE IMPROVED DECISION	ANNUAL VALUE
Allocate support to most valuable customers	Accounts manager	12	$100 000	$1 200 000
Predict call centre daily demand	Call centre management	4	150 000	600 000
Decide parts inventory levels daily	Inventory manager	365	5000	1 825 000
Identify competitive bids from major suppliers	Senior management	1	2 000 000	2 000 000
Schedule production to fill orders	Manufacturing manager	150	10 000	1 500 000
Allocate labour to complete a job	Production floor manager	100	4000	400 000

FIGURE 14-1 *Information requirements of key decision-making groups in a firm*

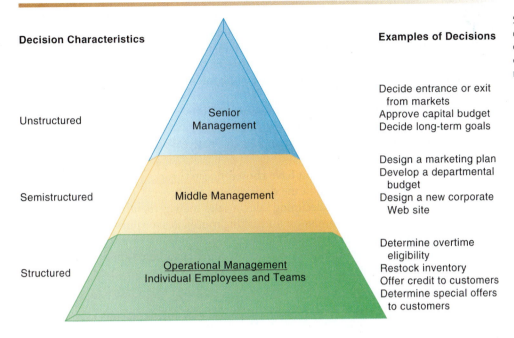

Decision Characteristics

Unstructured

Semistructured

Structured

Senior Management

Middle Management

Operational Management
Individual Employees and Teams

Examples of Decisions

Decide entrance or exit
from markets
Approve capital budget
Decide long-term goals

Design a marketing plan
Develop a departmental
budget
Design a new corporate
Web site

Determine overtime
eligibility
Restock inventory
Offer credit to customers
Determine special offers
to customers

Senior managers, middle managers, operational managers, and employees have different types of decisions and information requirements.

Many decisions have elements of both types of decisions and are **semistructured decisions**, where only part of the problem has a clear-cut answer provided by an accepted procedure. In general, structured decisions are more prevalent at lower organizational levels while unstructured problems are more common at higher levels of the firm.

Senior executives face many unstructured decision situations, such as establishing the firm's five- or ten-year goals or deciding on new markets to enter. Answering the question "Should we enter a new market?" would require access to news, government reports, and industry views as well as high-level summaries of firm performance. However, the answer would also require senior managers to use their own best judgment and poll other managers for their opinions.

Middle management faces more structured decision scenarios, but their decisions may include unstructured components. A typical middle-level management decision might be "Why is the reported order fulfillment report showing a decline over the past six months at a distribution centre in Kitchener?" This middle manager could obtain a report from the firm's enterprise system or distribution management system on order activity and operational efficiency at the Kitchener distribution centre. This is the structured part of the decision. But before arriving at an answer, this middle manager will have to interview employees and gather more unstructured information from external sources about local economic conditions or sales trends.

Operational management and rank-and-file employees tend to make more structured decisions. For example, a supervisor on an assembly line has to decide whether an hourly paid worker is entitled to overtime pay. If the employee worked more than eight hours on a particular day, the supervisor would routinely grant overtime pay for any time beyond eight hours that was clocked on that day.

A sales account representative often has to make decisions about extending credit to customers by consulting the firm's customer database that contains credit information. If the customer met the firm's pre-specified criteria for granting credit, the account representative would grant that customer credit to make a purchase. In both instances, the decisions are highly structured and are routinely made thousands of times each day in most large firms. The answer has been preprogrammed into the firm's payroll and accounts receivable systems.

Semistructured decisions

The Decision-Making Process

Making a decision is a multistep process. Simon (1960) described four different stages in decision making: intelligence, design, choice, and implementation (see Figure 14-2). These stages correspond to the four steps in problem-solving used throughout this book.

Intelligence consists of discovering, identifying, and understanding the problems occurring in the organization—why there is a problem, where, and what effects it is having on the firm.

Design involves identifying and exploring various solutions to the problem.

Choice consists of selecting from among solution alternatives.

Implementation involves making the chosen alternative work and continuing to monitor how well the solution is working.

What happens if the solution you have chosen doesn't work? Figure 14-2 shows that you can return to an earlier stage in the decision-making process and repeat it if necessary. For instance, in the face of declining sales, a sales management team may decide to pay the sales force a higher commission for making more sales to spur on the sales effort. If this does not produce sales increases, managers would need to investigate whether the problem stems from poor product design, inadequate customer support, or a host of other causes that call for a different solution.

Managers and Decision Making in the Real World

The premise of this book and this chapter is that systems to support decision making produce better decision making by managers and employees, above-average returns on invest-

Intelligence

Design

Choice

Implementation

FIGURE 14-2   *Stages in decision making*

The decision-making process can be broken down into four stages.

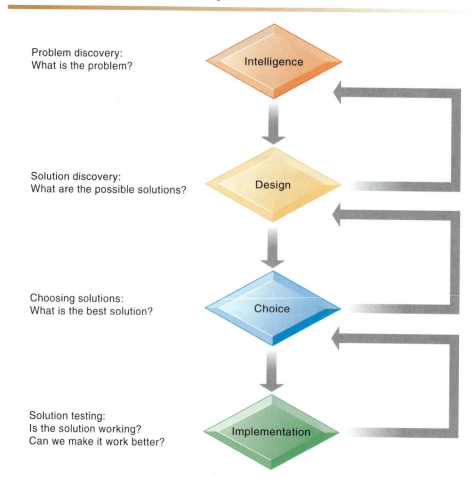

Problem discovery:
What is the problem?

Intelligence

Solution discovery:
What are the possible solutions?

Design

Choosing solutions:
What is the best solution?

Choice

Solution testing:
Is the solution working?
Can we make it work better?

Implementation

ment for the firm, and, ultimately, higher profitability. However, information systems cannot improve all the different kinds of decisions taking place in an organization. Let us examine the role of managers and decision making in organizations to see why this is so.

Managerial Roles Managers play key roles in organizations. Their responsibilities range from making decisions, to writing reports, to attending meetings, to arranging birthday parties. We can better understand managerial functions and roles by examining classical and contemporary models of managerial behaviour.

The **classical model of management**, which describes what managers do, was largely unquestioned from its inception in the 1920s until recent years. Henri Fayol and other early writers first described the five classical functions of managers as planning, organizing, coordinating, deciding, and controlling. This description of management activities dominated management thought for a long time, and it is still popular today.

The classical model describes formal managerial functions but does not address what exactly managers do when they plan, decide things, and control the work of others. For this, we must turn to the work of contemporary behavioural scientists who have studied managers in daily action. **Behavioural models of management** state that the actual behaviour of managers appears to be less systematic, more informal, less reflective, more reactive, and less well organized than the classical model would have us believe.

Observers find that managerial behaviour actually has five attributes that differ greatly from the classical description: First, managers perform a great deal of work at an unrelenting pace—studies have found that managers engage in more than 600 different activities each day, with no break in their pace. Second, managerial activities are fragmented; most activities last for less than nine minutes, and only 10 percent of the activities exceed one hour in duration. Third, managers prefer current, specific, and ad hoc information (printed information often will be too old). Fourth, they prefer oral forms of communication to written forms because oral media provide greater flexibility, require less effort, and bring a faster response. Fifth, managers give high priority to maintaining a diverse and complex web of contacts that acts as an informal information system and helps them execute their personal agendas and short- and long-term goals.

A second approach was taken by Mintzberg. Analyzing managers' day-to-day behaviour, Mintzberg found that it could be classified into 10 managerial roles. **Managerial roles** are expectations of the activities that managers should perform in an organization. Mintzberg found that these managerial roles fell into three categories: interpersonal, informational, and decisional.

Interpersonal Roles   Managers act as figureheads for the organization when they represent their companies to the outside world and perform symbolic duties, such as giving out employee awards, in their **interpersonal role**. Managers act as leaders, attempting to motivate, counsel, and support subordinates. Managers also act as liaisons between various organizational levels; within each of these levels, they serve as liaisons among the members of the management team. Managers provide time and favours, which they expect to be returned.

Informational Roles   In their **informational role**, managers act as the nerve centres of their organizations, receiving the most concrete, up-to-date information and redistributing it to those who need to be aware of it. Managers are therefore information disseminators and spokespersons for their organizations.

Decisional Roles   Managers make decisions. In their **decisional role**, they act as entrepreneurs by initiating new kinds of activities; they handle disturbances arising in the organization; they allocate resources to staff members who need them; and they negotiate conflicts and mediate between conflicting groups.

Table 14-2, based on Mintzberg's role classifications, is one look at where systems can and cannot help managers. The table shows that information systems do not yet contribute to some important areas of management life.

Classical model of management
Behavioural models of management
Managerial roles
Interpersonal role
Informational role
Decisional role

TABLE 14-2 *Managerial Roles and Supporting Information Systems*

ROLE	BEHAVIOUR	SUPPORT SYSTEMS
Interpersonal Roles		
Figurehead --------------------------→		None exist
Leader -------------- Interpersonal -----→		None exist
Liaison --------------------------------→		Electronic communication systems
Informational Roles		
Nerve centre ---------------------------→		Management information systems, ESS
Disseminator ---------Information -----→		Mail, office systems
Spokesperson --------processing ------→		Office and professional systems, workstations
Decisional Roles		
Entrepreneur --------Decision ---------→		None exist
Disturbance handler --making ---------→		None exist
Resource allocator --------------------→		DSS systems
Negotiator ----------------------------→		None exist

Sources: Kenneth C. Laudon and Jane P. Laudon; and Mintzberg, 1971.

Real-World Decision Making We now can see that information systems are not helpful for all managerial roles. And in those managerial roles where information systems can improve decisions, investments in information technology do not always produce positive results. There are three main reasons: information quality, management filters, and organizational culture (see Chapter 3).

Information Quality High-quality decisions require high-quality information. Table 14-3 describes information quality dimensions that can affect the quality of decisions.

If the output of information systems does not meet these quality criteria, decision making will suffer. Chapter 6 has shown that corporate databases and files have varying levels of inaccuracy and incompleteness, which in turn can degrade the quality of decision making.

Management Filters Even with timely, accurate information, some managers make bad decisions. Managers (like all human beings) absorb information through a series of filters to make sense of the world around them. Managers have selective attention, focus on certain kinds of problems and solutions, and have a variety of biases that make them reject information that does not conform to their prior conceptions.

TABLE 14-3 *Information Quality Dimensions*

QUALITY DIMENSION	DESCRIPTION
Accuracy	Do the data represent reality?
Integrity	Are the structure of data and relationships among the entities and attributes consistent?
Consistency	Are data elements consistently defined?
Completeness	Are all the necessary data present?
Validity	Do data values fall within defined ranges?
Timeliness	Are data available when needed?
Accessibility	Are the data accessible, comprehensible, and usable?

For instance, Cisco Systems Corporation, one of the most advanced users of online decision-support systems, nevertheless was forced to write off as a loss $3.5 billion in excess inventory in 2001 because management had not interpreted the information from systems correctly. The company's online sales order entry system throughout 1999 and 2000 showed exceptionally strong orders. However, customers, perceiving a shortage of routers and other networking equipment, were placing orders with multiple manufacturers, awarding the business to the first one who could deliver, and cancelling other orders. Cisco's systems were also recording high levels of order cancellation, but management ignored this "bad news" and emphasized the "good news": new orders were piling up (Laudon and Laudon, 2004).

Organizational Inertia and Politics   Organizations are bureaucracies with limited capabilities and competencies for acting decisively. When environments change and businesses need to adopt new business models to survive, strong forces within organizations resist making decisions calling for major change. Decisions taken by a firm often represent a balancing of the firm's various interest groups rather than the best solution to the problem.

Studies of business restructuring find that firms tend to ignore poor performance until threatened by outside takeovers, and they systematically blame poor performance on external forces beyond their control such as economic conditions (the economy), foreign competition, and rising prices, rather than blaming senior or middle management for poor business judgment (John, Lang, Netter, et al., 1992).

14.2   Systems for Decision Support

There are four kinds of systems for supporting the different levels and types of decisions we have just described. We introduced some of these systems in Chapter 2. *Management information systems* (*MIS*) provide routine reports and summaries of transaction-level data to middle and operational level managers to provide answers to structured and semistructured decision problems. *Decision-support systems* (*DSS*) provide analytical models or tools for analyzing large quantities of data for middle managers who face semistructured decision situations. *Executive support systems* (*ESS*) are systems that provide senior management, making primarily unstructured decisions, with external information (news, stock analyses, and industry trends) and high-level summaries of firm performance.

In this chapter, you will also learn about systems for supporting decision makers working as a group. Group decision-support systems (GDSS) are specialized systems that provide a group electronic environment in which managers and teams can collectively make decisions and design solutions for unstructured and semistructured problems.

Management Information Systems (MIS)

Management information systems (MIS), which we introduced in Chapter 2, help managers monitor and control the business by providing information on the firm's performance. They typically produce fixed, regularly scheduled reports based on data extracted and summarized from the firm's underlying transaction processing systems (TPS). Sometimes, MIS reports are exception reports, highlighting only exceptional conditions, such as when the sales quotas for a specific territory fall below an anticipated level or employees have exceeded their spending limits in a dental care plan. Today, many of these reports are available online through an intranet, and more MIS reports can be generated on demand. Table 14-4 provides some examples of MIS applications.

Decision-Support Systems (DSS)

Whereas MIS primarily address structured problems, DSS support semistructured and unstructured problem analysis. The earliest DSS were heavily model-driven, using some

TABLE 14-4 *Examples of MIS Applications*

COMPANY	MIS APPLICATION
Cartier Kitchens	Brampton, Ontario, firm that uses an MIS system to generate a report every morning on sales until they are completed, flagging any service issues or other reasons for incomplete installations.
Shoppers Drug Mart	Healthwatch MIS contains the pharmaceutical profiles of all the patients and informs the pharmacist who carries out the ordinance of any allergic reaction or possible interaction.
Environment Canada	National Enforcement Management Information System and Intelligence System allows tracking and management of pollution and wildlife enforcement activities and actions relating to legislation enforced by Environment Canada.
Taco Bell	Total Automation of Company Operations (TACO) system provides information on food, labour, and period-to-date costs for each restaurant.

type of model to perform "what-if" and other kinds of analyses. Their analysis capabilities were based on a strong theory or model combined with a good user interface that made the system easy to use. (Models are described below in more detail). The voyage-estimating DSS described in Chapter 2 and P&G's systems for supply chain restructuring in the chapter-opening case are examples of model-driven DSS.

Some contemporary DSS are data-driven. A **data-driven DSS** is a system that supports decision making by allowing users to extract and analyze useful information that was previously buried in large databases, often by using online analytical processing (OLAP) and data mining. The business intelligence applications described in Chapter 6 are examples of these data-driven DSS, as are the spreadsheet pivot table applications we describe in this section. Data-driven DSS support decision making by enabling users to extract useful information that was previously buried in large quantities of data.

Components of DSS Figure 14-3 illustrates the components of a DSS. They include a database of data used for query and analysis; a software system with models, data mining, and other analytical tools; and a user interface.

Data-driven DSS

FIGURE 14-3   *Overview of a decision-support system*

The main components of the DSS are the DSS database, the user interface, and the DSS software system. The DSS database may be a small database residing on a PC or a large data warehouse.

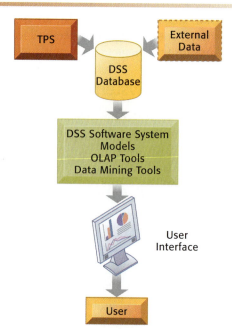

The **DSS database** is a collection of current or historical data from a number of applications or groups. It may be a small database, residing on a PC, and containing a subset of corporate data that has been downloaded and possibly combined with external data. Alternatively, the DSS database may be a massive data warehouse that is continuously updated by major corporate TPS (including enterprise applications and data generated by Web site transactions). The data in DSS databases are generally extracts or copies of production databases so that using the DSS does not interfere with critical operational systems.

The DSS user interface permits easy interaction between users of the system and the DSS software tools. Many DSS today have Web interfaces to take advantage of graphic displays, interactivity, and ease of use.

The **DSS software system** contains the software tools that are used for data analysis. It may contain various OLAP tools, data mining tools, or a collection of mathematical and analytical models that can easily be made accessible to the DSS user. A **model** is an abstract representation that illustrates the components or relationships of a phenomenon. A model can be a physical model (such as a model plane), a graphical model (such as a pie chart), a mathematical model (such as an equation), or a verbal model (such as a description of a procedure for writing an order).

Statistical modelling helps establish relationships, such as relating product sales to differences in age, income, or other factors between communities of customers. Optimization models determine optimal resource allocation to maximize or minimize specified variables, such as cost or time. A classic use of optimization models is to determine the proper mix of products within a given market to maximize profits. The chapter-opening case illustrates P&G's use of optimization models to determine how to maximize its return on investment in its supply chain.

Forecasting models often are used to forecast sales. The user of this type of model might supply a range of historical data to project future conditions and the sales that might result from those conditions. The decision maker could vary those future conditions (entering, for example, a rise in raw materials costs or the entry of a new, low-priced competitor in the market) to determine how new conditions might affect sales.

Sensitivity analysis models ask "what-if" questions repeatedly to determine the impact on outcomes of changes in one or more factors. *What-if analysis*—working forward from known or assumed conditions—allows the user to vary certain values to test results to better predict outcomes if changes occur in those values. What happens if we raise product price by 5 percent or increase the advertising budget by $100 000? What happens if we keep the price and advertising budgets the same? Desktop spreadsheet software, such as Microsoft Excel, is often used for this purpose (see Figure 14-4). Backward-sensitivity analysis software helps decision makers with goal seeking: If I want to sell one million product units next year, how much must I reduce the price of the product?

DSS database
DSS software system
Model
Sensitivity analysis

FIGURE 14-4   *Sensitivity analysis*

Total fixed costs	19000				
Variable cost per unit	3				
Average sales price	17				
Contribution margin	14				
Break-even point	1357				
			Variable Cost per Unit		
Sales	1357	2	3	4	5	6
Price	14	1583	1727	1900	2111	2375
	15	1462	1583	1727	1900	2111
	16	1357	1462	1583	1727	1900
	17	1267	1357	1462	1583	1727
	18	1188	1267	1357	1462	1583

This table displays the results of a sensitivity analysis of the effect of changing the sales price of a necktie and the cost per unit on the product's break-even point. It answers the question, "What happens to the break-even point if the sales price and the cost to make each unit increase or decrease?"

Using Spreadsheet Pivot Tables to Support Decision Making

Spreadsheet software is also useful for helping managers detect and understand patterns in data. For instance, let us a take a look at one day's worth of transactions at an online firm, Online Management Training Inc. (OMT Inc.), which sells online management training books and streaming online videos to corporations and individuals who want to improve their management techniques. On this day, the firm experienced 517 order transactions. Figure 14-5 shows the first 20 transaction records produced at the firm's Web site that day. The names of customers and other identifiers have been removed from this list.

You can think of this list as a database composed of transaction records (the rows). The fields for each customer record are as follows: customer ID, region of purchase, payment method, source of contact (e-mail versus Web banner ad), amount of purchase, the product purchased (either online training or a book), and time of day (in 24-hour time).

There is a great deal of valuable information in this transaction list that could help managers answer important questions and make important decisions:

- Where do most of our customers come from? The answer might tell managers where to spend more marketing resources or to initiate new marketing efforts.
- Where are the average purchases higher? The answer might tell managers where to focus marketing and sales resources or pitch different messages to different regions.
- What form of payment is the most common? The answer could be used to emphasize in advertising the most preferred means of payment.
- Are there any times of day when purchases are most common? Do people buy products while at work (likely during the day) or at home (likely in the evening)?
- Are there regional differences in the average purchase? If one region is much more lucrative, managers could focus their marketing and advertising resources on that region.
- Are there regional differences in the sources of our customers? Perhaps in some regions e-mail is the most effective marketing tool while in other regions Web banner ads are more effective. The answer to this more complicated question could help managers develop a regional marketing strategy.

FIGURE 14-5 *Sample list of transactions for Online Management Training Inc.*

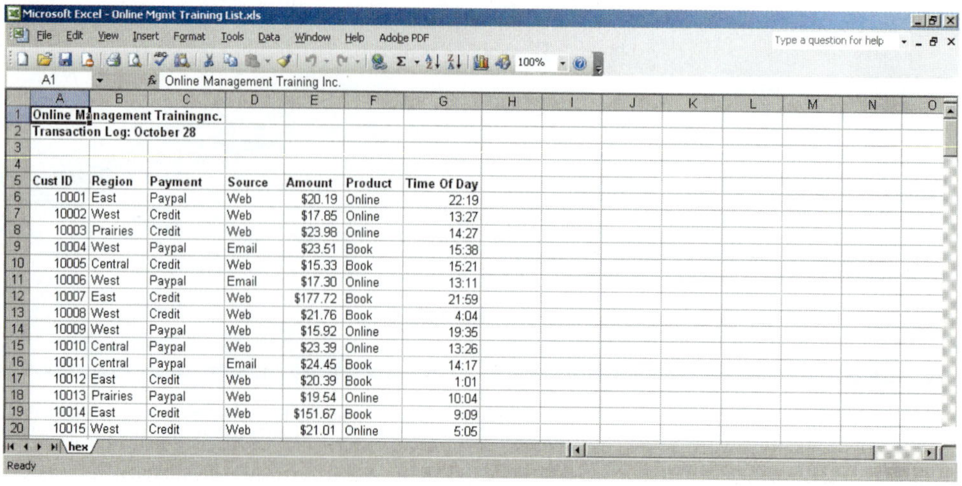

Row	A	B	C	D	E	F	G
1	Online Management Trainingnc.						
2	Transaction Log: October 28						
3							
4							
5	Cust ID	Region	Payment	Source	Amount	Product	Time Of Day
6	10001	East	Paypal	Web	$20.19	Online	22:19
7	10002	West	Credit	Web	$17.85	Online	13:27
8	10003	Prairies	Credit	Web	$23.98	Online	14:27
9	10004	West	Paypal	Email	$23.51	Book	15:38
10	10005	Central	Credit	Web	$15.33	Book	15:21
11	10006	West	Paypal	Email	$17.30	Online	13:11
12	10007	East	Credit	Web	$177.72	Book	21:59
13	10008	West	Credit	Web	$21.76	Book	4:04
14	10009	West	Paypal	Web	$15.92	Online	19:35
15	10010	Central	Paypal	Web	$23.39	Online	13:26
16	10011	Central	Paypal	Email	$24.45	Book	14:17
17	10012	East	Credit	Web	$20.39	Book	1:01
18	10013	Prairies	Paypal	Web	$19.54	Online	10:04
19	10014	East	Credit	Web	$151.67	Book	9:09
20	10015	West	Credit	Web	$21.01	Online	5:05

This list shows a portion of the order transactions for Online Management Training Inc. (OMT Inc.) on October 28, 2007.

Microsoft Excel spreadsheet software offers many tools that are helpful in answering these kinds of questions. If the list was small, you could simply inspect the list and try to get a sense of patterns in the data. But this is impossible when you have a list of over 500 transactions. Notice that these questions often involve two dimensions: region and average purchase, time of day and average purchase, payment type and average purchase. But the last question is more complex because it has three dimensions: region, source of customer, and purchase.

You could use Excel's charting capabilities, such as a bar chart, to answer some of these questions, but this would require you to sort the transactions on one dimension, calculate an average purchase price for each value of that dimension, manually create a new worksheet, and then create a bar chart. This would take a lot of time and be very inefficient.

Fortunately, spreadsheet software has a very powerful tool called a pivot table that categorizes and summarizes data very quickly. A **pivot table** is simply a table that displays two or more dimensions of data in a convenient format. Excel's PivotTable Wizard creates a pivot table for you. It is located in the drop-down Data menu. When you click on PivotTable and PivotChart Report in the Excel Data menu and tell Excel where your data are and what type of report your want (select PivotTable), the PivotTable and PivotChart Wizard screen appears (Figure 14-6). For precise instructions on how to create PivotTable reports, refer to MyMISLab section on PivotTables.

The PivotTable Wizard has three elements: an empty PivotTable with labels for rows, columns, and data areas; a PivotTable Field List that lists the fields in your list or database; and a PivotTable Toolbar. By dragging and dropping the fields you want to look at in your pivot table, you can analyze this list quickly and arrive at decisions quickly.

For instance, let us take the first question: "Where do our customers come from?" There are several answers to this question, but let us start with region and ask the question: "How many customers come from each region?" To find the answer, simply drag the Region field to the "Drop Row Fields Here" area of the empty pivot table, and drag Cust ID to the "Drop Data Items Here" areas of the empty pivot table. Figure 14-7 shows the results.

Pivot table

FIGURE 14-6 *The Excel PivotTable Wizard*

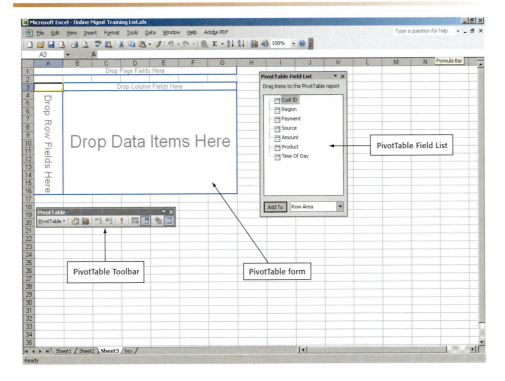

The PivotTable Wizard in Excel makes it easy to analyze lists and databases by simply dragging and dropping elements from the Field List to the PivotTable area.

By dragging and dropping fields to row and data areas of the pivot table form, you can quickly produce a table showing the relationship between region and number of customers. You will need to use the Field Settings button on the Toolbar to produce this table in order to redefine the Cust ID field as a count rather than a sum so Excel reports the number of customers, not the sum of their customer IDs, which would be meaningless.

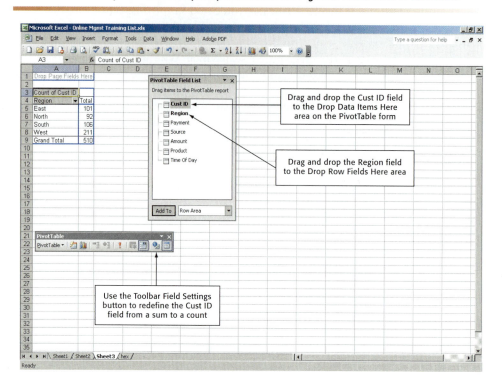

The PivotTable shows that most of our customers come from the Western region. So far we have looked at a single dimension, region, in understanding where our customers come from. Now let us take a more complicated question that involves two dimensions: Does the source of the customer make a difference in addition to region? We have two sources of customers: some customers respond to e-mail campaigns, and others respond to online banner advertising. In a few seconds you can find the answer shown in Figure 14-8. This pivot table shows that Web banner advertising produces most of the customers, and this is true for all the regions.

Could we analyze the average amount of the purchase to the table in Figure 14-8? The answer is yes, very easily: just drag the Amount field to the data area of the pivot table. If you do this, you will find that while the average purchase on this day was $38, the customers who responded to e-mail from the Western region had an average sale of nearly $49! As a manager you might want to use this knowledge and expand your e-mail campaigns to Western audiences and perhaps enlarge your banner advertising in other regions.

The complete Excel file for these examples is available on MyMISLab for Chapter 14. (Look for the file named OMT List.xls.) The Hands-On MIS Application Exercises section at the end of this chapter asks you to find answers to a number of other questions regarding this data file.

Business Value of DSS

DSS have become very powerful and sophisticated, providing fine-grained information for decisions that enable the firm to coordinate both internal and external business processes precisely. Some of these DSS are helping companies with decisions in customer relationship management or supply chain management (such as P&G's supply chain restructuring applications described in the chapter-opening case or Renault's DSS for supply chain planning described in the Window on Technology section on page 482). Some DSS take advantage of the company-wide data provided by enterprise systems. DSS today can also harness the interactive capabilities of the Web

FIGURE 14-8   *A pivot table that examines two dimensions*

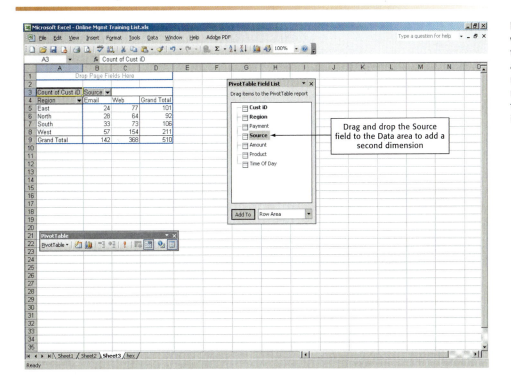

In this pivot table, we can examine where our customers come from in terms of two dimensions: region and advertising source. It appears nearly 40 percent of the customers respond to e-mail campaigns, and there are some regional variations in this theme.

to provide decision-support tools to both employees and customers. Table 14-5 lists some examples of DSS. Here are some additional examples that illustrate the range of DSS capabilities:

- Burlington Coat Factory has a DSS for pricing decisions. Many large retailers lose millions of dollars because their prices are "best guesses." If they wait too long to discount an item that is not selling well, they will be stuck with excess. If they discount too early, or discount too heavily, they lose profits because people buy goods they might have bought at a higher price. Burlington Coat Factory Warehouse has solved this problem by implementing price optimization software.

- Burlington Coat Factory uses ProfitLogic's Markdown Optimization Solution to manage pricing and inventory at all of its stores nationwide. ProfitLogic considers complex interdependencies between initial prices set for merchandise, prices for promotions, and prices for markdowns, including cross-item pricing effects and item seasonality. It enables Burlington to gain earlier visibility into the performance of merchandise in order to clear out underperforming items and free up inventory to stock fresher merchandise that is more in demand.

TABLE 14-5 *Examples of Decision-Support Systems*

ORGANIZATION	DSS APPLICATION
General Accident Insurance	Customer buying patterns and fraud detection
Canadian National Railway	Train dispatching and routing
Frito-Lay, Inc.	Price, advertising, and promotion selection
Burlington Coat Factory	Store location and inventory mix; pricing decisions
Royal Bank of Canada (RBC)	Customer profiles
Air Canada	Flight scheduling and passenger demand forecasting

WINDOW ON TECHNOLOGY

Renault Speeds Up Delivery with a New DSS

French auto maker Renault has been facing very intense competition in the Western European auto market. The time it takes to deliver a car after placing an order is a decisive factor in customer satisfaction. Renault wanted to turn it into a competitive weapon. The company decided to shorten the lead time between placement of the customer order and arrival in dealerships from six to two weeks.

This meant that Renault would have to transform its supply chain from a push to a pull model, in which cars are built to order. New information systems were required to speed up the entire planning and production process.

In Renault's old system, Renault's national sales companies throughout Europe predicted monthly sales for each model for the current and following year. The headquarters sales department reviewed the figures with industrial planners to make sure there was sufficient plant capacity to handle orders. This part of the planning process lasted nearly a month and took place each month.

In addition to planning data, customer orders taken at dealerships were transmitted daily to corporate headquarters, which dispatched them once a week to Renault's vehicle assembly plants. The plants then used these data to plan and schedule production. Except for this last step, the whole planning process was hampered by legacy mainframe systems, which could no longer handle all Renault's widening number of models and options available to customers. The old system took hours to perform all the computations in nightly batches. Simulations were impossible.

Renault's operations research (OR) team was charged with overhauling the company's supply chain planning systems and processes. The company had tried to use ERP software, but its generic tools could not handle the complex data describing Renault products. Consequently, the OR team had to develop the system in-house using goal-seeking software that seeks to optimize the mix of models, critical options (engine, gearbox), and secondary options that can meet sales forecasts within the constraints of the company's production capacity and product range. "Feasible" sales forecasts are sent to headquarters where industrial planners use goal-seeking software again to determine the optimal weekly output of car factories that meet the sales targets.

On the assembly plant floor, software directs production sequencing. The car sequence is built to smooth the workload on the assembly line and to minimize production costs when colours are changed during sequencing, which requires painting tubes to be washed.

The team worked with groups of users in Renault's sales and industrial department to define the planning problem, its constraints, the decision variables, the objectives to be optimized, and business rules to be followed. Each department selected the information it needed to meet its goals. For example, the sales department focused on the ability to produce the right mix of models, engines, equipment levels, colours, and options every month while industrial planners focused on weekly production volumes for each plant.

The team created a proof-of-concept prototype system for validation by end users before moving into full-scale software development. All the software tools for the New Delivery Project were rolled out between 1999 and 2003. Plant operators asked for some modifications to the software because it was not handling car sequencing well. (There were too many colour changeovers for assembly lines to handle.) Renault research teams from Canada, Europe, and Brazil competed to provide a solution. The software now performs more than 140 million evaluations in 10 minutes.

The changes introduced by the new system were accompanied by changes in related systems and business processes. Customer orders flow directly from dealers to assembly plants, bypassing corporate headquarters.

Renault's OR team is now working on new software to optimize the time for routing vehicles from plants to dealerships via intermediate dispatching centres. This requires building an extensive collection of paths through Renault's worldwide transportation network and assigning departure and arrival dates for every vehicle leaving the assembly line each day.

In addition to shortening delivery times and reducing inventory, Renault's New Delivery system helps ensure that each customer obtains exactly the car he or she wants. Under the old commitment model, customers were encouraged to buy what dealers had ordered and maintained in inventory. Dealers had to reduce prices to sell vehicles that remained in inventory too long. Additionally, the ability to sell customers the model and options they want and within a short delivery time gives Renault a more profitable product mix.

To Think About

1. How did this DSS improve decision making at Renault? Describe some of the decisions that were improved by using this system.

2. How much of an impact did this DSS have on business performance? Explain your answer.

3. What management, organization, and technology factors had to be addressed in order to make this system successful?

MIS in Action

Visit the Renault Canada Web site (**www.eurodrive.renault.com/cms/canada/en/**). Review the Renault passenger cars available for sale in Canada.

1. How many models are available for sale in the country you have chosen?

2. Select one model and explore its versions and prices. List the various options and accessories available for that vehicle.

3. If a customer were ordering a Renault car, what are some of the data that would have to be transmitted to suppliers?

Sources: Alain Nguyen, "Renault Speeds Up Delivery," *OR/MS Today*, April, 2006, and www.renault.com, accessed October 2, 2006.

DSS for Profitability Analysis Although a company has a high level of sales revenue, not all these sales may contribute to profits. A large customer with many requests for service or high-speed delivery of low-margin items may actually be costing the company money. The Brazilian unit of agricultural chemical maker Syngenta AG discovered in 2003 that it was losing money on some of its fastest-growing products. Syngenta's 200 salespeople were paid on how much they sold, and they had no way of calculating important cost components, such as expenditures for deliveries, rebates, and extended credit terms or the impact of currency shifts.

Syngenta built a DSS that estimates freight charges, employee commissions, currency shifts, and other costs to calculate a "pocket price" for a proposed sale. If the software determines the transaction is not profitable, the salesperson cannot enter the order unless that person has special permission from a manager. Company executives changed the incentive plan for the sales team to encourage sales that genuinely contributed to profits. In Mato Grosso state in western Brazil, the software helped managers learn that shipping costs were too high to sell low-margin products such as copper-based fungicide. Syngenta Brazil stopped selling these products to farmers in that area. In 2004, when Syngenta started using this DSS, profit margins climbed by 4 percent (Badal, 2006).

Data Visualization and Geographic Information Systems (GIS)

Data from information systems can be made easier for users to digest and act on by using graphics, charts, tables, maps, digital images, three-dimensional presentations, animations, and other data visualization technologies. By presenting data in graphical form, **data visualization** tools help users see patterns and relationships in large amounts of data, patterns that would be difficult to discern if the data were presented as traditional lists of text and numbers. Some data visualization tools are interactive, enabling users to manipulate data and see the graphical displays change in response to the changes they make.

Geographic information systems (GIS) are a special category of DSS that use data visualization technology to analyze and display data for planning and decision making in the form of digitized maps. The software assembles, stores, manipulates, and displays geographically referenced information, tying data to points, lines, and areas on a map. GIS have modelling capabilities, enabling managers to change data and automatically revise business scenarios to find better solutions. For example, the City of Hamilton uses a GIS to map the threat of West Nile Virus (see Figure 14-9).

GIS support decisions that require knowledge about the geographic distribution of people or other resources. For example, GIS might be used to help state and local governments calculate emergency response times to natural disasters, to help retail chains identify profitable new store locations, or to help banks identify the best locations for installing new branches or automatic teller machine (ATM) terminals.

The Window on Management section on page 484 describes an application of GIS in Sweden for planning the assignment of home health care aides who assist elderly people. Planners of elderly home health care must deal with a complex set of variables that include multiple tasks, many different caregivers and clients, and limited time frames for both caregiving and travel. This particular problem lends itself to geographic information system software because the locations of both the elderly clients and the home caregivers must be considered when planning daily schedules.

Data visualization

Geographic information systems (GIS)

FIGURE 14-9   *A geographic information system*

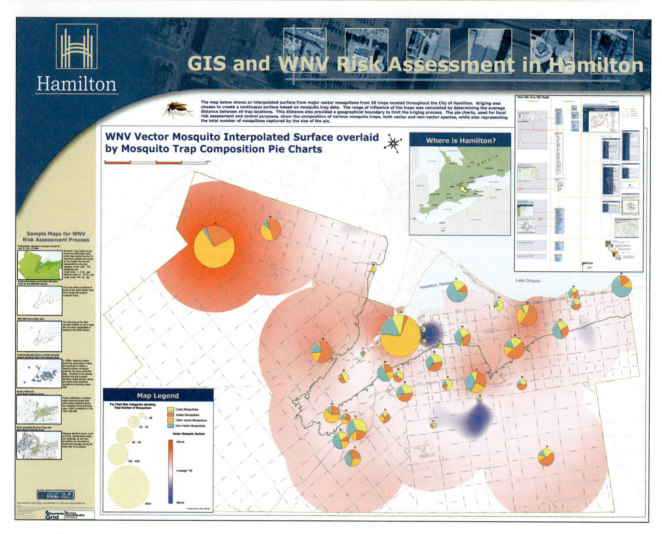

The City of Hamilton uses a geographic information system to examine West Nile Virus risk assessment within the city.

Source: City of Hamilton, Public Health Services, Health Protection Branch, West Nile Virus Program.

WINDOW ON MANAGEMENT

GIS Help the Elderly in Sweden

Caring for elderly people when they are too old to care for themselves is a growing concern in Canada, the United States, Japan, and other countries. In Sweden, elderly people in need of daily care can move to retirement homes or they can remain in their own home with caregiving assistance provided by the state. Today the trend is to encourage the elderly to stay in their own homes for as long as possible.

To bring support services into the home, an assessor working with Swedish local authorities determines what type and how much assistance the client needs. A typical care plan might call for two showers per week, weekly laundry, weekly cleaning,

a monthly doctor's visit, and 20 hours of additional care per month.

All this information serves as input to a visit plan stating when and where each caregiving visit should be performed. The visit plan can either be administered by the local government or, more commonly, by a private contractor.

The schedule for home health aide visits is normally planned several days in advance. However, plans may need to be revised if a staff member becomes ill or a client has to go to the hospital. Some visits may need to be shortened or postponed or have extra staff allocated. Last-minute changes are made to the plan each morning. Making these last-minute changes might consume 30 to 45 minutes per day, delaying the departure of a staff member until her daily assignments are finalized.

Ideally, the planning for elderly care should be as efficient as possible, distributing the workload evenly among the staff. Each visit has a window of time and requires a set of skills that the staff member must have. Sufficient travel time between visits must be allocated and each staff member must be given planned breaks for meals. Each elderly client has one or several preferred staff members who visit and certain visits require multiple staff members.

The problem of planning caregivers' schedules was similar to vehicle routing problems, which have been popular applications for geographic information systems. Elderly care planning must consider many different variables, including skills, time frame, locations, and the number of staff.

The Home Care Department of the Swedish city of Danderyd, the Linköping University, and the Linköping software company Optimal Solutions AB came up with a solution. They created a staff planning system called Laps Care that enables rapid and efficient planning of home care staff schedules. Laps Care has been used daily for elderly home care planning since November 2002.

Here's how the system works. The user inputs data about home health care employees, their clients, and the visits that are to be performed, as well as data about the time staff members must spend in transit to reach each client. Maps are included based on map data from Navigation Technologies, which contains a detailed description of the local road network. Using address matching, the system positions each customer on the map. The system uses these data to calculate travel time between visits, generating a plan that represents an optimal solution where the right person with the right skills provides the right care at the right time.

The resulting solution can be viewed as a text grid, in a Gantt chart, or on a map displaying the route of each staff member and the assigned visits. It takes the system about two minutes to generate each alternative solution. Users often use the system to create alternative solutions to evaluate, so within half an hour, 5 to 10 scenarios can be tested.

When the city of Danderyd started using Laps Care, it found that the system dramatically cut down the time to develop a daily visit plan. One person could create the plan within 15 minutes, and home health staff could leave for their assignments much earlier, saving about 7 percent of total working time. The system divides the workload much more evenly among caregivers than the earlier manual system and uses staff members' special skills more effectively. Although travel times have been reduced, the system is valued more for producing accurate travel time

estimates and good working schedules that leave enough time for travelling. There is much less early morning chaos.

Did the system provide an answer for everything? Not quite. There were some cases for which the system could not come up with a feasible solution, even though there were manual plans for home health care. Some home health aides were combining several tasks (e.g., doing laundry for three people at once).

Senior staff members initially created problems by trying to keep the more desirable tasks for themselves, leaving harder work for their newer colleagues. Laps Care eliminated this inequitable situation by creating the fairest possible schedule for everyone. Laps Care was so successful that it won the EURO Award 2003 for Excellence in Practice in Operations Research. Other organizations have adopted the system.

To Think About

1. How does Laps Care help home health care services make decisions?

2. What problems does it solve?

3. How does it provide value for these organizations and for their clients?

MIS in Action

Use Google, Yahoo!, or another search tool to find a listing for a home health agency in your city. Then visit the Web site for that agency. Next, use Google maps to determine the geographic area covered by that agency.

1. Considering the variety of services offered by the agency (gleaned from its Web site), how many health care workers do you think might be needed for one household that needed home health care?

2. Looking at the map of your city, do you feel there is value in a GIS like the Swedish one, for optimizing travel and care? Why or why not?

3. Develop a schedule for a home health care worker that would start with the worker at the agency's office picking up supplies and his schedule, and progressing through six home health care visits in an eight-hour workday. Describe how a GIS system could add value to an individual worker's day, and thus to the organization of home health-care workers in your city.

Sources: Patrik Eveborn, Patrik Flisberg, and Mikael Ronnqvist, "Laps," *European Journal of Operational Research*, pp. 962–976; and Optimal Solutions, "Laps Care," 2002, www.optimalsolutions.com, accessed September 15, 2007.

Web-Based Customer Decision-Support Systems

The growth of electronic commerce has encouraged many companies to develop DSS for customers who use Web information resources and capabilities for interactivity and personalization to help users select products and services. People are now using more information from multiple sources to make purchasing decisions (such as purchasing a car or computer) before they interact with the product or sales staff. For instance, nearly all automobile companies use customer decision-support systems that allow Web site visitors to configure their desired car. **Customer decision-support systems (CDSS)** support the decision-making process of an existing or potential customer. Computer companies such as Dell Computer do the same.

People interested in purchasing a product or service can use Internet search engines, intelligent agents, online catalogues, Web directories, newsgroup discussions, e-mail, and other tools to help them locate the information they need to help with their decision. Companies have developed specific customer Web sites where all the information, models, or other analytical tools for evaluating alternatives are concentrated in one location.

Web-based DSS have become especially popular in financial services because so many people are trying to manage their own assets and retirement savings. For example, RiskGrades.com, a Web site run by RiskMetrics Group, lets users input all their stock, bond, and mutual fund holdings to determine how much their portfolios might decline under various conditions. Users can see how the addition or subtraction of a holding might affect overall portfolio volatility and risk. Table 14-6 shows examples of Web-based DSS applications.

14.3 Executive Support Systems (ESS)

Executive support systems (*ESS*), which we introduced in Chapter 2, help managers with unstructured and semistructured problems by focusing on the information needs of senior management. Combining data from internal and external sources, ESS help senior executives monitor organizational performance, track activities of competitors, spot problems, identify opportunities, and forecast trends.

The Role of Executive Support Systems in the Firm

Use of ESS has migrated down several organizational levels so that the executive and subordinates are able to look at the same data in the same way. Today's systems try to avoid the problem of data overload because the data can be filtered or viewed in graphic format (if the user so chooses). ESS have the ability to **drill down**, moving from a piece of summary data to lower and lower levels of detail. The ability to drill down is useful not only to senior executives but also to employees at lower levels of the firm who need to analyze data. OLAP tools for analyzing large databases provide this capability.

Customer decision-support systems (CDSS)

Drill down

TABLE 14-6 *Examples of Web-Based DSS*

DSS	DESCRIPTION
Nikon Optical Canada	Web site allows a wide range of employees, including senior managers, marketing analysts, and sales representatives, to track sales activity of optical lenses purchased by practitioners, distributors, and optical laboratories across the Canadian territories. This enables Nikon to identify profitable customers for future sell-up opportunities, to track margins and areas of profitability, and to more effectively execute marketing campaigns.
TD Ameritrade	Web site features online, interactive tools application to help clients make decisions about bond investments. It provides information about bonds as investments and an interactive tool to show the effect of price and yield changes.
Bank of Montreal	Web site enables queries to run against the enterprise-wide database each day and delivers intuitive, drillable reports to senior executives, financial service managers, line-of-business mangers, branch employees, and HR personnel. The BMO MIND (Management Information-New Directions) CRM system can also perform CRM analyses to highlight accounts with low performance rates.

A major challenge of executive support systems has been to integrate data from systems designed for very different purposes so that senior executives can review organizational performance from a firm-wide perspective. Today, enterprise systems are able to provide managers with timely, comprehensive, and accurate firm-wide information. ESS based on such data can be considered logical extensions of enterprise system functionality.

Executives need a wide range of external data, from current stock market news to competitor information, industry trends, and even projected legislative action. Through their ESS, many managers have access to news services, financial market databases, economic information, and whatever other public data they may require.

Contemporary ESS include tools for modelling and analysis. With only a minimum of experience, most managers find they can use these tools to create graphic comparisons of data by time, region, product, price range, and so on. (While DSS use such tools primarily for modelling and analysis in a fairly narrow range of decision situations, ESS use them primarily to provide status information about organizational performance.)

ESS need to have some facility for environmental scanning. A key information requirement of managers at the strategic level is the ability to detect signals of problems in the organizational environment that indicate strategic threats and opportunities (Walls et al., 1992). The ESS need to be designed so that both external and internal sources of information can be used for environmental scanning purposes.

Business Value of Executive Support Systems

Much of the value of ESS is found in their flexibility and their ability to analyze, compare, and highlight trends. The easy use of graphics enables the user to look at more data in less time with greater clarity and insight than paper-based systems provide. Executives are using ESS to monitor key performance indicators for the entire firm and to measure firm performance against changes in the external environment. The timeliness and availability of the data result in needed actions being identified and carried out earlier than previously could have been done. Problems can be handled before they become too damaging; opportunities can also be identified earlier. These systems can thus help businesses move toward a "sense-and-respond" strategy.

A well-designed ESS could dramatically improve management performance and increase upper management's span of control. Immediate access to so much data increases executives' ability to monitor activities of lower units reporting to them. That very monitoring ability could enable decision making to be decentralized and to take place at lower operating levels. Executives are often willing to push decision making further down into the organization as long as they can be assured that all is going well. Alternatively, executive support systems based on enterprise-wide data could potentially increase management centralization, enabling senior executives to monitor the performance of subordinates across the company and to take appropriate action when conditions change.

Executive Support Systems and the Digital Firm

To illustrate the different ways in which an ESS can enhance decision making, we now describe important types of ESS applications for gathering business intelligence and monitoring corporate performance.

National Life: ESS for Business Intelligence Headquartered in Toronto, Canada, National Life markets life insurance, health insurance, and retirement/investment products to individuals and groups. The company has more than 370 employees in Toronto and its regional offices. National Life uses an executive information system based on Information Builders' WebFOCUS, which allows senior managers to access information from corporate databases through a Web interface. The system provides statistical reporting and the ability to drill down into current sales information, which is organized to show premium dollars by salesperson. Authorized users can drill down into these data to see the product, agent, and client for each sale. They can examine the data in many different ways—by region, by product, and by broker, accessing data for monthly, quarterly, and annual time periods (Information Builders, 2005).

Bonita Bay Properties and Nova Scotia Power: Monitoring Corporate Performance with Digital Dashboards and Balanced Scorecard Systems

ESS can be configured to summarize and report on key performance indicators for senior management in the form of a digital dashboard or "executive dashboard." The dashboard displays on a single screen all of the critical measurements for piloting a company, similar to the cockpit of an airplane or an automobile dashboard. The dashboard presents key performance indicators as graphs and charts in a Web browser format, providing a one-page overview of all the critical measurements necessary to make key executive decisions.

Bonita Bay Properties Inc., which develops planned communities centred around golf courses and fitness centres in southwest Florida, uses a digital dashboard to monitor daily business performance. Bonita Bay's managers are responsible for running the golf courses, clubhouses, restaurants, and fitness centres in these communities. Analytical tools from QlikTech International pull data from many different systems to populate dashboards with key performance indicators for senior executives and high-level operational managers. The dashboards display summaries from point-of-sale systems and general-ledger accounts to show how the business is performing on a daily basis and whether staffing levels are appropriate for the areas where the company is making its profits. Senior managers also drill down to compare the performance of fitness centres or to see whether activity on a golf course experiencing a slowdown has been picking up (Babcock, 2005).

Companies have traditionally measured value using financial metrics, such as return on investment (ROI), which we describe in Chapter 10. Many firms have implemented a **balanced scorecard** model that supplements traditional financial measures with measurements from additional perspectives, such as customers, internal business processes, and learning and growth. The goals and measures for the balanced scorecard vary from company to company. Companies are setting up information systems to populate the scorecard for management.

At Nova Scotia Power, Inc., the balanced scorecard (BSC) has been linked to many critical systems. For example, the annual business planning and budgeting process is now driven by the balanced scorecard. The new system is called the "Strategic Resource Allocation" because it provides the opportunity to display how resource allocation decisions directly influence the achievement of strategy. The scorecard is also linked to the incentive compensation system and has been cascaded throughout the company to ensure goal alignment at every level. Finally, and perhaps most importantly, the BSC is a powerful communication tool, signalling to everyone in the organization key success measures and how they can influence them.

Amsterdam-based ING Bank, which is part of the ING Group global financial services firm, adopted a balanced scorecard approach when it reorganized. Management wanted to shift from a product to a client orientation and develop appropriate performance indicators to measure progress in this new direction. In 1997, the bank built a Web-based BSC application using SAS tools for data warehousing and statistical analysis to measure 21 performance indicators. Data from the scorecard, from sources such as financial ledger applications and client retention and market penetration ratios, feed a central data warehouse. The data come from systems running on Lotus Notes, Microsoft Excel spreadsheets, and Oracle and DB2 databases. The data warehouse and BSC software run on IBM RS/6000 servers. ING initially made the BSC system available only to midrange executives in sales, but later extended it to 3000 users, including people at nearly every level of its relationship management group. Users regularly check progress with the scorecard. For example, by comparing how many visits they have made to different clients, sales people can make better decisions about how to allocate their time (Niven, 2006).

14.4 Group Decision-Support Systems (GDSS)

The DSS we have just described focus primarily on individual decision making. However, so much work is accomplished in groups within firms that a special category of systems called group decision-support systems (GDSS) has been developed to support group and organizational decision making.

Balanced scorecard

What Is a GDSS?

A **group decision-support system (GDSS)** is an interactive, computer-based system used to facilitate the solution of unstructured problems by a set of decision makers working together as a group. Tools for collaboration and Web-based conferencing described earlier in this text support some group decision processes, but their focus is primarily on communication. GDSS, however, provide tools and technologies geared explicitly toward group decision making and were developed in response to a growing concern over the quality and effectiveness of meetings. The underlying problems in group decision making have been the explosion of decision-maker meetings, the growing length of those meetings, and the increased number of attendees. Estimates on the amount of a manager's time spent in meetings range from 35 to 70 percent.

Components of GDSS GDSS make meetings more productive by providing tools to facilitate planning, generating, organizing, and evaluating ideas; establishing priorities; and documenting meeting proceedings for others in the firm. GDSS consist of three basic elements: hardware, software tools, and people. *Hardware* refers to the conference facility itself, including the room, the tables, and the chairs. Such a facility must be physically laid out in a manner that supports group collaboration. It also must include some electronic hardware, such as electronic display boards, as well as audiovisual, computer, and networking equipment.

GDSS *software tools* were originally developed for meetings in which all participants are in the same room, but they also can be used for networked meetings in which participants are in different locations. Specific GDSS software tools include the following:

- *Electronic questionnaires* aid the organizers in premeeting planning by identifying issues of concern and by helping to ensure that key planning information is not overlooked.
- *Electronic brainstorming* tools enable individuals, simultaneously and anonymously, to contribute ideas on the topics of the meeting.
- *Idea organizers* facilitate the organized integration and synthesis of ideas generated during brainstorming.
- *Questionnaire tools* support the facilitators and group leaders as they gather information before and during the process of setting priorities.
- *Tools for voting or setting priorities* make available a range of methods from simple voting, to ranking in order, to a range of weighted techniques for setting priorities or voting.
- *Stakeholder identification and analysis tools* use structured approaches to evaluate the impact of an emerging proposal on the organization and to identify stakeholders and evaluate the potential impact of those stakeholders on the proposed project.
- *Policy formation tools* provide structured support for developing agreement on the wording of policy statements.
- *Group dictionaries* document group agreement on definitions of words and terms central to the project.

People refers not only to the participants but also to a trained facilitator and often to a staff that supports the hardware and software. Together, these elements have led to the creation of a range of different kinds of GDSS, from simple electronic boardrooms to elaborate collaboration laboratories.

Overview of a GDSS Meeting

In a GDSS electronic meeting, each attendee has a workstation. The workstations are networked and connected to the facilitator's workstation and to the meeting's file server. All data that the attendees forward from their workstations to the group are collected and saved on the file server. Whiteboards are visible on either side of the projection screen. Many electronic meeting rooms have seating arrangements in semicircles and are tiered in legislative style to

Group decision-support system (GDSS)

FIGURE 14-10 *Group system tools*

The sequence of activities and collaborative support tools used in an electronic meeting system facilitate communication among attendees and generate a full record of the meeting.

Source: From Nunamaker et al., "Electronic Meeting Systems to Support Group Work," *Communications of the ACM*, July 1991. Reprinted by permission.

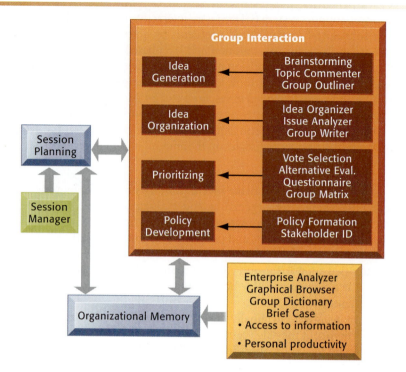

accommodate a large number of attendees. The facilitator controls the use of tools during the meeting.

Attendees have full control of their own desktop computers. During the meeting, all input to the integrated screens is saved on the file server, and participants' work is kept confidential. When the meeting is completed, a full record of the meeting (both raw material and resultant output) is available to the attendees and can be made available to anyone else with a need for access. Figure 14-10 illustrates the sequence of activities at a typical electronic meeting along with the types of tools used and the output of those tools.

Business Value of GDSS

Studies show that in traditional decision-making meetings without GDSS support, the optimal meeting size is three to five attendees. Beyond that size, the meeting process begins to break down. Studies show that, with the use of GDSS software, the number of attendees at a meeting can increase while productivity also increases. One reason for this is that attendees contribute simultaneously rather than one at a time, which makes more efficient use of meeting time.

A GDSS contributes to a more collaborative atmosphere by guaranteeing contributors' anonymity. Attendees can contribute without fear of personal criticism or that their ideas will be rejected because of the identity of the contributor. GDSS software tools follow structured methods for organizing and evaluating ideas and for preserving the results of meetings, enabling nonattendees to locate needed information after the meeting. The documentation of a meeting by one group at one site can also be used as input to another meeting on the same project at another site.

If properly designed and supported, GDSS meetings can increase the number of ideas generated and the quality of decisions while producing the desired results in fewer meetings in both face-to-face and distributed meeting environments (Anson and Munkvold, 2004). However, GDSS outcomes are not necessarily better than face-to-face meetings, and electronic brainstorming has not been widely adopted (Dennis and Reinicke, 2004). GDSS seem most useful for tasks involving idea generation, complex problems, and large groups (Fjermestad and Hiltz, 2000–2001, 1998–1999).

A GDSS can be configured in an almost infinite variety of ways, and the nature of electronic meeting technology is only one of a number of factors that affect meeting processes and output. The outcome of group meetings depends on the composition of the group, the manner in which the problem is presented to the group, the facilitator's effectiveness, the organization's culture and environment, the quality of the planning, the cooperation of the attendees, and the appropriateness of tools selected for different types of meetings and decision problems (Dennis and Wixom, 2001–2002; Dennis, Wixom, and Vandenberg, 2001; Hender, Dean, Rodgers, and Nunamaker, 2002).

Summary

1. Describe different types of decisions and the decision-making process.

The different levels in an organization (strategic, management, operational) have different decision-making requirements. Decisions can be structured, semistructured, or unstructured, with structured decisions clustering at the operational level of the organization and unstructured decisions at the strategic level. Decision making can be performed by individuals or groups and includes employees as well as operational, middle, and senior managers. There are four stages in decision making: intelligence, design, choice, and implementation. Systems to support decision making do not always produce manager and employee decisions that improve firm performance because of problems with information quality, management filters, and organizational inertia.

2. Assess how information systems support the activities of managers and management decision making.

Several different models of what managers actually do in organizations show how information systems can be used for managerial support. Early classical models of managerial activities stress the functions of planning, organizing, coordinating, deciding, and controlling. Contemporary research looking at the actual behaviour of managers has found that managers' real activities are highly fragmented, variegated, and brief in duration, with managers moving rapidly from one issue to another. Managers spend considerable time pursuing personal agendas and goals, and contemporary managers shy away from making grand, sweeping policy decisions.

Information technology provides new tools for managers to carry out both their traditional and newer roles, enabling them to monitor, plan, and forecast with more precision and speed than ever before and to respond more rapidly to the changing business environment. Information systems have been most helpful to managers by providing support for their roles in disseminating information, providing liaisons between organizational levels, and allocating resources. However, some managerial roles cannot be supported by information systems, and information systems are less successful at supporting unstructured decisions.

3. Demonstrate how decision-support systems (DSS) differ from MIS and how they provide value to the business.

Management information systems (MIS) provide information on firm performance to help managers monitor and control the business, often in the form of fixed regularly scheduled reports based on data summarized from the firm's transaction processing systems. MIS support structured decisions and some semistructured decisions.

Decision-support systems (DSS) combine data, sophisticated analytical models and tools, and user-friendly software into a single powerful system that can support semistructured or unstructured decision making. The components of a DSS are the DSS database, the user interface, and the DSS software system. There are two kinds of DSS: model-driven DSS and data-driven DSS. DSS can help support decisions for pricing, supply chain management, and customer relationship management as well as model alternative business scenarios. DSS targeted toward customers as well as managers are becoming available on the Web. A special category of DSS called geographic information systems (GIS) uses data visualization technology to analyze and display data for planning and decision making with digitized maps.

4. Demonstrate how executive support systems (ESS) help senior managers make better decisions.

Executive support systems (ESS) help senior managers with unstructured problems that occur at the strategic level of the firm. ESS provide data from both internal and external sources and provide a generalized computing and communications environment that can be focused and applied to a changing array of problems. ESS help senior executives monitor firm performance, spot problems, identify opportunities, and forecast trends. These systems can filter out extraneous details for high-level overviews, or they can drill down to provide senior managers with detailed transaction data if required. ESS take advantage of firm-wide data provided by enterprise systems.

ESS help senior managers analyze, compare, and highlight trends so that the managers may more easily monitor organizational performance or identify strategic problems and opportunities. They are very useful for environmental scanning, providing business intelligence to help management detect strategic threats or opportunities from the organization's environment. ESS can increase the span of control of senior management, allowing them to oversee more people with fewer resources.

5. *Evaluate the role of information systems in helping people working in a group make decisions more efficiently.*

People working together in a group can use group decision-support systems to help them in the process of arriving at a decision. Group decision-support systems (GDSS) have hardware, software, and people components. Hardware components consist of the conference room facilities, including seating arrangements and computer and other electronic hardware. Software components include tools for organizing ideas, gathering information, ranking and setting priorities, and documenting meeting sessions. People components include participants, a trained facilitator, and staff to support the hardware and software.

A GDSS helps decision makers meeting together to arrive at a decision more efficiently and is especially useful for increasing the productivity of meetings of more than four or five people. However, the effectiveness of a GDSS is contingent on the composition of the group, the task, appropriate tool selection and meeting support, and the organizational context of the meeting.

Key Terms

Balanced scorecard,   488

Behavioural models of management,   473

Choice,   472

Classical model of management,   473

Customer decision-support systems (CDSS),   486

Data visualization,   483

Data-driven DSS,   476

Decisional roles,   473

Design,   472

Drill down,   486

DSS database,   477

DSS software system,   477

Geographic information systems (GIS),   483

Group decision-support systems (GDSS),   489

Implementation,   472

Informational roles,   473

Intelligence,   472

Interpersonal roles,   473

Managerial roles,   473

Model,   477

Pivot table,   479

Semistructured decisions,   471

Sensitivity analysis,   477

Structured decisions,   470

Unstructured decisions,   470

Review Questions

1. *What are the different decision-making levels and decision-making constituencies in organizations? How do their decision-making requirements differ?*

2. *What is the difference between an unstructured, semistructured, and structured decision?*

3. *List and describe the stages in decision making.*

4. *Compare the descriptions of managerial behaviour in the classical and behavioural models.*

5. *Which specific managerial roles can information systems support? Where are information systems particularly strong in supporting managers, and where are they weak?*

6. *What is the difference between a decision-support system (DSS) and a management information system (MIS)?*

7. *What is the difference between a data-driven DSS and a model-driven DSS? Give examples.*

8. *What are the three basic components of a DSS? Briefly describe each.*

9. *How can DSS help firms with supply chain management and customer relationship management? How do DSS provide value for a business?*

10. *What is a geographic information system (GIS)? How does it use data visualization technology? How can it support decision making?*

11. *What is a customer decision-support system? How can the Internet be used for this purpose?*

12. *Define and describe the capabilities of an executive support system (ESS).*

13. *How do ESS enhance managerial decision making? How do they provide value for a business?*

14. *What is a group decision-support system (GDSS)? How does it differ from a DSS? What underlying problems in group decision making led to the development of GDSS?*

15. *Describe the three elements of a GDSS and five GDSS software tools.*

16. *How can GDSS provide value for a business?*

Discussion Questions

1. *As a manager or user of information systems, what would you need to know to participate in the design and use of a DSS or an ESS? Why?*

2. *If businesses used DSS, GDSS, and ESS more widely, would managers and employees make better decisions? Why or why not?*

3. *Do you believe your school uses any form of decision support systems? What are they? What do they do? Do you think they are data-driven or model-driven? How do they help your school achieve its objectives?*

4. *What do you think would be the obstacles to implementing group decision support systems? How can these obstacles be overcome?*

Teamwork: Designing a University GDSS

With three or four of your classmates, identify several groups in your university that could benefit from a GDSS. Design a GDSS for one of those groups, describing its hardware, software, and people elements. If possible, use electronic presentation software to present your findings to the class.

Learning Track Module

Building and Using Pivot Tables. This Learning Track Module is a full chapter with complete instructions on how to build and use Excel PivotTables. You can find it on MyMISLab for this chapter.

For online exercises, please visit www.pearsoned.ca/mymislab.

HANDS-ON MIS   Application Exercises

The projects in this section give you hands-on experience using spreadsheet software to analyze the impact of changes in prices of component parts on production costs for a real-world company, using a spreadsheet pivot table to analyze sales data and using online retirement planning tools for financial planning.

Improving Decision Making:
Analyzing the Impact of Component Price Changes

Software skills: Spreadsheet formulas, two-variable data table
Business skills: Manufacturing bill of materials sensitivity analysis

A bill of materials is used in manufacturing and production to show all the parts and materials required to manufacture a specific item or for the subassembly of a finished product, such as a motorcycle. The information in the bill of materials is useful for determining product costs, coordinating orders, and managing inventory. It can also show how product costs will be affected by price changes in components or raw materials. This project provides you with an opportunity to use spreadsheet software to perform a sensitivity analysis showing the impact of various prices for component parts on the total costs of a dirt bike. The bill of materials for this project has been simplified for instructional purposes.

Dirt Bikes Canada's management has asked you to explore the impact of changes in some of its parts components on production costs. Review the following bill of materials information for the brake system for Dirt Bikes Canada's Moto 300 model.

The completed bill of materials contains the description of the component, the identification number of each component, the supplier (source) of the component, the unit cost of each component, the quantity of each component needed to make each finished brake system, the extended cost of each component, and the total materials cost. The extended cost is calculated by multiplying the quantity of each component needed to produce the finished brake system by the unit cost. The prices of components are constantly changing, and you will need to develop a spreadsheet application that can show management the impact of such price changes on the cost to produce each brake system and on total production costs for the Moto 300 model.

1. Complete the bill of materials by calculating the extended cost of each component and the total materials cost for each brake system.
2. Develop a sensitivity analysis to show the impact on total brake system materials costs if the front brake calipers unit cost ranges from $103 to $107 and if the brake pipe unit cost ranges from $27 to $30.
3. The brake system represents 30 percent of the total materials cost for one Moto 300 motorcycle. Use sensitivity analysis again to show the impact of the changes in front brake caliper unit costs and brake pipe unit costs described previously on total materials costs for this motorcycle model.

Bill of Materials: Moto 300 Brake System

Component	Component No.	Source	Unit Cost	Quantity	Extended Cost
Brake cable	M0593	Nissin	$27.81	1	
Brake pedal	M0546	Harrison Billet	$6.03	2	
Brake pad	M3203	Russell	$27.05	2	
Front brake pump	M0959	Brembo	$66.05	1	
Rear brake pump	M4739	Brembo	$54.00	1	
Front brake caliper	M5930	Nissin	$105.20	1	
Rear brake caliper	M7942	Nissin	$106.78	1	
Front brake disc	M3920	Russell	$143.80	1	
Rear brake disc	M0588	Russell	$56.42	1	
Brake pipe	M0943	Harrison Billet	$28.52	1	
Brake lever cover	M1059	Brembo	$2.62	1	

Improving Decision Making: Using Pivot Tables to Analyze Sales Data

Software skills: Pivot tables
Business skills: Analyzing sales data

This project gives you an opportunity to learn how to use Excel's PivotTable functionality to analyze a database or data list.

Use the data list for Online Management Training Inc. described earlier in the chapter (OMT List.xls). This is a list of the sales transactions at OMT for one day. You can find this spreadsheet file on MyMISLab for this chapter.

Use Excel's PivotTable to help you answer the following questions:

1. Where are the average purchases higher? The answer might tell managers where to focus marketing and sales resources or pitch different messages to different regions.
2. What form of payment is the most common? The answer could be used to emphasize in advertising the most preferred means of payment.
3. Are there any times of day when purchases are most common? Do people buy products while at work (likely during the day) or at home (likely in the evening)?
4. What is the relationship between region, type of product purchased, and average sales price?

If you need instruction on how to use Excel PivotTables, see MyMISLab for Chapter 14.

Improving Decision Making:
Using a Web-Based DSS for Retirement Planning

Software skills: Internet-based software
Business skills: Financial planning

This project will help develop your skills in using Web-based DSS for financial planning. The Web site for TD Waterhouse (www.tdcanadatrust.com/planning/yrs.jsp) provides Web-based DSS for financial planning and decision making. Use this site to determine how much you need to save to have enough income for your retirement. Assume that you are 50 years old and plan to retire in 16 years. You have one dependent and $100 000 in savings. Your current annual income is $85 000. Your goal is to be able to generate an annual retirement income of $60 000, including all pension benefit payments. Use the Web site to determine how much money you need to save to help you achieve your retirement goal. Then critique the site—its ease of use, its clarity, the value of any conclusions reached, and the extent to which the site helps investors understand their financial needs and the financial markets.

CASE STUDY Can Decision Support Systems Make Your Health Care Better?

Imagine that you have just been admitted to the hospital with a blood clot in your leg. You are already taking Tagamet for treating ulcers. The hospital prescribes Coumadin to dissolve the clot. You refuse to take the medicine until someone double-checks the prescription to make sure there will be no adverse interaction with your other medication. In the end, you learn that you were correct. The Tagament interacts adversely with the Coumadin, leading to excess blood thinning and bleeding, and you must stop taking the Tagament until your blood clot has dissolved.

Or suppose you report to the emergency room (ER) of your local hospital because you feel very unwell. At the ER, a nurse or doctor (typically a nurse) assesses you to prioritize where in the roster of patients to place you. How does the nurse know what questions to ask you and which questions to ask as follow-up? What if the nurse is having a bad day and wrongly assesses your condition? You could be in the middle of a heart attack, or your ulcer could have just perforated—and in Canada's strapped medical system, you might wait hours to be seen by a physician.

Last summer, one author waited in an emergency room for seven and a half hours to be seen for acute abdominal pain. While she was waiting, a patient came in by ambulance who had only broken a finger (this patient was immobile due to having had a stroke several years previously, hence the ambulance). Because the other patient came in by ambulance, he went ahead in the queue. The doctor who finally saw the author told her that she had not been properly "triaged"—triage is the term for evaluating and ranking patients in order of severity of medical problem.

Shouldn't there be a system to assist triage nurses in evaluating patients and assigning places in the ER queue? It turns out there are such systems in Canada.

In Ottawa, a potential ER patient is urged to call a nurse, on call for the purpose, and describe symptoms. The "telenurse" then advises the patient on care, such as going to the ER, calling a personal physician, or reporting to a clinic the next day (if the call is at night, as many are).

Just last year, as part of a master's thesis, a computerized cardiac teletriage decision-support system was developed and tested at the University of Ottawa Heart Institute. There, nurse coordinators receive more than 1500 calls annually from patients requesting advice for cardiology and cardiac surgery concerns. Until last year, there was no standardized protocol to guide the nurse coordinators, nor did they receive any formal training.

To set up the DSS, cardiac best practice algorithms, or "rules-of-thumb," were programmed into a handheld device to be used by the telenurses. Before the DSS was introduced, the nurses used only a pen and pad of paper while on the phone with the patient. Using the DSS in the test experimental phase, the quality of assessment for each type of cardiac-related scenario improved significantly. Hopefully, a successful triage decision-support system can be developed soon to help in Canada's real emergency rooms. The worry of health care professionals is that they will rely too much on the DSS and not enough on their own training as to what questions to ask and what recommendations to make.

However, Canadian health care seems to be moving toward taking more advantage of decision-support systems across the realm of health care.

At five hospitals in Canada, children who use prosthetic arms and legs answer a DSS-based questionnaire as to how they use their prostheses. The DSS even uses an animated puffin ("PUFI") to offer encouragement, clarify words, and assure parents and children that they're "doing great." The DSS then aggregates the data so that clinicians can analyze how well the children are using their prosthetics and see whether more prosthetics training is required. More than 12 hospital sites around the world are using this system, including three in the U.K., and others in Australia, Holland, Sweden, and Slovenia. Children's answers from around the world are added to the database, enabling clinicians to better advise children and parents on how to maximize the functionality of their prostheses.

At Toronto's University Health Network (UHN), made up of Toronto General Hospital, Toronto Western Hospital, and Princess Margaret Hospital, Katherine Henning, head of performance measurement, and project manager Janine Kaye, use a data warehouse to make sense of reams of data from an assortment of databases, including hospital records, pathology, pharmacy, physician order entry, and patient satisfaction. UHN has used a data warehouse since 2000 and has data as old as 1987. "We now have data coming in from as many as 15 transactional systems," says Kaye. "And we have about 40 people accessing that data through an Oracle reporting tool." Henning says that UHN has only about one-third of the data inputs they hope to have in the system. Next to be added to the data warehouse are nursing data and operating room data.

Beverly Delaney, director of administrative informational systems at UHN, says: "We use our decision-support system (from Eclipsys) for all of our medical records reporting, for financial and performance analysis, for utilization management, for quality indicators, and essentially for any function that needs to look at integrated data. But the challenges we have faced in implementing all that have not been technical. We've rarely had a major technical issue. Most of our challenges have been cultural. . . . We've recently integrated with four other campuses. And most of them have long histories of doing things their own way. In the process, we've found that the ability and willingness of people to standardize their data is the biggest challenge. And they've got to be willing if a decision-support tool is to ever be truly useful to everybody."

UHN is in the process of "Webifying" their DSS, to give users faster access to data through the intranet. In doing so, administrators also hope to give users multiple views of the same data, so that they can confirm for themselves what the data show. The various views of the same data should also help to show any inaccuracies in the data, leading to correcting data and to a better overall DSS.

In Montreal, a system named MOXXI (Medical Offices of the XXIst Century) is also using integration to reduce adverse drug interactions. In 2003, Montreal physicians begin using Pocket PCs with high-speed wireless network cards to access patient charts and send drug prescriptions electronically to pharmacies, where the prescriptions are automatically integrated into the pharmacy software. The system connects more than 30 physicians, 12 000 patients, and 31 pharmacies in Montreal. "We've tried to set it up so that no matter what pharmacy the patient visited, the system would be able to retrieve electronic prescriptions and send information about prescriptions dispensed," says Dr. Robyn Tamblyn, director of the MOXXI project. Patients can pick at a moment's notice to which pharmacy they go. And because it is electronic, pharmacists do not receive illegible handwritten prescriptions, but instead receive encrypted documents with all the information they need. Of course, to facilitate this system, Quebec had to pass legislation making digital signatures legal. It is the ability of information systems to integrate data and to provide access to that data from a variety of places that permits the integration of health care information and health care services.

Sources: Kirsten C. Somoza, "A Computerized Cardiac Teletriage Decision Support System: Effects on Nurse Performance," **http://hot.carleton.ca/hot-topics/articles/cardiac-teletriage**, accessed May 8, 2007; Andy Shaw, "Organizations Work to Improve Coding of Clinical Data," **www.canhealth.com/nov03.html**, accessed May 8, 2007; Neil Zeidenberg, "New Software Tracks How Children Use Their Prosthesis Over Time," **www.canhealth.com/nov03.html**, accessed May 8, 2007; Andy Shaw, "Decision Support Systems Can Help Hospitals Reduce Costs amd Improve Patient Care," **www.canhealth.com/nov03.html**, accessed May 8, 2007; and Neil Zeidenberg, "Wireless Handheld Computers Enable Doctors to Prescribe at Point of Care," **www.canhealth.com/nov03.html**, accessed May 8, 2007.

CASE STUDY QUESTIONS

1. What problems are hospitals and physicians encountering in diagnosing diseases and prescribing medications? What management, organization, and technology factors are responsible for these problems?

2. Are DSS appropriate solutions? Why or why not? What management, technology, and organization issues are involved in the use of these systems?

3. What obstacles prevent computer systems from improving the medical industry? How can these obstacles be removed?

CHAPTER 15

Managing Knowledge

LEARNING OBJECTIVES

After completing this chapter, you will be able to do the following:

1. Assess the role of knowledge management and knowledge management programs in business.

2. Describe the types of systems used for enterprise-wide knowledge management and demonstrate how they provide value for organizations.

3. Describe the major types of knowledge work systems and assess how they provide value for firms.

4. Evaluate the business benefits of using intelligent techniques for knowledge management.

OPENING **CASE** | Content Management for the Royal Canadian Mint: How to Maximize Your Web Presence

The Royal Canadian Mint (RCM) does not just produce coins for Canada; it manufactures coins on contract for many other countries, too. The Mint also manufactures commemorative Canadian collector coins, a jewellery and watch collection, and customized products including medals and tokens. It sells these products through a variety of channels. Recently, the Mint recognized the need to market online through an e-commerce site and to integrate the diverse content found in its legacy enterprise resource planning (ERP) systems.

Operating since 1908 and employing more than 700 people today, the Mint is a for-profit Crown corporation. Toward this end, the Mint employs a network of dealers and distributors around the world.

Once the Mint's management decided on a Web site not only to promote its products but also to enhance the efforts of its sales force, the challenges were all too apparent. Not only did the site have to be technically sophisticated so that it could produce personalized content for a variety of visitors and administer product catalogues, the site would also have to integrate with the order fulfillment systems that were on a variety of platforms. To process orders and fulfill sophisticated reporting requirements, the Web site would need to link with legacy systems. Oh yes, and the system had to operate in both English and French.

"We wanted every visitor to the Mint's site to become a customer by [our] offering them a comfortable shopping experience with rich search offerings and intuitive transactional processing capabilities," said Diane Plouffe Reardon, executive director of communications at the Mint. Until this project, the Mint had used outsourcers to create, maintain, and

host their Web site, first developed in 1995. But working with outsourcers meant updates were costly and seldom done in a timely manner.

Content management is a substantial market, with about $1.16 billion in software globally and an extra $2.9 billion in services, according to the Gartner Group. As part of its traditional strategy of buying companies to acquire their technology, in 2001 Microsoft bought NCompass, a Vancouver-based Web content management company. NCompass' main product is Resolution, which has been rolled into Microsoft's Content Management Server.

Realizing it could not redevelop its Web site on its own, the Mint worked with Proximi-T, an IT consulting firm, to network with other vendors, primarily Microsoft, and develop an enterprise solution to manage the content of the redesigned Web site. Using Microsoft BizTake Server 2000, the Mint was able to use XML to extract and convert detailed

product information. Today, visitors access personalized pages that deliver only content that is based on their preferences. Microsoft's content management tools let non-technical writers and staff update online content easily.

Before being converted to the new, user-friendly edition, the Mint's Web site held 4000 pages, half in English and half in French. "Prior to the use of Web content management software, every page was hard-coded in HTML," says Michael Toope, Web site coordinator. "Even fixing a typo required the work of a programmer." Mint staff also had to pick up orders manually online, but today the orders are fed directly into an order-entry system.

Sources: Grace Casselman, "Growing Like a Weed," **www.backbonemag.com/ Magazine/E+Trends_07060601.asp**, accessed May 8, 2007; and Microsoft, "Case Study: The Royal Canadian Mint," **www.microsoft.com/ canada/casestudies/royal_canadian_mint.mspx?pf=true**, accessed May 8, 2007.

The Royal Canadian Mint's experience shows how organizational performance can benefit by making organizational knowledge more easily available. By organizing its knowledge about how to buy from the Mint, whether the buyer is a Canadian individual or a foreign government, the Mint has increased its efficiency and ability to serve customers.

The chapter-opening Business Challenges diagram calls attention to important points raised by this case and this chapter. The Mint is highly customer-focused. Much of the essential information and knowledge that should have been available to the customer was not easily accessible because it was stored in many different documents and legacy systems. Delays in accessing vital information created inefficiencies that impaired the Mint's business performance, including its response to customers. In order to benefit from enterprise content management technology, the Mint had to integrate its Web site and Web store with its legacy systems. This integration took a great deal of time and effort. By making content management user-friendly and efficient, the new system has made the Mint much more efficient and profitable.

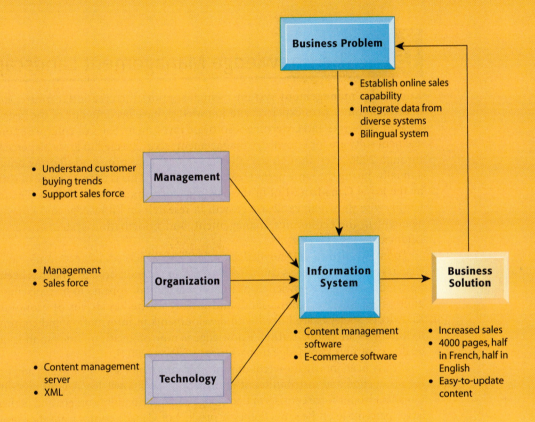

Business Problem
- Establish online sales capability
- Integrate data from diverse systems
- Bilingual system

Management
- Understand customer buying trends
- Support sales force

Organization
- Management
- Sales force

Technology
- Content management server
- XML

Information System
- Content management software
- E-commerce software

Business Solution
- Increased sales
- 4000 pages, half in French, half in English
- Easy-to-update content

HEADS UP

Collaborating and communicating with practitioners and experts, creating new knowledge, facilitating access to knowledge, and using that knowledge to improve business processes and decision making have become vital to organizational innovation and survival. This chapter shows how you and your firm can benefit from information systems for knowledge management.

- If your career is in finance and accounting, you may use rule-based expert systems for evaluating the credit risk of loan applicants and for investment portfolio selection, and you may use neural networks for securities trading and for detecting credit card fraud.

- If your career is in human resources, you will run employee training programs to help employees use knowledge management systems and may be responsible for operating the firm's learning management systems.

- If your career is in information systems, you will be evaluating software for knowledge management applications and intelligent techniques as well as helping business professionals classify and organize knowledge for knowledge management systems.

- If your career is in manufacturing, production, or operations management, you will use knowledge work and group collaboration tools for creating and sharing product design and manufacturing specifications, and you may also use expert and

case-based reasoning systems for diagnostic and repair work.

- If your career is in sales and marketing, you will use corporate portals and repositories for structured and unstructured knowledge to access and share information about customers, sales leads, competitors, and changes in product pricing and specifications.

15.1   The Knowledge Management Landscape

Knowledge management systems, which support the creation, capture, storage, and dissemination of firm expertise and knowledge, have become one of the fastest-growing areas of corporate and government software investment. Sales of enterprise content management software for knowledge management were expected to grow 35 percent annually through 2006, even though overall software sales are projected to grow only 6 percent annually during the same period (eMarketer, 2003). This is the same type of software used by the Royal Canadian Mint in the opening discussion for this chapter. The past decade has likewise shown an explosive growth in research on knowledge and knowledge management in the economics, management, and information systems fields (Alavi and Leidner, 2001; Cole, 1998).

Today we live in a "knowledge society" in which social, economic, and political changes are taking place as countries move from the industrial to what has been called the post-industrial age. Knowledge, or intellectual capital, appears to be replacing more tangible assets, such as labour, land, and money as the key driver of economic growth. Knowledge societies are linked with developments in information and communications technologies and globalization. Knowledge is now innovation, innovation is quality, and quality control is knowledge management (Gilbert, 2007).

We live in an information economy in which the major source of wealth and prosperity is the production and distribution of information and knowledge. A large percentage of the Canadian labour force consists of knowledge and information workers, and perhaps an even larger percentage of the gross domestic product of Canada comes from the knowledge and information sectors, such as banking and finance, accounting, insurance, and publishing.

Knowledge management has become an important theme at many large business firms as managers realize that much of their firm's value depends on the firm's ability to create and manage knowledge. Studies have found that a substantial part of a firm's stock market value is related to its intangible assets, of which knowledge is one important component, along with brands, reputations, and unique business processes (Gu and Lev, 2001). Well-executed knowledge-based projects have been known to produce extraordinary returns on investment although knowledge-based investments are difficult to measure (Blair and Wallman, 2001).

Important Dimensions of Knowledge

There is an important distinction between data, information, knowledge, and wisdom. Chapter 1 defines **data** as a flow of events or transactions captured by an organization's systems that, by itself, is useful for transacting but little else. To turn data into useful *information*, a firm must expend resources to organize data into categories of understanding, such as monthly, daily, regional, or store-based reports of total sales. To transform

Knowledge management
  systems
Data

information into **knowledge**, a firm must expend additional resources to discover patterns, rules, and contexts where the knowledge works. Finally, **wisdom** is thought to be the collective and individual experience of applying knowledge to the solution of problems. Wisdom involves where, when, and how to apply knowledge.

Knowledge is both an individual attribute and a collective attribute of the firm. Knowledge is a cognitive, even a physiological, event, that takes place inside peoples' heads. It is also stored in libraries and records, shared in lectures, and stored by firms in the form of business processes and employee know-how. Undocumented knowledge residing in the minds of employees is called **tacit knowledge** while knowledge that has been documented is called **explicit knowledge**. Knowledge can reside in e-mail, voice mail, graphics, and unstructured documents as well as structured documents. Knowledge is generally believed to have a location, either in the minds of humans or in specific business processes. Knowledge is "sticky" and not universally applicable or easily moved. Finally, knowledge is thought to be situational and contextual. For example, you must know when to perform a procedure as well as how to perform it. Table 15-1 reviews these dimensions of knowledge.

We can see that knowledge is a different kind of firm asset from, say, buildings and financial assets; that knowledge is a complex phenomenon; and that there are many aspects to the process of managing knowledge.

We can also recognize that knowledge-based core competencies of firms—the two or three things that an organization does best—are key organizational assets. Knowing how to do things effectively and efficiently in ways that other organizations cannot duplicate is a primary source of profit and competitive advantage that cannot be purchased easily by competitors in the marketplace.

For instance, having a unique build-to-order production system constitutes a form of knowledge and perhaps a unique asset that other firms cannot copy easily. With knowledge, firms become more efficient and effective in their use of scarce resources. Without knowledge, firms become less efficient and less effective in their use of resources and ultimately fail.

Organizational Learning and Knowledge Management Like humans, organizations create and gather knowledge using a variety of organizational learning mechanisms. Through collection of data, careful measurement of planned activities, trial and error (experimentation), and feedback from customers and the environment in general,

Knowledge
Wisdom
Tacit knowledge
Explicit knowledge

TABLE 15-1 *Important Dimensions of Knowledge*

KNOWLEDGE IS A FIRM ASSET	Knowledge is an intangible asset.
	The transformation of data into useful information and knowledge requires organizational resources.
	Knowledge is not subject to the law of diminishing returns as are physical assets, but instead experiences network effects as its value increases as more people share it.
KNOWLEDGE HAS DIFFERENT FORMS	Knowledge can be either tacit or explicit (codified).
	Knowledge involves know-how, craft, and skill.
	Knowledge involves knowing how to follow procedures.
	Knowledge involves knowing why, not simply when, things happen (causality).
KNOWLEDGE HAS A LOCATION	Knowledge is a cognitive event involving mental models and maps of individuals.
	There is both a social and an individual basis of knowledge.
	Knowledge is "sticky" (hard to move), situated (enmeshed in a firm's culture), and contextual (works only in certain situations).
KNOWLEDGE IS SITUATIONAL	Knowledge is conditional: Knowing when to apply a procedure is just as important as knowing the procedure (conditional).
	Knowledge is related to context: You must know how to use a certain tool and under what circumstances.

organizations gain experience. Organizations that learn will adjust their behaviour to reflect that learning by creating new business processes and by changing patterns of management decision making. This process of change is called **organizational learning**. Arguably, organizations that can sense and respond to their environments rapidly will survive longer than organizations that have poor learning mechanisms.

The Knowledge Management Value Chain

Knowledge management refers to the set of business processes developed in an organization to create, store, transfer, and apply knowledge. Knowledge management increases the ability of the organization to learn from its environment and to incorporate knowledge into its business processes. Figure 15-1 illustrates the five value-adding steps in the knowledge management value chain. Each stage in the value chain adds value to raw data and information as they are transformed into usable knowledge.

In Figure 15-1, a shaded box divides information systems activities and related management and organizational activities, with information systems activities on the top of the graphic and organizational and management activities below. One apt slogan of the knowledge management field is "Effective knowledge management is 80 percent managerial and organizational, and 20 percent technology."

In Chapter 1, we define *organizational and management capital* as the set of business processes, culture, and behaviour required to obtain value from investments in information systems. In the case of knowledge management, as with other information systems investments, supportive values, structures, and behaviour patterns must be built to maximize the return on investment in knowledge management projects. In Figure 15-1, the management and organizational activities in the lower half of the diagram represent the investment in organizational capital required to obtain substantial returns on the information technology (IT) investments and systems shown in the top half of the diagram.

Organizational learning
Knowledge management

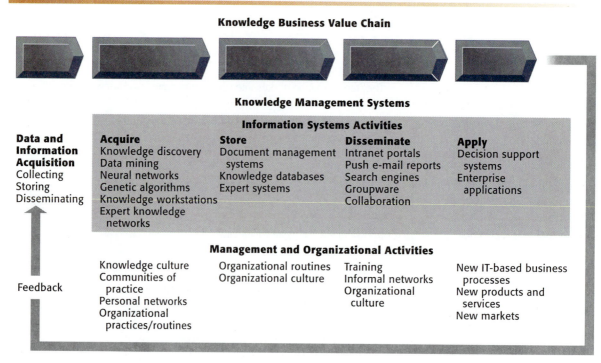

FIGURE 15-1   *The knowledge management value chain*

Knowledge management today involves both information systems activities and a host of enabling management and organizational activities.

Knowledge Acquisition Organizations acquire knowledge in a number of ways, depending on the type of knowledge they seek. The first knowledge management systems sought to build corporate repositories of documents, reports, presentations, and best practices. These efforts have been extended to include unstructured documents (such as e-mail). In other cases, organizations acquire knowledge by developing online expert networks so that employees can "find the expert" in the company who has the knowledge in his or her head.

In still other cases, firms must create new knowledge by discovering patterns in corporate data or by using knowledge workstations where engineers can discover new knowledge. These various efforts are described throughout this chapter. A coherent and organized knowledge system also requires systematic data from the firm's transaction processing systems that track sales, payments, inventory, customers, and other vital data, as well as data from external sources such as news feeds, industry reports, legal opinions, scientific research, and government statistics.

Knowledge Storage Once they are discovered, documents, patterns, and expert rules must be stored so they can be retrieved and used by employees. Knowledge storage generally involves the creation of a database. Document management systems that digitize, index, and tag documents according to a coherent framework are large databases adept at storing collections of documents. Expert systems also help corporations preserve the knowledge that is acquired by incorporating that knowledge into organizational processes and culture. Each of these is discussed later in this chapter.

Management must support the development of planned knowledge storage systems, encourage the development of corporate-wide schemas for indexing documents, and reward employees for taking the time to update and store documents properly. For instance, it would reward the sales force for submitting names of prospects to a shared corporate database of prospects where all sales personnel can identify each prospect and review the stored knowledge.

Knowledge Dissemination Portal, e-mail, instant messaging, and search engine technology have added to an existing array of collaboration technologies and office systems for sharing calendars, documents, data, and graphics (see Chapter 7). Contemporary technology seems to have created a deluge of information and knowledge.

How can managers and employees discover, in a sea of information and knowledge, that which is really important for their decisions and their work? Here, training programs, informal networks, and shared management experience communicated through a supportive culture help managers focus their attention on the important knowledge and information.

Knowledge Application Regardless of what type of knowledge management system is involved, knowledge that is not shared and applied to the practical problems facing firms and managers does not add business value. To provide a return on investment, organizational knowledge must become a systematic part of management decision making and become situated in decision-support systems (described in Chapter 14). Ultimately, new knowledge must be built into a firm's business processes and key application systems, including enterprise applications for managing key internal business processes and relationships with customers and suppliers. Management supports this process by creating—based on new knowledge— new business practices, new products and services, and new markets for the firm.

Building Organizational and Management Capital: Collaboration, Communities of Practice, and Office Environments In addition to the activities we have just described, managers can help by developing new organizational roles and responsibilities for the acquisition of knowledge, including the creation of chief knowledge officer executive positions, dedicated staff positions (knowledge managers), and communities of practice. The **chief knowledge officer (CKO)** is a senior executive who is responsible for the firm's knowledge management program. The CKO helps design programs and systems to find new sources of knowledge or to make better use of existing knowledge in organizational and management processes.

Chief knowledge officer (CKO)

Communities of practice (COPs) are informal social networks of professionals and employees within and outside the firm who have similar work-related activities and interests. The activities of these communities include self- and group education, conferences, online newsletters, and day-to-day sharing of experiences and techniques to solve specific work problems. Many organizations, such as IBM and the World Bank, have encouraged the development of thousands of online communities of practice.

COPs can make it easier for people to reuse knowledge by pointing community members to useful documents, creating document repositories, and filtering information for newcomers. COP members act as facilitators, encouraging contributions and discussion. COPs can also reduce the learning curve for new employees by providing contacts with subject matter experts and access to a community's established methods and tools. Finally, COPs can act as a spawning ground for new ideas, techniques, and decision-making behaviour.

Types of Knowledge Management Systems

There are essentially three major types of knowledge management systems: enterprise-wide knowledge management systems, knowledge work systems, and intelligent techniques. Figure 15-2 shows the knowledge management system applications for each of these major categories.

Enterprise-wide knowledge management systems are general-purpose firm-wide efforts to collect, store, distribute, and apply digital content and knowledge. Such systems provide databases and tools for organizing and storing the following: structured documents; unstructured documents; other knowledge objects; directories; tools for locating employees with expertise in a particular area; and, increasingly, Web-based tools for collaboration and communication. Section 15.2 discusses enterprise-wide knowledge management systems in more detail.

The development of powerful networked workstations and software for assisting engineers and scientists in the discovery of new knowledge has led to the creation of knowledge work systems such as computer-aided design, visualization, simulation, and virtual reality systems. **Knowledge work systems (KWS)** are specialized systems built for engineers, scientists, and other knowledge workers charged with discovering and creating new knowledge for a company. We discuss knowledge work applications in detail in Section 15.3.

Knowledge management also includes a diverse group of **intelligent techniques**, such as data mining, expert systems, neural networks, fuzzy logic, genetic algorithms, and

Communities of practice (COPs)
Knowledge work systems (KWS)
Intelligent techniques

FIGURE 15-2   *Major types of knowledge management systems*

Enterprise-Wide Knowledge Management Systems	Knowledge Work Systems	Intelligent Techniques
General purpose, integrated, firm-wide efforts to collect, store, disseminate, and use digital content and knowledge	Specialized workstations and systems that enable scientists, engineers, and other knowledge workers to create and discover new knowledge	Tools for discovering patterns and applying knowledge to discrete decisions and knowledge domains
Structured knowledge systems Semistructured knowledge systems Knowledge network systems	Computer-aided design (CAD) 3D visualization Virtual reality Investment workstations	Data mining Neural networks Expert systems Case-based reasoning Fuzzy logic Genetic algorithms Intelligent agents

There are three major categories of knowledge management systems, and each can be broken down further into more specialized types of knowledge management systems.

intelligent agents. These techniques have different objectives, from a focus on discovering knowledge (data mining and neural networks), to distilling knowledge in the form of rules for a computer program (expert systems and fuzzy logic), to discovering optimal solutions for problems (genetic algorithms). Section 15.4 provides more detail about these intelligent techniques.

15.2 Enterprise-Wide Knowledge Management Systems

Figure 15-3 provides an overview of the technologies and capabilities found in enterprise-wide knowledge management systems. They include capabilities for storing both structured and unstructured data; tools for locating employee expertise within the firm; and capabilities for obtaining data and information from key transaction systems, such as enterprise applications and from Web sites. They also include supporting technologies such as portals, search engines, and collaboration tools (including e-mail, instant messaging, groupware, blogs, wikis, and social bookmarking) to help employees search the corporate knowledge base, communicate and collaborate with others inside and outside the firm, and apply the stored knowledge to new situations. Systems for managing employee learning are emerging as another supporting technology for enterprise-wide knowledge management.

Managers and firms must deal with many different kinds of knowledge and knowledge issues. There are three major categories of enterprise-wide knowledge management systems for dealing with these different kinds of knowledge. Some knowledge exists already

FIGURE 15-3   *Enterprise-wide knowledge management systems*

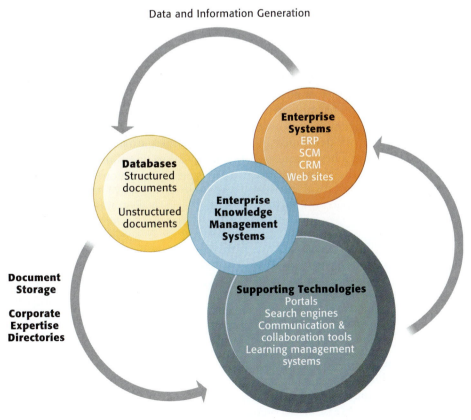

Enterprise-wide knowledge management systems use an array of technologies for storing structured and unstructured documents, locating employee expertise, searching for information, disseminating knowledge, and using data from enterprise applications and other key corporate systems.

TABLE 15-2 *Categories of Enterprise-Wide Knowledge Management Systems*

Type of Knowledge	Knowledge Content	Category of Enterprise Knowledge Management System
Structured knowledge	Formal documents	Structured knowledge systems
Semistructured knowledge	E-mail, voice mail, memos, brochures, digital pictures, bulletin boards, and other unstructured documents	Semistructured knowledge systems
Network (tacit) knowledge	Expertise of individuals	Knowledge networks

somewhere in the firm in the form of structured text documents, reports, and presentations, and the central problem is organizing this existing structured knowledge into a library and making it accessible throughout the firm. We will call this type of knowledge **structured knowledge**, and we can refer to these types of systems as **structured knowledge systems**.

Managers may also need information that may exist somewhere inside the firm in the form of less-structured documents, such as e-mail, voice mail, chat room exchanges, videos, digital pictures, brochures, or bulletin boards. We can call this knowledge **semistructured knowledge**, and we can refer to the systems that focus on this type of knowledge as **semistructured knowledge systems** (the industry name is *digital asset management systems*).

Systems for structured and semistructured knowledge function as knowledge repositories. A **knowledge repository** is a collection of internal and external knowledge in a single location for more efficient management and utilization by the organization. Knowledge repositories provide access through enterprise portals and search engine technology and may include tools for accessing information from corporate databases.

In still other cases, there are no formal or digital documents of any kind, and the knowledge resides in the heads of experienced employees somewhere in the company. Much of this knowledge is *tacit knowledge* and is rarely written down. Here, the problem faced by managers is building a network that connects knowledge demand with knowledge supply. **Knowledge network systems**, also known as *expertise location and management systems,* attempt to perform this function. Knowledge network systems provide an online directory of corporate experts in well-defined knowledge domains and use communication technologies to make it easy for employees to find the appropriate expert in a company. Some knowledge network systems go further by systematizing the solutions being developed by experts and then storing the solutions in a knowledge database as a best practices or frequently asked questions (FAQ) repository. Table 15-2 compares the major categories of enterprise-wide knowledge management systems.

Structured Knowledge Systems

The essential problem in managing structured knowledge is creating an appropriate classification scheme to organize information into meaningful categories in a knowledge database that can be easily accessed by employees. Once the categories for classifying knowledge have been created, each document needs to be "tagged," or coded, so that search engines can retrieve it and the quality of search results can be improved. Structured knowledge systems perform the function of implementing the tagging, interfacing with corporate databases where the documents are stored, and creating an enterprise portal environment for employees to use when searching for corporate knowledge.

All the major accounting and consulting firms have developed structured document and engagement-based (case-based) repositories of reports from consultants who are working with particular clients. The reports typically are created after the consulting engagement is completed and include detailed descriptions of the consulting objective,

Structured knowledge

Structured knowledge systems

Semistructured knowledge

Semistructured knowledge systems

Knowledge repository

Knowledge network systems

FIGURE 15-4 *KWorld's knowledge domains*

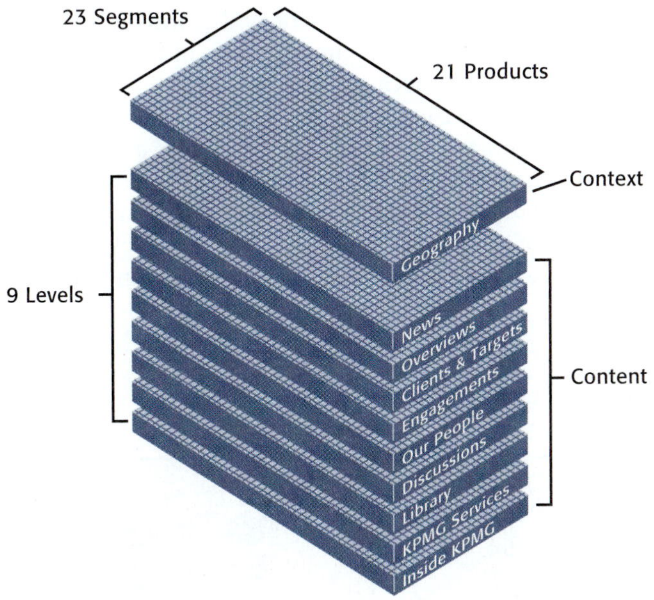

Content in Context

23 Segments

21 Products

Context

9 Levels

Geography

News
Overviews
Clients & Targets
Engagements
Our People
Discussions
Library
KPMG Services
Inside KPMG

Content

KPMG's KWorld is organized into nine levels of content that are further classified by product, market segment, and geographic area.

participants, and the practices used to achieve the client's objectives. These reports are placed in a massive database to be used later for training new consultants in the company's best practices and for preparing new consultants joining an existing on-site consulting team.

One of the world's largest structured knowledge systems is KPMG's KWorld. KPMG International is an international tax and accounting firm with 97 000 professionals serving clients through 1100 offices in 144 countries. With such a large global base of employees and clients, KPMG faced a number of problems in sharing knowledge, preventing the loss of knowledge as consultants retired or left the firm, disseminating best practices, and coping with information overload among individual consultants.

KWorld addresses these problems by providing an integrated set of knowledge content and collaboration tools for use worldwide. Although it is primarily a document repository, KWorld also provides online collaboration capabilities for the firm's consultants and an internal reporting system. KWorld stores white papers, presentations, best-practice proposals, articles, presentations, internal discussions, marketing materials, engagement histories, news feeds, external industry research, and other intellectual capital.

The content is organized into nine levels by KPMG products and market segments (see Figure 15-4). Within each of these levels are many subcategories of knowledge. For instance, the client knowledge domain includes entries on financials, industry dynamics, change dynamics, client organizations, client products and customers, and KPMG's history of engagements. Consultants use KWorld to coordinate their work as a team with a client, and the client is allowed access to the collaboration environment as well.

KPMG has invested heavily in the organizational and management capital required to make use of the millions of documents stored in KWorld. KPMG has created a division of knowledge management, headed by a chief knowledge officer. An extensive staff of analysts and librarians assesses the quality of incoming information, ensures its proper categorization, and provides some analysis of its importance.

Semistructured Knowledge Systems

Semistructured information is all the digital information in a firm that does not exist in a formal document or a formal report. It has been estimated that at least 80 percent of an organization's business content is unstructured—information in folders, messages, memos, proposals, e-mails, graphics, electronic slide presentations, and even videos created in different formats and stored in many locations.

Increasingly, firms are required to track and manage this semistructured content in order to comply with the CSOX Act (see Chapter 8) and other government legislation, and to manage their information assets more efficiently. Firms subject to Sarbanes-Oxley, for instance, must retain digital records of employee e-mail and phone conversations for a minimum of five years. Large firms such as Coca-Cola need to keep track of all the images of the Coca-Cola brand that have been created in the past at all their worldwide offices, both to avoid duplicating efforts and to avoid variation from a standard brand image.

A number of vendors have responded to this need with semistructured knowledge systems that track, store, and organize semistructured documents, as well as more structured traditional documents. For example, OpenText Livelink ECM™ specializes in "integrated knowledge management systems" (see Figure 15-5). In addition to providing centralized

FIGURE 15-5   *OpenText Livelink ECM integrated knowledge management system*

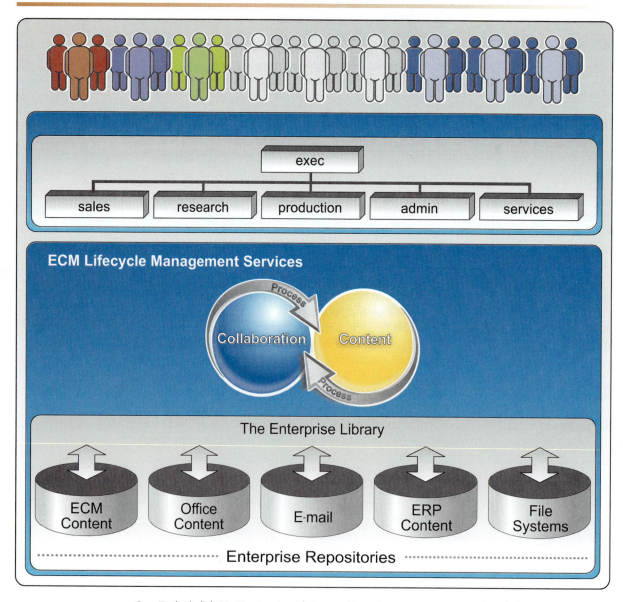

OpenText's Livelink ECM™ enterprise solution combines document management, knowledge management, business intelligence, and portal technologies and can be used for managing semistructured as well as structured knowledge.

WINDOW ON ORGANIZATIONS

Stikeman Elliott Computerizes Its Brainpower

Stikeman Elliott is an international business law firm based in Toronto, Ontario, noted for its work in mergers and acquisitions, antitrust, banking and finance, insolvency, intellectual property, and technology. The firm started with two lawyers in 1952 and today operates with more than 440 lawyers in eight offices in Canada, New York, London, and Sydney. It is one of the top business law firms in Canada.

Stikeman Elliott tries to promote a culture of initiative and high-performance standards. The key to creating and maintaining such a culture is in finding the best way to share the vast repositories of knowledge that reside in the brains of the lawyers and in the documents and files that the lawyers have been collecting throughout their careers. Foremost among the forms of knowledge critical to lawyers are precedents, which can include documents, forms, guidelines, and best practices.

Stikeman Elliott realized that an effective knowledge management (KM) system would enable the firm's lawyers to be more productive and contribute to sustaining the growth of the firm over the long term. In 2001, Stikeman Elliott selected Hummingbird's Enterprise Webtop to build a portal for the firm's corporate intranet. The portal officially launched in 2002 under the name STELLA, which is a play on the name of the firm.

With STELLA in place, all the firm's lawyers have easy access to the firm's knowledge assets, including important precedents, through a single access point using a Web browser. STELLA includes an expertise database, identifying lawyers with proficiency in specific areas. The portal also codifies the generation and organization of new precedents. Margaret Grottenthaler, the co-chair of Stikeman Elliott's national knowledge management committee, points out the importance of STELLA to the firm's junior employees: "It's the way to access all our research, all the legal how-tos. It's absolutely critical they use it. The more junior they are, the more likely they are to use it for those purposes."

An additional benefit of STELLA has been its ability to encourage the sense of community that Stikeman Elliott wishes to foster in its firm by growing organically rather than through mergers or acquisitions. Everyone in the firm, regardless of in which office they work, has access to the same resources. With everyone on equal footing, the multiple-office structure maintains the feel of a single organization. Stikeman Elliott believes that this working atmosphere positions the firm well among its competitors. The increased level of communication among the offices also prevents lawyers from duplicating work that has already been done. Lawyers can customize the portal's home page on their own computers so that they have quick access to the information they need most, whether it is their case files, news about their clients, or news about their clients' industries.

Stikeman Elliott integrated its portal closely with its document management (DM) system, which was also based on Hummingbird's DOCS Open software. (Hummingbird has since been acquired by OpenText). Stikeman employees use the Hummingbird SearchServer search engine to search through the firm's document repository and internal legal and business content, including e-mail, and some external resources, such as the LexisNexis database for legal, risk management, corporate, government, law enforcement, accounting, and academic information.

Of course, a KM system is only useful if it is populated with the knowledge of its users. Some firms have difficulty with partners who hoard their knowledge, it being a valuable commodity. At Stikeman Elliott, the greater obstacle has been time. Partners are often too busy to contribute their work to the system. To combat this problem, the firm is developing tools to automate the population of the knowledge database. With these tools, lawyers can easily create Web sites for their cases, clients, and industry research. STELLA has extranet capabilities that enable Stikeman Elliott to create sites on which clients can review and work with documents pertaining to their cases in a collaborative manner. Grottenthaler points out that the firm's KM system is actually geared toward the client, not the lawyer, because the ultimate goal is to serve the client better.

The KM team at Stikeman Elliott includes library staff and law clerks, in addition to lawyers. All three groups can add precedents, memos, and even meeting notes to the system. The team emphasizes the importance of the human presence in KM and keeps in close contact with the firm's lawyers to make sure they have access to the knowledge they need. A human subject matter expert also reviews content that has been added and categorized by automated procedures, which ensures the quality of the information.

To Think About

1. What are the problems and challenges that a law firm such as Stikeman Elliott faces?

2. What solutions are available to solve these problems?

3. How did implementing STELLA address these problems? How successful was the solution? Did Stikeman Elliott choose the best alternative?

MIS in Action

Visit the OpenText Livelink ECM™ Web site (www.opentext.com), and explore the sections on Hummingbird Enterprise Management and the ROI Case Studies. Then answer the following questions:

1. List and describe the components of OpenText Livelink ECM™ that are most useful for knowledge work. What

additional OpenText Livelink ECM™ capabilities might benefit a company such as Stikeman Elliott? Explain how each of these capabilities would help.

2. How did Hummingbird provide value for the companies discussed in the ROI case studies? How could OpenText Livelink ECM™ increase ROI for Stikeman Elliott?

Sources: Hummingbird, "Stikeman Elliott Collaborates with Hummingbird and ii3," www.hummingbird.com, accessed September 19, 2006; Judith Lamont, "Smart by Any Name—Enterprise Suites Offer Broad Benefits," *KMWorld Magazine*, April 2005; and Hugh McKellar, "Business and Practice: KM and the Law," *KM World*, October 2006.

repositories for document management, OpenText LiveLink ECM™ provides a rules-based e-mail management program that automatically profiles incoming and outgoing mail messages using rules developed by line managers.

One user of Hummingbird's enterprise knowledge management system is Canadian law firm Stikeman Elliott, which is described in the Window on Organizations section. Like other law firms, Stikeman Elliott is a knowledge-intensive company, but its employees, offices, and knowledge resources are distributed in many different locations. It implemented Hummingbird tools to help it leverage this knowledge and use it more efficiently.

Organizing Knowledge: Taxonomies and Tagging One of the first challenges that firms face when building knowledge repositories of any kind is the problem of identifying the correct categories to use when classifying documents. Firms are increasingly using a combination of internally developed taxonomies and search engine techniques. A **taxonomy** is a scheme for classifying information and knowledge in such a way that it can be easily accessed. A taxonomy is like a table of contents in a book or like a library's system for classifying books and periodicals according to subject matter and author. A business firm can access information much more easily if it devises its own taxonomy for classifying information into logical categories. The more precise the taxonomy, the more relevant are the search results produced by search engines. Once a knowledge taxonomy is produced, documents are all *tagged* with the proper classification.

Products such as Autonomy Taxonomy attempt to reduce the burden on users by categorizing documents using an existing corporate taxonomy. Such products consider the user's prior searches, the context of the search term in the document (the relationships between words in a document), related concepts the user may not have entered, as well as keyword frequency and the popularity of the document.

Several tools perform auto tagging and reduce the need for managers to develop their own unique taxonomies. Entrieva's SemioTagger software is a categorization and indexing engine that identifies key phrases in documents, assigns relevance factors to these phrases, and organizes the documents into categories, creating XML-based document tags using rules that users can see and modify. Users can add, delete, or merge categories after examining how the system responds.

One user of Semio's auto-tagging tools is Stanford University's HighWire Press, which publishes 324 online journals containing more than 12 million articles. HighWire needed a way to automate and expand its indexing process. It also needed to provide researchers with better browsing and searching capabilities to support the discovery of unexpected relationships, to link articles from a variety of disciplines, to identify concepts in articles, and to link these concepts in logical categories. Currently, the system has developed 22 000 categories and more than 300 000 concepts. The system supports 84 million hits each week with a database of 6 terabytes (Semio, 2006). The system requires some active management. HighWire Press reviews its classification scheme every quarter and makes changes based on user feedback and management insight.

Knowledge Network Systems

Knowledge network systems address the problem that arises when the appropriate knowledge is tacit knowledge residing in the memory of expert individuals in the firm. Because such knowledge cannot be conveniently found, employees expend significant resources

Taxonomy

rediscovering knowledge. An International Data Corporation (IDC) study estimated that the average cost of redundant effort in Fortune 500 companies exceeds $60 million per year per firm (AskMe, 2003).

Knowledge network systems provide an online directory of corporate experts in well-defined knowledge domains and use communication technologies to make it easy for employees to find the appropriate expert in a company. Some knowledge network systems go further by systematizing the solutions developed by experts and then storing the solutions in a knowledge database as a best-practices or frequently asked questions (FAQ) repository.

AskMe, Inc., offers a widely adopted enterprise knowledge network system. Its users include Procter & Gamble and Intec Engineering Partnership, a project management company with more than 500 employees worldwide serving the global oil and gas industry. The software, AskMe Enterprise, enables firms to develop a database of employee expertise and know-how, documents, best practices, and FAQs, and then to share that information across the firm using whichever portal technology the firm has adopted. Content can be further categorized through community spaces that organize expertise and knowledge around a common discipline. Federated search capabilities ensure the reuse of existing knowledge from internal repositories, third-party repositories, and external sources on the Web. Users can subscribe to RSS feeds to receive notifications about new content.

Figure 15-6 illustrates how AskMe Enterprise works. An Intec engineer with a question, for instance, could access relevant documents, Web links, and answers to previous

FIGURE 15-6   *AskMe Enterprise knowledge network system*

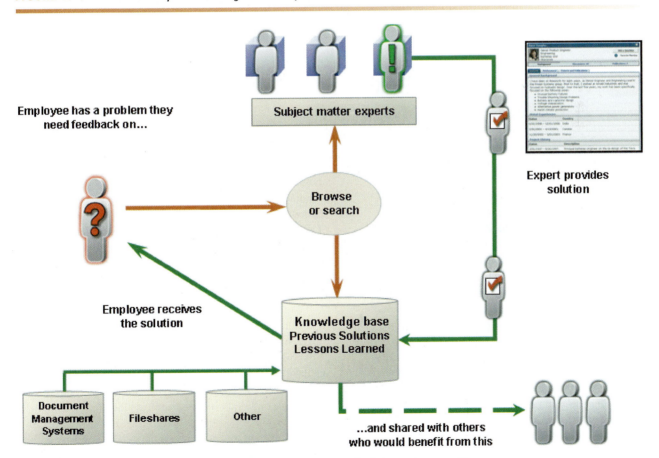

A knowledge network maintains a database of firm experts, as well as accepted solutions to known problems. The AskMe Enterprise system facilitates the communication between employees looking for knowledge and internal solution providers through the Web-based system, standard e-mail such as Outlook, PDAs, BlackBerry handhelds, or instant messaging. Solutions created in this communication are then added to a database of solutions in the form of FAQs, best practices, or other documents.

related questions by initiating a keyword search. If no answer was found, that person could post a general question on a Web page for categories, such as Pipeline or Subsea, for other engineers accessing that page to answer. Alternatively, the person could review the profiles of all company engineers with relevant expertise and send a detailed e-mail query to experts who might have the answer. All questions and answers are automatically incorporated into the knowledge database.

Supporting Technologies: Portals, Collaboration Tools, and Learning Management Systems

The major commercial knowledge management system vendors have integrated their content and document management capabilities with powerful portal and collaboration technologies. Enterprise knowledge portals can provide access to external sources of information, such as news feeds and research, as well as to internal knowledge resources along with capabilities for e-mail, chat/instant messaging, discussion groups, and videoconferencing.

Chapter 7 described the capabilities of groupware for organizational information— i.e., sharing and collaboration. Companies are now starting to use consumer Web technologies such as blogs, wikis, and social bookmarking for internal use to facilitate the exchange of information between individuals and teams.

Intel CEO Paul Otellini uses a blog for conveying his thoughts to employees and for soliciting their opinions. Internal teams at Ernst & Young use blogs to collaborate and share knowledge about clients and projects while French pharmaceutical company Ipsen uses blogs for reputation management and for gathering competitive intelligence.

WINDOW ON TECHNOLOGY

Sharing Knowledge with Social Bookmarking

Most Web users know the value of bookmarks, which allow Web surfers to store and annotate links to useful Web sites. Bookmarks make it much easier to relocate information. But they are tied to a single machine and Web browser, so you cannot bring them with you or share them easily with people in other locations.

Enter social bookmarking. Instead of storing bookmarks on desktops, users store them on shared sites, where they can be accessed from any location with Web access and also shared with other people. The shared sites can be sites for bookmarking pages on the public Web or internal corporate sites for bookmarking pages on the corporate intranet.

The bookmarks are "tagged" with key words to help organize and classify them. Other people can use these tags to find bookmarks relevant to their interests that may help them find information more easily, including new sources of information that might be missed by search engines.

For example, suppose you are on a corporate team doing research on wind power. If you did a Web search and found relevant Web pages on wind power, you would click on a bookmarking button on the social networking site and create a tag identifying each Web document in such a way that it would be linked to wind power. You can click on the "tags" button at the

social networking site to see a list of all the tags you created and select the documents you need.

Some even use these tags to identify other users with similar interests. Because social bookmarking sites indicate the author of each bookmark and provide access to that person's other bookmarked resources, users can make social connections with other individuals interested in a particular topic. This process allows like-minded individuals to find one another and create new communities of users.

It could be said that social bookmarking creates a network of resources and connections that represents the interests and judgments of a community of users.

Web-based social bookmarking sites are on the rise, including del.icio.us (pronounced delicious), which was acquired by Yahoo! in 2005. Del.icio.us is targeted at individual consumers, but there are other social bookmarking sites offering services to academic and business users. Academics use CiteULike.org to share and store academic papers while medical researchers and practitioners use Connotea.org to track references. Visitors to social bookmarking sites can search for resources by keyword, person, or popularity and see the public bookmarks, tags, and classification schemes that registered bookmark users have created.

IBM developed Dogear, a social bookmarking service for businesses. It includes a user authentication feature, which is important for ensuring only selected employees collaborate. Dogear allows users in a business to search and bookmark information on either the public Web or an internal corporate intranet. Users can decide whether to make all their tagged bookmarks public or only selected bookmarks, with the rest kept private. In addition to facilitating document-sharing, Dogear connects people in large organizations who would otherwise never meet and promotes information sharing between individuals in a team. According to David Millen, manager of IBM's Collaborative User Experience group, social bookmarking "allows you to see who is interested in the topics you're interested in." If you think a particular person's bookmarks are especially useful, you can subscribe to those bookmarks. Dogear users can subscribe to particular tags and have newly tagged items delivered automatically.

There are downsides. Public social bookmarking sites provide no oversight about how resources are organized or tagged. In some instances, this will lead to inconsistent or disorganized uses of tags. For example, if a user saves a bookmark for a site with information about wind power, but only tags the site with the term wind power and not with the terms alternative energy or renewable energy, that information might never be found by someone looking for information about wind power as a source of alternative energy. Social bookmarking reflects the values of a community of users, so there is always a chance they will present a skewed view of a particular topic.

To Think About

1. What are the advantages and disadvantages of using social bookmarking for knowledge management?

2. What management, organization, and technology issues should be addressed when considering whether to use social bookmarking for knowledge management at a business?

3. Should there be different standards for posting bookmarks to public Web pages at a public Web site versus posting bookmarks to internal corporate Web pages on a corporate social bookmarking site?

MIS in Action

Visit the social bookmarking site Del.icio.us (http://Del.icio.us), and search for bookmarks on a topic of your choice, such as global warming, bird flu, ethanol, or open-source. Then answer the following questions:

1. How easy was it to find bookmarks about your topic? How many bookmarks did you find?

2. Compare these bookmarks to the results of a search on your topic of choice using Google, Yahoo!, or another search engine. Which tools were the most useful in pointing you to good information?

3. Would you use Del.icio.us to find information for a research paper or business presentation? Why or why not?

Sources: Michael Totty, "Information Found — and Shared." *The Wall Street Journal*, September 11, 2006; Shamus McGillicudy, "Social Bookmarking: Pushing Collaboration to the Edge," SearchCIO.com, June 21, 2006; and Vauhini Vara, "Offices Co-Opt Consumer Web Tools Like 'Wikis' and Social Networking." *The Wall Street Journal*, September 12, 2006.

Wikis, introduced in Chapter 7, are inexpensive, easy to implement and use, and do not require a massive software rollout. They are meant to stimulate collaboration. Users determine the content, eliminating the need for a central distribution centre with extensive management. Wikis can centralize all types of corporate data that can be displayed in a Web browser, including Microsoft Word documents, spreadsheets, Microsoft PowerPoint slides, and electronic pages of documents, and wikis can embed e-mail and instant messages. Heavy-duty wikis are able to directly interface with corporate databases to import audio and picture files. Although users can modify wiki content contributed by others, wikis have some built-in version control. No changes can be made without recording the author of those changes, and it is possible to revert to an earlier version.

These features of wikis make them especially appealing to small businesses with limited technology staffs and budgets, but they are also being deployed by large enterprises. Nokia has been using Socialtext wiki software to facilitate information exchange within its Insight and Foresight Group. Intel Corp. created a wiki called Intelpedia that lets employees collect information and collaborate on projects instead of having to send countless e-mails (Vara, 2006). Socialtext, JotSpot, and Atlassian are leading wiki software vendors while Twiki and Perspective are non-commercial open-source tools.

Social bookmarking makes it easier to search for and also to share information by allowing users to save their bookmarks to Web pages on a public Web site and tag these bookmarks with keywords. These tags can be used to organize and search for the documents, and lists of tags can be shared with other people to help them find information of interest. The Window on Technology section on page 512 describes how this technology works and its benefits for knowledge management.

Social bookmarking

Learning Management Systems Companies need ways to keep track of and manage employee learning and to integrate it more fully into their knowledge management and other corporate systems. **Learning management systems (LMS)** provide tools for the management, delivery, tracking, and assessment of various types of employee learning and training.

Contemporary LMS support multiple modes of learning, including CD-ROM, downloadable videos, Web-based classes, live instruction in classes or online, and group learning in online forums and chat sessions. LMS consolidate mixed-media training, automate the selection and administration of courses, assemble and deliver learning content, and measure learning effectiveness.

For example, Royal LePage, the leading Canadian real estate broker, used SumTotal Systems for a redevelopment of its corporate university, increasing participation in the corporate learning management system by 150 percent within the first two years of redeployment. More than 40 percent of Royal LePage employees use the corporate university. The success of Royal LePage's corporate university motivated its parent company, Brascan Financial Corporation, to implement similar learning management systems by SumTotal in Royal LePage's sister companies (SumTotal Systems, 2007).

15.3 Knowledge Work Systems

The enterprise-wide knowledge systems we have just described provide a wide range of capabilities that can be used by many if not all the workers and groups in an organization. Firms also have specialized systems for knowledge workers to help them create new knowledge and to ensure that this knowledge is properly integrated into the business.

Knowledge Workers and Knowledge Work

Knowledge workers, which we introduced in Chapter 1, include researchers, designers, architects, scientists, and engineers who primarily create knowledge and information for the organization. Knowledge workers usually have high levels of education and memberships in professional organizations and are often asked to exercise independent judgment as a routine aspect of their work. For example, knowledge workers create new products or find ways of improving existing ones. Knowledge workers perform three key roles that are critical to the organization and to the managers who work within the organization:

- Keeping the organization current in knowledge as it develops in the external world—in technology, science, social thought, and the arts.
- Serving as internal consultants regarding the areas of their knowledge, the changes taking place, and opportunities.
- Acting as change agents, evaluating, initiating, and promoting change projects.

Requirements of Knowledge Work Systems

Most knowledge workers rely on office systems, such as word processors, voice mail, e-mail, videoconferencing, and scheduling systems, which are designed to increase worker productivity in the office. However, knowledge workers also require highly specialized knowledge work systems with powerful graphics, analytical tools, and communications and document management capabilities.

These systems require substantial computing power to handle the sophisticated graphics or complex calculations necessary for such knowledge workers as scientific researchers, product designers, and financial analysts. Because knowledge workers are so focused on knowledge in the external world, these systems also must give the worker quick and easy access to external databases. They typically feature user-friendly interfaces that enable users to perform needed tasks without having to spend a great deal of time learning how to use the system. Knowledge workers are highly paid—wasting a knowledge

Learning management
systems (LMS)

FIGURE 15-7 *Requirements of knowledge work systems*

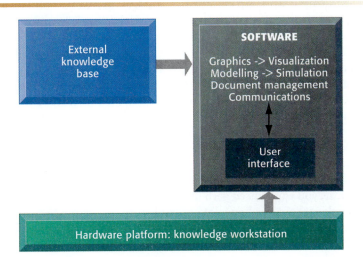

Knowledge work systems require strong links to external knowledge bases in addition to specialized hardware and software.

worker's time is simply too expensive. Figure 15-7 summarizes the requirements of knowledge work systems.

Knowledge workstations often are designed and optimized for the specific tasks to be performed. For example, a design engineer requires a different workstation setup than a financial analyst. Design engineers need graphics with enough power to handle three-dimensional computer-aided design systems. However, financial analysts are more interested in access to myriad external databases and technology for efficiently storing and accessing massive amounts of financial data.

Examples of Knowledge Work Systems

Major knowledge work applications include computer-aided design systems, virtual reality systems for simulation and modelling, and financial workstations. **Computer-aided design (CAD)** automates the creation and revision of designs, using computers and sophisticated graphics software. Using a more traditional physical design methodology, each design modification requires a mould to be made and a prototype to be tested physically. These steps must be repeated many times, which is a very expensive and time-consuming process. Using a CAD workstation, the designer need only make a physical prototype toward the end of the design process because the design can be easily tested and changed on the computer. The ability of CAD software to provide design specifications for the tooling and the manufacturing processes also saves a great deal of time and money while producing a manufacturing process with far fewer problems.

Computer-aided design (CAD)

Computer-aided design (CAD) systems improve the quality and precision of product design by performing much of the design and testing work on the computer.

For example, architects from Skidmore, Owings, & Merrill LLP used a 3-D design program called Revit to work out the creative and technical details of the design for the Freedom Tower at the site of the former World Trade Center. The software enabled the architects to strip away the outer layer to manipulate the shape of the floors. Changes appeared immediately in the entire model, and the software automatically recalculated the technical details in the blueprints (Frangos, 2004).

Virtual reality systems have visualization, rendering, and simulation capabilities that go far beyond those of conventional CAD systems. They use interactive graphics software to create computer-generated simulations that are so close to reality that users almost believe they are participating in a real-world situation. In many virtual reality systems, the user dons special clothing, headgear, and equipment, depending on the application. The clothing contains sensors that record the user's movements and immediately transmit that information back to the computer. For instance, to walk through a virtual reality simulation of a house, you would need garb that monitors the movement of your feet, hands, and head. You also would need goggles containing video screens and sometimes audio attachments and feeling gloves so that you can be immersed in the computer feedback.

Virtual reality is just starting to provide benefits in educational, scientific, and business work. For example, the Canadian Air Force uses quasi-realistic threat simulation to help pilots train for war. Ottawa-based PRIOR Data Services Ltd. developed tactical engagement display software for the Canadian Forces' Surface Threat Electronic Warfare System (STEW) at the air base in Cold Lake, Alberta. The system gives realistic ground radar signals that are used in the air crew's electronic warfare training. The system consists of five threat-emitters that can be reconfigured to imitate a number of threat systems. The system responds to jamming and manoeuvres, and automatically records events so that they may be played back and pilots can be debriefed (Balfour, 1999).

Virtual reality applications developed for the Web use a standard called **Virtual Reality Modelling Language (VRML)**. VRML is a set of specifications for interactive, three-dimensional modelling on the World Wide Web that can organize multiple media types, including animation, images, and audio, to put users in a simulated real-world environment. VRML is platform-independent, operates over a desktop computer, and requires little bandwidth.

DuPont, the global chemical company, created a VRML application called Hyperplant, which enables users to access three-dimensional data over the Internet using Web browser software. Engineers can go through three-dimensional models as if they were physically walking through a plant, viewing objects at eye level. This level of detail reduces the number of mistakes they make during construction of oil rigs, oil plants, and other structures.

The financial industry is using specialized **investment workstations** to leverage the knowledge and time of its brokers, traders, and portfolio managers. Firms such as TD Canada Trust and Assante have installed investment workstations that integrate a wide range of data from both internal and external sources, including contact management data, real-time and historical market data, and research reports. Previously, financial professionals had to spend considerable time accessing data from separate systems and piecing together the information they needed. By providing one-stop information faster and with fewer errors, the workstations streamline the entire investment process from stock selection to updating client records. Table 15-3 summarizes the major types of knowledge work systems.

Virtual reality systems

Virtual Reality Modelling Language (VRML)

Investment workstations

TABLE 15-3 *Examples of Knowledge Work Systems*

KNOWLEDGE WORK SYSTEM	FUNCTION IN ORGANIZATION
CAD/CAM (computer-aided design/ computer-aided manufacturing)	Provides engineers, designers, and factory managers with precise control over industrial design and manufacturing
Virtual reality systems	Provide architects, engineers, and medical workers with precise, photorealistic simulations of objects
Investment workstations	High-end PCs used in financial sector to analyze trading situations instantaneously and facilitate portfolio management

15.4 Intelligent Techniques

Artificial intelligence and database technology provide a number of intelligent techniques that organizations can use to capture individual and collective knowledge and to extend their knowledge base. Expert systems, case-based reasoning, and fuzzy logic are used for capturing tacit knowledge. Neural networks and data mining are used for **knowledge discovery**. They can discover underlying patterns, categories, and behaviours in large data sets that could not be discovered by managers alone or simply through experience. Genetic algorithms are used for generating solutions to problems that are too large and complex for human beings to analyze on their own. Intelligent agents can automate routine tasks to help firms search for and filter information for use in electronic commerce, supply chain management, and other activities.

Data mining, which we discussed in Chapter 6, helps organizations capture undiscovered knowledge residing in large databases, providing managers with new insight for improving business performance. It has become an important tool for management decision making, and we provided a detailed discussion of data mining for management decision support in Chapter 14.

The other intelligent techniques discussed in this section are based on **artificial intelligence (AI)** technology, which consists of computer-based systems (both hardware and software) that attempt to emulate human behaviour. Such systems are able to learn languages, accomplish physical tasks, use a perceptual apparatus, and emulate human expertise and decision making. Although AI applications do not exhibit the breadth, complexity, originality, and generality of human intelligence, they play an important role in contemporary knowledge management.

Capturing Knowledge: Expert Systems

An **expert system** is an intelligent technique for capturing tacit knowledge in a very specific and limited domain of human expertise. Expert systems capture the knowledge of skilled employees in the form of a set of rules in a software system that can be used by others in the organization. The set of rules in the expert system adds to the memory, or stored learning, of the firm.

Expert systems lack the breadth of knowledge and the understanding of fundamental principles of a human expert. They typically perform very limited tasks that can be accomplished by professionals in a few minutes or hours, such as diagnosing a malfunctioning machine or determining whether to grant credit for a loan. Problems that cannot be solved by human experts in the same short period of time are far too difficult for an expert system. However, by capturing human expertise in limited areas, expert systems can provide benefits, helping organizations make high-quality decisions with fewer people. Today expert systems are widely used in business in discrete, highly structured decision-making situations.

How Expert Systems Work Human knowledge must be modelled or represented in a way that a computer can process. Expert systems model human knowledge as a set of rules that collectively are called the **knowledge base**. Expert systems have from 200 to many thousands of these rules, depending on the complexity of the problem. These rules are much more interconnected and nested than in a traditional software program (see Figure 15-8). The strategy used to search through the knowledge base is called the **inference engine**. Two strategies are commonly used: forward chaining and backward chaining (see Figure 15-9).

In **forward chaining**, the inference engine begins with the information entered by the user and searches the knowledge base to arrive at a conclusion. The strategy is to fire, or carry out, the action of the rule when a condition is true. In Figure 15-9, beginning on the left, if the user enters a client's name with income greater than $100 000, the engine will fire all rules in sequence from left to right. If the user then enters information indicating

Knowledge discovery
Artificial intelligence (AI)
Expert system
Knowledge base
Inference engine
Forward chaining

FIGURE 15-8 *Rules in an expert system*

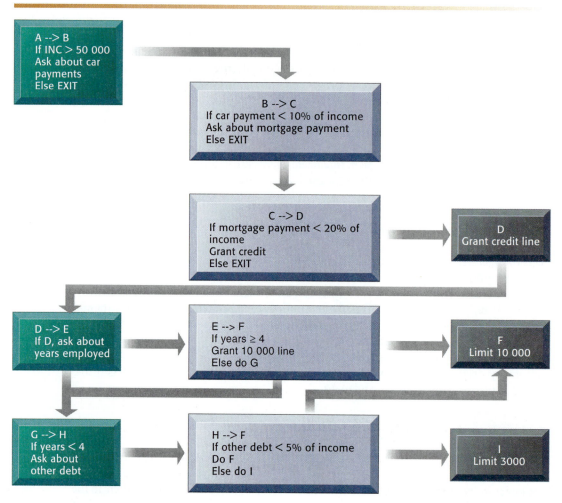

An expert system contains a number of rules to be followed. The rules are interconnected; the number of outcomes is known in advance and is limited; there are multiple paths to the same outcome; and the system can consider multiple rules at a single time. The rules illustrated are for simple credit-granting expert systems.

FIGURE 15-9 *Inference engines in expert systems*

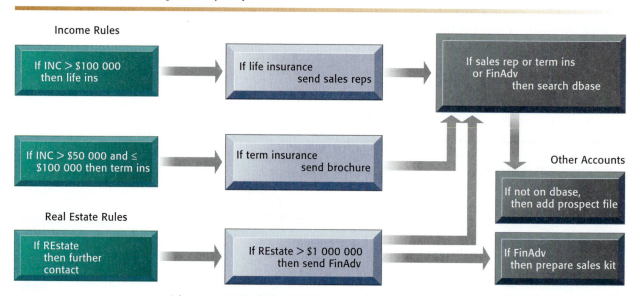

An inference engine works by searching through the rules and "firing" those rules that are triggered by facts gathered and entered by the user.

that the same client owns real estate, another pass of the knowledge base will occur and more rules will fire. Processing continues until no more rules can be fired.

In **backward chaining**, the strategy for searching the knowledge base starts with a hypothesis and proceeds by asking the user questions about selected facts until the hypothesis is either confirmed or disproved. In our example, in Figure 15-9, ask the question, "Should we add this person to the prospect database?" Begin on the right of the diagram and work toward the left. You can see that the person should be added to the database if a sales representative is sent, term insurance is granted, or a financial adviser visits the client.

Developing an expert system requires input from one or more experts who have a thorough command of the knowledge base, and one or more knowledge engineers who can translate the knowledge (as described by the expert) into a set of rules. A **knowledge engineer** is similar to a traditional systems analyst but has special expertise in eliciting information and expertise from other professionals.

Examples of Successful Expert Systems Expert systems provide businesses with an array of benefits including improved decisions, reduced errors, reduced costs, reduced training time, and higher levels of quality and service. Here are several examples:

The Learning Edge, a Toronto-based company, developed the IBM AS/400 Development Software Advisor as a marketing aid to help IBM's prospective customers better understand their application development needs and options. First the expert system gathers environmental and business process information; then it analyzes the data and recommends a programming language.

Countrywide Funding Corporation in Pasadena, California, uses an expert system to improve decisions about granting loans. This loan-underwriting firm employs about 400 underwriters in 150 offices around the country. The company developed a PC-based expert system in 1992 to make preliminary creditworthiness decisions on loan requests. The company had experienced rapid, continuing growth and wanted the system to help ensure consistent, high-quality loan decisions. Countrywide's Loan Underwriting Expert System (CLUES) has about 400 rules. Countrywide tested the system by sending every loan application handled by a human underwriter to CLUES as well. The system was refined until it agreed with the underwriters in 95 percent of the cases.

Countrywide does not rely on CLUES to reject loans because the expert system cannot be programmed to handle exceptional situations, such as those involving a self-employed person or complex financial arrangements. An underwriter must review all rejected loans and makes the final decision. CLUES has other benefits. Traditionally, an underwriter could handle six or seven applications a day. Using CLUES, the same underwriter can evaluate at least 16 per day. Countrywide now uses the rules in its expert system to answer inquiries from visitors to its Web site who want to know if they qualify for a loan.

Con-Way Transportation developed an expert system called Line-haul to automate and optimize planning of overnight shipment routes for its nationwide freight-trucking business. The expert system captures the business rules that dispatchers follow when assigning drivers, trucks, and trailers to transport 50 000 shipments of heavy freight each night across Canada and 25 states when plotting their routes. Line-haul runs on a Sun platform and uses data on daily customer shipment requests, available drivers, trucks, trailer space, and weight stored in an Oracle database. The expert system uses thousands of rules and 100 000 lines of program code written in C++ to crunch the numbers and create optimum routing plans for 95 percent of daily freight shipments.

Con-Way dispatchers tweak the routing plan provided by the expert system and relay final routing specifications to field personnel responsible for packing the trailers for their night-time runs. Con-Way recouped its $3.5 million investment in the system within two years by reducing the number of drivers, packing more freight per trailer, and reducing damage from rehandling. The system also reduces dispatchers' arduous nightly tasks (Pastore, 2003).

Although expert systems lack the robust and general intelligence of human beings, they can provide benefits to organizations if their limitations are well understood. Only certain classes of problems can be solved using expert systems. Virtually all successful

Backward chaining

Knowledge engineer

expert systems deal with problems of classification in limited domains of knowledge where there are relatively few alternative outcomes and these possible outcomes are all known in advance. Expert systems are much less useful for dealing with unstructured problems typically encountered by managers.

Many expert systems require large, lengthy, and expensive development efforts. Hiring or training more experts may be less expensive than developing an expert system. Typically, the environment in which an expert system operates is continually changing so that the expert system must also continually change. Some expert systems, especially large ones, are so complex that in a few years the maintenance costs equal the development costs.

Organizational Intelligence: Case-Based Reasoning

Expert systems primarily capture the tacit knowledge of individual experts, but organizations also have collective knowledge and expertise that they have built up over the years. This organizational knowledge can be captured and stored using case-based reasoning. In **case-based reasoning (CBR)**, descriptions of past experiences of human specialists, represented as cases, are stored in a database for later retrieval when the user encounters a new case with similar parameters. The system searches for stored cases with problem characteristics similar to the new one, finds the closest fit, and applies the solutions of the old case to the new case. Successful solutions are tagged to the new case, and both are stored together with the other cases in the knowledge base. Unsuccessful solutions also are appended to the case database along with explanations as to why the solutions did not work (see Figure 15-10).

Case-based reasoning (CBR)

FIGURE 15-10   *How case-based reasoning works*

Case-based reasoning represents knowledge as a database of past cases and their solutions. The system uses a six-step process to generate solutions to new problems encountered by the user.

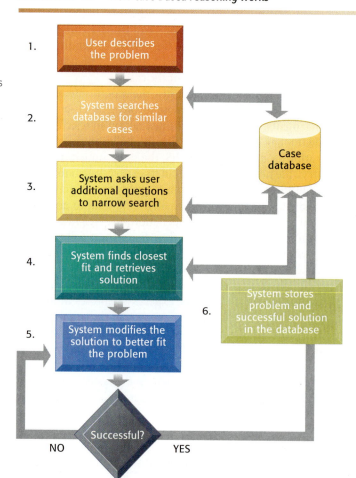

Expert systems work by applying a set of IF-THEN-ELSE rules extracted from human experts. Case-based reasoning, in contrast, represents knowledge as a series of cases, and this knowledge base is continuously expanded and refined by users. You will find case-based reasoning in diagnostic systems in medicine or customer support where users can retrieve past cases whose characteristics are similar to the new case. The system suggests a solution or diagnosis based on the best-matching retrieved case.

Fuzzy Logic Systems

Most people do not think in terms of traditional IF-THEN rules or precise numbers. Humans tend to categorize things imprecisely, using rules for making decisions that may have many shades of meaning. For example, a man or a woman can be *strong* or *intelligent*. A company can be *large*, *medium*, or *small* in size. Temperature can be *hot*, *cold*, *cool*, or *warm*. These categories represent a range of values.

Fuzzy logic is a rule-based technology that can represent such imprecision by creating rules that use approximate or subjective values. It can describe a particular phenomenon or process linguistically and then represent that description in a small number of flexible rules. Organizations can use fuzzy logic to create software systems that capture tacit knowledge where there is linguistic ambiguity.

Let us look at the way fuzzy logic would represent various temperatures in a computer application to control room temperature automatically. The terms (known as *membership functions*) are imprecisely defined so that, for example, in Figure 15-11, cool is between 50 degrees and 70 degrees, although the temperature is most clearly cool between about 60 degrees and 67 degrees. Note that cool is overlapped by *cold* or *norm*. To control the room environment using this logic, the programmer would develop similarly imprecise definitions for humidity and other factors, such as outdoor wind and temperature. The rules might include one that says: "If the temperature is *cool* or *cold* and the humidity is low while the outdoor wind is high and the outdoor temperature is low, raise the heat and humidity in the room." The computer would combine the membership function readings in a weighted manner and, using all the rules, raise and lower the temperature and humidity.

Fuzzy logic

FIGURE 15-11 *Implementing fuzzy logic rules in hardware*

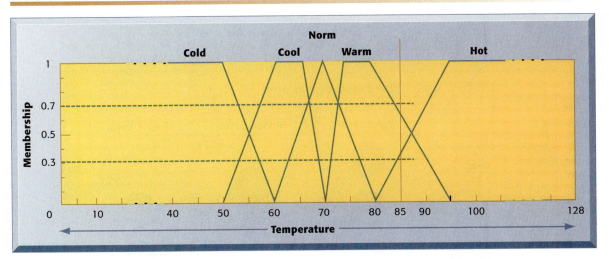

The membership functions for the input called temperature are in the logic of the thermostat to control the room temperature. Membership functions help translate linguistic expressions such as *warm* into numbers that the computer can manipulate.

Source: James M. Sibigtroth, "Implementing Fuzzy Expert Rules in Hardware," *AI Expert*, April 1992. © 1992 Miller Freeman, Inc. Reprinted with permission.

Fuzzy logic provides solutions to problems requiring expertise that is difficult to represent in the form of crisp IF-THEN rules. In Japan, Sendai's subway system uses fuzzy logic controls to accelerate so smoothly that standing passengers need not hold on. Mitsubishi Heavy Industries in Tokyo has been able to reduce the power consumption of its air conditioners by 20 percent by implementing control programs in fuzzy logic. The autofocus device in cameras is only possible because of fuzzy logic. In these instances, fuzzy logic allows incremental changes in inputs to produce smooth changes in outputs instead of discontinuous ones, making it useful for consumer electronics and engineering applications.

Management also has found fuzzy logic useful for decision making and organizational control. In Canada, researchers are using fuzzy logic systems to estimate declining fish populations so that fisheries management can take action where appropriate. Other Canadian researchers are working on fuzzy logic systems to help with forestry resource management. These fuzzy logic systems take current geographic information system data and project them into the future. Fuzzy logic is also useful in finance: A Wall Street firm created a system that selects companies for potential acquisition, using the language stock traders understand. In the insurance industry, a fuzzy logic system has been developed to detect possible fraud in medical claims submitted by health care providers anywhere in the United States.

Neural Networks

Neural networks are used for solving complex, poorly understood problems for which large amounts of data have been collected. They find patterns and relationships in massive amounts of data that would be too complicated and difficult for a human being to analyze. Neural networks discover this knowledge by using hardware and software that parallel the processing patterns of the biological or human brain. Neural networks "learn" patterns from large quantities of data by sifting through data, searching for relationships, building models, and correcting over and over again the model's own mistakes.

A neural network has a large number of sensing and processing nodes that continuously interact with one another. Figure 15-12 represents one type of neural network comprising an input layer, an output layer, and a hidden processing layer. Humans "train" the network by feeding it a set of training data for which the inputs produce a known set of outputs or conclusions. This helps the computer learn the correct solution by example. As the computer is fed more data, each case is compared with the known outcome. If it differs, a correction is calculated and applied to the nodes in the hidden processing layer. These steps are repeated until a condition, such as corrections being less than a certain amount, is reached. The neural network in Figure 15-12 has learned how to identify a fraudulent credit card purchase. Also, self-organizing neural networks can be trained by exposing them to large amounts of data and allowing them to discover the patterns and relationships in the data.

Neural networks

FIGURE 15-12   *How a neural network works*

A neural network uses rules it "learns" from patterns in data to construct a hidden layer of logic. The hidden layer then processes inputs, classifying them based on the experience of the model. In this example, the neural network has been trained to distinguish between valid and fraudulent credit card purchases.

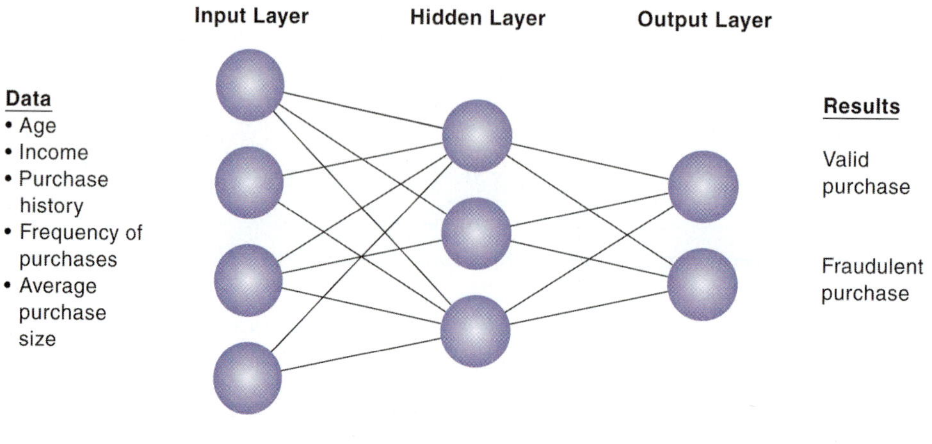

Input Layer   **Hidden Layer**   **Output Layer**

Data
• Age
• Income
• Purchase history
• Frequency of purchases
• Average purchase size

Results

Valid purchase

Fraudulent purchase

While expert systems seek to emulate or model a human expert's way of solving problems, neural network developers claim that they do not program solutions and do not aim to solve specific problems. Instead, neural network designers seek to put intelligence into the hardware in the form of a generalized capability to learn. In contrast, the expert system is highly specific to a given problem and cannot be retrained easily.

Neural network applications in medicine, science, and business address problems in pattern classification, prediction, financial analysis, and control and optimization. In medicine, neural network applications are used for screening patients for coronary artery disease, for diagnosing patients with epilepsy and Alzheimer's disease, and for performing pattern recognition of pathology images. The financial industry uses neural networks to discern patterns in vast pools of data that might help predict the performance of equities, corporate bond ratings, or corporate bankruptcies. Visa International uses a neural network to help detect credit card fraud by monitoring all Visa transactions for sudden changes in the buying patterns of cardholders.

There are many puzzling aspects of neural networks. Unlike expert systems, which typically provide explanations for their solutions, neural networks cannot always explain why they arrived at a particular solution. Moreover, they cannot always guarantee a completely certain solution, arrive at the same solution again with the same input data, or always guarantee the best solution. They are very sensitive and may not perform well if their training covers too little or too much data. In most current applications, neural networks are best used as aids to human decision makers instead of substitutes for them.

Genetic Algorithms

Genetic algorithms are useful for finding the optimal solution for a specific problem by examining a very large number of possible solutions for that problem. Their problem-solving techniques are conceptually based on the method that living organisms use to adapt to their environments—the process of evolution. They are programmed to work the way populations solve problems—by changing and reorganizing their component parts using processes such as reproduction, mutation, and natural selection.

Thus, genetic algorithms promote the evolution of solutions to particular problems, controlling the generation, variation, adaptation, and selection of possible solutions using genetically based processes. As solutions alter and combine, the worst ones are discarded and the better ones survive to go on to produce even better solutions.

A genetic algorithm works by representing information as a string of 0s and 1s. A possible solution can be represented by a long string of these digits. The genetic algorithm provides methods of searching all possible combinations of digits to identify the right string representing the best possible structure for the problem.

In one method, the programmer first randomly generates a population of strings consisting of combinations of binary digits (see Figure 15-13). Each string corresponds to

Genetic algorithms

FIGURE 15-13   *The components of a genetic algorithm*

		Colour	Speed	Intelligence	Fitness
1 0 1 1 0 1	1	White	Medium	Dumb	40
0 1 0 1 0 1	2	Black	Slow	Dumb	43
1 1 0 1 1 0	3	White	Slow	Very dumb	22
0 0 0 1 0 1	4	Black	Fast	Dumb	71
1 0 1 0 0 0	5	White	Medium	Very smart	53

A population of chromosomes | | | **Decoding of chromosomes** | | **Evaluation of chromosomes** |

This example illustrates an initial population of "chromosomes," each representing a different solution. The genetic algorithm uses an iterative process to refine the initial solutions so that the better ones, those with the higher fitness, are more likely to emerge as the best solution.

Source: Vasant Dhar and Roger Stein, *Seven Methods for Transforming Corporate Data into Business Intelligence*, p. 65, © 1997. Reprinted by permission of Prentice Hall, Upper Saddle River, New Jersey.

one of the variables in the problem. One applies a test for fitness, ranking the strings in the population according to their level of desirability as possible solutions. After the initial population is evaluated for fitness, the algorithm then produces the next generation of strings, consisting of strings that survived the fitness test plus offspring strings produced from mating pairs of strings, and tests their fitness. The process continues until a solution is reached.

Many business problems require optimization because they deal with issues such as minimization of costs, maximization of profits, efficient scheduling, and use of resources. If these situations are very dynamic and complex, involving hundreds or thousands of variables or formulas, genetic algorithms can expedite the solution because they can evaluate many different solution alternatives quickly to find the best one.

For example, General Electric engineers used genetic algorithms to help optimize the design for jet turbine aircraft engines, where each design change required changes in up to 100 variables. The supply chain management software from i2 Technologies uses genetic algorithms to optimize production-scheduling models incorporating hundreds of thousands of details about customer orders, material and resource availability, manufacturing and distribution capability, and delivery dates. International Truck and Engine used this software to iron out snags in production, reducing costly schedule disruptions by 90 percent in five of its plants. Genetic algorithms have also helped market researchers performing market segmentation analysis (Kuo, Chang, and Chien, 2004; Burtka, 1993; Wakefield, 2001).

Hybrid AI Systems

Genetic algorithms, fuzzy logic, neural networks, and expert systems can be integrated into a single application to take advantage of the best features of these technologies. These integrated systems are called **hybrid AI systems**. Hybrid applications in business are growing. In Japan, Hitachi, Mitsubishi, Ricoh, Sanyo, and others are starting to incorporate hybrid AI systems in products such as home appliances, factory machinery, and office equipment. Matsushita has developed a "neurofuzzy" washing machine that combines fuzzy logic with neural networks. Nikko Securities has been working on a neurofuzzy system to forecast convertible-bond ratings.

Intelligent Agents

Intelligent agent technology can help businesses navigate through large amounts of data to locate and act on information that is considered important. **Intelligent agents** are software programs that work in the background without direct human intervention to carry out specific, repetitive, and predictable tasks for an individual user, business process, or software application. The agent uses a limited built-in or learned knowledge base to accomplish tasks or make decisions on the user's behalf, such as deleting junk e-mail, scheduling appointments, or travelling over interconnected networks to find the cheapest airfare to California.

There are many intelligent agent applications today in operating systems, application software, e-mail systems, mobile computing software, and network tools. For example, the wizards found in Microsoft Office software tools have built-in capabilities to show users how to accomplish various tasks, such as formatting documents or creating graphs, and to anticipate when users need assistance.

Of special interest to business are intelligent agents for cruising networks, including the Internet, in search of information. Chapter 7 describes how shopping bots can help consumers find products they want and assist them in comparing prices and other features.

Many complex phenomena can be modelled as systems of autonomous agents that follow relatively simple rules for interaction. **Agent-based modelling** applications have been developed to model the behaviour of consumers, stock markets, and supply chains and to predict the spread of epidemics (Samuelson and Macal, 2006).

Procter & Gamble (P&G) used agent-based modelling to improve coordination among different members of its supply chain in response to changing business conditions

Hybrid AI systems
Intelligent agents
Agent-based modelling

FIGURE 15-14   *Intelligent agents in P&G's supply chain network*

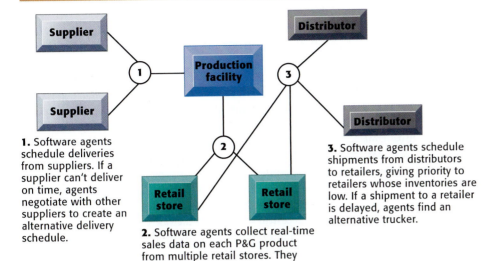

Intelligent agents are helping Procter & Gamble shorten the replenishment cycles for products such as a box of Tide.

1. Software agents schedule deliveries from suppliers. If a supplier can't deliver on time, agents negotiate with other suppliers to create an alternative delivery schedule.

2. Software agents collect real-time sales data on each P&G product from multiple retail stores. They relay the data to P&G production for replenishing orders and to sales and marketing for trend analysis.

3. Software agents schedule shipments from distributors to retailers, giving priority to retailers whose inventories are low. If a shipment to a retailer is delayed, agents find an alternative trucker.

(Sadeh, Hildum, and Kjenstad, 2003; Cavalieri, Cesarotti, and Introna, 2003). Figure 15-14 illustrates the use of intelligent agents in Procter & Gamble's supply chain network. The network models a complex supply chain as a group of semiautonomous "agents" representing individual supply chain components, such as trucks, production facilities, distributors, or retail stores. The behaviour of each agent is programmed to follow rules that mimic actual behaviour, such as "dispatch a truck when it is full." Simulations using the agents enable the company to perform what-if analyses on inventory levels, in-store stockouts, and transportation costs.

Using intelligent agent models, P&G discovered that trucks should often be dispatched before being fully loaded. Although transportation costs would be higher using partially loaded trucks because of both driver time and fuel to deliver fewer goods, the simulation showed that retail store stockouts would occur less often, thus reducing the amount of lost sales, which would more than make up for the higher distribution costs. Agent-based modelling has saved P&G $350 million annually on an investment of less than 1 percent of that amount (Anthes, 2003).

Summary

1. **Assess the role of knowledge management and knowledge management programs in business.**

   Knowledge management is a set of processes to create, store, transfer, and apply knowledge in the organization. Businesses need knowledge management programs because knowledge has become a central productive and strategic asset in today's information economy and a potential source of competitive advantage. Much of a firm's value depends on its ability to create and manage knowledge. Knowledge management promotes organizational learning by increasing the ability of the organization to learn from its environment and to incorporate knowledge into its business processes. Effective knowledge management systems require organizational and

   management capital to promote a knowledge culture and programs for knowledge management, including the creation of a chief knowledge officer. There are three major types of knowledge management systems: enterprise-wide knowledge management systems, knowledge work systems, and intelligent techniques.

2. **Describe the types of systems used for enterprise-wide knowledge management and demonstrate how they provide value for organizations.**

   Enterprise-wide knowledge management systems are firm-wide efforts to collect, store, distribute, and apply digital content and knowledge. Structured knowledge systems provide databases and tools for organizing and storing structured documents, while semistructured knowledge systems provide databases and tools for organizing and storing semistructured knowledge, such as e-mail or rich media. Knowledge network systems provide directories and tools for locating firm employees with special expertise who are important sources of tacit knowledge. Often these systems include group collaboration tools (including wikis and social bookmarking), portals to simplify information access, search tools, and tools for classifying information based on a taxonomy that is appropriate for the organization. Enterprise-wide knowledge management systems can provide considerable value if they are well designed and enable employees to locate, share, and use knowledge more efficiently.

3. *Describe the major types of knowledge work systems and assess how they provide value for firms.*

    Knowledge work systems (KWS) support the creation of new knowledge and its integration into the organization. KWS require easy access to an external knowledge base; powerful computer hardware that can support software with intensive graphics, analysis, document management, and communications capabilities; and a user-friendly interface. These capabilities can increase the productivity of highly paid knowledge workers. KWS often run on workstations that are customized for the work they must perform. Computer-aided design (CAD) systems and virtual reality systems, which create interactive simulations that behave like the real world, require graphics and powerful modelling capabilities. KWS for financial professionals provide access to external databases and the ability to analyze massive amounts of financial data very quickly.

4. *Evaluate the business benefits of using intelligent techniques for knowledge management.*

    Artificial intelligence lacks the flexibility, breadth, and generality of human intelligence, but it can be used to capture, codify, and extend organizational knowledge. Businesses can use artificial intelligence to help them capture and preserve tacit knowledge; for knowledge discovery; to generate solutions to specific problems that are too massive and complex to be analyzed by human beings on their own; and to help firms search for and filter information.

Expert systems capture tacit knowledge from a limited domain of human expertise and express that knowledge in the form of rules. The strategy employed to search through the knowledge base, called the inference engine, can use either forward or backward chaining. Expert systems are most useful for problems of classification or diagnosis. Case-based reasoning represents organizational knowledge as a database of cases that can be continually expanded and refined. When the user encounters a new case, the system searches for similar cases, finds the closest fit, and applies the solutions of the old case to the new case. The new case is stored with successful solutions in the case database.

Fuzzy logic is a software technology for expressing knowledge in the form of rules that use approximate or subjective values. Fuzzy logic has been used for controlling physical devices and is starting to be used for limited decision-making applications.

Neural networks consist of hardware and software that attempt to mimic the thought processes of the human brain. Neural networks are notable for their ability to learn and to recognize patterns that cannot be easily described by humans. They are being used in science, medicine, and business primarily to discover patterns in massive amounts of data.

Genetic algorithms develop solutions to particular problems using genetically based processes such as fitness, crossover, and mutation. Genetic algorithms are beginning to be applied to problems involving optimization, product design, and monitoring industrial systems where many alternatives or variables must be evaluated to generate an optimal solution.

Intelligent agents are software programs with built-in or learned knowledge bases that carry out specific, repetitive, and predictable tasks for an individual user, business process, or software application. Intelligent agents can be programmed to navigate through large amounts of data to locate useful information and in some cases act on that information on behalf of the user.

Key Terms

Agent-based modelling, 524

Artificial intelligence (AI), 517

Backward chaining, 519

Case-based reasoning (CBR), 520

Chief knowledge officer (CKO), 503

Communities of practice (COPs), 504

Computer-aided design (CAD), 515

Data, 500

Expert system, 517

Explicit knowledge, 501

Forward chaining, 517

Fuzzy logic, 521

Genetic algorithms, 523

Hybrid AI systems, 524

Inference engine, 517

Intelligent agents, 524

Intelligent techniques, 504

Investment workstation, 516

Knowledge, 501

Knowledge base, 517

Knowledge discovery, 517

Knowledge engineer, 519

Knowledge management, 502

Knowledge management systems, 500

Knowledge network systems, 506

Knowledge repository, 506

Knowledge work systems (KWS), 504

Learning management system (LMS), 514

Neural networks, 522

Organizational learning, 502

Semistructured knowledge, 506

Semistructured knowledge system, 506

Social bookmarking, 513

Structured knowledge, 506

Structured knowledge systems, 506

Tacit knowledge, 501

Taxonomy, 510

Virtual Reality Modelling Language (VRML), 516

Virtual reality systems, 516

Wisdom, 501

Review Questions

1. What is knowledge management? How does it promote organizational learning? Why is it of great interest to business?

2. Describe the important dimensions of knowledge. Distinguish between data, information, knowledge, and wisdom, and between explicit and tacit knowledge.

3. Describe the stages in the knowledge management value chain that add value as data and information are transformed into useful knowledge.

4. Describe the role played by organizational and management capital in knowledge management.

5. What are structured knowledge systems? Describe their capabilities.

6. What are semistructured knowledge systems? Describe their capabilities.

7. How do taxonomies and tools for tagging facilitate knowledge management?

8. Describe the capabilities of knowledge network systems.

9. Describe the role of the following in facilitating knowledge management: portals, wikis, blogs, social bookmarking, and learning management systems.

10. What are knowledge work systems? What role do they play in knowledge management? What are the generic requirements of knowledge work systems?

11. Describe how the following systems support knowledge work: CAD, virtual reality, and investment workstations.

12. What are intelligent techniques? Why are they of interest to businesses for knowledge management? How does artificial intelligence differ from human intelligence?

13. Define an expert system, describe how it works, and explain how it can contribute to knowledge management.

14. What is case-based reasoning? How does it differ from an expert system? How does it support knowledge management?

15. What is a neural network? How can neural networks help companies with knowledge management?

16. Define and describe fuzzy logic. For what kinds of applications is it suited?

17. What are genetic algorithms? How can they help organizations solve problems? For what kinds of problems are they suited?

18. What are intelligent agents? How can they be used to benefit businesses?

Discussion Questions

1. Knowledge management is a business process, not a technology. Discuss.

2. Describe various ways that knowledge management systems could help firms with sales and marketing or with manufacturing and production.

3. It has been said that knowledge management is about people, not technology or processes. Discuss this view.

4. What are some of the intelligent systems you use on a daily basis? Describe them and how they add value to your life, your work, or your schooling.

Teamwork: Rating Knowledge Network Systems

With a group of classmates, select two knowledge network system products, such as AskMe Enterprise and Tacit ActiveNet™. Compare their features and capabilities. To prepare your analysis, use articles from computer magazines and the Web sites for the knowledge network software vendors. If possible, use electronic presentation software to present your findings to the class.

Learning Track Module

Challenges of Knowledge Management Systems. If you want to learn more about the challenges of implementing and using knowledge management systems, you will find a Learning Track Module on this topic on MyMISLab for this chapter.

For online exercises, please visit www.pearsoned.ca/mymislab.

HANDS-ON **MIS**   Application Exercises

The projects in this section give you hands-on experience developing a knowledge management systems strategy for a real-world company, using expert system or spreadsheet tools to create a simple expert system and using intelligent agents to research products for sale on the Web.

Achieving Operational Excellence: Identifying Opportunities for Knowledge Management

Software skills: Web browser software, presentation software
Business skills: Knowledge management strategy formulation

This project provides an opportunity for you to identify applications for knowledge management at a real-world business and to suggest value-adding knowledge management applications.

Senior management has started reading about knowledge management and has asked you to explore opportunities for improving knowledge management at Dirt Bikes Canada. Write a report answering the following questions:

1. What are the most important knowledge assets at Dirt Bikes Canada? What functions and employee positions are responsible for creating, distributing, and using these knowledge assets? Are all these assets explicit knowledge?

2. What knowledge outside the organization is required by the company?

3. How could the following employee groups benefit from knowledge management: designers and engineers, product development specialists, marketing specialists, sales department staff and representatives, and managers.

4. Describe the kinds of knowledge management systems that would be most valuable for each of these groups. What information would each of these systems provide?

5. Use the Web to research how the company could make better use of the Internet for knowledge management. What Internet information resources (specific Web sites or Usenet groups) would be most useful to Dirt Bikes Canada?

6. Describe an enterprise portal for one of the employee groups listed above. To which knowledge resources would it link? What would the home page of this portal look like?

7. (Optional) Use electronic presentation software to summarize your findings for management.

Improving Decision Making: Building a Simple Expert System for Retirement Planning

Software skills: Spreadsheet formulas and the IF function or an expert system tool
Business skills: Benefits eligibility determination

Expert systems typically use a large number of rules. This project has been simplified to reduce the number of rules, but it will give you experience working with a series of rules to develop an application.

When employees at your company retire, they are given cash bonuses. These cash bonuses are based on the length of employment and the retiree's age. To receive a bonus, an employee must be at least 50 years of age and have worked for the company for five years. The following table summarizes the criteria for determining bonuses.

Using the information provided, build a simple expert system. Find a demonstration copy of an expert system software tool on the Web that you can download. Alternatively, use your spreadsheet software to develop the expert system. (If you are using spreadsheet software, we suggest using the IF function so you can see how rules are created.)

Length of Employment	Bonus
< 5 years	No bonus
5–10 years	20 percent of current annual salary
11–15 years	30 percent of current annual salary
16–20 years	40 percent of current annual salary
21–25 years	50 percent of current annual salary
26 or more years	100 percent of current annual salary

Improving Decision Making:
Using Intelligent Agents for Comparison Shopping

Software skills: Web browser and shopping bot software
Business skills: Product evaluation and selection

This project will give you experience using shopping bots to search online for products, find product information, and find the best prices and vendors.

You have decided to purchase a new digital camera. Select a digital camera you might want to purchase, such as the Canon PowerShot SD 700 or the Fuji FinePix E900. To purchase the camera as inexpensively as possible,

try several of the shopping bot sites, which do the price comparisons for you. Visit My Simon (**www.mysimon.com**), BizRate.com, and Froogle.com. Compare these shopping sites in terms of their ease of use, number of offerings, speed in obtaining information, thoroughness of information offered about the product and seller, and price selection. Which site or sites would you use and why? Which camera would you select and why? How helpful were these sites for making your decision?

CASE STUDY | Can Knowledge Systems Help Boeing Trounce Airbus?

With more than 150 000 employees worldwide, the Boeing Company is a giant producer of passenger airplanes, business jets, military aircraft, helicopters, flight instruments, and satellites. Until recently, Boeing was the world's number one commercial jet aircraft producer. It is now in a head-to-head struggle with Airbus for this position.

Airbus is 80 percent owned by European Aeronautic Defence & Space Co. (EADS) and 20 percent by the United Kingdom's BAE Systems, and receives subsidized loans from European governments. In 1996, Airbus decided to challenge Boeing for the jumbo jet market. Airbus management predicts air travel will expand rapidly, requiring many giant jumbo jets to carry the increased mass of passengers without hiking up operational costs. It envisions a hub-and-spoke model of air travel where jumbo jets transport passengers to a small number of hub cities, from which passengers transfer to smaller connecting flights to their ultimate destinations.

Boeing management has a very different vision.

It believes that most travellers prefer to fly from their own city nonstop to their destination, for example, Detroit to Shanghai rather than Detroit to Tokyo to Shanghai. Nonstop flights do not generally need jumbo jets. It foresees a turn to smaller airliners that will fly quickly and inexpensively, enabling passengers to fly nonstop from departure to destination, bypassing the overcrowded hubs. All in all, Boeing foresees a strong expansion of smaller jet sales rather than of jumbo jet sales. Both companies' business and product development strategies are based on these differing visions.

In addition to Airbus competition, Boeing faces difficult conditions because the market for commercial airplanes has been shrinking due to airline mergers and the downturn in air travel after the September 11, 2001, terrorist attacks. The company moved its global headquarters from Seattle to Chicago to focus on newer businesses based on information and communications technologies.

Boeing's management has been trying to lower costs by using technology to reform inefficient business processes. Boeing's airplane production process used to be highly paper-intensive, with a final design of the Boeing 747 consisting of approximately 75 000 paper engineering drawings. Boeing designers long ago realized they would save much production time if they reused existing designs rather than designing each aircraft from scratch. However, the process of design customization was manual and took more than 1000 engineers a year of full-time work to complete. For every customization choice on every airplane built, hundreds of pages of detailed drawings needed to be drawn manually.

To reuse old paper aircraft configurations and parts designs, the engineers first needed to search through an immense number of paper drawings to find appropriate designs to reuse for the specific configuration. They then laboriously copied the old designs to use for the new plane. Inevitably, errors crept into the new designs—large numbers of errors, given the large numbers of design sheets—because of unavoidable copying mistakes.

It used to take 800 computers to manage the coordination of engineering and manufacturing, and many of these did not communicate directly with each other. The list of parts produced by engineering for a given airplane was configured differently from the lists used by manufacturing and customer service. Ultimately, the parts list had to be broken down, converted, and recomputed up to 13 times during the production of a single plane.

Another problem with manual design was that the staff needed to create life-size mock-ups in plywood and plastic to ensure that everything fit and that the pipes and wires that run through the plane are placed properly and do not interfere with other necessary equipment. The mock-ups were also needed to verify the accuracy of part specifications. Building mock-ups was a slow, expensive, laborious process. At production time, errors would again occur when part numbers of specifications were manually copied and at times miscopied onto order sheets, resulting in the arrival of many wrong or mis-sized parts.

Engineers worked in separate fiefdoms based on their field of specialization. Some engineers designed the plane's parts, others assembled them, and others designed the parts' packing crates. They rarely compared notes. If production engineers discovered a part that did not fit, they sent a complaint back to the designers located in another plant. The designers then pulled out their drawings, reconfigured the part to make it match drawings of the surrounding parts, and sent the new design back to the plant. Warehouses were filled with paper.

In the early 1990s, Boeing began switching to a "paperless design" model, which it used to computerize the design and production of its 777 aircraft. The 777 aircraft carries 300 to 440 passengers and lowers operating, maintenance, and fuel costs because it uses lighter materials and can fly with only two pilots and two engines. The "paperless design" system employs Dassault Systems' CATIA computer-aided design software, nine IBM mainframes, a Cray supercomputer, and 2200 workstations, storing 3500 billion bits of information. It has enabled engineers to call up any of the 777's millions of parts, modify them, fit them into the surrounding structure, and put them back into the plane's "electronic box" so that other engineers can make their own adjustments.

Boeing assembled a single parts list that can be used by every division without modification. In addition, management established design-production teams that brought together designers and fabricators from a range of specialties throughout the whole process. Ultimately, the airplane was designed entirely on the computer screen and was initially assembled without expensive mock-ups. The company cut overall engineering design errors by 50 percent while designing and building a 777 in 10 months.

Although Boeing's 777 was a marketplace hit, Airbus continued to take market share from Boeing. The 9/11 terrorist attacks depressed demand for air travel, and Boeing's profits dropped 80 percent between 2001 and 2002. In 2002, Boeing's military division surpassed its commercial aviation division in revenue, despite Boeing's historic devotion to aircraft development. In 2003, for the first time in history, Airbus delivered more planes than Boeing. Boeing's market share had plunged from nearly 70 percent in 1996 to roughly 50 percent, and the company had to cut 60 000 employees.

Since then, Boeing has been on the rebound. Airbus stumbled in its launch of its giant A380 jumbo jet, which has two decks and is capable of flying 550 passengers. The A380 completed a successful maiden flight in April 2005, but Airbus announced that deliveries would be six months late due to the complexity of wiring the aircraft for sophisticated custom equipment such as in-flight entertainment and communications units requested by some airlines. Since the A380's electronic systems are highly integrated, a small change in one area ripples throughout the design. In July 2006, Airbus announced another six-month delay in A380 deliveries, again because of wiring problems. Inability to easily solve these problems caused Airbus to announce further delays the following September. At that time, EADS said it

was too early to say how long the latest delivery delay would last or how much it would cost.

Boeing, in the meantime, innovated again with its 787 "Dreamliner." The 787 is designed to carry 200 to 300 people on routes from North America to Europe and Asia. Boeing designed this plane to fly long distances economically while keeping passengers comfortable and economizing on fuel. About half of each plane will be made from carbon-fibre composite materials, which are lighter than aluminium and can be built in larger sections. The 787 offers more cabin pressure, humidity, headroom, and window space than comparable commercial planes. Its engines use about 20 percent less fuel per kilometre than similarly sized twin-engine planes. One version of the 787 is capable of flying 8300 nautical miles, long enough to fly nonstop from New York to Hong Kong. Boeing took only 4.5 years to bring the 787 to market, 16 to 18 months faster than most other models, and the 787 will enter service in 2008.

Boeing's 787 made all Airbus models on the market look outdated. To compete with the 787, Airbus, in the summer of 2004, offered the A350, a midsize plane for carrying 250 to 375 passengers that is basically a retooled version of its older A330 model. So far it has had little success, with a number of airlines stating that the A350's operating economies and comfort did not match those of the 787.

For Boeing, the 787 is a daring experiment because it is using a new production process. Instead of being produced under one roof, the 787 is being built in a modular assembly process. Boeing farmed out design and construction of about 80 percent of the aircraft to hundreds of other companies, many outside the United States.

Boeing Winnipeg is the largest aerospace composite manufacturer in Canada. The Winnipeg division designs, develops, and fabricates complex composite structures and sub-assemblies for its parent company, particularly for commercial airliners. The Canadian division is responsible for work on some of the wing structures, main landing gear doors, and vertical fins for the new 787 Dreamliner program. The Winnipeg plant will also furnish forward engine struts and aft pylons for the 787 project. Mitsubishi is in charge of the wings while Messier-Dowty of France is making the landing gear. Foreign suppliers have freedom to design the components, reducing Boeing's product development costs. Obviously, the Winnipeg division is working with both Mitsubishi and Messier-Dowty on the wings and landing gear assemblies.

Boeing and its key suppliers are using software that lets designers around the world electronically collaborate in designing components and manufacturing processes. Dassault Systems added features to its planning and design software to cope with Boeing's global supply chain. Boeing expanded its use of Dassault's version 5 Product Life Cycle Management software from 1000 to 6000 licences. This software suite includes CATIA design software, Enovia, a tool for managing design data, and Delmia, which simulates assembly and manufacturing processes. These software tools enable designers to use a single set of data and to simulate digitally the plane's life cycle from design through production, quickly modelling iterations in design to reduce errors and redundant work. CATIA V5 software makes it possible for Boeing's suppliers and subcontractors to have a bigger role in designing and developing the new jet. Boeing wants this technology to cut both recurring and non-recurring design and manufacturing costs in half compared with the 777.

Outsourcing the 787 required Dassault to improve integration of its CATIA, Enovia, and Delmia modules for Boeing. So Dassault created in Enovia a 3-D master file to serve as a single source for digital definitions across the software suite. Boeing also needed custom tools to handle designs with the carbon-fibre composite material.

As crucial deadlines loomed, Boeing engineers wrestled with several significant technical and production problems that could threaten delivery of the 787 in 2008. The fuselage section failed in company testing, forcing Boeing to make more sections than planned and to re-examine quality and safety. The overall weight of the plane was too high, especially the carbon-fibre wings. Suppliers struggled to meet Boeing's technical standards and ambitious production deadlines. Boeing would not accept the first two nose sections. Software programs designed by a variety of vendors had trouble "talking" to one another.

Airbus has also run into additional snags. In July 2006, Airbus announced further design changes to the A350 to widen its cabin and windows and provide adjustable cabin humidity. But it will not be able to enter service until 2012, four years after the 787. Airbus' problems with its A380 jumbo jet made it more difficult to make the design changes to the A350 required to match Boeing. Airbus also announced a long-term overhaul of its operations. To further cut costs, boost efficiency, and improve planning, Airbus needs to involve its suppliers more in the design process as Boeing has done. While Boeing started making the switch 10 years ago, Airbus was focused on merging its operations into a single company from its original structure as a diffuse consortium. According to Airbus Chairman Christian Streiff, "It will take about 10 years for us to get back to the level of Boeing in terms of development and efficiency."

The 787 has been central to Boeing's revival, racking up 350 orders in two years. It forced Airbus onto the defensive and to rethink its big plane strategy. Boeing calls the 787 its "game changer." Any major problems with the 787 would not only jeopardize sales, but Boeing's credibility and leading position in the passenger aircraft market.

Sources: Leslie Wayne, "Boeing Bets the House on Its 787 Dreamliner," *The New York Times*, May 7, 2006; Daniel Michaels and J. Lynn Lunsford, "Under Pressure, Airbus Redesigns a Troubled Plane," *The Wall Street Journal*, July 14, 2006; Simon Clow and Maeve Curtain, "EADS Sees Years of Work Ahead to Repair Airbus," *The Wall Street Journal*, October 5, 2006; Mark Landler, "Airbus Offers Up Redesigned A350 in a Challenge to Boeing," *The New York Times*, July 18, 2006; Stanley Holmes, "On a Wing and a Prayer at Boeing," *Business Week*, June 7, 2006; Daniel Michaels, "Airbus Opens Overhaul by Looking at Procurement," *The Wall Street Journal*, September 25, 2006; J. Lynn Lunsford and Daniel Michaels, "Bet on Huge Plane Trips Up Airbus," *The Wall Street Journal*, June 15, 2006, and "After Four Years in the Rear, Boeing is Set to Jet Past Airbus," *The Wall Street Journal*, June 10, 2005; Beth Bacheldor, "Boeing's Flight Plan," *Information Week*, February 16, 2004; Edward Wong, "For Jet Rivals, Caution Here, Swagger There," *The New York Times*, July 28, 2002; and "Boeing Winnipeg," **www.boeing.com/commercial/winnipeg**, accessed May 8, 2007.

CASE STUDY QUESTIONS

1. Analyze Boeing and its business strategy using the value chain and competitive forces models.

2. What is the relationship of knowledge management to Boeing's business strategy? How is Boeing using knowledge management systems to execute its business model and business strategy?

3. Evaluate Boeing's new business strategy. What management, organization, and technology issues will Boeing face as it attempts to implement the strategy? What role will knowledge management play in this strategy? How successful will Boeing be in pursuing that strategy?

4. Using the facts presented in this case, what role has knowledge management played in Airbus's business strategy and business performance?

Part IV CANADIAN CASE STUDY:
Second Life: A New Generation of Online Application

Imagine you are a business student attending a British Columbia university, majoring in management information systems. Now imagine that you enjoy logging on to a site known as Second Life (**www.secondlife.com**) to play around in a virtual animated environment. Your interests, in addition to business, are criminal justice and law enforcement.

While dabbling one afternoon in Second Life, you meet three other animated characters, who, it turns out, are actually members of Vancouver's Police Department. They are recruiting for new skilled technology workers to join the Vancouver Police Department. You decide to talk with these

police characters and apply for one of these new-generation police positions.

This scenario is not a fantasy. Second Life exists; it is a sophisticated, online three-dimensional virtual world. It is customizable; users can register for free and create their own characters, known as avatars; there are no assigned roles for these avatars. Your avatar can physically represent you or can look different. Your avatar may be an animal, a metaphysical character, a dragon—or almost anything else. You can customize your avatar's height, weight, skin colour, hair colour, and almost any physical characteristic. You can even name it with a pseudonym that represents whatever you desire. In Second Life, avatars can walk, run, dance, jump, fly, and even teleport to different environments. They can meet, interact, play with, and date other avatars, and they can also build, buy, and sell things.

"Buy and sell?" you ask. What can they buy and sell? Second Life users who register for free have a limited choice of clothes for their avatars. However, if you pay for a premium membership (US $6.00 per month, billed annually in advance, or US $9.95 per month, charged monthly), you have access to more costumes and accessories (such as boots, purses, and bookbags). Premium members can also buy virtual real estate to build a nightclub, gym, coffee house, school, resort, hotel, or even a home.

Second Life trade takes place in a virtual currency named Linden dollars (L $), named after Linden Labs, which developed Second Life. Premium users receive a one-time grant in Linden dollars of L $1250 plus a monthly stipend of L $300. There are systems for converting Linden dollars to real-world US dollars; as of July 2007, the exchange rate was L $265 to US $1.

Let's look deeper at what Second Life is and then at what it represents for the future of online applications and electronic commerce. Second Life requires a fairly fast computer and graphics card and a broadband Internet connection. Users who register (and are known as members or residents) download the Second Life user software and can then begin their Second Life travels. Users can also create multiple accounts, appearing as various avatars. There is an additional premium for these multiple accounts, but users commonly create multiple "first accounts," bypassing the need to pay the premium. It is interesting that Second Life was originally an undeveloped environment or grid, the equivalent of a wilderness waiting to be developed by users.

Second Life members develop their own "content" or environment and retain intellectual property rights to their creations in the real world. The content varies from the costumes members can purchase, to virtual shopping malls and gaming platforms. In addition to selling products, services are also available, such as classes in a variety of disciplines. Other members then buy this content, e.g., an avatar costume, with Linden dollars, and the creator receives payment in Linden dollars, which can eventually be converted to real-world cash. A small percentage of residents actually earn income from the Second Life economy, from a few hundred to even several thousand US dollars a month. A larger percentage of users make enough Linden dollars to offset most of their own Second Life expenditures. You may find it amusing that, in economic circles, the Linden currency has stimulated discussion regarding the possibility of taxing income earned in Linden dollars.

To facilitate the creation and sale of its virtual property, Second Life has a three-dimensional modelling tool enabling residents to create virtual landscapes, buildings, vehicles, furniture, costumes, machines—almost any thing the mind can invent. There is also a standard library of gestures and sounds that avatars can make. Second Life has its own scripting language, LSL, to add behaviours to objects, such as opening doors when approached. Creators of objects and behaviours can mark them as "no copy," "no mod" (cannot be modified by another), or "no trans" (meaning no transfer

to another avatar). Residents are even recording music and uploading the files to Second Life so other residents can enjoy the music.

Residents of Second Life can buy virtual real estate in 16-acre parcels, termed islands, and members can develop their islands as they see fit. Premium members can buy land up to 512 m² without paying an additional fee. Owning larger island areas requires the payment of additional premiums (from US $5 per month to US $295 per month). This virtual real estate can be sold to other residents for a profit—of course, a profit in Linden dollars. Some private Second Life islands, governed by residents, have covenants, limiting resale or commercial activity, or having other restrictions.

Be warned: There is adult content in Second Life; some islands are set up as brothels or pot shops. Mature content is separated from underage users: Teen Second Life was created in 2005 to permit teenagers to play in Second Life without having to falsify their personal information. Teen Second Life requires a valid cell phone number with SMS enabled (for the first time logon validation message) but no longer requires a parent's credit card number.

To communicate in a text-based mode, residents can use local chat or global instant messaging. Chatting is used for public conversation that can be heard within a local range of 25 virtual metres. Whispering may be heard within 18 virtual metres, while shouting may be heard up to 96 virtual metres away. Instant messaging is used for private conversations between only two avatars or the members of a group. Second Life is currently beta-testing voice communication.

Avatars can walk or run, but they can also fly more than 170 virtual metres above their current terrain and teleport to a specific virtual location. Avatars can ride in and even buy their own vehicles. Interestingly, an avatar can create a "personal landmark," a sort of home base, and teleport back to it at any time. They can also give the landmark away to another avatar.

The technology driving Second Life is very advanced. Using various server farms, Second Life stores data about its residents and their accounts, the products and services that have been created, and the geography of Second Life (i.e., real estate owned by its residents), all of which are known as "assets." Occasionally, the servers are overloaded and Second Life slows down, with some environments temporarily crashing. Linden Labs uses open-standards technologies, permitting users to create and improve software for the use of Linden Labs and Second Life. There are viewers, i.e., client software, for Microsoft Windows, Mac OS X, and most versions of Linux.

There is much to say about how Second Life works. You may also be wondering about how it got started, and what makes it so important for commerce.

In 2003, Philip Rosedale, a former chief technology officer at Real Networks, created Second Life as part of Linden Labs, the company he founded in 1999. Rosedale's investors included top technology gurus Mitch Kapor (creator of Lotus), Pierre Omidyar (founder of eBay), Jeff Bezos (founder of Amazon.com), and Ray Ozzie (Microsoft's technology architect). Interestingly, they can all be found in Second Life as avatars. Kapor also serves on Linden Lab's board of directors.

The founders of Second Life envisioned that Second Life would be important because its economy and its residents could provide a real marketplace for real-world companies. Let's look at how that happens, and how real-world companies and other organizations use Second Life.

In June 2007, Second Life had 8 297 295 members from more than 100 countries. Of these users, 1.5 million had logged on in the last 30 days. More than 40 000 users are logged on at almost any point during the day and into the night. More than 20 000 new members join Second Life every day. More than US $1.5 million is spent on Second Life in a 24-hour period. In June 2007, more than 300 000 residents spent Linden dollars, generating more than 14 million Linden dollar transactions. The Second Life economy has L$2.6 billion in circulation. The sheer volume of this virtual market has attracted a number of commercial, governmental, and not-for-profit organizations to try to use this market to further their goals.

As we saw at the beginning of this discussion, the Vancouver Police Department is recruiting on Second Life. The Vancouver Police Department held an information session for potential recruits in June 2007 on Second Life. After the information session, the Police Department received three resumes by e-mail and actually decided to interview a candidate who had attended the virtual information session while in Italy.

Like the Vancouver Police, Hewlett-Packard, Microsoft, and other technology companies are conducting initial interviews and participating in job fairs online at Second Life. Of course, follow-up interviews are held in person. Interestingly, certain online etiquette applies, even for avatars, during job interviews. Communication is by instant messaging, with real-world information, such as names, being exchanged. One candidate for a Hewlett-Packard job was a man whose avatar was female, but he felt that the Hewlett-Packard representative would understand that he was a man, since he had told the representative his real-world name. Gaffes such as having an avatar run into a wall or presenting a beer rather than a resume to the interviewer are usually laughed off by both the resident and the interviewer since both know that the Second Life technology can occasionally be tricky to manoeuvre.

Governmental agencies also take an interest in this online world. Sweden recently became the first country to open a Second Life embassy to promote Sweden's image and culture.

Second Life is also being used as a giant virtual classroom for major colleges and universities. Great Northern Way Campus is a collaboration between four Canadian schools: the University of British Columbia, Simon Fraser University, British Columbia Institute of Technology, and the Emily Carr Institute of Art and Design. This campus has a real-world presence just east of Vancouver. In Second Life, however, the campus erected a new virtual campus with a state-of-the-art virtual building on a Second Life island. Courses are offered through this online campus for the Masters in Digital Media program. Thompson Rivers University is another B.C. university using Second Life to deliver instruction. In Ontario, Mohawk College and Loyalist College offer classes through Second Life. In the U.S., the universities of Harvard, Princeton, and Stanford also teach through Second Life. Second Life is even used at a number of education institutions in Europe, and as far afield as Queensland University in Australia.

Late in 2006, a new trend occurred in Second Life. Large consortia of educational institutions have begun to purchase islands and then divide the "land" into smaller parcels to rent to colleges, universities, and educational projects and libraries. Land can be rented for as little as $200 per year, with permission to use common space for larger events. Some of these universities even host advertising for positions for faculty in Second Life. Other corporations doing business in Second Life include Microsoft, Warner Brothers, Nike, Major League Baseball, Dell Computer, Adidas, General Motors, and Circuit City. One way in which a corporation might use Second Life is as another marketing and promotion channel. For example, an avatar can buy a pair of Nike shoes and wear them; Nike hopes, of course, that the real-world resident will also buy a pair of their shoes.

Pontiac recently launched a Second Life presence by buying a six-region land mass called Motorati Island, which offers free virtual land to residents to create a car culture online. Pontiac hopes that these residents will create their own projects devoted to car culture.

The phrase "If you build it, they will come," from the movie *Field of Dreams*, has achieved wide cultural recognition. In terms of Second Life, these words have certainly been true. Online users by the millions have flocked to create the virtual environment that is Second Life. It is apparent that schools, organizations, and corporations all believe that if they build Second Life environments, not only will Second Life avatars come, but so will their real-world counterparts flock to these organizations' real-world environments.

To date, there has been no publicly available research to show that companies and other groups hosting a Second Life presence are increasing sales or memberships. In fact, some users who pay for premium membership resent the companies that ride their efforts for free without paying the premium. So it remains to be seen exactly how and how much Second Life will change the way we do business and receive education. But as the first such online environment with such a high volume of activity, it is possible that Second Life will present a new way of doing business.

Sources: Wency Leung, "Recruiting Real Talent in a Virtual World," *The Globe and Mail*, July 16, 2007; A Media Circus, "Pontiac Second Life Case Study," **http://amediacirc.us/2007/02/29/pontiac-second-life-case-studyraw-notes/**, accessed July 15, 2007; "Second Life," **http://en.wikipedia.org/wiki/Second_Life**, accessed July 15, 2007; Bob Rankin, "What is Second Life?" **http://askbobrankin.com/what_is_second_life.html**, accessed July 15, 2007; **www.secondlife.com**, accessed July 22, 2007; **http://simteach.com/wiki/index.php?title=Institutions_and_Organizations_in_SL#UNIVERSITIES.2C_COLLEGES_.26_SCHOOLS**, accessed July 22, 2007; and Second Life, "Economic Statistics," **www.secondlife.com/whatis/economy_stats.php**, accessed July 22, 2007.

Video Resource:

"Visiting Second Life's Virtual World." *News in Review*. Canadian Broadcasting Corporation. February 2007.

CASE STUDY QUESTIONS

1. Do you think Second Life is a new way of doing business? Why or why not?

2. Do you think Second Life will survive and thrive, or do you think other similar online sites will catch up and eventually surpass Second Life?

3. Second Life has had its share of technical glitches. Discuss whether you think the company owes it to its users to see that those do not recur, or whether you think the company should minimize expenses and only upgrade its technology when the system crashes become longer and more frequent.

4. Why would companies and other organizations choose to host a Second Life presence? How would a company make the decision to buy in to Second Life? Who would be assigned to work on creating and maintaining the company's presence on Second Life?

References

Chapter 1

"Adidas Goes for the Gold in Customer Service." www.ups.com (accessed June 14, 2006).

"Triumphs & Trip-Ups in 2004." *Baseline* (December 20, 2004).

Avison, David. "Information Systems in the MBA Curriculum: An International Perspective." *Communications of the AIS* 11. Article 6 (January 2003).

Barnes, Dave. "Delivering Corporate Citizenship." *Optimize Magazine* (September 2005).

Baskerville, Richard L., and Michael D. Myers. "Information Systems as a Reference Discipline." *MIS Quarterly* 26, no. 1 (March 2002).

Bautsch, H., J. Granger, T. Karnjate, F. Kahn, Z. Leveston, and G. Niehus. "An Investigation of Mobile Phone Use: A Sociotechnical Approach." *Socio-technical Systems in Industry*, Summer Session. Department of Industrial Engineering, University of Wisconsin, Madison (2001).

Bebasat, Izak, and Robert W. Zmud. "The Identity Crisis within the IS Discipline: Defining and Communicating the Discipline's Core Properties." *MIS Quarterly* 27, no. 2 (June 2003).

Brynjolffson, Erik. "The IT Productivity Gap." *Optimize Magazine* 21 (July 2003).

Brynjolfsson, Erik, and Lorin M. Hitt. "Beyond Computation: Information Technology, Organizational Transformation, and Business Performance." *Journal of Economic Perspectives* 14, no. 4 (2000).

Carr, Nicholas. "IT Doesn't Matter." *Harvard Business Review* (May 2003).

Davern, Michael J., and Robert J. Kaufman. "Discovering Potential and Realizing Value From Information Technology Investments." *Journal of Management Information Systems* 16, no. 4 (2000).

Davis, G. B., and M. H. Olson. *Management Information Systems: Conceptual Foundations, Structure, and Development*. New York: Mc Graw-Hill (1985).

Dedrick, Jason, Vijay Gurbaxani, and Kenneth L. Kraemer. "Information Technology and Economic Performance: A Critical Review of the Empirical Evidence." Center for Research on Information Technology and Organizations, University of California, Irvine (December 2001).

Duvall, Mel. "Kia Motors America: Lemon Aid." *Baseline* (June 2005).

eMarketer, Inc. "Canada Online." October 2006. www.emarketer.com/Reports/All/Em_canada_nov06.aspx?src=report_head_info_reports (August 1, 2007).

Environics. *Environics Communications*. October 10, 2006. http://eci.environics.net/news/Default.asp?articleID=1176 (accessed June 27, 2007).

Fairways Golf. "Stephen Ross Fired as RCGA Executive Director." March 9, 2007. www.fairwaysgolf.ca/news.php?id=290&what=news (accessed June 1, 2007).

Galliers, Robert D., and Maureen Meadows. "A Discipline Divided: Globalization and Parochialism in *Information Systems Research*." *Communications of the AIS* 11, Article 5 (January 2003).

Greenspan, Alan. "The Revolution in Information Technology." Boston College Conference on the New Economy (March 6, 2000).

Hacki, Remo, and Julian Lighton, "The Future of the Networked Company." *McKinsey Quarterly* 3 (2001).

Hines, Matt. "Case study: BI pulls its weight at heavy-hauler Trimac." *CRM News*. February 13, 2002. http://searchcrm.techtarget.com/originalContent/0,289142,sid11_gci801922,00.htm (accessed August 30, 2007).

Hymowitz, Carol. "Have Advice, Will Travel." *The Wall Street Journal* (June 5, 2006).

Industry Canada. "Canadian ICT Sector Profile." July 2007. http://strategis.ic.gc.ca/epic/site/ict-tic.nsf/en/h_it07229e.html (accessed August 30, 2007).

Jorgenson, Dale W. "Information Technology and Economic Performance: A Critical Review of Empirical Evidence." Center for Research on Information Technology and Organizations, University of California, Irvine (December, 2001).

Lamb, Roberta; Steve Sawyer, and Rob Kling. "A Social Informatics Perspective on Socio-Technical Networks." In *Proceedings of Americas Conference Information Systems*, edited H. Michael Chung. Long Beach, CA: UCLA (2004).

Laudon, Kenneth C. *Computers and Bureaucratic Reform*. New York: John Wiley and Sons (1974).

Lee, H. "Broadband and Mobile Opportunities: A Socio-technical Perspective." *Journal of Information Technology* 18 (2003).

Lev, Baruch. *Intangibles: Management, Measurement and Reporting*. The Brookings Institution Press (2001).

Marchand, Donald A. "Extracting the Business Value of IT: It Is Usage, Not Just Deployment that Counts!" *The Copco Institute Journal of Financial Transformation* (2004).

Martron.com. "RCGA Case Study." www.martron.com. April 21, 2005 (accessed June 1, 2007).

McGrath, Rita Gunther, and Ian C. McMillan. "Assessing Technology Projects Using Real Options Reasoning." Industrial Research Institute (2000).

Microsoft.com. "RCGA Cuts Costs and Improves Customer Service with Microsoft®.NET-based Online Tournament Program." www.microsoft.com/ canada/casestudies/rcga.mspx?pf=true (accessed June 1, 2007).

Mumford, Enid. "Socio-Technical Design: An Unfulfilled Promise or a Future Opportunity." In R. Baskerville, et. al. *The Social and Organizational Perspective on Research and Practice in Information Technology*. London: Chapman-Hall (2000).

Orlikowski, Wanda J. "The duality of technology: Rethinking the concept of technology in organizations." *Organization Science* 3, no.3 (1992).

Orlikowski, Wanda J., and J.J. Baroudi. "Studying Information Technology in Organizations: Research Approaches and Assumptions." *Information Systems Research* 2 (1991).

Orlikowski, Wanda J., and Stephen R. Bailey. "Technology and Institutions: What Can Research on Information Technology and Research on Organizations Learn from Each Other?" *MIS Quarterly* 25, no. 2 (June 2001).

Pew Research Center. "Trends 2005; Chapter 4: Internet: Mainstreaming of Online Life." (January 25, 2005).

Potterf, Katheryn. "Ready to Roll." *Profit Magazine* (May 2006).

Quinn, Francis J. "eBusiness Evangelist; An Interview with Erik Brynjolfsson." *Supply Chain Management Review* (May/June 2006).

Rosmarin, Rachel. "Accenture CIO Frank Modruson." *Forbes* (June 2, 2006).

Ross, Jeanne W., and Peter Weill. "Six IT Decisions Your IT People Shouldn't Make." *Harvard Business Review* (November 2002).

Rowley, Ian. "No Traffic Ahead for Toyota." *Business Week* (February 6, 2006).

Sawyer, S., and J. P. Allen. "Broadband and Mobile Opportunities: A Socio-technical Perspective." *Journal of Information Technology* 18 (June 2003).

Stiroh, Kevin. "The Economic Impact of Information Technology." Federal Reserve Bank of New York (2001).

Teece, David. *Economic Performance and Theory of the Firm: The Selected Papers of David Teece*. London: Edward Elgar Publishing (1998).

Triplett, Jack E., and Barry P. Bosworth. "Productivity in Services Industries: Trends and Measurement Issues." The Brookings Institution, Washington D.C. (2003).

United Parcel Service. *Round UPS* (Winter 2006).

Chapter 2

Choi, Soon-Yong, and Andrew B. Whinston. "Communities of Collaboration." *IQ Magazine* (July/August 2001).

Concur Public Relations. "All Air Canada Content Now Available Through Concur Technologies' Cliqbook Travel." March 22, 2007. www.concur.com/about/news/press.html?id=109 (accessed May 8, 2007).

Concur Public Relations. "Corporate Expense Management Case Study: MarketStar Stays Ahead of the ROI Curve with Concur Expense." - www.concur.com/about/customers/case_studies/marketstar.html (accessed June 28, 2006).

Ferdows, Kasra, Michael A. Lewis, and Jose A. D. Machuca. "Rapid-Fire Fulfillment." *Harvard Business Review* (November 2004).

Finney, Paul Burnham."Tools Can Catch Expense-Account Padders (and Make Filing Easier)." *The NewYork Times* (June 27, 2006).

Gruman, Galen. "Strategic HR Integration." *CIO Magazine* (August 15, 2005).

Kalakota, Ravi, and Marcia Robinson. *e-Business2.0: Roadmap for Success.* Reading, MA: Addison-Wesley (2001).

Keen, Peter G. W., and M. S. Morton. *Decision Support Systems: An Organizational Perspective.* Reading, MA: Addison-Wesley (1978).

Malone, Thomas M., Kevin Crowston, Jintae Lee, and Brian Pentland. "Tools for Inventing Organizations: Toward a Handbook of Organizational Processes." *Management Science* 45, no. 3 (March 1999).

Microsoft Corporation. "Hudson's Bay Company Gains More Accurate Business Snapshot of its Zellers Operations with Microsoft SQL Server 2000 Reporting Services." October 12, 2004. www.microsoft.com/canada/casestudies/hbc.mspx (accessed May 10, 2007).

Nolan, Richard, and F. Warren McFarland. "Information Technology and the Board of Directors." *Harvard Business Review* (October 1, 2005).

O'Leary, Daniel E. *Enterprise Resource Planning Systems: Systems Life Cycle, Electronic Commerce, and Risk.* New York: Cambridge University Press (2000).

Oracle Corporation. "Alcoa Implements Oracle Solution 20% below Projected Cost, Eliminates 43 Legacy Systems." www.oracle.com (accessed August 21, 2005).

Patrick, Ryan. "HBC Puts LID Technology on Zellers Inventory." *IT World Canada,* www.itworldcanada.com/Mobile/ViewArticle.aspx?title=&id=idgml-2726a919-81bd-4628&s=395692 (accessed May 10, 2007).

Picarelle, Lisa. Planes, Trains, and Automobiles. *Customer Relationship Management* (February 2004).

SAP. "Alcan Packaging Implements mySAP SCM to Increase Shareholder Value." www.mysap.com (accessed August 20, 2005).

Siebel Systems. "Saab Cars USA Increases Lead Follow-Up from 38 Percent to 50 Percent with Siebel Automotive." www.siebel.com (accessed October 15, 2005).

Simons, Craig. "Kia Makes U.S. Inroads and Builds for Future Growth." Cox News Service (March 14, 2006).

Sprague, Ralph H., Jr., and Eric D. Carlson. *Building Effective Decision Support Systems.* Englewood Cliffs, NJ: Prentice Hall (1982).

Sutton, Neil. "HBC Puts IT Smarts into its Merchandising Strategy." *IT Business Canada,* www.itbusiness.ca/it/client/en/Home/News.asp?id=40143&bsearch=True (accessed May 10, 2007).

Teuke, Molly Rose. "Sealing Success." *Profit Magazine* (February 2006).

Weill, Peter, and Jeanne Ross. "A Matrixed Approach to Designing IT Governance." *MIT Sloan Management Review* 46, no. 2 (Winter 2005).

Xtreme Retail 23. "Hudson's Bay Company Creates an Award-Winning Inventory Solution." www.xtremeretail.com/studies/hbcfinal.pdf (accessed May 10, 2007).

Chapter 3

7-Eleven Inc. "About 7-Eleven." www.7-eleven.com/about/history.asp,7-Eleven (accessed May 11, 2007).

Allison, Graham T. *Essence of Decision—Explaining the Cuban Missile Crisis.* Boston: Little Brown (1971).

Attewell, Paul, and James Rule. "Computing and Organizations: What We Know and What We Don't Know." *Communications of the ACM* 27, no. 12 (December 1984).

Beer, Michael, Russell A. Eisenstat, and Bert Spector. "Why Change Programs Don't Produce Change." *Harvard Business Review* (November–December 1990).

Bresnahan, Timothy F., Erik Brynjolfsson, and Lorin M. Hitt, "Information Technology, Workplace Organization, and the Demand for Skilled Labor." *Quarterly Journal of Economics* 117 (February 2002).

Camuffo, Arnaldo, Pietro Romano, and Andrea Vinellie. "Benetton Transforms Its Global Network." *MIT Sloan Management Review* 43, no. 1 (Fall 2001).

Canadian Tire Corporation. "Company Profile." www2.canadiantire.ca/CTenglish/h_ourstory.html (accessed August 3, 2007).

Christensen, Clayton. "The Past and Future of Competitive Advantage." *MIT Sloan Management Review* 42, no. 2 (Winter 2001).

Clemons, Eric K. "Competing on Analytics." *Harvard Business Review* (January 2006).

Clemons, Eric K. "Evaluation of Strategic Investments in Information Technology." *Communications of the ACM* (January 1991).

Clemons, Eric K. "Sustaining IT Advantage: The Role of Structural Differences." *MIS Quarterly* 15, no. 3 (September 1991).

Clemons, Eric K., Jeanne G. Harris, and Ajay K. Kohli, "How Do They Know Their Customers So Well?" *MIT Sloan Management Review* 42, no. 2 (Winter 2001).

Coase, Ronald H. "The Nature of the Firm." (1937) in Putterman, Louis, and Randall Kroszner. *The Economic Nature of the Firm: A Reader.* Cambridge University Press, 1995.

Crane, Mary. "Child's Play? Amazon Takes On Toys." Forbes.com (July 5, 2006).

Drucker, Peter. "The Coming of the New Organization." *Harvard Business Review* (January–February 1988).

Erasala, Naveen, and John "Skip" Benamati. "Understanding the Electronic Commerce Cycles of Change." *Journal of Organizational Computing and Electronic Commerce* 13, no.1 (2003).

Farhoomand, Ali, and Pauline S.P. Ng. "Creating Sustainable Competitive Advantage Through Internetworked Communities." *Communications of the ACM* 46, no. 9 (September 2003).

Feeny, David E., and Blake Ives. "In Search of Sustainability: Reaping Long-Term Advantage from Investments in Information Technology." *Journal of Management Information Systems* (Summer 1990).

Freeman, John, Glenn R. Carroll, and Michael T. Hannan. "The Liability of Newness: Age Dependence in Organizational Death Rates." *American Sociological Review* 48 (1983).

Fritz, Mary Beth Watson, Sridhar Narasimhan, and Hyeun-Suk Rhee. "Communication and Coordination in the Virtual Office." *Journal of Management Information Systems* 14, no. 4 (Spring 1998).

Gilbert, Clark, and Joseph L. Bower. "Disruptive Change." *Harvard Business Review* (May 2002).

Glaser, Mark. "Movie Download Services Still Need Work." PBS.org (June 30, 2006).

Greeson, Michael. "iTunes' Movie Downloads the 'Tipping Point' for Online Movie Distribution." DigitalTrends.com (June 22, 2006).

Gurbaxani, V., and S. Whang. "The Impact of Information Systems on Organizations and Markets." *Communications of the ACM* 34, no. 1 (January 1991).

Hansell, Saul. "At Last, Movies to Keep Arrive on the Internet." *The New York Times* (April 3, 2006).

Hinds, Pamela, and Sara Kiesler. "Communication across Boundaries: Work, Structure, and Use of Communication Technologies in a Large Organization." *Organization Science* 6, no. 4 (July–August 1995).

Hitt, Lorin M. "Information Technology and Firm Boundaries: Evidence from Panel Data." *Information Systems Research* 10, no. 2 (June 1999).

Hitt, Lorin M., and Erik Brynjolfsson. "Information Technology and Internal Firm Organization: An Exploratory Analysis." *Journal of Management Information Systems* 14, no. 2 (Fall 1997).

Holweg, Matthias, and Frits K. Pil. "Successful Build-to-Order Strategies Start with the Customer." *MIT Sloan Management Review* 43, no. 1 (Fall 2001).

Iansiti, Marco. "Managing the Ecosystem." *Optimize Magazine* (February 2005).

Iansiti, Marco, and Roy Levien, "Strategy as Ecology." *Harvard Business Review* (March 2004).

IBM Corporation. "Canadian Tire Fuels Business Innovation with Information on Demand Initiative." February 15, 2006. www-306.ibm.com/software/success/cssdb.nsf/CS/HSAZ-6M2UBV?OpenDocument&Site=software (accessed May 10, 2007).

Jensen, M. C., and W. H. Meckling. "Specific and General Knowledge and Organizational Science." In *Contract Economics*, edited by L. Wetin and J. Wijkander. Oxford: Basil Blackwell (1992).

Jensen, Michael C., and William H. Meckling. "Theory of the Firm: Managerial Behavior, Agency Costs, and Ownership Structure." *Journal of Financial Economics* 3 (1976).

Kanter, Rosabeth Moss. "The New Managerial Work." *Harvard Business Review* (November–December 1989).

Kauffman, Robert J., and Yu-Ming Wang. "The Network Externalities Hypothesis and Competitive Network Growth." *Journal of Organizational Computing and Electronic Commerce* 12, no. 1 (2002).

Kettinger, William J., Varun Grover, Subashish Guhan, and Albert H. Segors. "Strategic Information Systems Revisited: A Study in Sustainability and Performance." *MIS Quarterly* 18, no. 1 (March 1994).

Keyes, James. "Data on the Fly." *Baseline* (August 2005).

King, J. L., V. Gurbaxani, K. L. Kraemer, F. W. McFarlan, K. S. Raman, and C. S. Yap. "Institutional Factors in Information Technology Innovation." *Information Systems Research* 5, no. 2 (June 1994).

Kling, Rob. "Social Analyses of Computing: Theoretical Perspectives in Recent Empirical Research." *Computing Survey* 12, no. 1 (March 1980).

Koch, Christopher. "Who's Minding the Store?" *CIO* (May 15, 2005).

Kolb, D. A., and A. L. Frohman. "An Organization Development Approach to Consulting." *MIT Sloan Management Review* 12, no. 1 (Fall 1970).

Kontzer, Tony. "Data-Driven." *InformationWeek* (August 2, 2004).

Kopczak, Laura Rock, and M. Eric Johnson. "The Supply-Chain Management Effect." *MIT Sloan Management Review* 44, no. 3 (Spring 2003).

Kraemer, Kenneth, John King, Debora Dunkle, and Joe Lane. *Managing Information Systems*. Los Angeles: Jossey-Bass (1989).

Lamb, Roberta, and Rob Kling. "Reconceptualizing Users as Social Actors in *Information Systems Research*." *MIS Quarterly* 27, no. 2 (June 2003).

Laudon, Kenneth C. "A General Model of the Relationship between Information Technology and Organizations." Center for Research on Information Systems, New York University. Working paper, National Science Foundation (1989).

Laudon, Kenneth C. "Environmental and Institutional Models of Systems Development." *Communications of the ACM* 28, no. 7 (July 1985).

Laudon, Kenneth C. "The Promise and Potential of Enterprise Systems and Industrial Networks." Working paper, The Concours Group. Copyright Kenneth C. Laudon (1999).

Laudon, Kenneth C., and Carol G. Traver. *E-Commerce: Business, Technology, Society*. Upper Saddle River, N.J.: Prentice Hall (2006).

Laudon, Kenneth C., and Kenneth L. Marr, "Information Technology and Occupational Structure." (April 1995).

Laudon, Kenneth C. *Computers and Bureaucratic Reform*. New York: Wiley (1974).

Laudon, Kenneth C. *Dossier Society: Value Choices in the Design of National Information Systems*. New York: Columbia University Press (1986).

Lawrence, Paul, and Jay Lorsch. *Organization and Environment*. Cambridge, MA: Harvard University Press (1969).

Leavitt, Harold J. "Applying Organizational Change in Industry: Structural, Technological, and Humanistic Approaches." In *Handbook of Organizations*. Ed. James G. March. Chicago: Rand McNally (1965).

Levecq, Hugues, and Bruce W. Weber, "Electronic Trading Systems: Strategic Implication of Market Design Choices." *Journal of Organizational Computing and Electronic Commerce* 12, no. 1 (2002).

Malone, Thomas W., JoAnne Yates, and Robert I. Benjamin. "Electronic Markets and Electronic Hierarchies." *Communications of the ACM* (June 1987).

March, James G., and Herbert A. Simon. *Organizations*. New York: Wiley (1958).

Markus, M. L. "Power, Politics, and MIS Implementation." *Communications of the ACM* 26, no. 6 (June 1983).

Marlin, Steven. "The 24-Hour Supply Chain." *InformationWeek* (January 26, 2004).

McAfee, Andrew, and Francois-Xavier Oliveau. "Confronting the Limits of Networks." *MIT Sloan Management Review* 43, no.4 (Summer 2002).

McBride, Sarah. "Movie Debut: Films for Sale by Download." *The Wall Street Journal* (April 3, 2006).

Mendelson, Haim, and Ravindra R. Pillai. "Clock Speed and Informational Response: Evidence from the Information Technology Industry." *Information Systems Research* 9, no. 4 (December 1998).

Mintzberg, Henry, and Frances Westley. "Decision Making: It's Not What You Think." *MIT Sloan Management Review* (Spring 2001).

Mintzberg, Henry. *The Structuring of Organizations*. Englewood Cliffs, NJ: Prentice Hall (1979).

Mook, Nate. "Netflix Mulls Movie Download Service." BetaNews.com (June 21, 2006).

"More Canadians Taking Advantage of Paperless e-bills to Help Manage Household Finances." June 07, 2005, epost press release, retrieved August 3, 2007 from http://press.arrivenet.com/technology/article.php/649510.html.

"Online DVD Rental Guide." http://onlinedvdrentalguide.ca (accessed May 11, 2007).

Oracle Corporation. "Streamlining Convenience." 2006 Shared Strategy Study and "7-Eleven Inc." www.oracle.com (accessed July 15, 2006).

Orlikowski, Wanda J., and Daniel Robey. "Information Technology and the Structuring of Organizations." *Information Systems Research* 2, no. 2 (June 1991).

Pasha, Shaheen. "Amazon Has New Stories to Tell." *CNN Money* (August 22, 2005).

Pindyck, Robert S., and Daniel L. Rubinfeld. *Microeconomics*, Fifth Ed. Upper Saddle River, NJ: Prentice Hall (2001).

Porter, Michael E. *Competitive Advantage*. New York: Free Press (1985).

Porter, Michael E. "How Information Can Help You Compete." *Harvard Business Review* (August–September 1985a).

Porter, Michael E. "Strategy and the Internet." *Harvard Business Review* (March 2001).

Porter, Michael E., and Scott Stern. "Location Matters." *MIT Sloan Management Review* 42, no. 4 (Summer 2001).

Rae-Dupree, Janet. "Blockbuster: Movie Business Remains a Moving Target." *CIO Insight* (August 10, 2005).

RedHerring.com. "Guba Sells Sony Films." (July 11, 2006).

Reich, Blaize Horner, and Izak Benbasat. "Factors that Influence the Social Dimension of Alignment between Business and Information Technology Objectives." *MIS Quarterly* 24, no. 1 (March 2000).

Reinartz, Werner, and V. Kumar. "The Mismanagement of Customer Loyalty." *Harvard Business Review* (July 2002).

Reuters. "Guba to Distribute Warner Bros. Movies." (accessed via Yahoo! News, June 26, 2006).

Rivlin, Gary. "A Retail Revolution Turns 10." *The New York Times* (July 10, 2005).

Robey, Daniel, and Marie-Claude Boudreau. "Accounting for the Contradictory Organizational Consequences of Information Technology: Theoretical Directions and Methodological Implications." *Information Systems Research* 10, no. 42 (June 1999).

Shapiro, Carl, and Hal R. Varian. *Information Rules*. Boston, MA: Harvard Business School Press (1999).

Snider, Mike. "Movie Downloads Can Be Fun, and the Technology Is Advancing." *USA Today* (accessed via Citizen-Times.com, July 4, 2006).

Starbuck, William H. "Organizations as Action Generators." *American Sociological Review* 48 (1983).

Stross, Randall. "Trying to Get a Read on Amazon's Books." *The New York Times* (February 12, 2006).

Sullivan, Laurie. "Fine-Tuned Pricing." *InformationWeek* (August 15/22, 2005).

Tedeschi, Bob. "Making Several Stops at Shops Online, but Paying All at Google." *The New York Times* (July 17, 2006).

The Wall Street Journal. "Amazon Adds Groceries to Its Site." (June 15, 2006).

Tversky, A., and D. Kahneman. "The Framing of Decisions and the Psychology of Choice." *Science* 211 (January 1981).

Walker, Marlon A. "The Day the E-Mail Dies." *The Wall Street Journal* (August 26, 2004).

Weber, Max. *The Theory of Social and Economic Organization.* Translated by Talcott Parsons. New York: Free Press (1947).

Williamson, Oliver E. *The Economic Institutions of Capitalism.* New York: Free Press, (1985).

Chapter 4

Ambrosio, Johanna. "Connected to Nowhere." *InformationWeek* (May 1, 2006).

Association of Computing Machinery. "ACM's Code of Ethics and Professional Conduct." *Communications of the ACM* 36, no. 12 (December 1993).

Ball, Kirstie S. "Situating Workplace Surveillance: Ethics and Computer-based Performance Monitoring." *Ethics and Information Technology* 3, no. 3 (2001).

Barrett, Larry, and Sean Gallagher. "What Sin City Can Teach Tom Ridge." *Baseline* (April 2004).

Bellman, Steven, Eric J. Johnson, and Gerald L. Lohse. "To Opt-in or Opt-out? It Depends on the Question." *Communications of the ACM* 44, no. 2 (February 2001).

Bennett, Colin J. "Cookies, Web Bugs, Webcams, and Cue Cats: Patterns of Surveillance on the World Wide Web." *Ethics and Information Technology* 3, no. 3 (2001).

Bergstein, Brian. "Research Explores Data Mining, Privacy." Associated Press (June 17, 2006).

Bhattacharjee, Sudip, Ram D. Gopal, and G. Lawrence Sanders. "Digital Music and Online Sharing: Software Piracy 2.0?" *Communications of the ACM* 46, no. 7 (July 2003).

Bowen, Jonathan. "The Ethics of Safety-Critical Systems." *Communications of the ACM* 43, no. 3 (April 2000).

Brown Bag Software vs. Symantec Corp. 960 F2D 1465 (Ninth Circuit, 1992).

Burk, Dan L. "Copyrightable Functions and Patentable Speech." *Communications of the ACM* 44, no. 2 (February 2001).

Canadian Alliance Against Software Theft (CAAST). "Canadians Find Falsified Resumes a Bigger Offence than Using Pirated Software." 2006. www.caast.com/resources/2006_national_study.pdf (accessed June 1, 2007).

Canadian Alliance Against Software Theft (CAAST). "Fourth Annual BSA and ICD Global Software Piracy Study." 2007, www.caast.com/resources/piracy_study_2007.pdf (accessed June 1, 2007).

Canadian Alliance Against Software Theft (CAAST). "About CAAST." www.caast.com/about/default.asp?load=content (accessed June 1, 2007).

Carr, David F., and Sean Gallagher. "BofA's Direct-Deposit Debacle." *Baseline* (May 15, 2002).

"ChoicePoint Toughens Data Security." *CNN/Money* (July 5, 2005).

Day, George S., Adam J. Fein, and Gregg Ruppersberger. "Shakeouts in Digital Markets." *California Management Review* 45, no. 3 (Winter 2003).

Earp, Julia B., and David Baumer. "Innovative Web Use to Learn About Consumer Behavior and Online Privacy." *Communications of the ACM* 46, no. 4 (April 2003).

Farmer, Dan, and Charles C. Mann. "Surveillance Nation." *Part I Technology Review* (April 2003) and *Part II Technology Review* (May 2003).

Froomkin, A. Michael. "The Collision of Trademarks, Domain Names, and Due Process in Cyberspace." *Communications of the ACM* 44, no. 2 (February 2001).

Geitner, Paul. "Survey: 36 Percent of Software Pirated." Associated Press (July 7, 2004).

Gilhooly, Kym. "Dirty Data Blights the Bottom Line." *Computerworld* (November 7, 2005).

Hagerty, James R., and Dennis K. Berman. "New Battleground in Web Privacy War: Ads That Snoop." *The Wall Street Journal* (August 27, 2003).

Hansell, Saul. "The Internet Ad You Are About to See Has Already Read Your E-Mail." *The New York Times* (June 21, 2004).

Heingartner, Douglas. "Software Piracy is in Resurgence, with New Safeguards Eroded by File Sharing." *The New York Times* (January 19, 2004).

Holmes, Allan. "The Profits in Privacy." *CIO Magazine* (March 15, 2006).

Jackson, Linda A., Alexander von Eye, Gretchen Barbatsis, Frank Biocca, Hiram E. Fitzgerald, and Yong Zhao. "The Impact of Internet Use on the Other Side of the Digital Divide." *Communications of the ACM* 47, no. 7 (July 2004).

Jackson, Thomas W., Ray Dawson, and Darren Wilson. "Understanding Email Interaction Increases Organizational Productivity." *Communications of the ACM* 46, no. 8 (August 2003).

Kapner, Suzanne. "Internet Site, Fearing Suit over Content, Curbs Activity." *The New York Times* (March 14, 2003).

Katz, Yaakov. "Israeli 'Trojan Horse' Scandal Widens." Associated Press. June 1, 2005. www.msnbc.msn.com (accessed June 1, 2007).

Katz, Yaakov. "Trojan Horse Also Hit Major International Firms." *The Jewish Post.* May 30, 2005. www.jpost.com (accessed June 1, 2007).

Kling, Rob. "When Organizations Are Perpetrators: The Conditions of Computer Abuse and Computer Crime." In *Computerization & Controversy: Value Conflicts & Social Choices,* edited by Charles Dunlop and Rob Kling. New York: Academic Press (1991).

Kreie, Jennifer, and Timothy Paul Cronan. "Making Ethical Decisions." *Communications of the ACM* 43, no. 12 (December 2000).

Labossiere, Danielle. "The Hidden Cost of Piracy in Canada." *The Globe and Mail* (May 5, 2006).

Laudon, Kenneth C. *Dossier Society: Value Choices in the Design of National Information Systems.* New York: Columbia University Press (1986).

Laudon, Kenneth C. "Ethical Concepts and Information Technology." *Communications of the ACM* 38, no. 12 (December 1995).

Laudon, Kenneth C., and Carol Guercio Traver. *E-Commerce: Business, Technology, Society.* Third Edition. Upper Saddle River, N.J.: Prentice Hall (2006).

Lee, Jintae. "An End-User Perspective on File-Sharing Systems." *Communications of the ACM* 46, no. 2 (February 2003).

Lenhart, Amanda, John Horrigan, Lee Rainie, Katherine Allen, Angie Boyce, Mary Madden, and Erin O'Grady. "The Ever-Shifting Internet Population." *The Pew Internet and American Life Project* (April 16, 2003).

Lohr, Steve. "Software Group Enters Fray over Proposed Piracy Law." *The New York Times* (July 19, 2004).

Madden, Mary, and Lee Rainie. "Music and Video Downloading Moves Beyond P2P." *Pew Internet and American Life Project* (March 23, 2005).

Maltz, Elliott, and Vincent Chiappetta. "Maximizing Value in the Digital World." *MIT Sloan Management Review* 43, no. 3 (Spring 2002).

Mann, Catherine L. "What Global Sourcing Means for U.S. I.T. Workers and for the U.S. Economy." *Communications of the ACM* 47, no. 7 (July 2004).

Markoff, John. "Taking Snooping Further." *The New York Times* (February 25, 2006).

Martin, Jr. David M., Richard M. Smith, Michael Brittain, Ivan Fetch, and Hailin Wu. "The Privacy Practices of Web Browser Extensions." *Communications of the ACM* 44, no. 2 (February 2001).

McKim, Jennifer B. "Keep Your Child Safe from Online Predators." *Orange County Register* (July 18, 2006).

Microsoft Corporation. "Tech Data Canada Equips its Resellers and Employees with Tools to Help Fight Software Piracy." www.microsoft.com/canada/casestudies/techdata.mspx (accessed June 1, 2007).

Moores, Trevor, and Gurpreet Dhillon. "Software Piracy: A View from Hong Kong." *Communications of the ACM* 43, no. 12 (December 2000).

National Telecommunications & Information Administration, U.S. Department of Commerce. "Falling Through the Net: Defining the Digital Divide." (July 8, 1999).

Oz, Effy. "Ethical Standards for Information Systems Professionals." *MIS Quarterly* 16, no. 4 (December 1992).

Payton, Fay Cobb. "Rethinking the Digital Divide." *Communications of the ACM* 46, no. 6 (June 2003).

Pear, Robert. "Survey Finds U.S. Agencies Engaged in 'Data Mining.'" *The New York Times* (May 27, 2004).

Perez, Evan, and Rick Brooks. "For Big Vendor of Personal Data, A Theft Lays Bare the Downside." *The Wall Street Journal* (May 3, 2005).

Portfolio.com. "Tech Data Ranks 109th on 2007 Fortune 500." April 15, 2007. www.portfolio.com/resources/company-profiles/TECD/press/2007/04/16/tech-data-ranks-109th-on-2007-fortune-500r (accessed June 1, 2007).

Rainie, Lee, and Dan Packel. "More Online, Doing More." *The Pew Internet and American Life Project* (Febuary 18, 2001).

Reagle, Joseph, and Lorrie Faith Cranor. "The Platform for Privacy Preferences." *Communications of the ACM* 42, no. 2 (February 1999).

Redman, Thomas C. "The Impact of Poor Data Quality on the Typical Enterprise." *Communications of the ACM* 41, no. 2 (February 1998).

Rifkin, Jeremy. "Watch Out for Trickle-Down Technology." *The New York Times* (March 16, 1993).

Rigdon, Joan E. "Frequent Glitches in New Software Bug Users." *The Wall Street Journal* (January 18, 1995).

Rotenberg, Marc. "Communications Privacy: Implications for Network Design." *Communications of the ACM* 36, no. 8 (August 1993).

Samuelson, Pamela. "Computer Programs and Copyright's Fair Use Doctrine." *Communications of the ACM* 36, no. 9 (September 1993).

Sewell, Graham, and James R. Barker. "Neither Good, nor Bad, but Dangerous: Surveillance as an Ethical Paradox." *Ethics and Information Technology* 3, no. 3 (2001).

Sipior, Janice C., and Burke T. Ward. "The Dark Side of Employee Email." *Communications of the ACM* 42, no.7 (July 1999).

Smith, H. Jeff, Sandra J. Milberg, and Sandra J. Burke. "Information Privacy: Measuring Individuals' Concerns about Organizational Practices." *MIS Quarterly* 20, no. 2 (June 1996).

Straub, Detmar W., Jr., and William D. Nance. "Discovering and Disciplining Computer Abuse in Organizations: A Field Study." *MIS Quarterly* 14, no. 1 (March 1990).

Taylor, Curtis L. "Kids Swallowing Online Food Company Lures." *Newsday* (July 20, 2006).

Tech Data. "Welcome to Tech Data." www.techdata.com/content/cen/about/companyinfo.main.aspx (accessed June 1, 2007).

United States Department of Health, Education, and Welfare. *Records, Computers, and the Rights of Citizens.* Cambridge: MIT Press (1973).

United States Sentencing Commission. *Sourcebook of Federal Sentencing Statistics.* www.ussc.gov/ANNRPT/2004 (2004).

Urbaczewski, Andrew, and Leonard M. Jessup. "Does Electronic Monitoring of Employee Internet Usage Work?" *Communications of the ACM* 45, no. 1 (January 2002).

Volokh, Eugene. "Personalization and Privacy." *Communications of the ACM* 43, no. 8 (August 2000).

Wang, Huaiqing, Matthew K. O. Lee, and Chen Wang. "Consumer Privacy Concerns about Internet Marketing." *Communications of the ACM* 41, no. 3 (March 1998).

Wellman, Barry. "Designing the Internet for a Networked Society." *Communications of the ACM* 45, no. 5 (May 2002).

Whiting, Rick. "Who's Buying and Selling Your Data? Everybody." *InformationWeek* (July 10, 2006).

Wolf, Christopher. "Dazed and Confused: Data Law Disarray." *BusinessWeek* (June 8, 2006).

Zeller, Tom Jr. "The Fight Against V1@gra (and other Spam)." *The New York Times* (May 21, 2006).

Chapter 5

Akamai. "About Akamai." www.akamai.com/html/about/index.html (accessed February 27, 2007).

Akamai. "Akamai Remembers Danny Lewin." www.akamai.com/html/about/management_dl.html (accessed February 27, 2007).

Akamai. "Case Study: Akamai Helps Canadian Media Company Boost Traffic, Reduce Costs." www.streamingmedia.com/article.asp?id=9134&page=2&c=1 (accessed February 27, 2007).

Akamai. "Case Study: CGA-Canada Delivers 24/7 Interactive Online Learning to Students Worldwide While Reducing Infrastructure Costs by 40 percent." www.akamai.com/html/customers/case_study_cga_canada.html (accessed February 27, 2007).

Akamai. "Cathay Pacific Airways Increases Online Bookings and Extranet Adoption—Saving Over $1,000,000 Annually." www.akamai.com/html/customers/case_study_cathay.html (accessed February 27, 2007).

Akamai. "EdgeSuite Delivery." www.akamai.com/html/solutions/edgesuite_delivery.html (accessed February 27, 2007).

Akamai. "High Performance Streaming Increases Site Traffic and Reduces Costs." www.akamai.com/html/customers/case_study_chum.html (accessed February 27, 2007).

Aries, James A., Subhankar Banerjee, Marc S. Brittan, Eric Dillon, Janusz S. Kowalik, and John P. Lixvar. "Capacity and Performance Analysis of Distributed Enterprise Systems." *Communications of the ACM* 45, no. 6 (June 2002).

Babcock, Charles. "Virtualization's Next Stage." *InformationWeek* (March 20, 2006).

Barry, Douglas K. *Web Services and Service-Oriented Architectures: The Savvy Manager's Guide.* New York: Morgan Kaufman (2003).

Bell, Gordon, and Jim Gray. What's Next in High-Performance Computing? *Communications of the ACM* 45, no. 1 (January 2002).

Boake, Patrick. "Neoware Streamlines Air Canada Reservation System." *The Globe and Mail* (June 2, 2004).

Bracken, Laura. "Frenzy of Success for Frantic Films." *Playback.* May 24, 2004. www.playbackmag.com/articles/magazine/20040524/frantic.html (accessed February 23, 2007).

Bulkeley, William M. "Can LINUX Take Over the Desktop." *The Wall Street Journal* (May 24, 2004).

Bulkeley, William M. "New IBM Service Will Test Vision of Computing Power as Utility." *The Wall Street Journal* (July 1, 2002).

Bureau of Economic Analysis, National Income and Product Accounts, Table 5.3.5 Fixed Investment by Type. Washington, D.C. (2006).

Butler, Steve. "IT Spending and Trends." *eMarketer* (March 2005).

Butler, Steve. "Telecom Spending." *eMarketer* (April 2004).

Champy, James. "Re-examining the Infrastructure." *Optimize Magazine* 23 (September 2003).

Chari, Kaushal, and Saravanan Seshadri. "Demystifying Integration." *Communications of the ACM* 47, no. 7 (July 2004).

CHUM Limited. "CHUM Limited Overview." www.chumlimited.com (accessed February 27, 2007).

CHUM Limited. "Company Information." www.chumlimited.com/corporate/investorrelations.asp (accessed April 11, 2007).

Columbia University. "A Chronology of Computing." www.columbia.edu/acis/history/ (November 2006).

Conry-Murray, Andrew. "Grid Computing's Promises and Perils." Network Magazine.com (February 5, 2004).

Cuomo, Jerry, et. al., "WebSphere Capacity — On Demand: Developing Edge Computing Applications." IBM Corporation and Akamai (2003). www-106.ibm.com/developerworks/websphere/library/techarticles/0310_haberkorn/haberkorn.html.

David, Julie Smith, David Schuff, and Robert St. Louis. "Managing Your IT Total Cost of Ownership." *Communications of the ACM* 45, no. 1 (January 2002).

Dempsey, Bert J., Debra Weiss, Paul Jones, and Jane Greenberg. "What Is an Open Source Software Developer?" *Communications of the ACM* 45, no. 1 (January 2001).

DreamWorks Animation. www.dreamworksanimation.com (accessed September 29, 2005).

Dunn, Darell. "Intel 'Core' Focuses On Power Consumption." *InformationWeek* (March 7, 2005).

EDS. "BP Canada Energy Company Case Study." http://eds.com/services/casestudies/bp_energy.aspx (2007).

eMarketer. "IT Spending and Trends." (March 2005).

Frantic Films, www.franticfilms.com (accessed February 23, 2007).

Ganek, A. G., and T.A. Corbi. "The Dawning of the Autonomic Computing Era." *IBM Systems Journal* 42, no. 1 (2003).

Gates, Bill, Nathan Myhrvold, and Peter Rinearson. *The Road Ahead.* New York: Penguin (1996).

Gerlach, James, Bruce Neumann, Edwin Moldauer, Martha Argo, and Daniel Frisby. "Determining the Cost of IT Services." *Communications of the ACM* 45, no. 9 (September 2002).

Grey, Jim. "Learning from the Amazon Technology Platform." *ACM Queue* 4, no. 4 (May 2006).

Hagel III, John, and John Seeley Brown. "Your Next IT Strategy." *Harvard Business Review* (October, 2001).

IBM. "20th Century Disk Storage Technology." www-1.ibm.com/ibm/history/exhibits/storage/storage_chrono20.html (accessed July 2004).

IBM. "Camelot Stores More and Boosts Performance with IBM System Storage." ftp://ftp.software.ibm.com/common/ssi/rep_sp/n/TSC03011USEN/TSC03011USEN.PDF (accessed December 1, 2006).

IBM. "Gridlines: The Intersection of Technology and Business." www-1.ibm.com/grid/gridlines/January2004/feature/teamwork.shtml (July 2004).

IBM. "How Customers Are Making On Demand Real." www.ibm.com/news/us/2003/11/on_demand_real.html. July 2004 (accessed August 1, 2007).

IBM. "IBM Launches New Autonomic Offerings for Self-Managing IT Systems." IBM Media Relations (June 30, 2005).

IBM. "The Mainframe Family Tree and Chronology." www-1.ibm.com/ibm/history/exhibits/mainframe/mainframe_FT1.html (accessed July 2004).

Intel Corporation. "Expanding Moore's Law: The Exponential Opportunity." (Fall 2002).

Intel Corporation. "Microprocessor Quick Reference Guide." www.intel.com/pressroom/kits/quickreffam.htm, July 2004.

International Technology Roadmap for Semiconductors Committee. "The International Technology Roadmap for Semiconductors 2003 Edition." http://public.itrs.net/ (accessed July 2004).

IT Business.ca. "Five Vendors to Watch in 2007." www.itbusiness.ca/it/client/en/CDN/DetailNewsPrint.asp?id=42203 (accessed August 1, 2007).

Kephart, Jeffrey O., and David M. Chess, "The Vision of Autonomic Computing." *IEEE Computer* (January 2003).

Kern, Thomas, Leslie P. Willcocks, and Mary C. Lacity. "Application Service Provision: Risk Assessment and Mitigation." *MIS Quarterly* Executive 1, no. 2 (2002).

Kerstetter, Jim. "The Linux Uprising." *BusinessWeek* Online (March 2003).

Krazit, Tom. "HP Bolsters Utility Services." *Network World* (December 2005).

Kurzweil, Ray. "Exponential Growth an Illusion? Response to Ilkka Tuomi." KurzweilAI.net (September 23, 2003).

Lee, Jinyoul, Keng Siau, and Soongoo Hong. "Enterprise Integration with ERP and EAI." *Communications of the ACM* 46, no. 2 (February 2003).

Leonard, Ed. "I.T. Gets Creative at Dreamworks." *Optimize Magazine* (April, 2006).

Loo, Alfred W. "The Future of Peer-to-Peer Computing." *Communications of the ACM* 46, no. 9 (September 2003).

Lyman, Peter, and Hal R. Varian. "How Much Information, 2003." www.sims.berkeley.edu/how-much-info-2003 (accessed November 1, 2006).

Markoff, John, and Jennifer L. Schenker. "Europe Exceeds U.S. in Refining Grid Computing." *The New York Times* (November 10, 2003).

McDougall, Paul. "In Depth: Customers Analyze Outsourcing Vendors and Strategies." *InformationWeek* (June 19, 2006).

McDougall, Paul. "Seven Fearless Predictions for Outsourcing in 2006." *InformationWeek* (December 20, 2005).

Moore, Gordon. "Cramming More Components Onto Integrated Circuits." *Electronics* 38, no. 8 (April 19, 1965).

National Science Foundation, "Revolutionizing Science and Engineering Through Cyberinfrastructure: Report of the National Science Foundation Blue-Ribbon Advisory Panel on Cyberinfrastructure." Washington D.C. (January, 2003).

Neoware. "Case Study: Air Canada." www.neoware.com/solutions/canada.html (accessed August 1, 2007).

Niemeyer, Alex, Misok H. Pak, and Sanjay E. Ramaswamy. "Smart Tags for Your Supply Chain" *McKinsey Quarterly* 4 (2003).

O'Reilly, Tim. "What is Web 2.0: Design Patterns and Business Models for the Next Generation of Software." www.oreillynet.com/lpt/a/6228 (accessed August 1, 2005).

Open Source Development Lab. "The Linux Marketplace—Moving from Niche to Mainstream." Prepared by IDC for OSDL. www.osdl.org/docs/linux_market_overview.pdf (accessed December 14, 2004).

Patel, Samir, and Suneel Saigal. "When Computers Learn to Talk: A Web Services Primer." *McKinsey Quarterly*, no. 1 (2002).

Phillips, Charles. "Stemming the Software Spending Spree." *Optimize Magazine* (April 2002).

Ricadela, Aaron. "High-Tech Reveries." *InformationWeek* (May 23, 2005).

Ricadela, Aaron. "Living on the Grid." *InformationWeek* (June 17, 2002).

Rogow, Rruce. "Tracking Core Assets." *Optimize Magazine* (April 2006).

Salkever, Alex, with Olga Kharif. "Slowly Weaving Web Services Together." *Business Week* (June 24, 2003).

Schmerken, Ivy. "Girding for Grid." *Wall Street & Technology* (April 2003).

Schuff, David and Robert St. Louis. "Centralization vs. Decentralization of Application Software." *Communications of the ACM* 44, no. 6 (June 2001).

Shankland, Stephen. "IBM: On Demand Computing Has Arrived." *CNET News* (November 12, 2003).

Stango, Victor. "The Economics of Standards Wars." *Review of Network Economics* 3, no. 1 (March 2004).

Statistics Canada. "Gross Dometic Product at Basic Prices, Communications, Transportation, and Trade." www40.statcan.ca/101/cst01/trade26.htm. 2006a (accessed August 1, 2007).

Statistics Canada. "Business and Government Use of Information and Communication Technologies." www40.statcan.ca/101/cst01/econ146a.htm. 2006b (accessed August 1, 2007).

Statistics Canada. "Internet use by individuals, by selected frequency of use and age" www40.statcan.ca/101/cst01/comm19.htm. 2006c (accessed August 1, 2007).

Sun Microsystems. "Computing at the Edge." www.sun.com/software/grid/whitepaper.edge.pdf (accessed March 2, 2007).

Susarla, Anjana, Anitesh Barus, and Andrew B. Whinston. "Understanding the Service Component of Application Service Provision: An Emprical Analysis of Satisfaction with ASP Services." *MIS Quarterly* 27, no. 1 (March 2003).

Sutton, Neil. "Toronto Firm Creates Google Mashup." *Computing Canada* 32, no. 15 (October 20, 2006).

Tuomi, Ilka. "The Lives and Death of Moore's Law." *FirstMonday*, col 7, no. 11. www.firstmonday.org (November 2002).

Web 2.0. http://whatis.techtarget.com/definition/0,,sid9_gci1169528,00.html (2006).

Weill, Peter, and Marianne Broadbent. "Management by Maxim: How Business and IT Managers Can Create IT Infrastructures." *MIT Sloan Management Review* (Spring 1997).

Weill, Peter, and Marianne Broadbent. *Leveraging the New Infrastructure.* Cambridge, MA: Harvard Business School Press (1998).

Weill, Peter, Mani Subramani, and Marianne Broadbent. "Building IT Infrastructure for Strategic Agility." *MIT Sloan Management Review* 44, no. 1 (Fall 2002).

Weitzel, Tim. *Economics of Standards in Information Networks.* Springer (2004).

Chapter 6

"Caught Up in DNA's Growing Web," *The New York Times* (March 17, 2006).

Cappiello, Cinzia, Chiara Francalanci, and Barbara Pernici. "Time-Related Factors of Data Quality in Multichannel Information Systems." *Journal of Management Information Systems* 20, no. 3 (Winter 2004).

CBC News. "Wrongfully Convicted." www.cbc.ca/news/background/wrongfullyconvicted/ (accessed March 25, 2007).

Chen, Andrew N.K., Paulo B. Goes, and James R. Marsden. "A Query-Driven Approach to the Design and Management of Flexible Database Systems." *Journal of Management Information Systems* 19, no. 3 (Winter 2002–2003).

Eckerson, Wayne W. "Data Quality and the Bottom Line." The Data Warehousing Institute (2002).

Epic.org. "Genetic Privacy." www.epic.org (accessed August 3, 2006).

Fayyad, Usama, Ramasamy Ramakrishnan, and Ramakrisnan Srikant. "Evolving Data Mining into Solutions for Insights." *Communications of the ACM* 45, no.8 (August 2002).

Gage, Debbie, and John McCormick. "The Disconnected Cop." *Baseline* (September 10, 2002).

Gilhooly, Kym. "Dirty Data Blights the Bottom Line." *Computerworld* (November 7, 2005).

Government of Canada. "Bonjour Québec.com—E-Business Case Study." strategis.ic.gc.ca/epic/site/dsib-tour.nsf/en/qq00113e.html (accessed March 25, 2007).

Government of Quebec. "Reserve Québec with Bonjour Québec.com." July 7, 2004. www.bulletin.enligne.gouv.qc.ca/archives/2004/ 07_juillet_aout/english/print_en/p_index.html (accessed March 25, 2007).

Government Technology. "Case Study: Royal Canadian Mounted Police," available http://www.govtech.net/digitalcommunities/studies/ sybase_RCMPv2.pdf (accessed April 10, 2007).

IBM. "Case Study: Canadian Tire Fuels Business Innovation with Information On Demand Initiative." www-306.ibm.com/software/success/ cssdb.nsf/CS/HSAZ-6M2UBV?OpenDocument& Site=corp&cty=en_us (accessed March 29, 2007).

Jukic, Boris, Nenad Jukic, and Manoj Parameswaran. "Data Models for Information Sharing in E-Partnerships: Analysis, Improvements, and Relevance." *Journal of Organizational Computing and Electronic Commerce* 12, no. 2 (2002).

Klau, Rick. "Data Quality and CRM." Line56.com (March 4, 2003).

Kroenke, David. *Database Processing: Fundamentals, Design, and Implementation*, 10th ed. Upper Saddle River, NJ: Prentice Hall (2006).

Lee, Yang W., and Diane M. Strong. "Knowing-Why about Data Processes and Data Quality." *Journal of Management Information Systems* 20, no. 3 (Winter 2004).

McFadden, Fred R., Jeffrey A. Hoffer, and Mary B. Prescott. *Modern Database Management*, Sixth Edition. Upper Saddle River, NJ: Prentice Hall (2002).

MetroCanada.com. "Travel Canada." www.metrocanada.com/travelcanada. htm (accessed March 25, 2007).

Microsoft. "2005 *Computerworld* Honors Case Study: CADVIEW." www.cwhonors.org/laureates/government/20055332.pdf (accessed April 10, 2007).

Microsoft. "The Royal Canadian Mounted Police: Microsoft Software Helps Solve Crimes." www.microsoft.com/canada/casestudies/rcmp.mspx (accessed April 10, 2007).

Morrison, Mike, Joline Morrison, and Anthony Keys. "Integrating Web Sites and Databases." *Communications of the ACM* 45, no.9 (September 2002).

Munroe, Susan. "Canadian Murder Rate Stays Low without Capital Punishment." *Canada Online*. canadaonline.com/od/crime/a/ abolitioncappun.htm (accessed March 25, 2007).

National DNA Data Bank of Canada. "Privacy and Security." www.nddb-bndg.org/pri_secu_e.htm (accessed March 25, 2007).

National DNA Data Bank of Canada. www.nddb-bndg.org/images/ brochure_e.pdf (accessed March 25, 2007).

Pierce, Elizabeth M. "Assessing Data Quality with Control Matrices." *Communications of the ACM* 47, no. 2 (February 2004).

Sabourin, Vincent, Michel Vézina, and Louise Côté. "The Adoption of Electronic Affairs in the Tourism Industry: Success Key Factors and Barriers to Adoption." www.cefrio.qc.ca/english/projets/Documents/ bonjour_eng_fnl.pdf (accessed March 25, 2007).

Watson, Hugh J., and Barbara J. Haley. "Managerial Considerations." *Communications of the ACM* 41, no. 9 (September 1998).

Whiting, Rick. "Aaww, Rubbish!" *InformationWeek* (May 8, 2006).

Chapter 7

Bose, Indranil, and Raktim Pal. "Auto-ID: Management Anything Anywhere, Anytime in the Supply Chain." *Communications of the ACM* 48, no.8 (August 2005).

Brandt, Richard. "Net Assets." *Stanford Magazine* (November–December 2004).

Butler, Steve. "VoIP: Spending and Trends." *eMarketer* (June 2005).

Carr, David F. "How Google Works." *Baseline* (July 2006).

Claburn, Thomas. "Google Goes toWork," *Information Week* (February 27, 2006).

Claburn, Thomas. "Google Revealed." *Information Week* (August 28, 2006).

Delaney, Kevin J., and Mylene Mangalindan. "Google Plans Online-Payment Service." *The Wall Street Journal* (June 20, 2005).

Delaney, Kevin J. "Hoping to Overtake Its Rivals, Yahoo Stocks Up on Academics." *The Wall Street Journal* (August 25, 2006).

Delaney, Kevin J. "Search Engines Find a Role for Humans." *The Wall Street Journal* (May 11, 2006).

Delaney, Kevin J. "Web Start-Ups Vie to Detect 'Click Fraud.'" *The Wall Street Journal* (June 9, 2005).

Dignan, Larry. "RFID: Hit or Myth?" *Baseline* (February 2004).

Dunn, Darrell. "Who's Watching Now?" *InformationWeek* (February 27, 2006).

Elgin, Ben, and Jay Greene. "The Counterattack on Google." *BusinessWeek* (May 8, 2006).

Elkin, Noah. "Wireless Broadband: The Future Around the Corner." *eMarketer* (May 2005).

Evron. "Evron says." www.evron.com/Newsletters/survey2003.asp (2003).

Germain, Jack M. "Monitoring Employee Communications in the Enterprise." NewsFactor Network (April 10, 2006).

"Google Bundles Package of Tools for Business, Education Markets." *The Wall Street Journal* (August 28, 2006).

Greenstein, Howard. "Web 2.0 Meets the Enterprise." *Optimize Magazine* (May 2006).

Grover, Varun, and Khawaja Saeed. "The Telecommunication Industry Revisited." *Communications of the ACM* 46, no.7 (July 2003).

Hansell, Saul. "Your Ads Here (All of Them)." *The New York Times* (October 30, 2005).

Hof, Robert. "Web 2.0 Has Corporate America Spinning." *BusinessWeek* (June 5, 2006).

Hoover, J. Nicholas. "5 Things You Must Know About VoIP." *InformationWeek* (July 3, 2006).

Hoover, J. Nicholas. "In Your Face." *InformationWeek* (May 8, 2006).

Housel, Tom, and Eric Skopec. *Global Telecommunication Revolution: The Business Perspective.* New York: McGraw-Hill (2001).

Intel Corporation. "Pilot Project Using Mobile IP-Centrex to Build an Integrated Voice and Data Environment." www.intel.com (accessed August 14, 2006).

Intel Corporation. "VoIP Enables VIP Service at Hyatt Regency Osaka." (2006). www.intel.com (accessed August 14, 2006).

Johnson, Keith. "Europe Picks Up 3G, as Phone Hopes Lift." *The Wall Street Journal* (August 25, 2005).

LaFraniere, Sharon. "Cellphones Catapult Rural Africa to 21st Century." *The New York Times* (August 25, 2005).

Lohr, Steve, and Saul Hansell. "Microsoft and Google Set toWage Arms Race." *The New York Times* (May 2, 2006).

Macklin, Ben. "Broadband: Demographics and Usage." *eMarketer* (July 2005).

Madden, Mary, and Lee Rainie. "America's Online Pursuits." Pew Internet and American Life Project (April 25, 2004).

Malykhina, Elena. "Bold Bet on WiMax." *InformationWeek* (August 14, 2006).

Malykhina, Elena. "RFID: Beyond the Pallet." *InformationWeek* (June 19, 2006).

Malykhina, Elena, and J. Nicholas Hoover. "Clear Signal for Wimax." *InformationWeek* (July 3, 2006).

Markoff, John. "Google to Offer Instant Messaging and Voice Communications on Web." *The New York Times* (August 24, 2005).

Meru Networks. "Hyatt Regency Osaka Deploys Hotel-Wide Wireless VoIP System: New System Rivals Wired Dial-Tone Quality." (2005).

Mindlin, Alex. "You've Got Someone Reading Your E-Mail." *The New York Times* (June 12, 2006).

Nasaw, Daniel. "Instant Messages Are Popping Up All Over." *The Wall Street Journal* (June 12, 2003).

National Research Council. *The Internet's Coming of Age.* Washington, D.C.: National Academy Press (2000).

Netcraft. "Netcraft August 2005 Web Server Survey." (August 2005).

Nicopolitidis, Petros, Georgios Papademitriou, Mohammad S. Obaidat, and Adreas S. Pomportsis. "The Economics of Wireless Networks." *Communications of the ACM* 47, no. 4 (April 2004).

Niemeyer, Alex, Minsok H. Pak, and Sanjay E. Ramaswamy. "Smart Tags for Your Supply Chain." *McKinsey Quarterly* 4 (2003).

Niemeyer, Alex, Misok H. Pak, and Sanjay E. Ramaswamy. "Smart Tags for Your Supply Chain." *McKinsey Quarterly* 4 (2003).

Overby, Christine Spivey. "RFID at What Cost?" Forrester Research (March 1, 2004).

Papazoglou, Mike P. "Agent-Oriented Technology in Support of E-Business." *Communications of the ACM* 44, no. 4 (April 2001).

Richtel, Matt. "The Wi-Fi in Your Handset." *The New York Times* (July 29, 2006).

Roberti, Mark. "Wal-Mart Begins RFID Process Changes." *RFID Journal* (February 1, 2005).

Rothfeder, Jeffrey. "What's Wrong with RFID?" *CIO Insight* (August 1, 2004).

Roush, Wade. "The Internet Reborn." *Technology Review* (October 2003).

Statistics Canada. "Canadian Internet Use Survey." www.statcan.ca/Daily/English/060815/d060815b.htm (August 15, 2006).

Sullivan, Laurie. "Hey, Wal-Mart, New Case of Pampers Is on the Way." *InformationWeek* (January 23, 2006).

Talbot, David. "The Internet Is Broken." *Technology Review* (December 2005/January 2006).

Vogelstein, Fred. "Search and Destroy." *Fortune* (May 2, 2005).

Wailgum, Thomas. "Tag, You're Late." *CIO Magazine* (November 15, 2004).

Weier, Mary Hayes. "RFID: Hold the Revolution, Pass the Incremental Change." *InformationWeek* (April 2, 2007).

Werbach, Kevin. "Using VoIP to Compete." *Harvard Business Review* (September 2005).

Worthen, Ben. "The Enterprise Gets Googled." *CIO Magazine* (May 1, 2006).

Young, Shawn. "Market for Internet Calling, Once Tiny, Gets Crowded Fast." *The Wall Street Journal* (August 26, 2005)

Yuan, Li. "Text Messages Sent by Cellphone Finally Catch on in U.S." *The Wall Street Journal* (August 11, 2005).

Chapter 8

Anti-Phishing Working Group. "Phishing Activity Trends." (May 2006).

Arnfield, Robin. "Online Banking: How Safe Is Your Money?" NewsFactor Network (January 20, 2006).

Associated Press. "Worm Damage Could Have Been Reduced." (May 5, 2004).

Austin, Robert D., and Christopher A. R. Darby. "The Myth of Secure Computing." *Harvard Business Review* (June 2003).

Backhouse, James, Carol Hsu, and Aidan McDonnell, "Toward Public-Key Infrastructure Interoperability." *Communications of the ACM* 46, no. 6 (June 2003).

Bank, David. "Mydoom Worm Renews Debate On Cyber-Ethics." *The Wall Street Journal* (November 11, 2004).

Bank, David. "Outbreak!" *The Wall Street Journal* (November 15, 2004).

Bank, David, and Riva Richmond. "What's That Sneaking into Your Computer?" *The Wall Street Journal* (April 26, 2004).

Bank, David, and Riva Richmond. "Where the Dangers Are." *The Wall Street Journal* Technology Report (July 18, 2005).

Berghel, Hal. "The Discipline of Internet Forensics." *Communications of the ACM* 46, no. 8 (August 2003).

Biever, Celeste. "Instant Messaging Falls Prey to Worms." (May 14, 2005).

Borzo, Jeannette. "Something's Phishy." *The Wall Street Journal* (November 15, 2004).

Brenner, Susan W. "U.S. Cybercrime Law: Defining Offenses." Information Systems Frontiers 6, no. 2 (June 2004).

Bryan-Low, Cassell. "Tech-Savvy Blackmailers Hone a New Form of Extortion." *The Wall Street Journal* (May 5, 2005).

Byers, Simon, and Dave Kormann. "802.11b Access Point Mapping." *Communications of the ACM* 46, no. 5 (May 2003).

Cam Winget, Nancy, Russ Housley, David Wagner, and Jesse Walker. "Security Flaws in 802.11b Data Link Protocols." *Communications of the ACM* 46, no. 5 (May 2003).

Cavusoglu, Huseyin, Birendra Mishra, and Srinivasan Raghunathan. "A Model for Evaluating IT Security Investments." *Communications of the ACM* 47, no. 7 (July 2004).

Chawki, Mohamed. "Phishing in Cyberspace: Issues and Solutions." Computer Crime Research Center (August 19, 2006).

"Computer Attacks-Jason Salah Arabo." Federal Crimes Blog (April 13, 2006).

Cox, Mark. "Internet Security Threats Increasing in Maliciousness and Criminal Intent: CompTIA." eChannel Line Daily New (June 19, 2005).

D'Amico, Mary Lisbeth. "Call Security." *The Wall Street Journal* (February 13, 2006).

Darby, Christopher. "The Dollars and Cents of Security." *Optimize Magazine* 12 (October 2002).

Datz, Todd. "The Interactive Nightmare." *CSO Magazine* (April 2004).

De Guzman, Mari-Len. "Company Offers Canadian Field Workers Mobile Device." *Computerworld Canada* (November 30, 2005).

De Guzman, Mari-Len. "Security: Keeping Mobile Workers Safe from Highway Robbery," *CIO Canada* (October 1, 2006).

Delaney, Kevin J. "'Evil Twins' and 'Pharming'." *The Wall Street Journal* (May 17, 2005).

Di Pietro, Roberto, and Luigi V. Mancini. "Security and Privacy Issues of Handheld and Wearable Wireless Devices." *Communications of the ACM* 46, no. 9 (September 2003).

Evers, Joris. "Kevin Mitnick Web Site Hacked." ZDNet (August 21, 2006).

Foley, John. "You Call This Trustworthy Computing?" *InformationWeek* (February 14, 2005).

Fox, Armando, and David Patterson. "Self-Repairing Computers." *Scientific American* (May 2003).

Gage, Deborah. "Helping Customers Help Themselves." *Baseline* (May 15, 2006).

Gage, Deborah, and Kim S. Nash. "When Bots Attack." *Baseline* (April 2006).

Golden, G. Richard III, and Vassil Roussev. "Next-Generation Digital Forensics." *Communications of the ACM* 49, no. 2 (February 2006).

Gordon, Lawrence A., Martin P. Loeb, and Tashfeen Sohail. "A Framework for Using Insurance for Cyber-Risk Management. "*Communications of the ACM* 46, no. 3 (March 2003).

Gordon, Lawrence A., Martin P. Loeb, William Lucyshyn, and Robert Richardson, "2005 CSI/FBI Computer Crime and Security Survey." Computer Security Institute (2005).

Gordon, Lawrence A., Martin P., Loeb, William Lucyshyn, and Robert Richardson. "2006 CSI/FBI Computer Crime and Security Survey." Computer Security Institute (2006).

Hartman, Amir, with Craig LeGrande and Tom Goff. "Lock Out Business Risks." *Optimize Magazine* (December 2005).

Horowitz, Alan S. "Biting Back." *Computerworld* (January 13, 2003).

Housley, Russ, and William Arbaugh. "Security Problems in 802.11b Networks." *Communications of the ACM* 46, no. 5 (May 2003).

Hulme, George V. "Dial V for Virus." *InformationWeek* (December 6, 2004).

ICSA Labs. "Tenth Annual Computer Virus Prevalence Survey." www.icsalabs.com, www.cybertrust.com (accessed June 17, 2005).

Jones, George. "The Absolute Worst (So Far)." *InformationWeek* (July 10, 2006).

Joshi, James B.D., Walid G. Aref, Arif Ghafoor, and Eugene H. Spafford. "Security Models for Web-Based Applications." *Communications of the ACM* 44, no. 2 (February 2001).

Laudon, Kenneth C. "Data Quality and Due Process in Large Interorganizational Record Systems." *Communications of the ACM* 29 (January 1986a).

Leland, John, and Tom Zeller Jr.. "Technology and Easy Credit Give Identity Thieves an Edge." *The New York Times* (May 30, 2005).

Lemos, Robert. "Major Prison Time for Bot Master." *Security Focus* (May 9, 2006).

MacLean, Susan. "Preventing Mobile Data Theft." *IT Focus*, www.itworldcanada.com/a/IT-Focus/b5f55476-c2a3-47e1-949d-dba0166a88b0.html (accessed April 14, 2007).

McFadden, Beth. "Security from Scratch." *Baseline* (May 15, 2006).

Mercuri, Rebeca T. "Analyzing Security Costs." *Communications of the ACM* 46, no. 6 (June 2003).

Mercuri, Rebecca T. "The HIPAA-potamus in Health Care Data Security." *Communications of the ACM* 47, no. 7 (July 2004).

Meyerson, Bruce. "BackBerry Blackout Hits North America." *San Diego Tribune* (April 19, 2007).

Mitchell, Dan. "It's Here; It's There; It's Spyware." *The New York Times* (May 20, 2006).

Morrison, Kimberly. "Internet Sees Increase in 'Phishing' for Online Victims." *Knight Ridder Newspapers* (February 28, 2005).

Newman, Robert. *Enterprise Security*. Upper Saddle River, NY: Prentice Hall (2003).

NIST. "Software Vulnerabilities." Workshop on Software Security Assurance Tools, Techniques, and Metrics (November 2005).

Panko, Raymond R. *Corporate Computer and Network Security*. Upper Saddle River, N.J.: Pearson Prentice Hall (2004).

Phonebusters. "Year End Statistics" **www.phonebusters.com/english/ documents/Yearlyen0001_000.pdf** (accessed September 18, 2007).

Reuters. "Sasser Computer Worm Author Confesses in Trial." (July 5, 2005).

Richardson, Michael. "The Darker Side of Canadian Cyberspace." *Vanguard Issue 3*. **www.ewa-canada.com/news/Cyber.pdf** (1999).

Roberts, Paul. "Fake Microsoft Security Trojan on the Loose, Antivirus Firm Says." ID News Service (April 8, 2005).

Roche, Edward M., and George Van Nostrand. *Information Systems, Computer Crime and Criminal Justice*. New York: Barraclough Ltd. (2004).

Scalet, Sarah. "Two-Factor Too Scarce at Consumer Banks." *CIO Magazine* (July 2006).

Schwerha, Joseph J. IV. "Cybercrime: Legal Standards Governing the Collection of Digital Evidence." *Information Systems Frontiers* 6, no. 2 (June 2004).

Searcey, Dionne, and Shawn Young, "Arrests Indicate Vulnerability of Web Phone Service to Fraud." *The Wall Street Journal* (June 8, 2006).

Shaw, Gillian. "What Evil Twin Lurks at Your WiFi Café?" *The Vancouver Sun* (November 4, 2006).

Shukla, Sudhindra, and Fiona Fui-Hoon Nah. "Web Browsing and Spyware Intrusion." *Communications of the ACM* 48, no. 8 (August 2005).

Straub, Detmar W., and Richard J. Welke. "Coping with Systems Risk: Security Planning Models for Management Decision Making." *MIS Quarterly* 22, no. 4 (December 1998).

Thompson, Roger. "Why Spyware Poses Multiple Threats to Security." *Communications of the ACM* 48, no. 8 (August 2005).

Thomson, Iain. "Akamai Investigates Denial of Service Attack." vunet.com (June 17, 2004).

Todd Weiss, "Wi-Fi Phishing Scam Targets Business Travelers." *Computerworld* (May 10, 2005).

Vara, Vauhini. "Lurking in the Shadows." *The Wall Street Journal* Technology Report (July 18, 2005).

Vara, Vauhini. "Tech Companies Check Software Earlier for Flaws." *The Wall Street Journal* (May 4, 2006).

Volonino, Linda, and Stephen R. Robinson. *Principles and Practices of Information Security*. Upper Saddle River, NJ: Prentice Hall (2004).

Wang, Huaiqing, and Chen Wang. "Taxonomy of Security Considerations and Software Quality." *Communications of the ACM* 46, no. 6 (June 2003).

Warkentin, Merrill, Xin Luo, and Gary F. Templeton. "A Framework for Spyware Assessement." *Communications of the ACM* 48, no. 8 (August 2005).

Zeller, Tom Jr. "The Scramble to Protect Personal Data." *The New York Times* (June 9, 2005).

Zhou, Jianying. "Achieving Fair Nonrepudiation in Electronic Transactions." *Journal of Organizational Computing and Electronic Commerce* 11, no. 4 (2001).

Chapter 9

Agarwal, Ritu, Jayesh Prasad, Mohan Tanniru, and John Lynch. "Risks of Rapid Application Development." *Communications of the ACM* 43, no. 11 (November 2000).

Albert, Terri C., Paulo B. Goes, and Alok Gupta. "GIST: A Model for Design and Management of Content and Interactivity of Customer-Centric Web Sites." *MIS Quarterly* 28, no. 2 (June 2004).

Arinze, Bay, and Murugan Anandarajan. "A Framework for Using OO Mapping Methods to Rapidly Configure ERP Systems." *Communications of the ACM* 46, no.2 (February 2003).

Bannan, Karen J. "A Helping Hand." *Profit Magazine* (February 2006).

Barthelemy, Jerome. "The Hidden Costs of IT Outsourcing." *MIT Sloan Management Review* (Spring 2001).

Boehm, Barry W. "Understanding and Controlling Software Costs." IEEE Transactions on *Software Engineering* 14, no. 10 (October 1988).

Champy, James A. *X-Engineering the Corporation: Reinventing Your Business in the Digital Age*. New York: Warner Books (2002).

Curbera, Francisco, Rania Khalaf, Nirmal Mukhi, Stefan Tai, and Sanjiva Weerawarana. "The Next Step in Web Services." *Communications of the ACM* 46, no 10 (October 2003).

Davenport, Thomas H., and James E. Short. "The New Industrial Engineering: Information Technology and Business Process Redesign." *MIT Sloan Management Review* 31, no. 4 (Summer 1990).

Davidson, Elisabeth J. "Technology Frames and Framing: A Socio-Cognitive Investigation of Requirements Determination." *MIS Quarterly* 26, no. 4 (December 2002).

Den Hengst, Marielle, and Gert-Jan DeVreede. "Collaborative Business Engineering: A Decade of Lessons from the Field." *Journal of Management Information Systems* 20, no. 4 (Spring 2004).

Earl, Michael, and Bushra Khan. "E-Commerce Is Changing the Face of IT." *MIT Sloan Management Review* (Fall 2001).

Eidenai Innovations. "About EI: Clients." **www.eidenai.ca/EI/SiteContent/ About/Clients/** (accessed April 19, 2007).

Eidenai Innovations. "About EI: Vision." **www.eidenai.ca/EI/SiteContent/ About/Vision/** (accessed April 19, 2007).

Eidenai Innovations. "EI Case Studies: Lemontonic." **www.eidenai.ca/EI/ SiteContent/CaseStudies/Pages/LemontonicCaseStudy.html** (accessed April 19, 2007).

El Sawy, Omar A. *Redesigning Enterprise Processes for E-Business*. McGraw-Hill (2001).

Feeny, David, Mary Lacity, and Leslie P. Willcocks. "Taking the Measure of Outsourcing Providers." *MIT Sloan Management Review* 46, no. 3 (Spring 2005).

Ferris, C., and J. Farrell. "What Are Web Services." *Communications of the ACM* 46, no. 6 (2003).

Fingar, Peter. "Component-Based Frameworks for E-Commerce." *Communications of the ACM* 43, no. 10 (October 2000).

Gefen, David, and Catherine M. Ridings. "Implementation Team Responsiveness and User Evaluation of Customer Relationship Management: A Quasi-Experimental Design Study of Social Exchange Theory." *Journal of Management Information Systems* 19, no. 1 (Summer 2002).

Gemino, Andrew, and Yair Wand. "Evaluating Modeling Techniques Based on Models of Learning." *Communications of the ACM* 46, no. 10 (October 2003).

Grant, Delvin. "A Wider View of Business Process Engineering." *Communications of the ACM* 45, no. 2 (February 2002).

Grunbacher, Paul, Michael Halling, Stefan Biffl, Hasan Kitapci, and Barry W. Boehm. "Integrating Collaborative Processes and Quality Assurance Techniques: Experiences from Requirements Negotiation." *Journal of Management Information Systems* 20, no. 4 (Spring 2004).

Hagel, John III, and John Seeley Brown. "Your Next IT Strategy." *Harvard Business Review* (October, 2001).

Hammer, Michael, and James Champy. *Reengineering the Corporation*. New York: HarperCollins Publishers (1993).

Hammer, Michael. "Process Management and the Future of Six Sigma." *MIT Sloan Management Review* 43, no.2 (Winter 2002).

Hammer, Michael. "Reengineering Work: Don't Automate, Obliterate." *Harvard Business Review* (July–August 1990).

Hickey, Ann M. and Alan M. Davis. "A Unified Model of Requirements Elicitation." *Journal of Management Information Systems* 20, no. 4 (Spring 2004)

Hirscheim, Rudy, and Mary Lacity. "The Myths and Realities of Information Technology Insourcing." *Communications of the ACM* 43, no. 2 (February 2000).

Hoffer, Jeffrey, Joey George, and Joseph Valacich. *Modern Systems Analysis and Design*, Third ed. Upper Saddle River, NJ: Prentice Hall (2002).

Ivari, Juhani, Rudy Hirscheim, and Heinz K. Klein. "A Dynamic Framework for Classifying Information Systems Development Methodologies and Approaches." *Journal of Management Information Systems* 17, no. 3 (Winter 2000–2001).

Iyer, Bala, Jim Freedman, Mark Gaynor, and George Wyner. "Web Services: Enabling Dynamic Business Networks." *Communications of the Association for Information Systems* 11 (2003).

Kendall, Kenneth E., and Julie E. Kendall. *Systems Analysis and Design*, Fifth ed. Upper Saddle River, NJ: Prentice Hall (2002).

Klein, Gary, James J. Jiang, and Debbie B. Tesch. "Wanted: Project Teams with a Blend of IS Professional Orientations." *Communications of the ACM* 45, no. 6 (June 2002).

Lamont, Judith. "BPM: from the user's perspective." www.kmworld.com (accessed November 1, 2006).

Lee, Jae Nam, and Young-Gul Kim. "Effect of Partnership Quality on IS Outsourcing Success." *Journal of Management Information Systems* 15, no. 4 (Spring 1999).

Lee, Jae Nam, Shaila M. Miranda, and Yong-Mi Kim. "IT Outsourcing Strategies: Universalistic, Contingency, and Configurational Explanations of Success." *Information Systems Research* 15, no. 2 (June 2004).

Lee, Jae-Nam, Minh Q. Huynh, Ron Chi-wai Kwok, and Shih-Ming Pi. "IT Outsourcing Evolution-Past Present, and Future." *Communications of the ACM* 46, no. 5 (May 2003).

Lemontonic. "Lemontonic: The Revolution of Life Online." www.lemontonic.com, accessed April 19, 2007.

Levina, Natalia, and Jeanne W. Ross. "From the Vendor's Perspective: Exploring the Value Proposition in Information Technology Outsourcing." *MIS Quarterly* 27, no. 3 (September 2003).

Lientz, Bennett P., and E. Burton Swanson. *Software Maintenance Managment*. Reading, MA: Addison-Wesley (1980).

Limayem, Moez, Mohamed Khalifa, and Wynne W. Chin. "Case Tools Usage and Impact on System Development Performance." *Journal of Organizational Computing and Electronic Commerce* 14, no. 3 (2004).

Lombardi, Rosie. "From Paper Trail to Patient Care," www.itworldcanada.com/a/E-Government/78a168dc-e318-4702-ada5-0c93c482afca.html (accessed April 17, 2007).

Lunt, Penny. "Well-Oiled Machines. BPM Projects Point to Success." *Transform Magazine* (April 2003).

Martin, James. *Application Development without Programmers*. Englewood Cliffs, NJ: Prentice Hall (1982).

Mazzucchelli, Louis. "Structured Analysis Can Streamline Software Design." *Computerworld* (December 9, 1985).

Microsoft Corporation. "Online Daters Get Up Close and Personal at Microsoft.NET-based Lemontonic.com." www.microsoft.com/canada/casestudies/lemontonic.mspx (accessed April 19, 2007).

Nerson, Jean-Marc. "Applying Object-Oriented Analysis and Design." *Communications of the ACM* 35, no. 9 (September 1992).

Newswire.ca. "Lemontonic Appoints Kaleil Isaza Tuzman to Board." www.newswire.ca/releases/archive/February2005/24/c7770.html?view=print (accessed April 19, 2007).

Nidumolu, Sarma R. and Mani Subramani. "The Matrix of Control: Combining Process and Structure Approaches to Managing Software Development." *Journal of Management Information Systems* 20, no. 4 (Winter 2004).

Patel, Samir, and Suneel Saigal. "When Computers Learn to Talk: A Web Services Primer." *The McKinsey Quarterly*, no. 1 (2002).

Peffers, Ken, and Charles E. Gengler. "How to Identify New High-Payoff Information Systems for the Organization." *Communications of the ACM* 41, no.1 (January 2003).

Phillips, James, and Dan Foody. "Building a Foundation for Web Services." *EAI Journal* (March 2002).

Pitts, Mitzi G., and Glenn J. Browne. "Stopping Behavior of Systems Analysts During Information Requirements Elicitation." *Journal of Management Information Systems* 21, no. 1 (Summer 2004).

Prahalad, C. K., and M.S. Krishnan. "Synchronizing Strategy and Information Technology." *MIT Sloan Management Review* 43, no. 4 (Summer 2002).

Ravichandran, T., and Marcus A. Rothenberger. "Software Reuse Strategies and Component Markets." *Communications of the ACM* 46, no. 8 (August 2003).

Sabherwahl, Rajiv. "The Role of Trust in IS Outsourcing Development Projects." *Communications of the ACM* 42, no. 2 (February 1999).

Scott, Louise, Levente Horvath, and Donald Day. "Characterizing CASE Constraints." *Communications of the ACM* 43, no. 11 (November 2000).

Shank, Michael E., Andrew C. Boynton, and Robert W. Zmud. "Critical Success Factor Analysis as a Methodology for MIS Planning." *MIS Quarterly* (June 1985).

Sharma, Srinarayan, and Arun Rai. "CASE Deployment in IS Organizations." *Communications of the ACM* 43, no. 1 (January 2000).

Sircar, Sumit, Sridhar P. Nerur, and Radhakanta Mahapatra. "Revolution or Evolution? A Comparison of Object-Oriented and Structured Systems Development Methods." *MIS Quarterly* 25, no. 4 (December 2001).

Smith, Howard, and Peter Fingar. *Business Process Management: The Third Wave Tampa*. Florida: Meghan-Kiffer Press (2002).

Sprott, David. "Componentizing the Enterprise Application Packages." *Communications of the ACM* 43, no. 3 (April 2000).

SRA, Inc. "Small Business Administration Disaster Credit Management System Support." (October 2006).

Summit Magazine. "The Ottawa Hospital Launches an Instrument Tracking System." October 2005. www.summitconnects.com/In_the_News/ARCHIVE/2005_10.htm (accessed April 17, 2007).

Swanson, E. Burton, and Enrique Dans. "System Life Expectancy and the Maintenance Effort: Exploring their Equilibration." *MIS Quarterly* 24, no. 2 (June 2000).

Tam, Kar Yan, and Kai Lung Hui. "A Choice Model for the Selection of Computer Vendors and Its Empirical Estimation" *Journal of Management Information Systems* 17, no. 4 (Spring 2001).

TGX Medical Systems. "Alex Gold." www.tgxmedical.com/products_and_services/alex_gold.asp (accessed April 17, 2007).

Thormeyer, Rob. "SBA weathers storm of criticism over loan processing." October 5, 2006. *Government Computing News*, www.sra.com/about/index.asp?id=602 (accessed September 1, 2007).

Turetken, Ozgur, David Schuff, Ramesh Sharda, and Terence T. Ow. "Supporting Systems Analysis and Design Through Fisheye Views." *Communications of the ACM* 47, no. 9 (September 2004).

Van Den Heuvel, Willem-Jan, and Zakaria Maamar. "Moving Toward a Framework to Compose Intelligent Web Services." *Communications of the ACM* 46, no. 10 (October 2003).

Vitharana, Padmal. "Risks and Challenges of Component-Based Software Development." *Communications of the ACM* 46, no. 8 (August 2003).

Watad, Mahmoud M., and Frank J. DiSanzo. "Case Study: The Synergism of Telecommuting and Office Automation." *MIT Sloan Management Review* 41, no. 2 (Winter 2000).

Weinberg Allen, and William Forrest. "Infrastructure's Outer Limits." *Optimize Magazine* (April 2006).

Wikipedia. "Actor (UML)" http://en.wikipedia.org/wiki/Actor_%28UML%29 (accessed October 18, 2007).

Wikipedia. "Agile Software Development." http://en.wikipedia.org/wiki/Agile_software_development (accessed October 18, 2007).

Wikipedia. "Use case" http://en.wikipedia.org/wiki/Use_cases (accessed October 18, 2007).

Wulf, Volker, and Matthias Jarke. "The Economics of End-User Development." *Communications of the ACM* 47, no. 9 (September 2004).

Yourdon, Edward, and L. L. Constantine. *Structured Design*. New York: Yourdon Press (1978).

Zachman, J. A. "Business Systems Planning and Business Information Control Study: A Comparison." *IBM Systems Journal* 21 (1982).

Chapter 10

Agarwal, Ritu, and Viswanath Venkatesnh. "Assessing a Firm's Web Presence: A Heuristic Evaluation Procedure for the Measurement of Usability." *Information Systems Research* 13, no.3 (September 2002).

Aladwani, Adel M. "An Integrated Performance Model of Information Systems Projects." *Journal of Management Information Systems* 19, no.1 (Summer 2002).

Alleman, James. "Real Options Real Opportunities." *Optimize Magazine* (January 2002).

Andres, Howard P., and Robert W. Zmud. "A Contingency Approach to Software Project Coordination." *Journal of Management Information Systems* 18, no. 3 (Winter 2001–2002).

Asohan, A. "MDC launches two new APICTA initiatives." August 2, 2003. www.unrealmind.com/press_release_7.htm (accessed May 21, 2005).

Attewell, Paul. "Technology Diffusion and Organizational Learning: The Case of Business Computing." *Organization Science*, no. 3 (1992).

Banker, Rajiv. "Value Implications of Relative Investments in Information Technology." Department of Information Systems and Center for Digital Economy Research, University of Texas at Dallas (January 23, 2001).

Barki, Henri, and Jon Hartwick. "Interpersonal Conflict and Its Management in Information Systems Development." *MIS Quarterly* 25, no. 2 (June 2001).

Barki, Henri, Suzanne Rivard, and Jean Talbot. "An Integrative Contingency Model of Software Project Risk Management." *Journal of Management Information Systems* 17, no. 4 (Spring 2001).

Baudisch, Patrick, Doug DeCarlo, Andrew T. Duchowski, and Wilson S. Geisler. "Focusing on the Essential: Considering Attention in Display Design." *Communications of the ACM* 46, no. 3 (March 2003).

Beasty, Colin. "Barriers to CRM Success." *CRM Magazine* (May 1, 2006).

Benaroch, Michel, and Robert J. Kauffman. "Justifying Electronic Banking Network Expansion Using Real Options Analysis." *MIS Quarterly* 24, no. 2 (June 2000).

Benaroch, Michel, Sandeep Shah, and Mark Jeffrey. "On the Valuation of Multistage Information Technology Investments Embedding Nested Real Options." *Journal of Management Information Systems* 23, No. 1 (Summer 2006).

Benaroch, Michel. "Managing Information Technology Investment Risk: A Real Options Perspective." *Journal of Management Information Systems* 19, no. 2 (Fall 2002).

Bharadwaj, Anandhi. "A Resource-Based Perspective on Information Technology Capability and Firm Performance." *MIS Quarterly* 24, no. 1 (March 2000).

Bhattacherjee, Anol, and G. Premkumar. "Understanding Changes In Belief and Attitude Toward Information Technology Usage: A Theoretical Model and Longitudinal Test." *MIS Quarterly* 28, no. 2 (June 2004).

Boer, F. Peter. "Real Options: The IT Investment Risk Buster." *Optimize Magazine* (July 2002).

Bostrom, R. P., and J. S. Heinen. "MIS Problems and Failures: A Socio-Technical Perspective. Part I: The Causes." *MIS Quarterly* 1 (September 1977); "Part II: The Application of Socio-Technical Theory." *MIS Quarterly* 1 (December 1977).

Brooks, Frederick P. "The Mythical Man-Month." Datamation (December 1974).

Brynjolfsson, Erik, and S. Yang. "Intangible Assets: How the Interaction of Computers and Organizational Structure Affects Stock Markets." MIT Sloan School of Management (2000).

Brynjolfsson, Erik, and Lorin M. Hitt. "Beyond the Productivity Paradox." *Communications of the ACM* 41, no. 8 (August 1998).

Brynjolfsson, Erik, and Lorin M. Hitt. "Information Technology and Organizational Design: Evidence from Micro Data." (January 1998).

Brynjolfsson, Erik. "The Contribution of Information Technology to Consumer Welfare." *Information Systems Research* 7, no. 3 (September 1996).

Brynjolfsson, Erik. "The IT Productivity GAP." *Optimize Magazine* 21 (July 2003).

Brynjolfsson, Erik. "The Productivity Paradox of Information Technology." *Communications of the ACM* 36, no. 12 (December 1993).

CBC.ca. "Canadian Corporate Takeovers That Made News." February 27, 2007. www.cbc.ca/news/background/mergers (accessed April 20, 2007).

Chabrow, Eric. "IT Plays Linchpin Role in High-Stakes M&As." *InformationWeek* (June 26, 2006).

Chatterjee, Debabroto, Carl Pacini, and V. Sambamurthy. "The Shareholder-Wealth and Trading Volume Effects of Information Technology Infrastructure Investments." *Journal of Management Information Systems* 19, no. 2 (Fall 2002).

Chatterjee, Debabroto, Rajdeep Grewal, and V. Sabamurthy. "Shaping Up for E-Commerce: Institutional Enablers of the Organizational Assimilation of Web Technologies." *MIS Quarterly* 26, no. 2 (June 2002).

Chau, PatrickY. K. and Vincent S. K. Lai. "An Empirical Investigation of the Determinants of User Acceptance of Internet Banking." *Journal of Organizational Computing and Electronic Commerce* 13, no. 2 (2003).

Concours Group. "Delivering Large-Scale System Projects." (2000).

Cooper, Randolph B. "Information Technology Development Creativity: A Case Study of Attempted Radical Change." *MIS Quarterly* 24, no. 2 (June 2000).

Datz, Todd. "Portfolio Management: How to Do It Right." *CIO Magazine* (May 1, 2003).

Davern, Michael J., and Robert J. Kauffman. "Discovering Potential and Realizing Value from Information Technology Investments." *Journal of Management Information Systems* 16, no. 4 (Spring 2000).

Davis, Fred R. "Perceived Usefulness, Ease of Use, and User Acceptance of Information Technology." *MIS Quarterly* 13, no. 3 (September 1989).

De Meyer, Arnoud, Christoph H. Loch, and Michael T. Pich. "Managing Project Uncertainty: From Variation to Chaos." *MIT Sloan Management Review* 43, no. 2 (Winter 2002).

Delone, William H., and Ephraim R. McLean. "The Delone and McLean Model of Information Systems Success: A Ten-Year Update." *Journal of Management Information Systems* 19, no. 4 (Spring 2003).

Doll, William J., Xiaodung Deng, T. S. Raghunathan, Gholamreza Torkzadeh, and Weidong Xia. "The Meaning and Measurement of User Satisfaction: A Multigroup Invariance Analysis of End-User Computing Satisfaction Instrument." *Journal of Management Information Systems* 21, no. 1 (Summer 2004).

Donlan, Bill. "Anatomy of a Successful CRM Implementation." CIOupdate.com (July 11, 2005).

Ein-Dor, Philip, and Eli Segev. "Organizational Context and the Success of Management Information Systems." *Management Science* 24 (June 1978).

Fichman, Robert G. "Real Options and IT Platforms Adoption: Implications for Theory and Practice." *Information Systems Research* 15, no. 2 (June 2004).

Frank, Robert, and Robin Sidel. "Firms that Lived by the Deal in '90s Now Sink by the Dozens." *The Wall Street Journal* (June 6, 2002).

Gefen, David, and Catherine M. Ridings. "Implementation Team Responsiveness and User Evaluation of Customer Relationship Management: A Quasi-Experimental Design Study of Social Exchange Theory." *Journal of Management Information Systems* 19, no. 1 (Summer 2002).

Hitt, Lorin, D.J. Wu, and Xiaoge Zhou. "Investment in Enterprise Resource Planning: Business Impact and Productivity Measures." *Journal of Management Information Systems* 19, no. 1 (Summer 2002).

Housel, Thomas J., Omar El Sawy, JianfangJ. Zhong, and Waymond Rodgers. "Measuring the Return on e-Business Initiatives at the Process Level: The Knowledge Value-Added Approach." ICIS (2001).

HSBC. "Home: HSBC Bank Canada" www.hsbc.ca/hsbc (accessed May 22, 2005).

HSBC. "Welcome to HSBC in Mayalsia" www.hsbc.com.my (accessed July 11, 2004).

Iversen, Jakob H., Lars Mathiassen, and Peter Axel Nielsen. "Managing Risk in Software Process Improvement: An Action Research Approach." *MIS Quarterly* 28, no. 3 (September 2004).

Jackson, Dale. "You Can't Beat Barbarians, So Why Not Join the Invasion? A Money Manager Assesses Valuations to Predict Targets." *The Globe and Mail* (April 10, 2007).

Jeffrey, Mark, and Ingmar Leliveld. "Best Practices in IT Portfolio Management." *MIT Sloan Management Review* 45, no. 3 (Spring 2004).

Kalin, Sari. "Making IT Portfolio Management a Reality." *CIO Magazine* (June 1, 2006).

Keen, Peter W. "Information Systems and Organizational Change." *Communications of the ACM* 24 (January 1981).

Keil, Mark, and Daniel Robey. "Blowing the Whistle on Troubled Software Projects." *Communications of the ACM* 44, no. 4 (April 2001).

Keil, Mark, and Ramiro Montealegre. "Cutting Your Losses: Extricating Your Organization When a Big Project Goes Awry." *MIT Sloan Management Review* 41, no. 3 (Spring 2000).

Keil, Mark, Joan Mann, and Arun Rai. "Why Software Projects Escalate: An Empirical Analysis and Test of Four Theoretical Models." *MIS Quarterly* 24, no. 4 (December 2000).

Keil, Mark, Paul E. Cule, Kalle Lyytinen, and Roy C. Schmidt. "A Framework for Identifying Software Project Risks." *Communications of the ACM* 41, 11 (November 1998).

Keil, Mark, Richard Mixon, Timo Saarinen, and Virpi Tuunairen. "Understanding Runaway IT Projects." *Journal of Management Information Systems* 11, no. 3 (Winter 1994–95).

Kettinger, William J., and Choong C. Lee. "Understanding the IS-User Divide in IT Innovation." *Communications of the ACM* 45, no. 2 (February 2002).

Klein, Gary, James J. Jiang, and Debbie B. Tesch. "Wanted: Project Teams with a Blend of IS Professional Orientations." *Communications of the ACM* 45, no. 6 (June 2002).

Kolb, D. A., and A. L. Frohman. "An Organization Development Approach to Consulting." *MIT Sloan Management Review* 12 (Fall 1970).

Laudon, Kenneth C. "CIOs Beware: Very Large Scale Systems." Center for Research on Information Systems, New York University Stern School of Business, working paper (1989).

LeBlond, Raoul. "Time as a Strategic Tool." *CIO Asia* (March 2004).

Levinson, Meridith. "When Failure Is Not an Option." *CIO Magazine* (June 1, 2006).

Lientz, Bennett P., and E. Burton Swanson. *Software Maintenance Management.* Reading, MA: Addison-Wesley (1980).

Lipin, Steven, and Nikhil Deogun. "Big Mergers of 90s Prove Disappointing to Shareholders." *The Wall Street Journal* (October 30, 2000).

Logistics Management. "American Airlines Cargo to Join Unisys-Operated Cargo Portal Services." (May 2, 2005).

Mahmood, Mo Adam, Laura Hall, and Daniel Leonard Swanberg, "Factors Affecting Information Technology Usage: A Meta-Analysis of the Empirical Literature." *Journal of Organizational Computing and Electronic Commerce* 11, no. 2 (November 2, 2001).

Markus, M. Lynne, and Robert I. Benjamin. "The Magic Bullet Theory of IT-Enabled Transformation." *MIT Sloan Management Review* (Winter 1997).

McFarlan, F. Warren. "Portfolio Approach to Information Systems." *Harvard Business Review* (September–October 1981).

McGrath, Rita Gunther, and Ian C. McMillan. "Assessing Technology Projects Using Real Options Reasoning." Industrial Research Institute (2000).

McIlmurray, Spencer. "M&A Survival Kit: Relearning Enterprise Addition and Subtraction." *CIO Magazine* (October 24, 2006).

Moore, Nick. "The New Role of the CIO in M&A Due Diligence." Software Mag.com (July, 2006).

Mumford, Enid, and Mary Weir. *Computer Systems in Work Design: The ETHICS Method.* New York: John Wiley (1979).

Nambisan, Satish, and Yu-Ming Wang. "Web Technology Adoption and Knowledge Barriers." *Journal of Organizational Computing and Electronic Commerce* 10, no. 2 (2000).

Nidumolu, Sarma R., and Mani Subramani. "The Matrix of Control: Combining Process and Structure Approaches to Management Software Development." *Journal of Management Information Systems* 20, no. 3 (Winter 2004).

Olazabal, Nedda Gabriela. "Banking: The IT Paradox." *McKinsey Quarterly*, no. 1 (2002).

Palmer, Jonathan W. "Web Site Usability, Design and Performance Metrics." *Information Systems Research* 13, no. 3 (September 2002).

Patton, Susannah. "Customer Service: Answering the Call." *CIO Magazine* (June 1, 2006).

Premkumar, G. "A Meta-Analysis of Research on Information Technology Implementation in Small Business." *Journal of Organizational Computing and Electronic Commerce* 13, no. 2 (2003).

"PERT Chart" http://whatis.techtarget.com/wsearchResults/ 1,290214,sid9,00.html?query=Pert+chart (accessed October 18, 2007).

Quan, Jin "Jim," Quing Hu, and Paul J. Hart. "Information Technology Investments and Firms' Performance—A Duopoly Perspective." *Journal of Management Information Systems* 20, no. 3 (Winter 2004).

Robey, Daniel, and M. Lynne Markus. "Rituals in Information System Design." *MIS Quarterly* (March 1984).

Robey, Daniel, Jeanne W. Ross, and Marie-Claude Boudreau. "Learning to Implement Enterprise Systems: An Exploratory Study of the Dialectics of Change." *Journal of Management Information Systems* 19, no. 1 (Summer 2002).

Rockart, John F. "Chief Executives Define Their Own Data Needs." *Harvard Business Review* (March–April 1979).

Ross, Jeanne W., and Cynthia M. Beath. "Beyond the Business Case: New Approaches to IT Investment." *MIT Sloan Management Review* 43, no. 2 (Winter 2002).

Ryan, Sherry D., David A. Harrison, and Lawrence L Schkade. "Information Technology Investment Decisions: When Do Cost and Benefits in the Social Subsystem Matter?" *Journal of Management Information Systems* 19, no. 2 (Fall 2002).

Sambamurthy, V., Anandhi Bharadwaj, and Varun Grover. "Shaping Agility Through Digital Options: Reconceptualizing the Role of Information Technology in Contemporary Firms." *MIS Quarterly* 27, no. 2 (June 2003).

Santhanam, Radhika, and Edward Hartono. "Issues in Linking Information Technology Capability to Firm Performance." *MIS Quarterly* 27, no. 1 (March 2003).

Schmidt, Roy, Kalle Lyytinen, Mark Keil, and Paul Cule. "Identifying Software Project Risks: An International Delphi Study." *Journal of Management Information Systems* 17, no. 4 (Spring 2001).

Schwalbe, Kathy. *Information Technology Project Management,* Fourth ed. Course Technology (2005).

Siewiorek, Daniel P. "New Frontiers of Application Design." *Communications of the ACM* 45, no.12 (December 2002).

Sircar, Sumit, Joe L. Turnbow, and Bijoy Bordoloi. "A Framework for Assessing the Relationship between Information Technology Investments and Firm Performance." *Journal of Management Information Systems* 16, no. 4 (Spring 2000).

Smith, H. Jeff, Mark Keil, and Gordon Depledge. "Keeping Mum as the Project Goes Under." *Journal of Management Information Systems* 18, no. 2 (Fall 2001).

Speier, Cheri, and Michael. G. Morris. "The Influence of Query Interface Design on Decision-Making Performance." *MIS Quarterly* 27, no. 3 (September 2003).

Straub, Detmar W., Arun Rai and Richard Klein. "Measuring Firm Performance at the Network Level: A Nomology of the Business Impact of Digital Supply Networks." *Journal of Management Information Systems* 21, no. 1 (Summer 2004).

Swanson, E. Burton. *Information System Implementation.* Homewood, IL: Richard D. Irwin (1988).

Tallon, Paul P, Kenneth L. Kraemer, and Vijay Gurbaxani. "Executives' Perceptions of the Business Value of Information Technology: A Process-Oriented Approach." *Journal of Management Information Systems* 16, no. 4 (Spring 2000).

Thatcher, Matt E., and Jim R. Oliver. "The Impact of Technology Investments on a Firm's Production Efficiency, Product Quality, and Productivity." *Journal of Management Information Systems* 18, no. 2 (Fall 2001).

Tornatsky, Louis G., J. D. Eveland, M. G. Boylan, W. A. Hetzner, E. C. Johnson, D. Roitman, and J. Schneider. *The Process of Technological Innovation: Reviewing the Literature.* Washington, DC: National Science Foundation (1983).

Unisys. "Cargo Portal Services Launches Two New Services." Enterprise Networks and Servers, (October 2004).

Unisys. "Multi-carrier Web-Based Booking for Air Cargo." www.unisys.com/ transportation/clients/featured_case_studies/northwest_ airlines_c0_united_airlines_and_air_canada_case_study.htm (accessed May 22, 2005).

University Malaysia Sarawak. "eBario Wins AFACT's eASIA Award." - www.unimas.my/ebario/award4.htm (accessed May 21, 2005)

Venkatesh, Viswanath, Michael G. Morris, Gordon B Davis, and Fred D. Davis. "User Acceptance of Information Technology: Toward a Unified View." *MIS Quarterly* 27, no. 3 (September 2003).

Wallace, Linda, and Mark Keil. "Software Project Risks and Their Effect on Outcomes." *Communications of the ACM* 47, no. 4 (April 2004).

Wang, Eric T.G., Gary Klein, and James J. Jiang. "ERP Misfit: Country of Origin and Organizational Factors." *Journal of Management Information Systems* 23, no. 1 (Summer 2006).

Wikipedia. "Program Evaluation and Review Technique." http://en.wikipedia.org/wiki/Pert_chart (accessed October 18, 2007).

Xia, Weidong, and Gwanhoo Lee. "Grasping the Complexity of IS Development Projects." *Communications of the ACM* 47, no. 5 (May 2004).

Zhu, Kevin, and Kenneth L. Kraemer. "E-Commerce Metrics for Net-Enhanced Organizations: Assessing the Value of e-Commerce to Firm Performance in the Manufacturing Sector." *Information Systems Research* 13, no. 3 (September 2002).

Zhu, Kevin, Kenneth L. Kraemer, Sean Xu, and Jason Dedrick. "Information Technology Payoff in E-Business Environments: An International Perspective on Value Creation of E-business in the Financial Services Industry." *Journal of Management Information Systems* 21, no. 1 (Summer 2004).

Zhu, Kevin. "The Complementarity of Information Technology Infrastructure and E-Commerce Capability: A Resource-Based Assessment of Their Business Value." *Journal of Management Information Systems* 21, no. 1 (Summer 2004).

Chapter 11

Arellano, Nestor E. "Canadian IT Industry Needs Image Makeover, say Analysts." *ITWorld Canada* (January 24, 2007).

Associated Press. "Nestle Reports 14 Percent Rise in Sales." April 25, 2006 (accessed via MSNBC.com, October 11, 2006).

Baily, Martin N., and Diana Farrell. "Exploding the Myths of Offshoring." *McKinsey Quarterly* (July 2004).

Baker, Stephen, and Manjeet Kripalani. "Software: Will Outsourcing Hurt America's Supremacy?" *BusinessWeek* (March 1, 2004).

Bloch, Michael, and Marcus Schaper, "Building a Global IT Organization: An Interview with DPWN's Managing Director of IT." *McKinsley Quarterly* (May 2006).

Buckman, Rebecca. "H-P Outsourcing: Beyond China." *The Wall Street Journal* (February 23, 2004).

Canadian Chamber of Commerce. "Offshore Outsourcing: Opportunities and Challenges for the Canadian Economy." www.chamber.ca/cmslib/general/OutSourcing050113.pdf (January 2005).

Central Intelligence Agency. *The World Fact Book.* www.cia.gov/cia/publications/factbook (accessed September 12, 2006).

Cone, Edward. "Avnet Tries Buying Its Way to the Top." *CIO Insight* (February 1, 2006).

Davison, Robert. "Cultural Complications of ERP." *Communications of the ACM* 45, no. 7 (July 2002).

Deans, Candace P., and Michael J. Kane. *International Dimensions of Information Systems and Technology.* Boston, MA: PWS-Kent (1992).

Drucker, Jesse, and Ken Brown. "Press 1 for Delhi, 2 for Dallas." *Wall Street Journal* (March 9, 2004).

Ein-Dor, Philip, Seymour E. Goodman, and Peter Wolcott. "From Via Maris to Electronic Highway: The Internet in Canaan." *Communications of the ACM* 43, no. 7 (July 2000).

eMarketer, "Worldwide Sourcing IT Services Export Share, by Country/Region." (March 2004).

Engardio, Pete. "The Future of Outsourcing." *BusinessWeek* (January 30, 2006).

Farhoomand, Ali, Virpi Kristiina Tuunainen, and Lester W. Yee. "Barrier to Global Electronic Commerce: A Cross-Country Study of Hong Kong and Finland." *Journal of Organizational Computing and Electronic Commerce* 10, no. 1 (2000).

Forrester Research. "IT Outsourcing Shows Accelerating Growth." (December 2004).

Global Insight. "IT Outsourcing and the U.S. Economy." (October 2005).

Gross, Daniel. "Why 'Outsourcing' May Lose Its Power as a Scare Word." *The New York Times* (August 13, 2006).

Ives, Blake. "Global Information Technology: Some Lessons from Practice." *International Information Systems* 1, no. 3 (July 1992).

Ives, Blake, and Sirkka Jarvenpaa. "Applications of Global Information Technology: Key Issues for Management." *MIS Quarterly* 15, no. 1 (March 1991).

Ives, Blake, and Sirkka Jarvenpaa. "Global Business Drivers: Aligning Information Technology to Global Business Strategy." *IBM Systems Journal* 32, no. 1 (1993).

Ives, Blake, S. L. Jarvenpaa, and R. O. Mason, "Global business drivers: Aligning Information Technology to Global Business Strategy." *IBM Systems Journal* 32, no. 1 (1993).

Jarvenpaa, Sirkka L., Kathleen Knoll, and Dorothy Leidner. "Is Anybody Out There? Antecedents of Trust in Global Virtual Teams." *Journal of Management Information Systems* 14, no. 4 (Spring 1998).

Jarvenpaa, Sirkka L., Thomas R. Shaw, and D. Sandy Staples. "Toward Contextualized Theories of Trust: The Role of Trust in Global Virtual Teams." *Information Systems Research* 15, no. 3 (September 2004).

King, William R., and Vikram Sethi. "An Empirical Analysis of the Organization of Transnational Information Systems." *Journal of Management Information Systems* 15, no. 4 (Spring 1999).

Krishna, S., Sundeep Sahay, and Geoff Walsham. "Managing Cross-Cultural Issues in Global Software Outsourcing." *Communications of the ACM* 47, no. 4 (April 2004).

Lai, Vincent S., and Wingyan Chung. "Managing International Data Communication." *Communications of the ACM* 45, no. 3 (March 2002).

Liang, Huigang, Yajiong Xue, William R. Boulton, and Terry Anthony Byrd. "Why Western Vendors Don't Dominate China's ERP Market." *Communications of the ACM* 47, no. 7 (July 2004).

MacFarquhar, Neil. "Tunisia's Tangled Web Is Sticking Point for Reform." *The New York Times* (June 25, 2004).

Mann, Catherine L. "What Global Sourcing Means for U.S. I.T. Workers and for the U.S. Economy." *Communications of the ACM* 47, no. 7 (July 2004).

Mann, Catherine. "Globalization of IT Services and White Collar Jobs: the Next Wave of Productivity Growth." Institute for International Economics (December 2003).

Martinsons, Maris G. "ERP In China: One Package Two Profiles." *Communications of the ACM* 47, no. 7 (July 2004).

McCue, Andy. "Gartner: Outsourcing Costs More than In-House." *CNET News* (March 7, 2006).

Nestlé. "Nestlé Group in 2005: Record Sales and Profits—Higher Dividend Proposed." February 23, 2006. www.nestle.com (accessed March 1, 2006).

Overby, Stephanie, "The Hidden Costs of Offshore Outsourcing." *CIO Magazine* (Sept. 1, 2003).

Roche, Edward M. *Managing Information Technology in Multinational Corporations.* New York: Macmillan (1992).

Schultz, Charles. "Offshoring, Import Competition, and the Jobless Recovery." The Brookings Institute, Washington D.C. (June 2004)

Shore, Barry. "Enterprise Integration Across the Globally Dispersed Service Organization." *Communications of the ACM* 49, no. 6 (June 2006).

Soh, Christina, Sia Siew Kien, and Joanne Tay-Yap. "Cultural Fits and Misfits: Is ERP a Universal Solution?" *Communications of the ACM* 43, no. 3 (April 2000).

Steinert-Threlkeld, Tom. "Nestlé Pieces Together Its Global Supply Chain." *Baseline* (January 20, 2006).

Sullivan, Laurie. "DHL Taps Several Vendors For RFID Project." *TechWeb News* (March 8, 2006).

Tan, Zixiang, William Foster, and Seymour Goodman. "China's State-Coordinated Internet Infrastructure." *Communications of the ACM* 42, no. 6 (June 1999).

Tractinsky, Noam, and Sirkka L. Jarvenpaa. "Information Systems Design Decisions in a Global Versus Domestic Context." *MIS Quarterly* 19, no. 4 (December 1995).

Trichur, Rita. "Transworks Takeover of Minacs Could Result in Some Jobs Going to India: Analyst." CBC News. www.cbc.ca/cp/business/060626/b062652.html (June 26, 2006) (accessed August 11, 2007).

Watson, Richard T., Gigi G. Kelly, Robert D. Galliers, and James C. Brancheau. "Key Issues in Information Systems Management: An International Perspective." *Journal of Management Information Systems* 13, no. 4 (Spring 1997).

Chapter 12

Anderiz, Diego. "The Rebirth of CRM." *IT Adviser* 44 (July/August 2006).

Anderson, James C., and James A. Narus. "Selectively Pursuing More of Your Customer's Business." *MIT Sloan Management Review* 44, no. 3 (Spring 2003).

Babcock, Charles. "Customer-Data Hubs Inch Ahead." *InformationWeek* (April 25, 2005).

Beasty, Colin. "CRM Where You Least Expect It." *Customer Relationship Management* (March 2005).

D'Avanzo, Robert, Hans von Lewinski, and Luk N. Van Wassenhove. "The Link Between Supply Chain and Financial Performance." *Supply Chain Management Review* (November 1, 2003).

Davenport, Thomas H. "Putting the Enterprise into Enterprise Systems." *Harvard Business Review* (July–August 1998).

Davenport, Thomas H. *Mission Critical: Realizing the Promise of Enterprise Systems.* Boston, MA: Harvard Business School Press (2000).

Day, George S. "Creating a Superior Customer-Relating Capability." *MIT Sloan Management Review* 44, no. 3 (Spring 2003).

Deloitte. "Sony Canada Launches New High Velocity Supply Chain." www.deloitte.com/dtt/case_study/0,1005,sid%253D3648% 2526cid%352D32458,00.html (accessed May 1, 2007).

Dowling, Grahame. "Customer Relationship Management: In B2C Markets, Often Less is More." *California Management Review* 44, no. 3 (Spring 2002).

Dubrowski, Stefan. "CCL Relies on Web-based Consensus." *IT Focus.* www.itworldcanada.com/Pages/Docbase/ViewArticle. aspx?id=idgml-4d2eb4c0-fc13-4dd5-8e81-1080c036388d (accessed May 3, 2007).

Fleisch, Elgar, Hubert Oesterle, and Stephen Powell. "Rapid Implementation of Enterprise Resource Planning Systems." *Journal of Organizational Computing and Electronic Commerce* 14, no. 2 (2004).

Goodhue, Dale L., Barbara H. Wixom, and Hugh J. Watson. "Realizing Business Benefits through CRM: Hitting the Right Target in the Right Way." *MIS Quarterly* Executive 1, no. 2 (June 2002).

Gosain, Sanjay, Arvind Malhotra, and Omar A. ElSawy. "Coordinating for Flexibility in e-Business Supply Chains." *Journal of Management Information Systems* 21, no. 3 (Winter 2004–2005).

Handfield, Robert B., and Ernest L. Nichols. "Supply Chain Redesign: Transforming Supply Chains into Integrated Value Systems." *Financial Times Press* (2002).

Hitt, Lorin, D.J. Wu, and Xiaoge Zhou. "Investment in Enterprise Resource Planning: Business Impact and Productivity Measures." *Journal of Management Information Systems* 19, no. 1 (Summer 2002).

Kalakota, Ravi, and Marcia Robinson. *E-Business 2.0.* Boston: Addison-Wesley (2001).

Kalakota, Ravi, and Marcia Robinson. *Services Blueprint: Roadmap for Execution.* Boston: Kanakamedala, Kishore, Glenn Ramsdell, and Vats Srivatsan. "Getting Supply Chain Software Right." *McKinsey Quarterly*, no. 1 (2003).

Kopczak, Laura Rock, and M. Eric Johnson. "The Supply-Chain Management Effect." *MITSloan Management Review* 44, no. 3 (Spring 2003).

Lee, Hau, L., V. Padmanabhan, and Seugin Whang. "The Bullwhip Effect in Supply Chains." *MIT Sloan Management Review* (Spring 1997).

Lee, Hau. "The Triple-A Supply Chain." *Harvard Business Review* (October 2004).

Malhotra, Arvind, Sanjay Gosain, and Omar A. El Sawy. "Absorptive Capacity Configurations in Supply Chains: Gearing for Partner-Enabled Market Knowledge Creation." *MIS Quarterly* 29, no. 1 (March 2005).

Microsoft. "Manufacturer Improves Customer Communication and Supply Chain Flow with Web Services." http://download.microsoft.com/ documents/customerevidence/20407_CCLCustom_CaseStudy_ word.doc (accessed May 3, 2007).

Oracle. "Fresh Guest Data Helps IHOP Franchises Thrive." www.oracle.com (accessed September 5, 2006).

Overby, Stephanie. "Can't We All Just Get Along?" *CIO Australia* (March 10, 2004).

Rai, Arun, Ravi Patnayakuni, and Nainika Seth. "Firm Performance Impacts of Digitally Enabled Supply Chain Integration Capabilities." *MIS Quarterly* 30, no. 2 (June 2006).

Ranganathan, C., and Carol V. Brown. "ERP Iinvestments and the Market Value of Firms: Toward an Understanding of Influential ERP Project Variables." *Information Systems Research* 17, no. 2 (June 2006).

Ranganathan, C., Jasbir S. Dhaliwal, and Thompson S.H. Teo. "Assimilation and Diffusion of Web Technologies in Supply-Chain Management: An Examination of Key Drivers and Performance Impacts." *International Journal of Electronic Commerce* 9, no. 1 (Fall 2004).

Robey, Daniel, Jeanne W. Ross, and Marie-Claude Boudreau. "Learning to Implement Enterprise Systems: An Exploratory Study of the Dialectics of Change." *Journal of Management Information Systems* 19, no. 1 (Summer 2002).

"SAP Chosen by Novartis as a Major Building Block." *EETimes* (June 16, 2003).

Scott, Judy E., and Iris Vessey. "Managing Risks in Enterprise Systems Implementations." *Communications of the ACM* 45, no. 4 (April 2002).

Slone, Reuben E. "Leading a Supply Chain Turnaround." *Harvard Business Review* (October 2004).

Sony Canada. "Sony and SAP Team Up to Keep Ahead in Competitive Retail Market." www.sap.com/industries/hightech/pdf/CS_Sony_Canada. pdf (accessed May 1, 2007).

Sun Microsystems. "Customer Snapshot: Manufacturing: Sony of Canada." www.sun.com/customers/servers/sony_ca.html (accessed May 1, 2007).

Westervelt, Robert. "Customer Data Hub Keeps IHOP Stats Hot." www. searchoracle.techtarget.com (accessed June 7, 2005).

Whitecap Canada. "Case Studies: CCL Industries, Inc." www.whitecapcanada.com/client_cs_ccl.aspx (accessed May 3, 2007).

Whiting, Rick. "You Look Marvelous!" *InformationWeek* (July 24, 2006).

Winer, Russell S. "A Framework for Customer Relationship Management." *California Management Review* 43, no. 4 (Summer 2001).

Yu, Larry. "Successful Customer Relationship Management." *MIT Sloan Management Review* 42, no. 4 (Summer 2001).

Chapter 13

Adomavicius, Gediminas, and Alexander Tuzhilin. "Personalization Technologies: A Process-Oriented Perspective." *Communications of the ACM* 48, no. 10 (October 2005).

Ba, Sulin, and Paul A. Pavlou. "Evidence of the Effect of Trust Building Technology in Electronic Markets: Price Premiums and Buyer Behavior." *MIS Quarterly* 26, no. 3 (September 2002).

Bakos, Yannis. "The Emerging Role of Electronic Marketplaces and the Internet." *Communications of the ACM* 41, no. 8 (August 1998).

Bhargava, Hemant K., and Vidyanand Chourhary. "Economics of an Information Intermediary with Aggregation Benefits." *Information Systems Research* 15, no. 1 (March 2004).

Bright, Beckey. "Clip Quest." *The Wall Street Journal* (September 12, 2005).

Brynjolfsson, Erik, Yu Hu, and Michael D. Smith. "Consumer Surplus in the Digital Economy: Estimating the Value of Increased Product Variety at Online Booksellers." *Management Science* 49, no. 11 (November 2003).

Chaudhury, Abhijit, Debasish Mallick, and H. Raghav Rao. "Web Channels in E-Commerce." *Communications of the ACM* 44, no. 1 (January 2001).

Chopra, Anand. "Let Me Help You with That." *KMWorld* (September 2006).

Christiaanse, Ellen. "Performance Benefits Through Integration Hubs." *Communications of the ACM* 48, no.5 (April 2005).

Claburn, Thomas. "Analysis: eBay's Growth to Come from Community, Not Acquisitions." *InformationWeek* (June 19, 2006).

Claburn, Thomas. "eBay Is Sold on Wikis." *InformationWeek* (June 14, 2006).

CNBC. "Ten Things You Didn't Know About eBay." www.msnbc.com (accessed June 29, 2005).

ComScore Networks, "Digital Calculator Report: Top 100 List." www.Comscore.com (September 2005).

Cowley, Stacy. "eBay Opens More PayPal Tools to Developer Partners." *InformationWeek* (June 12, 2006).

Cowley, Stacy. "eBay Turns to Partners, ISPs to Jack Up Sales." *InformationWeek* (July 24, 2006).

Crockett, Roger O. et. al., "IPod Killers?" *BusinessWeek* Online (April 21, 2005).

Cuneo, Eileen Colkin. "Web Ads Upend Industry Practices." *InformationWeek* (June 13, 2005).

DeFelice, Alexandra. "A New Marketing Medium." *Customer Relationship Management* (January 2006).

Devaraj, Sarv, Ming Fan and Rajiv Kohli. "Antecedents of B2C Channel Satisfaction and Preference: Validating e-Commerce Metrics." *Information Systems Research* 13, no. 3 (September 2002).

Dewan, Rajiv M., Marshall L. Freimer, and Jie Zhang. "Management and Valuation of Advertisement-Supported Web Sites." *Journal of Management Information Systems* 19, no. 3 (Winter 2002–2003).

Elliott, Stuart. "Shopping by Phone, on the Move." *The New York Times* (June 24, 2006).

eMarketer, Inc. (Noah Elkin). "Mobile Marketing and M-Commerce: Global Spending and Trends." (February 2005).

eMarketer, Inc. "Comparative Estimates: B2C E-Commerce." (July 2004).

eMarketer, Inc., "E-Commerce Retail Trends." (January, 2006).

eMarketer, Inc., "Worldwide Online Access." (May 2006).

"E-Tailing's Next Lift." *Optimize Magazine* (July, 2005).

Evans, Philip, and Thomas Wurster. Blown to Bits: How the new economics of information Transforms Strategy. Boston, MA: Harvard Business School Press (2000).

Gardner, W. David. "Fans Say 'Take Me Out to the Web Site.'" *InformationWeek* (August 22, 2005).

Hansell, Saul. "eBay Gambles on Google Partnership for Success of Skype, the Internet Phone Service." *The New York Times* (August 29, 2006).

Holmes, Elizabeth. "On MySpace, Millions of Users Make 'Friends' with Ads." *The Wall Street Journal* (August 7, 2006).

Hoover, Nicholas. "eBay Bets on VoIP, but Do Sellers Want to Chat?" *InformationWeek.* (September 19, 2005).

Howe, Peter J. "Major League Baseball Pitches Cellphone Content." *Boston Globe* (March 14, 2005).

Huang, Gregory T. "The Web's New Currency." *Technology Review* (November 2003).

Hui, Kai Lung, and Patrick Y.K. Chau. "Classifying Digital Products." *Communications of the ACM* 45, no. 6 (June 2002).

Iansiti, Marco, F. Warren McFarlan and George Wesserman. "Leveraging the Incumbent's Advantage." *MIT Sloan Management Review* 44, no. 4 (Summer 2003).

Jesdanun, Anick. "Online Age Verification May Prove Complex." Associated Press (July 17, 2006).

Kaplan, Steven, and Mohanbir Sawhney. "E-Hubs: the New B2B Marketplaces." *Harvard Business Review* (May–June 2000).

Kauffman, Robert J., and Bin Wang. "New Buyers' Arrival Under Dynamic Pricing Market Microstructure: The Case of Group-Buying Discounts on the Internet, *Journal of Management Information Systems* 18, no. 2 (Fall 2001).

Kenny, David, and John F. Marshall. "Contextual Marketing." *Harvard Business Review* (November–December 2000).

Kesmodel, David. "More Marketers Place Web Ads by Time of Day." *The Wall Street Journal* (June 23, 2006).

Kingson, Jennifer A. "Wireless Moves the Cash Register Where You Are." *The New York Times* (November 26, 2005).

Koufaris, Marios. "Applying the Technology Acceptance Model and Flow Theory to Online Consumer Behavior." *Information Systems Research* 13, no. 2 (2002).

Laudon, Kenneth C., and Carol Guercio Traver. *E-Commerce: Business, Technology, Society.* Third Edition. Upper Saddle River, N.J.: Prentice Hall (2006).

Lee, Hau L. and Seungin Whang. "Winning the Last Mile of E-Commerce." *MIT Sloan Management Review* 42, no. 4 (Summer 2001).

Lim, Gyoo Gun, and Jae Kyu Lee. "Buyer-Carts for B2B EC: The b-Cart Approach." *Journal of Organizational Computing and Electronic Commerce* 13, no. 3 & 4 (2003).

Madden, Andrew P. "The Business of Blogging." *Technology Review* (August 2005).

Magretta, Joan. "Why Business Models Matter." *Harvard Business Review* (May 2002).

Mangalindan, Mylene. "eBay, Google Reach Overseas Text-Ad Alliance." *The Wall Street Journal* (August 28, 2006).

Mangalindan, Mylene. "eBay Merchants Seek Management Change." *The Wall Street Journal* (August 21, 2006).

Mangalindan, Mylene, and Jessica E. Vascellaro. "You've Got Money: Paying via Text Message." *The Wall Street Journal* (April 26, 2006).

Markillie, Paul. "A Perfect Market." *Economist* (May 15–21, 2004).

Markoff, John. "Apple Unveils a New IPod and a Phone Music Player." *The New York Times* (September 8, 2005.)

McKnight, D. Harrison, Vivek Choudhury, and Charlea Kacmar. "Developing and Validating Trust Measures for e-Commerce: An Integrative Typology." *Information Systems Research* 13, no. 3 (September 2002).

McWilliam, Gil. "Building Stronger Brands through Online Communities." *MIT Sloan Management Review* 41, no. 3 (Spring 2000).

Mossberg, Walter H. "Sprint Brings Music Direct to Cellphones, But Price Is Too High." *The Wall Street Journal* (November 17, 2005).

"The MySpace Generation." *BusinessWeek* (December 12, 2005).

"MySpace Plans New Age Restritions." Associated Press (June 21, 2006).

Needleman, Sarah. "Blogging Becomes a Corporate Job: Digital 'Handshake'?" *TheWall Street Journal* (May 31, 2005).

"Online Extra: Stonyfield Farm's Blog Culture." *BusinessWeek* (May 2, 2005).

Pavlou, Paul A., and David Gefen. "Building Effective Online Marketplaces with Institution-Based Trust." *Information Systems Research* 15, no. 1 (March 2004).

Peralty, David. "Blog Community Strong in Canada." www.bloggingpro.com/archives/2006/10/25/blog-community-strong-in-canada (2006).

Pew Internet and American Life Project. "The State of Blogging." Pew Internet & American Life Project (January 2005).

Pinker, Edieal, Abraham Seidmann, and Riginald C. Foster. "Strategies for Transitioning 'Old Economy' Firms to E-Business." *Communications of the ACM* 45, no. 5 (May 2002).

Prahalad, C.K., and Venkatram Ramaswamy. "Coopting Consumer Competence." *Harvard Business Review* (January–February 2000).

Riggins, Frederic J. "Market Segmentation and Information Development Costs in a Two-Tiered Fee-Based and Sponsorship-Based Web Site." *Journal of Management Information Systems* 19, no. 3 (Winter 2002–2003).

Rosenbush, Steve. "Fox to Make MySpace More Spacious." *BusinessWeek* (August 8, 2006).

Rosenbush, Steve. "Socializing for Dollars." *BusinessWeek* (April 10, 2006).

Roush, Wade. "Social Machines." *Technology Review* (August 2005).

Roy, Cayce. "E-tailing's Next Lift." *Optimize Magazine* (July 2005).

Sawhney, Mohanbir, Emanuela Prandelli, and Gianmario Verona. "The Power of Innomediation." *MIT Sloan Management Review* (Winter 2003).

Schultze, Ulrike, and Wanda J. Orlikowski. "A Practice Perspective on Technology-Mediated Network Relations: The Use of Internet-Based Self-Serve Technologies." *Information Systems Research* 15, no. 1 (March 2004).

Sebor, Jessica. "MySpace Cadets." *Customer Relationship Management* (September 2006).

Smith, Michael D., Joseph Bailey, and Erik Brynjolfsson. "Understanding Digital Markets: Review and Assessment." In Erik Brynjolfsson and Brian Kahin, ed. *Understanding the Digital Economy*. Cambridge, MA: MIT Press (1999).

Statistics Canada. "The Daily: Electronic Commerce and Technology." www.statcan.ca/daily/English/070420/d070420b.htm (April 20, 2007).

"Stonyfield Farm's Chief Blogger Leaves." Backbone Corporate Blogging Survey (March 24, 2006).

Sullivan, Laurie. "eBay to Go Head to Head Against Google for Online Ad Market." *InformationWeek* (June 12, 2006).

Sultan, Fareena, and Andrew Rohm. "The Coming Era of 'Brand in Hand' Marketing." *MIT Sloan Management Review* 47, no. 1 (Fall 2005).

Surmacz, Jon. "In a League of Its Own." *CIO Magazine* (April 15, 2005).

Tedeschi, Bob. "Like Shopping? Social Networking? Try Social Shopping." *The New York Times* (September 11, 2006).

Thomke, Stefan, and Eric von Hippel. "Customers as Innovators." *Harvard Business Review* (April 2002).

Urbaczewski, Andrew, Leonard M. Jessup, and Bradley Wheeler. "Electronic Commerce Research: A Taxonomy and Synthesis." *Journal of Organizational Computing and Electronic Commerce* 12, no. 2 (2002).

Werbach, Kevin. "Syndication: The Emerging Model for Business in the Internet Era." *Harvard Business Review* (May–June 2000).

Westland, J. Christopher. "Preference Ordering Cash, Near-Cash and Electronic Cash." *Journal of Organizational Computing and Electronic Commerce* 12, no. 3 (2002).

White, Bobby. "Major League Baseball Steps Out as Coach in the Game of Web Video." *The Wall Street Journal* (March 27, 2006).

Wireless Week. "World of Warcraft Hits 7 Million Players." Digital Trends (September 7, 2006).

Yen, Benjamin P.-C. and Elsie O. S. Ng. "The Impact of Electronic Commerce on Procurement." *Journal of Organizational Computing and Electronic Commerce* 13, no. 3 & 4 (2003).

Yoo, Byungjoon, Vidyanand Choudhary, and Tridas Mukhopadhyay. "A Model of Neutral B2B Intermediaries." *Journal of Management Information Systems* 19, no. 3 (Winter 2002–2003).

Yuan, Li. "Can't Talk Now, I'm Winning." *The Wall Street Journal* (October 11, 2005).

Yuan, Li. "Now, the Very Small Screen." *The Wall Street Journal* (September 22, 2005).

Yuan, Li. "TV-Anytime, Anywhere." *The Wall Street Journal* (September 12, 2005).

Yuan, Li, and Cassell Bryan-Low. "Coming Soon to Cellphone Screens-More Ads Than Ever." *The Wall Street Journal* (August 16, 2006).

Chapter 14

Anson, Rob, and Bjorn Erik Munkvold. "Beyond Face-to-Face: A Field Study of Electronic Meetings in Different Time and Place Modes." *Journal of Organizational Computing and Electronic Commerce* 14, no. 2 (2004).

Anthes, Gary H. "Modeling Magic," *Computerworld* (February 7, 2005).

Apte, Chidanand, Bing Liu, Edwin P.D. Pednault, and Padhraic Smith." Business Applications of Data Mining." *Communications of the ACM* 45, no. 8 (August 2002).

Babcock, Charles. "Smaller Businesses Try Analytics." *InformationWeek* (May 9, 2005).

Bacheldor, Beth. "Beating Down Inventory Costs." *InformationWeek* (April 21, 2003).

Bacheldor, Beth. "Nimble, Quick Supply Chains In Demand." *InformationWeek* (March 24, 2003).

Badal, Jaclyne. "A Reality Check for the Sales Staff." *The Wall Street Journal* (October 16, 2006).

Bannan, Karen J. "Smart Selling." *Profit Magazine* (May 2006).

Barkhi, Reza. "The Effects of Decision Guidance and Problem Modeling on Group Decision-Making." *Journal of Management Information Systems* 18, no. 3 (Winter 2001–2002).

Bazerman, Max H., and Dolly Chugh. "Decisions Without Blinders." *Harvard Business Review* (January 2006).

Briggs, Robert O., Gert-Jan de Vreede, and Jay. F. Nunamaker Jr.: "Collaboration Engineering with ThinkLets to Pursue Sustained Success with Group Support Systems." *Journal of Management Information Systems* 19, no. 4 (Spring 2003).

Cognos Incorporated. "Integrated CPM Solution from Cognos and SSA Global Drives Performance at Caesars Entertainment." (May 15, 2005).

Cone, Edward, and David F. Carr. "Unloading on the Competition." *Baseline* (October 2002).

De Vreede, Gert-Jan, Robert M. Daviso, and Robert O., Briggs. "How a Silvery Bullet May Lose Its Shine." *Communications of the ACM* 46, no. 8 (August 2003).

Dennis, Alan R., and Barbara H. Wixom, "Investigating the Moderators of the Group Support Systems Use with Meta-Analysis." *Journal of Management Information Systems* 18, no. 3 (Winter 2001–2002).

Dennis, Alan R., and Bryan A. Reinicke. "Beta Versus VHS and the Acceptance of Electronic Brainstorming Technology." *MIS Quarterly* 28, no. 1 (March 2004).

Dennis, Alan R., and Monica J. Garfield. "The Adoption and Use of GSS in Project Teams: Toward More Participative Processes and Outcomes." *MIS Quarterly* 27, no. 2 (June 2003).

Dennis, Alan R., Barbara H. Wixom, and Robert J. Vandenberg. "Understanding Fit and Appropriation Effects in Group Support Systems via Meta Analysis." *MIS Quarterly* 25, no. 2 (June 2001).

Dennis, Alan R., Craig K. Tyran, Douglas R. Vogel, and Jay Nunamaker, Jr. "Group Support Systems for Strategic Planning." *Journal of Management Information Systems* 14, no. 1 (Summer 1997).

Eveborn, Patrik, Patrik Flisberg, and Mikael Ronnqvist. "Laps." *European Journal of Operational Research*: 962–976. www.optimalsolutions.com (accessed May 5, 2004).

Few, Stephen. "Dashboard Confusion." *Intelligent Enterprise* (March 20, 2004).

Fjermestad, Jerry, and Starr Roxanne Hiltz. "An Assessment of Group Support Systems Experimental Research: Methodology and Results." *Journal of Management Information Systems* 15, no. 3 (Winter 1998–1999).

Fjermestad, Jerry, and Starr Roxanne Hiltz. "Group Support Systems: A Descriptive Evaluation of Case and Field Studies." *Journal of Management Information Systems* 17, no. 3 (Winter 2000–2001).

Fjermestad, Jerry. "An Integrated Framework for Group Support Systems." *Journal of Organizational Computing and Electronic Commerce* 8, no. 2 (1998).

George, Joey. "Organizational Decision Support Systems." *Journal of Management Information Systems* 8, no. 3 (Winter 1991–1992).

Gorry, G. Anthony, and Michael S. Scott Morton. "A Framework for Management Information Systems." *MIT Sloan Management Review* 13, no. 1 (Fall 1971).

Hender, Jillian M., Douglas L. Dean, Thomas L. Rodgers, and Jay F. Nunamaker Jr. "An Examination of the Impact of Stimuli Type and GSS Structure on Creativity." *Journal of Management Information Systems* 18, no. 4 (Spring 2002).

Information Builders Inc. "Information Builders Underwrites New Enterprise Reporting System for National Life." www.informationbuilders.com (accessed August 7, 2005).

John, Kose, Larry Lang, and Jeffry Netter. "The Voluntary Restructuring of Large Firms in Response to Performance Decline" *The Journal of Finance* (July 1992).

Kohavi, Ron, Neal J. Rothleder, and Evangelos Simoudis. "Emerging Trends in Business Analytics." *Communications of the ACM* 45, no. 8 (August 2002).

Kwok, Ron Chi-Wai, Jian Ma, and Douglas R. Vogel. "Effects of Group Support Systems and Content Facilitation on Knowledge Acquisition." *Journal of Management Information Systems* 19, no. 3 (Winter 2002–2003).

LaCroix, Benoit, and Jacques Desrosiers. "Altitude Manpower Planning." *OR/MS Today* (April 2004).

Latour, Almar. "After 20 Years, Baby Bells Face Some Grown-Up Competition." *The Wall Street Journal* (May 28, 2004).

Laudon, Kenneth C., and Jane P. *Management Information Systems: Managing the Digital Firm* Eighth edition. Upper Saddle River, NJ: Prentice Hall (2004).

Lilien, Gary L., Arvind Rangaswamy, Gerrit H. Van Bruggen, and Katrin Starke. "DSS Effectiveness in Marketing Resource Allocation Decisions: Reality vs. Perception." *Information Systems Research* 15, no. 3 (September 2004).

Nguyen, Alain. "Renault Speeds Up Delivery." *OR/MS Today* (April 2006).

Niven, Paul. "Cascading the Balanced Scorecard: A Case Study on Nova Scotia Power, Inc." www.balancedscorecard.biz/articles/Cascading%20the%20Balanced%20Scorecard_a%20case%20Study%20on%20Nova%20Scotia%20Power,%20Inc..pdf (2006).

Nunamaker, J. F., Alan R. Dennis, Joseph S. Valacich, Douglas R. Vogel, and Joey F. George. "Electronic Meeting Systems to Support Group Work." *Communications of the ACM* 34, no. 7 (July 1991).

Optimal Solutions. "Laps Care." www.optimalsolutions.com (accessed September 15, 2007).

Oracle Corporation. "Pharmacia Gains Discipline and Improves Corporate Performance Management Thanks to a Comprehensive, Strategic View of Research Operations." www.oracle.com (accessed August 31, 2003).

Palisade. "Procter & Gamble Uses @ RISK and PrecisionTree World-Wide." - www.palisade.com (accessed August 6, 2005).

Parlin, Kara, with Jennifer Hawthorne. "Coaxing Additional Sales from Clients." Internet World (April 2003).

PeopleSoft. "Spotlight on Performance at Detroit Edison." www.peoplesoft.com (accessed November 3, 2002).

Pinsonneault, Alain, Henri Barki, R. Brent Gallupe, and Norberto Hoppen. "Electronic Brainstorming: The Illusion of Productivity." Information Systems Research 10, no. 2 (July 1999).

Shaw, Andy. "Decision Support Systems Can Help Hospitals Reduce Costs and Improve Patient Care." www.canhealth.com/nov03.html (accessed May 8, 2007).

Shaw, Andy. "Organizations Work to Improve Coding of Clinical Data," www.canhealth.com/nov03.html (accessed May 8, 2007).

Siebel Systems. "Compass Bank Reduces Loan Write-Offs by 7 Percent Using Siebel Business Analytics." www.siebel.com/business-intelligence/success-stories.shtm (accessed August 14, 2005).

Simon, H. A. The New Science of Management Decision. New York: Harper & Row (1960).

Somoza, Kirsten C. "A Computerized Cardiac Teletriage Decision Support System: Effects on Nurse Performance," http://hot.carleton.ca/hot-topics/articles/cardiac-teletriage (accessed May 8, 2007).

Stodder, David. "True Tales of Performance Management." Intelligent Enterprise (June 1, 2004).

Walls, Joseph G., George R. Widmeyer, and Omar A. El Sawy. "Building an Information System Design Theory for Vigilant EIS." Information Systems Research 3, no. 1 (March 1992).

Wrazen, Ed. "UK Forces Cut Supply Chain Costs by $30 Million." Trillium Software. www.trillium.com (accessed May 26, 2004).

Yoo, Youngjin, and Maryam Alavi. "Media and Group Cohesion: Relative Influences on Social Presence, Task Participation, and Group Consensus." MIS Quarterly 25, no. 3 (September 2001).

Zeidenberg, Neil. "New Software Tracks How Children Use Their Prosthesis Over Time." www.canhealth.com/nov03.html (accessed May 8, 2007).

Zeidenberg, Neil. "Wireless Handheld Computers Enable Doctors to Prescribe at Point of Care. www.canhealth.com/nov03.html (accessed May 8, 2007).

Chapter 15

Alavi, Maryam, Timothy R. Kayworth, and Dorothy E. Leidner. "An Empirical Investigation of the Influence of Organizational Culture on Knowledge Management Practices." Journal of Management Information Systems 22, no. 3 (Winter 2006).

Anandarajan, Murugan. "Profiling Web Usage in the Workplace: A Behavior-Based Artificial Intelligence Approach." Journal of Management Information Systems 19, no. 1 (Summer 2002).

Anthes, Gary H. "Agents Change." Computerworld (January 27, 2003).

AskMe Corporation. "Select Customers: P&G Case Study." (August 2003). http://www.askmecorp.com/customers/default.asp.

Awad, Elias, and Hassan M Ghaziri. Knowledge Management. Upper Saddle River, NJ: Prentice Hall (2004).

Bacheldor, Beth. "Boeing's Flight Plan." Information Week (February 16, 2004).

Balfour, Gail. "Canadian Forces Train f or Combat with Virtual Reality." IT World Canada. www.itworldcanada.com/a/Computerworld/778ba108-61f2-4f42-8b7a-ad7eb9f41685.html (July 16, 1999).

Bargeron, David, Jonathan Grudin, Anoop Gupta, Elizabeth Sanocki, Francis Li, and Scott Le Tiernan. "Asynchronous Collaboration Around Multimedia Applied to On-Demand Education." Journal of Management Information Systems 18, no. 4 (Spring 2002).

Barker, Virginia E., and Dennis E. O'Connor. "Expert Systems for Configuration at Digital: XCON and Beyond." Communications of the ACM (March 1989).

Becerra-Fernandez, Irma, Avelino Gonzalez, and Rajiv Sabherwal. Knowledge Management. Upper Saddle River, NJ: Prentice Hall (2004).

Birkinshaw, Julian, and Tony Sheehan. "Managing the Knowledge Life Cycle." MIT Sloan Management Review 44, no. 1 (Fall 2002).

Blair, Margaret M., and Steven Wallman. "Unseen Wealth." Brookings Institution Press (2001).

Boeing. "Boeing Winnipeg. www.boeing.com/commercial/winnipeg (accessed May 8, 2007).

Booth, Corey, and Shashi Buluswar. "The Return of Artificial Intelligence." McKinsey Quarterly no. 2 (2002).

Burtka, Michael. "Generic Algorithms." The Stern Information Systems Review 1, no. 1 (Spring 1993).

Cannataro, Mario, and Domenico Talia. "The Knowledge Grid." Communications of the ACM 46, no. 1 (January 2003).

Casselman, Grace. "Growing Like a Weed." www.backbonemag.com/Magazine/E+Trends_07060601.asp (accessed May 8, 2007).

Cavalieri, Sergio, Vittorio Cesarotti, and Vito Introna. "A Multiagent Model for Coordinated Distribution Chain Planning." Journal of Organizational Computing and Electronic Commerce 13, no. 3 & 4 (2003).

Clow, Simon, and Maeve Curtain. "EADS Sees Years of Work Ahead to Repair Airbus." The Wall Street Journal (October 5, 2006).

Cole, R.E. "Introduction, Knowledge Management Special Issue." California Management Review (Spring 1998).

Cross, Rob, and Lloyd Baird. "Technology is Not Enough: Improving Performance by Building Organizational Memory." MIT Sloan Management Review 41, no. 3 (Spring 2000).

Cross, Rob, Nitin Nohria, and Andrew Parker. "Six Myths about Informal Networks-and How to Overcome Them." MIT Sloan Management Review 43, no. 3 (Spring 2002).

Davenport, Thomas H., Robert J. Thomas and Susan Cantrell. "The Mysterious Art and Science of Knowledge-Worker Performance." MIT Sloan Management Review 44, no. 1 (Fall 2002).

Desouza, Kevin C. "Facilitating Tacit Knowledge Exchange." Communications of the ACM 46, no. 6 (June 2003).

Desouza, Kevin C., and J. Roberto Evaristo. "Managing Knowledge in Distributed Projects." Communications of the ACM 47, no. 4 (April 2004).

Dhar, Vasant, and Roger Stein. Intelligent Decision Support Methods: The Science of Knowledge Work. Upper Saddle River, NJ: Prentice Hall (1997).

Du, Timon C., Eldon Y. Li, and An-pin Chang. "Mobile Agents in Distributed Network Management." Communications of the ACM 46, no.7 (July 2003).

Earl, Michael. "Knowledge Management Strategies: Toward a Taxonomy." Journal of Management Information Systems 18, no. 1 (Summer 2001).

Easley, Robert F., Sarv Devaraj, and J. Michael Crant. "Relating Collaborative Technology Use to Teamwork Quality and Performance: An Empirical Analysis." Journal of Management Information Systems 19, no. 4 (Spring 2003).

eMarketer, "Portals and Content Management Solutions." (June 2003).

Frangos, Alex." New Dimensions in Design." The Wall Street Journal (July 7, 2004).

Gelernter, David. "The Metamorphosis of Information Management." Scientific American (August 1989).

Gilbert, Jane. "Catching the Knowledge Wave: Redefining Knowledge for the Post-Industrial Age." Education Canada (Summer 2007).

Goodnoe, Ezra. "How to Use Wikis for Business." InformationWeek (August 8, 2005).

Gregor, Shirley, and Izak Benbasat. "Explanations from Intelligent Systems: Theoretical Foundations and Implications for Practice." MIS Quarterly 23, no. 4 (December 1999).

Grover, Varun, and Thomas H. Davenport. "General Perspectives on Knowledge Management: Fostering a Research Agenda." Journal of Management Information Systems 18, no. 1 (Summer 2001).

Gu, Feng, and Baruch Lev. "Intangible Assets. Measurements, Drivers, Usefulness." http://pages.stern.nyu.edu/~blev/ (2001).

Guerra, Anthony. "Goldman Sachs Embraces Rules-Based Solution." Wall Street and Technology (May 2001).

Hinton, Gregory. "How Neural Networks Learn from Experience." Scientific American (September 1992).

Holland, John H. "Genetic Algorithms." Scientific American (July 1992).

Hollis, Emily. "U.S. Navy: Smooth Sailing for Education." (2004). www.clomedia.com (accessed November 1, 2006).

Holmes, Stanley. "On a Wing and a Prayer at Boeing." *BusinessWeek* (June 7, 2006).

Housel Tom, and Arthur A. Bell. *Measuring and Managing Knowledge.* New York: McGraw-Hill (2001).

Hummingbird. "Stikeman Elliott Collaborates with Hummingbird and ii3." www.hummingbird.com (accessed September 19, 2006).

Jarvenpaa, Sirkka L. and D. Sandy Staples. "Exploring Perceptions of Organizational Ownership of Information and Expertise." *Journal of Management Information Systems* 18, no. 1 (Summer 2001).

Jeong, Woo Seok, Sun Gwan Han, and Geun Sik Jo. "Intelligent Cyber Logistics Using Reverse Auction." *Journal of Organizational Computing and Electronic Commerce* 13, no. 3 & 4 (2003).

Jones, Quentin, Gilad Ravid, and Sheizaf Rafaeli. "Information Overload and the Message Dynamics of Online Interaction Spaces: A Theoretical Model and Empirical Exploration." *Information Systems Research* 15, no. 2 (June 2004).

Kankanhalli, Atreyi, Frasiska Tanudidjaja, Juliana Sutanto, and Bernard C.Y Tan. "The Role of IT in Successful Knowledge Management Initiatives." *Communications of the ACM* 46, no. 9 (September 2003).

King, William R., Peter V. Marks, Jr., and Scott McCoy. "The Most Important Issues in Knowledge Management." *Communications of the ACM* 45, no. 9 (September 2002).

KPMG. "Insights from KPMG's European Knowledge Management Survey 2002/2003." KPMG (2003a).

Kuo, R. J., K. Chang, and S. Y. Chien. "Integration and Self-Organizing Feature Maps and Genetic-Algorithm-Based Clustering Method for Market Segmentation." *Journal of Organizational Computing and Electronic Commerce* 14, no. 1 (2004).

Lamont, Judith. "Communities of Practice Leverage Knowledge." *KMWorld* (July/August 2006).

Lamont, Judith. "Compliance: The Hazards of E-Mail." *KMWorld* (October 2006).

Lamont, Judith. "Smart by Any Name—Enterprise Suites Offer Broad Benefits." *KMWorld* (April 2005).

Landler, Mark. "Airbus Offers Up Redesigned A350 in a Challenge to Boeing." *The New York Times* (July 18, 2006).

Lee, Kyoung Jun, Yong Sik Chang, Hyung Rim Choi, Hyun Soo Kim, Young Jae Park, and Byung Joo Park. "A Time-Bound Framework for Negotiation and Decision Making of Virtual Manufacturing Enterprise." *Journal of Organizational Computing and Electronic Commerce* 14, no. 1 (2004).

Leonard, Dorothy, and Walter Swap. "Deep Smarts." *Harvard Business Review* (September 1, 2004).

Lev, Baruch, and Theodore Sougiannis. "Penetrating the Book-to-Market Black Box: The R&D Effect." *Journal of Business Finance and Accounting* (April/May 1999).

Lev, Baruch. "Sharpening the Intangibles Edge." *Harvard Business Review* (June 1, 2004).

Lunsford, J. Lynn, and Daniel Michaels. "After Four Years in the Rear, Boeing is Set to Jet Past Airbus." *The Wall Street Journal* (June 10, 2005).

Lunsford, J. Lynn, and Daniel Michaels. "Bet on Huge Plane Trips Up Airbus." *The Wall Street Journal* (June 15, 2006).

Maes, Patti. "Agents that Reduce Work and Information Overload." *Communications of the ACM* 38, no. 7 (July 1994).

Maglio, Paul P., and Christopher S. Campbell. "Attentive Agents." *Communications of the ACM* 46, no. 3 (March 2003).

Markus, M. Lynne, Ann Majchrzak, and Less Gasser. "A Design Theory for Systems that Support Emergent Knowledge Processes." *MIS Quarterly* 26, no. 3 (September 2002).

Markus, M. Lynne. "Toward a Theory of Knowledge Reuse: Types of Knowledge Reuse Situations and Factors in Reuse Success." *Journal of Management Information Systems* 18, no. 1 (Summer 2001).

McCarthy, John. "Generality in Artificial Intelligence." *Communications of the ACM* 30, no. 12 (December 1987).

McGillicudy, Shamus. "Social Bookmarking: Pushing Collaboration to the Edge." SearchCIO.com (June 21, 2006).

McKellar, Hugh. "Business and Practice: KM and the Law." *KMWorld* (October 2006).

Michaels, Daniel, and J. Lynn Lunsford. "Under Pressure, Airbus Redesigns a Troubled Plane." *The Wall Street Journal* (July 14, 2006).

Michaels, Daniel. "Airbus Opens Overhaul by Looking at Procurement." *The Wall Street Journal* (September 25, 2006).

Microsoft. "Case Study: The Royal Canadian Mint." www.microsoft.com/canada/casestudies/royal_canadian_mint.mspx?pf=true (accessed May 8, 2007).

Moravec, Hans. "Robots, After All." *Communications of the ACM* 46, no. 10 (October 2003).

Munakata, Toshinori, and Yashvant Jani. "Fuzzy Systems: An Overview." *Communications of the ACM* 37, no. 3 (March 1994).

Orlikowski, Wanda J. "Knowing in Practice: Enacting a Collective Capability in Distributed Organizing." *Organization Science* 13, no. 3 (May–June 2002).

Pastore, Richard. "Cruise Control." *CIO Magazine* (February 1, 2003).

Perry, Andrew. "KM in Review: Tracing the Value of Knowledge Assets." *KMWorld* (October 2002).

Rumelhart, David E., Bernard Widrow, and Michael A. Lehr. "The Basic Ideas in Neural Networks." *Communications of the ACM* 37, no. 3 (March 1994).

Sadeh, Norman, David W. Hildum, and Dag Kjenstad. "Agent-Based E-Supply Chain Decision Support." *Journal of Organizational Computing and Electronic Commerce* 13, nos. 3 and 4 (2003).

Samuelson, Douglas A., and Charles M. Macal. "Agent-Based Simulation." *OR/MS Today* (August 2006).

Semio Corporation. "Case Study: Leveraging the World's Largest Repository of Life Science Research With Entrieva's Semio Technology." www.semio.com (accessed September 5, 2006).

Sibigtroth, James M. "Implementing Fuzzy Expert Rules in Hardware." *AI Expert* (April 1992).

Spangler, Scott, Jeffrey T. Kreulen, and Justin Lessler. "Generating and Browsing Multiple Taxonomies over a Document Collection." *Journal of Management Information Systems* 19, no. 4 (Spring 2003).

Starbuck, William H. "Learning by Knowledge-Intensive Firms." *Journal of Management Studies* 29, no. 6 (November 1992).

SumTotal Systems. "Enterprise Learning Solutions for a Competitive Marketplace: Royal LePage Case Study." www.sumtotalsystems.com/success/loginhtml?id=23 (2007).

Tiwana, Amrit. "Affinity to Infinity in Peer-to-Peer Knowledge Platforms." *Communications of the ACM* 46, no. 5 (May 2003).

Totty, Michael. "Information Found-and-Shared." *The Wall Street Journal* (September 11, 2006).

Vara, Vauhini. "Offices Co-Opt Consumer Web Tools Like 'Wikis' and Social Networking." *The Wall Street Journal* (September 12, 2006).

Voekler, Michael. "Staying a Step Ahead of Fraud." *Intelligent Enterprise* (September 2006).

Wakefield, Julie. "Complexity's Business Model." *Scientific American* (January 2001).

Walczak, Steven. "Gaining Competitive Advantage for Trading in Emerging Capital Markets with Neural Networks. " *Journal of Management Information Systems* 16, no. 2 (Fall 1999).

Wang, Huaiqing, John Mylopoulos, and Stephen Liao. "Intelligent Agents and Financial Risk Monitoring Systems." *Communications of the ACM* 45, no. 3 (March 2002).

Wayne, Leslie. "Boeing Bets the House on Its 787 Dreamliner." *The New York Times* (May 7, 2006).

Wong, Edward. "For Jet Rivals, Caution Here, Swagger There," *The New York Times* (July 28, 2002).

Zack, Michael H "Rethinking the Knowledge-Based Organization." *MIT Sloan Management Review* 44, no. 4 (Summer 2003).

Glossary

2.5G networks Wireless cellular networks that are packet-switched and provide higher-speed data transmission rates ranging from 50 to 144 Kbps using the existing cellular network infrastructure.

3G networks Cellular networks based on packet-switched technology with speeds ranging from 144 Kbps for mobile users to more than 2 Mbps for stationary users, enabling users to transmit video, graphics, and other rich media, in addition to voice.

802.11b An IEEE standard for wireless fidelity (Wi-Fi) transmission; limited range of 30 metres.

acceptable use policy (AUP) Defines acceptable uses of the firm's information resources and computing equipment, including desktop and laptop computers, wireless devices, telephones, and the Internet, and specifies consequences for noncompliance.

acceptance testing Provides the final certification that the system is ready to be used in a production setting.

access control Policies and procedures a company uses to prevent improper access to systems by unauthorized insiders and outsiders.

access point Box in a wireless LAN consisting of a radio receiver/transmitter and antennae that link to a wired network, router, or hub.

accountability The mechanisms for assessing responsibility for decisions made and actions taken.

accounting rate of return on investment (ROI) Calculation of the rate of return on an investment by adjusting cash inflows produced by the investment for depreciation. Approximates the accounting income earned by the investment.

accumulated balance digital payment systems Systems enabling users to make micropayments and purchases on the Web, accumulating a debit balance on their credit card or telephone bills.

agency theory Economic theory that views the firm as a nexus of contracts among self-interested individuals who must be supervised and managed.

agent-based modelling Modelling complex phenomena as systems of autonomous agents that follow relatively simple rules for interaction.

Ajax Development technique for creating interactive Web applications capable of updating the user interface without reloading the entire browser page.

analog signal A continuous waveform that passes through a communications medium; used for voice communications.

analytical CRM Customer relationship management applications dealing with the analysis of customer data to provide information for improving business performance.

antivirus software Software designed to detect, and often eliminate, computer viruses from an information system.

application proxy filtering Firewall screening technology that uses a proxy server to inspect and transmit data packets flowing into and out of the organization so that all the organization's internal applications communicate with the outside using a proxy application.

application server software Software that handles all application operations between browser-based computers and a company's back-end business applications or databases.

application service provider (ASP) Company providing software that can be rented by other companies over the Web or a private network.

application software Programs written for a specific application to perform functions specified by end users.

application software package A set of prewritten, precoded application software programs that are commercially available for sale or lease.

artificial intelligence (AI) The effort to develop computer-based systems that can behave like humans, with the ability to learn languages, accomplish physical tasks, use a perceptual apparatus, and emulate human expertise and decision making.

asynchronous transfer mode (ATM) A networking technology that parcels information into 8-byte cells, allowing data to be transmitted between computers from different vendors at any speed.

attribute A piece of information describing a particular entity.

authentication The ability of each party in a transaction to ascertain the identity of the other party.

authorization management systems Systems for allowing each user access only to those portions of a system or the Web which that person is permitted to enter, based on information established by a set of access rules.

authorization policies Policies that determine differing levels of access to information assets for different levels of users in an organization.

automation Using the computer to speed up the performance of existing tasks.

autonomic computing Effort to develop systems that can manage themselves without user intervention.

backbone Part of a network handling the major traffic and providing the primary path for traffic flowing to or from other networks.

backward chaining A strategy for searching the rule base in an expert system that acts like a problem solver by beginning with a hypothesis and seeking out more information until the hypothesis is either proved or disproved.

balanced scorecard Model for analyzing firm performance which supplements traditional financial measures with measurements from additional business perspectives, such as customers, internal business processes, and learning and growth.

bandwidth The capacity of a communications channel as measured by the difference between the highest and lowest frequencies that can be transmitted by that channel.

banner ad A graphic display on a Web page used for advertising. The banner is linked to the advertiser's Web site so that a person clicking on it will be transported to the advertiser's Web site.

batch processing A method of collecting and processing data in which transactions are accumulated and stored until a specified time when it is convenient or necessary to process them as a group.

baud A change in signal from positive to negative or vice versa that is used as a measure of transmission speed.

behavioural models Descriptions of management based on behavioural scientists' observations of what managers actually do in their jobs.

benchmarking Setting strict standards for products, services, or activities and measuring organizational performance against those standards.

best practices The most successful solutions or problem-solving methods that have been developed by a specific organization or industry.

biometric authentication Technology for authenticating system users that compares a person's unique characteristics such as fingerprints, face, or retinal image, against a stored set profile of these characteristics.

bit A binary digit representing the smallest unit of data in a computer system. It can have only one of two states, representing 0 or 1.

blade server Entire computer that fits on a single, thin card (or blade) and that is plugged into a single chassis to save space, power, and complexity.

blog Popular term for Weblog, designating an informal, yet structured Web site where individuals can publish stories, opinions, and links to other Web sites of interest.

blogosphere Totality of blog-related Web sites.

Bluetooth Standard for wireless personal area networks that can transmit up to 722 Kbps within a 10-metre area.

botnet A group of computers that have been infected with bot malware without users' knowledge, enabling a hacker to use the amassed resources of the computers to launch distributed denial-of-service attacks, phishing campaigns, or spam.

broadband High-speed transmission technology. Also designates a single communications medium that can transmit multiple channels of data simultaneously.

bullwhip effect Distortion of information about the demand for a product as it passes from one entity to the next across the supply chain.

bus network Network topology linking a number of computers by a single circuit with all messages broadcast to the entire network.

business continuity planning Planning that focuses on how the company can restore business operations after a disaster strikes.

business driver A force in the environment to which businesses must respond and that influences the direction of business.

business ecosystem Loosely coupled but interdependent networks of suppliers, distributors, outsourcing firms, transportation service firms, and technology manufacturers.

business functions Specialized tasks performed in a business organization, including manufacturing and production, sales and marketing, finance and accounting, and human resources.

business intelligence Applications and technologies to help users make better business decisions.

business model An abstraction of what an enterprise is and how the enterprise delivers a product or service, showing how the enterprise creates wealth.

business process management (BPM) Methodology for revising the organization's business processes to use business processes as fundamental building blocks of corporate information systems.

business process reengineering The radical redesign of business processes, combining steps to cut waste and eliminating repetitive, paper-intensive tasks in order to improve cost, quality, and service, and to maximize the benefits of information technology.

business-to-business (B2B) electronic commerce Electronic sales of goods and services among businesses.

business-to-consumer (B2C) electronic commerce Electronic retailing of products and services directly to individual consumers.

byte A string of bits, usually eight, used to store one number or character in a computer system.

cable Internet connections Internet connections that use digital cable lines to deliver high-speed Internet access to homes and businesses.

call centre An organizational department responsible for handling customer service issues by telephone and other channels.

campus area network (CAN) An interconnected set of local area networks in a limited geographical area such as a college or corporate campus.

CA*net4 Canadian research network with new protocols and transmission speeds that provides an infrastructure for supporting high-bandwidth Internet applications; similar to Internet2 in the U.S.

capital budgeting The process of analyzing and selecting various proposals for capital expenditures.

carpal tunnel syndrome (CTS) Type of RSI in which pressure on the median nerve through the wrist's bony carpal tunnel structure produces pain.

case-based reasoning (CBR) Artificial intelligence technology that represents knowledge as a database of cases and solutions.

cellular telephone (cell phone) A device that transmits voice or data, using radio waves to communicate with radio antennas placed within adjacent geographic areas called cells.

central processing unit The part of the computer system where the manipulation of symbols, numbers, and characters occurs, and that controls the other parts of the computer system.

centralized processing Processing that is accomplished by one large central computer.

change agent In the context of implementation, the individual acting as the catalyst during the change process to ensure successful organizational adaptation to a new system or innovation.

change management Managing the impact of organizational change associated with an innovation, such as a new information system.

channel The link by which data or voice are transmitted between sending and receiving devices in a network.

chat Live, interactive conversations over a public network.

chief information officer (CIO) Senior manager in charge of the information systems function in the firm.

chief knowledge officer (CKO) Senior executive in charge of the organization's knowledge management program.

chief security officer (CSO) Head of a formal security function for the organization and is responsible for enforcing the firm's security policy.

choice Simon's third stage of decision making, when the individual selects among the various solution alternatives.

churn rate Measurement of the number of customers who stop using or purchasing products or services from a company. Used as an indicator of the growth or decline of a firm's customer base.

classical model of management Traditional description of management that focused on its formal functions of planning, organizing, coordinating, deciding, and controlling.

click fraud Fraudulently clicking on an online ad in pay per click advertising to generate an improper charge per click.

clicks-and-mortar Business model where the Web site is an extension of a traditional bricks-and-mortar business.

clickstream tracking Tracking data about customer activities at Web sites and storing them in a log.

client The user point-of-entry for the required function in client/server computing, normally a desktop computer, workstation, or laptop computer.

client/server computing A model for computing that splits processing between clients and servers on a network, assigning functions to the machine most able to perform the function.

coaxial cable A transmission medium consisting of thickly insulated copper wire; can transmit large volumes of data quickly.

Code Division Multiple Access (CDMA) Major cellular transmission standard in North America that transmits over several frequencies, occupies the entire spectrum, and randomly assigns users to a range of frequencies over time.

collaborative commerce The use of digital technologies to enable multiple organizations to collaboratively design, develop, build, and manage products through their life cycles.

collaborative filtering Tracking users' movements on a Web site, comparing the information gleaned about a user's behaviour against data about other customers with similar interests to predict what the user would like to see next.

collaborative planning, forecasting, and replenishment (CPFR) Firms collaborating with their suppliers and buyers to formulate demand forecasts, develop production plans, and coordinate shipping, warehousing, and stocking activities.

communications devices Devices which provide connections between the computer and communications networks.

communities of practice (COPs) Informal social networks of professionals and employees within and outside the firm who have similar work-related activities and interests.

competitive forces model Model used to describe the interaction of external influences, specifically threats and opportunities, that affect an organization's strategy and ability to compete.

complementary assets Additional assets required to derive value from a primary investment.

component-based development Building large software systems by combining pre-existing software components.

computer Physical device that takes data as an input, transforms the data by executing stored instructions, and outputs information to a number of devices.

computer abuse The commission of acts involving a computer that may not be illegal but are considered unethical.

computer crime The commission of illegal acts through the use of a computer or against a computer system.

computer forensics The scientific collection, examination, authentication, preservation, and analysis of data held on or retrieved from computer storage media in such a way that the information can be used as evidence in a court of law.

computer hardware Physical equipment used for input, processing, and output activities in an information system.

computer literacy Knowledge about information technology, focusing on understanding of how computer-based technologies work.

computer software Detailed, preprogrammed instructions that control and coordinate the work of computer hardware components in an information system.

computer virus Rogue software program that attaches itself to other software programs or data files in order to be executed, often causing hardware and software malfunctions.

computer vision syndrome (CVS) Eyestrain condition related to computer display screen use; symptoms include headaches, blurred vision, and dry and irritated eyes.

computer-aided design (CAD) Information system that automates the creation and revision of designs using sophisticated graphics software.

computer-aided software engineering (CASE) Automation of step-by-step methodologies for software and systems development to reduce the amounts of repetitive work the developer needs to do.

computer-based information systems (CBIS) Information systems that rely on computer hardware and software for processing and disseminating information.

connectivity The ability of computers and computer-based devices to communicate with one another and share information in a meaningful way without human intervention.

consumer-to-consumer (C2C) electronic commerce Consumers selling goods and services electronically to other consumers.

controls All the methods, policies, and procedures that ensure protection of the organization's assets, accuracy, and reliability of its records, and operational adherence to management standards.

conversion The process of changing from the old system to the new system.

cookies Tiny file deposited on a computer hard drive when an individual visits certain Web sites. Used to identify the visitor and track visits to the Web site.

cooptation Bringing the opposition into the process of designing and implementing a solution without giving up control of the direction and nature of the change.

copyright A statutory grant that protects creators of intellectual property against copying by others for any purpose for a minimum of 50 years.

core competency Activity at which a firm excels as a world-class leader.

core systems Systems that support functions that are absolutely critical to the organization.

cost transparency The ability of consumers to discover the actual costs merchants pay for products.

counterimplementation A deliberate strategy to thwart the implementation of an information system or an innovation in an organization.

cracker Hacker with criminal intent.

critical success factors (CSFs) A small number of easily identifiable operational goals shaped by the industry, the firm, the manager, and the broader environment that are believed to ensure the success of an organization. Used to determine the information requirements of an organization.

cross-selling Marketing complementary products to customers.

CSOX (Canadian Rules for Sarbanes-Oxley Act, Bill 198) The Canadian Act of Parliament that imposes responsibility on companies and their management to protect investors by safeguarding the accuracy and integrity of financial information that is used internally and released externally.

culture The set of fundamental assumptions about what products the organization should produce, how and where it should produce them, and for whom they should be produced.

customer decision-support system (CDSS) System to support the decision making process of an existing or potential customer.

customer lifetime value (CLTV) Difference between revenues produced by a specific customer and the expenses for acquiring and servicing that customer minus the cost of promotional marketing over the lifetime of the customer relationship, expressed in today's dollars.

customer relationship management (CRM) Business and technology discipline that uses information systems to coordinate all the business processes surrounding the firm's interactions with its customers in sales, marketing, and service.

customer relationship management systems Information systems that track all the ways in which a company interacts with its customers and analyze these interactions to optimize revenue, profitability, customer satisfaction, and customer retention.

customization (1) The modification of a software package to meet an organization's unique requirements without destroying the package software's integrity. (2) Changing a delivered product or service based on a user's preferences or prior behaviour.

cybervandalism Intentional disruption, defacement, or destruction of a Web site or corporate information system.

data Streams of raw facts (representing events occurring in organizations or the physical environment) before they have been organized and arranged into a form that people can understand and use.

data administration A special organizational function for managing the organization's data resources, concerned with information policy, data planning, maintenance of data dictionaries, and data quality standards.

data cleansing Activities for detecting and correcting data in a database or file that are incorrect, incomplete, improperly formatted, or redundant. Also known as data scrubbing.

data definition DBMS capability that specifies the structure and content of the database.

data dictionary An automated or manual tool for storing and organizing information about the data maintained in a database.

data-driven DSS A system that supports decision making by allowing users to extract and analyze useful information that was previously buried in large databases.

data element A field.

data entry operators IS staff whose main job is to enter data into information systems.

data flow diagram (DFD) Primary tool for structured analysis that graphically illustrates a system's component process and the flow of data between them.

data governance Policies and processes for managing the availability, usability, integrity, and security of the firm's data.

data inconsistency The presence of different values for the same attribute when the same data are stored in multiple locations.

data management technology The software governing the organization of data on physical storage media.

data manipulation language A language associated with a database management system that end users and programmers use to manipulate data in the database.

data mart A small data warehouse containing only a portion of the organization's data for a specified function or population of users.

data mining Analysis of large pools of data to find patterns and rules that can be used to guide decision making and predict future behaviour.

data quality audit A survey and/or sample of files to determine accuracy and completeness of data in an information system.

data redundancy The presence of duplicate data in multiple data files.

data visualization Technology for helping users see patterns and relationships in large amounts of data by presenting the data in graphical form.

data warehouse A database, with reporting and query tools, that stores current and historical data extracted from various operational systems and consolidated for management reporting and analysis.

data workers People such as secretaries or bookkeepers who process the organization's paperwork.

database A group of related files.

database (rigorous definition) A collection of data organized to service many applications at the same time by storing and managing data so that they appear to be in one location.

database administration Refers to the more technical and operational aspects of managing data, including physical database design and maintenance.

database management software Software used for creating and manipulating lists, creating files and databases to store data, and combining information for reports.

database management system (DBMS) Special software to create and maintain a database and enable individual business applications to extract the data they need without having to create separate files or data definitions in their computer programs.

database server A computer in a client/server environment that is responsible for running a DBMS to process SQL statements and perform database management tasks.

dataconferencing Teleconferencing in which two or more users are able to edit and modify data files simultaneously.

decisional roles Mintzberg's classification for managerial roles where managers initiate activities, handle disturbances, allocate resources, and negotiate conflicts.

decision-support systems (DSS) Information systems at the organization's management level that combine data and sophisticated analytical models or data analysis tools to support semistructured and unstructured decision making.

dedicated lines Telephone lines that are continuously available for transmission by a lessee. Typically conditioned to transmit data at high speeds for high-volume applications.

dedicated server computer A computer on a network that performs important network functions for client computers, such as serving up Web pages, storing data, and storing the network operating system (and hence controlling the network).

demand planning Determining how much product a business needs to make to satisfy all its customers' demands.

denial-of-service (DoS) attack Flooding a network server or Web server with false communications or requests for services in order to crash the network.

dense wavelength division multiplexing (DWDM) Technology for boosting transmission capacity of optical fibre by using many different wavelengths to carry separate streams of data over the same fibre strand at the same time.

Descartes' rule of change A principle that states that if an action cannot be taken repeatedly, then it is not right to be taken at any time.

design Simon's second stage of decision making, when the individual conceives of possible alternative solutions to a problem.

digital cash Currency that is represented in electronic form that moves outside the normal network of money.

digital certificate An attachment to an electronic message to verify the identity of the sender and to provide the receiver with the means to encode a reply.

digital chequing Systems that extend the functionality of existing checking accounts so they can be used for online shopping payments.

digital credit card payment system Secure services for credit card payments on the Internet that protect information transmitted among users, merchant sites, and processing banks.

digital dashboard Displays all of a firm's key performance indicators as graphs and charts on a single screen to provide a one-page overview of all the critical measurements necessary to make key executive decisions.

digital divide Large disparities in access to computers and the Internet among different social groups and different locations.

digital firm Organization where nearly all significant business processes and relationships with customers, suppliers, and employees are digitally enabled, and key corporate assets are managed through digital means.

digital goods Goods that can be delivered over a digital network.

digital market A marketplace that is created by computer and communication technologies that link many buyers and sellers.

Digital Millennium Copyright Act (DMCA) U.S. law that adjusts copyright laws to the Internet Age by making it illegal to make, distribute, or use devices that circumvent technology-based protections of copyrighted materials.

digital signal A discrete waveform that transmits data coded into two discrete states as 1-bits and 0-bits, which are represented as on-off electrical pulses; used for data communications.

digital signature A digital code that can be attached to an electronically transmitted message to uniquely identify its contents and the sender.

digital subscriber line (DSL) A group of technologies providing high-capacity transmission over existing copper telephone lines.

digital wallet Software that stores credit card, electronic cash, owner identification, and address information and provides this data automatically during electronic commerce purchase transactions.

direct cutover A risky conversion approach where the new system completely replaces the old one on an appointed day.

disaster recovery planning Planning for the restoration of computing and communications services after they have been disrupted.

disintermediation The removal of organizations or business process layers responsible for certain intermediary steps in a value chain.

distance learning Education or training delivered over a distance to individuals in one or more locations.

distributed database A database that is stored in more than one physical location. Parts or copies of the database are physically stored in one location, and other parts or copies are stored and maintained in other locations.

distributed denial-of-service (DDoS) attack Numerous computers inundating and overwhelming a network from numerous launch points.

distributed processing The distribution of computer processing work among multiple computers linked by a communications network.

documentation Descriptions of how an information system works from either a technical or end-user standpoint.

domain name English-like name that corresponds to the unique 32-bit numeric Internet Protocol (IP) address for each computer connected to the Internet.

Domain Name System (DNS) A hierarchical system of servers maintaining a database enabling the conversion of domain names to their numeric IP addresses.

domestic exporter Form of business organization characterized by heavy centralization of corporate activities in the home country of origin.

downsizing The process of transferring applications from large computers to smaller ones.

downtime Period of time in which an information system is not operational.

drill down The ability to move from summary data to lower and lower levels of detail.

DSS database A collection of current or historical data from a number of applications or groups. Can be a small PC database or a massive data warehouse.

DSS software system Collection of software tools that are used for data analysis, such as OLAP tools, data mining tools, or a collection of mathematical and analytical models.

due process A process in which laws are well-known and understood and there is an ability to appeal to higher authorities to ensure that laws are applied correctly.

dynamic pricing Pricing of items based on real-time interactions between buyers and sellers that determine what an item is worth at any particular moment.

edge computing Method for distributing the computing load (or work) across many layers of Internet computers in order to minimize response time.

efficient customer response system System that directly links consumer behaviour back to distribution, production, and supply chains.

e-government Use of the Internet and related technologies to digitally enable government and public sector agencies' relationships with citizens, businesses, and other arms of government.

e-learning Instruction delivered through purely digital technology, such as CD-ROMs, the Internet, or private networks.

electronic billing and payment presentation systems Systems used for paying routine monthly bills that allow users to view their bills electronically and pay them through electronic funds transfers from banks or credit card accounts.

electronic business (e-business) The use of the Internet and digital technology to execute all the business processes in the enterprise. Includes e-commerce as well as processes for the internal management of the firm and for coordination with suppliers and other business partners.

electronic commerce (e-commerce) The process of buying and selling goods and services electronically involving transactions using the Internet, networks, and other digital technologies.

electronic data interchange (EDI) The direct computer-to-computer exchange between two organizations of standard business transactions, such as orders, shipment instructions, or payments.

electronic payment system The use of digital technologies, such as credit cards, smart cards, and Internet-based payment systems, to pay for products and services electronically.

electronic records management (ERM) Policies, procedures, and tools for managing the retention, destruction, and storage of electronic records.

e-mail The computer-to-computer exchange of messages.

e-mail handheld Handheld device for wireless data transmission that includes a small display screen and a keypad for typing short e-mail messages.

employee relationship management (ERM) Software dealing with employee issues that are closely related to CRM, such as setting objectives, employee performance management, performance-based compensation, and employee training.

encryption The coding and scrambling of messages to prevent their being read or accessed without authorization.

end-user development The development of information systems by end users with little or no formal assistance from technical specialists.

end-user interface The part of an information system through which the end user interacts with the system, such as online screens and commands.

end users Representatives of departments outside the information systems group for whom applications are developed.

enterprise analysis An analysis of organization-wide information requirements by looking at the entire organization in terms of organizational units, functions, processes, and data elements; helps identify the key entities and attributes in the organization's data.

enterprise application integration (EAI) software Software that works with specific software platforms to tie together multiple applications to support enterprise integration.

enterprise applications Systems that can coordinate activities, decisions, and knowledge across many different functions, levels, and business units in a firm. These systems include enterprise systems, supply chain management systems, and knowledge management systems.

enterprise portal Web interface providing a single entry point for accessing organizational information and services, including information from various enterprise applications and in-house legacy systems so that information appears to be coming from a single source.

enterprise relationship management (ERM) ERM software deals with employee issues that are closely related to CRM, such as setting objectives, employee performance management, performance-based compensation, and employee training.

enterprise software Set of integrated modules for applications such as sales and distribution, financial accounting, investment management, materials management, production planning, plant maintenance, and human resources that allow data to be used by multiple functions and business processes.

enterprise systems Integrated enterprise-wide information systems that coordinate key internal processes of the firm.

entity A person, place, thing, or event about which information must be kept.

entity-relationship diagram A methodology for documenting databases illustrating the relationship between various entities in the database.

ergonomics The interaction of people and machines in the work environment, including the design of jobs, health issues, and the end-user interface of information systems.

ethical "no free lunch" rule Assumption that all tangible and intangible objects are owned by someone else, unless there is a specific declaration otherwise, and that the creator wants compensation for this work.

ethics Principles of right and wrong that can be used by individuals acting as free moral agents to make choices to guide their behaviour.

EV-DO Technology used in cellular network service for providing anytime, anywhere broadband wireless Internet access for PCs and other devices at average speeds of 300 to 500 Kbps. Stands for Evolution Data Optimized.

evil twin Wireless network that pretends to be legitimate to entice participants to log on and reveal passwords or credit card numbers.

exchange Third-party Net marketplace that is primarily transaction oriented and that connects many buyers and suppliers for spot purchasing.

executive support systems (ESS) Information systems at the organization's strategic level designed to address unstructured decision making through advanced graphics and communications.

expert system Knowledge-intensive computer application that captures the expertise of humans in limited domains of knowledge.

explicit knowledge Knowledge that has been documented.

external integration tools Project management technique that links the work of the implementation team to that of users at all organizational levels.

extranet Private intranet that is accessible to authorized outsiders.

Extreme Programming (XP) One of the methodologies used in agile software development that seeks to minimize the cost of changing requirements during systems development.

Fair Information Practices (FIP) A set of principles originally set forth in 1973 in the U.S. that governs the collection and use of information about individuals and forms the basis of most North American and European privacy laws.

fault-tolerant computer systems Systems that contain extra hardware, software, and power supply components that can back a system up and keep it running to prevent system failure.

feasibility study As part of the systems analysis process, the way to determine whether the solution is achievable, given the organization's resources and constraints.

feedback Output that is returned to the appropriate members of the organization to help them evaluate or correct input.

fibre-optic cable A fast, light, and durable transmission medium consisting of thin strands of clear glass fibre bound into cables. Data are transmitted as light pulses.

field A grouping of characters into a word, a group of words, or a complete number, such as a person's name or age.

file A group of records of the same type.

file transfer protocol (FTP) Tool (or protocol) for retrieving and transferring files from a remote computer.

finance and accounting information systems Systems that keep track of the firm's financial assets and fund flows.

firewall Hardware and software placed between an organization's internal network and external networks to prevent outsiders from invading private networks.

firewire A port known as IEEE1824 that can transfer data much faster than older ports. Available on newer Apple and now PCs as well.

focused differentiation Competitive strategy for developing new market niches for specialized products or services where a business can compete in the target area better than its competitors.

foreign key Field in a database table that enables users to find related information in another database table.

formal control tools Project management technique that helps monitor the progress toward completion of a task and fulfillment of goals.

formal planning tools Project management technique that structures and sequences tasks, budgeting time, money, and technical resources required to complete the tasks.

forward chaining A strategy for searching the rule base in an expert system that begins with the information entered by the user and searches the rule base to arrive at a conclusion.

fourth-generation language A programming language that can be employed directly by end users or less-skilled programmers to develop computer applications more rapidly than conventional programming languages.

frame relay A shared network service technology that packages data into bundles for transmission but does not use error-correction routines. Cheaper and faster than packet switching.

franchiser Form of business organization in which a product is created, designed, financed, and initially produced in the home country, but for product-specific reasons, relies heavily on foreign personnel for further production, marketing, and human resources.

fuzzy logic Rule-based artificial intelligence technique that tolerates imprecision by using nonspecific terms called membership functions to solve problems.

Gantt chart Visually represents the timing, duration, and resource requirements of project tasks.

genetic algorithms Problem-solving methods that promote the evolution of solutions to specified problems using the model of living organisms adapting to their environment.

geographic information system (GIS) System with software that can analyze and display data using digitized maps to enhance planning and decision-making.

global culture The development of common expectations, shared artifacts, and social norms among different cultures and peoples.

global positioning system (GPS) Worldwide satellite navigational system.

Global System for Mobile Communication (GSM) Major cellular transmission standard outside North America, with strong international roaming capability, operating primarily in the 900-MHz and 1.8-GHz frequency bands using time division multiple access (TDMA) in which each user is allocated a portion of time on the frequency.

Golden Rule "Do unto others as you would have them do unto you." The ethical principle that states that one should imagine oneself in the place of others and think of the self as the object of the decision.

graphical user interface (GUI) The part of an operating system users interact with that uses graphic icons and the computer mouse to issue commands and make selections.

grid computing Applying the resources of many computers in a network to a single problem.

group decision-support system (GDSS) An interactive computer-based system to facilitate the solution to unstructured problems by a set of decision makers working together as a group.

groupware Software that provides functions and services that support the collaborative activities of work groups.

hacker A person who gains unauthorized access to a computer network for profit, criminal mischief, or personal pleasure.

hertz Measure of frequency of electrical impulses per second, with 1 Hertz equivalent to 1 cycle per second.

high-availability computing Tools and technologies, including backup hardware resources, to enable a system to recover quickly from a crash.

home page A World Wide Web text and graphical screen display that welcomes the user and explains the organization that has established the page.

hotspot A specific geographic location in which an access point provides public Wi-Fi network service.

hubs Very simple devices that connect network components, sending a packet of data to all other connected devices.

human resources information systems Systems that maintain employee records, track employee skills, job performance and training, and support planning for employee compensation and career development.

hybrid AI systems Integration of multiple artificial intelligence technologies into a single application to take advantage of the best features of these technologies.

hypertext markup language (HTML) Page description language for creating Web pages and other hypermedia documents.

hypertext transfer protocol (HTTP) The communications standard used to transfer pages on the Web. Defines how messages are formatted and transmitted.

identity theft Theft of key pieces of personal information, such as credit card numbers or Social Insurance Numbers, in order to obtain merchandise and services in the name of the victim or to obtain false credentials.

Immanuel Kant's Categorical Imperative A principle that states that if an action is not right for everyone to take, it is not right for anyone to take.

I-mode Standard developed by Japan's NTT DoCoMo mobile phone network for enabling cell phones to receive Web-based content and services.

implementation (1) Simon's final stage of decision-making, when the individual puts the decision into effect and reports on the progress of the solution. (2) The stage in the systems development life cycle when a system is put into production mode.

industry structure The nature of participants in an industry and their relative bargaining power. Derives from the competitive forces and establishes the general business environment in an industry and the overall profitability of doing business in that environment.

inference engine The strategy used to search through the rule base in an expert system; can be forward or backward chaining.

information Data that have been shaped into a form that is meaningful and useful to human beings.

information appliance Device that has been customized to perform a few specialized computing tasks well with minimal user effort.

information asymmetry Situation where the relative bargaining power of two parties in a transaction is determined by one party in the transaction possessing more information essential to the transaction than the other party.

information density The total amount and quality of information available to all market participants, consumers, and merchants.

information policy Formal rules governing the maintenance, distribution, and use of information in an organization.

information requirements A detailed statement of the information needs that a new system must satisfy; identifies who needs what information, and when, where, and how the information is needed.

information rights The rights that individuals and organizations have with respect to information that pertains to themselves.

information system Interrelated components working together to collect, process, store, and disseminate information to support decision making, coordination, control, analysis, and visualization in an organization.

information systems department The formal organizational unit that is responsible for the information systems function in the organization.

information systems literacy A broad-based understanding of information systems that includes behavioural knowledge about organizations and individuals using information systems, as well as technical knowledge about computers.

information systems managers Leaders of the various specialists in the information systems department.

information systems plan A road map indicating the direction of systems development: the rationale, the current situation, the management strategy, the implementation plan, and the budget.

information technology (IT) All the hardware and software technologies a firm needs to achieve its business objectives.

information technology (IT) infrastructure Computer hardware, software, data, storage technology, and networks providing a portfolio of shared IT resources for the organization.

informational roles Mintzberg's classification for managerial roles where managers act as the nerve centres of their organizations, receiving and disseminating critical information.

informed consent Consent given with knowledge of all the facts needed to make a rational decision.

input The capture or collection of raw data from within the organization or from its external environment for processing in an information system.

input device Device such as a keyboard or mouse that converts data and instructions into electronic form for input into the computer.

instant messaging Chat service that allows participants to create their own private chat channels so that a person can be alerted whenever someone on his or her private list is online to initiate a chat session with that particular individual.

intangible benefits Benefits that are not easily quantified; they include more efficient customer service or enhanced decision making.

Integrated Services Digital Network (ISDN) International standard for transmitting voice, video, image, and data to support a wide range of service over the public telephone lines.

intellectual property Intangible property created by individuals or organizations that is subject to protections under trade secret, copyright, and patent law.

intelligence The first of Simon's four stages of decision making, when the individual collects information to identify problems occurring in the organization.

intelligent agents Software programs that use a built-in or learned knowledge base to carry out specific, repetitive, and predictable tasks for an individual user, business process, or software application.

intelligent techniques Knowledge management techniques with different objectives, from a focus on discovering knowledge (data mining and neural networks), to distilling knowledge in the form of rules for a computer program (expert systems and fuzzy logic), to discovering optimal solutions for problems (genetic algorithms).

internal integration tools Project management technique that ensures that the implementation team operates as a cohesive unit.

Internal Rate of Return (IRR) The rate of return or profit that an investment is expected to earn.

international information systems architecture The basic information systems required by organizations to coordinate worldwide trade and other activities.

Internet Global network of networks using universal standards to connect millions of different networks.

Internet Protocol (IP) address Four-part numeric address indicating a unique computer location on the Internet.

Internet service provider (ISP) A commercial organization with a permanent connection to the Internet that sells temporary connections to subscribers.

Internet telephony Technologies that use the Internet Protocol's packet-switched connections for voice service.

Internet2 Research network with new protocols and transmission speeds that provides an infrastructure for supporting high-bandwidth Internet applications.

internetworking The linking of separate networks, each of which retains its own identity, into an interconnected network.

interorganizational systems Information systems that automate the flow of information across organizational boundaries and link a company to its customers, distributors, or suppliers.

interpersonal roles Mintzberg's classification for managerial roles where managers act as figureheads and leaders for the organization.

intranet An internal network based on Internet and World Wide Web technology and standards.

intrusion detection system Tools to monitor the most vulnerable points in a network to detect and deter unauthorized intruders.

investment workstation Powerful desktop computer for financial specialists, which is optimized to access and manipulate massive amounts of financial data.

ISO 17799 International set of standards and best practices for security and control.

iterative A process of repeating over and over again the steps to develop a system.

Java Programming language that can deliver only the software functionality needed for a particular task, such as a small applet downloaded from a network; can run on any computer and operating system.

joint application design (JAD) Process to accelerate the generation of information requirements by having end users and information systems specialists work together in intensive interactive design sessions.

just-in-time Scheduling system for minimizing inventory by having components arrive exactly at the moment they are needed and finished goods shipped as soon as they leave the assembly line.

key field A field in a record that uniquely identifies instances of that record so that it can be retrieved, updated, or sorted.

key logger Spyware that records every keystroke made on a computer to steal personal information or passwords or to launch Internet attacks.

knowledge Concepts, experience, and insight that provide a framework for creating, evaluating, and using information.

knowledge base Model of human knowledge that is used by expert systems.

knowledge discovery Identification of novel and valuable patterns in large databases.

knowledge engineer A specialist who elicits information and expertise from other professionals and translates it into a set of rules, or frames, for an expert system.

knowledge management The set of processes developed in an organization to create, gather, store, maintain, and disseminate the firm's knowledge.

knowledge management system System that supports the creation, capture, storage, and dissemination of firm expertise and knowledge.

knowledge network systems Online directories for locating corporate experts in well-defined knowledge domains.

knowledge repository Collection of documented internal and external knowledge in a single location for more efficient management and utilization by the organization.

knowledge work systems (KWS) Specialized systems built for engineers, scientists, and other knowledge workers charged with discovering and creating new knowledge for a company.

knowledge workers People such as engineers or architects who design products or services and create knowledge for the organization.

knowledge- and information-intense products Products that require a great deal of learning and knowledge to produce.

learning management system (LMS) Tools for the management, delivery, tracking, and assessment of various types of employee learning.

legacy system A system that has been in existence for a long time and that continues to be used to avoid the high cost of replacing or redesigning it.

legitimacy The extent to which one's authority is accepted on grounds of competence, vision, or other qualities. Making judgments and taking actions on the basis of narrow or personal characteristics.

liability The existence of laws that permit individuals to recover the damages done to them by other actors, systems, or organizations.

Linux Reliable and compactly designed operating system that is an offshoot of UNIX and that can run on many different hardware platforms and is available free or at very low cost. Used as an alternative to UNIX and Windows NT.

local area network (LAN) A telecommunications network that requires its own dedicated channels and that encompasses a limited distance, usually one building or several buildings in close proximity.

mainframe Largest category of computer, used for major business processing.

maintenance Changes in hardware, software, documentation, or procedures to a production system to correct errors, meet new requirements, or improve processing efficiency.

malware Malicious software programs such as computer viruses, worms, and Trojan horses.

managed security service provider (MSSP) Company that provides security management services for subscribing clients.

management information systems (MIS) (1) The field of management information systems (MIS) deals with behavioural issues as well as technical issues surrounding the development, use, and impact of information systems used by managers and employees in the firm. (2) A specific category of information systems serving middle management, providing middle managers with reports on the organization's current performance to monitor and control the business and predict future performance.

management-level systems Information systems that support the monitoring, controlling, decision-making, and administrative activities of middle managers.

managerial roles Expectations of the activities that managers should perform in an organization.

man-month The traditional unit of measurement used by systems designers to estimate the length of time to complete a project. Refers to the amount of work a person can be expected to complete in a month.

manufacturing and production information systems Systems that deal with the planning, development, and production of products and services and with controlling the flow of production.

market entry costs The cost merchants must pay simply to bring their goods to market.

marketspace A marketplace extended beyond traditional boundaries and removed from a temporal and geographic location.

mashups Composite software applications that depend on high-speed networks, universal communication standards, and open-source code.

mass customization The capacity to offer individually tailored products or services using mass production resources.

megahertz A measure of cycle speed, or the pacing of events in a computer; one megahertz equals one million cycles per second.

menu costs Merchants' costs of changing prices.

metric A standard measurement of performance.

metropolitan area network (MAN) Network that spans a metropolitan area, usually a city and its major suburbs. Its geographic scope falls between a WAN and a LAN.

microbrowser Web browser software with a small file size that can work with low-memory constraints, tiny screens of handheld wireless devices, and low bandwidth of wireless networks.

micropayment Payment of a very small sum of money, often less than $10.

microprocessor Very large scale integrated circuit technology that integrates the computer's memory, logic, and control on a single chip.

microwave A high-volume, long-distance, point-to-point transmission in which high-frequency radio signals are transmitted through the atmosphere from one terrestrial transmission station to another.

middle management People in the middle of the organizational hierarchy who are responsible for carrying out the plans and goals of senior management.

middleware Software that connects two disparate applications, allowing them to communicate with each other and to exchange data.

midrange computer Middle-size computer that is capable of supporting the computing needs of smaller organizations or of managing networks of other computers.

minicomputer Middle-range computer used in systems for universities, factories, or research laboratories.

MIS audit Identifies all the controls that govern individual information systems and assesses their effectiveness.

MIS steering committee The group of top managers who oversee the MIS function, focusing primarily on policy, planning, and budgeting, and on prioritizing projects.

mobile commerce (m-commerce) The use of wireless devices, such as cell phones or handheld digital information appliances, to conduct both business-to-consumer and business-to-business e-commerce transactions over the Internet.

mobile wallets (m-wallets) Store m-commerce shoppers' personal information and credit card numbers to expedite the purchase process.

moblog Specialized blog featuring photos with captions posted from mobile phones.

model An abstract representation that illustrates the components or relationships of a phenomenon.

model-driven DSS Primarily stand-alone system that uses some type of model to perform "what-if" and other kinds of analyses.

modem A device for translating a computer's digital signals into analog form for transmission over ordinary telephone lines, or for translating analog signals back into digital form for reception by a computer.

module A logical unit of a program that performs one or several functions.

Moore's Law Assertion that the number of components on a chip doubles each year.

MP3 (MPEG3) Compression standard that can compress audio files for transfer over the Internet with virtually no loss in quality.

multicore processor Integrated circuit to which two or more processors have been attached for enhanced performance, reduced power consumption, and more efficient simultaneous processing of multiple tasks.

multimedia The integration of two or more types of media such as text, graphics, sound, voice, full-motion video, or animation into a computer-based application.

multinational Form of business organization that concentrates financial management and control out of a central home base while decentralizing other systems.

multiplexing Ability of a single communications channel to carry data transmissions from multiple sources simultaneously.

multitiered (N-tier) client/server architecture Client/server network in which the work of the entire network is balanced over several different levels of servers.

nanotechnology Technology that builds structures and processes based on the manipulation of individual atoms and molecules.

natural language Nonprocedural language that enables users to communicate with the computer using conversational commands resembling human speech.

net marketplace A single digital marketplace based on Internet technology linking many buyers to many sellers.

net present value (NPV) The amount of money an investment is worth, taking into account its cost, earnings, and the time value of money.

network The linking of two or more computers to share data or resources, such as a printer.

network address translation (NAT) Conceals the IP addresses of the organization's internal host computer(s) to prevent sniffer programs outside the firewall from ascertaining them and using that information to penetrate internal systems.

network economics Model of strategic systems at the industry level based on the concept of a network where adding another participant entails zero marginal costs but can create much larger marginal gains.

network interface card (NIC) Expansion card inserted into a computer to enable it to connect to a network.

network managers IS staff who manage the organization's networks.

network operating system (NOS) Special software that routes and manages communications on the network and coordinates network resources.

networking and telecommunications technology Physical devices and software that link various computer hardware components and transfer data from one physical location to another.

neural networks Hardware or software that attempts to emulate the processing patterns of the biological brain.

nonobvious relationship awareness (NORA) Technology that can find obscure hidden connections between people or other entities by analyzing information from many different sources to correlate relationships.

normalization The process of creating small stable data structures from complex groups of data when designing a relational database.

object Software building block that combines data and the procedures acting on the data.

object-oriented database management system (OODBMS) An approach to data management that stores both data and the procedures acting on the data as objects that can be automatically retrieved and shared; the objects can contain multimedia.

object-oriented development Approach to systems development that uses the object as the basic unit of systems analysis and design. The system is modelled as a collection of objects and the relationship between them.

object-oriented programming An approach to software development that combines data and procedures into a single object.

object-relational DBMS A database management system that combines the capabilities of a relational DBMS for storing traditional information and the capabilities of an object-oriented DBMS for storing graphics and multimedia.

offshore software outsourcing Outsourcing systems development work or maintenance of existing systems to external vendors in another country.

on-demand computing Firms off-loading peak demand for computing power to remote, large-scale data processing centres, investing just enough to handle average processing loads and paying for only as much additional computing power as the market demands. Also called utility computing.

online analytical processing (OLAP) Capability for manipulating and analyzing large volumes of data from multiple perspectives.

online processing A method of collecting and processing data in which transactions are entered directly into the computer system and processed immediately.

online transaction processing Transaction processing mode in which transactions entered online are immediately processed by the computer.

open-source software Software that provides free access to its program code, allowing users to modify the program code to make improvements or fix errors.

operating system The system software that manages and controls the activities of the computer.

operational-level systems Information systems that monitor the elementary activities and transactions of the organization.

operational CRM Customer-facing applications, such as sales force automation, call centre and customer service support, and marketing automation.

operational management People who monitor the day-to-day activities of the organization.

opt-in Model of informed consent prohibiting an organization from collecting any personal information unless the individual specifically takes action to approve information collection and use.

opt-out Model of informed consent permitting the collection of personal information until the consumer specifically requests that the data not be collected.

optical network High-speed networking technologies for transmitting data in the form of light pulses.

organization (behavioural definition) A collection of rights, privileges, obligations, and responsibilities that are delicately balanced over a period of time through conflict and conflict resolution.

organization (technical definition) A stable, formal, social structure that takes resources from the environment and processes them to produce outputs.

organizational and management capital Investments in organization and management such as new business processes, management behaviour, organizational culture, or training.

organizational impact analysis Study of the way a proposed system will affect organizational structure, attitudes, decision making, and operations.

organizational learning Creation of new standard operating procedures and business processes that reflect an organization's experience.

output The distribution of processed information to the people who will use it or to the activities for which it will be used.

Output devices Devices such as printers and video display terminals that convert electronic data produced by the computer system and display them in a form that people can understand.

outsourcing The practice of contracting computer centre operations, telecommunications networks, or applications development to external vendors.

P3P Industry standard designed to give users more control over personal information gathered on Web sites they visit. Stands for Platform for Privacy Preferences Project.

packet filtering Examines selected fields in the headers of data packets flowing between a trusted network and the Internet.

packet switching Technology that breaks messages into small, fixed bundles of data and routes them in the most economical way through any available communications channel, reassembling the packets when they have arrived at their destination.

paradigm shift Radical reconceptualization of the nature of the business and the nature of the organization.

Parallel port Sends a signal multiple bits at a time. Faster than a serial connection.

parallel strategy A safe and conservative conversion approach where both the old system and its potential replacement are run together for a time until everyone is assured that the new one functions correctly.

particularism Making judgments and taking action on the basis of narrow or personal characteristics, in all its forms (religious, nationalistic, ethnic, regionalism, geopolitical position).

partner relationship management (PRM) Software that enables automation of the firm's relationships with its selling partners using customer data and analytical tools to improve coordination and customer sales.

patch Small piece of software to repair the software flaws without disturbing the proper operation of the software.

patent A legal document that grants the owner an exclusive monopoly on the ideas behind an invention for between 17 and 20 years; designed to ensure that inventors of new machines or methods are rewarded for their labour while making widespread use of their inventions.

payback method A measure of the time required to pay back the initial investment on a project.

peer-to-peer Network architecture that gives equal power to all computers on the network; used primarily in small networks.

peer-to-peer payment systems Electronic payment systems for people who want to send money to vendors or to individuals who are not set up to accept credit card payments.

personal area network (PAN) Computer network used for communication among digital devices (including telephones and PDAs) that are close to one person.

personal digital assistant (PDA) Small handheld computer with built-in wireless telecommunications capable of entirely digital communications transmission.

personalization Ability of merchants to target marketing messages to specific individuals by adjusting the message for a person's name, interests, and past purchases.

PERT chart Network diagram depicting project tasks and their interrelationships.

pharming Phishing technique that redirects users to a bogus Web page, even when an individual enters the correct Web page address.

phased approach Introduces the new system in stages either by functions or by organizational units.

phishing Form of spoofing involving setting up fake Web sites or sending e-mail messages that resemble those of legitimate businesses that ask users for confidential personal data.

pilot study A strategy to introduce the new system to a limited area of the organization until it is proven to be fully functional; only then can the conversion to the new system across the entire organization take place.

pivot table Spreadsheet tool for reorganizing and summarizing two or more dimensions of data in a tabular format.

podcasting Publishing audio broadcasts via the Internet so that subscribing users can download audio files onto their personal computers or portable music players.

pop-up ad Advertising that opens automatically and does not disappear until the user clicks on it.

port Used to connect peripheral devices to the central computer unit. Ports determine which devices can be used based on connectors or drivers.

portal (1) Web interface for presenting integrated, personalized content from a variety of sources. (2) A Web site service that provides an initial point of entry to the Web.

portfolio analysis An analysis of the portfolio of potential applications within a firm to determine risks and benefits and to select among alternatives for information systems.

post-implementation audit Formal review process conducted after a system has been placed in production to determine how well the system has met its original objectives.

predictive analysis Use of data mining techniques, historical data, and assumptions about future conditions to predict outcomes of events.

present value The value, in current dollars, of a payment or stream of payments to be received in the future.

price discrimination Selling the same goods, or nearly the same goods, to different targeted groups at different prices.

price transparency The ease with which consumers can find out the variety of prices in a market.

primary activities Activities most directly related to the production and distribution of a firm's products or services.

primary key Unique identifier for all the information in any row of a database table.

primary storage Area of computer hardware that temporarily stores data and program instructions while computer is turned on.

privacy The claim of individuals to be left alone, free from surveillance or interference from other individuals, organizations, or the state.

private exchange Another term for a private industrial network.

private industrial networks Web-enabled networks linking systems of multiple firms in an industry for the coordination of trans-organizational business processes.

process specifications Describe the logic of the processes occurring within the lowest levels of a data flow diagram.

processing The conversion, manipulation, and analysis of raw input into a form that is more meaningful to humans.

procurement Sourcing goods and materials, negotiating with suppliers, paying for goods, and making delivery arrangements.

product differentiation Competitive strategy for creating brand loyalty by developing new and unique products and services that are not easily duplicated by competitors.

production The stage after the new system is installed and the conversion is complete; during this time the system is reviewed by users and technical specialists to determine how well it has met its original goals.

production or service workers People who actually produce the products or services of the organization.

profiling The use of computers to combine data from multiple sources and create electronic dossiers of detailed information on individuals.

program-data dependence The close relationship between data stored in files and the software programs that update and maintain those files. Any change in data organization or format requires a change in all the programs associated with those files.

programmers Highly trained technical specialists who write computer software instructions.

programming The process of translating the system specifications prepared during the design stage into program code.

project Planned series of related activities for achieving a specific business objective.

project management Application of knowledge, tools, and techniques to achieve specific targets within a specified budget and time period.

protocol A set of rules and procedures that govern transmission between the components in a network.

prototype The preliminary working version of an information system for demonstration and evaluation purposes.

prototyping The process of developing an experimental system quickly and inexpensively for demonstration and evaluation so that users can better determine information requirements.

public key encryption Uses two keys: one shared (or public) and one private.

public key infrastructure (PKI) System for creating public and private keys using a certificate authority (CA) and digital certificates for authentication.

pull-based model Supply chain driven by actual customer orders or purchases so that members of the supply chain produce and deliver only what customers have ordered.

pure-play Business models based purely on the Internet.

push-based model Supply chain driven by production master schedules based on forecasts or best guesses of demand for products; products are "pushed" to customers.

query language Software tool that provides immediate online answers to requests for information that are not predefined.

radio-frequency identification (RFID) Technology using tiny tags with embedded microchips containing data about an item and its location to transmit short-distance radio signals to special RFID readers that then pass the data on to a computer for processing.

random access memory (RAM) A computer's internal primary storage. It can directly access any location.

Rapid Application Development (RAD) Process for developing systems in a very short time period by using prototyping, fourth-generation tools, and close teamwork among users and systems specialists.

rational model Model of human behaviour based on the belief that people, organizations, and nations engage in basically consistent, value-maximizing calculations.

rationalization of procedures The streamlining of standard operating procedures, eliminating obvious bottlenecks, so that automation makes operating procedures more efficient.

read-only memory (ROM) Its contents are present even when the computer is turned off. ROM is nonvolatile and can only be read.

real options pricing models (ROPMs) Models for evaluating information technology investments with uncertain returns by using techniques for valuing financial options.

record A group of related fields.

recovery-oriented computing Computer systems designed to recover rapidly when mishaps occur.

reduced instruction set computing (RISC) Computer chips with only the most frequently used instructions embedded in them. Makes the microprocessors faster.

relational DBMS A type of logical database model that treats data as if they were stored in two-dimensional tables. It can relate data stored in one table to data in another as long as the two tables share a common data element.

repetitive stress injury (RSI) Occupational disease that occurs when muscle groups are forced through repetitive actions with high-impact loads or thousands of repetitions with low-impact loads.

request for proposal (RFP) A detailed list of questions submitted to vendors of software or other services to determine how well the vendor's product can meet the organization's specific requirements.

resource allocation The determination of how costs, time, and personnel are assigned to different phases of a systems development project.

responsibility Accepting the potential costs, duties, and obligations for the decisions one makes.

richness Measurement of the depth and detail of information that a business can supply to the customer as well as information the business collects about the customer.

ring network A network topology in which all computers are linked by a closed loop in a manner that passes data in one direction from one computer to another.

risk assessment Determining the potential frequency of the occurrence of a problem and the potential damage if the problem were to occur. Used to determine the cost/benefit of a control.

Risk Aversion Principle Principle that one should take the action that produces the least harm or incurs the least cost.

router Specialized communications processor that forwards packets of data from one network to another network.

routines (also known as *standard operating procedures*) Precise rules, procedures, and practices that have been developed to cope with expected situations.

RSS Technology using aggregator software to pull content from Web sites and feed it automatically to subscribers' computers.

safe harbour Private self-regulating policy and enforcement mechanism that meets the objectives of government regulations regarding privacy expectations but does not involve government regulation or enforcement.

sales and marketing information systems Systems that help the firm identify customers for the firm's products or services, develop products and services to meet their needs, promote these products and services, sell the products and services, and provide ongoing customer support.

Sarbanes-Oxley Act U.S. law passed in 2002 that imposes responsibility on companies and their management to protect investors by safeguarding the accuracy and integrity of financial information that is used internally and released externally.

satellite An orbiting relay station for transmitting microwave signals over very long distances. Used for the transmission of data.

scalability The ability of a computer, product, or system to expand to serve a larger number of users without breaking down.

scope Defines what work is and is not included in a project.

scoring model A quick method for deciding among alternative systems based on a system of ratings for selected objectives.

search costs The time and money spent locating a suitable product and determining the best price for that product.

search engine A tool for locating specific sites or information on the Internet.

search engine marketing Use of search engines to deliver, in their results, sponsored links for which advertisers have paid.

secondary storage Devices (magnetic and optical disks, magnetic tape) that store data and programs even when the computer is not turned on.

Secure Hypertext Transfer Protocol (S-HTTP) Protocol used for encrypting data flowing over the Internet; limited to individual messages.

Secure Sockets Layer (SSL) Enables client and server computers to manage encryption and decryption activities as they communicate with one another during a secure Web session.

security Policies, procedures, and technical measures used to prevent unauthorized access, alteration, theft, or physical damage to information systems.

security policy Statements ranking information risks, identifying acceptable security goals, and identifying the mechanisms for achieving these goals.

semistructured decisions Decisions in which only part of the problem has a clear-cut answer provided by an accepted procedure.

semistructured knowledge Information in the form of less structured objects, such as e-mail, chat room exchanges, videos, graphics, brochures, or bulletin boards.

semistructured knowledge system System for organizing and storing less structured information, such as e-mail, voice mail, videos, graphics, brochures, or bulletin boards. Also known as a digital asset management system.

senior management People occupying the topmost hierarchy in an organization who are responsible for making long-range decisions.

sensitivity analysis Models that ask "what-if" questions repeatedly to determine the impact of changes in one or more factors on the outcomes.

serial port Sends a signal along a cable one bit at a time.

server Computer specifically optimized to provide software and other resources to other computers over a network.

server farm Large group of servers maintained by a commercial vendor and made available to subscribers for electronic commerce and other activities requiring heavy use of servers.

service-oriented architecture Software architecture of a firm built on a collection of software programs that communicate with one another to perform assigned tasks to create a working software application.

service platform Integration of multiple applications from multiple business functions, business units, or business partners to deliver a seamless experience for the customer, employee, manager, or business partner.

shopping bot Software with varying levels of built-in intelligence to help electronic commerce shoppers locate and evaluate products or services they might wish to purchase.

short message service (SMS) Text message service used by digital cell phone systems to send and receive short alphanumeric messages less than 160 characters in length.

Simple Object Access Protocol (SOAP) Set of rules that allows Web services applications to pass data and instructions to one another.

six sigma A specific measure of quality, representing 3.4 defects per million opportunities; used to designate a set of methodologies and techniques for improving quality and reducing costs.

smart card A credit-card-size plastic card that stores digital information and that can be used for electronic payments in place of cash.

smart phone Wireless phone with voice, text, and Internet capabilities.

sniffer Type of eavesdropping program that monitors information travelling over a network.

social bookmarking Capability for users to save their bookmarks to Web pages on a public Web site and tag these bookmarks with keywords to organize documents and share information with others.

social engineering Tricking people into revealing their passwords by pretending to be legitimate users or members of a company in need of information.

social networking sites Online community for expanding users' business or social contacts by making connections through their mutual business or personal connections.

social shopping Use of Web sites featuring user-created Web pages for shoppers to share knowledge about items of interest to one another.

sociotechnical design Design to produce information systems that blend technical efficiency with sensitivity to organizational and human needs.

sociotechnical view Seeing systems as composed of both technical and social elements.

software package A prewritten, pre-coded, commercially available set of programs that eliminates the need to write software programs for certain functions.

spam Unsolicited commercial e-mail.

spamming Form of abuse in which thousands and even hundreds of thousands of unsolicited e-mail and electronic messages are sent out, creating a nuisance for both businesses and individual users.

spoofing The forgery of an e-mail header so that the message appears to have originated from someone or somewhere other than the actual source.

spyware Technology that aids in gathering information about a person or organization without their knowledge.

star network A network topology in which all computers and other devices are connected to a central host computer. All communications between network devices must pass through the host computer.

stateful inspection Determines whether network packets are part of an ongoing dialogue between a sender and receiver.

storage area network (SAN) A high-speed network dedicated to storage that connects different kinds of storage devices, such as tape libraries and disk arrays so they can be shared by multiple servers.

storage technology Physical media and software governing the storage and organization of data for use in an information system.

stored value payment systems Systems enabling consumers to make instant online payments to merchants and other individuals based on value stored in a digital account.

strategic information systems Computer systems at any level of the organization that change goals, operations, products, services, or environmental relationships to help the organization gain a competitive advantage.

strategic transitions A movement from one level of sociotechnical system to another. Often required when adopting strategic systems that demand changes in the social and technical elements of an organization.

structure chart System documentation showing each level of design, the relationship among the levels, and the overall place in the design structure; can document one program, one system, or part of one program.

structured Refers to the fact that techniques are carefully drawn up, step by step, with each step building on a previous one.

structured decisions Decisions that are repetitive, routine, and have a definite procedure for handling them.

structured knowledge Knowledge in the form of structured documents and reports.

structured knowledge systems Systems for organizing structured knowledge in a repository where it can be accessed throughout the organization. Also known as a content management system.

Structured Query Language (SQL) The standard data manipulation language for relational database management systems.

supply chain Network of organizations and business processes for procuring materials, transforming raw materials into intermediate and finished products, and distributing the finished products to customers.

supply chain execution systems Systems to manage the flow of products through distribution centres and warehouses to ensure that products are delivered to the right locations in the most efficient manner.

supply chain management Integration of supplier, distributor, and customer logistics requirements into one cohesive process.

supply chain management systems Information systems that automate the flow of information between a firm and its suppliers in order to optimize the planning, sourcing, manufacturing, and delivery of products and services.

supply chain planning systems Systems that enable a firm to generate demand forecasts for a product and to develop sourcing and manufacturing plans for that product.

support activities Activities that make the delivery of a firm's primary activities possible. Consist of the organization's infrastructure, human resources, technology, and procurement.

switch Device to connect network components that has more intelligence than a hub and can filter and forward data to a specified destination.

switching costs The expense a customer or company incurs in lost time and expenditure of resources when changing from one supplier or system to a competing supplier or system.

syndicators Businesses aggregating content or applications from multiple sources, packaging them for distribution, and reselling them to third-party Web sites.

system testing Tests the functioning of the information system as a whole in order to determine if discrete modules will function together as planned.

systems analysis The analysis of a problem that the organization will try to solve with an information system.

systems analysts Specialists who translate business problems and requirements into information requirements and systems, acting as liaisons between the information systems department and the rest of the organization.

systems design Details how a system will meet the information requirements as determined by the systems analysis.

systems development The activities that go into producing an information systems solution to an organizational problem or opportunity.

systems life cycle A traditional methodology for developing an information system that partitions the systems development process into formal stages that must be completed sequentially with a very formal division of labour between end users and information systems specialists.

systems operators IS staff who actually operate computers hands-on for tasks such as keeping systems running, changing paper on massive, high-speed printers, and loading hard drives.

T lines High-speed data lines leased from communications providers, such as T1 lines, which have a transmission capacity of 1.544 Mbps.

tacit knowledge Expertise and experience of organizational members that has not been formally documented.

tangible benefits Benefits that can be quantified and assigned a monetary value; they include lower operational costs and increased cash flows.

taxonomy Method of classifying things according to a predetermined system.

teamware Group collaboration software that is customized for teamwork.

technology standards Specifications that establish the compatibility of products and the ability to communicate in a network.

technostress Stress induced by computer use; symptoms include aggravation, hostility toward humans, impatience, and enervation.

telecommunications system A collection of compatible hardware and software arranged to communicate information from one location to another.

teleconferencing The ability to confer with a group of people simultaneously using the telephone or electronic-mail group communication software.

Telnet Network tool that allows someone to log on to one computer system while doing work on another.

test plan Prepared by the development team in conjunction with the users; it includes all the preparations for the series of tests to be performed on the system.

testing The exhaustive and thorough process that determines whether a system produces the desired results under known conditions.

token Physical device similar to an identification card that is designed to prove the identity of a single user.

topology The way in which the components of a network are connected.

total cost of ownership (TCO) Designates the total cost of owning technology resources, including initial purchase costs, the cost of hardware and software upgrades, maintenance, technical support, and training.

total quality management (TQM) A concept that makes quality control a responsibility to be shared by all people in an organization.

touch point Method of firm interaction with a customer, such as telephone, e-mail, customer service desk, conventional mail, or point-of-purchase.

trade secret Any intellectual work or product used for a business purpose that can be classified as belonging to that business, provided it is not based on information in the public domain.

transaction cost theory Economic theory stating that firms grow larger because they can conduct marketplace transactions internally more cheaply than they can with external firms in the marketplace.

transaction processing systems (TPS) Computerized systems that perform and record the daily routine transactions necessary to conduct the business; they serve the organization's operational level.

transborder data flow The movement of information across international boundaries in any form.

Transmission Control Protocol/Internet Protocol (TCP/IP) Dominant model for achieving connectivity among different networks. Provides a universally agreed-on method for breaking up digital messages into packets, routing them to the proper addresses, and then reassembling them into coherent messages.

transnational Truly global form of business organization with no national headquarters; value-added activities are managed from a global perspective without reference to national borders, optimizing sources of supply and demand to local competitive advantage.

transport layer security (TLS) Successor to SSL, which enables client and server computers to manage encryption and decryption activities while communicating during a secure Web session.

Trojan horse A software program that appears legitimate but contains a second hidden function that may cause damage.

tuple A row or record in a relational database.

twisted wire A transmission medium consisting of pairs of twisted copper wires; used to transmit analog phone conversations but can be used for data transmission.

Unified Modeling Language (UML) Industry standard methodology for analysis and design of an object-oriented software system.

uniform resource locator (URL) The address of a specific resource on the Internet.

unit testing The process of testing each program separately in the system. Sometimes called program testing.

Universal Description, Discovery, and Integration (UDDI) Allows a Web service to be listed in a directory of Web services so that it can be easily located by other organizations and systems.

universal serial bus (USB) port Port that permits up to 128 devices to be "daisy chained" through only one USB port or by use of USB hubs.

UNIX Operating system for all types of computers that is machine independent and supports multiuser processing, multitasking, and networking. Used in high-end workstations and servers.

unstructured decisions Nonroutine decisions in which the decision maker must provide judgment, evaluation, and insights into the problem definition; there is no agreed-upon procedure for making such decisions.

Usenet Forums in which people share information and ideas on a defined topic through large electronic bulletin boards where anyone can post messages on the topic for others to see and to which others can respond.

user-designer communications gap The difference in backgrounds, interests, and priorities that impede communication and problem solving among end users and information systems specialists.

user interface The part of the information system through which the end user interacts with the system; type of hardware and the series of on-screen commands and responses required for a user to work with the system.

Utilitarian Principle Principle that assumes one can put values in rank order and understand the consequences of various courses of action.

utility computing Model of computing in which companies pay only for the information technology resources they actually use during a specified time period. Also called on-demand computing or usage-based pricing.

value chain model Model that highlights the primary or support activities that add a margin of value to a firm's products or services where information systems can best be applied to achieve a competitive advantage.

value web Customer-driven network of independent firms that use information technology to coordinate their value chains to collectively produce a product or service for a market.

value-added network (VAN) Private, multipath, data-only, third-party–managed network that multiple organizations use on a subscription basis.

videoconferencing Teleconferencing in which participants see one another over video screens.

virtual company Organization using networks to link people, assets, and ideas to create and distribute products and services without being limited to traditional organizational boundaries or physical location.

virtual private network (VPN) A secure connection between two points across the Internet to transmit corporate data. Provides a low-cost alternative to a private network.

Virtual Reality Modelling Language (VRML) A set of specifications for interactive three-dimensional modelling on the World Wide Web.

virtual reality systems Interactive graphics software and hardware that create computer-generated simulations that provide sensations that emulate real-world activities.

virtualization Presenting a set of computing resources so that they can all be accessed in ways that are not restricted by physical configuration or geographic location.

Voice over IP (VoIP) Facilities for managing the delivery of voice information using the Internet Protocol (IP).

war driving Technique in which eavesdroppers drive by buildings or park outside and try to intercept wireless network traffic.

Web 2.0 Second-generation, interactive Internet-based services that enable people to collaborate and share information and to create new services online, including mashups, blogs, RSS, and wikis.

Web browser An easy-to-use software tool for accessing the World Wide Web and the Internet.

Web bugs Tiny graphic files embedded in e-mail messages and Web pages that are designed to monitor online Internet user behaviour.

Web hosting service Company with large Web server computers to maintain the Web sites of fee-paying subscribers.

Web master IS staff person responsible for the organization's Web site.

Web page Any of the World Wide Web pages maintained by an organization or an individual.

Web server A computer that uses Web server software to house Web pages for a Web site.

Web server software Software that manages requests for Web pages on the computer where they are stored and then delivers the page to the user's computer.

Web services Set of universal standards using Internet technology for integrating different applications from different sources without time-consuming custom coding. Used for linking systems of different organizations or for linking disparate systems within the same organization.

Web Services Description Language (WSDL) Common framework for describing the tasks performed by a Web service so that it can be used by other applications.

wide area network (WAN) Telecommunications network that spans a large geographical distance. May consist of a variety of cable, satellite, and microwave technologies.

Wi-Fi Standards for Wireless Fidelity, referring to the 802.11 family of wireless networking standards.

wiki Collaborative Web site where visitors can add, delete, or modify content, including the work of previous authors.

WiMax Popular term for IEEE Standard 802.16 for wireless networking over a range of up to 50 kilometres with a data transfer rate of up to 75 Mbps. Stands for World wide Interoperability for Microwave Access.

Windows Microsoft family of operating systems for both network servers and client computers. The most recent version is Windows Vista.

Wintel PC Any computer that uses Intel microprocessors (or compatible processors) and a Windows operating system.

Wireless Application Protocol (WAP) System of protocols and technologies that lets cell phones and other wireless devices with tiny displays, low-bandwidth connections, and minimal memory access Web-based information and services.

wireless NIC Add-in-card (network interface card) that has a built-in-radio and antenna.

wireless portals Portals with content and services optimized for mobile devices to steer users to the information they are most likely to need.

wireless sensor networks (WSNs) Networks of interconnected wireless devices with built-in processing, storage, and radio frequency sensors and antennae that are embedded into the physical environment to provide measurements of many points over large spaces.

wisdom The collective and individual experience of applying knowledge to the solution of problems.

WML (Wireless Markup Language) Markup language for Wireless Web sites; based on XML and optimized for tiny displays.

work flow management The process of streamlining business procedures so that documents can be moved easily and efficiently from one location to another.

World Wide Web A system with universally accepted standards for storing, retrieving, formatting, and displaying information in a networked environment.

worms Independent software programs that propagate themselves to disrupt the operation of computer networks or destroy data and other programs.

XML (Extensible Markup Language) General-purpose language that describes the structure of a document and supports links to multiple documents, allowing data to be manipulated by the computer. Used for both Web and non-Web applications.

Photo and Screen Shot Credits

Index

Note: *f* denotes a figure, and *t* denotes a table

Organization Index

Subject Index